The Complete Blueprint To Building A High-Scoring (Man-To-Man) Offensive System—Book 1 of 2 books

John Kimble

This book is dedicated to our grand-daughter, Lila Elizabeth who was born as this book was being written. This beautiful little girl has given her parents as well as us so much happiness, joy and love in such a short amount of time. This is to tell her how much her grandparents and parents love and appreciate her

ACKNOWLEDGMENT

This book is dedicated to all of those who have influenced my basketball coaching life and to all the committed basketball coaches that have spent countless hours at coaching clinics, reading books, and "X and Oing" it with their colleagues. I have been a player, a fan, a teacher of the game, a student of the game, a coach and a lover of the game. As a student and a coach of the game, there have been several influences that have impacted my coaching beliefs. These influences range from summer basketball camps, coaching clinics, coaching textbooks and written publications, video tapes, observing other coaches' practices, and the countless informal coaching clinics with many other coaches trying to learn just one more drill, defense, or play. Personal influences in my coaching life have been from many of the most top-notch coaches of the game: The Doug Collins Basketball Camp (Doug Collins and Bob Sullivan), The University of Illinois Basketball Camp (Dick Nagy and Lou Henson), The Indiana Basketball Camp (Bob Knight), The Dick Baumgartner Shooting Camp (Dick Baumgartner), The Iowa Basketball Camp (Lute Olson and Scott Thompson), The Washington State University Cougar Cage Camp (George Raveling, Tom Pugliese, Mark Edwards and Jim Livengood), The Snow Valley Basketball School (Herb Livesey), The Notre Dame University Basketball Camp (Digger Phelps and Danny Nee), The Illinois State University Basketball Camp (Tom Richardson), The Millikin University Basketball Camp (Joe Ramsey), Eastern Illinois University (Don Eddy), The Purdue University Basketball Camp (Lee Rose), The Oregon State University Basketball Camp (Ralph Miller and Lanny Van Eman), The Troy University Basketball Camp (Don Maestri), the Maryville (TN) College Basketball Camp (Randy Lambert) and the Kansas State University Basketball Camp (Jim Wooldridge, Mike Miller, and Chad Altadonna). Just a few of the most memorable and outstanding speakers I have heard at some of the many coaching clinics I have attended have been, Coach Doug Collins, Coach Hubie Brown, Coach Bob Knight, Coach Dick Nagy, Coach Don Meyers, Coach Lute Olson and Coach Rick Majerus. The most outstanding authors of coaching books have been Coach Del Harris, Coach Dean Smith, Coach Bob Knight, and Coach Fran Webster. Coach Lute Olson, Coach Hubie Brown. Coach Don Meyer and Coach Jerry Krause, Coach Del Harris, and Coach Dick Baumgartner have been authors of some of the most outstanding video tapes I have observed and learned a great deal. Coaching colleagues with whom I have worked are: Benny Gabbard, Doug Collins, Steve Gould, Bob Sullivan, Norm Frazier,Dave Toler, Brian James, Tom Wierzba, Steve Laur, Ron Roher, Will Rey, Mike Davis, Dennis Kagel, Don Eiker, Bob Trimble and Ed Butkovich. I was fortunate to always be involved with tremendous coaching staffs with outstanding coaches, who were even more outstanding as people and friends to me than as coaches. These good friends were outstanding people such as Benny Gabbard, Mitch Buckelew, Scott Huerkamp, Phil Barbara, Chris Martello, Don Tanney, Les Wilson, Al Cornish, Ron Lowery, John Lenz, Doug Zehr, and Ken Maye. To all of these people, I say "Thank you for your loyalty, commitment, hard work and effort!"

I would like to say "thanks" to the many players I have coached, to the extra-ordinary non-player students that were big parts of the basketball programs—the managers, the student statisticians, the film-takers, the student athletic trainers, and student helpers. I hope that I conveyed to each and every one of them the fact that they were important parts of the program and that they all deserved credit for the successes of their basketball programs that they were a part of.

I want to also say "thank you" to the special adults that I have met and become friends with in the different communities where I have coached. These are people that participated in the development and the successes of the basketball programs where I coached. These people were contributors, supporters of the program, faithful fans, and loyal friends. Some were parents of players, while some were parents of students and some were just fans of the game. These people are Bob and Ro Flannagan, Ed and Roseanne Moore, Ron and Mary Roher, Dick and Sharon Payne, Don and Bev Hiter, Dave Gregory, Norm Frazier, John and Pam Russell, Ken and Judy Sunderland, Fred Prager, Mark Henry, Carlan and Dee Dee Martin, George Stakely, Charles Owens, Dutch VanBuskirk, Kelly Stanford and so many other good people.

This book is dedicated to all of those who have influenced my personal life. I was brought up by inspirational parents who always taught me to go the extra step, to never be satisfied until the job was done right. I hope I have succeeded in accomplishing that goal with the writing of this book. My wife, Pat, was my biggest source of encouragement to write this book. She was my constant positive reinforcement and support. My daughter Emily and son Adam also were sources of personal encouragement that helped me continue this endeavor. My two brothers, Joe and Jim, who also offered support as I slowly progressed through the ordeal of organizing and writing. And also to my parents, who were always positive role models and constant sources of encouragement and support. Mr. Jerry Krause (friend, coach at Gonzaga University, author and an invaluable source of information) also was of great help and encouragement; as was Mr. Murray Pool (former high school coach and current publisher of Basketball Sense, friend, and source of information). Benny Gabbard was the one person who got me started in my junior college coaching career and showed great faith and confidence in me in my first years of coaching junior college basketball.

This book is dedicated to all of those "students of the game" who have the same love and passion for the game as I have always had.

FOREWORD

Coach John Kimble has once again written a basketball coaching book which stimulates thinking on how to utilize all types of fundamentally strong offensive techniques and methods within the framework and structure numerous offensive plays/entries from many different offensive alignments/sets that, if not producing a good shot will smoothly flow into the final phase of the offensive attack—various continuity offenses. Coach Kimble wrote this detailed and thorough book not to create an occasional winning season for one team but to create a fundamentally sound offensive system that will produce successful winning teams for all squads within the program. Those teams could include 6th, 7th, and 8th grade teams all the way through the entire high school levels both for all of the girls' as well as all the boys' teams, including possibly post high school teams.

Coach Kimble has integrated his overall plan of action with seamless transitions from each of the three progression and skill levels, which closely fit the characteristics and skill levels of those teams, whether the teams are elementary, middle school/junior high or high school to post high school teams.

This plan is designed to include identical offensive concepts, techniques, and methods at the appropriate skill levels, philosophies that can progress from the elementary phases into the highest levels within the entire program.

When players mature and improve their skills and understanding (in addition to the coaching staff also growing), so should the sophistication of the new team's playing and competition levels. Therefore, the fundamental skill levels should improve as well as the methods, techniques, and plans of action for all players as well as the coaching staff.

Coach Kimble has created a blue print for each level of development to have a seamless transition from one level (or squad/team) to the next level. Therefore, a program with the same offensive system will be able to maintain a high degree of consistency and therefore success.

In addition, Coach Kimble has included various man-to-man plays/entries (to be used by the specific level of talent) that are begun out of various man-to-man offensive sets/alignments. Each of those plays will have smooth and immediate conversions from this initial phase of the offense (the alignment and then the play) to the final offensive spot-ups that will allow a smooth flowing transition into the final phase of the attack—various offensive continuities that will also fit the specific team's offensive skill levels and the team's actual strengths and weaknesses being taken into account.

This is a system that players can continually progress and grow in. Successful coaches adapt their strategy to take advantage of their talent. This book demonstrates how to make adjustments, depending on that talent, while maintaining a solid system that players will know inside-out. The game has changed greatly over the past years and the *Designing a Blueprint to Building a Successful Man-to-Man Offensive System* book has ideas which keep pace with those changes. The book can be used for both men's and women's, boys' and girls' teams from elementary to post high school programs.

Bob Ociepka (Retired)

NBA Assistant Coach (25 years)

Los Angeles Clippers	Portland Trailblazers	Chicago Bulls	Minnesota Timberwolves
Milwaukee Bucks	Detroit Pistons	Cleveland Cavs	Detroit Pistons
Orlando Magic	Philadelphia 76ers	Los Angeles Clippers	Indiana Pacers

Head High School Coach at Gordon Tech High School

Chicago, Illinois And York High School

Elmhurst, Illinois

TABLE OF CONTENTS

CHAPTER 1
THE PRIMARY OBJECTIVES OF A SUCCESSFUL MULTIPLE-PHASE MAN-TO-MAN OFFENSIVE SYSTEM

While on the surface, this offensive system may appear to be complicated with the many details and nuances, once the coaching staff learns it; they will be able to effectively teach the system to their players.

Again, while the appearance leads to speculation the system is complex; this system has very simple primary objectives. The two objectives are that all of the various actions and schemes are to simply position (and continually reposition) individual players into situations where each player can have a maximum number of opportunities to succeed offensively. This can be accomplished first with careful evaluations of each individual player.

Each player must clearly have his individual skills assessed so that the more outstanding skills of each player can be utilized by placing that player in a situation where he/she can have the greatest opportunity to succeed. Players who have inferior skills must be individually worked with to improve those deficiencies with specific drills in practice, while also manipulating those players in games so that they will not be forced to execute those lesser skills during games. Specific situations must be created for individual players to be able to utilize their strengths while avoiding for the most part the offensive actions that have lesser chances for success. While eluding those types of situations in games, every individual player's lesser offensive skills and talents must be worked on in practices to build up those offensive weaknesses into strengths. The greater the number of offensive strengths a player has, the more weapons that offensive team has in its arsenal that can be used to attack opposing defenses. This can be even more effective when an opposing team's defensive weaknesses are discovered, a player's corresponding offensive strengths can be used to even exasperate the discovered defensive weaknesses. This obviously gives the offensive team a much greater probability of success.

An obvious and simplistic example would be for an offensive system not to create many opportunities and instances for a short offensive player that does not have the necessary offensive post-up skills. But a successful and well-thought out offensive system that has a presumed 'perimeter type player' possessing notable offensive post-up skills in addition to facing an inferior post-up defender should be placed in those types of offensive scenarios (without greatly disrupting the overall offensive plan of action.) This plan would benefit both the individual player as well as the overall offensive team's chances of success.

When an offensive system can have several individual players placed in offensive situations where success is more likely for the team. In addition, a team's overall offensive skills must also be observed and evaluated so that as a team, those skills should include in the design and blueprint of the offensive attack. Conversely, a team's overall general deficient skills must be avoided more often than they are used.

Another simplistic example would be a team that lacks team depth, overall ball-handling skills and perimeter shooting skills to implement a spread offense with many '3 point' shot scenarios.

As a team addresses and works to improve individual players' skills, so should that same team work on improving that same team's overall offensive deficiencies. The more overall offensive strengths a team possess, the more weapons that offensive team has in its arsenal that can be used to attack opposing team defenses. As an offense probes and discovers an opponent's general weaknesses, offensive system should have methods to take advantage of those team defensive weaknesses. This obviously gives the offensive team a much greater likelihood of success.

A simple and short way to address these primary objectives to players could be to state, "constantly attempt to put players in situations/scenarios/positions where they have the best chances for success and avoid those instances where players have a much lesser chance for overall offensive success."

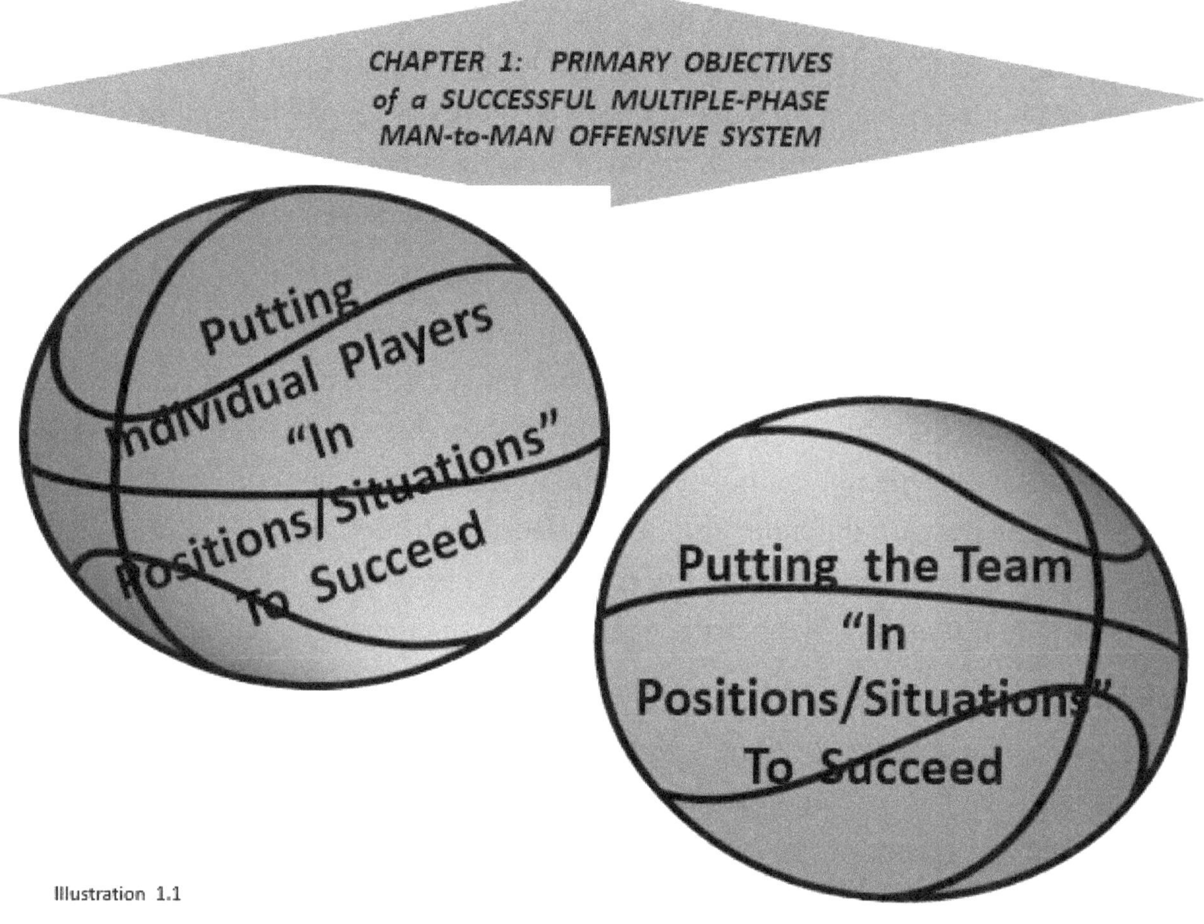

Illustration 1.1

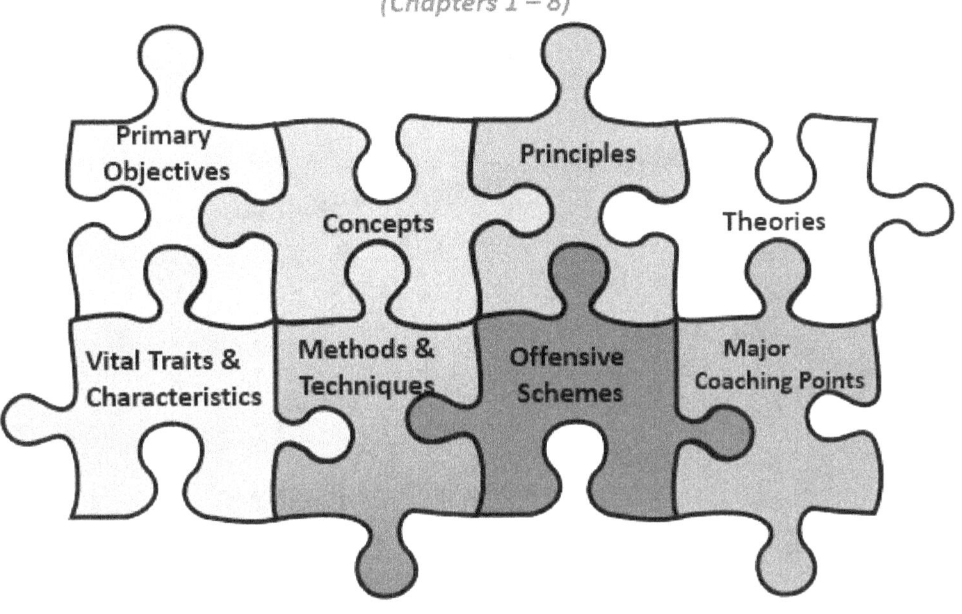

The BLUEPRINT Pieces of a Successful Multiple-Phase Man-to-Man Offensive System
(Chapters 1 – 8)

The Important Phases in a Successful Multiple-Phase Man-to-Man Offensive System

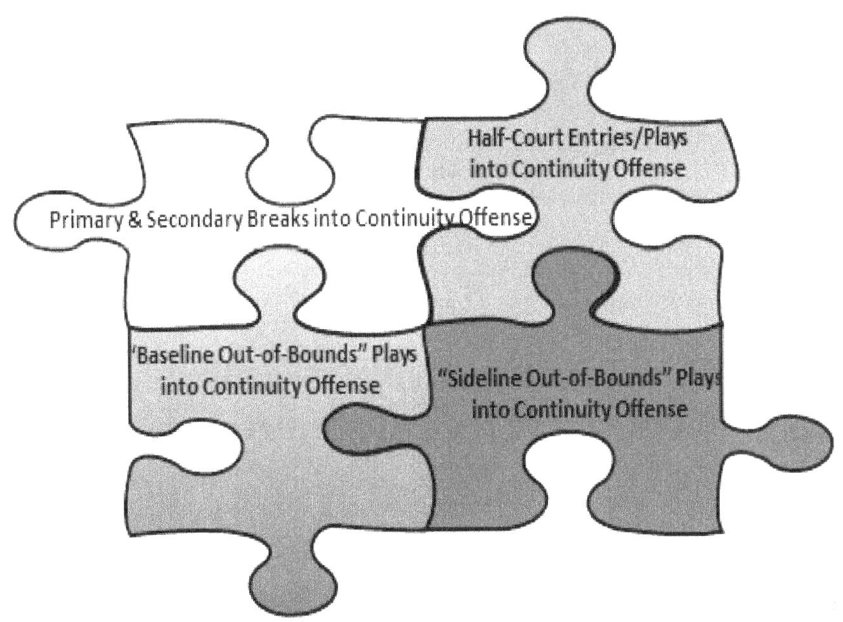

CONCEPT 1:

PRIMARY OBJECTIVES OF MULTIPLE-PHASE OFFENSIVE SYSTEMS
(FOR ALL FULL-COURT AND HALF-COURT OFFENSIVE SITUATIONS)

The Primary Objectives of a good offensive system are to "always place all individual offensive players in positions/locations and situations to succeed." This means that the initial objective of every play/entry is to immediately "place the right people in the right place" so that those players can utilize and highlight their specific strengths, minimize their individual Weaknesses and therefore have better opportunities to score quickly and directly off of the play. The offensive action is to allow that team to be the team that initiates the 'action' while also forcing the defense to always be the reactionary team and to adjust to the strategies and movement of both the ball and the offensive players. This is combined with another objective of always having any of the five possible basic phases or levels within the offensive system. Another major (but not immediate) objective of each play is that if the entry does not produce a shot, all five offensive players end up in what we call the "spot-ups" of the specific continuity offense that is utilized.

⊕ *CONCEPT 2:*

THE FIVE PHASES OF A MULTIPLE PHASE OFFENSIVE SYSTEM

The five basic ways that an offense can begin attacking the opposition's defense have been thoroughly discussed. During every game, each of these five methods, will be the initial attacking wave or phase of the offensive system. When shots are not taken from this particular phase but possession of the basketball is retained, there is always a smooth & seamless transition into the continuity phase of the offensive attack. Primary Fastbreaks that flow into Secondary Fastbreaks can have an extra phase of attack that flows into the designated continuity offense or the motion-type offense. Never do we want to run a Fastbreak or a half-court play and when no shots are taken, then back out of that phase to again restart or "set up" the offense. The Multiple-Phase Offensive System never gives the opposition's defense any breathing room and always maintains constant pressure on the opposition's defense.

The five main phases mean that an offense can begin attacking the opposition's defense by utilizing:

A. A Primary Fastbreak that should flow into a Secondary Break attack that could then possibly have various "Options" and "Counter-Options" that would then flow into the designated continuity offense or motion-type offense.
B. A Press Offense that could flow into (the same) Secondary Break attack. If there are no immediate scores or shots, the same "Secondary Break Options" could be executed that could then also flow into the designated continuity offense.
C. Half-court plays (also called entries or quick-hitters) that could also sometimes flow into some of the same "Secondary Break Options" that would then seamlessly transition into the desired continuity offense. Other half-court plays that immediately and fluidly flow into the continuity offense.

D. Baseline Out-of-Bounds (B.L.O.B.) plays could be the first wave or phase of attack that would then flow into the same designated continuity or motion-type offense.

E. Sideline Out-of-Bounds (S.L.O.B.) plays that could also be the initial phase of the attack. If no shots are produced could then also flow into the same continuity or motion-type offense.

⊕ *CONCEPT 3A:*

UTILIZE EVERY POSSIBLE FULL-COURT
DEFENSIVE SITUATION-TO-OFFENSIVE SITUATION

We want to utilize various first phases of our offensive attack, but always finish with the same last phase or wave of attack—a designated Continuity or Motion-type offense (that fits that specific season's offensive personnel's skill levels.) We want to implement an offensive scheme that can begin from several different beginning points before ending up seamlessly and smoothly flowing into a (half-court) continuity offense that maintains a continuous attack on the opposition's defense. The first group of starting points could/should begin from the defensive end of the court and can be incorporated from the team's defense into different offensive avenues of attack such as from all "Defense-to-Offense" conversions that begin with Primary Fastbreaks that transition into Secondary Fastbreaks and then flow into the desired continuity offense. Specifically, this could start out of Full Court Press Offenses into Primary Fastbreaks, on into Secondary Fastbreaks and then flow into the designated continuity offense.

⊕ *CONCEPT 3B:*

ALWAYS HAVE SMOOTH TRANSITIONS FROM ANY OFFENSIVE PHASE
INTO THE NEXT PHASE OF THE OVERALL OFFENSE

Coaches should continually be looking for new ways to place all of their offensive players "in positions to succeed." This means that every offensive play/entry out of every offensive set/alignment should have multiple objectives. The initial objective of every play/entry is to immediately "place the right people in the right place" so that those players can utilize their specific strengths, minimize their individual weaknesses and therefore have better opportunities to score quickly and directly off of the play. Another major (but not immediate) objective of each play is that if the entry does not produce a shot, all five offensive players end up in what is called "spot-ups." These "spot-ups" are the five specific locations/positions on the floor that allow the designated continuity (or motion) offense to immediately flow from the finished entry into the designated continuity offense—giving the opposition's defense absolutely no time to adjust or recover from their attempt of defending the offense's entry.

⊕ *CONCEPT 3C:*

ALWAYS HAVE SMOOTH TRANSITIONS FROM ANY OFFENSIVE PHASE INTO THE NEXT PHASE OF THE OVERALL OFFENSE

This philosophy of flowing smoothly and immediately from half-court entries/plays (that do not produce shots) should and is incorporated from the other offensive avenues of attack—Press Offenses flowing into Primary Fastbreaks that flow into Secondary Fastbreaks and eventually into the designated continuity offense. In addition, there should be a seamless conversion from "Defense-to-Offense" Primary Fastbreaks that flow into Secondary Fastbreaks and then into the desired continuity offense. In addition, all Baseline and Sideline Out-of-Bounds plays should also possess the ability of smoothly and instantly flowing into the continuity offense that is to be executed.

⊕ *CONCEPT 4:*

ALWAYS MAXIMIZE THE NUMBER OF "FASTBREAK OPPORTUNITIES WHICH ARE AVAILABLE"–

Full Court pressure defenses are practical weapons on the defensive side of the ball that can help control tempo of the game and can affect the physical, emotional and mental conditioning of the opposition. But there is no rule that says that a team cannot magnify that same weapon by "full court pressing on offense." That means that a team that is equipped to be able to pressure an opponent on defense should be able to apply that same degree of pressure with an organized fastbreak system that can not only attack after the opposition after turnovers and missed shots, but after made shots. This quick in-bounding after "their scores," can also be an effective deterrent against the opposition's defensive attempt to try to full-court pressure your team's offense.

ALWAYS HAVE A SMOOTH CONVERSION FROM EVERY PRIMARY AND SECONDARY FASTBREAK OPPORTUNITY INTO THE NEXT WAVE OR PHASE OF THE ATTACK--

Utilize full court press offensive attacks and a primary and secondary fast break system that is compatible with and that fully complements the overall man-to-man offense package. The continuity offenses that are selected should have the capabilities to be able to easily transition from the Primary Break immediately into the Secondary Break and on into the desired continuity offense. This gives the offense a perpetual attack on the opposition's defense and to maintain a constant attack on the opposition's defense, therefore preventing the opposition from ever recovering or reorganizing in its defensive transition phase. A key to winning is to control the tempo of the game. A team can control tempo when they have a smoother, quicker and more effective defense-to offensive transition than the opposition's offense-to defense transition.

Secondary Fastbreak Options are designed to be "accelerated full-court plays" that are similar to half-court plays/entries in several ways. Just like half-court plays/entries, the first objective of all Secondary Break Options is to place offensive personnel in situations where they can succeed. This can be done by utilizing offensive players' strengths and minimizing those player's weaknesses as well in different types of options out of the Break.

In addition, the Secondary Break Options will attack defensive weaknesses of individual defenders as well as the opposition's overall team defensive weaknesses.

A primary objective of the offensive attack is that if and when the Secondary Break Options have not created the shot desired, the Break has at least moved players and repositioned players into new locations where they can succeed. Those locations are the designated spot-ups of the Second Phase or Wave of Attack— the team's designated Continuity Offense. If the Primary Break does not produce the desired shot, the Primary Break flows effortlessly into the Secondary Break Option. If the selected Secondary Break Option does not create the shot wanted, the offense can then smoothly and fluidly flow into the next form (or phase) of attack—the designated Continuity Offense.

As is our philosophy in our half-court man (and zone) offensive philosophies, we would very much like to be multiple in the various methods of attacking defenses in the fastbreak part of our offensive attack. After determining our team's physical as well as mental strengths and weaknesses, we would like to have multiple weapons in our overall offensive scheme. We would like to have a balanced inside and perimeter attack as well as have plays or options that can highlight various individual players' offensive strengths. This can make the offensive attack less predictable and therefore more difficult to defend. This means that we could have specific Secondary Break Options to fit our offensive personnel's strengths and needs for both sides of the floor. Ideally, the Secondary Break could have separate and different options that start from each side of the floor to attack the defense possibly in entirely two different manners.

As stated previously, any one or two from this list of options could be actually used at the end of the Secondary Fastbreaks. Again, it must carefully be determined which should be used at the conclusion of Secondary Breaks from the left side of the floor and which one from the right side of the floor. These fundamentally sound and successful options include:

A. The "Bump & Flare-Cut" Option,
B. The "Back-Screen" & Quick Ball-Screen/Roll,"
C. The "Brush-Screen," the "Give-n-Go Cut,"
D. The "Iso Duck-In Cut,"
E. The "Veer Cut," the "Early Ball-Screen/Roll,"
F. The "Chase & Early Screen/Rim-Run,"
G. The "Chase & Early Screen/Down-Screen," the "Late Ball-Screen/Roll," and
H. The "Duck-In Cut & Late Ball-Screen/Rim-Run" and the "Flex & Weave."

⊕ *CONCEPT 6:*

UTILIZE VARIOUS "1ST PHASES" BUT ALWAYS USE
THE SAME LAST PHASE—
THE MAN CONTINUITY OFFENSE (OR MOTION-TYPE) OFFENSE PHASE---

One offensive philosophy is to implement an offensive scheme that can begin from various locations before ending up seamlessly and smoothly flowing into a continuity offense that maintains a continuous attack on the opposition's defense. The offense could begin from the full court location from the various types of conversion from defense to offense such as after turnovers, defensive rebounds after opponents' missed field goals and free throws, or after opponents' made field goals or free throws, or various Full-Court Press

Offenses. Other ways to implement the same offensive scheme could begin after offensive baseline and sideline out-of-bounds situations while the most frequent situation is after offensive half-court plays/entries that do not produce shots. With no shot taken or loss of possession of the ball, all five offensive players should be relocated into important locations or positions on the floor that are defined as the continuity offense's "spot-ups."

✿ CONCEPT 7A:

CHOOSING MOTION OFFENSES OR CONTINUITY OFFENSES AS THE FINAL PHASE OF THE OFFENSIVE ATTACK--

Some coaches believe in choosing various forms of motion offenses (when the play/entry does not create a shot) that will then give freedom to their offensive players and also create a high level of unpredictability to opposing defenses. Coaches disagreeing with this type of philosophy will state that unpredictable movement is good, but movement with no purpose or fundamental value is not good. It is difficult for the proper player to have proper movement at the proper time. This "motion" philosophy may also give individual offensive players so much freedom that their indecisiveness in choosing their movement may actually stifle the movement desired. Many offensive players (and teams) may need more structure in their offensive play and more help in their offensive decision-making.

Another group of coaches believe in maintaining a high level of controlling what their individual players can and cannot do, based on the coaching staff's evaluations of individual and team" offensive abilities. This can be achieved by utilizing half-court continuity offenses that provide structure to offensive players. Opponents of using the continuity offense philosophy complain that it makes the offensive players too predictable in their movements and the predictability makes it easier for opponents to defend. Additionally, some coaches believe that it makes offensive players "robots on specific tracks."

Other coaches adhere to the philosophy of choosing various forms of motion offenses that will then give freedom to their offensive players and also create a high level of unpredictability to opposing defenses. Opponents of using the continuity offense philosophy sometimes complain that it makes the offensive players too predictable in their movements and the predictability makes it easier for opponents to defend. Additionally, some coaches believe that it turns offensive players into "robots on specific tracks."

⊕ CONCEPT 7B:

CHOOSING MOTION OFFENSES OR CONTINUITY OFFENSES AS THE FINAL PHASE OF THE OFFENSIVE ATTACK— (WITH REASONS TO CHOOSE CONTINUITY OFFENSES):

Often times, coaches disagreeing with this last type of philosophy will state that unpredictable movement is good, but movement with no purpose or fundamental value is not good. It is sometimes difficult for the proper player to have proper movement at the proper time. This "motion" philosophy may also give individual offensive players so much freedom that their indecisiveness in choosing their movement may actually stifle the movement desired. Many offensive players (and teams) may need more assistance and organization in their offensive decision-making. And by using continuity offenses that are fundamentally sound in concept, these continuity offenses can then also serve as a "base offense" and a type of security to the offensive players (when other phases of the offensive attack have broken down or are not as successful as usual.) This gives that offensive team somewhat of a "security blanket" that they can always rely on when entries break down with no productive shot taken.

⊕ CONCEPT 8:

CREATING A MIXTURE OF BOTH CONTINUITY AND MOTION TYPES OF HALF-COURT OFFENSES (FOR THE SECOND PHASE OF ATTACK)

Coaches could institute somewhat of a blend of both philosophies and try to get the best of both worlds. And that is a continuity offense that can smoothly transition from one phase to the final phase, which is a continuity offense that has some freedom as well as a structure in the form of rules. Every time a player has the basketball and makes a pass to one of his other four teammates, there is a rule that provides structure and helps guide the movement of all five players. It is not a rigid offense because the player with the ball realistically has at least three (of his four) teammates that he can almost always pass the ball. Each pass from any of the five "spot-up" locations then has at least three potential pass receivers. Therefore, there is the freedom of making the pass to different players and thus a high degree of unpredictability of what movement takes place after the unpredictable pass is made.

⊕ *CONCEPT 9A:*

REQUIREMENTS OF ALL CONTINUITY OFFENSES: SMOOTH AND IMMEDIATE CONVERSION FROM PLAYS/ENTRIES TO CONTINUITY OFFENSE

Every continuity offense that is selected should have the capabilities to be able to flow seamlessly, smoothly and instantly from the initial phase/wave of attack into the final phase-the designated continuity offense. This gives the offense a perpetual attack on the opposition's defense and to maintain a constant attack on the opposition's defense, therefore preventing the defense from ever recovering or reorganizing in its defense.

⊕ *CONCEPT 9B:*

REQUIREMENTS OF ALL CONTINUITY OFFENSES: THE SELECTED CONTINUITY OFFENSE MUST FIT THAT TEAM'S SPECIFIC SKILL-LEVELS:

There are numerous continuity offenses that exist that a coaching staff can select. A coaching staff should carefully evaluate that season's team skill-levels in regards to the team's general ability, the overall talent level of its opponents for that year before then deciding on the appropriate continuity offense. The continuity offense must also fit the chosen style of play and the overall staff's coaching philosophy. In addition to selecting the appropriate team defense for the season as well as the specific style of play the staff wants the team to play, this could very well be the biggest and most important decisions a coaching staff will make for that specific season. Choosing the correct plays/entries from the right offensive set or alignment is another vital decision that must be made. But, offensively, the most crucial decision might be in picking the most efficient and productive continuity offense.

⊕ *Concept 9C:*

Requirements Of All Continuity Offenses: Continuity Offenses Must Execute Fundamentally Sound Passes Made From Each Spot-Up Location To The Other Four Spot-Up Locations Within The Continuity Offense:

Based on which continuity offense is utilized, there are many different types of movements that both the one 'on-the-ball player' and the four 'off-the-ball offensive players' could make before or after the various types of offensive pass is made. These fundamentally sound types of action all have specific purposes and objectives that will attack defenders both individually as well as an entire defensive group. The actions will literally reposition players into locations and situations that will give offensive players as well as the overall offensive team advantages to more easily attack and defeat the opposition's defense.

Once again, the opposition will have trouble recognizing and then actually defending the high volume of the types of offensive movements and actions that can exist within the structure of the continuity offense. These many types of movements and cuts, when controlled by the many types of passes that can be made will give the offense a degree of structure, but still provides freedom of fluid and unpredictable movement by all offensive players.

⊕ *Concept 10:*

"The Importance Of A Continuity Offense's Spot-Up Locations"— Provides An Instant And Fluid Transition From The 1st Phase To The Last Phase Of The Offensive Attack—

After a selected play/entry from a set/alignment is executed and the offensive team maintains control of the ball with no shot taken; the next phase of the offensive attack begins by smoothly and seamlessly flowing into a variety of continuity offenses or types of motion offenses. This next phase or wave of the attack from different types of offenses must begin with players beginning in specific locations on the court after the play/entry has been concluded (with no shot or loss of possession of the ball.) These important locations or positions are defined as the continuity offense's "spot-ups." The concern that a defensive opponent is able to predict the offensive action should be somewhat minimal, especially if there are multiple plays/entries that are used with some options and counter-options within the continuity offense. When plays or entries are run but the desired shot is not taken, but possession of the ball remains with the offensive team and then flows into the designated continuity offense, defenses will not be able to recognize the actual continuity offense because of the spot-ups of all five offensive players. And from those spot-ups, there will again be an immediate and fluid conversion into the continuity offense that actually is the second and final wave or phase of the overall offensive attack.

Spot-Ups of a continuity offense become a conduit between a team's plays/entries & the team's Second phase of attack—be it a continuity offense or a motion-type offense. It also becomes a means to be able to smoothly continue after Secondary Breaks, Baseline Out-of-Bounds, and Sideline Out-of-Bounds Plays that do not produce shots. 'Spot-Ups' are a way to camouflage a continuity offense because many times the offense will score or lose possession of the ball during the entry before the actual continuity is utilized. Therefore opposing teams will not even see the continuity offense many times and therefore, not necessarily be accustomed to defending it.

⊕ *CONCEPT 11A:*

"SPOT-UPS OF CONTINUITY OFFENSES" WILL CREATE AN EVENLY BALANCED AND THEREFORE AN UNPREDICTABLE AND CONTINUOUS SCORING ATTACK"—

Chuck Daly, once Head Coach of the Detroit Pistons, has stated, "Offense is spacing and spacing is offense."

Good man-to man offenses maintain good floor balance and good spacing between offensive players. (Appropriately 15 feet to 18 feet between most players.) Proper spacing will (vertically as well as horizontally) stretch the overall strength of the defense and helps make ball-reversals much easier and safer as well as skip passes. Spacing also discourages double-team traps both on the perimeter as well as "double-downs" when the ball is passed inside to an interior player.

This multi-phase offensive attack produces a potent and fluid type of offense that fits many types of philosophies and styles of offensive play. Using plays from various sets that then smoothly flow into this continuity offense can give the team various styles of offensive attack such as an up-tempo or a slower ball-control type of attack which can both be executed, making the attack a different kind of "balanced attack." Passing rules in this continuity offense allow an offensive team to have both an "inside oriented" as well as an outside or "3-pt. oriented" or a mixture of both—making it an even different type of balanced (and more difficult to defend) method of attack. In addition, various types of plays can provide a balanced scoring attack as well.

The concern that a defensive opponent is able to predict the offensive action should be somewhat minimal, especially if there are multiple plays/entries that are used with some options and counter-options within the continuity offense. When plays or entries are successfully executed with no shots taken and the play transitions into the continuity, the smooth beginning of the continuity is camouflaged by the play's action so that the continuity is not even recognized or distinguished as that continuity offense. Still, the spot-ups will smoothly flow into the designated continuity offense that becomes the second wave phase of the offensive attack.

As stated, every man-to-man offensive continuity can be a very effective and productive way to attack opposing man-to-man defenses. The selected continuity eventually gives every player equal opportunities both on the perimeter and on the interior to perform and utilize their offensive talents and skills. The continuity places individual offensive players in all of the various spot-up locations that can give every player a distinct and immediate "position advantage" that can be taken advantage of immediately. The continuity provides specific spot-ups so that each play can smoothly and seamlessly flow into that continuity to therefore become the final phase or wave of attack. It should be emphasized that each team must select the appropriate plays and just as importantly (or maybe even more so) the proper continuity or motion offense that is the right fit for their team.

✪ *CONCEPT 11B:*

"SPOT-UPS OF CONTINUITY OFFENSES" WILL CREATE
BALANCED LOCATIONS AND SPACING
FOR EVERY INDIVIDUAL OFFENSIVE PLAYER—

A Continuity Offense's Spot-Ups provide excellent positions for maximum offensive success by allowing for ideal spacing both on the perimeter as well as the interior, by spreading the opposition's defense both vertically and horizontally. The Spot-Ups of the designated continuity offense give offensive players good cutting, screening and passing angles to utilize in the offensive action. The continuity's spot-ups provide opportunities for inside and outside shots. The spot-ups of the continuity offense also provide spacing for aggressive (but under control) dribble-attacks to the basket. In addition, these Spot-Ups can offer the offensive team fundamentally sound opportunities for successful offensive rebounding and also for efficient defensive transition.

✪ *CONCEPT 11C:*

CONTINUITY OFFENSES MUST PROVIDE THE OFFENSIVE TEAM WITH AN
"EVENLY BALANCED INTERIOR AND PERIMETER SCORING ATTACK"—

Outstanding man offenses should have somewhat of a balanced attack by having an "inside-out" perimeter shooting attack as well as an "outside-in" type of attack. Starting an attack in one particular location to force opposing defenses to react, adjust and commit to stopping that form of attack before the offense itself countering to the other type of scoring attack is invaluable in keeping defenses off balance and off guard. Make the opposition "pick their poison" on which they attempt to defend—the inside or the perimeter.

"SPOT-UPS OF CONTINUITY OFFENSES"
WILL CREATE BALANCED FLOOR LOCATIONS FOR PLAYERS AND THEREFORE HELP CREATE MORE OF A
BALANCED AND UNPREDICTABLE AND CONTINUOUS SCORING ATTACK—

A Continuity Offense's Spot-Ups provide excellent positions for maximum offensive success by allowing for ideal spacing both on the perimeter as well as the interior, by spreading the opposition's defense both vertically and horizontally. The Spot-Ups of the designated continuity offense give offensive players good cutting, screening and passing angles to utilize in the offensive action. The continuity's spot-ups provide opportunities for inside and outside shots. The spot-ups of the continuity offense also provide spacing for aggressive (but under control) dribble-attacks to the basket. In addition, these Spot-Ups can offer the offensive team fundamentally sound opportunities for successful offensive rebounding and also for efficient defensive transition.

Each entry that does not produce a shot from the half-court alignment the play was executed from will at least place all five offensive personnel in either a (Balanced or Unbalanced) "4-Out/1-In" set of continuity spot-ups or from a (Balanced or Unbalanced) "3-Out/2-In" continuity spot-ups. These same spot-ups should be filled at the conclusion of any Secondary Fastbreaks, Baseline Out-of-Bounds (B.L.O.B.) or Sideline Out-of-Bounds (S.L.O.B.) plays. Again, players having repositioned into these designated spot-ups allows the offense to smoothly, seamlessly, and immediately flow into various continuity offenses or different forms of motion offenses. This makes the designated continuity offense even more crucial to the overall success of the offense.

⊕ *CONCEPT 12:*

CONTINUITY OFFENSES ARE ABLE TO AND WILL PROVIDE
AN OFFENSIVE TEAM WITH OFFENSIVE STABILITY THAT WILL THEN DELIVER
POTENTIAL OFFENSIVE SUCCESS-

Coaching staffs should use continuity offenses that are fundamentally sound in concept that can also serve as a "base offense" and a type of security to the offensive players (when other phases of the offensive attack have broken down or are not as successful as usual.)

This gives players somewhat of a "safety blanket" where confidence can again be instilled so that an offensive team can "weather the storm" and again become successful and productive.

✦ *CONCEPT 13:*

COACHES MUST ALSO SELECT THE MOST EFFECTIVE ENTRIES/PLAYS FOR EACH SPECIFIC TEAM-

Coaches must select the most effective entries/plays as well as the most effective continuity/motion offenses for each specific team. This is the philosophy behind each and every man-to-man continuity offense and its package of entries/plays that is firmly believed in. There are numerous continuity offenses that can possess families of plays/entries from various offensive alignments/sets that can have its plays quickly, easily and fluidly flow into the designated continuity offense's "spot-up" positions. It must also be emphasized that a team can have an excess of entries/plays as well as too many different continuity man offenses. Therefore, a coaching staff must study which continuity offense best suits their team's personnel and then pick the most productive and efficient plays that fit their players as well as the chosen continuity offense. In addition, the coaching staff should evaluate their personnel both physically and mentally to make sure the correct offenses and the correct plays and the appropriate number are chosen.

✦ *CONCEPT 14:*

COACHES SHOULD UTILIZE DIFFERENT ENTRIES/PLAYS THAT ARE EXECUTED FROM DIFFERENT SETS/ALIGNMENTS—

Possessing and executing multiple entries/plays from a variety of various alignments/sets can greatly improve the overall offensive package. Coaching staffs should be able to integrate different entries/plays out of various sets/alignments to be more varied to become less predictable to the opposition while still maintaining a degree of simplicity for their own team. An offensive package limited to just one primary scorer when other players could also become higher level scorers if given the proper scoring chances in specific plays gives the offensive team a greater level of balance and unpredictability as well as making the offensive package more of an "equal opportunity scoring attack."

COACHES SHOULD UTILIZE THE SAME OR
VERY SIMILAR ENTRIES/PLAYS THAT ARE EXECUTED
FROM DIFFERENT SETS/ALIGNMENTS—

Using multiple plays and also multiple sets can greatly improve the overall offensive package. Coaching staffs should be able to integrate similar or possibly identical entries/plays out of various sets/alignments to appear to be more complex to their defensive opponents while keeping it simplified to the offensive team. This can make the offense appear to be more unpredictable to the defense and easier for the offense to comprehend, understand and become more productive.

✦ *CONCEPT 16:*

COACHES SHOULD SELECT AND UTILIZE ENTRIES/PLAYS THAT WILL HIGHLIGHT
INDIVIDUAL OFFENSIVE PLAYERS' STRENGTHS AS WELL AS MINIMIZE THOSE SAME
PLAYERS' WEAKNESSES—

Capitalize on the strengths of the offensive alignment/set by distorting the shape of the original man defense to stretch it both vertically as well as horizontally, as well as to initially place individual defenders in potentially unsuccessful positions. Capitalize on various offensive player's individual strengths via various entries/plays or different alignments/sets while attacking weaknesses of both individual defenders as well as the overall team defense in the form of quick-hitting plays. These plays can also serve as a conduit to smoothly flow into the designated continuity offense. The entries can move the opposing man-to-man defenders as well as disguising how the offensive team is proceeding to attack the defense. This adds another layer of unpredictability to the overall offensive attack. The opponent's defense must first place all attention and effort into attempting to stop the entry/play and without any time for reorganization or regrouping to then attempt to defend the continuity man-to-man offense.

COACHES SHOULD SELECT AND UTILIZE ENTRIES/PLAYS AND CONTINUITY OFFENSES THAT WILL SUCCESSFULLY ATTACK OPPOSING TEAMS' OVERALL DEFENSIVE WEAKNESSES—

Every opposing man-to-man defense has inherent team weaknesses. Coaching staff should learn the opponents' particular styles of the defenses that are being used so that the offense may attack and take advantage of the general weaknesses of each defense. Every man-to-man defense has specific strengths and weaknesses of the overall opposition's man defense. Coaches should study and know the particular styles of the man-to-man defense being used against their team to avoid the strengths and probe the inherent weaknesses of that style of defense. An opponent's seemingly defensive strength might be able to be converted into a weakness with the proper offensive scheming. While also searching for that defensive weakness, the opposition's defensive transition skills might be the key weakness. Once discovered, those weaknesses can be attacked and capitalized on by the offense.

⊕ *CONCEPT 18:*

EVERY OFFENSIVE PLAY AND CONTINUITY OFFENSE MUST HAVE CLEARLY DEFINED RULES FOR EACH PLAYERS' DEFENSIVE TRANSITION RESPONSIBILITIES-

Make sure that defensive transition responsibilities (preventing opponents from getting into THEIR own fastbreak offense) are clear-cut and carried out by everyone after every single offensive possession. Not only should it be clearly defined as to whom "gets back," but what "getting back" really means—as far as "how far back and where (on the court.) We want that assigned defender to quickly sprint to the center jump circle, giving depth as well as balance to be able to cover both sides of the floor.

EVERY OFFENSIVE PLAY AND CONTINUITY OFFENSE MUST HAVE CLEARLY DEFINED RULES FOR EACH PLAYERS' OFFENSIVE TRANSITION RESPONSIBILITIES—

Just as important are the offensive rebounding responsibilities are also clear-cut and carried out by everyone. The three best qualified and most skilled offensive rebounders are called "fullbacks," to clearly describe their one and only assignment is to hit the offensive boards with a "full" commitment toward that assignment. It is important that all offensive rebounders understand that "long field goal misses" mean "long rebounds." "Fullbacks" must learn to read the angles of missed shots and the techniques of beating the opposition's defensive box-outs. The attitude should be instilled to those three offensive rebounders that they look as every offensive shot is "THEIR" offensive rebound ('Stick-back' opportunity.)

The fourth most qualified offensive rebounder is titled the "halfback" as he specifically splits his responsibilities as "half" offensive rebounder and "half" defensive transition.

The fifth offensive player is descriptively called the "tailback." Regardless of where he is located when the offensive shot is taken, the "tailback" must devote his full attention and energy to properly getting his "tail" back on defense.

🌐 *CONCEPT 20:*

COACHES SHOULD IMPLEMENT OFFENSIVE BOTH BASELINE AND SIDELINE OUT-OF-BOUNDS PLAYS-

Another initial phase of the offensive attack, while still finishing with the same designated Continuity or Motion-type offense (that matches offensive personnel's skill levels) could and should be from all Baseline Out-of-Bounds and Sideline Out-of-Bounds plays that are utilized. This would be only as long as these plays also possess the same ability of easily and instantaneously being able to immediately flow into the designated continuity offense.

EVERY OFFENSIVE PLAYER
SHOULD VALUE AND UTILIZE THE DRIBBLE PROPERLY—

Man-to-man offensive players should know the value of the dribble and utilize the dribble properly. They should utilize the dribble in an efficient manner to either advance the ball down-court, to attack the basket to score, to "drive & dump" to a teammate for an inside pass, for "penetrate & pitch" action to a perimeter teammate, to improve passing angles to make passes to teammates, to reverse the ball from one side of the floor to the other side or to escape defensive double-team traps.

⊕ *CONCEPT 22:*

ALL OFFENSIVE PLAYS AND CONTINUITY OFFENSES
MUST BE ABLE TO FLATTEN DEFENSES
AS WELL AS TO UTILIZE BALL-REVERSALS—

Flatten the defense by getting the basketball down to the baseline and then reverse the ball quickly to the opposite side of the floor. This is another way of stretching the defense first in a vertical manner and then in a horizontal manner. This movement of the ball from one side of the floor to the opposite side causes ballside defenders and helpside defenders to be in constant movement as well as to change defensive assignments, stances and locations. Ball reversals by means of reverse passes, skip passes or dribbles will force the opponents to defend both sides of the floor, thereby forcing all five defenders to move and forcing all defenders to become both ball defenders as well as off-ball defenders. This can exploit major weaknesses of all individual defenders. Ball-reversals are so revered by some coaching staffs that they keep a detailed statistic on how many ball reversals take place in their offensive schemes.

⊕ *CONCEPT 23:*

ALL SUCCESSFUL OFFENSES MUST UTILIZE VARIOUS METHODS TO ELIMINATE
OPPONENTS' HELPSIDE DEFENSES

A major objective of various types of continuity offenses (as well as offensive plays/entries/quick-hitters) can also be to eliminate or weaken helpside defenders to attack the opposition's post defenders as well as to isolate post defenders with either flash-post action and/or to occupy helpside defensive opponents with 2 or 3-man games on the offense's weakside.

✣ *CONCEPT 24:*

ALL SUCCESSFUL OFFENSES MUST UTILIZE VARIOUS "SKIP PASSES" IN VARIOUS LOCATIONS—

Perimeter players should not hesitate on making "skip-passes" across the court. "Skip-passes" are an instant method of reversing the ball from one side of the court to the other side. Reversing the ball is an integral concept for successful offenses to be able to attack both inside and also on the perimeter. "Skip-passes" will also discourage "man defenses" from providing good helpside defense in the lane from the weakside of the offense, off of the "skip pass." After "skip passes" are made, post players should seal off the post defenders that deny them the ball on the original ballside and be prepared to receive the pass from the original weakside. "Skip-passes" can provide offenses with open "catch & shoot 3's" or opportunities to "shot fake & create." When man-to-man defenders react to the "skip pass," a second "skip pass" back to the original ballside can be very effective. A phrase "One good skip pass deserves another" should be taught and utilized in every type of offense that is utilized.

✣ *CONCEPT 25:*

INSTRUMENTAL TO OFFENSIVE INDIVIDUAL AND OVERALL OFFENSIVE TEAM SUCCESSES ARE THE USE OF PASS FAKES AND SHOT FAKES--

Coaches should always stress to every offensive player to always use good passing and shot fakes against the opposition's defenders.

Basic passing fakes can sometimes move multiple defenders in their eagerness to play good defense, causing defensive problems for the opposing defenses.

Shot fakes can create many more opportunities to drive to the basket and to draw fouls on the opposition. To be successful, shot fakes do not have to cause the defender to leave the ground, but to just slightly move that defender or straighten the defender's legs. Defenders cannot play defense with their legs straight. Defenders will not be able to jump or make any quick lateral defensive moves. Shot fakes made earlier in the game will give shooters more space to take those jump shots later in the course of the game.

⚆ CONCEPT 26:

SUCCESSFUL MAN OFFENSIVE PLAYS AND CONTINUITY OFFENSES
MUST HAVE PRESSURE RELEASE OPTIONS TO
COMBAT OPPOSITION'S DENIAL PRESSURE--

Teams should have simple and easily understood methods to combat aggressive defensive overplays and denials (both on the perimeter and in the post) for their entries as well as their Second Phase/Wave of Attack—whether it is a continuity or motion type offense. "Backdoor Cuts," "Give-n-Go Cuts," "Blind Pig" Actions, "Iverson Cuts," "Barkley Cuts" (defined as "Iverson Cuts" by the offensive team's Post Players,) "Dribble Hand-Offs," "Fake Dribble Hand-Offs," "Counter Options" and other actions are ways to eliminate opponents' denial pressure on the perimeter. High-Low Flash post overloads and off-ball screens on the weakside are viable options to counter opponents' Helpside Defenses that are necessary in the opposition's aggressive and interior man-to-man defensive action.

⚆ CONCEPT 27:

COACHES AND PLAYERS MUST BELIEVE THAT
OFFENSIVE PATIENCE IS INVALUABLE TO OFFENSES--

Offensive players should be patient and move the ball as well as themselves. They should force the defense to move, to react, and to work for extended periods of time to wear down opponents and provide more opportunities for defensive mistakes. Offensive players should always remember that "THEY" cannot score if "WE" have the ball. A team's patience on offense will ultimately affect both the opposition's defense as well as their own offense (by fatigue as well as offensive impatience.)

SUCCESSFUL OFFENSIVE SYSTEMS MUST
INCORPORATE AND UTILIZE A WIDE VARIETY OF OFFENSIVE CUTS--

Attack opposing man defenses with various types of offensive cuts both on the ballside and the weakside. Use a mixture of the different kinds of cuts by off-the-ball offensive players such as: "V-Cuts," "Pipe or Zipper Cuts," "Shuffle Cuts," "Duck-In Cuts," "Iverson Cuts," "Barkley" Cuts, "Michigan" Cuts, "Shuffle Cuts," "Scissors" Cuts, "Flex Cuts," "Veer Cuts," "Bump Cuts," "Curl Cuts," "Give-n-Go Cuts," "Backdoor Cuts," "Blind-Pig" Cuts, "Flare Cuts," "UCLA Rub-Off Cuts," "Bruin" Bump Cuts," "Flash Post Cuts," "Slash Cuts," "Blur Cuts," (Post) "Spin-Screen Cuts," and "Basket Cuts" (Ball-Screen Rolls and Rim-Runs).

⊕ *CONCEPT 29:*

SUCCESSFUL OFFENSIVE SYSTEMS MUST
INCORPORATE AND UTILIZE A WIDE VARIETY OF "OFF-THE-BALL" SCREENS--

Integrate the many different types of "off-the-ball screens" in the offense so that your team can to either completely eliminate or at least move the "helpside" defense, or to have personnel cutting towards the ball either on the perimeter or the interior. These "off-the-ball screens" could be in the form of "Big-on-Small," "Small-on-Big," "Small-on-Small" or "Big-on-Big" types of "off-the-ball screens." Another form of an "off-the-ball screen" is called a "Ram Screen" that makes the up-coming Ball-Screen even tougher to predict when it will develop and therefore more difficult to defend. Screens set by a different sized player on a different sized teammate helps discourage defensive switching or can quickly put defensive players in drastic mismatches that can and should be capitalized on.

⊕ *CONCEPT 30A:*

SUCCESSFUL OFFENSIVE SYSTEMS MUST
INCORPORATE AND UTILIZE A VARIETY OF "ON-THE-BALL-SCREENS"—

An offensive scheme should/could include "on-the-ball" screens with three different starting points and the six or more different "follow-up methods/techniques" that can effectively be executed. The locations of the initial ball-screen can also be on different locations of the court. Therefore having different starting points and locations, different types of ending action and different players setting as well receiving the actual ball-screen, in addition to the different combinations of players involved, can result in numerous offensive ball-screening scenarios that would be very difficult for defensive teams to adequately defend.

⊕ *CONCEPT 30B:*

SUCCESSFUL OFFENSIVE SYSTEMS MUST INCORPORATE AND UTILIZE A VARIETY OF "ON-THE-BALL-SCREENS"—

There are five different fundamentally sound methods to initiate the ball-screen action. These ways are:

A. The traditional stationary ball-screen usually set near the top of the key or halfway from the top of the key and the high elbow areas,
B. The "Long Ball-Screen" where the designated ball-screener breaks into the designated screening location,
C. The "Flat Screen" action usually set somewhere near the middle "alley" just inside the 10-second timeline with the ball-screener setting the stationary ball-screen with his butt pointing directly towards the basket or
D. The "Double Wide" Ball-Screen (utilizing two offensive players side by side that set a wider ball-screen,)
E. The Ghost Ball-Screens that can start at various locations on the floor and can be set by all types of personnel,
F. The "Inside Ball-Screens" that are set at the high post elbow area for middle penetration drives.

⊕ *CONCEPT 31:*

SUCCESSFUL OFFENSIVE SYSTEMS MUST INCORPORATE AND UTILIZE A VARIETY OF WAYS TO CONCLUDE THEIR "ON-THE-BALL-SCREENS"--

Various types of actions that could be utilized after executing 'Following (the-pass) Ball-screens'; could be any of the following such as:

A. The "Ball-Screen/Roll,"

B. "Ball-Screen/Rim-Run,"

C. "Ball-Screen/Slip" (Picking and Popping),

D. "Ball-Screen/Flare-Cut,"

E. "Ball-Screen/Re-Screen" or

F. Various forms of "Screen-the-Screener" action on either the interior or the perimeter player.

✦ *CONCEPT 32:*

SUCCESSFUL OFFENSIVE SYSTEMS MUST INCORPORATE AND UTILIZE A VARIETY OF "COMBO SCREENS"--

A now popular offensive concept that is being applied is the series of action where the initial screener sets two (or more) different types of screens in a very short, smooth and fluid series of offensive action. Another newer type of action (called the "Chin Screen" action) is a reverse pass that initiates a back-screen for the ball reversal passer that is immediately followed by a ball-screen(with various types of action that could then follow that ball-screen.) Other forms of Combo Screens could be started with an off-ball screen and then finished with a second off-ball screen. Many types of Combo Screens can start with a ball-screen that is then followed with a second off-ball screen on a second teammate. These are fluid forms of action that give the screener's defender no time to read the type of screen and prepare to defend it.

✦ *CONCEPT 33:*

SUCCESSFUL OFFENSIVE SYSTEMS MUST INCORPORATE AND UTILIZE VARIOUS FORMS OF BOTH THE WEAVE/DRIBBLE HAND-OFF AND FAKE DRIBBLE HAND-OFF ACTIONS--

There are many forms of offensive Weave/Dribble Hand-Off actions that can be integrated into a successful offense. The ball can easily be handed off before then dribbled towards the middle of the floor as a form of ball reversal. In addition, centering the basketball in the middle of the floor eliminates the defense's definition of a "ballside" and a "helpside." That means there will be a large decrease in defensive support. Utilize "weave/dribble hand-off action" can also highlight offensive players' dribbling and driving skills and talents. It can also invert post players into becoming perimeter players, which means opposing post defenders are forced to defend in possibly unfamiliar areas where they could very easily have weaknesses. The weave/dribble hand-offs can also provide opportunities in creating "big on small" or "small on big" mismatches that can be capitalized on by discovering individual defenders' weaknesses as well as utilizing individual offensive players' offensive strengths. To counter "Dribble Hand-Off" action, an offensive team can also have an option that incorporates "Fake Dribble Hand-Offs."

⊕ *CONCEPT 34A:*

SUCCESSFUL OFFENSIVE SYSTEMS MUST INCORPORATE AND UTILIZE VARIOUS FORMS OF "FLIP-PASSES" (ALSO CALLED "PASS HAND-OFFS")

There are several ways that an offensive "Flip Pass" action can be integrated to attack opposing defenses within the framework of several different offensive plays/entries. This action, that could also be called "Pass Hand-offs" (or PHOs) can have the same results as many Dribble Hand-Offs (DHOs) previously discussed. The ball can move in the direction both towards and away from the center of the floor. When the ball is dribbled towards the wing with the initial Passer following his "Wing Pass, " there will be indecision and a delay by the defense to read if the ball and the play continue in the same direction, if the ball remains at the FT Line extended or if the direction of the play is changed to move back towards the middle of the floor. This hesitation by the defense can often give the offense enough time to take advantage of that delay and be able to successfully attack the defense and the many disadvantages this type of action can provide for the offense. This action could be used as a counter to any of the countless times in a game when there is a "Wing Pass" that was made from the top of the key. After the use of a couple of "Flip Passes" are made, every "Wing Pass" is made afterwards, there could be a slight moment of doubt by the defense. When this action is used with a mixture of (traditional) 'big' and a 'small' players, defensive switching strategies would cause all types of defensive switches. These defensive switches could cause various types of defensive problems that the offense could take advantage of.

⊕ *CONCEPT 34B:*

SUCCESSFUL OFFENSIVE SYSTEMS MUST INCORPORATE AND UTILIZE VARIOUS FORMS OF "FAKE FLIP-PASSES" (ALSO CALLED "FAKE PASS HAND-OFFS")

While integrating "Flip Pass" actions within the offensive structure of the system, a form of deception and misleading of the defense in partnership with this type of action comes the use of the "Fake Flip Pass." There are several ways that after using the "Flip Pass" action, an offensive team can switch up its attack with faking the actual "Flip Pass" and following up with a different form of attack. When defensive opponents attempt to adjust their defensive "REACTION" to the initial offensive "ACTION" of the "Flip Pass," they will remain a step behind and forcing the defense to remain in that same 'reactionary mode of thinking and acting.' As in any "Flip-Pass" action, the same possibilities of misdirection, the covering up the actual objectives, the increase of confusion and hesitancy by the opposition, and the possible creation of 'position player mismatches' will also be created for the offense to make the most of.

⊕ *CONCEPT 35:*

SUCCESSFUL OFFENSIVE SYSTEMS MUST INCORPORATE AND UTILIZE VARIOUS WAYS TO IMPLEMENT AND UTILIZE THE CREATION OF "POSITION MISMATCHES"--

All continuity offenses can implement an offensive plan of attack that can be defined as creating "position mismatches." This means that the offense can force opposing defenders into having to defend offensive players they were not initially assigned to guard. This can be done by integrating "Big-on-Small" or "Small-on-Big" off-ball and/or on-ball screens within the rules of the continuity or very easily in the design of specific quick-hitting plays/entries. This could also be a form of forcing defenders to be inverted, while offensive players remain in their normal and customary locations.

✦ <u>*CONCEPT 36:*</u>

SUCCESSFUL OFFENSIVE SYSTEMS MUST INCORPORATE AND UTILIZE VARIOUS WAYS TO INVERT OFFENSIVE PERSONNEL TO CREATE "POSITION MISMATCHES"--

Coaches should constantly look to invert offensive personnel to create "position advantages," such as a perimeter player ending up in the post area to have a possible "position advantage." These advantages could be one or more or a combination of height, strength, quickness and/or inside scoring skills advantages (through experience and training.) These types of action can be created by carefully designed plays as well as the continuity offense that is decided upon. Perimeter Players could be inverted with certain perimeter players repositioning themselves inside and Post Players could also be inverted to also take advantages of their offensive skills and the possible weaknesses of their opponents.

✦ <u>*CONCEPT 37:*</u>

SUCCESSFUL OFFENSIVE SYSTEMS MUST INCORPORATE AND UTILIZE VARIOUS WAYS TO INVERT PERIMETER-TYPE OFFENSIVE PLAYERS--

One simple, but sound method of attack that can be a part of this offensive system is to "invert" perimeter players. This means that so-called "perimeter players" can be placed into post-up locations. After perimeter players have been taught and trained how to successfully post up their perimeter defenders inside, there are plays designed that will take advantage of those possible "position mismatches." The coaching staff takes the challenge of preparing "perimeter players" to be more prepared as offensive post players than opponents' perimeter players to be good post defenders and vice versa with the traditional "post players." Specific offensive plays, rules or special options within the continuity can then provide various players with "position advantages" by taking advantage of newly-found offensive strengths and newly discovered individual defensive weaknesses both on the interior as well as on the perimeter.

SUCCESSFUL OFFENSIVE SYSTEMS MUST INCORPORATE AND UTILIZE VARIOUS WAYS TO INVERT OFFENSIVE POST PLAYERS–

A Continuity offense (as well as many plays) not only can invert perimeter players "down on the blocks," but can also move and reposition certain offensive post players away from the basket; so that they can attack their defender on the perimeter as well. This attack could be because of that player's dominating quickness, ball-handling and/or perimeter shooting skills (or because of a specific defender's overall perimeter defensive weakness.) Inverting offensive post players could also be to pull defensive "bigs" away from the basket to take away defensive strengths, such as defensive rebounding and shot-blocking skills. This can give that designated player (be it a traditional so-called perimeter player or a post player out on the perimeter) an opportunity to use his driving, passing and/or perimeter shooting skills, as well as his offensive creative skills. These methods could be incorporated within the general rules of the continuity, in the counter-options or in specific plays executed for that primary reason.

CONCEPT 39A:

SUCCESSFUL OFFENSIVE SYSTEMS MUST INCORPORATE AND UTILIZE VARIOUS WAYS TO ISOLATE OFFENSIVE POST PLAYERS—

One way to attack opposing team's defenders is to place both the traditional as well as the so-called inverted perimeter players in the post with little or no interior support for those specific defenders. When opposing post players play behind the offensive post players, those "Inside Passes" should be able to easily be made to that particular post player. The properly selected continuity offense should have a plan of attack to neutralize double-teams from perimeter defenders with perimeter movement so that post players can then "kick the ball back out" for open perimeter shots. If post defenders try to full-front or three quarter front post players to deny them the ball, we want our offenses to be able to take away weakside defensive help so that lob passes can be made to the fronted post player. The positioning, repositioning and moving of offensive players can be accomplished within the framework of the selected continuity offense. This can give a coaching staff the ability to be able to not only place a designated player into the mid-post area, but to isolate that particular player so that he can attack a lone defender from a high percentage shot location.

⊕ *CONCEPT 39B:*

SUCCESSFUL OFFENSIVE SYSTEMS MUST INCORPORATE AND UTILIZE VARIOUS WAYS TO ISOLATE OFFENSIVE POST PLAYERS--

Still another method used to attack opposing defenders is to position both the traditional as well as inverted perimeter players in the post with little or no interior support for those defenders. If defensive post players play behind, we should be able to easily make the inside pass to that designated post player. We want to have a plan of attack to neutralize double-teams from perimeter defenders with perimeter movement so that post players can then "kick the ball back out" for open perimeter shots. If post defenders try to full-front or three quarter front post players to deny them the ball, we want our offenses to be able to take away weakside defensive help so that lob passes can be made to the fronted post player. The positioning, repositioning and moving of offensive players can be accomplished within the framework of the selected offensive plays/entries. This can give a coaching staff the ability to be able to not only place a designated player into the mid-post area, but to isolate that particular player so that he can attack a lone defender from a high percentage shot location.

⊕ *CONCEPT 40:*

SUCCESSFUL OFFENSIVE SYSTEMS MUST INCORPORATE AND UTILIZE VARIOUS WAYS TO ISOLATE OFFENSIVE PERIMETER PLAYERS--

If an offensive team can isolate players "in the post," that type of attack should be able to also isolate certain offensive players on the perimeter. Those players can attack their defenders on the perimeter as well, with those defenders able to receive much help from defensive teammates. This attack could be executed because of an offensive player's advantage in quickness, ball-handling and/or perimeter shooting skills (or because of a specific defender's overall perimeter defensive weakness.) This would provide that designated offensive player (be it a traditional so-called perimeter player or a post player out on the perimeter) an advantage and a chance to use his driving abilities, his passing and/or perimeter shooting skills, as well as his offensive creative skills. Various forms of off-ball screening on the weakside or overloading the ballside with offensive players can help eliminate helpside defenders to force the opposition into "one-on-one" defensive assignments on the interior. These methods could just as well be integrated somewhere within the structure of the continuity.

⊕ *CONCEPT 41:*

SUCCESSFUL OFFENSIVE SYSTEMS MUST INCORPORATE AND UTILIZE VARIOUS WAYS TO UTILIZE "FALSE (BALL OR PLAYER) MOTION"—

If an offensive team is mentally able to handle it, some offensive sets can be camouflaged by actually beginning in one alignment, then using a form of "false (ball) movement;" before "shifting" the location of both the ball and offensive personnel into the actual desired start point of the offensive attack. With some offensive sets, begin certain offensive plays/entries with "false (ball) movement" and/or "false (player) movement." The "false (player) movement" concept is somewhat comparable to a football team "shifting" from one offensive formation and actually ending up in a different offensive formation before the action actually begins. This somewhat simple action can cause a delay in the defense's read of the offense's objectives. The "(False) Motion" concept is when offensive personnel move from their original locations (on a designated time) after the ball and player movement—disguising what the offense's final alignment and intended action (to confuse and weaken the defense.)

⊕ *CONCEPT 42:*

SUCCESSFUL OFFENSIVE SYSTEMS MUST INCORPORATE AND UTILIZE THE "SHIFTING CONCEPT"—

The "shifting" concept is simply when offensive personnel move or shift (on cue) from their original locations to different locations before the play/entry/quick-hitter actually begins—changing the offensive set to a different offensive set. (Before the defense can adjust.)

$$\oplus \quad \textit{CONCEPT 43:}$$

SUCCESSFUL OFFENSIVE SYSTEMS MUST INCORPORATE AND UTILIZE VARIOUS WAYS TO IMPLEMENT THE "COMBO OFFENSE" CONCEPT—

The "Combo Offense" Concept is executing one continuity offense and when at a designated "trigger point," the offense simply converts to a compatible; but entirely different continuity offense with no delays or interruptions. This causes the opposition's defense to try to read and then react to a different set of offensive actions.

$$\oplus \quad \textit{CONCEPT 44:}$$

SUCCESSFUL OFFENSIVE SYSTEMS MUST INCORPORATE AND UTILIZE THE "DO-SOMETHING-DIFFERENTLY-THAN-WHAT-OTHER-TEAMS-DO" CONCEPT—

This may be construed as an unusual concept, but it is felt that it can be a very valuable concept to implement. It is believed that a portion of the offensive scheme that is used should be somewhat unique and different from the majority of teams (as long as it is still fundamentally sound and not a huge portion of the overall offensive scheme.) Regardless of how minor the action is, doing something different offensively than most teams means that the opposition has not seen the action from other teams and therefore not had the experience in defending that specific type of action or style. This then makes it more difficult for the opposing defenses to defend.

$$\oplus \quad \textit{CONCEPT 45:}$$

SUCCESSFUL OFFENSIVE SYSTEMS MUST INCORPORATE AND UTILIZE VARIOUS WAYS TO IMPLEMENT DECEPTION & DISGUISES—

Keeping the opposition off balance by not showing the defense the offense's actual plan of attack can be accomplished by executing plays/entries/quick-hitters from different alignments/sets and running counters to the plays that are most frequently used.

Showing different looks offers the offense even more deception and having "counter plays" can make the offensive action more deceiving, causing the defense doubt (and slower) in their (defensive) reaction times to the overall (offense's) actions.

✸ <u>*CONCEPT 46:*</u>

SUCCESSFUL OFFENSIVE SYSTEMS MUST INCORPORATE AND UTILIZE A WIDE VARIETY OF SCORERS
(AS WELL AS THE LOCATIONS OF THOSE SCORERS)—

Preventing the opposition's defense from knowing the offense's actual plan of attack can be accomplished by executing a play/entry that either attacks various particular defensive weakness or highlights/utilizes any number of different offensive player's dominant skills. Those skills of the various players could produce shots from various locations on the floor where those players are more efficient and skilled. If the desired shot is not taken, there still could then exist a smooth transitioning into the continuity offense that then either attacks the defense possibly with a different offensive scorer from a different location within the framework of the continuity offense.

✸ <u>*CONCEPT 47:*</u>

SUCCESSFUL OFFENSIVE SYSTEMS MUST INCORPORATE AND UTILIZE VARIOUS WAYS TO IMPLEMENT A WIDE VARIETY OF STYLES
(AS WELL AS THE LOCATIONS OF THOSE SCORERS)—

An offensive team that has the flexibility and the type of players that can thrive in various styles of play as well as the ability to use different game speeds in both the half court and the full-court phases of the game will have a tremendous opportunity for more offensive success. Different offensive styles of play that can be executed by an offensive team not only allow the team to highlight both individual and team offensive playcrs as well as take advantage of defensive weaknesses. Having multiple styles and tempos of play that all can be successfully executed gives the offense another opportunity to succeed as well as also increasing the amount of unpredictability the defense must deal with.

COACHES AND PLAYERS SHOULD
BELIEVE IN, VALUE AND UTILIZE FUNDAMENTAL DRILLS"—

Every athletic team has practice to prepare for their games. What takes place is practice can and will make the difference in whether that team will succeed in the game or fail. It is very likely that a large portion of each of these daily practices will be the fundamental drills. Drills, the way those drills are taught and how they are incorporated in the daily practices will determine whether a coach is a good coach or not and whether the team has a chance to succeed in actual competition or not.

Drills, the way the drills are taught and how they are incorporated in the daily practices will determine whether a coach is a good coach or not and whether the team has a chance to succeed in actual competition or not. "Game-realistic" scenarios must be implemented to simulate "game-like" conditions in the form of drills. Drills must be created to practice the many necessary fundamental skills and techniques. The old cliché, "practice makes perfect" should not apply. A better philosophy that should be used in practices is this: "Perfect practice makes perfect!" That must come through "game-realistic" drills and conditions under a very watchful and scrutinizing coaching staff. Success must come in small consistent increments so that players' confidence in themselves, in their teammates, and in the "system" will slowly and gradually develop.

⊕ *CONCEPT 49:*

COACHES SHOULD BELIEVE IN, VALUE AND ALWAYS UTILIZE
THE CORRECT TEACHING/COACHING METHODS"—

Good coaches are outstanding teachers and motivators. In order for a basketball program to be successful, that coaching staff must demand that every player be fundamentally sound in how to perform all techniques in each of the many phases of the game. That staff then must be able to motivate every player in performing those fundamentals at their highest level of intensity. The staff's attention to detail must be crucial, as well as the positive and constructive criticism that must come with the teaching and the drill work. One successful method of teaching basketball skills is the "whole-part-whole" method with a great emphasis on the how and the why on every technique, every skill, on offense, defense, transition, or whatever technique is being taught to every player as well as the overall team. Players must have confidence in the coaching staff that the methods and the techniques that they are being taught are crucial to the improvement of each player as well as to the overall success of the basketball team.

⊕ *CONCEPT 50:*

COACHES SHOULD BELIEVE IN, AND ALWAYS VALUE THE IMPORTANCE OF DAILY PRACTICE PLANS:--

Good teachers have efficient lesson plans. Good coaching staff must have daily practice plans that are time efficient and productive so that all fundamental offensive and defensive skills, physical conditioning, as well as overall team offenses, defenses, special situations, the understanding of rules. These practice plans must be followed closely but coaches must still be flexible enough to modify the time frames that are pre-planned in the practices. An overall Master Practice Plan must also be designed, recorded, and evaluated for the staff to stay "on track."

⊕ *CONCEPT 51:*

COACHES SHOULD BELIEVE IN, VALUE AND ALWAYS UTLIZE STATISTICS IN PLAYER EVALUATIONS—

An old cliché "if it is worth doing, it is worth measuring" should be used to measure athletic performances both in athletic practices as well as in games. To maintain a good offensive system, that system must be constantly observed and evaluated not only by the number of wins and losses and by passing the "eye test," but also by an objective comparison to previous games, previous season and by opponents' performances. Stats and data analysis are becoming increasingly more important in many sports and basketball must follow that trend. While many of the traditional statistics are still of great value, there are other statistics that can also help a staff get a more accurate read on not only the performance of the system, but also of the current team as well as current individual players' performances. Using many of the traditional data, several ratios and frequencies can be implemented to give the coaching staff more assessment data and a clearer and objective evaluation tool in performances.

✦ *CONCEPT 52:*

COACHES AND PLAYERS SHOULD BELIEVE IN AND VALUE BOTH INDIVIDUAL PLAYERS' OFFENSIVE AND DEFENSIVE GAME PERFORMANCE GRADES ALONG WITH THE OVERALL TEAM'S OFFENSIVE AND DEFENSIVE GRADES BY UTILIZING THE PERFORMANCE GRADING SYSTEM"—

To instill a team-first atmosphere (and not individual glory in the most common statistics such as "most points scored or most rebounds") and to motivate players as well as the overall team; both an Offensive and a Defensive Performance Grading System can and should be implemented. When a coaching staff builds its grading system, it can place a greater emphasis on what they value the most to fit their system and philosophy. Players should not only understand what the coaching staff values the most during games as well as in practices. Individual offensive and defensive grades on every player (regardless of the position and the amount of playing time) can be accumulated as well as overall team grades for both their own team as well as the opposition's grades. These team grades can be compared from game to game as well as from season to season; giving the coaching staff concrete evidence in the evaluation of players, teams and the overall performance of the system. When players see what types of offensive and defensive statistics are of the highest value to the coaching staff by their grades and how those highest grade leaders are recognized in the form of rewards; players will adjust their focus to the same values the coaching staff places on those specific aspects of the game. When those individual statistics are then integrated into the overall team's offensive and defensive grades, the team's attitudes will improve and success will then come to the team.

These are the concepts that serve as the foundation and the building blocks that can establish an effective and productive man-to-man offensive system that can withstand the weather of time. As players and their respective ability levels of both strengths and weaknesses change from one season to the next, in addition to opponents changing; a fundamentally sound offensive system can adjust accordingly without major disruptions or changes to the overall program. This consistency gives both the players and the coaching staff faith and confidence in the system.

Chapter 3
Fundamental Theories
Applied In A Successful Multiple-Phase Man-To-Man Offensive System

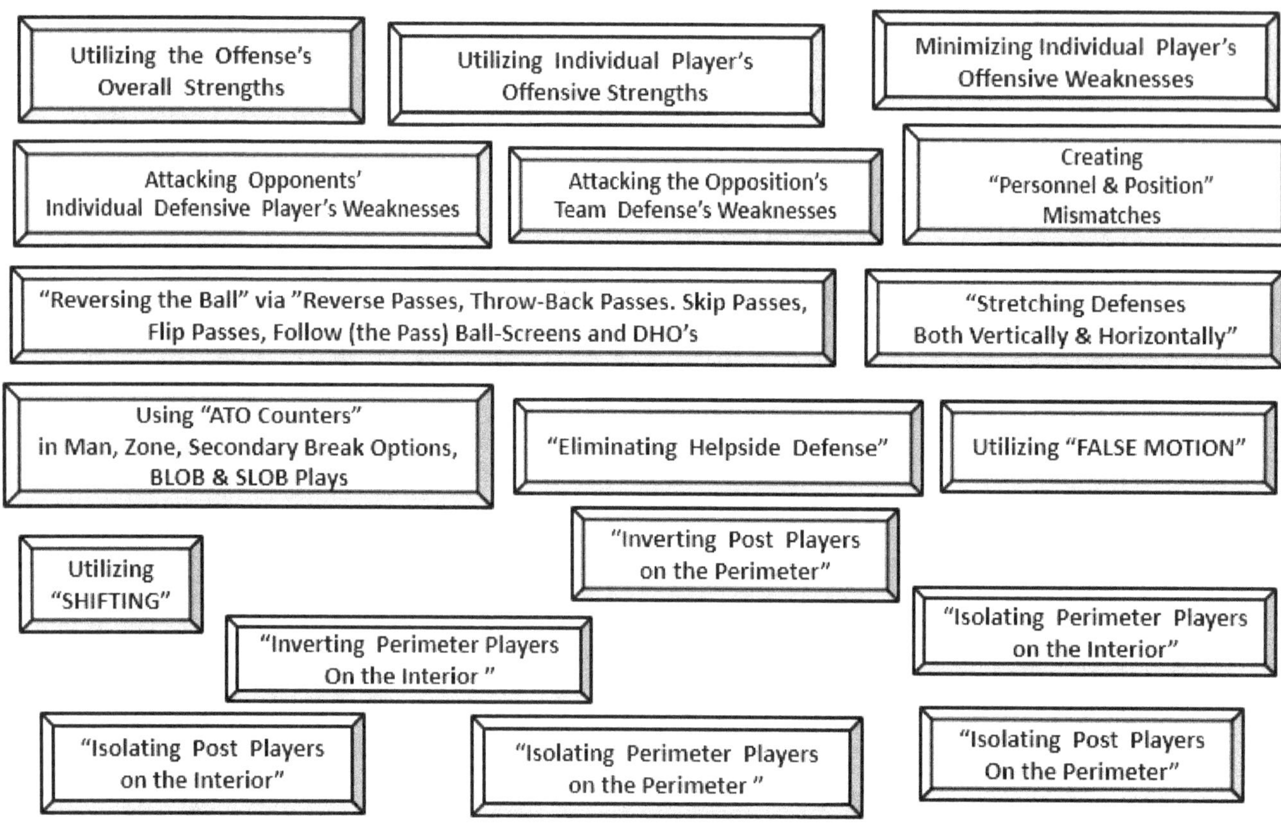

Utilizing the Offense's Overall Strengths
Utilizing Individual Player's Offensive Strengths
Minimizing Individual Player's Offensive Weaknesses
Attacking Opponents' Individual Defensive Player's Weaknesses
Attacking the Opposition's Team Defense's Weaknesses
Creating "Personnel & Position" Mismatches
"Reversing the Ball" via "Reverse Passes, Throw-Back Passes. Skip Passes, Flip Passes, Follow (the Pass) Ball-Screens and DHO's
"Stretching Defenses Both Vertically & Horizontally"
Using "ATO Counters" in Man, Zone, Secondary Break Options, BLOB & SLOB Plays
"Eliminating Helpside Defense"
Utilizing "FALSE MOTION"
Utilizing "SHIFTING"
"Inverting Post Players on the Perimeter"
"Isolating Perimeter Players on the Interior"
"Inverting Perimeter Players On the Interior "
"Isolating Post Players on the Interior"
"Isolating Perimeter Players on the Perimeter "
"Isolating Post Players On the Perimeter"

After the list comes the actual examples of the theories that is the text used in conjunction with the PowerPoint diagrams.

⊕ *THEORY 1:*

UTILIZING THE OFFENSE'S OVERALL STRENGTHS–

When the coaching staff determines the biggest strengths the team possesses should create plays/entries and a continuity offense(s) to then incorporate those strengths as much as possible.

⊕ *THEORY 2:*

UTILIZING INDIVIDUAL PLAYER'S OFFENSIVE STRENGTHS—

After the coaching staff analyzes and evaluates every player's top strengths, players' strengths should also be incorporated within the framework of plays/entries as well as the continuity offense that is to be executed. Individual offensive strengths used will give the overall offense even more weapons to utilize.

⊕ *THEORY 3:*

MINIMIZING INDIVIDUAL PLAYER'S OFFENSIVE WEAKNESSES—

Conversely, every player's weaknesses and offensive deficiencies should be avoided as much as possible within the offensive attack. Those deficiencies should not be ignored in practice sessions but worked on constantly to turn those weaknesses into strengths that can then be utilized more. Those newly developed and improved upon weaknesses can now become offensive strengths that produce even more benefits to the offense.

⊕ *THEORY 4:*

ATTACKING OPPONENTS' INDIVIDUAL DEFENSIVE PLAYER'S WEAKNESSES

After discovering the weaknesses of individual defenders, those should be attacked within the basic overall structure of the offensive attack, giving the offense another type of advantage over the defense.

🏀 <u>THEORY 5:</u>

ATTACKING THE OPPOSITION'S TEAM DEFENSE'S WEAKNESSES—

Just like the individual flaws in the structure and objectives of the opposition's defense, the offense should take advantage of that discovery and attack within the framework of the overall offense.

🏀 <u>THEORY 6:</u>

CREATING "PERSONNEL & POSITION" MISMATCHES—

Within the structure of the plays and the continuity offense(s), the offense looks to discover how offensive players can place themselves in offensive various types of advantages. See Play # 1.

🏀 <u>THEORY 7:</u>

"REVERSING THE BALL" VIA" REVERSE PASSES, THROW-BACK PASSES.
SKIP PASSES, FLIP PASSES, FOLLOW (THE PASS) BALL-SCREENS AND DHO'S—

The quicker and more often an offensive team can change the "defensive ballside" into the "defensive weakside" and vice versa; the more opportunities of success the offense will have available. See Play # 2.

🏀 <u>THEORY 8:</u>

"STRETCHING DEFENSES BOTH VERTICALLY & HORIZONTALLY"—

The more an offense can stretch an opposing defense, the thinner and weaker the defense becomes. This new weaknesses creates even more opportunities for offensive success. See Plays # 3 & 8.

🏀 <u>THEORY 9:</u>

USING "ATO COUNTERS" IN MAN, ZONE, SECONDARY BREAK OPTIONS,
BLOB & SLOB PLAYS—

Using After Time-Out Counter Plays within the overall offensive system gives offensive teams moments to communicate and organize a play/entry that appears to the defense to be known and recognized, when in fact, has similarities with a drastic difference somewhere in the Counter Plays' action. This gives the offense still another offensive advantage. See Play # 5.

🏀 <u>THEORY 10:</u>

"ELIMINATING HELPSIDE DEFENSE"—

When an offense wants to attack a defense on the interior, opposing defenses will want to "load up" their interior defense with extra defenders. Offensive players on the "Ballside" are obviously bigger threats to the defense since they are closer to the ball, so defenses cannot adjust and move those "Ballside defenders" closer to the offensive post players. But offensive players that are on the opposite side of the ball are further away from the ball and are not as viable scoring threats because of their increased distance from the actual basketball. See Plays # 1, 2, 3, 4, 6, 7, & 8.

🏀 <u>THEORY 11:</u>

UTILIZING "FALSE MOTION"—

"When an offense needs to move and adjust specific player's positions and locations from its initial offensive set/alignment, to different locations that are necessary for the continuation of the play; this action (called "False Motion") is vital. See Play # 7.

🏀 <u>THEORY 12:</u>

UTILIZING "SHIFTING"—

This procedure has players shift from one location in an offensive set into a new location. This "shifting" from one set into another set before there is actual offensive action begins helps give the offense still additional offensive advantages by making offensive actions less predictable.

⊕ *THEORY 13:*

"INVERTING POST PLAYERS ON THE PERIMETER"—

When a defined offensive post-player is discovered with so-called "above average offensive talents" that can lead to advantages for that offensive player and the team via offensive players/entries, those situations should be used often. See Play # 8.

⊕ *THEORY 14:*

"INVERTING PERIMETER PLAYERS ON THE INTERIOR"—

Conversely, when a defined offensive perimeter-type player can use his discovered "above average offensive skills" in different locations such as in the Mid or Low post areas, other plays/entries should be built and utilized within the offensive package. In addition, moving so-called "perimeter-type defenders" that are forced to defend someone in the "post areas" should have distinct disadvantages such as lack of experience, training, height, weight, strength, etc. These all could be weaknesses that the offense should and could take advantage of. See Play #2, # 8 & 9

⊕ *THEORY 15:*

"ISOLATING PERIMETER PLAYERS ON THE INTERIOR"—

In addition to placing opposing defenders that are more of a "perimeter-type defenders" that have greater deficiencies and weaknesses in these abnormal situation, when these so-called weaker defenders would need extra help in the form of "double-down traps" or extra interior support. See Play # 8.

🏀 <u>*THEORY 16:*</u>

"ISOLATING POST PLAYERS ON THE INTERIOR"—

When offensive 'post-type players" are placed in these close-to-the-basket and high percentage scoring areas with no extra support defense, the advantages clearly would go to the offensive team. See Plays # 1, 3, 4, 5, 6, 7 and 9.

🏀 <u>*THEORY 17:*</u>

"ISOLATING PERIMETER PLAYERS ON THE PERIMETER"—

To simplify things, "isolating any defender on their so-called "perimeter-type" player in the wide open spaces of the perimeter places the defense in disadvantages for the defense which creates tremendous advantages for the offensive players. See Plays 6 & 8.

🏀 <u>*THEORY 18:*</u>

"ISOLATING POST PLAYERS ON THE PERIMETER"—

Isolating any type of opposing defender in interior areas that are close to the basket and are in high percentage scoring areas is a very difficult task for any type of defender in one-on-one settings. See Play 10.

CHAPTER 4

PRINCIPLES OF A SUCCESSFUL MULTIPLE-PHASE MAN-TO-MAN OFFENSIVE SYSTEM

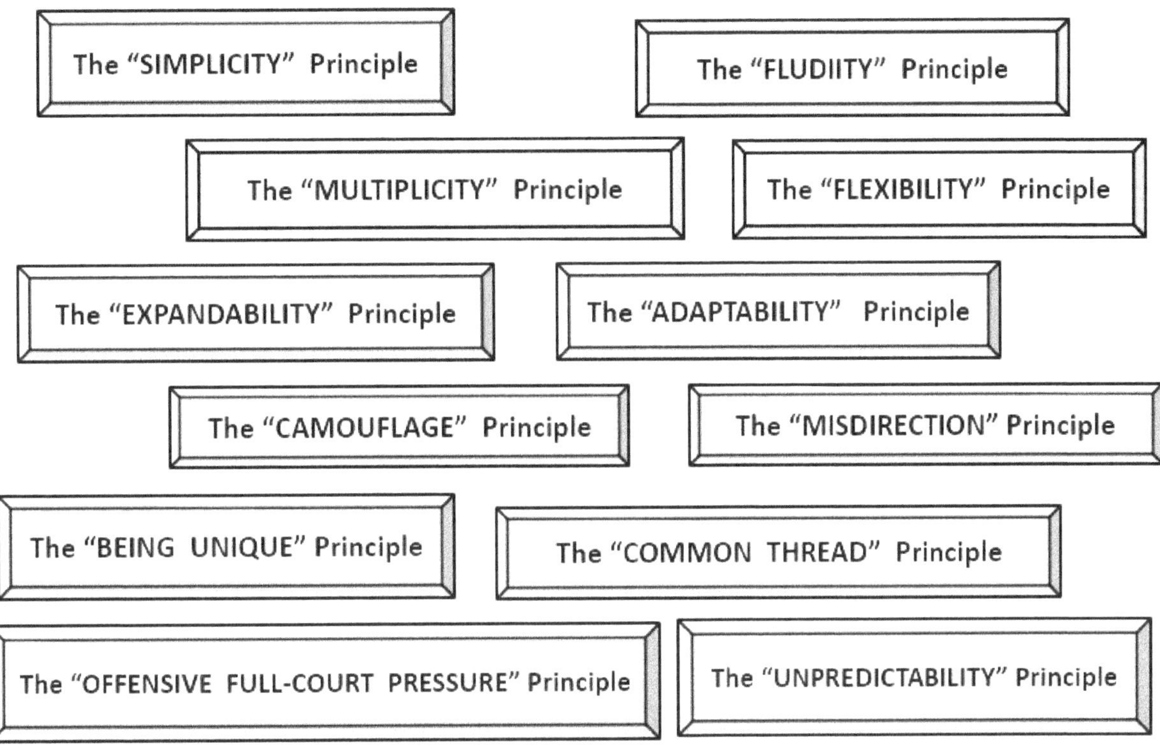

✤ *PRINCIPLE 1—*

THE "SIMPLICITY" REQUIREMENT:

A successful man offensive package must require simplicity (for its own offensive players) possibly as its main component. Players must know what their assignments and responsibilities are in each phase of the overall offensive attack. Coaching staff must evaluate their team's mental abilities as much or more than their squad's physical skills and talents to determine its mental capacity and how much that team can utilize other important offensive characteristics and traits. The level of *"Simplicity"* is different in each specific team. This belongs in the same group of requirements that a successful team's man offense should possess, such as the "Simplicity," the "Fluidity," the "Multiplicity," the "Flexibility," the "Expandability," the "Adaptability" and the "Unpredictability" principles. From these comes the ability for man offenses to be so unpredictable to opposing man defenses that a team's man offensive scheme can be very productive, efficient and successful.

🌐 *PRINCIPLE 2—*

THE "FLUIDITY" REQUIREMENT:

Regardless of the number of offensive sets utilized and the number of offensive plays/entries/quick-hitters that are implemented; each play must have the ability to instantly, seamlessly and fluidly flow into the chosen continuity offense. This gives the offensive package separate (on paper) phases of offensive attack that blend so smoothly that it appears on the court to be one long continuous offensive assault on the opposition's man-to-man defense. This is the very important "Fluidity" requirement that each phase of the offense needs to be successful.

🌐 *PRINCIPLE 3—*

THE "MULTIPLICITY" REQUIREMENT:

Once the "Simplicity" and the "Fluidity" principles have been integrated into the multiple-phase offensive system, many other very important principles can be implemented, with the "Multiplicity" trait quite possibly being the next most important. This is because the "Multiplicity" principle is the bridge to many other more valuable principles. Being able to have multiple plays out of multiple sets/alignments and multiple continuities is invaluable to an offensive system. This allows the offense to be more varied and less predictable to opposing defenses, while still maintaining a degree of simplicity for your own team, but it must be stressed to NOT have too many plays or alignments. Being multiple offensively allows an offensive team to possess more "weapons" and more ways to attack and defeat opposing defenses. Some teams could also have more than one continuity offense; but again, too much could mentally hamper and diminish an offensive team's effectiveness. Each team will have its own set of limitations on how multiple it can be offensively. Having the correctly chosen continuity offense that every play in the offensive arsenal can smoothly transition into not only gives the offensive team still another vehicle to attack the defense, but a form of a security blanket. If the play breaks down, the team can go back to its continuity offense that a team has been accustomed to and can maintain its attack. Each play that does not create the desired shot can seamlessly flow into the (fundamentally sound) continuity offense that has its own methods and ways to successfully attack the defense. This would be a tremendous advantage to the offense and a huge disadvantage to the opposition's defense.

 PRINCIPLE 4—

THE "FLEXIBILITY" REQUIREMENT:

An offensive package that is "Multiple" also allows the offense to be "Flexible," "Expandable," and "Adaptable." If an offensive team has the ability to change its method of attack because of its own specific strengths and weaknesses along with the opposition's defensive strengths and weaknesses, it will be a much more successful offense and add more ways to attack the opposition's defense. This "Flexibility" characteristic increases a team's offensive strengths exponentially.

🏀 *PRINCIPLE 5—*

THE "EXPANDABILITY" REQUIREMENT:

An overall offensive scheme that possesses the strength of also being expandable always gives the offensive team the potential to add other forms of attack as the season progresses to become a more explosive offensive team. This could be by adding extra plays either out of the same offensive set or out of an entirely different offensive alignment. The number of options and/or counter-options to the designated continuity offense could be expanded to give the continuity offense more fire-power.

🏀 *PRINCIPLE 6—*

THE "ADAPTABILITY" REQUIREMENT:

If an offensive team has the ability to change or vary its plan of attack because of middle-of-the-game "time and score" situations, because of its own personnel changes or the opposition's defensive actions and adjustments; then it increases a team's chance for a more successful season. This important requirement is called *"Adaptability"* Principle.

🏀 *PRINCIPLE 7—*

THE "CAMOUFLAGE" REQUIREMENT:

Offensive teams in every sport are constantly attempting to fool its competitive defensive opponents to force those defenses into being more vulnerable and susceptible to the offense's actual plan of attack. Offensive teams try to also conceal their actual objectives until the very last moment in order to gain as much of an advantage as well possible over the opposition's defense. When offensive teams hide its own objectives, its strengths and its team weaknesses while at the same time looking to attack the opponents' weaknesses by camouflaging their methods of attack, it will always keep the opposition off-balance, confused and hesitant. This gives the offense advantages over the defense and allows the offense to be even more unpredictable. Deceiving the opposition can occur in the beginning parts of plays/entries by incorporating *"shifting" and "false motion" actions.* This allows the offense to utilize and take advantage of one of the more important principles in every offensive scheme and attack—and that is called the *"Unpredictability"* Principle.

⊕ *PRINCIPLE 8—*

THE "MISDIRECTION" REQUIREMENT:

In addition to concealing until the last possible moment of what an offensive team is attempting to do and how it is attempting to attack an opposing defense at the beginning of the offensive action, an offensive team can also attempt to confuse and fool a defense by utilizing additional "false motion" further into the offensive movement and also by utilizing planned *"misdirection actions"* by using different techniques and methods. This can often help neutralize defensive strengths and actually turn those strengths into defensive weaknesses. This offensive principle also helps effectively utilize possibly the most important offensive principles that is needed in every offensive scheme and plan of attack—once again, the *"Unpredictability"* Principle.

⊕ *PRINCIPLE 9—*

THE "BEING UNIQUE" REQUIREMENT:

As stated previously, offensive basketball teams are constantly attempting to gain advantages over their defensive opponents. One principle that can be applied to for an offensive coach to thoroughly evaluate his/her own team's overall offensive skills and talents as well as the opposition. If a coach has very similar forms and methods of the offensive attack that his/her team's opponent utilizes. That means that defensive opponents that are accustomed to defending very similar offensive actions will become more proficient in defending those similar attacks and methods. Therefore, if a coach decides to use different methods of offensive attacks that defenses are not accustomed to seeing, not knowing how to properly defend those unique offensive actions, the defensive opponents will have a much more difficult time in understanding, preparing for and correctly defending those different types of offensive actions. A coaching staff should not make drastic changes to be different for the sake of being different, but if those changes will accent his/her team's skills, minimize his/her team's weaknesses and also force the opposition into preparing for and playing against those changes; the offense will be more successful. These changes in the offensive scheme can often help neutralize defensive strengths and highlight defensive weaknesses. This will help the offense with the *"Unpredictability"* Principle.

⊕ *PRINCIPLE 10—*

THE "FULL-COURT OFFENSIVE PRESSURE PLACED ON THE OPPOSITION'S DEFENSES" REQUIREMENT:

Full Court pressure defenses are practical weapons on the defensive side of the ball that can help the opposition control the tempo of the game and can affect the physical, emotional and mental conditioning of offenses. But there is no rule that says that a team cannot magnify that same weapon by applying offensive pressure and stress on the opponent's defensive team at the full court level. Our belief is to apply "full court offensive pressure on the opposition's defense." This means that a coach's offensive team could apply a large degree of pressure on the opposition's defense by utilizing every possible fastbreak opportunity that is created. These could take place immediately not only after the opposition's turnovers and missed shots, but also after opponent's 'made' shots. This quick in-bounding after "their scores," can also be an effective deterrent against the opposition's defensive attempt to try to full-court pressure your team's offense.

⊕ *PRINCIPLE 11—*

"COMMON THREADS IN ALL THE VARIOUS FORMS OFFENSIVE ATTACK" REQUIREMENT:

The full utilization and integration of all forms/methods of offensive attacks; be it half-court offensive attacks, offensive out-of-bounds attacks, full-court offensive attacks off of Full-Court Press Offensive attacks, as well as all transitions attacks must all have the same common threads that integrate the same offensive concepts and philosophies. These various forms of attacks begin at different points of time in all offensive/defensive positions that also begin in different locations of the court. While there are different origins and different times of initiation, the common threads will help make all of these attacks a more effective and successful attacks against the opposition's defenses.

⊕ *PRINCIPLE 12—*

THE "UNPREDICTABILITY" REQUIREMENT:

A Multiple-Phase Offensive System that is "Multiple," and/or "Flexible," and/or "Expandable" and/or "Adaptable" as well as able to "Camouflage" its objectives and often make it appear the offensive action is going in one particular direction before suddenly switching directions provides even more potential advantages and benefits to the offensive team. Conversely, those also create disadvantages and problems for the opposing defenses. These principles helps create the single most advantage for any and every offensive scheme and attack—the *"Unpredictability"* Principle. If an offensive team can make changes in how it attacks opposition's defenses from game to game and even from quarter to quarter of the same game, it makes it extremely difficult for any defense to attempt to solve the offensive plan that can constantly change. A defensive team that does not know what to expect from the offense has a much more difficult time to defend any offensive attack.

CHAPTER 5
VITAL TRAITS AND CHARACTERISTICS USED IN A SUCCESSFUL MULTIPLE-PHASE OFFENSIVE SYSTEM

⊕ *TRAIT 1:*

THE "SIMPLICITY" TRAIT/CHARACTERISTIC—

A successful man offensive package must require simplicity (for its own offensive players) possibly as its main component. Players must know what their assignments and responsibilities are in each phase of the overall offensive attack. Coaching staff must evaluate their team's mental abilities as much or more than their squad's physical skills and talents to determine its mental capacity and how much that team can utilize other important offensive TRAITS and CHARACTERISTICS. This trait belongs to the same group of concepts of a successful team's man offense should possess, such as: "Simplicity," "Fluidity," "Multiplicity," "Flexibility," "Expandability," "Adaptability" and "Unpredictability." From these characteristics comes the ability for man offenses to be so unpredictable to opposing man defenses that a team's man offensive scheme can be very productive, efficient, and successful.

⊕ *TRAIT 2:*

THE "FLUIDITY" TRAIT/CHARACTERISTIC--

Regardless of the number of offensive alignments/sets utilized and the number of offensive plays/entries/quick-hitters that are implemented; each play must have the ability to instantly, seamlessly and fluidly flow into the designated continuity offense. On paper, this gives the offensive package separate phases or layers of offensive attack that blend and transition so seamlessly and smoothly that it appears on the court to be one long continuous offensive assault on the opposition's man-to-man defense. This is the very important *"Fluidity"* characteristic.

⊕ *TRAIT 3A:*

THE "MULTIPLICITY" TRAIT/CHARACTERISTIC–

Once the "Simplicity," the "Fluidity," along with the "Deception & Misdirection" TRAITS and CHARACTERISTICS have been integrated into the man offensive package, many other very important characteristics/TRAITS and CHARACTERISTICS can be implemented, with the "Multiplicity" trait quite possibly being the next most important. This is because the "Multiplicity" characteristics are the bridge to many other more valuable TRAITS and CHARACTERISTICS. Being multiple in the number of plays, sets/alignments and possibly other continuities is an invaluable trait of an offensive system. This allows the offense to be more varied and less predictable to opposing defenses, while still maintaining a degree of simplicity for your own team. A philosophy is that an offensive team can have multiple plays/entries and can run out of multiple sets/alignments, but it must be stressed to NOT have too many plays or alignments.

⊕ _TRAIT 3B:_

THE "MULTIPLICITY" TRAIT/CHARACTERISTIC--

Being multiple offensively allows an offensive team to possess more "weapons" and more ways to attack and defeat opposing defenses. Some teams could also have more than one continuity offense; but we believe that no more than two continuities. Each team will have its own set of limitations on how multiple it can be offensively. Having the correctly chosen continuity offense that every play in the offensive arsenal can smoothly transition into not only gives the offensive team still another vehicle to attack the defense, but a form of a security blanket. If the play breaks down, the team can go back to its continuity offense that the team has been accustomed to and can maintain its attack. Each play that does not create the desired shot can seamlessly flow into the (fundamentally sound) continuity offense that has its own methods and ways to successfully attack the defense. This would be a tremendous advantage to the offense and a huge disadvantage to the opposition's defense. Therefore, the _"Multiplicity"_ trait is an invaluable weapon to all offensive packages/schemes.

⊕ _TRAIT 4:_

THE "FLEXIBILITY" TRAIT"--

An offensive package that is "Multiple" also allows the offense to be "Flexible," "Expandable," and "Adaptable." If an offensive team has the ability to change its method of attack because of different opponents having varying strengths and weaknesses, the offensive package will be much more successful and add more ways to attack the opposition's defense, it increases its offensive strengths exponentially. This is the offensive package's important characteristic called the _"Flexibility"_ trait.

⊕ _TRAIT 5:_

THE "EXPANDABILITY" TRAIT/CHARACTERISTIC--

An overall offensive scheme that possesses the strength of also being expandable always gives the offensive team the potential to add other types or forms of attack as the season progresses to become a more explosive offensive team. This characteristic is what we call the *"Expandability"* trait.

⊕ *TRAIT 6:*

THE "ADAPTABILITY" TRAIT/CHARACTERISTIC--

If an offensive team has the ability to change or vary its plan of attack because of game "time and situation" factors in the middle of a game or season because of personnel changes during a game or the season, then it increases a team's chance for a more successful season. Unexpected changes in personnel clearly could call in changes in styles, tempo of games, offensive plays, and/or continuity offenses. This is the important *"Adaptability"* characteristic that is a necessary trait for all successful offensive systems.

⊕ *TRAIT 7:*

THE "UNPREDICTABILITY" TRAIT/CHARACTERISTIC--

An offensive package that is "Multiple," and/or "Flexible," and/or "Expandable" and/or "Adaptable" and possesses "Deception & Misdirection" characteristics will very much possess the all-important weapon of being unpredictable to all opposing defenses. If an offensive team can make changes in how it attacks opposition's defenses from game to game and even from quarter to quarter of the same game, it makes it extremely difficult for any opposition to attempt to solve the offensive plan that can constantly change and adjust to the defense. This is the all-important *"Unpredictability"* offensive characteristic.

⊕ *TRAIT 8:*

THE "CAMOUFLAGING AND DECEIVING OF THE OPPOSITION" TRAIT/CHARACTERISTIC--

Offensive systems that can effectively deceive opposing defenses will increase defensive mistakes, confusion, breakdowns, and hesitancy. These defensive results will provide great amounts of offensive productivity, efficiency, and success in the offense's actions, plays, and continuity offenses. Many of the offensive sets/alignments discussed in this book are symmetrically balanced; each play could initially attack either side of the floor. This makes each play ambidextrous and therefore even more unpredictable for the opposition until the very last instant. Another method for offenses is to implement offensive counters, counter-options and/or ATOs. These organized and pre-planned, pre-taught, pre-coached actions by the offensive team will maintain the offensive advantage of preserving the unpredictability factor. This sustains the "offensive actions that attack defensive reactions" factor. "Shifting" and "False Motion" can also be integrated to add to the camouflaging, the hiding of the plays' objectives court just before the beginning actions of the entry/play/quick-hitter starts. It takes place after the ball has crossed the timeline but before there are passes by the Point Guard or before screens are set for that same Point Guard. We define the "False Motion" within offensive systems as the actual movement of both the ball and players that can also help deceive opponents in the ways an offensive team is attempting to attack the opposition's defense.

✪ *TRAIT 9:*

THE "DISGUISE/HIDING/COVERING" TRAIT--

This important trait can be used so that every entry/play could be camouflaged in the same offensive set or in other alignments. This makes many offensive actions more unpredictable and therefore, tougher to defend; almost every entry could be executed with or without "Iverson Cuts." There can be very simple and basic offensive actions that can be implemented off and on that can change the entire cosmetic appearance of various offensive sets/alignments in addition to many plays/entries. Some entries could substitute Iverson Cuts with "L-Cuts" where both 03 and 02 break up and out from their initial Deep Corner locations to the FT Line extended, but remain on the same side of the floor. When and if "Iverson Cuts" are appropriate for a play, the designated "high cutter" (03 for example) and the "low cutter" (02) can be easily switched to give each play a different cosmetic look. Mixing in each play with "L-Cuts, with a crossing of the two players through the lane, or executing "Iverson Cuts" and switching whether 03 or 02 is the high Iverson Cutter and the opposite player being the low (Iverson) Cutter gives each individual play/entry many more different 'looks' that will momentarily cause the defense to hesitate at the initial action of the play/entry and therefore allow the offense to deceive defenses even more so. Opposing defenses may have to compete and defend these different ways the offense may attack defenses. Executing basically the same play, but out of various offensive sets, is another easy and simple method for the offense to utilize in the overall offensive system.

⊕ ***TRAIT 10:***

THE "VARIETY" TRAIT/CHARACTERISTIC--

The more opportunities an offensive team can have in implementing various players that also have different levels of athleticism and different offensive strengths, the more legitimate offensive weapons an offensive team can have. The more multiple the offense can be within its wide variety of offensive entries and also in the final phase of the offensive attack—be it a Motion Offense or a Continuity Offense, the more methods a team can successfully attack a defense. A successful offensive system can include a range of offensive phases, levels or waves of attack that all have the unique ability to be able to flow smoothly from one part to the next part of the offensive attack. A coaching staff cannot just become more multiple for the sake of being more multiple. A team's offensive system must be compatible with the coaching staff's philosophies as well as fitting the team's offensive personnel's overall basketball strengths and skills as well as its basketball intelligence. Too much of anything good can be bad. An offensive team cannot be bogged down mentally with too many offensive sets, too many offensive plays, too many continuity offenses, too many counter-options, etc. Another factor that can be implemented within an offensive system is a coaching staff that properly selects the proper style of play to maximize that particular team's success. Within reason, there can be a range of styles of play that meet an offensive team's overall strengths that can be chosen, changed, and modified from one season to the next. Adjusting and modifying the different varieties of tempo and style of play can play a vital role in the success of an offensive team. Implementing a wide range of methods to attack defenses with primarily inside oriented or perimeter oriented attacks can (and should be) altered to fit each team's needs for that specific season. The methods to attack the presumed opponents' defensive weaknesses with the current team's offensive strengths will have to be diversified from season to season and possibly from shorter time periods. The *"Variety"* trait is also a very important component of successful offensive packages/schemes.

⊕ *TRAIT 11:*

THE "MISDIRECTION" TRAIT/CHARACTERISTIC—

The offensive teams in every sport are constantly attempting to fool its competitive defensive opponents to make them vulnerable and susceptible to the offense's actual plan of attack. With deception, the offensive team is trying to disguise its own strengths while hiding its team weaknesses while at the same time looking to attack the opponents' weaknesses. This trait is tied directly to the offensive scheme of "Unpredictability," again making the offense a more efficient form of attack. Deception can occur in the beginning parts of plays/entries by incorporating the invaluable *"Misdirection"* trait. This trait in the offensive scheme can often help neutralize defensive strengths and actually turn those strengths into defensive weaknesses. The *"Misdirection"* trait helps institute one of the other more important TRAITS and CHARACTERISTICS in every offensive (as well as defensive) schemes and attacks—the *"Unpredictability"* Trait.

⊕ *TRAIT 12:*

THE USE OF UNIQUE ACTIONS/SCHEMES DIFFERENT THAN MOST OPPONENTS' ACTIONS.

A successful offensive system does not have to be the same as most other offensive systems. In fact, the more unique an offensive system is in relationship to its opponents; the greater chance it can become a dominant and successful system. That is only when that specific offensive system actually fits not only the coaching staff's philosophies and beliefs but that it corresponds to the actual talent levels, strengths and weaknesses of the offensive personnel on that season's team. An offensive system that is unique for the sake of being unique will not make an offensive system successful or productive. But when philosophies and personnel strengths match and can fit in with that different type of offensive style, its tempo and its ways to attack the opposition's defenses; it can be a very successful system. Because of the uniqueness of the offense, opposing defenses will not have been able to acquire a knowledge of the system, will not have the experience to understand strengths, weaknesses, and objectives. To opposing defenses, this different offensive system will be more difficult to understand, harder to prepare opposing players to defend it and much more difficult to be able to predict the actions of the offense. These reasons simply start adding to more and more offensive advantages and widen the gap between an offense's "actions" that are attempted to be defended by an opposing team's "reactions."

CHAPTER 6

METHODS AND TECHNIQUES USED IN A SUCCESSFUL MULTIPLE-PHASE MAN-TO-MAN OFFENSIVE SYSTEM

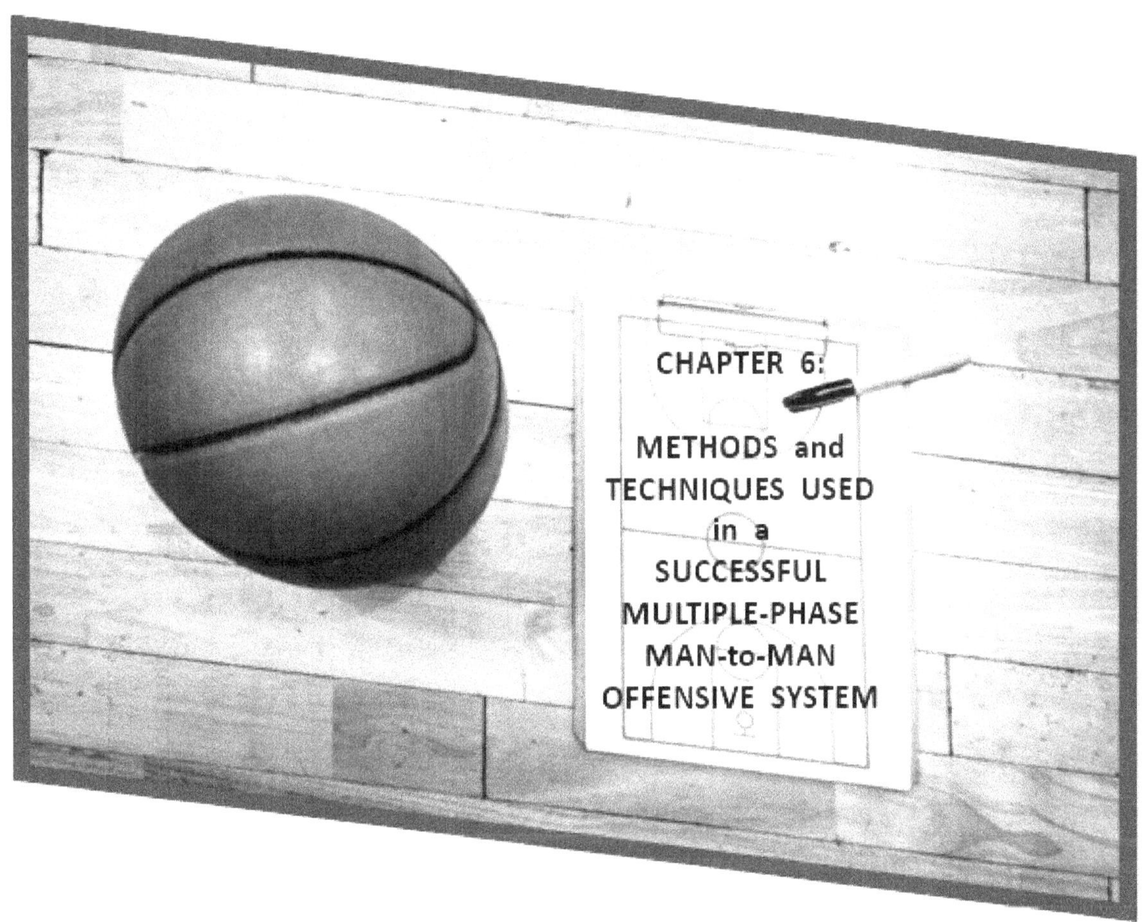

There are many techniques that could and should be implemented in some manner within the framework of both the package of offensive plays as well as within the offensive continuity or motion offense's scheme. The more of these techniques used and applied by the offense's entries as well as the continuities used; the more weapons that offensive team can possess. More weapons help an offensive team probe opponent's defenses for both individual as well as overall team defensive weaknesses. These techniques could be categorized as either various types of cuts, various types of off-ball screens and diverse types of ball-screens that have ending types of actions following those different types of ball-screens. An offensive team wants to maximize those fundamentally sound techniques without overloading a team with too many techniques incorporated within the offense. The package of various entries/plays should be able to implement more of a variety of these techniques than the desired continuity or motion offense.

✪ *TECHNIQUE 1:*

**ALL OFFENSIVE PLAYERS SHOULD REALIZE THE
OFFENSIVE EFFECTIVENESS AS
WELL AS TO BE ABLE TO EXECUTE THE "INSIDE PASS"—**

Offensive players should make bounce-passes "away" from the defenders of their interior pass receiver unless the post player is fronted. If the offensive post player is fronted, the passer should then lob the ball "away" from the fronting defender towards the corner of the backboard. We want all "inside passes" to be "bounce passes" except for "lob passes" when playing against fronting interior defenders.

✪ *TECHNIQUE 2:*

**ALL OFFENSIVE PLAYERS SHOULD REALIZE
OFFENSIVE EFFECTIVENESS AS WELL AS TO BE ABLE TO
EXECUTE THE PROPER "INSIDE PASS" TECHNIQUES—**

Offensive players should make bounce-passes to their post-up teammate's hand that is "AWAY" from that interior defender unless the post player is fronted. If the post defender is ¾ fronting on the offensive post player's "high" side, the ball should be passed to the outstretched "low" hand of the post player. If the defender is ¾ fronting on the "low" side, the ball should be passed to the post player's "high" hand of that teammate. If the defender is winning the "battle of the feet" and is effectively denying the inside pass, a quick pass to another perimeter teammate should have a much better passing angle to make that successful inside pass. If the offensive post player is fronted defensively, the passer should then lob the ball "away" from the fronting defender towards the corner of the backboard. Another method would be to make a quick, accurate and safe "skip pass" and have the interior player then "seal off" his fronting defender. If the post defender is playing completely behind, the perimeter passer should make a hard bounce pass and slightly shade the pass either low or high to set the post player up for maximum shot effectiveness.

ALL OFFENSIVE PLAYERS SHOULD REALIZE
OFFENSIVE EFFECTIVENESS AS WELL AS TO BE
ABLE TO EXECUTE "SKIP PASSES"—

Perimeter players should not hesitate on making "skip-passes" across the court. "Skip-passes" are an instant method of reversing the ball from one side of the court to the other side. Reversing the ball is an integral concept for successful offenses to be able to attack both inside and also on the perimeter. "Skip-passes" will also discourage "man defenses" from providing good helpside defense in the lane from the weakside of the offense, off of the "skip pass." After "skip passes" are made, post players should seal off the post defenders that deny them the ball on the original ballside and be prepared to receive the pass from the original weakside. "Skip-passes" can provide offenses with open "catch & shoot 3's" or opportunities to "shot fake & create." When MAN defenders react to the "skip pass," a second "skip pass" back to the original 'ballside' can be very effective. A phrase "One good skip pass deserves another" should be taught and utilized in every type of offense that is utilized.

🏀 *TECHNIQUE # 4A:*

ALL OFFENSIVE PLAYERS SHOULD REALIZE
OFFENSIVE EFFECTIVENESS AS WELL AS TO BE ABLE TO
UTILIZE THE "THROW-BACK REVERSE PASS"--

Perimeter players should be able to execute the all-important 'Throw-back (Reverse) Pass' that could/should be used off of the dribble. This pass being made off of the dribble makes an even quicker misdirection actions that can surprise both the on-ball defender but also all of the off-ball defenders. With it being off of the dribble and reversing the ball, it prevents all defenders from being able to react as quickly to the pass. This immediate and most likely surprising pass makes it more difficult for the initial 'helpside defenders' to adjust and become the new 'ballside defenders,' as well as making it tougher from those initial 'ballside defenders' to adjust to become the new 'helpside defenders.' The likely surprise and the quickness of being able to execute the pass to a new offensive threat can create several types of defensive weaknesses, both on the interior as well as in the interior.

ALL OFFENSIVE PLAYERS SHOULD REALIZE
OFFENSIVE EFFECTIVENESS AS WELL AS TO BE ABLE TO
EXECUTE THE "HAMMER PASS"--

Perimeter players should also be able to execute a somewhat newer type of pass that is gaining popularity in the NBA and major college basketball. This pass comes after a ball-handler drives the baseline and when a 'helpside defender' rotates over to stop the ball, a weakside offensive player drifts down towards the Weakside Deep Corner behind the '3 Pt.' Line to receive the so-called "Hammer Pass." This driving action stretches the defense both vertically as well as horizontally. Even when the opposing defenders execute the fundamentally sound defensive rotations, there very likely will be an offensive player available for an open '3.' Again, with the "Hammer Pass" being executed off of the dribble and reversing the ball in a very unique manner, it keeps the opposition from being able to react as quickly to the pass. Just as the "Throw-back Pass" can attack defenses in somewhat of a unique way, the "Hammer Pass" will also cause the opposition's defense problems in the conversion from initial 'helpside defenders' becoming new 'ballside defenders' and vice versa.

⊕ *TECHNIQUE # 5A:*

ALL OFFENSIVE PLAYERS SHOULD REALIZE
OFFENSIVE EFFECTIVENESS AS WELL AS TO BE ABLE TO EXECUTE THE PROPER
DRIBBLING TECHNIQUES—

Another objective of this continuity offense is to have the capability for players at times to have the freedom within the structure of the offense to be able to attack individual defenders off of the dribble. This is done partially by giving offensive players the proper spacing to be able to create within the structure of the offense. Even though both dribbling techniques are primarily zone offense dribbling both the ball defender as well as helping defenders to create both high percentage inside shots as well as open "3s" as well as other pass receivers being able to drive to the basket. Any dribbler can either attack the initial on-ball defender and when that defender needs help, that dribble/driver can "penetrate & pitch" to a receiver on the perimeter for open shots or another driving opportunity or he can "drive & dump" to a post player close to the basket. Even if the shot is missed by the driver or the pass-receiving teammate, the "stick-back" opportunities are greatly enhanced because of less successful defensive box-outs by the defense's forced scrambling rotations.

⊕ *TECHNIQUE # 5B:*

**ALL OFFENSIVE PLAYERS SHOULD REALIZE
OFFENSIVE EFFECTIVENESS AS WELL AS TO BE ABLE TO
EXECUTE THE VARIOUS FORMS OF "PERIMETER PULL" DRIBBLES"--**

Offensive players must at times, have the freedom within the structure of the offense to be able to attack individual defenders off of the dribble. This is done partially by giving offensive players the proper spacing to be able to create within the structure of the offense. Offenses must constantly move both the basketball and offensive personnel quickly and efficiently. The more frequent and the quicker the movement of both the ball and personnel, the greater the chance for defensive breakdowns. Even though this dribbling technique is thought of primarily as a zone offensive dribbling technique, these 'perimeter pull' dribbles will attack both the ball defender as well as attacking all off-the-ball defenders. These various types of 'perimeter pull' dribbles will create both high percentage inside shots as well as open "3s" for off-the-ball offensive teammates. as well as other pass receivers being able to drive to the basket.

⊕ *TECHNIQUE # 5C:*

**ALL OFFENSIVE PLAYERS SHOULD REALIZE
OFFENSIVE EFFECTIVENESS AS WELL AS TO BE ABLE
TO EXECUTE ALL OF THE VARIOUS FORMS OF "PERIMETER PULL" DRIBBLES"--**

When an offensive player dribbles vertically down from the 'Wing' area down towards the 'Deep Corner' area, this particular 'Perimeter Pull' Dribbles could be specifically called 'Down-Dribbles.' 'Up-Dribbles' are vertical dribbles in the opposite direction, from the initial 'Deep Corner' up towards the 'Wing' area. Both of these types of dribbles can also serve as a method of improving the passing angle so as to deliver the ball to a Post player near the 'Ballside Block.' Both of these types of dribbles can stretch the defense vertically and therefore weaken the defense's interior. These dribbles also of these particular types of dribbles definitely force opponents' helpside defenders to move as the ball is moved either down towards the baseline or up towards the timeline. When helpside defenders have to provide interior support defense. When a ball-handler makes a 'perimeter pull' dribble across the top of the defense (called a 'Drag Dribble), the action not only reverses the ball to the opposite side of the floor, which causes opposing defenders to adjust to the movement of the ball, to switch their individual positioning, stances, and defensive responsibilities from 'helpside to ballside' or 'ballside to helpside' responsibilities. With all five defenders having to make those major types of changes and adjustments (with the offense possibly only moving one player that has the ball), the opportunities for the offense to capitalize on possibly several breakdowns is great. This simple 'Drag Dribble' also stretches the defense horizontally, and therefore again weakens the defensive interior.

⊕ *TECHNIQUE # 5D:*

ALL OFFENSIVE PLAYERS SHOULD REALIZE
OFFENSIVE EFFECTIVENESS AS WELL AS TO BE ABLE TO
EXECUTE THE VARIOUS FORMS OF "PENETRATION" DRIBBLES"--

Any dribbler can either attack the initial on-ball defender and when he slightly penetrates into one of the gaps between the ball and the next closest defender on either side of the ball. That action can force a defensive teammate to not only help but to then end up in a location and/or stance disadvantage when and if the ball is then passed to his specific man. That can then cause a defensive breakdown where a second defensive opponent must attempt to help the new ball-defender that is in trouble. This chain reaction can continue until the offense can attack the weakened and scrambling and out-of-position defense with an inside shot or an open perimeter shot. A situation can also take place where the on-ball defender does not have a perimeter teammate that can help out. That dribbler can then dribble and make an even deeper penetration and when that defender needs help, that dribble/driver can "penetrate and pitch" to a receiver on the perimeter for open shots or another driving opportunity or he can "drive and dump" to a post player close to the basket. Even if the shot is missed by the driver or the pass-receiving teammate, the "stick-back" opportunities are greatly enhanced because of less successful defensive box-outs by the defense's forced scrambling rotations.

$$\oplus \quad \textit{T\scriptsize{ECHNIQUE}} \textbf{\textit{\# 6:}}$$

ALL POST PLAYERS SHOULD REALIZE OFFENSIVE EFFECTIVENESS
AS WELL AS TO BE ABLE TO EXECUTE
THE VARIOUS LOW AND HIGH POST FLASH-CUTS—

All offensive players operating in the low post areas should understand the importance and how to execute flash post cuts to both the low post and the high post with or without the aid of off-ball screens. If screens are set for the flashing post player, that player should first set his defender up with more than one-step V-Cuts and then scraping shoulder to shoulder with the screener. In addition, the actual screener should be prepared to counter defensive switches by sealing off the new defender and also becoming a flash-post player.

$$\oplus \quad \textit{T\scriptsize{ECHNIQUE}} \textbf{\textit{\# 7:}}$$

ALL POST PLAYERS SHOULD REALIZE
OFFENSIVE EFFECTIVENESS AS WELL AS TO BE
ABLE TO EXECUTE THE "DUCK-IN CUT"—

Post players should use the "Duck-In" Cut and be ready to then use either a "power" move or a "face-up" move. This is particularly effective when the ball is passed inside from the top of the key. Regardless of how the opposition's post defender tries to defend the "Duck-In" Cut, the offense has an effective method of defeating the defensive action. The "Spin-Screen and Post Up" move should also be implemented when the defense is fronting the "Duck-In" move (with help from a screen from a second interior player.)

$$\oplus \quad \textit{T\scriptsize{ECHNIQUE}} \textbf{\textit{\# 8A:}}$$

ALL POST PLAYERS SHOULD REALIZE OFFENSIVE EFFECTIVENESS AS WELL AS TO BE
ABLE TO EXECUTE THE LOW-POST, THE HIGH POST FLASH-CUTTING AND THE
"DUCK-IN" CUTTING TECHNIQUES--

All offensive players operating in the low post areas (including "inverted" perimeter players) should understand the importance and how to execute flash post cuts to both the low post and the high post with or without the aid of off-ball screens. If screens are set for the flashing post player, that player should first set his defender up with multi-step V-Cuts and then scraping shoulder to shoulder with the screener. in addition, the actual screener should be prepared to counter defensive switches by sealing off the new defender and also becoming a flash-post player.

When the defense tries to play on the side of the offensive post player, those post players should be able to use the "Show & Go Opposite" Power Move and the "Olajuwon Whirl Move"

When the defense presents ¾ or full denial in the post, the offense should execute the "Seal & Lob Pass" action between passer and post player.

When the defense plays directly behind, the "Duck-In" Cut the "Sikma Move" should be executed o square up to the basket (before then executing the (perimeter) "Blast" or "Cross-Over" Move to attack the defender.

If there are defensive "Double-Down" traps executed, the offensive post player must be aware of offensive perimeter players that are making "Drift Cuts" to get open and be able to make the "Kick-Out" Pass to the open perimeter teammate.

⊕ *TECHNIQUE # 8B:*

**ALL PERIMETER PLAYERS SHOULD REALIZE
OFFENSIVE EFFECTIVENESS AS WELL AS TO BE ABLE
TO EXECUTE THE 'DRIFT CUTS' AFTER INSIDE PASSES ARE MADE--**

If the ball is passed inside to a post player, all each perimeter player should rotate ½ of an offensive spot-up location either towards the Ballside Baseline or away from that same Baseline that will neutralize the various types of double-teams and rotations that defensive teams could utilize to combat the offensive team's "inside game." Each perimeter player should immediately "get his feet and hands ready" and already "cheat" to begin getting his shoulders and toes squared up to the basket. He should prepare to catch the 'Kick-out Pass' and be able to shoot quickly off of that pass as well as to drive to the basket or to immediately make the 'extra pass' to a perimeter teammate or to make a second inside pass back to the same post player.

ALL OFFENSIVE PLAYERS SHOULD REALIZE OFFENSIVE EFFECTIVENESS AS WELL AS TO BE ABLE TO EXECUTE THE VARIOUS PERIMETER CUTS–

Teams that use a variety of different types of offensive cuts by all types of offensive players from different locations on the floor during the many phases of the offense makes the offense much less predictable and ultimately much more difficult to defend by both individual defenders as well as the overall opponents' team defense. These types of cuts force individual defenders to defend their men more often as well as to occupy themselves to help reduce the effectiveness of the opposition's ballside and helpside defense on support defense. These offensive cuts that could be utilized within the offense's frameworks are:

A. "V" Cuts,

B. "Pipe" or "Zipper" Cuts,

C. "Shuffle" Cuts,

D. "Flex" Cuts,

E. "Scissors" Cuts,

F. "Veer" Cuts,

G. "Flex Bump" Cuts,

H. "Curl" Cuts,

I. "Backdoor" Cuts,

J. "Give-n-Go" Cuts,

K. "Flare-Cuts,

L. "UCLA Rub-Off" Cuts,

M. "Bruin" Bump Cuts,

N. "Ghost-Screen" Cuts,

O. "Brush" Cuts,

P. "Iverson" Cuts and

Q. "Barkley" Cuts.

In addition, the traditional "Post Players" types of cuts that "inverted perimeter" players should be able to execute are:

A. "Duck-In" Cuts,

B. "Lob" Cuts, (High or Low)

C. "Flash-Post" Cuts,

D. "Slash" Cuts,

E. "Spin-Screen" Cuts,

F. "Basket Cuts ("Slip" Cuts, "Rolls," or "Rim-Runs.")

G. "Backdoor" Cuts,

H. "Blind-Pig" Cuts,

I. Give-n-Go" Cuts,

J. "V"-Cuts,

K. "L"-Cuts,

L. "Lift" Cuts,

M. "Drift" Cuts,

N. "Pipe" Cuts,

O. "Shuffle" Cuts,

P. "Iverson" Cuts,

Q. "Barkley" Cuts,

R. "Flare" Cuts,

S. "Lob" Cuts,

T. "Flex" Cuts,

U. "Bump Flex" Cuts,

V. "Veer" Cuts,

W. "Scissors" Cuts,

X. "Flash Post" Cuts,

Y. "Slash" Cuts,

Z. "UCLA" Cuts,

AA.   "Bruin" Bump Cuts,

BB. "Michigan" Cuts,

CC. "Blur" Cuts,

DD.   "Duck-In" Cuts,

EE.   "Flash-Post" Cuts,

FF.   "Spin-Screen" Cuts, and

GG. "Basket" Cuts (Ball-Screen Rolls or Rim-Runs)

✪ *TECHNIQUE # 10:*

ALL OFFENSIVE PLAYERS SHOULD REALIZE OFFENSIVE EFFECTIVENESS AS WELL AS TO BE ABLE TO EXECUTE THE VARIOUS TYPES OF PIVOTS

Offensive players must understand the value of basketball and how devastating turnovers can be to the offensive production of both individual players as well as the overall offensive team. Pivots are needed with offensive players on the perimeter as they prepare to shoot off of the dribble, as well as off of the pass and cutting from either side of the court. The perimeter player's foot closest to the basket is called the 'Inside Foot' and that 'Inside Foot' should be the designated 'Pivot Foot' (for both players cutting and catching the pass before shooting off of the pass. Dribblers should also pivot off of their 'Inside Foot' as they are about to shoot off of the dribble. Post players that receive 'Inside Passes' and prepare to execute their offensive post moves must heavily depend on the proper pivot in different directions, with either foot being the designated pivot foot. Offensive rebounders need to be able the same type of pivots as all other offense players. When the opposition shoots the ball, those defensive players are about to become offensive players in transition. Therefore defensive players must first know how to execute front and reverse pivots with either foot being the pivot foot so as to defensively 'box-out' the opponent to defensively rebound the ball. They then must proficiently execute both types of pivots with either foot being that pivot foot to successfully outlet the ball to being their team's transition offense. Offensive players must also be able to successfully execute all types of pivots versus opponent's defensive double-team traps.

✪ *TECHNIQUE # 11:*

ALL OFF-THE-BALL OFFENSIVE PLAYERS SHOULD REALIZE OFFENSIVE EFFECTIVENESS AS WELL AS TO BE ABLE TO EXECUTE THE PROPER TECHNIQUES OF CATCHING THE PASS (AND QUICKLY ATTACKING WITH A SHOT OR WITH DRIBBLE PENETRATION) ---

When catching the basketball, perimeter players should always be ready to become immediate offensive threats as shooters, passers, or driving threats. Off-ball receivers should always be prepared to receive the pass, immediately attack the basket with a dribble or be ready to shoot quickly and accurately off of the pass. They should always "have their feet and hands ready." They should always keep their shoulders at least partially squared up to the basket as well as facing the passer. Receiving the pass could come off of solo cuts, cutting off of the various types of screens available or floating on the weakside perimeter.

⊕ *TECHNIQUE # 12:*

ALL OFFENSIVE PLAYERS SHOULD REALIZE
OFFENSIVE EFFECTIVENESS AS WELL AS TO BE ABLE TO
EXECUTE ALL FORMS OF PASS FAKE AND SHOT FAKE TECHNIQUES–

All offensive players should realize the importance of good pass against defenders. A coaching point of emphasis can be taught with the phrases:

A. "Fake a pass to make a pass."
B. "Fake high and pass low or fake low and pass high."

Passing fakes should be as realistic as possible and that means the fakes should be executed at game speed. Basic realistic passing fakes helps relieve defensive pressure as well as reduce interceptions and deflections.

All offensive players should also realize the importance of good shot fakes against defenders. A coaching point of emphasis can be to look at the rim while making a shot fake and making the fake look as close to an actual shot is vital. The ball should be brought up through the nose and face with the eyes on the rim. The ball should then be yanked back down on the side in a protective location while the drive to the basket begins. Shot fakes can create many more opportunities to drive to the basket and to draw fouls. To be successful, shot fakes do not have to cause the defender to leave the ground, but to just slightly move him or straighten his legs. Defenders cannot play defense with their legs straight. Basic realistic passing fakes help relieve defensive pressure as well as reduce interceptions and deflections.

ALL OFFENSIVE PLAYERS SHOULD UNDERSTAND AND BE ABLE TO PERFORM THE TECHNIQUES OF HOW TO 'OBTAIN & MAINTAIN' "BODY POSITION ADVANTAGES" IN THE POST—

Coaches should teach every one of their post players (as well as their so-called "perimeter" players) the techniques of how to obtain and then maintain "body position advantages" over their post defenders. "Arm bars" and "target hands" should be used to obtain the inside pass from teammates. "Sealing" off an interior defender after pin-screening for a teammate, after skip passes or ball-reversals or defensive overplays. Versus interior defensive overplay such as ¾ or full fronting can be defeated by movement of the basketball along with the interior player then obtaining and then maintaining the position advantage over the aggressive defense.

Along with various methods of eliminating the opposition's helpside defense, offenses can get the ball inside to effectively attack the opponent's interior defense.

⊕ *TECHNIQUE # 13B:*

ALL OFFENSIVE PLAYERS SHOULD REALIZE OFFENSIVE EFFECTIVENESS AS WELL AS TO BE ABLE TO EXECUTE THE BASIC POST PLAYERS' MOVES AFTER RECEIVING THE INSIDE PASS–

If the post player catches the ball in the post area without any physical contact by the post defender; he should "bunny-hop and land on both feet simultaneously" as the ball is being caught. This enables either foot to be used as a pivot foot for the offensive post player.

Four effective offensive post moves that every offensive player should work on are:

A. the "Show-and-Go-Opposite" move,
B. the "Square-up & Up-and-Under" move,
C. the "Whirl" move and
D. The "Spin Screen" Action.

Each of these moves could/should have different types of shots that can be taken at the end of any of these offensive post moves.

⊕ *TECHNIQUE # 14:*

**ALL OFFENSIVE PLAYERS SHOULD BE ABLE TO
INTEGRATE VARIOUS METHODS TO
ELIMINATE OPPONENTS' HELPSIDE DEFENSES**

Vertically stretching as well as horizontally stretching defenses can take away many of the opposition's strengths and defensive reactions. Overloading the post with both high post and low post players with flash posts can also take away defensive help.

In addition, using 2 or 3-man weakside actions will help occupy or eliminate opponent's helpside defenses that are necessary to defend almost all offensive interior games.

This weakens the overall defense, giving the offense more opportunities to score from the interior. Reading helpside defenders properly can also give offenses possibilities to score from the perimeter as well. This action can give offenses a two-pronged attack that is very difficult to stop both forms of action.

⊕ *TECHNIQUE # 15A:*

**ALL OFFENSIVE PLAYERS SHOULD REALIZE
OFFENSIVE EFFECTIVENESS AS WELL AS THE TECHNIQUES OF
SETTING AND RECEIVING 'ON-THE-BALL-SCREENS'—**

Offensive plays and possibly continuity offenses should/could include "on-the-ball" screens with several of the different starting points and many of the different "follow-up ball-screening actions" that can effectively be executed. The actual offensive ball-screeners should be well-versed in performing the various individual offensive techniques that are needed to be successful in the different ball-screens, particularly the action just after the actual ball-screen has been set. The actual 'on-the-ball screeners' always should have a wide base and make sure they keep the legal distance from the defender as well as not reach out to hold or illegally hinder the defender.

There are many types of ball-screens that can be introduced, in addition to where those screens should be set. Also, there are many forms of action that follow these different ball-screens and the strengths and weaknesses of these. Many of these ball-screens should also be introduced before a coaching staff determines which types and locations should be integrated into their current season's offensive scheme. The starting points of the initial ball-screen can vary from different locations of the court.

Receiving as well setting the actual ball-screens from different starting points and different types of ending action as well as the different combinations of players involved can result in numerous offensive ball-screening scenarios that would be very difficult for defensive teams to adequately defend.

Dribblers that receive ball-screens must be able to set up and then attack the ball-defender with the proper angles before then "dribble-scraping" off of the screening teammate. After taking advantage of the ball-screen, dribblers should also be able to anticipate and attack the next wave of defense whether it is the initial ball-defender that is trailing him, or a switching defender that could be in the form of a defensive mismatch (in speed or height), or a double-team or a rotating defender and be effective as a driver, shooter and passer.

These different methods or types of ball-screens that could be utilized within each offensive team's frameworks are defined as:

A. "Big-on-Small" Ball-Screens,
B. "Small-on-Big" Ball-Screens,
C. "Long" Ball-Screens,
D. "Flat" Ball-Screens,
E. "Double" Ball-Screens,
F. "Twisted Double" Ball-Screens,
G. "Inside" Ball-Screens,
H. "Pistol Ball-Screens,
I. "Follow (the Pass) Ball-Screens,"
J. "Ram" Ball-Screens,
K. "Consecutive" Ball-Screens, and
L. "Stagger" Ball-Screens.

These most common and likely starting locations where "On-the-Ball-screens" can successfully be set are:

A. At the top of the key (for "Long Ball-Screens and any type of Double Wide Ball-Screens,
B. Near the elbow area on both sides of the floor (for "Inside Ball-Screens and "Pistols Ball-Screens,
C. Near the Wing areas for "Follow (the Pass" Ball-Screens and
D. Sometimes further out between the time-line and the top of the key for a (Ball) Flat-Screen."

The many and various types of actions that could be utilized that can follow any of the 'on-the-ball screens could be any of the following such as:

A. The "Ball-Screen/Roll,"
B. "Ball-Screen/Rim-Run,"
C. "Ball-Screen/Slip" (Pick and Pop),
D. "Ball-Screen/Flare-Cut,"
E. "Ball-Screen/Re-Screen" or
F. "Various forms of 'Screen-the-Screener' action on either the interior and the perimeter."

🏀 *TECHNIQUE # 16A:*

**ALL OFFENSIVE PLAYERS SHOULD BE ABLE TO
EXECUTE ALL OF THE TECHNIQUES OF
SETTING AND ALSO RECEIVING 'OFF-THE-BALL SCREENS'—**

With ball-screens being a huge part of the offensive system, even more so should the large variety off-ball screens be an integral part of the offense. Every offensive player should thoroughly be able to execute the proper those off-ball screening techniques. They also should have a wide base and make sure they maintain the legal distance from the defender and not hold or illegally hinder the defender. The skills of the different options that can follow the off-ball screening action should also be emphasized and acquired. Cutters that receive screens must be able to set up and then attack the defender with the proper angles before then "scraping" off of the shoulder of the screening teammate with their "feet and hands ready." Cutters should be prepared to receive the ball and instantly become a threat to shoot off of the pass, to drive or to make the next pass to a teammate.

Integrate these many different types of "off-the-ball screens" within the framework of the designated continuity offense so that your team can either completely eliminate or at least move the "helpside" defense, or to have offensive personnel cutting towards the ball either on the perimeter or the interior. These "off-the-ball screens" could be in the form of "Big-on-Small," "Small-on-Big," "Small-on-Small" or "Big-on-Big" types of "off-the-ball screens." Screens set by a different sized player on a different sized teammate helps discourage defensive switching or can quickly put defensive players in drastic mismatches that can and should be capitalized on.

These off-ball screens could also be combined with other types of off-ball screens discussed to become a two-part form of screening action. Some of these screens can be called:

A. "Down-Screens" (with or without 'Seals' or Flash Post action,)
B. "Stagger-Screens," (Twisted or Not)
C. "Shuffle-Screens,"
D. "Chin Back-Screens,"
E. "Flare-Screens,"
F. "UCLA-Screens," (with or without UCLA Bumps Actions)
G. "UCLA-Screens," (With or Without 'Bump' Cuts,)
H. "Pin-Screens," (With or Without Seal-Offs)
I. "Interior "Spin-Screens,"
J. "Brush-Screens,"
K. "Elevator-Screens" or "Twisted Elevator" Screens,
L. "Interior Lane Exchange Cross-Screens,"
M. "Down-Screens,"
N. "Screen-the-Screener Screens,"
O. "Ram-Screens,"
P. Various "Combo-Screens,"
Q. "Dribble Hand-Offs,"
R. "Dribble Hand-Offs & Off-Ball Screens," and
S. "Dribble Hand-Offs & Rolls or Rim-Runs."
T. "Ghost Down-Screens,"
U. "Pin-Screens" (with or without Post Seal-offs,)
V. "Stagger-Screens" (Twisted or Not),
W. "Ghost Flare-Screens",

X. "Iverson,"
Y. "Barkley" Screens,
Z. "UCLA-Screens," (with or without Bump Cut Options)
AA. "Brush-Screens," and
BB.(Interior) Spin-Screens"

A now popular offensive series of action is where the initial screener sets two (or more) different types of screens in a very short, smooth and fluid series of offensive action. Another newer type of action is a reverse pass that initiates a back-screen for the ball reversal passer that is immediately followed by a ball-screen (with various types of action that could then follow that ball-screen.)

Other forms of Combo Screens could be started with an off-ball screen and then finished with a second off-ball screen. Many types of 'Combo Screens' can start with a ball-screen that is then followed with a second off-ball screen on a second teammate. These are fluid forms of action that give the screener's defender no time to read the type of screen and prepare to defend it.

✪ *TECHNIQUE # 17A:*

ALL OFFENSIVE PLAYERS SHOULD REALIZE
OFFENSIVE EFFECTIVENESS AS WELL AS TO BE ABLE TO
UTILIZE THE VARIOUS FORMS OF THE
'DRIBBLE HAND-OFF' AND THE POSSIBLE ACTIONS TO FOLLOW—

There are different manners that an offensive ball-handler can exchange the ball with one of his teammates. One method of giving up the ball to a teammate is by the dribbler simply handing the ball to a teammate. From there, the initial ball-handler now is the new off-the-ball teammate and the initial off-the-ball teammate becomes the new ball-handler who has the same three basic offensive possible roles: to become a dribbler/driver, a passer and/or a shooter. These three DHO options will be difficult for opposing defenses to defend, particularly when there are multiple options and each of the actions are similar but yet different, not easy to detect and therefore difficult to defend. The initial ball-handler making the hand-off becomes an offensive player without the ball and becomes a different threat to the defense. The offensive player that receives the DHO is now the offensive player with the ball and becomes a more dangerous type of player once having possession of the ball. All of the various types of drives to the basket, the passes to teammates and the wide range of shots falls into the hands of the new ball-handler.

✪ *TECHNIQUE # 17B:*

**ALL OFFENSIVE PLAYERS SHOULD REALIZE
OFFENSIVE EFFECTIVENESS AS WELL AS TO BE ABLE TO
UTILIZE THE VARIOUS FORMS OF THE
'FAKE DRIBBLE HAND-OFF' AND THE POSSIBLE ACTIONS TO FOLLOW—**

A counter to the previously discussed offensive action is for two offensive players to fake the actual Dribble Hand-Off. This simple method of the two players exchanging their actions can very easily mislead and confuse the opposing defense. The initial ball-handler and teammate still must make the same close connection, but because there is no actual exchange of the ball; the dribbler must retain his dribble. Therefore, after deceiving the defenders; the initial ball-handler remains the ball-handler with the same three potential offensive threats that can be used against the defender. In addition, after faking the actual hand-off, the initial off-ball teammate retains the same off-ball offensive possible actions— making the various cuts, the possible setting of the various possible screens and the possibility of receiving screens from any of his offensive teammates.

There is still another effective method of executing another swift, short and safe offensive exchanges of the ball between the initial ball-handler and another one of his teammates. One method is the simple return of the ball from the initial Pass Receiver 'flipping' the ball back to the initial Passer, who has followed his pass to cut near the receiver and the ball. From there, the initial ball-handler again becomes the ball-handler with the same three basic offensive options: a dribbler/driver, a passer and/or a shooter.

These three options are again unpredictable to the opposing defense. The initial ball-handler is now the teammate that does not have the ball and has the same options as all other off-the-ball offensive players—making any of the possible cuts, setting screens or receiving screens. All the various types of cuts and different methods of screens are all possible.

The initial off-the-ball teammate has gained possession of the ball by receiving the 'Flip Pass' and now has the same options of all ball-handlers. All the various types of dribbles and dribbling attacks are open for the new dribbler/driver.

80

ALL OFFENSIVE PLAYERS SHOULD REALIZE
OFFENSIVE EFFECTIVENESS AS WELL AS TO BE ABLE TO
UTILIZE THE VARIOUS FORMS OF THE 'FAKE FLIP PASS'
(OR 'FAKE PASS HAND-OFF') AND THE POSSIBLE ACTIONS TO FOLLOW—

There is still another effective method of executing another swift, short and safe offensive exchanges of the ball between the initial ball-handler and another one of his teammates. To counter the "Flip Pass" action, the pass receiver can simply fake the expected 'Flip Pass' back to the initial passer and maintain the same stance so as to become the same 'Triple Threat' offensive player, with the initial 'Passer' now being the off-ball teammate that has the same off-ball actions.

☻ *TECHNIQUE # 18:*

ALL OFFENSIVE PLAYERS SHOULD REALIZE
OFFENSIVE EFFECTIVENESS AS WELL AS TO BE ABLE TO
EXECUTE THE TECHNIQUES OF ANY OF THE SECONDARY BREAK
SCREENING AND CUTTING OPTIONS

Any one or two from this list of options could be actually used at the end of the Secondary Fastbreaks. Again, it must carefully be determined which should be used at the conclusion of Secondary Breaks from the left side of the floor and which one from the right side of the floor:

A. "The Techniques of the Bump & Flare-Cut" Option,
B. "The Techniques Back-Screen" & Quick Ball-Screen/Roll,"
C. "The Techniques Brush-Screen,"
D. "The Techniques Give-n-Go Cut,"
E. "The Techniques Iso Duck-In Cut,"
F. "The Techniques Veer Cut,"
G. "The Techniques Early Ball-Screen/Roll,"
H. "The Techniques Chase & Early Screen/Rim-Run,"
I. "The Techniques Chase & Early Screen/Down-Screen,"
J. "The Techniques Late Ball-Screen/Roll,"

K. "The Techniques Duck-In Cut & Late Ball-Screen/Rim-Run."

CLOSING

These are the proper fundamental offensive techniques and the correct techniques that serve as the fundamentally sound building blocks that can help establish an effective and productive man-to-man offensive system that will withstand the test of time. As players and their respective ability levels of both strengths and weaknesses change from one season to the next, in addition to opponents' skills and talents changing; a fundamentally sound offensive system can adjust accordingly without major disruptions or changes to the overall program. This consistency gives both the players and the coaching staff faith and confidence in each other and in the overall system.

CHAPTER 7

USING VARIOUS OFFENSIVE SCHEMES AND FORMS OF OFFENSIVE ATTACKS IN A SUCCESSFUL MULTIPLE-PHASE MAN-TO-MAN OFFENSIVE SYSTEM

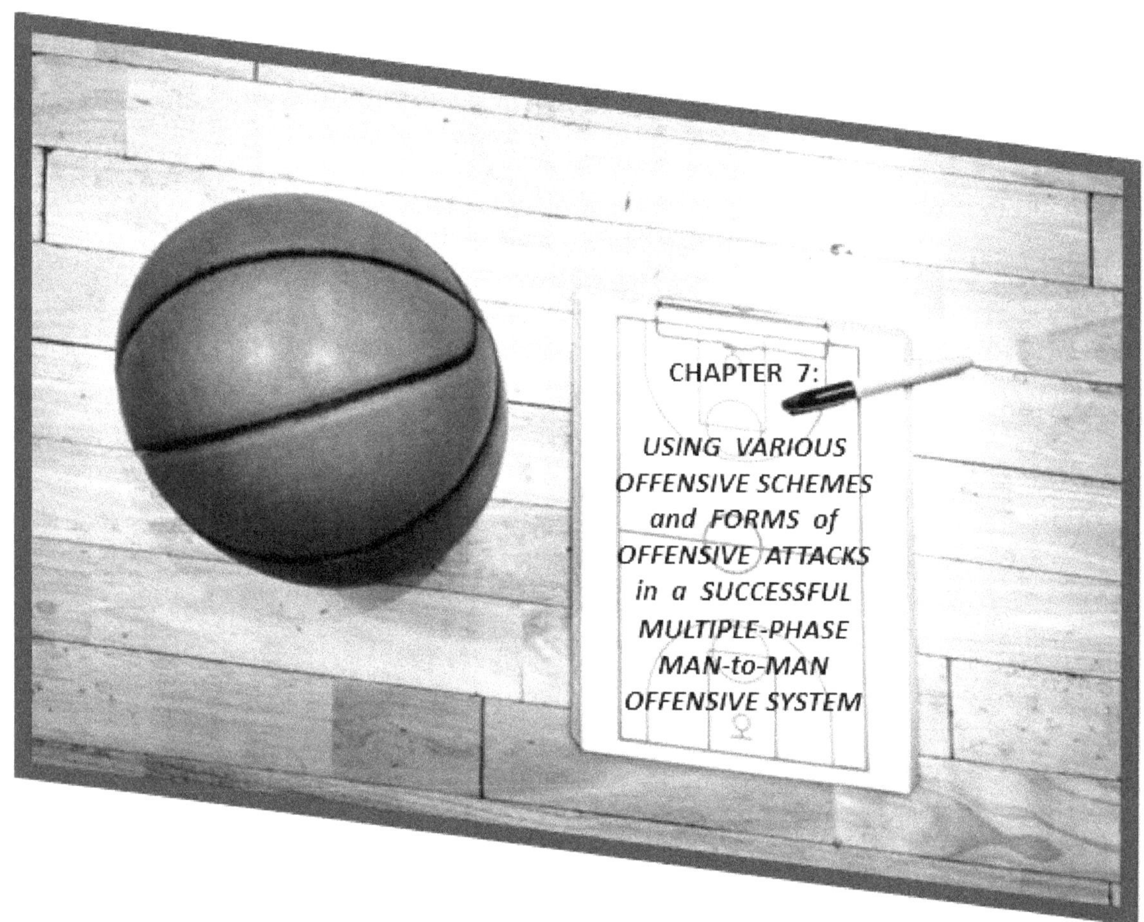

There are many different philosophies on how to attack opposing defenses. This multiple-phase offensive system uses more than one phase/layer/wave of attack, with each phase/wave having a seamless and immediate conversion into the next phase/wave. While this system can be confusing to defenses and difficult to defend, this system can be properly taught and coached so that it can be easily understood and ultimately executed by players of many different levels of (physical talent, mental understanding, and playing experience.)

In addition, there are several types of offensive schemes and different ways within this system that offenses can attack their defensive counter-parts. Many of these can be

integrated within the same offensive system that can attack defenses in various ways. The larger the number of schemes that can be successfully utilized and integrated within the same system, the greater the opportunity an offensive team can find the most efficient and productive schemes that can place both individual and the overall team in the best and most frequent "positions to succeed."

Each play has been carefully studied and evaluated to determine which level of talent and experience (for both players and coaching staffs) must be possessed for that specific team to be able to successfully execute the play. If players do not know how or are physically unable to execute the skills within plays, the play will not be able to be productive. Likewise, if coaching staffs do not or cannot effectively teach the skills, that play will not be productive. While it is obvious that the physical skills and talents must be possessed by the players, but the mental understanding of the game by all players and coaching staffs is mandatory for both. If either group fails, the offensive play will also fail.

The most sophisticated plays/entries would fall into one of the three levels all based on the team's physical talents and skills, the mental capacities and the overall team's game experience. In addition, the coaching staff must have a high degree of basketball knowledge as well as very high teaching and coaching skills to educate his/her entire basketball team. The proper breakdown drills must be thoroughly utilized to hone the fundamental skills and techniques needed for individual players and the overall team to execute plays that can be efficient, productive and successful. We define this family of plays as the "Level 3 category" of plays. This "Level 3" family of plays will have a much more complex offensive scheme that would require a very high amount of physical talent as well as requiring a greater amount of the players (to execute) and the coaches (to teach and coach) mental capacities and experience needed for the offense to be efficient, productive and successful. We feel plays in our defined "Level 3" category could possibly be successful for NBA teams, definitely for college teams and also for many high schools and older AAU teams.

The next classification or level of plays would be possibly slightly lower as far as sophistication, complexity and the actual 'length' of the play (and the number of passes, cuts, and screens used) in the play's overall scheme. While all "Level 2" plays in each of the chapters in this book remain to be fundamentally sound, these plays may lack the actual number of techniques/methods that are implemented within that play in comparison to the more advanced "Level 3" plays/entries. Therefore any team that successfully executes the highest "Level 3" plays/entries could/should easily be able to execute any of these so-called lower "Level 2" plays/entries, if so desired. Almost all high school teams should be able to execute successfully all aspects of the "Level 2" plays.

The final grouping of plays would be called "Level 1" plays and are not as difficult for offensive players to master the execution of them, both physically as well as mentally. Even though the techniques are still fundamentally, they may not be as complex to learn and understand in addition to being easier to physically execute.

"Level 1" plays would be lower in the scheme's complexities and the number of techniques used in the execution of this category of plays. Obviously, since these "Level 1" plays are still sound, but lack some of the methods used in the two previous more sophisticated and complex levels; these more elementary plays should be able to be utilized by any teams that use either of the two higher level plays. We feel that Middle School/Junior High teams as well as younger AAU teams or organizations should be able to utilize any of the "Level 1" plays successfully, with a possibility that some of those teams that are slightly more advanced (than other teams) could possibly use some plays located in the immediate next immediate level.

Ideas, concepts, and techniques from actual plays from teams of all three levels have been used to modify or to create different combinations of the various techniques and schemes used that will help prove these entries can be successfully used. This allows the author to create numerous plays that use the various schemes to build a library of fundamentally sound plays that will be unique and will be appropriate for the wide range of teams with the various ages and skill levels.

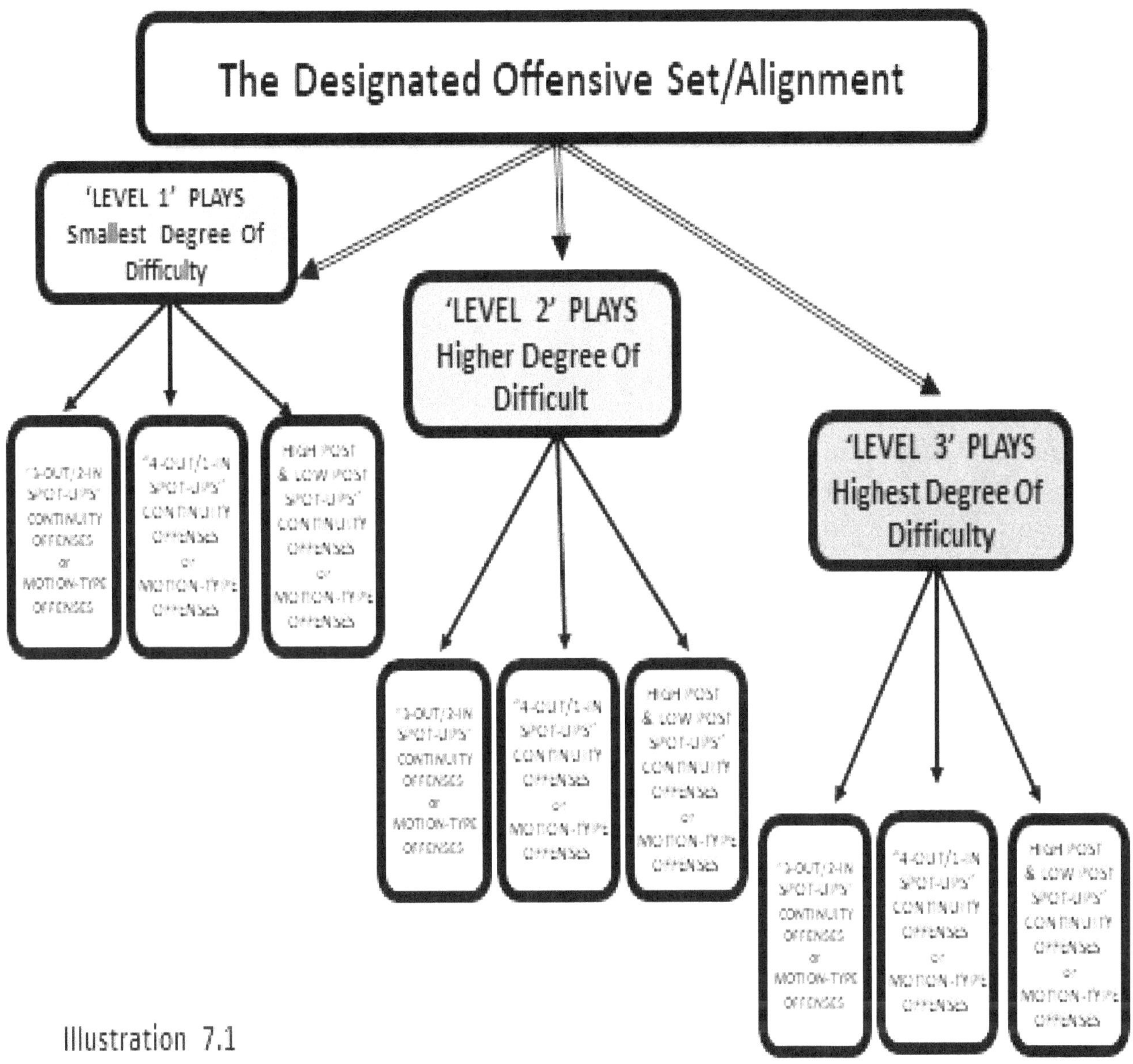

Illustration 7.1

In addition to the multiple-phase concept of this system, there are several types of offensive schemes and different ways that offenses can attack their defensive counter-parts. Many of these can be integrated within the same offensive system that can attack defenses in various ways. The larger the number of schemes that can be successfully utilized and integrated within the same system, the greater the opportunity an offensive team can find the most efficient and productive schemes that can place both individual and the overall team in the best and most frequent "positions to succeed."

Some of these offensive schemes that could be easily integrated include:

A. "Ball-Screen" Actions from Various Locations,
B. Different 'Off-the-Ball Screening" Action from Various Locations,
C. "Pistols" Action,
D. "Penetrate and Pitch" Actions,
E. "Drive and Dump" Actions,
F. "Dribble Hand-Off" Action Followed by "On-the-Ball" or "Off-the-Ball" Actions,
G. "Fake Dribble Hand-Off" Actions,
H. "Flip Pass Hand-Off" Action Followed by "On-the-Ball" or "Off-the-Ball" Action,
I. "Fake Flip-Pass Hand-Off" Actions,
J. "Chin-Screen and Cut" Actions,
K. "Flex-Screen and Various Cuts" Actions,
L. "Shuffle-Screen and Various Cuts" Actions,
M. "UCLA-Screen and Various Cuts" Actions,
N. "(Off-the-Ball) Screen the (Ball-)Screener" Actions,
O. "Consecutive Combination Screen" Actions,
P. "Mismatch On-the-Ball Screen" Actions,
Q. "Mismatch Off-the-Ball Screen" Actions,
R. "Blind Pig" and Other Types of "Basket Cuts" Actions,
S. "Hammer" (Drive/Pass/Flare-Cut) Baseline" Actions,
T. "Ghost Ball-Screens with various types of action following the screen and
U. "Ghost Off-Ball-Screens with the various types of action following the screen.

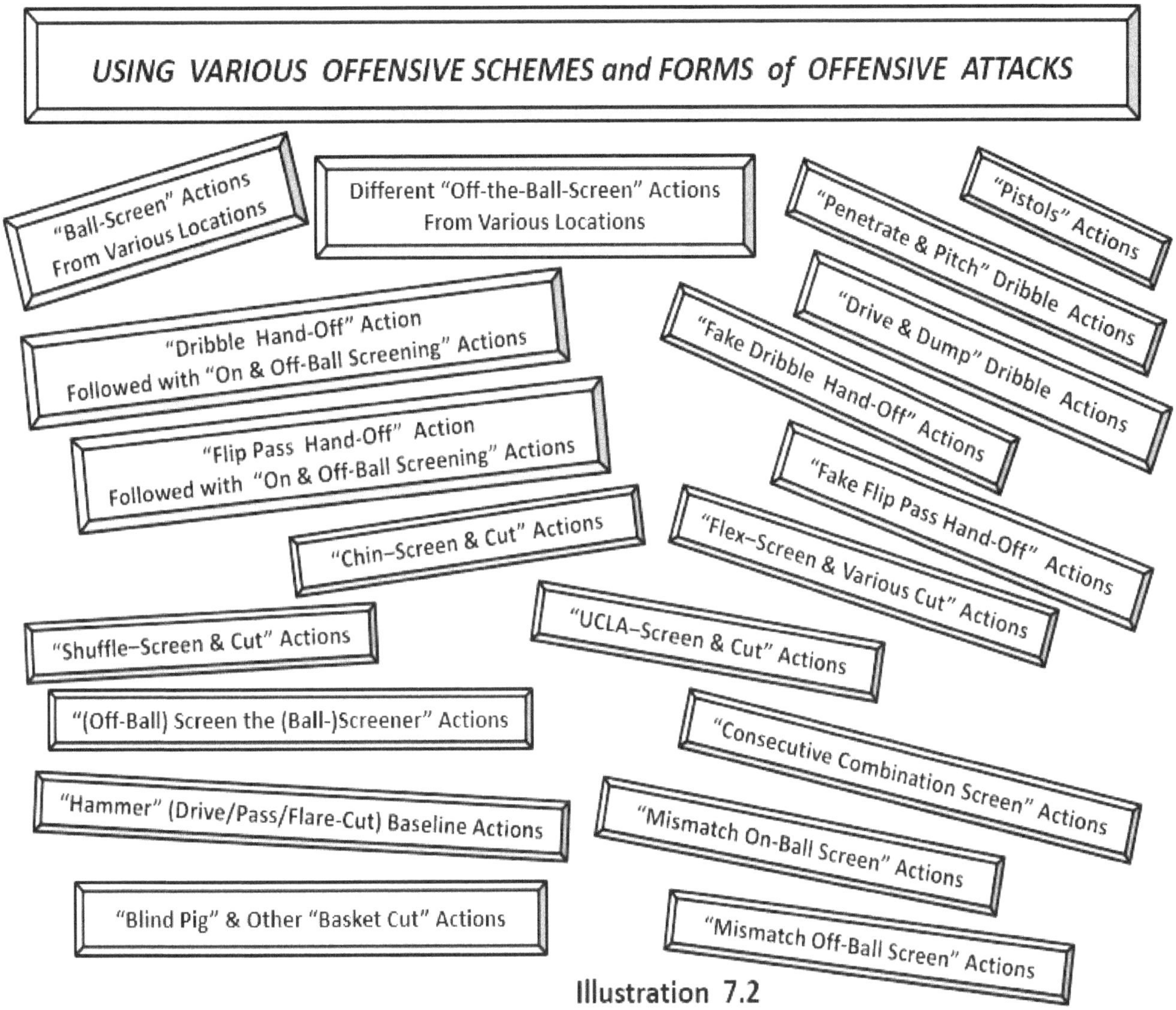

USING VARIOUS OFFENSIVE SCHEMES and FORMS of OFFENSIVE ATTACKS

"Ball-Screen" Actions From Various Locations

Different "Off-the-Ball-Screen" Actions From Various Locations

"Pistols" Actions

"Penetrate & Pitch" Dribble Actions

"Drive & Dump" Dribble Actions

"Dribble Hand-Off" Action Followed with "On & Off-Ball Screening" Actions

"Fake Dribble Hand-Off" Actions

"Flip Pass Hand-Off" Action Followed with "On & Off-Ball Screening" Actions

"Fake Flip Pass Hand-Off" Actions

"Chin–Screen & Cut" Actions

"Flex–Screen & Various Cut" Actions

"UCLA–Screen & Cut" Actions

"Shuffle–Screen & Cut" Actions

"(Off-Ball) Screen the (Ball-)Screener" Actions

"Consecutive Combination Screen" Actions

"Hammer" (Drive/Pass/Flare-Cut) Baseline Actions

"Mismatch On-Ball Screen" Actions

"Blind Pig" & Other "Basket Cut" Actions

"Mismatch Off-Ball Screen" Actions

Illustration 7.2

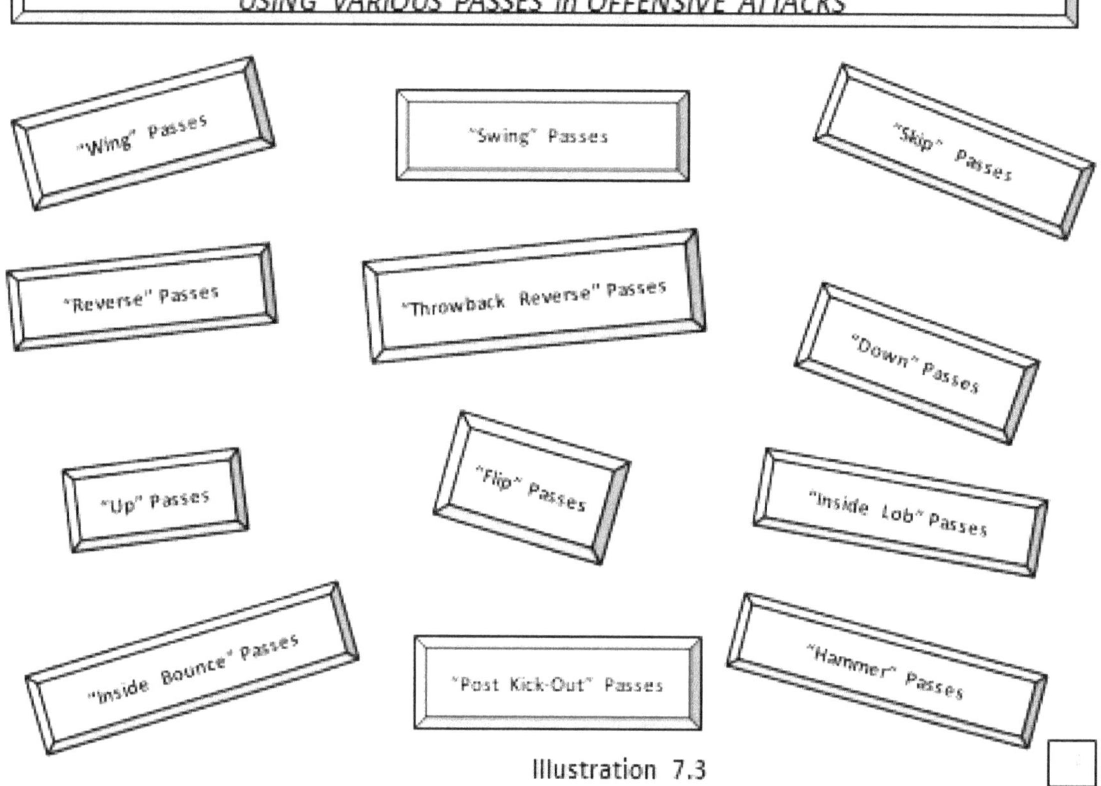

Illustration 7.3

MAJOR COACHING POINTS OF EMPHASIS IN A SUCCESSFUL MULTIPLE-PHASE MAN-TO-MAN OFFENSIVE SYSTEM

✇ *COACHING POINT 1:*

OFFENSES MUST VERTICALLY & HORIZONTALLY STRETCH THE OFFENSIVE FLOOR IN EVERY PHASE OF THE OVERALL OFFENSIVE ATTACK

By stretching the offensive floor both horizontally as well as vertically, offenses force opposing defenses to guard and defend a wider and longer area of the floor. This stretching, pulling and thinning the defense can only weaken the defense; giving offense great advantages in the different phases of the offensive system. The stretching concept should be applied in the Full-Court part of the offense. Primary Fastbreaks, Full-Court Press Offenses, half-court plays/entries, Sideline and Baseline Out-of-Bounds plays in addition to the final level that each of these phases will eventually flow into—the designated continuity offense will all benefit with the stretching and weakening of the overall opposition's defense.

⊕ *COACHING POINT 2:*

COACHES MUST USE A
SYMMETRICALLY BALANCED OFFENSIVE ALIGNMENT

If the particular set/alignment is perfectly symmetrical, each entry can then possess the capabilities of being able to attack either side of the floor. Therefore, with each play being "ambidextrous," each play can be a duel threat as being able to initially attack both sides of the floor. In addition, each play could be inside-oriented or perimeter-oriented. A team can also create plays for every player that will capitalize on that player's strengths. So after plays and the desired side are called out, players will have time to comprehend their responsibilities and assignments for that play and then begin to execute those assignments in an efficient and productive manner.

⊕ *COACHING POINT 3:*

COACHES MUST HAVE A BALANCED AND UNPREDICTABLE ATTACK

This multi-phase offensive attack produces a potent and fluid type of offense that fits many types of philosophies and styles of offensive play. Using different plays from different sets can give the team various styles of offensive attack such as an up-tempo or a slower ball-control type of attack. Both styles could be utilized and executed, making the attack a different kind of "balanced attack."

Plays from this set can be "inside oriented" as well as outside or "3-pt. oriented" or a mixture of both—making it an even different type of balanced (and more difficult to defend) method of attack. Still, if the play/entry does not create a shot, the offense will always be able to smoothly and easily transition to the designated continuity offense.

COACHES MUST UTILIZE OFFENSIVE PLAYERS' STRENGTHS AND MINIMIZE THOSE SAME OFFENSIVE PLAYERS' WEAKNESSES

Different plays/entries designed especially for specific players can also utilize various offensive strengths that different offensive players can possess in addition to minimizing that player's offensive players' weaknesses. In addition, the correctly selected play can also attack both the opposition's individual as well as team defensive weaknesses, before then capitalizing and attacking those discovered defensive weaknesses. Various parts of the selected play/entry can also have their own general strengths and characteristics that make the play unique in its own way. The play can be utilized to not only accentuate individual offensive players' special skills and talents, but to also to attack both individual defenders' specific deficiencies as well as take advantage of the opposition's overall defensive weaknesses.

✪ *COACHING POINT 5:*

OFFENSES MUST DISCOVER AND THEN ATTACK INDIVIDUAL OPPONENT'S DEFENSIVE WEAKNESSES

In addition to overall defensive weaknesses, coaching staffs should constantly be probing and searching for defensive weaknesses of individual opponents that they can attack. Those weaknesses could be in the form of a defender that cannot match up to his offensive responsibility because of a lack of height, strength, quickness, or knowledge/training in defending his man in a certain area of the offense. That opponent might be hurting your team by being an important offensive scorer, rebounder, ball-handler or play-maker. Attacking that player and getting him in foul trouble or even fouled out of the game could very well decrease or completely diminish his overall contributions to his team. Specific plays called to attack that opponent or using specific options of the continuity could allow the offense to attack that newly discovered defensive weakness and reduce that opponent's overall contributions.

 COACHING POINT 6:

OFFENSES MUST CREATE VARIOUS "POSITION MISMATCHES"

Another objective of different types of offensive action can be to create "position mismatches." This purpose is to force opposing defenders into having to defend offensive players they were not initially assigned to guard, mainly because those opponents are not matched with the defensive skills, strengths and experience to successfully be able to defend that specific offensive players. This objective can often be accomplished by the offensive team executing "Big-on-Small" or "Small-on-Big" off-ball or on-ball screens.

These offensive actions could also be a method of inverting opposing defenders while (from their normal and custom 'perimeter areas' or their 'interior areas;' while keeping offensive players in their normal and customary locations.

 COACHING POINT 7:

OFFENSES MUST INVERT OFFENSIVE PERIMETER PLAYERS

A fundamentally sound method of attack often used in this offensive attack is to "invert" perimeter players. This means that entries/plays can be created that include placing so-called "perimeter players" into post-up locations. After perimeter players have been taught and trained how to successfully post up their perimeter defenders inside, there are plays designed that will take advantage of those possible "position mismatches." The coaching staff takes the challenge of preparing "perimeter players" to be more prepared as offensive post players than opponents' perimeter players to be good post defenders and vice versa with the traditional "post players." Specific offensive plays can then provide various players with "position advantages" by taking advantage of newly-found offensive strengths and newly discovered individual defensive weaknesses both on the interior as well as on the perimeter. These created plays should utilize these concepts by giving every offensive player the opportunities to be positioned at both perimeter & post-up spot-up locations, so that those players can utilize their offensive skills in various manners.

⊕ COACHING POINT 8:

OFFENSES MUST INVERT OFFENSIVE POST PLAYERS IN VARIOUS MANNERS

Not only do we want to invert perimeter players "down on the blocks," we also want to be able to move and reposition certain offensive post players <u>away</u> from the basket; so that they can attack their defender on the perimeter as well. This attack could be because of that player's dominating quickness, ball-handling and/or perimeter shooting skills (or because of a specific defender's overall perimeter defensive weakness.) Inverting offensive post players could also be to pull defensive "bigs" away from the basket to take away defensive strengths, such as defensive rebounding and shot-blocking skills. This can give that designated player (be it a traditional so-called perimeter player or a post player out on the perimeter) an opportunity to use his driving, passing and/or perimeter shooting skills, as well as his offensive creative skills. These methods could be implemented in many different man-to-man plays/entries/quick-hitters.

⊕ COACHING POINT 9:

OFFENSES MUST ATTACK THE OPPONENT'S OVERALL TEAM DEFENSIVE WEAKNESSES

Coaching staffs should study and know the particular styles of the man-to-man defense being used against their team, so that those inherent weaknesses of that specific style of defense can be discovered, attacked and then capitalized on by the offense in the proper fundamentally sound methods and techniques. Those techniques should already be built into various plays that can be used. In addition, those weaknesses can be taken advantage of within the framework of the designated continuity offense via options and counter-options.

⊕ COACHING POINT 10:

OFFENSES MUST ELIMINATE HELPSIDE DEFENDERS IN THEIR OFFENSIVE ACTIONS AND MOVEMENT

A fundamentally sound objective of various types of offensive action is to eliminate or weaken helpside defenders that can help provide extra defensive support for interior post defenders. By minimizing or eliminating helpside defenders initially on the weakside of the defense away from the basketball, the offensive action can more effectively attempt to attack the opposition's ballside post defenders and to isolate those opposing post defenders. Offensive actions can be accomplished with either flash-post action (both high-post and low-post action) and/or with '2 or 3-man' games on the offense's weakside. Other offensive actions could be by executing Diagonal down-screens and stagger-screens could be utilized on the weakside to occupy helpside defenders and prevent those defenders to being involved with helping their interior ballside defenders.

⊕ *COACHING POINT 11:*

**OFFENSES MUST ISOLATE OFFENSIVE PERIMETER PLAYERS
IN THE MANY VARIOUS MANNERS**

If an offensive team can isolate players "in the post," we also want to reverse that type of attack by being able to also isolate certain offensive perimeter players out on the perimeter. Those players can attack their defenders on the perimeter as well, with those defenders not able to receive much help from defensive teammates. This attack could be executed because of an offensive perimeter player's advantage in quickness, ball-handling and/or perimeter shooting skills (or because of a specific defender's overall perimeter defensive weakness.) This can give that designated offensive player an opportunity to use his overall advantages in driving, passing and/or perimeter shooting skills, as well as his offensive creative skills. These methods could just as well be integrated within the framework of the correctly chosen offensive play or somewhere within the structure of the continuity that is used.

⊕ *COACHING POINT 12:*

**OFFENSES MUST ISOLATE OFFENSIVE POST PLAYERS
IN DIFFERENT MANNERS**

Still another method way we want to attack opposing defenders is to position both the traditional as well as inverted perimeter players in the post with little or no interior support for those particular defenders. If defensive post players play behind, we should be able to easily make the inside pass to that designated post player. We want to have a plan of attack to neutralize double-teams from perimeter defenders with perimeter movement so that post players can then "kick the ball back out" for open perimeter shots.

If post defenders try to full-front or three quarter front post players to deny them the ball, we want our offenses to be able to take away weakside defensive help so that lob passes can be made to the fronted post player. The positioning, repositioning and moving of offensive players can be accomplished within the framework of the selected offensive plays/entries.

This can give a coaching staff the ability to be able to not only place a designated player into the mid-post area, but to isolate that particular player so that he can attack a lone defender from a high percentage shot location.

⊕ *COACHING POINT 13:*

COACHES SHOULD IMPLEMENT "SHIFTING" WITHIN THE OFFENSIVE SYSTEM

Hiding from opponents the actual plan of attack until the last possible moment can be achieved in basketball by using a form of what football offenses also try to do. One of these simple methods of deception is what we call "shifting." Our definition of "shifting" is simply that offensive players can move or shift to a new location when the ball is in play just before it reaches the timeline, but obviously, before the first pass is made and the entry/play actually begins. This last second movement of one or more offensive players actually changes the cosmetic appearance of the offense by "shifting" from one offensive set /alignment to a new and possibly much different one that is the actual set/alignment that is desired. This keeps defenses from being able to predict and therefore know how to defend the offensive action. There is less time for the opposing defenses to react to the offensive alignment and before the offense executes the desired play/entry—thereby giving the offense another huge advantage.

⊕ *COACHING POINT 14:*

COACHES MUST IMPLEMENT "FALSE MOTION" WITHIN THE OFFENSIVE SYSTEM

The second technique or method of deception is what we call "false motion." We define "false motion" as the offense actually making cuts, setting screens and passing the ball before then truly attacking in the desired manner. This could possibly take place when the ball is reversed, the true offensive action that is designed to attack the defense in the true manner then begins. Again, this is done to prevent defenses from being able to predict specific offensive action. The "false motion" is fundamentally sound and still makes the defense move, work & defend, but its goal is to deceive and camouflage the offense's true objectives. This is the other manner that disguises the true intentions and action of the offense and therefore giving the offense still another advantage for successful execution.

⊕ *COACHING POINT 15:*

OFFENSES MUST IMPLEMENT ONLY PLAYS/ENTRIES THAT FIT THE TEAM'S SKILL LEVELS

Coaching staffs should study which plays/entries (as well as the continuity or motion offense) that best suit their team's personnel and subsequently select the most productive and efficient plays and continuity offense that fit their players. There are numerous plays/entries from this offensive set or alignment that can possess families or groups of plays in which every entry can quickly, easily and fluidly flow into the designated continuity offense's "spot-up" positions. Each play can be executed to highlight an individual offensive player's skills, to attack an individual defender's weakness(es) or a discovered overall team defensive weakness. Each entry can be categorized by players' initial actions to begin the play. These various fundamentally sound categories include:

"Iverson" Cuts, "Barkley" Cuts, "Backdoor" Cuts, "Give-n-Go" Cuts, "Flex & Veer" Cuts, "Flex" Bump Cuts, "UCLA Rub-Off Action," "Bruin" Bump Cuts, "Wing Passes," "Post Pop-Out Passes," different types of "On the Ball-Screens," "Wing Pass & Follow (Ball-)Screens, various "Off-Ball-Screens," "Dribble Weave Hand-Offs," "Fake DHO" Action, "Low-Post & "High-Post" Flash Cuts" and "Inverting & Isolating" Perimeter and Post Players.

⊕ *COACHING POINT 16:*

PLAYERS MUST USE THE PROPER TECHNIQUES
WHILE EXECUTING ALL PLAYS/ENTRIES

There are many techniques that could and should be implemented in some manner within the framework of both the package of offensive plays as well as within the offensive continuity or motion offense's scheme. The more of these techniques that are used and applied by the offense's entries and by the continuities used; the more weapons that offensive team can possess. More weapons help an offensive team probe opponent's defenses for both individual as well as overall team defensive weaknesses. These techniques could be categorized as either various types of cuts, different kinds of off-ball screens and a wide range of ball-screens that have ending types of actions following those ball-screens. An offensive team wants to maximize those fundamentally sound techniques without overloading a team with too many techniques incorporated within the offense. The package of various entries/plays should be able to implement more of a variety of these methods than the desired continuity or motion offense.

⊕ *COACHING POINT 17:*

OFFENSIVE PLAYS/ENTRIES AND CONTINUITY OFFENSES
MUST HAVE THE PROPER FLOOR BALANCE AND PROPER SPACING

Good man offenses maintain good floor balance and good spacing between offensive players (About 15 feet to 18 feet between most perimeter players). Proper spacing will horizontally and also vertically stretch the overall strength of the defense and helps make ball-reversals and skip passes much easier and safer to use. Proper spacing isolates defenders both on the perimeter and the interior. Proper floor spacing reduces the amount of pressure on the ball because there is less defensive help that can support ball-defenders and actually reduce the pressure that 'one-pass-away defenders' can apply to their offensive responsibility. Proper floor spacing aids in preventing defensive "help & recovers" on offensive dribble penetrations as well as also discourages double-team traps both on the perimeter as well as "double-downs" when the ball is passed inside to an interior player.

🌐 COACHING POINT 18:

OFFENSIVE PLAYERS MUST ALWAYS USE THE DRIBBLE TO ATTACK DEFENSES

Another objective of various types of offensive action is to not only attack individual defenders but to also attack overall opponents' team defenses by forcing defenders to have to give help to their defensive teammates. This can be done giving offensive players the proper spacing and freedom and then have offensive players utilize their dribble to attack individual defenders to force off-the-ball defenders to have to help, creating openings for their own opponent they were guarding.

One of these two types of attacks could be called the "Drive & Dump." The dribbler drives into the lane and if there is interior vertical defensive rotation that arrives on time to stop the drive, an 'inside pass' can be made to the open man in the lane.

The second type of dribble-attack could be called the "Penetrate & Pitch." The dribbler drives into the lane and if there is outside defensive help, the dribble/driver "pitches" the ball out on the perimeter to the open teammate for an open "3." These dribble attacks that isolate defenders can be executed still within the structure of the offense.

🌐 COACHING POINT 19:

OFFENSIVE PLAYERS MUST ALWAYS USE REALISTIC BALL FAKES AND SHOT FAKES

Coaches should constantly stress to offensive players that they always should use good ball-fakes as well as realistic shot-fakes against the opposition's man-to-man (or zone) defenses. A coaching point phrase could be "fake a pass to make a pass." In addition, it must be emphasized that shot fakes are extremely important before a shooter drives to the basket as well as after he has killed his dribble (particularly in the lane.) One part of a shot fake that is easily forgotten is for the offensive player with the ball to actually look at the rim during his shot fake and to bring the ball up through his nose for a more realistic-looking shot fake.

OFFENSES MUST ALWAYS USE VARIOUS CUTS IN THEIR PLAYS/ENTRIES

Teams that use a variety of different types of offensive cuts by all types of offensive players from different locations on the floor during the many phases of the offense makes the offense much less predictable and ultimately much more difficult to defend by both individual defenders as well as the overall opponents' team defense. These types of cuts force individual defenders to defend their men more often as well as to occupy themselves to help reduce the effectiveness of the opposition's ballside and helpside defense on support defense. These offensive cuts that should be utilized within the offense's frameworks are defined as:

A) "V" Cuts,
B) "Pipe" or "Zipper" Cuts,
C) "Shuffle" Cuts,
D) "Flex" Cuts,
E) "Flex Bump" Cuts,
F) "Flex Veer" Cuts,
G) "UCLA Rub-Off Cuts,
H) "UCLA Bump" Cuts,
I) "Curl" Cuts,
J) "Backdoor" Cuts,
K) "Give-n-Go" Cuts,
L) "Flare-Cuts,
M) "Iverson" Cuts,
N) "Barkley" Cuts,
O) "Duck-In" Cuts,
P) "Lob" Cuts,
Q) (High or Low) "Flash-Post" Cuts,
R) "Slash" Cuts,
S) "Spin-Screen" Cuts, and
T) "Basket Cuts (including cuts such as "Slip" Cuts, "Rolls," "Rim-Runs," "Ghost Ball-Screen Cuts," "Ghost Flare-Screen Cuts," "Ghost Diagonal Down-Screen Cuts," or "Ghost Pin-Down Screen Cuts.")

OFFENSIVE PLAYERS MUST ALWAYS USE THE PROPER ANGLES TO IMPROVE PASSING TO THEIR TEAMMATES

Utilizing the proper angles in basketball is a very underrated concept in basketball. The proper angles in executing several different techniques and methods is a lost art. One example would be when a perimeter player with the ball is on a higher plane than his teammate that is posting up a defender on the "Block" is being front or ¾ fronted with that same defender shading the offensive player on the high side. If the ball can switch to become on the plane lower than the post defender, the offensive post player will be able to have a "position advantage" over his opponent. It is the post player's responsibility to maintain that new-found advantage with the proper pivoting, footwork and using his body to 'seal' off and keep that defender on the so-called high side of him (when the ball is lower than the defender.) Adjusting to the proper angle may simply require a quick pass to a perimeter teammate that is in better location to be able to have that improved "passing angle." Another method may simply require a short perimeter 'pull dribble' that not only improves the angle, but also stretches opposing defenses that will weaken the opposition's interior support defense.

◉ *COACHING POINT 22:*

OFFENSIVE DRIBBLERS, CUTTERS AND SCREENERS SHOULD USE THE PROPER ANGLES TO IMPROVE ALL TYPES OF SCREENING ACTIONS

Both 'on-the-ball' and 'off-the-ball' offensive screens are implemented between (at least one screener) and the designated cutter that is to use the screen to free himself from his individual defender. Good defenders are conscious and aware of many upcoming screens that will be used to slow down or impair their defending their offensive opponent. It is imperative that the screener always set the legal screen with the legal distance between he and the defender with a wide base and to expect contact. The invaluable technique that seems to not be stressed enough is that the screener must also set the screen to offer the largest and widest "wall" or obstacle to prevent or slow down the defender's progress. The most forgotten technique is for that screener to have his butt directly pointing to the spot on the floor where his teammate needs to pass through on his cut or on his dribble.

The receivers of all 'off-the-ball' offensive screens must remember initially to set up their defender for the coming (various types of) off-ball screen being set for him. He then must make sure that he makes as close of contact as possible with the proper side of the screener before then turning to make the slight "angle" to square up to both the passer with the ball and also with the basket. In addition, we have the off-ball cutters prepare for the actual catch with hands in position and for the proper footwork (to stop the cutter's momentum to be able to quickly take the shot under control) and be ready for a possible immediate 'catch and shoot' or 'catch and create' offensive action. We use three phrases to emphasize and constantly remind offensive players to always execute those techniques:

A) "Scraping off of the (screener's) outside shoulder,"
B) "Getting your feet and hands ready (for the pass)" as well as
C) "Cheating your inside shoulder to square up to the ball and the basket."

Dribblers that are to receive 'on-the-ball' offensive screens must remember should also initially set up their ball-defender for the coming ball-screen. That dribbler must also make as close of contact as possible with the proper side of the ball-screener before then "turning the corner" to attack the basket. While the dribbler already in in possession of the ball, we still have the driver/dribbler prepare for the receiving of the ball with the hands in already in position in the 'shooting pocket.' In addition, we have the dribbler get his timing down to also prepare his 'Inside pivot heel' to square up to the basket as he makes the last dribble (the lowest and the hardest dribble that flows directly and quickly into the shooting pocket) just before his 'lift off.' We also stress getting the 'inside shoulder already starting its turn towards the basket even as the last dribble is being made. The same three phrases can be made to constantly remind offensive players to always execute those techniques "Dribble-scraping off of the (screener's) shoulder" and "getting your feet and hands ready" as well as "cheating your inside shoulder to square up (to the basket earlier)."

⊕ COACHING POINT 23:

ALL OFFENSIVE PLAYERS MUST ALWAYS USE THE PROPER ANGLES
TO IMPROVE 'DRIVES TO THE BASKET'

Football coaches constantly coach and emphasize their running backs to sometimes run "east and west," but mostly to run "north and south" or "downhill." While the phrase is coming into the basketball world, it still can be emphasized more so. We try to show players that on drives to the basket out from the perimeter, that the angle they begin with can reduce their driving distance and therefore driving time. We try to show players the imaginary 45 degree angles from each sideline diagonally towards the basket as being the perfect lay-up path. We then try to emphasize that unless a driver is vertically and horizontally trying to (passively) 'Perimeter Pull Dribble'" the ball to stretch interior defenders or is ultimately trying to drive the baseline; the best bet is to drive within the imaginary "cone" for more direct (and shorter/quicker) penetrations to the basket. Therefore, those driving angles should also be emphasized.

ALL OFFENSIVE PLAYERS MUST UTILIZE
A WIDE VARIETY OF "ON-BALLSCREENS"

Offensive schemes should/could include "on-the-ball" screens with as many as five different starting points and a maximum of six or so different "follow-up methods or techniques" that can effectively be executed. The starting points of the initial ball-screen can vary from different locations of the court. Therefore having different players receiving the ball-screen in addition to setting the actual ball-screens from different starting points and different types of ending action as well as the different combinations of players involved can result in a multitude of offensive ball-screening scenarios. These various scenarios could be applied to specific players that fit their offensive strengths and allow certain players to avoid some scenarios where there can be individual weaknesses. In addition to playing to individual players' strengths, to avoiding individual players' weaknesses, the various scenarios can be used to attack individual defenders' weakness. The various scenarios will also can a higher degree of unpredictability for opposing teams, making it even more difficult for defensive teams to adequately defend.

⊕ *COACHING POINT 25:*

OFFENSES MUST UTILIZE THE VARIOUS LOCATIONS FOR ALL "ON-BALL SCREENS"

These basic starting locations where the ball-screen can effectively be set are at the top of the key, an area between the top of the key and the elbow area on both sides of the floor, (for the ball-screener to set "Inside Ball-Screens" at the high post elbow area or for the ball-screener to attack the defender and the overall defense down the middle of the lane,) and near both wide deep corner areas.

Another area could be further out between the time-line and the top of the key for a "Big" to set a "Flat (Ball)-Screen" for the dribbler to shed his defender higher up, further from the basket and attack the middle interior of the floor.

⊕ *COACHING POINT 26:*

COACHES SHOULD UTILIZE OFFENSES THAT UTILIZE THE VARIOUS WAYS TO INITIATE "ON-BALL SCREENS"

These various types of (fundamentally sound) on the ball-screens that should/could be utilized within each offensive team's frameworks are defined as:

A) "Big-on-Small" Ball-Screens,
B) "Small-on-Big" Ball-Screens,
C) "Inside" Ball-Screens,
D) "Follow" (the Pass & Ball-) Screens,
E) "Long" Ball-Screens,
F) "Ram" Ball-Screens,
G) "Ghost" Ball-Screens,
H) "Flat" Ball-Screens,
I) "Double" Ball-Screens,
J) "Twisted Double" Ball-Screens,

K) "Consecutive" Ball-Screens,

L) "Stagger" Ball-Screens and

M) "Spain" Ball-Screen Action.

N) A fundamentally sound way to initiate the ball-screen action could be the traditional stationary ball-screen usually set near the top of the key or halfway from the top of the key and the high elbow areas.

O) Another method (the "Flat Screen") is action when the somewhat traditional stationary ball-screener sets his screen somewhere near the middle "alley" just inside the 10-second time-line with his back directly towards the basket—allowing the dribbler to dribble-scrape off of either of the screener's shoulder and directly in a straight line towards the rim.

P) Different or more modern methods of setting ball-screens could be the "Long Ball-Screen" where the designated ball-screener breaks from an initial low post position up to the designated screening location.

Q) Another method could be the "Ram-Screen" where one offensive player sets a a form of a "Down-Screen" for that specific cutter to use to break towards the ball (initially as a possible pass receiver), before then continuing towards the ball (and ball-handler) to then set an on-ball screen.

R) A third method (called the "Follow (ball-) Screen which is when a passer completes a pass to a teammate and immediately "follows" his pass to set an immediate ball-screen on the new ball-handler/dribbler.

⊕ *COACHING POINT 27:*

COACHES SHOULD UTILIZE OFFENSIVE ACTION THAT ALWAYS USE THE VARIOUS WAYS TO FINISH THE VARIOUS TYPES OF "ON-BALL SCREENS

Various finishes to the different types of 'ball-screens' that could/should also be integrated (dependent upon each team's strengths, weaknesses, style and staff's philosophies) could be any of the following such as the:

A) "Screen-Roll,"

B) "Rim-Run,"

C) "Lob-Cut" after Screen-the-(Ball-)Screener action,

D) "Flare-Cut (also called "Pick & Pop"),

E) Various "Off-the-Ball" Screening Actions after the initial Ball-Screen

F) "Back-screen the Ball-Screen on his roll" ("Spain" action.)

❊ COACHING POINT 28:

COACHES SHOULD UTILIZE OFFENSES THAT UTILIZE A VARIETY OF THE DIFFERENT OFF-THE-BALL-SCREENS

Integrate these many different types of "off-the-ball screens" within the framework of the offense so that your team can either completely eliminate or at least move the "helpside" defense, or to have offensive personnel cutting towards the ball either on the perimeter or the interior. These could be in the form of "Big-on-Small," "Small-on-Big," "Small-on-Small" or "Big-on-Big" types of "off-the-ball screens." Screens set by a different sized player on a different sized teammate helps discourage defensive switching or can quickly put defensive players in drastic mismatches that can and should be capitalized on. These off-ball screens could also be combined with other types of off-ball screens discussed to become a two-part form of screening action.

❊ COACHING POINT 29:

COACHES SHOULD UTILIZE OFFENSES THAT UTILIZE A VARIETY OF THE DIFFERENT OFF-THE-BALL-SCREENS

These various types of (fundamentally sound) off-the-ball-screens that should/could be utilized within each offensive team's frameworks are defined as:

Some of these "Off-the-Ball-Screens can be called:

A) "Diagonal Down-Screens" (with or without Flash Post action,)
B) "Pin-Screens" (with or without Post Seal-offs,)
C) "Stagger-Screens" (Twisted or Not),
D) "Elevator-Screens" (Twisted or Not),
E) "Shuffle-Screens,"
F) "Back-Screens,"
G) "Flare-Screens,"
H) "Flex-Screens" (with or without Bump Cuts or Veer Cuts,)
I) "Iverson Screens,"

j) "Barkley Screens,"

K) "Chin Back-Screens,

L) "UCLA-Screens," (with or without Bump Cuts),

M) "Brush-Screens,"

N) "Ram-Screens,"

O) (Interior) "Lane Exchange Cross-Screens,"

P) (Interior) Spin-Screens"

Q) "Various Ghost Off-the-Ball Screens,"

R) "Various (Off-Ball) "Screen & Re-Screen" Combo Actions.

Each of the following screens could be set with different types of offensive personnel both setting the screen and receiving the screen. These screens could involve either "Big-on-Small" screens, "Small-on-Big" screens, "Big-on-Big, screens" or "Small-on-Small Off-the-Ball-Screens." These four various combinations can cause opposing defenses problems if defensive switches are involved.

⊕ *COACHING POINT 30:*

COACHES SHOULD EXECUTE OFFENSES THAT UTILIZE A VARIETY OF "COMBO-SCREENS"

A popular offensive series of action now is where the initial screener sets two (or more) different types of screens in a very short, smooth and fluid series of offensive actions. The initial screener then screens a second teammate which gives the passer multiple pass receiving targets and therefore provides the offense with more scoring threats.

Some of these "Combo-Screens" could be:

A) Shuffle Back-Screen into a Ball-Screen,

B) Shuffle Back-Screen into a Stagger-Screen,

C) UCLA Back-Screen into an Inside Ball-Screen & Roll,

D) UCLA Back-Screen into an Inside Ball-Screen & Flare-Cut,

E) Ball-Screen into a Down-Screen,

F) Other Combos that can be created.

COACHES SHOULD VALUE THE IMPORTANCE OF A
CONTINUITY OFFENSE'S "SPOT-UPS"

After a selected play/entry from a designated offensive set/alignment is executed and the offensive team maintains control of the ball with no shot taken; the next phase of the offensive attack begins by smoothly and seamlessly flowing into a designated continuity offense or a particular type of motion offense. This next phase or wave of the attack from a wide type of offense must begin with players beginning in specific locations on the court after the play/entry has been concluded (with no shot or loss of possession.)

We define these important locations or positions as the continuity offense's "spot-ups." Each play in the team's arsenal must have the very same "spot-ups," so that the next phase of the offense will begin with all five players having filled those same "spot-up" locations.

The concern that a defensive opponent would be able to predict the offensive action should be somewhat minimal, especially if there are multiple plays/entries to be used and that there are options and counter-options within the framework of the continuity offense. When plays or entries are successfully executed, but with no shots taken and the play then transitions into the continuity offense; the smooth beginning of the actual continuity is actually camouflaged by the plays' action. Therefore, the continuity offense is not even recognized or distinguished as that continuity offense. Still, players in the correct spot-up locations will smoothly and easily flow into the designated continuity offense which then instantly becomes the second wave of the overall offensive attack.

Each entry/play/quick-hitter that does not produce a shot from the alignment/set will at least place all five offensive personnel specifically in either (Even-Front or Odd-Front) "4-Out/1-In" or (Balanced or Unbalanced) "3-Out/2-In" spot-ups. Particular groups of these spot-ups should also be filled at the conclusion of any Secondary Fastbreak actions, from every Baseline Out-of-Bounds (B.L.O.B.) or from each of the Sideline Out-of-Bounds (S.L.O.B.) plays. Again, this allows the offense to smoothly, seamlessly and immediately flow from an offensive play into various continuity offenses or different forms of motion offenses. This makes the designated continuity or motion offense even more crucial to the overall success of the offense.

Each entry/play/quick-hitter that does not produce a shot from the alignment/set will at least place all five offensive personnel specifically in either (Even-Front or Odd-Front) "4-Out/1-In" or (Balanced or Unbalanced) "3-Out/2-In" spot-ups. Particular groups of these spot-ups should also be filled at the conclusion of any Secondary Fastbreak actions, from every Baseline Out-of-Bounds (B.L.O.B.) or from each of the Sideline Out-of-Bounds (S.L.O.B.) plays. Again, this allows the offense to smoothly, seamlessly and immediately flow from an offensive play into various continuity offenses or different forms of motion offenses. This makes the designated continuity or motion offense even more crucial to the overall success of the offense. "Spot-Ups" of a continuity offense become a conduit between a team's plays/entries and the team's 2nd phase of attack—be it a continuity offense or a motion-type offense. It also becomes a means to be able to smoothly continue not only after half-court plays that did not produce a shot; but just as importantly after all Secondary Break actions, all Baseline Out-of-Bounds Plays and every Sideline Out-of-Bounds Play in the team's arsenal in which the action did not generate a shot. "Spot-Ups" are a way to also camouflage a continuity offense because many times the offense will score or lose possession of the ball during the entry before the actual continuity can begin and be utilized. Out of all of an offensive team's possessions, opposing teams often will not even face the continuity offense and therefore not necessarily be accustomed to defending it. These are the major points of focus that coaches should stress to all players to establish an effective and productive man-to-man offensive system that can withstand the weather of time. As players and their respective ability levels of both strengths and weaknesses change from one season to the next, in addition to opponents changing; a fundamentally sound offensive system can adjust accordingly without major disruptions or changes to the overall program. This consistency gives both the players and the coaching staff faith and confidence in the system.

CHAPTER 9

ON-BALL SCREENS USED IN A SUCCESSFUL MULTIPLE-PHASE MAN-TO-MAN OFFENSIVE SYSTEM

These thirty offensive actions all involved the use of the fundamentally sound and extremely successful action of the traditional "ball-screen" modified in various manners from the many different plays/entries (out of the many different offensive sets/alignments.)

Notice that the overall action of each quick-hitter/play/entry, regardless of what specific level the play is, repositions each offensive to move into one of the proper spot-ups of the designated continuity or motion-type offense. Therefore, if the various ball-screening actions of the play does not immediately create the desired shot, the action will at least allow for a smooth, immediate and fluid transition into that last phase of the offensive attack—the continuity or motion-type offense. This gives the opposition no opportunity to recover or regroup after just preventing a shot from initial entry.

The "Ball-Screen" action has long been a staple to offenses of levels of competition. From elementary teams to the NBA, the many ways that the various types of ball-screens are set, the different types of players that use the screen, various players that set the screens; the action can produce shots. In addition, defenses will have increasingly difficulties with the unpredictability factor, because of the many combinations of players that could be involved in the action. In addition, with the many different locations that the ball-screens could be executed increase that large amount of unpredictability. In addition, there are countless types of action that can be executed following the actual ball-screen.

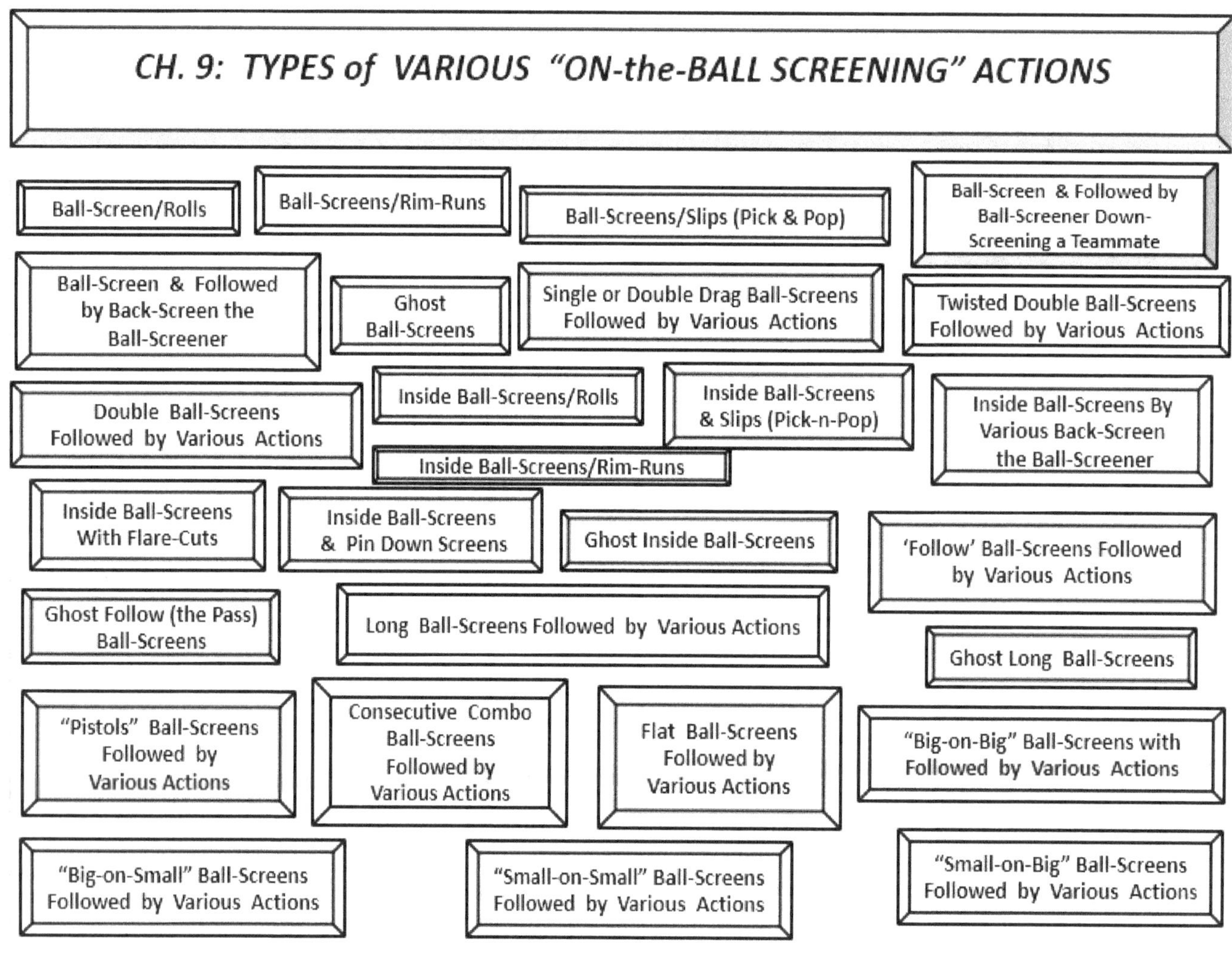

Diagram 9.1

⊕ PLAY # 1: "BIG-ON-SMALL BALL-SCREEN/ROLL" ACTION

Diagram 9.1 illustrates the very basic, but still extremely successful "Ball-Screen/Roll." This action can and should be included within the free-flowing but organized structure of several quick-hitting plays/entries from every level of play. This action could begin out of almost every offensive alignment, but this example is taken from an Offensive Baseline Out-of-Bounds (BLOB) situation, called "Jam."

The play begins with 05 back-pedaling out to the 'High Post Elbow' location and receiving 01's inbounds "Lob Pass." 03 immediately lifts to the FT Line extended to receive a Dribble Hand-Off from 05 and for 01 to have space to break towards the new "Ballside Deep Corner." As 03 receives the ball, 04 diagonally breaks up to set a "Big-on-Small Ball-Screen" to perimeter drag dribble across towards the opposite side's perimeter "Slot." As 03 "dribble-scrapes" off of 04's top (left) shoulder, 04 makes a reverse pivot off of his lower right foot to open up to the ball and rolls down the lane and looks for a possible "Inside Pass" from 03 (or possibly from 02 or 05). With 05 remaining near the new "Weakside Slot," the presumed biggest defender, X5, is taken away from the play and cannot help out his isolated defensive teammate, (either X4 or possibly X3). With 01 and 02 spotted up in the perimeter "Deep Corners" on both sides of the floor, 03 and 05 on the two perimeter "Slots," the initial "Ball-Screener," 04 will enjoy a dominating "position advantage" by completing isolating his defender in the vulnerable highest scoring area on the court.

Regardless of how the "Ball-Screen/Roll" action is played by the defense, whether it be: a) "straight up," "hedge" or "hard hedge," "switch," "trap" or "drop;" the offense should be able to capitalize on what the defense gives up and be able to create either "position advantages" or "player advantages" to get the desired shot by the desired player(s) directly from the entry.

Still, if the desired shot is not taken, all five players are in the "4-Out/1-In" Spot-Ups for the designated 2nd Phase of the attack to seamlessly begin. The defense cannot recover from defensive switches or being out of position attempting to defend the initial action of the play.

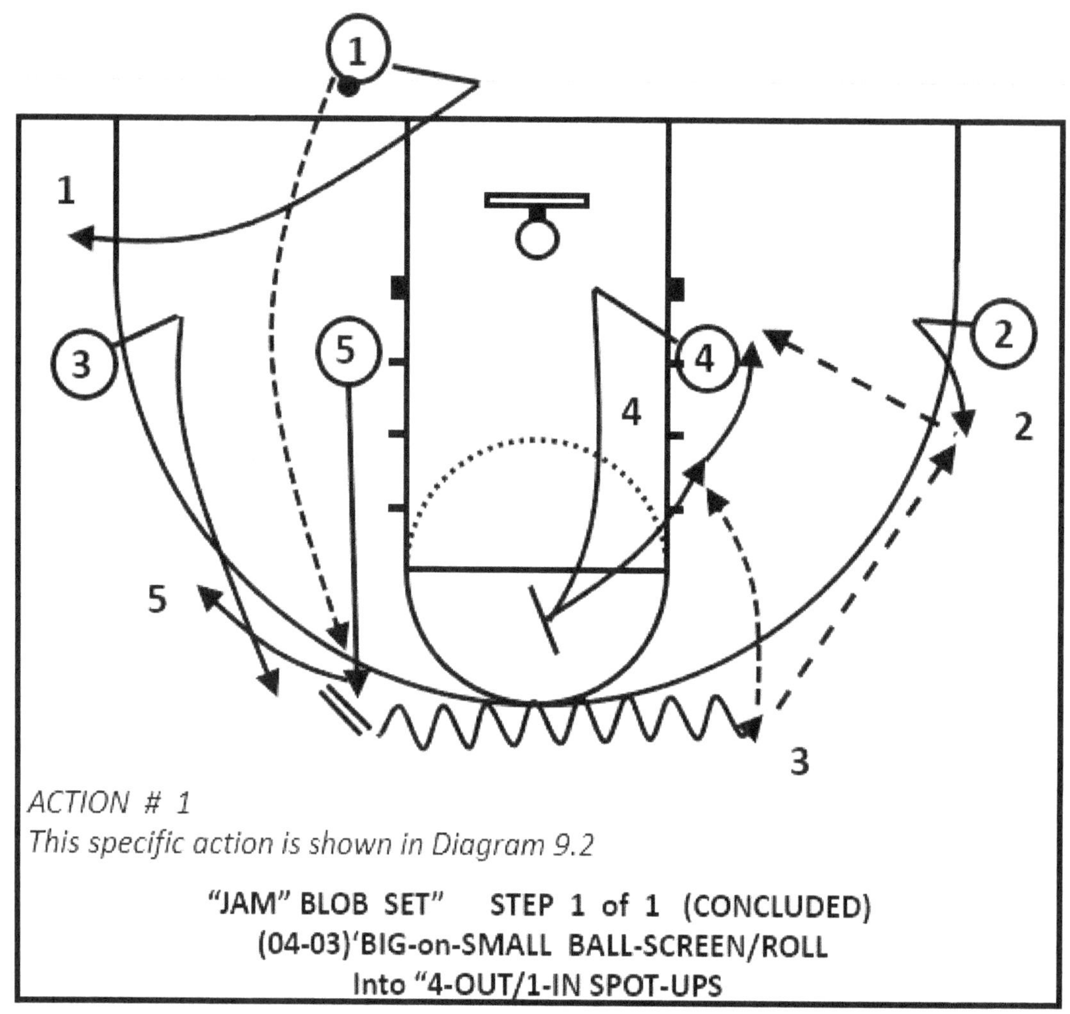

Diagram 9.2

🏀 PLAY # 2: "BIG-ON-SMALL BALL-SCREEN/RIM-RUN" ACTION

Out of the "Twins" Set, Diagram 9.3 illustrates another "Big-on-Small Ball-Screen," but this time with the action by the screener (04) setting the same screen near the top of the key. As the designated ball-handler (01) "dribble-scrapes" off of 04's top left shoulder and breaks contact with the screener, this time 04 makes a front pivot off of the same lower right foot to make a "Rim-Run" towards the basket and looks for 01's "Lob Pass."

As 01 starts dribbling towards 04, 05 makes a diagonal "Slash Cut" diagonally across the basket to the newly designated "Ballside Mid-Post Notch (above-the-Block.) 02 and 03's initial locations vertically stretch the defense and as 01 approaches the right "Slot," 02 breaks out to his "Deep Corner" to also then horizontally stretch the defense; further weakening the defensive interior for both 05 and his "Slash Cut" and then for 04 on his

"Rim-Run." 03 breaks up to the newly declared "Weakside Slot" with 01 filling the new "Ballside Slot." Interior shots first by 05 and then by 04, followed by perimeter shot options by 01, 02 and also by 03 can all be viable shot for this Play # 2.

Once again, all five players have attacked their individual defenders and weakened the overall team defense; with players in the correct spot-up positions for a seamless and fluid beginning to the designated continuity or Motion-type offense.

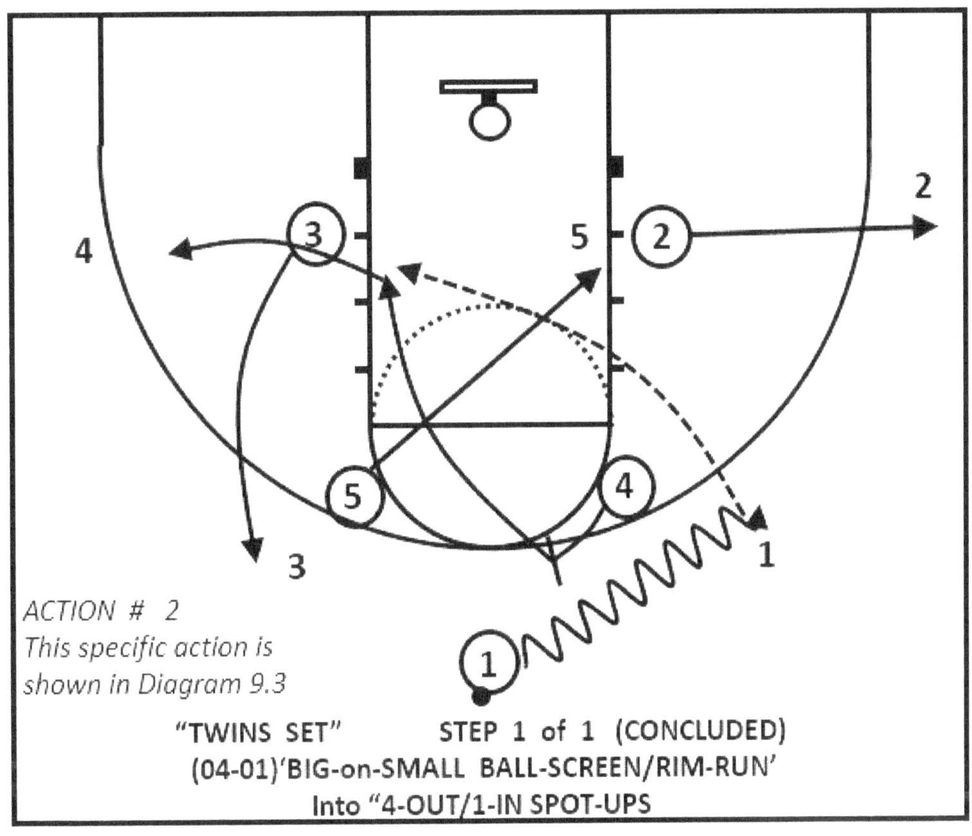

Diagram 9.3

🌐 PLAY # 3: "BIG-ON-SMALL BALL-SCREEN SLIP" ACTION

Diagram 4 illustrates another version of the "Ball-Screen," out of "2-Down Flat" Set. With 01 at the top of the key, 04 makes a strong and aggressive "Duck-In" Cut from his initial location. 01 looks to capitalize on making the pass to 04 on his cut as he dribbles towards 05, located at the high "Elbow" area on the left side of the floor. At the same time, 03 "drift cuts" towards his "Deep Corner," vertically and horizontally stretching the defense. 01 "dribble-scrapes" off of 05's top right shoulder. When defenses attempt to defend the ball-screen by "dropping (X5), "hard hedging" or "switching:' 05 can then "slip his screen and flare as far as to the opposite "Slot." This action is commonly also called "Pick and Pop" and was made popular with Bill Laimbeer and the Detroit Pistons years ago. It has been copied by many teams from all three Levels of play since then. If 05 has perimeter scoring skills, particularly "catch and shoot" skills from behind the arc; this action will be very successful. Keep in mind that even if 05 turns down his shot, 04 has still gained a "Position advantage" by isolating his lone defender in the highest scoring area on the floor—the lane just in front of the basket.

If no shots are taken, (particularly by 05 or 04) all players are once again in the "4-Out/1-In" Spot-Ups for the final phase of the offense, able to smoothly and immediately begin; giving the defense no time to regroup or recover.

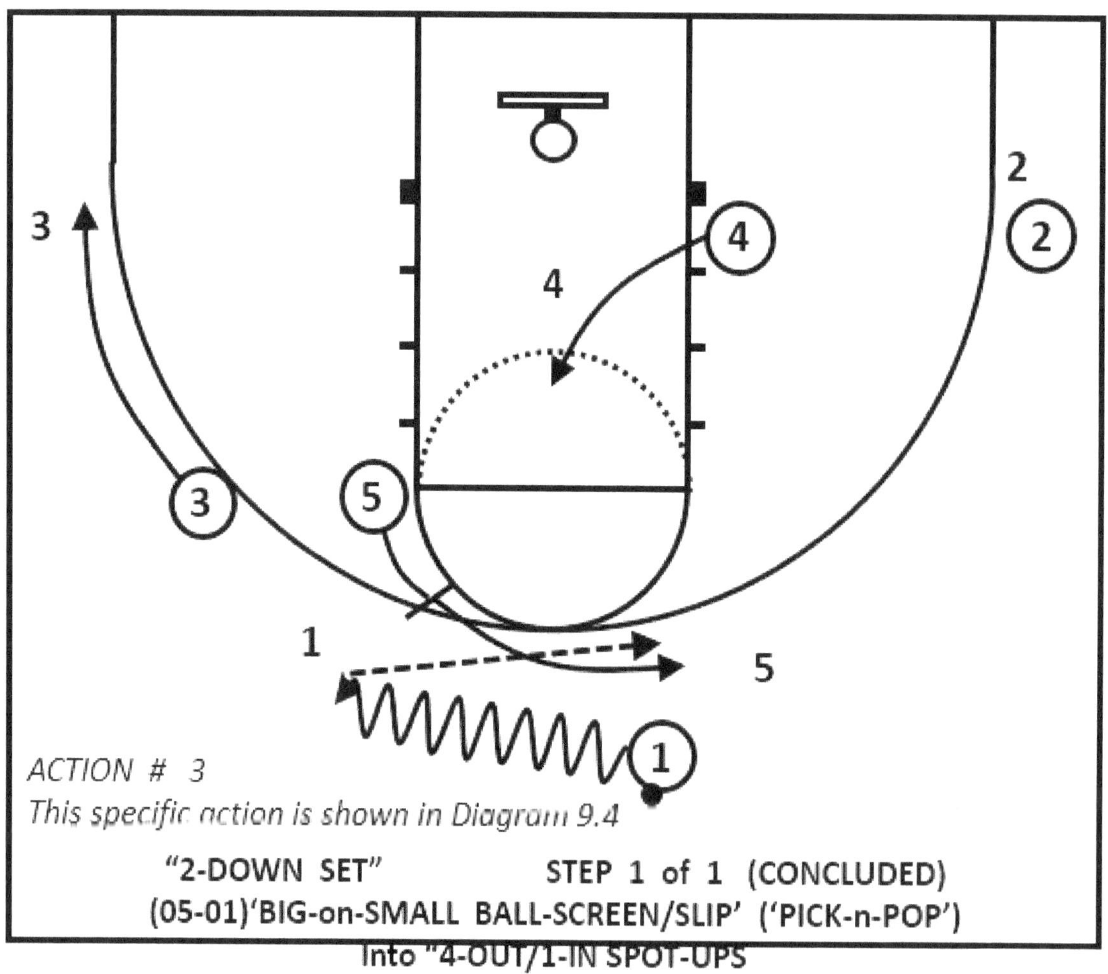

Diagram 9.4

✦ Play # 4: "Big-on-Small Ball-Screen Pin-Down" Action

Diagram 9.5 illustrates an entry out of the "Horns" Set when it is felt that 05 is not an overwhelming perimeter scoring threat. To capitalize on 04's interior scoring skills, 05's lack of scoring skills and 02's perimeter scoring skills, this play utilizes players' strengths while avoiding other player's weaknesses. Another "Big-on-Small" (05-01) Ball-Screen initiates the action of this play.

01 again "dribble-scrapes" off of 05's top right shoulder and 04 immediately diagonally "Slash Cuts" across the lane to post up his defender in another isolation situation. With 03 and 02 both starting in their respective "Deep Corners," the defense is already stretched into a weakened condition. As 01 breaks contact with 05's top shoulder, 05 makes another front pivot off of his left lower foot to then go set a "Big-on-Small" (this helps discourage defensive switching) Screen for 02 to use to rub his defender off and break to the newly declared "Weakside Slot" for a "catch and shoot" shot behind the arc. 05's action not only frees up 02 for the open shot, but also pulls the most likely biggest defender (X5) away from the basket; to help further X4's situation. "4-Out/1-In" Spot-Ups are again easily and quickly filled; not only for another fluid transition into the next phase of the offensive attack, but also helping to contribute for better offensive rebounding opportunities as well as defensive transitioning success.

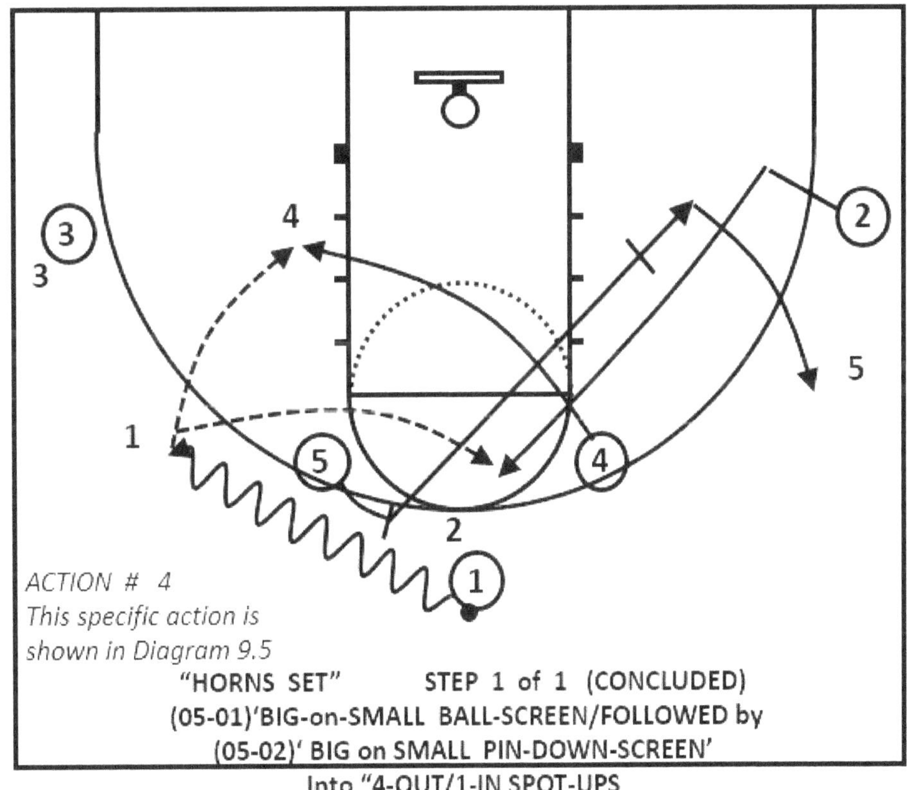

Diagram 9.5

⊕ Play # 5: "(Small-on Big Back-)Screen the (Ball-)Screener"

ACTION

Out of the "Hi-Lo Stax" Set, this quick-hitter starts with another "Big-on-Small Ball-Screen" with 01 closely dribbling off of 05's top shoulder while 03 "flare-cuts" to his "Deep Corner." At the same time, 04 flashes across the lane to isolate his post defender on the opposite side of the lane.

Another method of attacking opponent's "ball-screening" defenses is using different forms of "screening the (ball-)screener" action. Play # 5 has 02 diagonally make a long break to set a (02-05) "Small-on-Big Diagonal Back-Screen' for 05 to peel off 02's outside left shoulder and make a "Lob Cut" to the basket. With 02 screening for a "Big" (05), if defenses would switch this very difficult screen to defend; it would place a perimeter player (X2) on an offensive "Big" (05) near the basket. This gives the offense not only a "player advantage" but a "position advantage." 01 would still have an inside scoring option in looking to hit 04 on his isolation action. 01 and 03 both should have primary perimeter scoring opportunities.

If the play has not created the desired shots, it still has accomplished repositioning all five offensive players in the proper "4-Out/1-In" Spot-Up locations for an immediate transition into the last phase of the offensive attack.

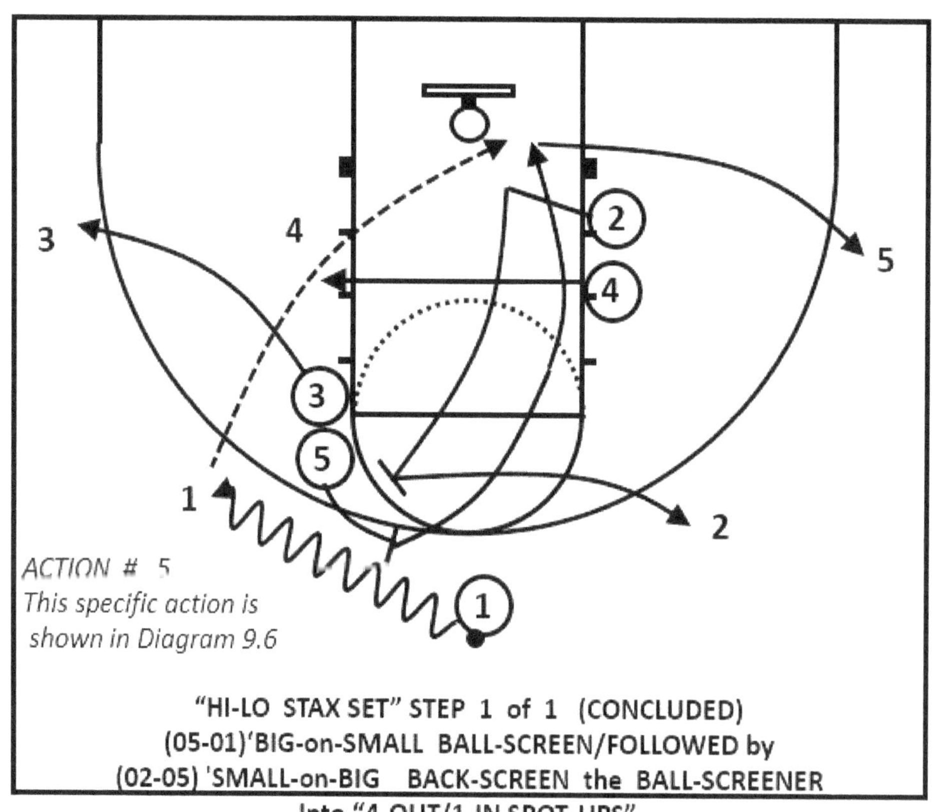

"HI-LO STAX SET" STEP 1 of 1 (CONCLUDED)
(05-01)'BIG-on-SMALL BALL-SCREEN/FOLLOWED by
(02-05) 'SMALL-on-BIG BACK-SCREEN the BALL-SCREENER
Into "4-OUT/1-IN SPOT-UPS"

Diagram 9.6

Play # 6 out of the "1-Down" Set is an illustration of another type of (counter-)attack to disrupt opposing defenses attempting to defend ball-screens. With 02 bringing the ball across the line himself or by receiving an early (01-02) "Reverse Pass," 02 starts towards 04. At the same time 04 breaks up as if to set a "Big-on-Small Ball-Screen" at the Slot. With X4 anticipating the screen, 04 breaks off of his screening path and makes a "Rim-Run" to the basket. To occupy his defender, 05 either flashes from across the left side of the lane to "Iso Post-Up" his defender or he begins on the same side of the floor as 04. This option of starting on either side of the lane gives the offense more looks and more deception and less predictability for the opposition. To occupy any possible weakside help defense, 03 steps up to set a (03-01) "Big-on-Small Flare-Screen." This gives 02 two possible '3 Pt. Scoring' Pass Receivers besides a back-up interior receiver in 05. If 05 is not immediately hit by 01, he should break out to the vacant "Deep Corner." This stretches and pulls the presumed biggest defender (X5) further away from the basket, leaving X4 in a more isolated and weakened defensive position/location.

If no shots are taken, all players are in the "4-Out/1-In" Offensive Spot-Ups—the initial starting locations for various other continuity offenses.

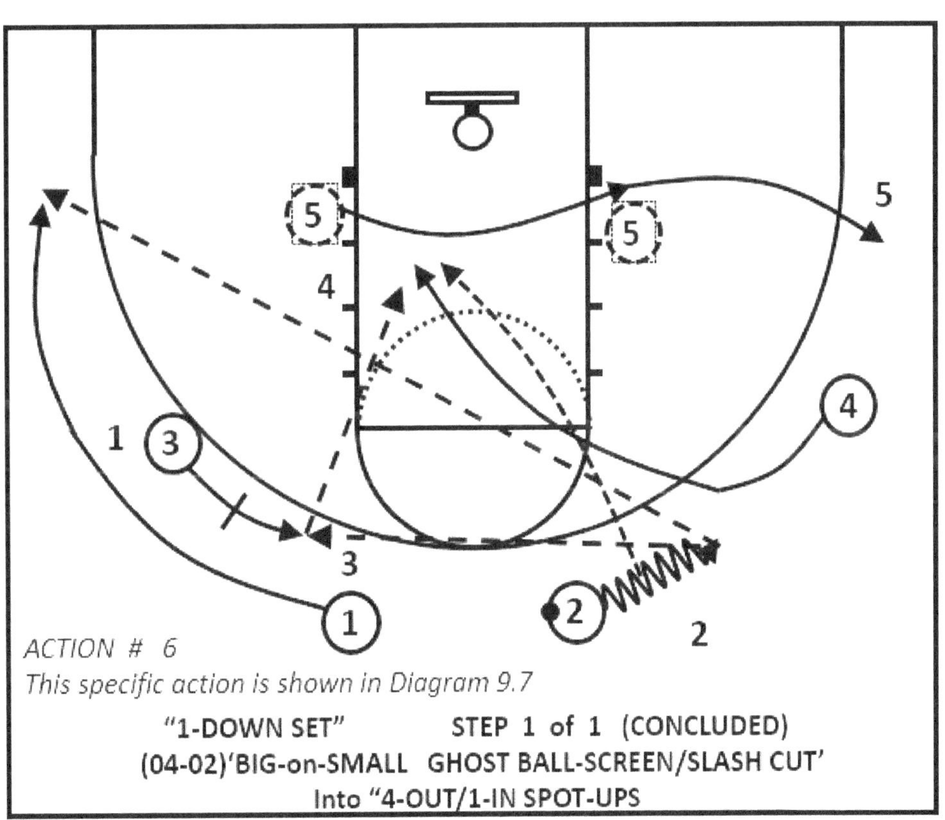

Diagram 9.7

⊕ PLAY # 7: "BIG-ON-SMALL DOUBLE BALL-SCREEN (WITH SLIP AND RIM-RUN)" ACTION.

Out of the "3-UP" Set Play # 7, 01 uses the Double "Big-on-Small Ball-Screen" set by both 05 and 04. After scraping and breaking contact with 04's top left shoulder, 01 dribbles towards the inside of the offense's right "Slot." If he can turn the corner and make a full dribble penetration, he should look to score, or to make a "Drive & Dump" pass to 04 or a "Penetrate and Pitch" pass to 02, flattened and spread out in the "Deep Corner. If 01 is "walled" off and cannot fully penetrate, he should make his dribble more of a "dribble pull" and stay out towards the "Slot."

With 04 making a "Rim-Run" and 05 making a "Slip" (again, sometimes called "Pick & Pop), the offense has stretched the defense both vertically and horizontally—further weakening the overall defense. If 05 is a strong perimeter scoring threat and/or X5 is a weak perimeter defender; 01 could reverse the ball to 05. 05 could look to score off of the "catch and shoot" or make interior or perimeter passes to his four teammates. This gives the offense not only immediate scoring threats but also places all players into the same "4-Out/1-In" Spot-Ups (for an immediate and fluid transition into the designated Continuity offense.)

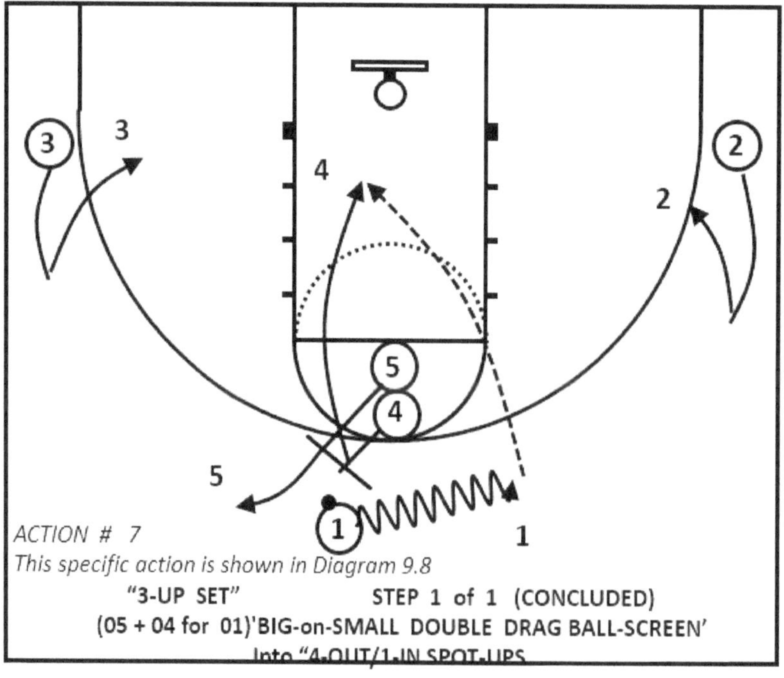

Diagram 9.8

⊕ PLAY # 8: "BIG-ON-SMALL TWISTED DOUBLE BALL-SCREEN (WITH SLIP AND RIM-RUN)" ACTION.

Diagram 9.9 illustrates a play out of the unique set, called the "Nail" Set. With 03 and 02 at the Free Throw line extended on their respective sides of the floor, 05 begins on the "Nail" with 04 stacked vertically just above 05.

This action could easily be executed out of the same "3-Up" Set (Diagram 9.8) and it simply has 05 step vertically above the stack to set the ball-screen with 04. This action is simply called the "Twisted (Big-on-Small) Ball-Screen. "Rolls" down the lane by 05 and "Slips" by 04 could be executed or 05 and 04 could reverse the rolls and slips; making the play even more unpredictable as well as giving 05 and/or 04 opportunities to accent their offensive advantages over their individual opponent.

This diagram illustrates Play # 8 with 01 "dribble-scraping off of 05's top left shoulder before 05 slips to the "Slot." This action then has 04 making a "Rim-Run" to the basket just as 01 breaks contact with 05 on his perimeter (or penetrating into the lane) dribble towards the right side of the floor. Both 03 and 02 drift down to their "Deep Corners" to vertically stretch the floor as their initial locations have already horizontally pulled their defenders further out of the middle. The "4-Out/1-In" Spot-Ups are once again filled so that the advantage of the fluid and immediate transition into the final phase of the attack remains.

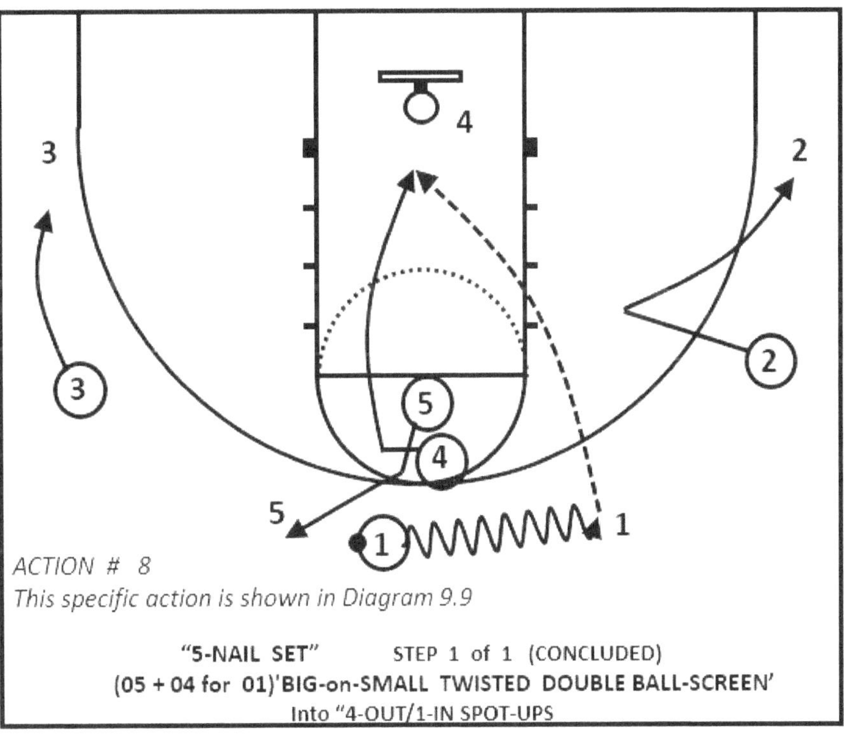

Diagram 9.9

⊕ Play # 9: "Big-on-Small Double Ball-Screen (with Slip and Rim-Run)" Action.

Diagram 9.10 illustrates a play out of the "5-SQUEEZE" Set where 01 starts towards the right "Slot" area with 03 and 02 both making "Iverson Cuts" to the opposite "Wing" Spot-Up locations. As 01 then begins his change of direction with a cross-over dribble, both 05 and 04 break up to the top of the key to set their ball-screen action.

When 01 "dribble-scrapes" towards the offense's left "Slot" location off of 05's outside right shoulder 05 makes a front pivot off of his left foot to continue slipping to the newly designated weakside "Slot" position. At the same time, 04 makes a reverse pivot off of his inside right pivot to make an aggressive (and isolated) "Rim-Run" to the basket, looking for a "Lob Pass" from 01 or an "Inside Pass" from 02 on an "Isolated Post-Up."

If nothing is available on the left side of the floor, 01 could reverse the ball to 05, particularly if 05 has strong offensive perimeter skills from behind the arc. If the ball is reversed to 05 and/or 03 (with a 01-03 "Skip Pass" or a 05-03 "Down Pass,") 04 should "chase the ball to post up on the new "Ballside Mid-Post." With 02 and 03 both spotting up in the "Deep Corners," the interior support defense is again stretched vertically and horizontally to further isolate X4. In addition, the "4-Out/1-In" Spot-Ups are again filled for the same seamless and fluid conversion into the last phase of the attack.

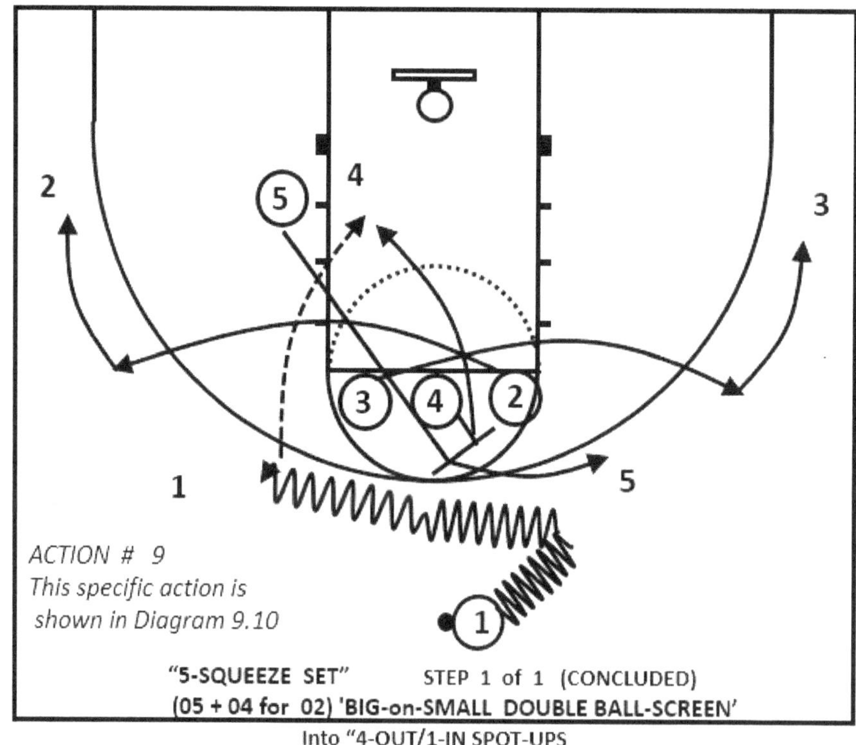

Diagram 9.10

⊕ Play # 10: "Big-on-Small Inside Ball-Screen/Roll" Action.

Diagram 9.11 illustrates a play out of the "2-SQUEEZE" Set. 02 breaks diagonally out from his initial "Mid-Post" location to the "Wing" spot on his initial side of the floor. As 01 makes the "Wing Pass" to 02, 05 quickly slashes to the new "Ballside Mid-Post," looking for a quick "Iso Post-Up." 03 breaks out to the FT Line extended and 01 flare-cuts to the new "Weakside Slot to both stretch the weakside defense.

If 05 does not receive an immediate pass from 01, 04 cuts towards 02 and the ball to set a "Big-on-Small Inside Ball-Screen" for 02 to use to either make a strong "penetrating dribble" into the lane or a "perimeter pull dribble" to move the ball to the other side of the floor and to stretch the defense even further. 05 steps out to the "Deep Corner" to pull his "defensive Big" away from the basket. After 01 "dribble-scrapes" off of 04's top right shoulder, 04 reverse pivots off of his lower left shoulder and rolls through the lane in his isolation cut towards the basket. 04 looks to receive the ball from either 02, 01 or 03. If 02 throws the ball back to 05, 04 should again "chase the ball and flash to the new "Ballside Mid-Post" location. If no shots are taken, regardless of the perimeter location of the ball; the "4-Out/1-In" Spot-Ups are filled for a smooth conversion into the next phase of the offensive attack.

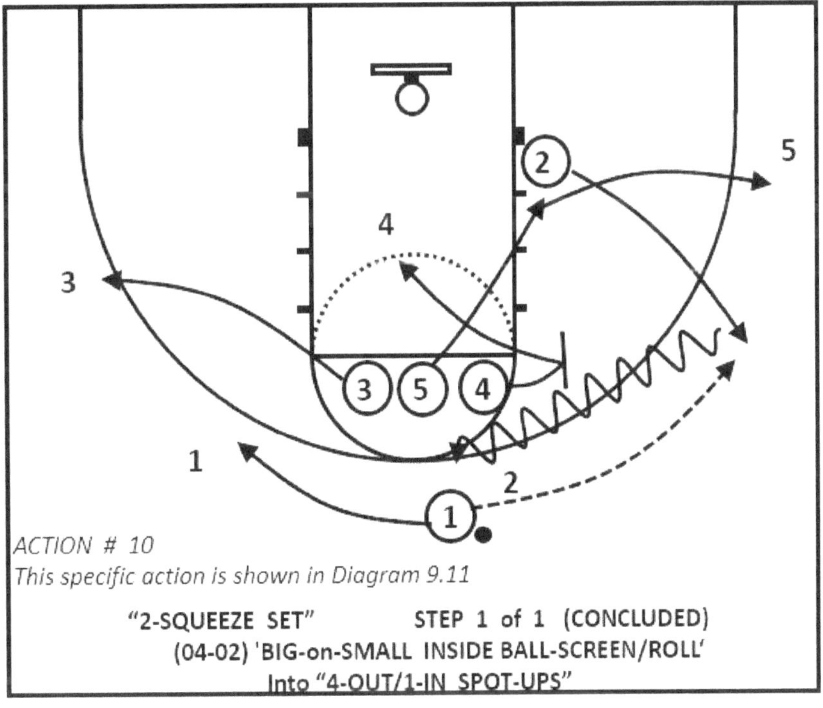

Diagram 9.11

⊕ PLAY # 11: "BIG-ON-SMALL INSIDE BALL-SCREEN/RIM-RUN" ACTION

Diagram 9.12 shows a play that has already been initiated out of the "3-ACROSS" Set with 04 starting on the left side of the lane. With 02 having the ball at the top of the key making a "Wing Pass" to 03, 01 has set a (01-02) "Flare-Screen" 02 to use to stretch his defender towards the new "Weakside Deep Corner." After screening for 02, 01 slips his screen and remains near the "Weakside Slot."

At the same time, 05 breaks from his initial "Nail" spot towards 03 and the ball to set a "ball-screen" for 03 to attack his defender out near the top of the key area. After 03 "dribble-scrapes" off of 05's top right shoulder, 05 then makes a front pivot off of his left foot to "Rim-Run" to the basket. 03 looks to either make a "Lob Pass" to 05. If 05 does not receive 03's "Lob Pass," 05 empties out of the lane to the vacant "Deep Corner." If 03 retains his dribble, he looks to make, a "penetrating dribble" into the lane (where he could "penetrate and pitch" to either 01 or 03 or make a "penetrating drive and dump" to 04.

If the desired shot is not found from the many options available, the "4-Out/1-In" Spot-Ups are once again to allow the offense to continue its relentless attack on the opposition's defense.

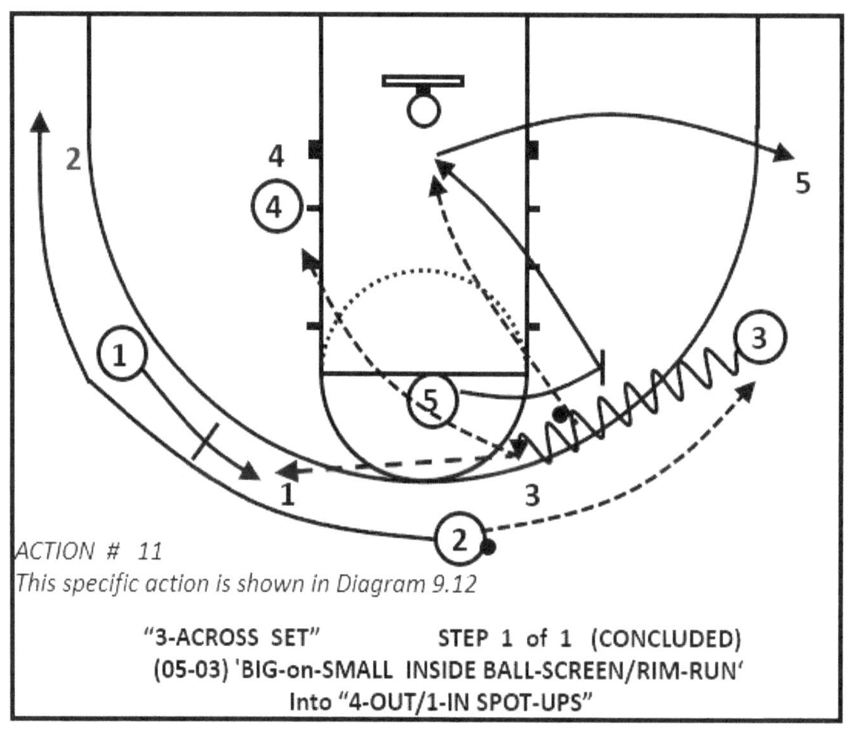

Diagram 9.12

⊕ PLAY # 12: "BIG-ON-SMALL INSIDE BALL-SCREEN/SLIP" ACTION

Diagram 9.13 shows a play that has already been started with 02 having the ball on the FT Line extended, 03 at the "Weakside Slot," and 01 also on the weakside at the FT Line extended. 04 has isolated his defender on the "Ballside Block," and 05 stepping out from the "Ballside High Post" area. As always, when using ball-screens, 02 sets his defender up with jab steps and fakes before then "dribble-scraping" off of 05's to right shoulder. In this instance, two teammates other than 05 are going to attack the interior defense. 04 will make a strong Iso Duck-In Cut while 03 crosses his defender up from the appearance of a (03-01) Pin-Down Screen by "ghosting" the perceived action and diving to the basket. To make way for less congestion, 05 makes a front pivot off of his right foot and steps to the perimeter area that 02 has just vacated. This helps 04 on his isolation action and also for 03 on his surprise inside cutting action.

It is also even more effective when 05 has good offensive perimeter skills, such as "catch and shoot" (off of the pass) skills and/or perimeter passing skills. 05 could receive 02's "Reverse Throwback Pass," turn down a shot and then look to hit 04 isolated on the "Ballside Block."

A unique feature in this particular play is that a new set of offensive spot-ups are used—the "3-Out/2-In" Spot-Ups. This gives the offense a whole new set of continuity offenses that could be used as well as different Motion-types of offenses (with their own different set of rules).

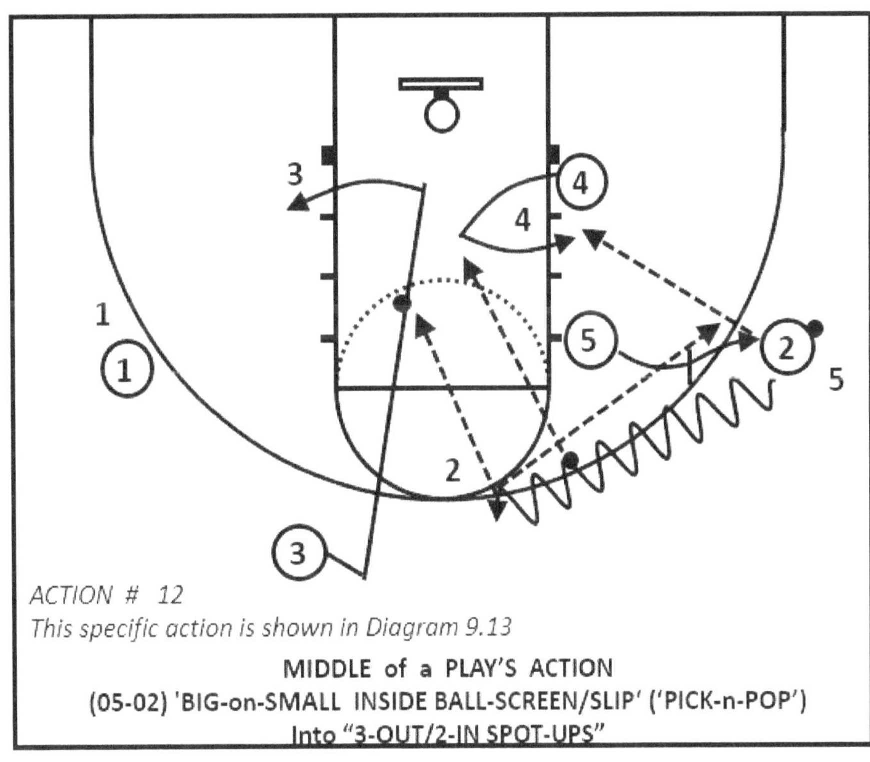

Diagram 9.13

PLAY # 13: "BIG-ON-SMALL INSIDE BALL-SCREEN FOLLOWED BY "SMALL-ON-BIG (BACK-) SCREEN THE (BALL-) SCREENER" ACTION

Diagram 9.14 shows a middle of a play where 01 has possession of the basketball on the offense's right side of the floor. 02 has isolated and inverted his perimeter-type defender with 05 at the Ballside High Post, 04 inverted out on the now designated "Weakside Slot" and 03 spotted up on the "Weakside Wing."

After 01 turns down the interior pass to 02, 05 again steps out on the perimeter to set his "Big-on-Small Inside Ball-Screen" for 01 to utilize his dribble with either "perimeter penetration" or "perimeter pull-dribbling" action. After "dribble-scraping" off of 05's top right shoulder and breaking contact with 05, 02 steps up to set a "Small-on-Big (Back-)Screen the (Ball-)Screen" for 05 to use. 05 front pivots off of his lower left foot and "scrapes" off of 02's left shoulder to then make a "Rim-Run" cut to the basket. After setting the screen, 02 slips his screen to reposition himself in the "Deep Corner" on the same side of the floor.

To provide the offense with scoring threats on the weakside of the floor as well as to occupy weakside defenders to further isolate 05 on his "Rim-Run," 04 cuts over to set a "Big-on-Small Pin Down-Screen" for 03 to break up to the "Slot" After screening, 04 drifts further into the "Deep Corner" area to further stretch the opposition's defense. When no desired shots are taken, the offense has still attacked various individual defenders and repositioned every offensive player so that the designated continuity offense associated with the "4-Out/1-In" Spot-ups can fluidly begin.

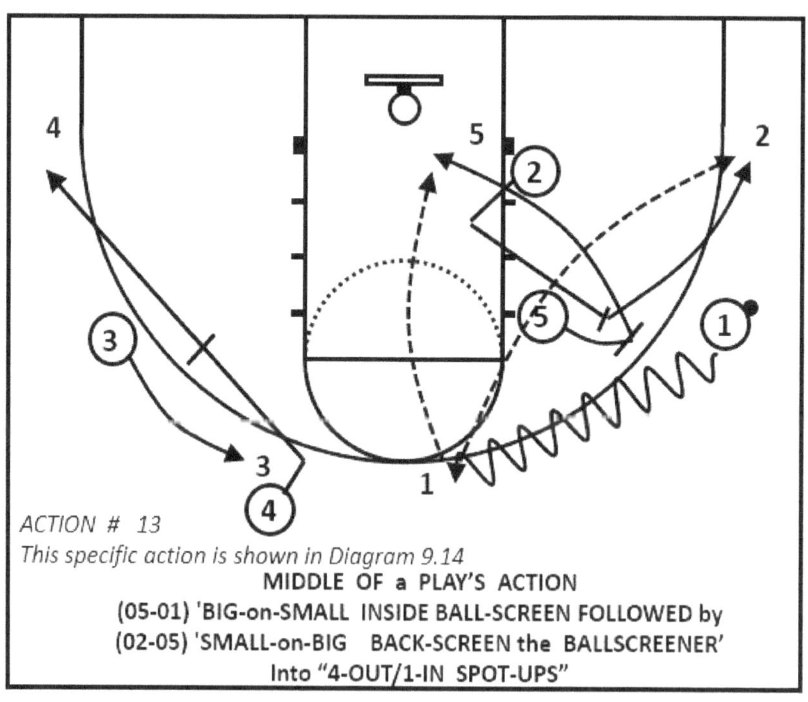

ACTION # 13

This specific action is shown in Diagram 9.14

MIDDLE OF a PLAY'S ACTION
(05-01) 'BIG-on-SMALL INSIDE BALL-SCREEN FOLLOWED by
(02-05) 'SMALL-on-BIG BACK-SCREEN the BALLSCREENER'
Into "4-OUT/1-IN SPOT-UPS"

Diagram 9.14

Diagram 9.15 illustrates the middle of a play that again places the ball in the hands of 01 at the FT Line extended on the right side of the floor. 05 is the player that has the advantage of posting up his isolated defender, X5, on the "Ballside Block" with 04 at the "Ballside High Post." 03 has ended up on the "Weakside Slot" and 02 at the "Weakside Wing."

When 01 turns down the interior pass to 05, 04 again steps out to set his "Big-on-Small Inside Ball-Screen" for 01 to use to make various passes to teammates or to look to use his "penetration dribble" into the lane or to use his "perimeter pull dribble" to vertically stretch the defense.

The weakside action of this particular play has 02 step up to set a "Small-on-Big Flare Screen" for 03. This gives 01 not one, but two perimeter scoring threats on the weakside while having a potential "Reverse Throwback" Pass opportunity to 04. This pass can be especially effective using misdirection and taking advantage of 04's possible perimeter scoring talents. In addition, it can be a way for the offense to attack X4's lack of perimeter defensive skills. 04 could also be the perimeter player that has an improved passing angle to deliver the ball to 05, isolated in the post.

If shots are not taken from the many options, all players are again repositioned into the "4-Out/1-In" Spot-Ups for the offense to continue its constant attack on the defense.

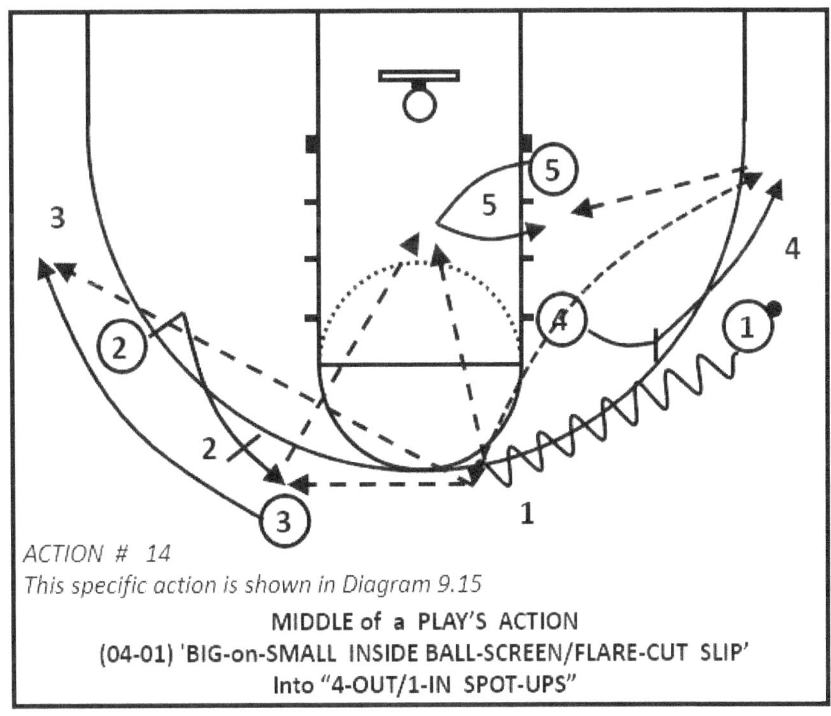

Diagram 9.15

⚽ PLAY # 15: "BIG-ON-SMALL INSIDE BALL-SCREEN/

FOLLOWED BY "PIN-DOWN SCREEN" ACTION

From the middle of the play, this diagram shows 03 having the basketball at the FT Line Extended, with 05 at the "Ballside High Post," 02 stretched out into the "Deep Corner, 01 at the "Weakside Slot" and 04 at the "Weakside FT Line extended.

When 03 "dribble-scrapes" off of 05's top right shoulder, 05's option in this play is to immediately break down to set a "Big-on-Small (05-02) Pin Down-Screen for 02 to fill the newly vacated wing area. After setting the screen for 02, 05 and slip his screen and "Rim-Run" (looking for interior passes from either 03 or from 02.

Weakside action has 04 start up to set a "Flare-Screen" for 01, but instead "ghosts the screen and continues to the "Weakside Block." 01 continues with his own "Flare-Cut" to the weakside.

02 has penetrating and perimeter scoring options off of his dribble, passing options to 02, to 05 to 04 or to 01. If these scoring options do not create the desired shot, the five offensive players have attacked and moved their own individual defenders as well as repositioned themselves into another set of offensive spot-ups. This is where a continuity or motion-type offense can begin out of these somewhat different "3-Out/2-In" Spot-Ups.

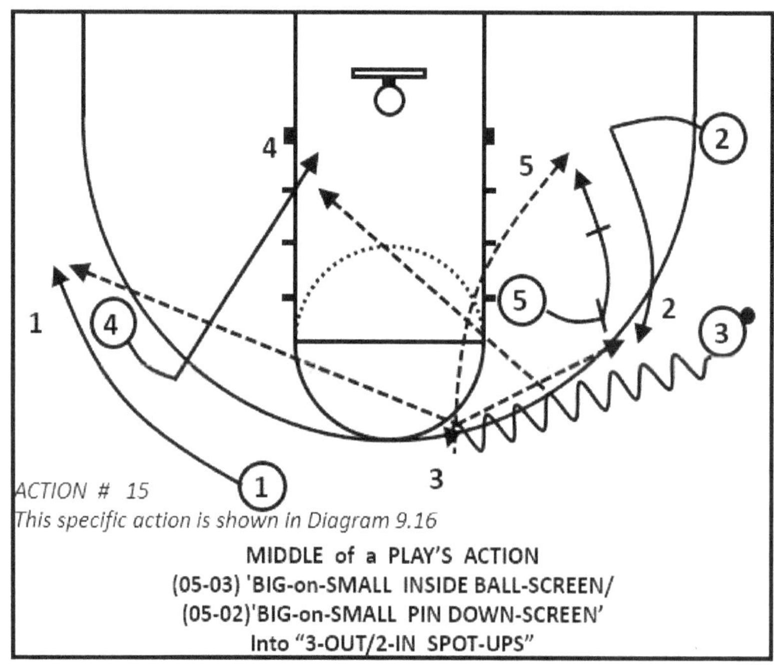

Diagram 9.16

⊕ PLAY # 16: "BIG-ON-SMALL GHOST INSIDE BALL-SCREEN" ACTION

From the middle of the play, this diagram shows 03 having the basketball at the FT Line Extended, with 05 at the "Ballside High Post," 02 stretched out into the "Deep Corner, 01 at the "Weakside Slot" and 04 at the "Weakside FT Line extended.

This play is unique in that there is a different form of deception in this play because 04 does not actually step out to set the "Inside Ball-Screen." Instead 04 sets a "Ghost Inside Ball-Screen" and quickly slashes to the basket, while looking for the quicker, earlier surprise pass from 01. If 01 still makes his "perimeter penetration dribble" or "perimeter pull dribble" (as he always has done in the previous plays) he looks again to make the pass to 04, a possible "Reverse Throwback Pass" to 03, who has lifted up to fill 01's initial "Wing" spot. 01 could look to hit 05 making a "Backdoor Cut" to the basket or to 02 on his "Flare-Cut" to the FT Line extended.

If shots are not created with all of the action described, the offensive players have forced their defenders to react and to move; while repositioning themselves into the proper "3-Out/2-In" Spot-Ups for a different type of Continuity or Motion Offenses than "4-Out/1-In" Spot-Ups utilize.

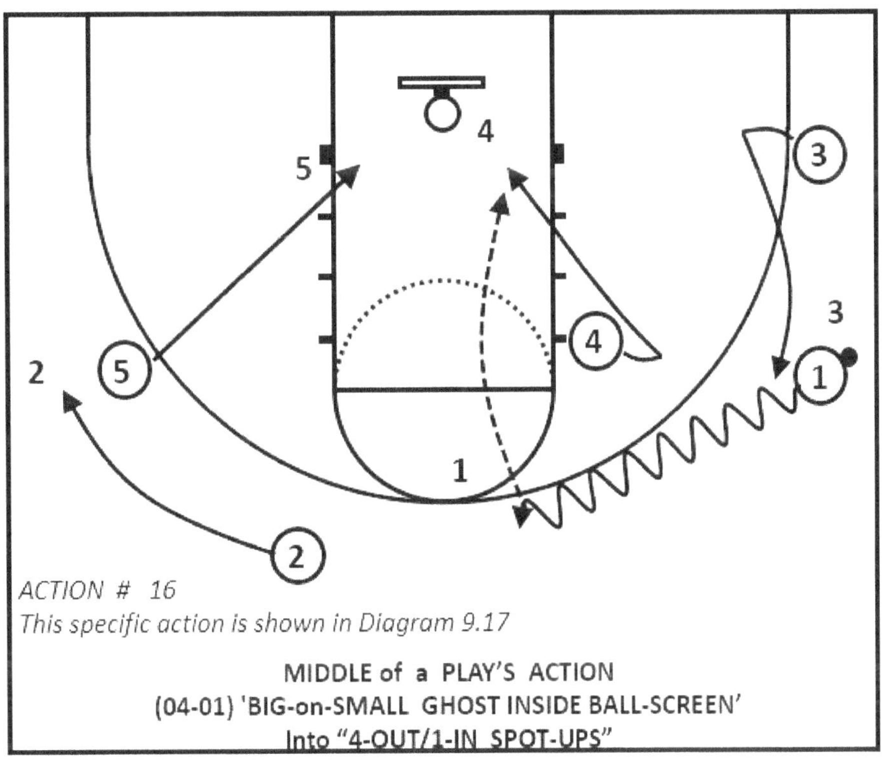

⦿ PLAY # 17: "FOLLOW-(THE-PASS) BALL-SCREEN/RIM-RUN" ACTION

Diagram 9.18 illustrates the entire Play # 17 that begins from the "2-TWIST" Set.

This entry starts with 01 bringing the ball across the time-line and making the 01-02 "Reverse Pass." 01 immediately follows his pass by cutting across to set a "Ball-Screen" for 02 to use and he "dribble-scrapes" off of 01's top right shoulder to proceed with his "perimeter pull dribble." As 01 breaks contact with 02, 01 makes a front pivot off of his left foot to then "scrape" off of 05's "Big-on-Small Back-Screen the Ball-Screener" to then make an inverted "Rim-Run to the basket. 05 breaks then slips his screen and slides out to the new "Weakside Slot." At the same time, 03 makes a "Flare-Cut" to the new Ballside Deep Corner" while 04 makes an aggressive "Iso Duck-In Cut" on his side of the lane.

01 looks to highlight his inverted leaping and post-up scoring skills and/or to attack X1's individual interior defensive skills. If 01 does not receive 02's "Lob Pass," he then empties out to the new "Weakside Deep Corner." This places the final offensive player into the correct "4-Out/1-In" Spot-Up locations, allowing the offense to maintain a constant pressure on the defense.

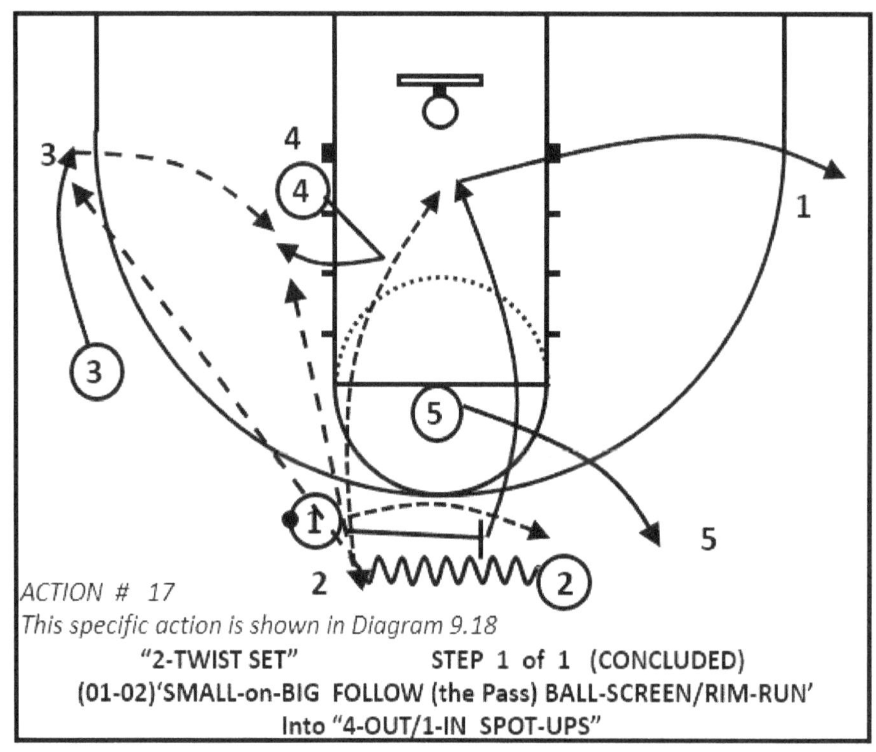

Diagram 9.18

⊕ Play # 18: "SMALL-on-BIG FOLLOW-(the-PASS) BALL-SCREEN/ROLL"

ACTION

From the "2-UP" Set, this play/entry shows the same type of ball-screen from a similar location, but with a different set of actions that follow the screen. 02 is the designated player to make the (02-01) "Reverse Pass" to 01 and then follows his pass to set a "Ball-Screen" for 01 to use. 01 then "dribble-scrapes" off of 02's top left shoulder. At the same time, 05 steps up and out to get out of the way of 02's following action. When 01 dribbles tightly off of 02's top shoulder to deflect his defender, 02 makes a "Reverse Pivot" off of his lower right foot. From there, he can open up to the ball and to 01 as he rolls down the lane to invert and isolate his perimeter-type defender, X1.

With 05 inverting the presumed biggest opposing defender away from the basket and occupying his weakside defender with a "Drift Cut" down towards the new "Weakside Deep Corner;" these actions not only stretch the defense vertically as well as horizontally, but also occupy them (so that 02 can further isolate his perimeter-type defender sliding down the lane.

If 02's skills and position advantage" does not help create the ideal shot, the "4-Out/1-In" Spot-Ups so that the offense can remain in fluid movement and attack mode.

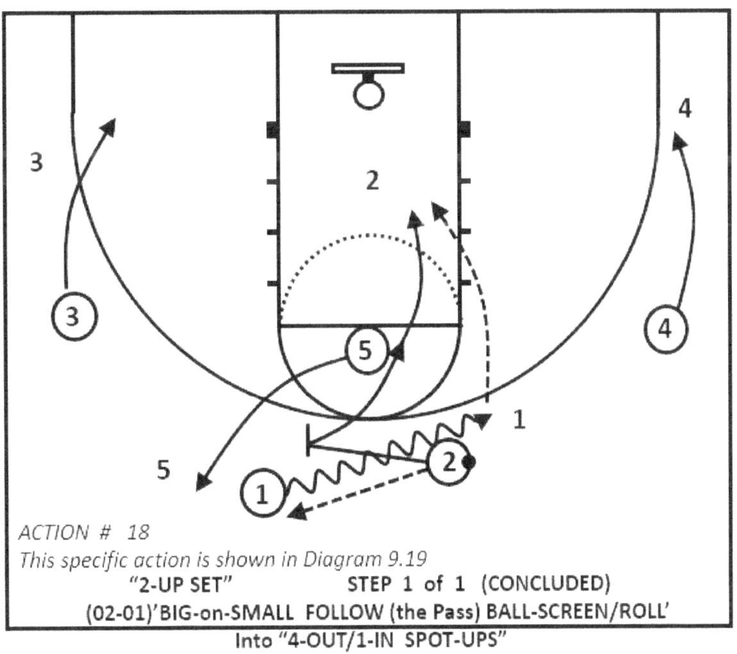

Diagram 9.19

ACTION

Diagram 19.20 shows another play/entry out of the same symmetrically balanced "2-UP" Set with making the initial "Wing Pass" to 04. Instead of going to set a "Follow-the-Pass Ball-Screen, 02 uses conception and fakes the action by simply making the Ghost action and immediately cuts to the basket. This action is actually a simple "Give-n-Go" Cut with a fake "Follow the Pass Ball-Screen" towards 04. 01 rotates over with 05 inverting to the new "Weakside Slot" area and 03 "Drift Cutting, positioning all five players into the proper "4-Out/1-In" Spot-Ups.

This play could easily be executed with a 02-01 "Reverse Pass," that is followed by a quick (1-03 Wing Pass." The next action would be for 01 to disguise his "Follow-the Pass Ball-Screen" presumed action with his own "Ghost" action.

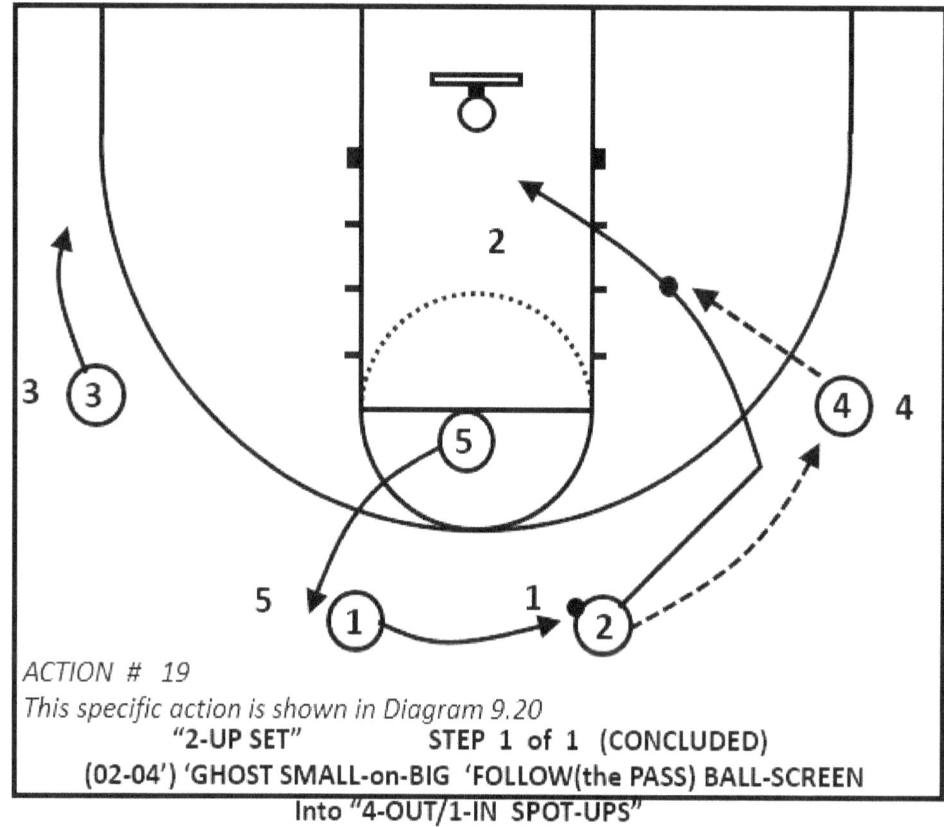

Diagram 9.20

Diagram 9.21 shows another form of ball-screening action that is different and can be more effective than the traditional ball-screen action for several reasons. This action could obviously be used in the half-court play setting as all other examples have been in this chapter. But to expand, we chose to show it as a Secondary Fastbreak setting.

After using other Secondary Break options that have 04 "chase the ball across the lane" while looking for the perimeter pass first from 02, then 01, then 05 at the top of the key and finally from 03 on the opposite Wing (from 01); this Secondary Break option uses deception by first having 05 and 03 change locations at the very end of the Primary Break.

During this Secondary Break, when 03 ends up at the top of the key at the very end of the Primary Break, he is the player that receives the "Reverse Pass" from 01. 02 immediately runs the baseline from one "Deep Corner" to the opposite "Deep Corner," looking for a possible (03-02) "Lob Pass."

Instead of 03 looking to make the "Inside Pass" to 04 cutting through the lane and/or to continue the swing of the ball to 05, 04 changes his route and breaks diagonally up towards 03 and the ball. Initially, this action appears to be and could actually be an aggressive "Duck-In Cut into the lane. If 03 cannot make that pass to 04 during his different cut, 04 continues into the direction of 03 to then set his "Big-on-Small Long Ball-Screen. 03 then fakes a drive or a pass towards 05 and "re-reverses" the ball via dribble. 03 should then "dribble-scrape" off of 04's

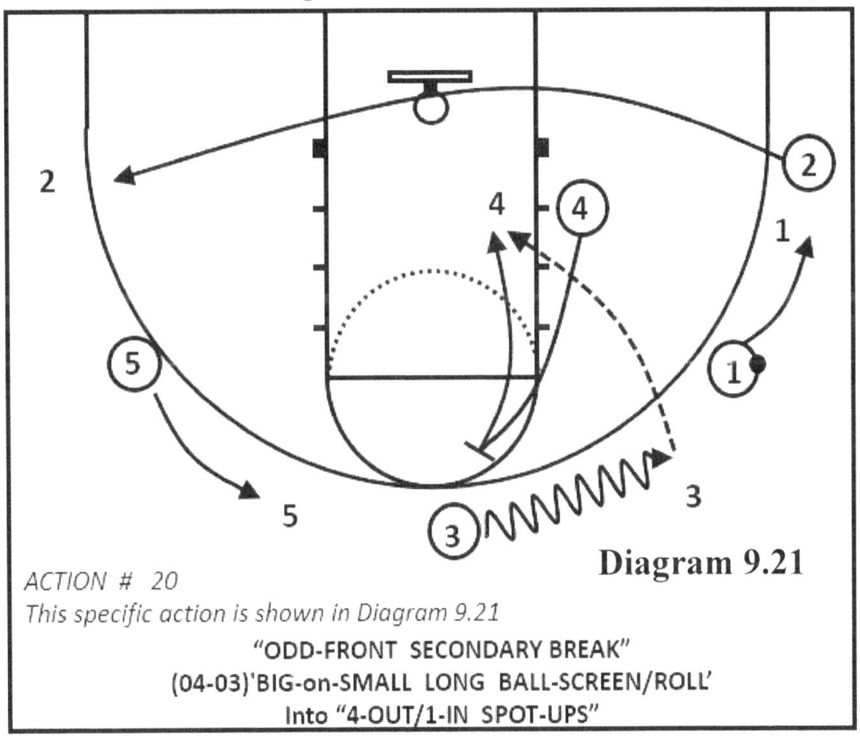

top outside left shoulder as he advances the ball towards the initial "Ballside Slot." As contact is broken, 04 "reverse pivots" off of his top left shoulder to open up to the ball, to 03 and to 01 as he makes a "Drift Cut" down the sideline. This gives 03 space to dribble towards the "FT Line Extended" for a better passing angle and can also create a new and improved passing angle for 01 to make the interior pass to 04 as he rolls down the lane. If the passes are not there, players have attacked and moved their individual defenders as well as repositioned themselves not in random locations, but in the same "4-Out/1-In" Spot-Ups that will allow the offense to seamlessly flow into the Continuity Offense that is wanted.

⊕ PLAY # 21: "BIG-ON-SMALL LONG BALL-SCREEN/RIM-RUN" ACTION

Diagram 9.22 illustrates another half-court play from beginning to end out of the "1-DOWN" Set with 02 making the "Reverse Pass" to 01 and immediately making a "Give-n-Go" Cut to the basket. If 02 does not receive the ball from on the 01-02 pass, 02 empties out to the sideline as he then drifts down to the new "Weakside Deep Corner." 04 breaks up to the now vacant "Slot."

As this action takes place on the new "Weakside," 05 breaks up from the new "Ballside Block" to set a "Big-on-Small Long Ball-Screen" for 01 to use. As 01 "dribble-scrapes" off of 05's outside right shoulder, 05 makes a front pivot off of his inside left foot to then "Rim-Run" to the basket.

04 now spots up at the "Slot" behind the arc, stretching the defense vertically. 03 "Drift Cuts" towards the new "Ballside Deep Corner," becoming a strong '3 Pt.' Shooting threat. In addition, 03 becomes a potential and likely threat to be the actual player to make the "Inside Pass" to 05 on his "Iso Post-Up (after finishing his "Rim-Run" to the basket. 01 has the ball outside of the arc and 02 ends up in the "Weakside Deep Corner." This action places four players outside of the arc with 05 completely isolating his lone defender.

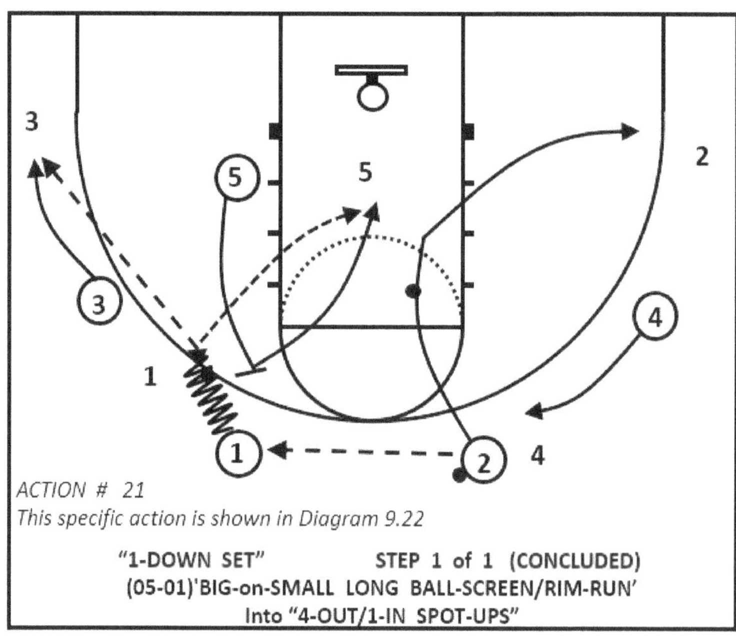

Diagram 9.22

If shots are not created, the offense once again has attacked various individual defenders and have repositioned each offensive player so that the designated Continuity

Offense that can smoothly and instantly begin once the "4-Out/1-In" Spot-Ups have been filled.

🏀 Play # 22: "BIG-ON-SMALL GHOST LONG BALL-SCREEN/RIM-RUN"

ACTION

Diagram 9.23 illustrates an entry out of the "4-DOWN" Set that could be executed after the action illustrated in Play # 21 has been executed two or three times in a game. With 01 centering up the ball at the top of the key, he could elect to drive towards either 05 and his side of the floor or towards 04 and the "Slot" on his side of the floor.

In this example, 01 dribbles towards 04's side of the floor. This keys that 05 immediately makes a "Vertical Elbow" Cut outside of the arc. 04 immediately breaks up as if to begin his "Big-on-Small Long Ball-Screen" (as done in various plays executed before.) But in this specific play, there is deception with 04 breaking off his route towards 01 as 04 actually sets a "Ghost Ball-Screen" and "Rim-Runs" to the basket much sooner than usual, catching X4 off guard. This is especially effective against teams that like to either "hard hedge," "trap" or "switch" all ball-screens.

04 and 05's actions isolate X4 and with 03 and 02 spotted up in their respective "Deep Corners;" the floor and the opposing defense has been stretched both vertically and horizontally-further weakening the overall defense.

In addition, the "4-Out/1-In" Spot-Ups are instantly filled; so that the designated 2nd Phase of the offense can also instantly begin its constant attack on the defense.

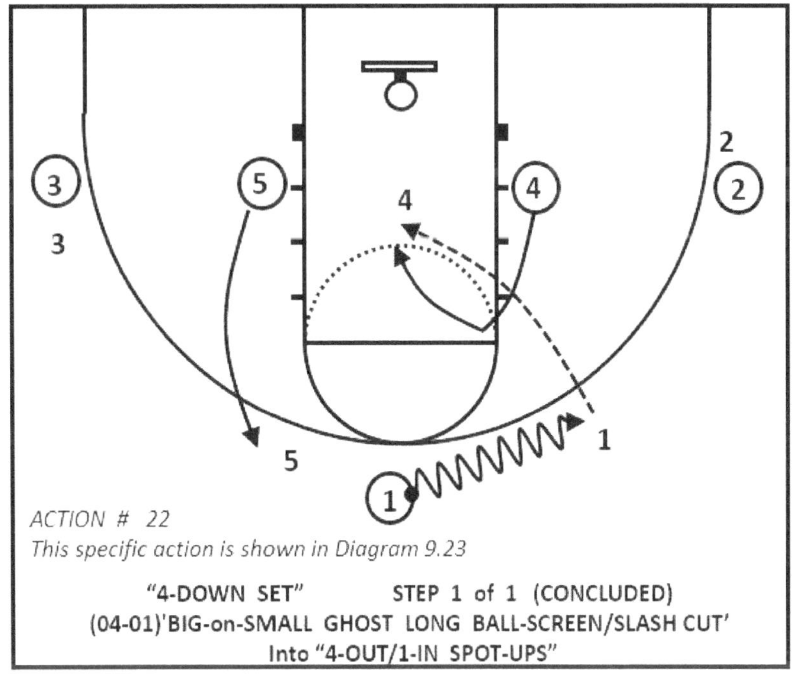

Diagram 9.23

⊕ **P**LAY **# 23: "BIG-ON-SMALL PISTOLS BALL-SCREEN/ROLL" ACTION**

Diagram 9.24 illustrates a half-court entry/play that begins from the "Nail" Offensive Set/Alignment—a symmetrically balanced alignment where each play could be executed towards either side of the floor. In this example, 01 starts the action by dribbling towards 02. With 02 faking a "Backdoor Cut" to relieve the denial pressure, he then reverses direction to receive the ball on the (01-02) Dribble Hand-Off. As the ball exchanges hands, 04 slashes to the initial "Ballside Block," while 05 steps up and over to immediately set his "Ball-Screen" for 02 to get his defender X2, lost in the offensive maze between 01, 05 and his man.

As 02 "dribble-scrapes" off of 05's top right shoulder, 05 then "reverse pivots" off of his left foot to open up to the ball and to 02 as he rolls through the lane; searching for the pass from 02 (or from 03 (who has drifted down into his "Deep Corner." As the ball is dribbled across the (imaginary) center line by 02, 04 should empty out to the new "Weakside Deep Corner" and 01 should step back up to fill the new "Weakside Slot" location. This action not only isolates 05 and his vulnerable defender, X5 but also repositions all offensive players into the "4-Out/1-In" Spot-Ups. Again, the offense has the position advantage of all five players to immediately flow into the designated 2nd Phase of the offense.

P**LAY # 24: "BIG-ON-SMALL BALL-SCREEN** FOLLOWED BY A **"BIG-ON-SMALL PIN DOWN-SCREEN" ACTION**

Diagram 9.25 illustrates another Primary Fastbreak situation that has smoothly flowed into a specific "Even Front Secondary Fastbreak" Option. With 01 possessing the ball at the Ballside Slot, the "First Trailer," (04) on the new "Ballside Block," 02 spotted up in the "Ballside Deep Corner, 05 settling in as the "Second Trailer" at the new "Weakside Slot," and 03 stretched out on the "Weakside Deep Corner;" both 01 and 02 look for the best possible passing angle to deliver the ball to 04 on the "Block."

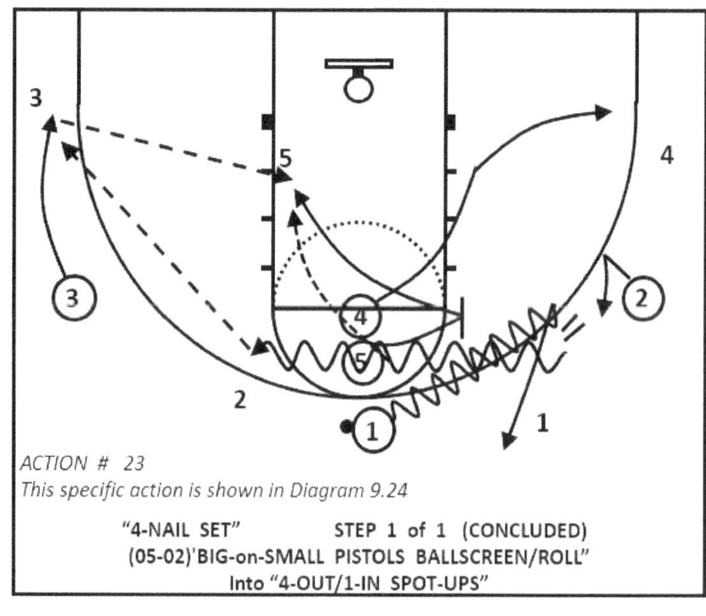

Diagram 9.24

The ball could be both "Down-Passed from 01 to 02 and then also "Up-Passed" from 02 to 01. When 01 receives the "Up-Pass," 05 should step over to set a "Big-on-Small Ball-Screen" for 01 to be able to freely move the ball on the perimeter to the opposite side of the floor. When the ball crosses the (imaginary) center line, 04 works aggressively hard to "chase the ball across the lane while actively looking to receive 01's "Inside Pass."

To occupy the presumed biggest defender, X5, and to eliminate the only other helpside defender (X2), as well as to free up one the presumed better perimeter shooters (02); 02 should scrape off of 05's outside right shoulder to break up to the new "Weakside Slot" for an open '3.'

05's screen for 01 should free 01 up to make an easier "Inside Pass" to either the isolated 04 on the interior or the wide open 02 on the perimeter. The "4-Out/1-In" Spot-Ups are once again filled so that immediately after the Primary Fastbreak flows into the Secondary Break Options and from there, the designated continuity offense can then smoothly begin.

PLAY # 25: "BIG-ON-SMALL FLAT BALL-SCREEN/SLIP" ACTION

Diagram 9.26 illustrates another half-court entry out of the "3-DOWN" Set with 01 attacking his defender by "dribble-scraping" off of either shoulder of 04 and looking for a hard penetrating dribble towards the lane and the basket. 05 should read his defender and when X5 steps up to help X1, 01 should look to make the "Lob Pass" to 05. During his penetrating dribble from the top of the key, he looks for "penetrate and pitch" pass receivers on both sides of the lane. As 01 gets into his lane, 03 and 02 can both slightly lift from their initial "Deep Corner" locations. This makes it more difficult for X3 and X2 to help out X1 on the dribble penetrating drive as well as to protect shots outside of the arc. After screening for 01, 04 drifts slightly to the side of the floor opposite of the side 01 has chosen. The "4-Out/1-In" Spot-Ups are

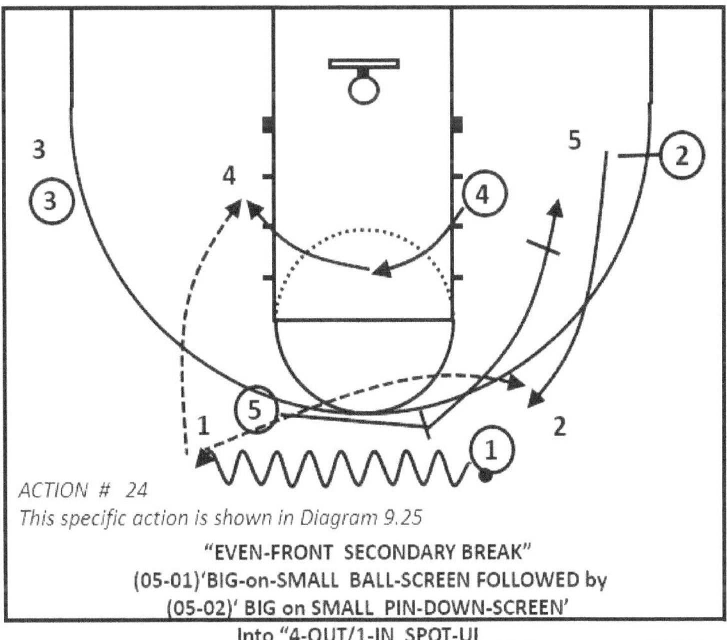

Diagram 9.25

somewhat filled for the designated continuity offense to smoothly and instantly begin its own fundamentally sound fluid (but structured) offensive attack.

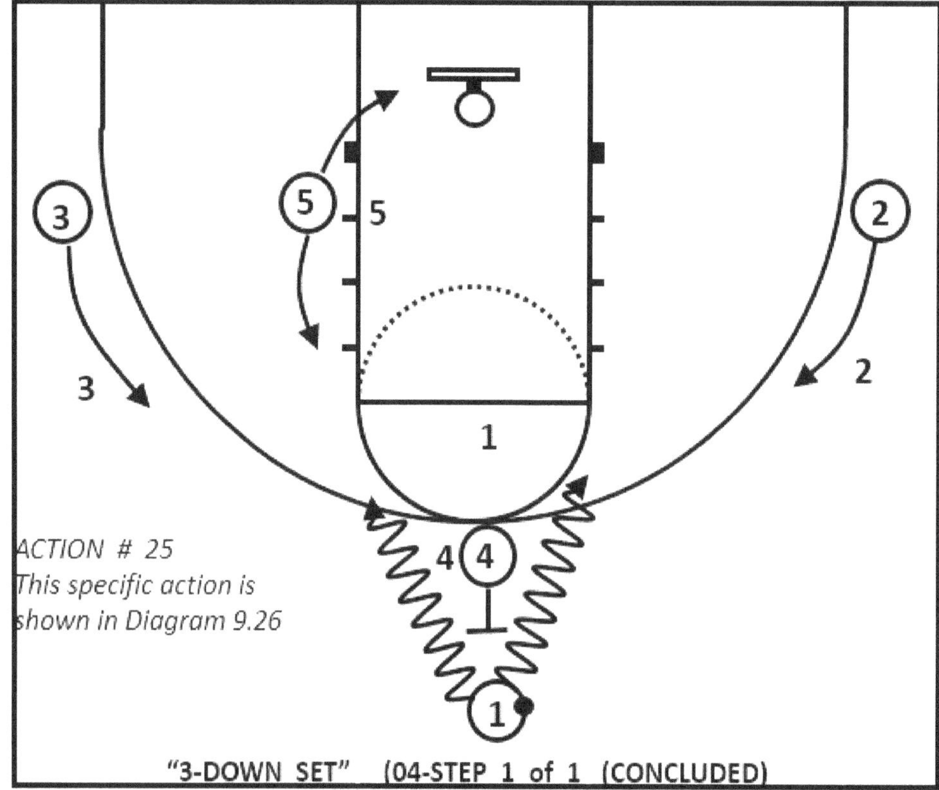

01)'BIG-on-SMALL FLAT BALL-SCREEN/SLIP' by 04 (01) 'PENETRATING DRIBBLE'
Into "4-OUT/1-IN SPOT-UPS"

Diagram 9.26

✦ PLAY # 26: "BIG-ON-BIG HIGH BALL-SCREEN/ROLL" ACTION

Diagram 9.27 illustrate a quick-hitting entry out of the "5-UP" Set—another symmetrically balanced offensive set. This means the play could be "mirrored" and run to either side of the floor.

Even though 05 and 03 could be the players on the initial side to attack, it has been designated that the right side would be the beginning action side. 04 is the player that steps out just outside of the arc to receive 01's initial pass. As 04 catches the ball, 02 should immediately make a hard "Backdoor Cut" to the basket and look for the quick bounce pass from 04. If 02 does not receive the quick and deceptive pass, he should then pop back out to his beginning spot-up location.

As soon as the pass is made, 03 should break up quickly to set a "Big-on-Small Flare-Screen" for 01 to use to "Flare-Cut" to the area outside of the arc between the FT Line Extended and the "Deep Corner" on the new "Weakside" of the floor. 03 then slips his "Flare-Screen" to break to the new "Weakside Slot," stretching the overall defense and giving 04 two legitimate '3 Pt.' scoring threats.

At the same time of the action of 01, 03 and 02; 05 cuts across the FT Line to set a "Big-on-Big High Ball-Screen" for 04 to use to attack the perimeter defensive skills of his defender. 04 dribbles across the floor by "dribble-scraping" off of 05's top right shoulder and looks to penetrate-dribble or to make passes to any of his four teammates. As 04 breaks contact with 05's top shoulder, 05 should reverse pivot off of his left foot to open up to the ball and to 04 and roll through the lane looking for an "Inside Pass" from whomever has possession of the ball.

This action can isolate both X4 and X5 and look for defensive weaknesses as well as utilize offensive strengths possessed by either 04 or 05.

If shots are not taken, the "4-Out/1-In" Spot-Ups are again filled for an immediate and smooth conversion from the half-court play/entry instantly into the designated continuity offense.

Not shown or discussed, but a Counter Play to Play 26 could be 05 making the same "Ball-Screen" for 04 and then make a "Rim-Run" to the basket. Executing "Rim-Runs" when the defense attempts to defend "Rolls" can give the offensive team several "position advantages."

1
3
5
5
4
4
3
1
2
2
ACTION # 26
This specific action is shown in Diagram 9.27
"5-UP SET"   STEP 1 of 1 (CONCLUDED)
(05-04) 'BIG-on-BIG HIGH BALL-SCREEN/ROLL' by 05
(01) 'PASS & FLARE-CUT'
Into "4-OUT/1-IN SPOT-UPS"

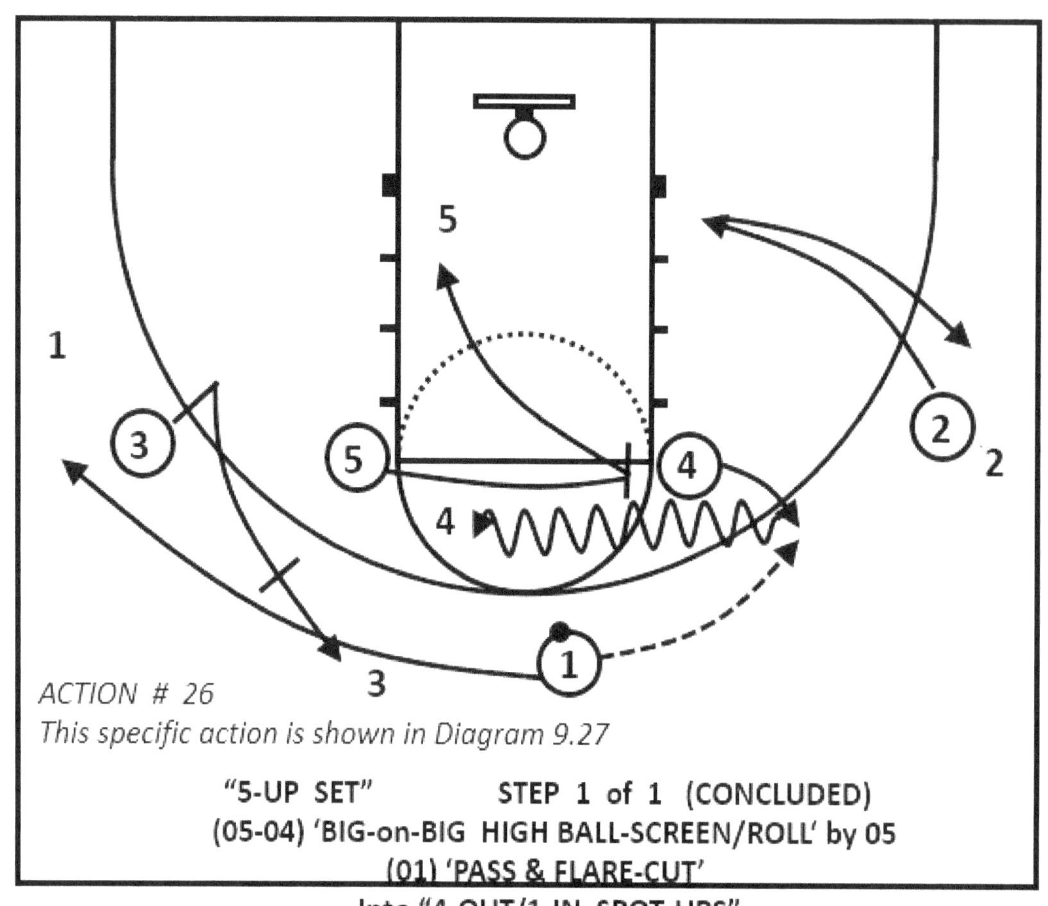

Diagram 9.27

Diagram 9.28 illustrates an entry out of the "HORNS" Set—another symmetrically balanced offensive set/alignment. This again means that any entry shown could be "mirrored" to the other side of the floor.

It appears that 01 has decided to attack the side of the floor so that 04 steps up to set his "Big-on-Small Ball-Screen" At the same time, 05 makes his "Diagonal Slash Cut" across the lane to the new "Ballside Block" to isolate his defender, X5. At the same time, 02 drifts and moves his defender for X2 to lose sight of him. On the new Weakside of the floor, 03 "Lift" Cuts up, while staying outside of the arc to become an immediate "catch and shoot off of the pass" threat.

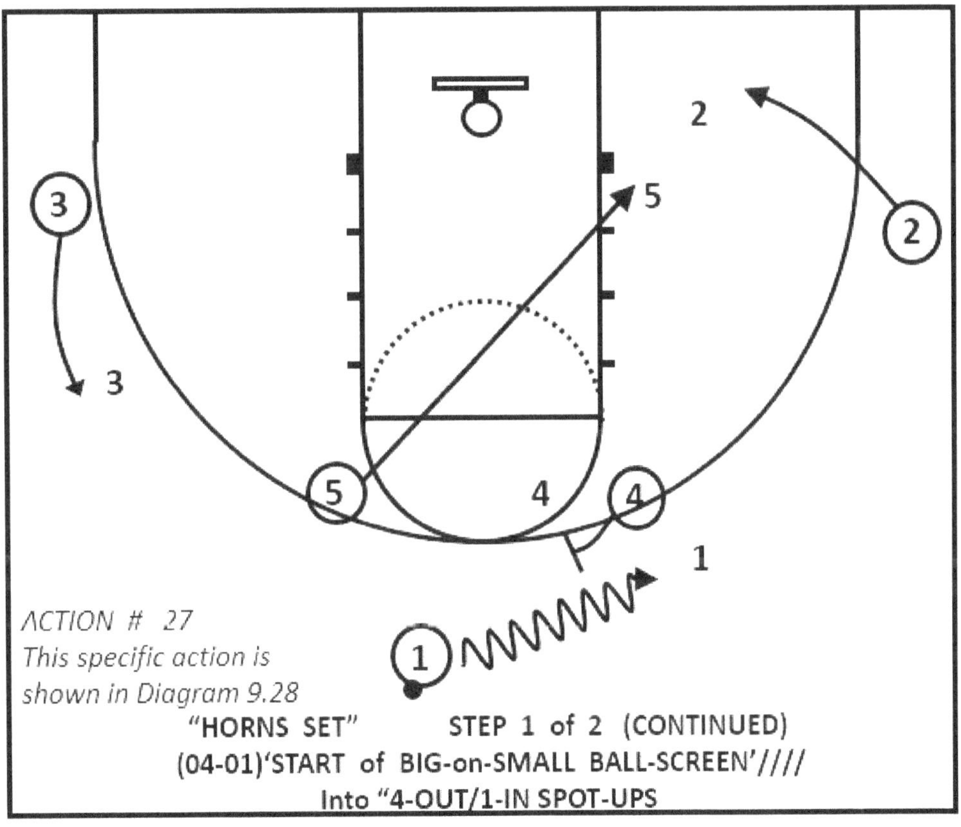

Diagram 9.28

ACTION

As 01 approaches 04 at the beginning of the action in Play # 27 players are in the locations shown in Diagram 9.29. With planned deception, 01 suddenly rejects the expected (04-01) Ball-Screen and reverses the direction he started and was expected to go to make a hard aggressive "perimeter penetration dribble" towards the open-spaced opposite side of the floor.

At that time, 03 puts his defender in a bind by making a "Drift Cut" towards the "Deep Corner, while remaining outside of the arc. 03 puts his defender in a defensive bind, in that X3 does not know whether to help out on his isolated teammate, X1 or to stay with his man to prevent the "penetrate and pitch" action between 01 and his own man. 02 remains along the baseline to set up his next offensive move—to then break up off of the "Big-on-Small Stagger Screen" set by 05 and 04.

This action not only occupies all three defenders on the offense's new weakside of the floor but also gives 01 on his penetrating drive to the basket a "Drive and Dump" passing option to 05, a "Reverse Throwback" option to 02 near the "Ballside Slot," and a "Penetrate and Skip Pass" option to 04 near the "Weakside Wing."

On the ballside of the floor, 01 has "Pull-up Jumper" or "Power Lay-up" scoring options as well as a closer and safer pass option to 03.

It seems unlikely that any one of the five offensive players would not get off an open shot from this (two diagrammed series of actions), but the "4-Out/1-In" Spot-Ups are again filled for the next wave of offensive attacks to continue smoothly.

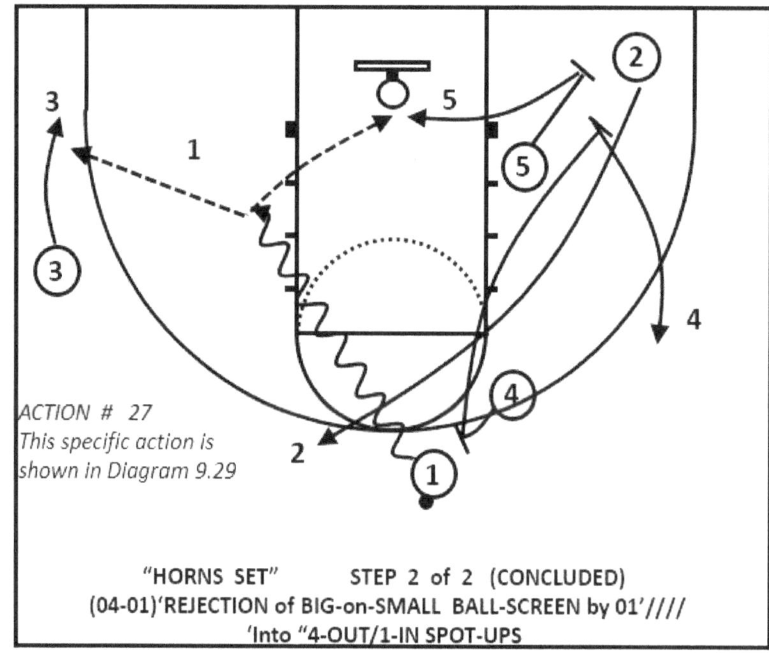

Diagram 9.29

⊕ PLAY # 28: "SMALL-ON-SMALL BALL-SCREEN/FLARE-CUT SLIP" ACTION

Diagram 9.30 shows this offensive action that begins out of the "5-TIGHT" Offensive Set/Alignment. This is another perfectly symmetrically balanced offensive alignment that will allow every play to be able to be executed on either side of the floor. This makes the plays even more unpredictable and therefore more difficult to defend.

This action has 02 be the designated perimeter player (either 02 or 03) to be the player that breaks up to the top of the key to set the "Small-on-Small Ball-Screen" for 01 to "dribble-scrape: off of his top left shoulder. 03 cuts through the lane to "invert and isolate" his perimeter-type defender, X3, on the opposite side's new "Ballside Block."

As 01 breaks contact with 02, 02 continues cutting across to the opposite side's now vacant "Weakside Wing" spot-up area. 05 curls over the top of 04 to cut to the "Ballside High Post Elbow" area; while 04 then pops to spot up at the top of the key. 01 finishes his dribble near the "FT Line Extended," looking to make "Inside Passes" first to 03, then to 05, a possible (01-04) "Reverse Pass" or a possible (01-02) "Skip Pass."

Players are now in a different set of offensive Spot-Ups, called the "High-Post/Low-Post" Spot-Ups" These spot-up locations will then allow other different continuity offenses to immediately begin and continue the pressure on the opposition.

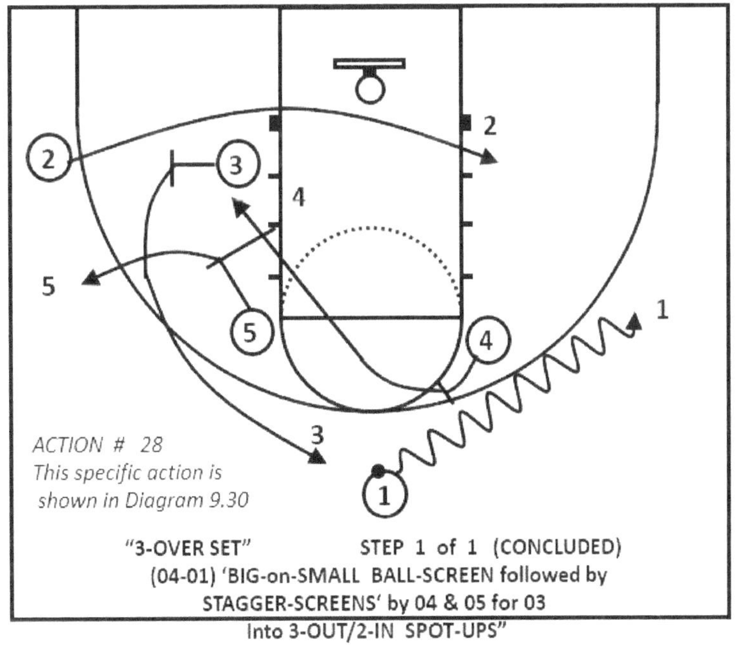

Diagram 9.30

Diagram 9.31 shows an example of an entry out of the "3-OVER" Set where 01 immediately takes advantage of attacking his defender on the more open side of the court with a (04-01) "Big-on-Small Ball-Screen."

In this particular alignment, as soon as 01 starts towards 04, 02 cuts off of the "Big-on-Small Flex Back-Screen" Set by 03 on the new weakside of the floor. After 01 "dribble-scrapes" off of 04's top left shoulder to drive to the FT Line extended, he looks to make the Interior Pass to the now inverted and isolated perimeter player, 02. After 01 breaks contact with 04, 04 makes a front pivot off of his lower right foot to then diagonally break down (with 05) to set a "Big-on-Small (Diagonal Stagger-)Screen the (Flex-)Screener. 03 "scrape-cuts' off of 05's outside left shoulder and prepares for a quick "catch and shoot" pass from 01 by "getting his feet and hands ready" before and during his cut to the top of the key. After screening, 05 slips out to the new "Weakside Wing" area and 04 remains on the new "Weakside Block." This places all five offensive players in the "3-Out/2-In" Spot-Ups for the various continuity offenses that are "family" to these spot-ups. The designated continuity or motion offense will be able to seamlessly begin as soon as 01 delivers the ball to a teammate. This quick conversion puts even more pressure on the opposition's defense.

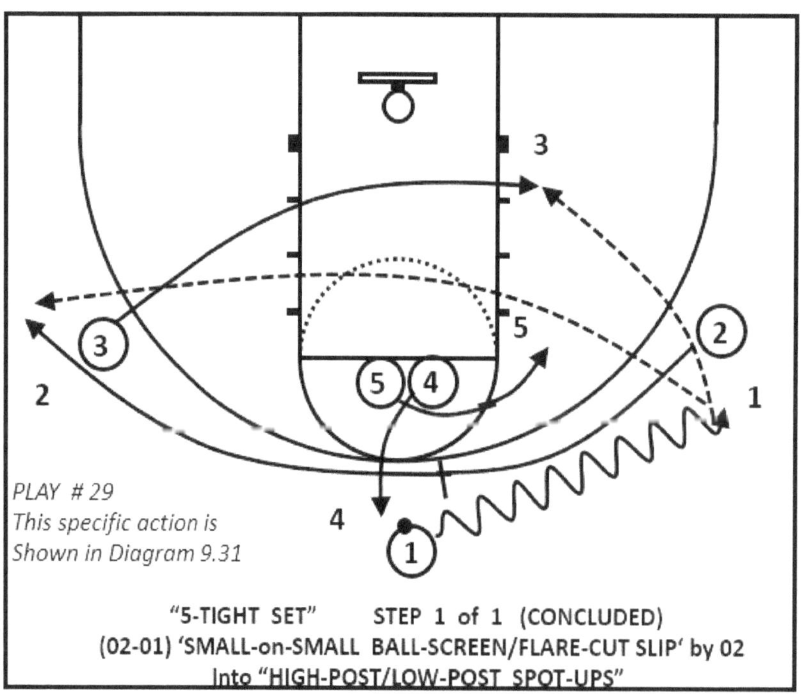

Diagram 9.31

PLAY # 30: "SMALL-ON-BIG BALL-SCREEN/SLIP" ACTION

Diagram 9.32 shows action in the middle of a play where all five offensive players have moved to various different locations and the plan was to then get the ball into 05's hands out at the top of the key.

With perimeter-type players, 02 and 03, at both "Wing" locations, either player could become the designated screener. In this illustration, 02 steps up to become the actual "Small-on-Big" Ball-Screener for 05 to attack his defender. After screening for 05, 02 makes a front pivot off of his inside right foot to instantly spot-up at the top of the key "with his feet and hands ready" for a quick "Reverse Throwback" Pass from 05. This action has also been traditionally called the "Pick and Pop" and when the 'picker' is a legitimate perimeter-type player with perimeter scoring skills and the defense switches the screen (with a presumed slower and less experienced perimeter defender, X5); there can be an immediate "position and player advantage" for 02.

This type of isolation on the perimeter is created with 03 setting a "Big-on-Small Pin Down-Screen on the one side of the floor with 04 making an "Iso Duck-In Cut" on the opposite side. With 05 having the ball at the "Wing" Spot-Up location, he has pulled the presumed biggest defender away from the basket, allowing 04 to also be able to isolate his own defender in a very vulnerable area-the "Ballside Block." Many scoring advantages can be created in the middle of this play, with the final advantage being that all players are in the "3-Out/2-In" Spot-Ups. As always, these and the other two types of spot-up discussed give the offensive team immediate advantages by being able to flow into the last phase of the offensive attack.

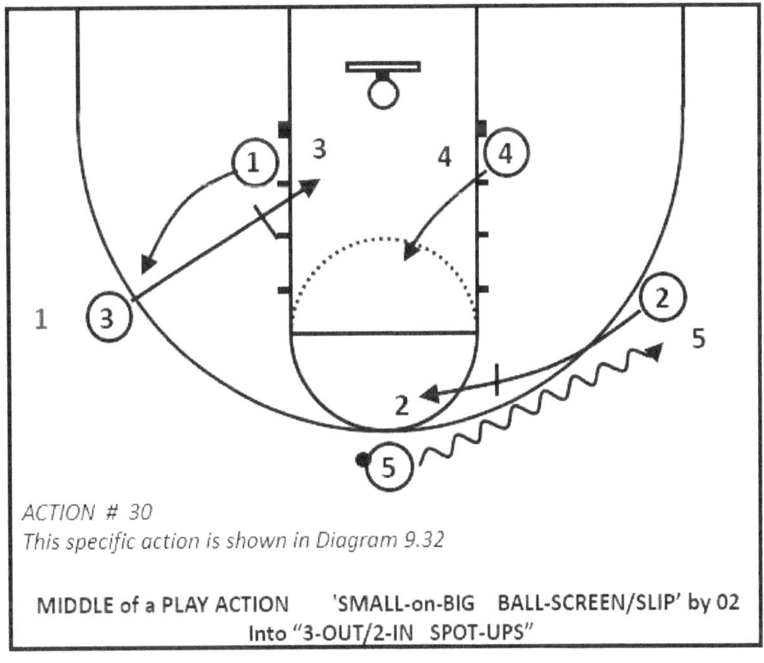

ACTION # 30
This specific action is shown in Diagram 9.32

MIDDLE of a PLAY ACTION   'SMALL-on-BIG   BALL-SCREEN/SLIP' by 02
Into "3-OUT/2-IN   SPOT-UPS"

Diagram 9.32

144

CLOSING

These thirty Ball-Screening types of action are all fundamentally sound and can be executed by various combinations of players in various locations on the floor and with countless finishing forms of action (after the actual screen has been set.)

These actions are shown out of various offensive sets/alignments and they all end in one of the three groups of offensive spot-ups. There are different continuity offenses or motion-type offenses that exist than can easily and fluidly begin from those offensive spot-ups.

Coaches should be able to pick and choose the right combinations from this chapter that fit the staff's philosophies, personalities and most of all the team's talent and skill levels to help improve the team's offensive production and efficiency.

These thirty-five plus offensive plays that use the fundamentally sound different types of screens dealing with off-ball teammates can be successful in the overall family of offensive actions.

As in all the various offensive actions that are valuable components of every quick-hitting play or entry, if and when these actions do not produce the shot that the coaching staff wants; will at least move every offensive player into the proper spot-up locations so that the designated continuity or motion-type offense can have a seamless and instant conversion from the end of the play immediately into this last phase of the overall offensive attack. This gives opposing defenses no time to breath, no time to recover or regroup after the actual play has ended.

"Off-the-Ball-Screens can take place in countless locations by any of the five offensive players that could be used by any of the five offensive teammates. From elementary teams to middle school to high school to college teams all the way up to the NBA, these many off-ball-screens can be utilized. Opposing defenders will have many defensive problems will have many defensive problems with the large amount of unpredictability that can take place. The many combinations of players that could be involved in the action as well as the various locations these screens could be used help with the unpredictability factor. There are countless types of action that can be executed following the various initial type of off ball-screens.

After contact is broken between the cutter and the designated shoulder of the screener, the screener should be able to use both front and reverse pivots (off of either foot) to initiate the following action of that screener.

The cutter that effectively uses the screen should be ready to immediately pivot off of either foot, with the ball clearly in possession and be able to dribble towards any direction or instantly pull up with "catch and shoot" or "catch and pass" stances, reads (on the defense) and actions.

With the various mixtures of off-ball screens set by different types of players from the many locations these screens can be set merged with the diverse actions that can be used after the actual screen is set, these combinations make up a huge number of offensive weapons that opposing defenses will have a difficult time in predicting and also defending.

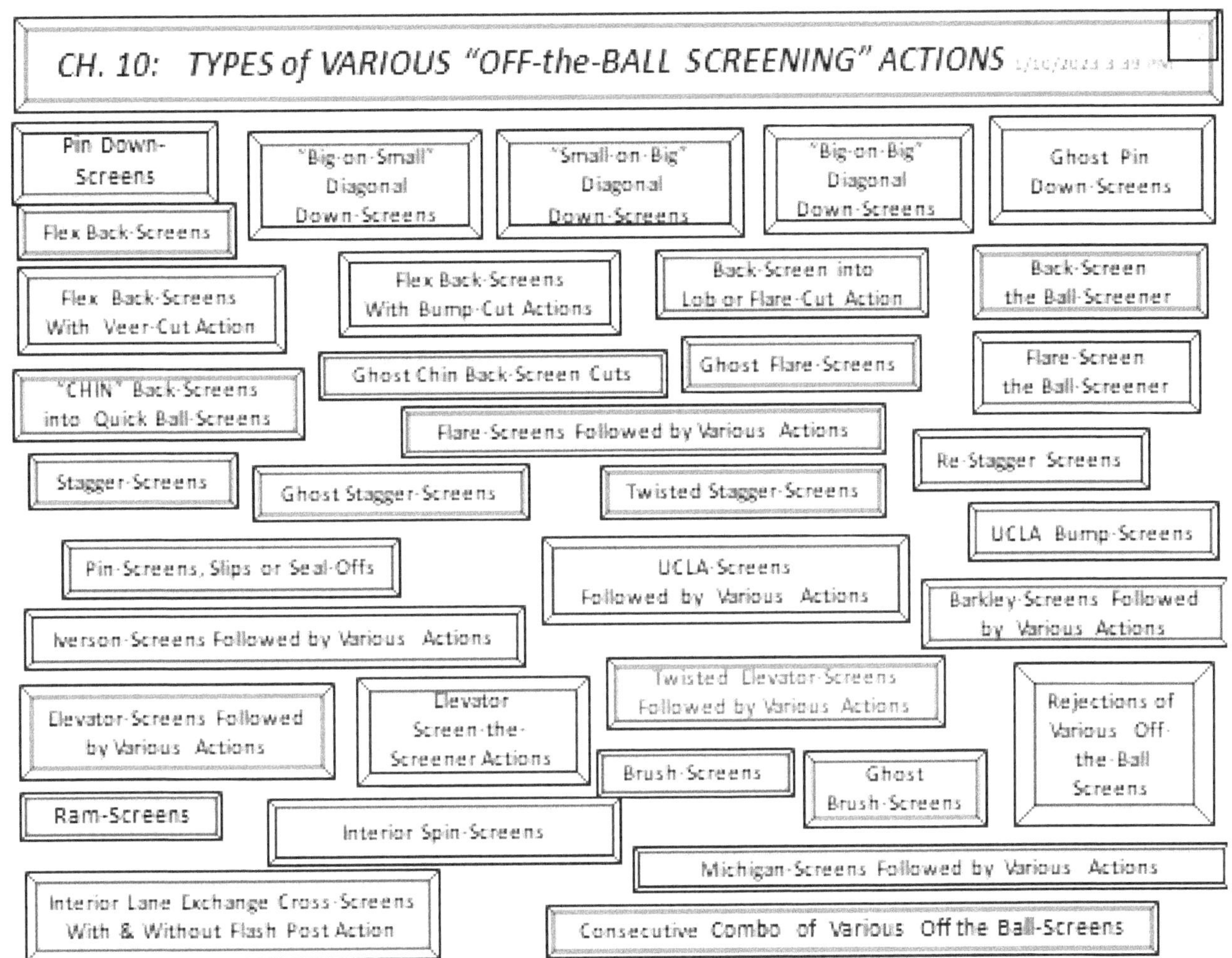

Illustration 10.1

✦ PLAY # 1: "BIG-ON-SMALL PIN DOWN-SCREEN" ACTION

Diagram 10.2 illustrates most likely the most common and the very basic, but still extremely utilized "Pin Down-Screen." This action is used so often that it is easy for offensive players and coaches to allow "game slippage" in which the fundamentals in executing the screen are allowed to become less sharp and crisp. In addition, defensive teams face the action so often that they can become used to defending the action and become very proficient at defending it.

Offensive teams must revisit the fundamentals so that this action can become more productive and effective in the overall use of the action.

The receiver of this screen must set his defender up by first moving aggressively in the opposite direction where the screen is coming and ideally get the defender to turn his head so the screener is not seen cutting toward the defender. When the cutter changes direction towards the screener, he must "get his feet and hands ready" to prepare for the "catch and shoot" opportunities he will receive (particularly after good Pin Downs are executed). The next primary technique is that the cutter should make immediately make contact with the screener's shoulder as he continues cutting towards the open spot to receive the pass.

In addition, the screener should legally set the screen with a wide base and have the proper angle so that his backside is pointing directly at where the cutter should break towards. When these screens are properly set, the mismatch screens ("big-on-small" or the "small-on-big" screens) can create numerous types of "position mismatch advantages" that will often force defenses to switch cutters and screeners will place themselves in possibly even more difficult defensive situations. As mentioned previously, the different locations and different pairs of personnel will present the defense with many types of headaches.

Diagram 10.2 illustrates the full Play # 1 initially executed out of the "3-OVER" Set with 04 stepping up to set a "Big-on-Small Ball-Screen" followed by his slipping of the ball-screen to remain at the top of the key to become the "ball-reversal" player. As 01 "dribble-scrapes" off of 04's outside left shoulder and approaches the "Ballside Wing" location, 03 flashes across the lane on his "Iso Duck-In Cut." At the same time, 05 gets into proper positioning to begin his "Big-on-Small Pin Down-Screen" for 02 to use to break up to the new "Weakside Slot."

With 04 inverted out to the top of the key and the (05-02) off-the-ball action taking place, this not only gives 02 an outstanding '3 Pt.' shot opportunity but also eliminates all possible helpside defensive support that the inverted perimeter-type defender (X3) needs to successfully deny 03 his outstanding shot opportunity.

If shots are not created by the action, the "3-Out/2-In" Spot-Ups are easily and quickly filled so that there will be a fluid and immediate transition into the designated final phase of the offensive attack. This phase could be one of many type of continuity offenses or one of many forms of motion offenses that could maintain the constant offensive pressure and attack on the opposition. See Diagram 10.2

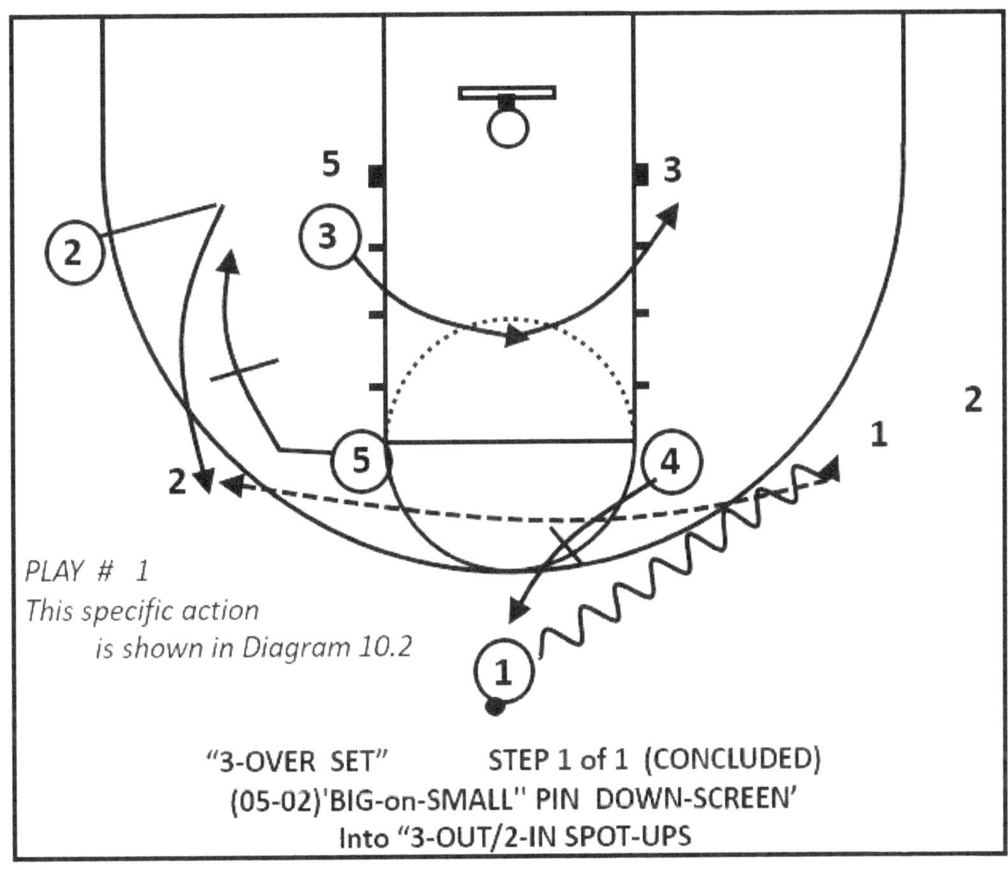

Diagram 10.2

✪ PLAY # 2: "BIG-ON-SMALL BALL-SCREEN/RIM-RUN" ACTION

Diagram 10.3 shows the entire entry out of the "HORNS" Set, where 01 elects to "dribble-scrape" off of the 05-01 screen and dribble towards the "Ballside Slot." 04 immediately "slash cuts" across the lane to post up on the new "Ballside Block," while 05 follows up his screening action for 01 with his "Big-on-Small Diagonal Pin Down-Screen" for 02 to break open at the top of the key.

02 scrapes off of 05's new outside right shoulder, "getting his feet and hands ready" as he prepares for a "catch and shoot" pass from 01 near the new "Weakside Slot. This action gives the play an outstanding opportunity for an open '3 Pt.' shot by a player who has the skills to repeatedly score from that area-02.. 03 spots up in the immediately new "Ballside Deep Corner," stretching the defense and becoming a perimeter scoring threat. In addition, the offensive screening action by 05 first frees 01 up for possible perimeter shots but also gives him opportunities to successfully make an "Inside Pass" after the presumed biggest opposing defender (X5) starts on the perimeter and eventually ends up on the defensive weakside perimeter, far from the basket. After setting his two screens, 05 drifts out to the new "Weakside Deep Corner," further stretching the defense both vertically and horizontally.

This fundamentally sound and simple-to-execute actions by all five players primarily attacks four possible immediate scorers before then placing all five players in the "4-Out/1-In" Spot-Ups where all five players again have the opportunity to attack their individual defender and become a primary scoring threat. See Diagram 10.3

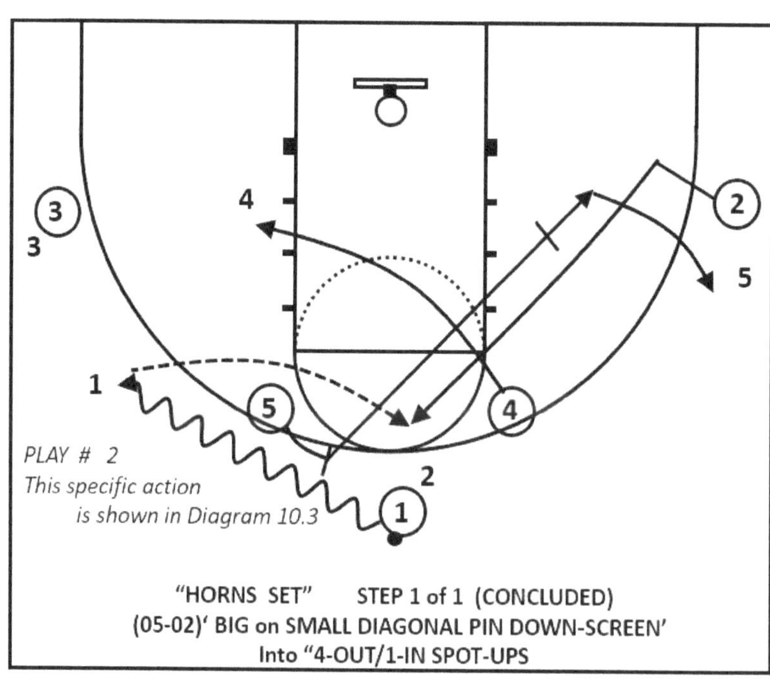

Diagram 10.3

Diagram 10.4 shows Play # 3 being executed out of the "HI-LO STAX" Set. As 01 approaches the top of the key, 02 breaks out to the right wing off of 04's "Big-on-Small Pin Down-Screen. 05 steps up to initiate this entry with another "Big-on-Small Ball-Screen for 01 to use to dribble towards the left "Wing" spot-up location. Also at the same time, 03 breaks across the lane to diagonally set a (03-04) "Small-on-Big Diagonal Down-Screen" for 04 to use to complete the cut to the new "Ballside Block." To eliminate any "big" defensive help, 05 continues to the weakside wing area to set a "Big-on-Small" Pin Down-Screen" for 02 to use to get open at the top of the key for an outstanding '3 Pt.' Shot opportunity. This action also gives a post-type player to further isolate his defender down on the new "Ballside Block." With 04 and 02 being the primary scoring threats, the "3-Out/2-In" Spot-Ups are easily filled; providing another quick conversion into the designated ("3-Out/2-In" type of) Continuity or Motion-type offense to immediately begin. See Diagram 10.4

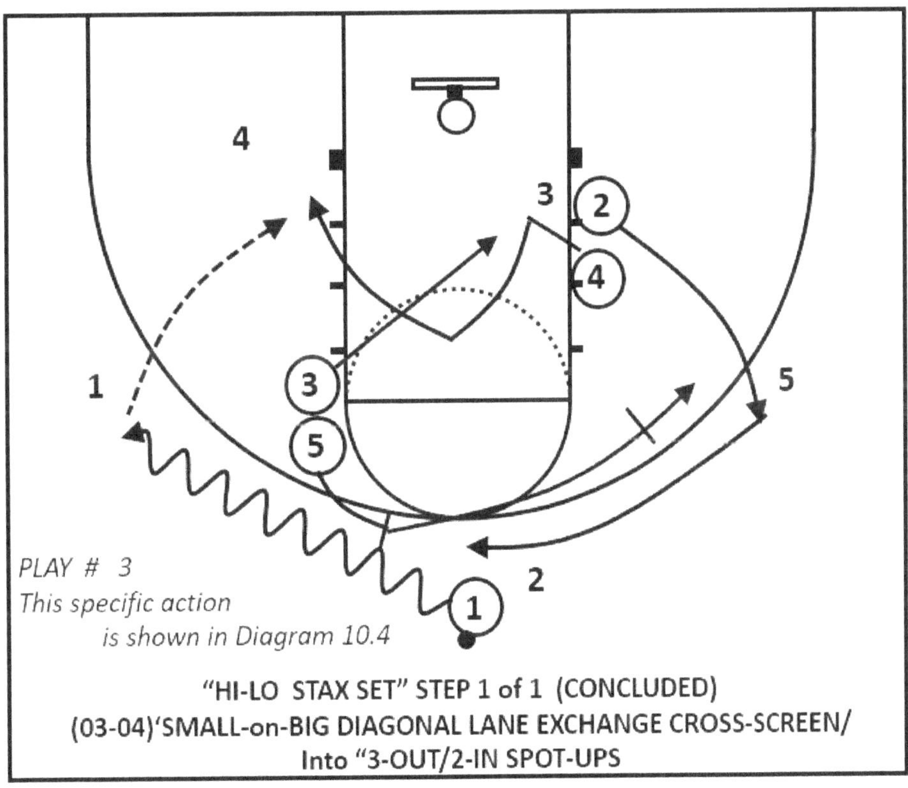

Diagram 10.4

This play and its action is executed out of the offensive set called the "2-TWIST" Set and Diagram 10.5 illustrates the same screen set near the same location but this time by two "offensive bigs." Having two players of the same type can encourage defenses to make the switch, but offenses can counter the defensive switch with the offensive screener reverse pivoting and turning to flash back to the ball to open (high or low) post area. This action also included eliminating helpside defense and therefore not only isolates one offensive post player but the second post player also and filling both the "Ballside High Post," but also the "Ballside Low Post." These screens followed by a quick pivot and "Iso-Cut" back towards the ball can very easily eliminate defenses from wanting to use defensive switches on "Big-on-Big Diagonal Down-Screens." In this entry/play, 02 steps over over to set a "Big-on-Small" Ball-Screen for 01 and the ball to smoothly and safely be reversed to the other side of the floor at the new "Ballside Slot." At the same time that this action is taking place, 05 sets a (05-03) "Iverson Screen" for 03 to to make his "Iverson Cut" to the opposite "Wing" area. After screening for 03, 05 then "banana cuts" to loop around (to achieve the proper screening angle) to set the (05-04) "Big-on-Big Diagonal Down-Screen." 04 sets his defender up before then "scraping off of 05's outside left shoulder for 04 to make his "Iso Flash Cut" to the new "Ballside Block." After dribbling

to the "Slot," 01 then makes the "Wing Pass" to 03 for 03 to then look immediately for the "Iso Post-Up" by 04. 03 could also look to make a "Skip Pass" to 02 on the opposite side of the floor, if 03 reads extra 'bad guys' helping out in the lane. The "3-Out/2-In" Spot-Ups are filled so that once again, no shots taken gives the offense a simple effective and immediate conversion into the designated Continuity Offense. See Diagram 10.5

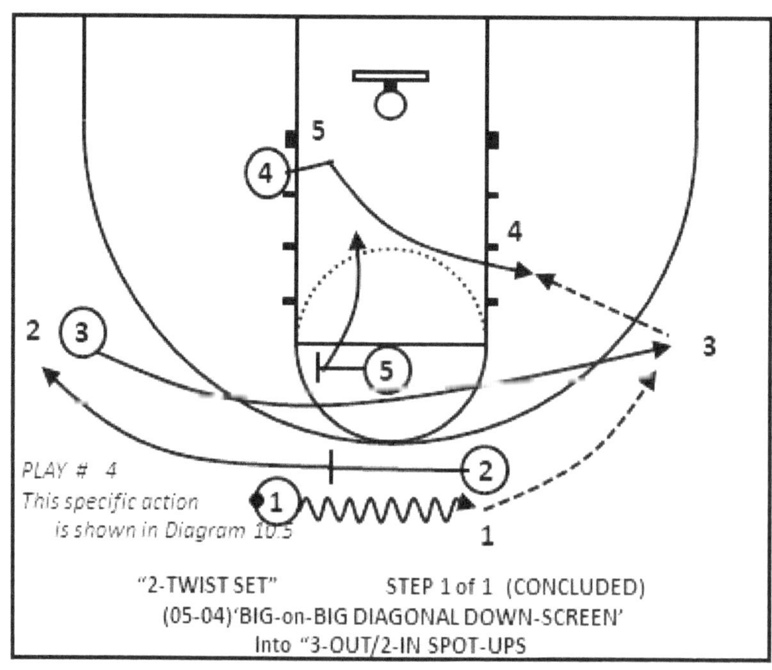

Diagram 10.5

Diagram 10.6 illustrates the next action from the entire Sideline Out-of-Bounds Play with 01 "triggering" the basketball from the left sideline. 05 starts on the "Ballside Elbow" location and 04 on the opposite sides "Elbow" location. Both immediately break down towards their teammates that is vertically below them. It would appear that both "Bigs" will set "Pin Down-Screens" for their perimeter-type teammates, but both set "Ghost Pin Down-Screens" for them. This makes not only their offensive teammates immediate pass receivers (and therefore potential scorers, but also themselves as reliable receivers/scorers as they break off their screening routes and become the threats.

05 cuts down towards 03 before flaring out towards the deeper sideline to become an immediate pass receiver. 03 continues his vertical cut up towards the "Ballside Slot" (but without the help of a screen), while 04 breaks his screening route to make an "Iso Flash-Cut" across the lane to post up his surprised defender. 02 starts up towards 04 before then reversing his direction to break back down towards the new "Weakside Deep Corner."

Regardless of whether the initial action is a half-court entry/play or a BLOB or SLOB play, one objective of all three types of offensive actions is to vertically and horizontally spread the floor to stretch and weaken the opponent's overall defense. 01 looks to directly hit 04 on his "Iso Cut" or to make a pass to 05 for a quick "Inside Pass" to 04 (with only a slight possibility of helpside defense in X2 spread out on the other side of the floor. If 03 receives the ball and he does not make the pass to 04 (or a pass to 05 that goes on to 04); he "perimeter pull dribbles" or makes an aggressive "penetrating dribble towards the inside of the offense's right "Elbow." With that side of the floor vacant except for 02, 02 has lay-up possibilities, pull-up jump shot opportunities, "penetrate and pitch" chances to 02 or "drive and dump" passes to 04.

If none of the several opportunities leads to the shot the offense wants to take, the offense still is in full control by moving all players into the "4-Out/1-In" Spot-Ups" for the continuous attacking offense to fluidly and smoothly begin. See Diagram 10.6

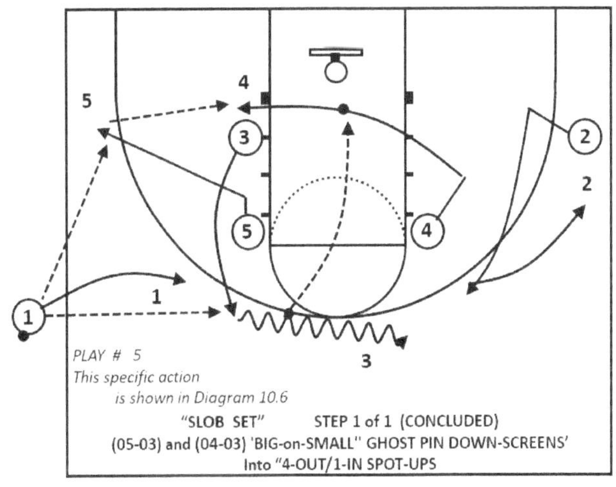

Diagram 10.6

Out of the "3-DOWN" Set, a fundamentally sound play has 01 "dribble-scrape" off of 04's top left shoulder and approach the newly declared "Ballside Slot." As the play begins, 03 sets his defender up by either "faking low and scraping high" or "faking high and scraping low" off of 05's stationary "Big-on-Small" Flex Back-Screen. 03 cuts across the lane ready to receive 01's pass the moment that 03 breaks contact with 05. After 04 sets his initial screen, 04 then diagonally cuts down towards 05's location to then set a "Big-on-Big (Diagonal Down-)Screen the (Flex-)Screener. This action gives this play a wide open "3 Pt.' shot for 05 at the "Weakside Slot" (if he is capable). Even if 05 is not a strong shooting threat, the action between 04 and 05 have moved both of the two largest defenders away from the basket to further isolate 03's perimeter-type defender in an uncomfortable and (possible unfamiliar) area to defend. With 03 isolating and inverting X3, this gives 03 a tremendous "position advantage" over his defender. 02 has stayed wide and deep to further stretch the defense and also give 01 another perimeter passing threat.

No shots taken give the offense the "4-Out/1-In" Spot-Ups so that the offensive continuity can begin (and continue until the designated shot is taken.) See Diagram 10.7

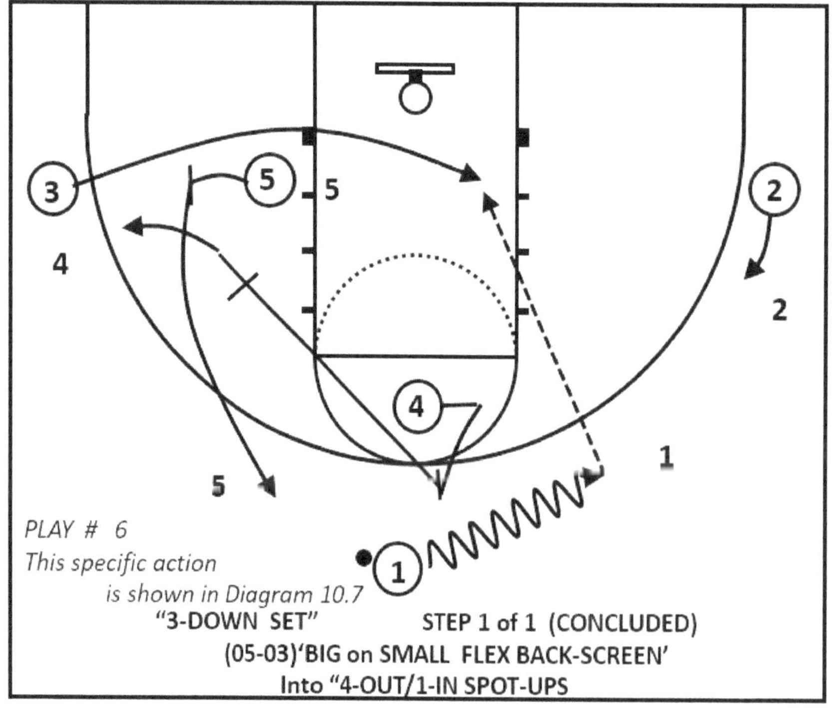

Diagram 10.7

⊕ Play # 7: "Big-on-Small Flex Back-Screen/Veer Cut" Action

Play # 7 can be used as a great counter to Play # 6 in that the same offensive set, the "3-DOWN" Set, can be used with very similar beginning action used to start the play. 01 "dribble-scrapes" off of the same "Big-on-Small Ball-Screen set by 04 but 04 makes a "Front Pivot" and slips the screen to spot-up on the newly declared "Weakside Slot." 05 sets the same type of "Big-on-Small Flex Back-Screen (as he does in Play # 6.) But in this action, 03 steps up higher before (always) making the "Flex-Cut" off of 05's lower right shoulder.

As 03 rubs his defender, X3, off of the lower side of 05; X5 could either switch or hedge (to help out his teammate attempting to defend 03). Lowering below the level of 05's horizontal positioning gives 05 a "position advantage" to then make a "reverse pivot" off of his lower right foot and to then make an aggressive "Iso Duck-In Cut" into the "Dotted Circle" area. On his "dribble-scrape" off of 04, 01 perimeter drag dribbles towards the new "Ballside Slot" and looks to first hit 03 on his inverted and isolated "Flex Cut."

If not open, 01 could "down pass" the ball to 02, spotted up in his flattened and spread out "Deep Corner" spot-up (who could have a better passing angle to deliver the ball to 03, now posting up.) 01 could also look to make the pass to 05 in the middle of the lane.

Also, 01 could make a "Reverse Throwback Pass" to 04, who should have an improved passing angle to make the "Inside Pass" to 05, mostly isolated from all defensive help. If 05 does not receive a quick "Inside Pass" from either 01 or 04, he returns to his initial "Mid-Post' spot-up with 03 running the baseline (possibly off of 05) to spot-up back in the same "Deep Corner" location he began. This places all players back in the same "4-Out/1-In" Spot-Ups for the same continuity offense to again maintain the consistent and constant attack on the opposition. See Diagram 10.8

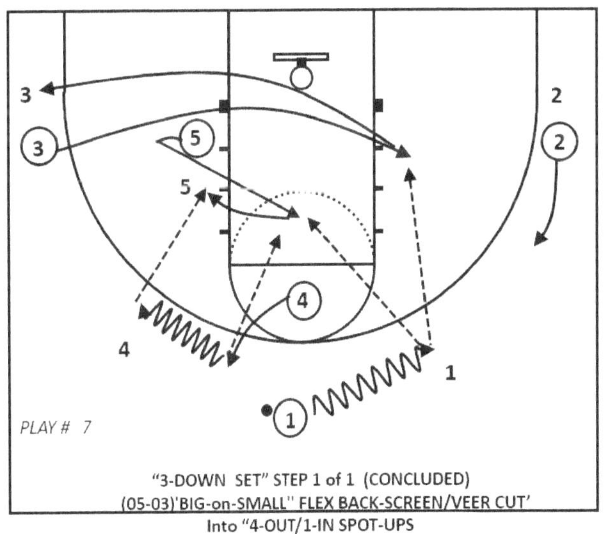

"3-DOWN SET" STEP 1 of 1 (CONCLUDED)
(05-03)'BIG-on-SMALL" FLEX BACK-SCREEN/VEER CUT'
Into "4-OUT/1-IN SPOT-UPS

Diagram 10.8.

Play # 8 is another play that can be included in the "Flex-Screen & Cut" family in which Plays 6 and 7 can be integral parts. Play # 8 could also be a counter to either play, making all three all the more unpredictable and therefore more efficient.

Out of the same "3-DOWN" Set, 01 again comes off of the "Big-on-Small Ball-Screen" set by 04 at the top of the key. 03 sets his defender up, especially how he does in Play # 6, (faking low and cutting high or faking high and cutting low.) But instead of actually scraping off of 05's shoulder, 03 "bumps 05 in the chest" and pushes 05 into the lane to have 05 actually make the "Flex-Cut" while 03 then uses the route that 05 takes in Play # 6. And that route is that 03 now "scrapes" off of 04's outside left shoulder. This deceptive "Big-on-Small Pin Down-Screen" should not only get 03 some wide open '3 Pt.' shots at the "Weakside Slot," but it also clears out to minimize any possible interior defensive support that X5 would need as he tries to defend 05, now isolated on the "Ballside Block."

Both 01 at the "Ballside Slot" and 02, spotted up at the new "Ballside Deep Corner" should have possible '3 Pt. shot opportunities plus outstanding "Inside Pass" opportunities available to 05 to them. If shots are not created, the same "4-Out/1-In" Offensive Spot-Ups are filled to maintain the constant offensive assault on the opposition's defense. See Diagram 10.9

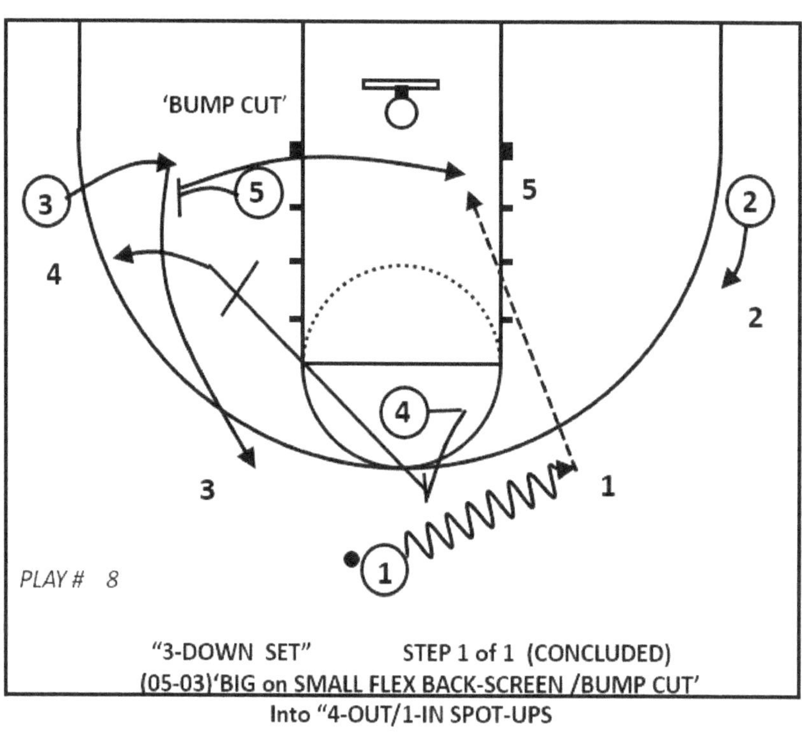

Diagram 10.9

Diagrams 10.10 and 10.11 show the entire play that can be executed out of the "3-ACROSS" Set where there exists a (02-04) "Small-on-Big Back-Screen" followed by a "Lob-Cut" and pass by 05 for an easy high percentage shot for 04.

Diagram 10.10 starts with 01's simple "Perimeter (Drag) Pull Dribble' from the top of the key towards the right side "Slot." As 01 starts to approach the "Slot," 02 sets his defender up and then makes a hard "Back-Door Cut" to end up as an "inverted and isolated perimeter post-up" scoring threat. At the same time, 03 rotates up and over to the new "Weakside Slot" and 05 pops out to fill the now vacant "Wing" spot-up at the FT Line extended. This action moves potential weakside defenders that X2 may need to defend 02. See Diagram 10.10

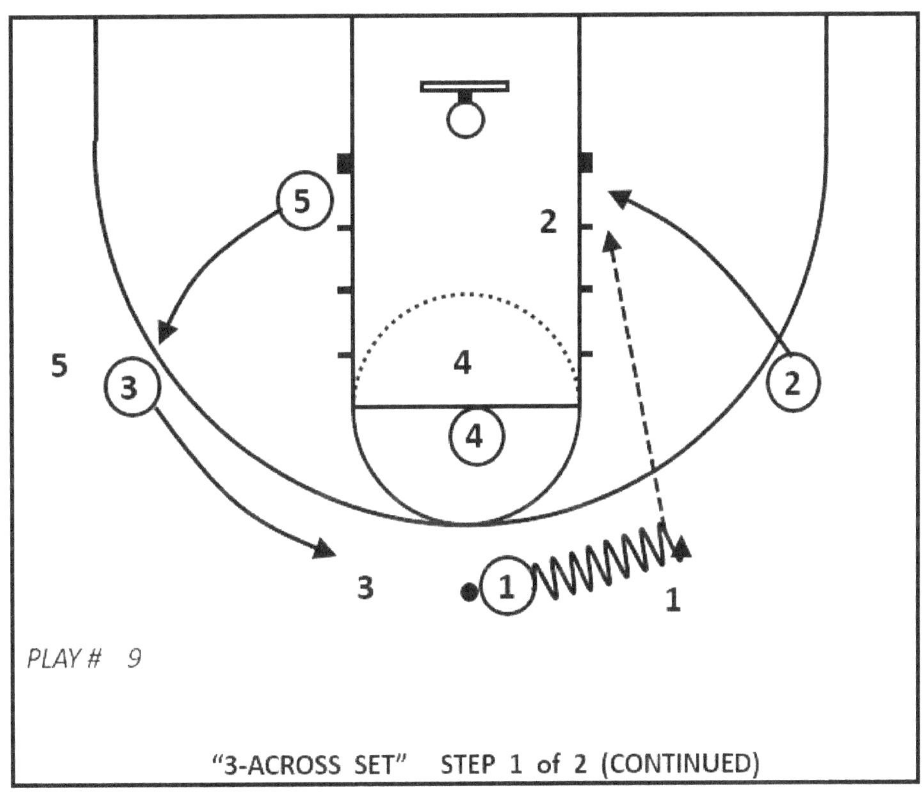

Diagram 10.10

Diagram 10.11 illustrates 01 turning down the pass to 02 and instead reversing the ball to 03. 03 should then make a quick "Wing Pass" to the now 'inverted and isolated-on-the-perimeter' teammate (05.) As the ball leaves 03's hands towards 05, 02 steps up diagonally to set a "Small-on-Big (Diagonal) Back-Screen" for 04 to spin off and scrape off of 02's outside left shoulder. On his "Lob Cut" to the basket, he should look over his left shoulder for 05's "Lob Pass."

Immediately after making the (03-05) "Wing Pass," 01 steps over to set a "Small-on-Big Flare-Screen" for 03 to "Flare-Cut" to the new "Weakside Wing" spot-up location. 01 then remains at the top of the key while 02 remains at the "Nail." There, all five players have ended up in different set of offensive spot-ups. These different spot-ups are called the "High Post/Low Post" Spot-Ups for an even different type of continuity or motion-type offense to be able to immediately begin. See Diagram 10.11

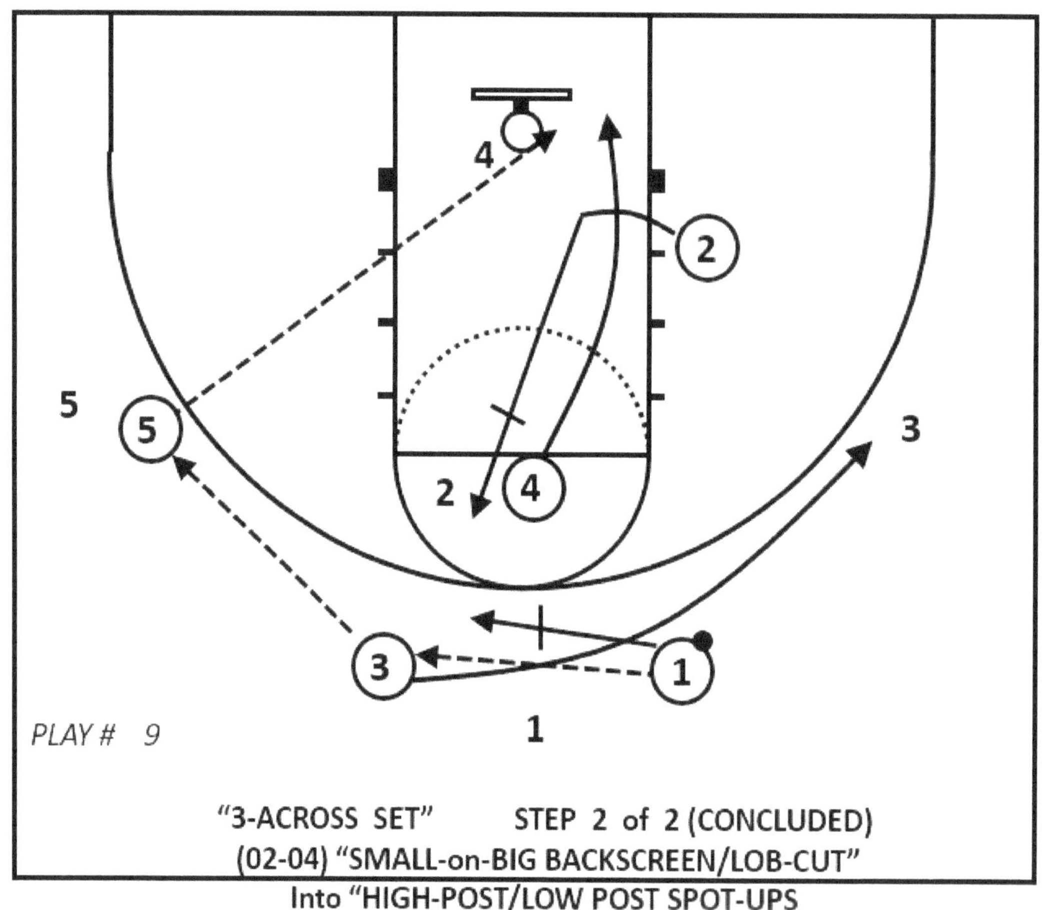

Diagram 10.11.

ACTION

Diagram 10.12 illustrates an entry that begins out of the "TWINS" Set, with 01 electing to use 04's "Big-on-Small Ball-Screen" for 01 to dribble to the new "Ballside Slot." 02 widens out to the "Deep Corner" on his side of the floor. 05 slashes across the lane to post up on the new "Ballside Block, while on the opposite side, 03 steps up from behind 04 and his defender to set a blind "Small-on-Big (Back-)Screen the (Ball-)Screener" for 04 to scrape his defender off of 03's outside right shoulder. 04 continues making somewhat of a "banana cut" towards the rim for 01's "Lob Pass." If 04 does not receive the ball, he then empties out to the "Deep Corner on his side of the floor to stretch the helpside defender (X4) away from 05 and his isolated defender, X5. This makes 05 the primary receiver for either 01 or 02. After turning down 04, 01 could also look to reverse the ball to 03 on the "Weakside Slot," making him the primary perimeter scoring threat.

If shots are not taken, the "4-Out/1-In" Spot-Ups are filled for a smooth conversion into the next phase of the offensive attack. See Diagram 10.12

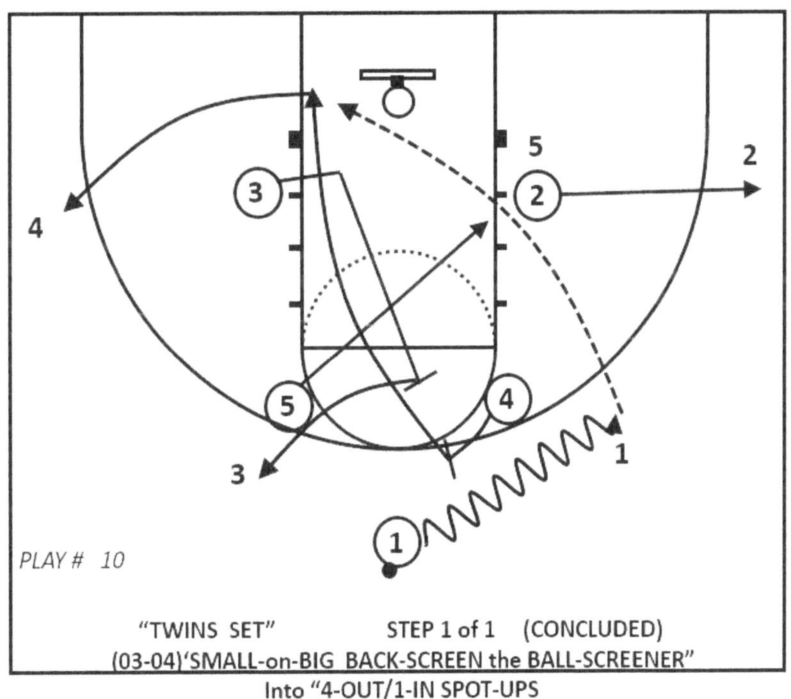

Diagram 10.12

Diagrams 10.13 and 10.14 show the entire action of Play # 11 (that begins out of the "5-SQUEEZE" Set. With 05 having the option to align on either side of the lane, 01 always dribbles to the "Slot" that is opposite of 05's initial side of the floor. 05 breaks up to fill the opposite side's "Slot" location. At the same time, 02 and 03 both make "Iverson Cuts" off of 04 and break to the "Wing "locations on the opposite side of the floor that they also started. After those cuts, 04 slides over to the new "Ballside High Post." See Diagram 10.13

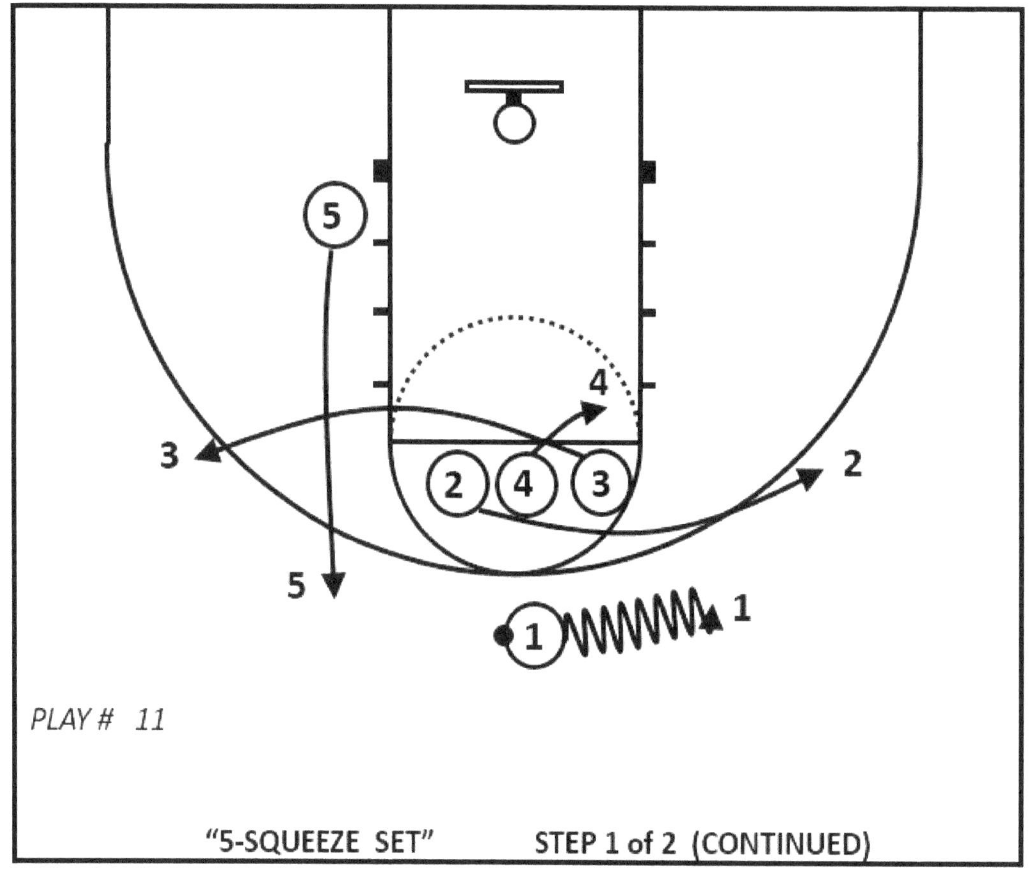

Diagram 10.13

Diagram 10.14 shows the conclusion of this fundamentally sound entry with 01 reversing the ball to 05. 04 immediately steps up to set his "Big-on-Small Chin Back-Screen" for 01 to utilize. 01 follows his pass with one jab step before then rubbing off of 04's outside left shoulder and curling through the lane looking for a pass from 05.

After screening for 01, 04 steps up and over to set a "Big-on-Big Inverted Ball-Screen" for 05 to attack his post-type defender, X5, with a "perimeter (Drag) Pull Dribble" towards the now vacant "Slot" location on the opposite side of the floor. After screening first for 01, then for 05, 04 continues with a "Big-on-Small Pin Down-Screen" for 03 to use to break up to the now vacant new "Weakside Slot." This gives 05 a potential for a highly successful "Throwback Reverse Pass" that makes 03 the most logical '3 Pt.' scoring threat in this play.

As 05 dribbles across the imaginary center line, 01 leaves his post up to flash across the lane to make his second "Inverted Flash-Cut" to the new "Ballside Block." This is the second time that 01 will enjoy "position advantages" over his perimeter-type defender with these "inverted and isolated post-up' scenarios. To flatten out the defense and to move off-the-ball defenders, both 04 and 02 make "Drift Cuts" to their respective "Deep Corners."

If shots are still not taken, the "4-Out/1-In" Spot-Ups are once again filled for an immediate and fluid transition into the offense's last phase of the attack. See Diagram 10.14

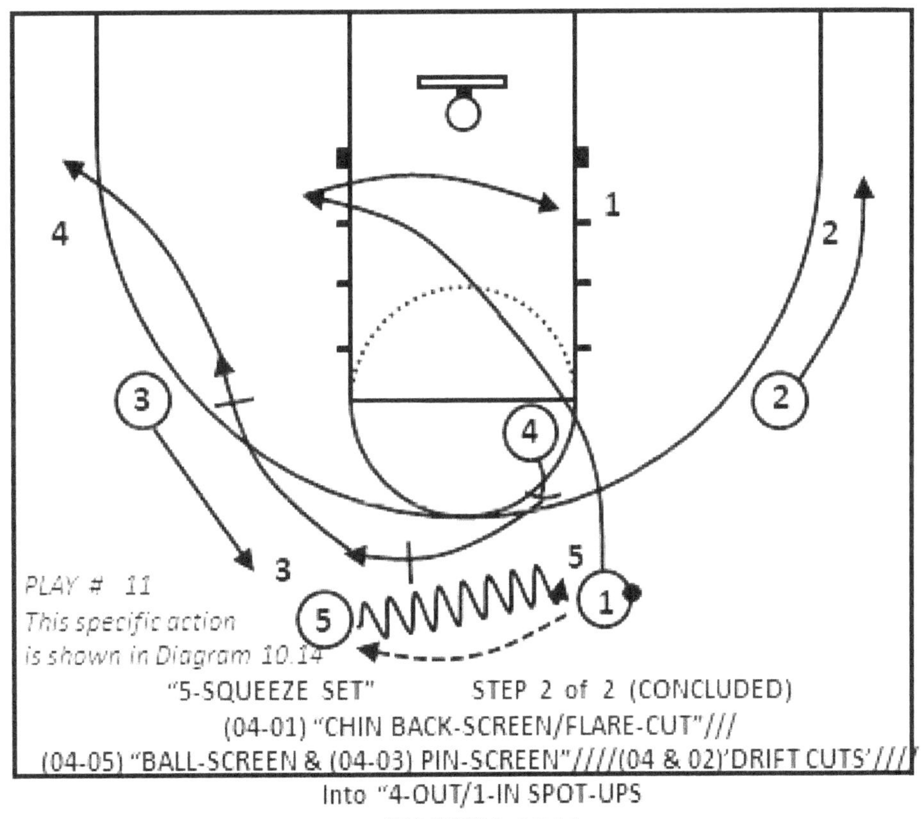

"5-SQUEEZE SET"   STEP 2 of 2 (CONCLUDED)
(04-01) "CHIN BACK-SCREEN/FLARE-CUT"///
(04-05) "BALL-SCREEN & (04-03) PIN-SCREEN"/////(04 & 02)'DRIFT CUTS'////
Into "4-OUT/1-IN SPOT-UPS
DIAGRAM 10.14

⊕ PLAY # 12: "BIG-ON-SMALL GHOST CHIN BACK-SCREEN/SLASH CUT"

ACTION

Diagram 10.15 illustrates the full entry/play that begins out of the "5-UP" Set. 01 dribbles towards 02 to the "Slot" with 05 popping out to the newly designated "Weakside Slot." 01 reverses the ball to the inverted 05 now out at the "Weakside Slot." 04 starts to step up as if to set a (04-01) "Big-on-Small Chin Back-Screen." Instead, 04 stops and becomes the actual "Chin Cutter" (instead of the actual Chin Screener.") 04 then is the player that diagonally slashes through the lane all the while looking for the pass from 05. At the same time, 02 steps up to set a "Flare-Screen" for 01 to use to "Flare-Cut" to the new "Weakside Deep Corner." 02 slips his "Flare-Screen" and remains at the "Slot" position opposite of 05. start drifting down to their respective "Deep Corners." 05 has the options to either make the "Inside Pass" to the inverted and isolated 01 now down on the "Ballside Block." If no shots are taken, the same "4-Out/1-In" Spot-Ups are filled for an immediate transition into the last phase of the offense—the continuity offense. See Diagram 10.15

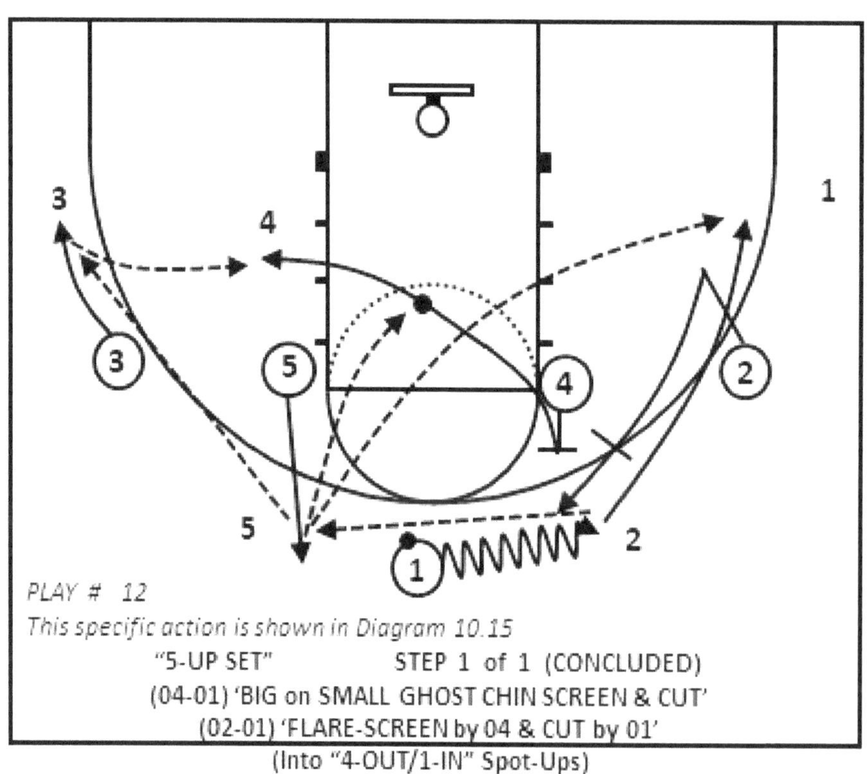

⊕ PLAY # 13: "BIG-ON-SMALL GHOST FLARE-SCREEN" ACTION

This play out of the "2-UP" Set takes place with 01 dribbling towards 05 "slash-cutting" to the presumed new "Ballside Block." After making a DHO with 02, 04 then starts to step up to set a presumed "Flare-Screen" for 01 to use. As 04 starts to set the (04-01) "Flare-Screen" and he see the middle of the floor emptied out (by 05's cut,) 04 should instead "Ghost Flare-Screen" 01 and slash across the lane towards the opposite side of the floor and away from 05. 01 would continue with his "Flare-Cut" without the 04 "Flare-Screen."

As 02 dribbles towards the "Slot," 03 should "Drift Cut" to the "Deep Corner" to flatten out the defense. 05 should then empty out to the new "Weakside Deep Corner" as 04 tries to "Iso Post-Up his defender." This places players in the "4-Out/1-In" Spot-Ups for a smooth conversion into the last phase of the attack. See Diagram 10.16

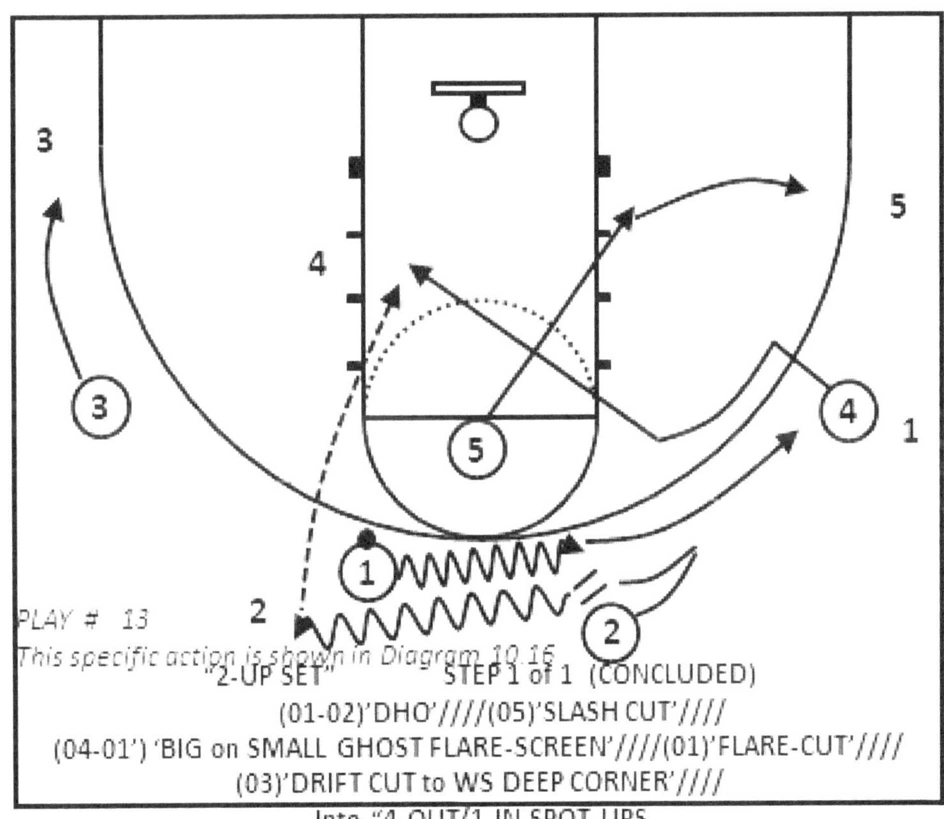

With the play being executed out of the "2-DOWN FLAT" Set, Diagrams 10.17 and 10.18 illustrate the complete execution of Play # 14, which utilizes the (01-02) "SMALL-ON-BIG FLARE-SCREEN and CUT. This entry is executed out of the "2-DOWN FLAT" Set, with 01 making the initial action with a "perimeter pull dribble" to the FT Line extended on the right side of the floor. As 01 starts his approach, 02 runs the baseline until he gets to 04 and then makes a "Pipe Cut" up to the vacant "Ballside Slot." At the same time, 05 sets a "Big-on-Small Pin Down-Screen for 03 to cut off of 05's outside left shoulder to the new "Weakside Slot." This action eliminates two of the three probably biggest defenders X3, X4 and X5) so that 04 can fully isolate his defender, X4. See Diagram 10.17

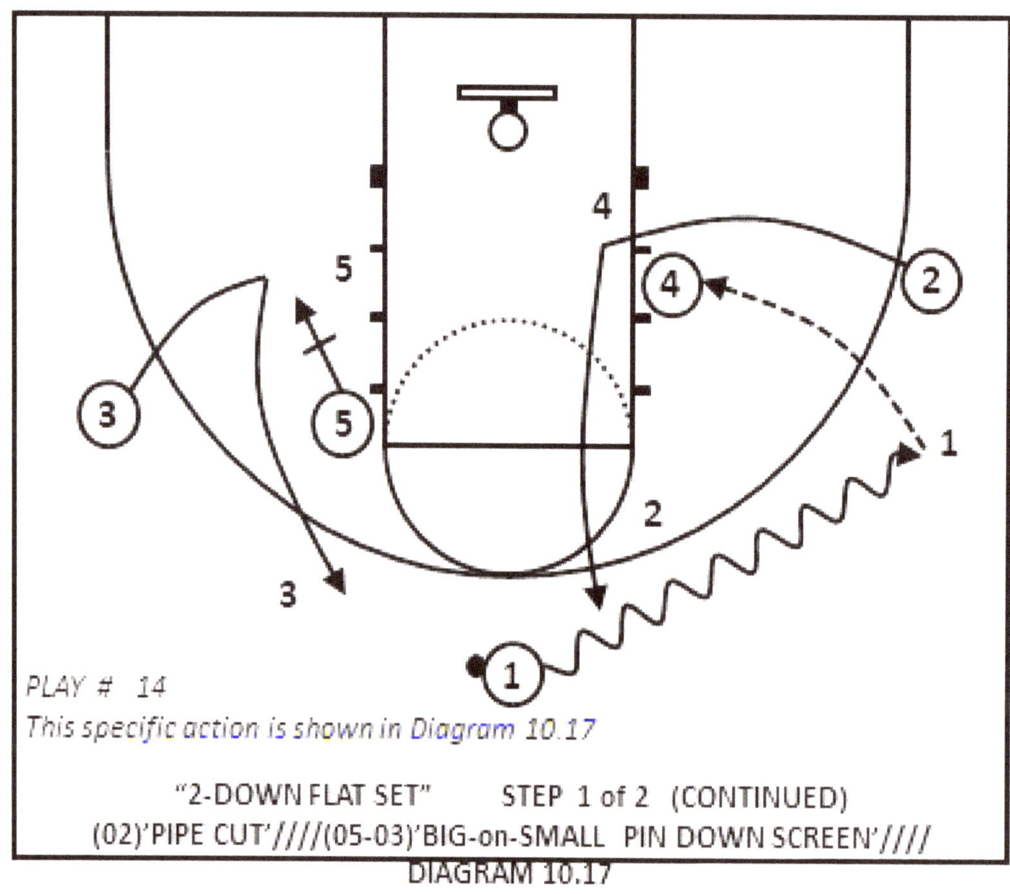

Diagram 10.18 illustrates 01 turning down the "Inside Pass" to 04 and reversing the ball to 02 and on over to 03. After making the pass to 03, 02 receives 01's "Flare-Screen" and makes his "Flare-Cut" towards the "Deep Corner" on his side of the floor 03 may have

a wide open '3 Pt.' shot at the "Slot" and gains more space to create by 05 drifting down into his "Deep Corner," flattening and vertically stretching the defense.

04 immediately "chases the ball" across the lane in no pre-determined route. He is just supposed to find the way to get open to receive the pass from 03 or 05 (or from teammates on the perimeter on either side of the floor.).

This action gives 04 an excellent opportunity for "Inside Shots" and possible perimeter shots for 01, 02 or 03. Still, if no shots are taken, the "4-Out/1-In" Spot-Ups are filled for an instant continuation of the attack on the defense. See Diagram 10.18

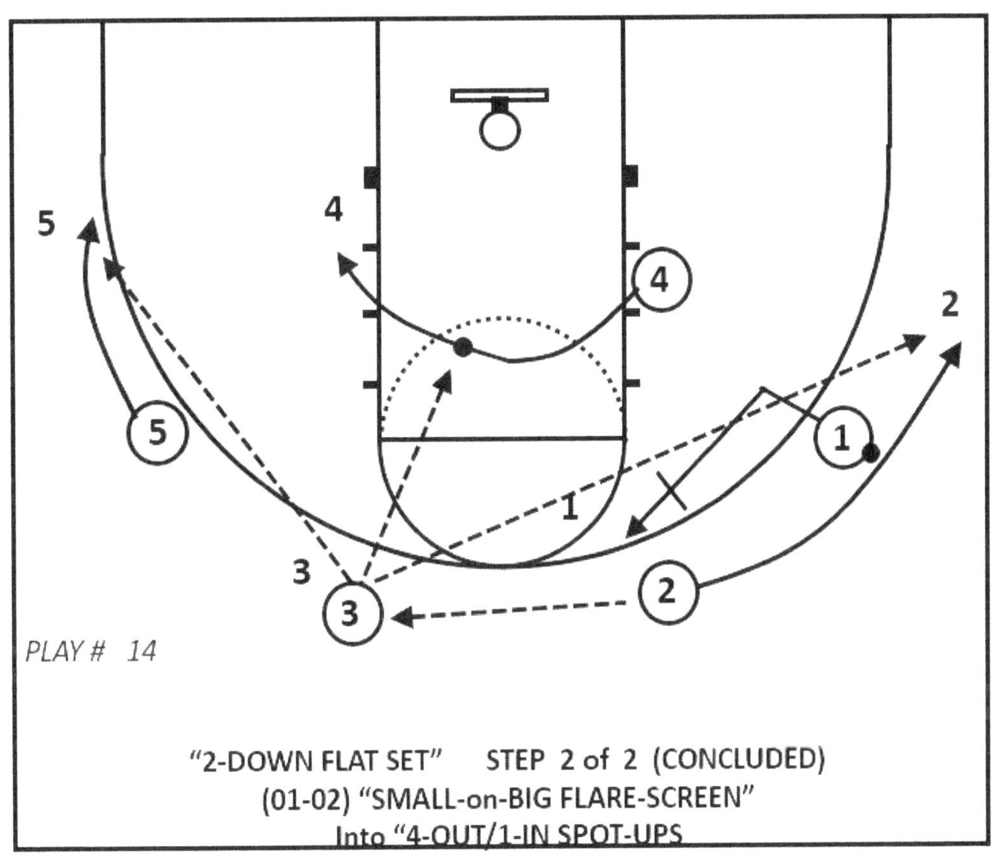

Diagram 10.18.

ACTION

Diagram 10.19 shows an example of the (03-04) "Small-on-Big Flare-Screen the Ball-Screener Action," with the play beginning out of the "HORNS" Set. 01 declares the right side of the floor as the initial action side by having 04 step up to set the 04-01 "Big-on-Small Ball-Screen" and 05 diagonally cutting across the lane before posting up on the opposite side of the in the new "Ballside Block." While 02 stays deep and wide in his initial "Deep Corner" spotted up and ready for a quick "catch and shoot/pass/create" pass from 01, 03 sprints along the baseline into the lane before he then diagonally runs up to set a "(Small-on-Big Flare)-Screen the (Ball-)Screener Screen on 04's defender. 04 sets his ball-screen for 01, front pivots off of his lower right foot and rubs his (post-type) defender off of 03's outside right shoulder to make a wide "Flare-Cut" midway between the "Weakside Wing" and "Weakside Deep Corner" locations. This action completely isolates 05 down on the "Block" with the next presumed defensive "Big," X4 spread out on the wide weakside of the floor; looking for 01's "Skip Pass."

If 04 has offensive perimeter skills (shooting, passing and/or driving) and/or if X4 has deficient perimeter defensive skills; 04 must benefit those advantages in one form or another, while allowing 05 to use the isolation scenario in the "Ballside Block" area. Players are spotted up in the proper "4-Out/1-In" Spot-Ups for the offense to continue into the last wave of the attack. See Diagram 10.19

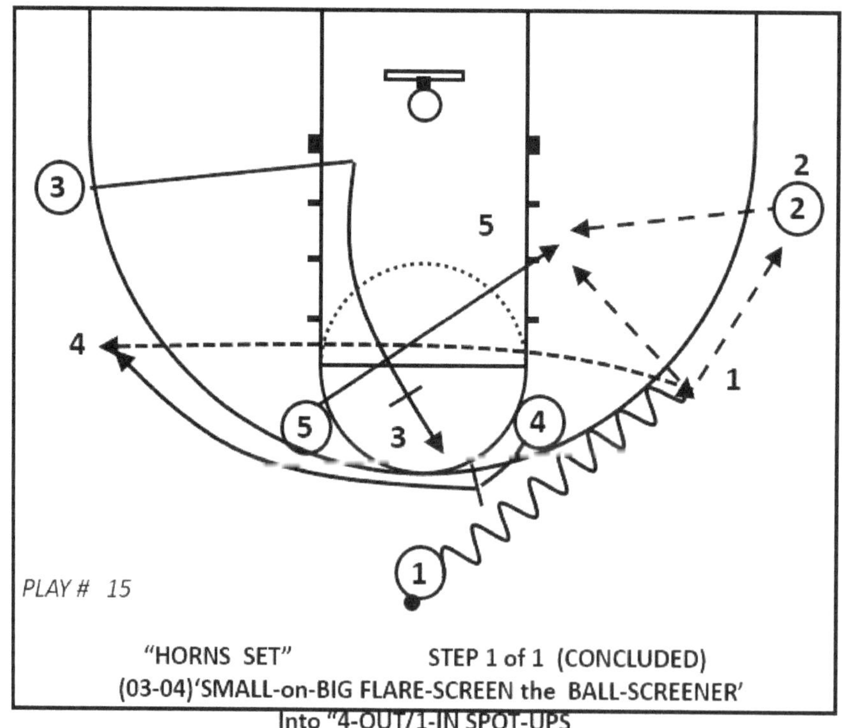

Diagram 10.19

Diagram 10.20 shows Play # 16 in its entirety from the initial "2-SQUEEZE" Set to its last phase of the attack. With 02 starting on the left side of the offense at the "Block," (when 02 could have also started on the other side of the lane), 01 dribbles toward the "Wing" spot-up opposite of 02's initial side of the floor.

At the same time, 03 makes an "Inverted and Iso Slash-Cut" to the newly declared "Ballside Block," while both 05 and 04 break diagonally down across the lane to set a "Big-on-Small Stagger-Screen" for 02 to use to break to the top of the key for an open '3 Pt.' shot opportunity. After the screen, 05 slides out to the "Wing" Spot-Up and 04 remains on the new "Weakside Block" area. This is to help eliminate possible helpside defense for 03 to be able to isolate his defender. In addition both 04 and 05 are in their new locations for offensive rebounding purposes.

All players are now in the "3-Out/2-In" Spot-Ups for the next wave of the offensive attack to begin. See Diagram 10.20

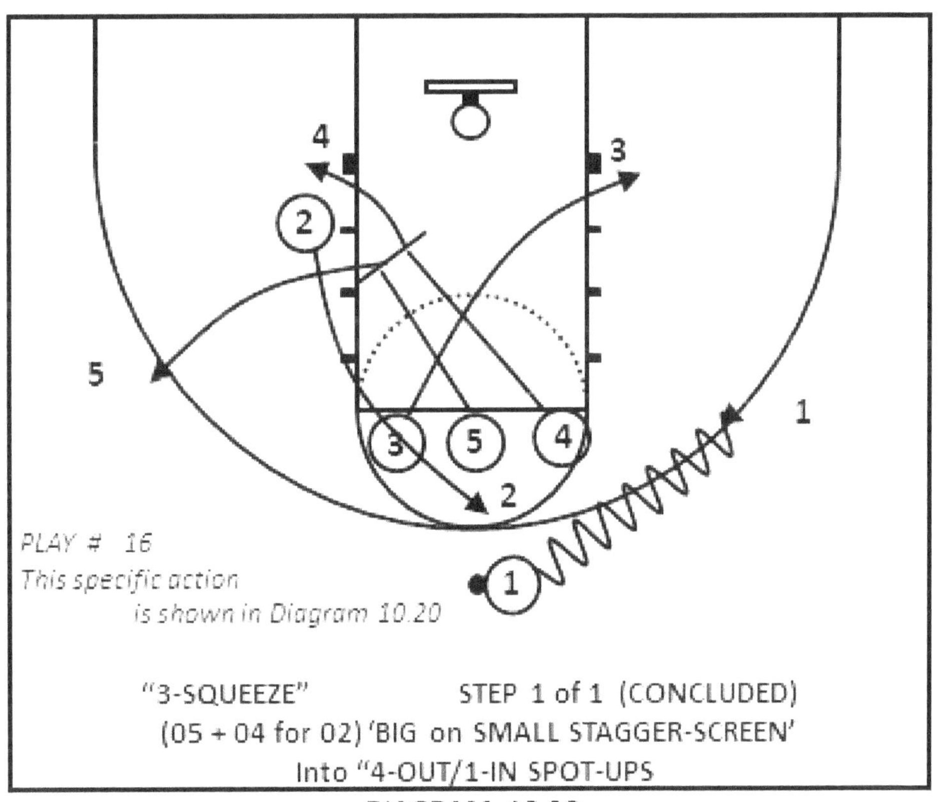

DIAGRAM 10.20

This action is shown to be executed out of the "3-UP" Set with 03 sprinting out of his "Deep Corner" to set a "Big-on-Small Long Ball-Screen" for 01. At the same time, 05 and 04 start to break diagonally down to set a "Big-on-Small Stagger-Screen" for 02 on the "Weakside." This action is a decoy and actually becomes a "Ghost Stagger-Screen" with 05 changing directions to "slash diagonally across the lane to the new "Ballside Bock. " 04 breaks his "stagger-screen" route off and simply cuts to the new "Weakside Block." 02 continues lifting to remain at the top of the key while 03 slips his screen and cuts to the FT Line extended. 01 looks to drive/create/shoot off of 03's "Ball-Screen" and then looks to hit 05 "Iso Posting Up his defender on the new "Ballside Block." After screening for 01, 03 looks to receive the quick "Reverse Throw-Back Skip-Pass" for an open shot. If not, 02 could continue the swing of the ball to 03 for his own "catch/shoot/create/pass" options that would definitely include hitting 04 on his own "post-up on his side of the lane."

If no shots are taken, the "3-Out/2-In" Spot-Ups are filled for a smooth continuation of the offensive attack. See Diagram 10.21

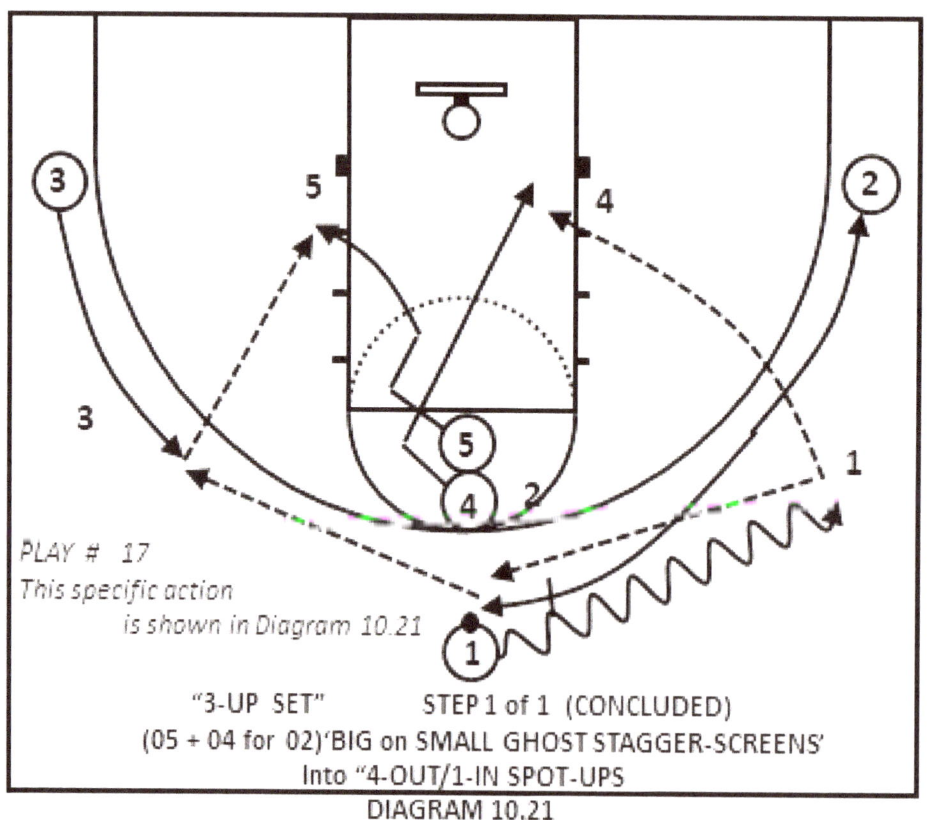

DIAGRAM 10.21

Diagram 10.22 illustrates a play very similar to the previous offensive set with this alignment called the "4-SQUEEZE" Set. With players exchanging various locations, 04 is now the player on the offense's left "Mid-Post Block" area, 02 on the left "Elbow, 03 on the right "Elbow" and 05 remaining at the "Nail."

01 again dribbles away from the overloaded side of the floor to the same "Wing" Spot-Up. 05 becomes the player that makes the diagonal "Iso Slash-Cut" to the new "Ballside Block," with 03 and 02 the designated players that make the "Small-on-Big" Stagger-Screen" for 04 to be the player to break to the top of the key for an open perimeter shot. If 04 has a specific strength in perimeter shooting or his defender, X4, has a particular defensive weakness in attempting to guard offensive perimeter players; this part of the play can be very successful. Regardless of the skills of 04, the action fully isolates 05 for outstanding scoring opportunities on the "Block."

After the stagger-screen is set with 04 scraping off of 02's outside left shoulder, and cutting to the top of the key, 02 empties out to the "Wing" location while 03 remains on the new "Weakside Block." The "3-Out/2-In" Spot-Ups are easily and immediately filled for the "Level 3" play to conclude with an easy transition into the designated continuity offense.

To create an easy counter to this play, 02 and 03 could change their routes to create a "Small-on-Big Stagger-Screen" that is now "twisted." The twist action forces 02 and 03 to change the route and final location of their actual stagger-screening action. This would reposition both players into the opposite weakside positions— 03 now on the "Weakside Wing" and 02 now on the "Weakside Block." See Diagram 10.22

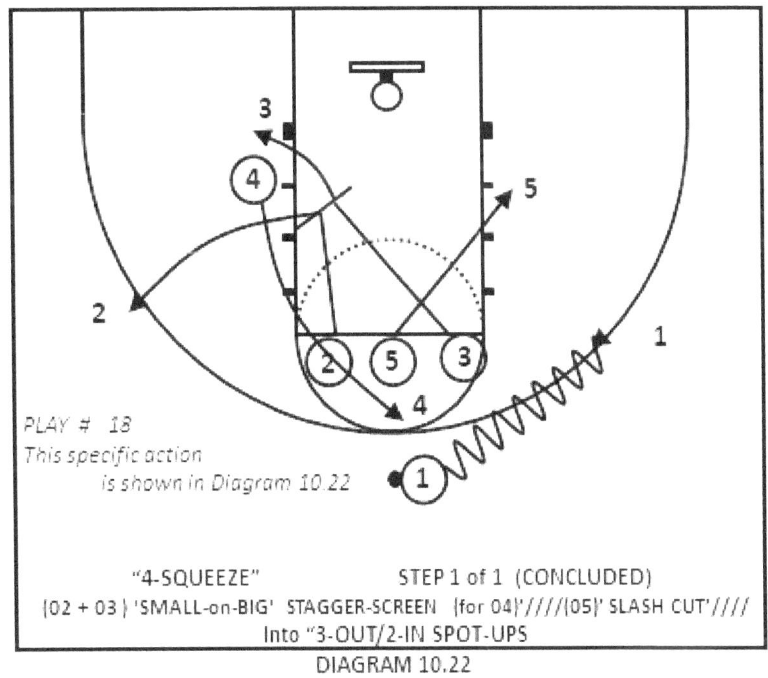

DIAGRAM 10.22

Diagram 10.23 illustrates a play out of the "2-TWIST" Set with 01 dribbling directly at 02, causing 02 to make a "Backdoor Cut" to the new "Ballside Block." At the same time, 03 and 04 rotate up and out to fill the vacant spots at the new "Weakside Slot" and "Weakside Wing." 05 remains spotted up at the "Nail." See Diagram 10.23

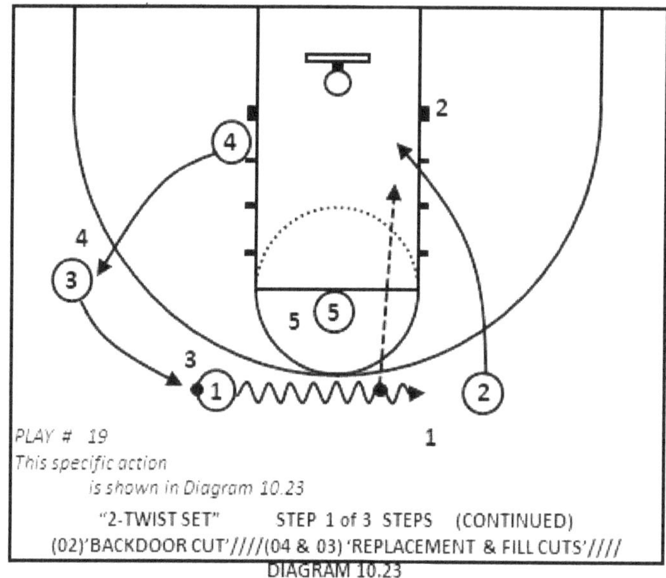

DIAGRAM 10.23

If 01 elects to not make passes to either 02 or 05, he should reverse the ball to 03 who quickly swings the ball over to 04 on the new "Ballside Wing." 04 looks to make the pass to 01 breaking to the top of the key off of the (05 & 03) "Stagger-Screen" for 01. See Diagram 10.24

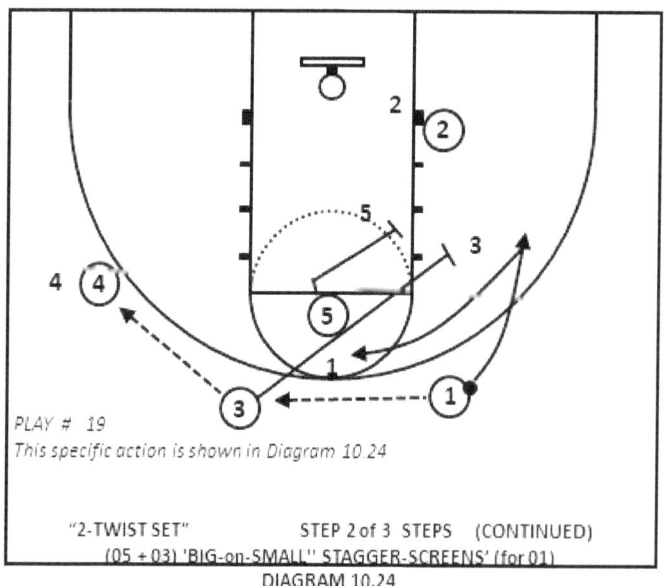

DIAGRAM 10.24

Most defenses would most likely then expect 02 to flash across the lane as 01 pops out to the top of the key off of the stagger-screen. In this particular play, instead, if 01 does not receive the ball, he makes a hard (diagonal) "Backdoor Cut" directly to the new "Ballside Block." 05 and 03 break down together to set their second "Big-on-Small Stagger-Screen" this time for 02 to use to break up to the top of the key. After screening, 05 slips to the rim while 03 curls out to the new "Weakside Wing" area. 04's new passing targets shift to becoming 01 on the interior, 02 out on top, 05 at the rim and 03 on the "Weakside Wing" for a possible (04-03) "Skip Pass."

Defenders have been attacked and moved and the offensive players are now in the "3-Out/2-In" Spot-Ups for a smooth transition into the designated continuity offense. See Diagram 10.25

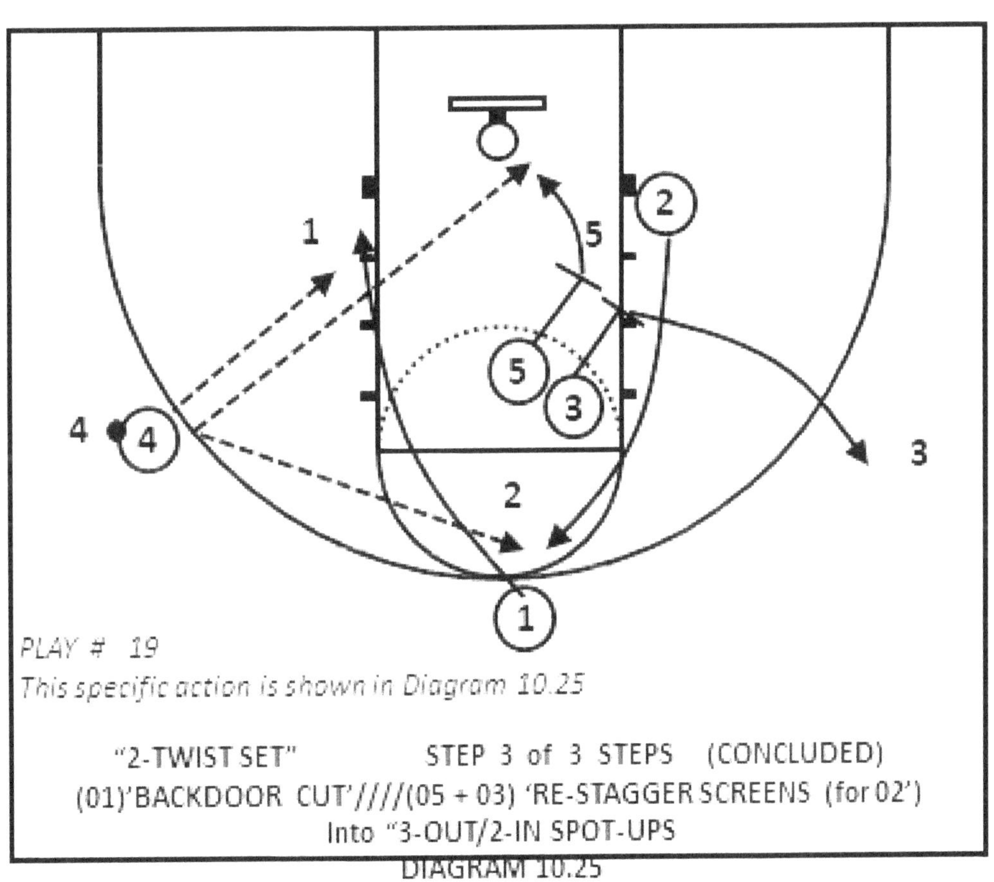

⊕ PLAY # 20: "SMALL-ON-BIG PIN DOWN-SCREEN" ACTION

Diagram 10.26 shows Play # 20 out of the "2-UP" Set, another symmetrically balanced offensive set. While the play could begin with 01 and 03, this occasion has 04 be the player that steps up to set a "Big-on-Small Ball-Screen" for 02 to use to dribble to the "Wing" area on the right side of the floor. To improve the passing angle to 05 or to create other offensive actions, 02 has the freedom to drive below the FT Line extended for as 04 approaches 02 to set the screen, 05 slashes diagonally to the new "Ballside Block" to isolate his defender.

To occupy the weakside during the beginning of this action, 01 breaks down to set a "Small-on-Big Pin Down-Screen" for 03 to use to exchange locations with 01 further drifting down towards the new "Weakside Deep Corner. This further aids 05 to isolate his defender, X5, on the "Ballside Block." This action spreads the floor both vertically as well as horizontally to attack the opposition's defense as well as to reposition players into the "4-Out/1-In" Spot-Ups so there is no interruption or delay from the entry to the last phase of the offense. See Diagram 10.26

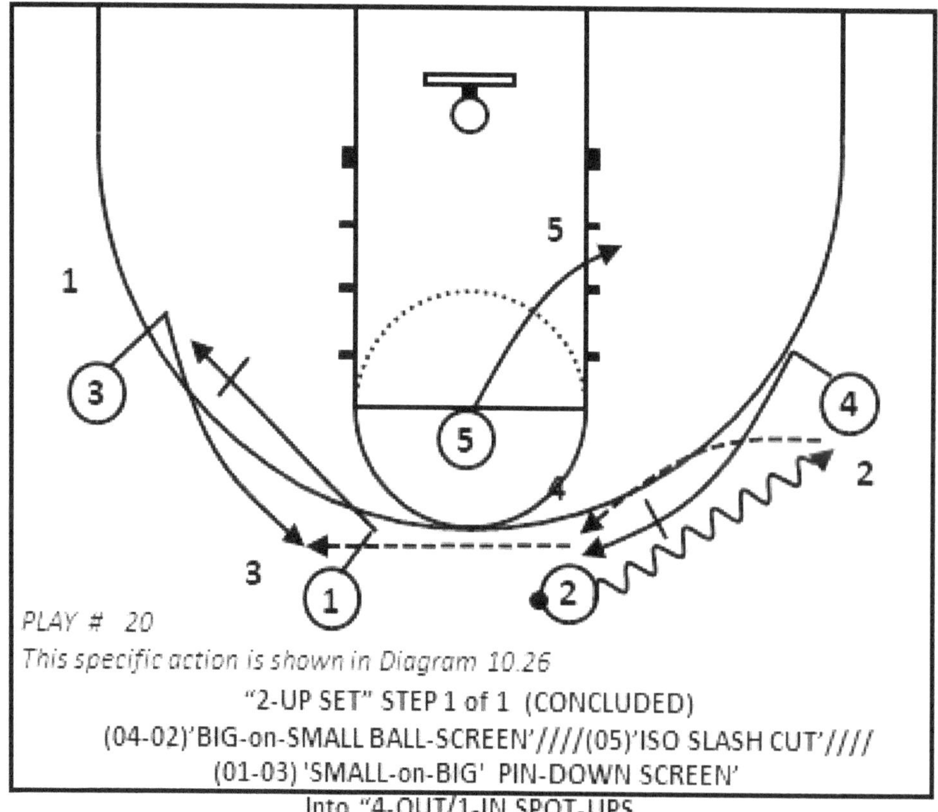

DIAGRAM 10.26

Diagram 10.27 is a diagram of Play # 21 out of the "1-DOWN" Set, with 05 having the option of posting up on the "notch above the Block" on either side of the lane. With just 05 switching sides of the lane gives the offensive alignment a different cosmetic look and position of strength. In this situation, 05 starts on the right side of the lane the play actually begins whenever 02 has possession of the ball. This could take place with a (01-02) "Reverse Pass" or with 02 actually bringing the ball across the timeline on the dribble. When 02 does approach the "Slot" area, 04 breaks down to set a "Big-on-Big Pin Down-Screen" for 05 to invert his defender and break out (off of 04's outside right shoulder) to the "Wing" area. After screening for 05, 04 replaces 05 with an "Iso Post-Up" on the "Ballside Block."

To occupy any possible weakside defenders that exists, 01 sets a "Small-on-Big" Pin Down-Screen" for 03 to use to break to the new "Weakside Slot." Both 05 and 01 can spot-up lower than the FT Line extended so they can vertically stretch and weaken the strength of the defense. If 05 has above average perimeter skills, (or X5 has below average perimeter defensive skills), 05 should attempt to benefit of those personnel advantages by using them. In addition, 04 may have personnel plusses over his defender that can be utilized.

If no shots are elected to be taken, all players are very close to being in the proper "4-Out/1-In" Spot-Ups so that the offense can continue. From there, the advantage of having a quick and easy conversion into the designated continuity offense can be utilized. See Diagram 10.27.

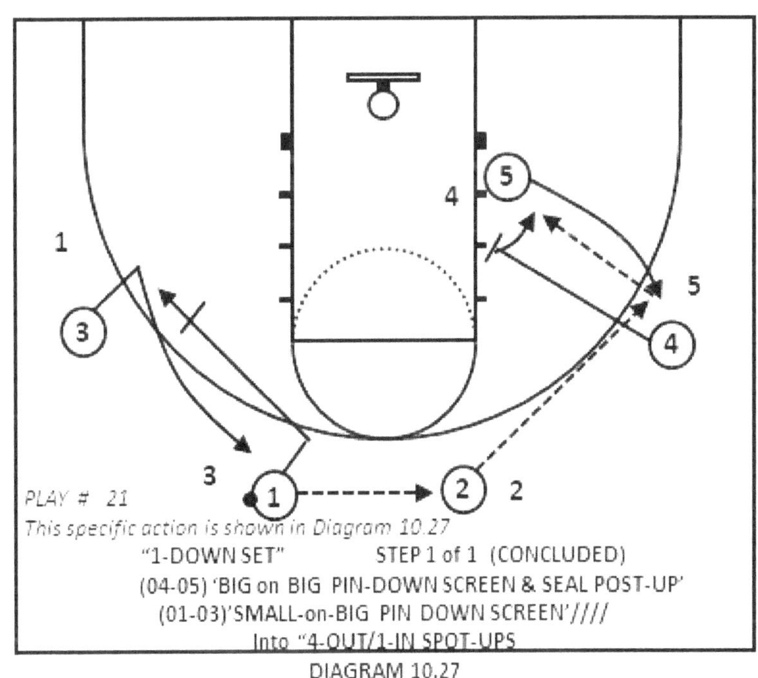

DIAGRAM 10.27

Play # 22 begins with the offense starting in a "4-DOWN" Set and all four off-the-ball players blasting out high towards 01 and the ball. 03 and 02 break directly to their "Wing" areas while 05 and 04 both "X-Cut" diagonally across the lane to the far-sided "Elbow" areas. This could be defined as "False Motion" where the players actually end up in the "5-UP" Offensive Set. This extra movement gives the opposition less time to identify the offensive set and guess what entry is about to be sprung upon them. This is just another advantage the coaching staff can create for their offense. See Diagram 10.28

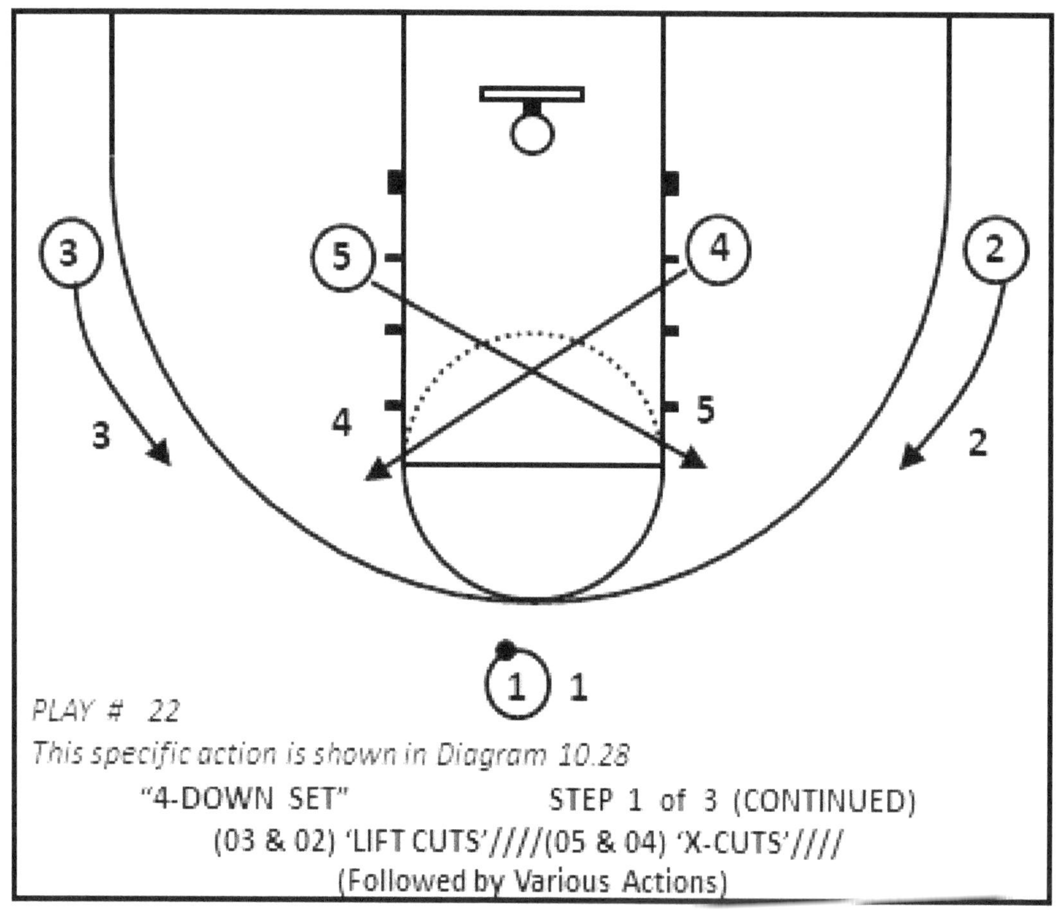

Diagram 10.28

With the offensive team having moved into another symmetrically balanced set, 01 could easily attack the defense immediately from either side. This diagram shows 01 initiating the action by making the pass to 03 on the left side of the floor. 01 reads how X1 plays the (01-03) "Wing Pass" and adjusts accordingly by rubbing off the appropriate shoulder of 04 as he makes his "UCLA" Cut to the "Ballside Block."

To occupy the weakside of the defense, 05 sets a diagonal "Pin Down-Screen" for 02 to us to break to the new "Weakside Slot." This gives 01 the opportunity to both invert and isolate his perimeter-type defender on the "Block." See Diagram 10.29

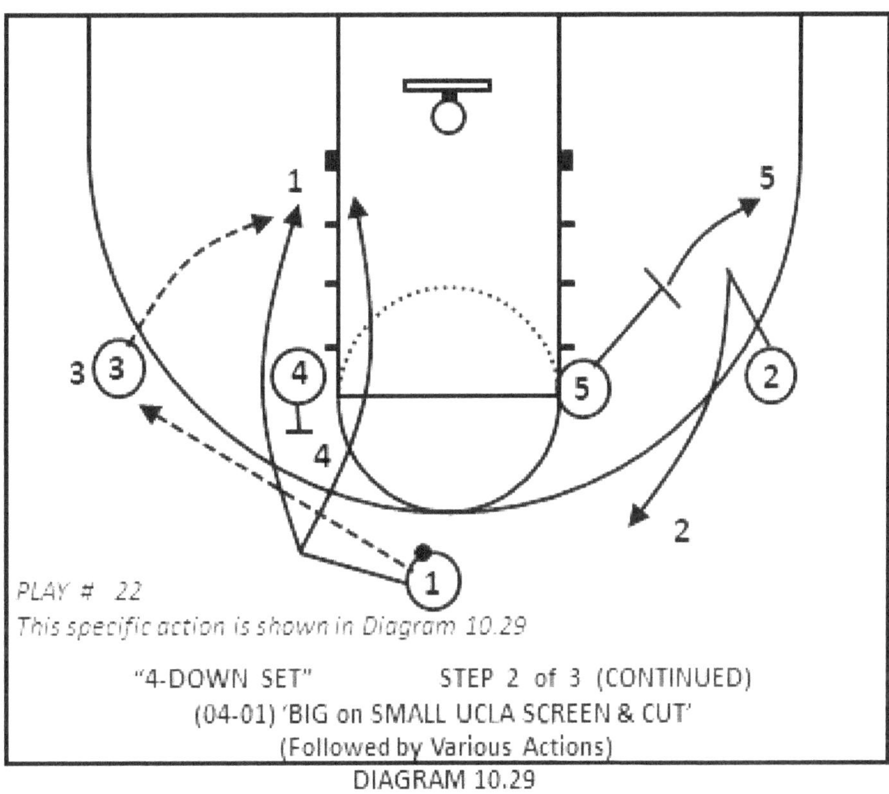

DIAGRAM 10.29

If 03 cannot make the pass to 01, 04 steps up and out to the empty "Slot" to receive 03's "Reverse Pass." 01 then adjusts his position and attacks his lone defender with some kind of a "Iso Duck-In Cut" into the middle of the lane.

If 04 cannot deliver the ball to 01 from the "Slot" location, he "Perimeter (Drag) Pull Dribbles" across the top of the key towards 02, who is cutting towards him.

04 and 02 fake a "Big-on-Small DHO" and 02 replaces 04 at the initial "Slot" position and then continues to set a "Pin Down-Screen" for 03 to use on the weakside. After screening for 03 on the "Weakside," 02 "Flare-Cut" towards the "Deep Corner" on his new side of the floor.

On the new "Ballside," 05 drifts wide and down towards his own "Deep Corner" to occupy his own defender, while 01 continues "to chase the ball as it circles the perimeter" and maintains good "post-up" positioning and stance.

If shots are not created for 01 on the interior or not produced for any of the perimeter players, the "4-Out/1-In" Spot-Ups are filled for the maintaining of the offensive attack. See Diagram 10.30

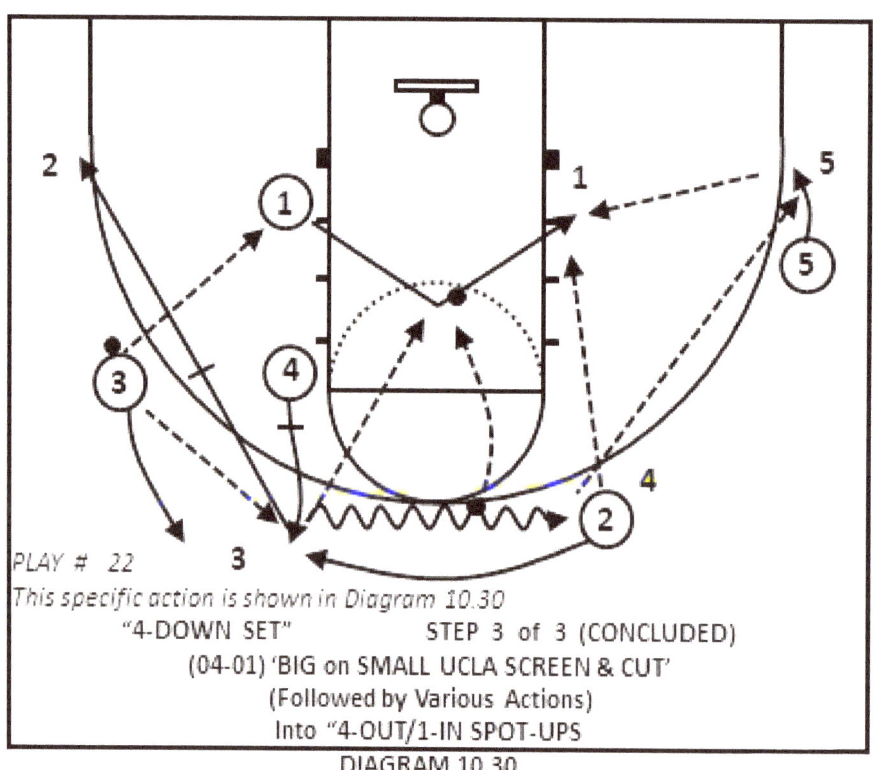

DIAGRAM 10.30

⊕ Play # 23: "Big-on-Small UCLA Screen & Cut" Action

Play # 23 is a Counter play to Play/Action 22. The first action is identical with Action 22 –"Lift Cuts" again by both 03 and 02 and "X-Cuts" by both 05 and 04. Again, out of the "4-DOWN" Set, 01 could again start the action on the right side of the floor, but for simplicity's sake, 01 will make the same (01-03) "Wing Pass" as he did in Play # 22. See Diagram 10.31

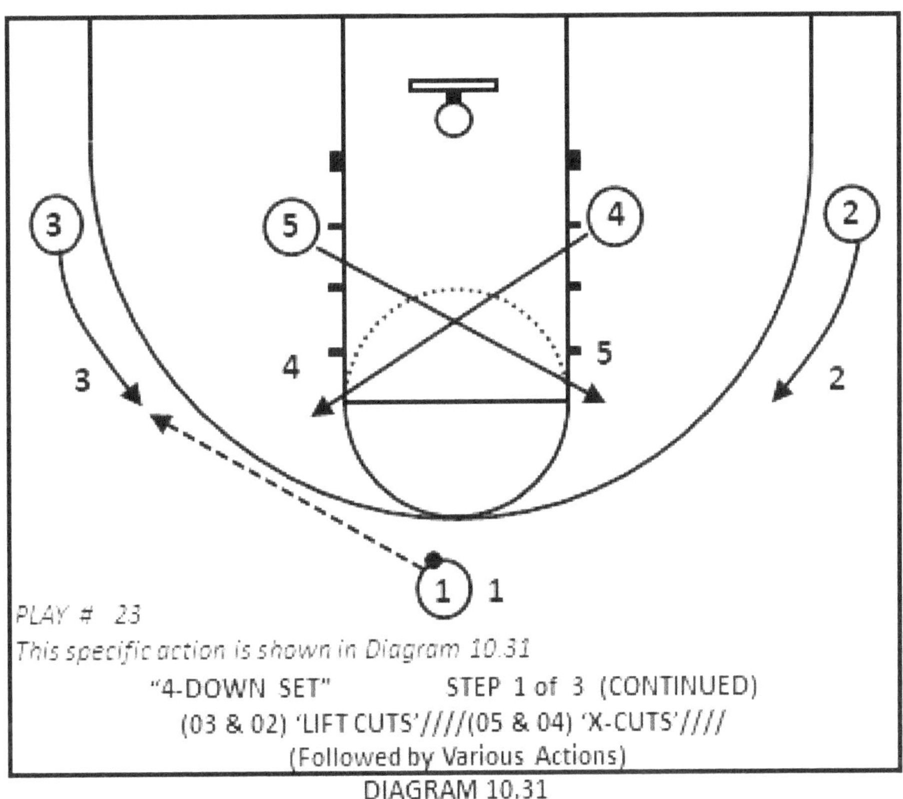

DIAGRAM 10.31

As 01 again sets his defender up for the (04-01) "UCLA Screen and Cut," he makes the same contact with 04 and then the action drastically changes. 05 again breaks down and over to "Pin-Screen" 02's defender to occupy weakside defenders and to place 02 at the new "Weakside Slot. See Diagram 10.32

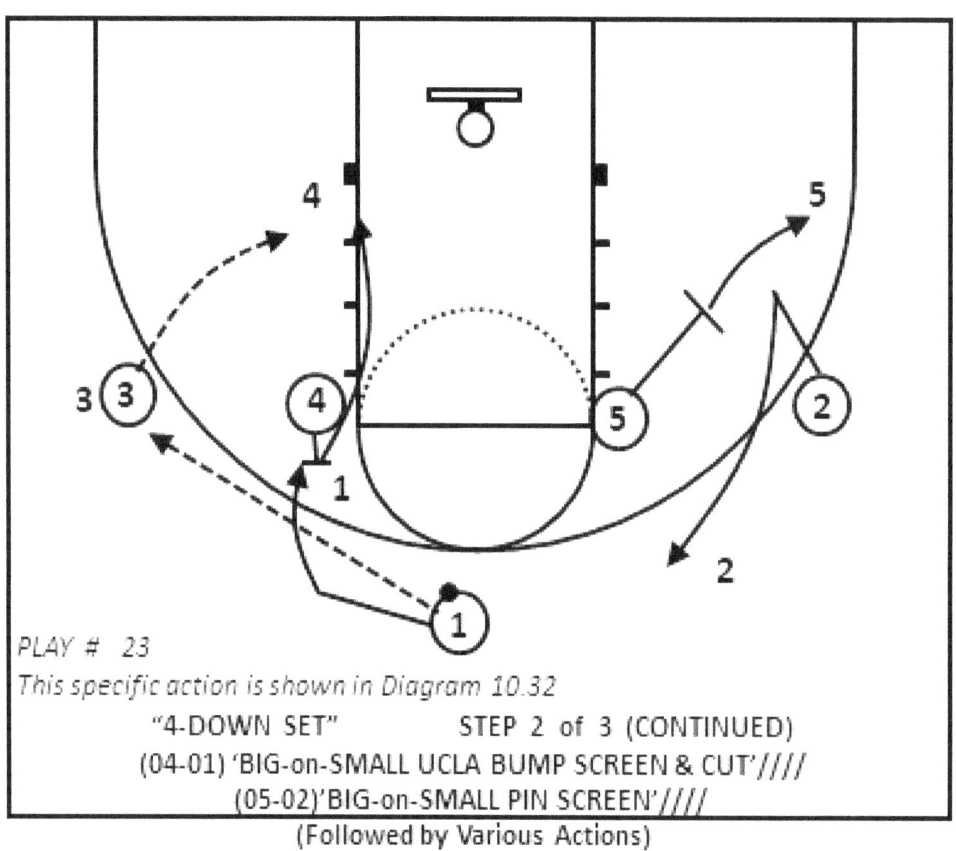

DIAGRAM 10.32

Just as 01 is about to scrape shoulders with 04 to rub X1 off, 01 "bumps" 04 to dictate that 04 make the so-called "UCLA Cut" and posting up on the new "Ballside Block." If 03 elects not to make the pass to 04, he reverses the ball 01 who has also stepped into the vacant "Slot" position. 01 immediately looks to hit 04 on his "Iso Duck-In Cut" and if not open inside, 01 starts his "Perimeter Pull (Drag) Dribble" across the top of the key, looking to make the "Inside Pass" to 04 on his "Duck-In Cut."

This action appears to be identical with the previous action on the "Drag Dribble" action. It quickly changes when 02, in this action, receives the (01-02) DHO and changes the direction of the ball. With the ball being "re-reversed," 04 stops his "Duck-In Cut" in the middle of the Dotted Circle and then cuts back towards the offensive left side of the lane where he started.

After 01 makes the handoff, 05 steps up to set his "Big-on-Small Flare-Screen" for 01 to use to "Flare-Screen" towards the opposite side's wide open area. On the ballside, as 02 approaches the empty "Slot" position, 03 makes his own "Flare-Cut" towards his "Deep Corner." 02 now looks to attack his defender off the dribble, to make the "Inside Pass" to 04 back on the initial side of the floor or to make the (02-03) "Down Pass" for 03 to have any of the possible offensive actions: "catch and shoot/inside pass to 04/skip pass to 01/create off of his own shot fake and dribble." If shots are not created, the "4-Out/1-In" Spot-Ups are once again filled for a smooth conversion into the next phase of the attack. See Diagram 10.33.

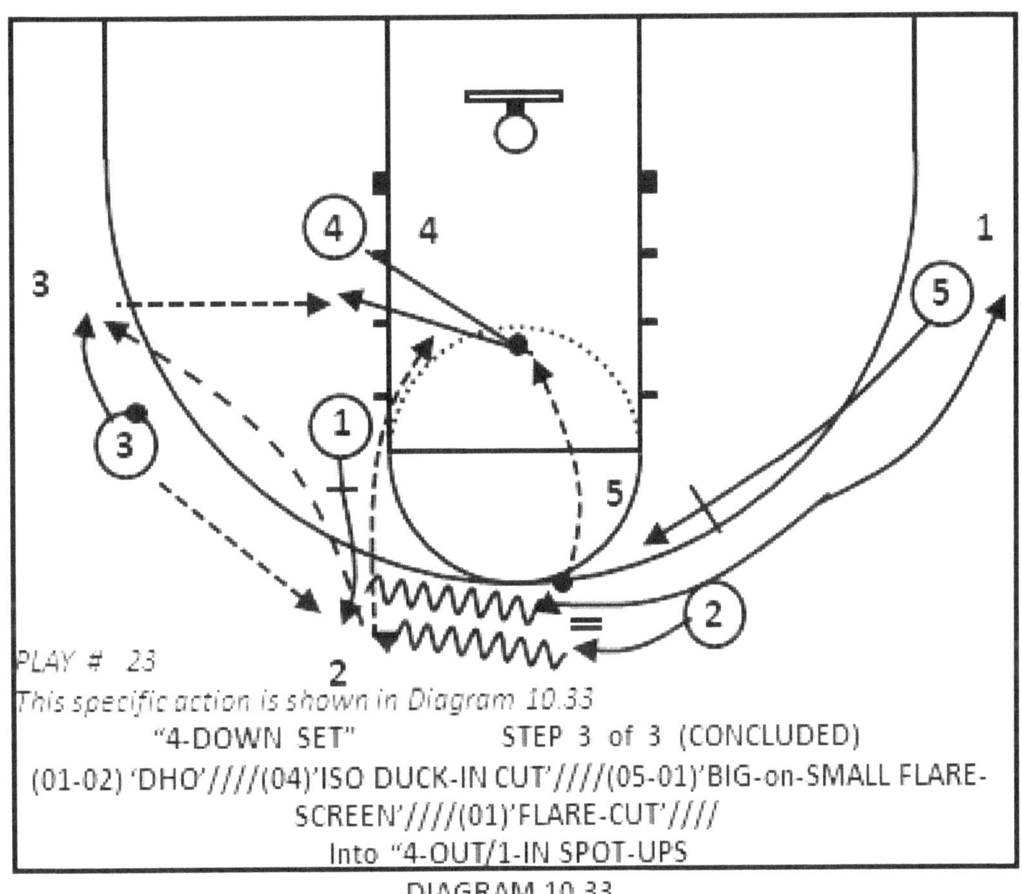

DIAGRAM 10.33

⊕ Play # 24: "Big-on-Small UCLA Screen & Bump- Cut" Action

Play # 24 is executed out of the "2-SQUEEZE" Set and is explained in Diagrams 10.34 through 10.36. In this first diagram, as 01 brings the ball down the floor , 02 starts on the left "Mid-Post" area and makes an "L-Cut" up and out" to the FT Line extended on his initial side of the floor. At the same time, 03 makes an "Iverson Cut" either under or over the top of both 05 and 04's Iverson Screens to the right "Wing" area opposite of 02's last position. See Diagram 10.34

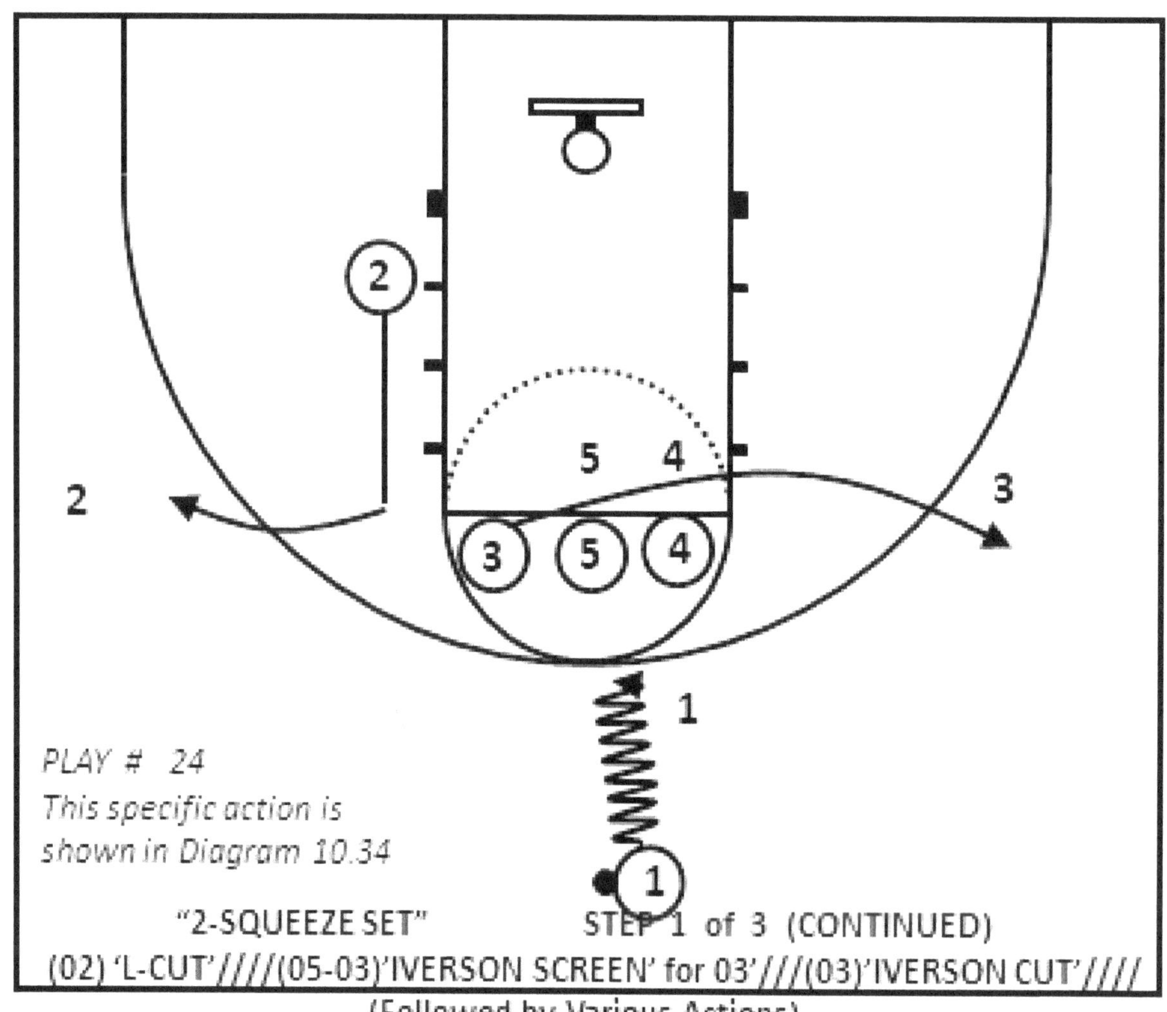

(Followed by Various Actions)
DIAGRAM 10.34

Having the option to making the initial "Wing Pass" to either 02 on the left or to 03 on the right side, 01 has elected to pass the ball to 03 on the right side of the floor. 01 then starts to set his defender up to execute (04-01) "UCLA Screen/Cut" action. At the last moment, 01 bumps his teammate so that 04 is the player that actually makes his "Iso Cut" towards the basket. To further isolate 04 and his defender, 05 steps out to the new "Weakside Slot," further spreading the floor and stretching the defense. See Diagram 10.35.

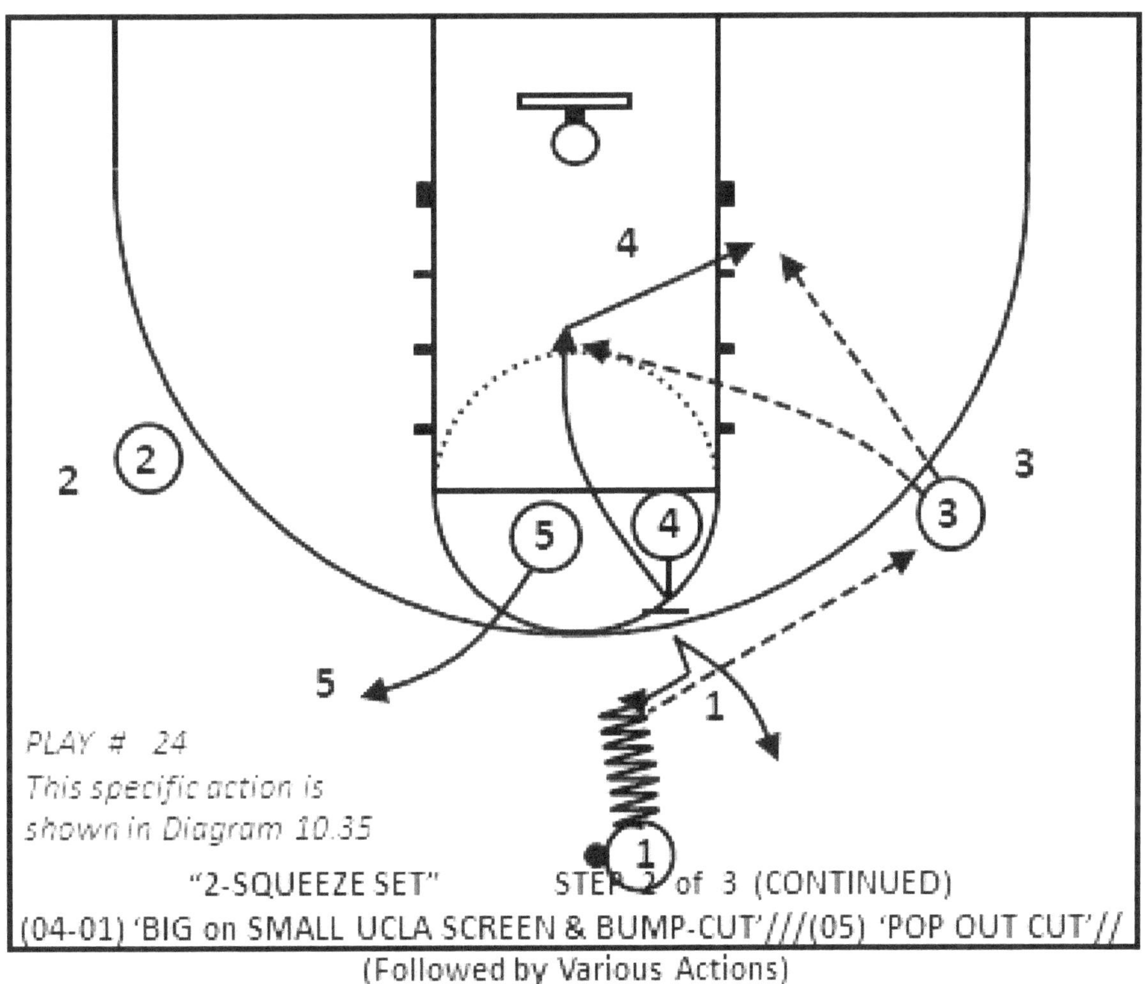

DIAGRAM 10.35

If 04 cannot get open on the "Ballside Block," 03 should reverse the ball to 01 with 04 then stepping back into the lane to "chase the outside passes made around the perimeter." If 01 cannot deliver the ball to 04 again at the "Dotted Circle", 05 cuts across to set a "Big-on-Small Ball-Screen" that is then followed by 05 continuing to set a "Big-on-Small Pin Down-Screen" for 03 to use to get open for a perimeter shots at the new "Weakside Slot." 05 ends up slipping his second screen and drifts down to the new "Weakside Deep Corner."

As 01 "dribble-scrapes" off of 05's top shoulder, he continues looking to make the "Inside Pass" to 04, still "chasing the ball" (around the perimeter.) To get open, 02 drifts a little lower to receive the pass from 01 and have opportunities for "catch/shoot or inside pass or create" off of 01's "Wing Pass."

01 should have "Inside Pass" opportunities to 04 on either side of the floor as well as a possible "Down Pass" to 02 or a "Throwback Reverse Pass" to 03. Both 02 and 03 would have "Inside Pass" opportunities to the isolated and constant moving 04 in the lane. Still, if no shots are taken, the "4-Out/1-In" Spot-Ups are filled for the next phase of the attack. See Diagram 10.36

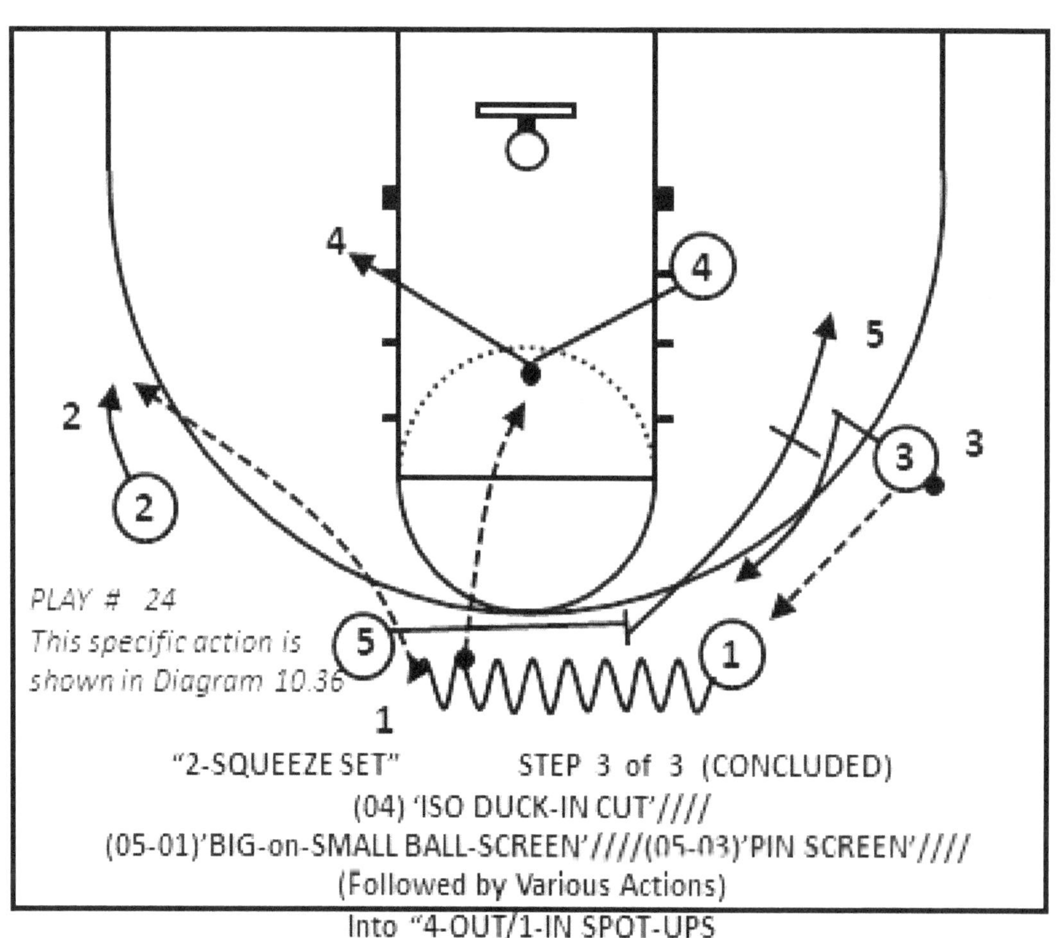

⊕ Play # 25: "Iverson Screens & Cuts" Action

Play # 25 is another specific play out the "3-ACROSS" Set with 05 having the freedom to start on either side of the lane. 03 and 02 both execute "Iverson Cuts" over and under 04 as they make their respective cuts across to the opposite sides of the floor. See Diagram 10.37

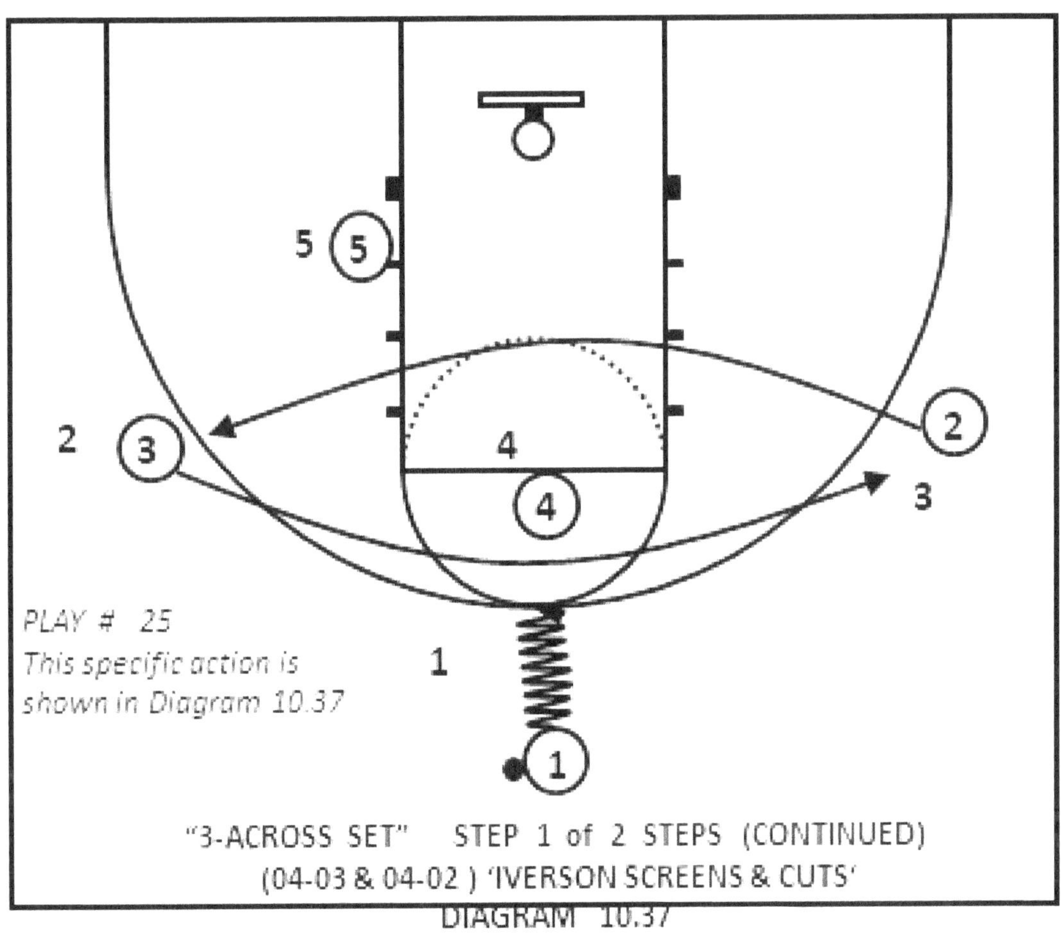

01 makes the (01-03) "Wing Pass" and immediately receives a (02-01) "Flare-Screen" for 01 to then "Flare-Cut" to the new "Weakside Wing" while 02 slips his screen and spot-ups at the "Top of the Key." As 03 receives the ball from 01, 04 attacks his defender and flashes to the new "Ballside Block" while 05 sets his defender up before flashing diagonally up and across the lane to the new "Ballside High Post" on the opposite side of the floor. These actions by all players eliminates any possible chance of interior support defense that 05 and particularly 04 needs.

If shots are not produced and taken, the new "HIGH-POST/LOW-POST" Spot-Ups are filled for the specific continuity offenses associated with these spot-ups to be able to fluidly begin. See Diagram 10.38

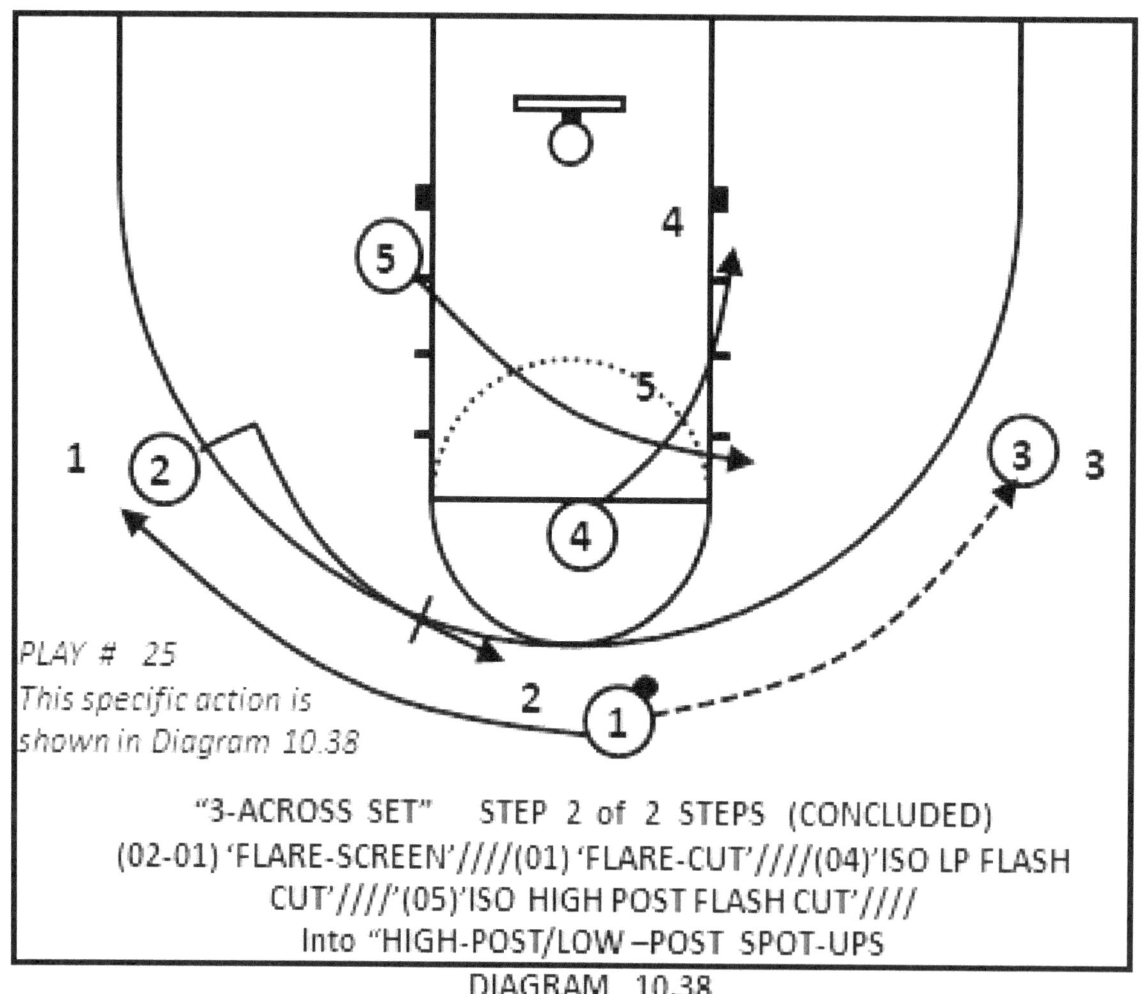

DIAGRAM 10.38

Out of the "HORNS" Set comes Play # 26 with 05 stepping over to set a "Big-on-Small Barkley Screen" for 04 to use to break to the offensive left "Wing" area. At the same time, 02 breaks up to make a "Replacement Fill Cut" for to 04's initial location. See Diagram 10.39

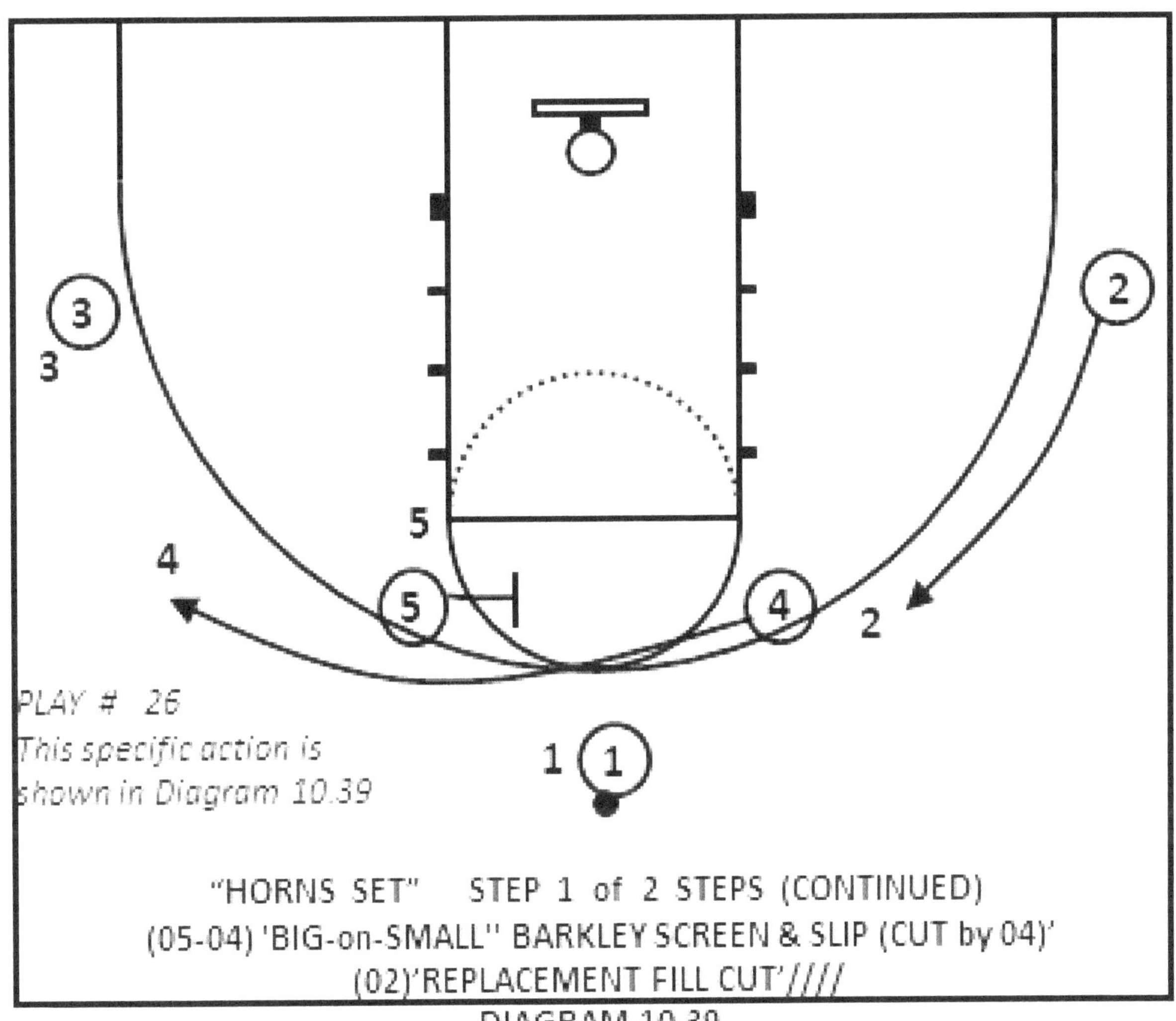

When 01 makes the "Wing Pass" to 04, 02 immediately steps up to set a "Flare-Screen" for 01 to use to "Flare-Cut" towards the new "Weakside Deep Corner." 02 then slips his screen to step up to the new "Weakside Slot." At the same time, 05 slips his (05-04) "Barkley Screen," and makes a "Rim-Run" to the basket while looking over his inside left shoulder for 04's "Lob Pass."

04 could make possible "Skip Passes" to 01 in the "Weakside Deep Corner" or to 02 at the "Weakside Slot." In addition, 03 may have possibilities for a (04-03) "Down Pass" that could provide 03 with "catch/shoot or catch/inside pass or catch/create opportunities" from his "Deep Corner" location.

If shots are not taken, the stable "4-Out/1-In" Spot-Ups are filled so that the designated continuity offense can quickly and smoothly maintain the attack. See Diagram 10.40

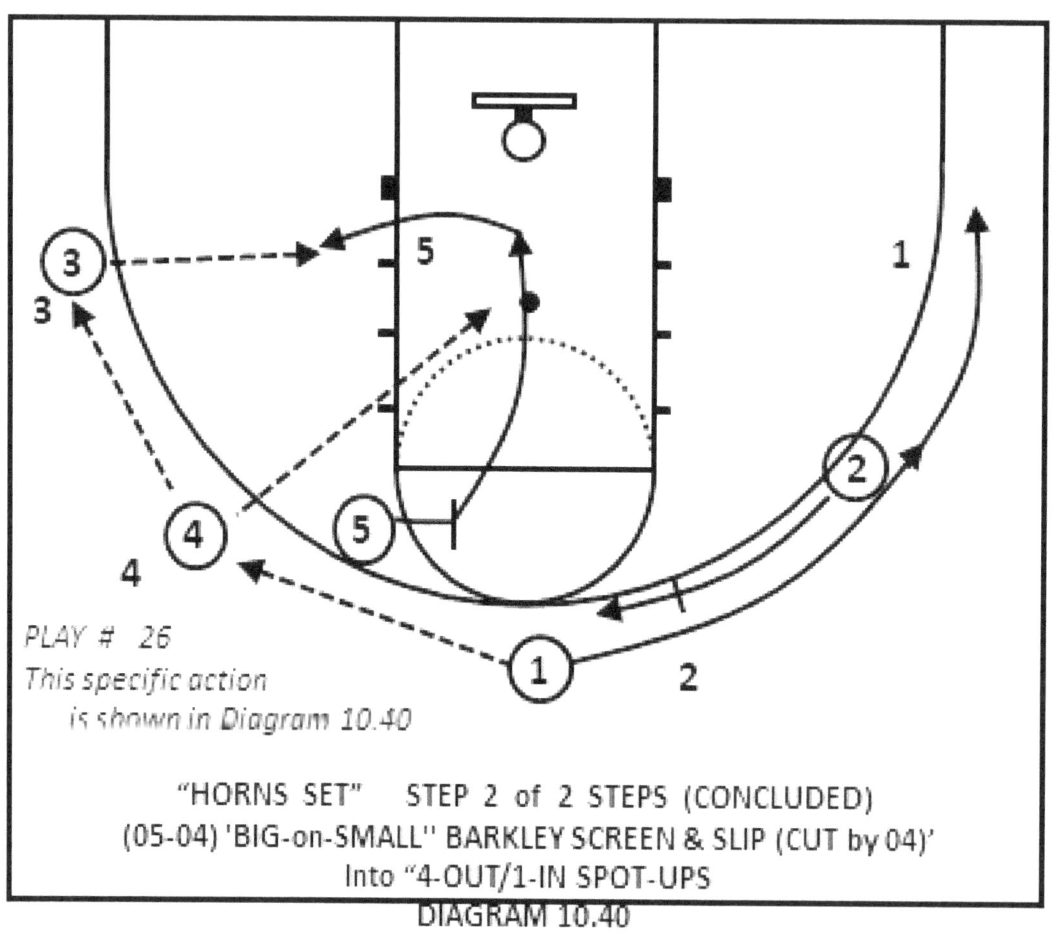

Diagram 10.41 shows the entire execution of Play # 27 out of the "HORNS" Set. Since this alignment/set is another one of the purely symmetrically balanced alignments, each play could be run to either side of the floor; making it much more difficult to defend.

With 01 deciding to "Perimeter Pull Dribble" to the left "Wing" area, causing 03 to be the player that sprints to the "Block" and then vertically straight up the middle of the lane to the "Nail" and then between the inside shoulders of 05 and 04 to use their "Big-on-Small Elevator Screen" to the top of the key. This should give 03 an excellent '3 Pt.' Shot opportunity behind the arc. At the same time, 02 breaks vertically up to the "Wing" area on his own side of the floor.

After 03 breaks contact with both 05 and 04, both post players slip their "Elevator Screens" and "Diagonally Slash Cut" to the "Mid-Post" area on their respective sides of the floor. If 03 does not have an open shot, the "3-Out/2-In" Spot-Ups are filled and the designated continuity offense can immediately begin with the next passing action by 03. See Diagram 10.41

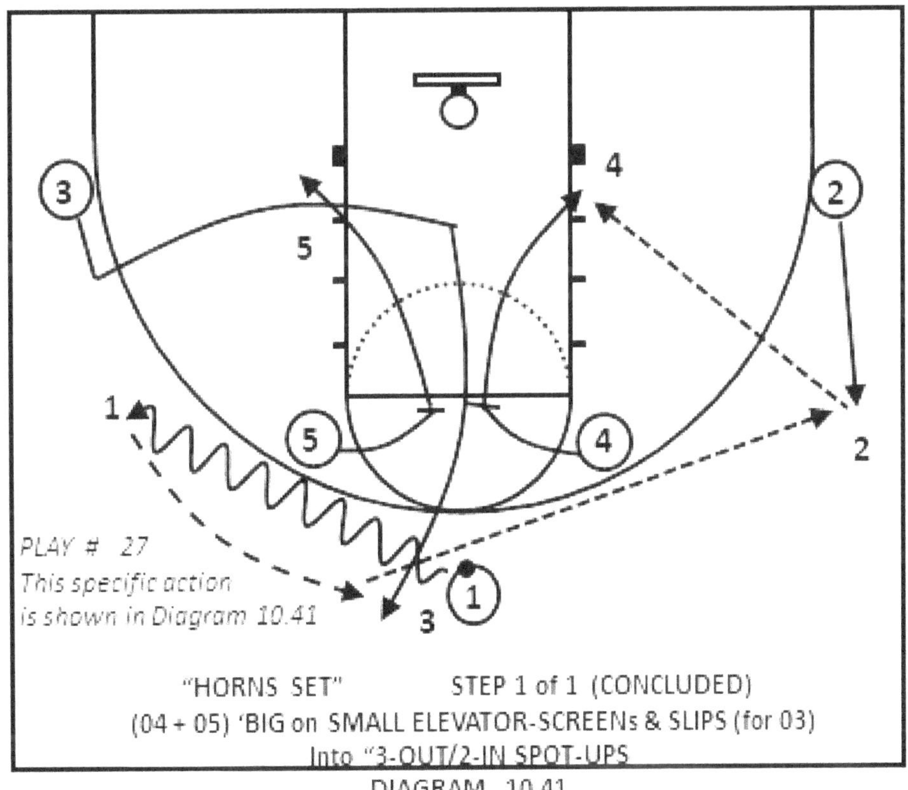

DIAGRAM 10.41

Diagrams 10.42 and 10.43 shows the entire execution of Play # 28 out of the "5-UP" Set. This alignment/set is still another one of the purely symmetrically balanced alignments, so each play could be run to either side of the floor; making it much more difficult for the opposition to defend.

Both 05 and 04 step up to set a "Big-on-Small Ball-Screens" for 01 to use. 01 elects to "dribble-scrape" off of the outside left shoulder of 04 and approach 02 near the right "Wing" area. As 01 approaches 02, 02 reverses the direction of his cut and instead makes a hard "Backdoor Cut" to the vacant "Ballside Block" area. See Diagram 10.42

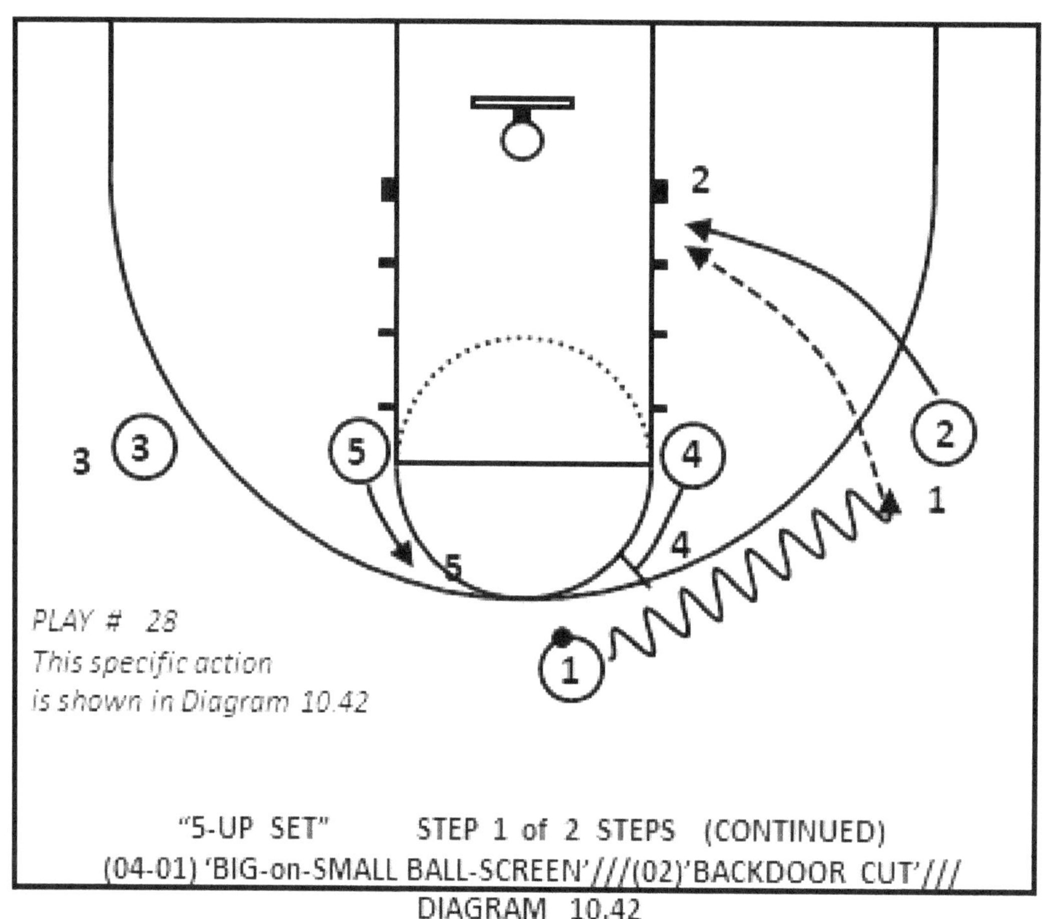

Diagram 10.43 shows 01 not making the pass to 02 because he is defended too closely. This then forces 02 to quickly read the defender and change directions to make an "Elevator Cut" up through the lane between the shoulders of both 04 and 05. To confuse the defense and cause defensive problems, both 04 and 05 make small "X-Cuts" to set their screens on both sides of the "Nail." 04 would end up on the left side of the "nail" and 05 on the right side of the "nail." That means that 02 would scrape off of 04's right shoulder and off of 05's left shoulder (after their "twisting of the Elevator Screen.")

After setting the screens for 02 to get open at the top of the key, both 04 and 05 slip down to the near "Mid-Post" areas to post their defenders up. This movement repositions players into the customary "3-Out/2-In" Spot-Ups for the next wave of attack to quickly begin. See Diagram 10.43

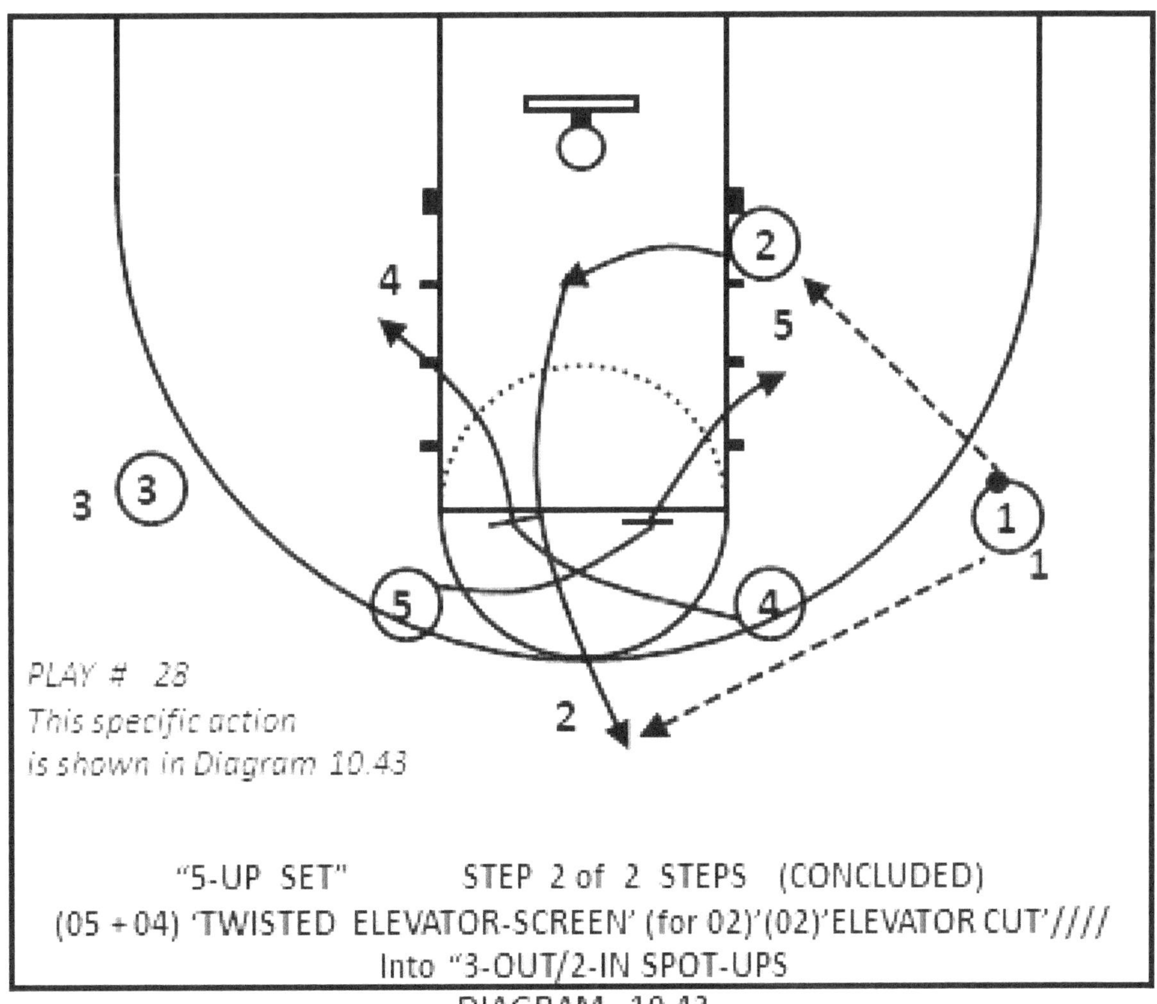

Diagrams 10.44 and 10.45 illustrate Play # 29 out of the "5-OUT" Set. On the left side of the floor, 03 steps up to set a "Small-on-Big" Back-Screen" for 05 to make a hard "Backscreen Shuffle Cut to the basket. After screening for 05, 03 slips his screen and breaks out to a location slightly higher and wider than the customary "Slot" position. On the opposite side of the floor 04 breaks down to set a "Big-on-Small" Pin-Screen for 02 to break up at the same location opposite of 03. See Diagram 10.44

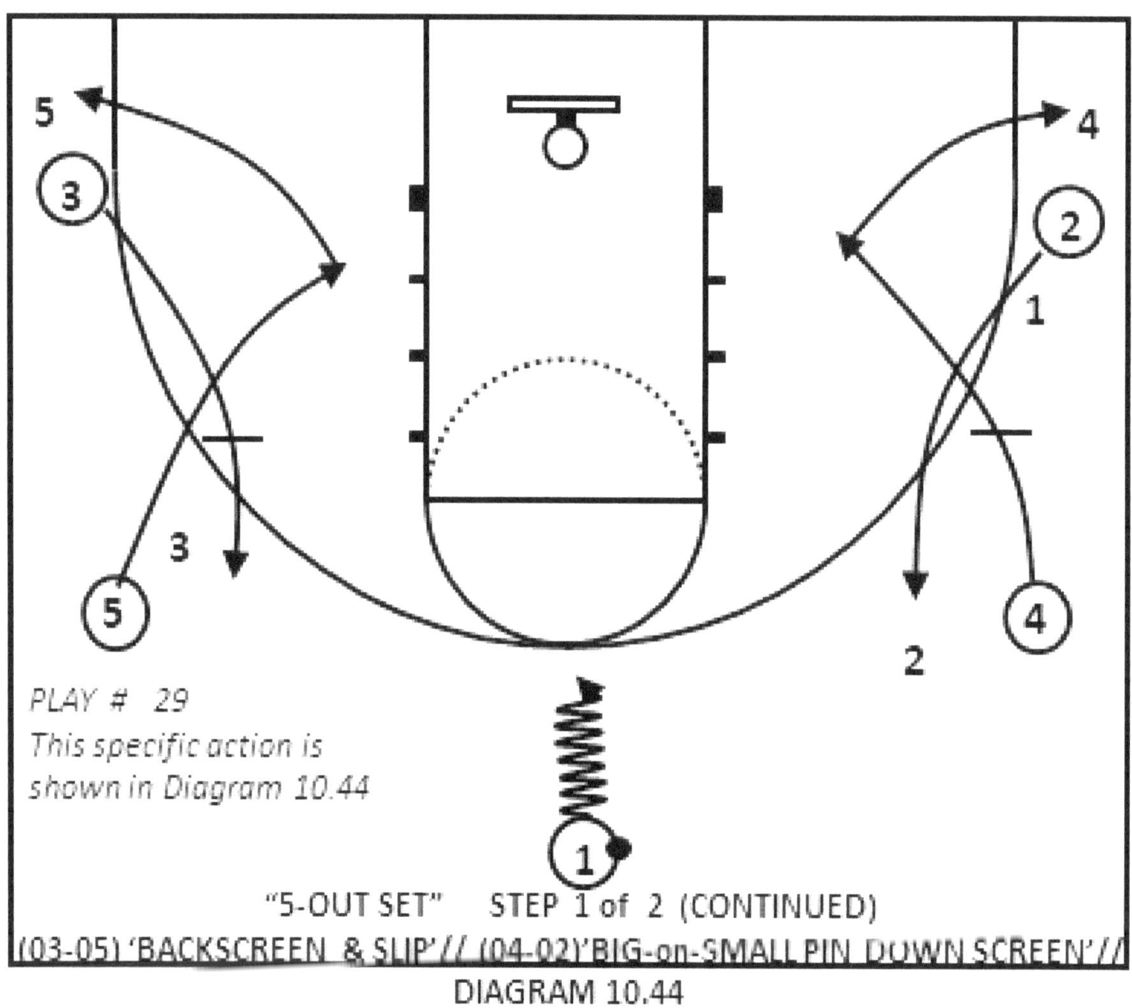

DIAGRAM 10.44

Diagram 10.45 demonstrates 01 making the (01-02) "Wing Pass" to 02 and then immediately breaking away from the ball to first set a "Small-on-Big Brush Screen" for 03 to use to diagonally "Slash Cut" across the lane to the opposite side of the lane. 01 then continues cutting down to then set a "Small-on-Big Pin Screen" for 05 to break up to the new "Weakside Slot" area. This action allows 03 to completely isolate his perimeter-type defender on the new "Ballside Block."

This action spreads the defense and repositions all players into the "4-Out/1-In" Spot-Ups for the offense to have the opportunity to continue the offensive attack. See Diagram 10.45

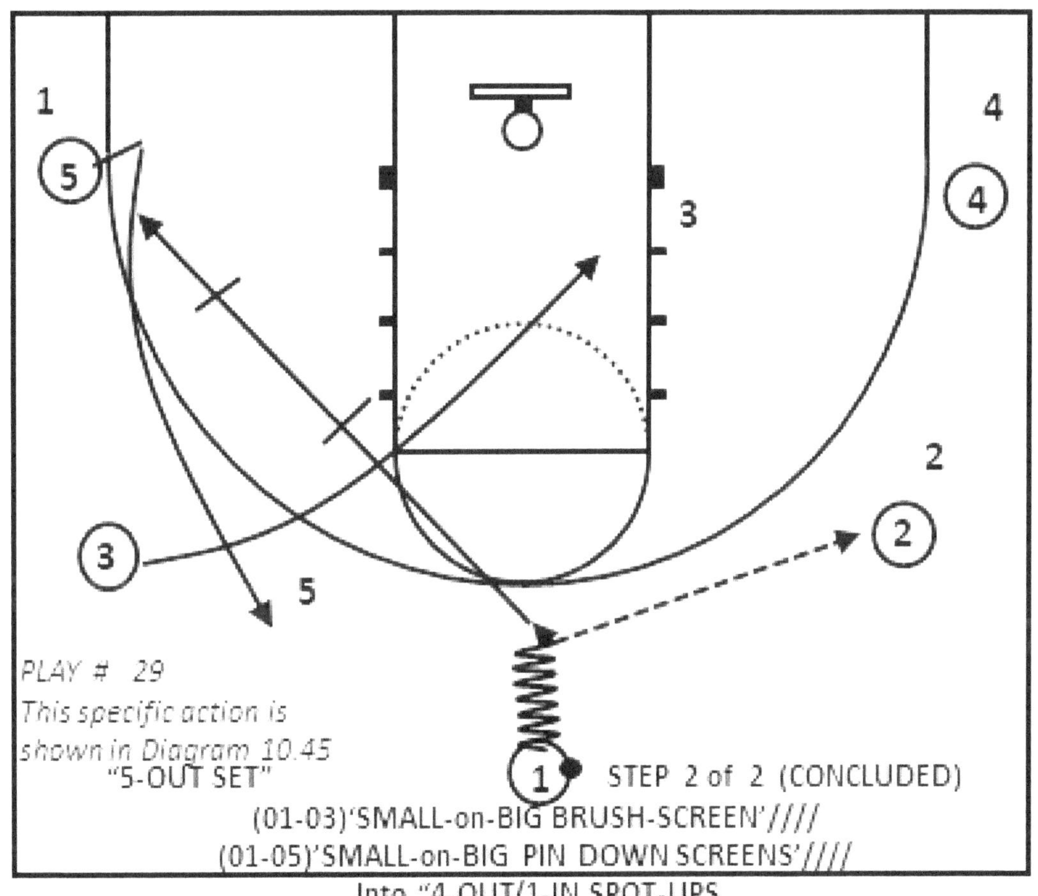

Diagrams 10.46 and 10.47 illustrate Play # 30 out of the "HORNS" Set. This play is a "Counter" to Play # 30 and its "Brush-Screen" action with 01 and 03 or with 01 and 02. On the left side of the floor, 05 steps out high and wide near the sideline area near where the old sideline 'hash-marks' used to be. 04 breaks out to the same position on the other side of the floor. See Diagram 10.46

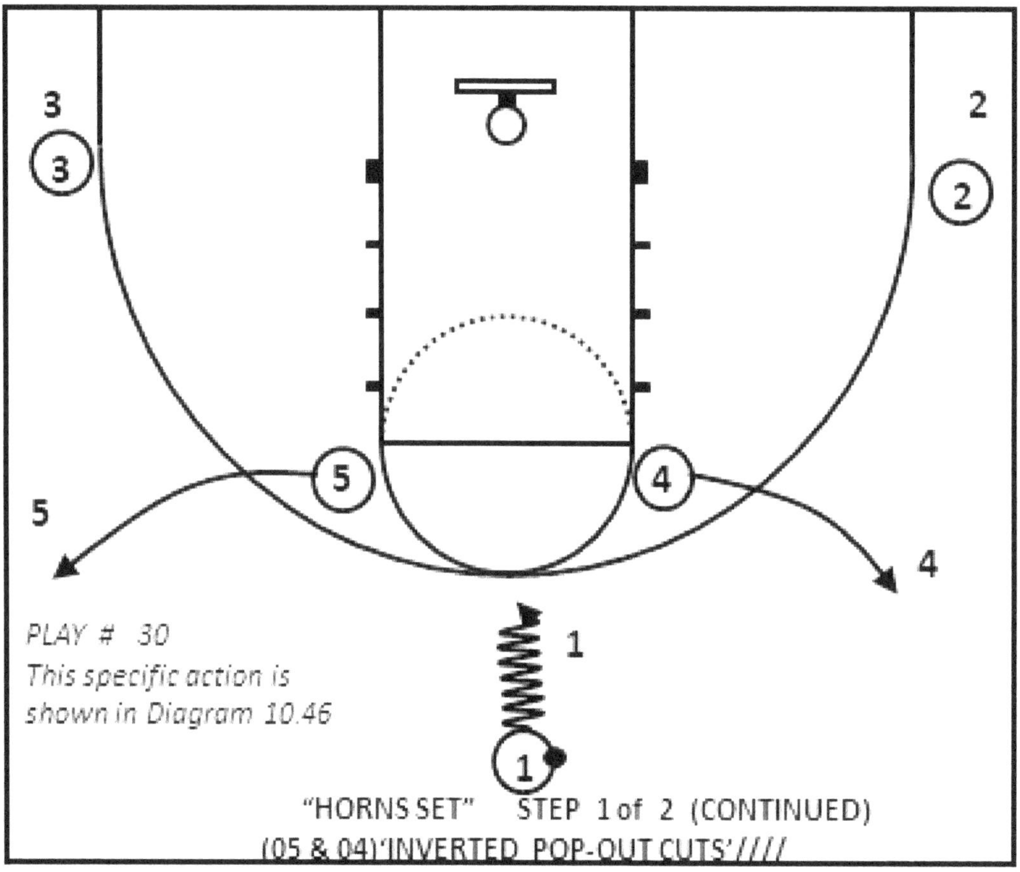

DIAGRAM 10.46

Diagram 10.47 shows the action after 01 has elected to make the pass to 05 on the left side of the floor. 01 then breaks away from the ball and 05 as if to go to set a (01-04) "Brush-Screen" for 05 to use. Instead, 01 breaks off of that route and 01 is the player that "Diagonally Slash Cuts" across the lane to the new "Ballside Block."

Instead of cutting off of 01, 04 turns and breaks down to set a "Big-on-Small Down-Screen" for 02 to break up to an area higher than the "Slot" on his side of the floor.

With four players spread out behind the arc in addition to 01 on the "Ballside Block" who has inverted and isolated his man, X1, the offensive action has moved the players into an extra wide set of "4-Out/1-In" Spot-Ups. The next phase of the offense can easily continue with all players simply tightening up their new locations. See Diagram 10.47

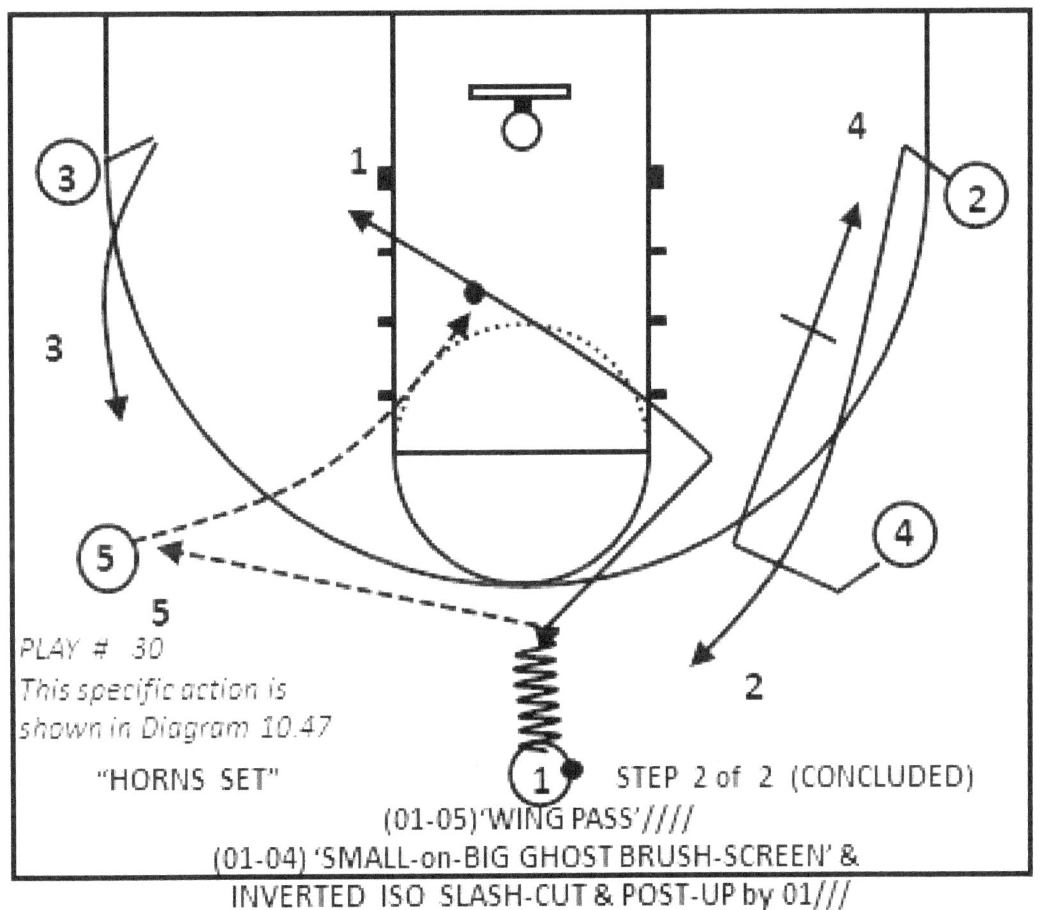

Diagram 10.47

Diagrams 10.48, 10.49 and 10.50 illustrate Play # 31 out of the "HI-LO STAX" Set. 04 makes a vertical "Up-Cut" to the nearest "Elbow" area. This immediately continues with "Iverson Cuts" over the top of 05 and 04 by 03 and with 02 running along the baseline to the opposite "Deep Corner" area. See Diagram 10.48

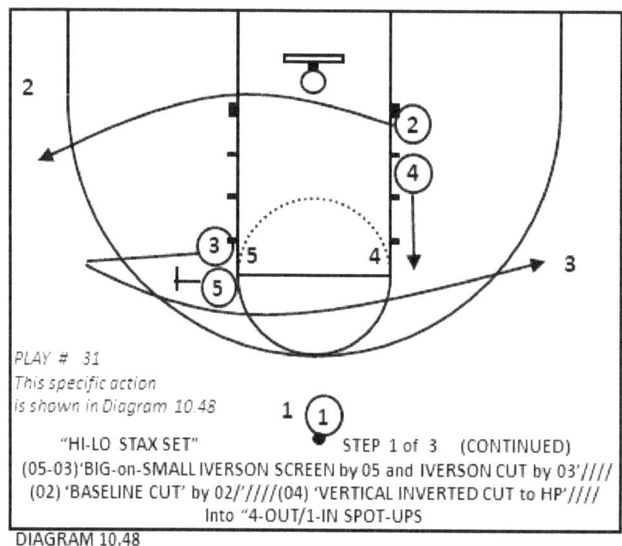

01 looks to make the "Wing Pass" and when it is being denied, 01 makes the pass to 04 so that 03 can make the "Blind Pig Cut" to the basket.

After making the pass to 04, 05 steps up to set a "Big-on-Small Flare-Screen" for 01 to use to start his "Flare-Cut" away from 04 and the ball. See Diagram 10.49

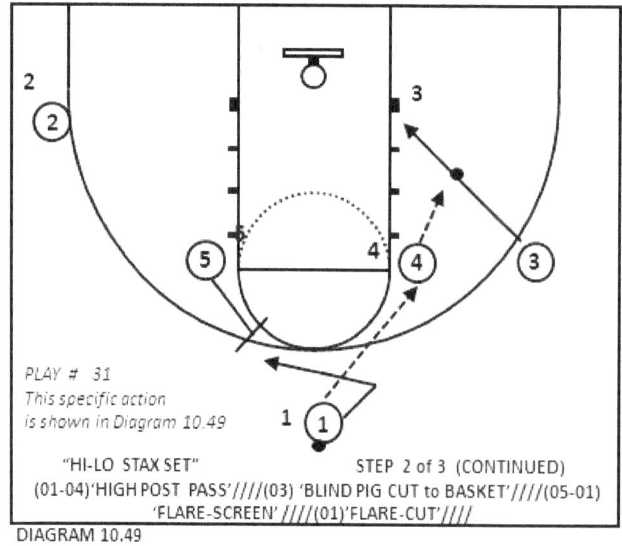

If 03 doesn't receive the quick pass from 04, 03 then slips out to the near "Deep Corner" area. Instead of "Flare-Cutting" off of 05's screen, 01 reverses directions and cuts back behind 04 to receive a "Flip Pass" back from 04. After the "Flip Pass" to 01, 04 "Rolls" or "Rim-Runs" to the basket and looks for some type of an "Inside Pass" from 01 or from 03.

After 01 rejects the (05-01) "Flare-Screen," 05 then changes directions to turn and make a (05-02) "Big-on-Small Pin Screen" for 02 to break up to the new "Weakside Slot." This action not only gives 01 another perimeter shot pass receiver but also helps 04 isolate his defender on his cut towards the basket. 03 is another pass receiver for 01 that should have "catch and shoot/create/pass" opportunities.

Not only giving the offense several pass receiving threats, but also giving the offense an excellent opportunity to flow into the designated continuity offense; all five players are in the correct "4-Out/1-In" Spot-Ups. See Diagram 10.50

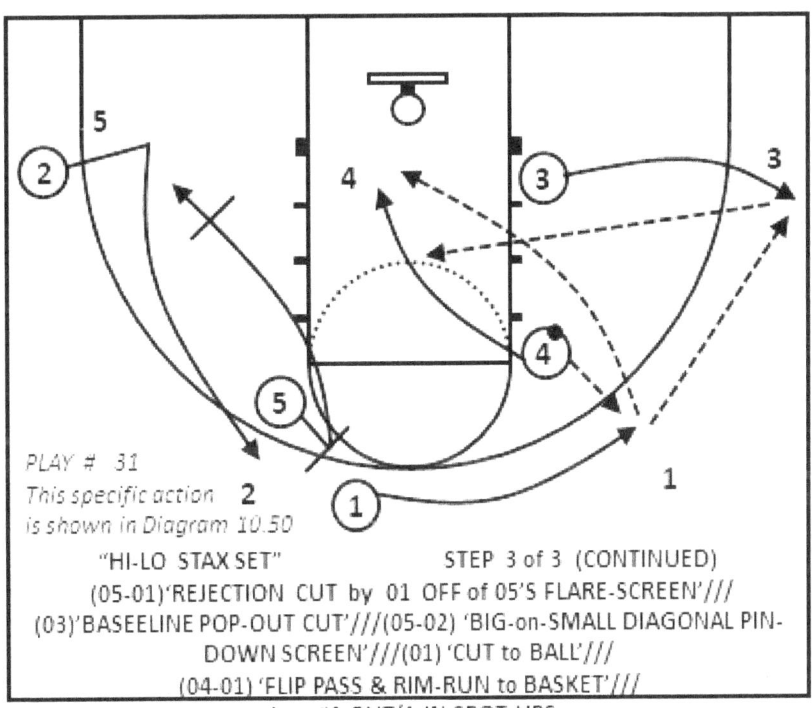

DIAGRAM 10.50

Diagrams 10.51 and 10.52 illustrate Play # 32 out of the "HI-LO STAX" Set. Both 05 and 04 set the "Big-on-Small Pin Screens for 03 and 02 to use to break to the "Wing" areas at the FT Line extended on their side of the floor. After 01 makes the "Wing Pass" to 03, 02 then breaks up to set a "Big-on-Small Flare Screen" for 01 to use to make his "Flare-Cut" to the new "Weakside Wing" area. 02 slips his screen and then remains at the "Weakside Slot." See Diagram 10.51

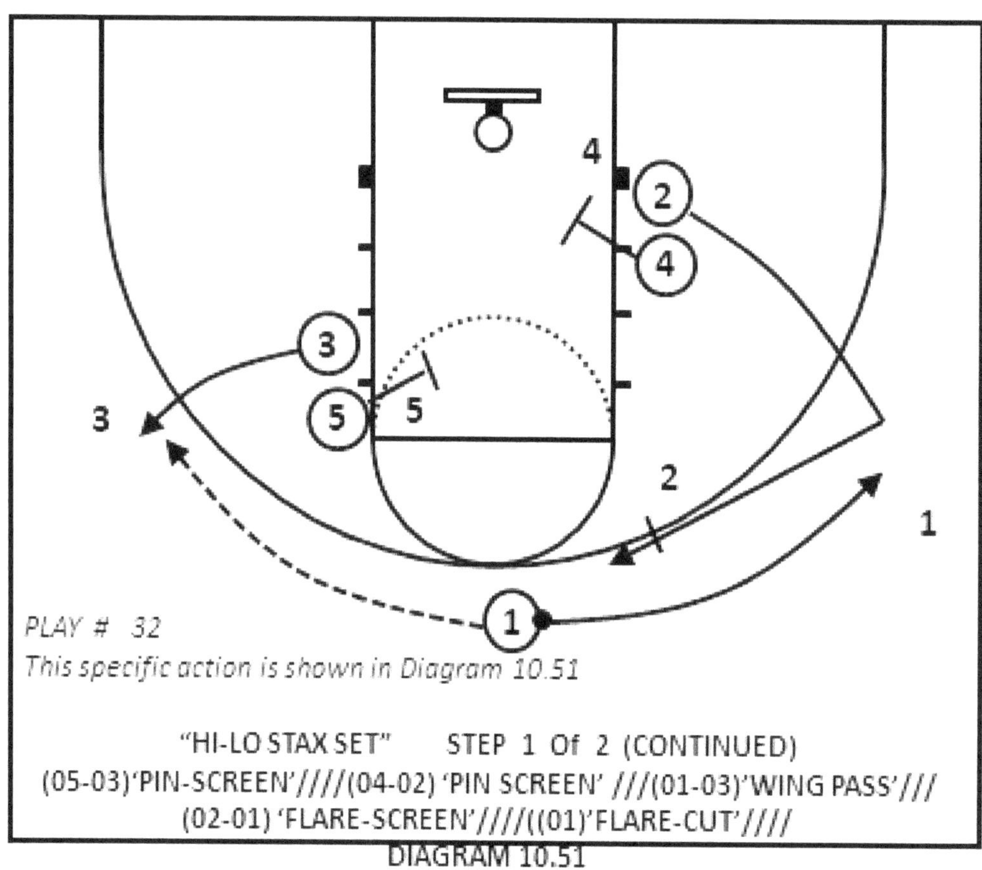

DIAGRAM 10.51

After the (05-03) "Pin-Screen," 05 diagonally breaks down to set a "Ram-Screen" for 04 to use to break directly towards 03 and the ball. 05 remains at the new "Weakside Block" area while 04 continues to break towards 03 to set a "Big-on-Small Long Inside Ball-Screen." 03 "dribble-scrapes" off of 04's top left shoulder to either "perimeter pull or penetrate dribble" while 04 then "front pivots" off of his lower right foot and "Rim-Runs" to the basket and looks for a (03-04) "Lob Pass." If no pass from 03 to 04 is available, 04 then empties out to the nearest "Deep Corner." At the same time, 01 makes a "Drift Cut" towards the "Deep Corner" on his side of the floor to stretch the defense both vertically and horizontally. This action could lead to a (03-01) or a (03-02) "penetrate and pitch" action. See Diagram 10.52

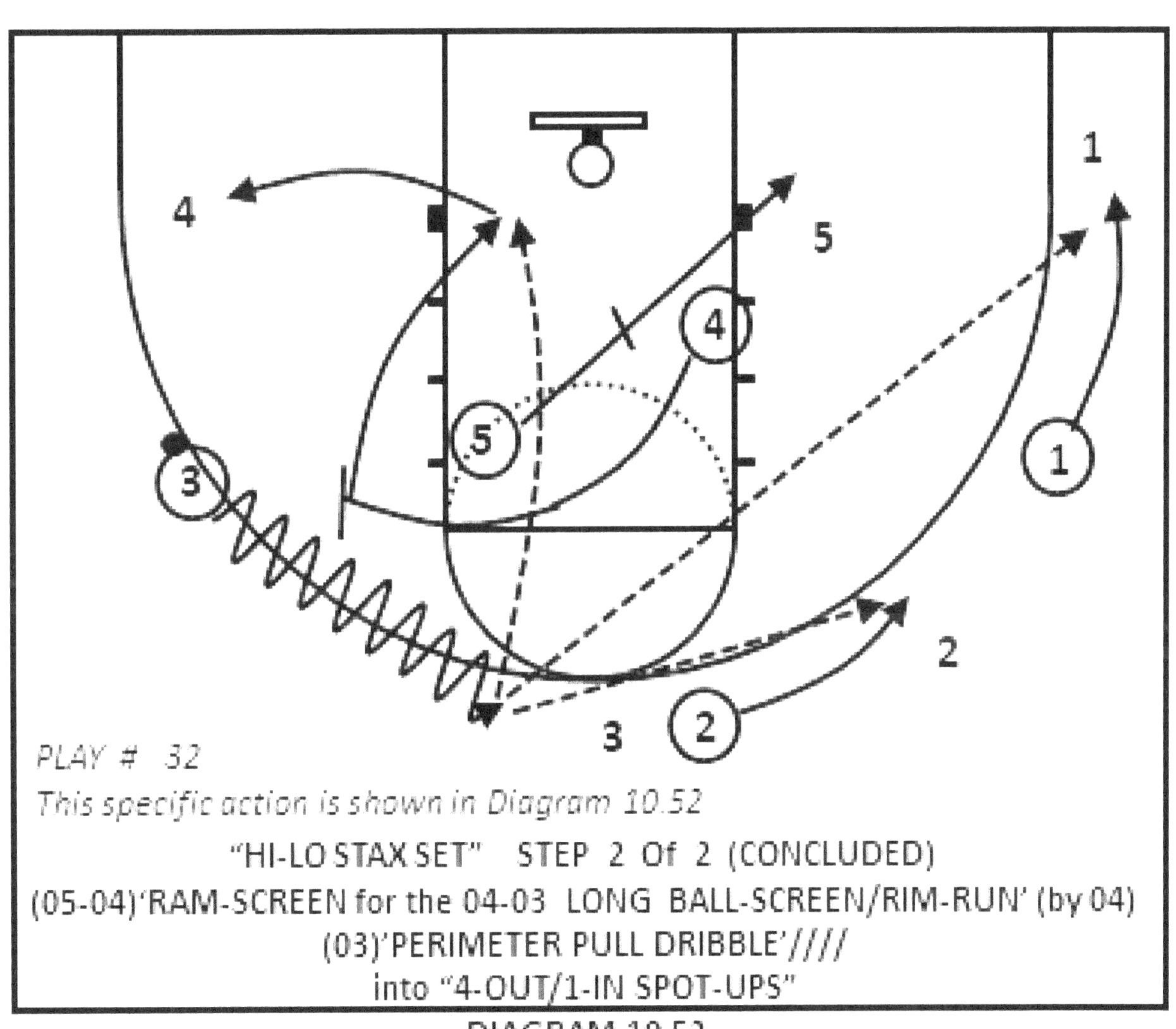

DIAGRAM 10.52

Diagrams 10.53 through 10.56 illustrate Play # 33 out of an "ODD-FRONT SECONDARY FASTBREAK" Option. Both 03 and 02 both sprint the floor in their assigned lanes and when they reach the FT Line extended, both diagonally dive to the basket. If there is no "Inside Pass" made to either 03 or 02 for a possible "lay-up," both players pop out to their respective "Deep Corner" areas and look for a "Down Pass." set the "Big-on-Small Pin Screens for 03 and 02 to use to break to the "Wing" areas at the FT Line extended on their side of the floor. After 01 makes the "Wing Pass" to 03, 02 then breaks up to set a "Big-on-Small Flare Screen" for 01 to use to make his "Flare-Cut" to the new "Weakside Wing" area. 02 slips his screen and then remains at the "Weakside Slot."

The Primary Fastbreak consists of a "3 on 0" or "3 on 1" or "3 on 2" offensive advantage. When there are no "number advantages," 01 declares a strong side by dribbling over to the "Wing" area. This dictates that 04, as the "1st Trailer," veers off to the new "Weakside Elbow" area before then slashing diagonally across to the new "Ballside Block." As the "2nd Trailer," 05 sprints under the proper timing to end up at the top of the key.

Once the ballside has been declared, the "Weakside Wing" breaks out from the "Weakside Deep Corner" to spot up at the FT Line extended. This action helps eliminate the opposition's weakside defense, giving 04 a much larger advantage of isolating his defender, X4. See Diagram 10.53

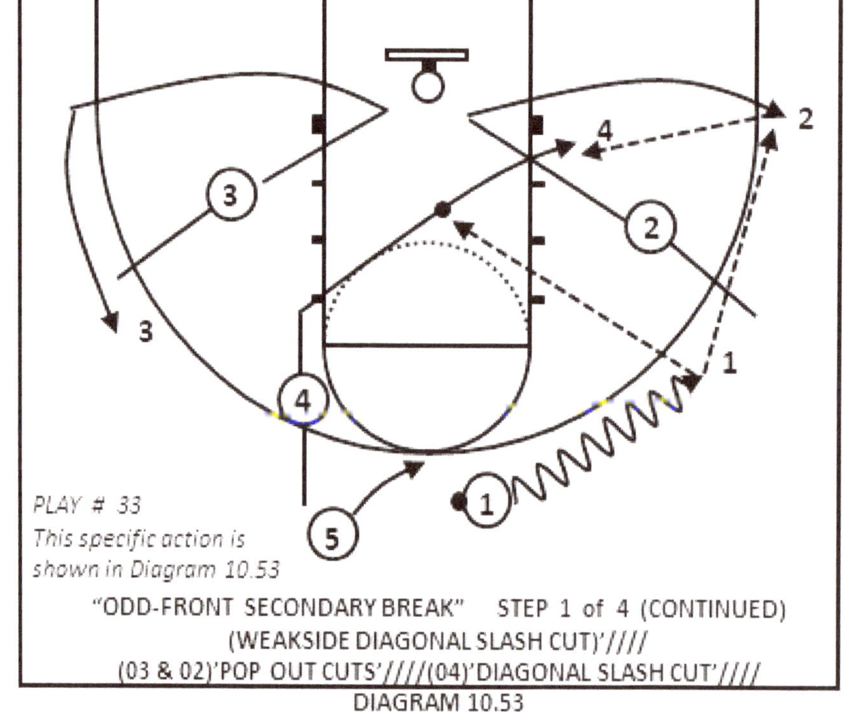

If 01 cannot make passes for "numbers lay-ups" and he cannot make the "Inside Pass" to 04, 01 looks to make a "Down Pass" to 02. 02 could have passing (to 04 or to 05 or 03), shooting (off of the pass or the dribble) or other creating possibilities. If 02 cannot make the pass to 04 and elects to "Up Pass" to 01, 04 and 01 work together to see if there now is a better passing angle for 01 to complete the pass to 04.

If 04 is not open on his "Iso Duck-In" Cut, 01 could "Reverse Pass" to 05 who also could have his own passing targets (such as 04, a "Lob Pass" to 02, a pass over to 03 or a pass back to 01), or 05 could look to shoot over the top the smaller defenders out on top. See Diagram 10.54

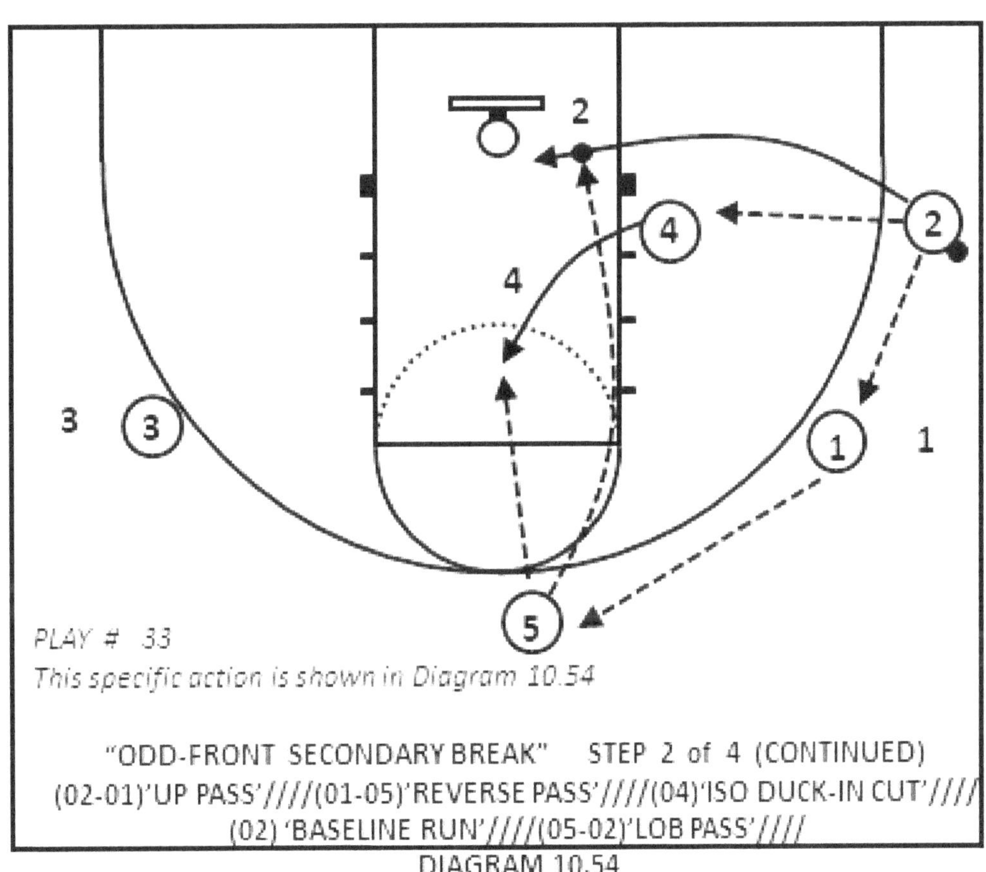

DIAGRAM 10.54

Diagram 10.55 shows 05 continuing the swing of the ball over to 03, with 04 "chasing the perimeter passes" and following the ball through the lane. By the time 03 receives the ball, 04 is about to "Iso post up" his defender and 02 is starting to diagonally break up to set a "Small-on-Big Back-Screen" for 05 to scrape off of 02's outside left shoulder and make a "Lob Cut" to the basket. After setting the screen, 02 slips his screen and remains at the top of the key. See Diagram 10.55

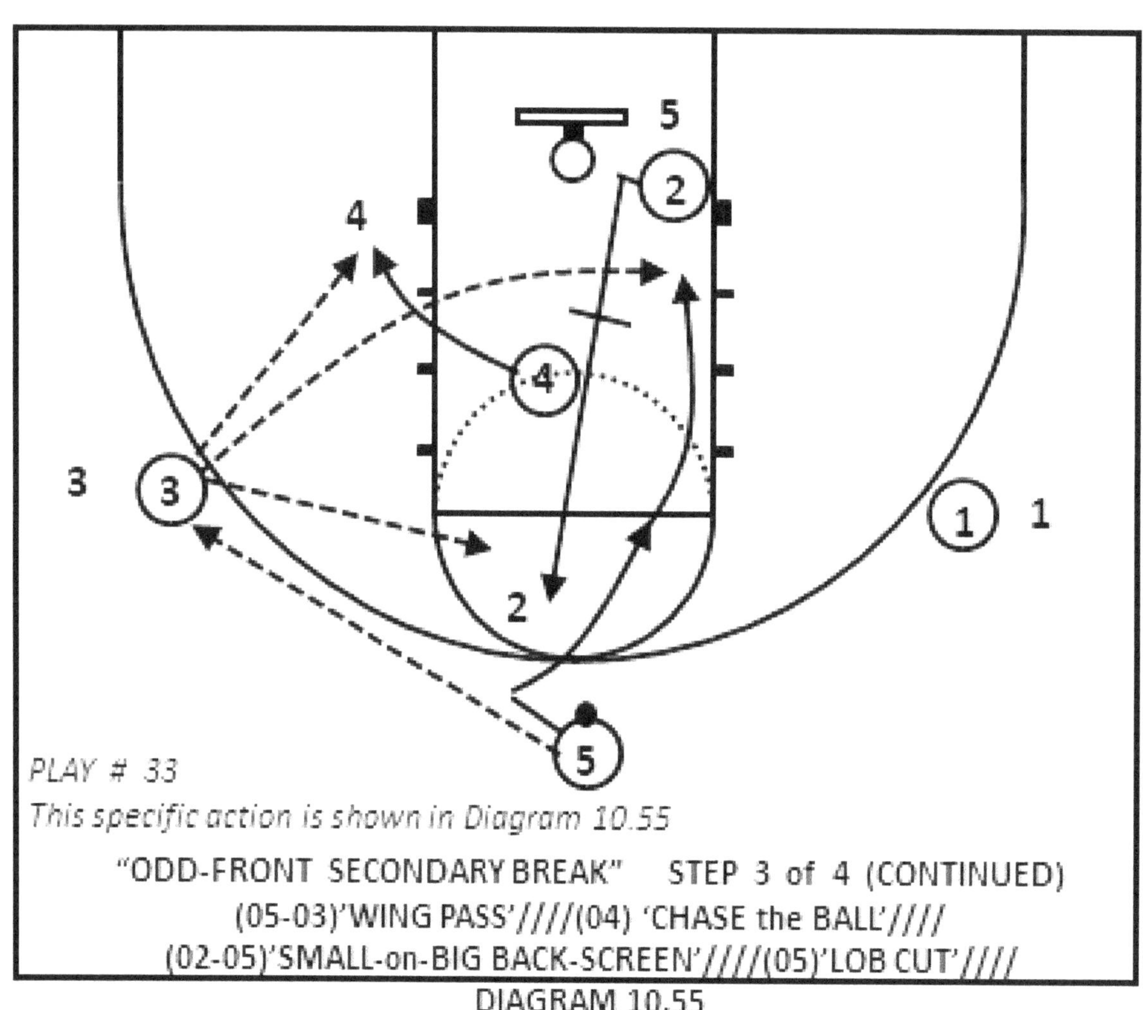

If 03 cannot make passes to 04, 05 or to 01; 03 looks to make the "Re-Reverse Pass" to 02, now at the top of the key. As 02 receives the ball from 03, 04 makes another "Iso Duck-In Cut" and X4 tries to defend him when 05 breaks from underneath the basket to set the blind "Back-Screen" for 04 to use as he "spins off" of 05's lower right shoulder and then curls around to step back towards the "Dotted Circle" area again. After screening for 04, 05 makes a "Front Pivot" and also steps diagonally into the same "Dotted Circle" area and looks for the ball (from either 02 or 01).

As the intense action goes on in the paint between 05 and 04, the defensive perimeter is attacked with the three perimeter-type players equally spread out behind the arc at the "Wing" areas and the "Top of the key" area—the "3-Out/2-In" Spot-Ups.

If there are no shots taken, the Primary Break has flowed into this Secondary Break and now has placed players in position to immediately flow into the designated continuity offense. See Diagram 10.56.

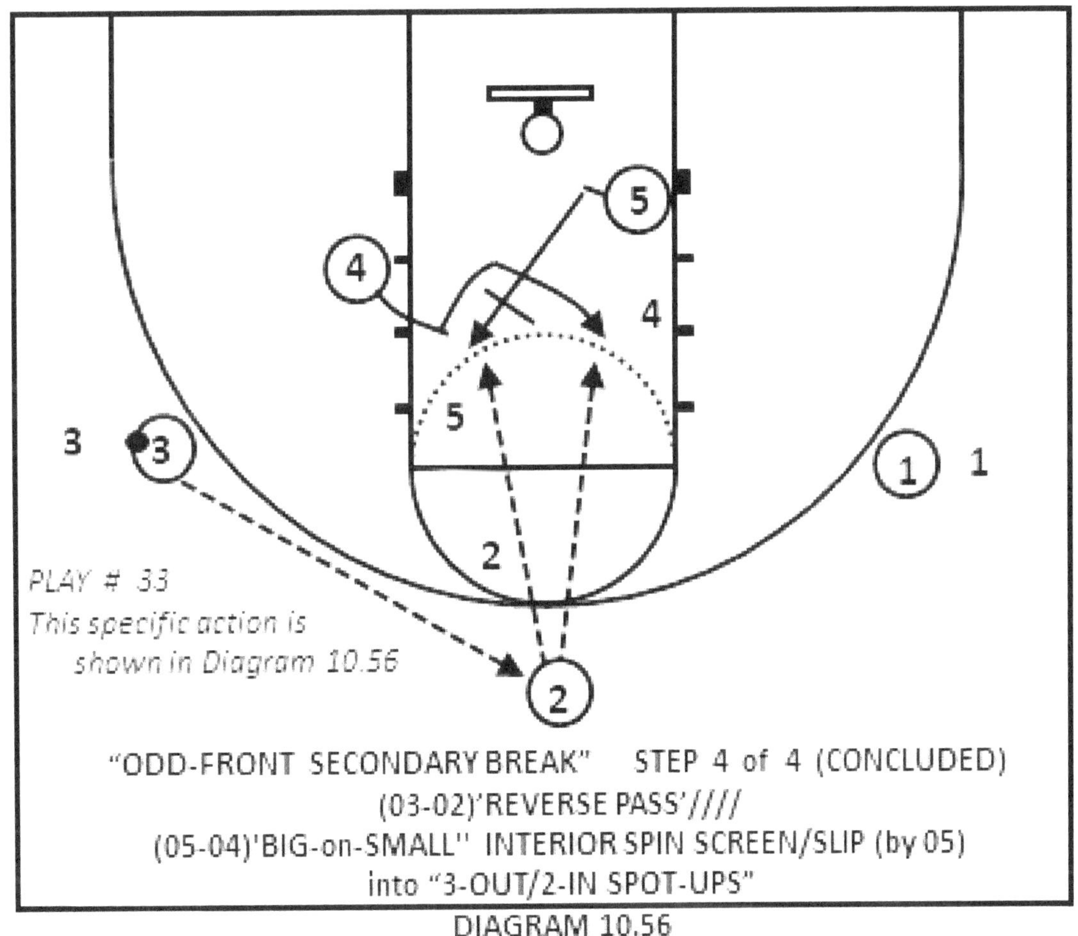

DIAGRAM 10.56

As in many plays/entries, 05 and 04 both set the same types of "Big-on-Small Pin-Screens" for 03 and 02 respectively. 02 breaks out near the FT Line extended followed by 04 breaking up to the "Elbow" area on his side of the floor.

On the other side of the floor, 03 breaks out to his "Wing" area before then breaking out further to set a "Big-on-Small Ball-Screen" for 01 to dribble to the FT Line extended on the left side of the floor. After setting his screen, 05 remains at the "Elbow" area on his initial side of the floor. See Diagram 10.57

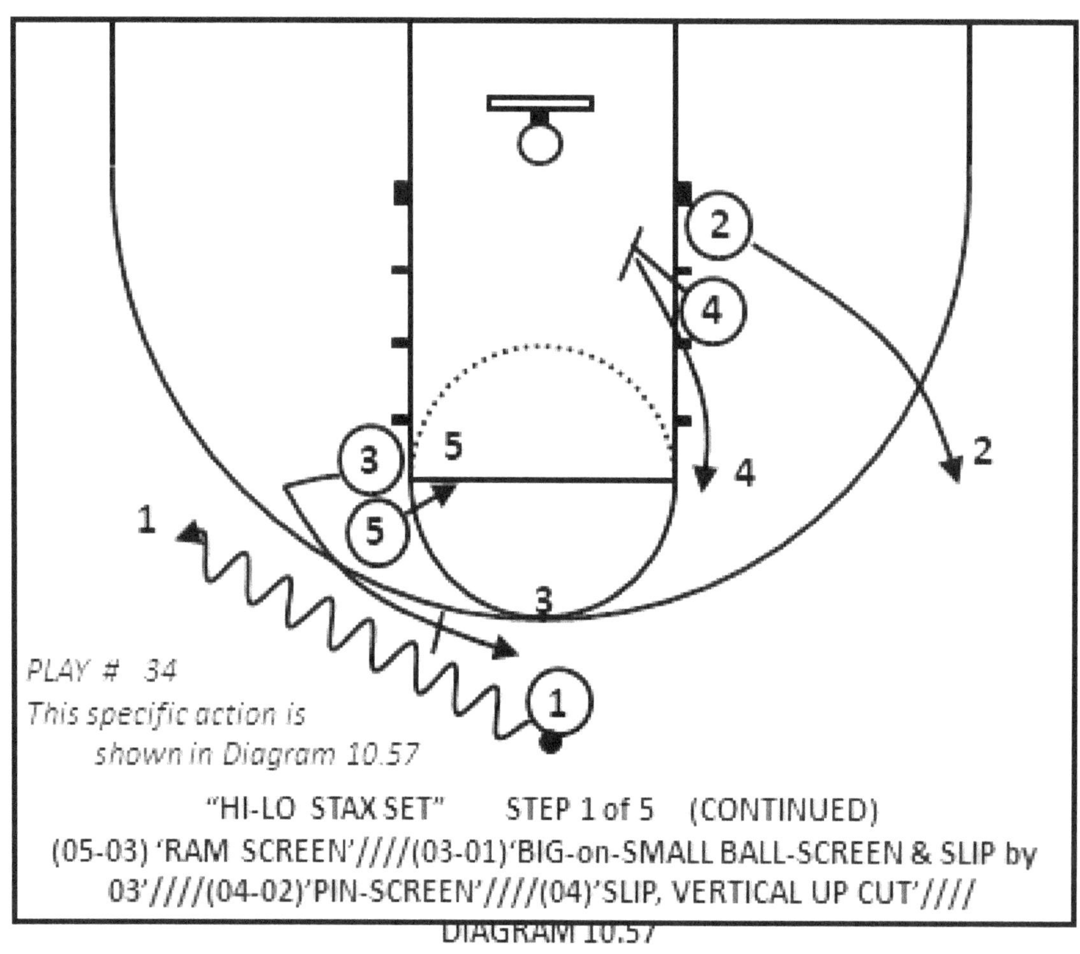

Diagram 10.58 shows 01 reversing the ball to 03 at the top of the key. 03 dribbles towards the "Slot" area and towards 02 on the opposite side of the floor. 04 breaks towards 02 to set a "Big-on-Small Pin-Screen" for 02 to break up and out. 03 then makes the "Wing Pass" to 02 and immediately receives the ball back to 03. 02 then immediately makes a quick and short "Backdoor Cut" to the basket. With all five players spread out and outside of the arc, 02 should be able to get open on his cut to the basket. See Diagram 10.58

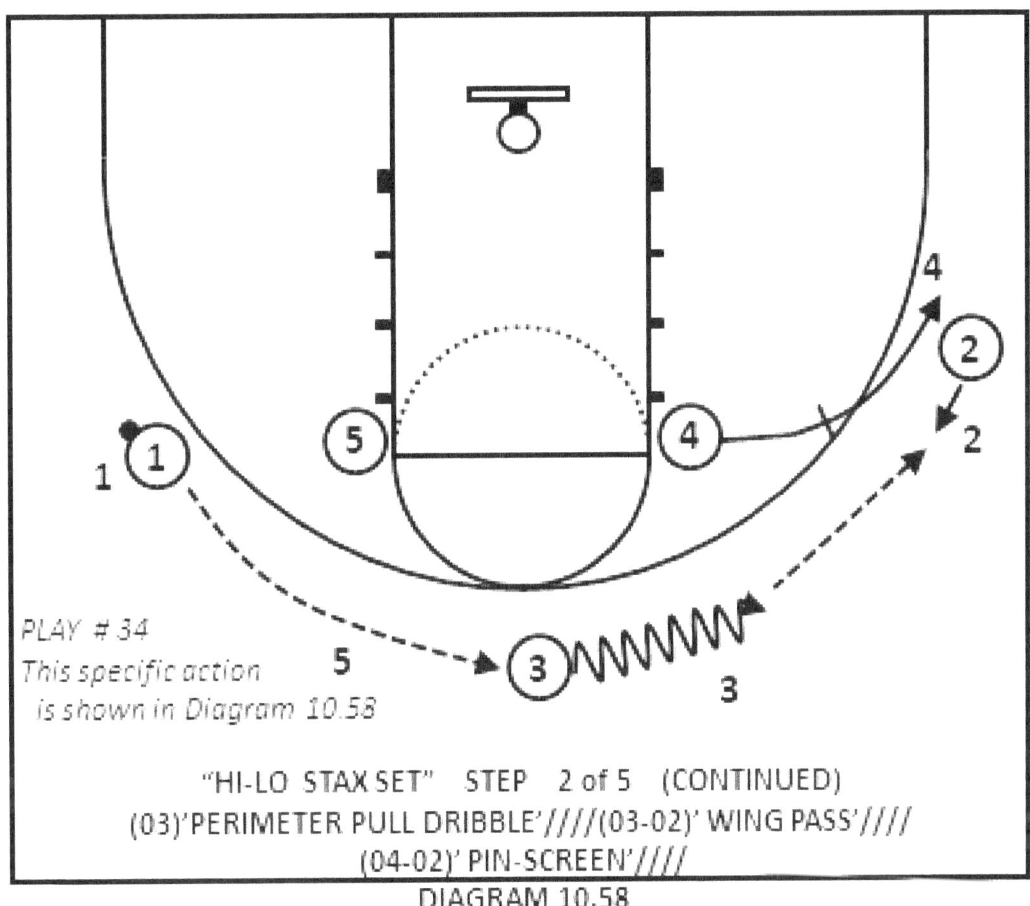

"HI-LO STAX SET" STEP 2 of 5 (CONTINUED)
(03)'PERIMETER PULL DRIBBLE'////(03-02)' WING PASS'////
(04-02)' PIN-SCREEN'////
DIAGRAM 10.58

Diagram 10.59 shows 05 popping out to the "Weakside Slot" and 02 looking to make an "Up Pass" back to 03 and immediately making a quick and short "Give-n-Go Cut" towards the basket. See Diagram 19.59

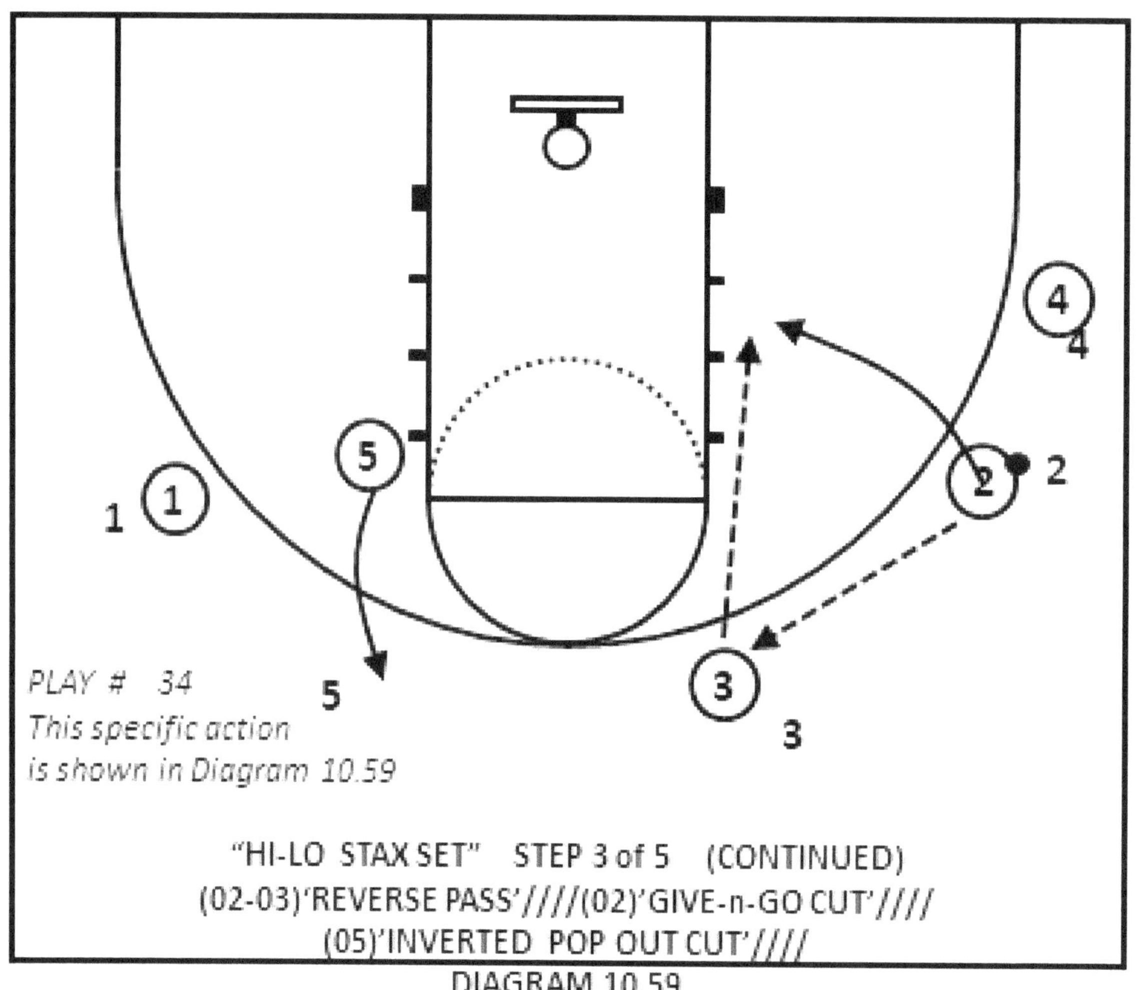

If 02 is not open, 03 reverses the ball to the inverted 05 on the opposite "Slot." As 01 steps in to the "Weakside Elbow," 02 breaks back up and over to cut over the top of 01's "Pin-Screen." We call this type of "Pin-Screen" with the preceding action a "Michigan Screen." We define this action as basically a horizontal "Pin-Screen" set by 01 and an "Iverson Cut" by 02 with the screener staying at the "Elbow" after the screen. See Diagram 10.60.

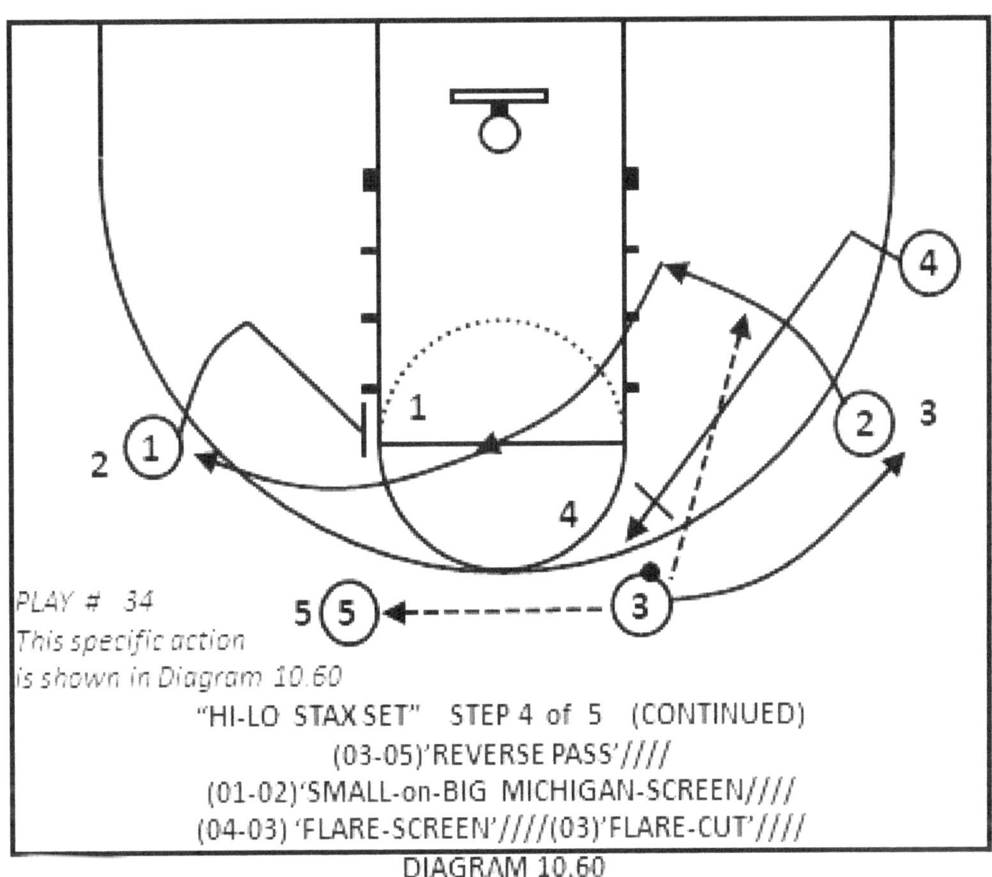

DIAGRAM 10.60

05 should be able to then make the "Wing Pass" to 02 now at the "Wing" area on the opposite side of the floor. 05 immediately reads his "post-type defender" who is inverted and trying to become an instant "perimeter-type" defender (who is inexperienced and lacking in skill). 05 can scrape off of either shoulder of 01 before then cutting to the "Ballside Block." This "Small-on-Big UCLA Backscreen" by 01 and "UCLA Cut" by 05 is attacking the opposition in a very unique manner that may not be able to be properly defended.

With 03 and 04 both on the weakside and outside of the arc, there can only be minimal weakside defense that X5 needs to successfully defend 05 in the isolated post area. 02 has the freedom to dribble lower to look to create or to have an improved angle to make the "Inside Pass" to 05. Both 04 and 03 could also drift slightly over towards the weakside sideline and baseline to horizontally and vertically stretch (and therefore weaken the interior defense.) 03 could make possible "Skip Passes" to 04 or 03 or an "Up Pass" to 01 (who has stepped out to the "Ballside Slot" after setting his screen for 05.

This action also repositions all five players into the "4-Out/1-In" Spot-Ups" so that the offensive attack has no interruptions or delays. See Diagram 10.61

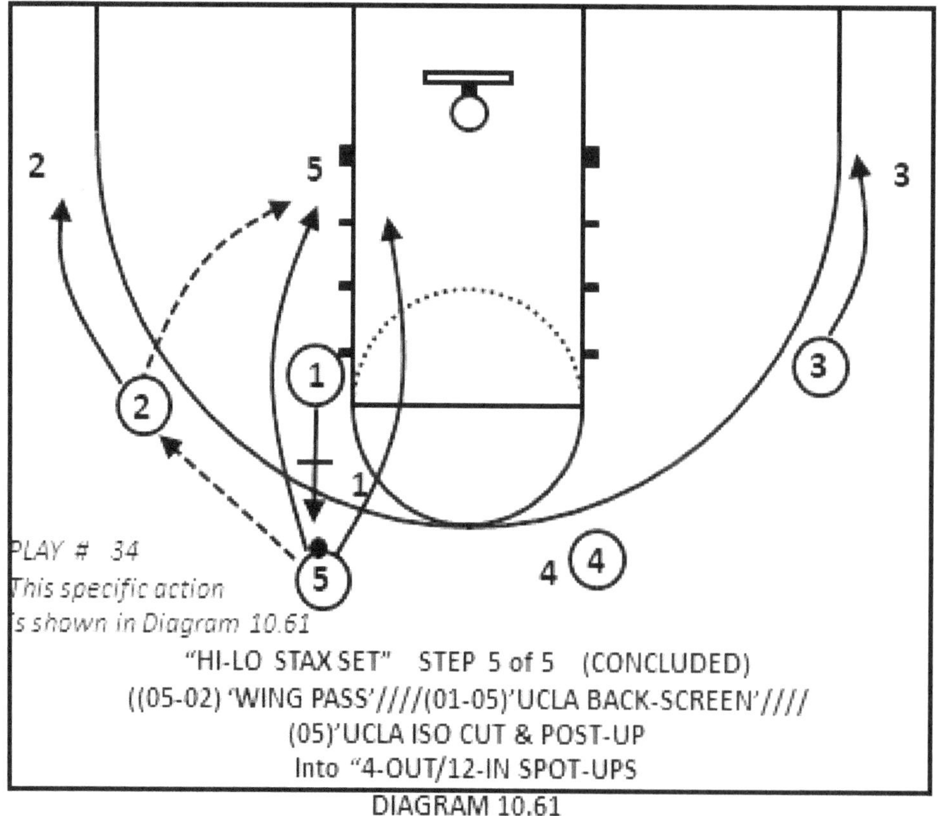

DIAGRAM 10.61

Diagrams 10.62 and 10.63 show the entire Play # 35. It is executed out of the "5-UP" Set, another symmetrically balanced offensive set. Again, this means that any play that is executed from this set could be started from either side of the floor.

Diagram 10.62 shows 01 dribbling towards the right side of the floor, seemingly indicating that the play will attack the offensive right side of the floor. As 01 reaches the approximate "Slot" position, he turns to make a "Throwback Reverse Pass" to 05 (who has popped out to his side of the floor's "Slot" location. 01 immediately cuts off of 04's outside left shoulder and curl tightly through the lane to the new "Ballside Block." 01 reverses the ball to 05 and quickly looks to make the "Inside Pass" to 01. As the ball reaches 05's hands, both 03 and 02 both "Flare-Cut" towards their respective "Deep Corners." See Diagram 10.62

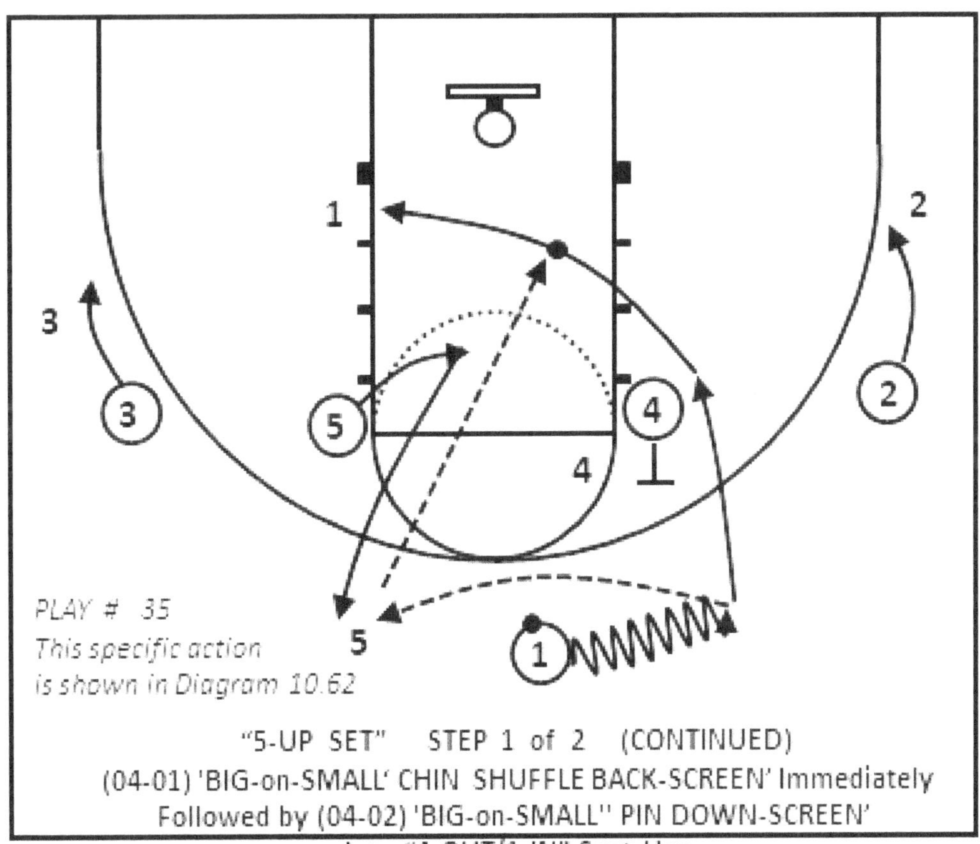

"5-UP SET"   STEP 1 of 2   (CONTINUED)
(04-01) 'BIG-on-SMALL' CHIN SHUFFLE BACK-SCREEN' Immediately
Followed by (04-02) 'BIG-on-SMALL'' PIN DOWN-SCREEN'
Into "4-OUT/1-IN" Spot-Ups
DIAGRAM 10.62

05 has other options besides making the pass to 01. 05 could make a "Down Pass" to 03 for 03 to have "catch and shoot," "catch and create" and "catch and pass" options (to various teammates.) To open up a "reverse pass" option, 04 should then turn and cut to set a "Big-on-Small Down-Screen" for 02 to break back up to move the ball to the opposite side of the floor. 04 then slips his screen and remains in his new "Deep Corner" location.

As the ball leaves 05's hands, 01 attacks his inverted and isolated perimeter-type defender with another "chase of the ball" as the ball swings around the perimeter in no prescribed method or route. In addition, 05 then breaks down to set another "Big-on-Small Pin Down Screen" for 03 to use to break up to the new "Weakside Slot."

This action helps eliminate "weakside interior defense" that X1 would need to successfully defend 01. In addition, this action on both sides of the floor has repositioned all five players into the "4-Out/1-In" Spot-Ups" for the offensive attack to be maintained. See Diagram 10.63

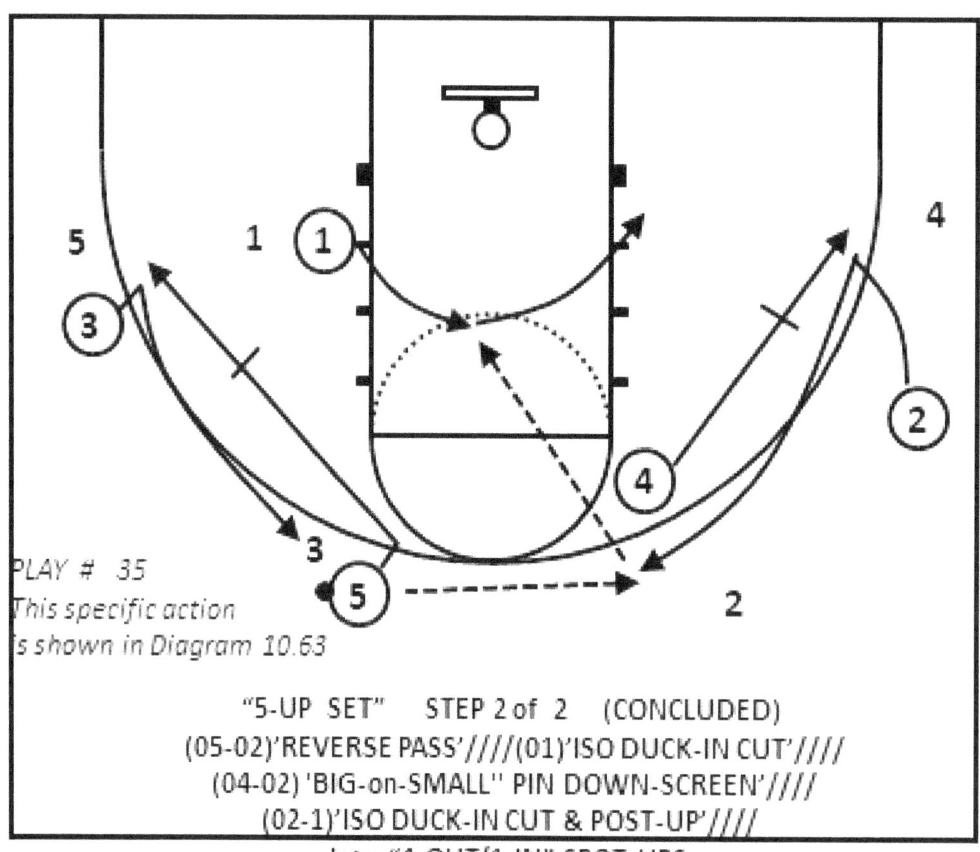

Into "4-OUT/1-IN" SPOT-UPS
DIAGRAM 10.63

Diagram 10.64 demonstrates the entire Play # 36 that is executed out of the "4-DOWN" Set/Alignment. Even though 01 could "perimeter pull dribble" towards either side of the floor to begin the play, 01 elects to dribble towards the right side of the floor. 02 breaks up from his "Deep Corner" to set a "Long Ball-Screen" for 01 to use to reach the designated "Wing" area. As 02 sets the screen for 01, 03 breaks up from his side of the floor to set a "Big-on-Small Long Flare-Screen the Ball-Screener" for 02 to use on his "Flare-Cut" to the new "Weakside Wing."

At the same time, 04 empties out to go across the lane to set a (04-05) "Lane Exchange Cross-Screen" for 05 to break across to post up on the new "Ballside Block." After 04 breaks contact with 05, 04 changes direction, seals off his defender and flashes back to the new "Ballside High Post."

With 05 and 04 posting up at the two "Ballside Post" areas, 01 at the "Ballside Wing," 02 now at the "Weakside Wing" and 03 now at the "Point," the "HIGH-POST/LOW-POST" Spot-Ups are filled for the designated continuity offense to then be ready to begin. See Diagram 10.64.

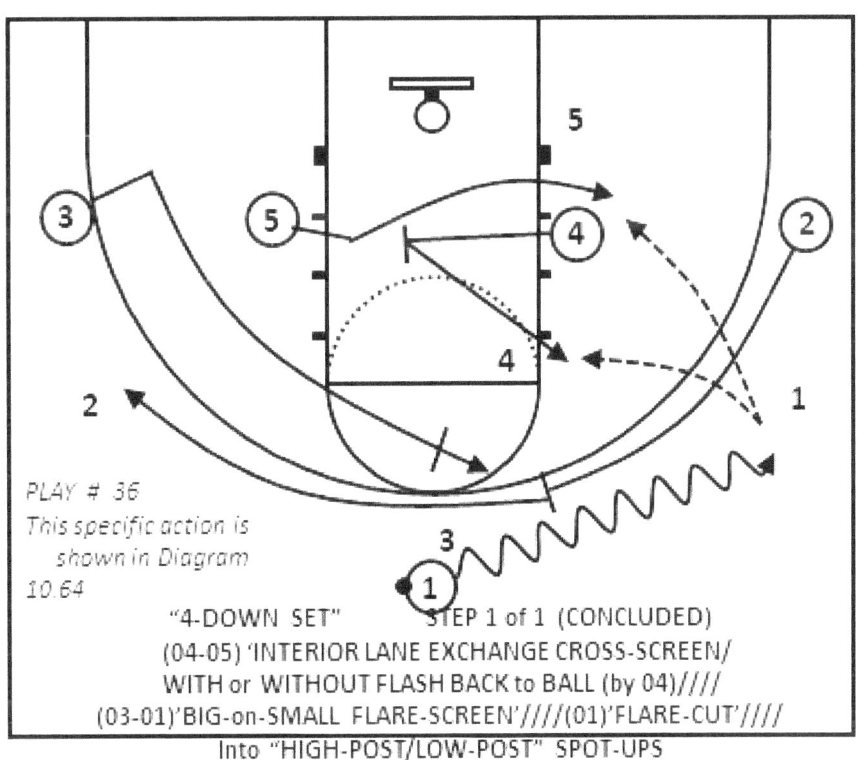

This chapter covers the various types of screens, the different cuts, the many different passes and the various kinds of dribbles within the framework and structure of the 36 plays/entries/quick-hitters out of 19 different offensive sets/alignments. These various plays can then flow into either the "3-Out/2-In" Spot-Ups, the "4-Out/1-In" Spot-Ups or the "High-Post/Low-Post" Spot-Ups. From these three different groups of spot-ups comes the many different continuity offenses that can and will utilize the same types of passes, screens, cuts and dribbles.

Creative coaches can and should develop many more types of plays that fit their own philosophies and the personnel (as long as they always can result in the proper spot-up locations for a seamless transition into the proper continuity or motion-type offense.

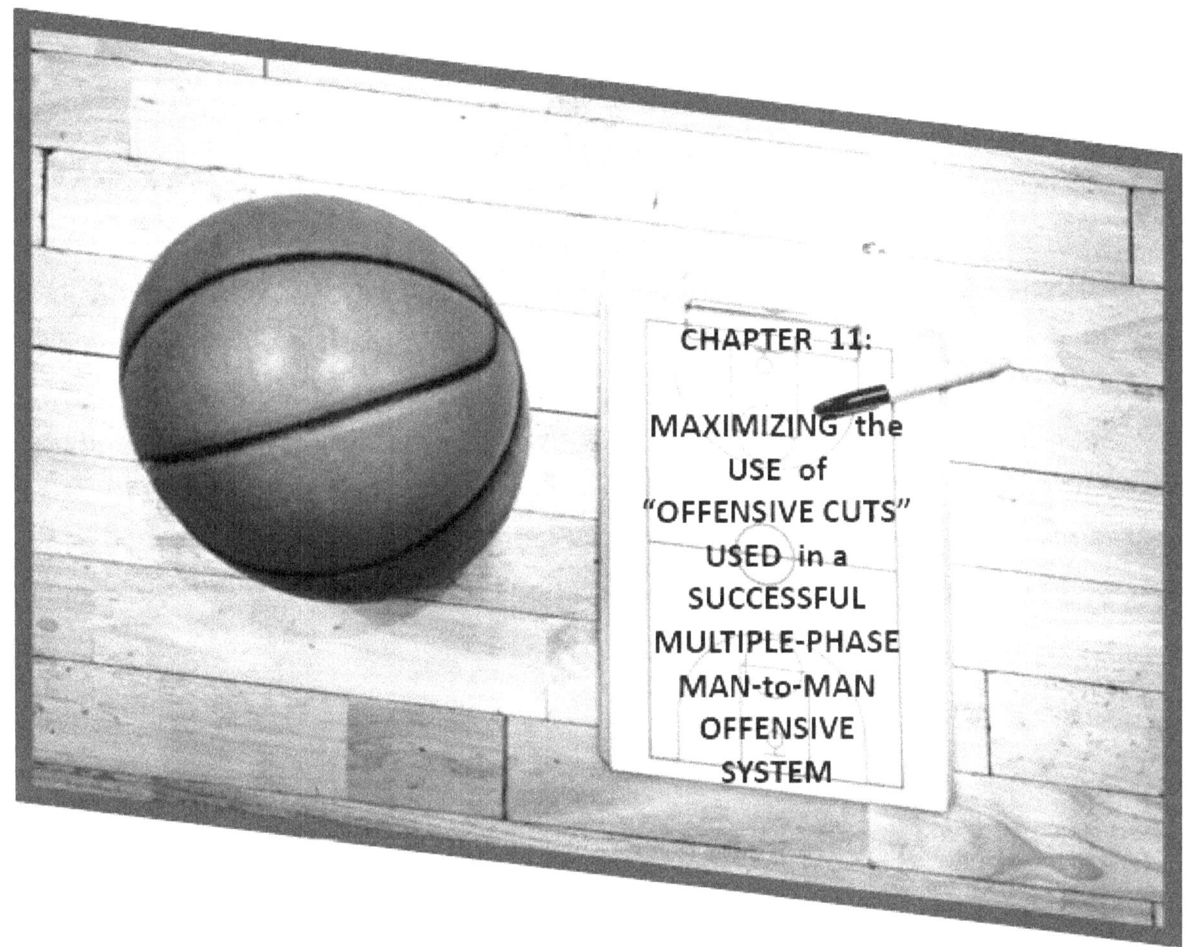

These forty-plus offensive actions all involving of the various types of offensive cuts that can be made from the many different locations on the floor. All are fundamentally sound and can be successful in achieving the various types of objectives within the overall structure and framework of not only half-court plays, but out-of-bounds plays, secondary fastbreak options and also the actual continuity offensive actions.

Regardless of what specific level each action of the three different modes of attack (secondary breaks, half-court plays, out-of-bounds play), the actions will challenge and reposition all opposing defenders as well as move each offensive player into one of the proper spot-ups of the designated continuity or motion-type offense. Many different offensive cuts can be integrated within each step of every offensive action, whether the action is being executed in any of the three different modes. Regardless of the fact that any one individual offensive cut could result in the designated shot, all different offensive cuts may not immediately create the desired shot, the cutting action(s) will at least allow for a smooth, immediate and fluid transition into that last phase of the offensive attack—the continuity or motion-type offense. This gives the opposition no opportunity to recover or regroup after just preventing a shot from initial entry.

Some of the various "cutting" actions have probably been the longest forms and natural forms of offensive attacks, be it for man-to-man offenses, zone offense, out-of-bounds actions and all full-court actions. Associated with the various cuts are a short and deceptive shorter cut that is designed to persuade or cause the defense to move in the opposite direction as the actual offensive cut that is to be used. Realistic "V-Cuts" at game speed that are executed while under control will cause individual defenders to have difficulties with the unpredictability factor, because of the many combinations of fakes and cuts that players could use. In addition, with the many different locations and types of the offensive cuts that could be executed increase that large levels of unpredictability. Large levels of unpredictability to defenses makes offensive actions much more efficient and productive.

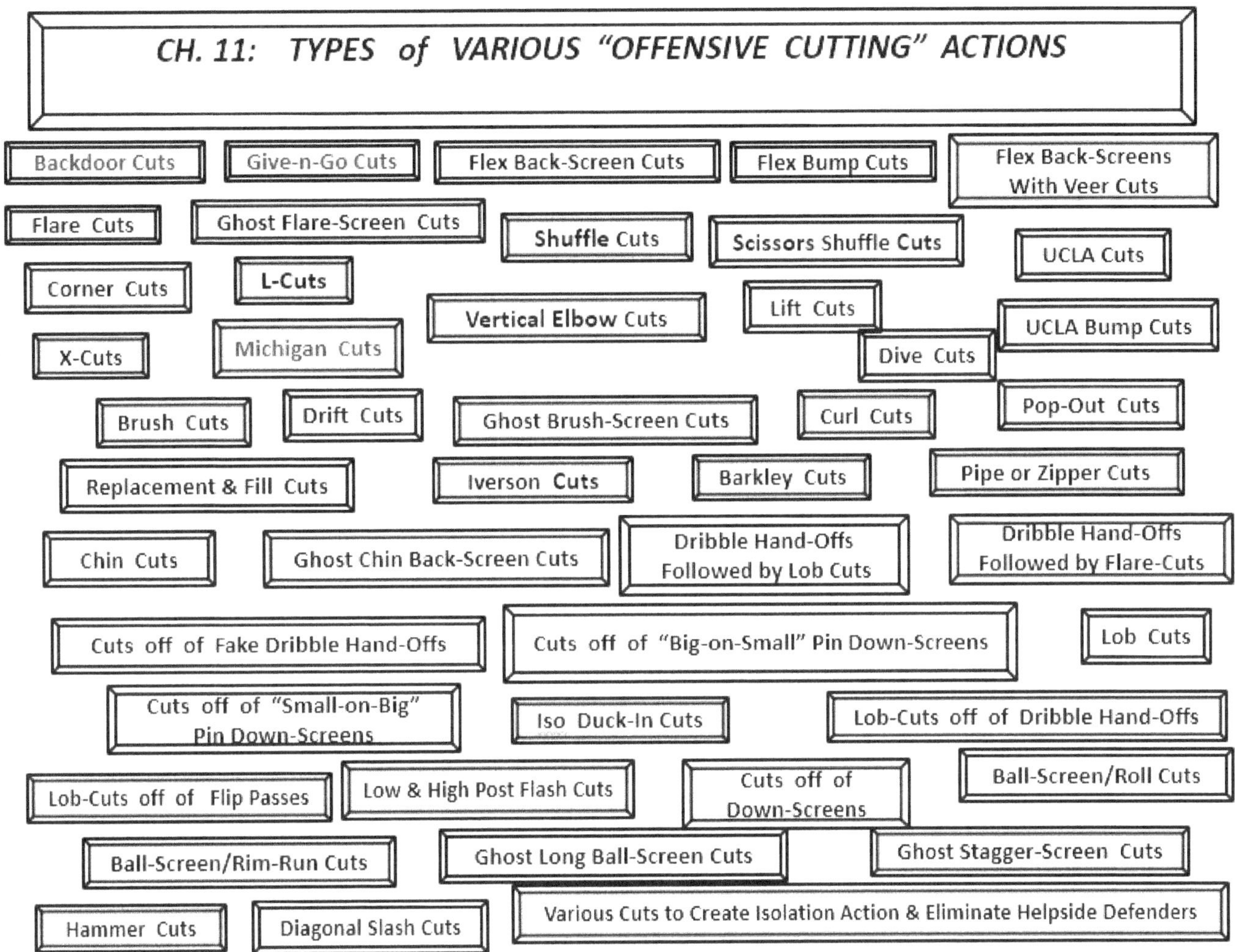

Illustration 11.1

Action # 1: "BACKDOOR CUT" ACTION (Moved down to be on same page as diagram)

Diagram 11.2 illustrates the very basic, but still extremely successful "Backdoor Cut." This traditional action, can be executed within the free-flowing but organized structure of several quick-hitting plays/entries from every level of play, is also called the "Basket Cut." In addition, this action could begin out of almost every offensive alignment, but this Action # 1 is executed out of the "3-OVER" Set.

This entry begins with 01 dribbling towards the strong side of the alignment. This initiates 03 to make a "Zipper Cut" vertically up the lane and cutting through the middle of the "05 and 04" "Elevator Screen" towards the top of the key. At the same time, 02 is the player that makes the highlighted "Backdoor Cut" to the basket. 01 looks to make the pass to 02, who has cut to the basket in a now vacant area near the basket. Notice in the diagram that 02's first action is to step towards 01 to make his "V-Cut" (in the opposite direction of his actual intended ""Backdoor Cut.") If an immediate pass to 02 is not made, the next passing option is to 03 out on top. If shots are not taken, this play would have other actions that take place to take the desired shot or to complete the play. See Diagram 11.2

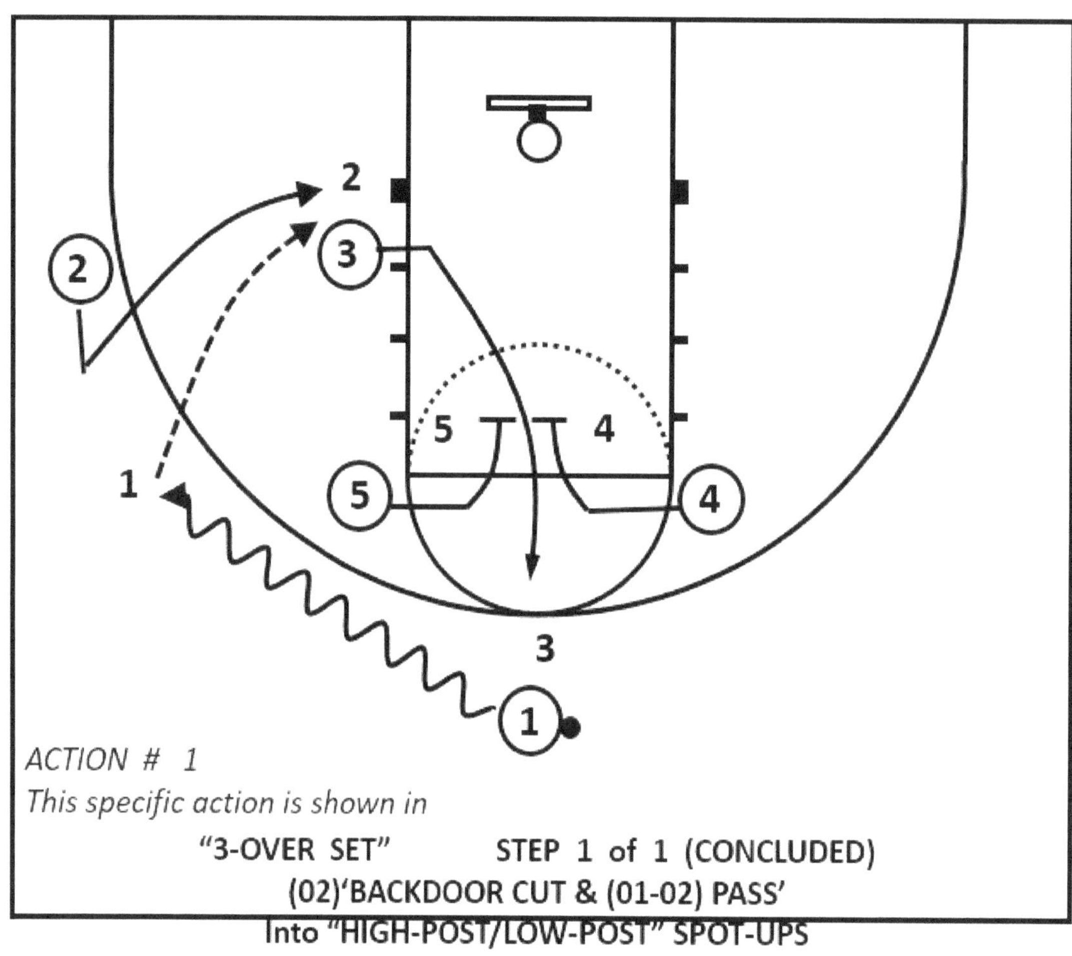

Diagram 11.2

Diagram 11.3 illustrates Action # 2 where a long-standing successful type of cut is shown by 01 attacking his defender when he executes the "more of a perimeter-type cut"—the "Give-n-Go Cut."

A "Give-n-Go Cut" is basically the same as a "Backdoor Cut" immediately after making a pass to a teammate and then cutting to the basket while looking for a return pass from the initial pass receiver.

After making the pass to 05, 01 first makes his obligatory "V-Cut" opposite of the direction he intends to make in his actual "Give-n-Go Cut." In this diagram, 01 plants his right foot (that is away from the ball) then stepping directly towards both the passer and the basket. After snapping his head and looking for 05, 01 should have his hands up, ready to receive a quick and hard pass. 01 should be prepared to catch and shoot the (likely) lay-up with resistance from the opposition.

This action then leads to an "inverted and isolated" position advantage for 01 and with 04 screening 02 on the weakside of the floor, this action further occupies two off-the-ball defenders that could possibly help out 01's defender, X1.

If no shots are taken, further offensive action (that could include other types of offensive cuts) in addition to screening, passing, and dribbling to further complete offensive play. See Diagram 11.3

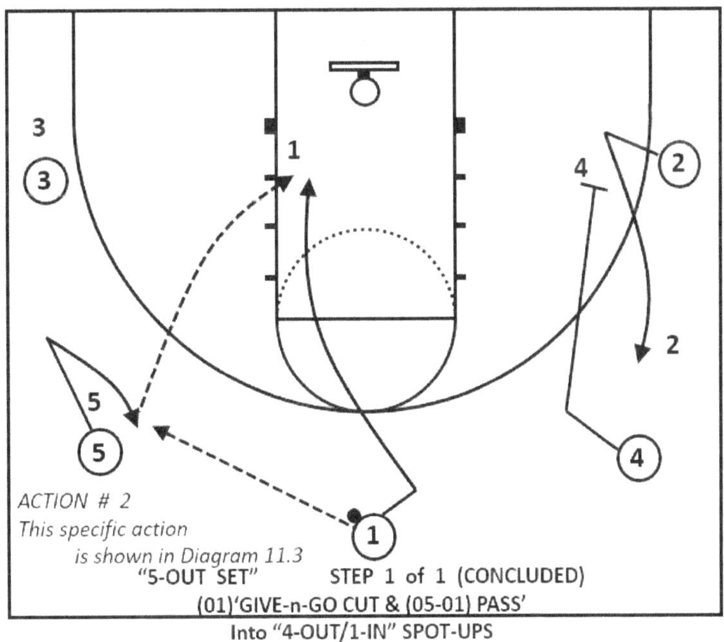

Diagram 11.3

Action # 3 shows the "Flex Back-Screen Cut' that is the receiving part of a two-man game between 04, the "Flex Screener" and 02, the "Flex Cutter." This action takes place out of the 2-DOWN FLAT" Set. 01 dribble-scrapes off of 05's "Big-on-Small Ball-Screen." To further isolate and invert 02's defender, X2; 05 then cuts down to set a "Big-on-Small (Pin Down-)Screen the (Flex-)Screener."

There would be movement after no shots are created if nothing has been created. See Diagram 11.4

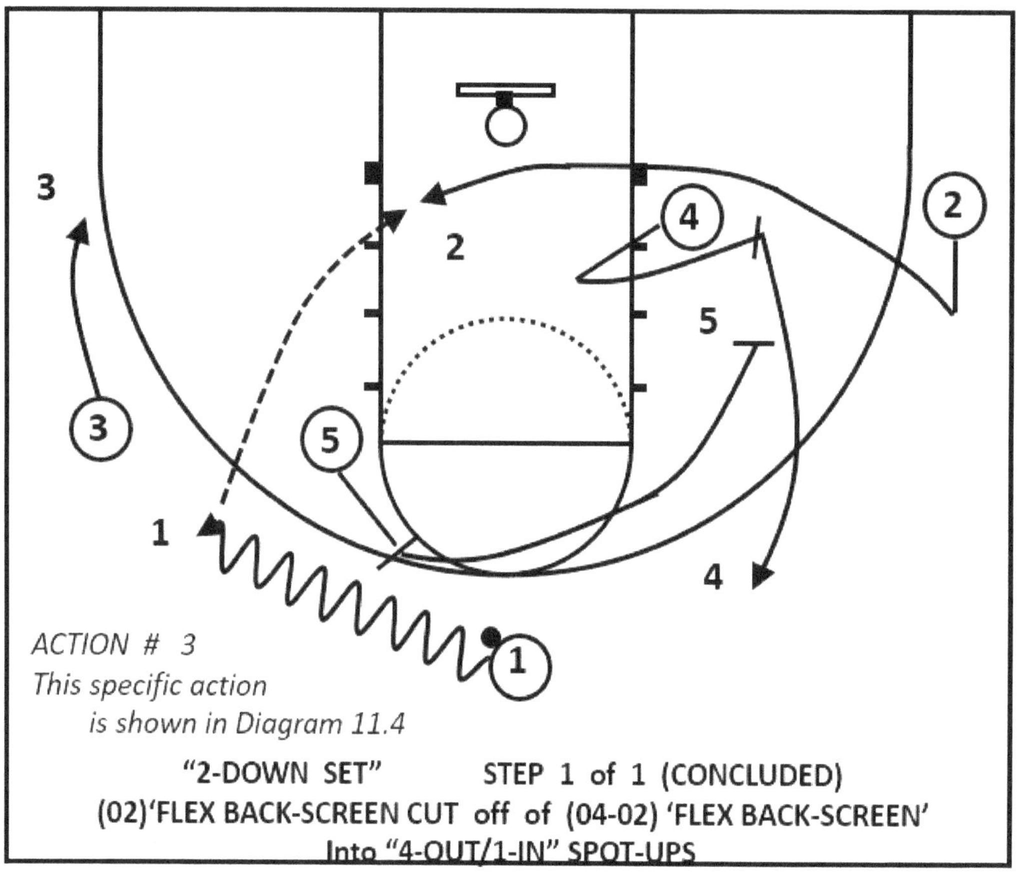

Diagram 11.4

Action # 4 shows complimentary action from Action # 3. This diagram has 03 start with his "V-Cut" before then starting the "Flex Cut" (off of 05's Flex Back-Screen). But 03 bumps 05 to cause 05 then to make another type of cut—a "Duck-In Cut" into the middle of the lane.

Using the "Flex Cut" with the "Flex Bump Cut" can cause confusion with the defenders trying to guard who is going to be the final cutter that cuts into the lane near the basket, while looking for the pass from 01, (in this instance.)

After 01 has dribble-scraped off of 04's "Big-on-Small Ball-Screen," he should have an open passing lane to deliver the ball to 05 on his "Bump Cut." Whether the pass to 05 is made or not and whether the shot is taken, players are in the "4-Out/1-In Spot-Ups" for the designated continuity offense to fluidly begin. See Diagram 11.5

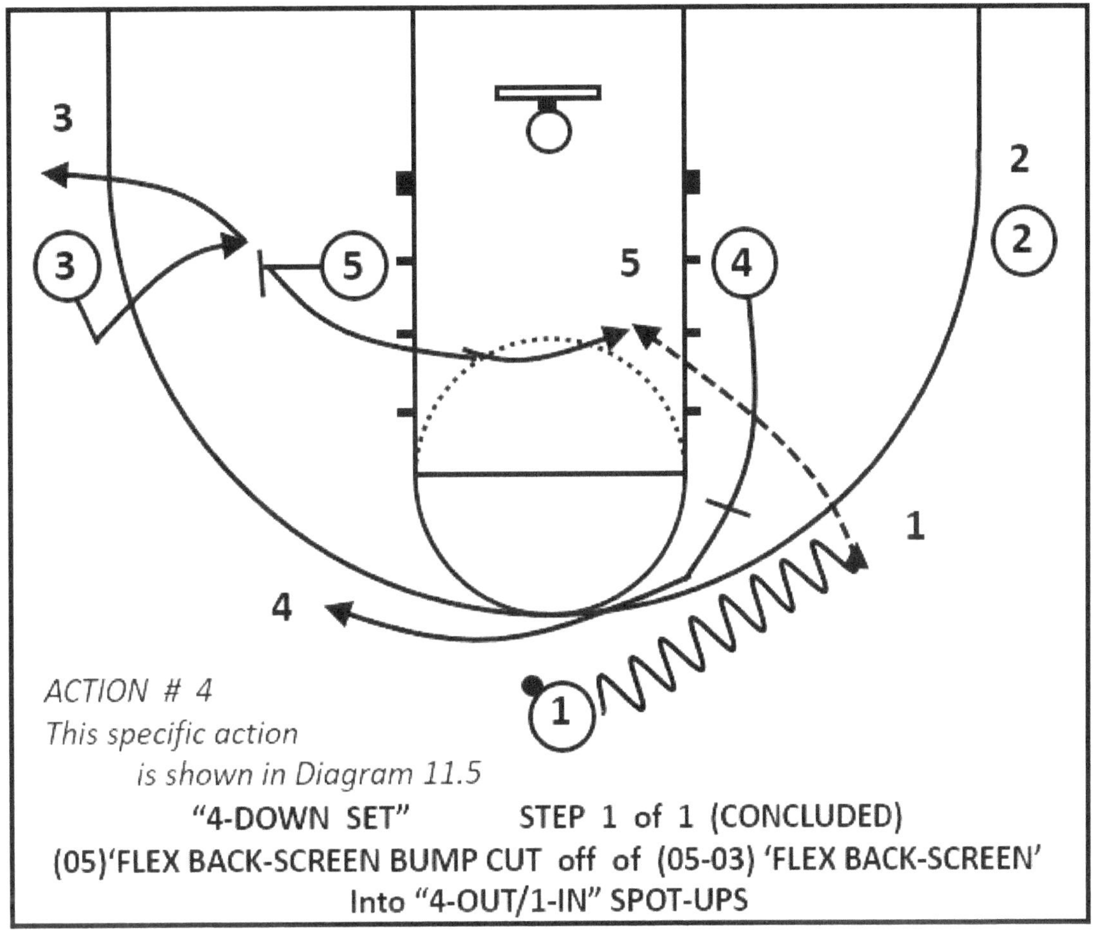

Diagram 11.5

Action # 5 shows another complimentary type of action in Diagram 11.6 where after 03 makes his "Flex Cut" off of the 05-03 "Flex Back-Screen," 01 has moved the ball to the opposite side's "Ballside Elbow" area. After 03 has scraped off of 05's lower baseline shoulder. In this action, it is mandatory that 03 cut low, so that X5 would have to slide lower in order to hedge or switch on to the cutter, 03.

Drifting lower will then give 05 the "position advantage" to make his own cut—"an Iso Duck-In Cut" into the Dotted Circle area in another "Iso" advantage for 05 over X5 or the possible switching X3.

If shots are not created by this action, this action also completes the entire play and places all players into the proper "4-Out/1-In" Spot-Ups for a designated continuity offense to smoothly and instantly begin. See Diagram 11.6

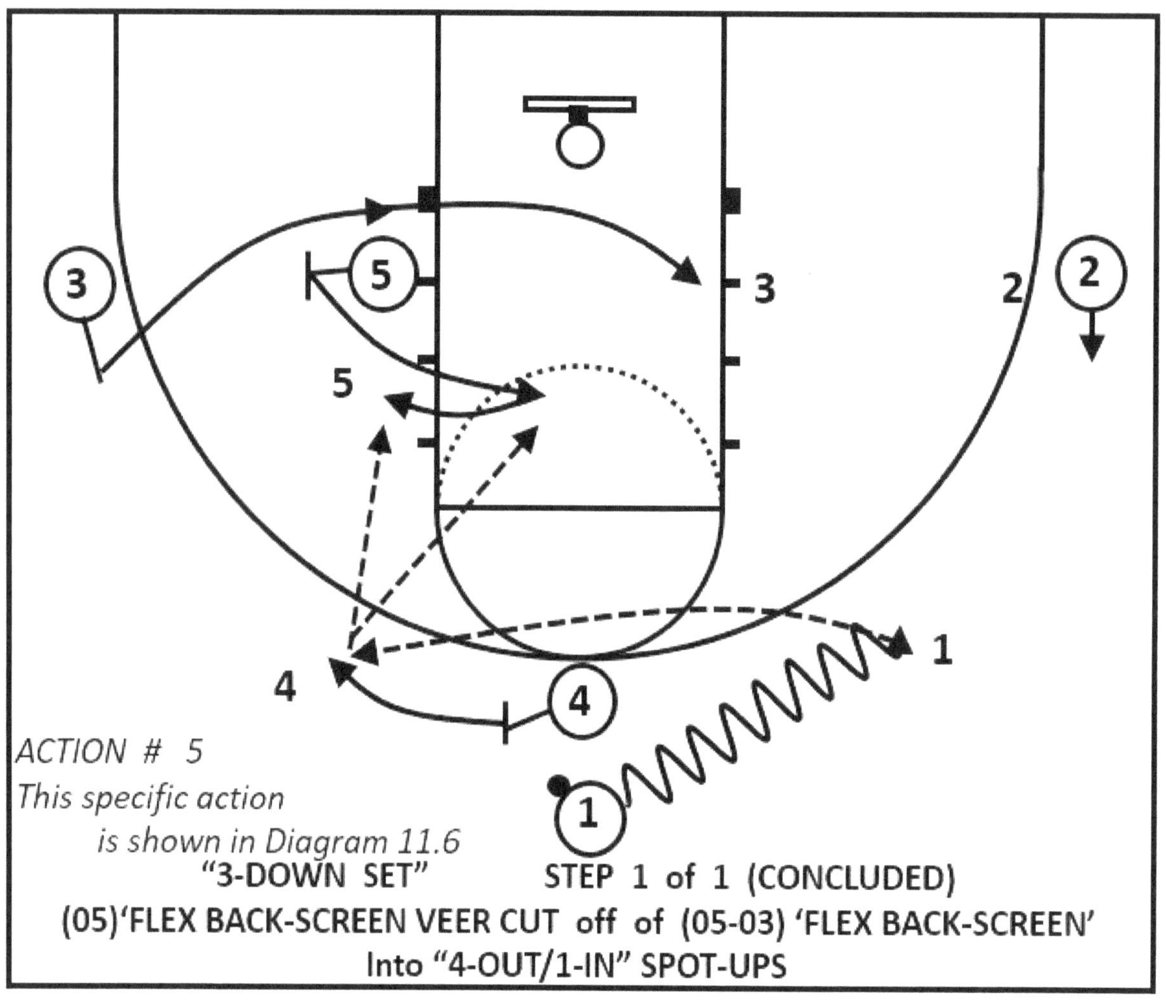

Diagram 11.6

Action # 6 illustrates a cut (that often times can also follow the actual "Flare-Screen) that is becoming more and more important in offensive schemes and therefore more and more frequently used. The action can result in becoming in a primary perimeter scoring option. Because of that, this "Flare Cut" action (that can also can become such a threat that it can draw attention to multiple defenders, obviously multiple off-ball defenders and thus creating better interior scoring opportunities on the actual Ballside.

Out of the "1-DOWN" Set, 01 reverses the ball to 02 and immediately 01 makes a "Flare Cut" by scraping off of 03's outside right shoulder to end in the "Wing" area. 01 would be aided by 03's "Flare-Screen." He should have his "feet and hands ready" to prepare for a possible (02-01) "Skip Pass." This could lead to a high percentage "catch and shoot" or "Inside Passes" to either 05 now on the new "Ballside Mid-Post" or to 04 flashing to the new "Ballside High Post."

It should be noted that if 02 returns the ball to 01 with a (02-01) "Skip Pass," 02 would immediately make his own "Flare-Cut" to the opposite wing area. It is also emphasized that 01 and 02 would make strong (and 'sellable') "V-Cuts" before they make their own "Flare-Cuts."

No shots created would place the offensive players into the "High Post/Low Post Spot-Ups" for the continuity offense to begin. See Diagram 11.7

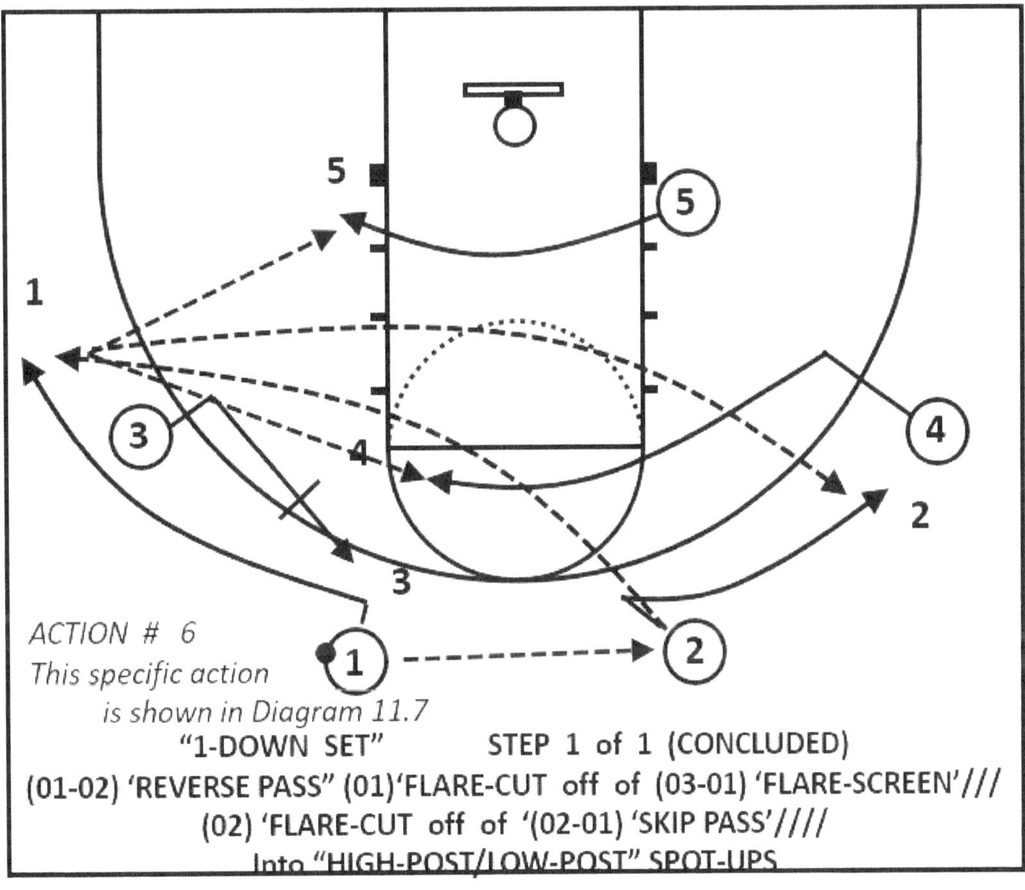

Diagram 11.7

Diagram 11.8 illustrates a complimentary action for the previous action described. The action starts with a half-court play that is run out of the "3-ACROSS" Set. As 01 dribbles towards 03, he makes a "Throwback Reverse Pass" to 04, who has popped out to the opposite "Slot" location. 03 "V-Cuts" before stepping up as if to "Flare-Screen" for 01. With 04 now having the ball, 01 starts to cut towards 03 as if to "Flare-Cut" off of 03's supposed "Flare-Screen." Instead, 03 breaks off of his route to then make a "Ghost Flare-Screen Cut" (basically it becomes a "Backdoor Cut" to the basket.

On the opposite side of the floor, 02 scrapes off of 05's outside shoulder on his "Big-on-Small Flare-Screen" for 02 to use when he makes his own "Flare Cut" to the new "Backside Deep Corner." If no shots are taken, there will be more offensive action to continue attacking defenders and to end up in the proper spot-ups for the continuity offense to fluidly begin. See Diagram 11.8

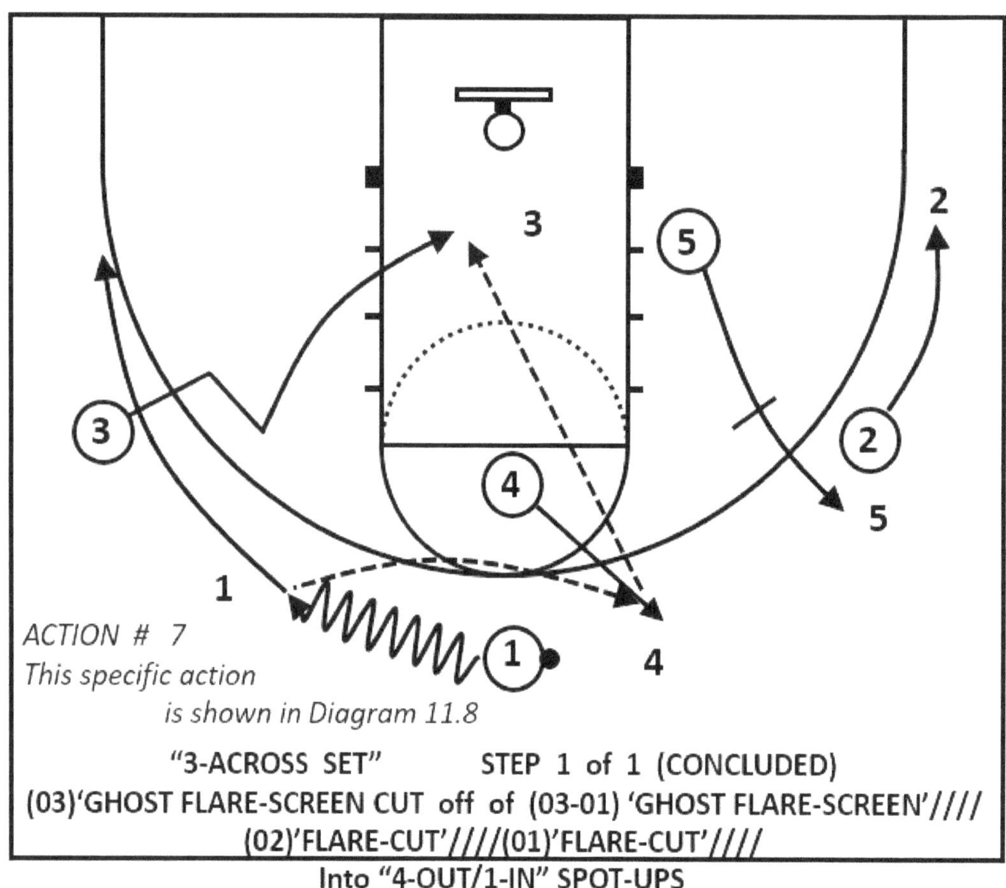

Diagram 11.8

Diagram 11.9 of Action # 8 demonstrates the beginning of a play that must be executed out of the "2-TWIST" Set. When 01 reverses the ball from the strong side of the floor to 02, 05 "Slash Cuts" to the opposite side of the floor's Mid-Post area. 01 makes a cut towards 02 as if to follow his pass, while 03 steps up to make a "Replacement Cut" to the new "Weakside Slot." 04 remains on his initial side of the lane. See Diagram 11.9

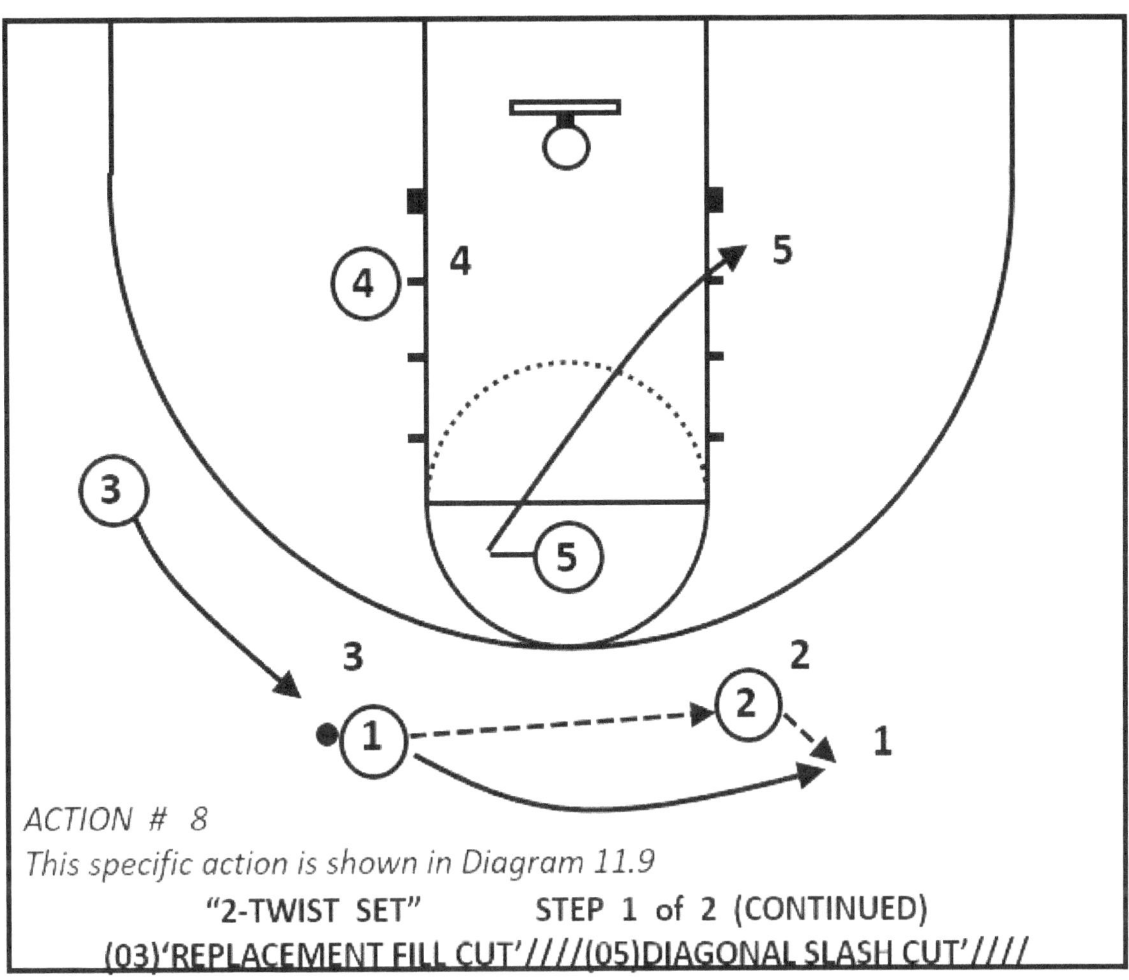

Diagram 11.9

Diagram 11.10 shows the following situation in Action # 8 with 02 making a "Flip Pass" back to 01 and 01 then reversing the ball to 03 on the opposite "Slot." As the 01-03 "Reverse Pass" is started, 04 breaks diagonally up to the middle of the FT Line at the "Nail" spot. This is called 04's "Nail Cut" and with it 02 scrapes off of 04's right shoulder to make his "Shuffle-Cut" off of 04's "Shuffle Back-Screen." This action isolates and inverts 01's defender in a very vulnerable area for the opposition's defense.

Other action will have to follow if no shots are taken so that the proper spot-ups are filled to conclude the actual play and to smoothly begin the continuity offense. See Diagram 11.10

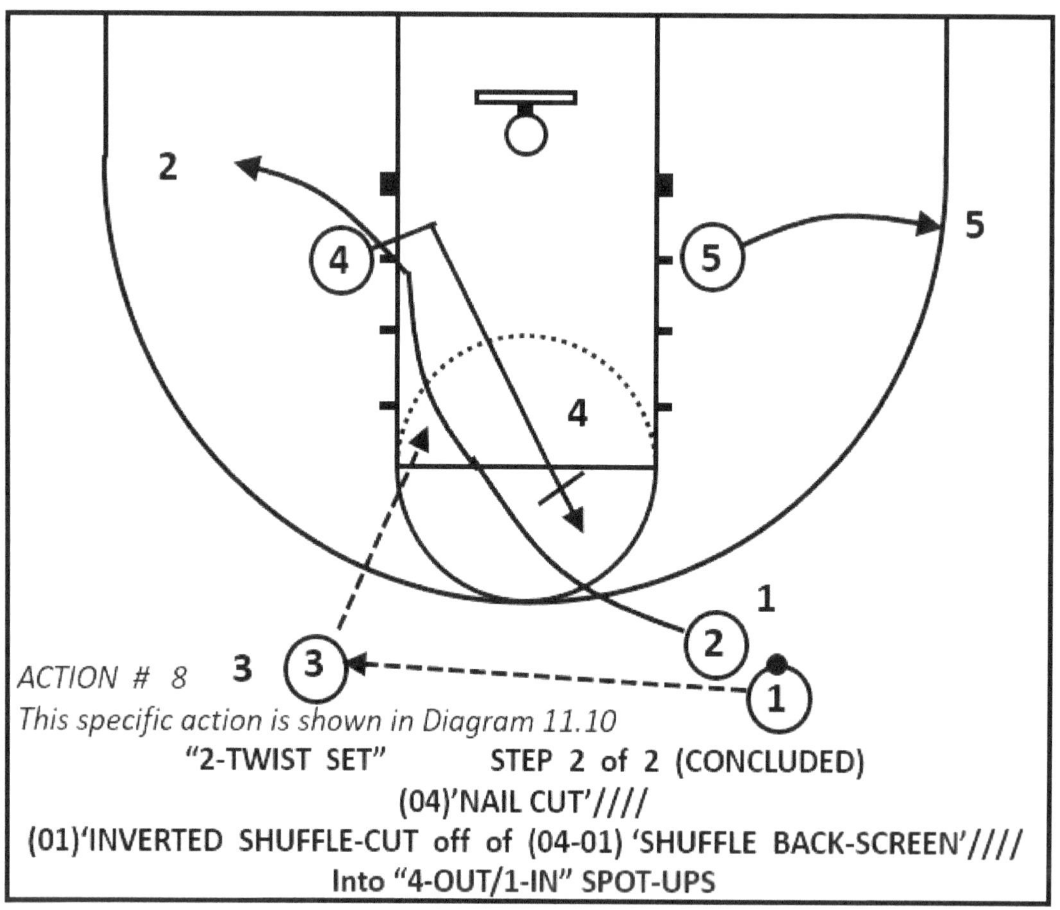

Diagram 11.10

Action #9 is shown in Diagrams 11.11 and 11.12. The action begins with an entry/play run out of the "1-DOWN" Set. With a (01-02) "Reverse Pass," 03 steps up to set a "Big-on-Small Flare-Screen" for 01 to use to make a "Flare-Cut" off of 03's outside shoulder. 01 ends up on the new "Weakside Wing," while 02 dribbles directly at 04 on the new "Ballside Wing." See Diagram 11.11

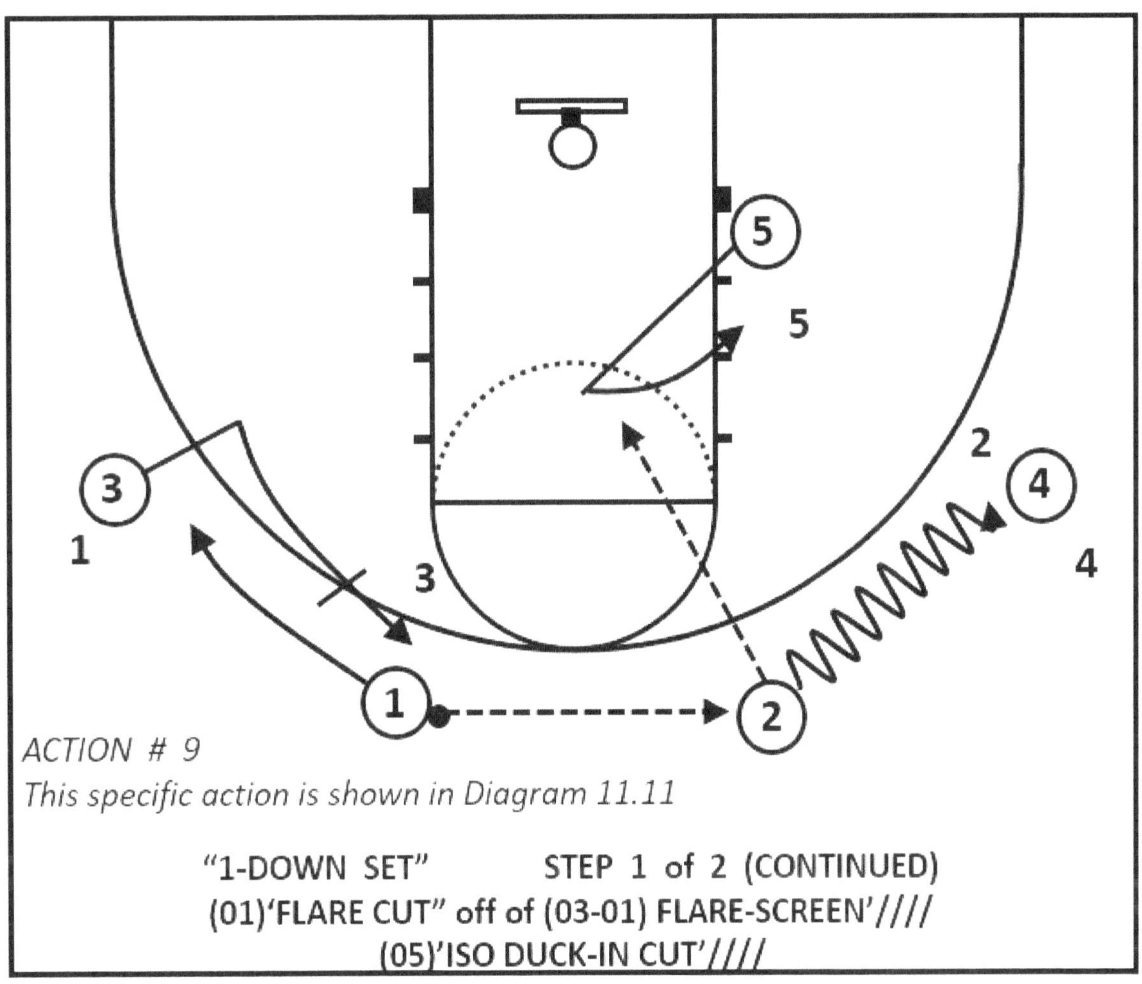

Diagram 11.11

As 02 receives the **ball** from 01, 05 steps into the "Dotted Circle" area by making his "Iso Duck-In Cut" and looks to receive the "Inside Pass" from 02 during his "perimeter pull dribble" towards 04. 02 could also make a "Skip Pass" to 01 after his "Flare-Cut." 02 could also look to make a pass back to 03 after he has slipped his "Flare-Screen" (for 01).

Diagram 11.12 shows the action after 04 receives the DHO from 02. 04 then "perimeter pull dribbles" towards the nearest "Slot" before making a (04-03) "Reverse Pass." 01 would have to make a strong "V-Cut" to get open to receive 03's "Wing Pass."

As the ball actually leaves 03's hands, 05 is already making his "Nail Cut" to then be able to set his "Big-on-Small Scissors Shuffle Back-Screen" first for 04 and then for 03 to both make their "Scissors Shuffle-Cuts" to the "Blocks" on both sides of the lane. 05 then slips his screens and pops to the top of the key.

01 looks to make for "Inside Passes" to both 03 and 04, a possible "Skip Pass" to 02 or a "Reverse Pass" to 05. These cuts, screens, DHO's, passes and dribbles have now placed all players in the proper "3-Out/2-In" Spot-Ups for the designated continuity offense to smoothly. See Diagram 11.12

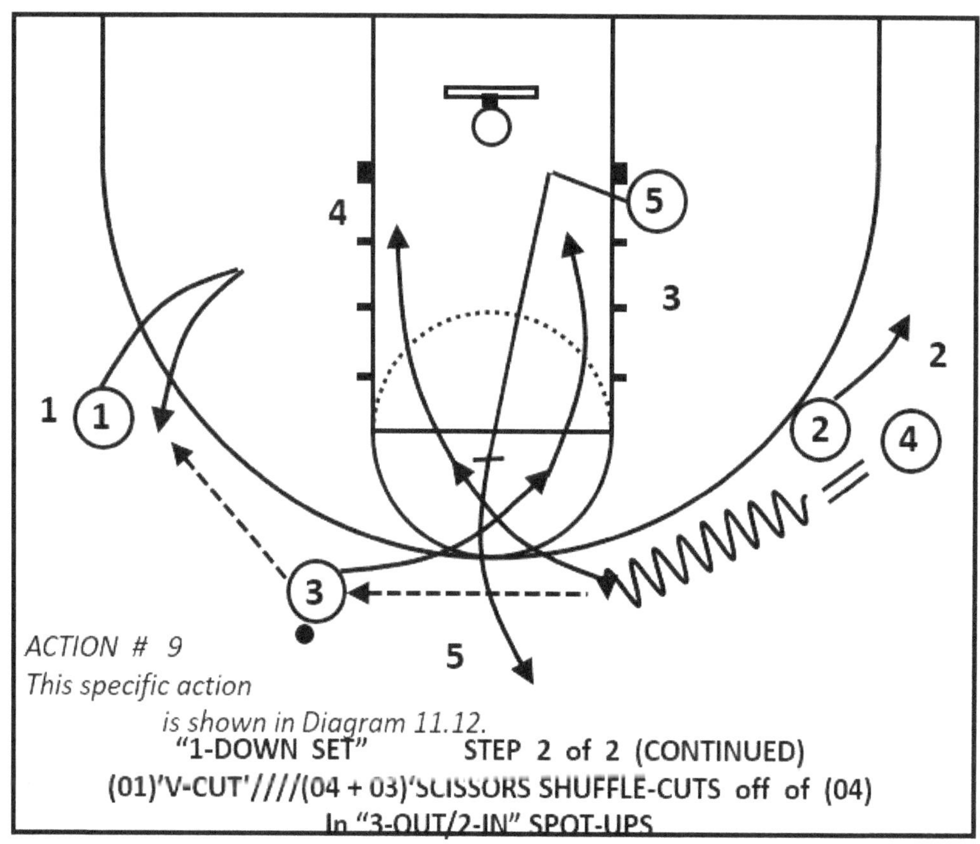

Diagram 11.12

Action # 10 is shown in Diagram 11.13 with another offensive action made famous by Coach John Wooden and his UCLA Bruins in the 1960's. The cut is made immediately after a pass is made from near the top of the key and "Slot" area to a "Wing" area. There a player sets a back-screen from the "High Post Elbow" area. It is basically a "Give-n-Go Cut" with a blind "High Post Shuffle Back-Screen" that cuts vertically down the lane to then post up on the new "Ballside Block."

We feel this action can be much more effective when the screener and cutter are mismatched—that is "Big-on-Small UCLA Shuffle Back-Screen" or a "Small-on-Big UCLA Shuffle Back-Screen." Since this action is initiated with a "Wing Pass" from the perimeter, we also believe that when a so-called "post-type Big Defender" is the initial passer/cutter that the chances that his individual is as efficient as a "perimeter-type Small Defender" are much smaller. In addition, the "UCLA Cutter" is moving to the area where he is most comfortable—in the "paint."

The screening mismatch then discourages defensive switches, because the switch would leave a "Small Defender" being forced to attempt to guard an offensive "Big" down on the "Block." That provides the offense with a "position and personnel advantage."

This diagram shows the action beginning out of what is called the "2-SQUEEZE" Set. When 01 approaches the top of the key, 02 first makes an "L-Cut" up and out from the "Block" to the "Wing" area at the FT Line extended. At the same time, 03 makes an "Iverson Cut" over the top of 05 with 04 making a "Barkley Cut" below 05, followed by 05 making a short "High Post" cut. See Diagram 11.13

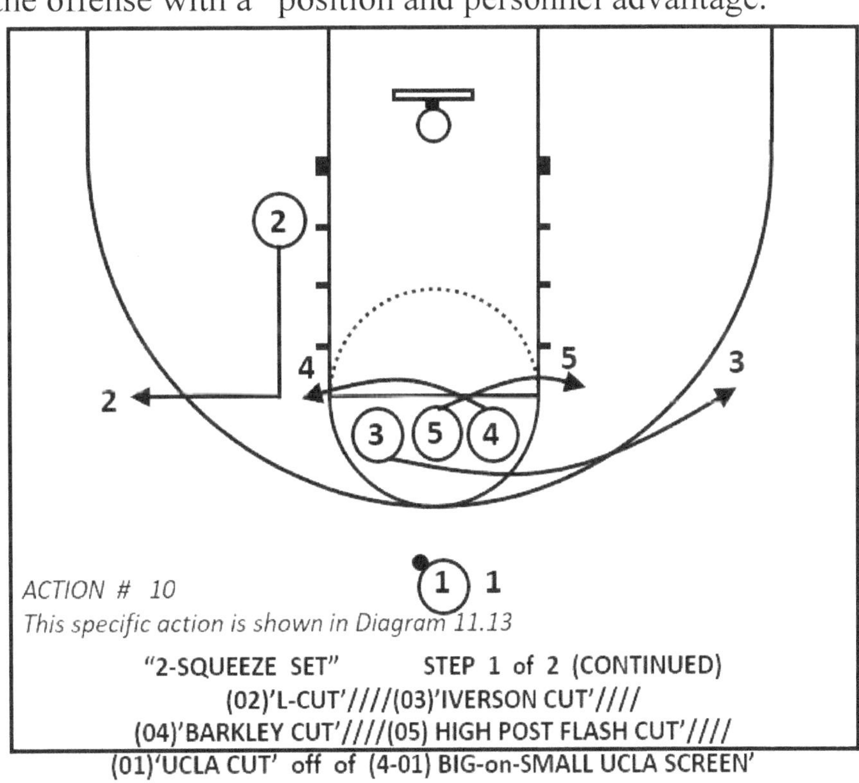

Diagram 11.13

Diagram 11.14 shows the action after the four different cuts have been made to place all four off-the-ball players actually into a totally different offensive alignment—we call the "5-UP" Set. Therefore this play could actually start out of either offensive set, giving the offense another weapon to attack the opposition.

In addition, 01 could make the initial "Wing Pass" to either 02 or to 03 on the opposite side of the floor. This gives the offense still another method to use the "UCLA Shuffle Back-Screen and Cut" Action. In this diagram, 01 makes the "Wing Pass" to 02. After making a strong "V-Cut" to set up his defender and to read the defender's reaction to the "V-Cut," 01 could run and scrape off of either shoulder of (04), before then cutting to the new "Ballside Block." This "UCLA Cut" by 01 also repositions 01 not only into an inverted situation, but because of the 2-man action of 05 and 03 on the weakside and because of 04 then slipping his screen to step out further to the perimeter, places 01 and X1 into a completely isolated situation and giving 01 a "Position advantage to capitalize on.

If 01 cannot get a shot from this action, the play can continue with other offensive action so all advantages would go to the offensive team. Eventually when no shots are taken, the specific spot-ups will be filled for the designated continuity offense. See Diagram 11.14

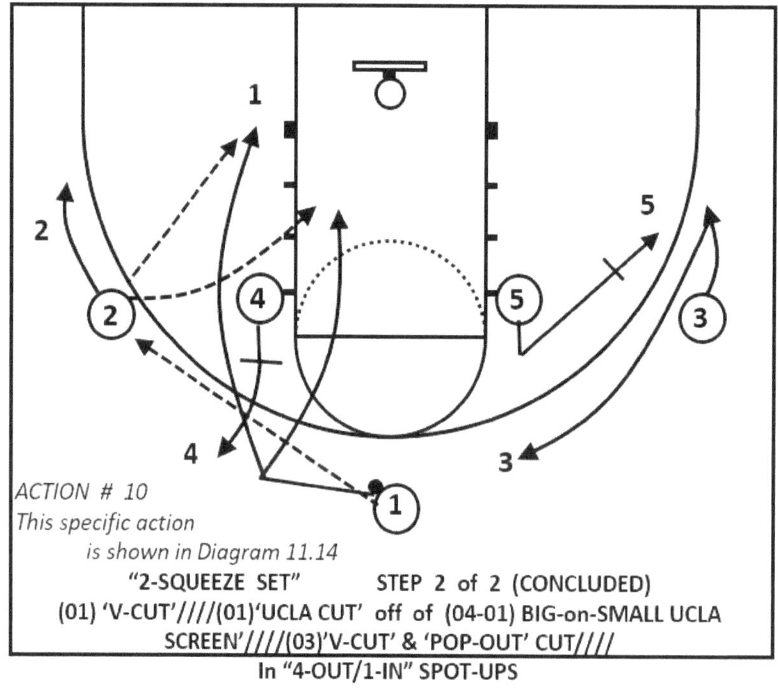

Diagram 11.14

The majority of basketball plays/entries/quick-hitters out of the many different offensive alignments/sets must have the ball first entered near the "Wing" area (via pass or dribble.) Defenses understand that and attempt to deny those passes. Action #11 shows examples of "L-Cuts" made by both 03 and 02 to defeat that type of ball denial pressure and receive the ball at either "Wing" area at the FT Line extended.

03 and 02 walk their defenders vertically straight up the Free Throw Lane Line to near the "Elbow" area before exploding out to the imaginary "FT Line extended. On their break up and out, they have their eyes on the passer and "their feet and hands ready for a catch and attack." See Diagram 11.15

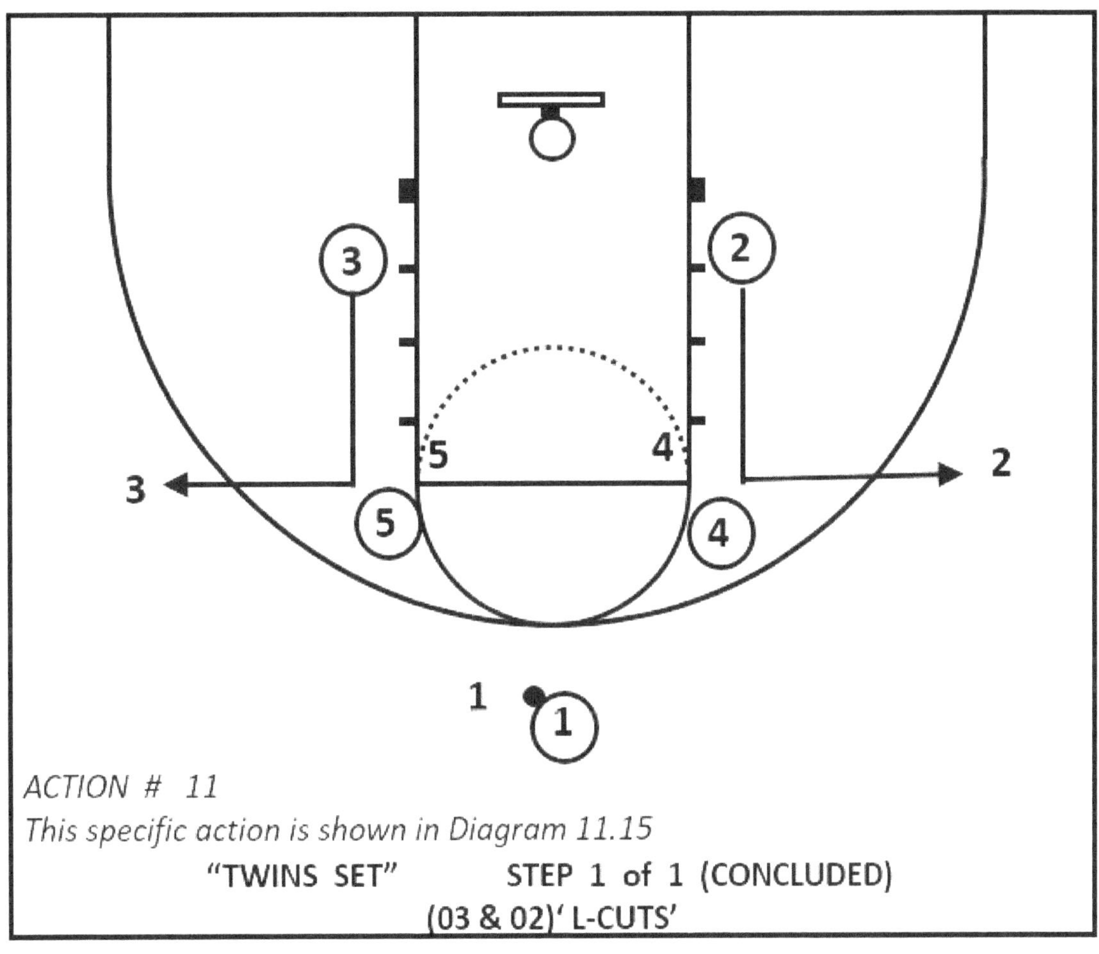

Diagram 11.15

Action # 12 illustrates a completed play out of the "3-DOWN" Set, with the alignment spreading the defense both vertically and horizontally. 01 and 04 both keep their defenders occupied their defenders, while 03 and 02 occupy their individual defenders with their "Lift Cuts." With the help of 04's "Big-on-Small Ball-Screen," 01 should have the opportunity to attack X5 with his "Iso Duck-In Cut" into the middle of the lane. If shots are not taken, all five players are already in the "4-Out/1-In" Spot-Ups for an immediate transition from this play into the continuity offense. See Diagram 11.16

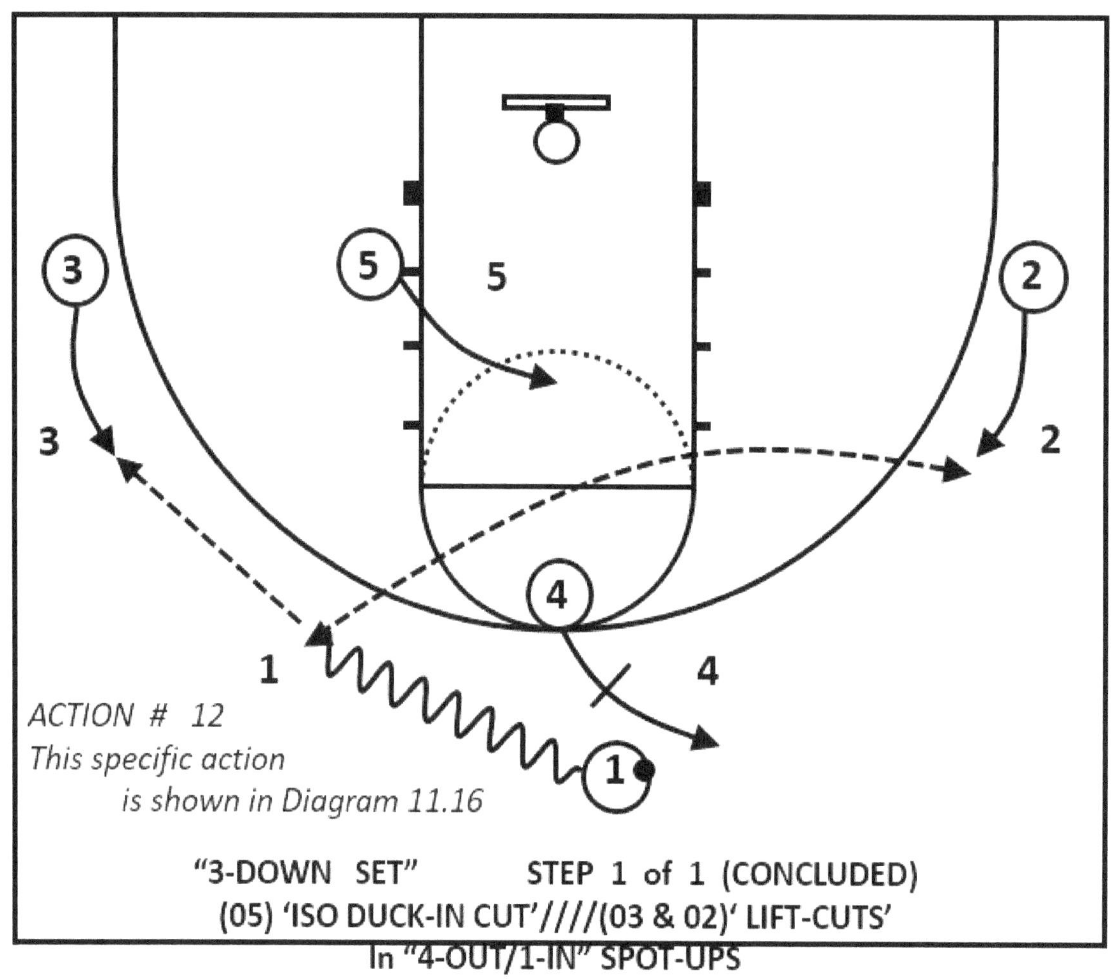

Diagram 11.16

Action # 13 illustrates the full play that begins out of the "3-ACROSS" Set. The play could begin with 01 making a "Slot Pass' to either 03 or to 02. Both players pop out to their respective "Slot" locations to receive the potential pass. In this case, 01 passes the ball to 03 and immediately makes a hard cut diagonally to the newly declared "Ballside Deep Corner." 04 always sets a "Big-on-Small Pin Down-Screen" on the perimeter play on the new "Weakside Wing," (in this case for 02 to make a cut higher off of 04's outside right shoulder to the empty "Slot." 05 makes a "Low Post Flash" across the lane to always end up on the new "Ballside Block." See Diagram 11.17

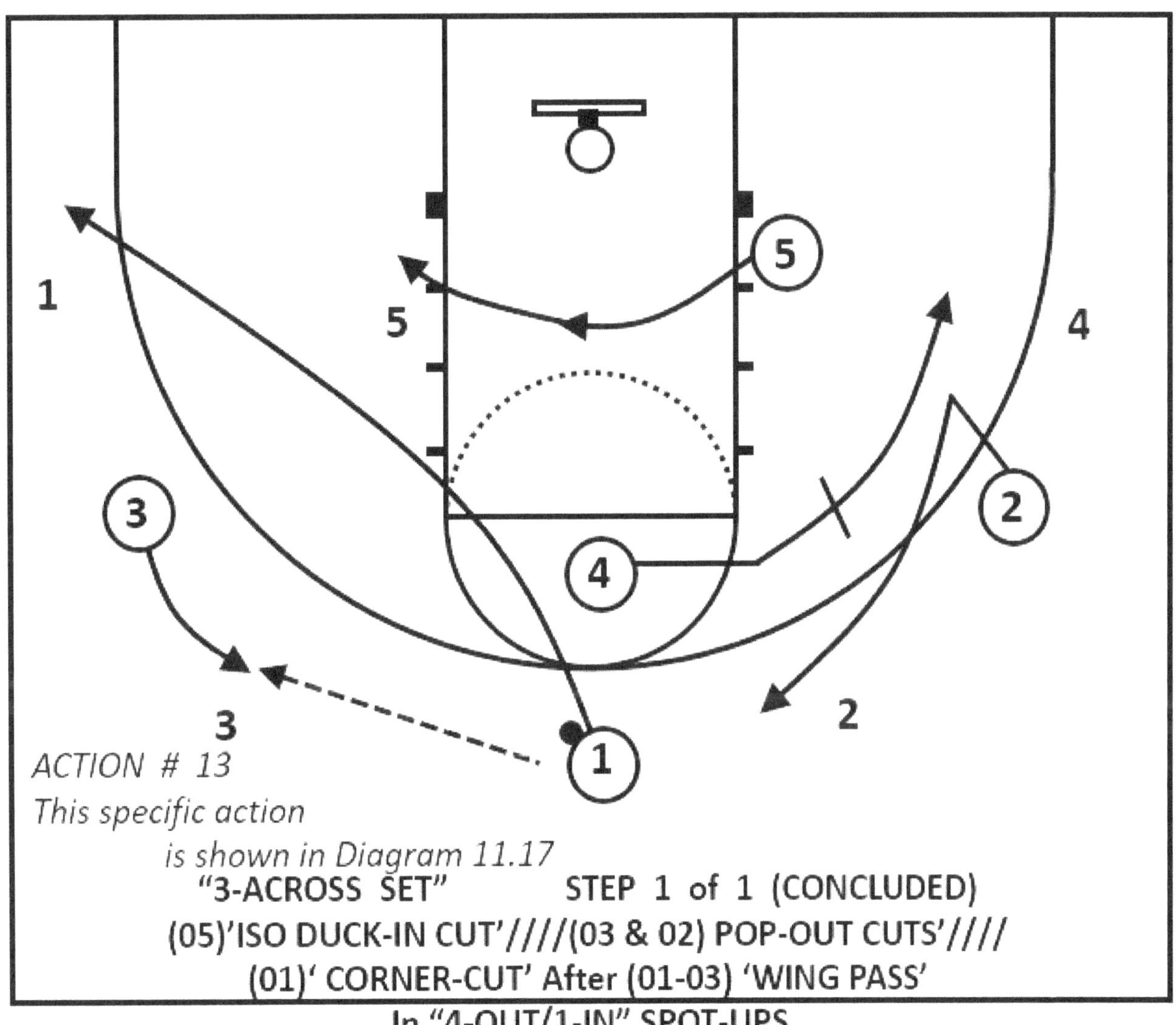

Diagram 11.17

Action # 14 illustrates the beginning of a play out of the "2-UP" Set where 01 makes the (01-02) Reverse Pass" and immediately 03 steps up to set a "Big-on-Small Flare-Screen" for 01 to use to make his "Flare-Cut" to the now vacant "Wing" area. At the same time, 05 first steps up towards 01's initial "Slot" location before he then makes a "Slash Cut" in the opposite direction towards the new "Ballside Mid-Post." See Diagram 11.18

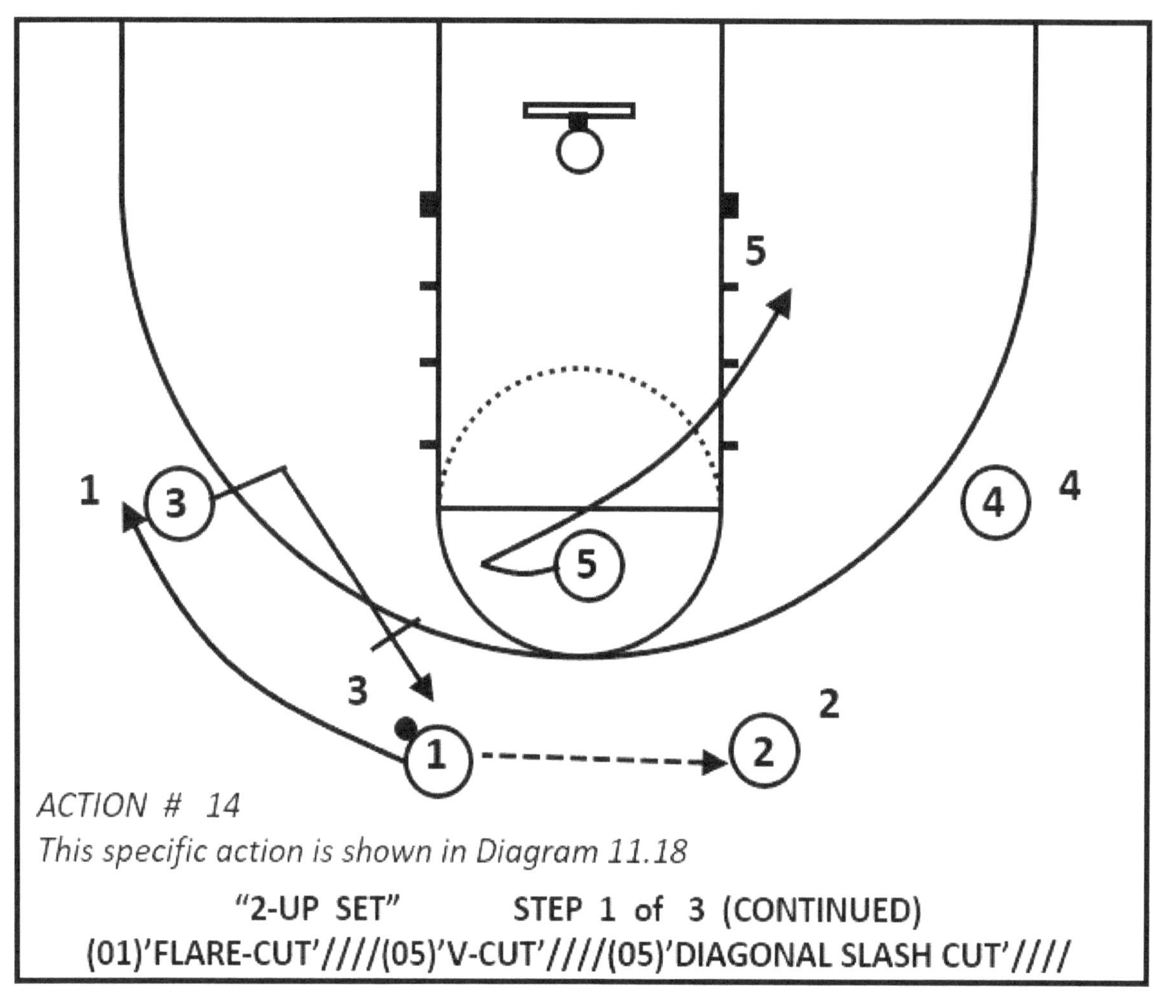

Diagram 11.18

The next step in this play has 02 swing the ball over to 04 before then making a "Corner Cut" to the "Deep Corner" on that side of the floor. 03 moves over to the top of the key (on his "Replacement Fill Cut") while 04 looks to make an "Inside Pass" to 04, a possible "Down Pass" to 02 or a "Skip Pass" to 01 or a "Reverse Pass" to 01. See Diagram 11.19

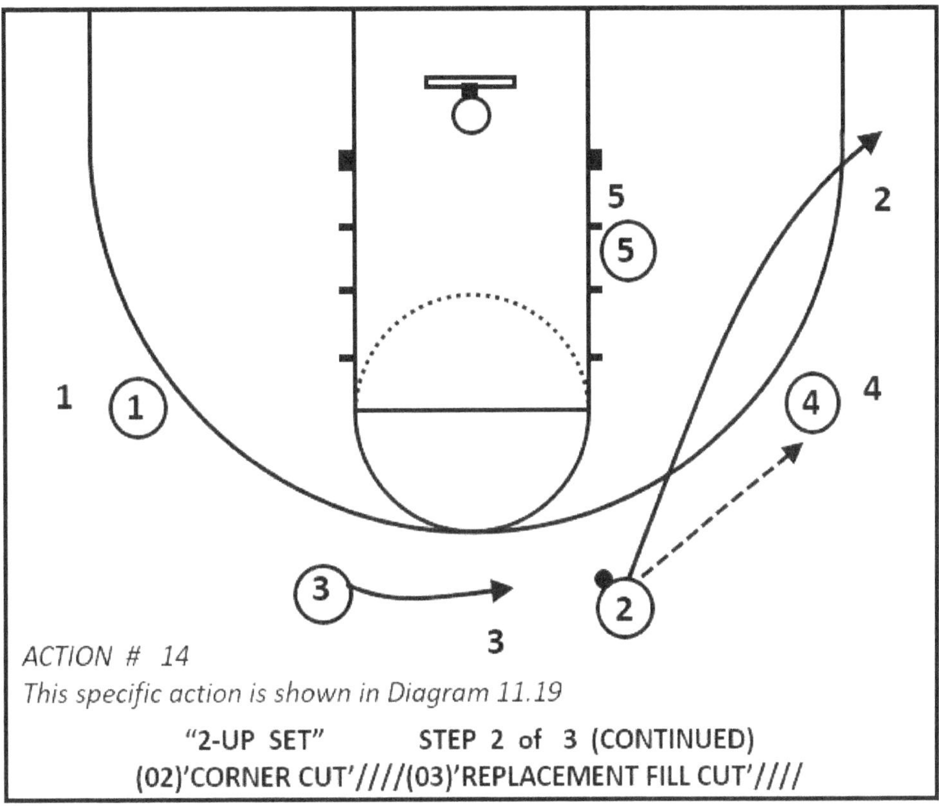

Diagram 11.19

Action # 14 continues in Diagram 11.20 with 04 turning down passes to 04 and 02 and instead making a "Reverse Pass" to 03. As the ball leaves the hands of 04, 04 cuts across the FT Line and off of 01's screen by scraping off of 01's top right shoulder. This action is almost identical to an "Iverson Screen and Cut," but because of the location of the screen, it is what we call a "Small-on-Big Michigan Screen" with 04 making the corresponding "Michigan Cut."

After making the 03-04 "Wing Pass," 02 breaks up to set a "Small-on-Big Flare-Screen" for 03 to then make a "Flare-Cut" to the new "Weakside Wing" area. If the action in the last three diagrams does not create a shot that is wanted, the action places players in the proper "High-Post/Low-Post" Spot-Ups for the specific continuity offense to begin instantly and smoothly. See Diagram 11.20

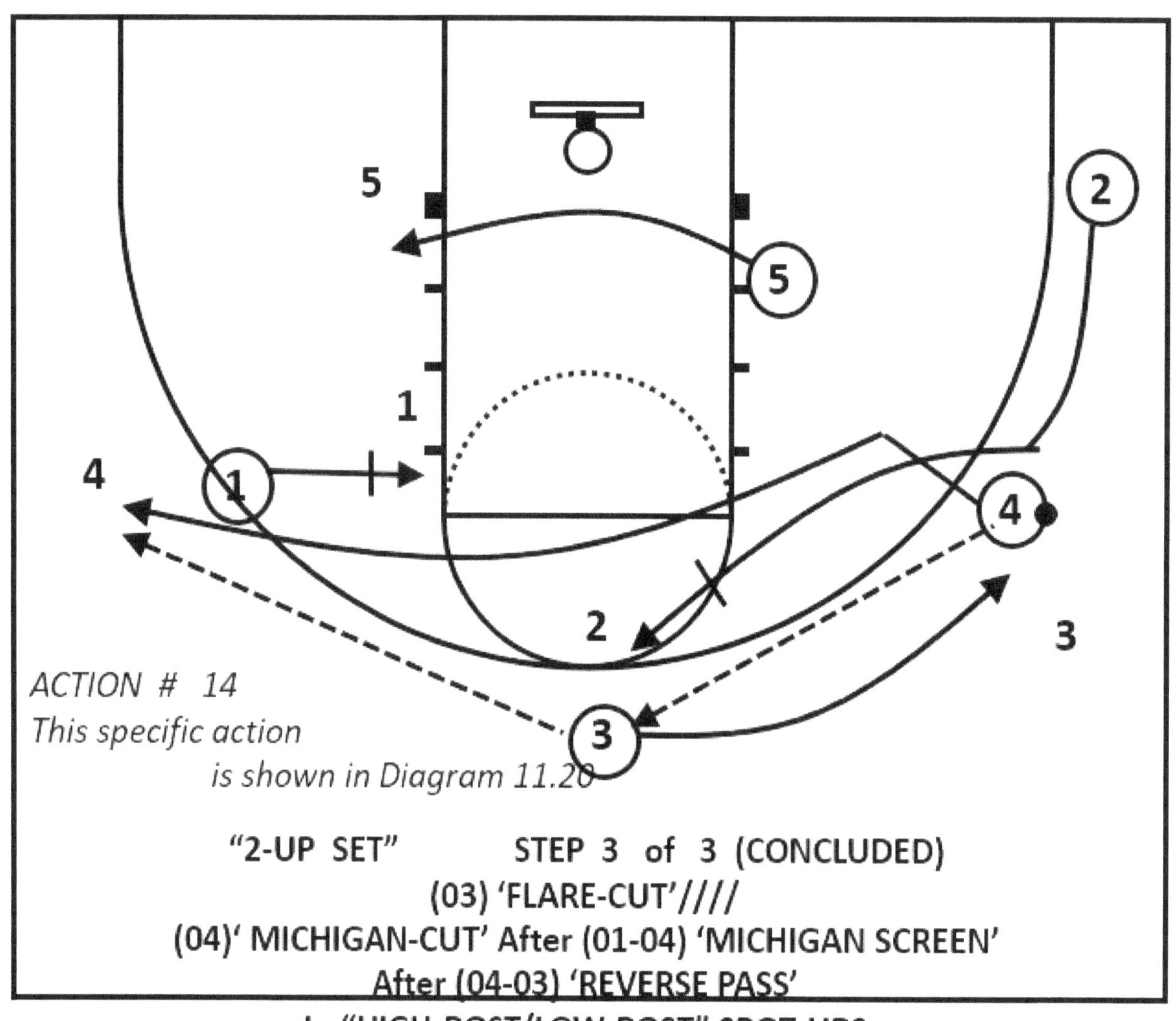

Diagram 11.20

Diagram 11.21 illustrates the entire play that is executed out of the "3-ACROSS" Set. 01 must dribble towards the opposite side where 05 starts and 03 sets his "Big-on-Small Ball-Screen." As 01 breaks contact with 03's outside right shoulder, 04 makes a strong and convincing "V-Cut" away from the screen before reversing directions and making a "Post X-Cut" towards the new "Ballside Mid-Post" area. At the same time, 05 makes a "V-Cut" before then making a "Diagonal High Post Flash Cut." After 03 screens for 01, 02 steps up to set a "Small-on-Big (Flare-)Screen the (Ball-)Screener" action for 03 to then make a "Flare-Cut" to the new "Weakside Wing" area. This action will challenge individual defenders and ultimately move all offensive players into the proper "High-Post/Low-Post" Spot-Ups for the designated continuity offense to fluidly begin at the conclusion of this entry. See Diagram 11.21

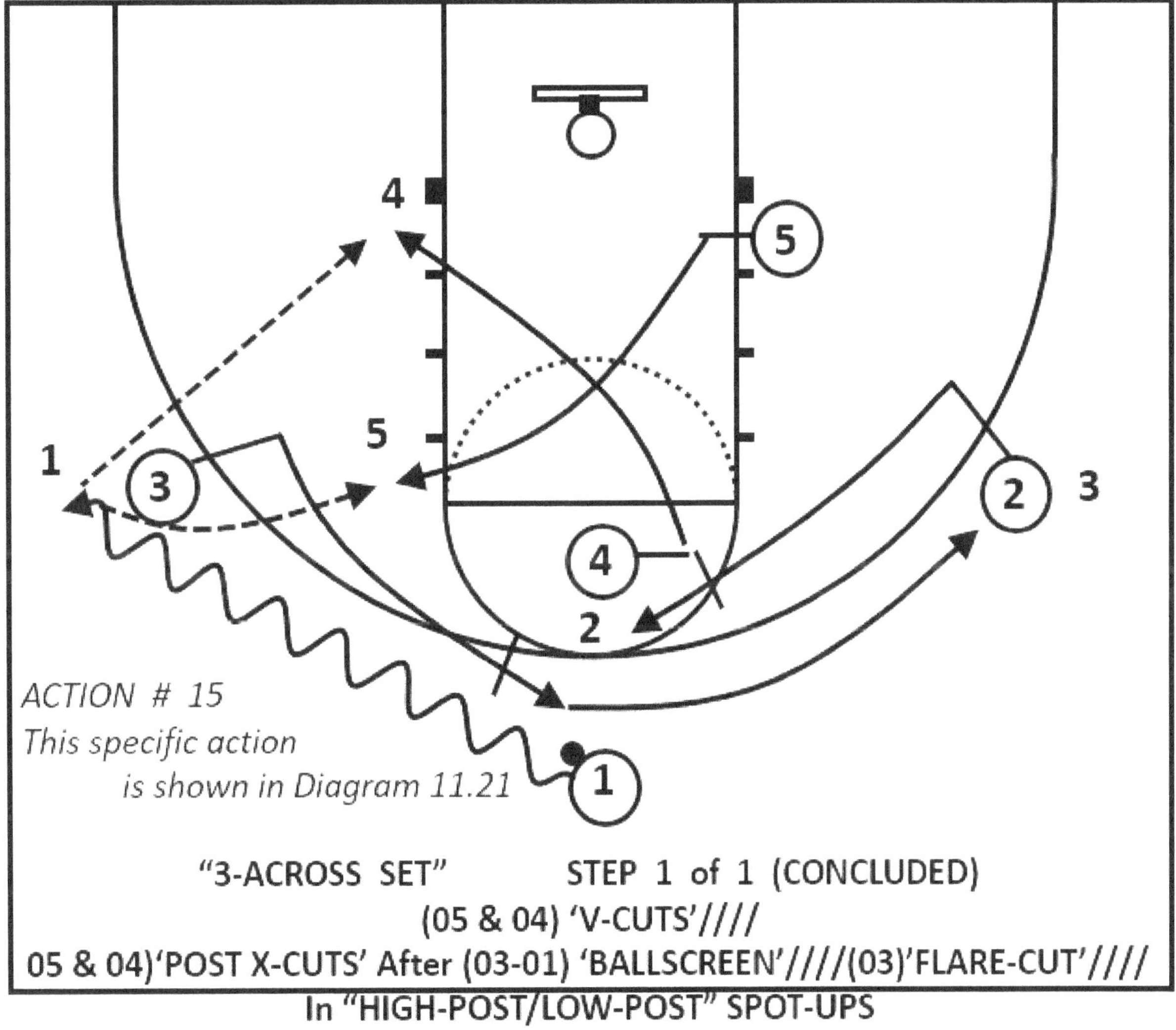

Diagram 11.21

Diagram 11.22 shows Action # 16 that is initiated out of the "4-SQUEEZE" Set. With 02, 05, and 03 all "squeezed" in together at the FT Line, with 05 at the "Nail;" 03 makes his "Iverson Cut" over the top of 05 to break to the "Wing" area on the left side of the floor while 02 makes his "Iverson Cut" below 05 to end up on the "Wing" area on the right side of the floor.

When 01 makes the "Wing Pass" to 03 on the left side of the floor (and on the same side of the floor where 04 has started,) 05 makes his short "High Post Flash Cut" toward the same side of the floor; 02 then steps up to set a "Flare-Screen" for 01 to then make a "Flare-Cut" to the newly declared "Weakside Wing" area.

With 03 receiving the ball, 04 starts to step out away from the new "Ballside Block" area before then making a hard "Post Dive-Cut" to the basket. This cut is simply a shorter "Backdoor Cut" made by a post-type player close to the basket versus the traditional longer cut out on the perimeter by a perimeter-type player. If 04 does not receive 03's quick pass, 04 stops in the lane to turn to then post up again on the "Ballside Block." With 02 and 01 making their screen and cut action on the weakside, 04 becomes an "Isolated Post Player" with 05 at the new "Ballside High Post" area. This action places all five players in the proper "High-Post/Low-Post" Spot-Ups for the desired continuity offense to be easily and quickly transitioned into. See Diagram 11.22

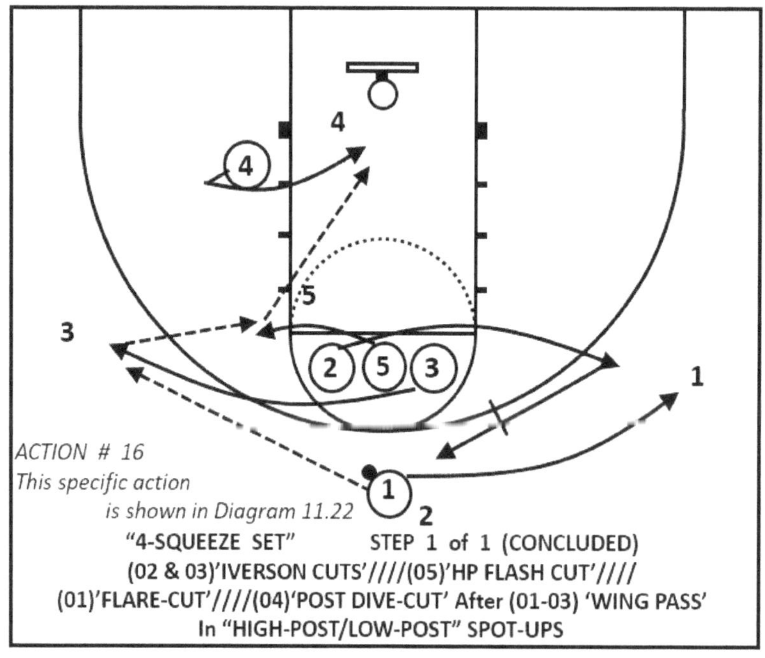

Diagram 11.22

Action # 17 shows the one step offensive play that is shown in Diagram 11.23 and is executed out of the "HORNS" Set. As 01 brings the ball near the top of the key, both 05 and 04 make "Inverted Pop-Out Cuts" just outside of the arc and slightly wider than the two "Slot" locations.

Either 05 or 04 could receive 01's initial pass, but the diagram has 01 making the pass to 04. As both 03 and 02 make their "Lift Cuts" to become perimeter passing targets, their actions also pull their individual defenders away from the basket. After 01 makes the pass to 04, he then makes a "V-Cut" towards the ball before then cutting towards 05 to set a "Small-on-Big" Brush Screen for 05 to scrape off of 01's back to make his own "Isolated Brush Cut" that becomes a "Diagonal Slash Cut" across the lane to the offense's right side of the lane to make an "Isolated Post-Up."

The several cuts, passes, and screens have repositioned all offensive players into the proper "4-Out/1-In" Spot-Ups for a designated continuity offense. See Diagram 11.23

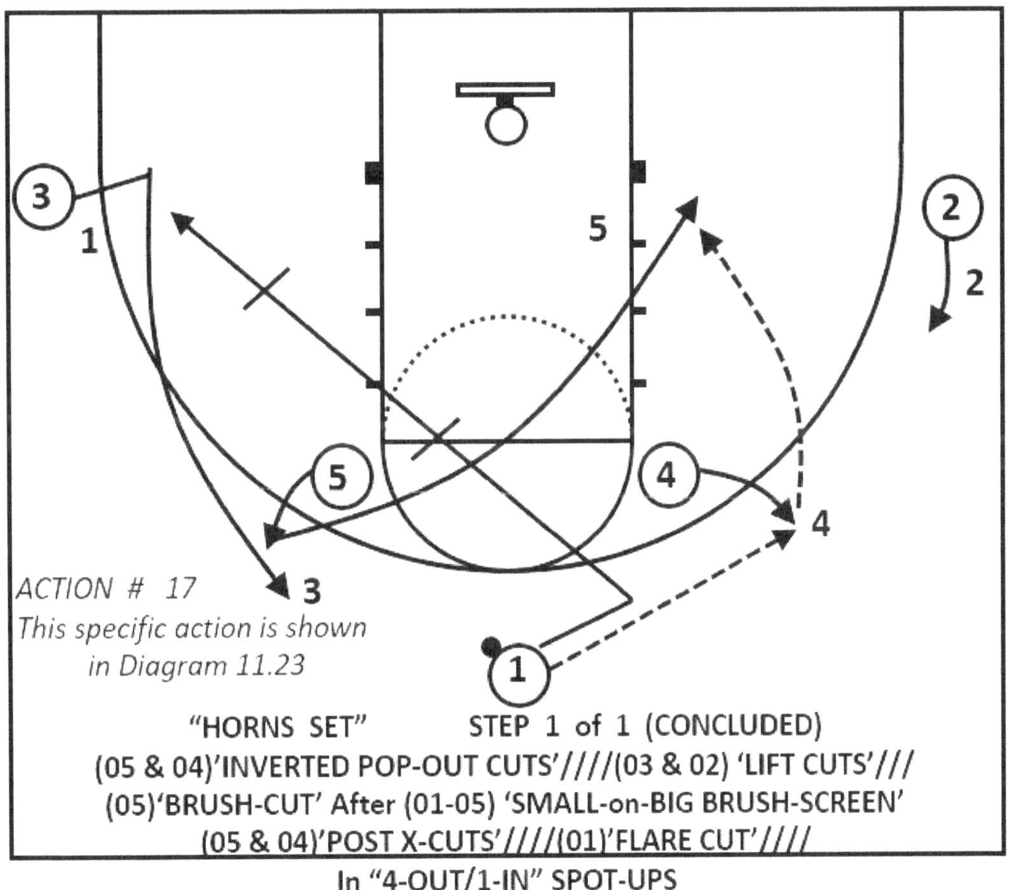

Diagram 11.23

Still another one step offensive action is shown in Diagram 11.24 and is executed out of the "HI-LO STAX" Set. As 01 brings the ball towards the top of the key, both 03 and 02 make their "Pop-Out" Cuts horizontally straight out from their initial locations. In addition, 04 breaks diagonally up to the FT Line extended on the same side of the floor. After 01 makes the "Wing Pass," he sets his defender up first with a "V-Cut" towards 04 and the ball. Then 01 changes the direction he is starting to go to then make a "Small-on-Big" Diagonal Pin Down-Screen for 05 to use to make his "Inverted Pop-Out Cut." See Diagram 11.24

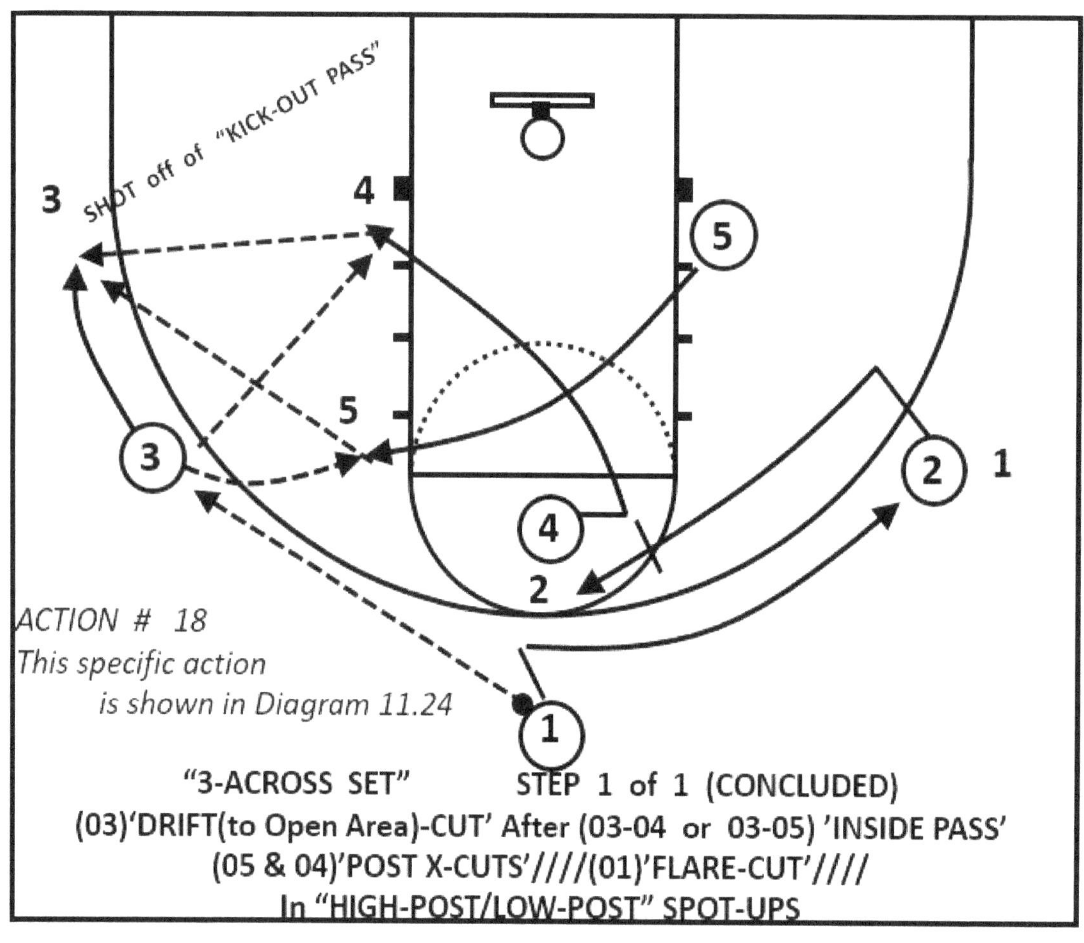

Diagram 11.24

After screening for 04, 01 slips his screen to make a quick and short "Inverted and Isolated Post-Up Cut. This action places all players into any and all of the "Secondary Break" Spot-Ups. From there, any of the Secondary Break Options could be executed immediately. This will add another phase to the offensive attack and if that action still does not create a shot, the action will at least place offensive players into the proper spot-ups for a designated continuity offense to fluidly begin. See Diagram 11.25

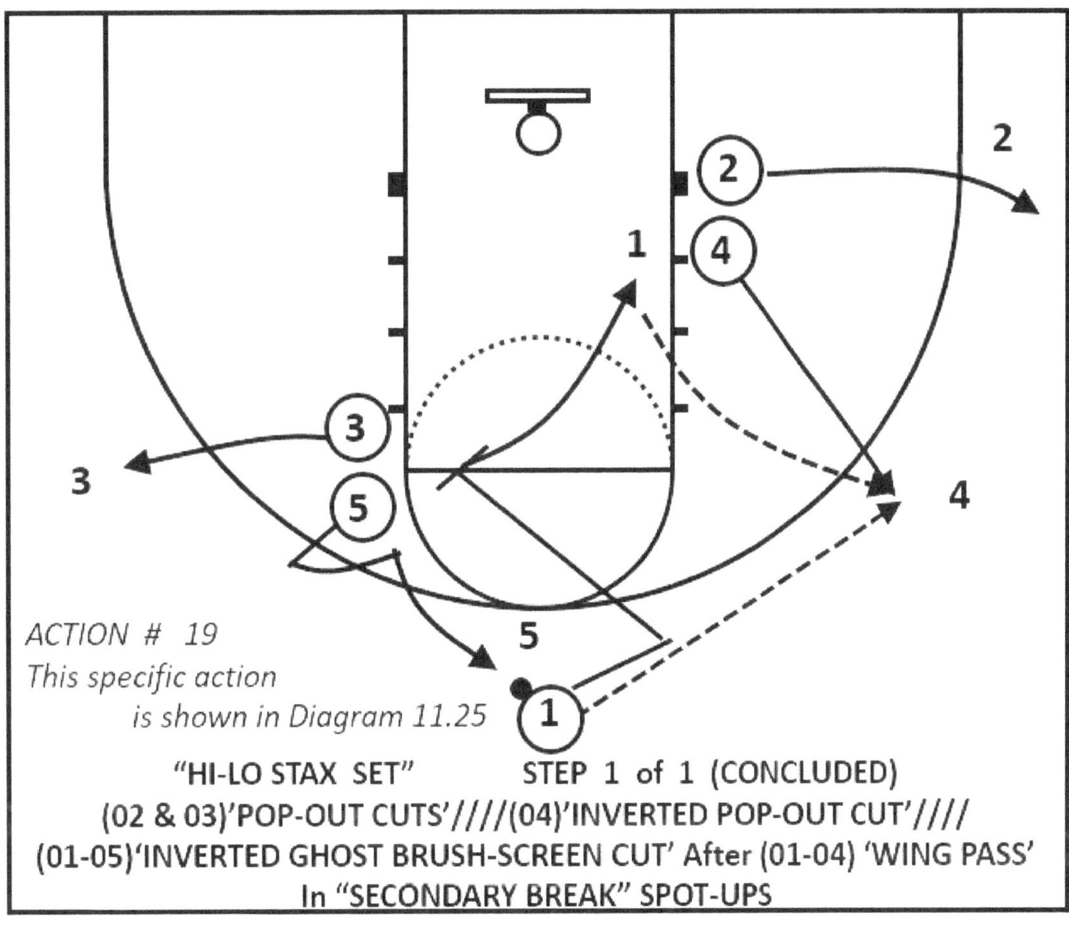

Diagram 11.25

Diagram 11.26 shows another action out of the same "HI-LO STAX" Set in which 01 "Perimeter Pull Dribbles" towards the vacant FT Line extended on the right side of the floor. At the same time, 04 sets a "Pin Down-Screen" for 02 to start to break out before then making a tight "Curl Cut" around and over 04 before then cutting across the lane to the opposite side's "Mid-Post" area. At the same time, 03 horizontally pops out to the FT Line extended and 05 makes an inverted "Pop-Out Cut" to the new "Weakside Slot." The play is designed for either 01, 05 or for 03 to make the "Inside Pass" to the "Inverted and Isolated" 02. Both 01 and 03 could have potential "Skip Passes" made to each other in addition to 05 at the top of the key. This action stretches and pulls the defense to isolate 02 down in the lane or on the "Block." In addition, the "3-Out/2-In" Spot-Ups are filled for a different designated continuity offense to seamlessly begin. See Diagram 11.26

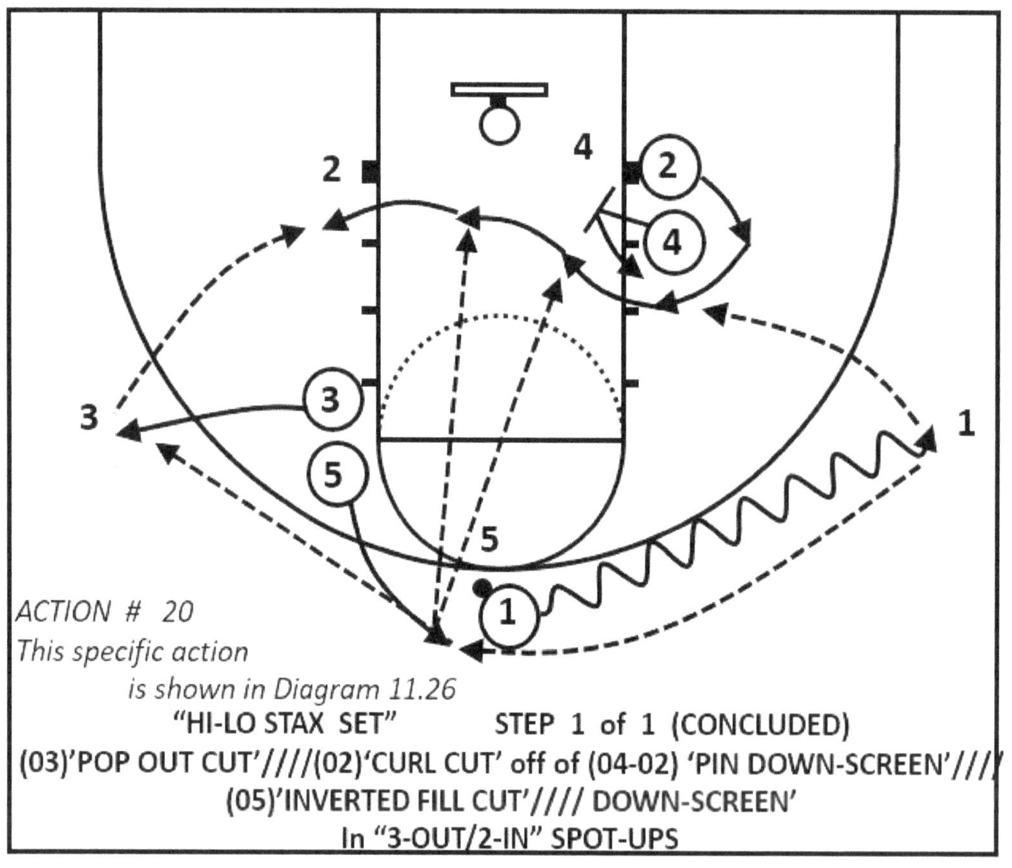

Diagram 11.26

Diagram 11.27 shows another action that can serve as a one-step play (out of the same "HI-LO STAX" Set. Both 03 and 02 set up their defenders with "V-Cuts" before making their "Pop-Out Cuts' out to their respective "Wing" areas (off of the "Pin Down-Screens" set by 05 and 04 respectively. Both 04 and 05 set their screens and when the ball is passed to either wing, the post-player that is initially on the new weakside of the floor (05 is the ball was passed to 02 or 04 if the ball is passed to 03); that player then makes his "Flash Post Cut" across the lane.

With 01 having the choice to making the initial pass to either side of the floor but still being able to execute the play allows for higher levels of structured freedom and unpredictability for the opposition's defense. After making the pass, 01 makes a "Flare-Cut" off of the "Flare-Screen" from the new "Weakside Wing" (03 in this diagram).

This diagram has 01 make the (01-02) "Wing Pass," with 04 remaining at his "Mid-Post" on the Block and 05 making the "High Post Flash Cut" to the new ballside of the court. If "Inside Shots" are not taken by 04 or 05 and perimeter shots are not taken by 02, 01 or 03; the "HIGH-POST/LOW-POST" Spot-ups are filled. The designated continuity offense could then begin in a seamless and instant manner. See Diagram 11.27

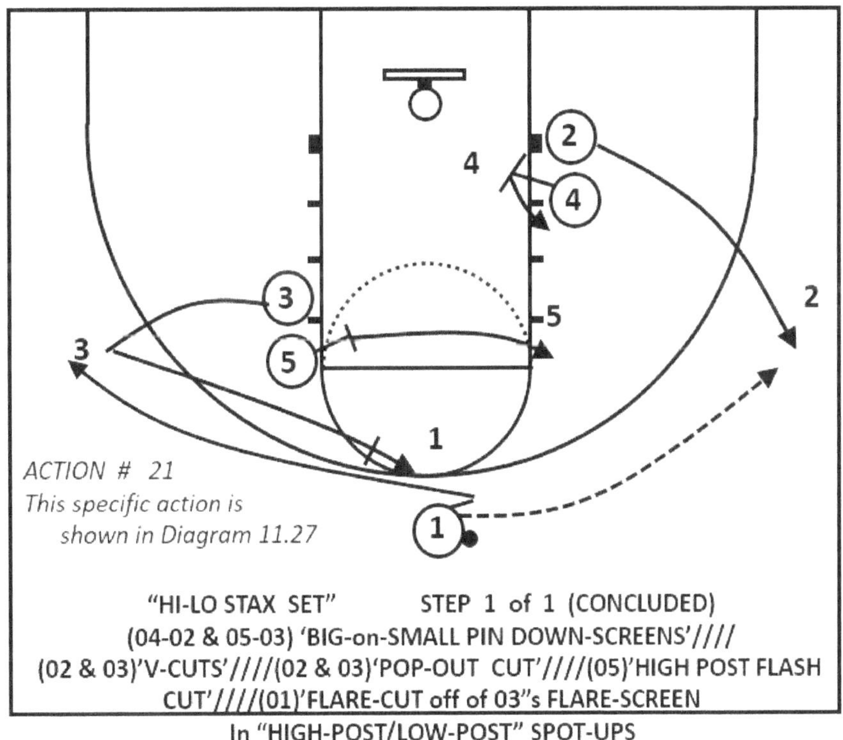

Diagram 11.27

Diagram 11.28 demonstrates the first step of Action # 22 out of "1-DOWN" Set. 01 makes the "Reverse Pass" to 02 and immediately 04 makes an "Iso Duck-In Cut" into the middle of the lane while 03 and 04 first make a "Fake Backdoor Cuts" before popping out to the FT Line extended. See Diagram 11.28

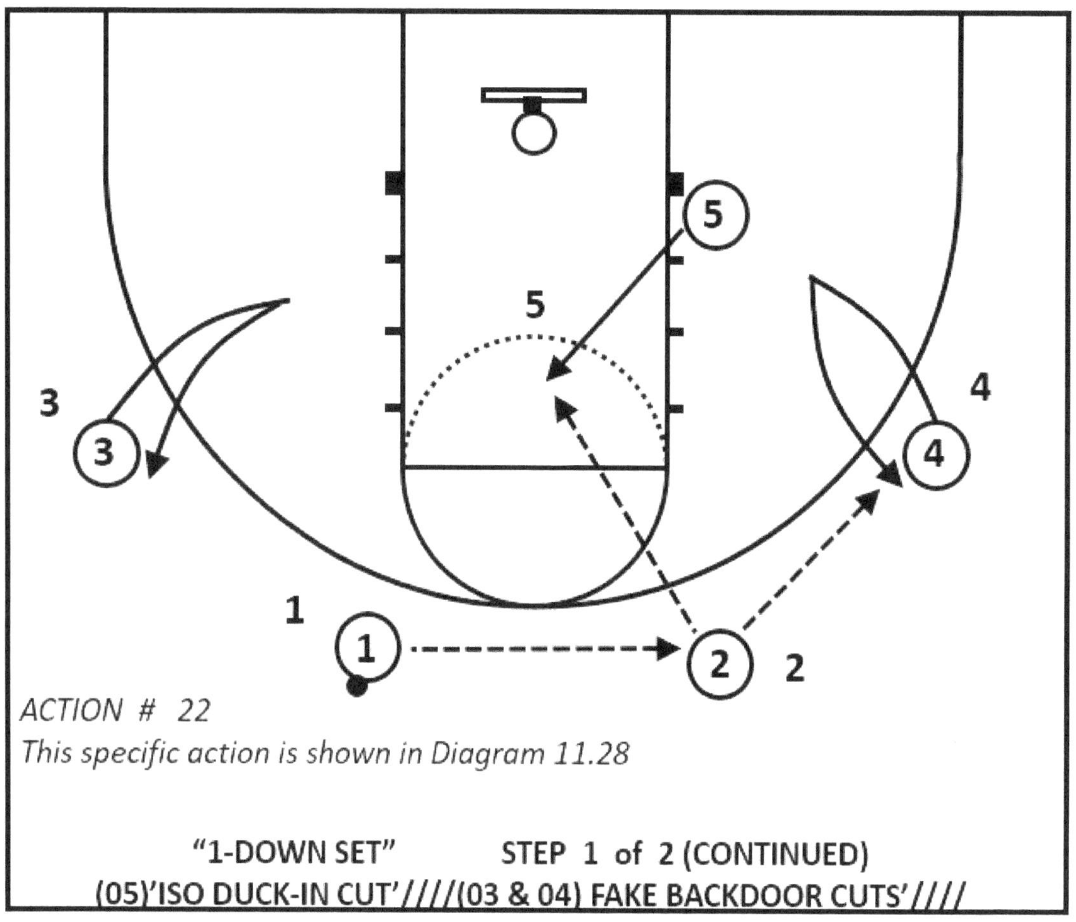

Diagram 11.28

Diagram 11.29 shows 02 turning down the pass to 05 and receiving the 04-02 "Big-on-Small Ball-Screen" dribbling to the "Wing" area. As 02 dribble-scrapes off of 04's outside left shoulder, 01 sets his defender up before then scraping off of 05's left shoulder on his "Big-on-Small Shuffle Back-Screen" and making a "Shuffle Cut" to the new "Ballside Block." To occupy any potential helpside defense, 03 "V-Cuts" his defender before then making a "Replacement Cut & Fill" to the now vacant "Weakside Slot." See Diagram 11.29

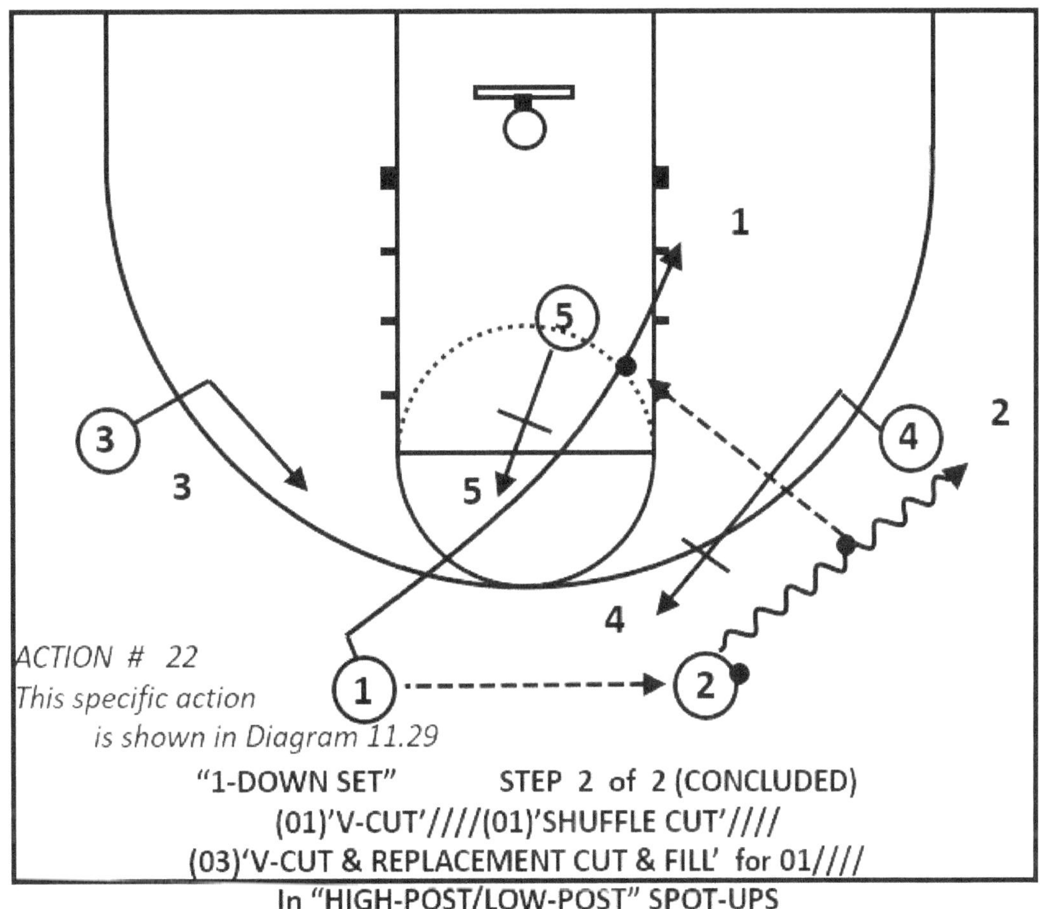

Diagram 11.29

Diagram 11.30 initiates the single step of this play that is being executed out of the "3-OVER" Set. After 02 makes his "Iverson Cut" off of the "Iverson Screens" set by 05 and 04, 01 makes the "Wing Pass" to 02. After "V-Cutting," 01 then makes a "Flare-Cut" off of 03's "Flare-Screen. After the pass is made to 02, 05 makes a "Diagonal Slash Cut" across the lane to the new "Ballside Block," while 04 then makes a "Lob Cut" to the new "Weakside Block."

If the designated shot is not taken, the "3-Out/2-In" Spot-Ups are filled and the designated continuity offense can seamlessly begin. See Diagram 11.30

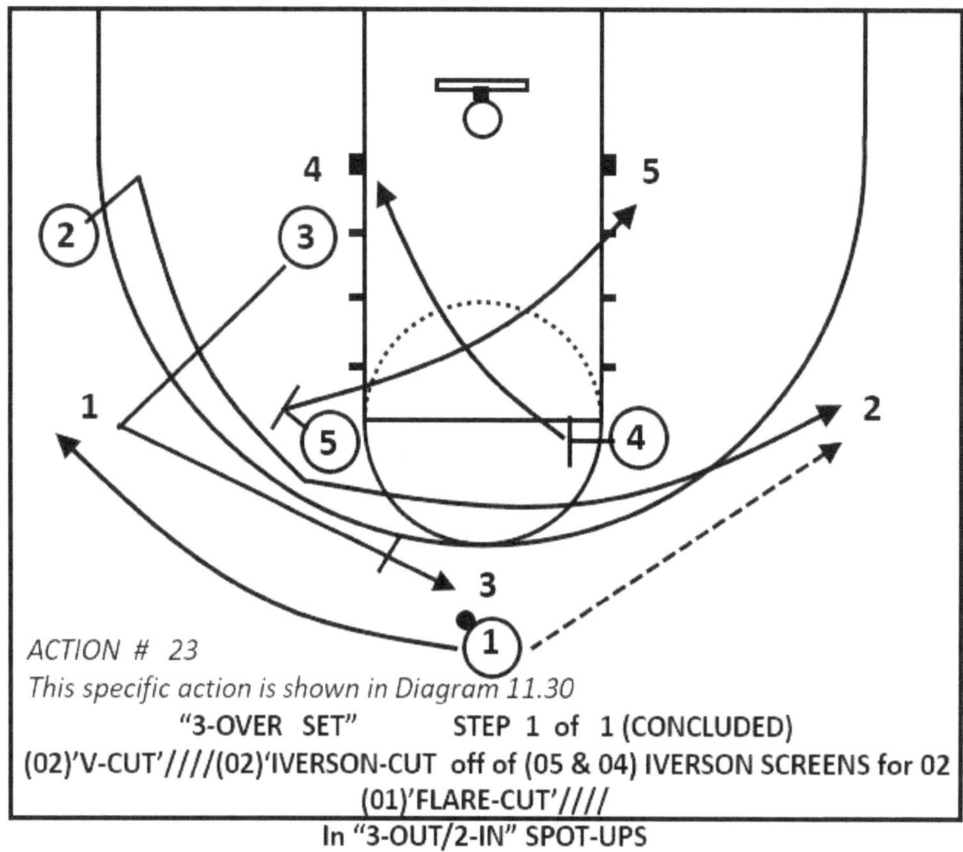

Diagram 11.30

The "HORNS" Set is shown again to show the entire play in Diagram 11.31. 05 is the designated offensive "Big" that sets his defender up with a "V-Cut" before then making his "Barkley Cut" off of 04's "Barkley Screen" After making the pass to 05 on the right wing, 03 breaks up to set his "Big-on-Small Flare-Screen" for 01 to use to make his "Flare-Cut" to the new weakside "Wing" area.

At the same time, 02 makes a "V-Cut" towards 05 and then makes a hard "Backdoor Cut" to the basket. If 02 does not receive the 05-02 Pass, 02 then stops his cut to then make an "Iso Post-Up" on the new "Ballside Block." With 04 remaining on the new "Ballside High Post," the "High-Post/Low-Post" Spot-Ups are filled for the designated continuity offense to immediately begin to maintain its attack on the opposition's defense. See Diagram 11.31

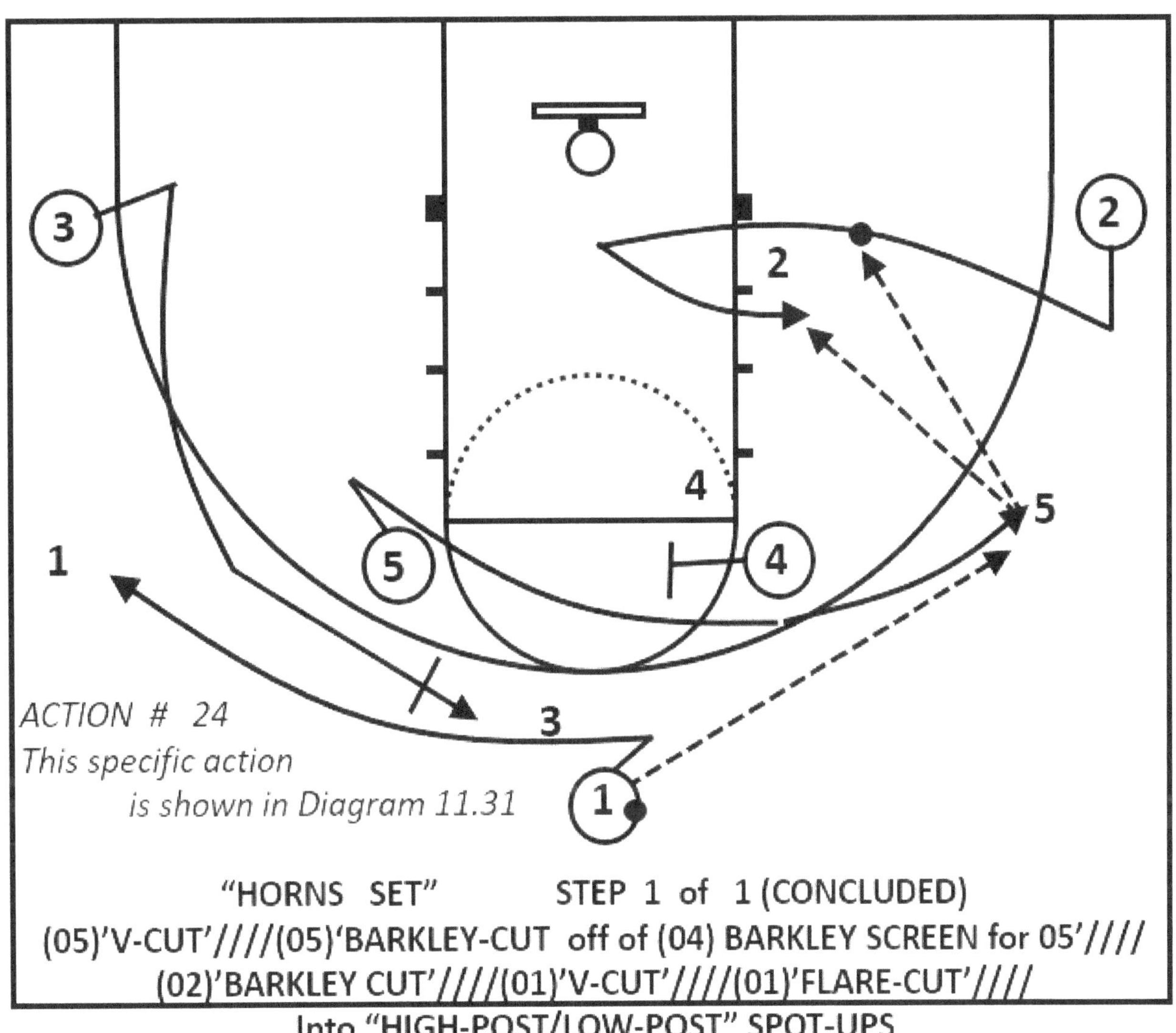

Diagram 11.31

Action # 25 is illustrated in Diagram 11.32 with two steps of offensive action. The action begins with a "Sideline Out-of-Bounds" Play. 02 initiates the action with a "Zipper Cut" up the lane to the "Ballside Slot. 04 immediately makes a "Diagonal Slash Cut" to the new "Ballside Block," while 03 makes a "Lift Cut" to the FT Line extended. See Diagram 11.32

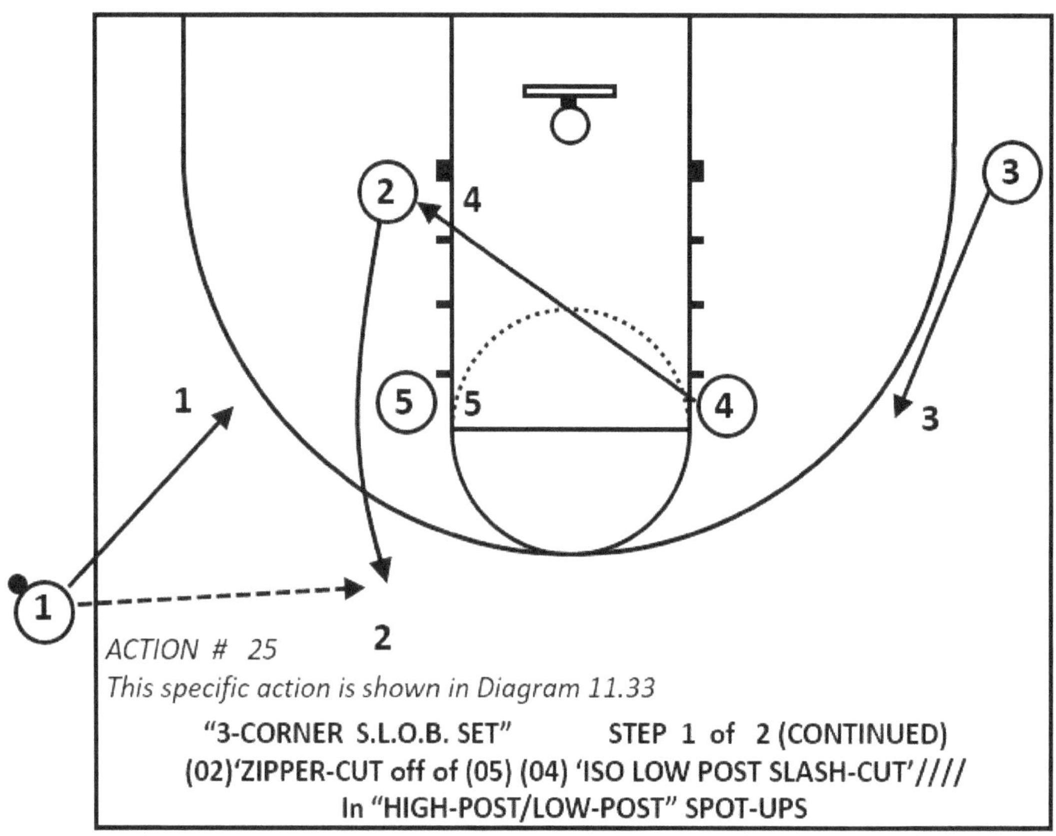

Diagram 11.32

Diagram 11.33 shows the action when no shots are taken and 02 elects to dribble the ball across the top of the key. 03 steps up to set his "Ball-Screen" for 02 to continue the dribble to the FT Line extended. After screening for 02, 01 steps up to set a "Small-on-Big (Flare-)Screen the (Ball-)Screener" for 03 to then execute his "Flare-Cut" (off of 01's outside right shoulder.) Also during the dribble, 05 makes his "Diagonal Slash-Cut" from the High Post area to across the lane to the new "Ballside Mid-Post." At the same time, 04 makes his "V-Cut" by stepping towards the basket before then making his "High Post Flash Cut" across the lane to the new "Ballside High Post."

After inbounding the ball, 01 steps inbounds to the FT Line extended, putting all five players into the "High-Post/Low-Post" Spot-Ups, 05 at the "Low Post," 04 at the "High Post, 02 at the "Ballside Wing," 03 at the "Weakside Wing" and 01 (after slipping his "Flare-Screen") ending up at the top of the key. This will allow this SLOB Play to easily and seamlessly flow into the designated continuity offense. See Diagram 11.33

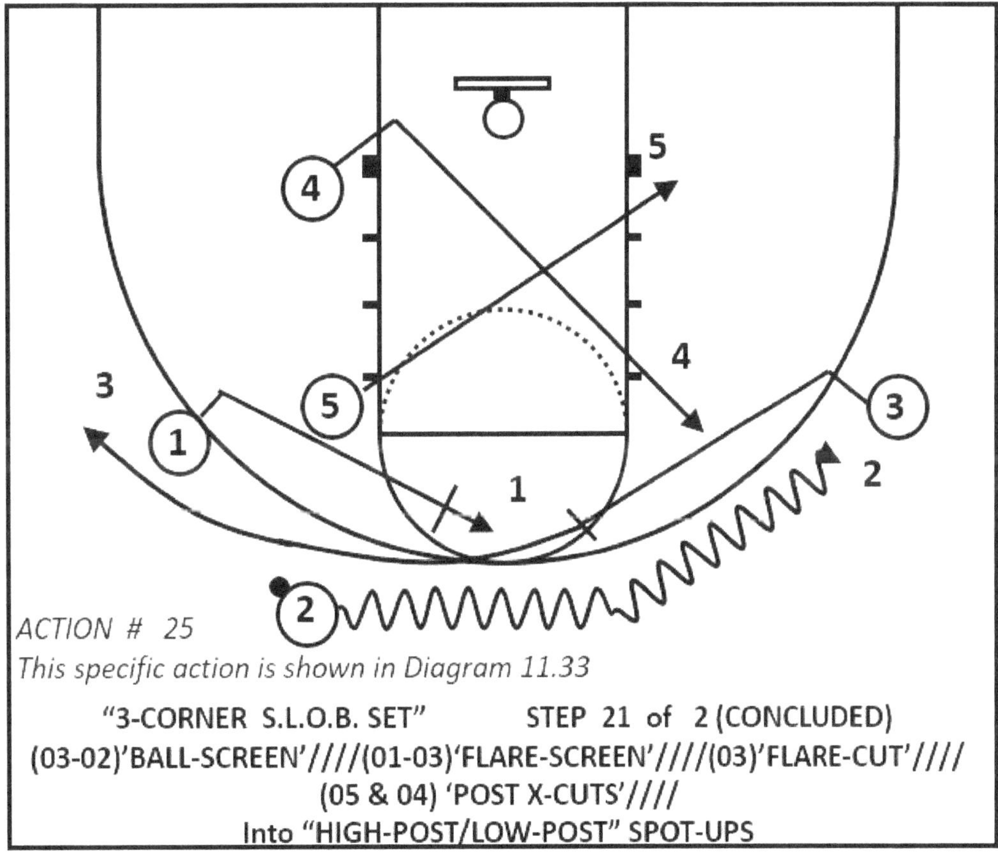

Diagram 11.33

Diagram 11.34 demonstrates a "Baseline Out-of-Bounds Play" with 01 taking the ball out-of-bounds from underneath the basket. 02 starts to break up away from the ball before then reversing directions and making a hard "Backdoor Cut" to the basket, through the lane and eventually out to the opposite side's "Deep Corner.

At the same time, 05 steps up to set a "Big-on-Small Flare-Screen" for 03 to "Flare Cut" towards the "Ballside Deep Corner." 03 must first make a strong "V-Cut" to influence his defender in the opposite direction from 05.

After 05 sets the screen for 03, 04 then breaks up to set a "(Back-)Screen the (Flare-)Screener for 05 to cut towards the "High Post" diagonally opposite of 01, the "Trigger." See Diagram 11.34

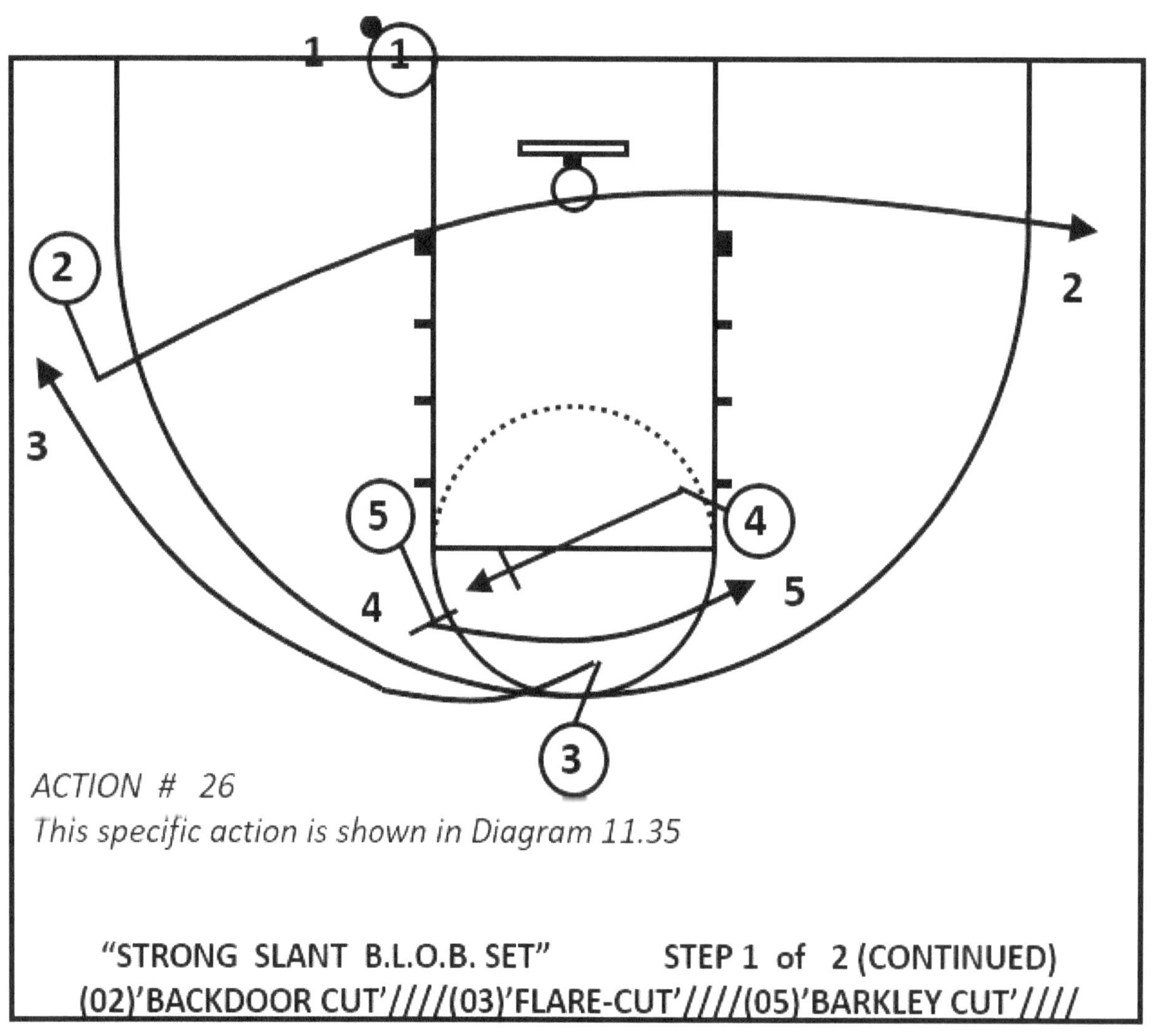

Diagram 11.34

Diagram 11.35 illustrates the last step of the BLOB with 01 "triggering" the ball inbounds to 03. (03 should then make an "Up Pass" to 04, who quickly swings the ball over to the inverted 05 on the 04-05 "Reverse Pass."

As the ball is in the air from 04 to 05, 01 steps inbounds to then set a "Small-on-Big Chin Back-Screen for 04 to make his "Chin Cut" through the lane and on to the new "Ballside Block. If shots are not taken, the "4-Out/1-In" Spot-Ups are filled for the third and final phase of this out-of-bounds play—the specific continuity offense. See Diagram 11.35

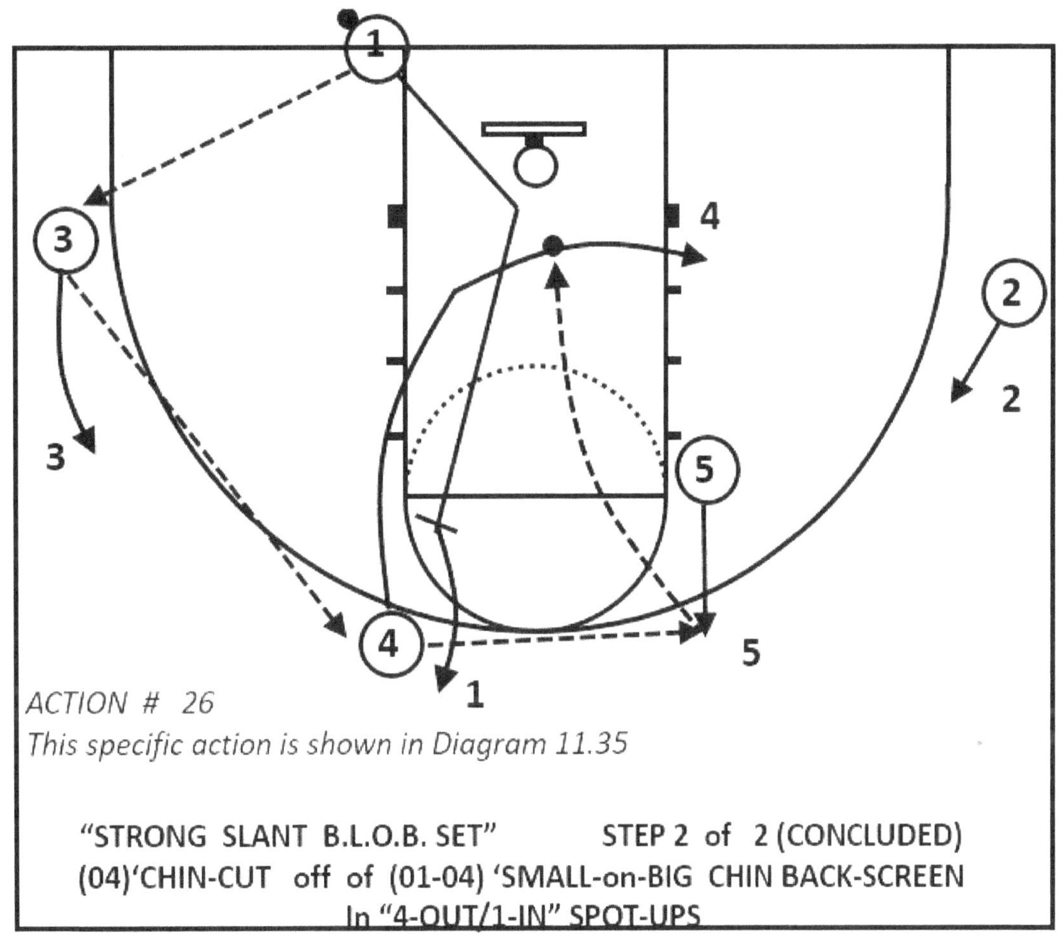

Diagram 11.35

Demonstrated in Diagram 11.36 is Action # 27 which shows the full play/entry that is executed out of the "5-TIGHT" Set. While 01 has the option of dribbling towards either "Slot" location, he has chosen the right side of the floor. At the same time, 05 pops out to the opposite "Slot" location and 02 breaks out as if to receive the ball on a 01-02 DHO. Instead, 01 reverses the ball to 05 and 04 starts his break out as if to set a "Chin Back-Screen." Instead, 04 breaks his route and executes a "Ghost Chin Back-Screen" and actually becomes the player to make the actual "Chin Cut." With all four teammates outside of the arc and above the FT Line extended, 04's cut diagonally across the lane to the opposite side of the lane becomes an "Isolated Chin Cut" after setting the so-called "Ghost Chin Screen."

After 05 receives the "Reverse Pass," both 03 and 01 make "Flare-Cuts" to their respective "Deep Corners" to flatten and stretch the defense. Both could be potential passers to help deliver the ball to 04. This action places all players in the "4-Out/1-In" Spot-Ups for the designated continuity offense to smoothly begin. See Diagram 11.36

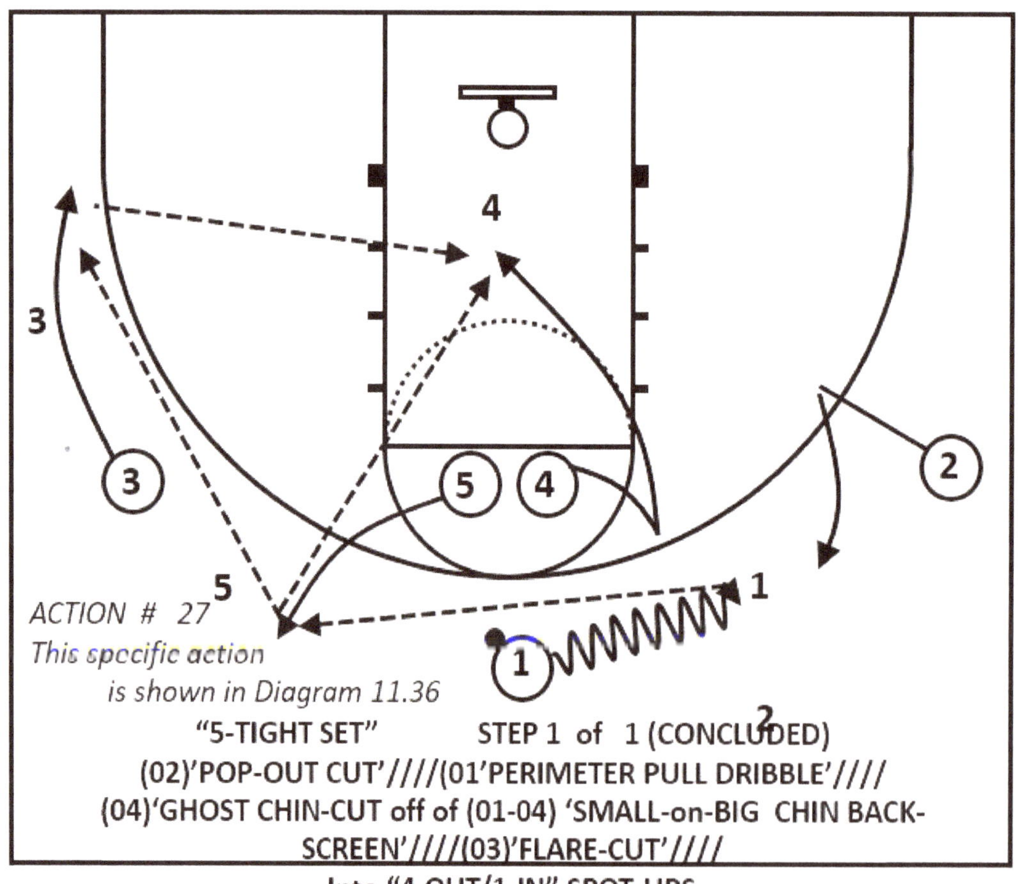

Diagram 11.36

Diagram 11.37 shows the initial part of a play/entry executed out of the "3-DOWN" Set. 01 starts with "dribble-scraping" off of the top right shoulder of 04 while 04 then slips his ball-screen. This action is frequently called "Pick and Pop" and is simply making a short "Flare-Cut" or slip after the ball-screen. At the same time that 01 breaks contact with 04, 05 makes a strong and aggressive "Iso Duck-In Cut" while 03 and 02 make their respective "Lift Cuts," occupying their perimeter defenders and keeping them away from attempting to help his isolated defender. In addition, 01 and 04 have kept their defenders outside of the arc giving 05 even more of an isolated and position advantage over X5. See Diagram 11.37

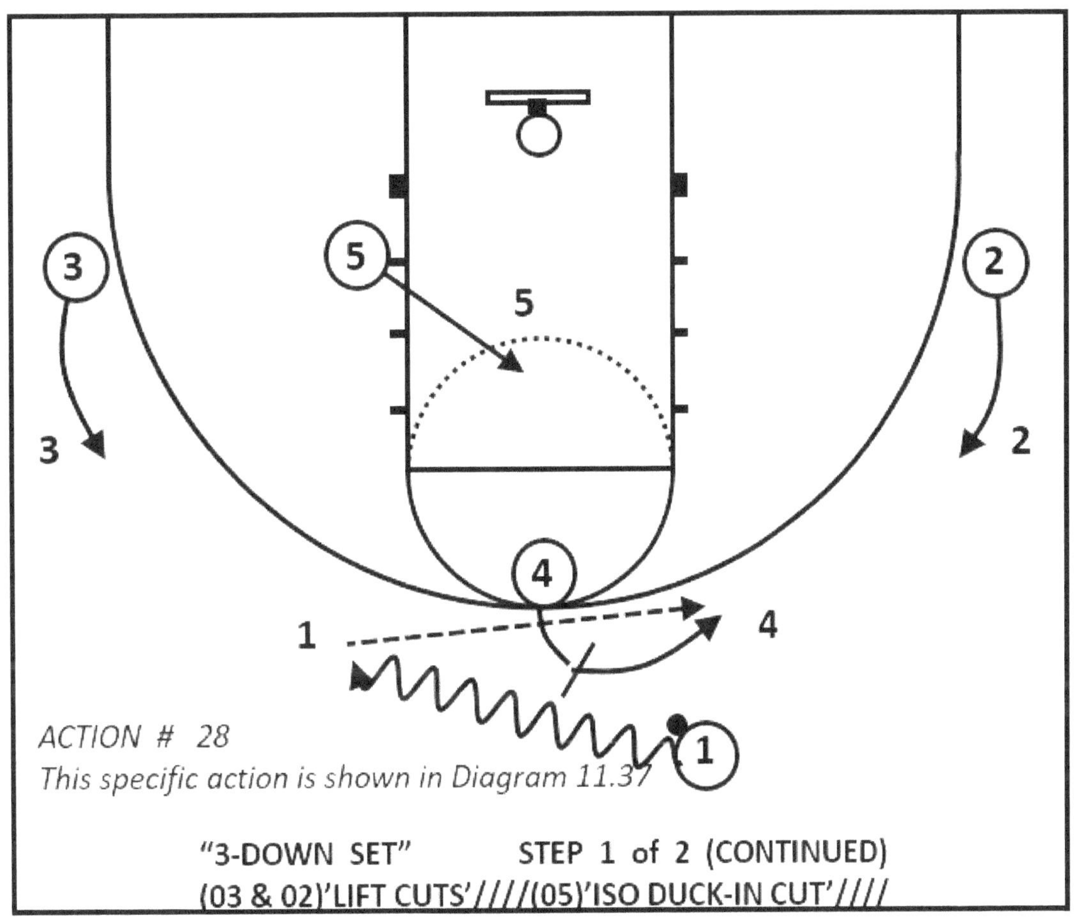

Diagram 11.37

Diagram 11.38 shows the conclusion of the play that was started in the previous diagram. When 04 receives the 01-04 "Reverse Pass" and turns down passes to 05, 01 and 03; he then starts his dribble towards 02 for 02 to receive the DHO.

When 05 does not receive the pass from 01 or 02, he empties out of the lane away from 04 and the ball. After giving up the ball to 02, 04 makes a "Rim-Run" Cut to the basket with a front pivot off of his lower left foot. On the opposite side of the ball, 05 and 01 meet near the "Weakside Elbow" area to converge on 03's defender to set a Stagger-Screen for 03 to use to break up to the new "Weakside Slot" for an open '3 Pt.' shot. 03's cut off of 01's outside left shoulder is preceded (obviously) by his own "V-Cut" to set his defender up, force him to turn his head before the defender gets "stagger-screened." 02 has a primary interior target, 04 and a primary perimeter target in 03. If shots are not taken, the players have repositioned themselves into the proper "4-Out/1-In" Spot-Ups for the specific designated continuity offense to seamlessly and effortlessly begin. See Diagram 11.38

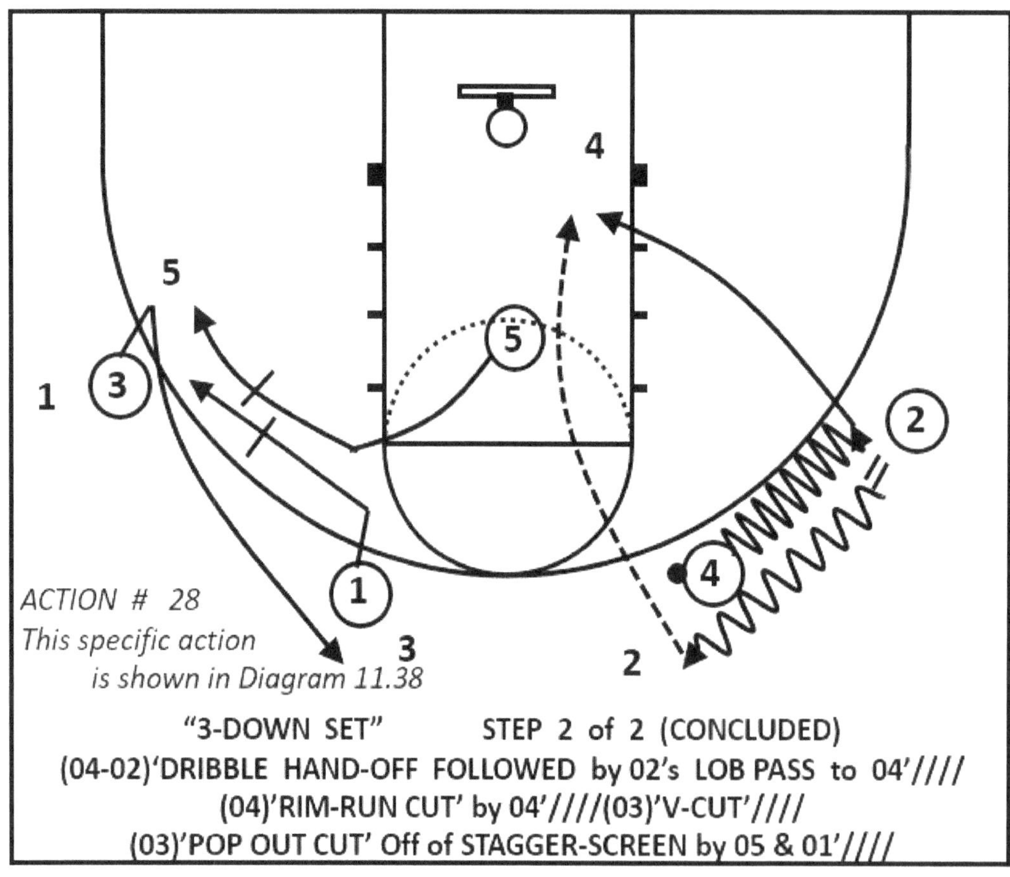

Diagram 11.38

The entire play shown in Diagram 11.39 and labelled as Action 29 begins with 01 dribbling the ball towards 02, with 05 and 04 breaking across to allow 03 to make a "Shuffle-Cut" off of the "Big-on-Small Staggered Back-Screen." After the Stagger-Screen, 05 slips to the slightly lower new "Weakside Wing" and 04 slips his screen by stepping out to the new "Weakside Slot."

After handing the ball off to 02 on the DHO, 01 then slips the hand-off to make "Flare-Cut" to the new "Ballside Deep Corner." 01 could make the "Inside Pass" to 03 or 02 could make passes to any of the open teammates. If shots are not created, the offense is in the proper "4-Out/1-In" Spot-Ups for that particular continuity offense to instantly begin. See Diagram 11.39

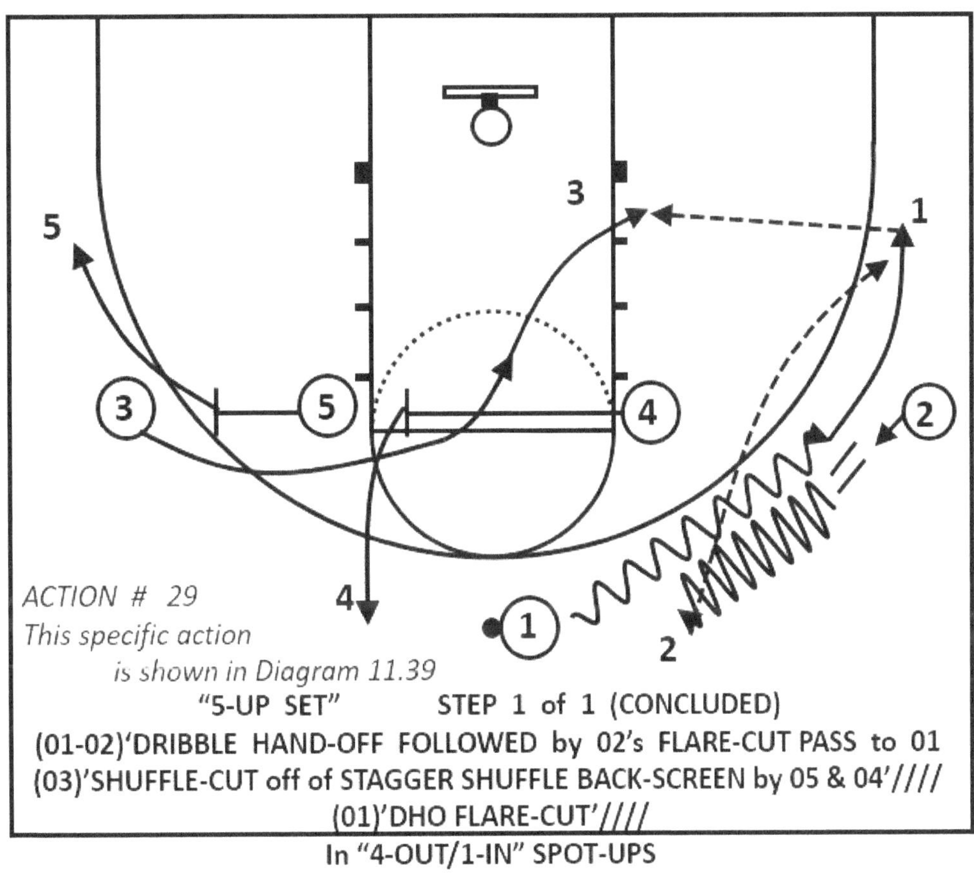

Diagram 11.39

Diagrams 11.40 and 11.41 demonstrate a play in its entirety that is called Action 30. It is executed out of an alignment that is called the"5-TIGHT" Set. With this alignment being a perfectly symmetrical alignment, each play could be executed towards either side of the floor. But in this case, 01 chose to dribble directly at 03 on the left side of the floor. This keys 05 to set a "Brush Screen" for 04 to make his "Brush Cut" into the Dotted Circle towards the basket. 02 makes a "Pop-Out Cut" to the new "Weakside Slot." After screening, 05 clears out to make an inverted "Replacement Fill Cut" to the FT Line extended on the newly defined weakside of the floor. See Diagram 11.40

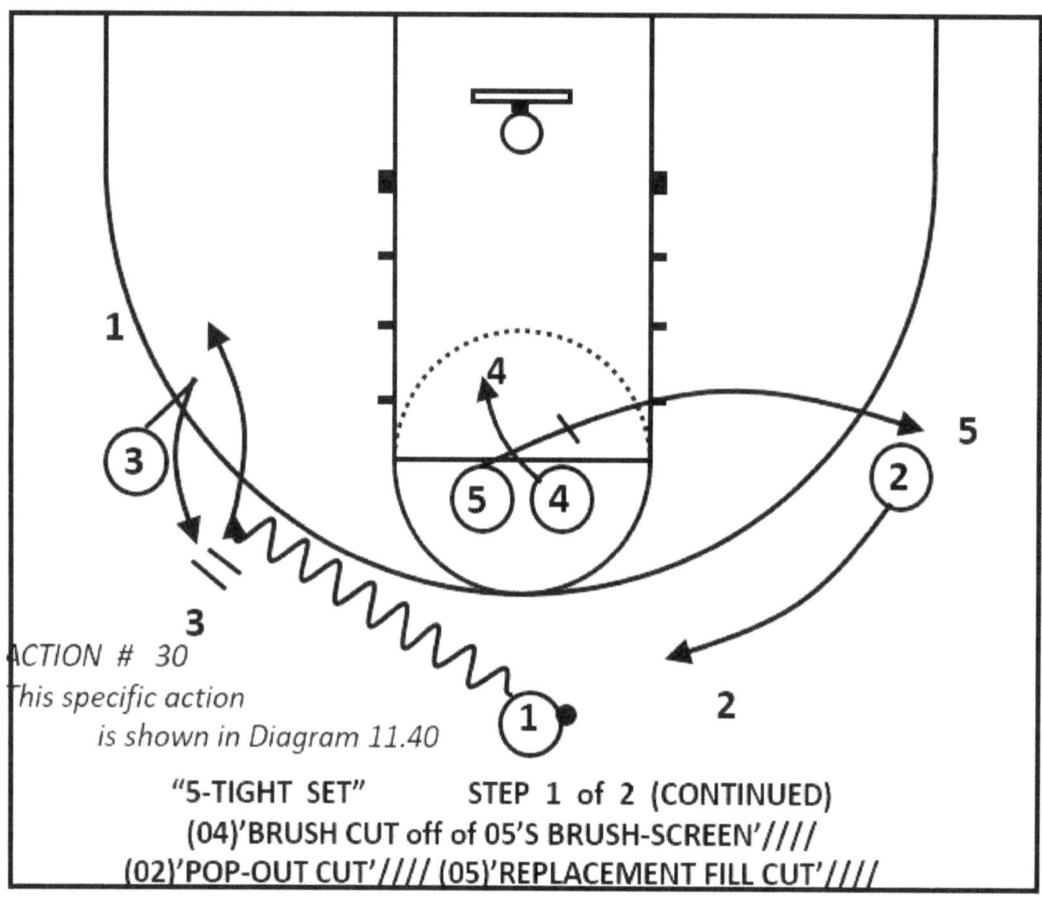

Diagram 11.40

Diagram 11.41 shows both 01 and 03 turning down the quick pass to 04 on his "Brush Cut" and 03 taking the DHO to dribble up towards the new "Ballside Slot with 01 giving up the ball and then making a "Flare-Cut." 03 then makes a "Reverse Pass" to 02 who then dribbles towards 05 on the opposite wing area and exchanges with 01. As 02 approaches 05, 02, and 05 both fake the DHO and 04 curls around off of 04's right shoulder to make a "Lob Cut" to the basket. 02 looks to make the "Lob Pass" to 05 or passes to 04, a "Reverse Pass" to 01 or a "Skip Pass" to 03. Regardless, the "4-Out1-In" Spot-Ups are filled and the designated continuity offense should easily be ready to begin and maintain the attack on the opposition. See Diagram 11.41

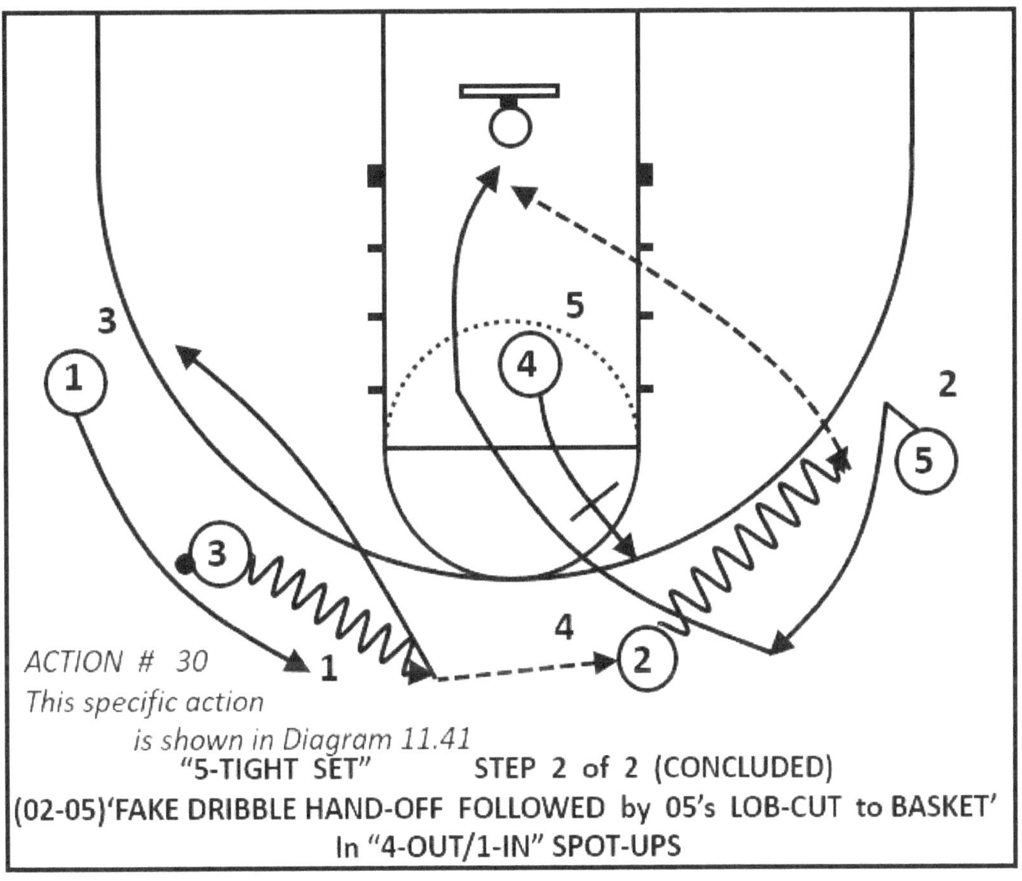

Diagram 11.41

Action 31 is shown as a two-step play executed out of the "HI-LO STAX" (but with cuts by the same players starting from different locations, could be run from the "5-Up" Set. As 01 approaches the top of the key on the dribble, 04 fakes a pin-screen for 02 and makes an "Inverted Pop-Out Cut" to the FT Line extended on his initial side of the floor. On the opposite side, 05 actually does make a "Big-on-Small Pin Down-Screen" for 03 to make a "Pop-Out Cut" to the FT Line extended on the left side of the offense. 03 must make a convincing "V-Cut" before scraping off of 05's lower left shoulder.

01 makes the "Wing Pass" to 04 and starts to follow his pass with his own "V-Cut." After two to three steps, he changes direction to rub his defender off of 05 outside right shoulder near the actual top of the key. From there, 01 continues with his "Inverted Lob Cut" to the basket. 05 slips his screen and makes a "Replacement Fill Cut" at the top of the key.

This action has pulled presumably the three defensive "Bigs" out above or near the FT Line extend and past the arc, giving 01 the space and opportunity to use his "position advantage." See Diagram 11.42

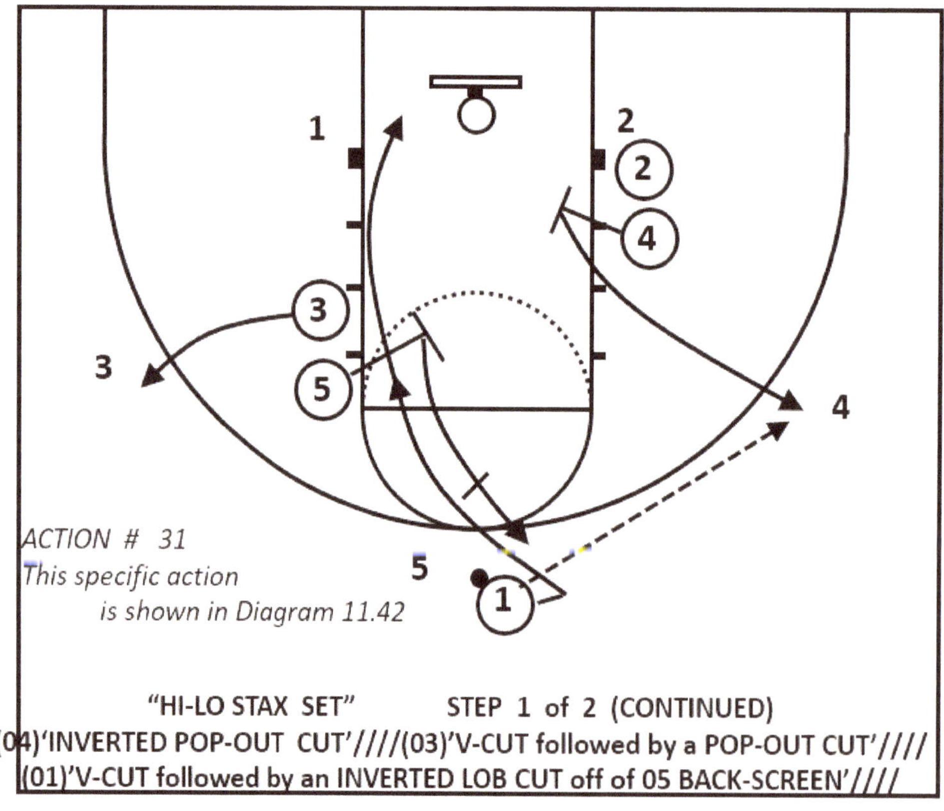

Diagram 11.42

Diagram 11.43 shows 04 turning down the "Lob Pass" to 01 and to 02 posted up on the new "Ballside Mid-Post." Instead, 04 reverses the ball to 05, inverted at the top of the key. 05 quickly reverses the ball to 03 on the opposite side of the floor. 05 then steps towards the ball to actually "V-Cut" before then setting a "Big-on-Small Diagonal Down-Screen" for 02. During this time, 02 walks his defender under the basket before changing directions to scrape off of 05's right shoulder. We describe this action as "sticking your head under the basket," and then "shoulder-scraping off of 05" while immediately "getting your feet and hands ready" for the 03-02 "Reverse Pass." While this makes 02 a viable offensive scoring threat, it also helps 01 to further isolate his perimeter-type defender on his "position advantaged" post-up.

If shots are not taken, the "3-Out/2-In" Spot-Ups are filled for the proper continuity offense to fluidly and immediately begin its last phase of the offensive attack. See Diagram 11.43

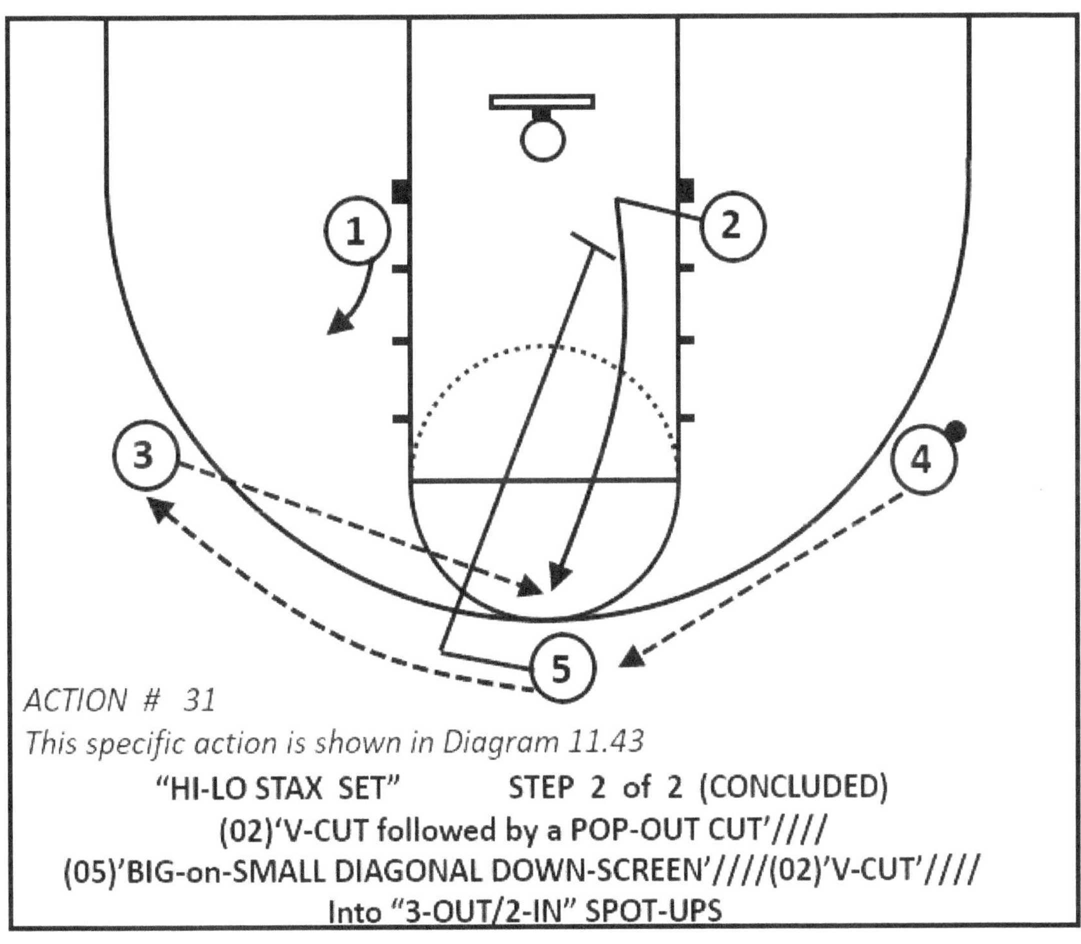

Diagram 11.43

Diagram 11.44 illustrates a one-step play in its entirety out of the "2-DOWN FLAT" Set with 02 making a "V-Cut" towards the baseline before "lifting" to the FT Line extended. At the same time, 04 makes a "Duck-In Cut" before then breaking to the "High Post" area on his side of the ball.

01 makes the "Wing Pass" to 02 before then making a "V-Cut" towards the ball and then breaking and scraping off of 05's outside right shoulder to make a "Lob Cut" to the basket. After setting the "Big-on-Small Back-Screen" for 01, 05 makes a "Replacement Fill Cut" to replace 01 at the top of the key.

If 02 does not hit 01 on the "Inverted Lob Cut," 04 makes a "Post Dive Cut" back to the vacant "Ballside Block." If "Inside Passes" are not made to either 01 or 04, the remaining three perimeter spots are filled for the "3-Out/2-In" Spot-Ups are properly filled. This allows for a smooth and instant transition from the end of the play to the very beginning of the continuity offense to be able to continuously be executed. See Diagram 11.44

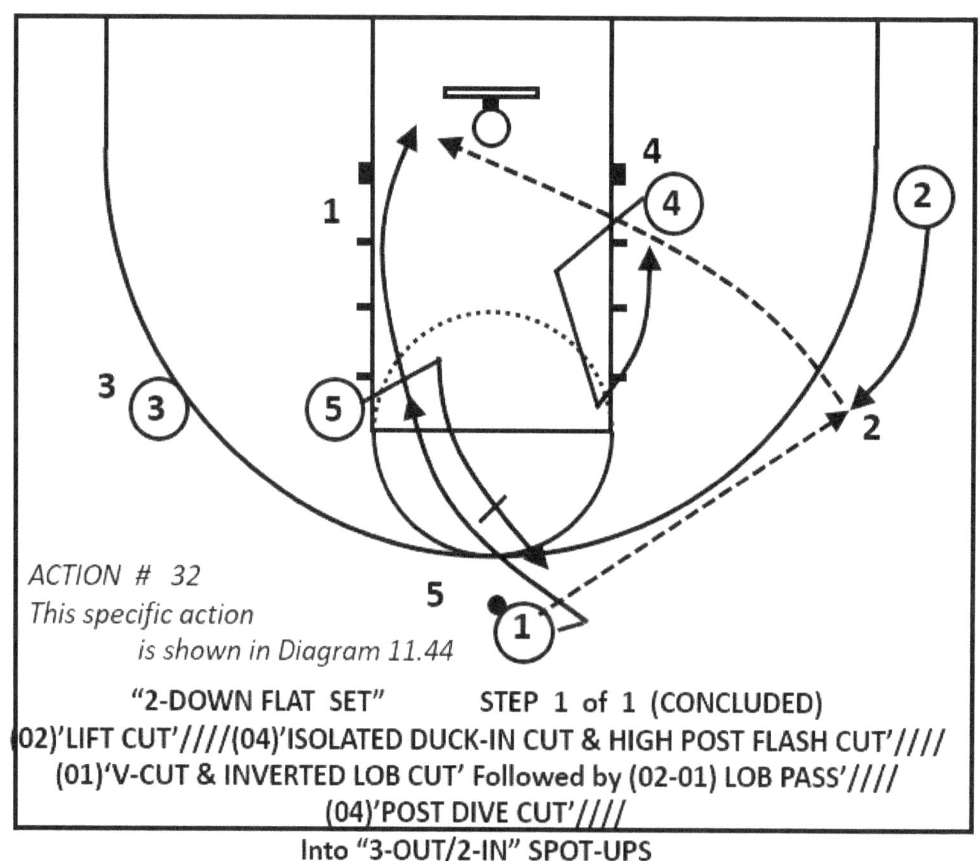

Diagram 11.44

Out of the "HI-LO STAX" Set, this two-step play starts in Diagram 11.45 with 01 "perimeter pull dribbling" towards the vacant "Wing" area on the left side of the floor. As 01 makes his dribble, 03 sets his "Small-on-Big Back-Screen" for 05 to first set his defender up before then scraping off of 03's outside right shoulder and make his "Lob Cut" to the basket.

To further isolate X5, 04 has set a "Big-on-Small Pin Down-Screen" for 02 to use when he makes his "Pop-Out Cut" to the newly declared "Weakside Wing."

01 looks to make the "Lob Pass" to 05, a "Reverse Pass" to 03 or a "Skip Pass" to 02 on the opposite side of the floor. See Diagram 11.45

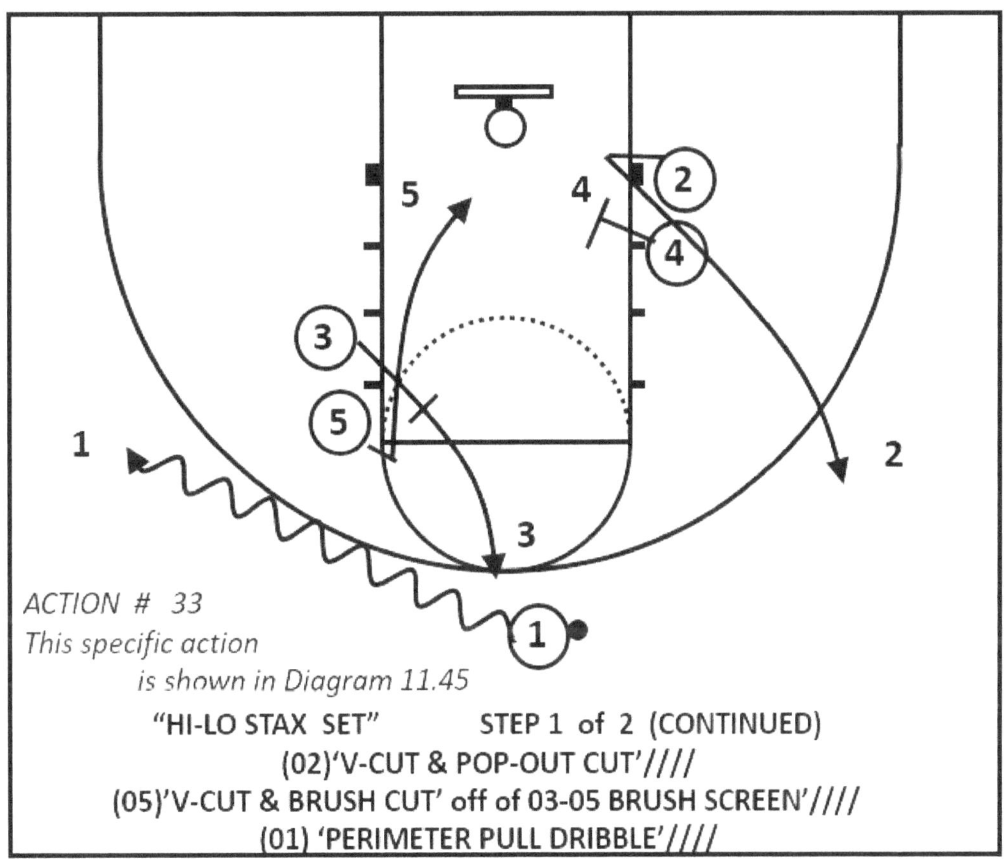

Diagram 11.45

Diagram 11.46 shows the continuation of this play that is called Action # 33. This diagram shows 01 electing to make the 01-03 "Reverse Pass" and 03 swinging the ball on over to 02. After making the pass, 03 elects to step over towards the ball (his own "V-Cut") before reversing the direction and cutting diagonally down to set a "Small-on-Big Diagonal Down-Screen" for 05 to use.

05 prepares for the screen by first setting his "V-Cut" with "sticking his head" under the basket before then "shoulder scraping" off of 03's outside left shoulder. 05 prepares for the pass by "getting his feet and hands ready" as he continues to the top of the key. This action not only attacks a post-type defender, presumably the opponent's biggest defender, by pulling his defender away from the basket and also giving 05 a wide open '3 Pt." shot opportunity. In addition, this action helps 04 to isolate his defender on the new "Ballside Block."

If shots are not taken, the "3-Out/2-In" Spot-Ups are filled for a designated continuity offense to fluidly and seamlessly begin. See Diagram 11.46

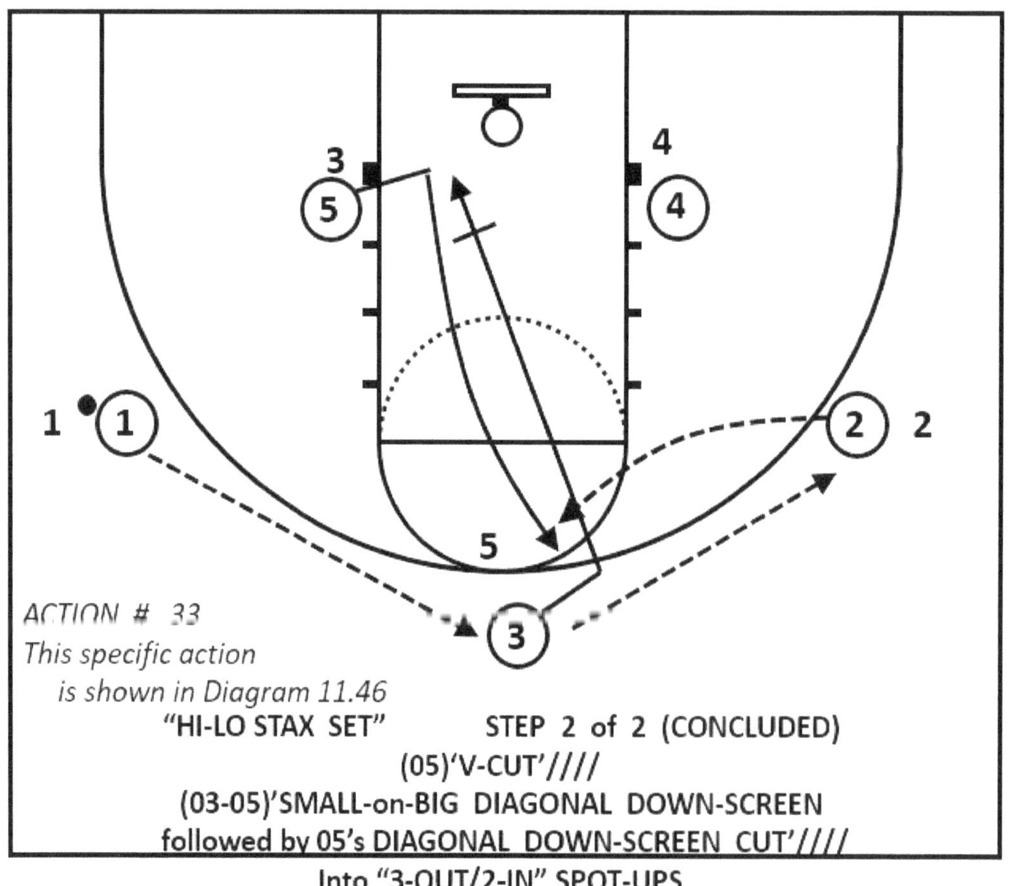

Diagram 11.46

Diagram 11.47 begins a two-step offensive play, called "Action # 34, that is executed out of the "3-UP" Set. As 01 brings the ball across the timeline, both 03 and 02 makes "V-Cuts" towards the basket before reversing their cuts to make the second cut—"Pop-Out Cuts" higher than the normal "Wing" areas and wider than the two "Slot" positions. 01 dribbles off of 05's top right shoulder towards 03. As 01 breaks contact with 04, 05 makes a "Slash Diagonal Cut" towards the new "Ballside Block. At the same time, 04 makes a front pivot off his lower foot to then go set a "Big-on-Small Pin Down-Screen for 02 (to scrape off of 04's outside shoulder) and to make a "Pop-Out Cut" to the new "Weakside Slot." After making his second screen for his second teammate, 04 slips down to the new "Weakside Deep Corner." See Diagram 11.47

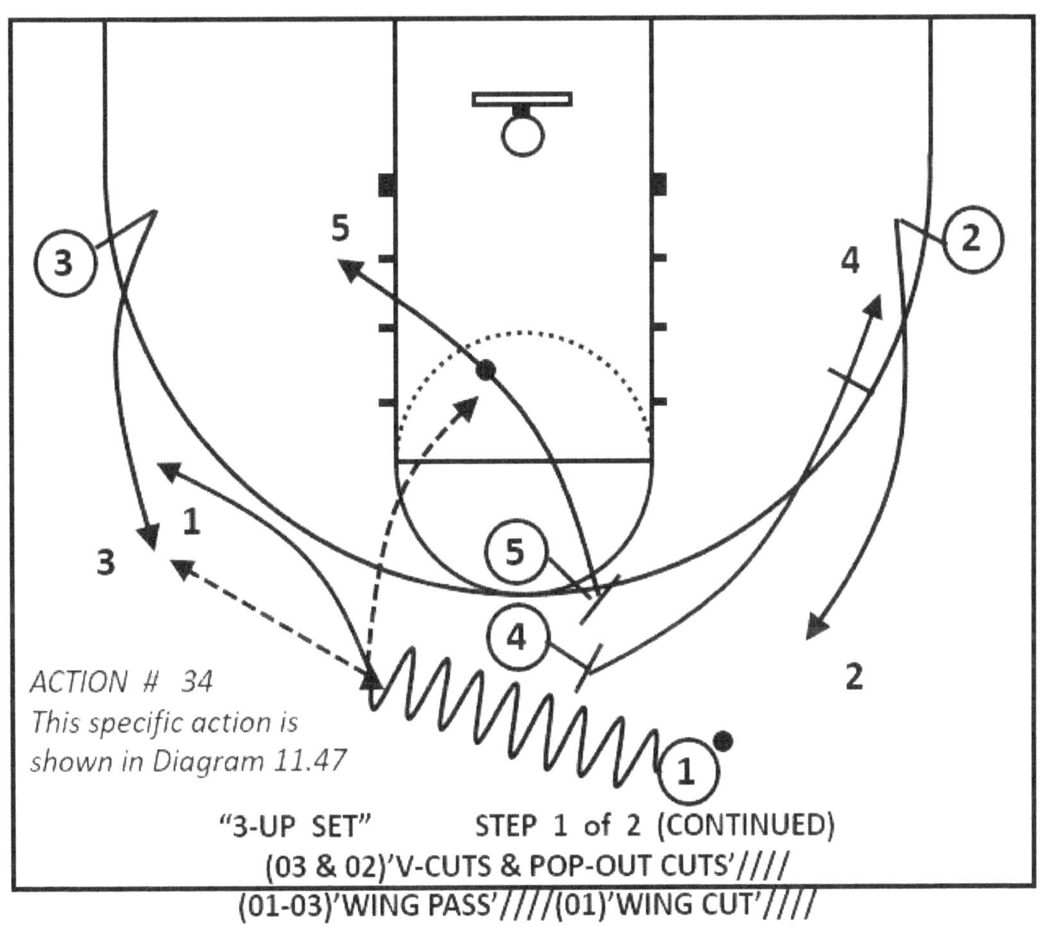

Diagram 11.47

The conclusion of this play (Action # 34) that begins with the previous diagram and ends in Diagram 11.48 has 03 make an immediate 03-02 "Reverse Pass" that triggers 05 to make an "Iso Duck-In Cut" into the "Dotted Circle" area. At the same time both 01 and 04 widen out to their respective sidelines and deep corner areas. This action horizontally and vertically further weakens the interior defense, allowing 05 to have more of an "isolation advantage" in a high percentage scoring area.

Still, if no shots are taken; the "4-Out/1-In" Spot-Ups are filled so that the proper designated continuity offense can immediately begin. See Diagram 11.48

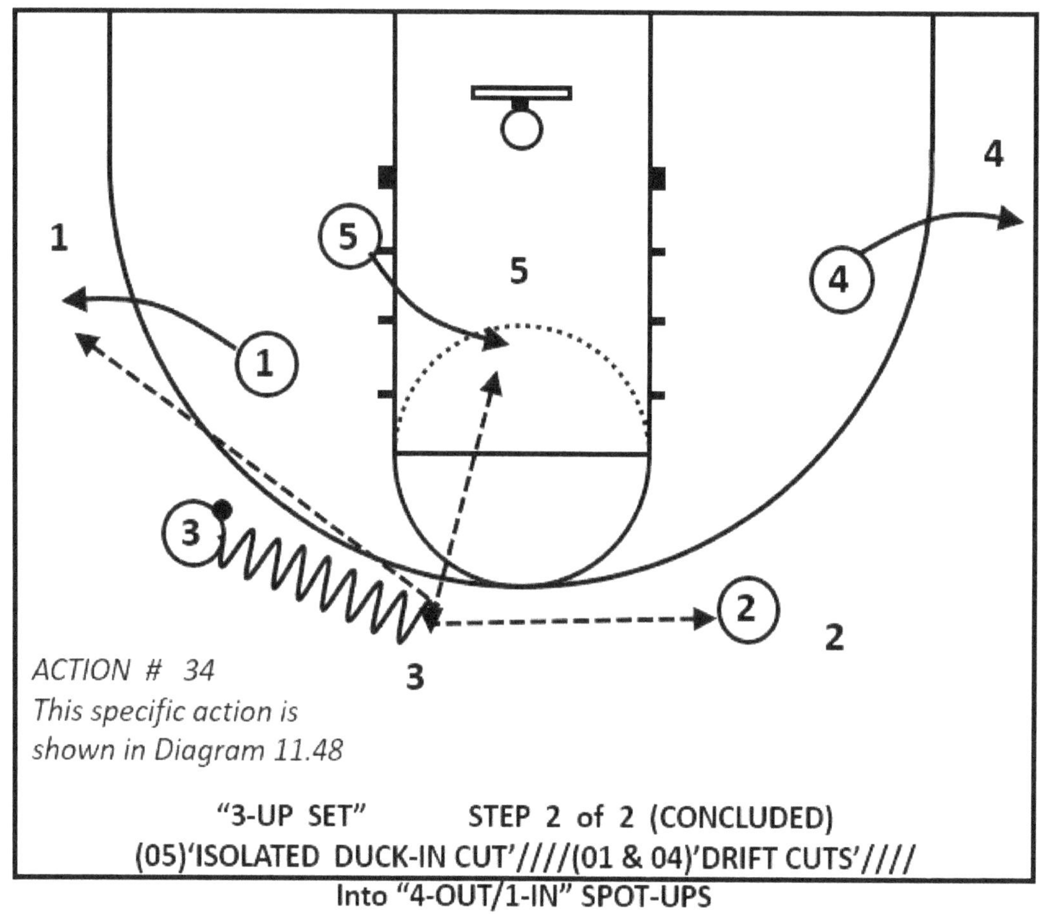

Diagram 11.48

Diagram 11.49 shows Action # 35, a one-step play, with 05 making an "Iso Duck-In Cut" while 01 has possession of the ball. After not receiving the pass from 01 or 02, 05 continues to then make a "Nail Cut" at the FT Line. 01 then makes a "Reverse Pass" to 02, where 02 then dribbles towards 04. 04 makes a "V-Cut" towards the basket before then breaking back towards 02 and the ball. If 02 does not make the pass to 04 on his "Fake Backdoor Cut" and 04 breaks back out; 04 then receives the 02-04 DHO.

After receiving the DHO, 04 starts dribbling out towards the near "Slot" and looks for 02 on his "Lob Cut." At the same time, 02 makes a "Lob Cut" to the basket. Also at the same time of this action, 03 steps up to set a "Big-on-Small Flare-Screen" for 01 to "shoulder scrape" off of 03's outside right shoulder on his "Flare-Cut" to the "Deep Corner" on his side of the floor. If shots are not taken by any of 04's teammates, the "4-Out/1-In" Spot-Ups are filled for the specific desired continuity offense to instantly begin. See Diagram 11.49

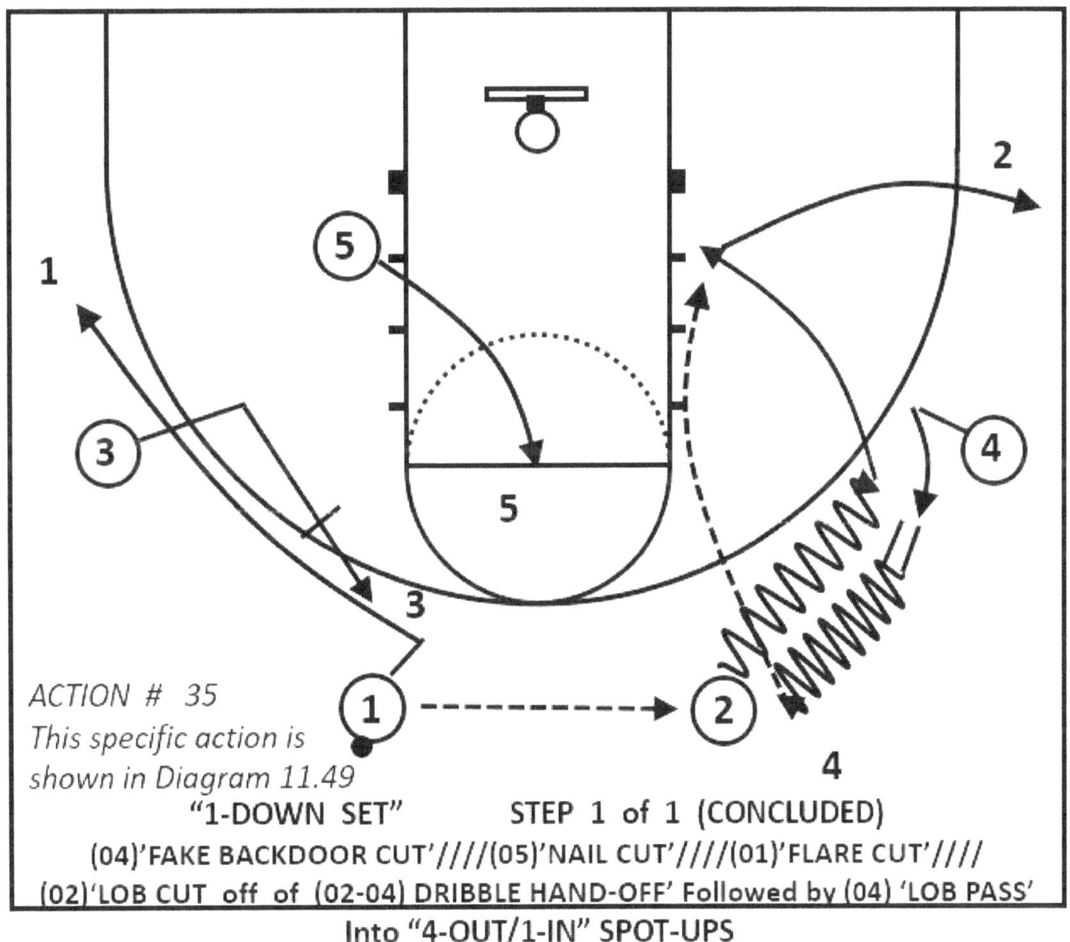

Diagram 11.49

Diagram 11.50 shows the beginning of this two-step play/entry with 01 bringing the ball across the timeline and then dribbling towards the "Slot" area on the right side of the floor. 05 makes a "Barkley Cut" off of 04's "Small-on-Big Barkley Screen" to end up on the "Wing" area on the opposite side of the floor. 03 makes his "Pop-Out Cut" diagonally to the newly declared "Weakside Wing" area on his side of the floor. At the same time, 02 makes a "V-Cut" before then making a "Pop-Out Cut" to the "Weakside Slot" opposite of 01's "Ballside Slot." See Diagram 11.50

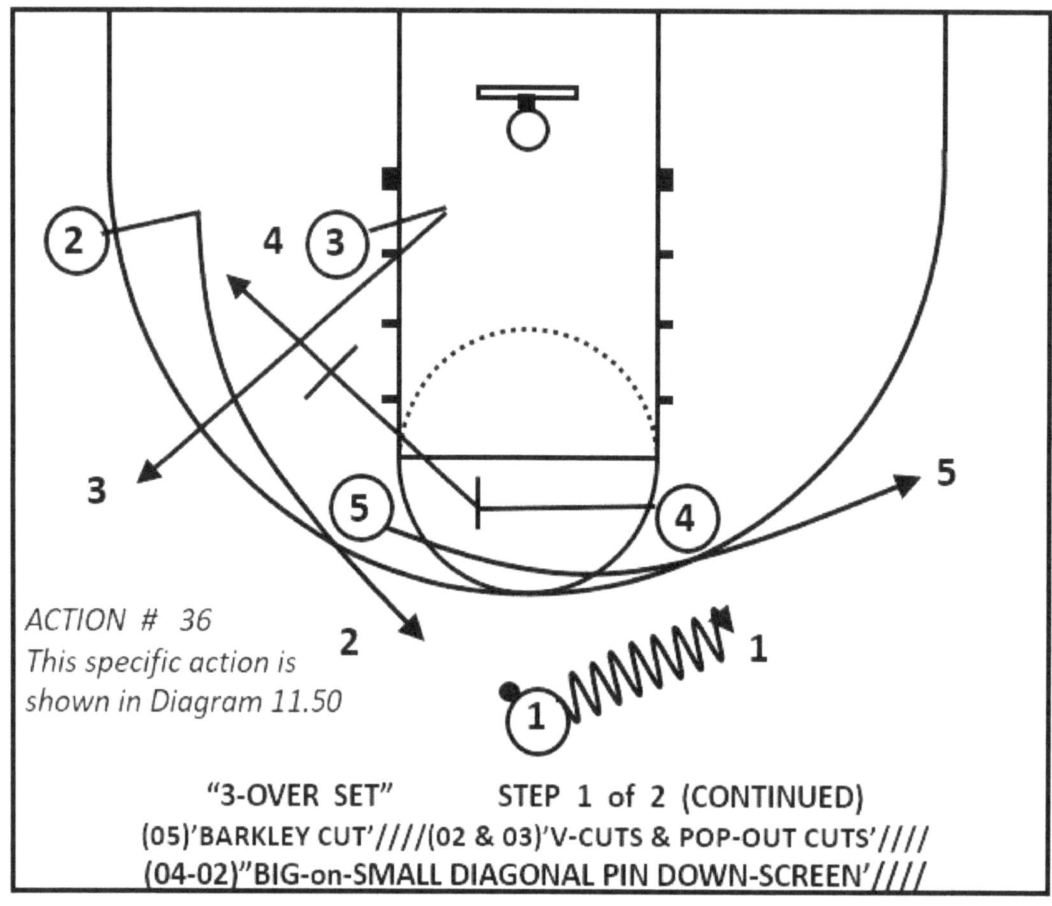

Diagram 11.50

Diagram 11.51 shows the second and final step of Action # 36 with 01 continuing his dribble towards 05 for a "Wing Pass," followed by a 05-01 return "Flip Pass." 05 then executes a "Rim-Run" to the basket while looking over the inside left shoulder for 01's Lob Pass." With 02 making a "Replacement & Fill Cut" to the top of the key and 03 and 04 making small "Drift Cuts" on the far sideline (to occupy their defenders and to further isolate X5).

If no shots are taken, 04 makes a "Post Dive" to fill the "3-Out/2-In" Spot-Ups for the next and final phase of the offense to smoothly begin—the continuity offense. See Diagram 11.51

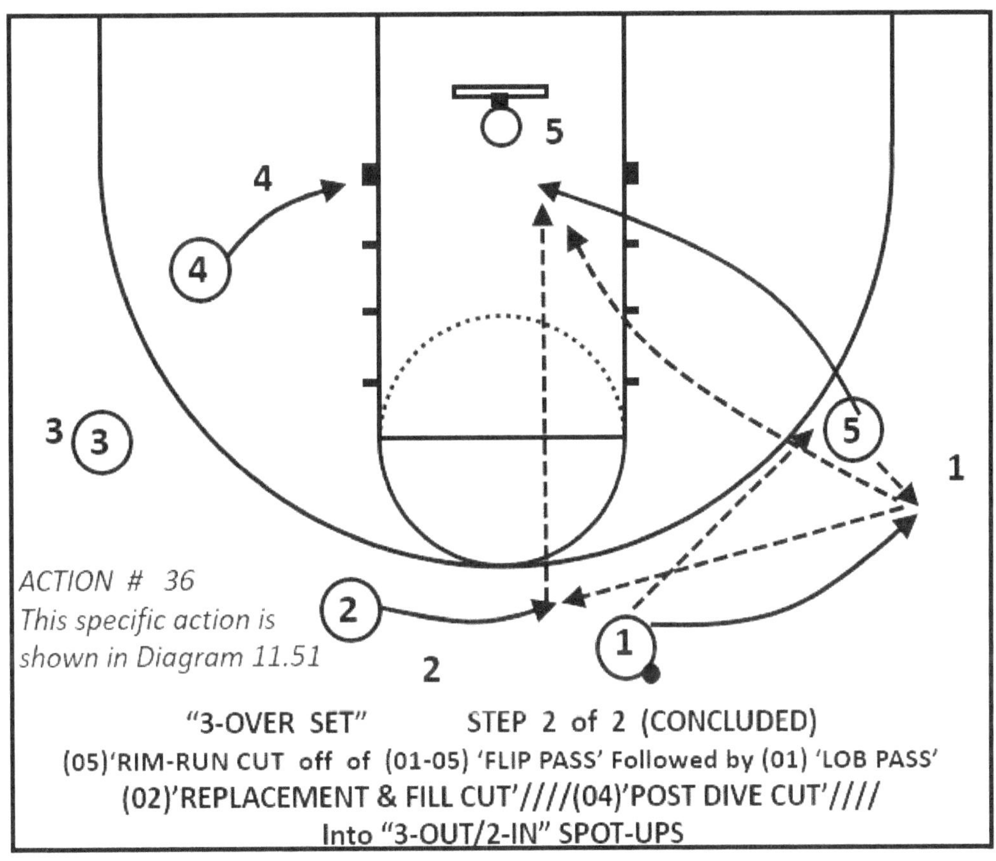

Diagram 11.51

Diagram 11.52 illustrates the initial step of Action # 37 that is started out of the "4-DOWN" Set. This alignment is symmetrically balanced so that any play could be executed towards either side of the floor. In this instance, it has been designated that 02 is the perimeter player to set the "Long Ball-Screen" for 01 to use as he dribbles towards the FT Line extended on the right side of the floor. After "dribble-scraping" off 02's outside left shoulder and halfway towards the "Wing" area, 04 makes a strong "Iso Duck-In Cut" into the "Dotted Circle" area before returning to his "Block." When 01 reaches the "Wing" area and kills his dribble, 05 sets his defender up with a "V-Cut," followed by a "High-Post Flash Cut."

To give the entry potentially a very strong perimeter scoring threat, 02 slips his ball-screen and continues over to set a "Small-on-Big Pin Down-Screen" for 03 to use to break to the top of the key. This gives the play an outstanding perimeter threat besides giving both 04 and 05 both isolated post-ups at their respective locations. See Diagram 11.52

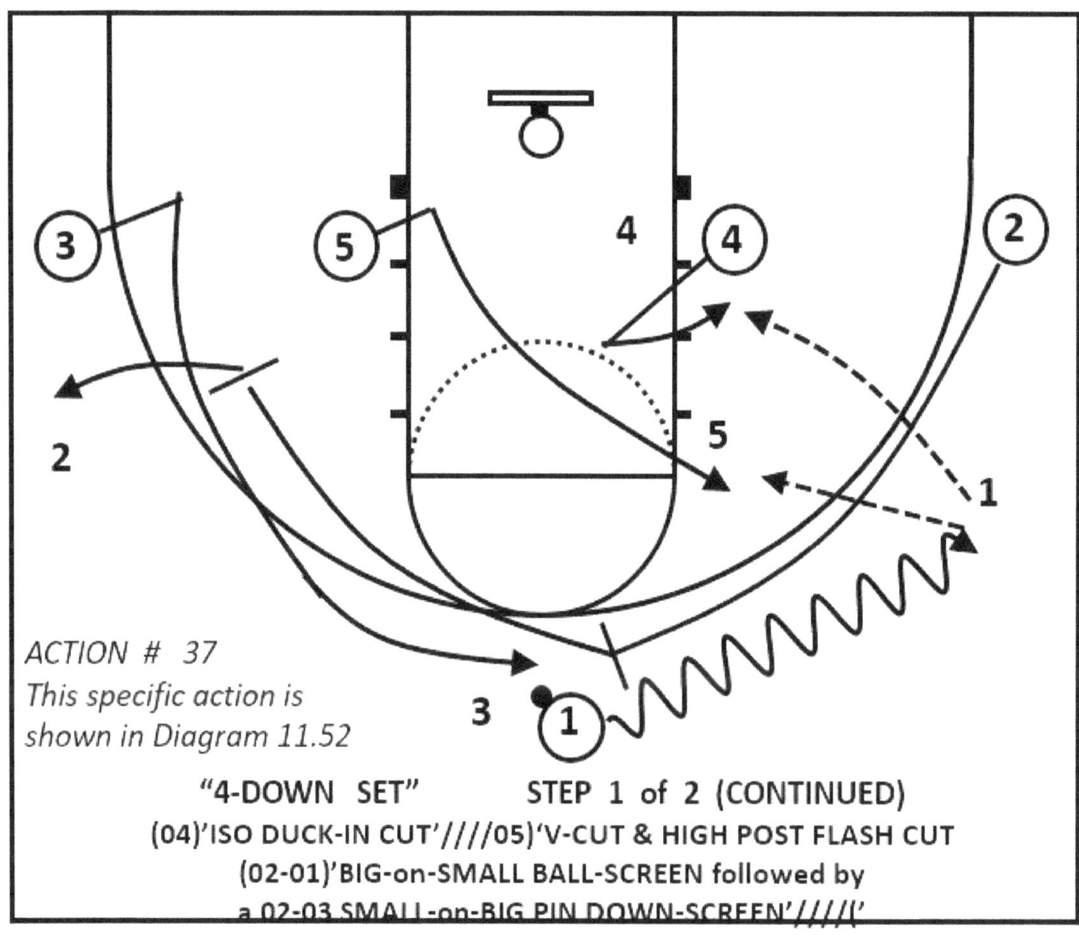

Diagram 11.52

Diagram 11.53 shows the latter part of the play when 01 turns down "Inside Passes" to 04 and 05 as well as a possible "Skip Pass" to 02. Instead, 01 reverses the ball to 03 out on top. If 03 turns down his perimeter shot, 05 and 04 execute their "Post X-Cuts" and diagonally cross the lane to the opposite two post positions, all the while looking for passes from either 03 or 02. This diagram has 03 continue the swing of the ball on to 02. 03 sets his defender up before "shoulder scraping off of 01's outside left shoulder as he "Flare-Cuts" to the new "Weakside Wing."

If shots are not taken, the "High-Post/Low-Post" Spot-Ups are filled for the particular continuity offense to fluidly and instantly begin. See Diagram 11.53

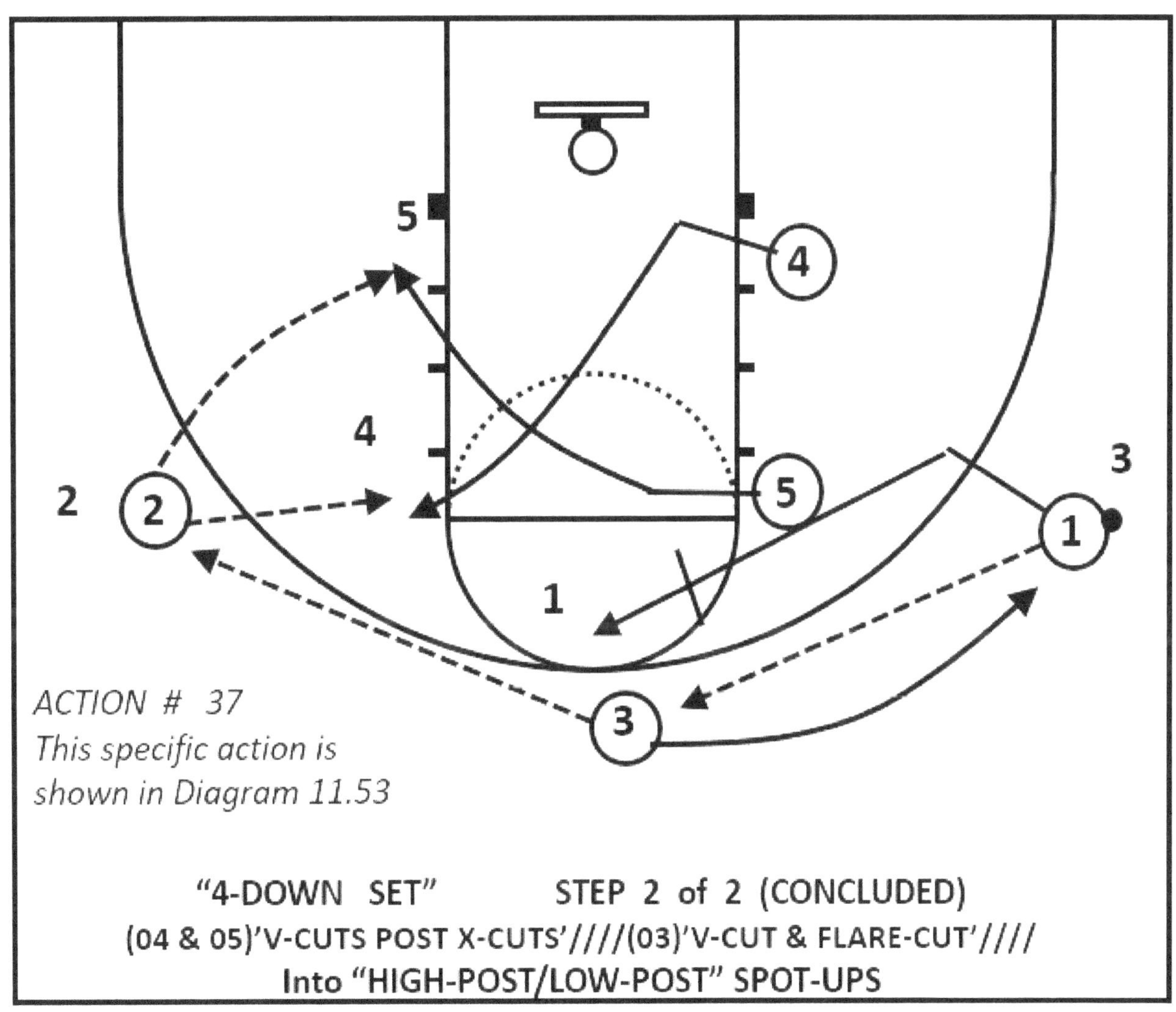

Diagram 11.53

Diagram 11.54 shows the beginning of a two-step play out of the "2-DOWN FLAT" Set with 01 dibble-scraping off of 05's top right shoulder to the new "Ballside Slot," while 05 then front pivots (off of his inside left foot) to set a "Long Pin Down-Screen" for 02 to use. 02 "V-Cuts" toward the baseline and then "shoulder scrapes" off of 05's outside right shoulder. 02 breaks up towards the newly declared "Weakside Slot" with his "feet and hands ready" for a "catch and shoot" pass from 01. 03 makes a shallow "Drift Cut" towards the "Deep Corner" for spacing purposes and to make sure he can get open to receive 01's "Wing Pass." Action # 38. See Diagram 11.54

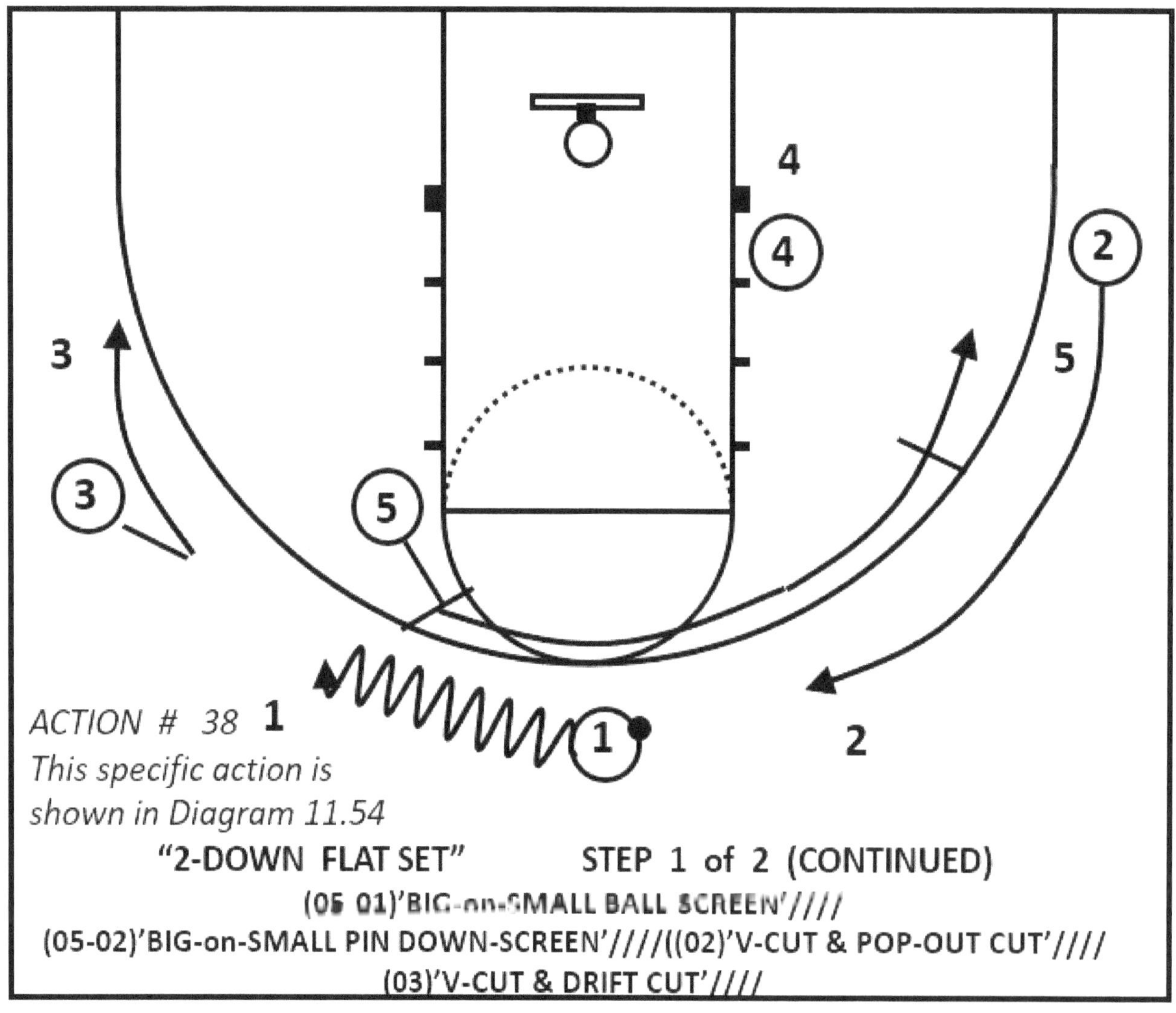

Diagram 11.54

Diagram 11.55 shows the second step in this play/entry for Action # 38. 01 makes the "Wing Pass" to 03 and immediately makes a cut towards 03 and the ball (to set the "Small-on-Big Diagonal Down-Screen" with the proper screening angle. After 04 scrapes off of 01's inside right shoulder and continues flashing to the new "Ballside High Post," 01 should either front or reverse pivot (off of his lower left foot) to then "Iso Post up" his perimeter-type defender on the new "Ballside Mid-Post." If shots are not taken, particularly by 01 and 04 or by 02; the "High-Post/Low-Post" Spot-Ups are immediately filled for another smooth conversion from the end of this play directly into the designated continuity offense. See Diagram 11.55

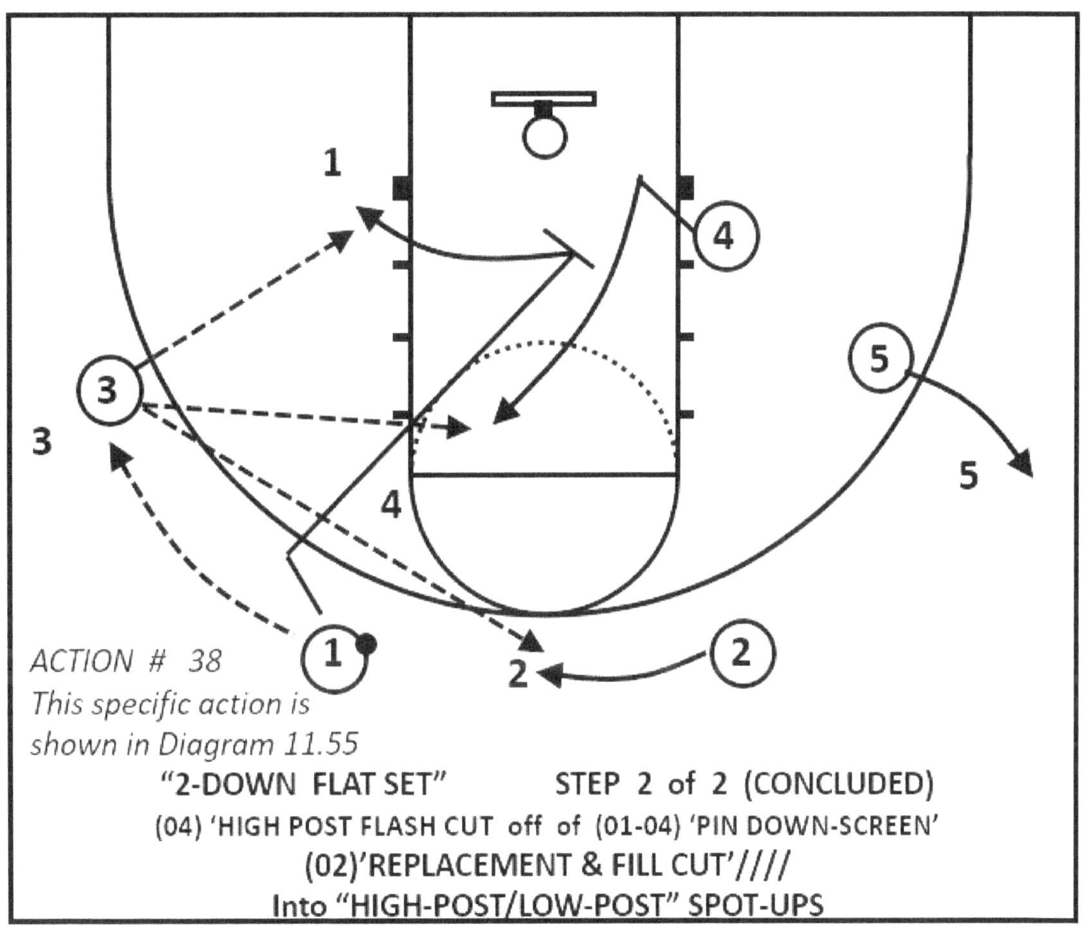

Diagram 11.55

Diagram 11.56 shows the complete play shown in Action # 39 out of the '4-DOWN"
Set. With options to call for either 04 or 05 to step up to ball-screen, 01 has 05 be the player
to do so. 01 then dribble-scrapes off of 05's top right shoulder and as 01 break contact with
05, 05 then makes a "Reverse Pivot" off of his lower left shoulder to "Roll" through the
lane down to the new "Ballside Block. 03 remains "spotted up" in his initial "Deep Corner"
area (looking "like a shooter" with his feet and hands ready). On the new weakside of the
floor, 02 makes a "V-Cut" before scraping off of the top right shoulder 0f 04 and making
his "Pop-Out Cut" to the new "Weakside Slot." This action between 04 and 02 occupies
any possible interior support defense and with both 03 and 01 stretching the defense out
behind the arc on the ballside allows 05 to fully isolate his defender "down on the Block."
If shots are not taken, the second phase of the offense can immediately begin with the "4-
Out/1-In" Spot-Ups correctly filled. See Diagram 11.56

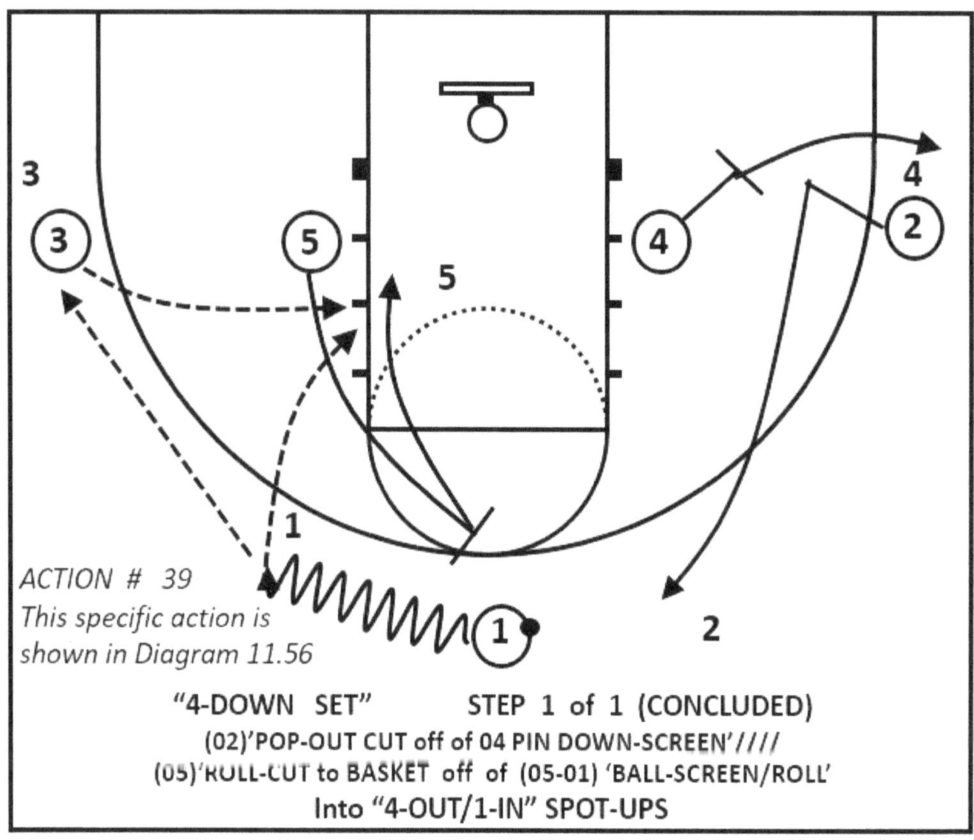

Diagram 11.56

Diagram 11.57 shows Action # 40, describing another 1-step offensive play/entry out of the "2-TWIST" Set with 04 electing to start on the left side of the lane. 02 makes an aggressive "V-Cut" towards 01 and the ball before then making a "Flare-Cut" to the "Wing" area on his initial side of the floor. 05 immediately steps up to set a "Big-on-Small" Ball-Screen" for 01 to use to make his "perimeter pull dribble" to the "Slot" on the opposite side of the floor.

As 01 breaks contact with 05's top left shoulder, 04 makes a "Low Post Flash Cut" across the lane to post up on the opposite side of the floor. At the same time, 05 makes a "Front Pivot" off of his lower right foot to make his probable successful "Rim-Run" to the basket. If interior shot opportunities are not taken by 04 and 05, all three perimeter players have all rotated to the "3-Out/2-In" Spot-Ups for possible perimeter shots. If none are taken, the "3-Out/2-In" Spot-Ups are filled for the offense to maintain its assault on the defense. See Diagram 11.57

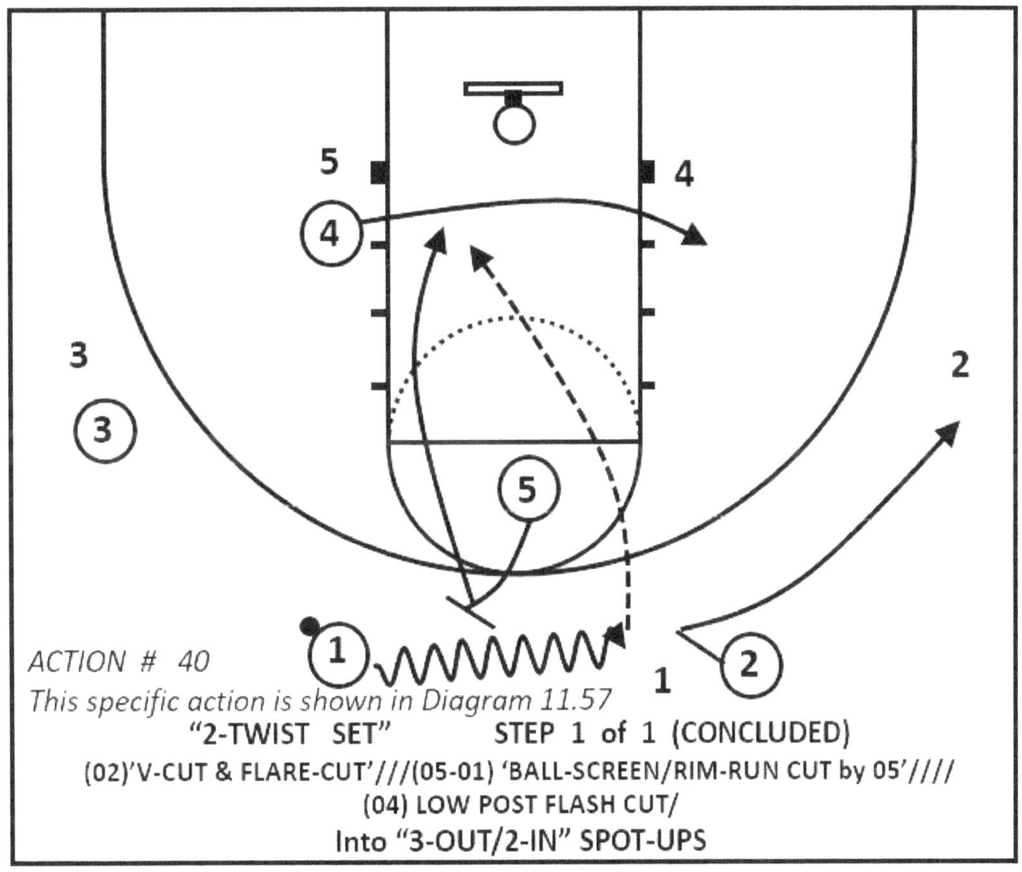

Diagram 11.57

Out of the "3-ACROSS" Set comes a one-step play shown in Diagram 11.58. With 05 starting on the right side of the lane, 01 makes a pass to the left side of the floor, to 03. 04 and 01 both break to get the proper screening angles to set a "Stagger-Screen" for 02 to use. 02 first "V-Cuts" before then becoming the primary perimeter scoring threat at the top of the key. As the ball is received, 05 breaks diagonally across the lane as if preparing to set a "Long Ball-Screen" for 03. Instead, he breaks off of his route to make a "Ghost Long Ball-Screen" and "Iso Posts up" his defender.

To help remove more helpside defense, 04 seals off his defender and flashed back to the new "Ballside High Post." The only possible remaining helpside defender would be X1, the smallest defender on the court trying to help X5 and X4 in the lane.

If shots are not created, the spot-ups for the "HIGH-POST/LOW-POST" Continuity Offense are filled and there can be smooth conversion from play to last phase of the attack. See Diagram 11.58

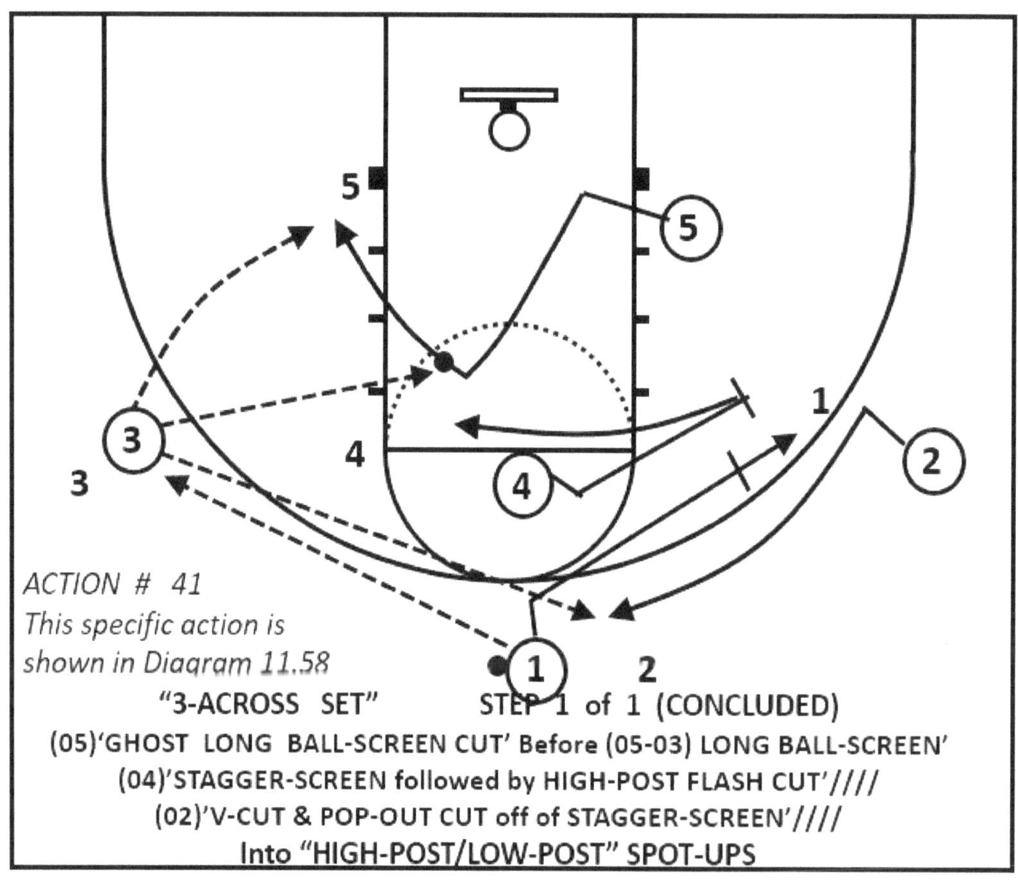

Diagram 11.58

Diagram 11.59 shows the beginning of a two-step play out of the "2-TWIST" Set. With 04 starting on the left side of the lane, 02 must dribble towards 01. At the same time, 03 makes a "V-Cut" before using 05 to set a "Big-on-Small Iverson Screen" and for 03 to "Iverson Cut" over the top to the opposite side's "Wing" area. At the same time, 01 makes his strong "V-Cut" away from the approaching 02 (with the ball) and reverses direction to receive the DHO. 01 then "perimeter pull dribbles" to the opposite "Slot," while 02 remains on the new "Weakside Slot." See Diagram 11.59

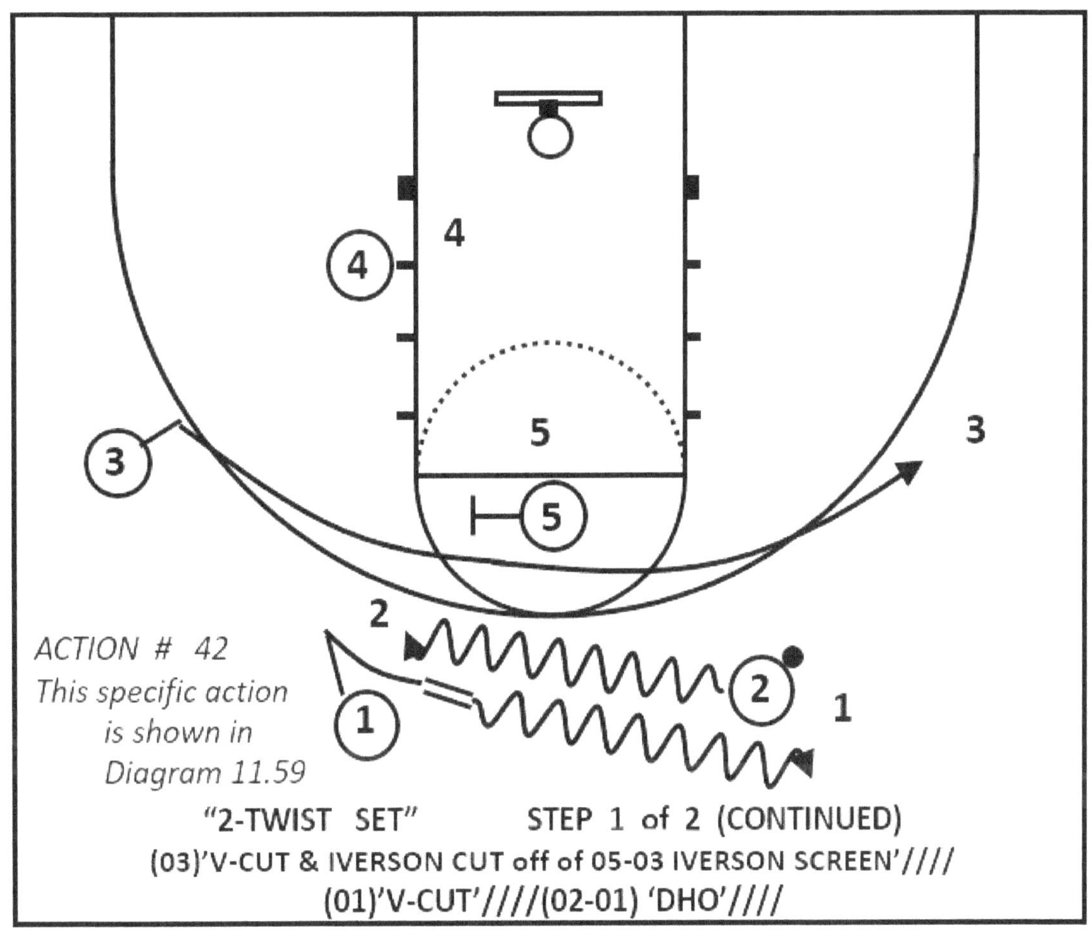

Diagram 11.59

01 then makes the "Wing Pass" to 03 with both 04 and 01 appearing to cut towards 03 and the ball as if to get the proper angle to go set a "Diagonal Stagger-Screen" for 04 to use. During their screening paths, 01 continues his route while 05 breaks his off and "Slash Cut" to the newly declared "Ballside Block." This action in essence now becomes a deceptive combination of a (01-04) "Small-on-Big Diagonal Down-Screen" and an isolated "Slash-Cut Post-Up" By 05.

If shots are not created for 05 on the "Block," by 04 at the top of the key, for 02 off of a possible "Skip Pass"; the "3-Out/2-In" Spot-Ups" are filled for a smooth transition into the designated continuity offense to immediately begin. See Diagram 11.60

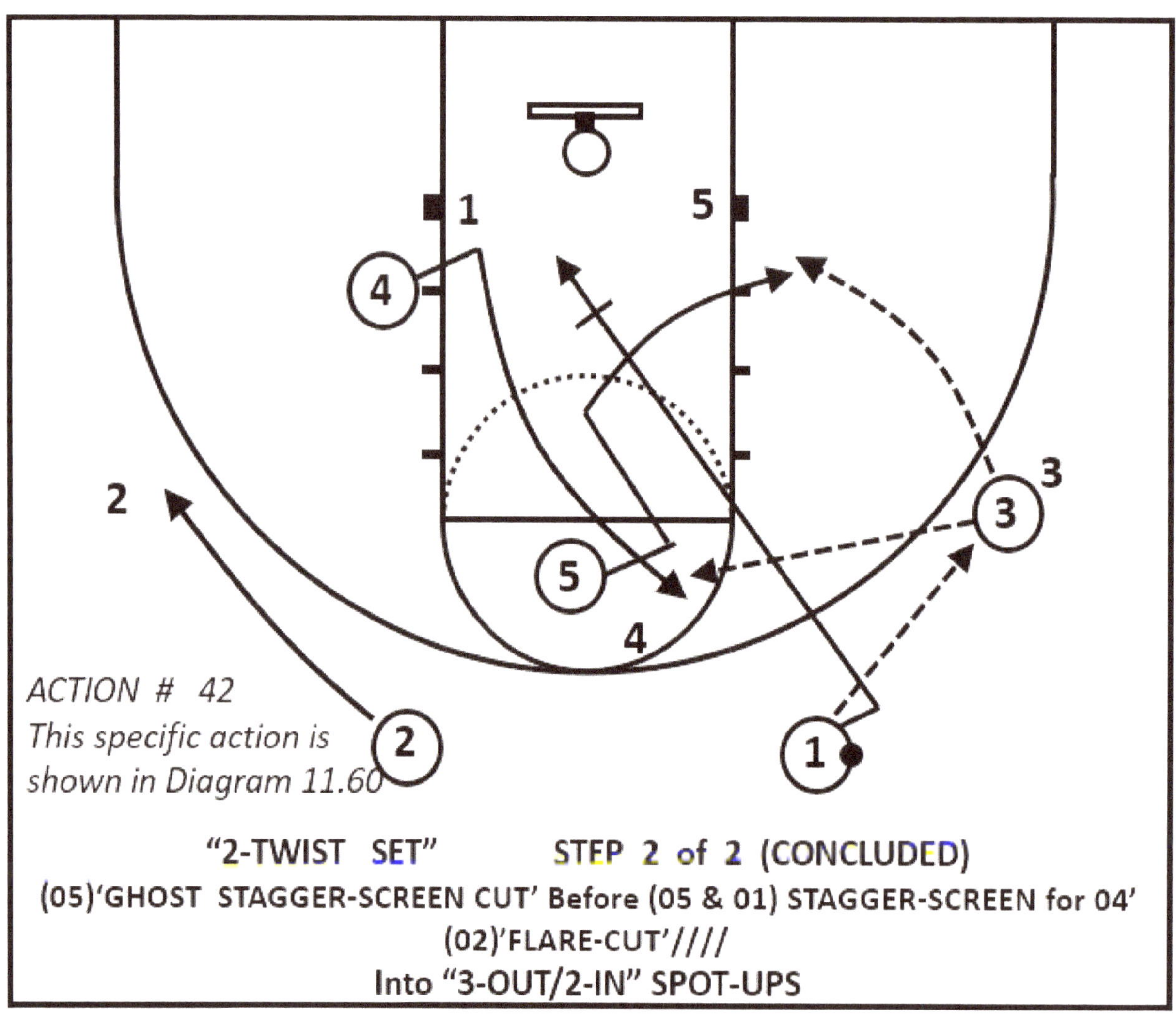

Diagram 11.60

Diagram 11.61 illustrates the beginning of Play # 43 out of the "5-SQUEEZE" Set with both 02 and 03 making "Iverson Cuts" over the top and underneath the "Iverson Screener," (04) at the "Nail." See Diagram 11.61

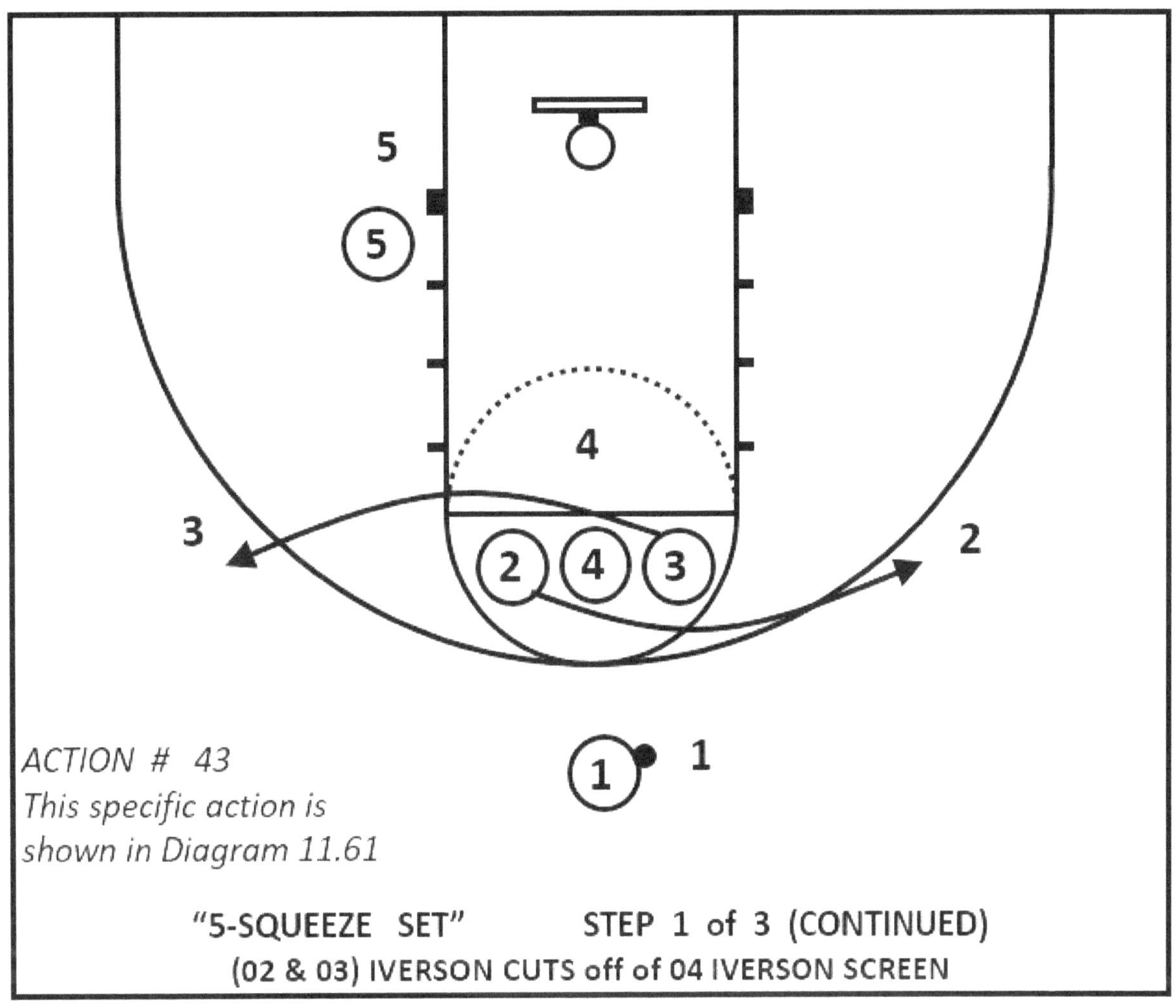

Diagram 11.61

Diagram 11.62 shows the continuation of the play with 01 then making a "Wing Pass" to 03, receiving 02's "Flare-Screen" and making a "Flare-Cut" to the new "Weakside Wing." At the same time, 05 makes a "Slip Cut" out to the "Short-Corner" on the same side of the floor while 04 flashes to the newly designated "Ballside High Post." 02 then slips his "Flare-Screen to end up at the "Weakside Slot" location. See Diagram 11.62

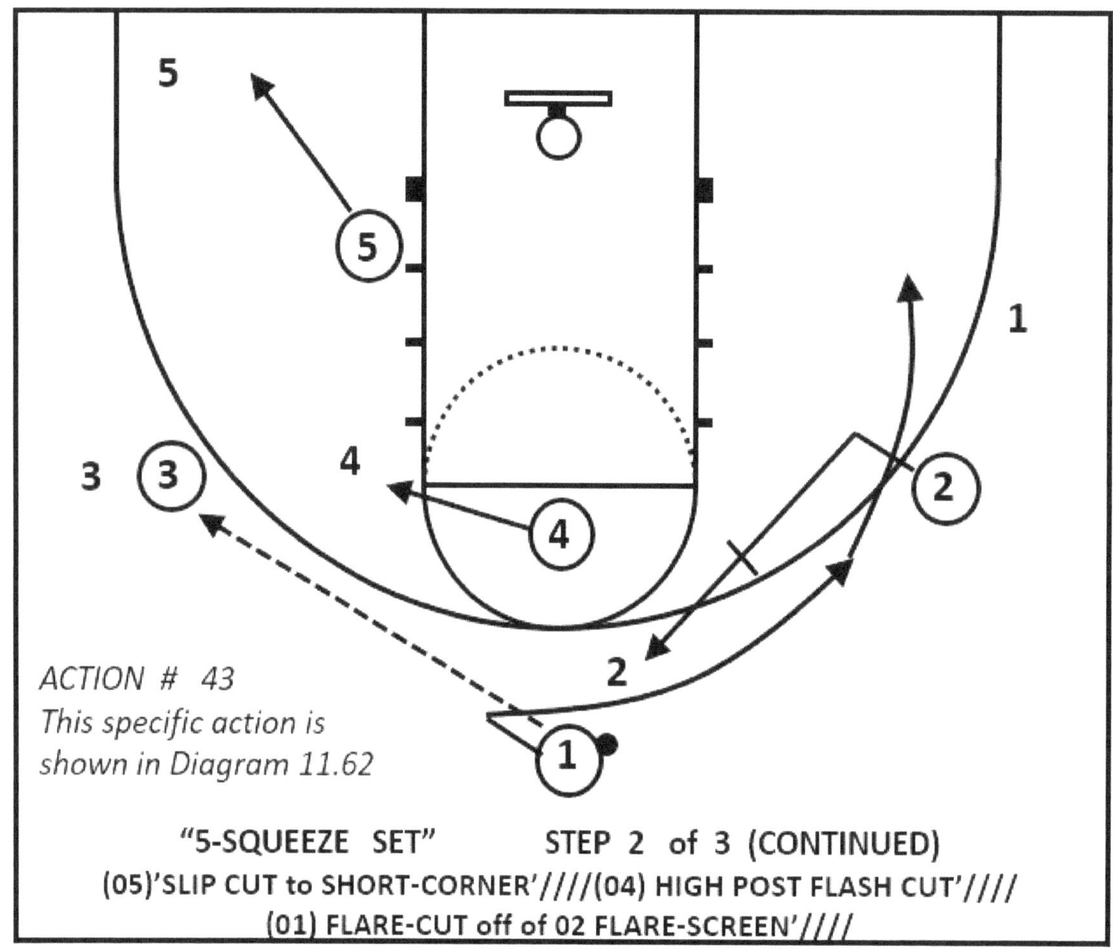

Diagram 11.62

Diagram 11.63 shows the continuation and the ending of Play # 43 with 05 stepping out and up to set a "Big-on-Small" Ball-Screen" for 03 to drive towards the baseline. 05 then makes a shallow Slip into the middle of the "Dotted Circle" area, with 04 influencing his defender further from the basket by slipping to the new "Ballside Slot."

With no offensive players but 03 below the FT Line extended, there can be no "helpside defenders" to help X3 out on 03's baseline drive. As 03 "Perimeter Pull (Down) Dribbles," 01 "Hammer Cuts" to the "Weakside Deep Corner" and looks for 03's "Hammer Pass" if he cannot finish with a lay-up. See Diagram 11.63

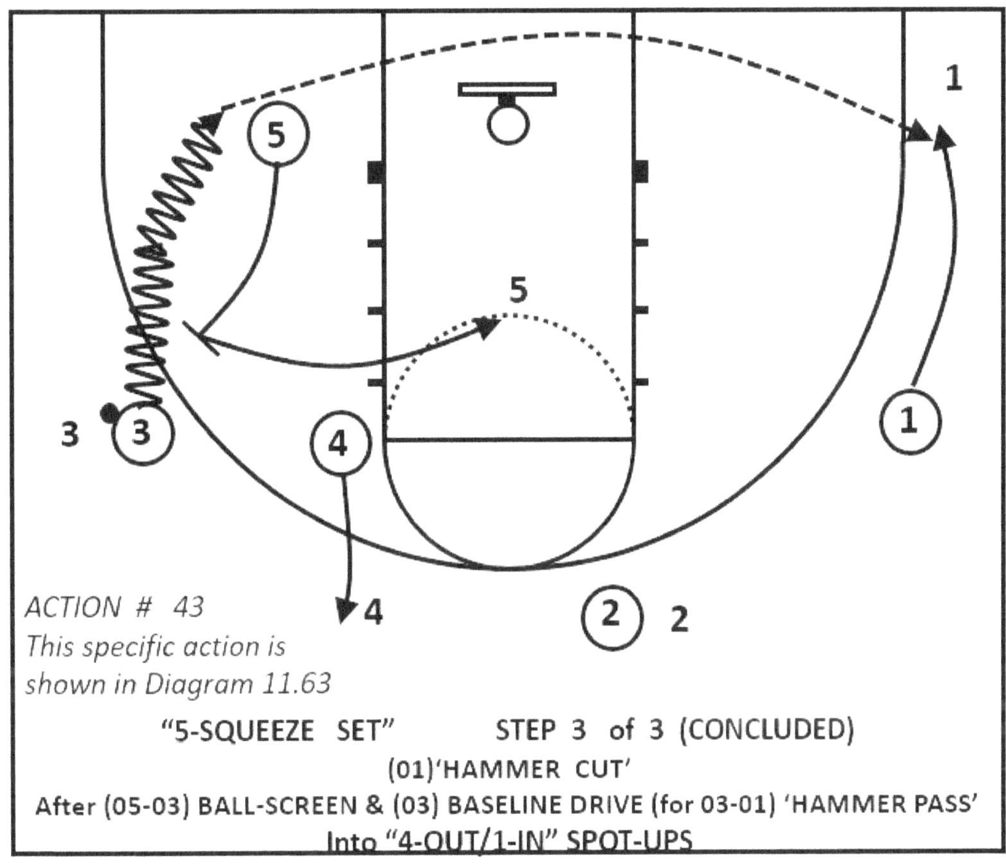

Diagram 11.63

Diagrams 11.64 and 11.65 illustrate the beginning and conclusion of Play # 44 that begins out of the "5 SQUEEZE" Set. 04 makes a "Barkley Cut" underneath 05 while 02 makes an "Iverson Cut" over the top of 05, located at the "Nail" spot. See Diagram 11.64

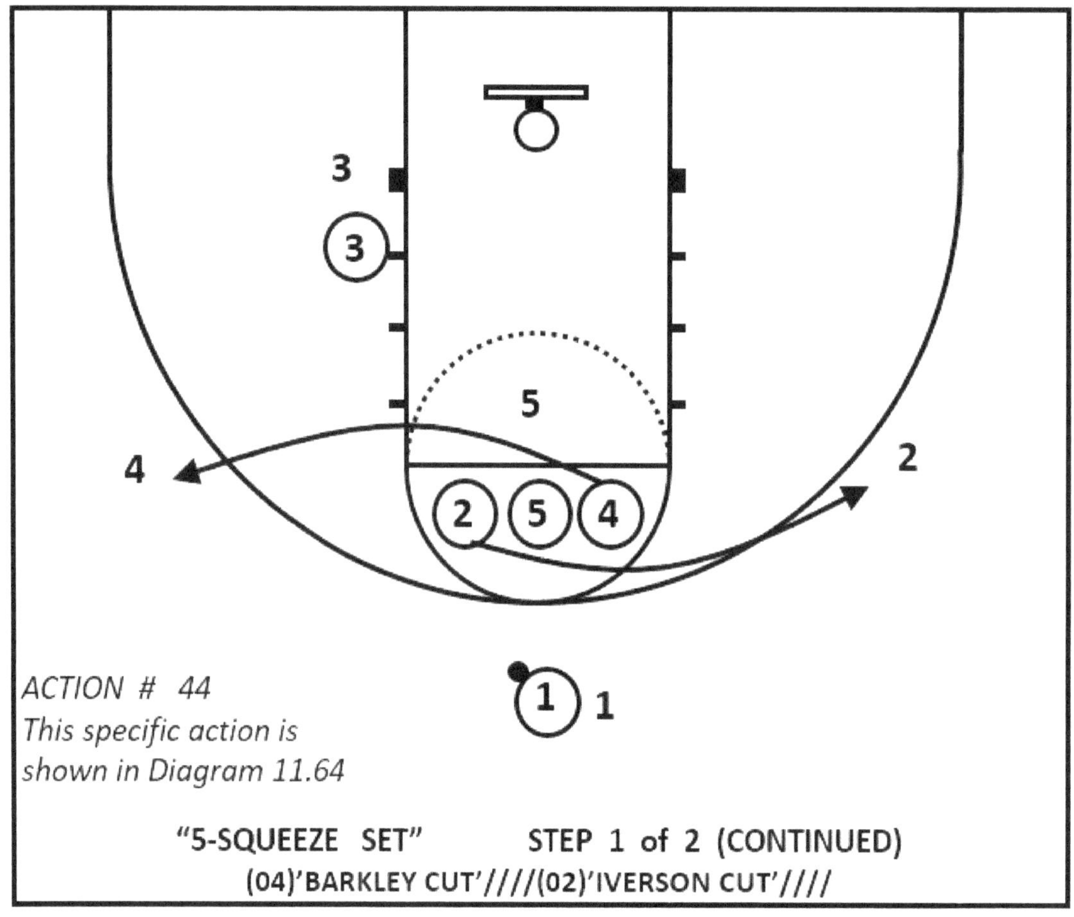

Diagram 11.64

Diagram 11.65 shows 01 making the "Wing Pass" to 02 and 05 immediately making a "Diagonal Slash Cut" to the newly declared "Ballside Block." At the same time 03 flashes to the new "Ballside Slot," with 04 setting a "Big-on-Small Flare-Screen" for 01 to "Flare-Cut" towards that side of the floor's "Deep Corner (after making his pass.) To improve the chances of better making the "Inside Pass" to 05, 02 makes a "Perimeter Pull (Down) Dribble" towards the "Deep Corner.

This action completes the play with all offensive players having moved and changing locations while attacking the individual defenders and the overall team defense. If shots are not taken, the "4-Out/1-In" Spot-Ups are filled for an immediate transition into the final phase of the offensive attack. See Diagram 11.65

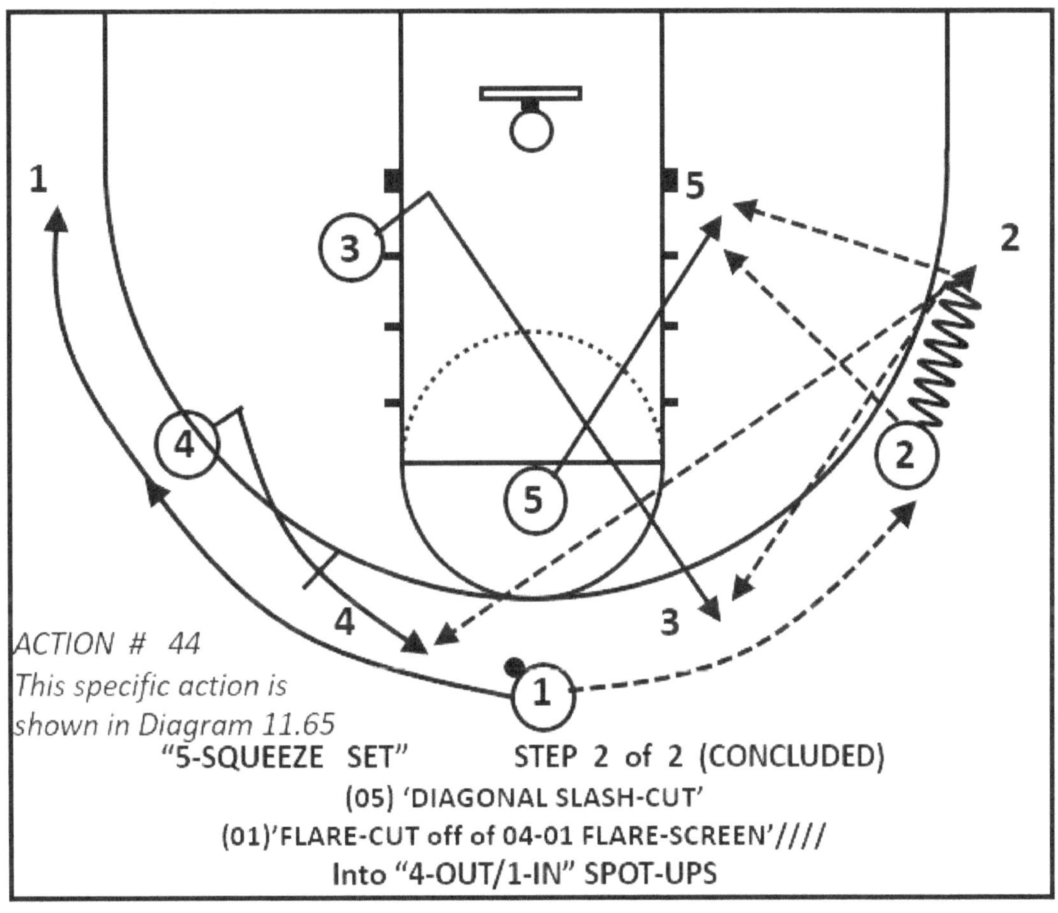

Diagram 11.65

Diagram 11.66 shows the entire Play # 45 that begins out of the "3-OVER" Set. As 01 "dribble-scrapes" off of 04's outside left shoulder, 05 then steps up to set a "(Back-)Screen the ("Ball-)Screener Action. 04 then "Flare-Cuts" to the new "Weakside Wing" and 05 slips his screen and steps to the top of the key.

At the same time that 01 breaks contact with 04, 02 makes a "Flex-Cut" off of 03's lower (this time for a reason) right shoulder and continues across the lane to post up his inverted perimeter-type defender, X2. After screening for 02, 03 then makes a long "Veer Cut" into and through the "Dotted Circle" area all the way to the new "Ballside High Post" area. 01 has multiple pass receiving options and if no shots are taken, the "High-Post/Low-Post" Spot-Ups are filled for a seamless conversion from the play directly into the designated continuity offense can begin.

While these cuts are all valuable, each one does not have to be implemented within the system. Each coaching staff can determine the number that can be used and which specific cuts can be incorporated within their own offensive system. See Diagram 11.66

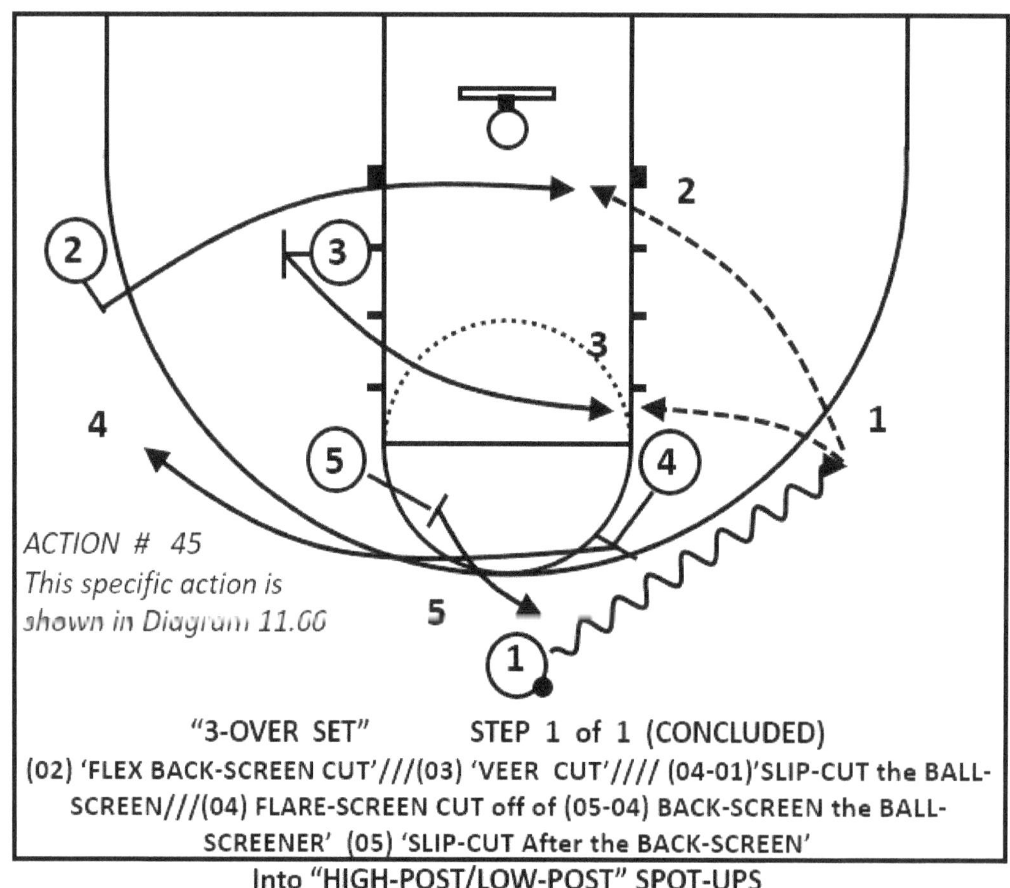

Diagram 11.66

It is imperative to know that these six dribble-actions can and should involve all five offensive players from the many different locations on the floor. Each dribble is fundamentally sound and can be used to execute the different purposes of the offense while still maintaining the overall structure and framework of half-court plays, out-of-bounds plays, secondary fastbreak options including the actual continuity offensive actions.

Regardless of what particular level each action of the three different modes of attack (secondary breaks, half-court plays, out-of-bounds play), these dribbles will be able to attack opponents individually as well as reposition each offensive player into one of the proper spot-ups of the designated continuity or motion-type offense. These various dribbles can be incorporated within each step of every offensive action, whether the action is being executed in any of the three different modes. Despite the fact that any offensive dribble from any offensive player could create the desire shot, the dribble will produce instant conversions into the designated continuity or motion-type offense. This provides an advantage for the offensive team in that the opposition will have no chance to recover and reorganize from any of the six dribbles that were utilized.

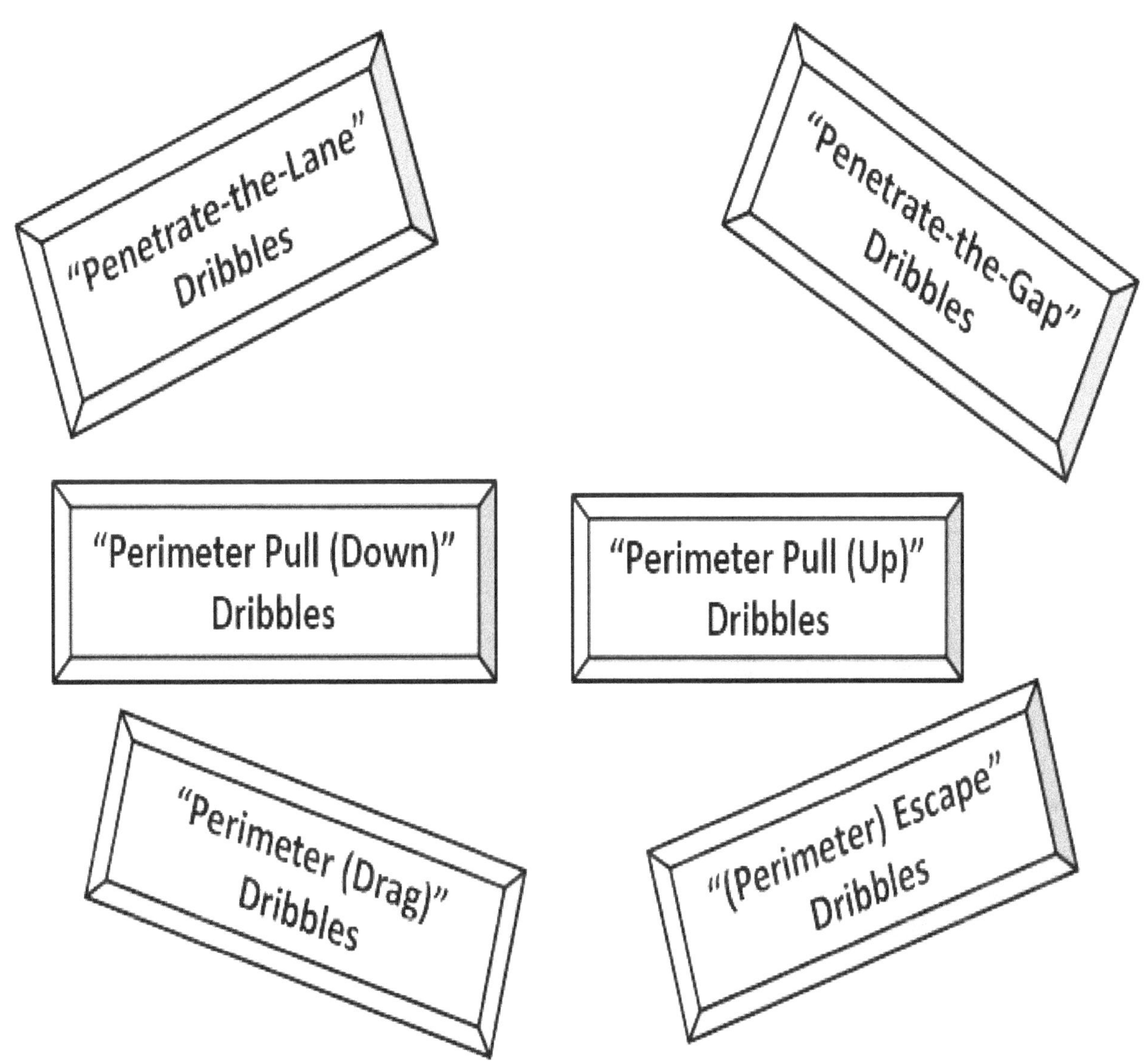

Illustration 12.1

Action # 1: "PENETRATE-the-LANE DRIBBLE" ACTION

Diagram 11.2 illustrates one of the most common and definitely the most aggressive dribble that has existed from the beginning of basketball-the "Penetrate-the-Lane" Dribble. This traditional action and even more common and popular dribble in today's game can be implemented within the free-flowing but organized attack of several quick-hitting plays/entries from any of the three levels of offensive plays/entries. This action is executed out of the "1-DOWN" Offensive Set.

This entry/play starts with 01 reversing the ball to 02 towards the strong side of the alignment. 03 then steps up as if to set a "Flare-Screen" for 01 before reversing the direction of his cut to then make a "Flare-Cut" of his own towards the "Deep Corner" on his side of the floor. 01 starts to make his "Flare-Cut" off of the presumed "Flare-Screen" before also changing directions to then step back to fill his initial "Slot" location. Both could immediately become pass receivers for 02 to move the ball to the opposite side of the floor.

Instead, 02 then swings the ball over to the inverted post-type player, 04, on the offensive right side of the floor. 02 immediately follows his pass to make a "Small-on-Big Ball-Screen" for 04 to use. This action immediately attacks the post-type defender, X4, and forces him to defend "perimeter-type offensive action." If the defense switches this screen, 04 will have a "player advantage." If the defense does not switch the screen, there could possibly be a "position advantage," whether X4 has above-average offensive perimeter skills or X4 has deficiencies in his perimeter defensive skills. 04 then "dribble-scrapes" tightly off of 02's outside right shoulder to drive towards the "Nail" location, while 05 is

ready to receive the ball on 04's "Drive and Dump," while 03 "spots up in the "Deep Corner" for a possible "catch and shoot" off of 04's "Penetrate and Pitch" action.

If shots are not taken, the "4-Out/1-In" Spot-Ups are filled for the desired continuity offense to immediately and fluidly begin. See Diagram 12.2

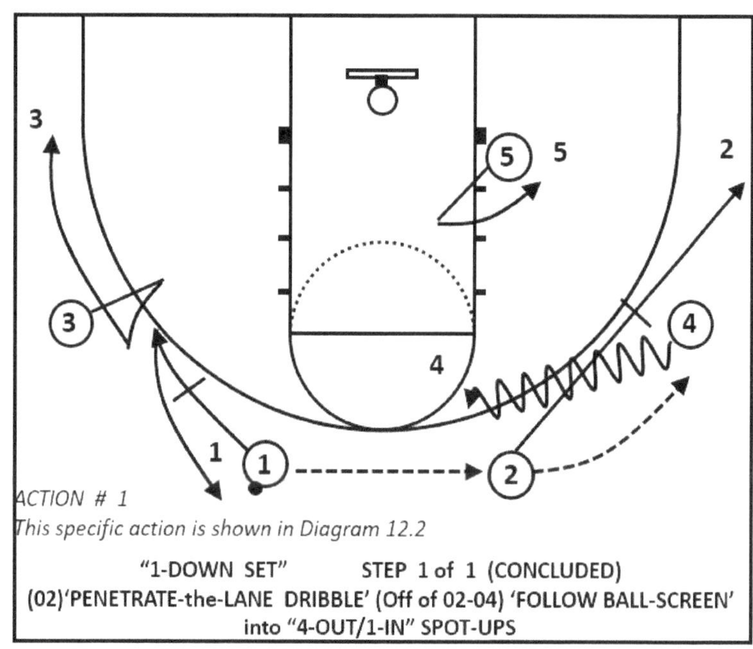

Diagram 12.2

Diagram 12.3 illustrates a slightly less aggressive dribble called, "Penetrate-the-Gap" Dribble. This dribble could actually have been intended to be a "Penetrate-the-Lane" Dribble, but a second defender stepped into the gap and stopped the initial penetration.

Out of the "2-TWIST" Set, this play starts with 03 cutting down to set a "Small-on-Big Pin Down-Screen" for 04 to break out to the "Wing" area. 05 then diagonally cuts down to set a "Big-on-Small (Pin Down-)Screen the ("Pin Down-)Screener for 03 to curl tightly off of 05's outside left shoulder. At the same time, 01 dribbles towards the top of the key, forcing X2 to help out his ball-defender teammate, X1. During the "Gap Dribble," 02 "Flare-Cuts" towards the wide open wing area, looking for the pass from 01.

After screening for 03, 05 then slashes across the lane to post up on the new "Ballside Block," while 03 curls his screen and flashes to the new "Ballside High Post." With 04 pulling his defender away from the ball and the basket, 05 should enjoy the isolated post-up action and look for 02's "Inside Pass." If 02 does not have the shot or the drive, he looks to make "Inside Pass" to either 05 or 03. This dribble action repositions all five players into the "High-Post/Low-Post" Spot-Ups for the continuity offense to smoothly begin. See Diagram 12.3

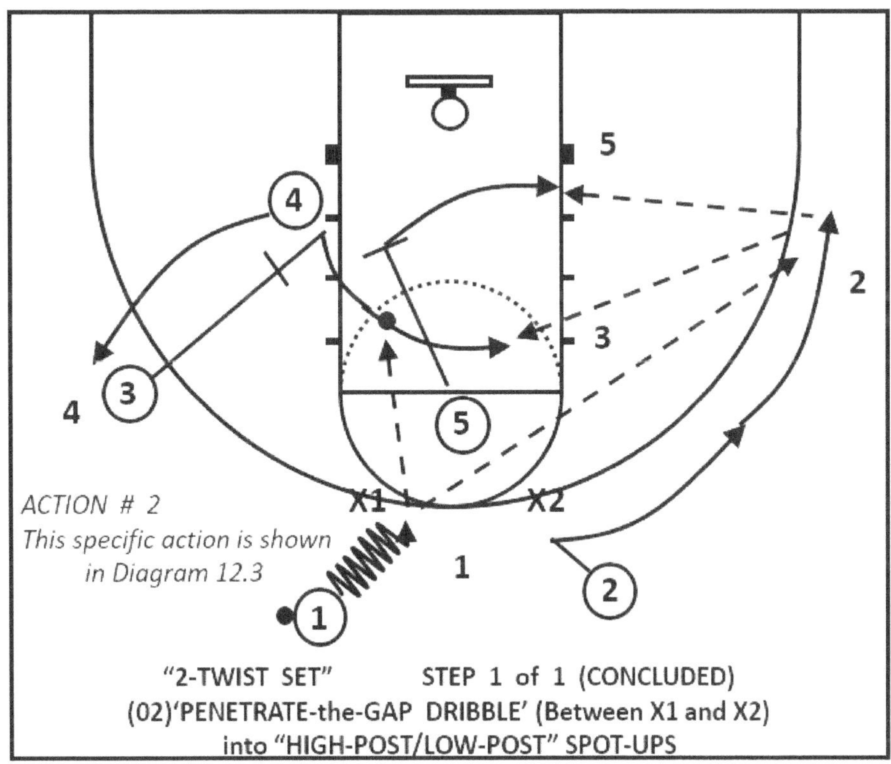

Diagram 12.3

Diagram 12.4 illustrates the beginning action of paly where there exists a "(Perimeter-Pull) Down" Dribble eventually by 03 down to the "Deep Corner" in his side of the floor.

02 first could make a "Penetrate-the-Gap" Dribble before reversing the ball over to 01, who quickly swings the ball over to 03. 01 then scrapes off of 05's left shoulder to make a "Lob Cut" to the basket. 01 bounces out to replace 01 at his initial "Slot" location. 05 then slides down the lane to look for the "Inside Pass" from 03. To minimize Opponent's "Helpside Defense," 04 replaces 02 at the new "Weakside Slot." See Diagram 12.4

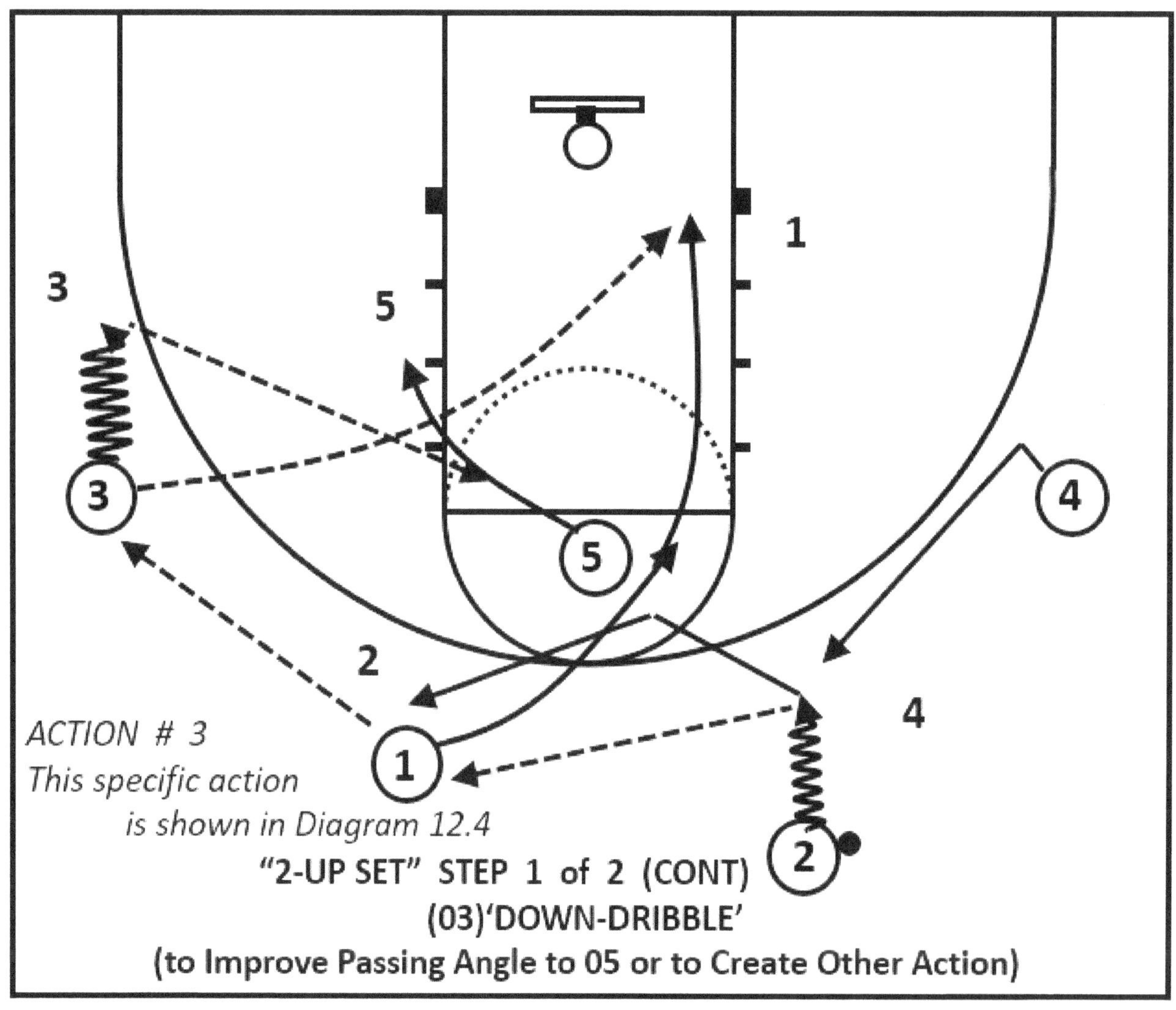

Diagram 12.4

Diagram 12.5 shows the conclusion of the Play. 05 should have caught X5 on his high side on his sliding down the lane. 03 could make the "Down Dribble" to the "Deep Corner" to improve the passing angle to 05, with 05 executing the proper footwork to keep X5 "sealed off" on the high side of him. With 01 stepping out on the perimeter's new "Weakside Deep Corner" and 04 pulling and stretching his defender out to the new "Weakside Slot," 05 has completely eliminated any possible "helpside defensive support." In addition, the "4-Out/1-In" Spot-Ups are immediately filled for an instant conversion into the desired continuity offense. See Diagram 12.5

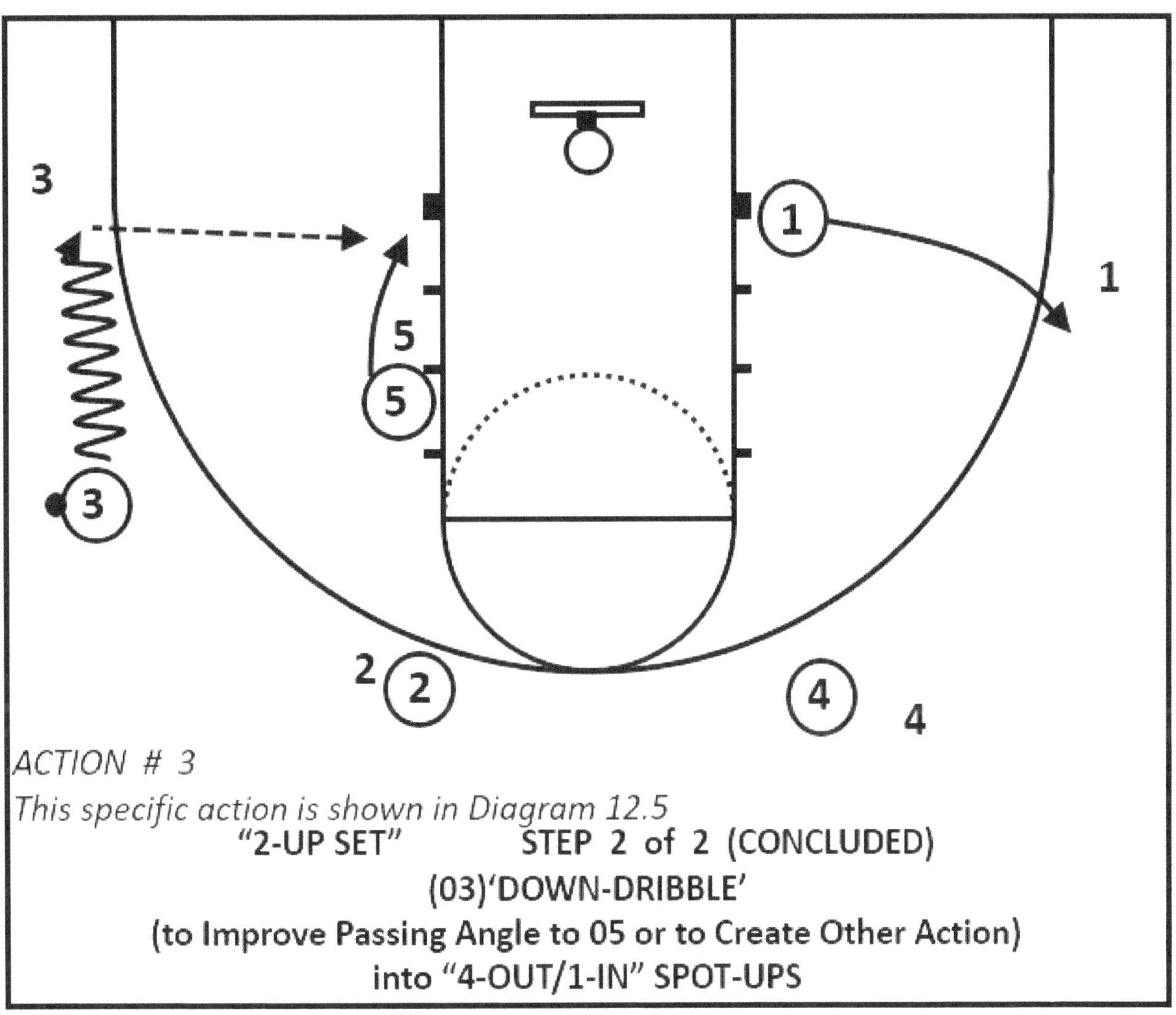

Diagram 12.5.

Diagram 12.6 shows the beginning of a fourth play out of the "HORNS" Set with 01 using a "Big-on-Small Ball-Screen" to initiate the play with a "Perimeter Pull" Dribble. The purpose of this (more of a passive) dribble is move all five defenders while safely relocating the location of the basketball. At the same time, 05 slashes diagonally through the lane to post his defender up on the new "Ballside Block." After screening for 04, 04 cuts down to then set a "Big-on-Small Pin Down-Screen" for 03 to use to break up to the now empty "Slot." This action between 04 and 03 provides the play with an open perimeter shot for 03 and even more of an "Isolation Post-Up" for 05. The dribble by 01 horizontally stretches and occupies the defense while also giving 01 the improved passing angles and opportunities to make passes to 05, 02, and 03. See Diagram 12.6

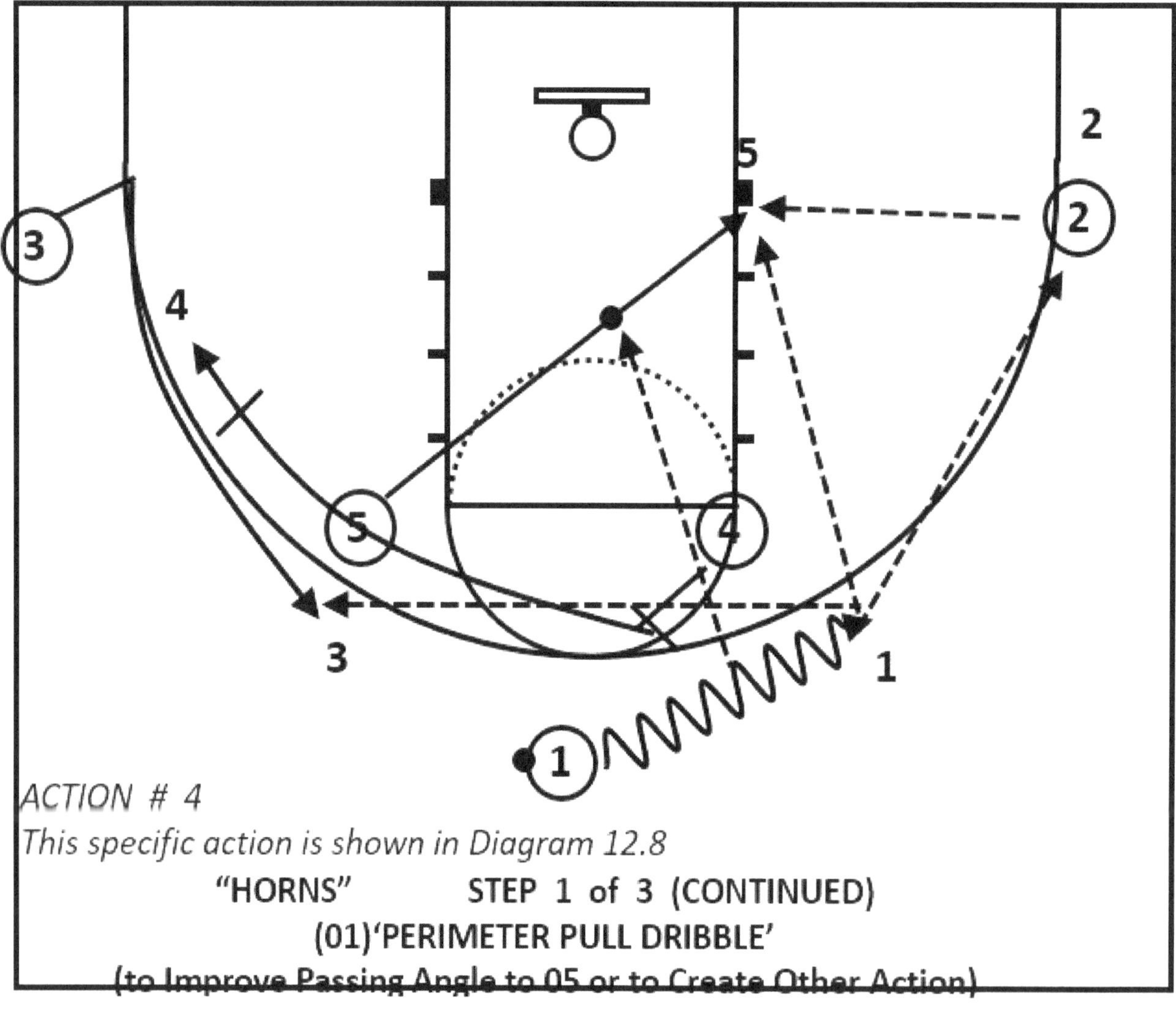

Diagram 12.6

If 01 does not have the shot or the passing angles to make the pass to 05, he can make a "Down Pass" to 02; where 02 may have the shot or a much improved passing angle to deliver the ball to 05. On the 01-02 "Down Pass," 01 makes a "Diagonal Rotation Cut" through the lane to the opposite "Deep Corner," while 03 and 01 make "Replacement Fill Cuts" to load up the two "Slot" locations. See Diagram 12.7

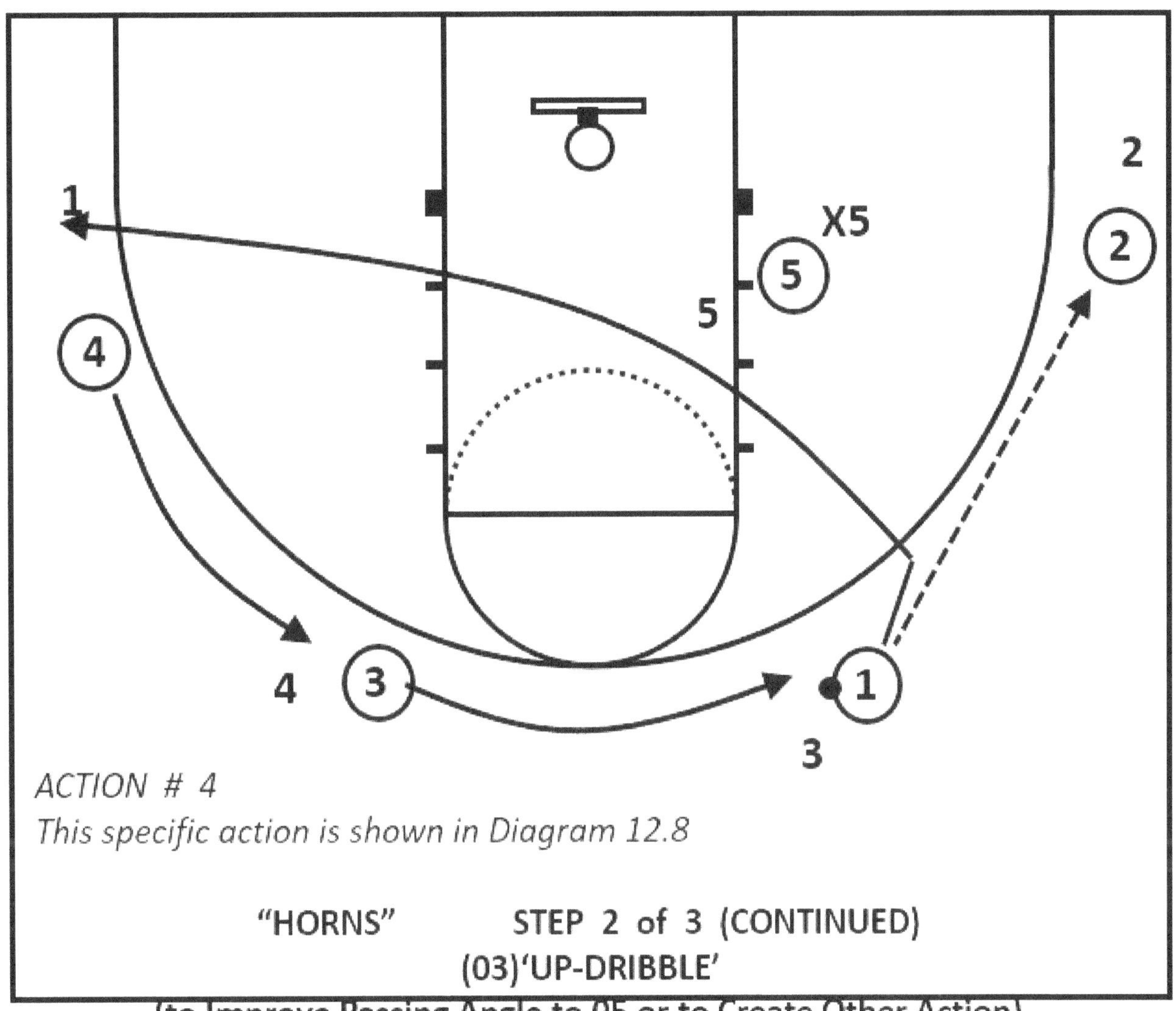

Diagram 12.7

Diagram 12.8 shows that X5 has denied the ball to 05 by moving to the baseline (or low) side of 05 and therefore shutting off the offense's "Inside Game." Either an 02-03 "Up Pass" or a 02 "Up Dribble" will regain the passing angle advantage that 02 should have to make the pass to 05.

Even if the "Inside Pass" to 05 is not made and shots are not taken, all five offensive players are again in the "4-Out/1-In" Spot-Ups for the designated continuity offense to smoothly begin. See Diagram 12.8

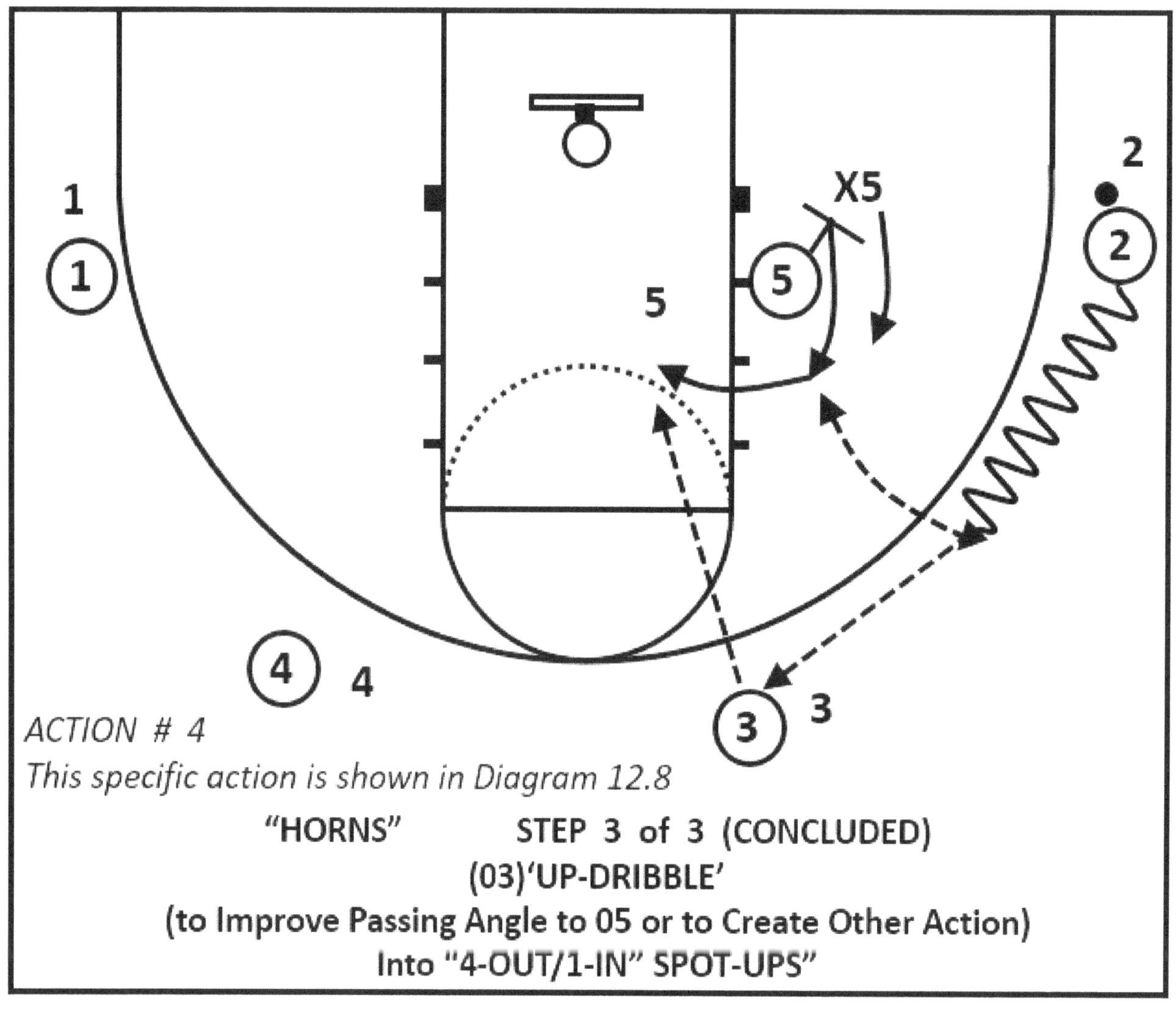

Diagram 12.8

An "Even Front Secondary Break" Option in Diagram 12.9 demonstrates 01 making a "Perimeter Pull Dribble going from right to left to attack the opposition. This dribble moves all the defenders and creates open driving, cutting, and passing lanes for all teammates. See Diagram 12.9

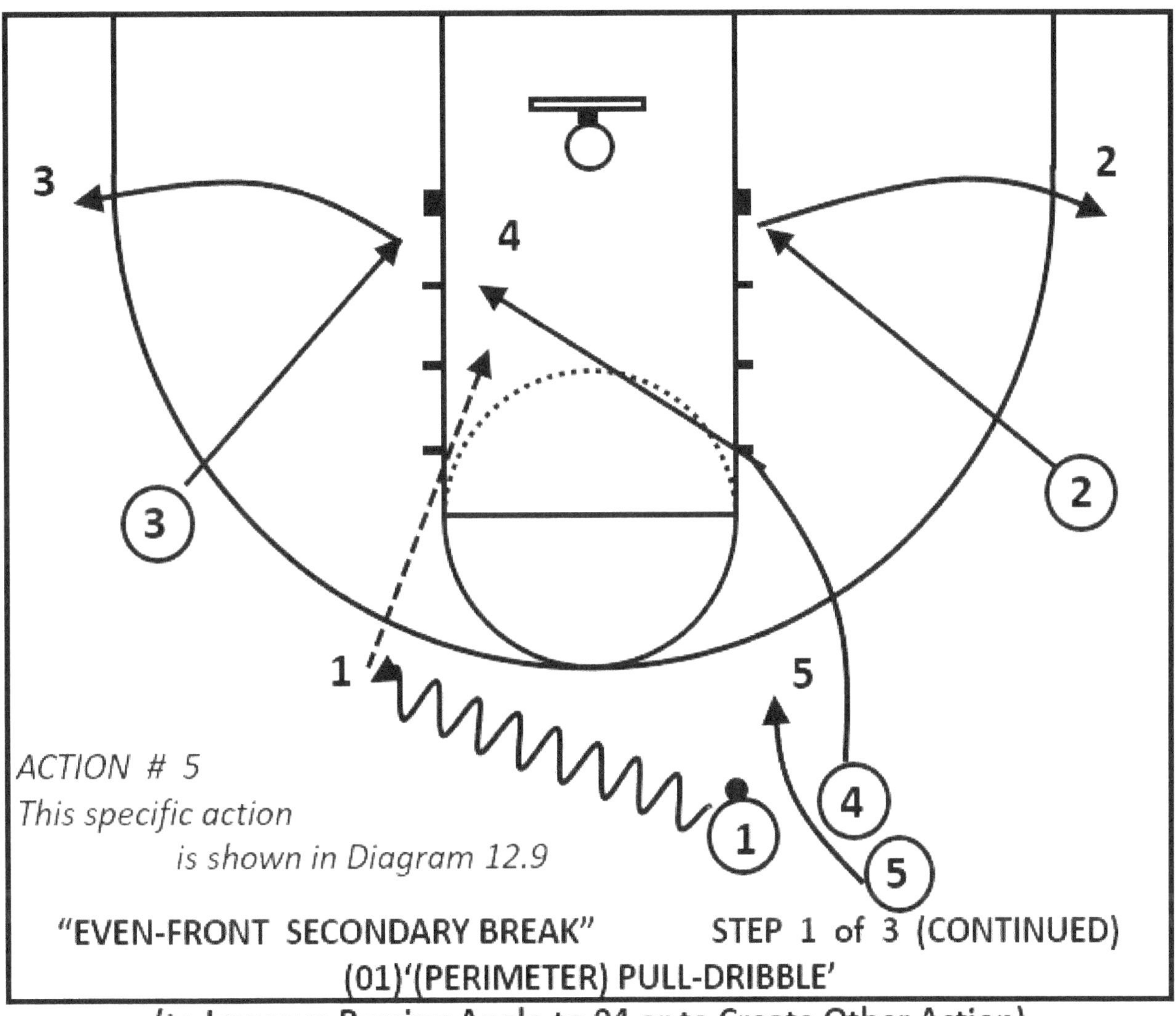

Diagram 12.9

Diagram 12.10 shows 01 continuing his dribble and reversing directions after 04, the designated "1st Trigger" has "Slash Cut" diagonally through the lane with both 03 and 02 flattening out the defense by running to their respective "Deep Corner" areas.

Instead of 01 making the "Reverse Pass" to 05, the "Trigger/2nd Trailer;" 05 makes a "Backdoor Cut" through the lane that then serves as a "Big-on-Small Stagger-Screen" with 04 so that 03 can make his "Flex Cut" off of the two screeners. With the "Weakside Slot" now empty, 01 maintains his dribble and makes a horizontal "Perimeter Pull (Drag)" Dribble across the top of the key to move the ball to the opposite side of the floor. This dribble occupies the attention of all the defenders as well as moves both defensive and offensive personnel (the same way a "Reverse Pass" would. This gives 01 an improved passing angle to hit 03 on his "Flex Cut" as well as making 02 a passing target threat. See Diagram 12.10

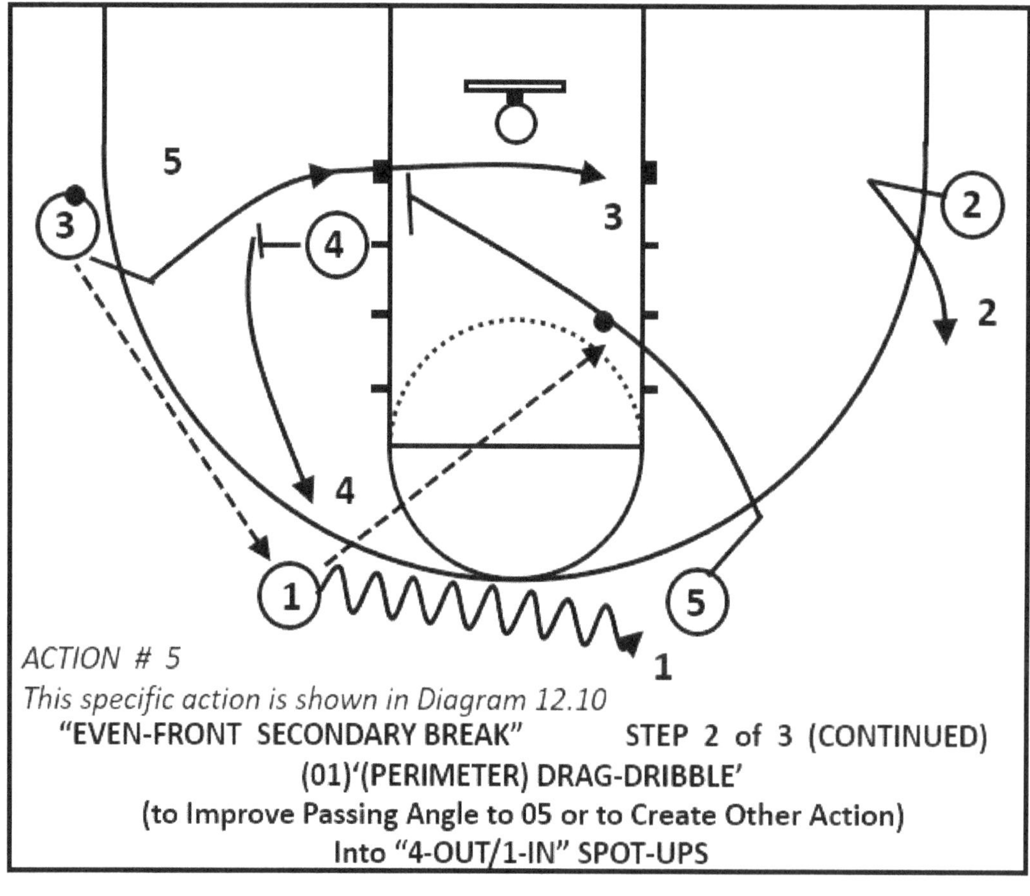

Diagram 12.10

Diagram 12.11 shows the continuation of the Secondary Break Option with 04 setting the first of the "Flex Screen" and then making a "Vertical Up Cut" to the now empty "Slot." After 03 scrapes off of 05, the second screener, that screener also breaks horizontally out towards the now empty "Deep Corner."

If no shots are taken, the Secondary Break Option is over and the "4-Out/1-In" Spot-Ups are once again filled, allowing for an immediate conversion into the designated continuity offense. See Diagram 12.11

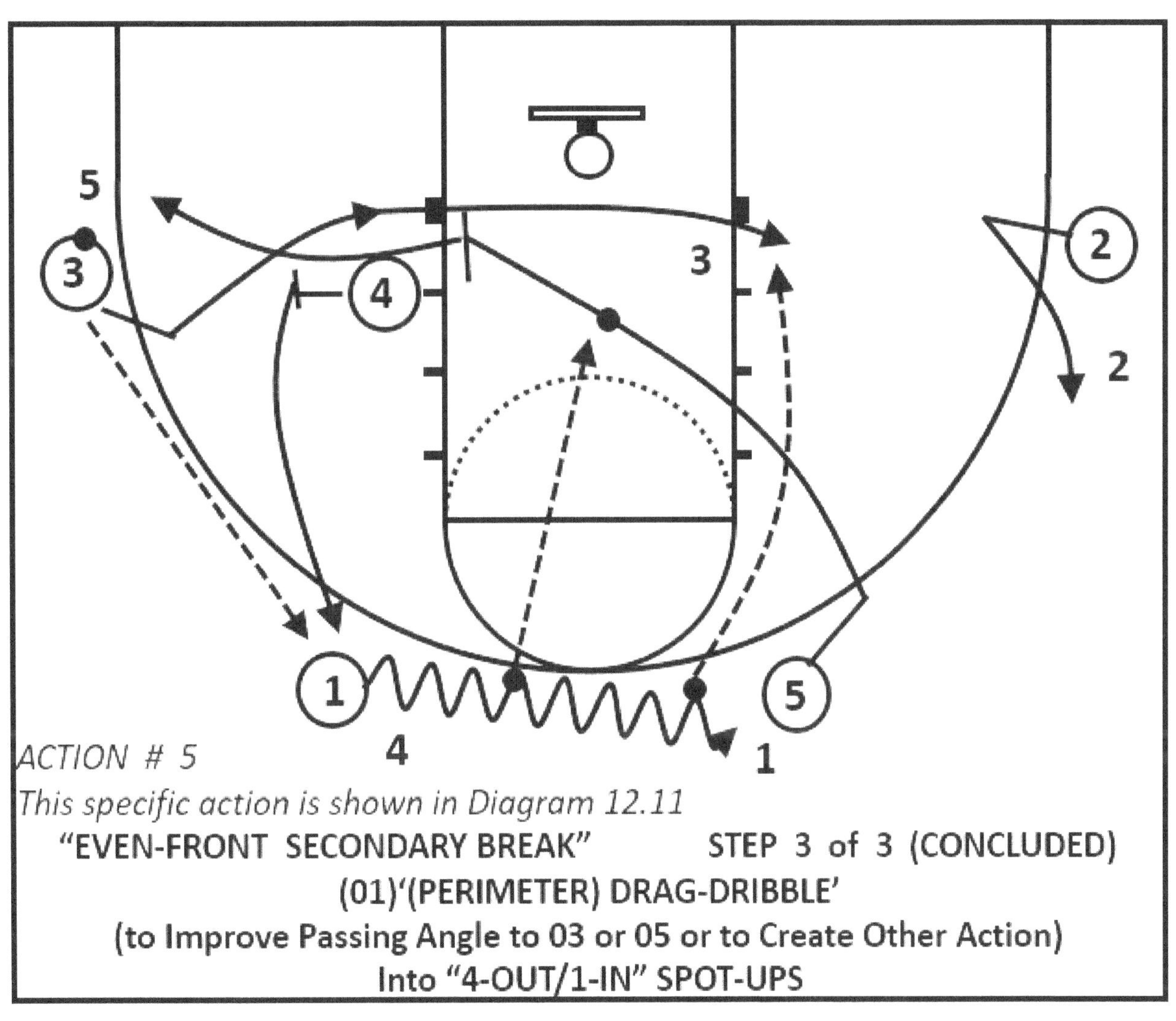

Diagram 12.11

Diagram 12.12 illustrates the entire half-court play/entry (Play # 6) that begins out of the "3-DOWN" Set. 04 steps up to set "Big-on-Small Ball-Screen" with the defense deciding to double-team trap the dribbler as he comes off of the screen. With two defenders (X1 and X4) trapping the ball, 04 slips his screen towards the empty "Slot" and 05 flashing to the middle of the floor (as he most likely would do against almost all half-court trap defenses.) This allows 03 to dive to the basket with 02 breaking up to become another safe outlet pass receiver. 01 "Escape Dribbles" out of the tight confines and then pulls one or both defenders out on the high "Slot" area where he has room to further escape the trap as well as to vertically and horizontally stretch the off-ball defenders that only number three defenders (against the four offensive players that are now spread out in shorter and safer passing lanes.)

The "Escape Dribble" not only evades the double-team trap but encourages the trap by spreading the floor before then attacking the disadvantaged defense. See Diagram 12.12

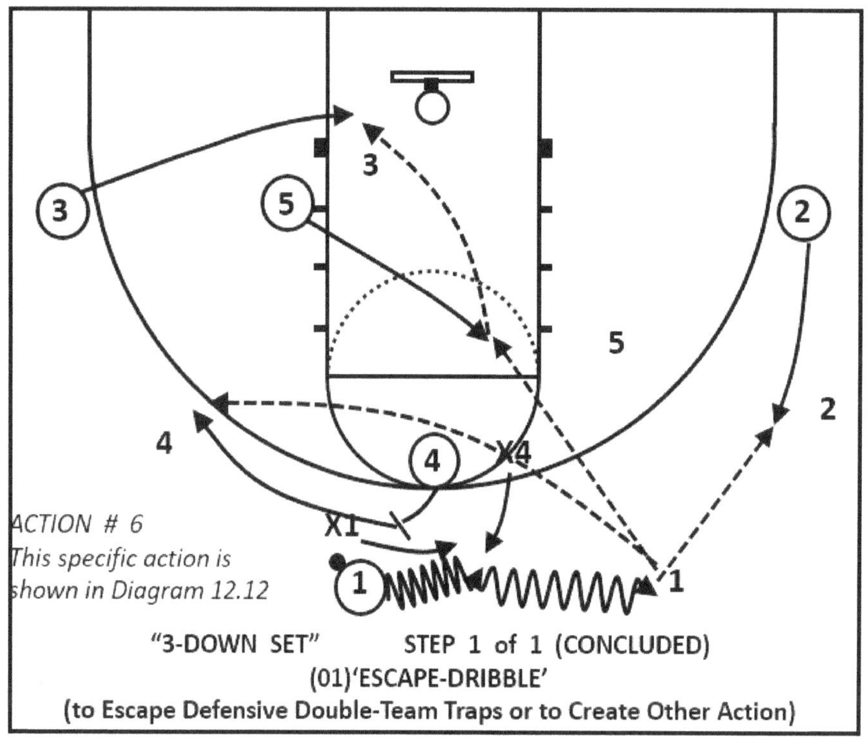

Diagram 12.12

With only six types of dribbles discussed, each dribble should be taught and coached by the coaching staff and it should be stressed that every player should be able to properly execute each of these fundamentally sound forms of dribbles.

It is very important to know that these 14 different types of passes can and should involve all five offensive players from the various locations on the floor. Each type of pass is fundamentally sound and can be executed for the success of each individual possession.

Every pass not only moves the ball but allows offensive players to move and create various types of actions that can attack both individual defenders as well as the overall team defense.

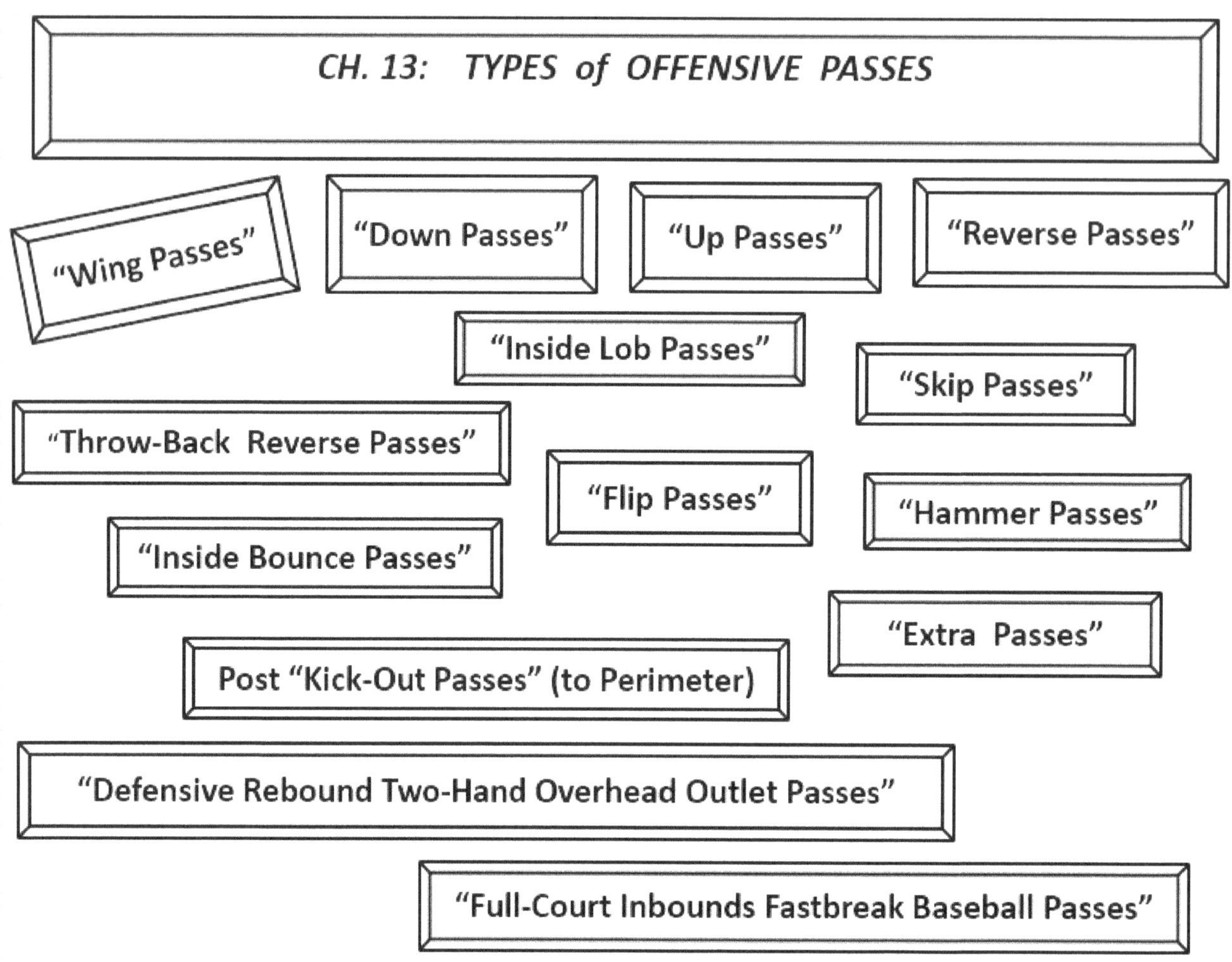

Illustration 13.1

Action # 1: "WING PASSES" ACTION

Diagram 13.2 shows an example of probably the most frequently used pass that immediately declares the offense's new "Ballside" and that most often is the method of beginning every half-court entry/play. Because of that frequency, opposing defenses often attempt to deny the offense's "Wing Pass." To counter the defensive pressure, various offensive cuts must be implemented to counter the defensive denial pressure, such as "Backdoor Cuts," "Zipper Cuts," "Pipe Cuts," "L-Cuts," "Pop-Out Cuts," "Iverson Cuts" or "Barkley Cuts."

This Play # 1 is started out of the "HI-LO STAX" Set with 03 popping out off of 05's "Pin Down-Screen" to the FT Line extended on his side of the floor, with 02 breaking straight out to the "Deep Corner" on his side of the floor and 04 making a diagonal inverted "Pop-Out Cut" to the FT Line extended on his side of the court.

01 makes the "Wing Pass" to 04 and then "Flare-Cuts" off of 05's "Flare-Screen" to the new "Weakside Wing." After setting his screen for 03, 05 continues across the FT Line to the opposite "Elbow" area. See Diagram 13.2

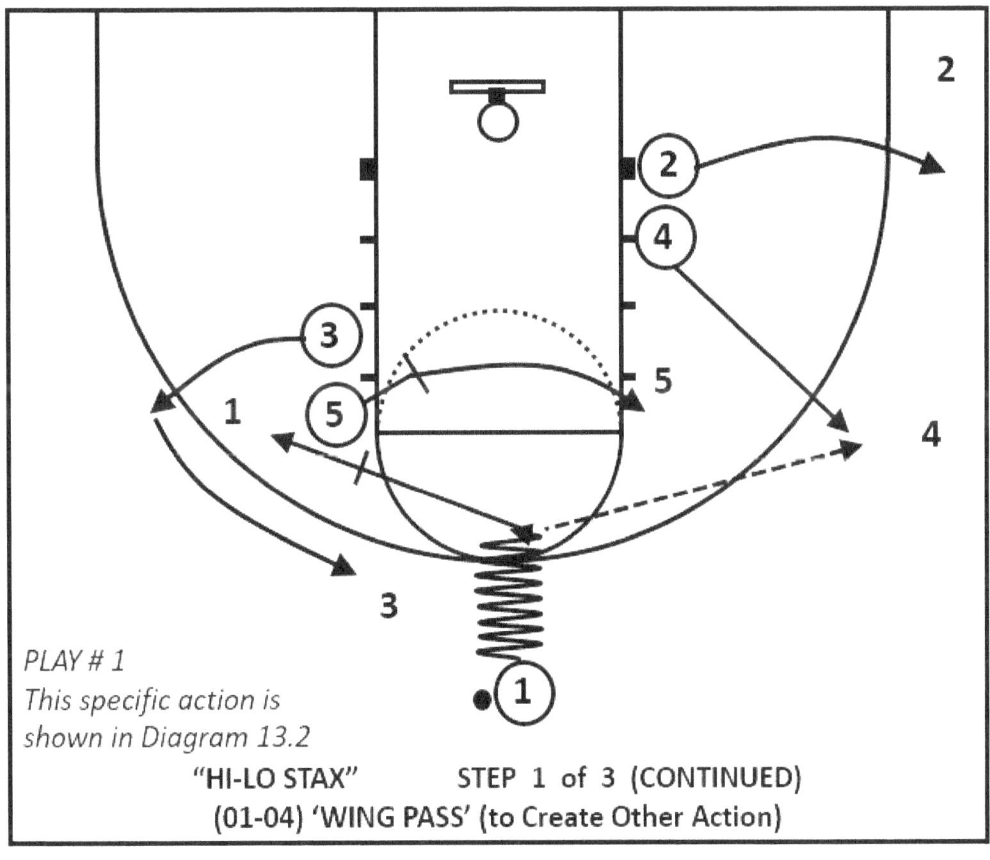

Diagram 13.2

Diagram 13.3 shows 04 looking to make the pass to 05 before then making a "Down Pass" to 02 in the "Deep Corner." 04 immediately attacks his "post-type defender," X4, with a "perimeter-type offensive cut,"- a "Give-n-Go Cut" (to the Block) and then to empty out to the opposite side of the lane. As soon as 04 starts to empty out of the lane, 05 times his cut to slide down the lane to post up on the "Ballside Block."

At the same time 04 and 05 make their cuts, both 03 and 01 make "Replacement Fill Cuts" to the two offensive "Slot" Spot-Ups locations. See Diagram 13.3

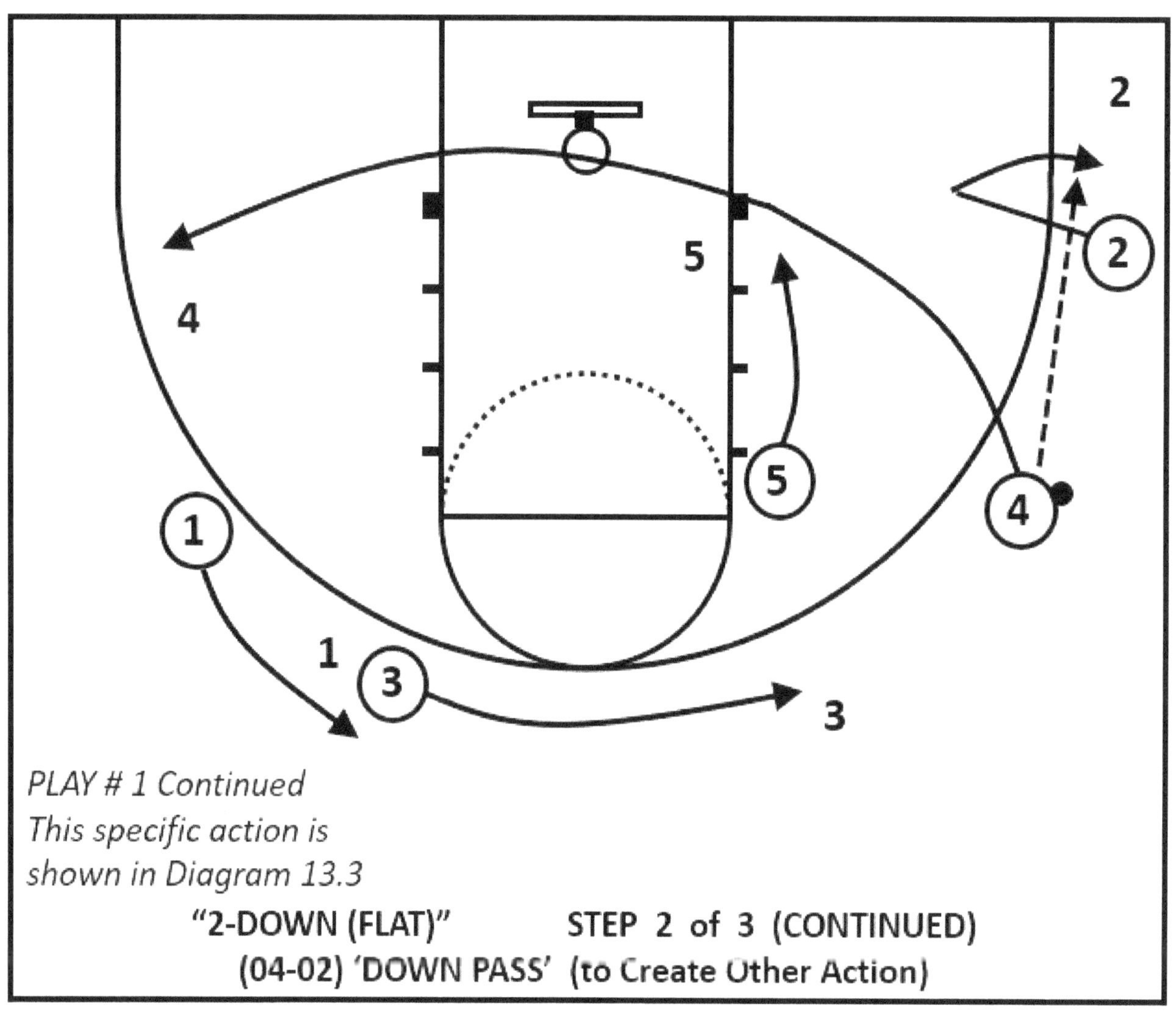

Diagram 13.3

If 02 cannot make passes to either 04 or 05 or a "Skip Pass" to 01; 02 makes the "Up Pass" to 03. If 03 cannot punch the ball inside to 05, 03 makes a "Reverse Pass" to 01 on the other side of the floor.

Upon making the pass to 01, 03 makes a diagonal "Give-n-Go Cut" through the lane to the opposite "Mid-Post Block" area. 01 looks to make the "Inside Pass" to 03, the "Down Pass" to 04, the "Reverse Pass" 05 or the "Skip Pass" to 02. While any of these passes can be made, all five players have repositioned themselves into the "4-Out/1-In" Spot-Ups so that the designated continuity offense can smoothly begin. See Diagram 13.4

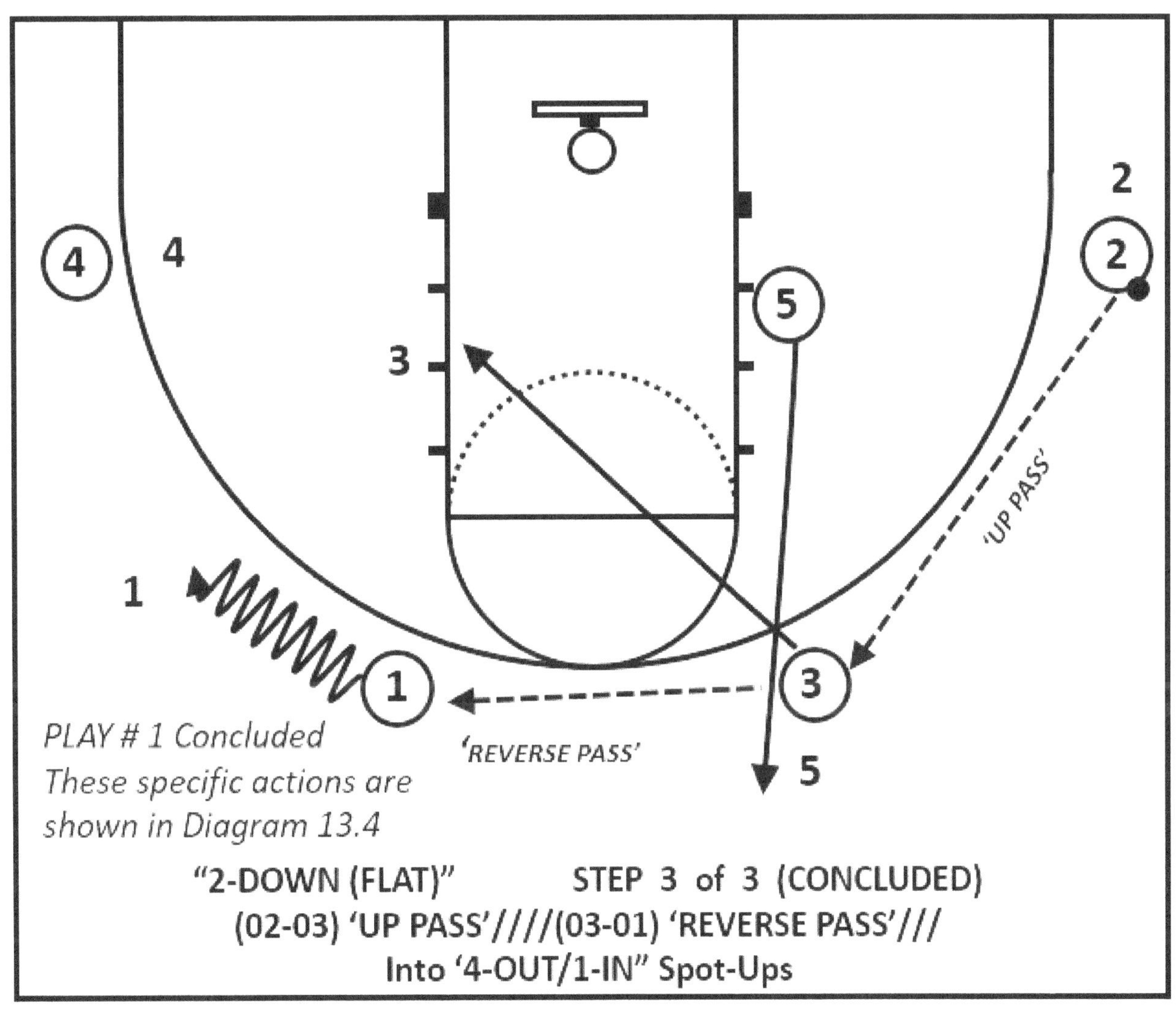

Diagram 13.4

Diagram 13.5 illustrates Play # 2 out of the "1-DOWN" Set. The play begins with an 02-01 "Reverse Pass" that is immediately followed by 04 stepping up to set a "Big-on-Small Flare-Screen," allowing 02 to make a "Flare-Cut" to the new "Weakside Wing" area. At the same time, 05 makes an aggressive "Iso Duck-In Cut" into the middle of the lane. With all four of 05's teammates outside of the arc and all at or above the FT Line extended, his "Duck-In Cut" should allow him to not only receive the ball but then attack his lone defender in the high percentage scoring area.

01 could also have a "Down Pass" opportunity to 03 who has drifted down to his "Deep Corner" area, a "Skip Pass" to 02 in his own "Deep Corner" or a possible "Reverse Pass" to 04 on the opposite "Slot" area. The "4-Out/1-In" Spot-Ups are properly filled so that the designated continuity offense can fluidly begin. See Diagram 13.5

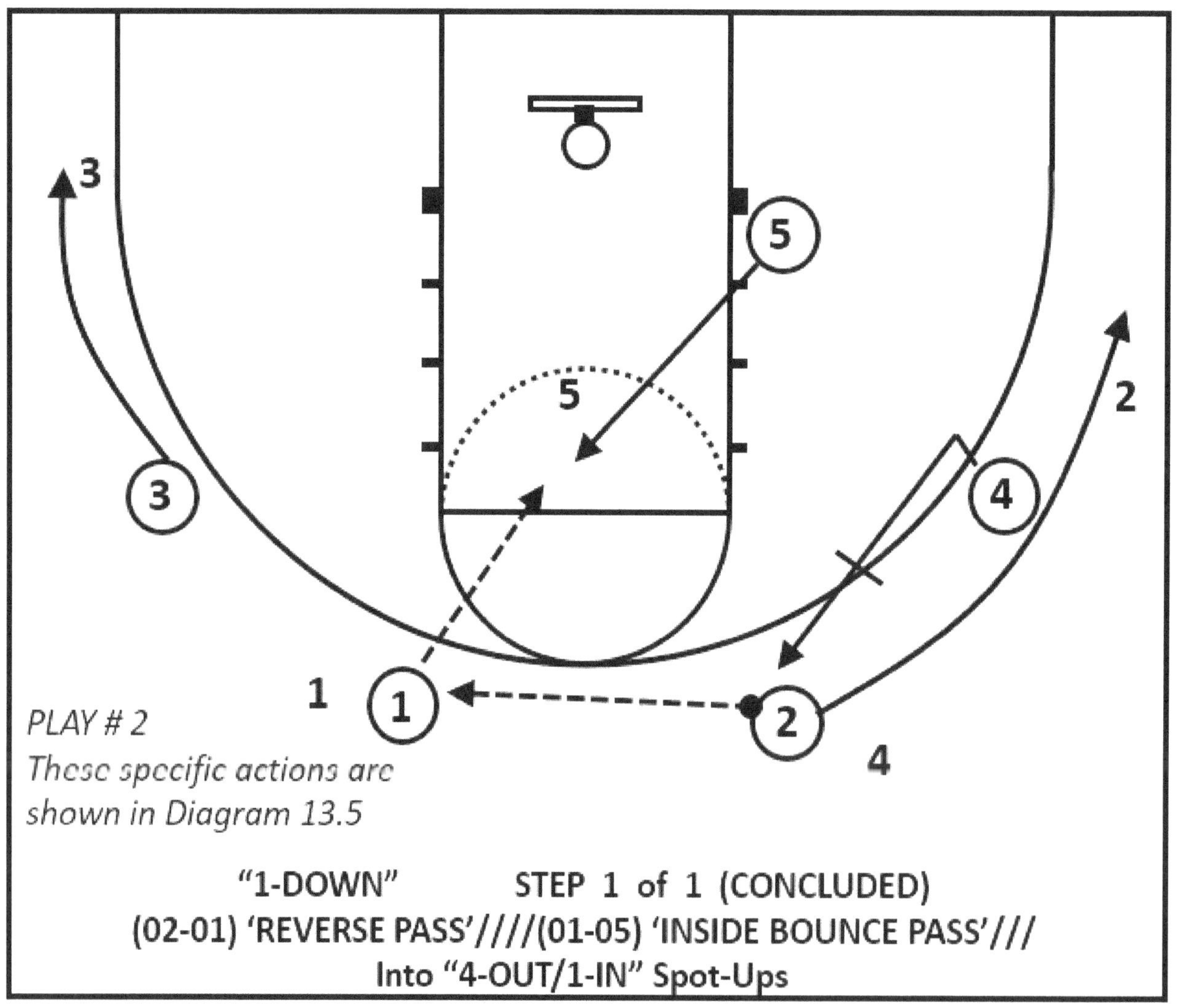

Diagram 13.5

Diagram 13.6 illustrates an entire play that begins out of the "2-UP" Set. This play could begin on either side of this symmetrically balanced offensive alignment, but this shows 01 making the "Wing Pass" to 03 and immediately following his pass with a cut towards 03.At the same time, 05 breaks from his initial "Nail" location to a "notch" below the new "Ballside Elbow" area.

At the same time, 01 makes his pass, 04 steps up to set a "Big-on-Small Flare-Screen" for 02 to make a "Flare-Cut" to a spot lower than the FT Line extended. 04 slips his screen and steps up to the new "Weakside Slot."

03 then makes a quick "Flip Pass" to 01 for 01 to make his "Perimeter Pull (Down) Dribble" towards the baseline. As he dribbles down towards the "Deep Corner," he looks to make an "Inside Pass" to 05, a baseline drive lay-up, a pull-up jump shot along the perimeter or a "Hammer Pass" to 02 along the Weakside Baseline. If shots are not created, the "4-Out/1-In" Spot-Ups are basically filled for an easy transition into the designated continuity offense. See Diagram 13.6

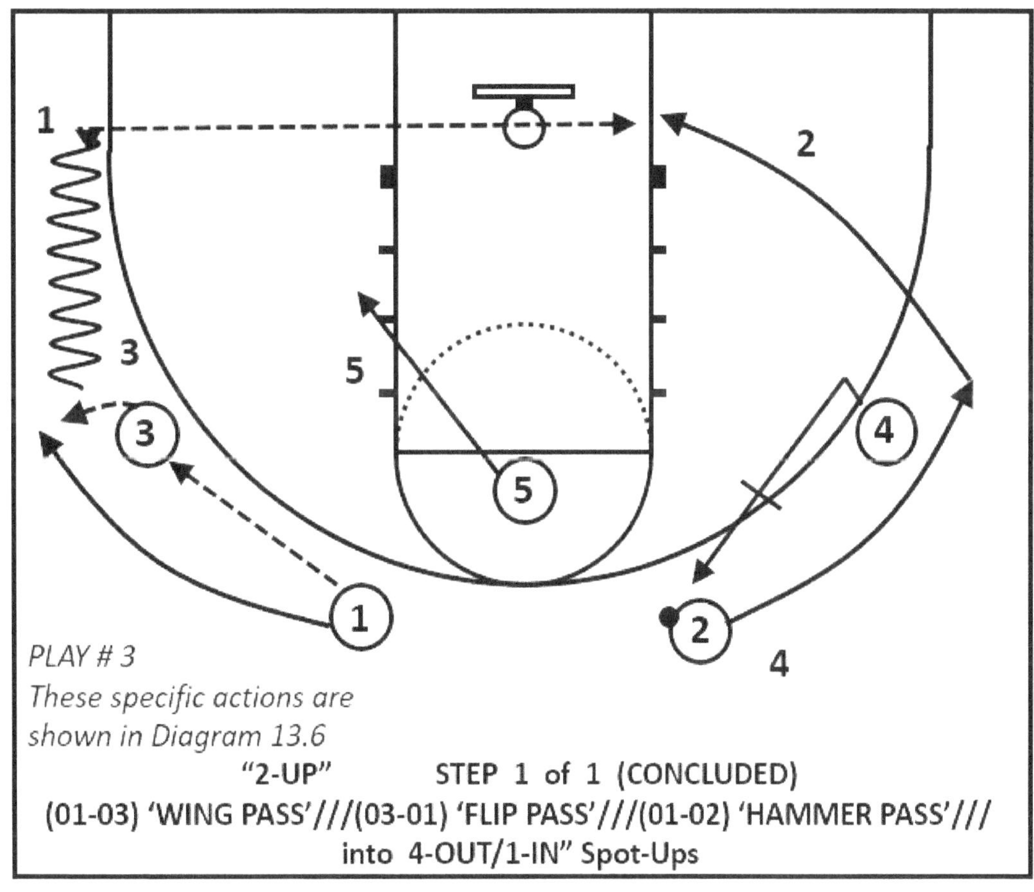

Diagram 13.6

Diagram 13.7 shows the entire Play # 4 where several types of passes are utilized in its attack on the opposition's defense. The play, out of the "3-ACROSS" Set, begins with 01 making a "Wing Pass" to 02 and 04 making a "Diagonal Slash Cut" to the newly declared "Ballside Block," while 05 makes an "Extended Elbow Vertical Up Cut" to the new "Weakside Slot." At the same time, 03 "Flare-Cuts" to his "Deep Corner" area and 01 rotates over to the new "Ballside Slot" location.

Diagram 13.7 then shows 02 making an "02-03" Skip Pass or another option of making an "Inside Pass" to 04.

After making the 02-04 "Inside Pass," 02 makes a "Drift Cut" towards his "Deep Corner." 04 looks to make "Post Kick-Out Passes" to either 02 or 01 on the initial ballside and possible passes to either 03 or 05. All five players have repositioned themselves into the popular "4-Out/1-In" Spot-Ups where any number of continuity offenses could immediately and fluidly begin. See Diagram 13.7

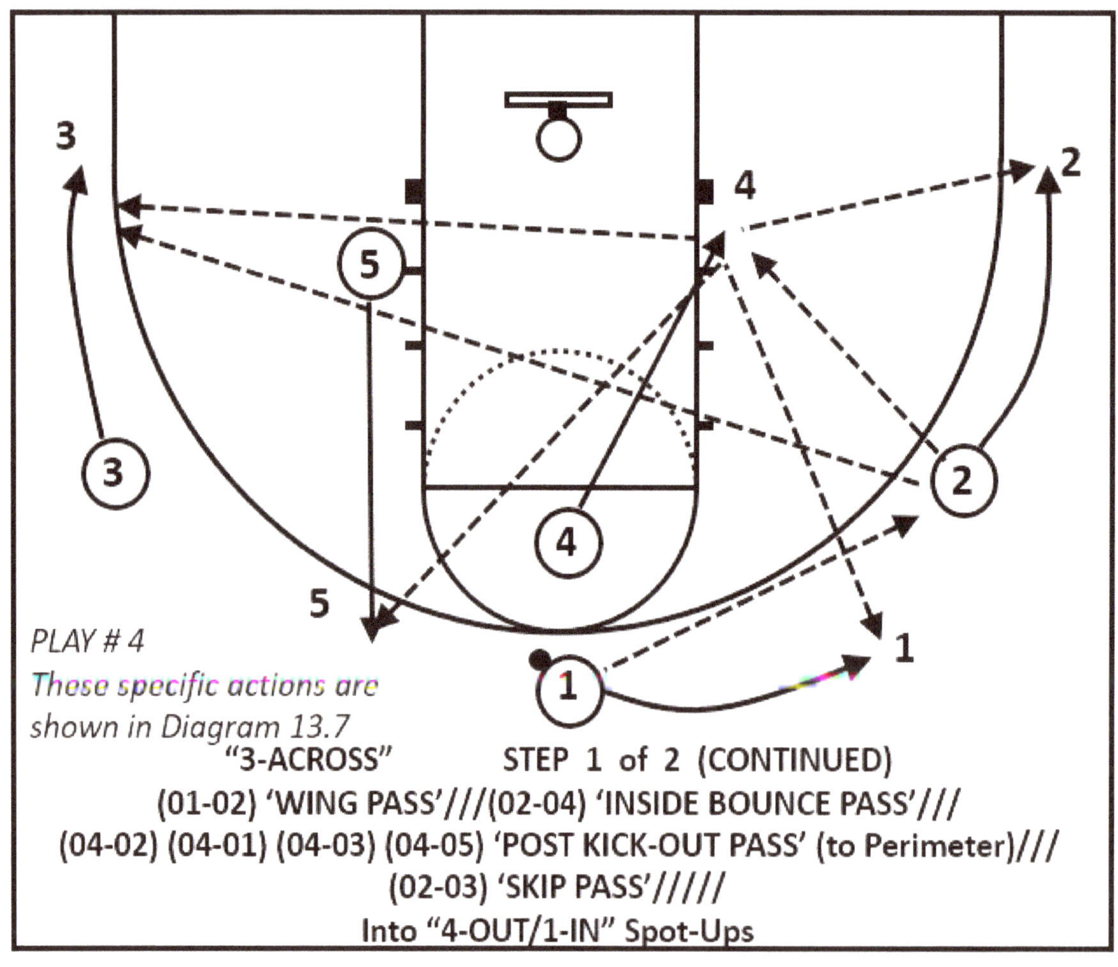

Diagram 13.7

Diagram 13.8 illustrates a different offensive scenario that illustrates a different type of pass. This action begins with the team starting on defense and obtaining possession of the ball with a defensive rebound. After successful defensive box-puts, 04 grabs the defensive rebound and looks to make the initial "Outlet Pass" ideally to the presumed best ball-handler, 01.

01 moves to an area where 04 can make a successful "Outlet Pass" while other players start to position themselves into their assigned Fastbreak running lanes. See Diagram 13.8

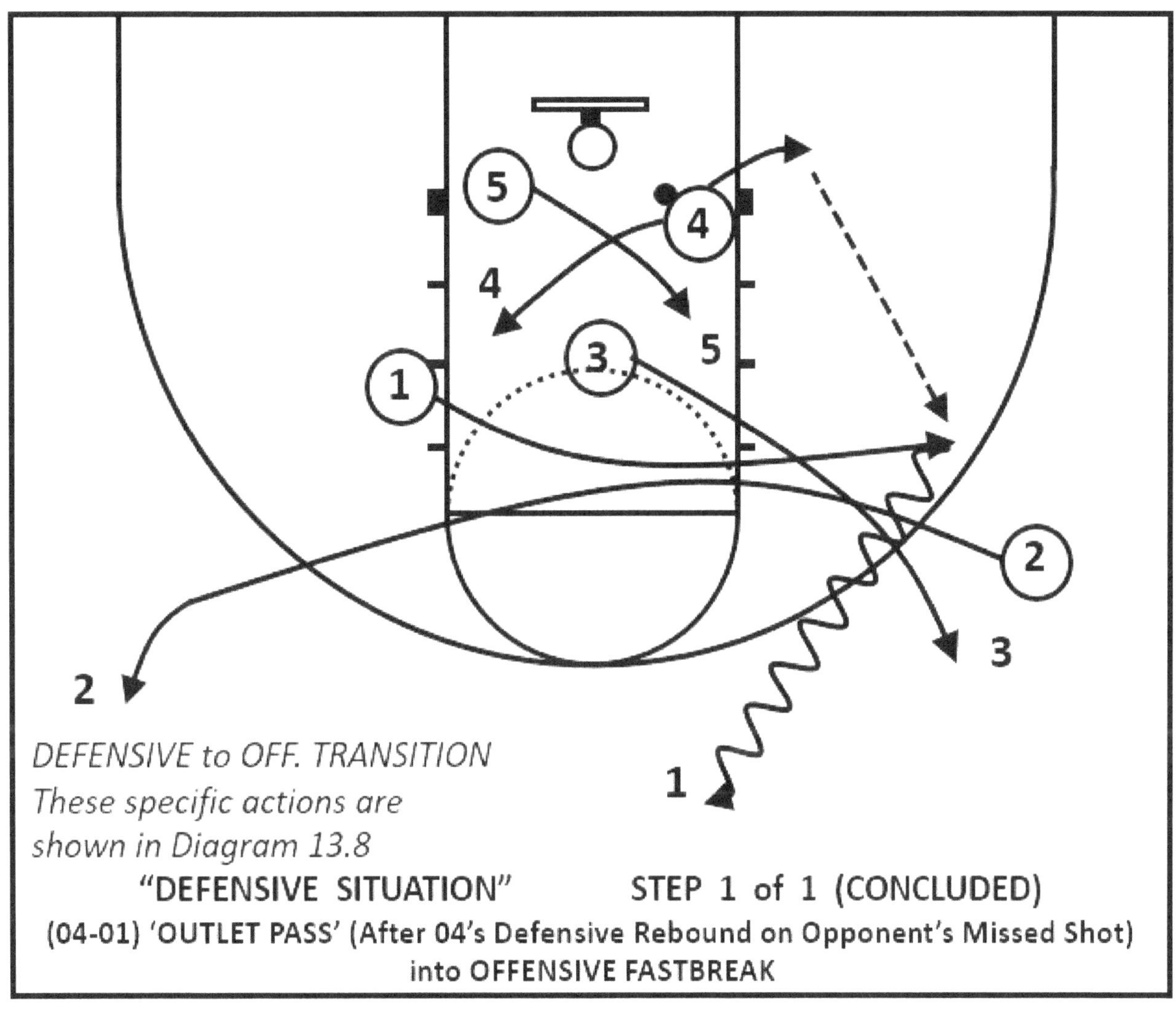

Diagram 13.8

Diagram 13.9. shows a similar situation where the opposing team has just scored and the defensive team turned offense immediately starts the repositioning of offensive players into their specific offensive positions. 05, called the "Trigger," is the player assigned to always take the ball out of bounds and look to make the passes to start the Primary Break. With 01 as the presumed designated primary ball-handler, 01 works hard to break towards 05 to receive the all-important "In-Bounds Pass."

Once the ball is in-bounded from 05 to 01, all players then look to get into their running lanes to start their Primary Break. See Diagram 13.9

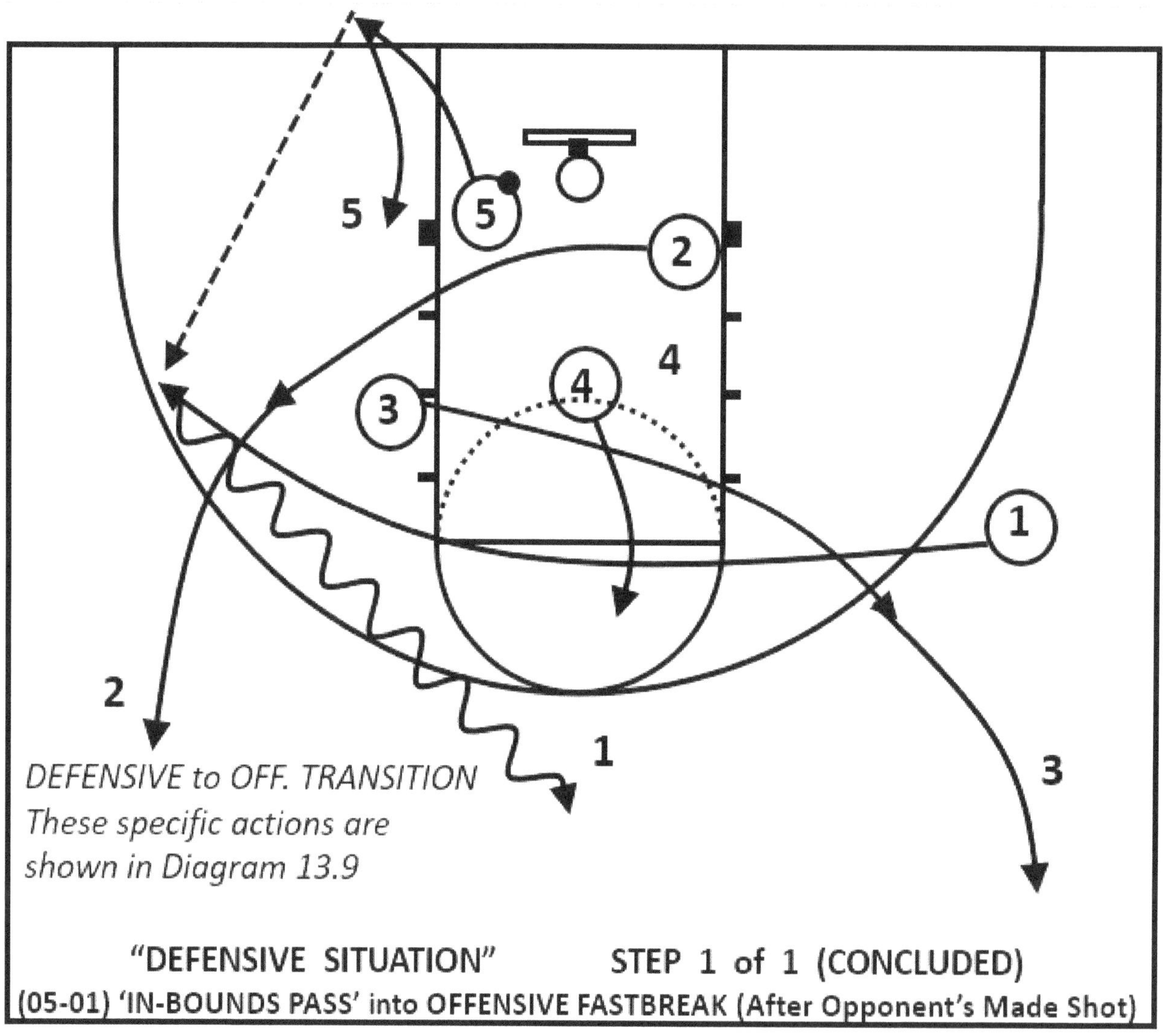

Diagram 13.9

With dribbling being the only other method of advancing the ball, it has already been stated how important these categories of passes are. Each offensive player, regardless of what position(s) each can play must be able to properly and successfully execute every kind of pass.

Each pass can help advance the ball, can place the ball in more advantageous positions, can place the ball in players' hands that have different and/or better offensive skills; making it more advantageous for those players to gain possession of the ball. As stated, each pass can change the location of the ball and give those offensive players ways to attack defenses in a myriad of ways.

With the final phase of all offensive attacks being the continuity or motion offense, it is extremely important that a coaching staff choose the most efficient and productive continuity offense. Most likely, the chosen continuity offense must agree with the staff's philosophy as well as coincide with the team's overall offensive strengths and avoid the majority of the team's weaknesses. The continuity offense must have a pre-determined set of offensive personnel spot-ups that allow the designated to seamlessly and immediately begin. With the continuity offense being able to then begin, the passing rules of the continuity offense then give the offense the means to fluidly begin and continue for indefinite periods of time.

The continuity offense and its rules must be simple enough for all players to understand and comprehend but be difficult for opposing defenses to predict the movements and actions. One possibility is to have one or two possible options or counter-options that could be integrated after the offense has been established.

Every offensive play/entry executed from each offensive alignment/set that is used that does not produce the desired shot but retains possession of the ball should always end up in the specific spot-ups where the designated continuity offense is able to immediately and smoothly begin. In addition, every Secondary Break Option that also is used but does not create the desired shot, the action should be able to reposition players into the same offensive spot-ups of the continuity offense.

In addition, every Baseline Out-of-Bounds play as well as each Sideline Out-of-Bounds play must also reposition players so that they fill the same continuity offense spot-ups. This allows the same continuity offense to again seamlessly begin.

Therefore, every type of offensive attack that does not produce the desired shot will at least place all five offensive players into the same spot-ups so that the designated continuity offense can begin.

Illustration 14.1 shows a flow-chart of how all half-court entries/plays will smoothly transition from one phase to the final phase of a designated continuity offense or motion-type offense for this Multiple-Phase Offense System. The first layer of the offense would be the specific offensive set/alignment an offensive team could use as it begins to then execute the various types of offensive plays/entries. When those entries do not create the desired shot that the coaching staff wants, at least the play will have repositioned all five players into the desired and correct spot-ups for the designated next phase of the offense; whether the staff believes in a motion-type offense or one (or more) types of continuity offenses which would include passing rules, counters and possible options to make the continuity offense less predictable and more fluid. This type of final phase of the offensive attack will give offensive players, as well as the overall team, additional advantages that can be used to successfully attack opposing defenses.

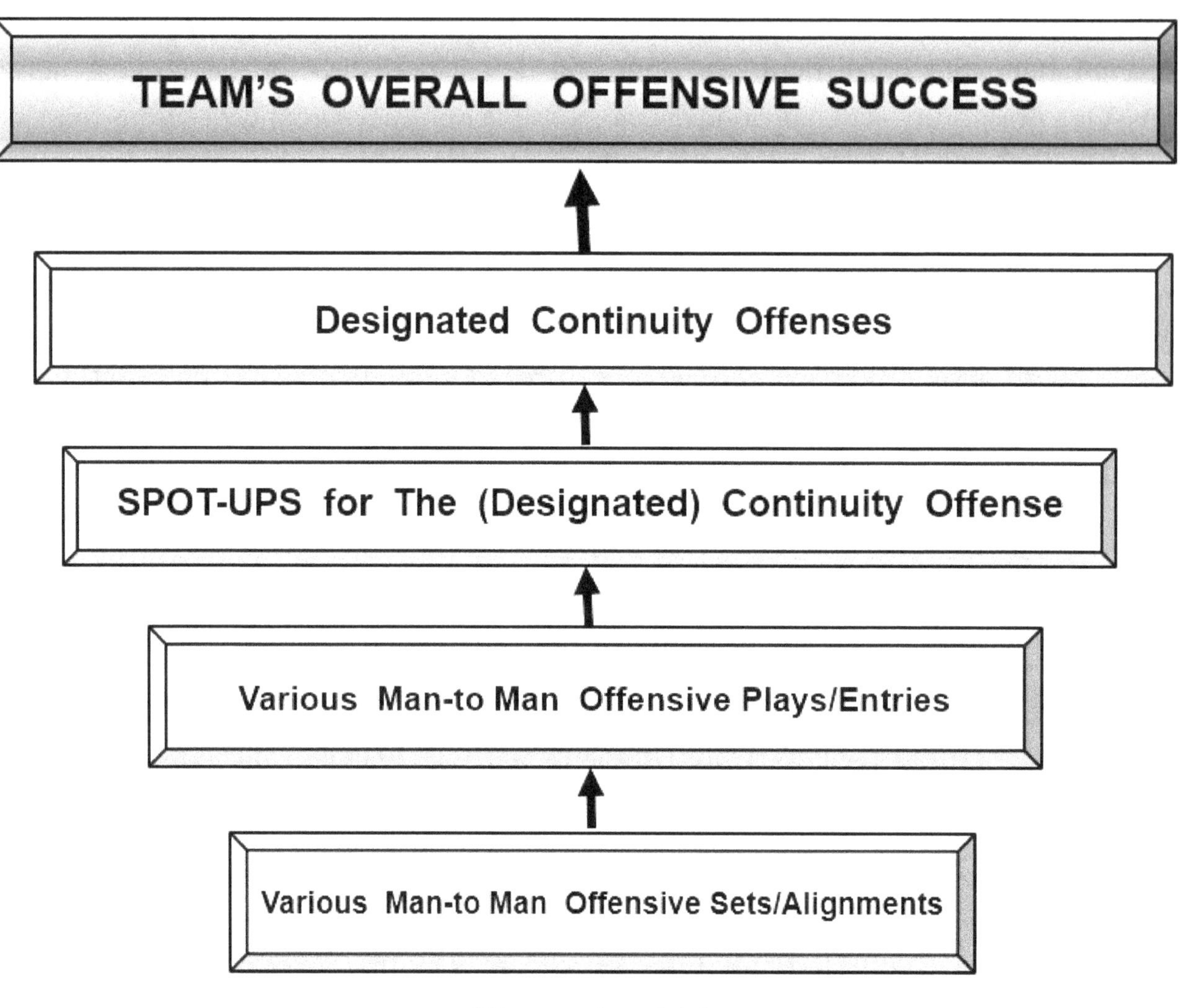

Illustration 14.1

Illustration 14.2 shows three different sets of spot-ups for various continuity offenses and/or for different motion offenses. These spot-ups could reposition players into either "4-Out/1-In Spot-Ups" that are almost symmetrically balanced so even though there is always an "Offensive Ballside" and an "Offensive Weakside," just the one player on the interior is the only player that prevents the offensive spot-ups to be perfectly symmetrical. These spot-ups could allow teams to have the smooth and immediate conversion (from the executed play/entry into either the desired continuity or the motion-type offense as the final offensive wave of attack.

Another set of spot-ups could place both a combination of one perimeter player and one interior post player on each side of the floor, with the fifth player exactly centered up in the middle of the floor at the top of the key. This makes the ending spot-ups in "3-Out/2-In Spot-Ups, where once again, the coaching staff can choose the last phase/wave of attack to be a (slightly more structured) continuity offense or a possible (more free-lance type of) motion offense.

The third type could be offensive spot-ups that have a "Ballside Block," a "Ballside High Post," a "Ballside Wing," a "Weakside Wing" and a player again centered up at the top of the key just outside of the arc. These spot-ups could be called the "1-3-1 High Post/Low Post" Spot-Ups that would allow the offensive team to immediately be able to execute its last wave of attack with its own continuity or motion-type offense.

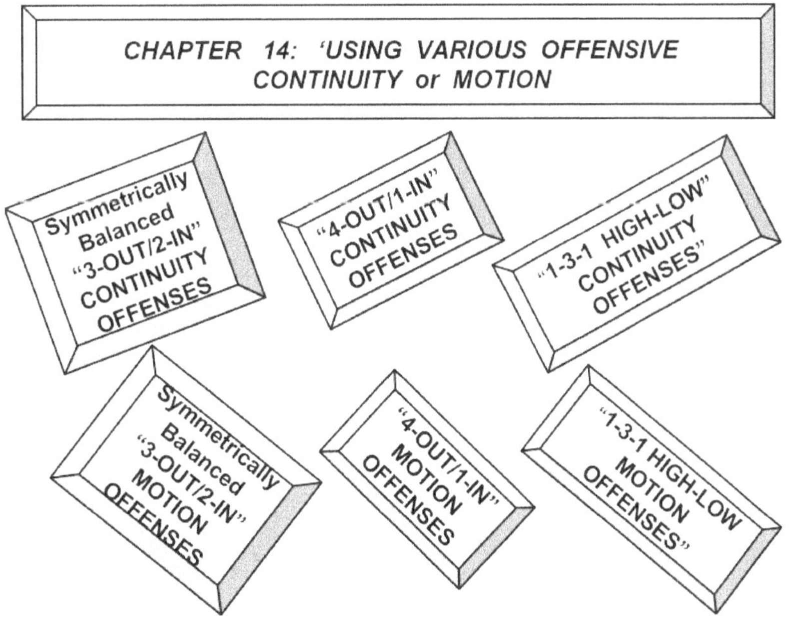

Illustration 14.2

Illustration 14.3 illustrates the simple and fundamentally sound Passing Rules of the "Triangle Power Game Continuity Offense": This continuity offense, with its actual (symmetrically balanced 3-Out/2-In Spot-Ups) would have five different types of passes that could be made within the structure of this "Triangle Power Game Continuity Offense." Each specific type of pass that could be made by any particular player from the selected spot-ups are: A) The "Wing Pass,"('Point to Wing' Pass) B) the "Skip Pass ('Wing to Wing' Pass,)" C) the "Reverse Pass," ('Wing to Point' Pass), D) the "Inside Pass (from any of the three perimeter spot-ups to a player spotted up on either interior position," and E) the "Kick-Out Pass (from a player in the post to any of the three perimeter players 'drifting' from their initial "3-Out/2-In perimeter Spot-ups" locations.

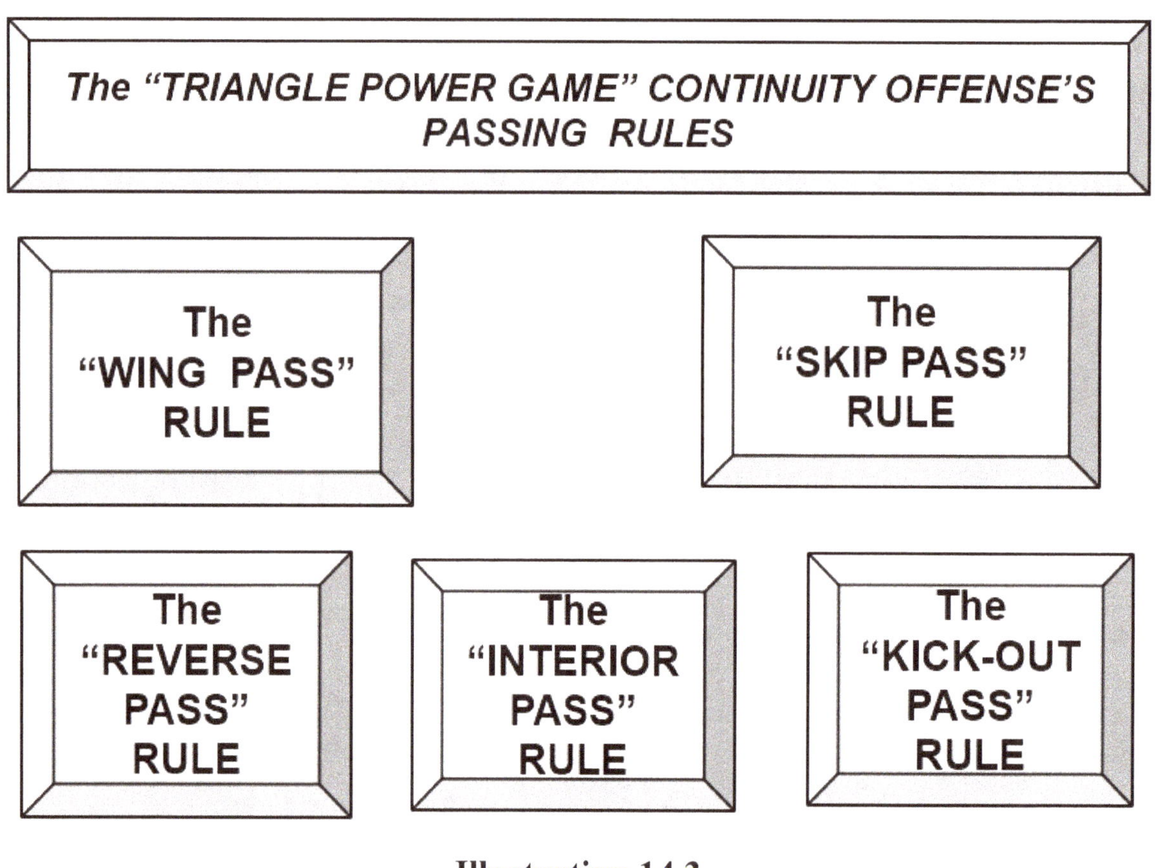

Illustration 14.3

The "TRIANGLE POWER Continuity Offense" (with "3-Out/2-In Spot-Ups")

Diagrams 14.1 and 14.2 illustrate just one example of an entry that begins out of an offensive alignment/set called "Horns." When the play does not produce the shot wanted, Diagram 14.2 shows the offensive action has repositioned all five players into the (symmetrically balanced) "3-Out/2-In Spot-Ups" for the designated continuity offense to be able to immediately begin. The next-phase continuity offense is called the "Triangle Power Continuity Offense."

Diagram 14.1 illustrates both 03 and 02 make their "Iverson Cuts," with 02 making the high cut first over the top of 04 and then 05. 02 ends up at the FT Line extended on the opposite side of the floor, while 03 makes the lower cut along the baseline up to the FT Line extended on the right side of the floor.

See Diagram 14.1

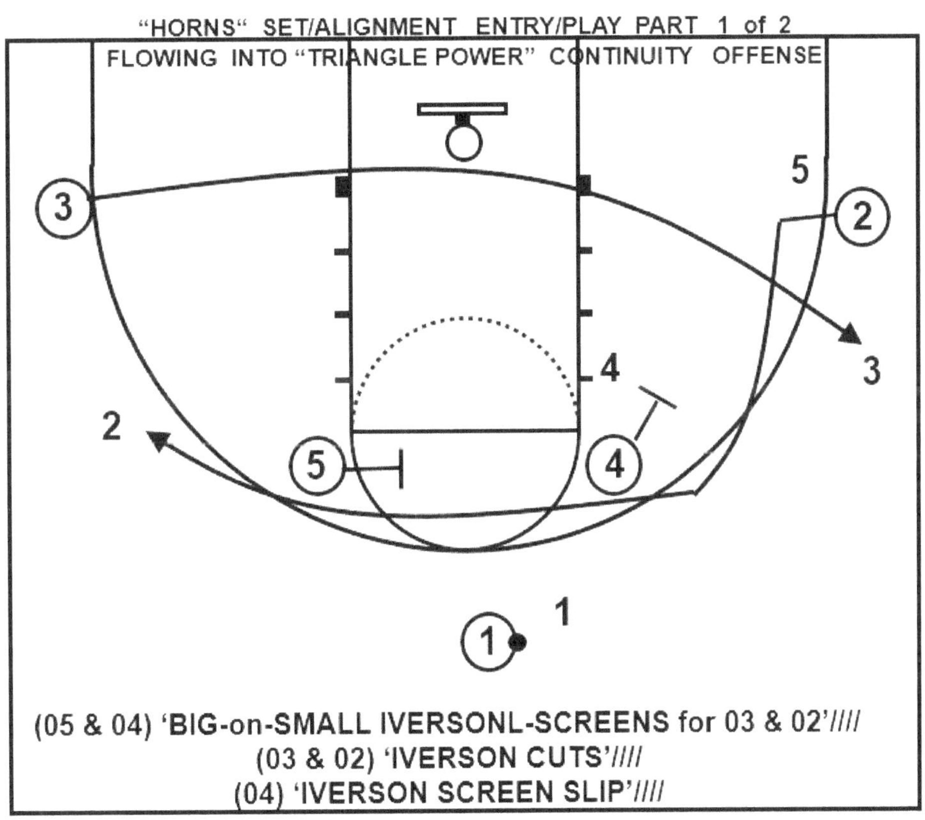

Diagram 14.1

With the "HORNS" Set initially being a symmetrically balanced offensive set and both 03 and 02 making the same "Iverson Cuts," players basically end up being in what we call the "5-UP" Set. This set/alignment also is a symmetrically balanced alignment that provides the offensive team with the benefit of 01 being able to make the initial "Wing Pass" to either 02 on the left side or to 03 on the right side of the floor.

The initial "HORNS" Set and the "Iverson Cuts" give the offense an advantage of being able to maximize the amount of being unpredictable to the opposing defense. In this instance, Diagram 14.2 shows the initial "HORNS" Set transforming into the "5-UP" Set (after the "Iverson Cuts" are made) and 01 electing to make the pass to 02 (instead of to 03) now at the "Wing" on the left side of the floor.

04 immediately slashes diagonally across the lane to post-up his defender in an isolated situation. After 01 makes the pass to 02, 05 has finished setting his "Iverson Screen" for 02, he slips his screen and makes a "Rim-Run Lob Cut" to the basket and waiting for 02's possible "Lob Pass." 03 should first look to make the "Inside Pass" to 04 on the "Ballside Block." As soon as the ball is out of 01's hands, 03 steps up to set his "Big-on-Small Flare-Screen." 01 sets up his defender and scrapes off of 03's top left shoulder and makes his Flare-Cut" to the now completely empty weakside perimeter area. 01 immediately starts to "get his feet and hands ready" for a possible "Skip Pass" from 02. 01e would have the possible "catch and shoot," a "catch and create" or "catch and pass (to 05)" possibilities. After screening for 01, 03 then slips his "Flare-Screen" and steps towards the top of the key, also prepared for a pass from 02. All five players have moved from their initial locations in the "HORNS" Set and have repositioned themselves in the proper "3-Out/2-In Spot-Ups," which are the "TRIANGLE POWER CONTINUITY OFFENSE." See Diagram 14.2

"HORNS" SET/ALIGNMENT ENTRY/PLAY PART 2 of 2
FLOWING INTO "TRIANGLE POWER" CONTINUITY OFFENSE
4
5
1
2
3
5
4
2
3
1
(01-02) 'WING PASS'////
(04)'IVERSON SCREEN & SLIP to SLASH to LOW POST'///
(05)'IVERSON SCREEN SLIP & LOB CUT to RIM'////
(03-01) 'BIG-on-SMALL FLARE-SCREEN for 01'////
(01) FLARE-CUT'////
into "3-OUT/2-IN SPOT-UPS"

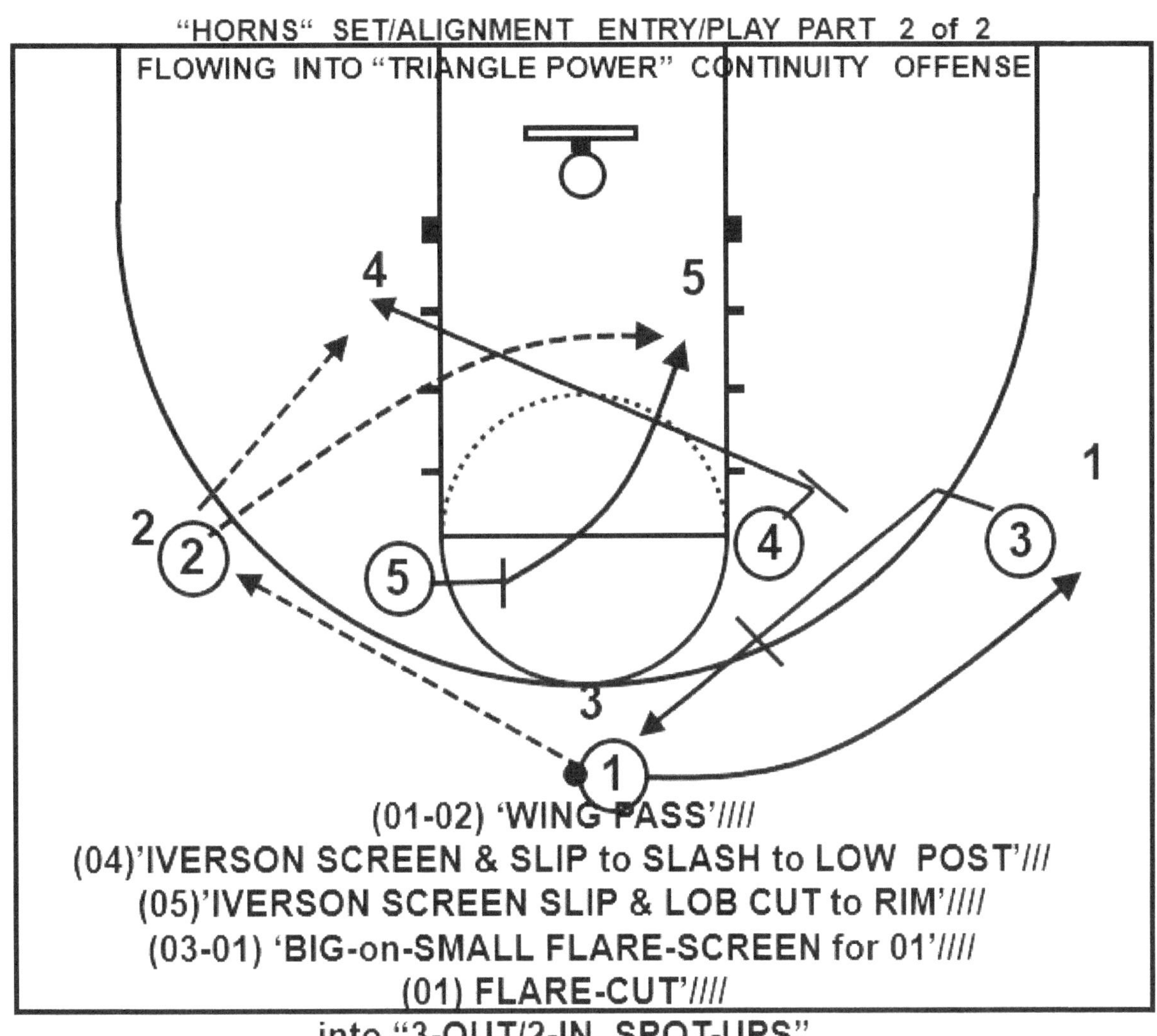

Diagram 14.2

Diagram 14.3 illustrates 02 looking for his possible pass-receivers in the proper priority order (04, 05 01 and then 03) as well as his own shooting and creating possibilities. When 02 elects to reverse the ball to 03, the "TRIANGLE POWER GAME CONTINUITY OFFENSE" immediately begins with the "Reverse Pass" first taking place. The "Reverse Pass Rule" is that when the "Reverse Pass" is made (from 02 to 03 in this instance), the actual "Ballside Post" (04 in this instance) always seals off his defender and makes a short diagonal "Lob Cut" to the rim. At the same time, 03 receives the "Reverse Pass," the "Weakside Post Player (05 in this diagram) makes a hard and aggressive "Iso Duck-In Cut" into the 'Dotted Circle' area.

This passing rule states that both players in the two post locations (04 and 05 in this instance) make their respective cuts and if neither receives the ball, both stop their respective cuts and immediately return to their initial locations on the same sides of the lane.

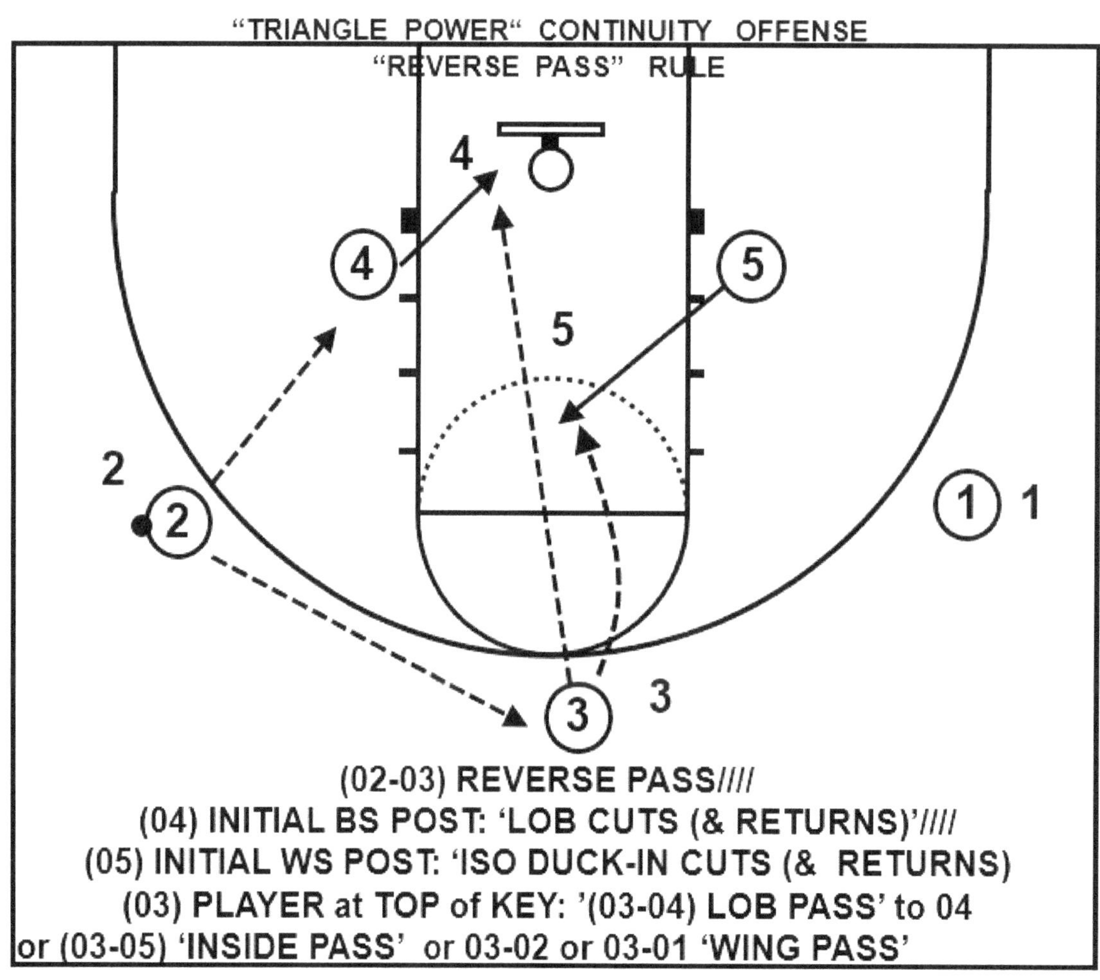

Diagram 14.3

Diagram 14.4 illustrates 03 having the ball at the top of the key, with the opportunities to make "Inside Passes" to either 04 or 05 or "Wing Passes" to either 02 or 01. This diagram shows 03 electing to make the "Wing Pass" to 01, activating the "Wing Pass Rule." As the pass is made, both players in the post locations (04 and 05) have returned to their initial post-up "spot-up" positions. After making the pass, 03 takes two steps towards his pass before then diagonally breaking down away from the ball to set a (in this case, a "Small-on-Big") Diagonal Down-Screen. This action is to not only help eliminate or minimize the helpside defense that X5 would need to successfully defend 05 (now on the Ballside Post), but to give 04 an open shot possibility on his cut off of 03's Diagonal Pin-Down Screen. 04 should scrape off of 03's outside left shoulder and break up through the lane to the top of the key. After immediately cutting off of the screen 04 should be prepared to receive 01's pass anywhere in the lane or as far out outside of the '3 Pt. arc at the top of the key (for a possible '3 Pt. shot.) At the same time, 02 should float behind the arc on the weakside wing area and be prepared for 01's "Skip Pass." 02's location and movement action also should horizontally stretch the defense and help minimize the opposition's helpside defense. This will give 05 a better isolation post-up opportunity on the "Ballside Block." See Diagram 14.4

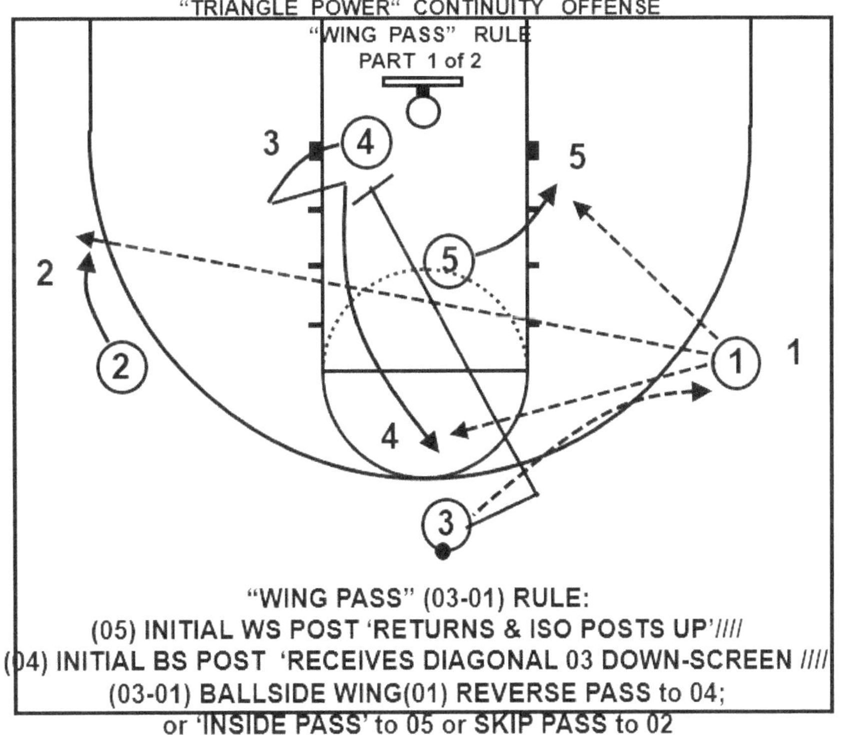

Diagram 14.4

After two counts and 05 not receiving 01's "Inside Pass," 05 turns to empty out and cut across the lane. It is 03's responsibility to set his defender up before using 05 as a "Lane Exchange Cross-Screener," electing to scrape off of either shoulder of 05 on his cut across the lane. This action is the last action of the "Wing Pass Rule." See Diagram 14.5

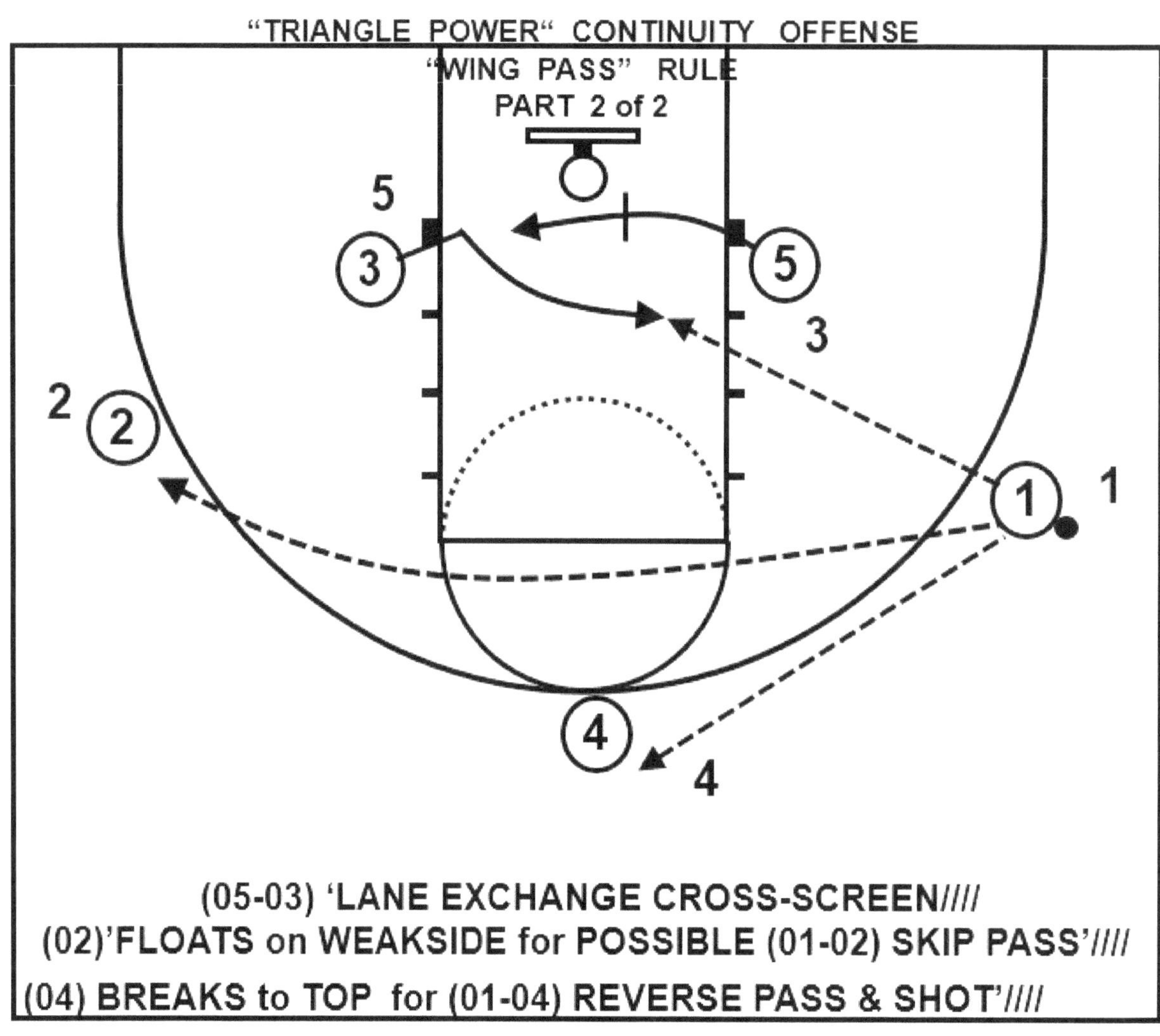

Diagram 14.5

After receiving 03's "Wing Pass" and turning down all of his possible offensive choices, 01 could make the pass out to 04 at the top of the key. This activates the (01-04) "Reverse Pass Rule." With the exception that the ball is reversed from the opposite side of the floor, Diagram 14.6 shows the action that follows the "Reverse Pass" just as Diagram 14.3 illustrates the same action, from the opposite side of the floor. In this instance, the new "Ballside Post" (03) makes the same "Rim-Run/Lob Cut" with 05 making the same type of "Iso Duck-In Cut" (as 04 and 05 actually did, respectively in Diagram 14.3).

When 04 does not make any "Inside Passes" to 03 or to 05, 04 has the freedom and choice to make a "Wing Pass" to either side of the floor. This again gives the offense the advantage of not only being able to attack the interior this time with two different inside scoring threats (against two different opponents) as well as being able to attack both perimeter sides of the floor with new offensive players spotted up on the perimeter. See Diagram 14.6

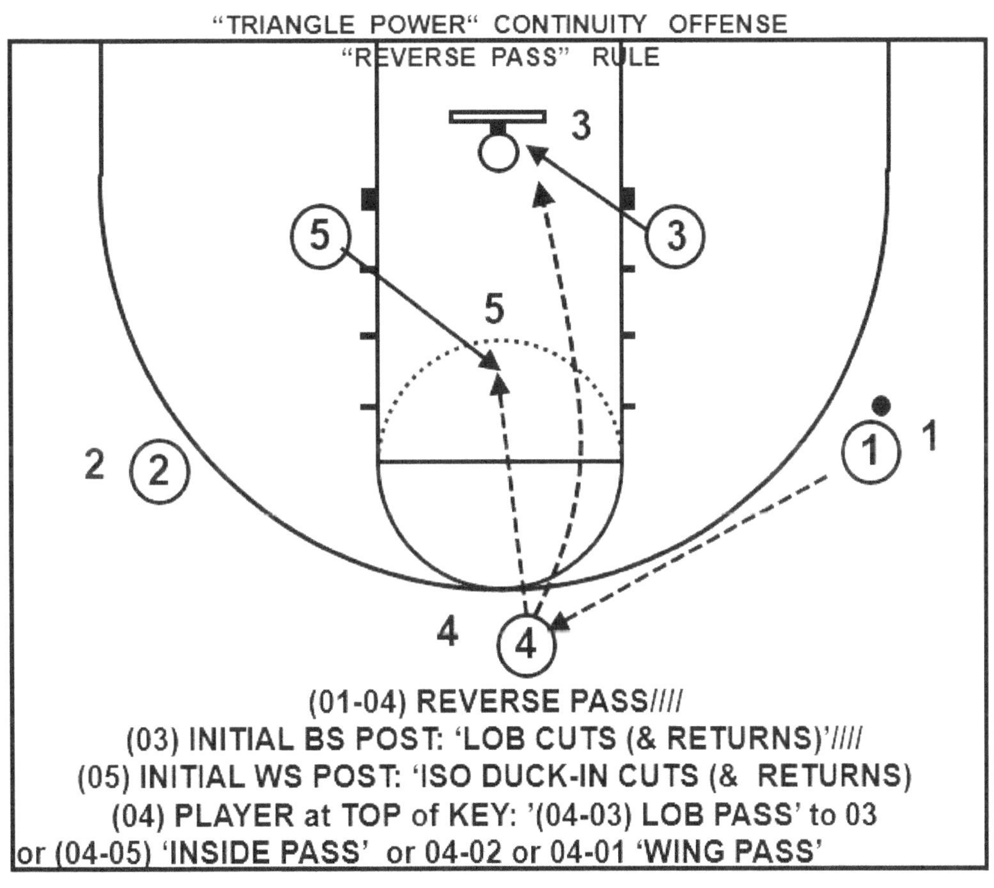

Diagram 14.6

Diagram 14.7 shows 04 continuing the swing of the ball by making his "Wing Pass" over to 02 on the left side of the floor. As 05 posts up his defender, 04 then cuts down to set the "Big-on-Small" Diagonal Down-Screen for 03 to use to break up to the top of the key. This action again helps eliminate the opposition's helpside defense that X5 needs to be effective in denying 02's "Inside Pass" to 05. In addition, 03 should be a legitimate scoring threat at the top of the key. These actions stretch the defense both vertically and horizontally as well as attacking the interior and the perimeter and on both sides of the floor. See Diagram 14.7

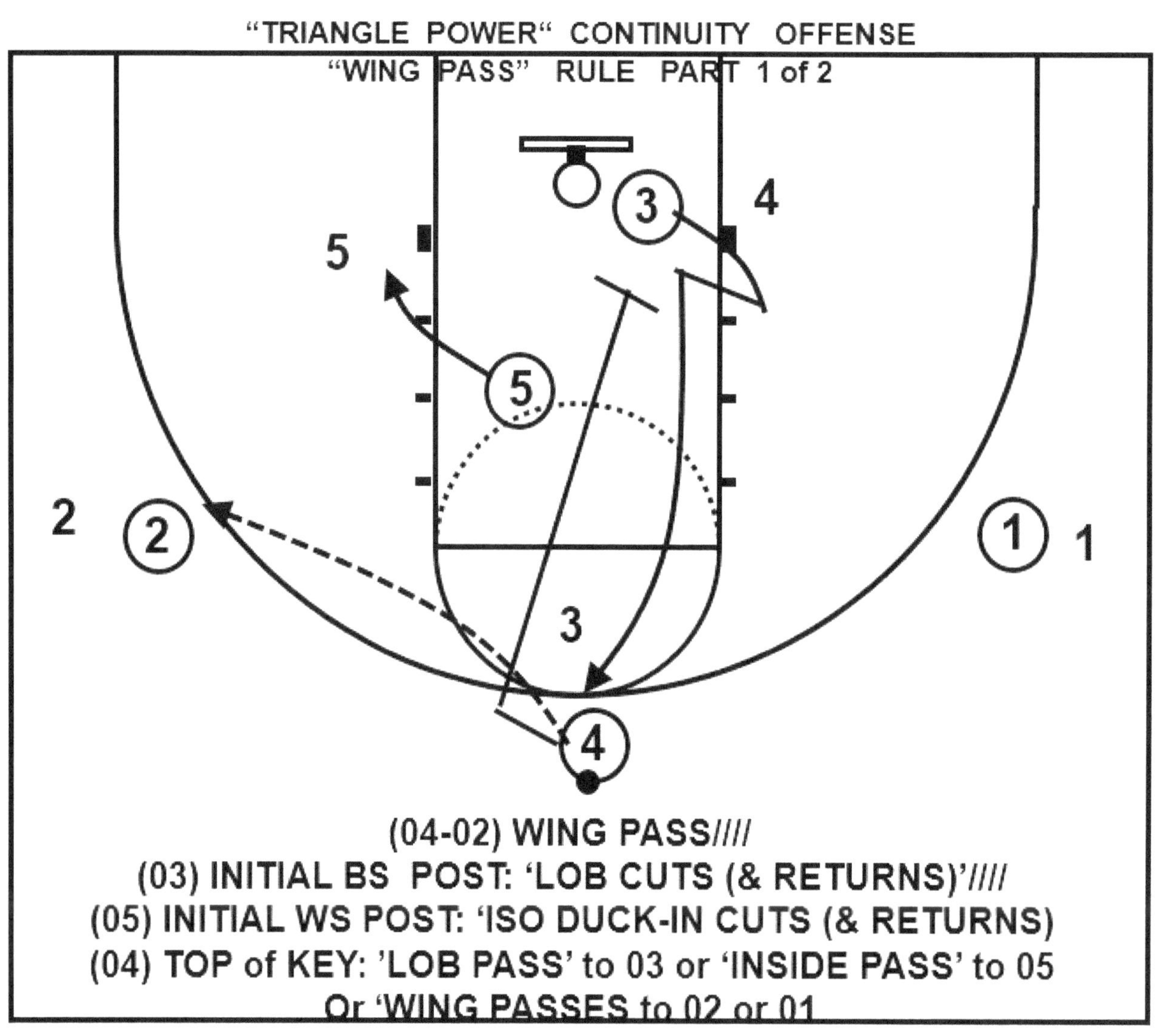

Diagram 14.7

After two counts of 02 not making the "Inside Pass" to 05, 05 then pivots and turns to empty out across the lane. 04's responsibility is to then search for 05 and to then scrape off of either shoulder to make his "Lane Exchange Cross-Screen" and to become the new "Ballside Post." 02 looks to then make the "Inside Pass" to 04 as he flashes across the lane, after freeing himself of X4 (with the 05-04 Cross-Screen.) 02 also has two perimeter pass opportunities, with 01 drifting behind the defense on the weakside and preparing for a "Skip Pass." 03 also could and should be a very legitimate scoring threat at the top of the key. See Diagram 14.8

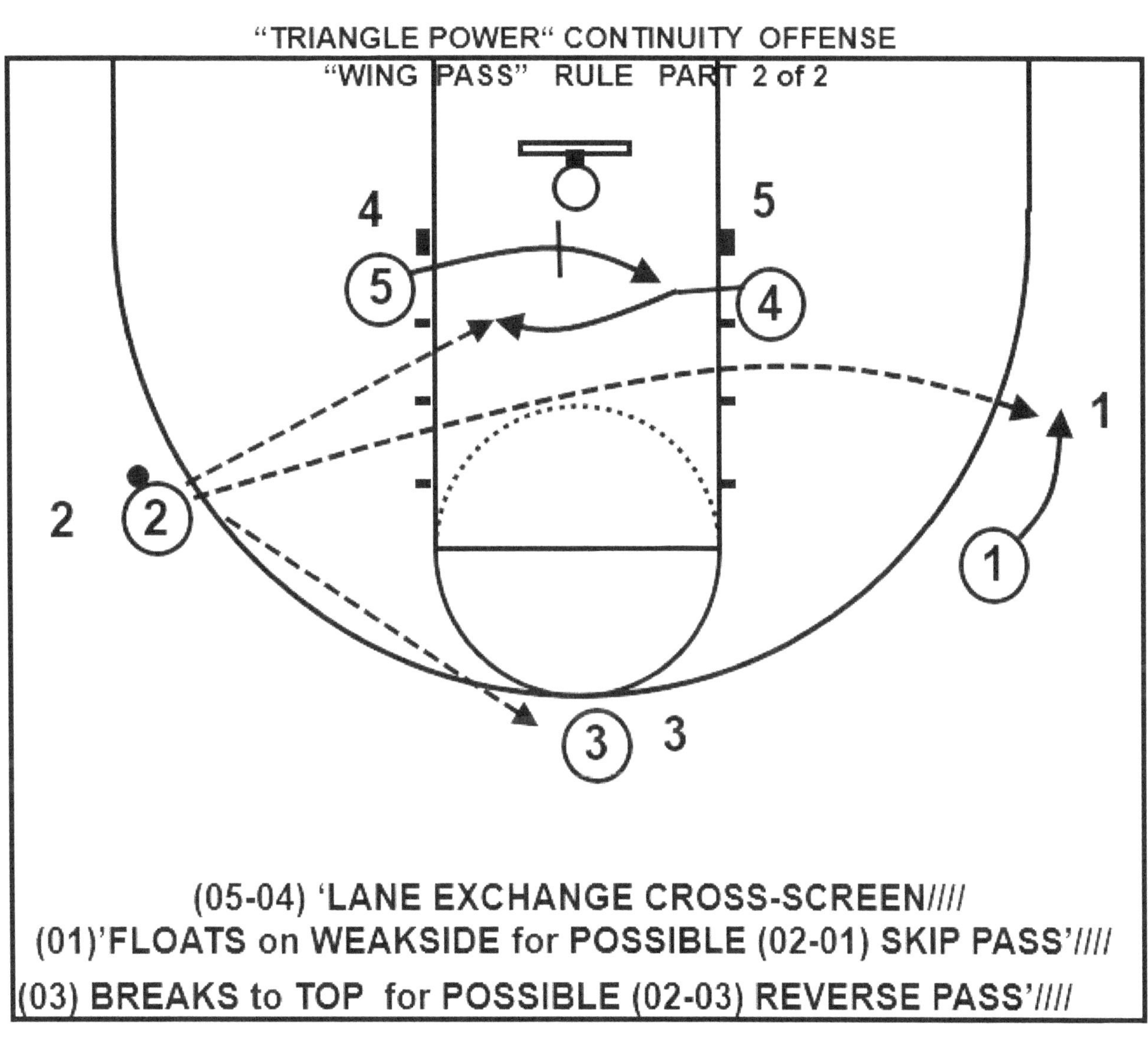

Diagram 14.8

Diagram 14.9 shows 02 making an "Inside Pass" to 04. To discourage defensive double-down traps on the ball in the post, all three players (regardless of whether they are classified as 'true perimeter players' or true 'offensive bigs,' are taught to always make "Drift Cuts" one half of an offensive spot-up TOWARDS the Ballside and away from their initial positioning. In addition, they are coached to immediately "get their feet and hands ready" for a quick "catch and shoot" or "catch and create" opportunities when the ball is kicked out by the player receiving the initial "Inside Pass." This action will either create offensive opportunities on the perimeter throughout the entire floor or discourage defenses from double-teams; giving more isolation post moves and attacks.

This diagram shows 02 drifting towards the "Deep Corner," with 03 rotating over towards the new "Ballside Slot" area and 01 moving over to the new "Weakside Slot" location. Perimeter players have basically rotated momentarily into "4-Out/1-In Spot-Ups." If any individual perimeter defender turns his head to drop into the post, his own individual offensive opponent will have moved from his initial location. If the ball is shot or if the ball is passed out, those defenders that committed to stopping the inside threat will not be able to quickly find and defend their own man. See Diagram 14.9

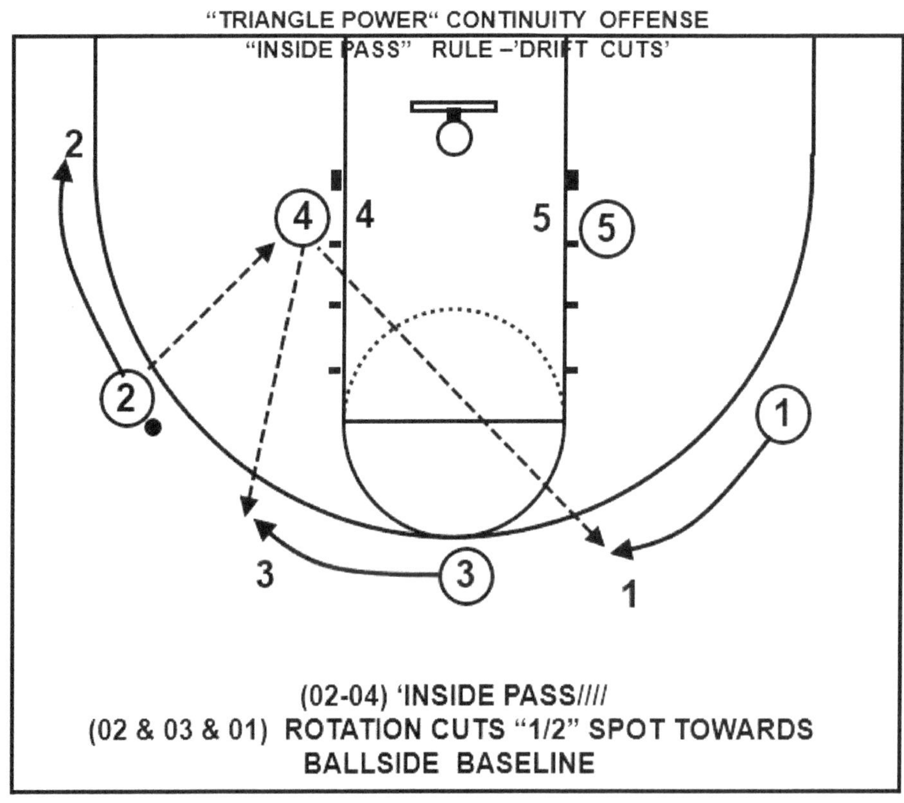

Diagram 14.9

After the "Inside Pass" is made to 04 and the "Drift Cuts" are made; all players that made their "Drift Cuts" *towards* the Ballside, now make the same "Drift Cut" back away from the "Ballside" and to their initial "3-Out/2-In Spot-Ups" positions. If 04 reads the defense collapsing on him or he finds an open teammate on the perimeter, he should make the "Kick-Out Pass" to his open teammate (whether it is 02, 03 or 01).

In this example, 04 makes the pass back out to 02 (after X2 has tried to 'double-down on the ball,' Being prepared before the pass has even been made, 02 has the same opportunities as a player receiving a "Skip Pass." 02 could immediately "catch and shoot," or "catch and make another pass" to another open teammate or he could attack his defender with his dribble." If no shots are taken after this offensive action is used to counter the defensive double-team adjustment; all five players are back in their proper "3-Out/2-In Spot-Ups" for the designated continuity offense to immediately maintain the offensive attack. See Diagram 14.10

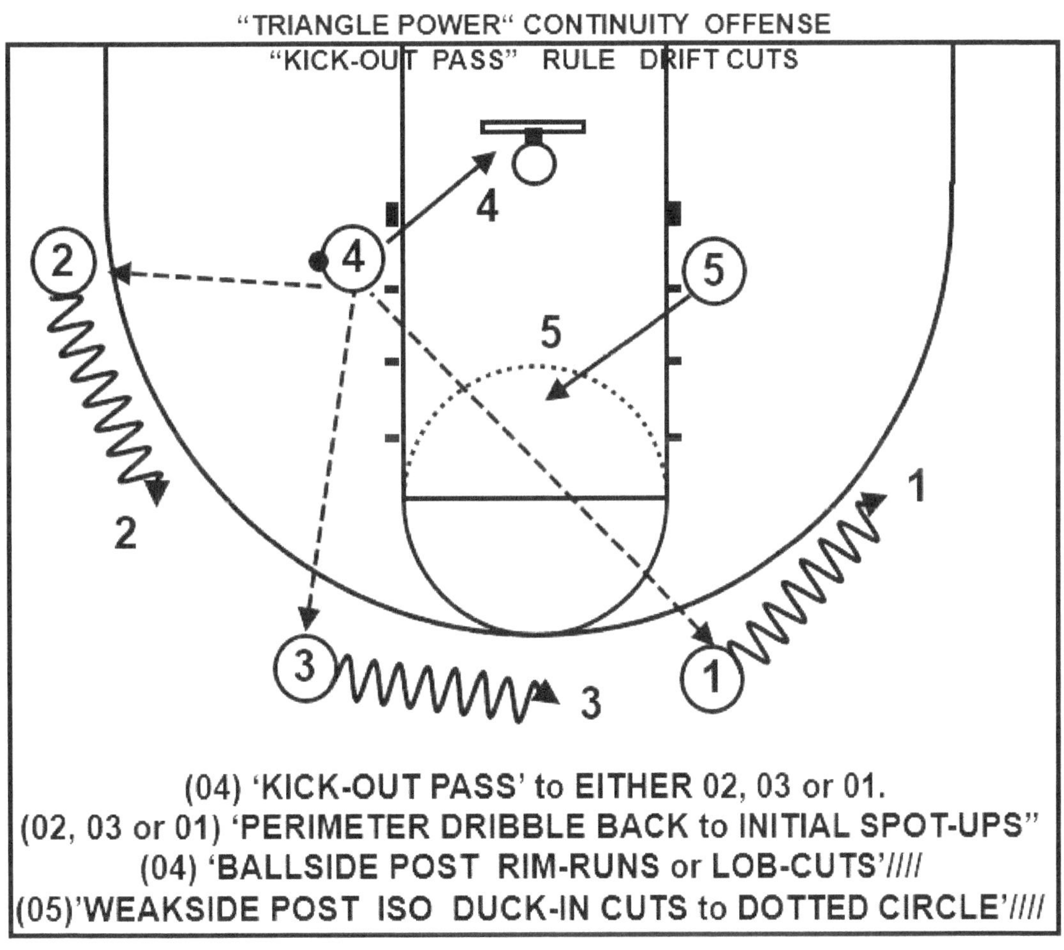

Diagram 14.10

The "Triangle Power Game" Continuity Offense could continue indefinitely and to use both sides of the floor, making this continuity offense a valuable, fundamentally sound and final-phase offensive attack.

The "VEER Continuity Offense" (with "4-Out/1-In Spot-Ups")

Illustration 14.4 illustrates the simple and fundamentally sound Passing Rules of the "VEER Continuity Offense." This continuity offense, with its (almost symmetrically balanced 4-Out/1-In Spot-Ups) would also have five different types of passes that could be made within the structure of this particular continuity offense. Any of these passes would be made by any player from that specific spot-up position. The "VEER Continuity Offense's" passes include: A) The "Down Pass," (from the 'Ballside Slot to the Deep Corner' Pass) B) from the "Skip Pass ('Ballside Slot' or 'Deep Corner' to the Weakside's Slot or Deep Corner' Pass,)" C) the "Reverse Pass," ('from 'Ballside Slot to initial Weakside Slot'), D) the "Inside Pass (from any of the four perimeter spot-ups to the lone player spotted up on either interior position," and E) the "Kick-Out Pass (from the player in the post to any of the four perimeter players that would be 'drifting' from their initial "3-Out/2-In perimeter Spot-ups" locations.

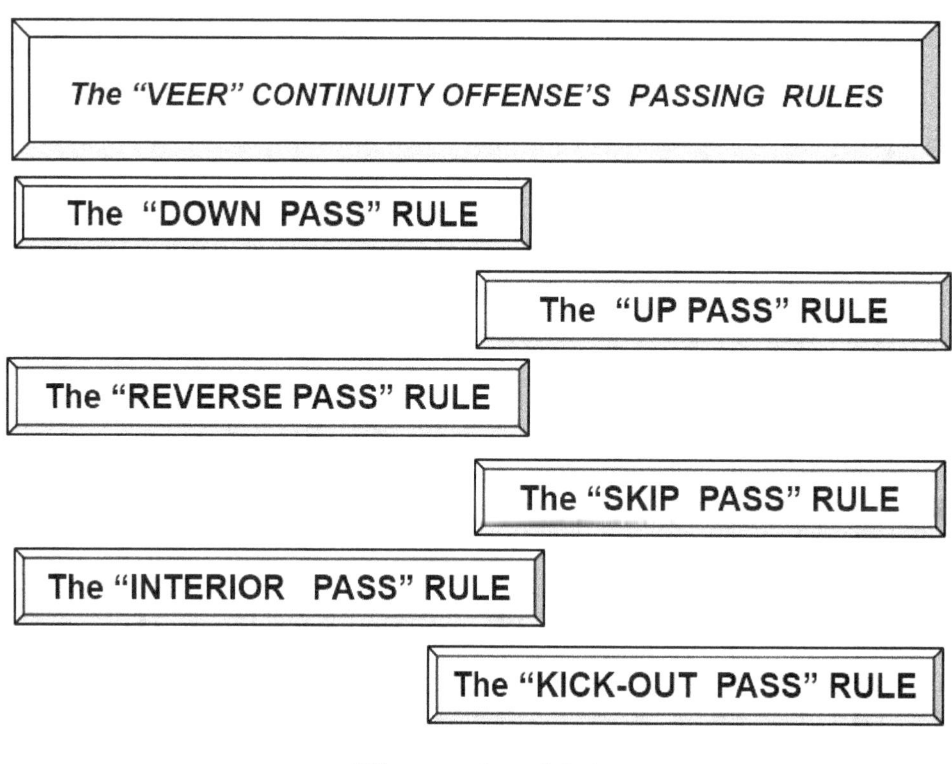

Illustration 14.4

Diagram 14.11 illustrates another play out of the "HORNS" Set, but ending up in "4-Out/1-In Spot-Ups. Therefore, a different continuity offense would be able to immediately begin. Again, by a team using this alignment, the offense has the luxury of being able to attack either side of the floor. In this case, 05 steps up to set a "Big-on-Small" Ball-Screen for 01 to "dribble-scrape" off of as he approaches the "Slot" location on the left side of the floor. As 01 breaks contact with 05's outside right shoulder, 04 then makes a diagonal "Slash Cut" across the lane to the newly designated "Ballside Block." After screening for 01, 05 then cuts across the perimeter to then set a "Big-on-Small" Diagonal Pin-Down Screen for 02 to use to break up to the empty "Weakside Slot" location. With 03 remaining in his initial Deep Corner location and "getting his feet and hands ready" (for his 'triple-threat opportunities), he waits for a possible 01-03 "Down Pass." This action from this play not only attacks the defense in different manners and on different sides of the floor, it also places all five players in the "4-Out/1-In Spot-Ups." These spot-up locations then allow the offense to seamlessly flow immediately into the "VEER" Continuity Offense. See Diagram 14.11

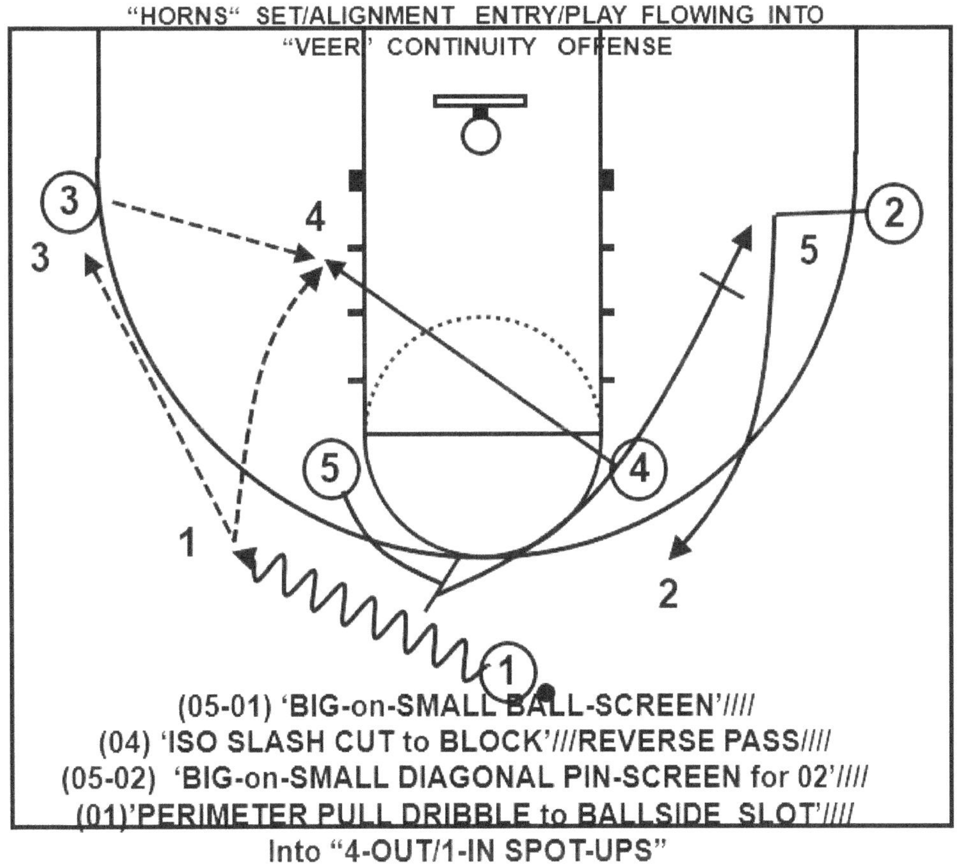

Diagram 14.11

Diagram 14.12 illustrates 01 turning down his primary pass receiver (04) and both possible pass receivers on the weakside perimeter (02 and 05) and his own shots. 01 may not be able to deliver the ball to 04 because of how 04 is being defended. He may not have the ideal passing angle to make the "Inside Pass" to 04, So, instead, 01 elects to make the pass to a teammate that is open for his own offensive options or has a much better passing angle to deliver the ball inside to the now open 04.

When 01 makes the "Down Pass" to 03, he must immediately rotate diagonally through the lane to fill 05's initial "Weakside Deep Corner" spot-up, while 02 rotates over to fills 01's "Ballside Slot." 05 would then move up to fill 02's initial "Weakside Slot" spot-Up. It must be emphasized to all players that each of the three off-the-ball perimeter players immediately make their "Rotation (and Replacement) Cuts," so that their respective off-the-ball defenders also immediately move their defensive locations. The object of this action is to specifically move X5 up and out of the lane as quickly as possible, while X3 must also be forced to leave the lane. These two defenders would be the only two possible helpside defenders the opposition would have to aid X4 in his defensive dilemma. It cannot be stressed enough that while 01 must immediately start his cut, he must make his cut the slowest of the three perimeter cuts. We do not want to force or encourage 01's defender, X1 to quickly replace X5 (as he moves up and out from the primary Helpside Defensive Position). Therefore, we feel that if 01 'idles down' on his cut, that will slow his defender down and prevent X1 from immediately getting into the most effective helpside position. After all three players have properly timed their cuts, it should give 03 and 04 time to capitalize on the opposition's defense. If no shots are produced, all five players have again filled the proper "VEER" Continuity Offense's Spot-Ups (to continue the structured but fluid offensive attack.) See Diagram 14.12

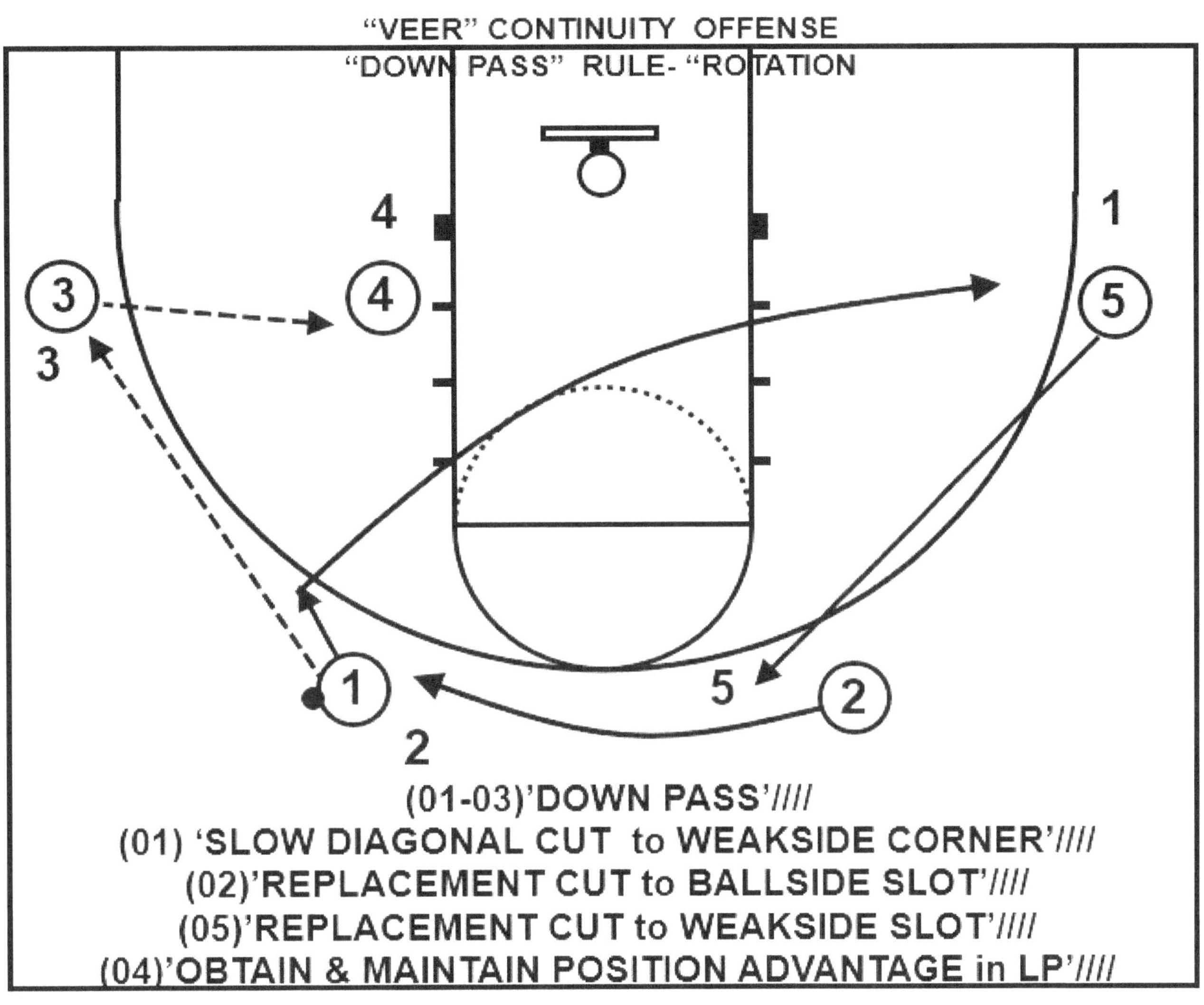

Diagram 14.12

Diagram 14.13 illustrates an example of 04 possibly losing his "position advantage" when the (01-03) "Down Pass" was made, with 03 unable to make the pass to 04. This could be because X4 somehow corrected his defensive fronting position and stance and moved to the lower baseline side of 04. Another possibility is that the offensive rotation movements did not force the defensive actions needed to eliminate 'Helpside Defense.'

Conversely, with the ball lower and the opposition's post defender (X4) now being on the low (or baseline) side of 04; if the ball were quickly moved higher than 04 and his defender (to 02 now the offensive "Ballside Slot"), 04 would now have "obtained the (new) position advantage over his defender. It would now be 04's responsibility to "maintain that new position advantage" by sealing off his defender, keep X4 on the low side of him and giving 02 (higher at the "Ballside Slot" location)an open passing lane to deliver the ball to 04. See Diagram 14.13

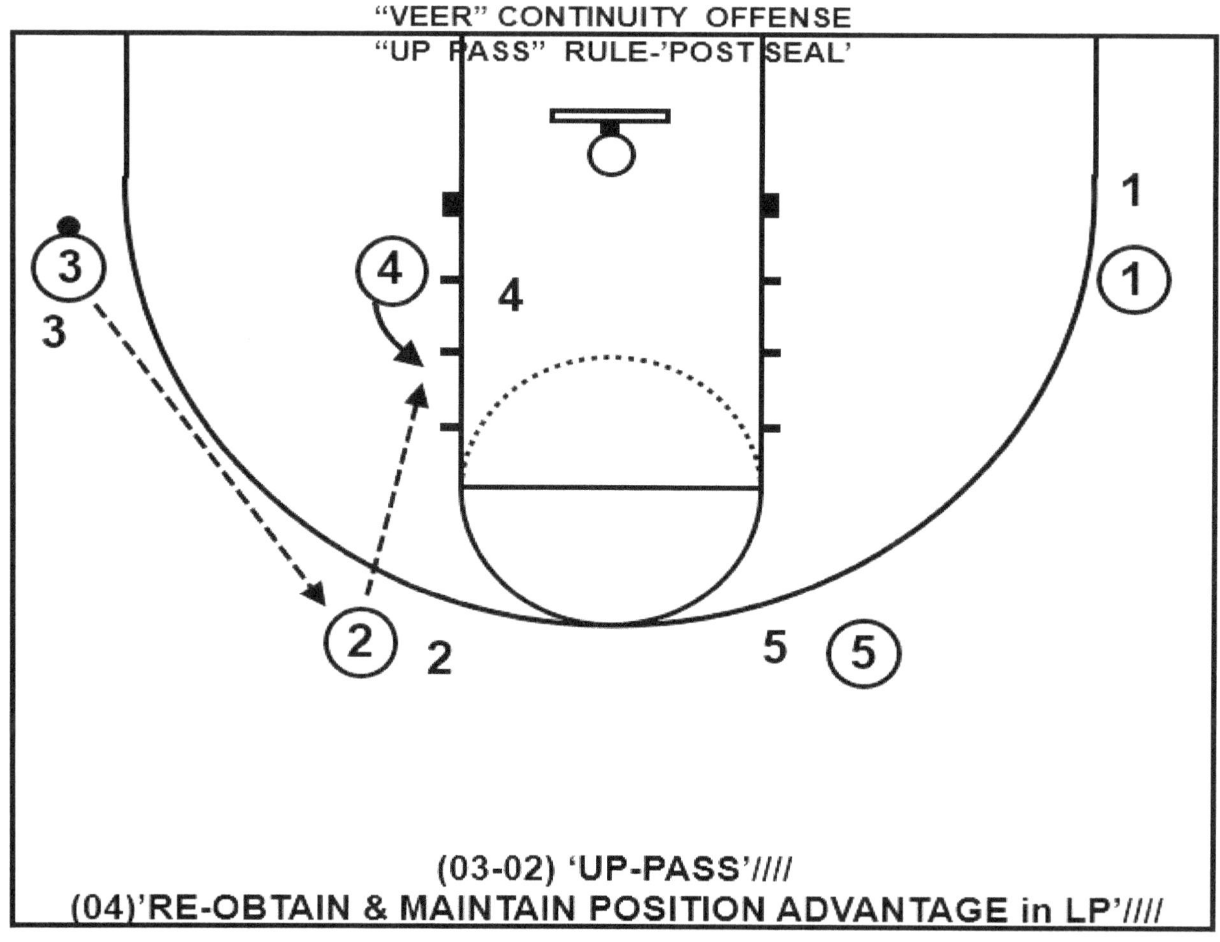

Diagram 14.13

Diagram 14.14 shows 02 electing to make a (02-05) "Reverse Pass" across to the opposite side of the floor. As soon as the ball leaves 02's hands, 02 makes a "Flare-Cut" towards the "Weakside Wing and Deep Corner" area and looks for a possible 05-02 "Skip Pass."

At the same time, 03 makes a hard "Flex Cut by cutting off of the low side of his "Flex-Screener" (04) 03 should scrape off of 04's lower baseline (right) shoulder and continue through the lane. 03 should be prepared to receive 05's "Inside Pass" for a quick close shot near the basket. With 03 cutting on the low side, it should force X4 to slide lower to possibly help out X3 on his man's cut. With X4 lowering his location, it will give 04 an advantage of being able to obtain a "position advantage over his lone defender." As soon as 03 breaks contact with 04, 04 makes a strong and aggressive "Iso Duck-In Cut" into the Dotted Circle area. 05 has shooting and driving opportunities as well as having "Inside Pass" opportunities both to 03 as well as to 04. In addition, 05 could make a (05-02) "Skip Pass" or a (05-1) "Down Pass" with the "Down Pass Rule" giving 01 scoring, driving and (inside) passing options that will allow the continuity offense to continue its attack on the opposition's defense.

See Diagram 14.14

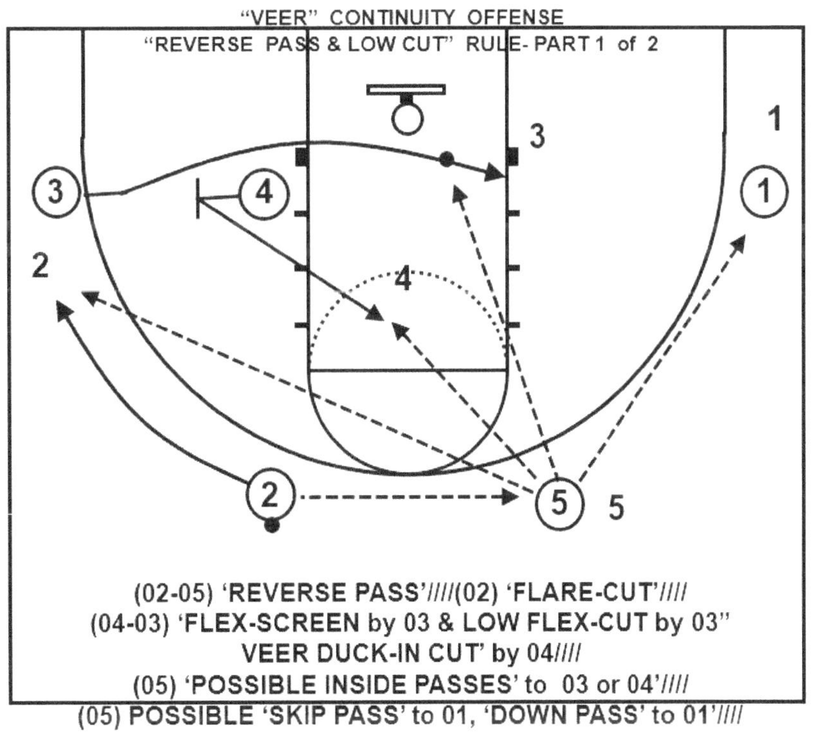

Diagram 14.14

Diagram 14.15 illustrates one of 05's options of continuing the attack and the continuity offense. If 05 turned down passes to his four teammates, 05 could "Perimeter Pull Dribble" across to the now vacant "Weakside Slot." 04 would attempt to seal off his defender in the middle of the lane, while 02 spots up in the new "Deep Corner." If 03 does not receive the pass from 05, 03 makes a vertical "Up-Cut" to the newly vacated and newly created "Weakside Slot." With 05 having inverted his 'post-type' defender out on the perimeter, all five players are now back in the "Flex Continuity Offense Spot-Ups." Whatever 05's pass is made, the corresponding passing rule would dictate movement by all offensive teammates and therefore continue the continuity offense. See Diagram 14.15

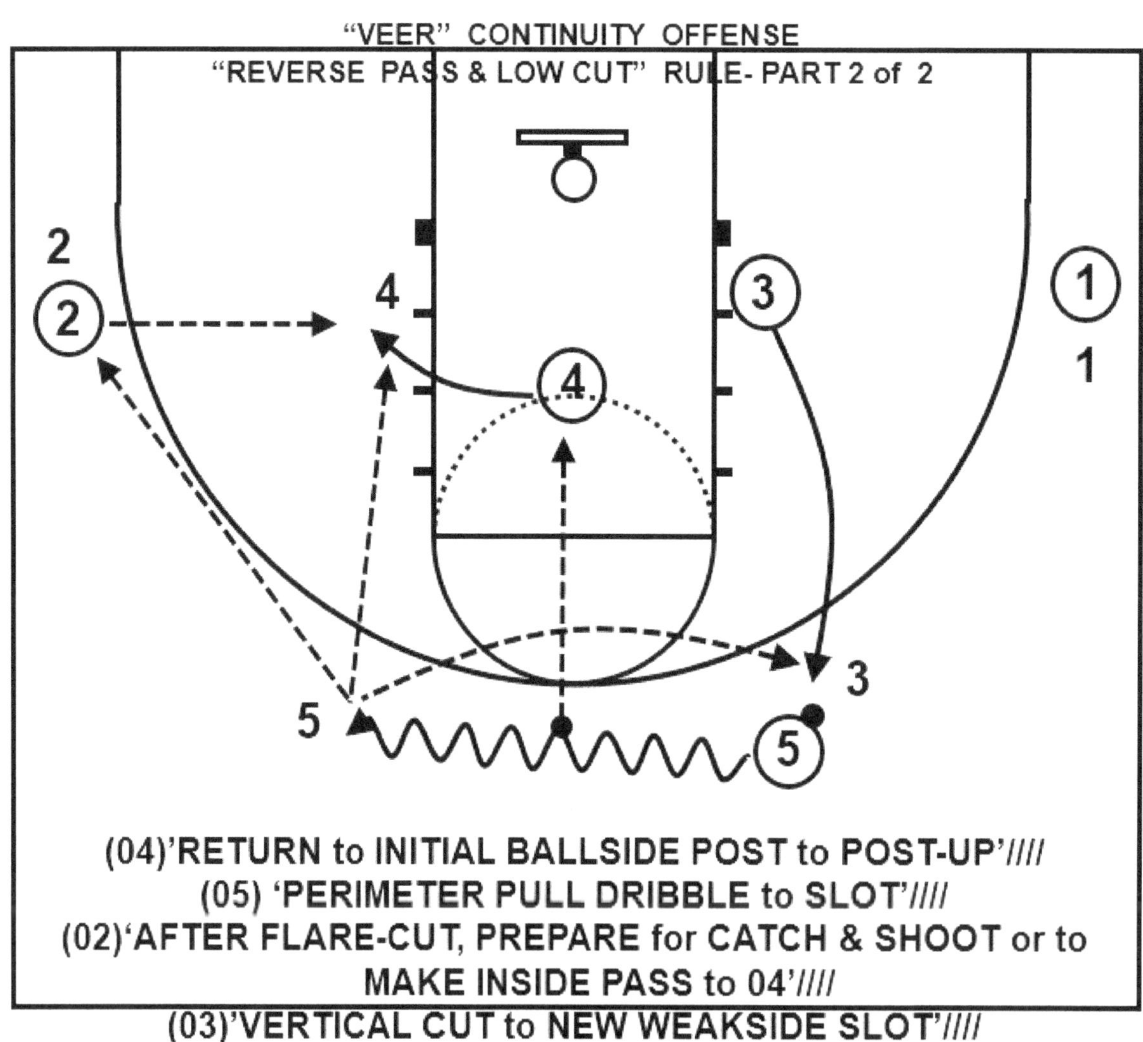

Diagram 14.15

Diagram 14.16 illustrates 02 making the same "Reverse Pass" as in Diagram 14.14, but with 03 reading his defender and knowing he can gain a "position advantage" on his defender with a high "Flex-Cut" over the top of 04. 02 again scrapes off of 04's shoulder, but this time it would be the top (left) shoulder as he cuts through the lane to again post up his defender on the opposite side of the lane. In this instance, after setting his screen for 03, 04 makes a vertical "Up-Cut" right up the lane to be a potential ("Reverse Pass") Receiver from 05. As before, after 02 makes his initial "Reverse Pass" to 05, 02 makes the same "Flare-Cut" to the same newly declared "Weakside Deep Corner" area. 05 has the same pass receivers with 01 spotted up in the "Deep Corner, 03 at the "Ballside Block," 04 now at the "Weakside Slot" and 02 now in the new "Weakside Deep Corner." This fills the proper spot-up locations so that the "VEER Continuity Offense" can continue attacking the opposition's defense, while maintaining a secure possession of the ball. See Diagram 14.16

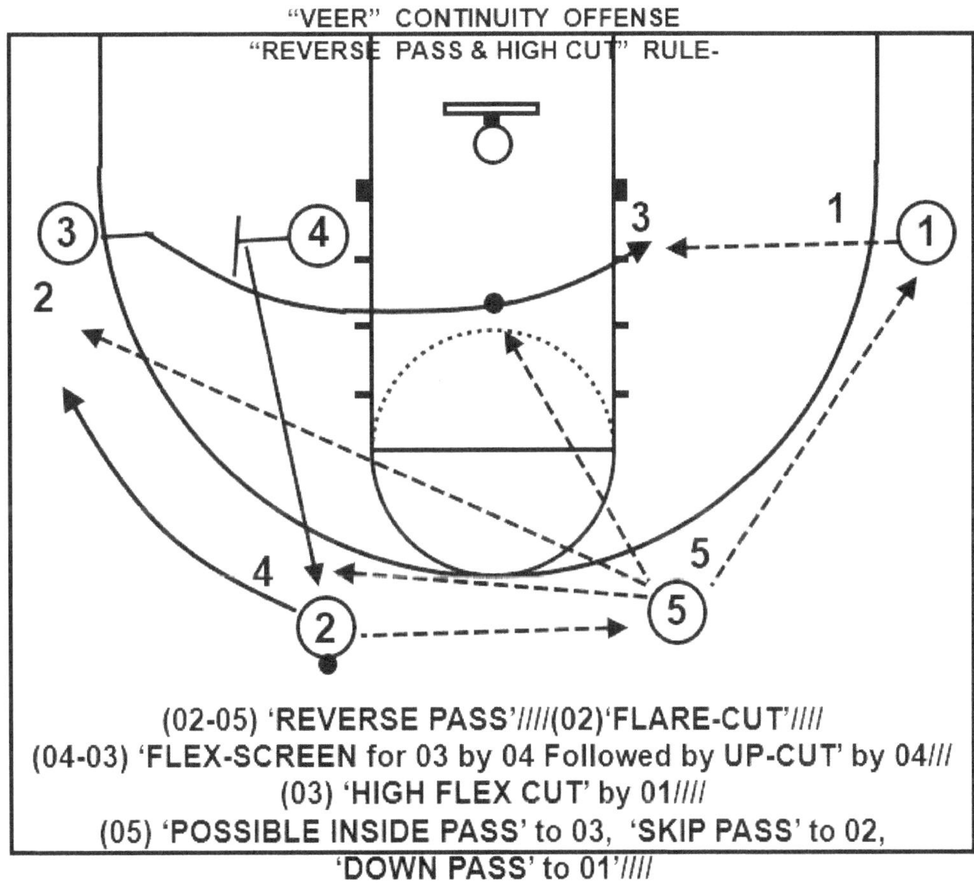

Diagram 14.16

Diagram 14.17 illustrates the beginning locations of all five players in Diagram 14.14 before 02 reversed the ball to 05. Instead, in this diagram, the option was for the offense to make the (02-03) "Down Pass." This pass would initiate the "Down Pass Rule" that is also demonstrated and discussed in Diagram 14.12 with different players involved.

This then would require that after making the "Down Pass" to 03, 02 again must immediately swing through the lane to fill 01's initial "Weakside Deep Corner" Spot-Up, while 05 moves from his "Weakside Slot" spot-up to quickly fill 02's now empty "Ballside Slot." 01 would then rotate up to fill 05's initial "Weakside Slot" Spot-Up.

This three-man rotation rule is to move three perimeter defenders and to eliminate or minimize the two potential 'helpside defenders' (X1 and X5 in this instance) by forcing them to adjust to their offensive players' new offensive locations. It is extremely important that each of the three off-the-ball perimeter players (02, 05 and 01) immediately make their "Rotation (and Replacement) Cuts," so that their respective off-the-ball defenders also immediately move their defensive locations. The object of this action is to specifically move X1 up and out of the lane as quickly as possible, while X5 must also be forced to leave the lane to defend his man (05) now on the perimeter outside of the arc on the side of the court where they ball is located. It also must be emphasized that while 02 must immediately start his cut after making the "Down Pass," he must make his cut the slowest of the three perimeter cuts, to hopefully slow down his defender's cut to the new primary 'helpside defender's best location. We want 01 'to slow down his diagonal cut through the lane so that it should also slow his defender down and prevent X2 from becoming a valuable 'helpside defender.' After 02, 05, and 01 all have properly timed their cuts, it should give 03 and 04 time to capitalize on the opposition's interior defense. Still, if no shots are taken, all five players have again filled the proper "VEER" Continuity Offense's Spot-Ups so that the offensive attack can be maintained. See Diagram 14.17

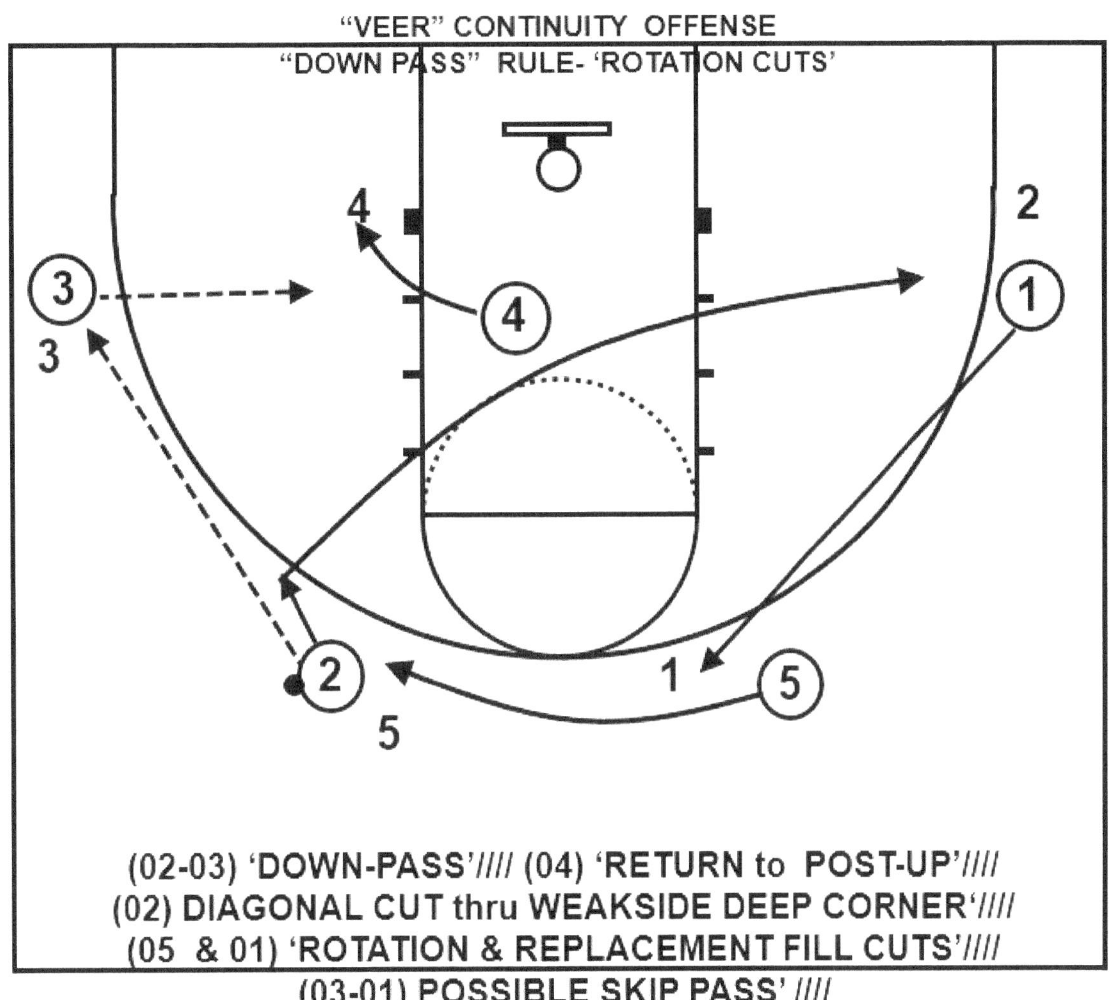

(02-03) 'DOWN-PASS'//// (04) 'RETURN to POST-UP'////
(02) DIAGONAL CUT thru WEAKSIDE DEEP CORNER'////
(05 & 01) 'ROTATION & REPLACEMENT FILL CUTS'////
(03-01) POSSIBLE SKIP PASS' ////

Diagram 14.17

Diagram 14.18 illustrates that the "Down Pass Rule" successfully allowed 03 to deliver the ball into 04. The defensive team countered by trying to execute one of several possible "double-down traps" on 04 and the ball. Even though the "Down Pass Rule" being effectively executed with the three offensive perimeter cuts, defenses may try to add extra pressure on the post with the ball with any of the three defenders collapsing on the interior (X3, X5, X1 or X2.) That is why 03, 05 and 01 all rotate a one-half spot-up location (in this particular continuity offense) *away* from the Ballside.

Any defender that turns his head away from his man and tries to trap the ball will not see (and therefore) successfully be able to react to 04's "Kick-Out Pass." This gives the "VEER" Continuity a great 'inside-out shooting opportunity for three possible offensive players on the perimeter. All players should again make their short cut and have their "feet and hands ready" for

the "Kick-Out Pass from 04 and have an open '3 Pt. Shot' opportunity. This offensive action counters the defensive reaction to the "Inside Pass" and attack and can give the offensive team multiple open shot opportunities outside of the arc. See Diagram 14.18

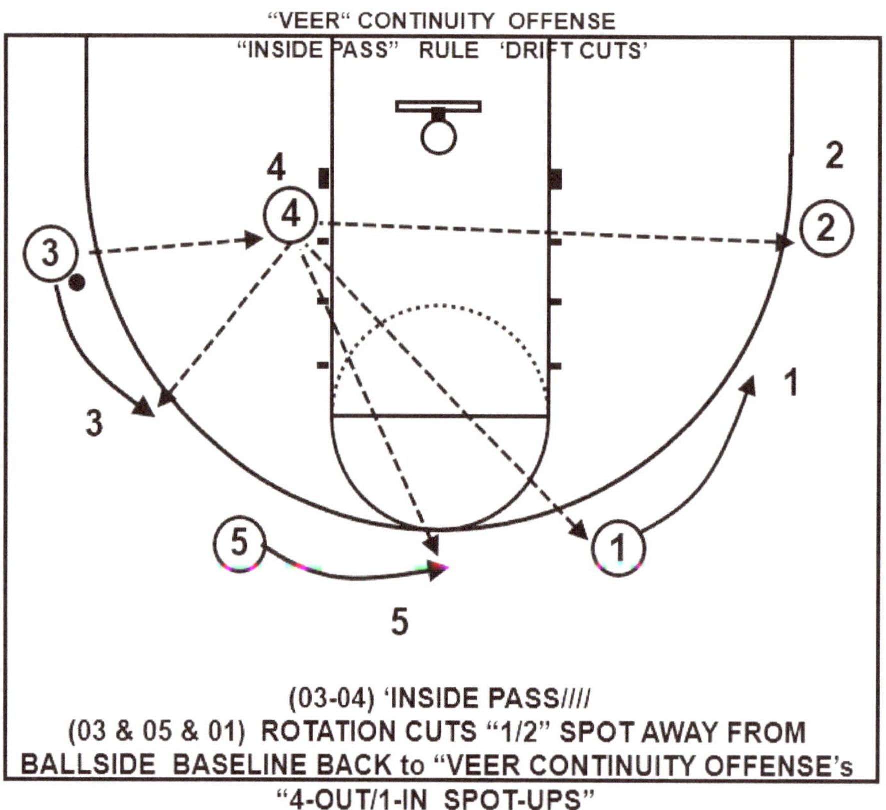

Diagram 14.18

Diagram 14.19 shows 04 receiving 03's "Inside Pass" before the three perimeter "Drift Cuts" are executed and 04 then making the "Kick-Out Pass" to 05. That could be because 05's defender, X5, is most likely the opposition's biggest defender and therefore would be the expected 'double-down defender' in this scenario. If 04 makes the pass to 05 and 05 does not have the skills for a perimeter shot or just simply elects not to take that shot, 05 makes a "perimeter pull dribble back to his initial "Ballside Slot" Spot-Up. He would have the same interior and perimeter passing threats will 04 "re-posting up" his defender as well as 05's three perimeter teammates drifting back to their own initial perimeter Spot-Up locations. This places all players back in the "4-Out/1-In Spot-Ups" so that the "VEER" Continuity Offense can maintain its attack on the opposition's defense when 05 makes any of the four possible types of passes (that include the corresponding rules to each of those types of passes.) See Diagram 14.19

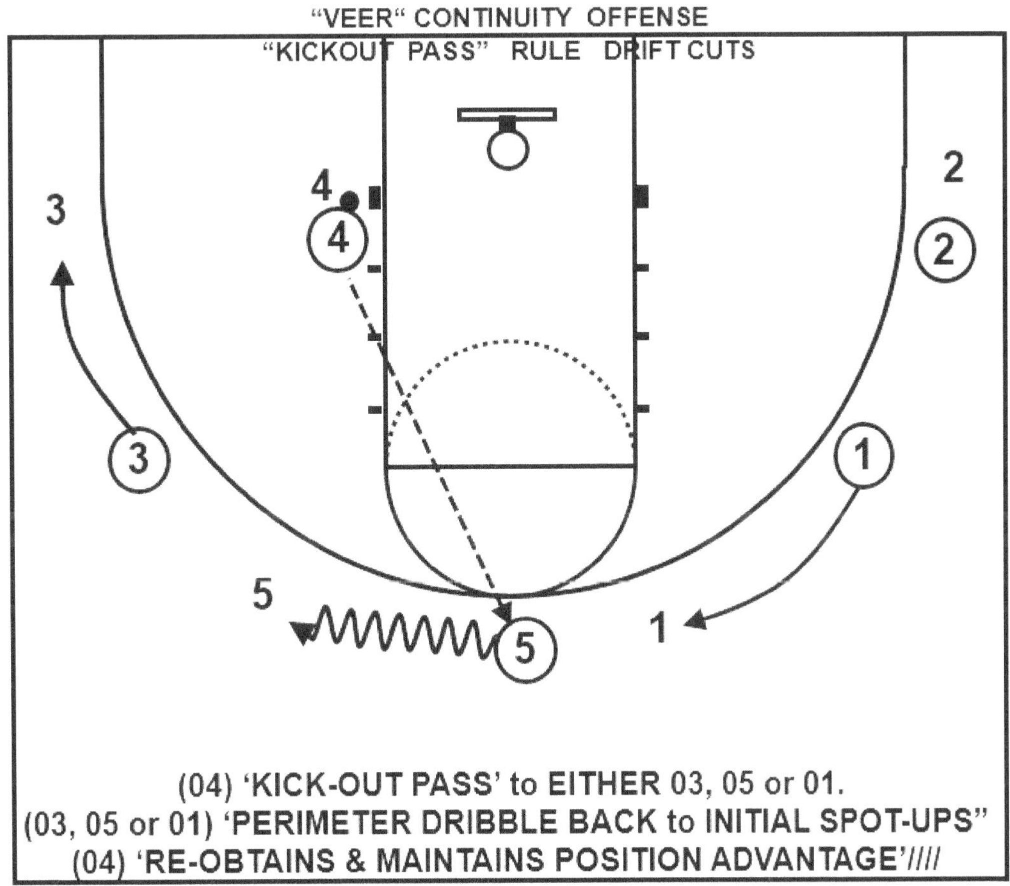

Diagram 14.19

The "HIGH-LOW Continuity Offense" (with "High Post & Low Post Spot-Ups")

Illustration 14.5 illustrates the simple and fundamentally sound Passing Rules of the "HIGH-LOW Continuity Offense." This continuity offense, with its (somewhat symmetrically balanced 3-Out/2-In Spot-Ups that are different than the other "3-Out/2-In Spot-Ups) would also have five different types of passes that could be made within the structure of this particular continuity offense. Any of these passes would be made by any player from that specific spot-up position. The "HIGH-LOW Continuity Offense's" passes include: A) the "Reverse Pass," (from the 'Ballside Wing' to the 'Point' at the top of the key) B) The "Wing Pass," (from the 'Point' at the top of the key to either Wing) C) the "Skip Pass," (from the 'Ballside Wing' to the opposite 'Weakside Wing,') D) the "Inside Pass," (from the 'Point' at the top of the key or the 'Ballside Wing' to either the 'Low Post' or the 'High Post' player) and E) the "Kick-Out Pass" (from either 'Post' that has the ball to any of the three perimeter players.

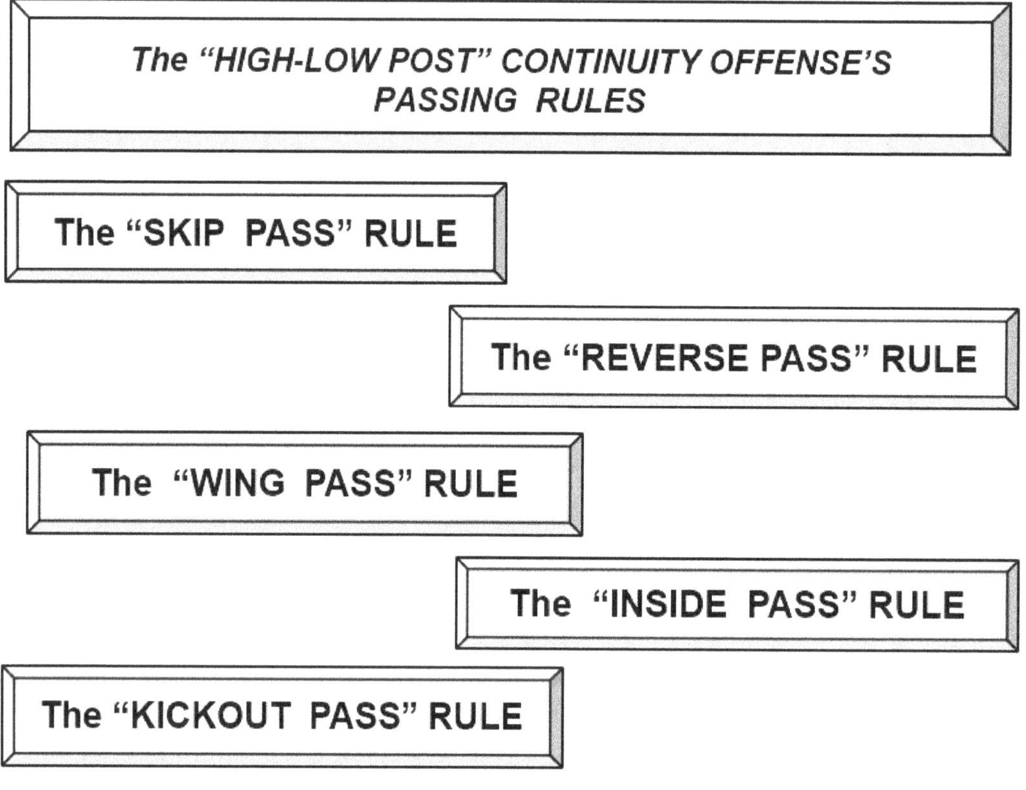

Illustration 14.5

Diagrams 14.20 and 14.21 illustrate an effective entry/play that can be executed out of the "HI-LO STAX" Offensive Set/Alignment. It starts with 03 stacked immediately below 05 at the offense's left High Post/Elbow area. On the opposite side of the floor, 04 starts on the 'first notch' above the Block just outside of the lane and 02 stacked up closely behind him. 01 is the Point Guard that brings the ball towards the top of the key to initiate all entries.

As 01 approaches the top of the key on his dribble, 04 sets a "Big-on-Small Pin-Down Screen" for 02 to use to break out to the FT Line extended on his side of the floor. 05 sets the same type of "Big-on-Small Pin-Down Screen" for 03 to use to break out to the corresponding FT Line extended on his own side of the floor. Both 04 and 05 then immediately look to seal off their defender to post up their man (with little or no possible interior defensive support nearby.

With the offensive alignment having a designated Perimeter Player stacked closely below a designated Post Player on both sides of the (symmetrically balanced offensive) set, the offense could wait until the last possible moment to make easy passes to either side of the floor. This immediately gives the offense an initial advantage of being unpredictable until the very last moment before declaring its intentions. See Diagram 14.20

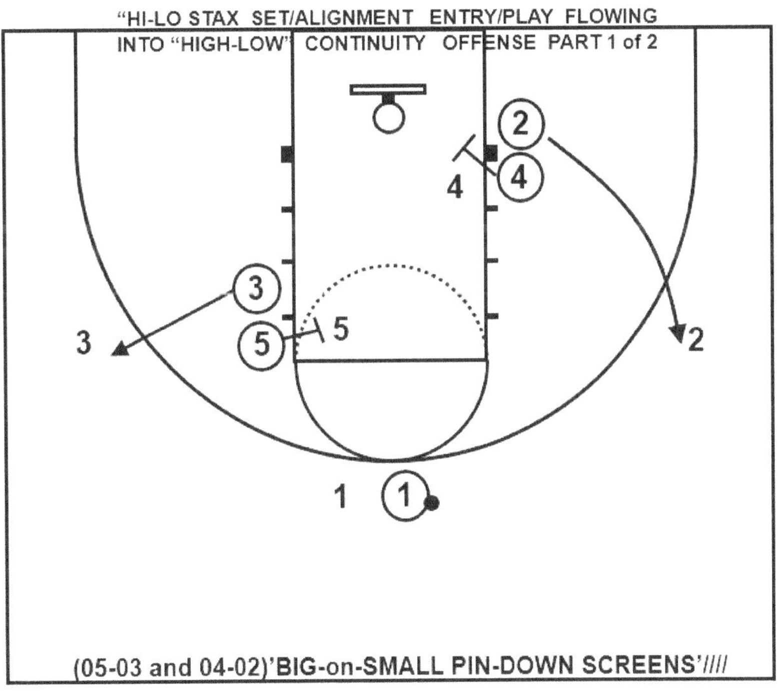

Diagram 14.20

Diagram 14.21 illustrates 01 choosing to make the first pass in the entry to 02 at the FT Line extended on his side of the floor. 03 immediately steps up to set a "Big-on-Small Flare-Screen" for 01 to scrape off of 03's right outside shoulder and to 'spot-up' on the left side of the floor. After screening for 02, 04 tries to "obtain a position advantage" on his defender. If not immediately open, he cuts diagonally up and across the lane to set a "Lane Exchange Cross-Screen" for 05 to use to then post up on the newly declared "Ballside Block." After 05 scrapes off of 04, 04 turns and flashes back to the new "Ballside High Post." This action should totally eliminate any possible helpside defense, giving 05 an immediate "position advantage" on his defender. 02 should have four possible targets, two inside and two on the perimeter. See Diagram 14.21

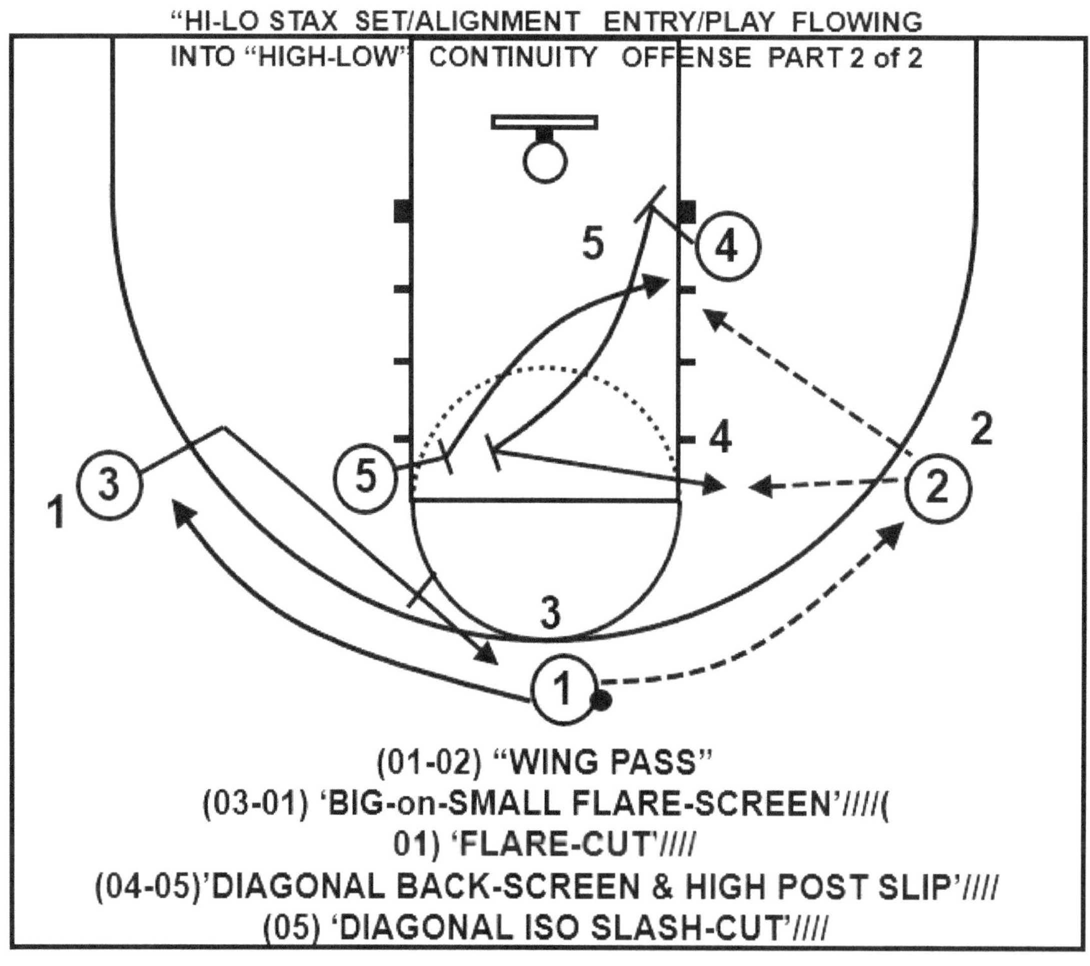

Diagram 14.21

Diagram 14.22 shows that the actual play is over with the ending spot-ups of all five players in the proper spot-ups for the designated "HIGH LOW POST" Continuity Offense to immediately begin with 02's pass and the Continuity Offense's corresponding Passing Rule dictating the specific movements of all five players. With 02 reading that there is an extra defender in the lane, (X1) trying to help discourage an Inside Pass to either 05 or 04, 02 can attack the new weakness of the defense- a perimeter player being more open than usual. 02 then makes the (02-01) "Skip Pass" over the top of the defense to 01, spotting up on the vacant weakside perimeter. 01 has the same options of attacking his close-out defender with a quick "catch and shoot," a "catch and drive (after a possible shot) or a possible "catch and pass" (to any of his four teammates. As the ball goes over their head, both 05 and 04 pivot and seal off their post defenders and look to receive a pass from 01. With 02 now being on the new "Weakside Wing" area, 02 can float and drift behind the defense while "getting their feet and hands ready" for a second "Skip Pass." The "spot-ups" are filled so that the continuity offense will continue with the next pass by 01 dictating the action. See Diagram 14.22

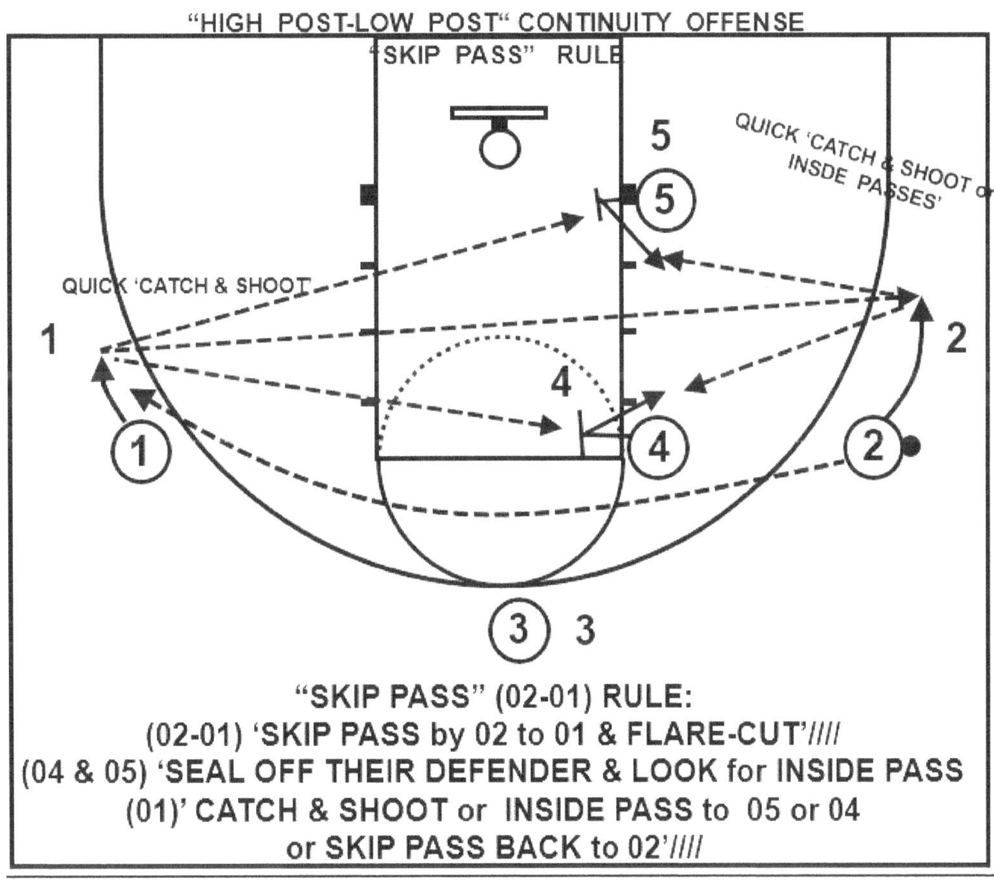

Diagram 14.22

Diagram 14.23 illustrates 02 not making the "Skip Pass," but instead, electing to make the (02-03) "Reverse Pass." The "Reverse Pass Rule" then dictates that both players in the post areas (05 and 04) attempt to seal off their defenders and get the inside position advantage on their defender just inside the lane and look for a quick touch pass from 03 out on top. See Diagram 14.23

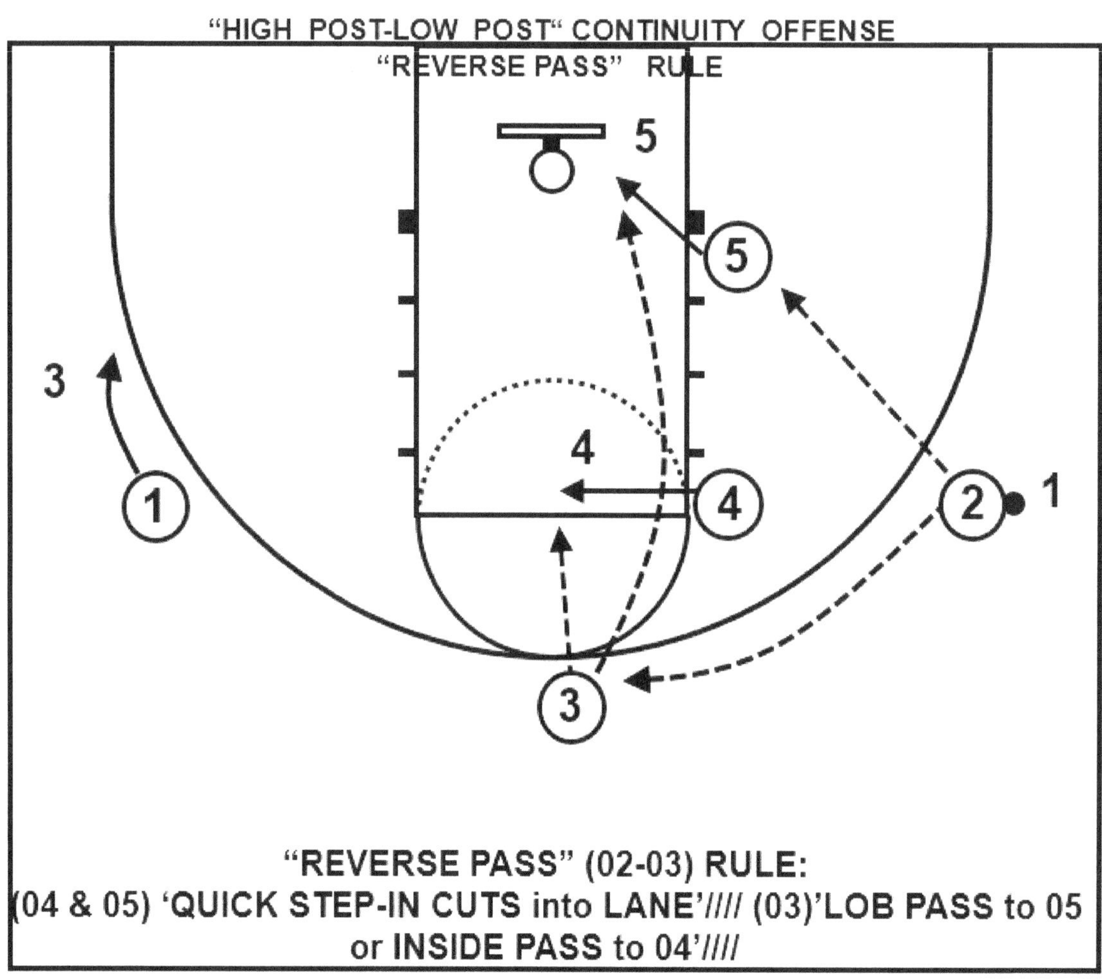

Diagram 14.23

The ball is now centered up and in the hands of 03 and with 03 not making the quick pass inside to either 04 or 05; the ball could be passed to either perimeter wing location. With 01 on the left side of the floor and 02 on the right side of the floor, 03 could easily move the ball to either side of the floor to continue moving the ball, all defenders and looking for various defensive breakdowns. In Diagram 14.24, 03 has chosen to make the "Wing Pass" to 01 on the left side of the floor. The corresponding passing rule then has both 04 and 05 extend their short cuts from their initial High and Low Post Spot-Up positions respectively and to "follow the direction of the ball. This means that 04 would diagonally slash through the lane to the newly declared "Ballside Block," while 05 steps out from near the basket to flash diagonally across the lane to the new "Ballside High Post" area. After making the (03-01) "Wing Pass," 03 then scrapes off of 02's outside left shoulder to make his "Flare-Cut" to the new "Weakside Wing" while 02 then slips his screen to fill in at the top of the key. Once again, the spot-ups are filled and the continuity offense will continue based on 01's actions with the ball. See Diagram 14.24

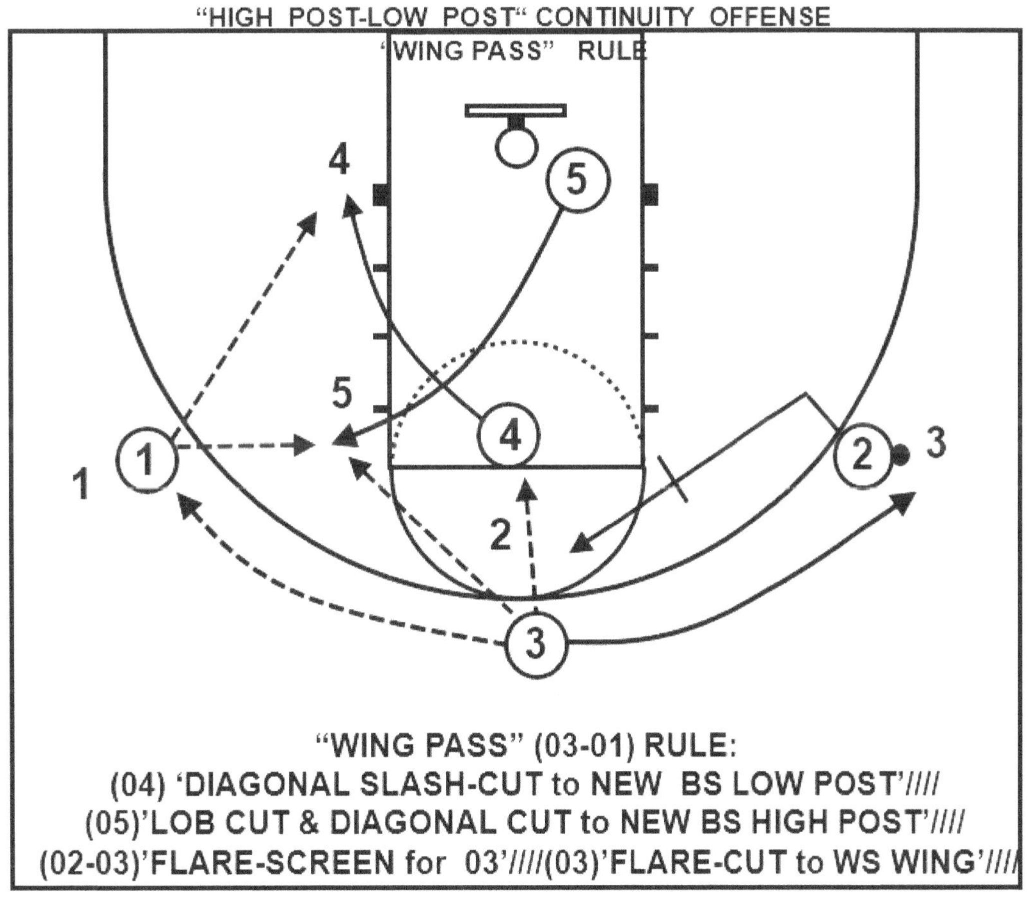

Diagram 14.24

Diagram 14.25 shows the possible continuation of the (03-01) "Wing Pass," without 01 attacking his defender. Instead, this diagram shows (04) "obtaining and maintaining his position advantage" over his post defender. With X4 being isolated with all of the actions and movements by his off-the-ball teammates, 01 makes the "Inside Pass" to 04. Opposing defenses could possibly attempt to trap the post with a perimeter 'double-down' from any of the perimeter-type defenders. Not knowing which defender could or would trap, the "Inside Pass Rule" has all four off-the-ball offensive players make the appropriate "Drift Cuts." In this particular "HIGH-LOW" Continuity Offense, the rule has all three perimeter players rotate a 'so-called' one half of a spot-up position towards the baseline on the ballside of the floor. Therefore, in Diagram 14.25, regardless of who makes the "Inside Pass" to 04, 01 makes his "Drift Cut" to the "Ballside Deep Corner," 02 rotates over to the "Ballside Slot" and 03 moves up and over to fill the "Weakside Slot." The Post Player (05) that does not receive the "Inside Pass" dives immediately to the rim, looking for the quick pass from his teammate. All three perimeter players must "get their feet, hands and their (inside) shoulder ready for a quick "Catch and Shoot" off of 04's "Kick-Out Pass." See Diagram 14.25

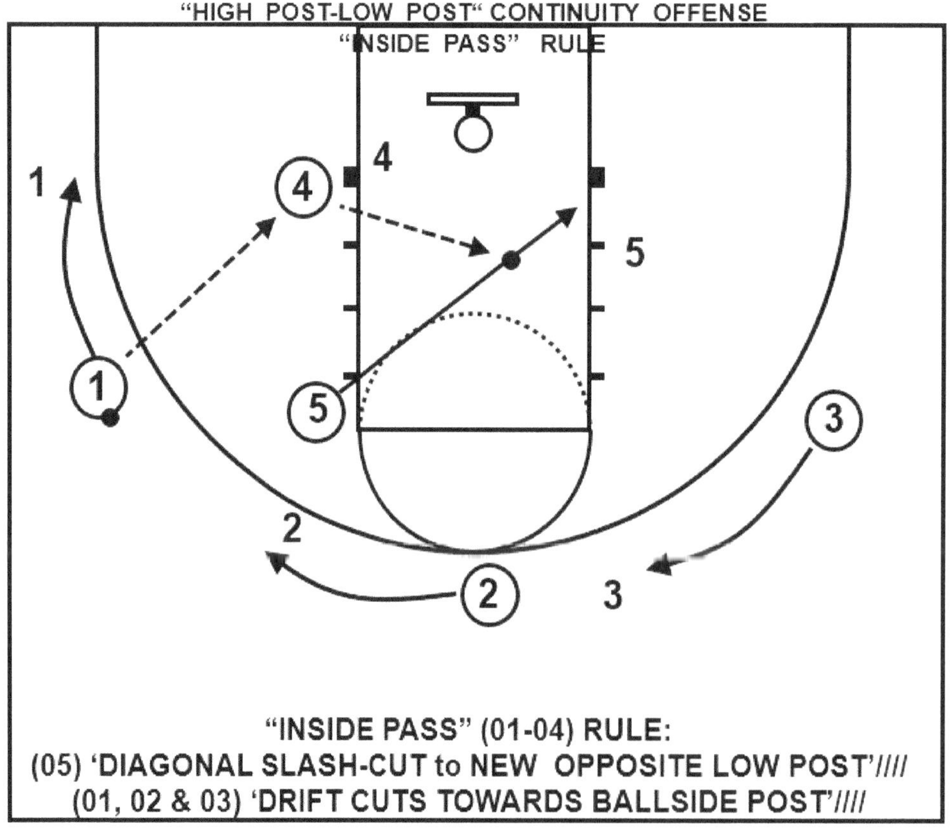

Diagram 14.25

Diagram 14.26 illustrates that 04 chose to make his "Kick-Out Pass" to 02, now spotted up at the "Ballside Slot." When the pass is made, all three players that have made their perimeter "Drift Cuts," should then move back (while again being prepared to receive the ball) to their initial perimeter locations. This means that 02 must make a "Perimeter Pull Dribble" back to the top of the key. The actual player that makes the "Kick-Out Pass" (04) should follow his pass and flash to the 'nail.' If no shots result from the "Inside Pass Rule" and "Kick-Out Pass Rule" actions, all five players have spotted back up into the continuity offense's locations. This allows the offensive attack to continue without any delays or interruptions; giving the opposition's defense no time to recover or regroup. See Diagram 14.26

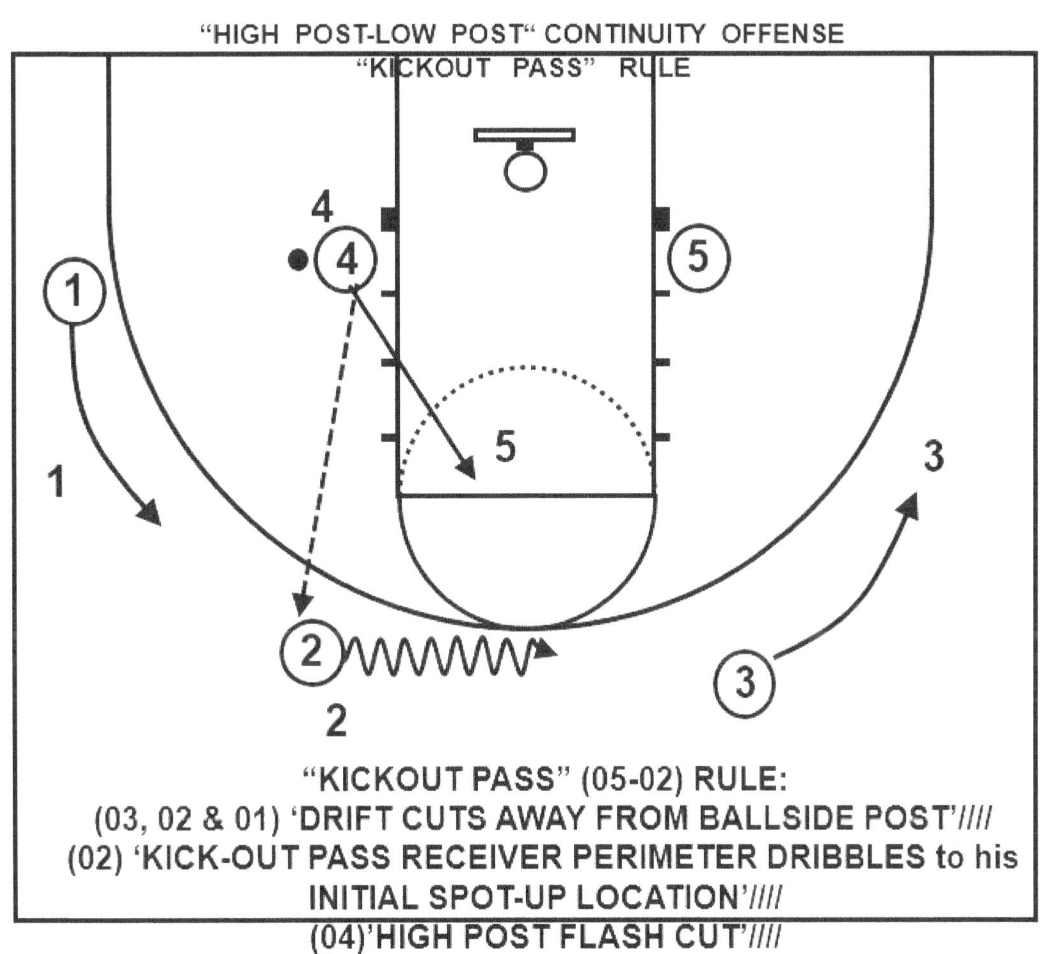

Diagram 14.26

CHAPTER 15
USING DIFFERENT OFFENSIVE SETS/ALIGNMENTS IN A SUCCESSFUL MULTIPLE-PHASE MAN-TO-MAN OFFENSIVE SYSTEM

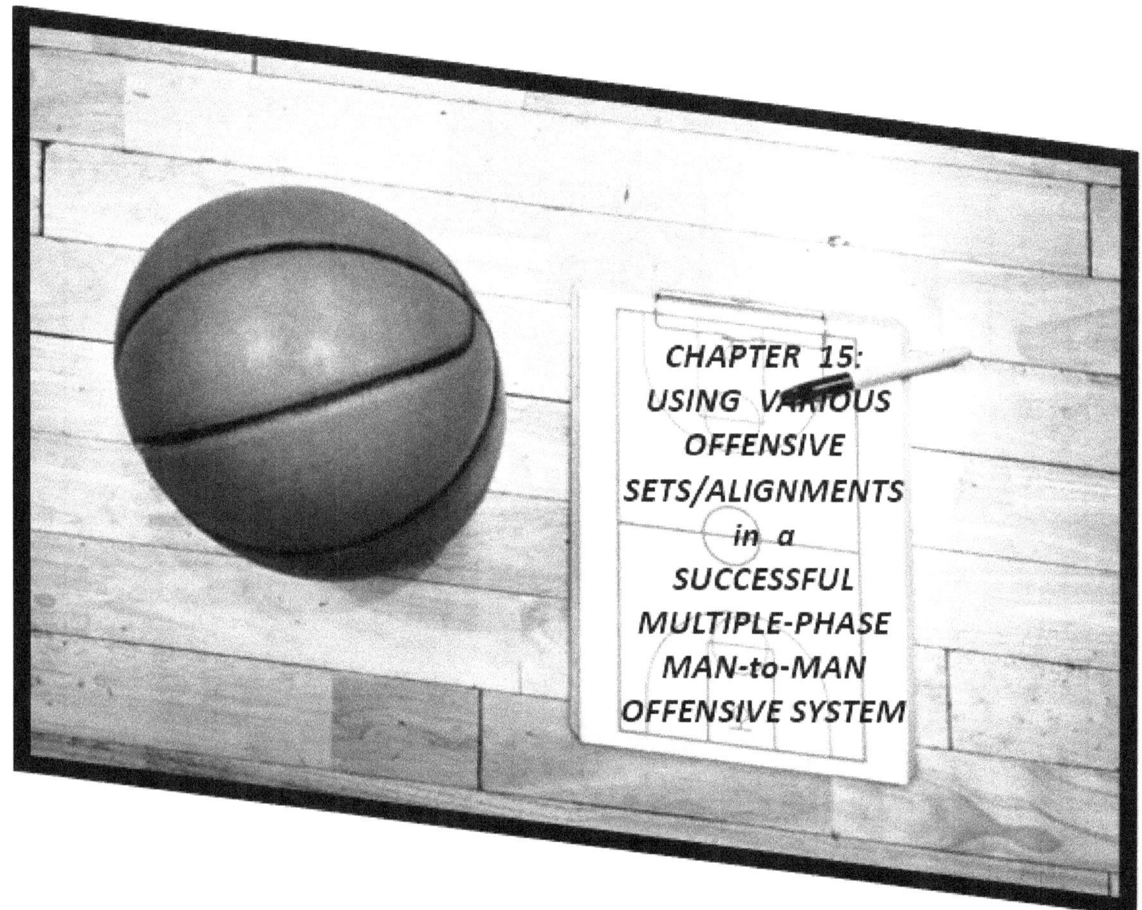

Illustration 15.1 illustrates a flow chart of every possible way a Multiple Offensive System can utilize to succeed with numerous methods of attacking and scoring. When an offensive team has the team personnel which physically and mentally allows a team to be able to successfully utilize multiple offensive alignments, that team can gain many advantages over the opposing defenses.

Illustration 15.1

Those advantages include being able to place different personnel into different locations on the floor that can allow those players to utilize an individual player's offensive skills more often while also being able to attack an individual defender's particular defensive weaknesses. This can also allow multiple players or the entire team to utilize their skills and talents more frequently and also attack the opposing team's overall defensive team's deficiencies. Another advantage is being able to execute different offensive plays/entries out of the different sets so that different advantages can be utilized. Still an obvious advantage is the fact that using multiple alignments/sets can give the offensive team a huge advantage in being unpredictable in the different actions.

It is imperative that each team's limitations and strengths be carefully evaluated by a coaching staff's in its number of offensive sets as well as its actual selection of alignments. Included below are several offensive sets/alignments that could be integrated within the offensive system. Again, it is stressed to not have an abundance of different alignments.

Illustration 15.2 shows the specific flow chart that can be adapted to execute any number of entries/plays out of any type and any number of offensive sets. When any of the entries do not produce the wanted shot, those entries that seemingly are "failed entries" (because of no shots taken), can still be a productive entry by placing all five offensive players in the proper "spot-up" locations for the designated continuity (or motion) offense to seamlessly and swiftly begin the next wave of attack that will always have the potential to produce the shot the offensive team wanted. As the Illustration also demonstrates, there are other ways that the offensive team can transition fluidly into the continuity offense. These methods will be shown in later illustrations in this chapter.

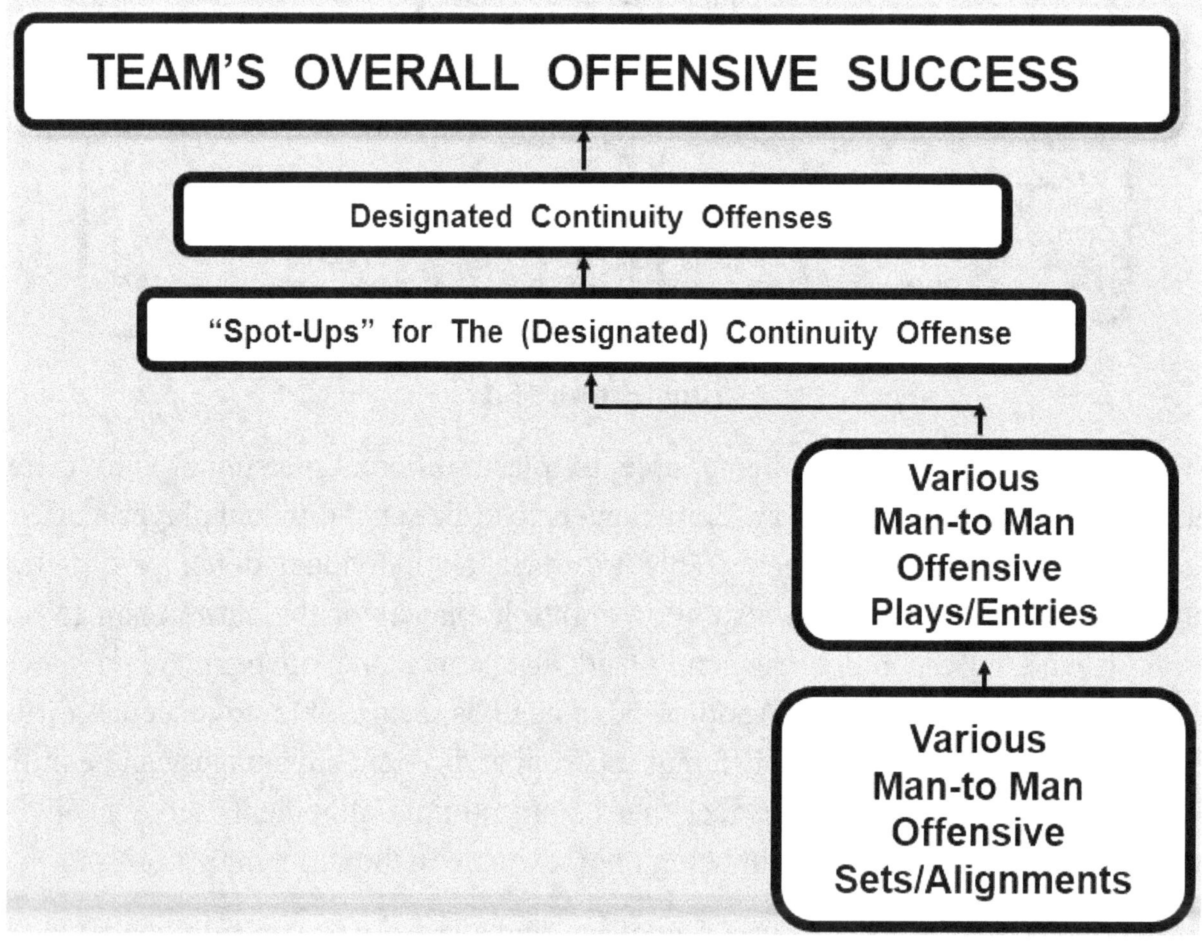

Illustration 15.2

The "1-DOWN SET"

Diagram 15.1 illustrates this set with it having a two-guard front of 01 and 02 at the two 'Slot' positions. 03 aligns at the FT Line extended just outside of the '3 Pt. Line' and 04 aligning on the other side of the floor, opposite of 03. One huge advantage is that the offense can position 05 on either side of the lane. This simple movement can give the offense a drastic and different cosmetic look to defenses that will affect defenses more than the offense. 05 is to align on the 'Notch above the Block.' on the side of the lane the offense wants to declare as the initial strong-side.

This alignment allows many plays to be executed and also has the flexibility to have different continuity offenses as the final phase of the attack. The personnel in this offensive set/alignment spreads the floor both horizontally as well as vertically, further weakening the defense.

Many types of plays can be executed from this set for any of the five offensive players. The plays can feature inside and outside scoring threats as well as various types of attacks on the defense, that could include dribble penetrations, various types of post-ups, ball screens with different types of actions that follow the ball screen, various types of off-the-ball screening actions. The number of plays can vary based on the mental and physical skill level of the team.

As in every offensive alignment/set that could be implemented, if the play does not produce the shot that is wanted; the entry will have probed defenders for weaknesses and repositioned each offensive player into the designated spot-ups of the desired continuity offense to be able to smoothly and instantly continue the overall offensive attack. See Diagram 15.1

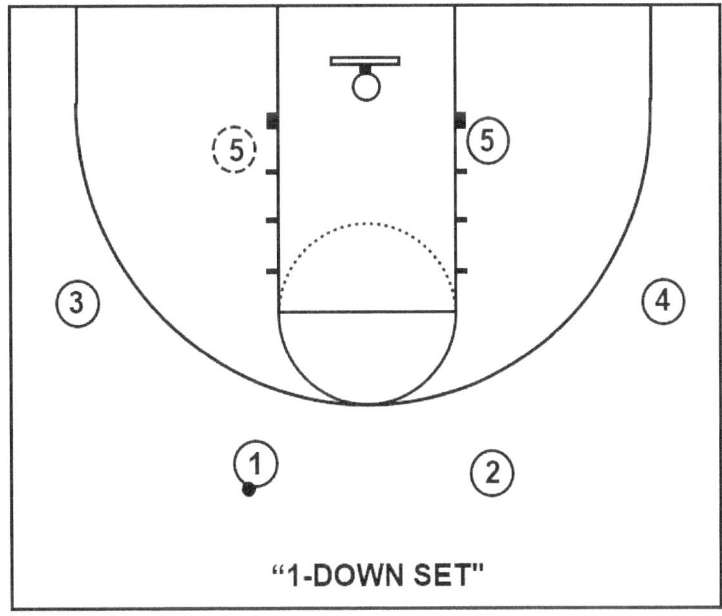

Diagram 15.1

The "2-DOWN SET

Diagram 15.2 shows the "2-DOWN SET with 01 being the long Guard bringing the ball across the timeline and 03 starting at the FT Line extended on the left side of the floor with 05 starting on the "High Post Elbow" position on the same side of the floor with 03. On the opposite side, 04 starts on the 'Notch above the Block.' with 02 aligned on the same side and the same plane as 04. This alignment also pulls stretches and thins the floor both horizontally as well as vertically, further weakening the defense. Again, if the wanted shot is not available, the continuity offense's correct spot-ups will have been filled so the final phase of the overall offensive attack can seamlessly and fluidly maintain the pressure on the opposition's defense.

Plays can be executed from this half-court offensive set for any player. There can be a balance of plays that can attack both on the interior as well as on the perimeter. Offensive actions such as dribble penetrations, various types of post-ups, ball screens with different types of actions that follow the ball screen, various types of off-the-ball screening actions and other more unique offensive schemes. The number of plays can vary based on the mental and physical skill level of the team.

As in every offensive alignment/set that could be implemented, if the play does not produce the shot that is wanted; the entry will have probed defenders for weaknesses and repositioned each offensive player into the designated spot-ups of the desired continuity offense to be able to smoothly and instantly continue the overall offensive attack. See Diagram 15.2

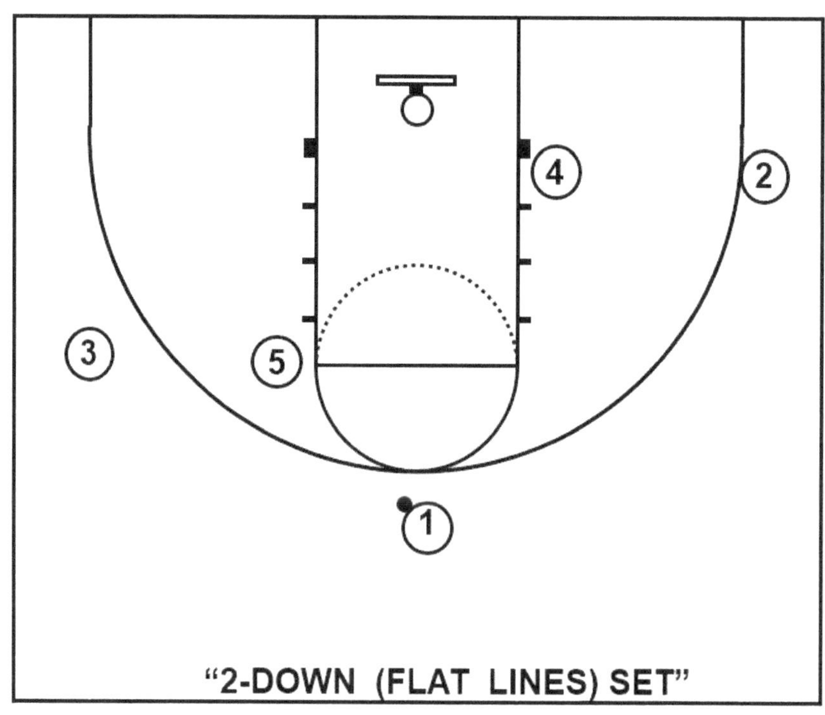

Diagram 15.2

The "2-SQUEEZE SET"

Diagram 15.3 is more of a unique alignment with 03, 05, and 04 horizontally tightly stacked and 'squeezed' together at the FT Line. 02 can align on either side of the lane on the first 'Notch above the Block,' giving the offense the flexibility of having either side of the floor to cosmetically appear to be the strong side of the alignment. The alignment stretches the defense from baseline to timeline. This alignment is very similar to another offensive set that will be later discussed. If a shot is not taken, the designated continuity offense will be able to instantly start.

Numerous plays can be executed to highlight specific skills and talents for any of the five offensive players. As in every alignment/set discussed, this offensive set will be composed of plays/entries that include a balance of both inside and outside scoring threats as well as various types of attacks on the defense previously discussed. The number of plays can vary based on the mental and physical skill level of the team.

As always, if the play does not produce the shot that is wanted; the entry will have probed defenders for weaknesses and repositioned each offensive player into the designated spot-ups of the desired continuity offense to be able to smoothly and instantly continue the overall offensive attack. See Diagram 15.3

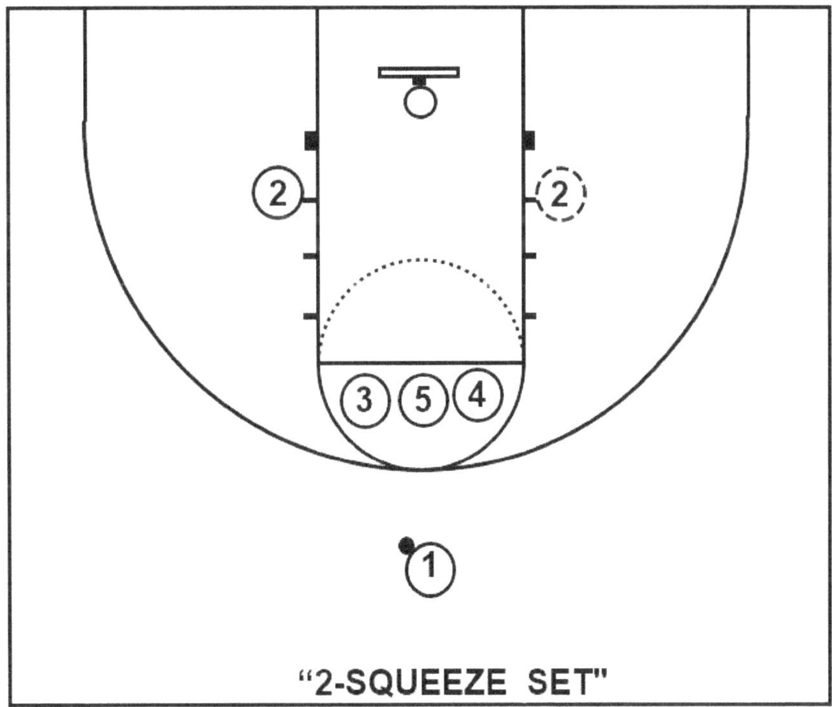

Diagram 15.3

The "2-UP SET"

Diagram 15.4 demonstrates an offensive that is a popular and commonly used set that we call the "2-UP." This alignment possesses a two-guard front, using 01 and 02 as the players to bring the ball across the timeline and start each play. 03 and 04 occupy the two 'Wing' positions at the FT Line extended on the left and right sides of the floor, respectively. 05 starts directly on the 'nail,' at the center of the actual FT Line. One immediately obvious advantage is that the alignment is completely symmetrically balanced with two players on both sides of the floor and 05 exactly centered up. This permits the offense the flexibility and unpredictability to be able to execute any chosen play on either side of the floor. This allows the offense to be able to highlight a player's skills or attack a defender's weaknesses that starts on either side of the floor. The floor is evenly spread and the alignment stretches the defense from sideline to sideline. See Diagram 15.4

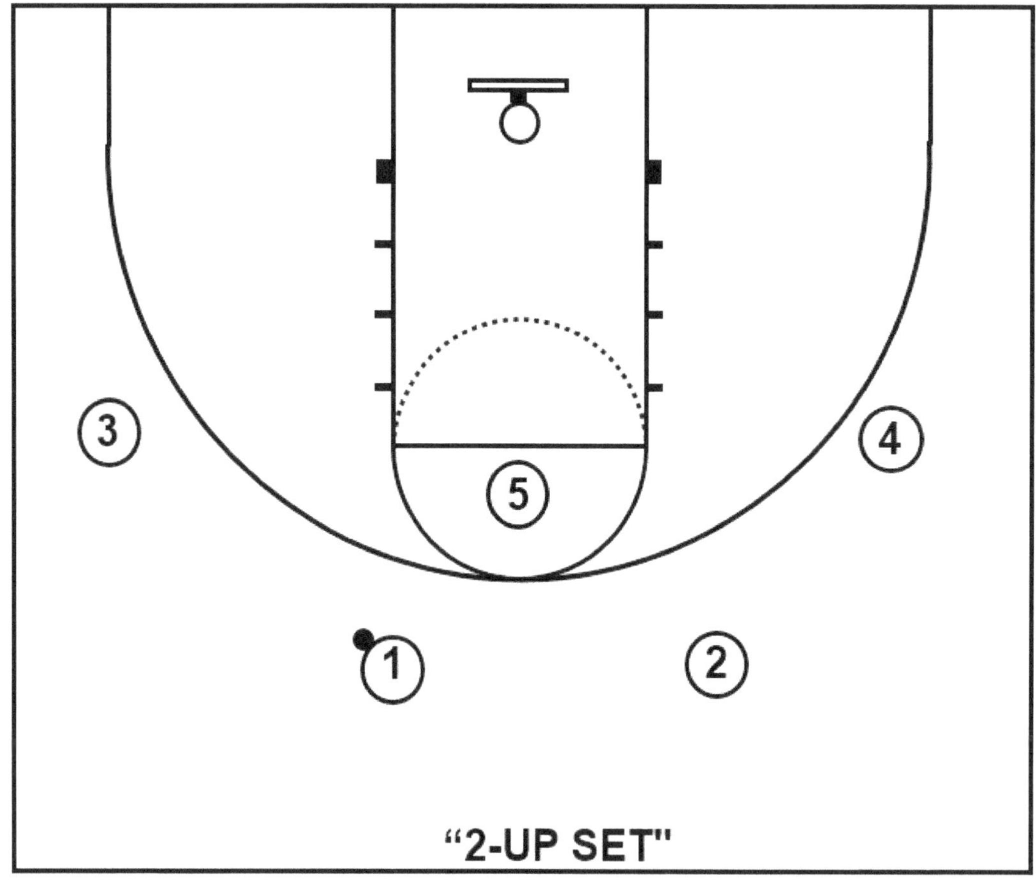

Diagram 15.4

The "2-TWIST SET"

Diagram 15.5 explains the "2-TWIST SET, which is a spin-off from the "2-UP SET." The only difference between these two alignments is the initial positioning of just one player—04. 04 moves from the perimeter wing position on the right side of the floor to down on the first 'Notch above the Block" on either side of the floor. As in every offensive alignment discussed except for the "2 UP SET," each alignment begins with at least one player starting on one side of the lane. The uniqueness of the set and the fact there is an immediate 'Low Post' presence can help stretch the floor both horizontally as well as vertically. If the desired shot is not discovered, the designated continuity offense will be able to immediately begin.

Creative entries/plays can be executed from this half-court offensive set for any player to have the opportunity to highlight specific offensive skills and/or to take advantage of individual defender's defensive weaknesses. A steady balance of inside scoring and perimeter scoring plays should be in this set's offensive package. Offensive actions such as dribble penetrations, various types of post-ups, ball screens with different types of actions that follow the ball screen, various types of off-the-ball screening actions and other more unique offensive schemes. The number of plays can vary based on the mental and physical skill level of the team. See Diagram 15.5

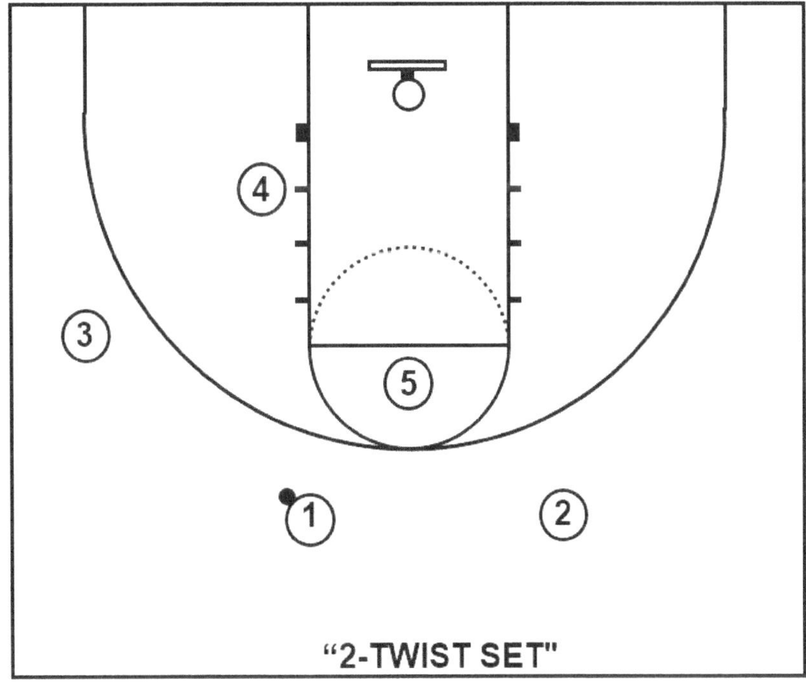

Diagram 15.5

The "3-ACROSS SET"

Diagram 15.6 shows the "3-ACROSS SET" with 03 and 02 spotted up at the two "Wing" locations (at the FT Line extended) on the same left hand an right hand sides of the floor. 01 is the lone Pt. Guard, 05 at the 'Nail' and 05 posted up on the 'Notch above the Block.' For the same reasons previously discussed, the offense could start 05 on either side of the lane, again giving the offense a drastic different looking appearance.

Entries/plays can be designed, taught and then executed from this half-court offensive set for any player to take advantage of outstanding offensive skills. Included in this package of plays for the "3-ACROSS SET" should be an equal balance of inside scoring and perimeter scoring plays. Dribbling actions, post-ups by any type of player in addition to the various types of screening actions, should be utilized. Again, if shots are not taken, players will have moved from their initial locations in the alignment to the continuity offense's correct spot-ups for an immediate start of the last phase of the offense. See Diagram 15.6

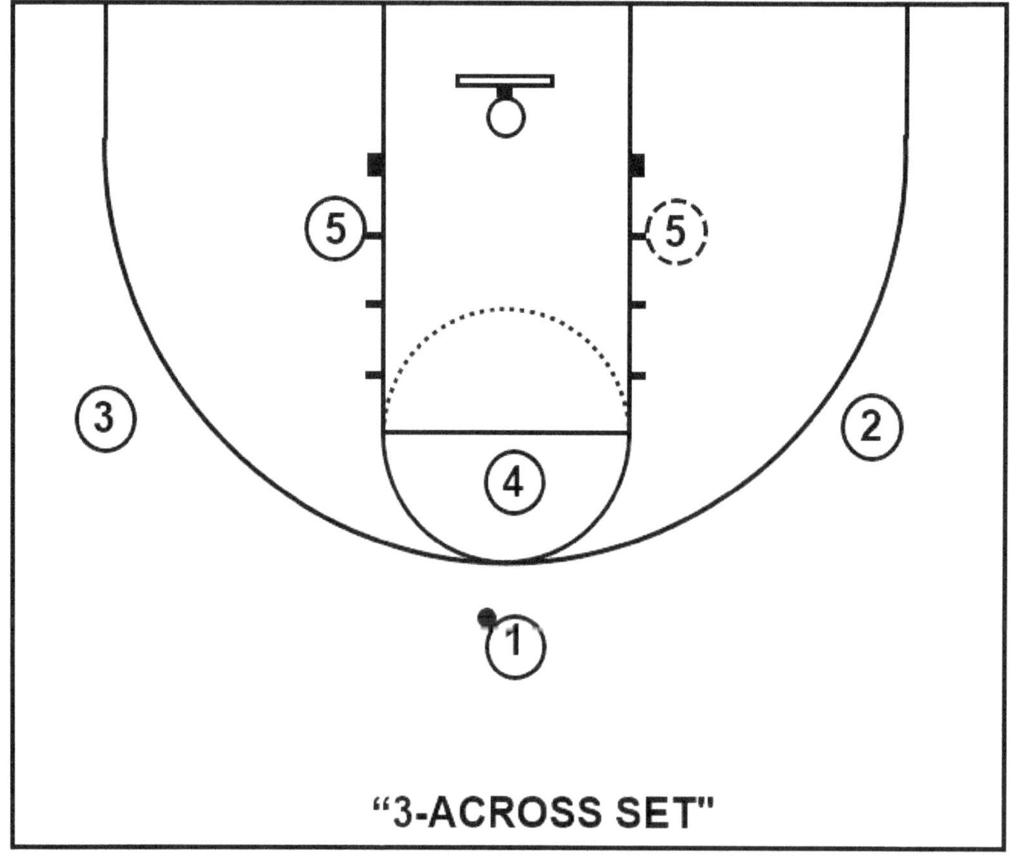

Diagram 15.6

The "3-DOWN SET"

Diagram 15.7 shows the "3-DOWN SET," yet another offensive set that can successfully stretch defenses both horizontally as well as vertically. This set/alignment 05 on either side's 'Notch above the Block' and both 03 and 02 on the same plane in their respective "Deep Corner" positions. 04 starts at the top of the key straddling the '3 Pt. Line. With three off-the-ball players flattened out near the basket and the baseline, 04 out at the top of the key and 01 with the ball; 01 has the space and freedom to attack his defender both with perimeter and also shots in the lane off dribble penetration. Having 05 on one or the other 'Low Post' positions, there is always an immediately 'inside scoring threat' with many different 'perimeter scoring threats.' With all of the various types of scoring threats by several different players that are available in the various areas of the floor, just the alignment can possibly cause defensive problems.

Entries/plays could be devised to that individual players' unique offensive skills as well as the team's overall scoring talents and skills should be important components of the "3-DOWN SET." To become multi-faceted, plays should consist of both inside scoring and perimeter scoring plays in this set's offensive package. Dribbling, passing, screening on the ball and off the ball with various types of offensive cuts should be some of the tools in this offensive set's 'toolbox.'

It bears repeating again that if the actual entry/play in the set does not produce the desired shot; the play will have attacked several different defenders as well as moved offensive players into the proper spot-ups of the designated continuity offense. See Diagram 15.7

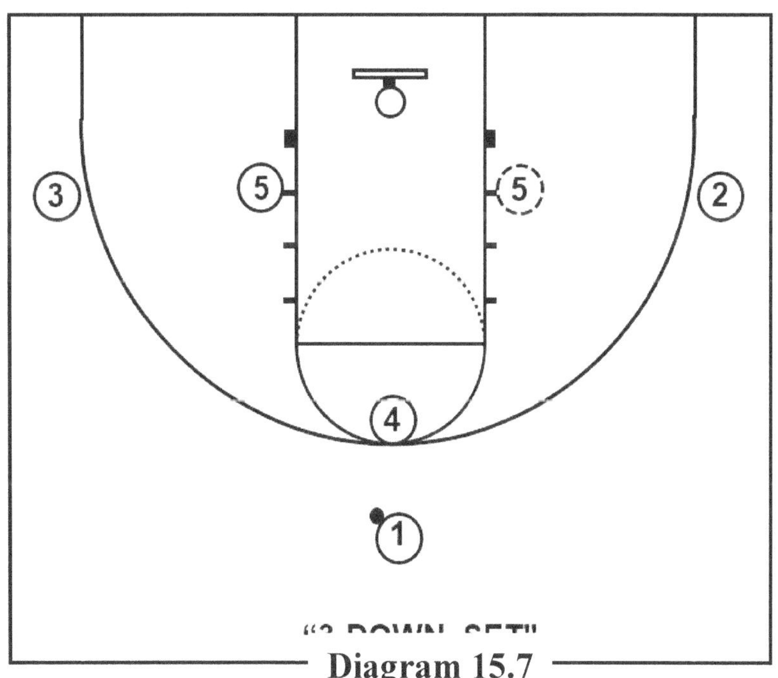

Diagram 15.7

The "3-OVER SET"

Diagram 15.8 shows a somewhat different offensive alignment called the "3-OVER SET." This set is very similar to a very common offensive set that will be described later. The offensive set has a lone Point Guard (01) bring the ball across the timeline into the frontcourt and begin each entry. 05 and 04 align just outside of the FT Circle and slightly higher up on the circle. 03 starts on the left side of the lane at the 'Notch above the Block' with 02 spotted up on the same side of the floor with 03 but in the "Deep Corner." There is an obvious overload on this set's left side of the floor with the right side having a great deal of space that any player having the opportunity to isolate his defender and attack him. Either side can be used for different plays that can use those specific attributes to its advantage.

Entries/plays could be integrated so that specific individual players that possess certain unique offensive skills are utilized in this offensive set. The same types of weapons that are used in the previous offensive alignments/sets should also be used for offensive success from the "3-OVER SET."

While the primary goal of every entry from every offensive set is to score, the very important secondary goal is that if the actual entry/play in the set does not produce the desired shot; the play will have attacked several different defenders as well as moved offensive players into the proper spot-ups of the designated continuity offense. See Diagram 15.8

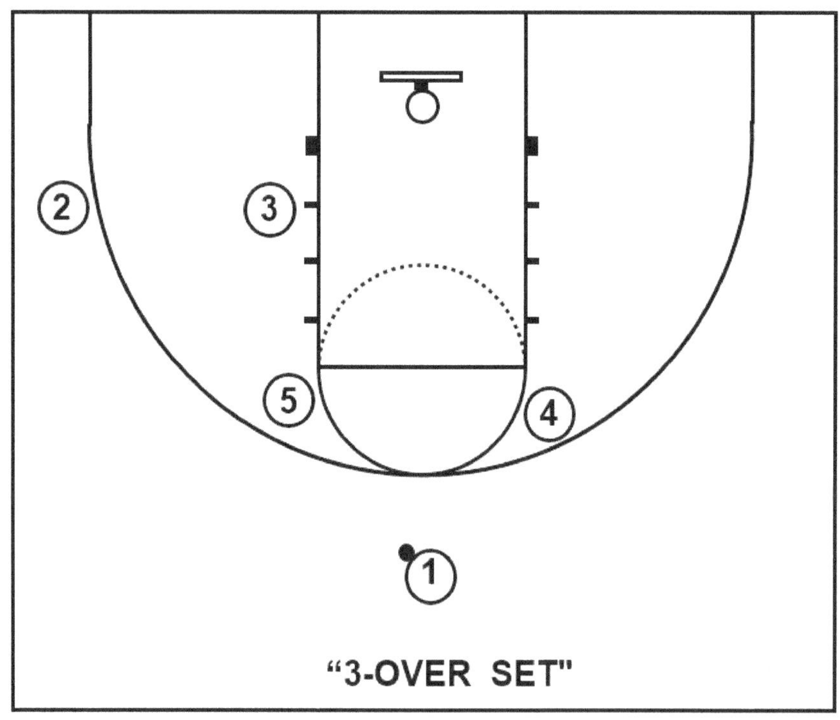

Diagram 15.8

The "3-SQUEEZE SET"

Diagram 15.9 is more of another unique alignment very similar to the "2-SQUEEZE SET," previously discussed. This offensive alignment is only different in that 03 is the designated 'inverted perimeter player' to isolate his perimeter-type defender on either side of the lane. 04 moves to the opposite side of the horizontal tightly squeezed stack with 02 now on the offense's left side and 05 remaining at the 'Nail' location. 05 and 04 are horizontally tightly stacked and 'squeezed' together at the FT Line. The offensive set allows 03 also has to be able to align on the first 'Notch above the Block,' on either side of the lane. This simple shifting of 02 will also make the set appear drastically different and switch the attention of the opposition's interior defense to the other side. As in the "3-Squeeze Set," just the alignment weakens the defense from baseline to timeline. This alignment will have numerous opportunities to provide 02 with 'position advantages' over his perimeter-type defender while also minimizing interior support defense. In addition, it also again forces two post-type opponents into most likely unfamiliar perimeter-type locations that either 04 and 05 can use their possible unique perimeter-type offensive skills against defenders that may have actual perimeter-type defensive skills.

When the entry's action and the movement of personnel does not produce the wanted shot, each player is repositioned into the correct "spot-ups" for an immediate conversion into the designated continuity offense. See Diagram 15.9

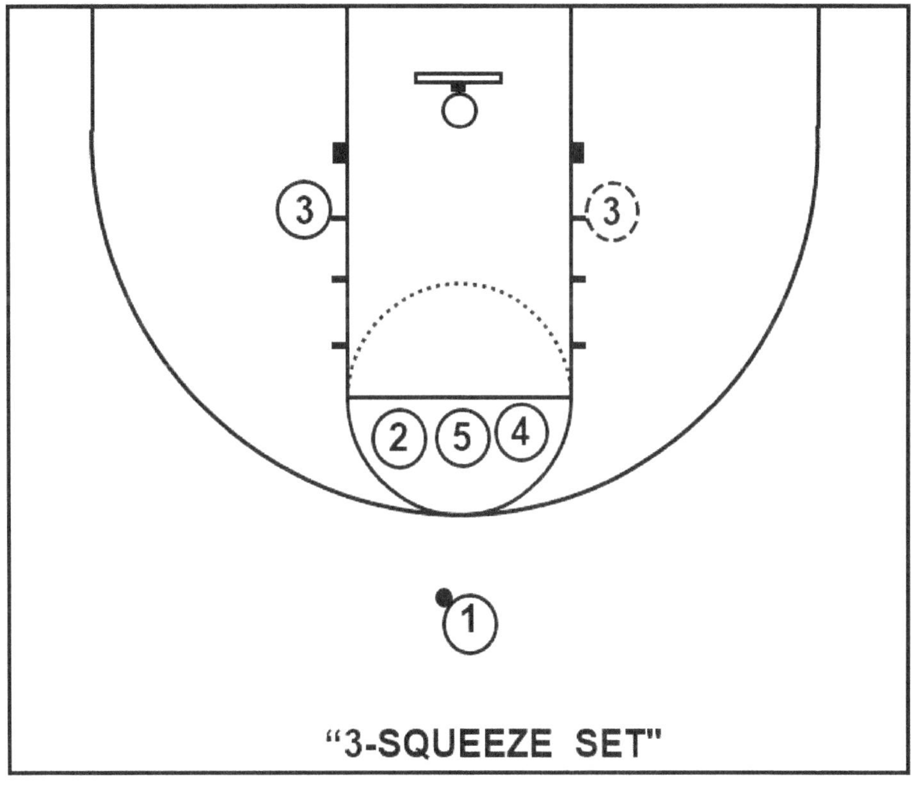

Diagram 15.9

The "3-UP SET"

Diagram 15.10 shows the "3-UP SET" with 03 and 02 spotted up in their respective "Deep Corner" locations (outside of the '3 Pt.' Line and on a horizontal plane level with first 'notch' just above the 'Block.' These locations are slightly higher than other offense's positions and the reason is that it gives both 03 and 02 some spacing to be able to dribble penetrate along the baseline after now having the option of being able to attack the baseline shoulder of their individual defender and not dribbling out of bounds. 04 and 05 stack up at the top of the key with 04 just outside of the arc and 05 just inside the line. Both players could face straight ahead or towards either sideline. To offer some minor differences in the appearance of the Set, 04 and 05 could also switch locations and place 04 at the top of the stack.

Placing the two post players in these locations allows for immediate "Big-on-Small On-Ball Screens" that could be followed with the ball-screener(s) then attacking the basket or remaining out on the perimeter. If either or both remain on the perimeter, that action could either highlight their perimeter-type offensive skills, attack their opponent's perimeter-type defensive skills and/or just simply keep an opposing 'big' defender away from the basket. With 03 and 02 closer to the basket, either perimeter-type player could easily get to the lane to capitalize on any post-type position advantages that may be discovered and then utilized.

Once it has been discovered that specific offensive players have the skills and talents that should be taken advantage of and used more frequently, plays to highlight those players' talents should be invaluable weapons in this set's arsenal. As always, if shots are not taken, each entry will have repositioned players from their initial locations in the alignment to the continuity's spot-ups for a fluid conversion into last phase of the offense. See Diagram 15.10

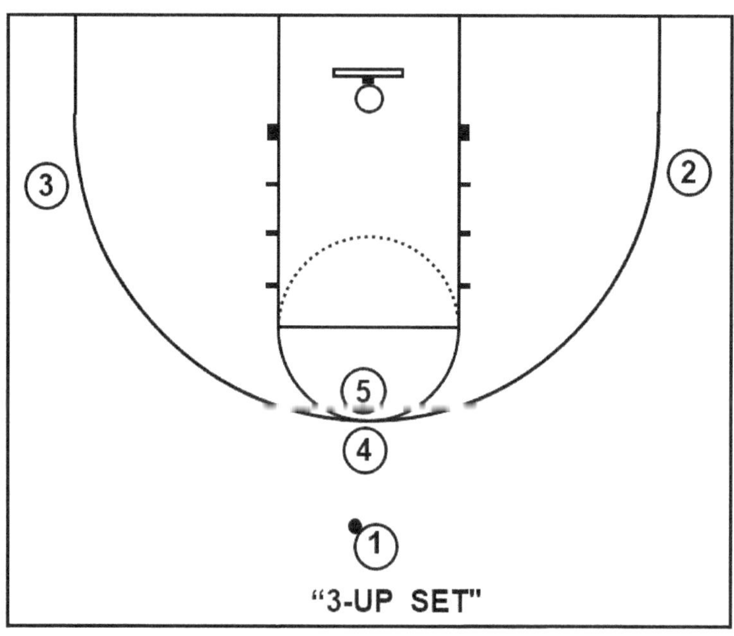

Diagram 15.10

The "3-OUT SET"

Diagram 15.11 shows the "3-OUT SET," mainly used for 'Last Second Shots,' 'Delay Games,' or all out 'Stalls/Freezes.' Both 03, 01, and 02 align out between the 10-second time line and the (now imaginary) traditional hash-marks. Both 05 and 04 spot up in the "Deep Corners" outside of the line and at the same horizontal plane level with the 'Notches above the Blocks.' Any defenders that have defensive weaknesses could be attacked easily. If the purpose of using this offensive set is to maintain the ball for a specific shot by a particular player at a specific time, this alignment can be very advantageous to use. Actual plays could be designed with players being eventually moved to the designated spot-ups for a continuity offense. But if the alignment is simply used for maintaining possession of the ball (while having the lead), no continuity offense would be needed. See Diagram 15.11

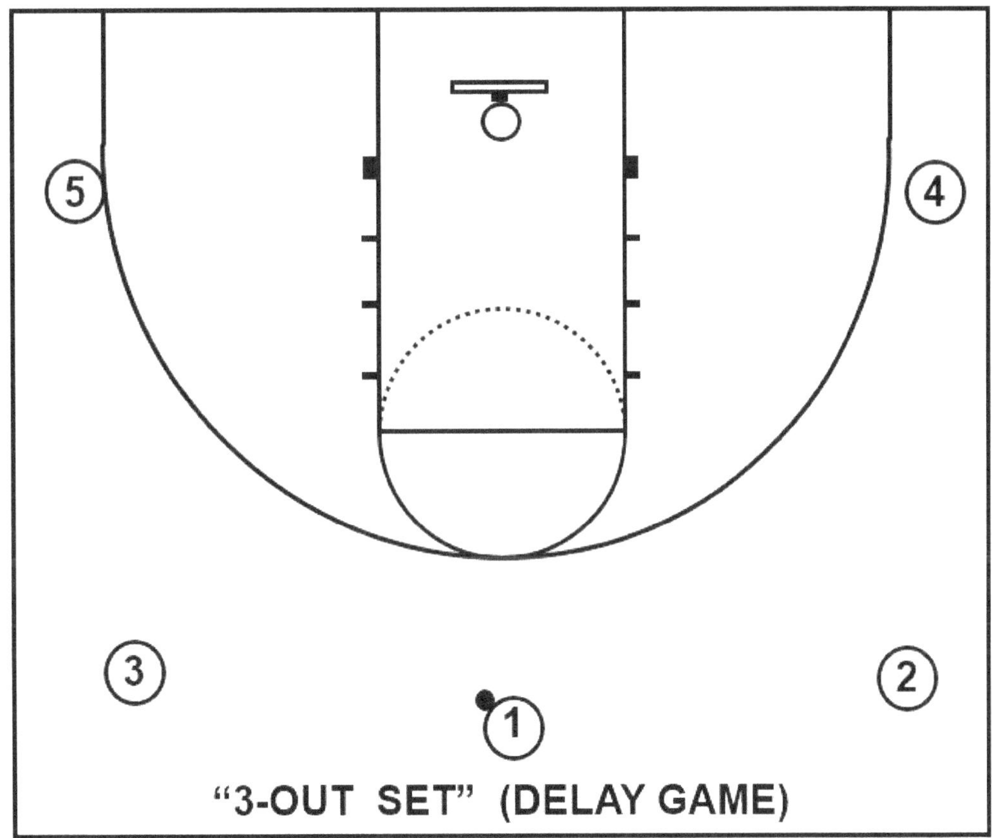

Diagram 15.11

The "4-DOWN SET"

Diagram 15.12 shows another fully symmetrically balanced alignment that also completely stretches the offense both vertically from the baseline to the timeline as well as horizontally from sideline to sideline. The alignment alone can thin and weaken the defense even before the actual entry/play begins to move defenders. Each entry could be executed from either side of the floor, so there is a high level of unpredictability with each entry able to highlight individual offensive players' strengths and/or attack specific defenders.

The alignment places 05 and 04 on their respective side's 'Notch above the Block' and both 03 and 02 on the same plane in their respective "Deep Corner" positions. With all four off-the-ball players flattened out near the basket and the baseline, 01 has the space and freedom to isolate and attack his defender both with perimeter and also shots in the lane off dribble penetration. As in all offensive alignments/sets, if the play does not produce a shot; the play will have moved offensive players into the proper spot-ups of the designated continuity offense. See Diagram 15.12

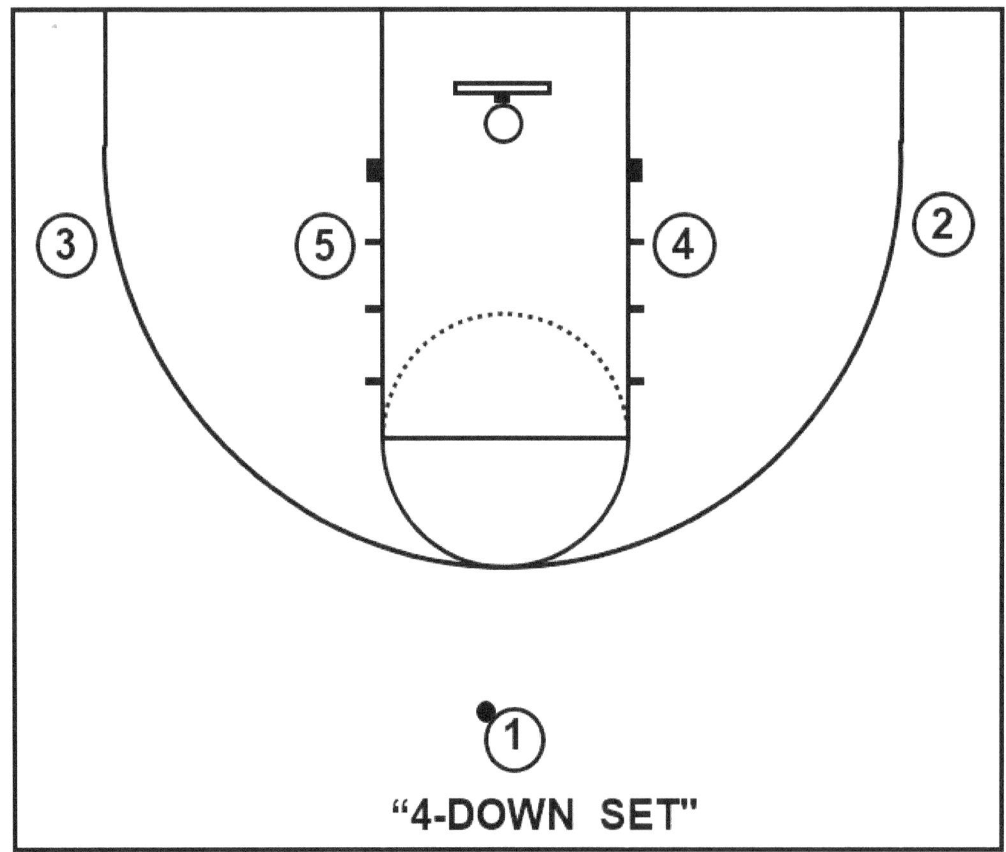

Diagram 15.12

The "4-SQUEEZE SET"

Diagram 15.13 shows another offensive set that is very similar to two other sets previously discussed. The main difference between these three unique sets/alignments is the designated player that is isolated in the post.

As the name suggests, 04 is now the player that has the chance to fully isolate his defender on the "Block." In addition, 05's location at the 'Nail,' keeps the most likely biggest defender away from 04 and the basket. 01, 02, and 03 are also spaced a good distance away from 04 when he receives the ball. Every player will end up in the correct spot-ups for another fluid and instant conversion into the designated continuity offense. This action continually gives individual players and the overall offensive team more and more advantages to succeed with various methods. See Diagram 15.13

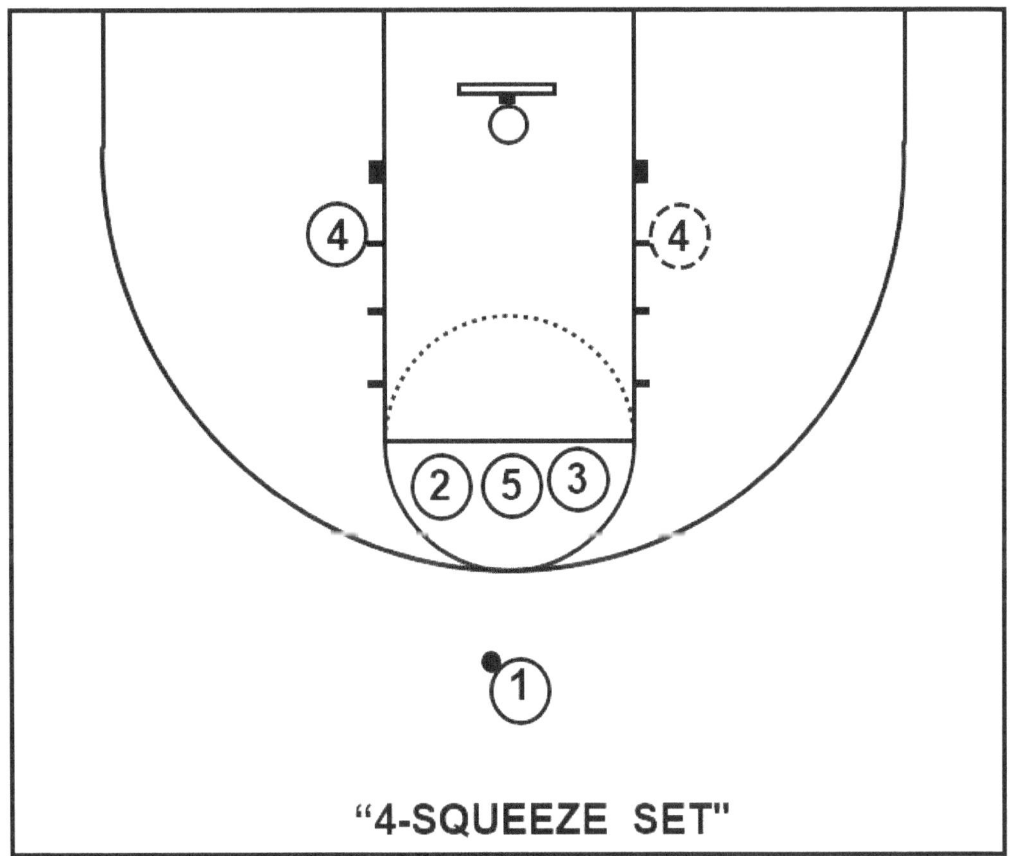

Diagram 15.13

The "5-SQUEEZE SET"

Diagram 15.14 shows the fourth offensive set in the family of "Squeeze Sets." In this instance, 05 is the player that has the opportunity to immediately isolate his defender in the post. This set is the only time that 04 starts at the 'Nail' with 03 squeezing in on 04 on the offense's right side opposite of his normal left "Wing" position. Conversely, 02 pinches in on the opposite side of 04, which is opposite of 02's normal right "Wing" position.

05 is very likely the best offensive post player and this set will give him immediate opportunities to capitalize on the "position advantage" that the "5-SQUEEZE SET" immediately provides for him. With 04 pulling the most likely second largest defender, X4, further away from the basket; 05 should have even better opportunities to successfully isolate and attack his defender.

Plays/entries from the "5-SQUEEZE SET" will also give players as well as the team further advantages and opportunities to succeed with various methods and types of action. But, if desired shots are not manufactured by the entries, the entries will at least move every player into the correct spot-ups for an immediate and smooth conversion into the designated continuity offense. See Diagram 15.14

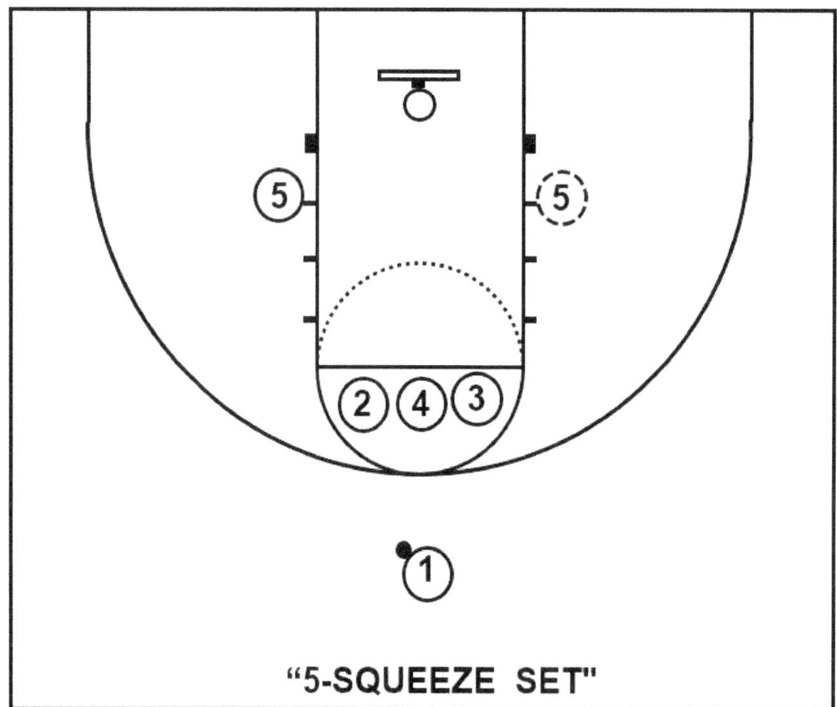

Diagram 15.14

The "5-WIDE SET"

Diagram 15.15 demonstrates an offensive set that is very similar to the "3-OUT SET" in its initial placement of offensive personnel, but has very different objectives. This alignment again has 01 in the center of the floor, but has 05 and 04 inverted out towards the two sideline (05 on the left and 04 on the right side).

These two post-type players (05 and04) do not start as high as 03 and 02 started in the "3-OUT Set"; but a little lower than the same imaginary sideline hash-marks. This gives 01 some additional space to be able to individually isolate his defender and break him down. These lower positions also gives both 05 and 04 better angles for possible "Big-on-Small Ball-screens" for 01. In addition, both are closer to their respective "Deep Corner" teammate and also to the basket. These lower positions will both allow quicker routes to the basket if 'Backdoor Cuts,' 'Ghost Ball-screens' (for 01), quicker 'Pin-Down Screens' or 'Ghost Pin-Down Screens.'

03 and 02 start in the "Deep Corners" and for the same reasons as discussed before, again spot-up on the same horizontal plane with the 'Notch above the Blocks' locations. This doubles the chances for 03 and/or 02 when they have the ball to successfully dribble penetrate to the basket from those initial corner locations. If shots are not taken, the entries will at least reposition every offensive player into the necessary spot-ups for a quick transition into the designated continuity offense-the final phase of the offensive attack. See Diagram 15.15

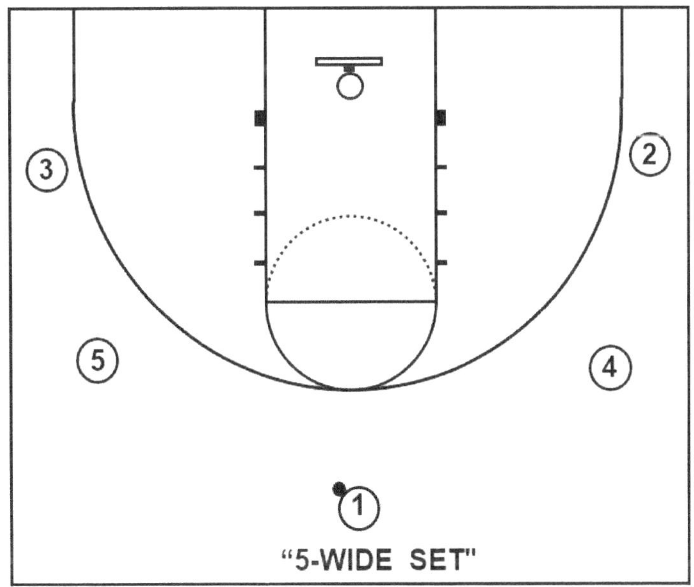

Diagram 15.15

The "5-TIGHT SET"

Diagram 15.16 demonstrates an offensive set that not only pulls the offensive post-type players (and their corresponding post-type defenders) initially away from the basket. This set is very similar to the "3-OUT SET" in its initial placement of offensive personnel, but has very different objectives. This alignment again has 01 in the center of the floor, places 03 and 02 respectively at the left and right "Wing" locations at the FT Line extended. 05 and 04 both align at the Free Throw Line and have only a 2-3 foot separation.

The emptiness of the Low Post on both sides of the lane allows any offensive player several opportunities to fill those locations and attack his defender. The opponent's defense is obviously spread thin from sideline to sideline with the post areas vacant, leaving opposing team's defenses vulnerable for various types of action they must defend. Each play from the "5-TIGHT SET" must meet the same requirement of all players ending up in the correct "spot-ups" for the same type of immediate and fluid conversion into the continuity offense that is to be executed. See Diagram 15.16

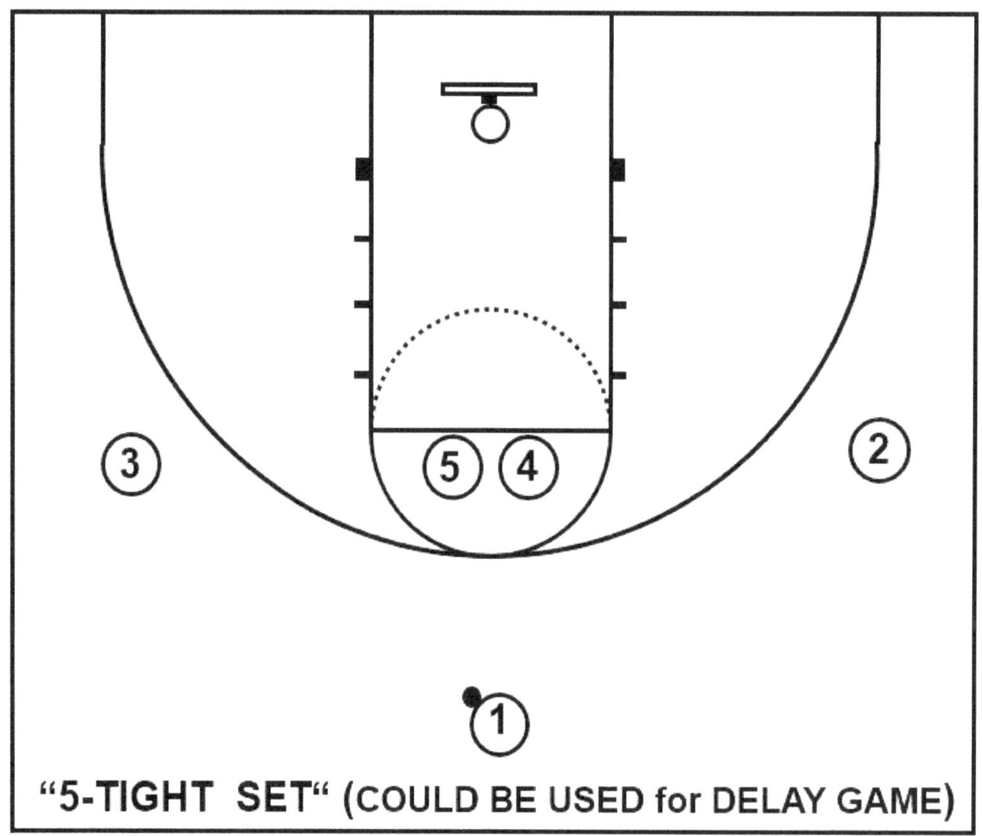

Diagram 15.16

The "5-UP SET"

Diagram 15.17 demonstrates an offensive set very similar to the "5-TIGHT SET" just discussed. The only difference is that both 05 and 04 widen out to their respective "High Post Elbow" locations. This alignment again has 01 in the center of the floor, places 03 and 02 respectively at the left and right "Wing" locations at the FT Line extended.

Again, with both Low Post positions initially being vacant, any offensive player will have openings to fill those locations and attack his defender (be it a perimeter-type or a post-type defender). With the defense again spread from sideline to sideline, but still having to defend the possibility of the post area being attacked, opposing team's defenses are stretched and vulnerable for different kinds of offensive actions that can be utilized in this set. Each play from the "5-UP SET" will still have every offensive player ending up in the continuity offense's correct "spot-ups" for maintaining the overall offensive attack. See Diagram 15.17

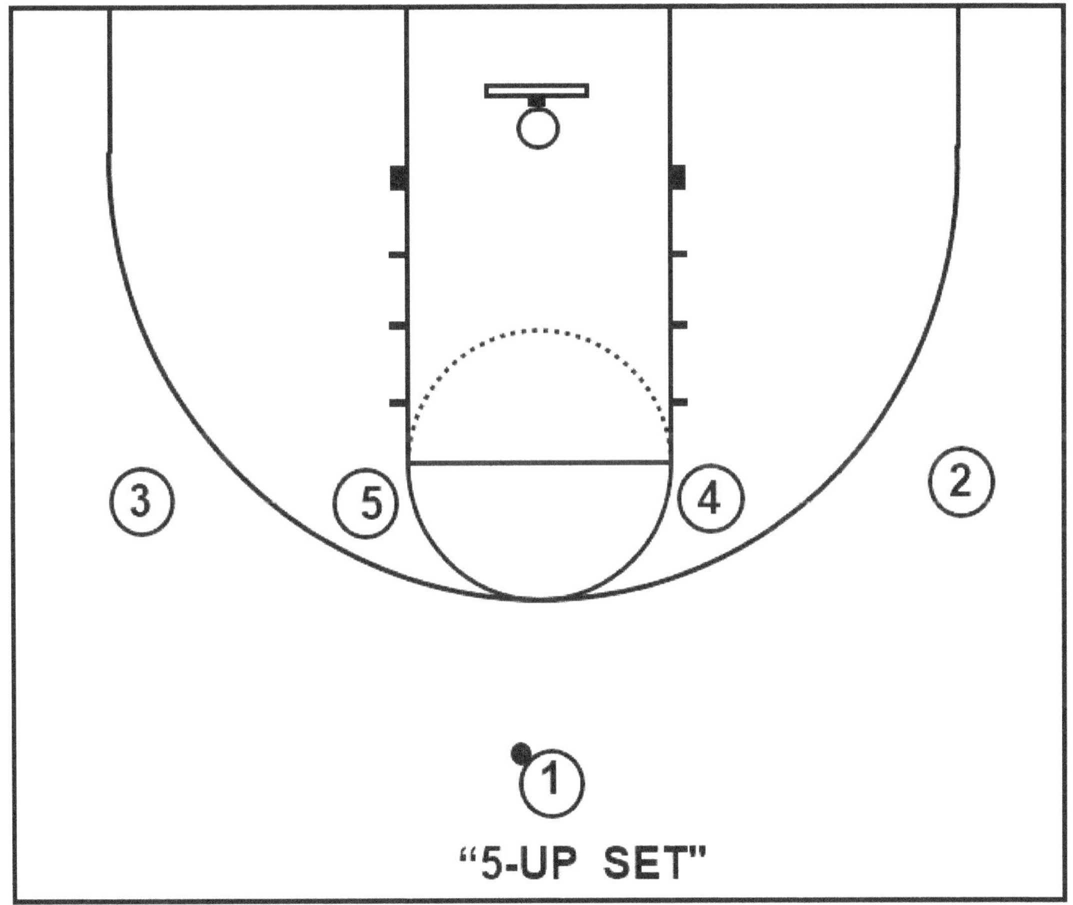

Diagram 15.17

Diagram 15.18 demonstrates somewhat of an offensive set that has some common ideas and techniques. While there are offensive sets that have offensive stacks, sometimes with both stacks starting near the "Blocks" and sometimes with both starting on the two "High Post Elbow" area. This alignment simply uses two stacks but one at the left "High Post Elbow" (05 ad 03) area and a second stack of 04 and 02 on the offense's right side at the "Low Post Block" area. There are obvious "Big-on-Small Pin Down Screens available on both sides of the floor. In addition, the alignment appears to be more of a perimeter scoring type offense on the left side of the lane while being more of an inside-oriented scoring type on the right side of the floor. This alignment again has 01 in the center of the floor, places 05 and 03 respectively stacked on the left and 04 and 02 stacked lower on the right side of the offense.

While there are numerous plays that can highlight individual players' skills, attack individual defenders' weaknesses; each entry that does not create the shot wanted will have successfully moved defenders, probed defenders for weaknesses and repositioned all offensive players to be in the designated continuity offense's correct spot-ups. See Diagram 15.18

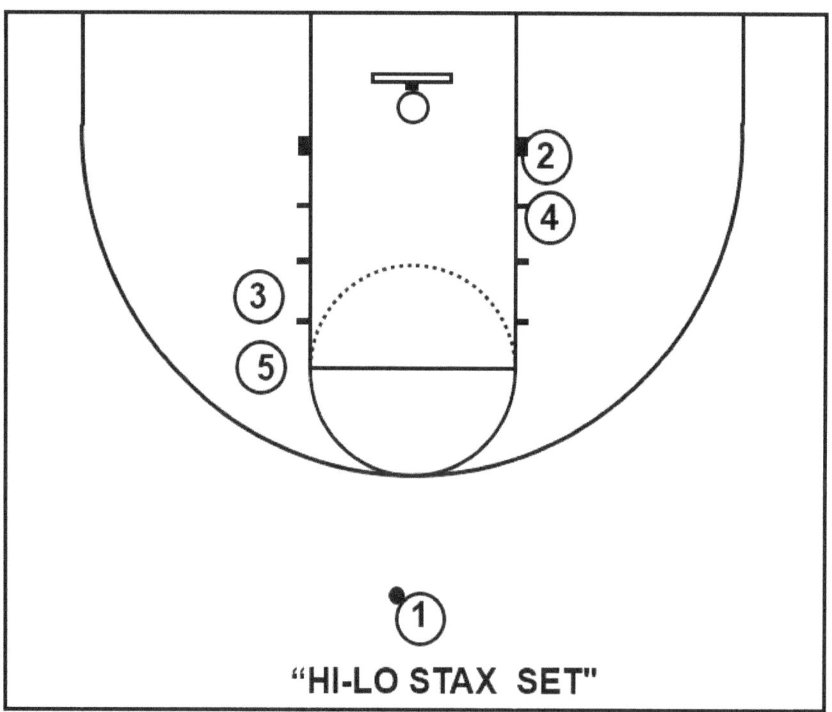

Diagram 15.18

The "HORNS SET"

Diagram 15.19 demonstrates probably the most popular offensive set/alignment in today's offenses. The alignment is symmetrically balanced, giving the offense an immediate advantage, in that each play can be ambidextrous and used to attack either side of the floor. Specific offensive players could be used in particular plays that could highlight their individual outstanding skills as well as attacking a particular opponent's weaknesses.

05 and 04 align a step higher and just slightly higher than the "High Post Elbow" area on the left and right sides of the lane respectively. 03 and 02 stretch the defense both vertically as well as horizontally by spotting up at the same "Deep Corner" spot-up locations as described in several of the other offensive sets.

This alignment is immediately conducive for 01 to shed his defender with the use of a "Big-on-Small Ball-Screen on either side of the floor. The ball-screener then has numerous actions that can take place either as a decoy, a screener for another teammate or the immediate primary receiver for 01 either on the perimeter (if his skills exist there) or in the lane (if his strongest skills exist in that area.) 01 could then become a primary scorer/creator/passer on his somewhat isolated dribble penetrations after receiving that ball-screen. See Diagram 15.19

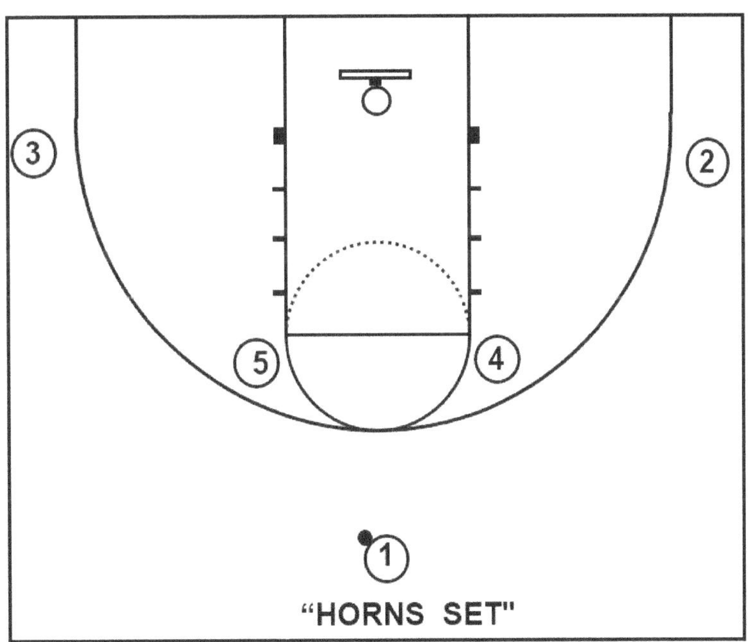

Diagram 15.19

Both 03 and 02 could then become the immediate '3 Pt.' scoring threats after 01 penetrates the lane and becomes more of a "penetrator and pitcher" (when the defense must have 'outside-in vertical defensive rotations to stop the ball.

Specific entries/plays can be executed from the "HORNS SET" for each player to have the occasion to highlight his own specific offensive skills as well as to take advantage of individual defender's defensive weaknesses that have been exposed. A steady balance of inside scoring and perimeter scoring plays should be in this set's offensive package, including dribble penetrations, various types of post-ups by both the traditional post-type players as well as by 'perimeter-type' players in the lanes. In addition, a variety of ball screens with different types of actions that follow the ball screen, various types of off-the-ball screening actions and other unique offensive schemes should be incorporated within this offensive set. The number of plays can vary based on the mental and physical skill level of the team.

Meeting the requirements of every entry from every offensive set/alignment in this Multiple Phase Offensive System, entries have to have filled the required offensive spot-ups of the designated offensive continuity that is to become the final phase of the offensive attack.

The "TWINS SET"

Diagram 15.20 demonstrates probably one of the older offensive sets/alignments that has been used by in many offenses over the years. The alignment is symmetrically balanced, giving the offense the same immediate advantage (as in the "HORNS SET," in that each play can be ambidextrous and used to attack both sides of the floor and use the individual offensive skills of certain offensive players. As in all offensive sets that are ambidextrous, defensive opponents will not know ahead of time which side of the floor will be attacked, making each player/entry less predictable and thereby giving another advantage to the offense.

05 and 04 align at the same locations as in the "HORNS SET," --a step higher and just slightly higher than the "High Post Elbow" area on the left and right sides of the lane respectively. But 03 and 02 change their locations and start tighter, just outside of the lane near the 'Notch above the Block.' This makes them an immediate scoring threat on the interior while still being able to stretch the defense horizontally with an easy break-out cut

to the same "Deep Corner" spot-up locations as described in several other offensive alignments.

This alignment can also be used so that 01 can quickly gain 'position advantages' on his defender with the use of a "Big-on-Small Ball-Screen by either 05 or 04. Again, the ball-screener then has the same countless actions that can be employed to attack the overall defense.

Each entry from this "TWINS SET" also has the ability and the responsibility to reposition players into the designated Continuity Offense's Spot-ups, again allowing for a seamless transition from entry to the last wave of the offensive attack. See Diagram 15.20

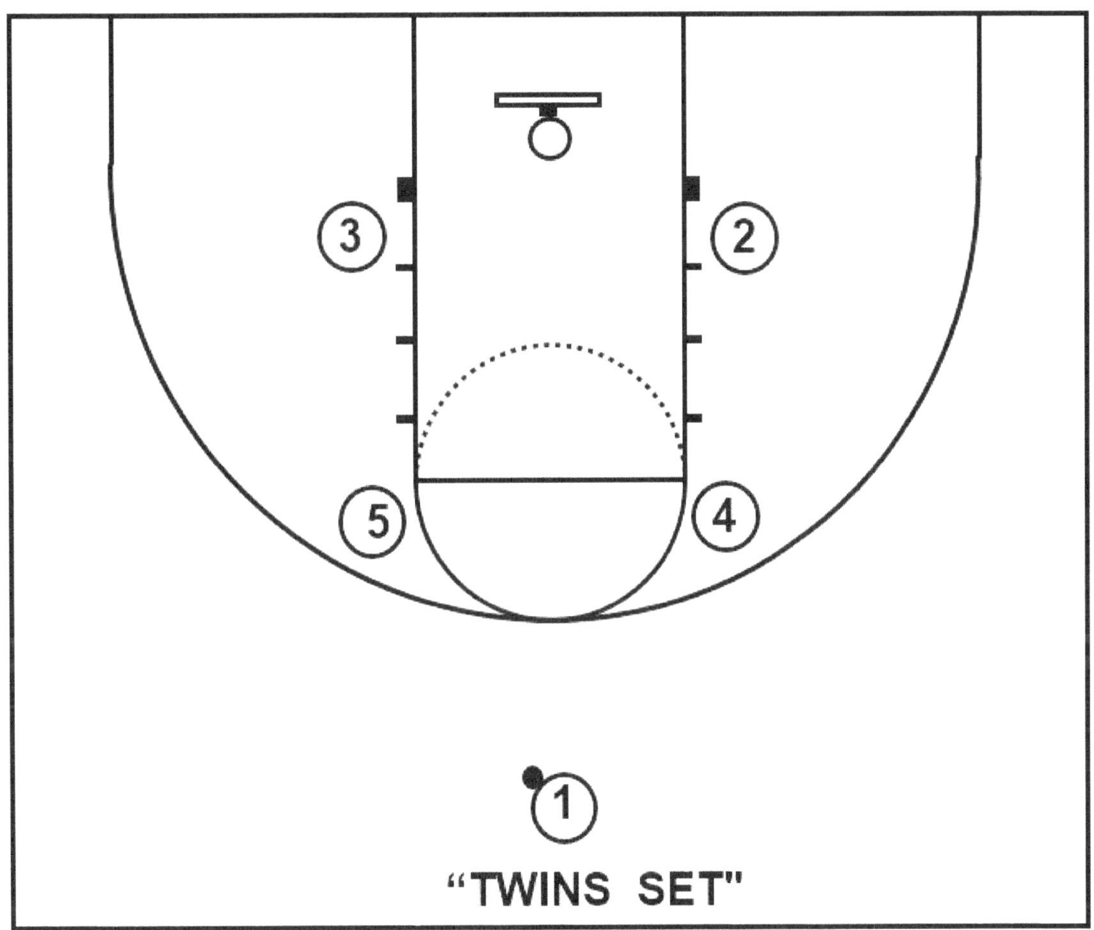

Diagram 15.20

The "BIG STACK SET"

Diagram 15.21 demonstrates an offensive set/alignment that balances the three designated perimeter players equally spaces them outside of the arc from the offense's left wing at the FT Line extended (03),the top of the key (01) and the right wing location at the FT Line extended (02.) 04 starts on the same 'Notch above the Block' with 05 vertically stacked closely above and in front of 04. To change the complexion of this offensive set to the defense or for other reasons, this 'big stack' of both post players could start on either side of the lane.

If shots that are wanted are not produced during the execution of the entries, the entries will have at least allowed each player to move his defender and to have repositioned himself into the accurate spot-ups for another instant and fluid transformation to start the designated continuity offense. See Diagram 15.21

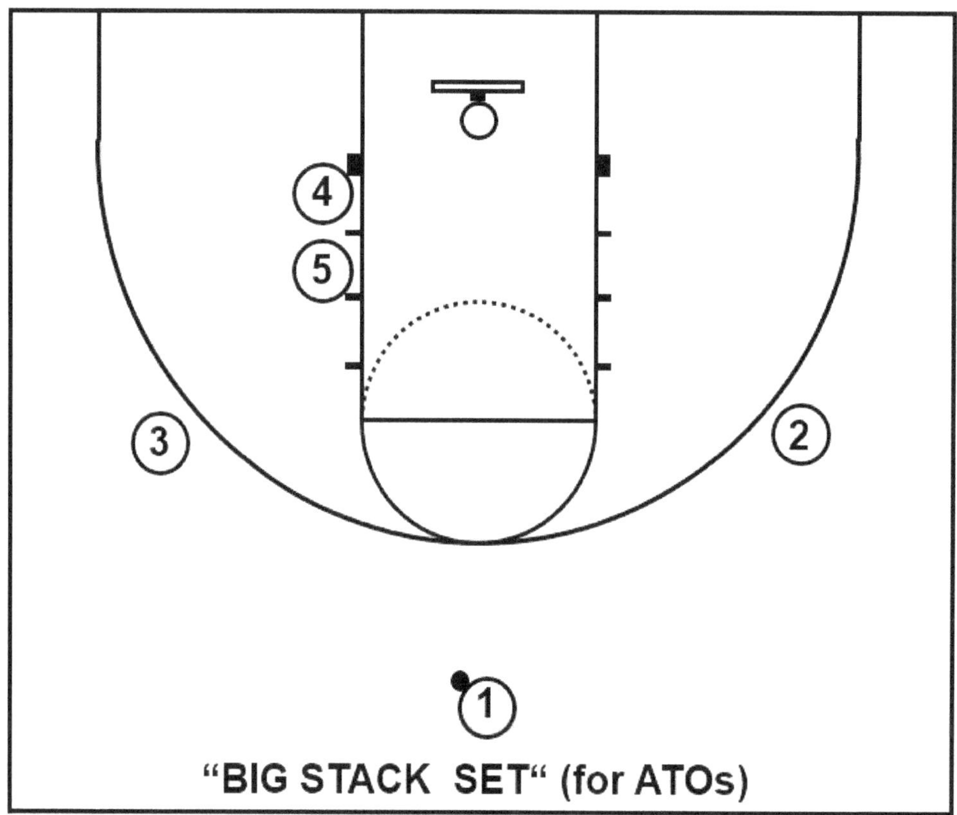

Diagram 15.21

The "SINGLE STACK SET"

Diagram 15.22 demonstrates an offensive set/alignment that is somewhat unique and could catch an opposing defense unprepared for its package of plays. 04 and 02 stack up in the same positions that they do in the "HI-LO STAX" SET--04 on the same 'Notch above the Block' with 02 vertically stacked closely behind 04. 05 starts his initial position at the 'Nail' spot on the floor with 03 aligned on the left wing outside of the arc at the FT Line extended. As always in an odd-front/one guard offensive set, 01 centers the ball in the middle 'alley' of the floor to bring the ball down the floor and jump-start each offensive play.

The right side of the offense will give 01 the space and freedom to attack his defender on the right side's perimeter area, while also having an immediate 'inside shot scorer in 04 and a perimeter-type player (02) that could pop out to the empty perimeter area or could end up at the top of the key or on the weakside. Plays from this different set/alignment could be used more as ATO (After Time-Outs special plays) where hidden substitutes could be brought in during the time-out to catch a defense napping. The actual play(s) could possibly never have been used during the course of the game until there is a special need for a surprise.

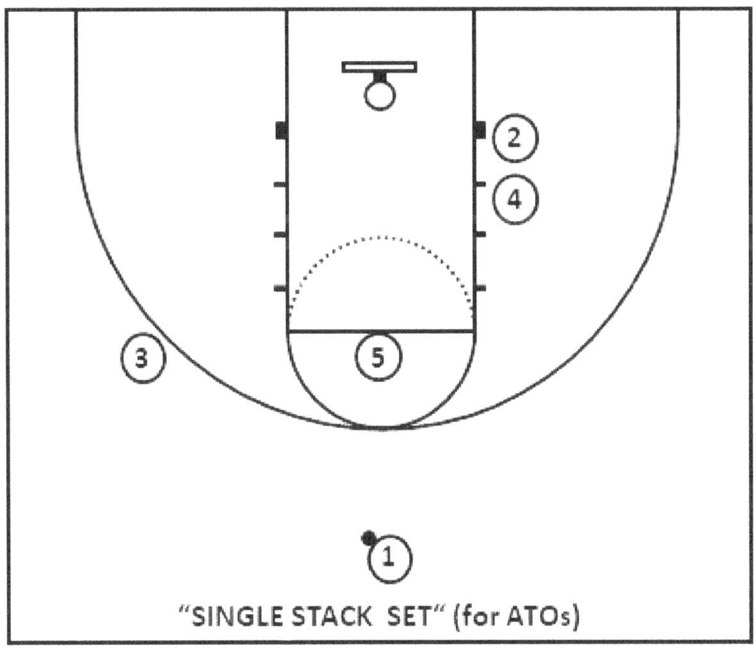

Diagram 15.22

Regardless of the reasons or the frequency of the play, these entries still must meet the requirement that if the designated shot is not taken, the entries will have at any rate repositioned all players into the continuity offense's spot-ups for another speedy start into the designated continuity offense.

With this Multiple-Phase Offensive System also providing Primary Fastbreaks the capabilities of being able to seamlessly and quickly transition into any of the possible Secondary Break alignments and options, this system is designed so that every single Secondary Break Option/Action will also have been built to be able to also have an instant and fluid transition into the next phase/level of overall attack. See Diagram 15.22

"EVEN-FRONT SECONDARY BREAK OPTIONS"

This multiple offensive system defines multiple secondary fastbreaks as 'accelerated and full court plays' that also can use specific talents and skills of specific players or the overall offensive team.

Primary Fastbreaks could begin from a defensive rebound after an opponent's made or missed field goal or free throw; after breaking an opponent's Full Court Press (after the opposition has scored) or after the opposition has committed a turnover. When there are 'no numbers' advantages in the Primary Break, there should be an instant and fluid conversion from the Primary Break into the Secondary Break.

Just as half-court plays can be executed more successfully out of certain half-court offensive alignments/sets, so could Secondary Break Options start from different 'looks.' Just as half-court plays probe and help discover individual defensive as well as overall team defensive weaknesses that the offensive team can take advantage of, so should Secondary Break Options. These reasons are just a few of the reasons (just as half-court plays have the exact reasons) to use both half-court plays as well as Secondary Break Options. The most obvious commonality between Secondary Break Options and Half-Court Plays/Entries is that both types of attacks that do not produce the shot wanted will reposition all five offensive players into the correct spot-up locations for an immediate conversion into the final wave of attack—the designated continuity offense.

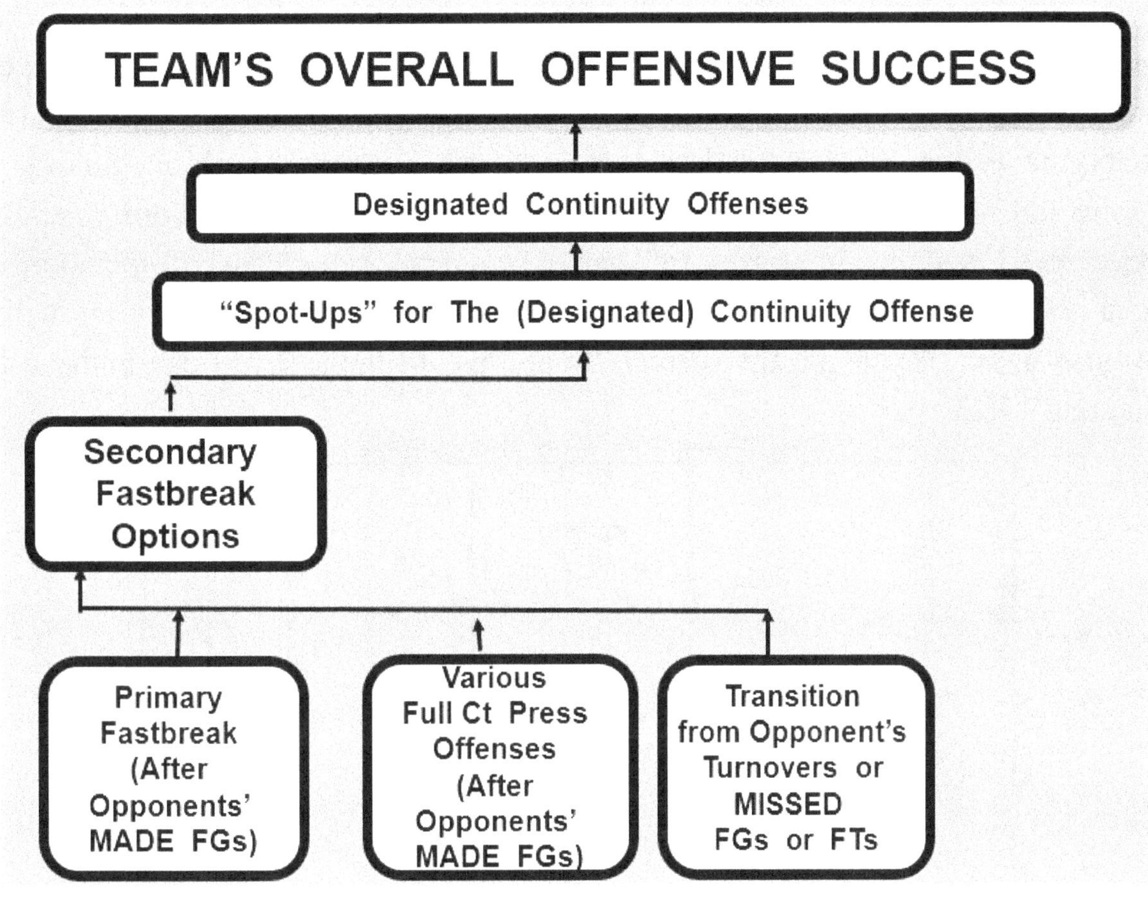

Illustration 15.3

Diagram 15.23 demonstrates an offensive team whose first wave or phase of their attack is an ' 'Even-Front' Primary Break that did not enjoy a 'numbers advantage' over the transition defense. The Primary Break is ambidextrous and could quickly push the ball down the floor, there is another high degree of the attack being unpredictable.

This example has 01 electing to push the ball to the 'Slot' on the right side of the floor, with both 02 and 03 running their outside lanes, diagonally diving to the basket (for possibly an 01 pass and an immediate lay-up) and then breaking out to their respective "Deep Corner" locations.

As 04 sprints the floor as the assigned "First Trailer," after reading 01 declare a current "Ballside Slot," he veers off to the newly declared "Weakside Elbow" area (to remove himself from the narrowed vision of all opposing defenders as they concentrate on the location of the ball and the action if front of them. From there, with no delay; 04 fluidly continues with a diagonal 'Slash Cut' across the lane to the newly declared "Ballside Block" area (actually the same "Notch above the Block" locations constantly discussed.)

05, the designated "Trigger/Second Trailer" runs the floor and remains slightly behind the level of the ball. When 04 slashes through the lane, 05 should be arriving at the empty "Weakside Slot," just outside of the arc and opposite of 01. From there, the first wave of the attack-the Primary Fastbreak has looked to take advantage of out-running, out-numbering and 'out-organizing' the opposition's transition defense with possible lay-ups, perimeter shots and inside passes to various players. Regardless of the number of Secondary Break Options used, when shots are not taken, each 'Break Option' will have repositioned every player into the correct "Spot-Ups" of the selected continuity offense. See Diagram 15.23

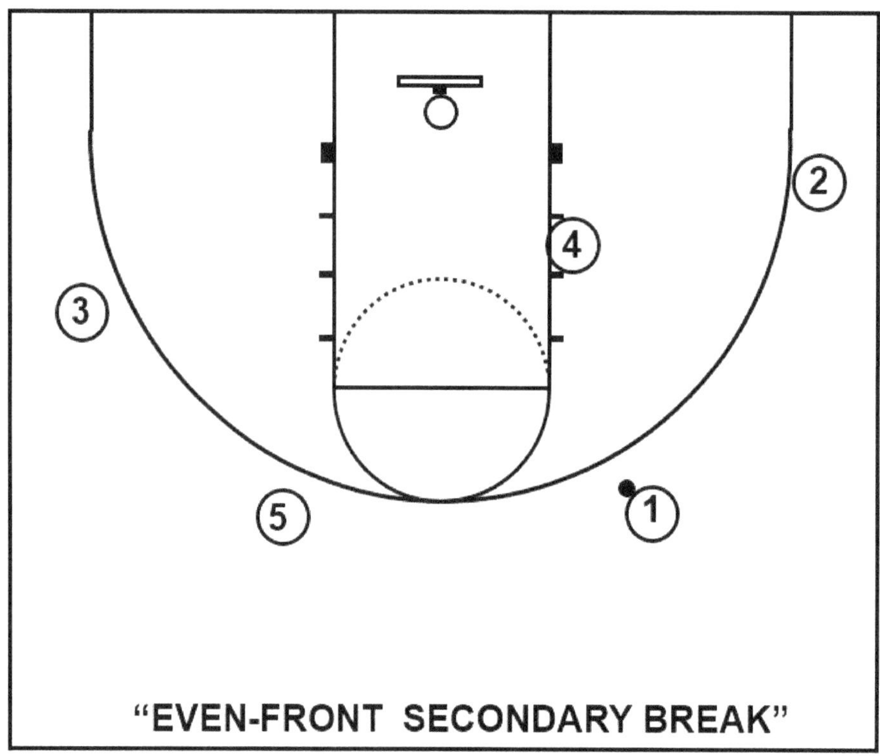

Diagram 15.23

Diagram 15.24 demonstrates another possible type of a first wave transition attack, but this time out of an 'Odd-Front' Primary Break that apparently did not succeed with a 'numbers advantage' over the transition defense. Even though the initial Primary Break could be executed towards either side of the floor, this diagram illustrates 01 electing to push the ball to the offense's right side of the floor with his perimeter pull dribble extending all the way to the FT Line extended. After both 03 and 02 have sprinted their respective outside lanes before diving to the basket for a potential pass from 01 for a potential lay-up; both pop out to their "Deep Corner" positions. When 01 has declared the ballside on the offense's right side of the floor, 04 again diagonally slashes from the newly declared "Weakside High Post Elbow" area behind interior defenders across the lane to the new "Ballside Block," while 03 then lifts to the FT Line extended. This will help eliminate the most likely 'helpside defenders,' which will allow 04 to 'iso post-up' his defender. The most likely biggest opposing defender will probably pick up 05, the "Trigger-Second Trailer," who will settle in behind the arc at the top of the key. This action and positioning of 01 and 03 horizontally stretch the already weakened transition defense, while 04 and 05 vertically stretch the defense. In addition, with 05 outside of the arc, a specifically assigned defensive opponent (X5) is forced to either stay with his man on the perimeter or abandon him to try to support his isolated interior defender, X4.

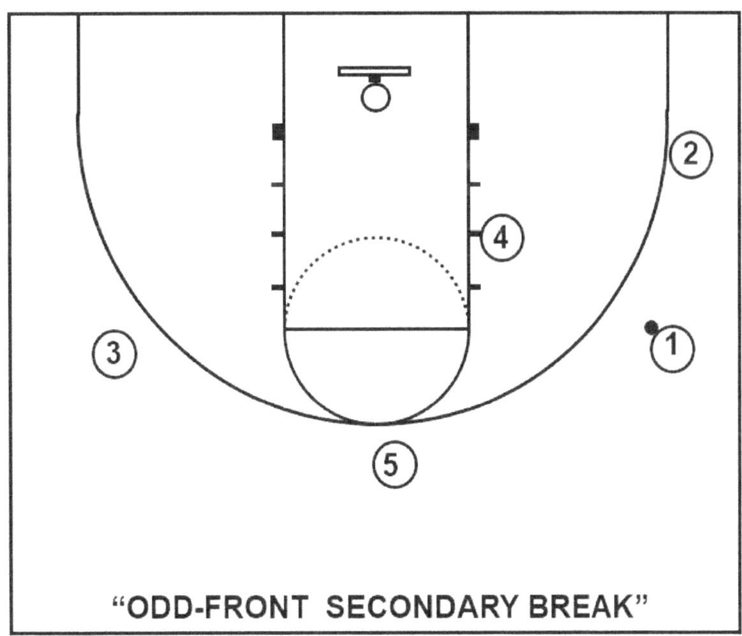

Diagram 15.24

As a matter of fact, an option of the actual Primary Break that flows directly into any of both the "Even Front" as well as the "Odd Front" Breaks could have the "Trigger/Second Trailer' (05) sprint the same path, but (instead of stopping at the "Weakside Slot" for "Even Front" Breaks and at the top of the key for all "Odd Front" Breaks) continue running directly at the weakside perimeter player (03 in this case) to exchange positions with that teammate.

When the offense looks to flatten out the defense by moving the ball to the "Deep Corner" with the possible creation of perimeter shots, inside passes to 04 or baseline drives, there can be as many options that can then take place when the ball is eventually passed back out to the top of the key.

After the designated Secondary Break also does not produce the desired shot, the ending actions will still reposition all players into the "4-Out/1-In" or the "3-Out/2-In" Spot-Ups for the continuity offense that is to be executed.

"BASELINE OUT-of-BOUNDS PLAYS"

Since the creation and the making of this offensive system is to have smooth conversions from the different beginning components of the offense (with possible use of multiple offensive sets/alignments) that will start the different types of plays can be very productive and successful; there is no reason that this concept should not also be applied in still another vehicle to score---all out-of-bounds plays. These includes both "Baseline Out-of-Bounds" Plays (and its corresponding alignments) and "Sideline Out-of-Bounds" Plays (and their alignments.) These alignments can also be multiple and will be the conduit of these out-of-bounds plays. As in the other two vehicles ("Primary/Secondary Breaks" and "Half-Court Plays/Entries") these "Out-of-Bounds Plays" would also be able to minimally reposition all five offensive players in the correct spot-ups of the same (or perhaps different) continuity offense.

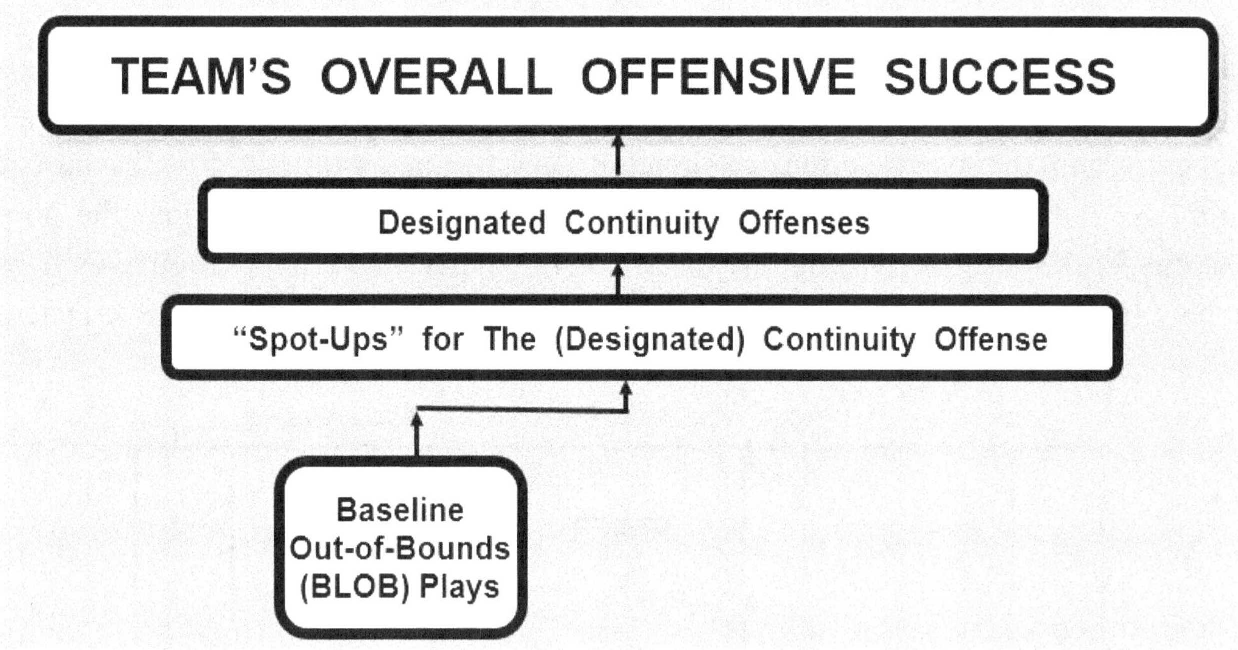

Illustration 15.4

The "JAM BASELINE OUT-of-BOUNDS SET"

Diagram 15.25 illustrates the first Baseline Out-of-Bounds Play Alignment in this chapter. With 01 the player that begins all half-court and Primary/Secondary Breaks as well as being the 'quarterback' of the team and presumably being the best passer on the team, 01 is always the player that takes the ball out of bounds on the designated side of the baseline. 05 and 04 always start on the 'Notch above the Block' with 05 always being on the left side when facing the basket and 04 on the right side. Both 03 and 02 align on the same horizontal plane with 03 on the same side with 05 and 02 paired up with 04. Both 03 and 02 start just outside of the arc with their "feet and hands ready" for a "quick catch and attack (catch and shoot, catch and drive or catch and pass.").

Different kinds of plays can be executed from this "JAM SET" for any offensive player. These BLOB plays can incorporate various actions and movements that will provide inside and outside scoring threats in different ways. Those methods could and should include various types of dribble penetrations, various types of post-ups, ball screen actions that precede various types of actions after the ball screen, in addition to the various types of off-the-ball screening actions. The number of plays can vary based on the mental and physical skill level of the team.

Once again, as in all offensive plays/entries from the countless offensive set/alignments that are used, each offensive play (half-court or from these out-of-bounds scenarios) or form of action (Secondary Break Options) the ultimate objective is to score off of the play that begins with the specific offensive situation. As stated many times before (because it is extremely important,) the secondary objective is to reposition players into the proper positions for the designated continuity to have an immediate and seamless conversion from the play (started in the specific offensive set) that does not create the shot. See Diagram 15.25

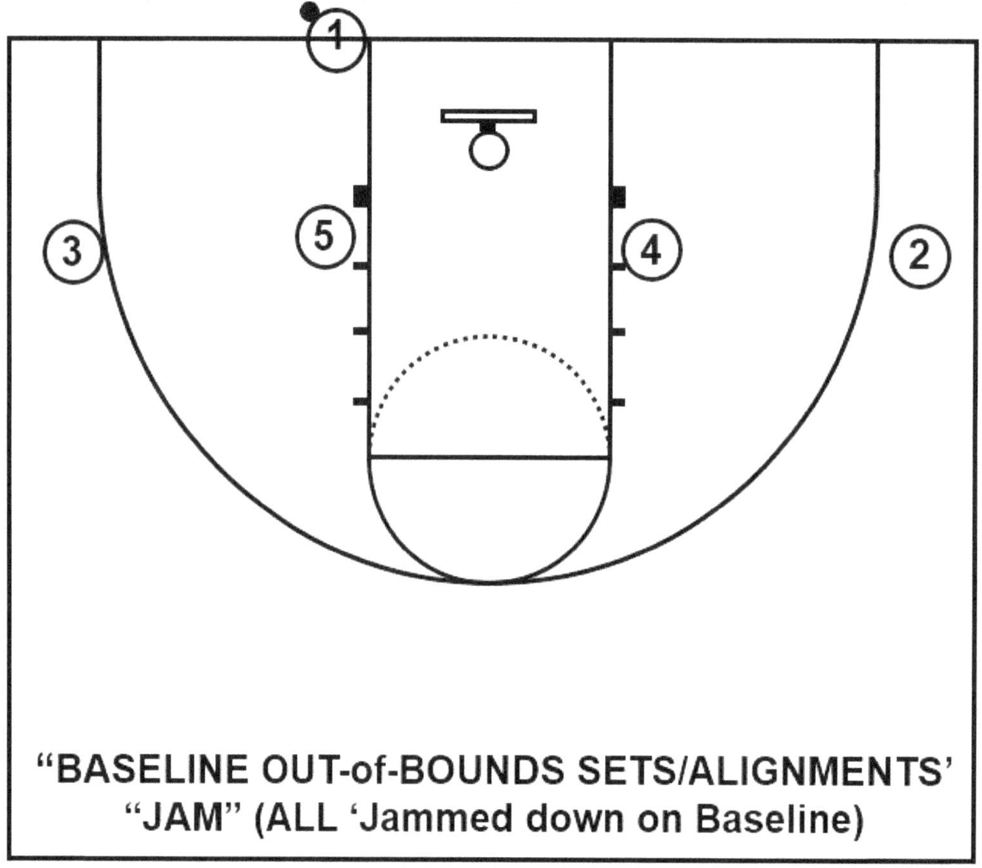

Diagram 15.25

The "STRONG(-SIDE) SLANT" BASELINE OUT-of-BOUNDS SET

Diagram 15.26 illustrates a second BLOB Set that could be called "STRONG(-SIDE) SLANT." For the same reasons previously discussed, 01 again is the automatic "BLOB Trigger." 05 and 04 align on the two "High Post Elbow" positions and 03 starting at the top of the key outside of the "3 Pt." arc and 02 beginning on the offense's left "Deep Corner."

This alignment could also allow an assortment of various ways to attack specific defenders or highlight offensive skills and talents of particular players so that the actual BLOB Play not only creates shots but actual points. But if the play does not produce the shot wanted, the next top priority is for the action to at least move all five offensive players into the correct spot-up positions so that there is no delay between the end of the play (that did not take a shot) and the immediate beginning of the designated continuity offense. See Diagram 15.26

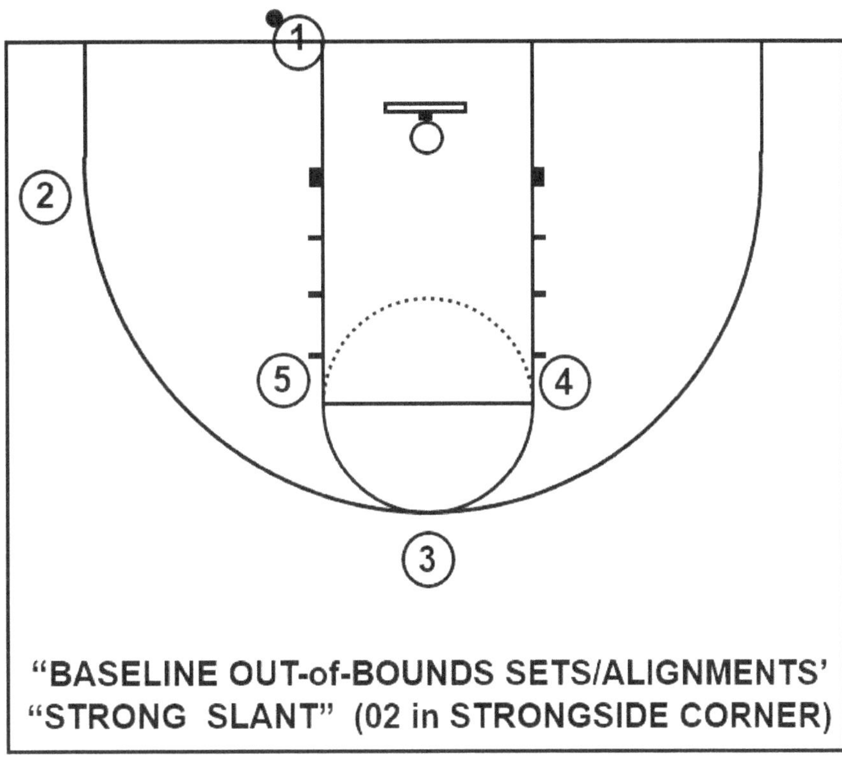

Diagram 15.26

The "WEAK(-SIDE) SLANT" BASELINE OUT-of-BOUNDS SET

Diagram 15.27 is a diagram of another BLOB Set called "WEAK(-SIDE) SLANT." Again, 01 is the automatic "BLOB Trigger" with 05 and 04 aligned on the same two "High Post Elbow" positions and 03 at the same top of the key outside of the "3 Pt." arc. The only difference between the two BLOB Sets is where 02 starts. In this "WEAK SLANT SET," 02 starts on the offense's right "Deep Corner."

The same two priorities exist for this alignment as well as any other alignments. If no shots are taken, the continuity offense will be able to immediately begin since those necessary spot-up locations will be filled. Defenses must stop the play before immediately then having to defend the continuity offense's various types of attacks. See Diagram 15.27

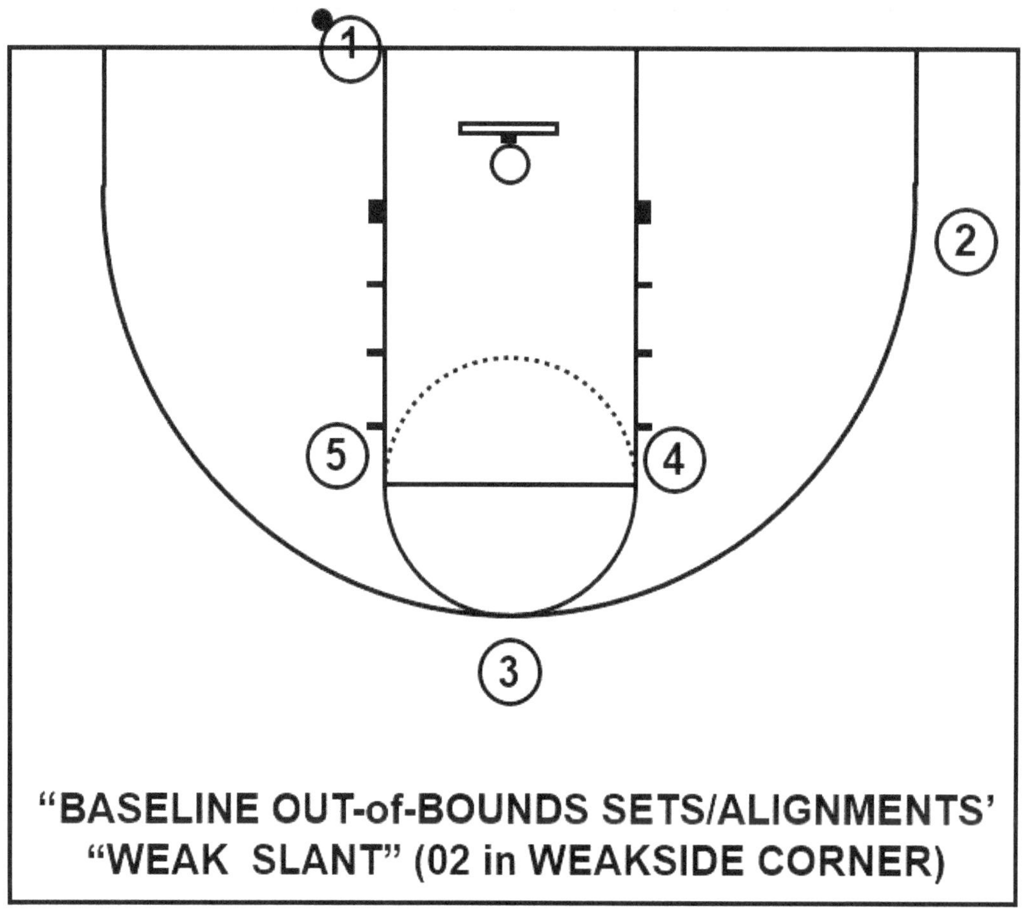

Diagram 15.27

The "VICTORY" BASELINE OUT-of-BOUNDS SET

Diagram 15.28 shows a different alignment, called the "VICTORY" BLOB SET, that can create different types of offensive actions, with each action being potential shot producers. In addition, the same requirement exists that each play must reposition each offensive player into the proper locations for the same smooth and instant conversion into the system's final phase of attack.

01 becomes the "Trigger" on the designated new "Ballside" of the play. 05 starts on the 'Notch above the Block' position on his usual half-court side of the lane with 04 on his normal right side of the floor. 02 starts on the "Nail" with 03 tightly stacked directly behind 02 with both perimeter players facing 01 and the basket.

Plays should integrate different types and kinds of movement that will create inside and outside scoring threats. Different types of dribbling actions, ball screen actions, off-the-ball screening actions, post-ups by both post-type and perimeter-type players, DHO actions and 'iso' actions could be integrated. See Diagram 15.28

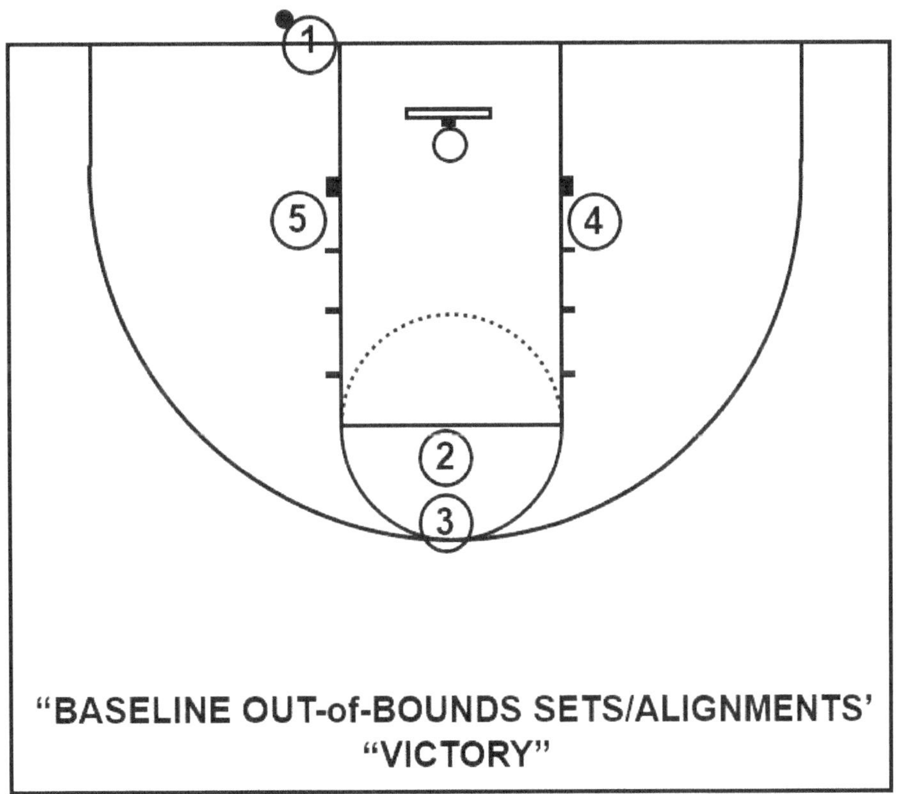

Diagram 15.28.

"SIDELINE OUT-of-BOUNDS PLAYS"

If "Baseline Out-of-Bounds Plays" can implement an organized and successful attack that serves as another vehicle that can smoothly flow into the continuity offense, so should "Sideline Out-of-Bounds Plays" be able to productively utilize that same concept. Various offensive alignments for SLOB Plays could and should be utilized with the same methods of attacks that are used in Secondary Break Options, Half-Court Plays/Entries and BLOB Plays. These could also include some of the many types of on-ball screens (with the various types of action that follow the on-ball screens), various off-the-ball types of screening actions, the different off-the-ball types of cuts and other productive actions. This could include Dribble Hand-Offs, fake DHOs, Pass Hand-Offs and Fake PHOs. When the use of Primary/Secondary Breaks and Half-Court Plays/Entries and BLOB Plays have immediate conversions into the desired continuity offense is an outstanding offensive weapon, it would only make sense that every SLOB play should have the capabilities of the same type of seamless conversions by moving every player into the proper spot-ups of the same (or possibly even different) continuity offense.

A team that could mentally handle the uniqueness of multiple continuity offenses could possibly and potentially have a second continuity offense (or a variation of the one designated offense) that was used only for BLOB and SLOB Plays.

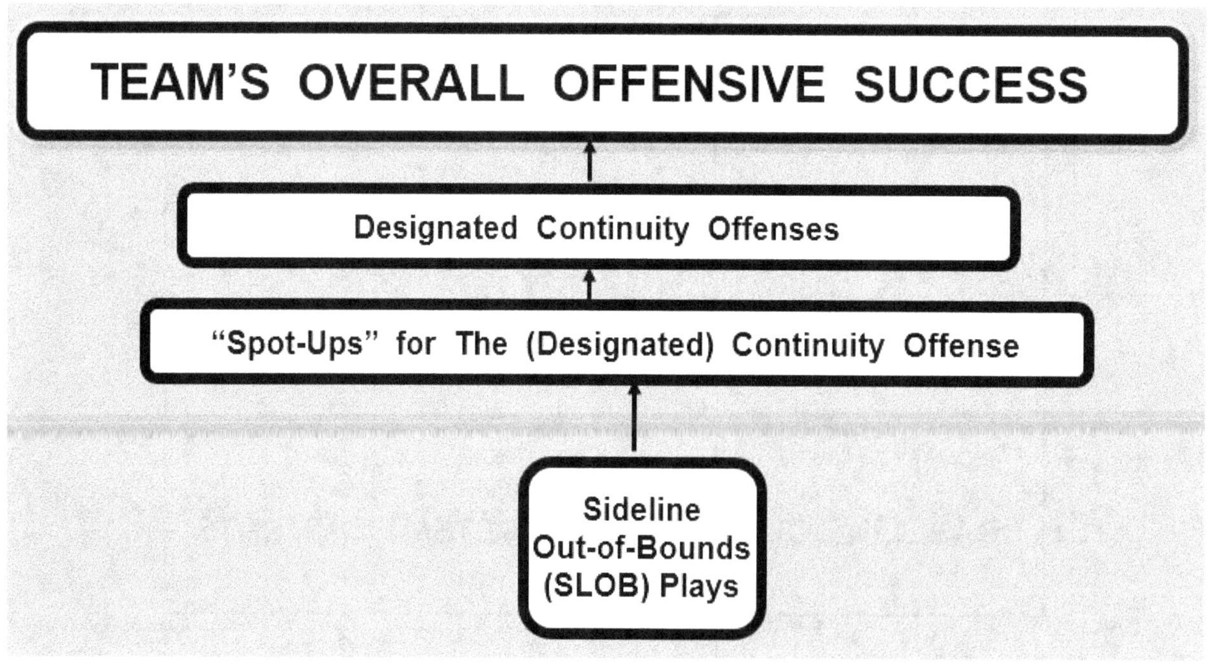

Illustration 15.5.

The "3-CORNER" SIDELINE OUT-of-BOUNDS SET

Diagram 15.29 illustrates a sideline out-of-bounds offensive alignment with 01 triggering the ball out of bounds, 05 and 04 both at the two "High Post Elbow" areas, 02 on the "Ballside Block" and 03 flattened out and horizontally spread out on the offensive "Weakside Deep Corner."

This alignment has various possibilities in getting any number of players open to receive the in-bounds pass as well as immediate scoring threats both on the interior as well as the perimeter. See Diagram 15.29

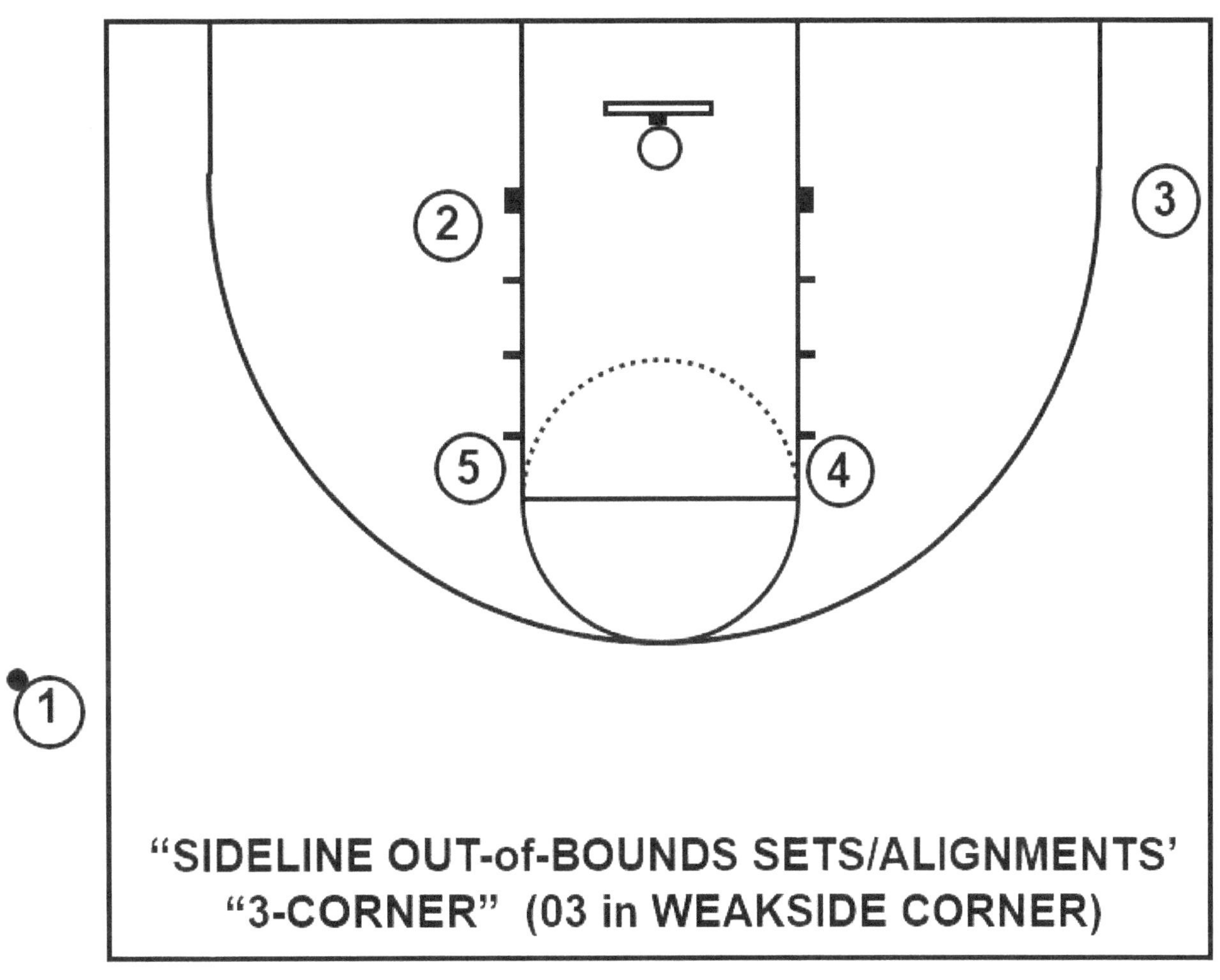

Diagram 15.29

Diagram 15.30 shows another SLOB Set/Alignment, called the "3-KEY SET" that is very similar to the previous alignment. 01, 05, 04 and 02 align in the very same locations as before. The only change is that 03 moves from the previous alignment's initial "Deep Corner" position to the very top of the key, just outside of the '3 Pt.' arc. While this alignment is slightly different, each play in this SLOB SET'S Package could add to or delete some of the same offensive techniques the previous package of plays uses. See Diagram 15.30

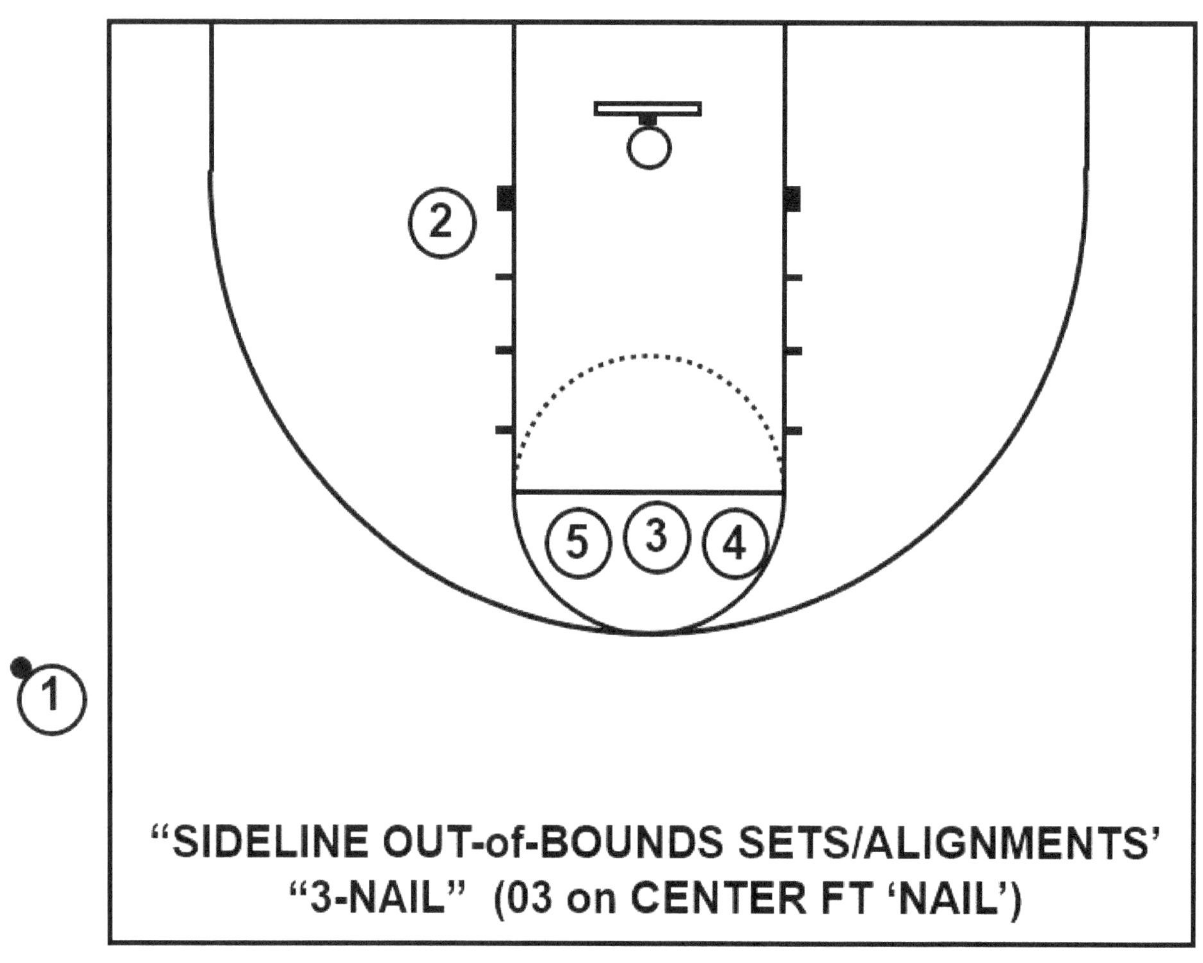

Diagram 15.30

Diagram 15.31 illustrates another SLOB Alignment/Set almost identical with the previous sets with the exception of just one player again—03. This time, 03 aligns at the top of the key. His change in his initial location can give not only himself but other pass receiving options for the remaining three players. This would lead to new primary and secondary scoring threats after the beginning cuts and screens take place. See Diagram 15.31

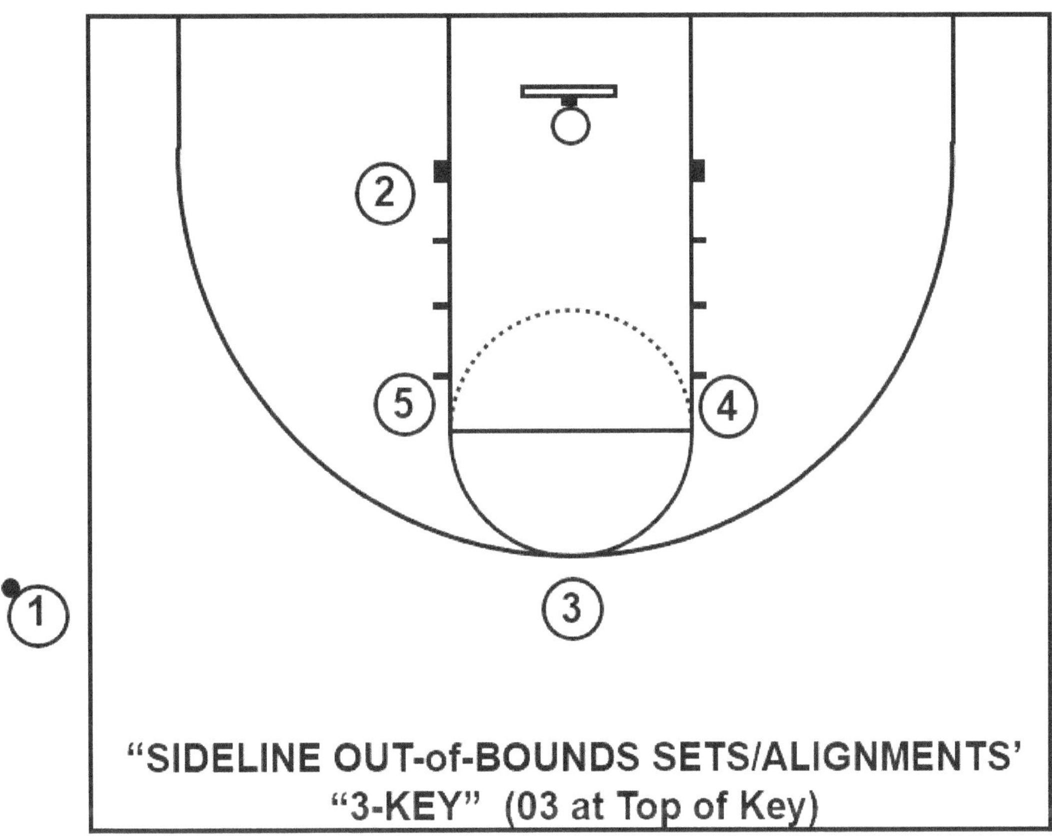

Diagram 15.31

Regardless of the beginning alignments and the similarity of the initial positioning of almost all players, as well as the specific schemes that are used, a major similarity is that each play that does not produce the desired shot the offense wants; the final positioning of all five players are the designated continuity offense's exact "spot-ups." This allows the plays started from the sideline to immediately and fluidly transition into the desired continuity offense.

There are many different philosophies on how to attack opposing defenses. This multiple-phase offensive system uses more than one phase/layer/wave of attack, with each phase/wave having a seamless and immediate conversion into the next phase/wave. While this system can be confusing to defenses and difficult to defend, this system can be properly taught and coached so that it can be easily understood and ultimately executed by players of many different levels of (physical talent, mental understand and playing experience.)

In addition, there are several types of offensive schemes and different ways within this system that offenses can attack their defensive counter-parts. Many of these can be integrated within the same offensive system that can attack defenses in various ways. The larger the number of schemes that can be successfully utilized and integrated within the same system, the greater the opportunity an offensive team can find the most efficient and productive schemes that can place both individual and the overall team in the best and most frequent "positions to succeed."

The plays/entries carefully diagrammed down to the small and seemingly unimportant 'V-Cuts' made by countless players before making their more important following cut are also described in detail.

Each play has been carefully studied and evaluated to determine which level of talent and experience must be possessed for that specific team to be able to successfully execute the play. This includes all players' physical skills as well as their mental understanding of the game. Coaches must also have the experience and the associated level of understanding of the game as well as their coaching/teaching of the nuances of each play.

The most sophisticated plays/entries would fall into the first of the three levels all based on the team's physical talents and skills, the mental capacities and the overall team's game experience. In addition, the coaching staff must have a high degree of basketball knowledge as well as very high teaching and coaching skills to educate his/her entire basketball team. The proper breakdown drills must be thoroughly utilized to hone the fundamental skills and techniques needed for individual players and the overall team to execute plays that can be efficient, productive, and successful. We define this family of plays as the "Level 3 category" of plays. This "Level 3" family of plays will have a much more complex offensive scheme that would require a very high amount of physical talent as well as requiring a greater amount of the players (to execute) and the coaches (to teach and coach) mental capacities and experience needed for the offense to be efficient, productive and successful. We feel plays in our defined "Level 3" category could possibly be successful for NBA teams, definitely for college teams and also for many high schools and older AAU teams.

The next classification or level of plays would be possibly slightly lower as far as sophistication, complexity and the actual 'length' of the play (and the number of passes, cuts, and screens used) in the play's overall scheme. While all "Level 2" plays in each of the chapters in this book remain to be fundamentally sound, these plays may lack the actual number of techniques/methods that are implemented within that play in comparison to the "Level 1" plays/entries. Therefore any team that successfully executes the highest "Level 1" plays/entries could/should easily be able to execute any of these so-called lower "Level

2" plays/entries, if so desired. Almost all high school teams should be able to execute successfully all aspects of the "Level 2" plays.

The final grouping of plays would be called "Level 1" plays are not as difficult for offensive players to master the execution of them, both physically as well as mentally. Even though the techniques are still fundamentally, they may not be as complex to learn and understand in addition to being easier to physically execute.

"Level 1" plays would be lower in the scheme's complexities and the number of techniques used in the execution of this category of plays. Obviously, since these "Level 1" plays are still sound, but lack some of the methods used in the two previous more sophisticated and complex levels; these more elementary plays should be able to be utilized by any teams that use either of the two higher level plays. We feel that Middle School/Junior High teams as well as younger AAU teams or organizations, should be able to utilize any of the "Level 1" plays successfully, with a possibility that some of those teams that are slightly more advanced (than other teams) could possibly use some plays located in the immediate next immediate level.

Ideas, concepts, and techniques from actual plays from teams of all three levels have been used to modify or to create different combinations of the various techniques and schemes used that will help prove these entries can be successfully used. This allows the author to create numerous plays that use the various schemes to build a library of fundamentally sound plays that will be unique and will be appropriate for a wide range of teams with various ages and skill levels.

With this book having plays in these three presumed categories or levels, the book will reach out and benefit a much larger group of serious basketball coaches from elementary school age to the highest skilled levels that exist.

In addition, an experienced and resourceful coach may be able to mold some plays that include all of the offensive techniques that he/she desires could reshape a specific play that begins in one specific offensive set/alignment and reshape it so that it could begin in a different offensive/set that is more favorable to that coach and his/her coaching staff's liking.

Conversely, that innovative and creative coach may completely like the specific offensive set/alignment and favor the very same offensive actions included in a certain play, but can modify that play so that the ending spot-ups of all five players are conducive

to being able to begin the final phase of the offensive attack by using a more favorable offensive continuity offense.

The "1-DOWN SET"

PLAYS/ENTRIES THAT END in the "3-OUT/2-IN" OFFENSIVE SPOT-UPS

After the entry/play/quick-hitter has been executed but no shots have been taken, all five players will end up in a different group of offensive spot-ups. These "3-Out/2-In Spot-Ups" will have players moved about the court with any of the five ending up in the "Ballside Block," the "Ballside Wing," the "Weakside Block," the "Weakside Wing," and the "Point" (at the top of the key). These five positions can provide the offense with safe and easy types of ball-reversals, large gaps for dribble penetration, opportunities to deliver the ball inside to whomever (perimeter-type or post-type players) is posting up their defender on the "Ballside Block," and a player that can be a perimeter-scoring threat and a legitimate offensive rebounding threat from outside of the arc on his "offensive crashing of the boards." The "3-Out/2-In Spot-Ups also provide ample opportunities for constant and effective defensive transition responsibilities.

Diagram 16.1 illustrates the "1-DOWN SET." 05 is the designated player that has the ability to post up on the 'Mid-Post' on either side of the lane. 01 and 02 are the guards that bring the ball down the floor to initiate the offense and the designated play/entry. The two remaining players (03 and 04) are "spotted up on the "Wing" locations, on both sides of the lane outside of the arc at the FT Line extended. With 05 being able to post up on either side of the lane and therefore start on either side of the lane, the offense will have two diverse cosmetic looks and therefore gives the offense a higher level of unpredictability. In this diagram, 05 posts up on the offense's right side of the lane, below 04's initial right "Wing" spot-up location.

There is a significant number of philosophies on how to attack the various types of opposing defenses. This multiple-phase offensive system uses more than one phase/layer/wave of attack, with each phase/wave having a seamless and immediate conversion into the next phase/wave. While this system can be confusing to defenses and difficult to defend, this system can be properly taught and coached so that it can be easily understood and ultimately executed by players of many diverse levels of (physical talent, mental understand, and playing experience.)

In addition, there are several types of offensive schemes and different ways within this system that offenses can successfully attack their defensive counter-parts. Many of these can be integrated within the same offensive system that can attack defenses in various ways. The larger the number of schemes that can be successfully integrated within the same system, the greater the opportunity an offensive team can find the most efficient and productive schemes that can place both individual and the overall team in the best and most frequent "positions to succeed."

The plays/entries carefully diagrammed down to the small and seemingly unimportant 'V-Cuts' made by countless players before having those same players then make their more important cuts are also described in detail.

Each play has been carefully studied and evaluated to determine which level of talent and experience must be possessed for that specific team to be able to successfully execute the play. The most sophisticated plays/entries would fall into the latter of the three levels all based on the team's physical talents and skills, the mental capacities and the overall team's game experience. In addition, the coaching staff must have a high degree of basketball knowledge as well as very high teaching and coaching skills to educate his/her entire basketball team. The proper breakdown drills must be thoroughly utilized to hone the fundamental skills and techniques needed for individual players and the overall team to execute plays that can be efficient, productive, and successful. In addition to the sophistication of the plays as far as the various offensive techniques used, it is almost certain there is a larger number of the various offensive techniques that are weaved into the offensive entry or play. Therefore, there will be additional steps of parts of the higher sophisticated "Level 3" plays.

We define this family of plays as the "Level 3 category" of plays. As just stated, this "Level 3" family of plays will have a much more complex offensive scheme that would require high amounts of physical talent as well as requiring a greater amount of the players (to execute) and the coaches (to teach and coach) mental capacities and experience needed for the offense to be efficient, productive and successful. We feel plays in our defined "Level 3" category could possibly be successful for NBA teams, definitely for college teams and also for many high schools and more experienced AAU teams.

The next lower classification or level of plays would be somewhat lower as far as sophistication, complexity and the actual 'length' of the play (including the number of passes, cuts, screens and other techniques used) in the one particular play's overall series of actions. While all "Level 2" plays in each of the chapters in this book remain to be fundamentally sound, these plays may lack the actual number of techniques/methods that are implemented within that play in comparison to the "Level 3" plays/entries. Therefore, any team that successfully executes the highest "Level 3" plays/entries should easily be able execute any of these so-called lower "Level 1 and 2" plays/entries, if so desired. It appears most high school teams should be able to execute successfully all aspects of all of the "Level 1 and 2" plays.

The final grouping of plays would be called "Level 1" plays and are not as difficult for offensive players to master their execution of the plays, both physically as well as mentally. Even though the techniques are still fundamentally sound, they may not be as complex to learn and understand in addition to being easier to physically execute. These plays will not take as long of a time to execute the full play because of the lesser number of actual offensive actions implemented within the play.

"Level 1" plays would be lower in the scheme's complexities and the number of techniques used in the execution of this category of plays. This means that these plays will be executed in shorter periods of time before the end of the play and therefore the beginning of the designated continuity offense. More than likely, the fewer number of diagrams will relate to the number of offensive techniques and actions; therefore the lower level of complexity in that particular play/entry.

Obviously, since these "Level 1" plays are still sound, but lack some of the methods used in the two previous more sophisticated and complex levels; these more elementary plays should be able to be utilized by any teams that use either of the two higher level plays. We feel that Middle School/Junior High teams as well as younger AAU teams or organizations should be able to utilize any of the "Level 1" plays successfully, with a possibility that some of those teams that are slightly more advanced (than other teams) could possibly use some plays located in the immediate next immediate level.

Various concepts, techniques and methods taken from other plays/entries from teams ranging in all three levels could be utilized to produce other plays with the various combinations of those concepts to create different plays. This provides the imaginative and resourceful coach endless boundaries to be different and creative in developing newer plays for his system.

Any team that has the capabilities of executing "Level 3" plays (sometimes called quick-hitters or entries) would then be able to execute the somewhat less complicated and complex plays categorized in both the "Level 2 and Level 1" groups.

Also, any offensive team that can execute "Level 2" plays should then be able to incorporate and implement (the somewhat lower) "Level 1" plays/entries.

The "Level 3" plays that are discussed in this chapter should most likely be slightly too complex for teams that use the Level 1 and 2 plays. Some teams may be able to handle some particular plays that are just a step up from their normal family of plays, such as a team that predominately implements "Level 1" plays may have the capabilities of adding a very small number of "Level 2" plays. Or a team that has a majority of "Level 2" plays may only on rarely have instances to successfully incorporate a "Level 3" play.

With this book having plays, in these three presumed categories or levels, the book will reach out and benefit a much larger group of serious basketball coaches from elementary school age to the highest skilled levels that exists.

In addition, an experienced and resourceful coach may be able to mold some plays that include all of the offensive techniques that he/she desires could reshape a specific play that begins in one specific offensive set/alignment and reshape it so that it could begin in a different offensive/set that is more favorable to that coach and his/her coaching staff's liking.

Conversely, that innovative and creative coach may completely like the specific offensive set/alignment and favor the very same offensive actions included in a certain play, but can modify that play so that the ending spot-ups of all five players are conducive to being able to begin the final phase of the offensive attack by using a more favorable offensive continuity offense.

PLAYS/ENTRIES THAT END in the "3-OUT/2-IN" OFFENSIVE SPOT-UPS

After the entry/play/quick-hitter has been executed but no shots have been taken, all five players will end up in a different group of offensive spot-ups. These "3-Out/2-In Spot-Ups" will have players moving about the court with any of the five ending up in the "Ballside Block," the "Ballside Wing," the "Weakside Block," the "Weakside Wing," and the "Point" (at the top of the key). These five positions can provide the offense with safe and easy types of ball-reversals, large gaps for dribble penetration, opportunities to deliver the ball inside to whomever (perimeter-type or post-type players) is posting up their defender on the "Ballside Block," and a player that can be a perimeter-scoring threat and a legitimate offensive rebounding threat from outside of the arc on his "offensive crashing of the boards." The "3-Out/2-In Spot-Ups also provide ample opportunities for constant and effective defensive transition responsibilities.

Diagram 16.1 shows Play # 1 with 05 on the right side of the lane and 01 initiating the play with a simple and safe 01-02 "Reverse Pass," that is immediately followed with a quick "Give-n-Go Cut diagonally through the lane. If 02 does not return the pass quickly to 01, 02 makes his "perimeter pull dribble across the top of the key to the newly vacated "Slot" location. At the same time, 01 starts to empty out of the lane and cut towards 05. 05 uses 01's cut to scrape off of either the high or low shoulder of 01 for a "Small-on-Big Lane Exchange Cross-Screen." This drastic player personnel change between 01 and 05 should eliminate defensive switches and therefore cause more problems for the defense by eliminating one possible defensive option.

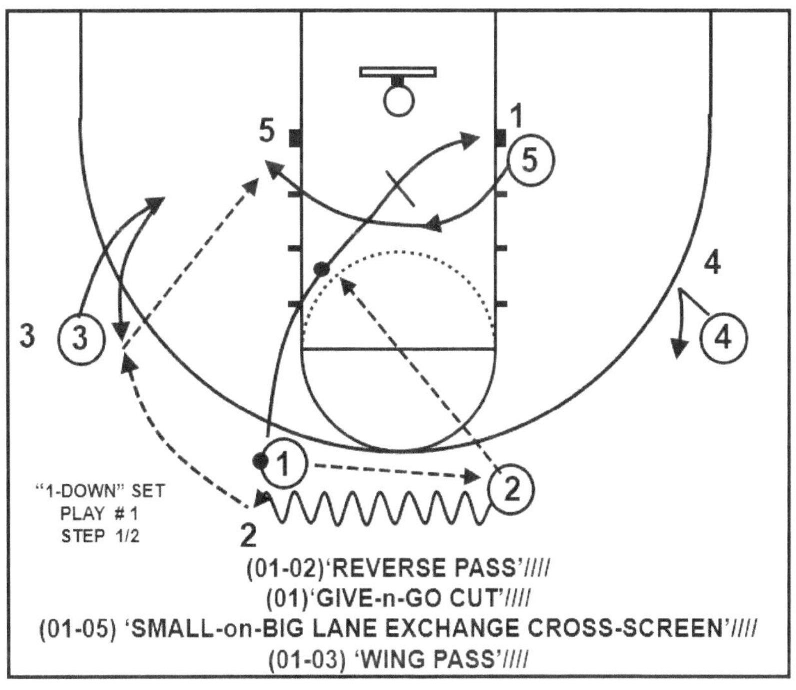

Play # 1   Diagram 16.1

Diagram 16.2 shows 02 making the "Wing Pass" to 03 and 03 immediately looks to make the pass to 05, now posting up on the new "Ballside Block." After passing the ball to 03, 02 then follows the pass to start the (02-03) "Follow the Pass Ball-Screen." This action should give 03 the opportunity to first deliver the ball to 05 on his cut across the lane to attack his defender. 03's second option is then quickly followed with 03 being able to dribble the ball across the center of the floor (to the opposite "Slot." As 03 crosses the imaginary 'center line,' 04 breaks down to set a "Big-on-Down" Pin Down-Screen for 01 to use to pop out to the FT Line extended. After screening for 01, 04 continues across the lane to set (a second) "Lane Exchange Cross-Screen" for 05 to again attack his individual defender. 03 is the only player that is not precisely in the correct "3-Out/2-In" Spot-ups, but the designated continuity offense that can be executed from these spot-ups is ready to continue the attack on the defense. See Diagram 16.2

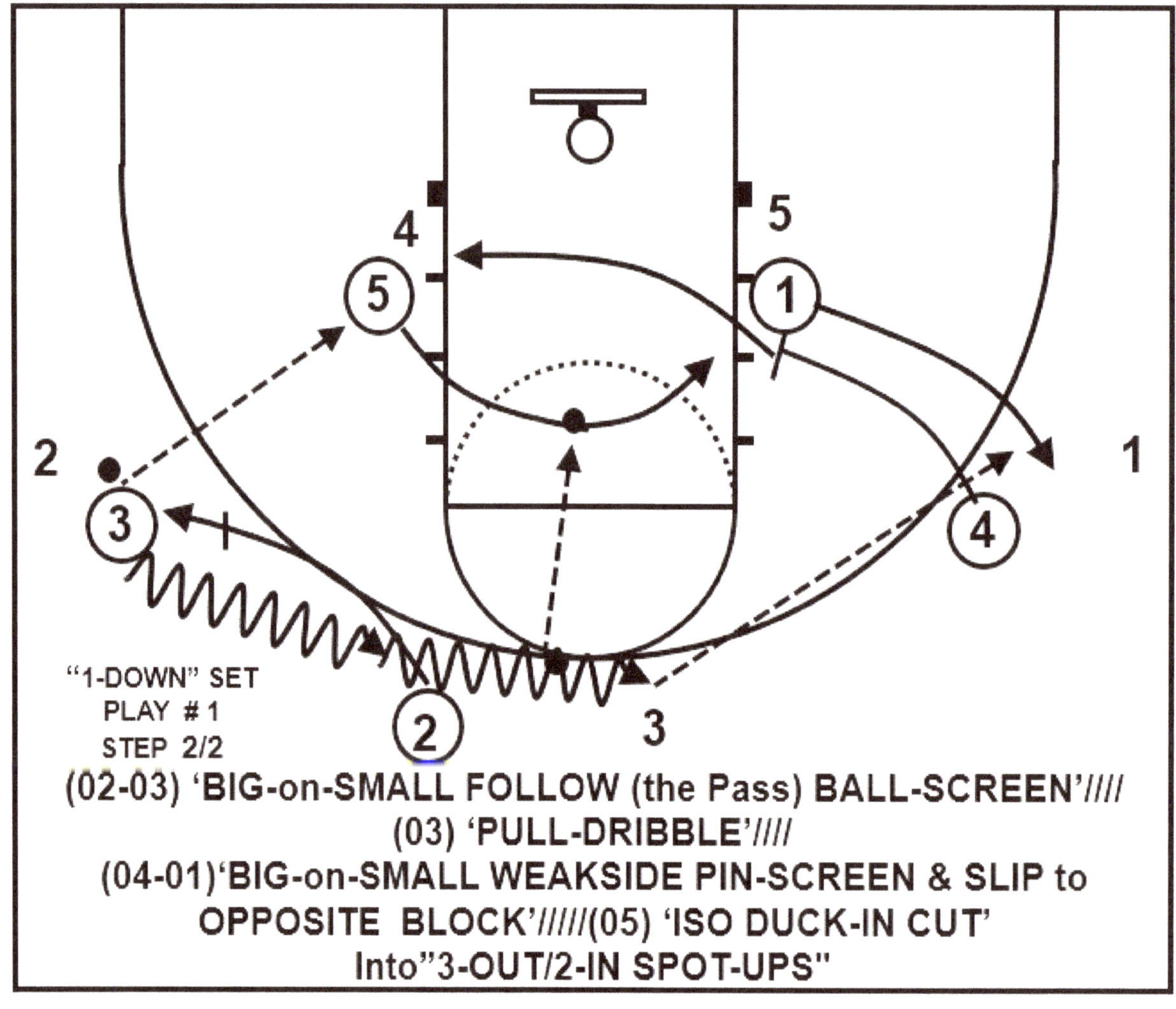

Diagram 16.2

Diagram 16.3 illustrates Play # 2 with the ball being in 01's hands (via a "Reverse Pass" from 02 or 01 bringing the ball across the timeline on the dribble.) IF 02 reverses the ball to 01, 04 then steps up to set a "Big-on-Small Flare-Screen" for 02 to use to the new "Weakside Wing" Spot-Up.

Cosmetic variations could be integrated to give the entry a somewhat different look such as 01 making a DHO with 02 and 02 ending up with the ball on 01's initial "Slot." A possible (01-02) "(Follow the Pass) Ball-Screen with 02 again having possession of the ball at the offense's left "Slot" (ready to start the actual play) could be another option for disguising the play.

Regardless, when the pass is made to 03, the passer (01 or 02) makes another "Give-n-Go" Cut, looking for a return pass from 03. If 01 does not receive the ball, he continues diagonally through the lane to the opposite side of the lane. From the initial "Weakside Block," 05 then uses 01 as a "Lane Exchange Cross Screen Cutter" to flash to the new "Ballside High Post Elbow." See Diagram 16.3.

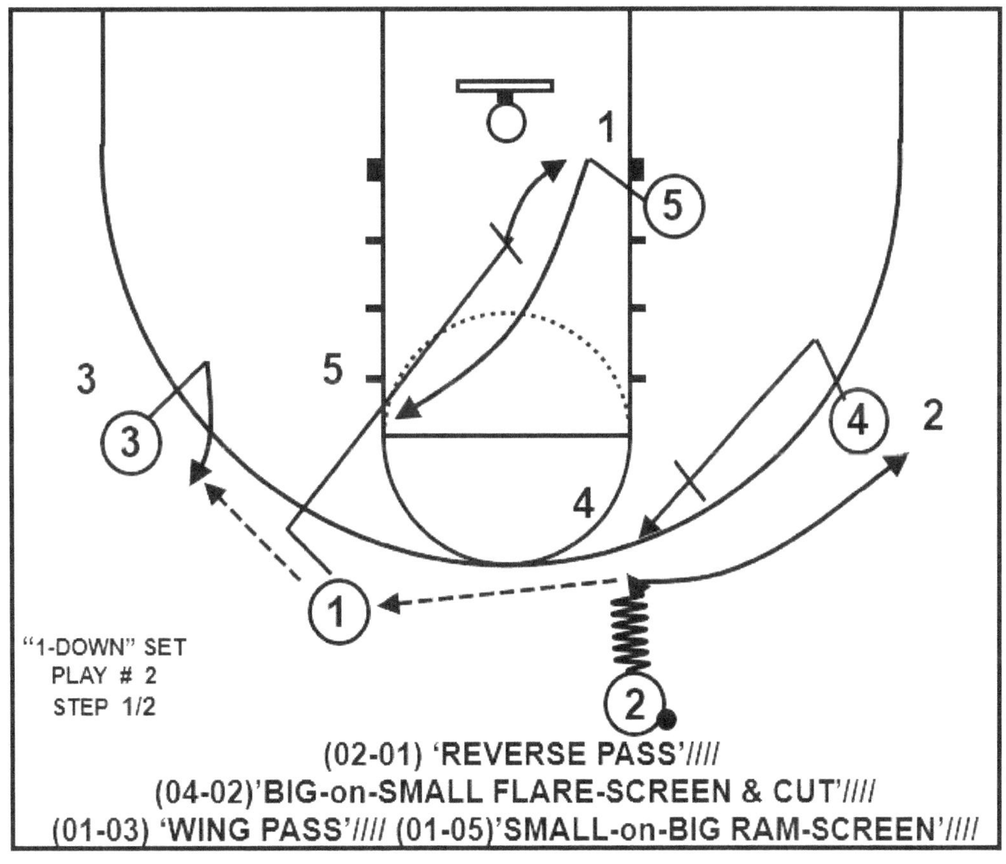

Play # 2   Diagram 16.3

If 05 does not receive the pass from 03, (05) steps out to set a "Big-on-Small Inside Ball-Screen." 03 then "dribble-scrapes" off of 05's top left shoulder, 05 makes a front pivot off of his right foot and makes his "Rim-Run" to the basket. To eliminate any chance of interior support defense, 02 cuts to the "Weakside Block" to set a (Slightly) "Big-on-Small Pin Down-Screen for 01 to break out to the FT Line extended. From near the top of the key, 04 then sets a "Pistols Ball-Screen" for 03 to more easily dribble to the top of the key. Once the ball is centered up, 03 could have four different pass receivers, two on each side of the floor with two on the perimeter (01 and the inverted 04) and two (05 and the inverted 02). This accurately moves and repositions all five players into the proper "3-Out/2-In" Spot-Ups again for the designated continuity offense to fluidly begin. See Diagram 16.4

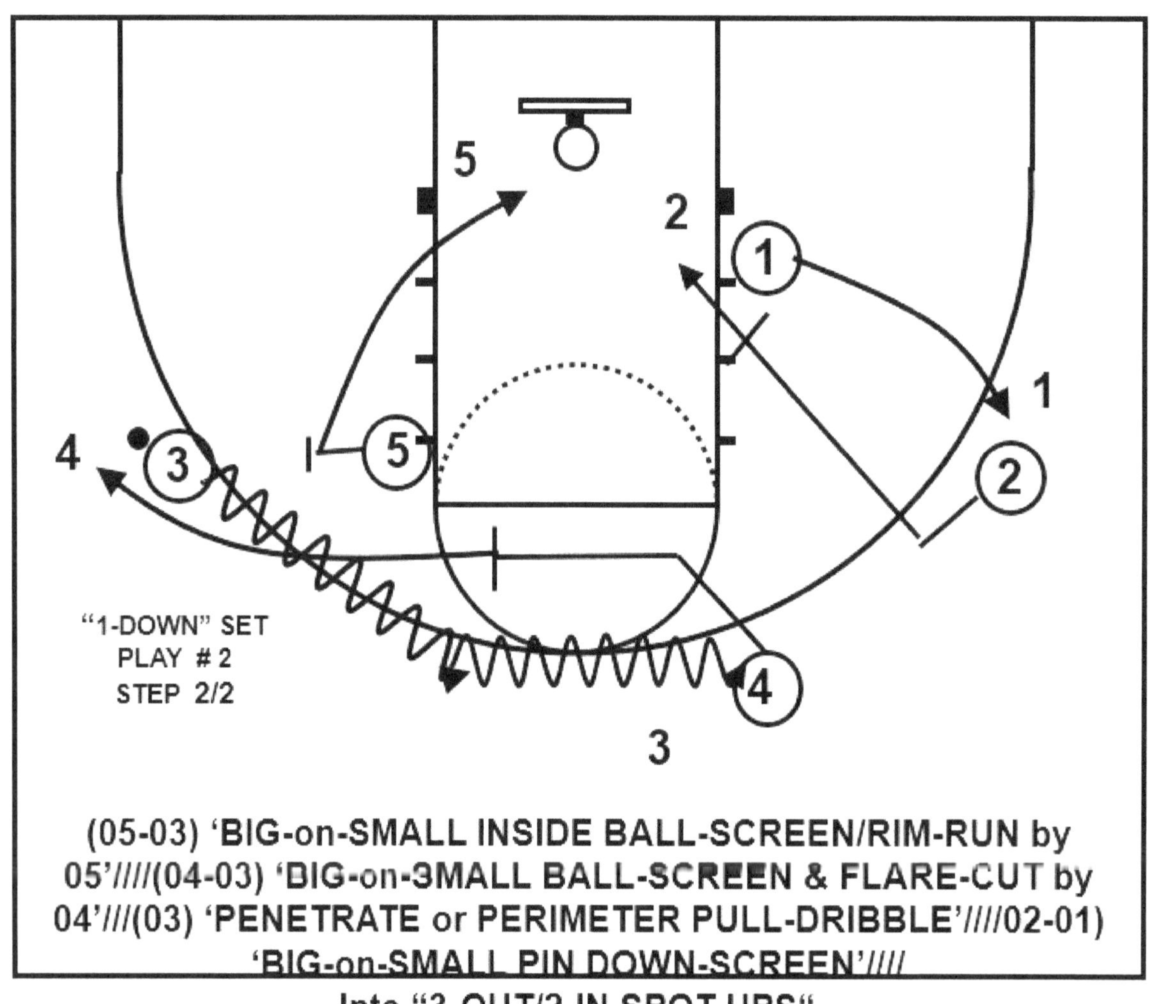

(05-03) 'BIG-on-SMALL INSIDE BALL-SCREEN/RIM-RUN by 05'/////(04-03) 'BIG-on-SMALL BALL-SCREEN & FLARE-CUT by 04'////(03) 'PENETRATE or PERIMETER PULL-DRIBBLE'/////02-01) 'BIG-on-SMALL PIN DOWN-SCREEN'////
Into "3-OUT/2-IN SPOT-UPS"

Diagram 16.4

Diagram 16.5 illustrates the beginning of Play # 3 with 05 deciding to start on the offense's left side of the lane. With 01 dribbling the ball across the timeline, 01 makes the 01-02 "Reverse Pass." 01 then immediately receives a "Big-on-Small Flare-Screen" for 01 to then "Flare-Cut" to the new "Weakside Wing." At the same time, 05 makes an "Iso Duck-In Cut" into the middle of the lane, looking for a pass from 01 or 02. If not open, 05 continues across the lane to post up on the opposite side of the floor. 02 looks to make the "Inside Pass" and then dribbles towards 04. See Diagram 16.5

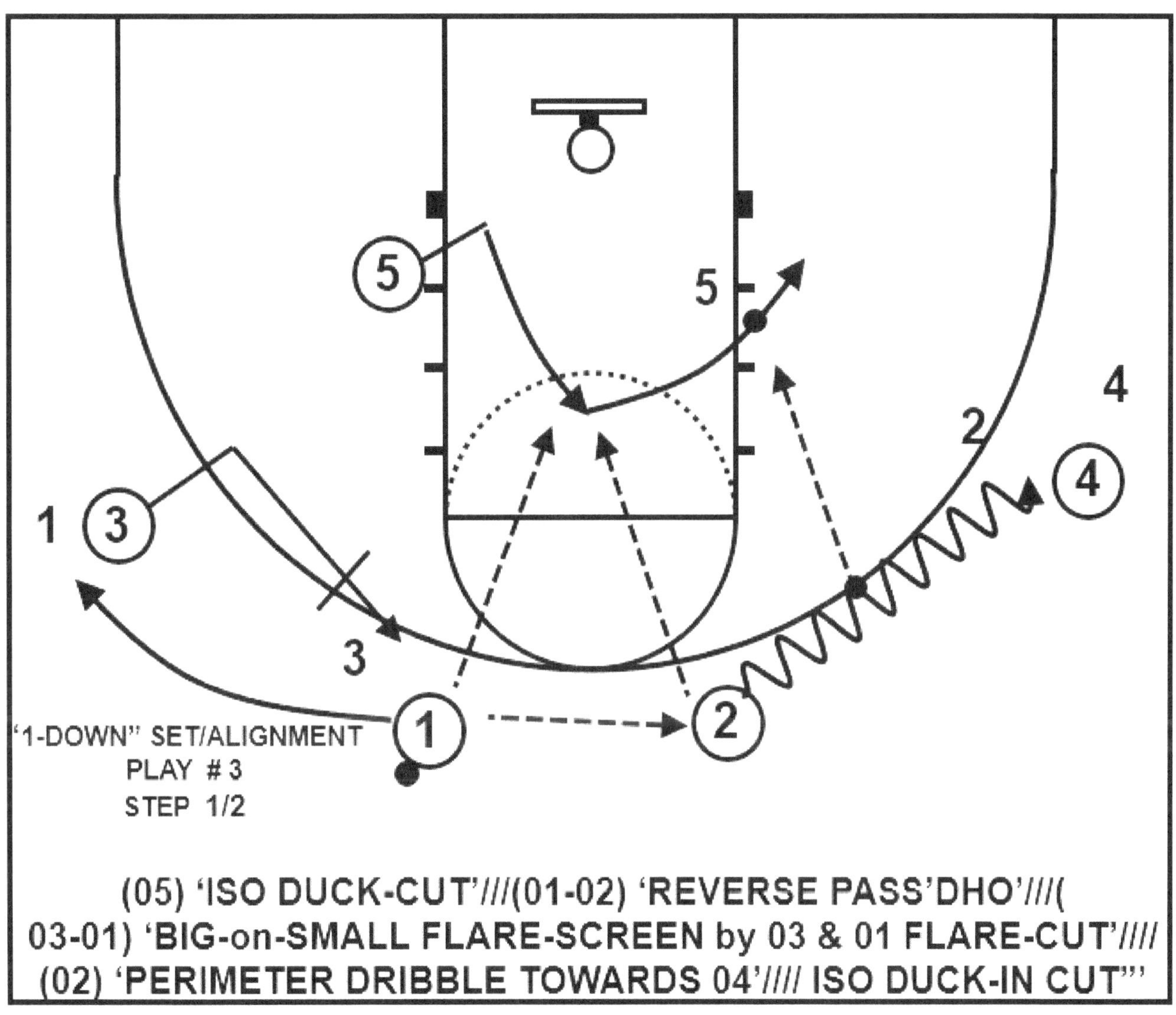

Play # 3   Diagram 16.5

Diagram 16.6 illustrates 02 then making a (02-04) "Small-on-Big Dribble Hand-off" for 04 to use to dribble the ball to the top of the key. At the same time, 05 steps up to set a "Big-on-Small Back-Screen" for 02 to make a front pivot off of his inside left foot and "scrape" off of 05's outside left shoulder on his (inverted) cut to the basket. 05 then fills the "Wing" spot-up location while 02 fills the empty "Block."

If 04 does not make the "Lob Pass" to 02 or a "Throwback Reverse Pass" to 05, 04 dribbles towards the top of the key. As that offensive action takes place, 03 is spotted up at the opposite side's slot and makes one or two steps towards 04 and the ball, before then making a "Backdoor-Cut" towards the left side of the lane. If 03 does not receive the pass, 03 empties out to the vacant "Block" on the same side of the floor. 01 remains spotted up on his side's "Wing" area.

In addition to attacking specific defenders as well as moving every offensive and defensive player, all the "3-Out/2-In" Spot-Ups are filled. With 04 making potential passes to any of his four teammates, the next pass made by 04 will initiate the last phase of the overall attack—the designated continuity offense. See Diagram 16.6

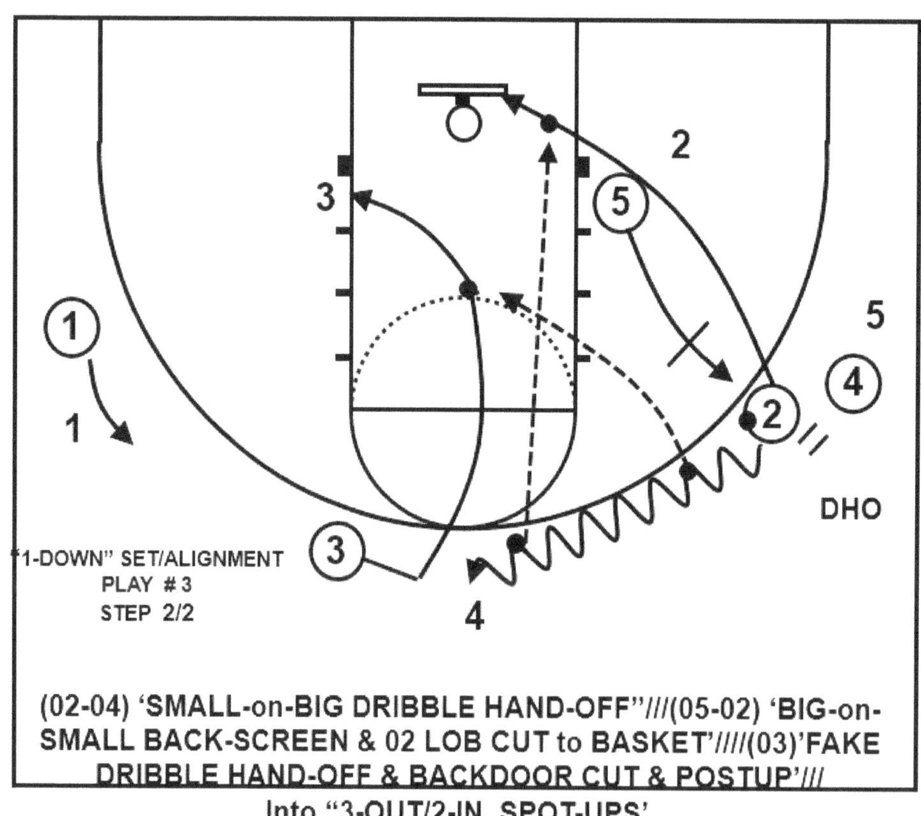

Diagram 16.6

Diagram 16.7 illustrates the first component of Play # 4—a high Level 3 play, due to its several fundamentally solid offensive actions that will attack various individual defenders.

The play/entry begins with 02 making a "perimeter pull dribble" (or "drag dribble") across the top of the key toward 01. As 02 approaches 01, 01 cuts towards him as if to receive an (02-01) DHO, but instead cuts closely off of 02's outside left shoulder, with 04 stepping up and out to set a "Big-on-Small Flare-Screen" for 01 to continue with a "Flare-Cut" to the FT Line extended on the opposite side of the floor. At the same time, 05 steps up to set a "Big-on-Small Back-Screen" (before then slipping the screen and stepping to the "Wing" on that same side of the floor.) 03 makes his inverted cut to the basket. If 03 does not receive the 02-03 "Inside Pass," he continues through the lane to the opposite side of the floor. See Diagram 16.7

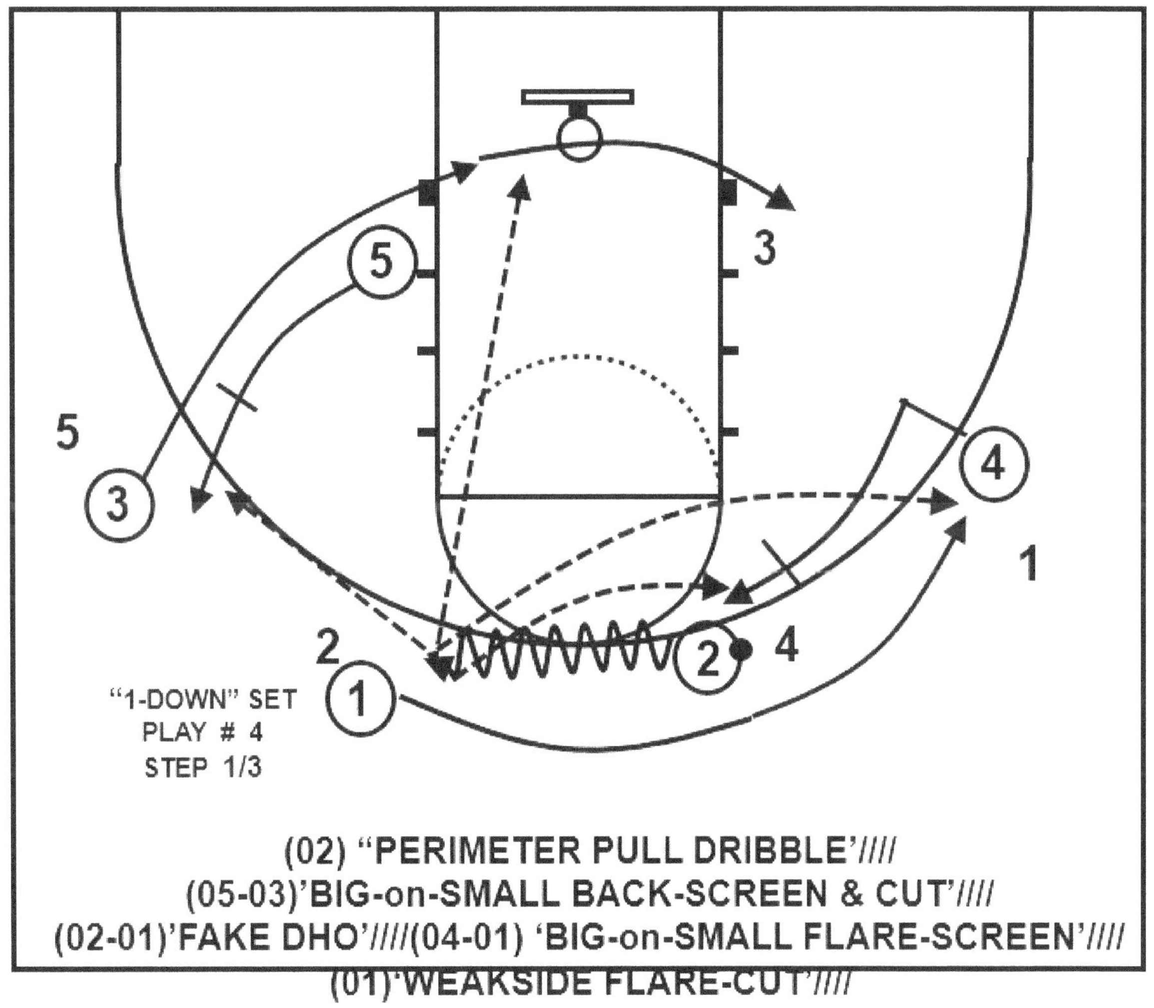

Play # 4   Diagram 16.7

Diagram 16.8 shows the next phase of the play with 02 turning down passes to 03, 01, 04 and 05. When 02 then makes the 02-04 "Reverse Pass," 03 makes his "Inverted and Isolated Duck-In Cut" into the Dotted Circle. Regardless of how X3, a perimeter-type defender, tries to defend 03 on his "Duck-In Cut," 03 should have the methods and techniques to counter the defender's attempts to guard 03. To further isolate 03 as well as to give 04 another outstanding perimeter scoring threat, 05 steps up and over to set a "Big-on-Small Flare-Screen" for 02 to "Flare-Cut" to the weakside of the floor. At this point of the play, the two presumed defensive 'Bigs," (X4 and X5) are now forced out away from the basket in the two offensive "Slot" locations. These two post-type defender are taken away from interior support responsibilities as well as now forced out behind the arc. Therefore 04 and 05 both could use their presumed "above average" offensive perimeter skills and attack their opponents' presumed "below average perimeter-type defensive skills." See Diagram 16.8

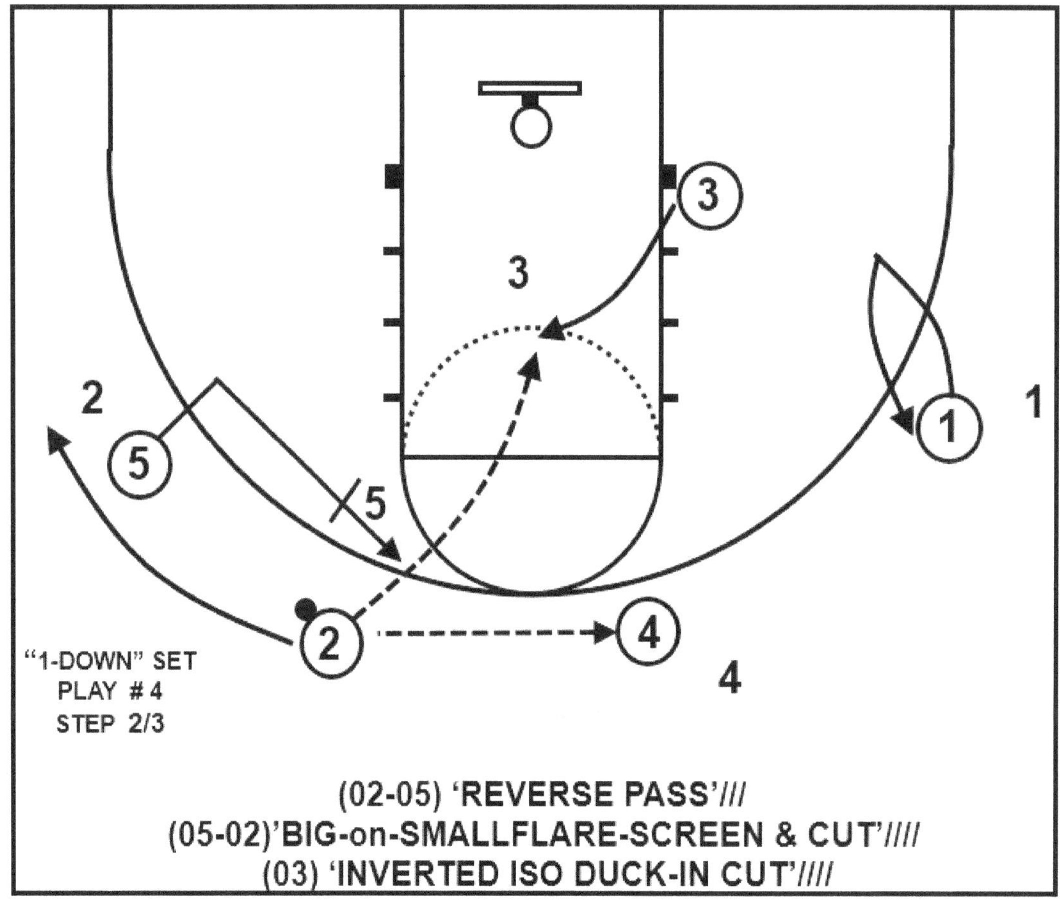

Diagram 16.8

Diagram 16.9 illustrates the action where 04 does not make the pass to 03 and instead, passes the ball to 01. Immediately, 03 steps out of the "Dotted Circle" area to the "Nail" location. 05 is the first cutter to rub his defender off by "scraping" off of 03's left shoulder and cut to the new "Ballside Block." 04 then scrapes off of 03's right shoulder and makes the "Lob-Cut" for a possible "Lob Pass" from 01. After "Scissor Back-Screening" first for 05 and then for 04, 03 pops out to the top of the key. If shots are not taken at this point of the play, the play is over and the "3-Out/2-In" Spot-Ups are filled for the continuity offense to fluidly begin. See Diagram 16.9

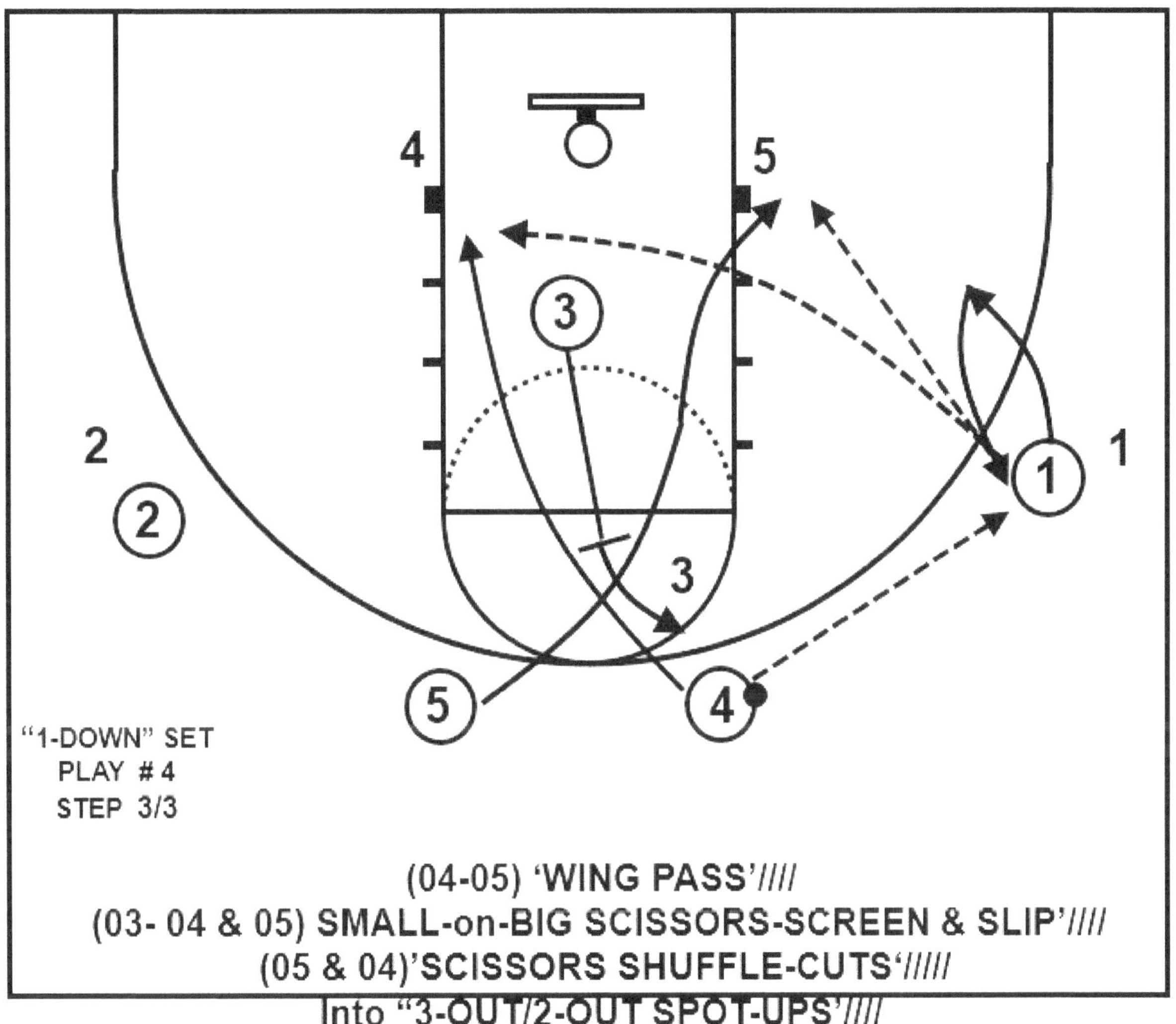

Diagram 16.9

Diagram 16.10 illustrates the beginning of Play # 5 with 02 bringing the ball across the timeline and looking to make the "Inside Pass" to 05 on his "Iso Duck-In Cut" into the Dotted Circle. At the same time, 01 steps over to set a "Small-on-Big Pin Down-Screen" for 03 to break up to 01's initial "Slot" location. If 02 does not make the pass to 05, 05 continues across the lane and 02 then looks to make the perimeter pass to 03. When 02 makes the (02-03) "Reverse Pass," 04 then steps up and over to set a "Big-on-Small Flare-Screen" for 02 to attack his defender and "Flare-Cut" to the "Weakside Wing" area. 02 scrapes off of 04's outside left shoulder and immediately "gets his feet and hands ready" for a "Catch-and-Shoot Skip Pass" from 03. See Diagram 16.10

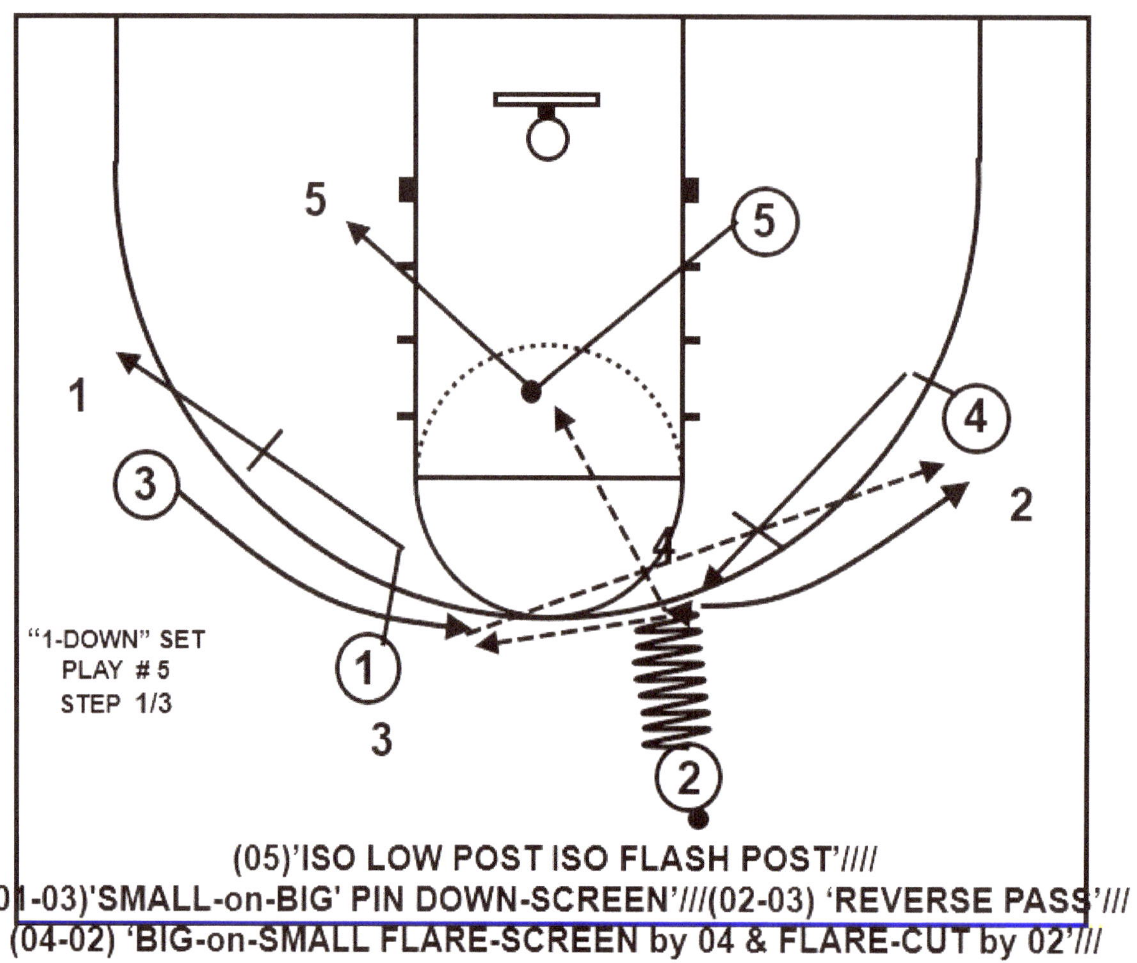

Play # 5   Diagram 16.10

Diagram 16.11 illustrates the continuation of Play # 5 with 03 not making the passes to any of his teammates, but instead starting his "perimeter pull-dribble" to drag the ball across the top of the key. 04 breaks towards and behind 03 as if to receive a hand-off from 03. Instead, this particular play (with 03 likely being the better ball-handler), 04 fakes the hand-off, so that 03 reverses the ball to the opposite side of the floor via dribble. As 03 crosses the imaginary center line, 05 makes his second "Iso Duck-In Cut" into the same Dotted Circle area (but starting from the opposite side of the lane.) If 03 cannot make the pass to 05 or if he cannot improve the passing angle (to make the pass to 05, now on the "Block,") 03 can look to make the "Wing Pass to 02, (who should have an excellent passing angle to deliver the ball to 05.) See Diagram 16.11

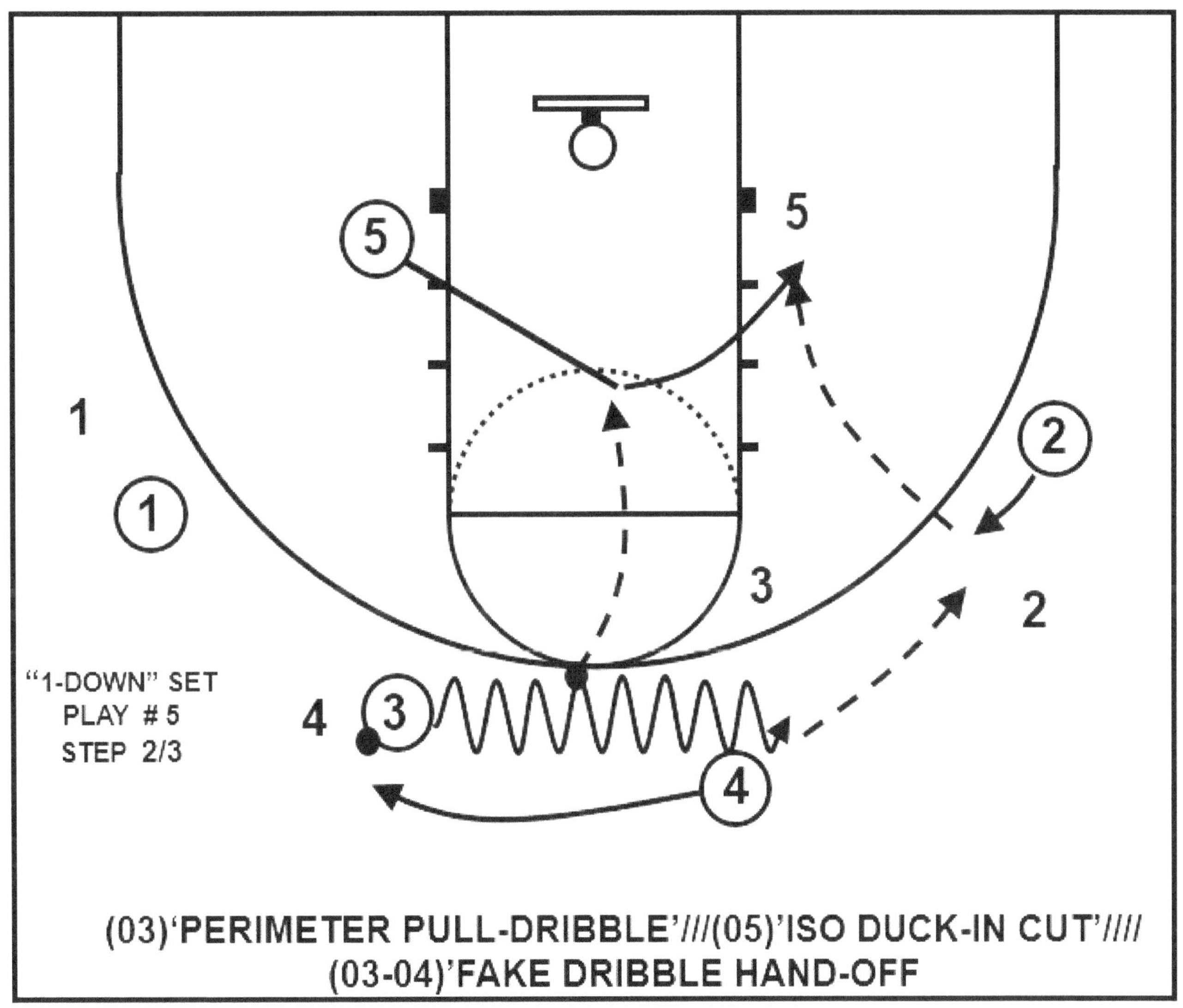

Diagram 16.11

Diagram 16.12 shows the last component of the play with 03 or 02 not being able to make the "Inside Pass" to 05. 03 reverses the ball to 04 with 05 immediately stepping up and out to set a "Big-on-Small Back-Screen" for 02 to rub his defender off of 05 as he cuts through the lane to the opposite side of the lane. 05 then continues his cutting action with stepping further out to set a (05-03) "Big-on-Small Flare-Screen" for 03 to use to make a "Flare-Cut" to the now vacant new "Weakside Wing" area.

With 04 having the ball out on the perimeter and 05 moving out on the perimeter, both defensive "Bigs" are vertically stretched out away from the interior. This gives 02 an "inverted and isolated" post-up advantage on his perimeter-type defender. If 04 cannot make that "Inside Pass" to 02 on his cut through the lane, he can swing the ball over to 01, who presumably should be an outstanding passer and should possess an improved passing angle (to deliver the ball to the isolated and inverted 02). After making the pass to 01, 04 should receive the (05-04) "Diagonal Back-Screen" for 04 to make a "Lob-Cut" to the basket. If 04 does not receive the "Lob Pass" from 01, 04e stays at to the "Weakside Block" (for two major reasons.)

One reason is to prevent X4 from attempting to "double-down" on the ball to 02 in the post. X4 must honor 04's cut to the basket and know that 01 should have the ability to make that pass to 04. The second reason is that with 04's cut, all five players are now in the proper "3-Out/2-In" Spot-Ups so that the next pass made will smoothly and instantly begin the designated continuity offense. See Diagram 16.12

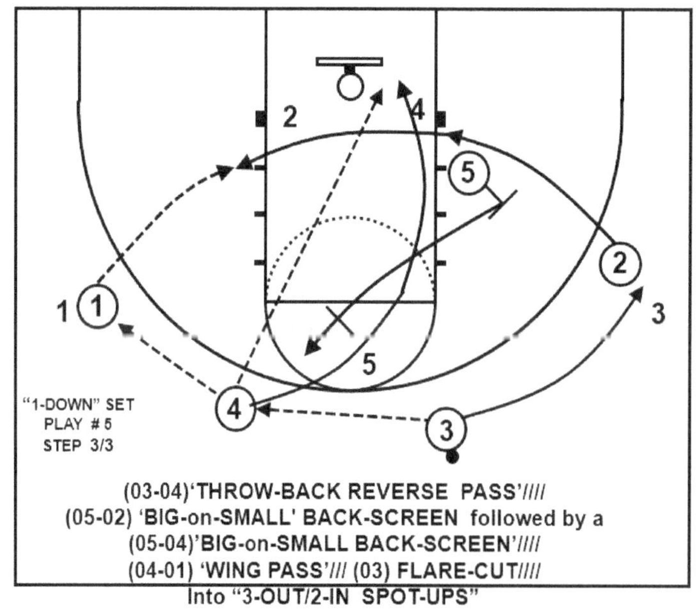

Diagram 16.12

This play has added value in that there can be subtle, simple, easy, and minor changes to the play to have multiple counter plays that all can be married to this particular play.

Diagram 16.13 demonstrates the beginning of Play # 6. As 01 brings the ball across the timeline, 03 steps up as if to set a "Big-on-Small Ball-Screen." Instead, 03 "ghosts" the action and breaks off his screening route to make a hard and aggressive cut towards the basket. After killing his dribble, 01 looks to make the pass to 03 before then making a "Reverse Pass" to 02. If 03 does not receive the pass, 03 then pops out to the FT Line extended on the same side of the floor. After passing the ball to 02, 02 looks to make an "Inside Pass" to 05 on his "Iso Duck-In Cut." 01 follows his pass to set a "Small-on-Big Follow-the Pass Ball-Screen." See Diagram 16.13

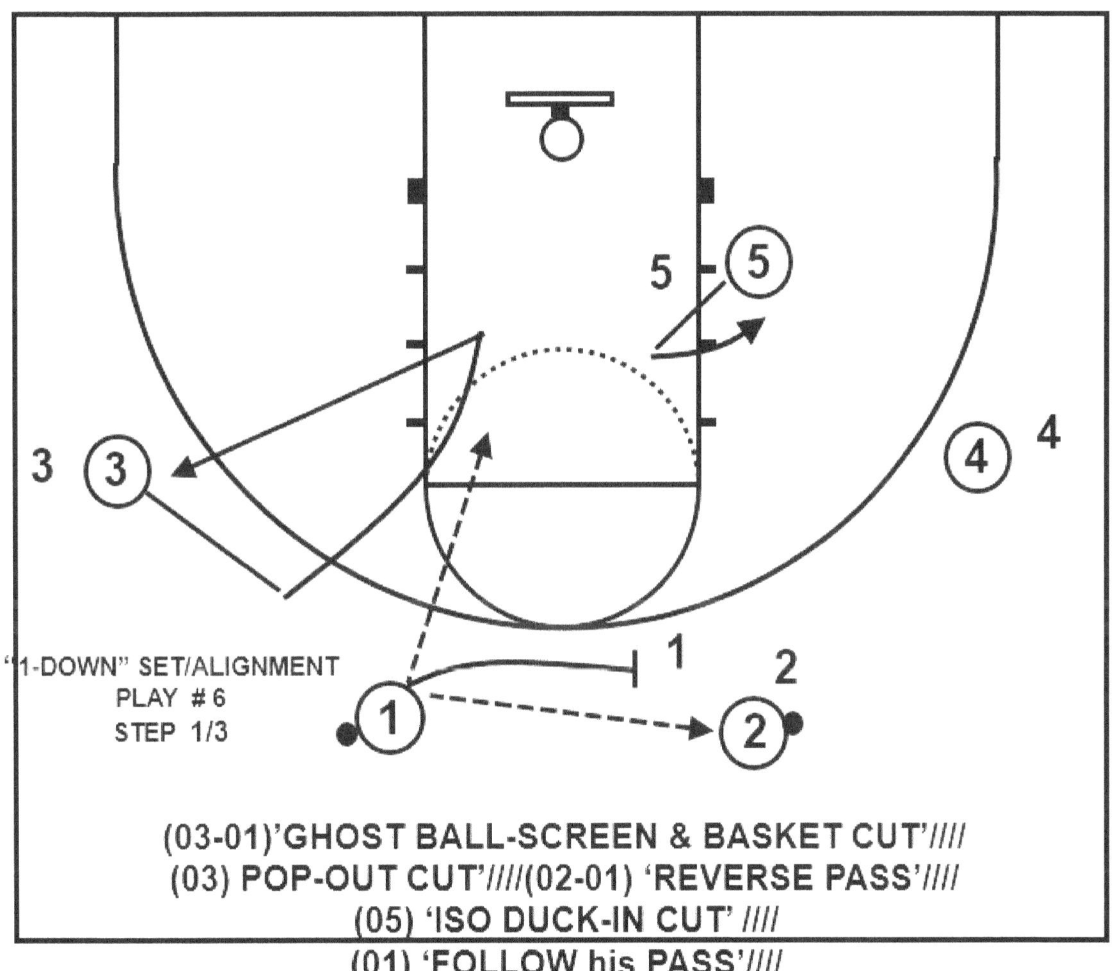

Play # 6   Diagram 16.13

After making the (01-02) "Reverse Pass, 01 follows his pass to set his (01-02)"Small-on-Big Ball-Screen." After 02 crosses the imaginary center line, 04 uses 05 as a "Big-on-Small Back-Screen." 02 then "dribble-scrapes" off of 01's outside top right shoulder towards the opposite side's "Slot."

After (01-02) "Ball-Screen," is set, 05 then steps up to set a "Big-on-Small (Back-)Screen the (Ball-)Screener" for 01 to make his "Flare-Cut" to the new "Weakside Wing." On 02's dribble, 02 looks to make the "Inside Pass" to 04, a "Throwback Reverse Pass" to 05 or a "Skip Pass" to 01, who is now spotted up on the new "Weakside Wing." See Diagram 16.14

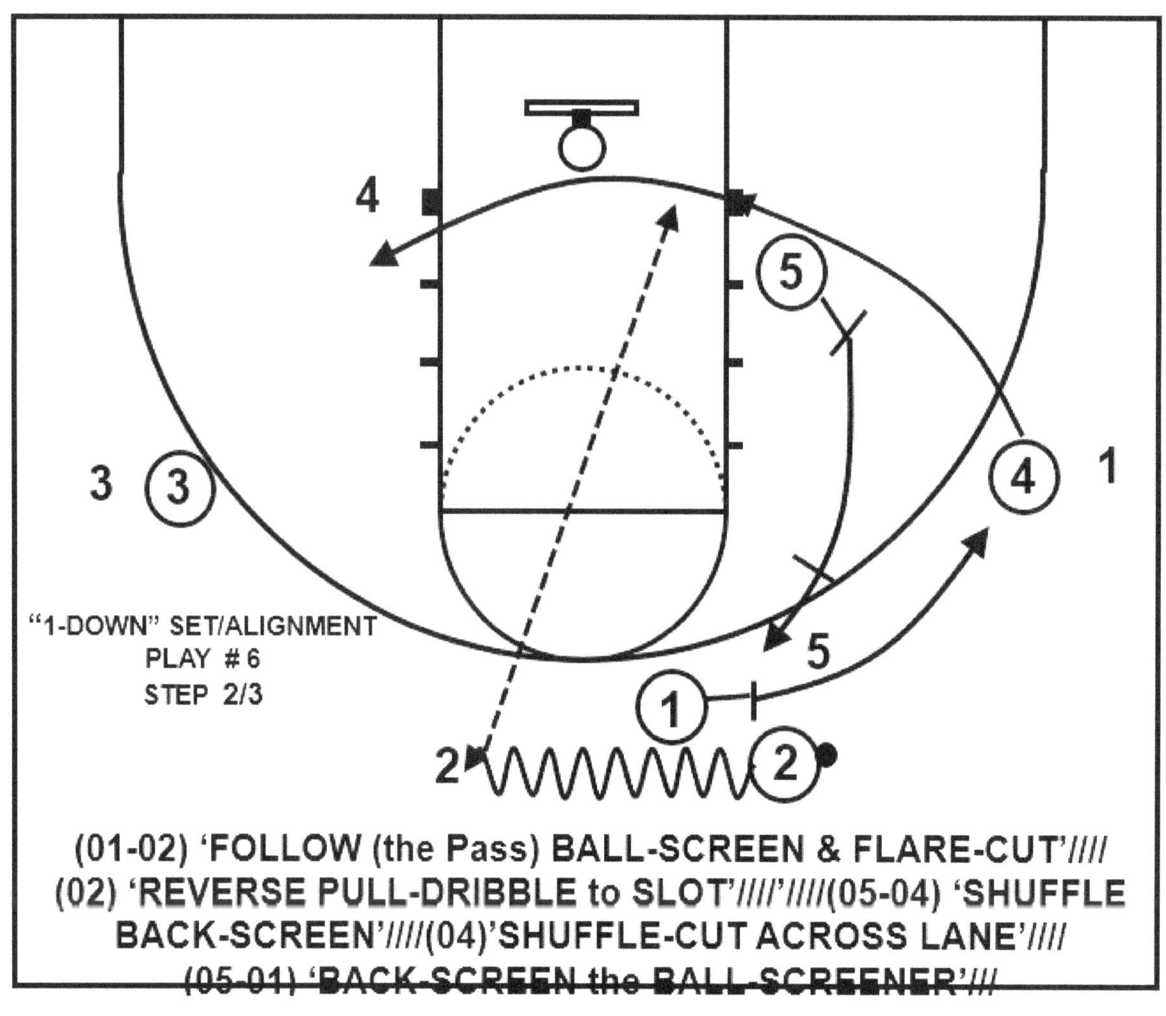

Diagram 16.14

Diagram 16.15 illustrates the end of the entry with 02 turning down all passes until he makes the "Wing Pass" to 03. With an improved passing angle, 03 looks to make the "Inside Pass" to 04. With the pass to 03, both 02 and 05 break diagonally over to set a "Twisted Stagger-Screen" for 01 to use. Setting stagger-screens on the weakside of the court helps to eliminate helpside defense as well as the twisted action helps confuse defenders and helps prevent defensive switches. This gives 04 an outstanding isolation post-up opportunity, particularly with 05 and his defender, X5, (presumably the biggest opposing defender) further from 04 and the basket. This action also makes 01 the primary receiver on the perimeter with 04 remaining as the primary interior receiver. If shots are not taken, this action attacks and moves individual defenders as well as placing all five offensive players in the proper "3-Out/2-In" Spot-Ups for the designated continuity offense to seamlessly begin. See Diagram 16.15

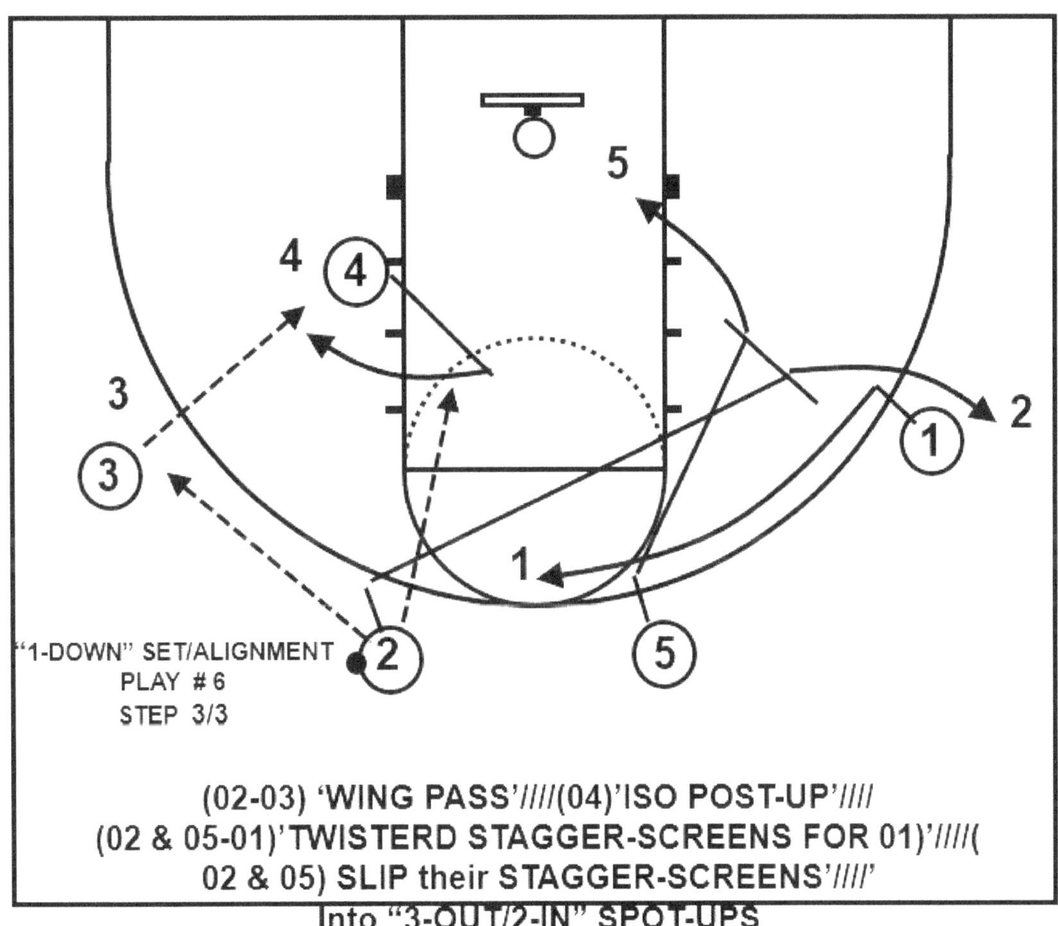

Diagram 16.15

CLOSING

These six entries/plays are a group of entries all executed out of the "1-DOWN" set and they include all three levels of skills. Therefore, any coach of any level of completion and age would have the opportunity to take "as is" plays from this chapter or to modify any play to fit his/her needs. Each of the entries will properly reposition all five offensive players into the specific spot-ups of the desired continuity offense to be able to immediately and effortlessly begin, giving the offense still another advantage over the opposition's scrambling defense.

CHAPTER 17
PLAYS/ENTRIES EXECUTED FROM
THE "2-DOWN FLAT SET/ALIGNMENT"

There are many different philosophies on how to attack opposing defenses. This multiple-phase offensive system uses more than one phase/layer/wave of attack, with each phase/wave having a seamless and immediate conversion into the next phase/wave. While this system can be confusing to defenses and difficult to defend, this system can be properly taught and coached so that it can be easily understood and ultimately executed by players of many different levels of (physical talent, mental understand and playing experience.)

In addition, there are several types of offensive schemes and different ways within this system that offenses can attack their defensive counter-parts. Many of these can be

integrated within the same offensive system that can attack defenses in various ways. The larger the number of schemes that can be successfully utilized and integrated within the same system, the greater the opportunity an offensive team can find the most efficient and productive schemes that can place both individual and the overall team in the best and most frequent "positions to succeed."

The plays/entries carefully diagrammed down to the small and seemingly unimportant 'V-Cuts' made by countless players before making their more important following cut are also described in detail.

Each play has been carefully studied and evaluated to determine which level of talent and experience must be possessed for that specific team to be able to successfully execute the play. This includes all players' physical skills as well as their mental understanding of the game. Coaches must also have the experience and the associated level of understanding of the game as well as their coaching/teaching of the nuances of each play.

The most sophisticated plays/entries would fall into the first of the three levels all based on the team's physical talents and skills, the mental capacities and the overall team's game experience. In addition, the coaching staff must have a high degree of basketball knowledge as well as very high teaching and coaching skills to educate his/her entire basketball team. The proper breakdown drills must be thoroughly utilized to hone the fundamental skills and techniques needed for individual players and the overall team to execute plays that can be efficient, productive, and successful. We define this family of plays as the "Level 3 category" of plays. This "Level 3" family of plays will have a much more complex offensive scheme that would require a very high amount of physical talent as well as requiring a greater amount of the players (to execute) and the coaches (to teach and coach) mental capacities and experience needed for the offense to be efficient, productive and successful. We feel plays in our defined "Level 3" category could possibly be successful for NBA teams, definitely for college teams and also for many high schools and older AAU teams.

The next classification or level of plays would be possibly slightly lower as far as sophistication, complexity and the actual 'length' of the play (and the number of passes, cuts and screens used) in the play's overall scheme. While all "Level 2" plays in each of the chapters in this book remain to be fundamentally sound, these plays may lack the actual number of techniques/methods that are implemented within that play in comparison to the "Level 1" plays/entries. Therefore any team that successfully executes the highest "Level

1" plays/entries could/should easily be able execute any of these so-called lower "Level 2" plays/entries, if so desired. Almost all high school teams should be able to execute successfully all aspects of the "Level 2" plays.

The final grouping of plays would be called "Level 1" plays and are not as difficult for offensive players to master the execution of them, both physically as well as mentally. Even though the techniques are still fundamentally, they may not be as complex to learn and understand in addition to being easier to physically execute.

"Level 1" plays would be lower in the scheme's complexities and the number of techniques used in the execution of this category of plays. Obviously, since these "Level 1" plays are still sound, but lack some of the methods used in the two previous more sophisticated and complex levels; these more elementary plays should be able to be utilized by any teams that use either of the two higher level plays. We feel that Middle School/Junior High teams as well as younger AAU teams or organizations should be able to utilize any of the "Level 1" plays successfully, with a possibility that some of those teams that are slightly more advanced (than other teams) could possibly use some plays located in the immediate next immediate level.

Ideas, concepts, and techniques from actual plays from teams of all three levels have been used to modify or to create different combinations of the various techniques and schemes used that will help prove these entries can be successfully used. This allows the author to create numerous plays that use the various schemes to build a library of fundamentally sound plays that will be unique and will be appropriate for a wide range of teams with the various ages and skill levels.

With this book having plays in these three presumed categories or levels, the book will reach out and benefit a much larger group of serious basketball coaches from elementary school age to the highest skilled levels that exists.

In addition, an experienced and resourceful coach may be able to mold some plays that include all of the offensive techniques that he/she desires could reshape a specific play that begins in one specific offensive set/alignment and reshape it so that it could begin in a different offensive/set that is more favorable to that coach and his/her coaching staff's liking.

Conversely, that innovative and creative coach may completely like the specific offensive set/alignment and favor the very same offensive actions included in a certain

play, but can modify that play so that the ending spot-ups of all five players are conducive to being able to begin the final phase of the offensive attack by using a more favorable offensive continuity offense.

The "2-DOWN FLAT SET"
PLAYS/ENTRIES THAT END in the "3-OUT/2-IN" OFFENSIVE SPOT-UPS

After the entry/play/quick-hitter has been executed but no shots have been taken, all five players will be repositioned in "3-Out/2-In Spot-Ups" that will have players moved about the court with any of the five ending up in the "Ballside Block," the "Ballside Wing," the "Weakside Block," the "Weakside Wing," and the "Point" (at the top of the key).

These five positions can provide the offense with safe and easy types of ball-reversals, large gaps for dribble penetration, opportunities to deliver the ball inside to whomever (perimeter-type or post-type players) is posting up their defender on the "Ballside Block," and a player that can be a perimeter-scoring threat and a legitimate offensive rebounding threat from outside of the arc on his "offensive crashing of the boards." The "3-Out/2-In Spot-Ups also provide ample opportunities for constant and effective defensive transition responsibilities. There will be three assigned "Full-Backs" (full offensive rebounding responsibilities), one assigned "Tail-Back" (to always get his tail back to be the primary defensive "goalie" until other teammates quickly arrive to protect the basket) and one "Half-Back" that is 'half offensive rebounder on the perimeter and 'half defensive transition defender.' Against certain teams, he could adjust and commit to even more of a rebounder or more of a defender.

Diagram 17.1 illustrates the "2-DOWN FLAT SET" with 01 bringing the ball down the floor and moving towards the top of the key. 03 aligns at the FT Line extended just outside of the '3 Pt. Line' and 05 aligning on the same side of the floor, at the "High Post Elbow' location. 04 begins at the mid-post location on the opposite side of the floor with 02 aligned on the same side of the floor as 04 in the "Deep Corner," just outside of the arc.

This offensive set/alignment allows various types of plays to be executed and also can flow seamlessly into different continuity offenses so that the continuity can be the final phase of the attack. The personnel of the "2-DOWN FLAT SET" is able to spread the floor both horizontally as well as vertically, making it easier to attack the interior of the opposition's defense with offensive post-ups and/or hard dribble penetrations that could lead to "drive and dump-offs and/or "penetration and perimeter pitch" out passes.

Every offensive player can have different plays/entries/ quick-hitters suited for them that allow that specific player to attack his defender and his weaknesses as well as allowing him to utilize his own unique scoring skills. The plays/entries from this set will be able to provide both inside and outside scoring opportunities. These plays could incorporate many different kinds of attacks that could include dribble penetrations, pull dribbles on the perimeter, numerous kinds of post-ups by all types of players (whether they are true post-type players or even inverted perimeter-type players.) Various kinds of ball screens with different types of actions that follow the ball screen, in addition to the several different kinds of off-the-ball screening actions. After the off-ball screens are set, the action can include a large variation of slips and cuts out on the perimeter or also towards the basket. The types and the number of plays/entries will be dependent upon the overall mental and physical skill levels of the team as well as the coaching staff.

As always, if any entry/quick-hitter does not result in the desired shot, the action will have explored the weaknesses of individual defenders as well as the overall team's weaknesses. In addition, the action has moved defenders and repositioned every offensive player into the proper spot-ups so that several continuity offenses could have an immediate smooth transition after the conclusion of the play.

Diagram 17.1 illustrates both 05 and 03 stepping up to set a "Big-on-Small Double Ball-Screen" for 01 to use to dribble to the FT Line extended on the left side of the floor. At the same time, 04 makes an "Iso Flash Cut" across the lane to post up his defender. As 01 "dribble-scrapes" off of 03's outside right shoulder, both 05 and 03 break contact with 05 the "rim-running" to the newly vacated "Weakside of the basket." 03 continues looping around the top of the key to then set a "Big-on-

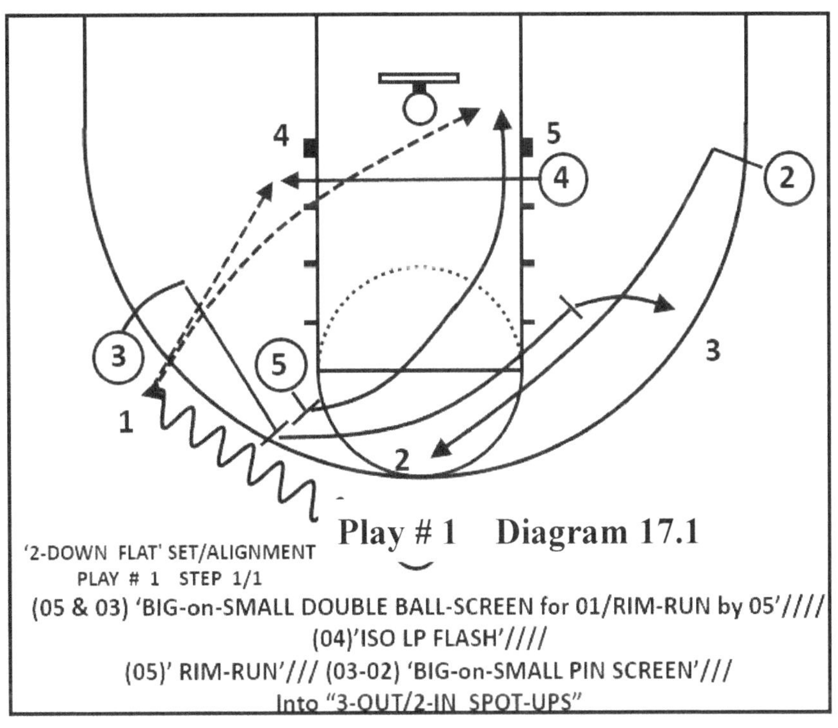

Small" Pin Down-Screen for 02 to use to break up to the top of the key. 03 settles in at the

new "Weakside Wing." This action momentarily occupies all weakside defenders for 01 and 04 to run their "2-Man Inside Game." See Diagram 17.1

Primary shooters are 04 on the interior post-up, 05 on the "Lob Cut," then 02 at the perimeter top of the key and 03 for a possible "Skip Pass." If shots are not taken out of this "Level 1" play, all players are in the "3-Out/2-In" Spot-ups for a smooth and instant transition into the designated continuity offense.

Diagram 17.2 illustrates another "Level 1" play called Play # 2. This action appears to be the same play as Play # 1 with 05 and 03 stepping up to set the same "Big-on-Small Double Ball-Screen" with 01 again dribble-scraping off of 03.

As contact is broken with 03, 05 makes a "Reverse Pivot" off of 05's lower left foot to roll down the lane to post up his defender. At the same time, 04 has diagonally stepped up to set a "Big-on-Small (Back-)Screen the (Ball-)Screener for 03 to run to the basket and look for a "Lob Pass" near the basket. To give 03 more space to attack his "perimeter-type" defender, 02 "lift-cuts" to the new "Weakside Wing." After screening, 04 inverts his defender by stepping out to the top of the key. This gives 01 a perimeter pass receiver as well as properly positioning the last player (04) into the "3-Out/2-In" Spot-Ups for the designated continuity offense to begin. See Diagram 17.2

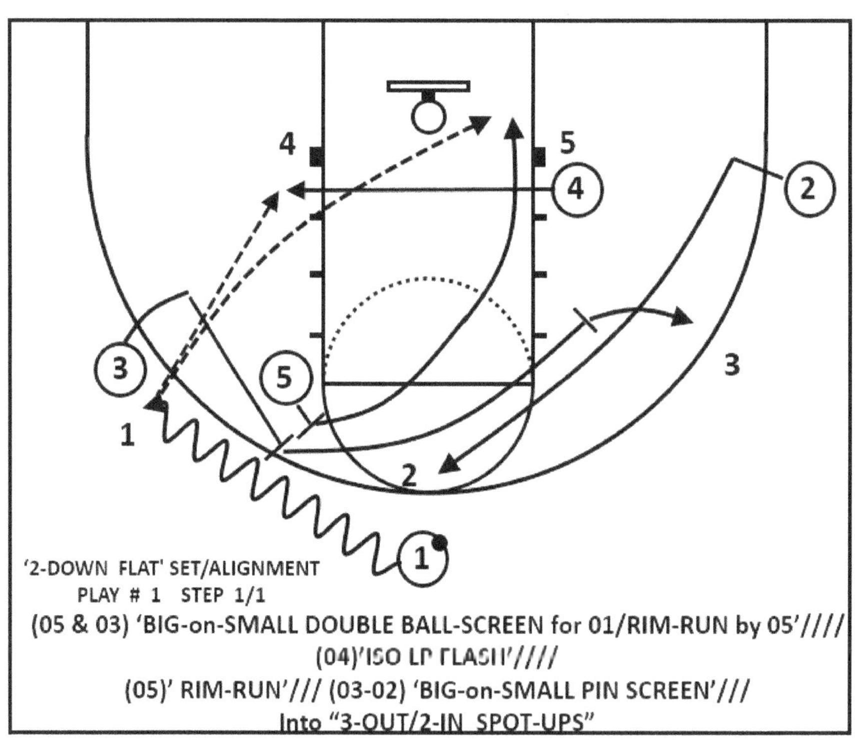

Diagram 17.2

Diagram 17.3 illustrates a third Level 1 play that is in the group of plays in which any two could be "counter plays" to the so-called designated "primary play." The play begins with 01 again "dribble-scraping" off of 03's top right shoulder after 05 and 03 have set the same type of screen at the same location.

As in Play # 1, 04 flashes across the lane to post up his defender in an isolated situation with 05 and 03 again first screening for 01 and then diagonally cutting down to set a "Big-on-Small Stagger-Screen" for 02 to use for an open '3 Pt.' shot at the top of the key.

After screening, 05 slips to the basket and 03 slips out to the "Wing." This gives this "Level 1" play a double-edged sword—an interior threat for 04 and an excellent perimeter threat in 02 at the top of the key. This action also places players in the "3-Out/2-In" Spot-Ups for a smooth and fluid conversion into the final phase of the attack. See Diagram 17.3

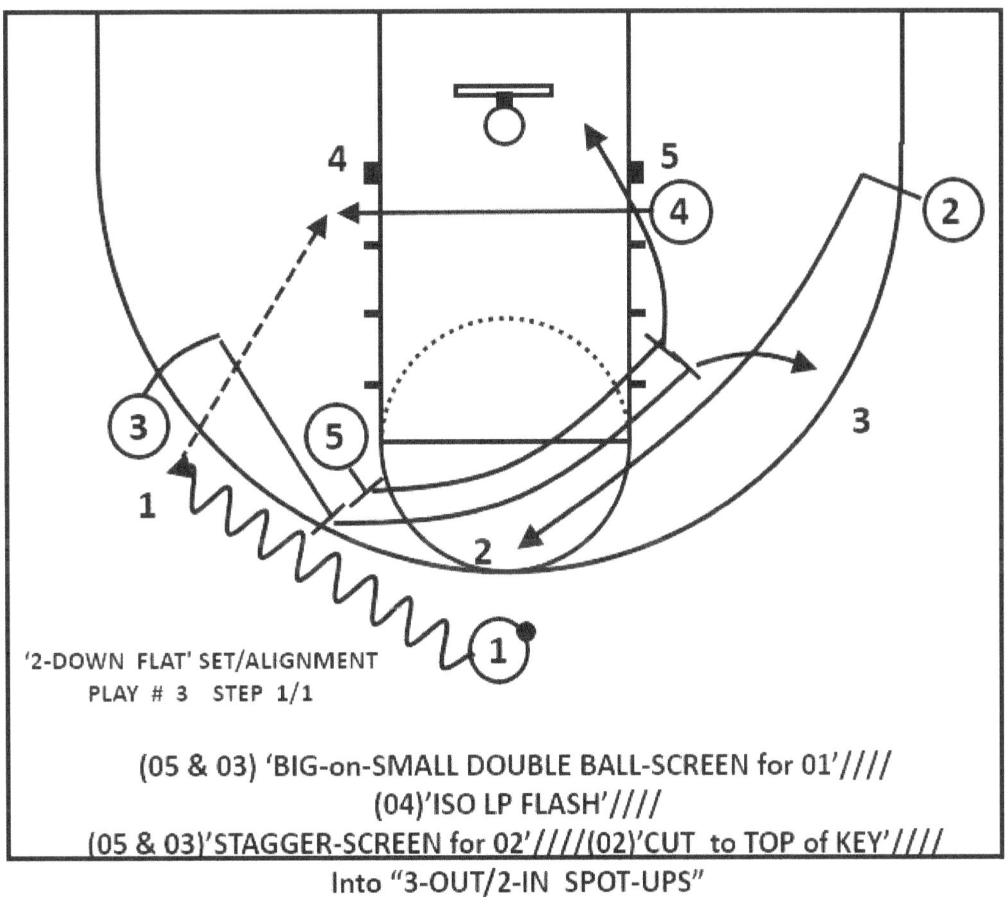

Play # 1   Diagram 17.3

Diagram 17.4 is an example of this group jumping from "Level 1" plays directly to "Level 3" plays/entries. As 01 approaches the top of the key, 04 makes his "Iso Duck-In

Cut" into the "Dotted Circle" Area and looks to gain a "position advantage" over his lone isolated defender. At the same time, 05 steps out to set a "Big-on-Small Iverson Screen" for 03 to "Iverson Cut" through the "Nail" spot and on to the opposite side's "Wing" area. See Diagram 17.4

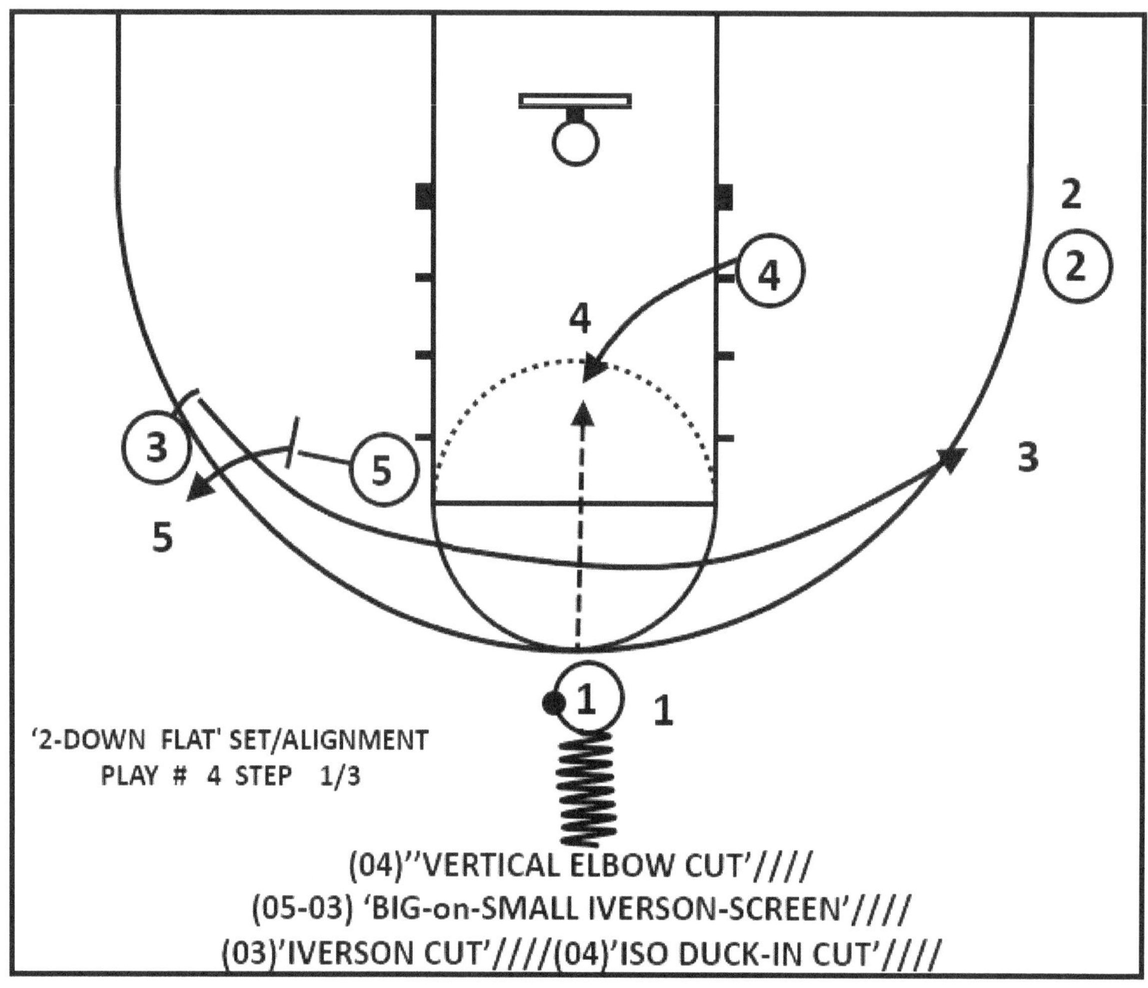

Play # 4   Diagram 17.4

01 could make an immediate "Inside Pass" to 04 in the middle of the lane, or he could make a "Wing Pass" to 03 for three possible options. Both 03 or 02 could have better passing angles to deliver the ball to 04 or they both could have their own scoring options of shooting off of the pass or driving to the basket. If 01 makes the pass to 03, 05 quickly steps up to set a "Big-on-Small Flare-Screen" for 01 to then "Flare-Cut" to the new "Weakside Wing" while 05 slips his screen and stays at the top of the key. See Diagram 17.5

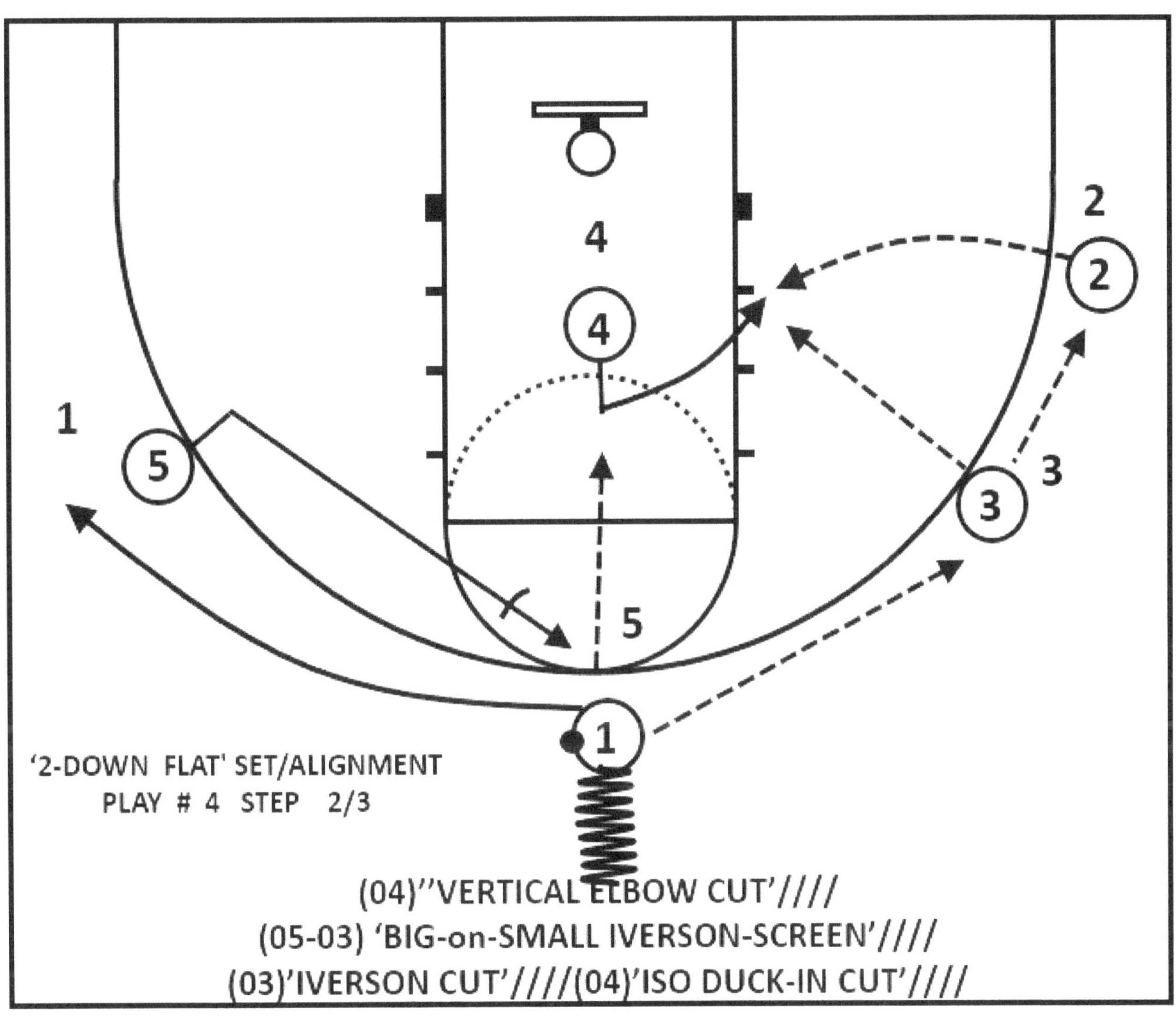

Diagram 17.5

With 02 in the "Ballside Deep Corner," 04 now posted up at the "Ballside Block," 05 inverted at the top of the key, with 03 at the "Ballside Wing" and 01 at the new "Weakside Wing" all players are in the same (with the exception of 01 and 03 exchanging locations and assignments) "Odd Front Secondary Break" Spot-Ups for any of those options that are used to. Any or all of the Break Options could be the second phase of the offense to this play. If no shots are taken, the continuity offense could then begin (as it always does in the previous and future plays discussed.) See Diagram 17.6

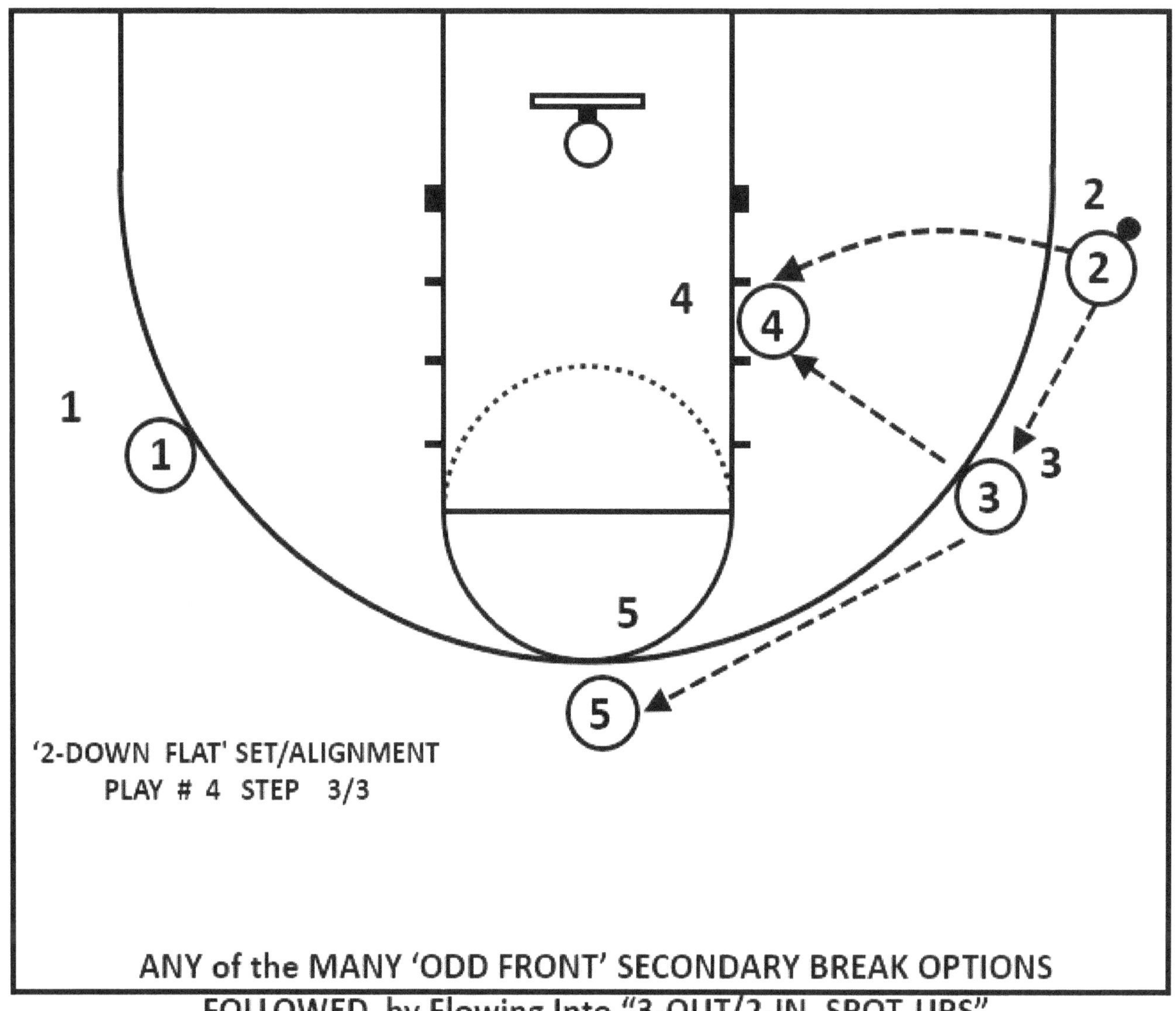

Diagram 17. 6

Diagrams 17.7 and 17.8 show another "Level 3" play that could be a great 'Counter-Play" to Play # 4 with the exact action of all five players in the first two diagrams.

With 01 bringing the ball down, 03 makes an "Iverson Cut" across the FT Line with 05 then slipping his screen and filling 03's initial "Wing" position. As 01 approaches the top of the key after 03 has passed across the "Nail" to the opposite "Wing", 04 makes a strong "Iso Duck-In Cut" to attack his isolated defender, X4. See Diagram 17.7

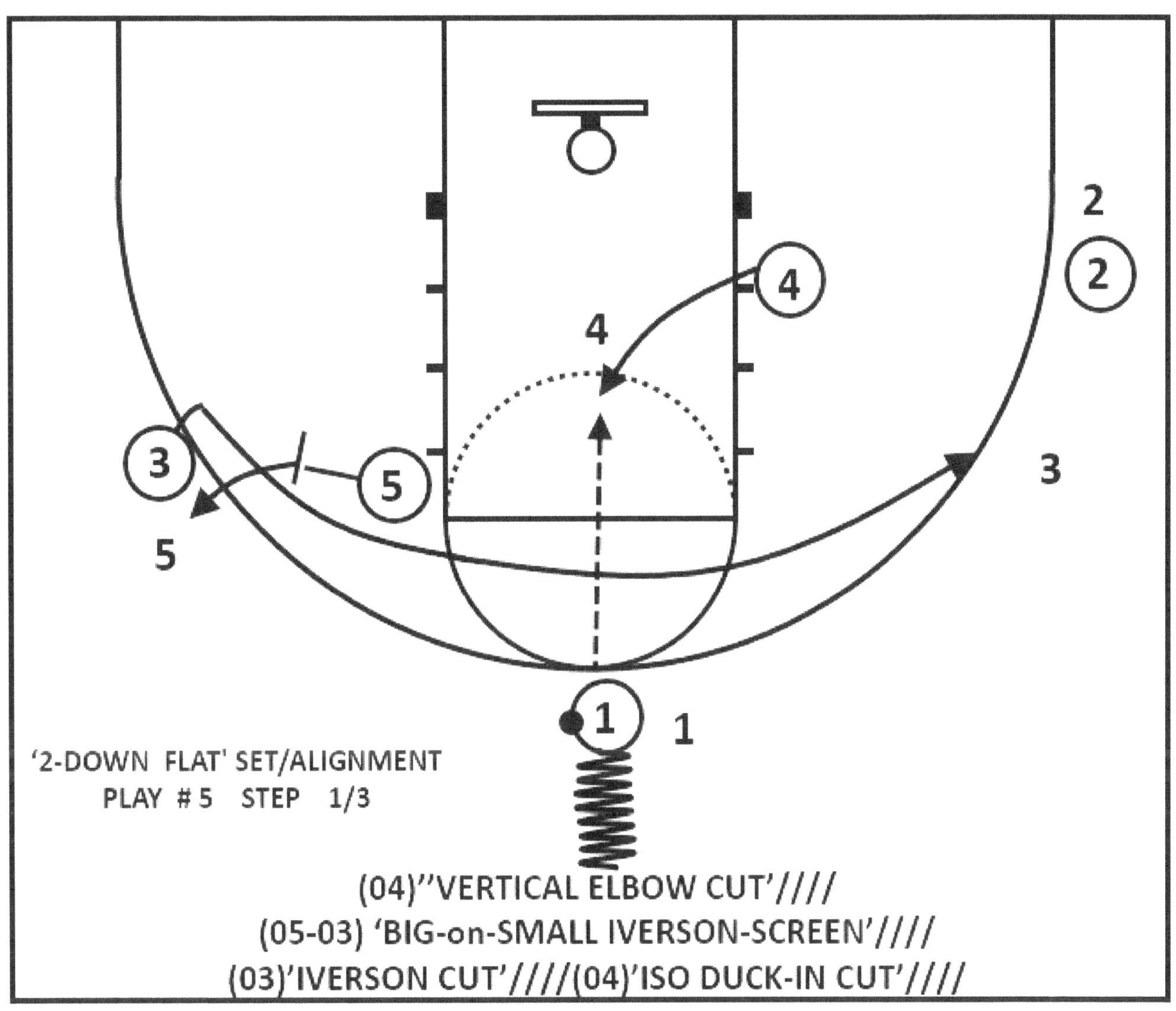

Play # 5   Diagram 17.7

Diagram 17.8 shows 01 looking to make the "Inside Pass" to 04 near the "Dotted Circle" area and also to 03 now at the "Wing" area. In this diagram, 01 makes the "Wing Pass" to 03 and immediately receiving a "Big-on-Small Flare-Screen" by 05. 01 "Flare-Cuts" to the wing, looking for a possible "Skip Pass" from 03 for an open '3.' 03 and 02 both should have outstanding passing angles for either to successfully deliver the ball to 04 now posted up on the new Ballside Block." See Diagram 17.8

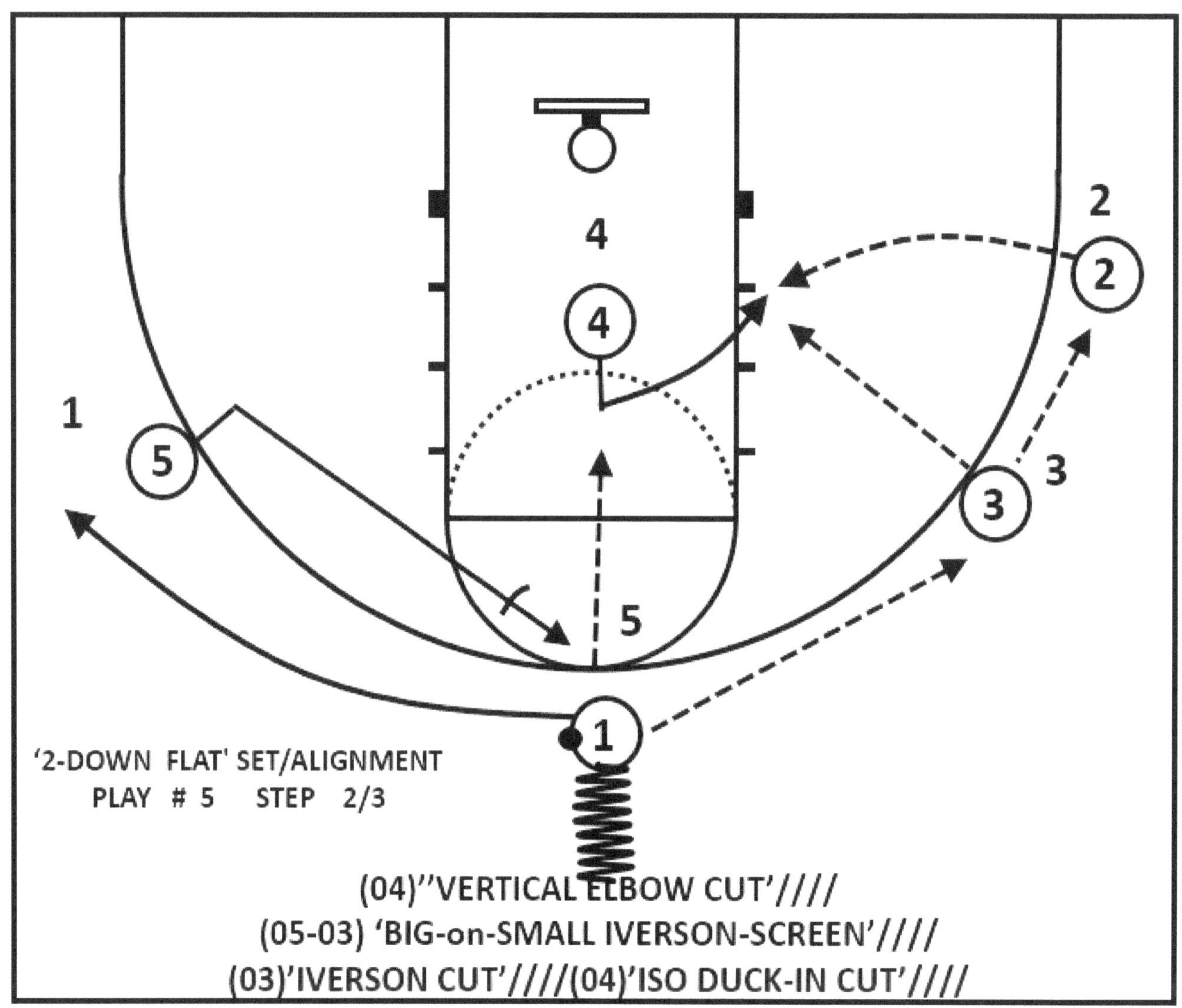

Diagram 17.8

Diagram 17.9 shows the differences between the two plays where the ball is "Up Passed" from 02 to 03 and reversed to 05. As 05 swings the ball over to 01, 02 sets his defender up by moving higher before then scraping off 04's lower left shoulder and on his "Flex Cut" continues across the lane to invert and isolate his perimeter-type defender.

After 02 breaks contact with 04, 04 then walks his defender up to receive the (05-04) (Diagonal Down-) Screen the (Flex-)Screener" to break up to the top of the key for an open '3 Pt.' Shot. This action gives the play a good perimeter threat besides helping to minimize interior defensive support for the inverted perimeter-type defender, X2.

This action also accomplishes a third major goal and that is to place all in the proper "3-Out/2-In" Spot-Ups. From there, any of the many continuity offenses or motion-type offenses can seamlessly begin with the next pass being made by 05 at the top of the key. See Diagram 17.9

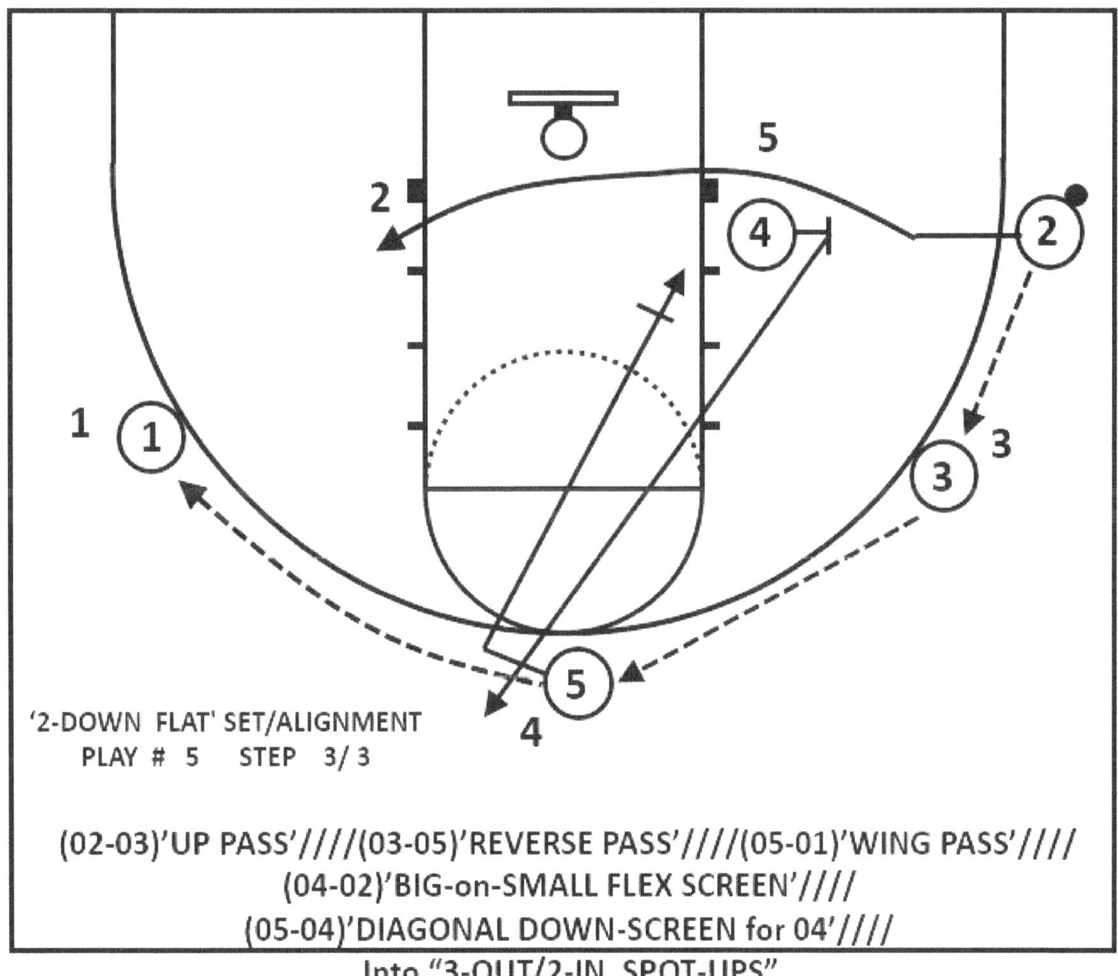

Diagram 17.9

Diagram 17.10 begins Play # 6 with the play appearing to be either Play # 4 or # 5. And that is 04 again ducking into the "Dotted Circle" as 01 approaches the top of the key, followed quickly by 05 and 03 with the same "Iverson Screen & Cut" action. See Diagram 17.10

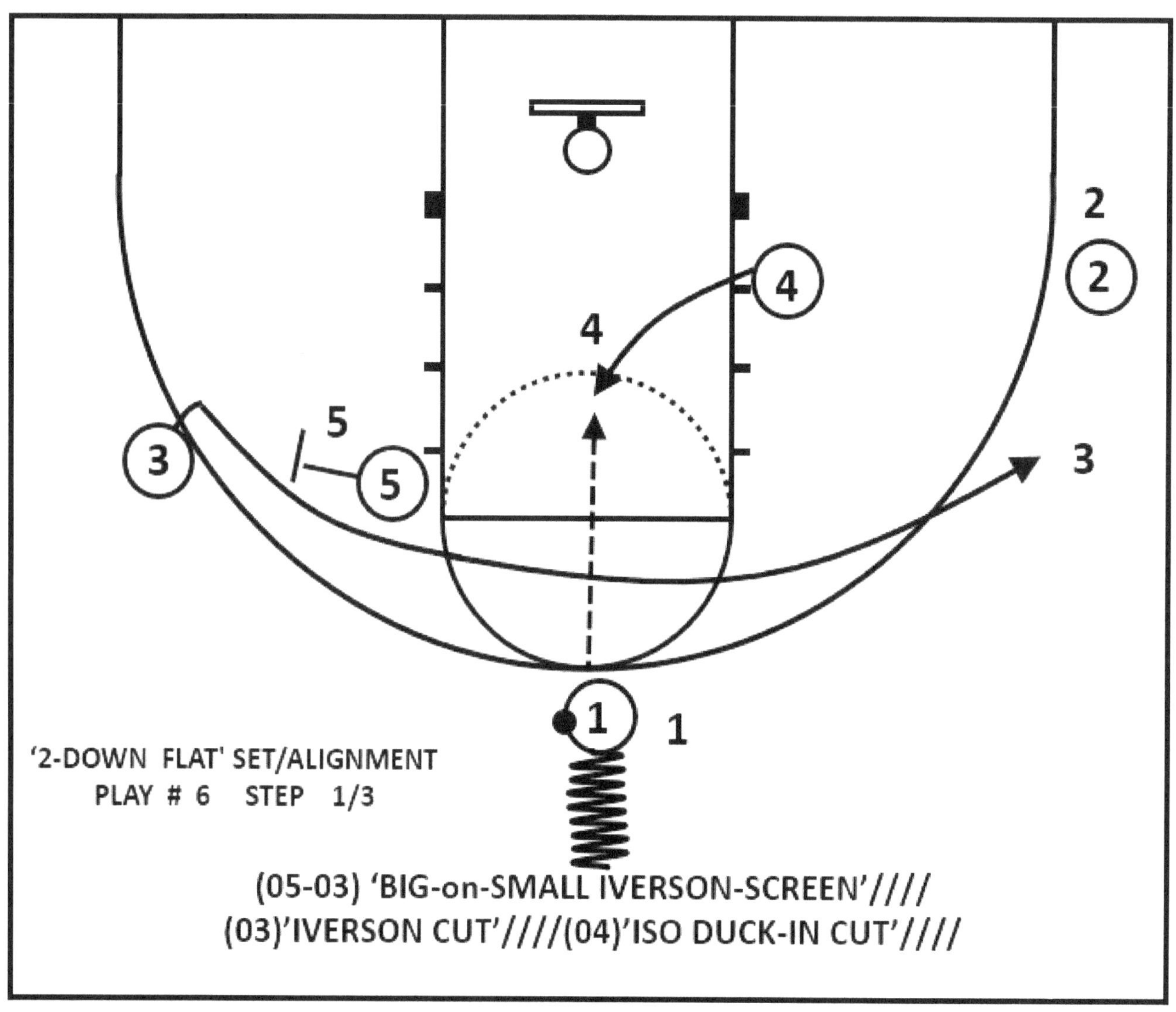

Play # 6   Diagram 17.10

Diagram 17.11 shows 04 breaking back out of the lane (after his usual "Duck-In Cut) when 01 dribbles off of the imaginary center line to approach 05. As 01 breaks contact with 05's outside right shoulder, 05 slips his screen and stays at the top of the key. At the same time, 02 steps in as if to make the same "Flex Cut" as in Play # 5. But 02 makes contact with 04 to push him across the lane on the "Bump-Cut" for 04. 02 then remains at the vacant "Block" while 04 cuts across the lane to the opposite side of the lane. See Diagram 17.10 All Diagrams should have a white background

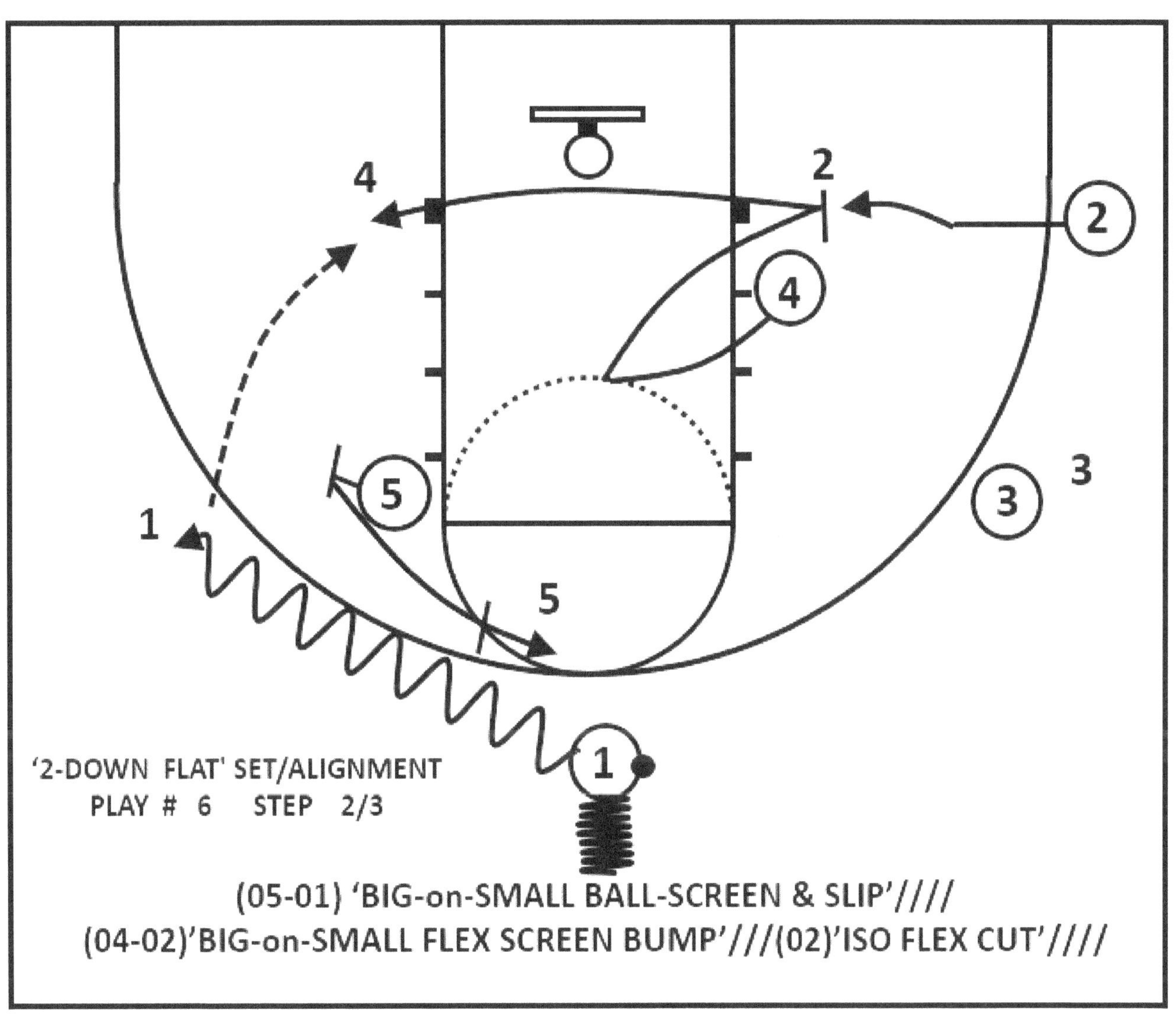

Diagram 17.11

Diagram 17.12 illustrates the action with 03 reversing the ball to 05. If 05 does not make "Inside Passes" to either 04 or 02, 05 should swing the ball over to 01 at the "Wing" area on the FT Line extended.

After making the "Wing Pass" to 01, 05 sets himself up to get the proper screening angle to set the "Diagonal Pin Down-Screen" for 02 to use to break up to the top of the key. This action allows not only frees 02 up for an open '3 Pt. Shot' at the top of the key, but occupies the opponent's most likely biggest defender (X5) to prevent him from being involved in helpside support for his teammate, X4, getting isolated on the new "Ballside Block." 01 can look to make the "Inside Pass" to 04, to the "Reverse Pass" to the probably open 02 or the "Skip Pass" to 03 (especially if X3 tries to get involved with the interior support defense that X4 needs.)

This also repositions players into the proper "3-Out/2-In" Spot-Ups for the designated last phase of the offense to be able to seamlessly start. See Diagram 17.12

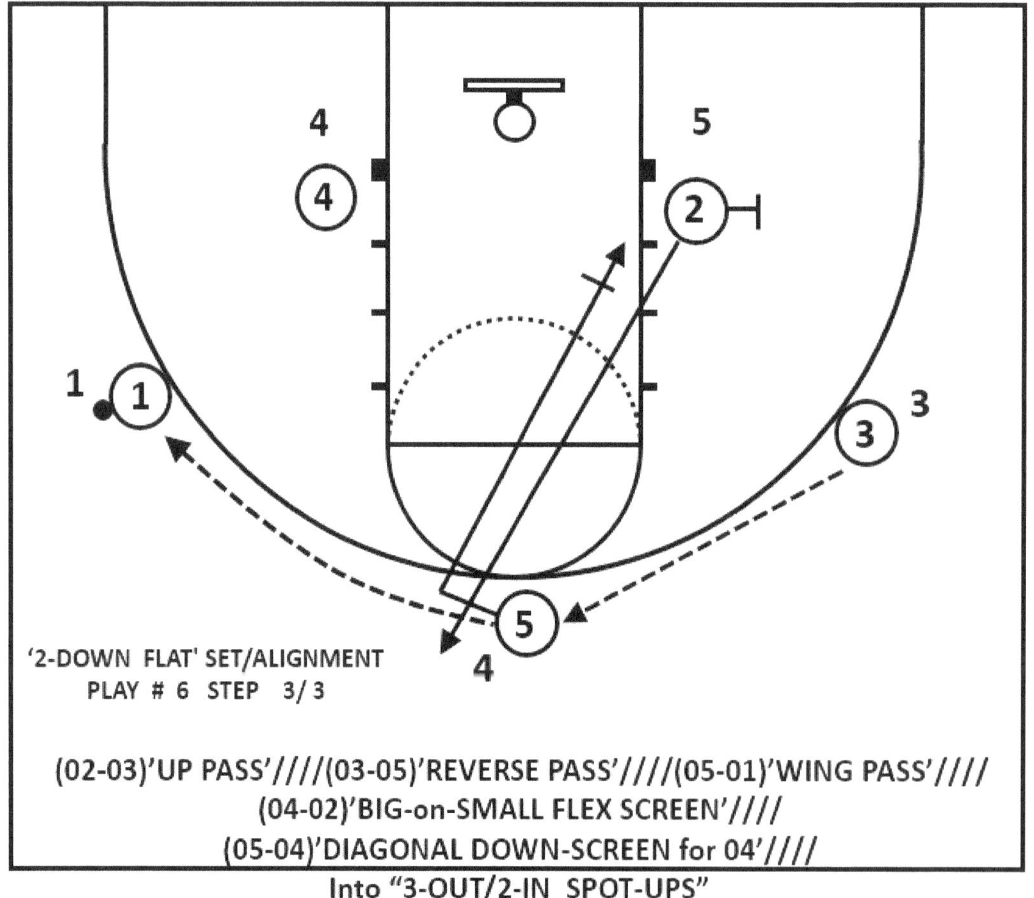

Diagram 17.12

These six entries out of the "2-DOWN FLAT" Set all flow into the "3-Out/2-In" Spot-Ups for the specific continuity offense to fluidly begin. This package of plays includes three "Level 1" (basic) plays plus three "Level 3" plays that are the more complex and sophisticated plays in this group of plays.

PLAYS/ENTRIES THAT END in the "4-OUT/1-IN" OFFENSIVE SPOT-UPS

The difference in the following plays/entries in this chapter are that all five players will end up in a different group of offensive spot-ups. These "4-Out/1-In Spot-Ups" will have players moved about the court with any of the five ending up in the "Ballside Deep Corner," the "Ballside Slot," the "Weakside Slot," the "Ballside Post," and the "Weakside Deep Corner." These five positions can provide the offense with safe and easy types of ball-reversals, large gaps for dribble penetration, opportunities to deliver the ball inside to whomever (perimeter-type or post-type players) is posting up their defender on the "Ballside Block," and a player that can be a perimeter-scoring threat and a legitimate offensive rebounding threat from outside of the arc on his "offensive crashing of the boards." The "4-Out/1-In Spot-Ups also provide ample opportunities for constant and effective defensive transition responsibilities.

Play # 7 shows the entire play where 01 initiates the play with a "Wing Pass" to 03 and immediately follows his pass for a presumed "Flip Pass" or a "Pass Hand-Off." Instead, 01 fakes the hand-off and cuts down to the new "Ballside Deep Corner." At the same time, 05 starts his slide down the lane, before giving up and emptying out of the lane. At the same time, 04 sets his defender up before then scraping off of either shoulder of 05 to flash across the lane to the new "Ballside Mid-Post." 02 rolls up to the new "Weakside Slot" to move a potential helpside interior support defender as well as to give 03 or 01 a potential "Skip Pass Receiver" on the opposite side of the floor. If 04 does not receive the ball on the 05-04 "Lane Exchange Cross-Screen, 03 makes a "Perimeter Pull Dribble" out to the "Slot." This dribble stretches and pulls the defense as well as possible improving passing angles particularly to 04 and 02. 03's "Dribble Throw-Back Reverse Pass" to 01 is another possible pass and potential scoring opportunity.

If not shots are taken, the "4-Out/1-In" Spot-Ups are filled for a seamless conversion from half-court play into continuity offense. See Diagram 17.13

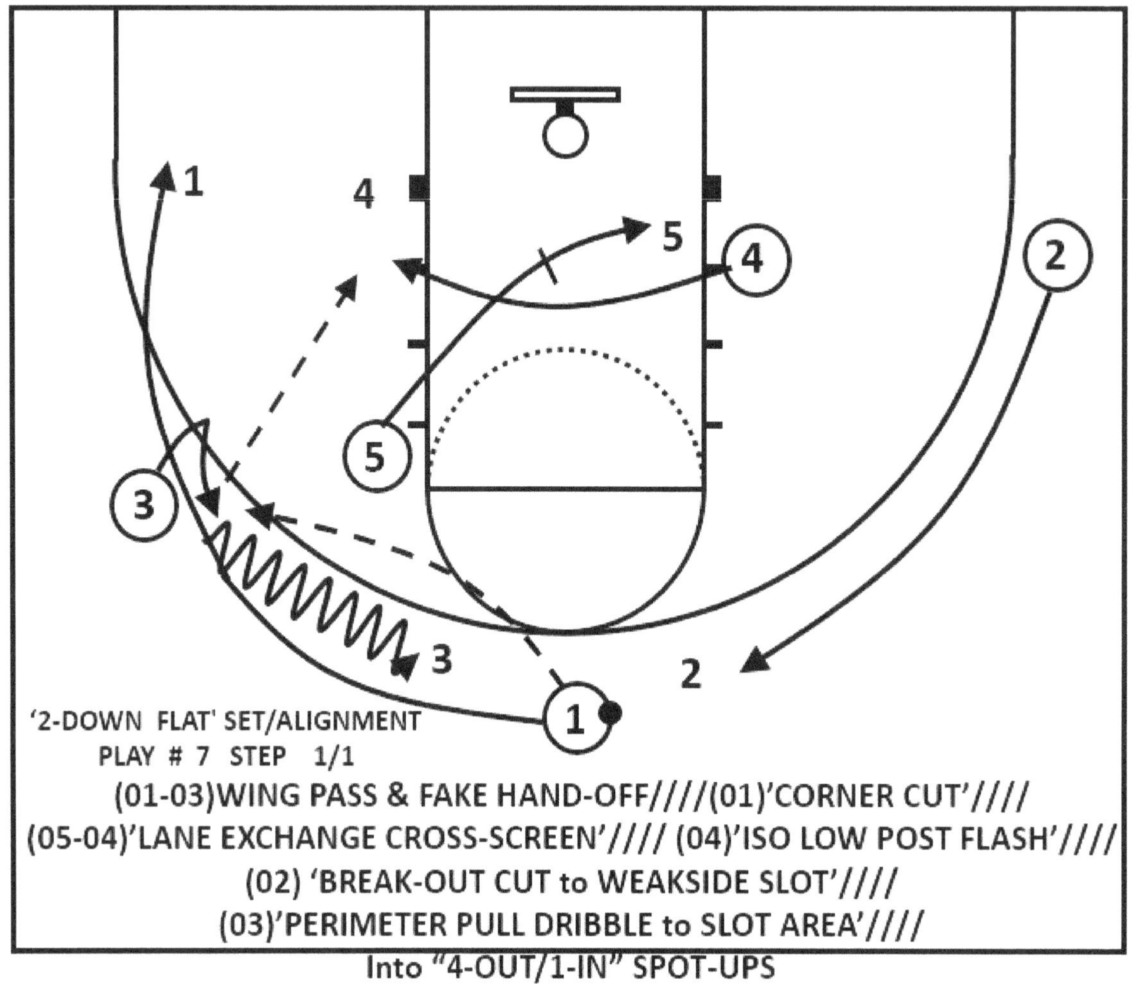

Play # 7   Diagram 17.13

Plays # 8 through 12 are a package of plays that all have 03 rejecting a "Big-on-Small Pin Down-Screen by 05 with 03 then moving towards the "Weakside Wing" and 05 always ending up on the "Weakside Slot." The action always has 01 "perimeter pull dribbling" towards the FT Line extended on the right side of the floor and 02 always making a "Pipe Cut" first towards the basket and then vertically straight up the 'lane line' to the newly declared "Ballside Slot."

Diagrams 17.14 and 17.15 illustrate Play # 8 with 01 starting the play with 01 making a "perimeter pull dribble" towards the FT Line extended on the right side of the floor. At the same time, 02 cuts towards 04 and then makes a "Pipe Cut" vertically up the lane to the new "Ballside Slot." At the same time, 03 moves down towards the Deep Corner on his side of the floor, as if to set his defender up for 05's 'Pin Down-Screen. Instead, 03 reverses his cut's direction as does 05 for the supposed screen. 03 ends up at the FT Line extended on the new weakside of the floor and 05 ends up inverting the presumed opponent's biggest defender, X5, by being the offensive player that breaks up to the new "Weakside Slot." This action totally removes any possible 'helpside defense.' so that 04 can fully isolate his defender on the new "Ballside Mid-Post." 01 then first looks to make the "Inside Pass" to 04 or to make the pass to 02 at the "Slot" or possible "Skip Passes" to either 03 or 05 on the opposite side of the floor. See Diagram 17.14

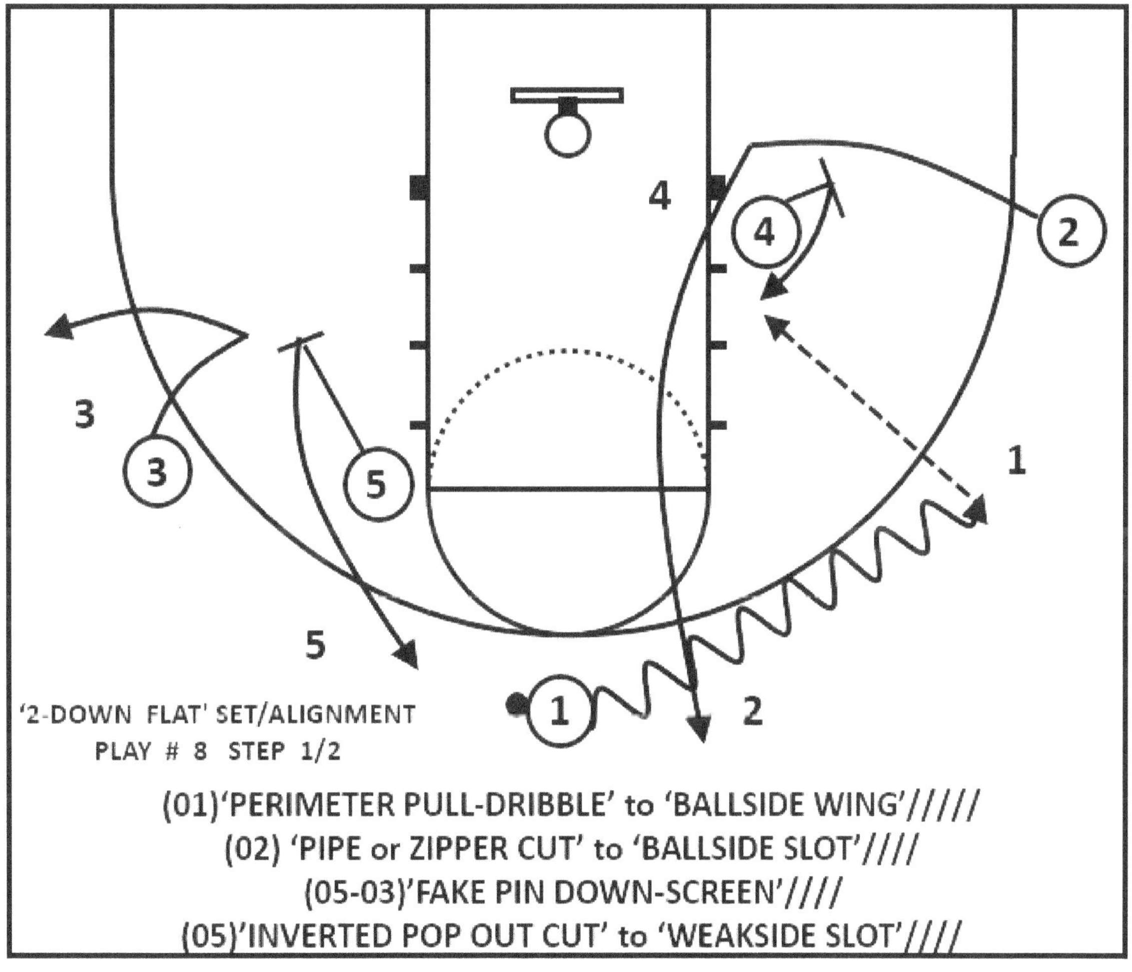

Play # 8   Diagram 17.14

Diagram 17.15 illustrates 01 making the "Up Pass" to 02 and immediately "Flare-Cutting" to the "Deep Corner" and preparing for a quick return pass from 02. At the same time, 05 breaks over to set a "Big-on-Small Ball-Screen" for 02 to use. 02 then "dribble-scrapes" off of 05's top right shoulder. As 02 breaks contact with 05, 05 slips his screen and remains on the "Slot" on the opposite side of the floor." As 02 crosses the imaginary center line of the half-court, 04 "chases the ball" through and across the lane, looking for an "Inside Pass" from 02. At the same time, 03 starts to break up towards 02, but then reverses direction to "Flare-Cut" to the "Deep Corner" on his side of the floor. With 03 and 01 both making cuts towards their own baseline, this action occupies their respective defenders and allows 04 to further isolate his defender, X4. This also flattens out the defense and places all five offensive players in the proper "4-Out/1-In" Spot-Ups for an immediate conversion from the play into the designated continuity offense.

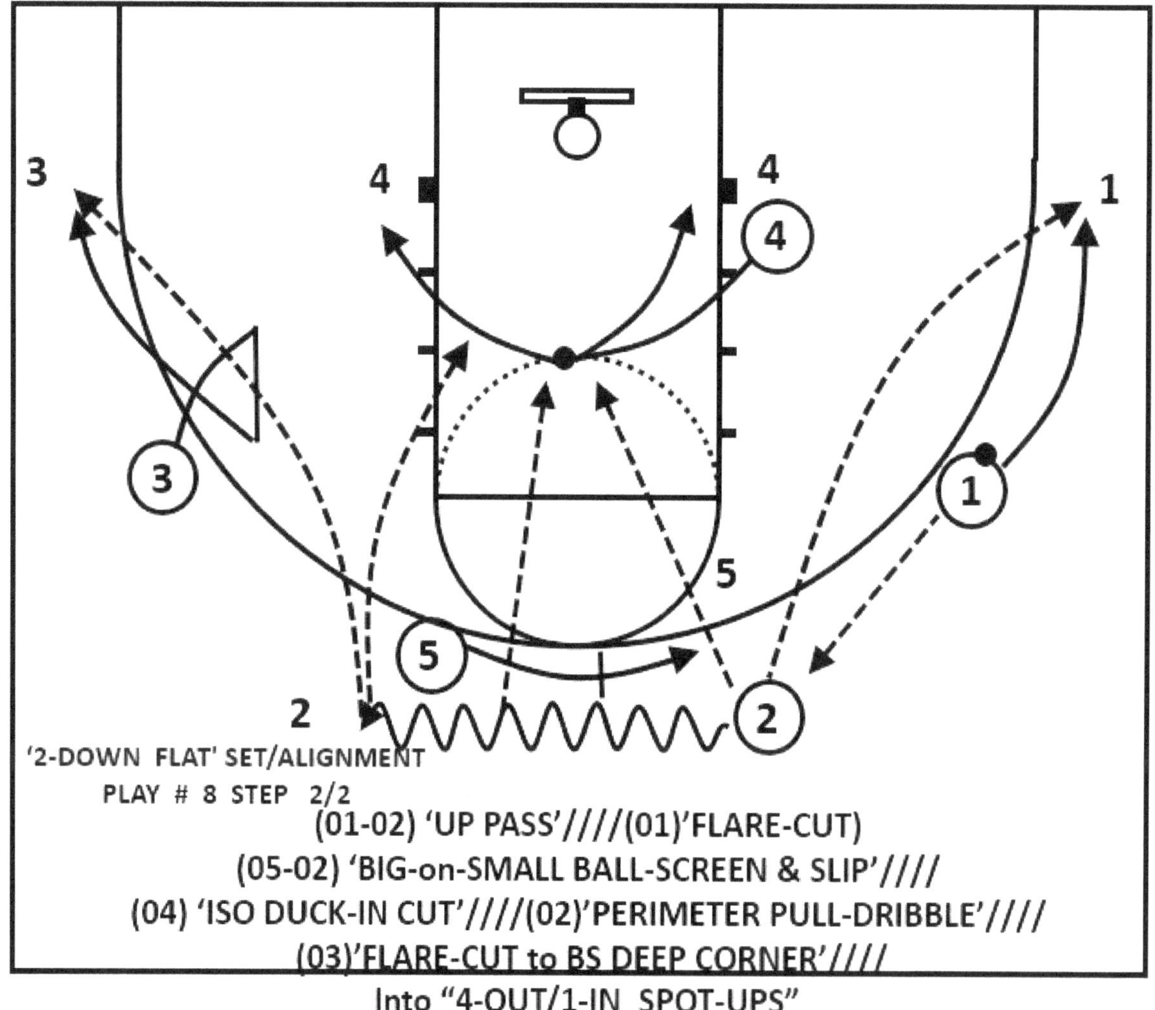

Diagram 17.15

Diagrams 17.16 and 17.17 show the second "Rejection Play," a two step play that appears to be the same play previously discussed. But this Play #9 has a counter action to attack the defense with 05's (better than average) offensive post up skills (or X5 with below average defensive post-up skills or in foul trouble.) With the same dribble made by 01 and the same 'Pipe Cut" by 02, 05 appears to again set a "Pin Down-Screen" for 03. But again, 03 rejects the screen and flares back out behind the arc on the FT Line extended, while 05 then reverses direction to again invert his post-type defender by breaking out to the new "Weakside Slot." See Diagram 17.16

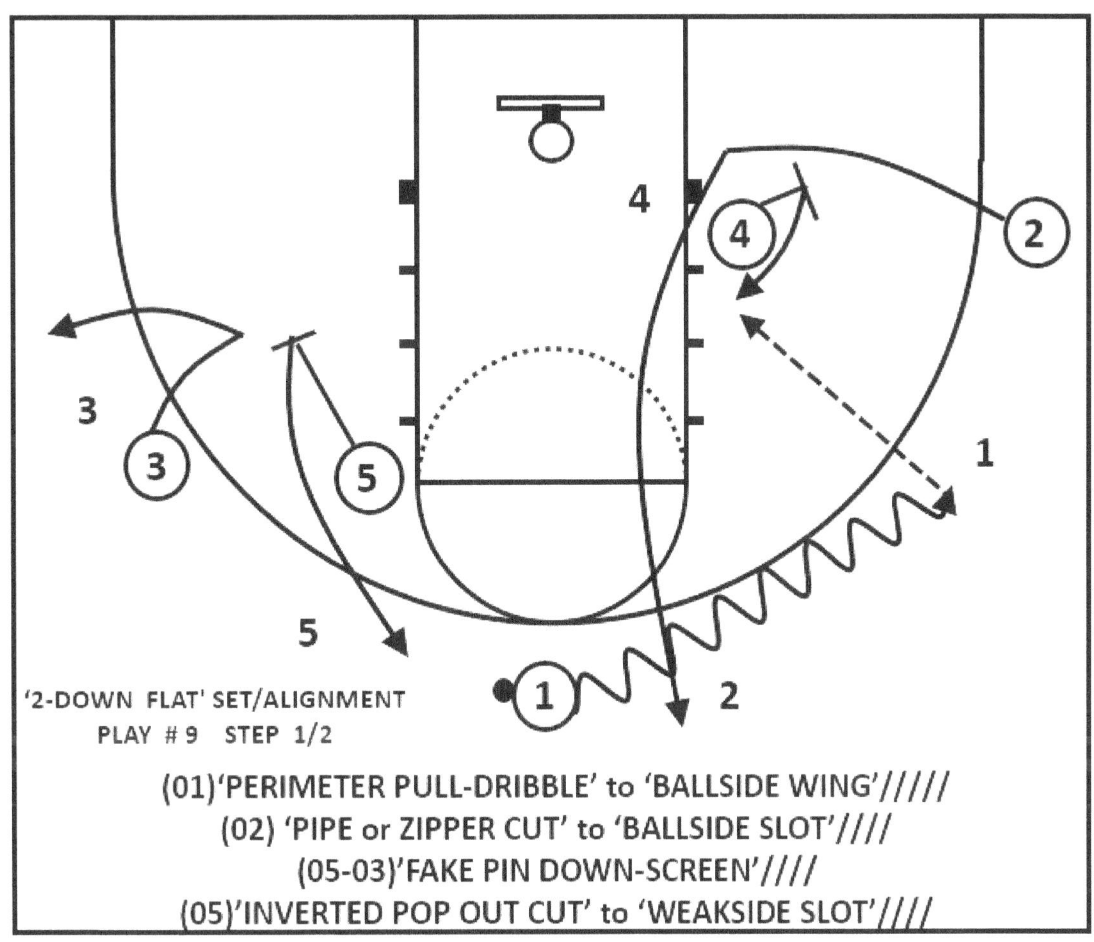

Play # 9   Diagram 17.16

Diagram 17.17 shows 01 again turning down the "Inside Pass" to 04 and moving the ball up to 02. 05 again cuts over to set the same "Big-on-Small Ball-Screen" for 02 to again move the ball across the top of the key. 03 again "Flare-Cuts" to his "Deep Corner" area, preparing for another "catch and shoot" pass from 02. This action still appears to be the initial play previously discussed. When 05 has outstanding post-up skills and/or X5 has inferior defensive skills, the action changes. When 02 "dribble-scrapes" off of 05's top right shoulder, 05 reverse pivots off of his lower left foot and rolls down the lane to post up his defender. 05 will have a huge advantage when X5 switches or hard hedges on the 05-02 Ball-Screen." To further gain advantages, 04 breaks vertically up to the new "Weakside Elbow" area instead of chasing the ball across the lane. This places 05 into the primary interior scorer while the previous play has 04 as that main scorer. Both plays become similar again in that the same "4-Out/1-In" Spot-Ups are filled for another smooth transition from half-court play to designated continuity offense. See Diagram 17.17

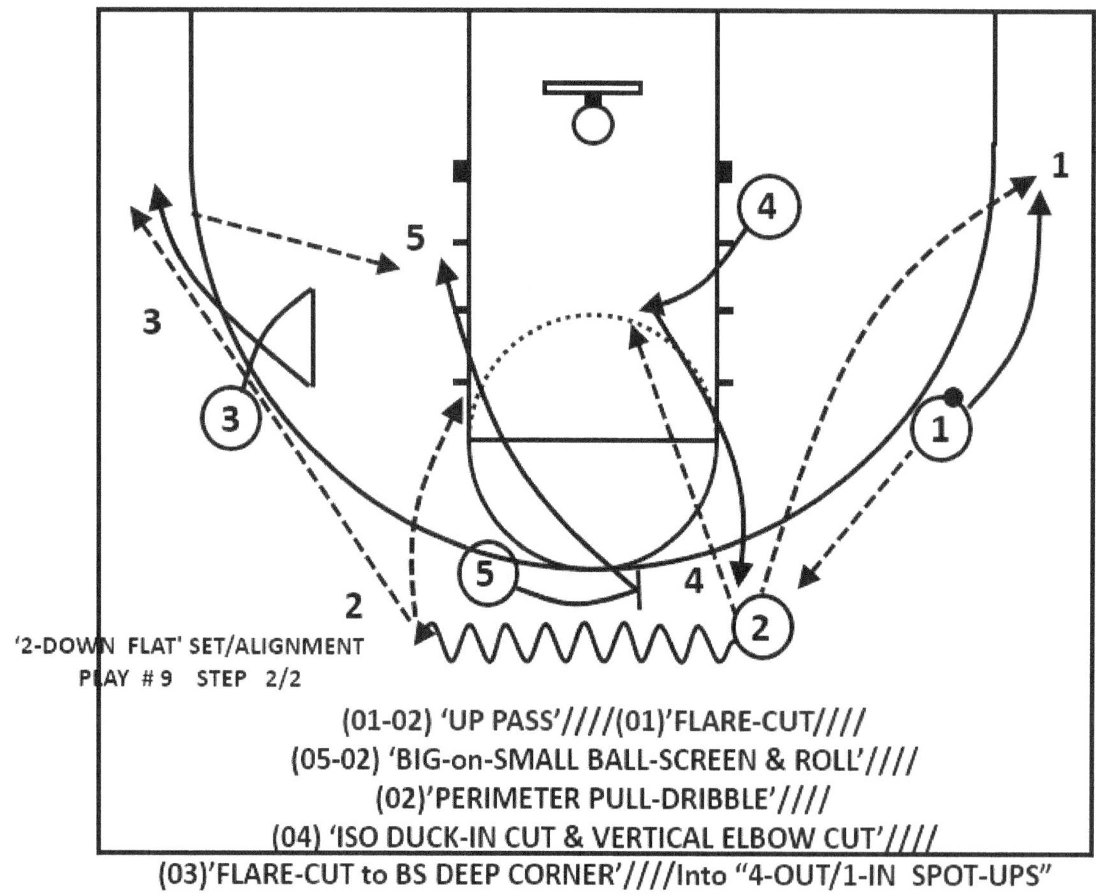

Diagram 17.17

This "2-DOWN FLAT" Set alignment is very similar to the "HI-LO STAX" Set and with minor adjustments, most offensive plays/entries from one offensive set can be utilized into the other offensive set. This gives either offensive package numerous more offensive actions that can attack the opposition's defense. Extra plays plus Counter Plays can confuse opposing defenses and give the offense extra advantages to attack the opposition.

There are many different philosophies on how to attack opposing defenses. This multiple-phase offensive system uses more than one phase/layer/wave of attack, with each phase/wave having a seamless and immediate conversion into the next phase/wave. While this system can be confusing to defenses and difficult to defend, this system can be properly taught and coached so that it can be easily understood and ultimately executed by players of many different levels of (physical talent, mental understand and playing experience.)

In addition, there are several types of offensive schemes and different ways within this system that offenses can attack their defensive counter-parts. Many of these can be integrated within the same offensive system that can attack defenses in various ways. The larger the number of schemes that can be successfully utilized and integrated within the same system, the greater the opportunity an offensive team can find the most efficient and productive schemes that can place both individual and the overall team in the best and most frequent "positions to succeed."

The plays/entries carefully diagrammed down to the small and seemingly unimportant 'V-Cuts' made by countless players before making their more important following cut are also described in detail.

Each play has been carefully studied and evaluated to determine which level of talent and experience must be possessed for that specific team to be able to successfully execute the play. This includes all players' physical skills as well as their mental understanding of the game. Coaches must also have the experience and the associated level of understanding of the game as well as their coaching/teaching of the nuances of each play.

As in the other offensive sets/alignments discussed, the most sophisticated plays/entries would fall into the first of the three levels all based on the team's physical talents and skills, the mental capacities and the overall team's game experience. In addition, the coaching staff must have a high degree of basketball knowledge as well as very high teaching and coaching skills to educate his/her entire basketball team. The proper breakdown drills must be thoroughly utilized to hone the fundamental skills and techniques needed for individual players and the overall team to execute plays that can be efficient, productive and successful. We define this family of plays as the "Level 3 category" of plays. This "Level 3" family of plays will have a much more complex offensive scheme that would require a very high amount of physical talent as well as requiring a greater amount of the players (to execute) and the coaches (to teach and coach) mental capacities and experience needed for the offense to be efficient, productive and successful. We feel plays in our defined "Level 3" category could possibly be successful for NBA teams, definitely for college teams and also for many high schools and older AAU teams.

The next classification or level of plays would be possibly slightly lower as far as sophistication, complexity and the actual 'length' of the play (and the number of passes, cuts and screens used) in the play's overall scheme. While all "Level 2" plays in each of the chapters in this book remain to be fundamentally sound, these plays may lack the actual number of techniques/methods that are implemented within that play in comparison to the "Level 1" plays/entries. Therefore any team that successfully executes the highest "Level 1" plays/entries could/should easily be able to execute any of these so-called lower "Level

2" plays/entries, if so desired. Almost all high school teams should be able to execute successfully all aspects of the "Level 2" plays.

The final grouping of plays would be called "Level 1" plays and are not as difficult for offensive players to master the execution of them, both physically as well as mentally. Even though the techniques are still fundamentally, they may not be as complex to learn and understand in addition to being easier to physically execute.

"Level 1" plays would be lower in the scheme's complexities and the number of techniques used in the execution of this category of plays. Obviously, since these "Level 1" plays are still sound, but lack some of the methods used in the two previous more sophisticated and complex levels; these more elementary plays should be able to be utilized by any teams that use either of the two higher level plays. We feel that Middle School/Junior High teams as well as younger AAU teams or organizations should be able to utilize any of the "Level 1" plays successfully, with a possibility that some of those teams that are slightly more advanced (than other teams) could possibly use some plays located in the immediate next immediate level.

Ideas, concepts, and techniques from actual plays from teams of all three levels have been used to modify or to create different combinations of the various techniques and schemes used that will help prove these entries can be successfully used. This allows the author to create numerous plays that use the various schemes to build a library of fundamentally sound plays that will be unique and will be appropriate for the wide range of teams with the various ages and skill levels.

With this book having plays in these three presumed categories or levels, the book will reach out and benefit a much larger group of serious basketball coaches from elementary school age to the highest skilled levels that exists.

In addition, an experienced and resourceful coach may be able to mold some plays that include all of the offensive techniques that he/she desires could reshape a specific play that begins in one specific offensive set/alignment and reshape it so that it could begin in a different offensive/set that is more favorable to that coach and his/her coaching staff's liking.

Conversely, that innovative and creative coach may completely like the specific offensive set/alignment and favor the very same offensive actions included in a certain play, but can modify that play so that the ending spot-ups of all five players are conducive

to being able to begin the final phase of the offensive attack by using a more favorable offensive continuity offense.

The "2-SQUEEZE" Set

PLAYS/ENTRIES THAT END in the "3-OUT/2-IN" OFFENSIVE SPOT-UPS

After the entry/play/quick-hitter has been executed but no shots have been taken, all five players will end up in a different group of offensive spot-ups. These "3-Out/2-In Spot-Ups" will have players moved about the court with any of the five ending up in the "Ballside Block," the "Ballside Wing," the "Weakside Block," the "Weakside Wing," and the "Point" (at the top of the key). These five positions can provide the offense with safe and easy types of ball-reversals, large gaps for dribble penetration, opportunities to deliver the ball inside to whomever (perimeter-type or post-type players) is posting up their defender on the "Ballside Block," and a player that can be a perimeter-scoring threat and a legitimate offensive rebounding threat from outside of the arc on his "offensive crashing of the boards." The "3-Out/2-In Spot-Ups also provide ample opportunities for constant and effective defensive transition responsibilities.

Diagram 18.1 illustrates the "2-SQUEEZE SET." As the name implies, 02 is the designated player that has the ability to post up on the 'Mid-Post' on either side of the lane. 01 is always the only guard that brings the ball down the floor to initiate the offense and the designated play/entry. The three remaining three players (04, 05 and 03) are "horizontally squeezed" together on the Free Throw Line. With their backs toward their offensive basket, 05 always aligns at the "Nail" position with 04 on the outside of 05's right shoulder and 03 on the outside of 05's left shoulder. With 02 being able to post up on either side of the lane and therefore start on either side of the lane, the offense will have two diverse cosmetic looks and therefore gives the offense a higher level of unpredictability. In this diagram, 02 posts up on the offense's right side of the lane, below 03's initial left 'elbow' location.

There is a significant number of philosophies on how to attack the various types of opposing defenses. This multiple-phase offensive system uses more than one phase/layer/wave of attack, with each phase/wave having a seamless and immediate conversion into the next phase/wave. While this system can be confusing to defenses and difficult to defend, this system can be properly taught and coached so that it can be easily understood and ultimately executed by players of many diverse levels of (physical talent, mental understand, and playing experience.)

In addition, there are several types of offensive schemes and different ways within this system that offenses can successfully attack their defensive counter-parts. Many of these can be integrated within the same offensive system that can attack defenses in various ways. The larger the number of schemes that can be successfully integrated within the same system, the greater the opportunity an offensive team can find the most efficient and productive schemes that can place both individual and the overall team in the best and most frequent "positions to succeed."

The plays/entries carefully diagrammed down to the small and seemingly unimportant 'V-Cuts' made by countless players before making those same player then make their more important cuts are also described in detail.

Each play has been carefully studied and evaluated to determine which level of talent and experience must be possessed for that specific team to be able to successfully execute the play. The most sophisticated plays/entries would fall into the latter of the three levels all based on the team's physical talents and skills, the mental capacities, and the overall team's game experience. In addition, the coaching staff must have a high degree of basketball knowledge as well as very high teaching and coaching skills to educate his/her entire basketball team. The proper breakdown drills must be thoroughly utilized to hone the fundamental skills and techniques needed for individual players and the overall team to execute plays that can be efficient, productive and successful. In addition to the sophistication of the plays as far as the various offensive techniques used, it is almost certain there is a larger number of the various offensive techniques that are weaved into the offensive entry or play. Therefore, there will be additional steps of parts of the higher sophisticated "Level #3" plays.

We define this family of plays as the "Level 3 category" of plays. As just stated, this "Level 3" family of plays will have a much more complex offensive scheme that would require high amounts of physical talent as well as requiring a greater amount of the players (to execute) and the coaches (to teach and coach) mental capacities and experience needed for the offense to be efficient, productive and successful. We feel plays in our defined "Level 3" category could possibly be successful for NBA teams, definitely for college teams and also for many high schools and more experienced AAU teams.

The next lower classification or level of plays would be somewhat lower as far as sophistication, complexity and the actual 'length' of the play (including the number of passes, cuts, screens and other techniques used) in the one particular play's overall series of actions. While all "Level 2" plays in each of the chapters in this book remain to be fundamentally sound, these plays may lack the actual number of techniques/methods that are implemented within that play in comparison to the "Level 3" plays/entries. Therefore, any team that successfully executes the highest "Level 3" plays/entries should easily be able to execute any of these so-called lower "Level 1 and 2" plays/entries, if so desired. It appears most high school teams should be able to execute successfully all aspects of all of the "Level 1 and 2" plays.

The final grouping of plays would be called "Level 1" plays and are not as difficult for offensive players to master their execution of the plays, both physically as well as mentally. Even though the techniques are still fundamentally sound, they may not be as complex to learn and understand in addition to being easier to physically execute. These plays will not take as long of a time to execute the full play because of the lesser number of actual offensive actions implemented within the play.

"Level 1" plays would be lower in the scheme's complexities and the number of techniques used in the execution of this category of plays. This means that these plays will be executed in shorter periods of time before the end of the play and therefore the beginning of the designated continuity offense. More than likely, the fewer number of diagrams will relate to the number of offensive techniques and actions; therefore the lower level of complexity in that particular play/entry.

Obviously, since these "Level 1" plays are still sound, but lack some of the methods used in the two previous more sophisticated and complex levels; these more elementary plays should be able to be utilized by any teams that use either of the two higher level plays. We feel that Middle School/Junior High teams as well as younger AAU teams or organizations should be able to utilize any of the "Level 1" plays successfully, with a possibility that some of those teams that are slightly more advanced (than other teams) could possibly use some plays located in the immediate next immediate level.

Ideas, concepts, and techniques from actual plays from teams of all three levels have been used to modify or to create different combinations of the various techniques and schemes used that will help prove these entries can be successfully used. This allows the author to create numerous plays that use the various schemes to build a library of fundamentally sound plays that will be unique and will be appropriate for a wide range of teams with the various ages and skill levels.

Any team that has the capabilities of executing "Level 3" plays (sometimes called quick-hitters or entries) would then be able to execute the somewhat less complicated and complex plays categorized in both the "Level 2 and Level 1" groups.

Also, any offensive team that can execute "Level 2" plays should then be able to incorporate and implement (the somewhat lower) "Level 1" plays/entries.

The "Level 3" plays that are discussed in this chapter should most likely be slightly too complex for teams that use the Level 1 and 2 plays. Some teams may be able to handle some particular plays that are just a step up from their normal family of plays, such as a team that predominately implements "Level 1" plays may have the capabilities of adding a very small number of "Level 2" plays. Or a team that has a majority of "Level 2" plays may only on rarely have instances to successfully incorporate a "Level 3" play.

With this book having plays in these three presumed categories or levels, the book will reach out and benefit a much larger group of serious basketball coaches from elementary school age to the highest skilled levels that exists.

In addition, an experienced and resourceful coach may be able to mold some plays that include all of the offensive techniques that he/she desires could reshape a specific play that begins in one specific offensive set/alignment and reshape it so that it could begin in a different offensive/set that is more favorable to that coach and his/her coaching staff's liking.

Conversely, that innovative and creative coach may completely like the specific offensive set/alignment and favor the very same offensive actions included in a certain play, but can modify that play so that the ending spot-ups of all five players are conducive to being able to begin the final phase of the offensive attack by using a more favorable offensive continuity offense.

Diagram 18.1 shows Play # 1 that has 02 on the left side of the lane and 03 steps up to set the "Big-on-Small Ball-Screen" for 01. 01 then dribble-scrapes off of 03's outside (left) shoulder with 03 making a reverse pivot off of his inside (right) pivot foot so that he can roll down the lane and post up his (perimeter-type) defender up on the new "Ballside Block." This action can be very effective, especially if 03 has individual advantages in posting up X3, who may be a weaker post defender, an inexperienced post defender, a defender that is in foul trouble, or if 03 has exceptional offensive post-up skills. To add to 03's potential 'position advantages,' both 05 and 04 quickly break down to set a "Big-on-Small Elevator-Screen" on 02's defender. This presents 02 with a likely successful '3 Pt.' shooting threat at the top of the key. This action gives the offense opportunities for the offense's presumably best passer (01) to deliver the ball to 03 in an isolated and inverted post-up situation as well as providing the offense with an outstanding '3 Pt.' scoring threat (for 02) at the top of the key.

After his part of the 'Elevator-Screen,' 04 flares out to the new "Weakside Wing" and 05 remains close to the basket on the weakside of the lane (for possible weakside offensive rebounding opportunities). In addition, the movements of all of the offensive players also reposition those players into the correct "3-Out/2-In Spot-Ups; providing the offense an instant and smooth transition into the next layer of attack. Play # 1 falls only into the Level 1 with the lowest level of sophistication and the easiest degree of difficulty, meaning all teams of any levels experience and skill should be able to successfully implement this play within its arsenal. See Diagram 18.1

Play # 1

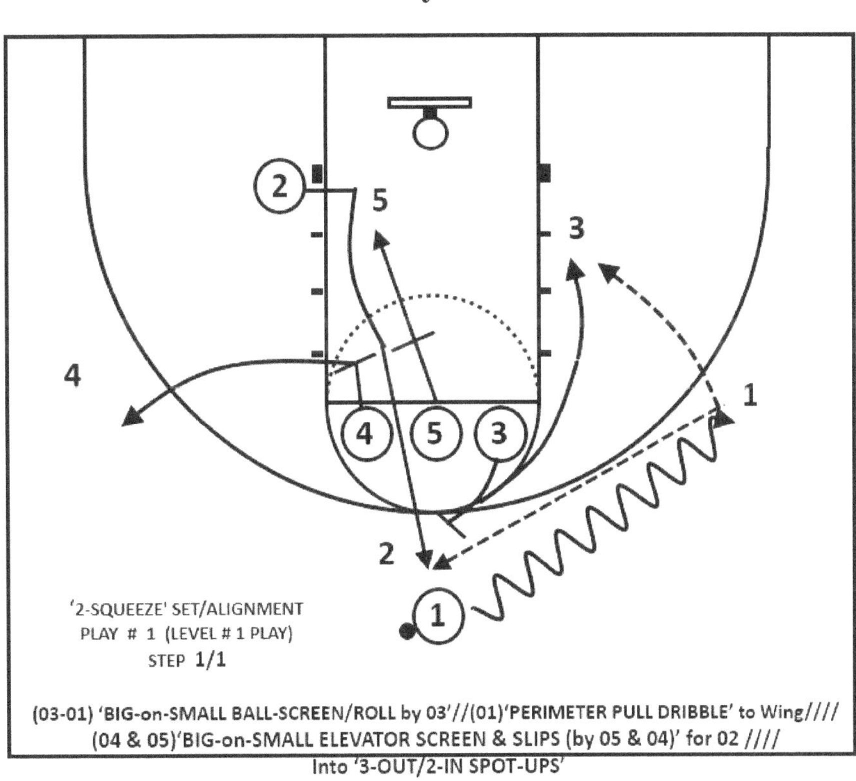

Play # 1   Diagram 18.1.

Diagram 18.2 illustrates the entire Play # 2 with 02 starting on the left side of the lane and 01 electing to use the 03-01 "Big-on-Small Ball-Screen." As 01 "dribble-scrapes" off of 03's top shoulder and breaks contact with him, 05 is the selected player to diagonally slash-cut to the new "Ballside Block" to post up his defender. To fully isolate X5 as well as to give the play an outstanding '3-Pt.' shot opportunity by a good shooter, 03 and 04 then break down diagonally down to set a "stagger-screen" for 02 to use for an open '3 Pt.' shot at the top of the key.

After screening for 02, 04 slides out to the new "Weakside Wing" and 03 settles in to the new "Weakside Block" area. With 04 stepping out on the perimeter instead of 03, the action should stretch and pull the presumed second biggest defender (X4) further from the basket for 05 to further attack his defender. If shots are not taken, the "3-Out/2-In Spot-Ups" are filled for the continuity offense to immediately begin with the next pass from 01. Play # 2 falls into the Level 1 Category for most instances, again meaning every team that possesses any degree of experience and skill should be able to successfully implement this play within its offensive playbook. See Diagram 18.2

Play # 2.

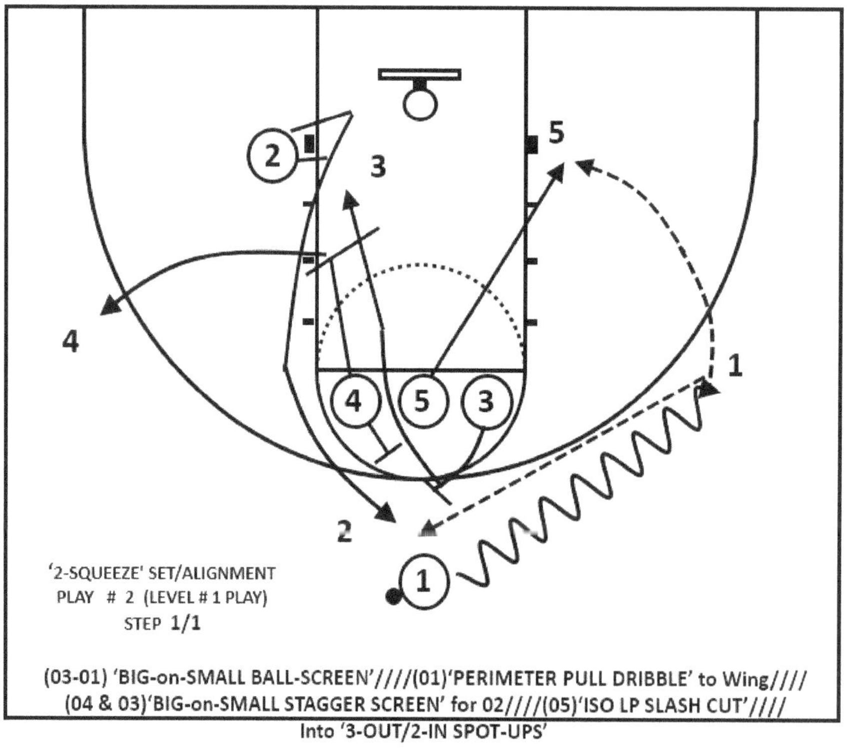

'2-SQUEEZE' SET/ALIGNMENT
PLAY # 2 (LEVEL # 1 PLAY)
STEP 1/1

(03-01) 'BIG-on-SMALL BALL-SCREEN'/////(01)'PERIMETER PULL DRIBBLE' to Wing////
(04 & 03)'BIG-on-SMALL STAGGER SCREEN' for 02////(05)'ISO LP SLASH CUT'////
Into '3-OUT/2-IN SPOT-UPS'

Play # 2   Diagram 18.2.

Diagram 18.3 illustrates Play # 3 with 02 starting on the offense's right side of the lane. In this play, 01 "dribble-scrapes" off of 04's outside shoulder to the FT Line extended on as 02 makes an "L-Cut" up and out to the FT Line extended on his current side of the floor. Again in Play #3, 05 is the newly designated player that attacks his defender by "slash-cutting" diagonally to the new "Ballside Mid-Post" area while 03 again remains at the '"Nail" position. See Diagram 18.3

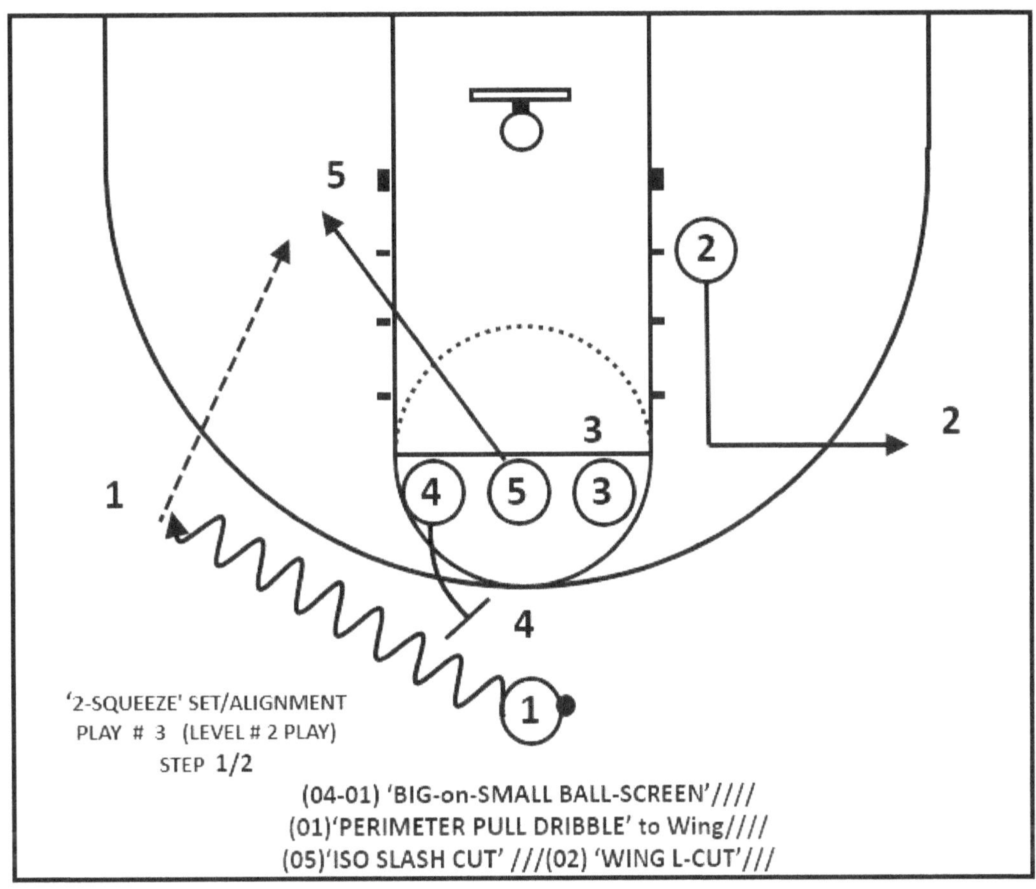

Play # 3   Diagram 18.3

Diagram 18.4 shows the continuation and conclusion of Play # 3 with 01 killing his dribble at the FT Line extended. He looks for his own perimeter shot, but primarily he first looks to make the "Inside Pass" to the isolated 05 posted up on the new "Ballside Block." At the same time, 03 has stepped up from his initial location to then set a (03-04) "Small-on-Big (Back-)Screen the (Ball-)Screener. 04 sets his defender up and then rubs his defender off by scraping off of 03's outside (left) shoulder and makes a "Lob Cut" to the basket, looking for 01's "Lob Pass" near the basket. After back-screening for 04, 03 also slips his screen and steps out to the top of the key.

After setting his "Big-on-Small Ball-Screen" for 01 to shed his defender, 04 is the designated "Lob Cutter" that cuts off of 03's outside (left) shoulder and "rim-runs" to the basket while looking for 01's pass. The horizontal action by 01 and 02 horizontally stretch the defense while the action of both 05 and 04 vertically stretches the overall defense. The "Small-on-Big (Back-)Screen the (Ball-)Screener action between 03 and 04 provides the offense with a second interior scoring threat and continues to isolate X5 on the new "Ballside Mid-Post." After screening for 04, 03 slips his screen and steps out to the top of the key.

05 and 04's cuts into the lane keep the presumed two best interior scoring threats (O5 and O4) near the basket with high percentage scoring opportunities, while 01, 03 and 02 become legitimate scoring threats on the perimeter's "3-Out/2-In Spot-Up" locations 01 looks inside for 05, then looks for the pass to 04 and then for perimeter passes to either 03 out on top or a "Skip Pass" to 02 on the weakside of the floor. If shots do not materialize, the designated continuity offense (that always start out of the regular "3-Out/2-In Spot-Ups") can immediately and smoothly begin. Play # 3 is considered to fit the first two levels, meaning that for the most part, teams belong in the first two levels of experience, mental and physical skills, should be successfully able to implement this play. See Diagram 18.4

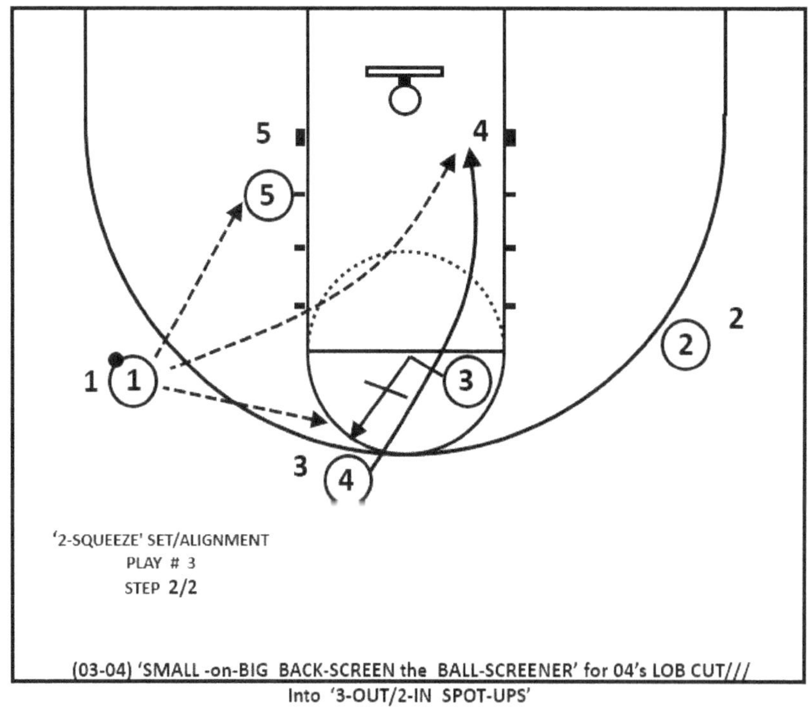

Diagram 18.4

Play # 4, shown in Diagram 18.5, illustrates another play from the same offensive set and the initial action appears to be identical to the action of Play # 3. In this play, 02 is on the same side of the lane as the previous play, with 01 again dribble-scraping off of the outside shoulder of 04's "Big-on-Small Ball-Screen" to the offense's left side of the floor away from 02. As 01 breaks contact with 04's outside right shoulder, 03 is now the new player that slashes diagonally to the new empty "Ballside Block," while 04 makes a front pivot and again slips his screen to break to the top of the key. 05 remains at the 'Nail,' which pulls the presumed two biggest defenders (X4 and X5) away from the basket. 01 then looks to make the pass to the now 'isolated and inverted perimeter player' (03) on the "Ballside Block." See Diagram 18.5

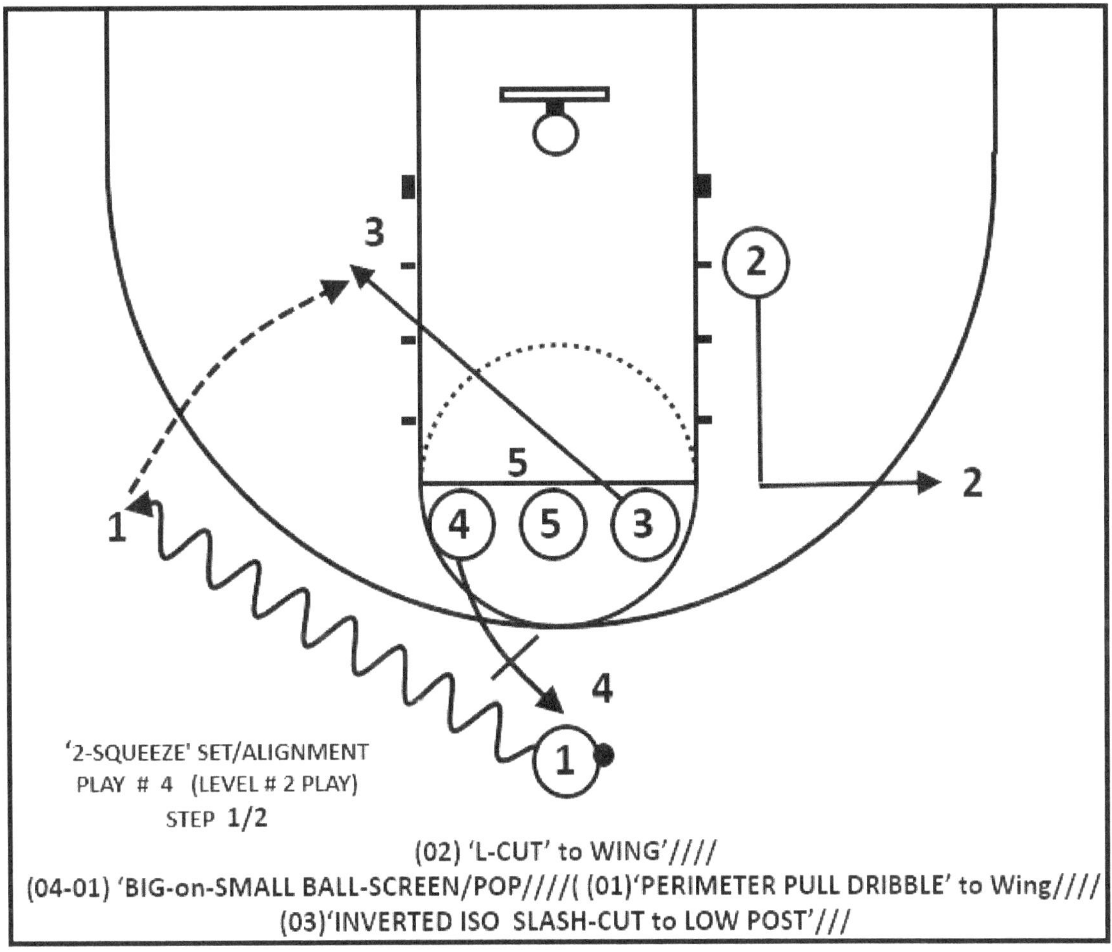

Play # 4   Diagram 18.5

If 01 turns down the "Inside Pass" to 03, 01 reverses the ball out to 04 now at the top of the key. From the initial "Ballside Block," 03 starts his "chase of the ball" as 04 swings the ball on over to 02 on the opposite "Wing" area, 04 and 05 diagonally cut over to then set a "Big-on-Small Stagger Screen" for 01. 01 should then be able to use the stagger-screen to break up (off of 05's outside (left) shoulder for an open '3 Pt.' shot at the now vacant top of the key. After finishing his part of the screen, 05 slips out to the new "Weakside Wing" area (to become an inverted post-type player), while 04 remains at the new "Weakside Block" area. The same (isolated and inverted) "Inside Shot" opportunity for 03 exists on the opposite side of the floor in addition to 01 now having an open perimeter shot at the top of the key. If 02 turns down the passes to either 03 cutting across the lane or to 01 now at the top of the key, the "3-Out/2-In Spot-Ups" are filled so that the offensive action can smoothly continue and maintain the attack in the final phase of the offense. Play # 4 is considered to also fit the first two levels, again stating that Play # 4 also falls into the first two levels of experience, mental and physical skills, should be able to successfully implement this play. See Diagram 18.6

Play # 4.

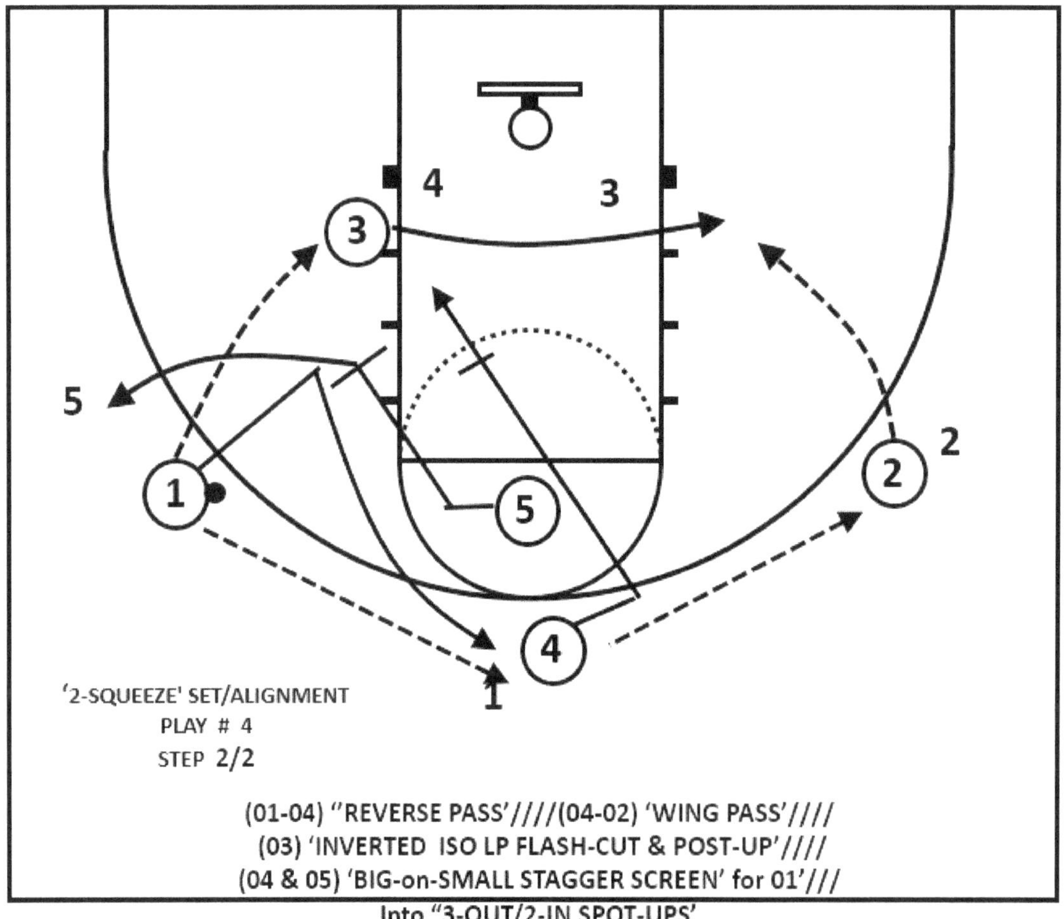

Diagram 18.6.

Play # 5 (in Diagram 18.7) starts with 04 again stepping up from his initial position to set a (04-01) "Big-on-Small Ball-Screen" for 01 to attempt to shed his defender and to continue to the Free Throw Line extended on the left side of the floor. As 01 breaks contact with 04's outside (right) shoulder, 05 again is the player that now slashes diagonally down to the newly declared "Ballside Block." 01's primary target is to make the pass to 05, the presumed offense's best interior scorer. In addition, when 04 slips his ball-screen and steps to the top of the key, the defense's presumed second largest post defender (X4) has now been stretched vertically to the top of the key and further from the basket and from the defender that needs him the most—X5. See Diagram 18.7

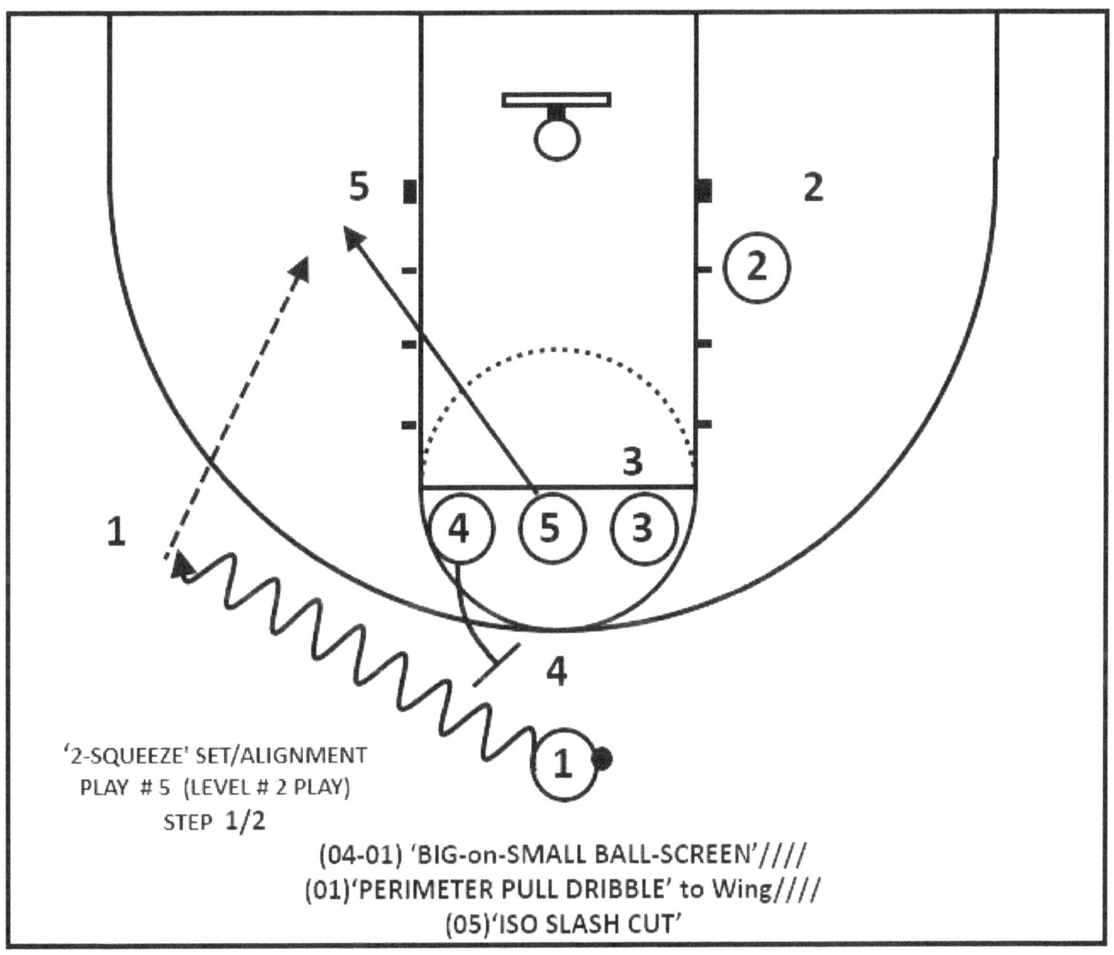

Play # 5   Diagram 18.7.

To eliminate possible helpside defense and to reposition 05 in an even more advantageous isolated post-up situation, both 04 and 03 then break down diagonally to set a "Big-on-Small Stagger-Screen" that will also give 02 an outstanding opportunity for an open '3' at the top of the key. 02 sets his defender up and then breaks up diagonally to scrape off of 03's outside (right) shoulder to the top of the key.

After the stagger-screen for 02, 04 remains near the "Weakside Block" while 03 curls out to the "Weakside Wing." 05 and 02 become the primary possible scorers in this quick-hitter, (one being an interior scoring threat and the other a '3 Pt.' scoring threat). Still, if shots are not taken; the "3-Out/2-In Spot-Ups" are filled for a smooth and immediate conversion into the desired continuity offense.

Play #5 is also considered to fit the Level 2 Category allowing every team that possesses certain degrees of experience and skill (such as the so-called "Level 1" and 2 types of teams) to be able to successfully incorporate this play within its offensive playbook and make it a productive part of its arsenal. See Diagram 18.8

Play # 5

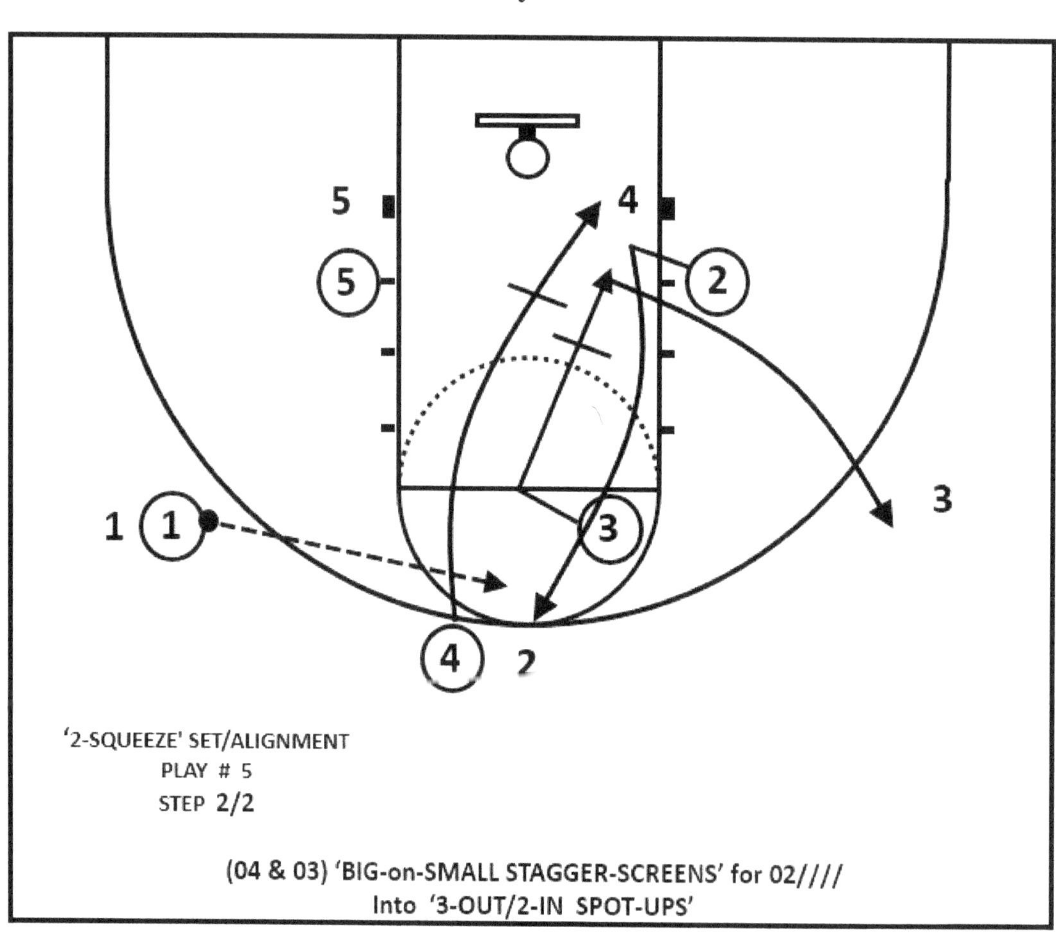

Diagram 18.8

Diagram 18.9 illustrates the beginning of Play # 6 with 02 on the right side of the lane and 01 dribbling away from 02 towards the "Wing" area on the left side of the floor. 04 diagonally cuts under 05 to first "Brush-Screen" 05's defender and then stops in the 'Dotted Circle' area. 05 uses 04's screen to diagonally 'slash cut" to the new "Ballside Block" to isolate his defender on a post-up. 04 then steps out of the lane to the 'Nail.' This action also keeps his post-type defender (X4) out higher and further away from the basket and from helping his post defender, X5.

During 01's dribble away from both 03 and 02, from his initial location, 03 then sets a stationary "Pin Down-Screen" for 02 to use to break to the top of the key. After setting the screen, 03 slips the screen to float over to the new "Weakside Wing" area. . 05 posts up and continues to isolate his defender on the "Ballside Block." while 04 remains at the "Nail." The actions of 05 and 02 have vertically extended the floor from the top of the key to the baseline, while 01 and 04 have stretched the defense from sideline to sideline. Interior shots should be available for the isolated 05 and a likely open '3 Pt.' shot for 02 at the top of the key and also possibly for 03 at the new "Weakside Wing" area.

If no shots are produced, the "High-(Post)/Low-(Post) Spot-Ups are filled for that particular type of continuity offense to immediately begin. See Diagram 18.9

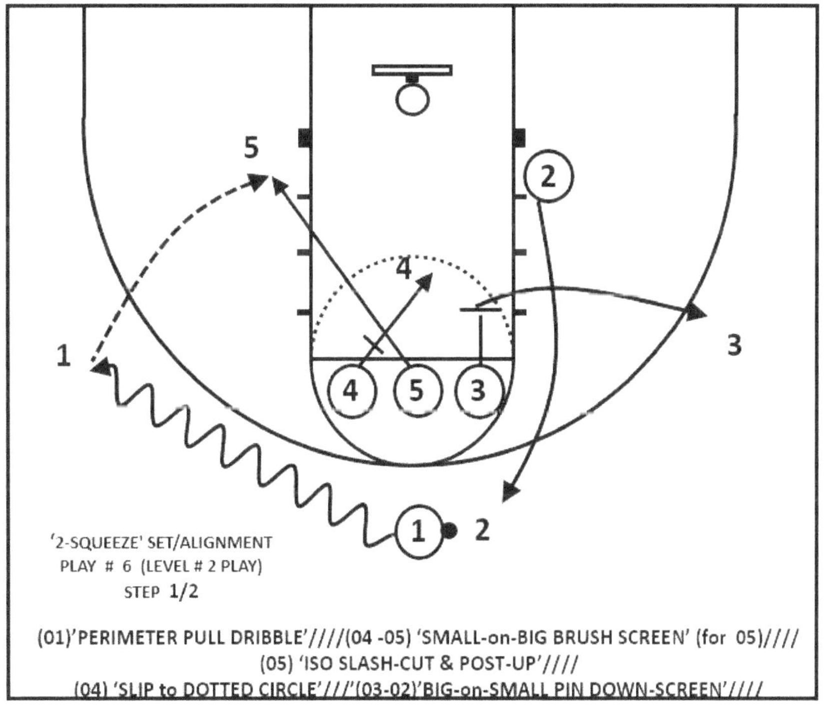

Play # 6   Diagram 18.9

Diagram 18.10 illustrates the action that would immediately follow the action in Diagram 18.9 if the coaching staff wanted to execute a continuity offense that requires "3-Out/2-In Spot-Ups." If 01 turns down the "Inside Pass" to 05 and makes the 01-02 "Reverse Pass" to 02 with no shot taken by 02; 04 diagonally cuts down to set a "Diagonal Brush Screen" for 05 to use as 05 "chases the ball around the perimeter." 02 continues the swing of the ball on over to the 03 and 05 continues cutting to the new "Ballside Block." At the same time, 01 steps up to set a "Small-on-Big Flare-Screen for 02 to scrape off of 01's outside right shoulder on his "Flare-Cut" to the new "Weakside Wing." 01 then slips his (01-02) "Flare-Screen" to become an immediate scoring threat at the top of the key. 04 remains down on the new "Weakside Block," with 05 being the primary interior scoring threat and 02 and 01 being the main perimeter scoring threats. If shots are not created, the "3-Out/2-In Spot-Ups" are filled for a smooth and fluid transition into the designated continuity offense. Play # 6 is an entry that probably should remain in the Level 2 Category, allowing any team that possesses the so-called "Level 1 and Level 2 (physical and mental) capabilities" to be able to integrate this entry into its offensive system. See Diagram 18.10

Play # 6

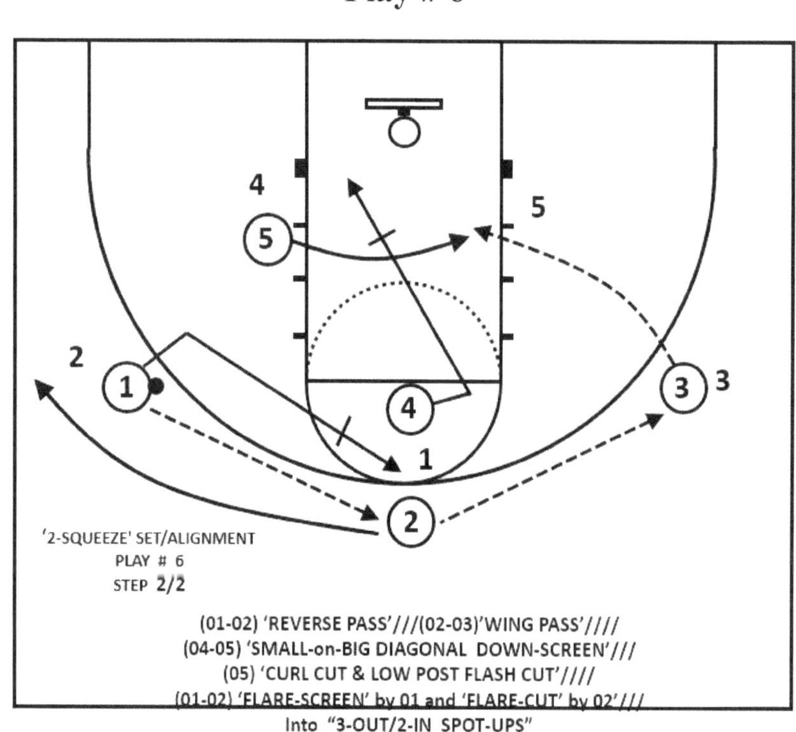

Diagram 18.10

Diagram 18.11. illustrates the beginning of Play # 7 which appears to actually be Play # 18. With 02 again on the right side of the lane and 01 again dribbling away from 02 towards the "Wing" area on the left side of the floor, 05 makes a "Barkley Cut" over 03 and 04 dives to the newly declared "Ballside Block." 03 sets the same stationary "Pin Down-Screen" for 02 to use on his cut off of the screen to the top of the key. 02 again scrapes off of 03's outside (right) shoulder and breaks to the top of the key outside of the arc. After setting the screen, 03 slips the screen and looks to dive to the basket. If 03 is not open, he steps back out to the "Nail" at the FT Line. As this action takes place away from 01 and the ball, 04 continues to isolate his defender on the "Ballside Block," while 03 remains at the "Nail." 05's extended cut then will pull his post-type defender (X5) out to the FT Line extended away from the basket and the ball. On this occasion, the actions of 04 and 02 have vertically extended the floor from the top of the key to the baseline, while the cuts made by 01 and 05 have horizontally stretched the defense from sideline to sideline. Whenever an offense can stretch the defense both vertically as well as horizontally, these actions completely weaken the interior defense and further allows the isolated 04 on the new "Ballside Block" more shot opportunities. In addition, there should more likely open '3 Pt.' shot opportunities for 02 at the top of the key. If no shots are produced, the "High-(Post)/Low-(Post) Spot-Ups are filled for that particular type of continuity offense to immediately begin. See Diagram 18.11

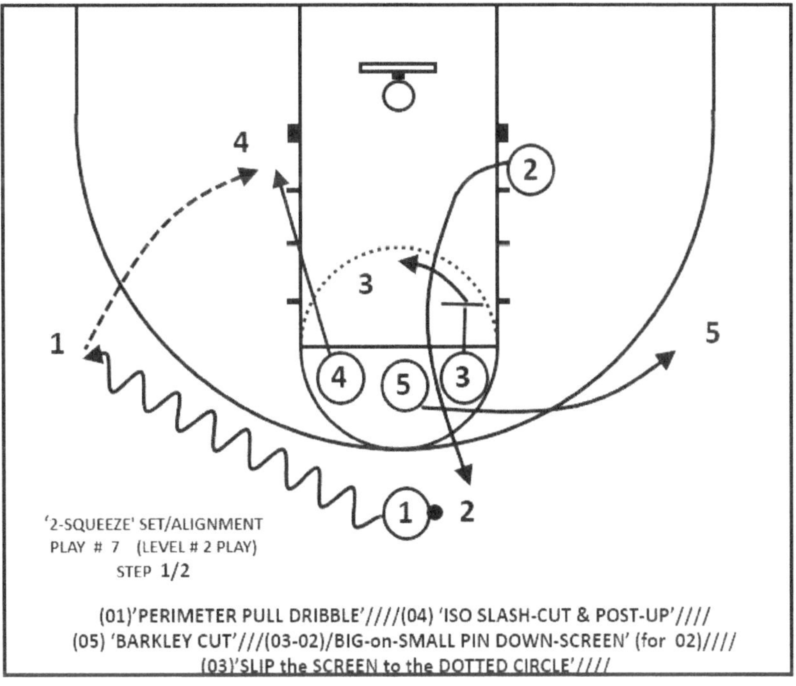

Play # 7   Diagram 18.11

This illustrates the action that would immediately follow the action in Diagram 18.17 if the coaching staff wanted to execute a continuity offense that requires "3-Out/2-In Spot-Ups." At the beginning of the play, if 01 turns down the "Inside Pass" to 04 and makes the 01-02 "Reverse Pass" to 02 (with no shot taken by 02); 03 diagonally cuts down to set a "Small-on-Big Brush Screen" for 04 to use as he "chases the (01-02) "Reverse Pass." 02 can continue the swing of the ball on over to the inverted 05 with 04 continuing his cut across the lane to the new "Ballside Block." After the 02-05 "Wing Pass," 01 steps up to set a "Small-on-Big Flare-Screen" for 02 to scrape off of 01's outside (right) shoulder on his "Flare-Cut" to the new "Weakside Wing," looking for a possible 05-02 "Skip Pass." After screening, 01 then slips his (01-02) "Flare-Screen" to become an immediate scoring threat at the top of the key. After screening for 04, 03 remains down on the new "Weakside Block," with 04 still being the primary interior scoring threat. 02 and 01 are the main perimeter scoring threats. If shots are not created, the "3-Out/2-In Spot-Ups" are filled for a smooth and fluid transition into the designated continuity offense. Play # 7 falls into the Level 2 category of plays/entries, again allowing. See Diagram 18.12. Play # 7 is a play that also is in the Level 2 Category, allowing any team that has the so-called "Level 1 and Level 2 capabilities" to make this entry a productive and efficient offensive play. See Diagram 18.12

Play # 7

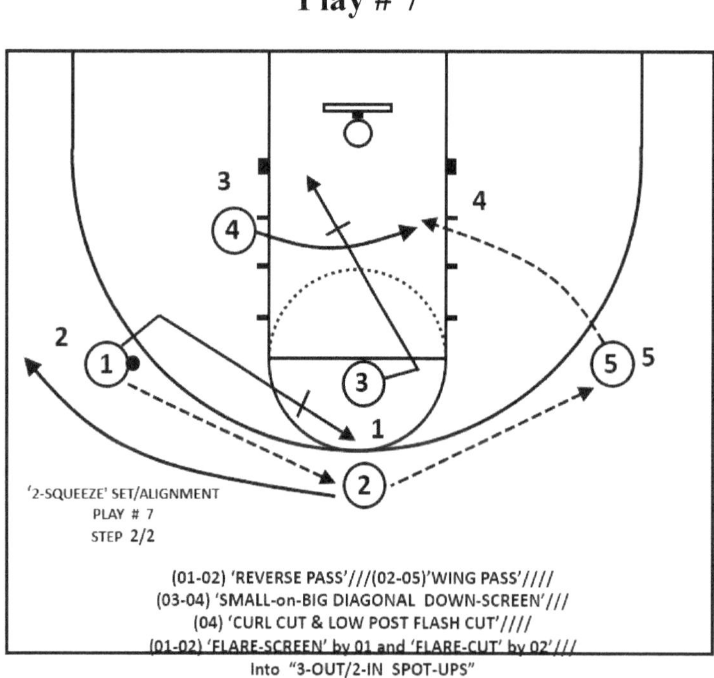

Diagram 18.12

These twenty plays all from the same "2-SQUEEZE" Set can all be very effective forms of action that will use every form of fundamental offensive techniques to gain offensive position and personnel advantages. The practices of inverting and/or isolating post-players out on the perimeter or inverting and/or isolating perimeter players on the interior are used frequently. Different types of ball screens with numerous kinds of actions after the actual screen as well as the many various types of off-ball screens and the countless methods of the action of finishing those screens, are designed within the framework and structure of these plays.

With the different types of fluid movement that each play possesses and the different players that are the primary pass-receivers/potential scorers; there is one constant similarity in each of these plays. And that is the ability of each play that does not produce the desired shot will always reposition all five players into the required and necessary offensive spot-ups that allows the offensive attack to have an immediate and fluid conversion from the actual entry/play into the continuity offense that is to become the last wave of attack. Within the package of plays out of this set/alignment are counters and counter-options to base plays that can cross up and attack defenses that expect certain actions from plays that have been executed. In addition, within the rules and the framework of the continuity offense, it can also possess options to modify specific movements of the continuity. Each continuity offense will have Secondary Break Options, entries/plays from more than one offensive set as well as BLOB and SLOB plays that can immediately flow into those continuity offenses. Additionally, each designated continuity offense will have specific offensive rebounding and defensive transition schemes that assign particular players to execute the required tasks for excellent offensive and defensive results.

Chapter 19
Plays/Entries Executed From The "2-Up Set/Alignment"

There are many different philosophies on how offenses can successfully go about attacking (delete to attack opposing) opponent's man-to-man defenses. This multiple-phase offensive system uses more than one phase/layer/wave of attack, with each phase/wave having a seamless and immediate conversion into the next phase/wave. While this system can be confusing to defenses and difficult to defend, this system can be properly taught and coached so that it can be easily understood and ultimately executed by players of many different levels of (physical talent, mental understand, and playing experience.)

In addition, there are several types of offensive schemes and different ways within this system that offenses can attack their defensive counter-parts. Many of these can be

integrated within the same offensive system that can attack defenses in various ways. The larger the number of schemes that can be successfully utilized and integrated within the same system, the greater the opportunity an offensive team can find the most efficient and productive schemes that can place both individual and the overall team in the best and most frequent "positions to succeed."

The plays/entries carefully diagrammed down to the small and seemingly unimportant 'V-Cuts' made by countless players before making their more important following cut are also described in detail.

Each play has been carefully studied and evaluated to determine which level of talent and experience must be possessed for that specific team to be able to successfully execute the play. This includes all players' physical skills as well as their mental understanding of the game. Coaches must also have the experience and the associated level of understanding of the game as well as their coaching/teaching of the nuances of each play.

The most sophisticated plays/entries would fall into the first of the three levels all based on the team's physical talents and skills, the mental capacities and the overall team's game experience. In addition, the coaching staff must have a high degree of basketball knowledge as well as very high teaching and coaching skills to educate his/her entire basketball team. The proper breakdown drills must be thoroughly utilized to hone the fundamental skills and techniques needed for individual players and the overall team to execute plays that can be efficient, productive and successful. We define this family of plays as the "Level 3 category" of plays. This "Level 3" family of plays will have a much more complex offensive scheme that would require a very high amount of physical talent as well as requiring a greater amount of the players (to execute) and the coaches (to teach and coach) mental capacities and experience needed for the offense to be efficient, productive and successful. We feel plays in our defined "Level 3" category could possibly be successful for NBA teams, definitely for college teams and also for many high schools and older AAU teams.

The next classification or level of plays would be possibly slightly lower as far as sophistication, complexity and the actual 'length' of the play (and the number of passes, cuts, and screens used) in the play's overall scheme. While all "Level 2" plays in each of the chapters in this book remain to be fundamentally sound, these plays may lack the actual number of techniques/methods that are implemented within that play in comparison to the "Level 1" plays/entries. Therefore any team that successfully executes the highest "Level

1" plays/entries could/should easily be able to execute any of these so-called lower "Level 2" plays/entries, if so desired. Almost all high school teams should be able to execute successfully all aspects of the "Level 2" plays.

The final grouping of plays would be called "Level 1" plays and are not as difficult for offensive players to master the execution of them, both physically as well as mentally. Even though the techniques are still fundamentally, they may not be as complex to learn and understand in addition to being easier to physically execute.

"Level 1" plays would be lower in the scheme's complexities and the number of techniques used in the execution of this category of plays. Obviously, since these "Level 1" plays are still sound, but lack some of the methods used in the two previous more sophisticated and complex levels; these more elementary plays should be able to be utilized by any teams that use either of the two higher level plays. We feel that Middle School/Junior High teams as well as younger AAU teams or organizations should be able to utilize any of the "Level 1" plays successfully, with a possibility that some of those teams that are slightly more advanced (than other teams) could possibly use some plays located in the immediate next immediate level.

Ideas, concepts and techniques from actual plays from teams of all three levels have been used to modify or to create different combinations of the various techniques and schemes used that will help prove these entries can be successfully used. This allows the author to create numerous plays that use the various schemes to build a library of fundamentally sound plays that will be unique and will be appropriate for the wide range of teams with the various ages and skill levels.

With this book having plays in these three presumed categories or levels, the book will reach out and benefit a much larger group of serious basketball coaches from elementary school age to the highest skilled levels that exists.

In addition, an experienced and resourceful coach may be able to mold some plays that include all of the offensive techniques that he/she desires could reshape a specific play that begins in one specific offensive set/alignment and reshape it so that it could begin in a different offensive/set that is more favorable to that coach and his/her coaching staff's liking.

Conversely, that innovative and creative coach may completely like the specific offensive set/alignment and favor the very same offensive actions included in a certain

play, but can modify that play so that the ending spot-ups of all five players are conducive to being able to begin the final phase of the offensive attack by using a more favorable offensive continuity offense.

The most sophisticated plays/entries would fall into the first of the three levels all based on the team's physical talents and skills, the mental capacities and the overall team's game experience. In addition, the coaching staff must have a high degree of basketball knowledge as well as very high teaching and coaching skills to educate his/her entire basketball team. The proper breakdown drills must be thoroughly utilized to hone the fundamental skills and techniques needed for individual players and the overall team to execute plays that can be efficient, productive and successful. We define this family of plays as the "Level 3 category" of plays. This "Level 3" family of plays will have a much more complex offensive scheme that would require a very high amount of physical talent as well as requiring a greater amount of the players (to execute) and the coaches (to teach and coach) mental capacities and experience needed for the offense to be efficient, productive and successful. We feel plays in our defined "Level 3" category could possibly be successful for NBA teams, definitely for college teams and also for many high schools and older AAU teams.

The next classification or level of plays would be possibly slightly lower as far as sophistication, complexity and the actual 'length' of the play (and the number of passes, cuts and screens used) in the play's overall scheme. While all "Level 2" plays in each of the chapters in this book remain to be fundamentally sound, these plays may lack the actual number of techniques/methods that are implemented within that play in comparison to the "Level 1" plays/entries. Therefore any team that successfully executes the highest "Level 1" plays/entries could/should easily be able execute any of these so-called lower "Level 2" plays/entries, if so desired. Almost all high school teams should be able to execute successfully all aspects of the "Level 2" plays.

The final grouping of plays would be called "Level 1" plays and are not as difficult for offensive players to master the execution of them, both physically as well as mentally. Even though the techniques are still fundamentally, they may not be as complex to learn and understand in addition to being easier to physically execute.

"Level 1" plays would be lower in the scheme's complexities and the number of techniques used in the execution of this category of plays. Obviously, since these "Level 1" plays are still sound, but lack some of the methods used in the two previous more sophisticated and complex levels; these more elementary plays should be able to be utilized by any teams that use either of the two higher level plays. We feel that Middle School/Junior High teams as well as younger AAU teams or organizations should be able to utilize any of the "Level 1" plays successfully, with a possibility that some of those teams that are slightly more advanced (than other teams) could possibly use some plays located in the immediate next immediate level.

Ideas, concepts and techniques from actual plays from teams of all three levels have been used to modify or to create different combinations of the various techniques and schemes used that will help prove these entries can be successfully used. This allows the author to create numerous plays that use the various schemes to build a library of fundamentally sound plays that will be unique and will be appropriate for the wide range of teams with the various ages and skill levels.

With this book having plays in these three presumed categories or levels, the book will reach out and benefit a much larger group of serious basketball coaches from elementary school age to the highest skilled levels that exists.

In addition, an experienced and resourceful coach may be able to mold some plays that include all of the offensive techniques that he/she desires could reshape a specific play that begins in one specific offensive set/alignment and reshape it so that it could begin in a different offensive/set that is more favorable to that coach and his/her coaching staff's liking.

Conversely, that innovative and creative coach may completely like the specific offensive set/alignment and favor the very same offensive actions included in a certain play, but can modify that play so that the ending spot-ups of all five players are conducive to being able to begin the final phase of the offensive attack by using a more favorable offensive continuity offense.

The "2-UP SET"

PLAYS/ENTRIES THAT END in the "3-OUT/2-IN" OFFENSIVE SPOT-UPS

After the entry/play/quick-hitter has been executed but no shots have been taken, all five players will end up in a different group of offensive spot-ups. These "3-Out/2-In Spot-Ups" will have players moved about the court with any of the five ending up in the "Ballside Block," the "Ballside Wing," the "Weakside Block," the "Weakside Wing," and the "Point" (at the top of the key). These five positions can provide the offense with safe and easy types of ball-reversals, large gaps for dribble penetration, opportunities to deliver the ball inside to whomever (perimeter-type or post-type players) is posting up their defender on the "Ballside Block," and a player that can be a perimeter-scoring threat and a legitimate offensive rebounding threat from outside of the arc on his "offensive crashing of the boards." The "3-Out/2-In Spot-Ups also provide ample opportunities for constant and effective defensive transition responsibilities.

Diagram 19.1 illustrates the "2-UP SET." As the name implies, 01 and 02 are the players located in the two "Slot" locations with 03 and 04 on the two "Wing" positions located at the FT Line extended on both sides of the floor. 05 is the player that that begins at the "nail" location and should possess the abilities to post up on the 'Mid-Post' on either side of the lane.

There are many different philosophies on how to attack opposing defenses. This multiple-phase offensive system uses more than one phase/layer/wave of attack, with each phase/wave having a seamless and immediate conversion into the next phase/wave. While this system can be confusing to defenses and difficult to defend, this system can be properly taught and coached so that it can be easily understood and ultimately executed by players of many different levels of (physical talent, mental understand and playing experience.)

In addition, there are several types of offensive schemes and different ways within this system that offenses can attack their defensive counter-parts. Many of these can be integrated within the same offensive system that can attack defenses in various ways. The larger the number of schemes that can be successfully utilized and integrated within the same system, the greater the opportunity an offensive team can find the most efficient and productive schemes that can place both individual and the overall team in the best and most frequent "positions to succeed."

The plays/entries carefully diagrammed down to the small and seemingly unimportant 'V-Cuts' made by countless players before making their more important following cut are also described in detail.

Each play has been carefully studied and evaluated to determine which level of talent and experience must be possessed for that specific team to be able to successfully execute the play. This includes all players' physical skills as well as their mental understanding of the game. Coaches must also have the experience and the associated level of understanding of the game as well as their coaching/teaching of the nuances of each play.

The most sophisticated plays/entries would fall into the first of the three levels all based on the team's physical talents and skills, the mental capacities and the overall team's game experience. In addition, the coaching staff must have a high degree of basketball knowledge as well as very high teaching and coaching skills to educate his/her entire basketball team. The proper breakdown drills must be thoroughly utilized to hone the fundamental skills and techniques needed for individual players and the overall team to execute plays that can be efficient, productive and successful. We define this family of plays as the "Level 3 category" of plays. This "Level 3" family of plays will have a much more complex offensive scheme that would require a very high amount of physical talent as well as requiring a greater amount of the players (to execute) and the coaches (to teach and coach) mental capacities and experience needed for the offense to be efficient, productive and successful. We feel plays in our defined "Level 3" category could possibly be successful for NBA teams, definitely for college teams and also for many high schools and older AAU teams.

The next classification or level of plays would be possibly slightly lower as far as sophistication, complexity and the actual 'length' of the play (and the number of passes, cuts, and screens used) in the play's overall scheme. While all "Level 2" plays in each of the chapters in this book remain to be fundamentally sound, these plays may lack the actual number of techniques/methods that are implemented within that play in comparison to the "Level 1" plays/entries. Therefore, any team that successfully executes the highest "Level 1" plays/entries could/should easily be able execute any of these so-called lower "Level 2" plays/entries, if so desired. Almost all high school teams should be able to execute successfully all aspects of the "Level 2" plays.

The final grouping of plays would be called "Level 1" plays and are not as difficult for offensive players to master the execution of them, both physically as well as mentally. Even though the techniques are still fundamentally, they may not be as complex to learn and understand in addition to being easier to physically execute.

"Level 1" plays would be lower in the scheme's complexities and the number of techniques used in the execution of this category of plays. Obviously, since these "Level 1" plays are still sound, but lack some of the methods used in the two previous more sophisticated and complex levels; these more elementary plays should be able to be utilized by any teams that use either of the two higher level plays. We feel that Middle School/Junior High teams as well as younger AAU teams or organizations should be able to utilize any of the "Level 1" plays successfully, with a possibility that some of those teams that are slightly more advanced (than other teams) could possibly use some plays located in the immediate next immediate level.

Ideas, concepts and techniques from actual plays from teams of all three levels have been used to modify or to create different combinations of the various techniques and schemes used that will help prove these entries can be successfully used. This allows the author to create numerous plays that use the various schemes to build a library of fundamentally sound plays that will be unique and will be appropriate for the wide range of teams with various ages and skill levels.

With this book having plays in these three presumed categories or levels, the book will reach out and benefit a much larger group of serious basketball coaches from elementary school age to the highest skilled levels that exists.

In addition, an experienced and resourceful coach may be able to mold some plays that include all of the offensive techniques that he/she desires could reshape a specific play that begins in one specific offensive set/alignment and reshape it so that it could begin in a different offensive/set that is more favorable to that coach and his/her coaching staff's liking.

Conversely, that innovative and creative coach may completely like the specific offensive set/alignment and favor the very same offensive actions included in a certain play, but can modify that play so that the ending spot-ups of all five players are conducive to being able to begin the final phase of the offensive attack by using a more favorable offensive continuity offense.

The "2-UP SET"

PLAYS/ENTRIES THAT END in the "3-OUT/2-IN" OFFENSIVE SPOT-UPS

After the entry/play/quick-hitter has been executed but no shots have been taken, all five players will end up in a different group of offensive locations. These "3-Out/2-In Spot-Ups" will have players moved about the court with any of the five ending up in the "Ballside Block," the "Ballside Wing," the "Weakside Block," the "Weakside Wing," and the "Point" (at the top of the key). These five positions can provide the offense with safe and easy types of ball-reversals, large gaps for dribble penetration, opportunities to deliver the ball inside to whomever (perimeter-type or post-type players) is posting up their defender on the "Ballside Block," and a player that can be a perimeter-scoring threat and a legitimate offensive rebounding threat from outside of the arc on his "offensive crashing of the boards." The "3-Out/2-In Spot-Ups also provide ample opportunities for constant and effective defensive transition responsibilities.

Diagram 19.1 illustrates the "2-UP" Set with both 01 and 02 always being the two primary ball-handlers bringing the ball into the front court toward the top of the key area. They both start the offensive play/quick-hitter/play at the two 'slot' positions. 03 always starts at the "Wing" area on the left side of the floor just outside of the arc at the FT Line extended with 04 always opposite of 03 on the right side of the floor and with 05 always beginning at the 'Nail' in the center of the FT Line.

This alignment is perfectly balanced symmetrically, allowing either 01 or 02 to begin any entry/play/quick-hitters towards either side of the floor.

As in every offensive set/alignment, each offensive play/entry will use the various types of offensive actions consisting of different cuts, various types of ball-screens, different types of off-the-ball screens, different kinds of dribbles and the various types of passes that all can be used by different players and from various locations on the floor. If the various types of actions used do not create the shot that is wanted, the movement of the offensive players will always reposition them into the necessary locations, called 'spot-ups.' Those designated 'spot-ups' for all five players will then allow the designated continuity offense(s) chosen to be able to smoothly and instantly flow into that specific continuity offense. Without any hesitation, this multiple phase attack will prevent any opposing defense from being able to regroup, reorganize or readjust, giving the offense another edge to take advantage of.

Diagram 19.1 shows 01 making the "Reverse Pass" to 02 as the beginning of Play # 1. 04 immediately makes his "Backdoor Cut" to the basket and if he does not receive the quick pass from 02, 04 continues across the lane to the opposite side of the lane. As 04 empties out of the lane and 02 dribbles to the FT Line extended, 01 makes his "Shuffle-Cut" off of 05's "Big-on-Small Shuffle-Screen." After setting the screen, 05 steps out to fill the empty 'Point' position at the top of the key. 02 looks to make the pass to 01 on his inverted cut through the lane to post up his perimeter-type defender, X1 on the new "Ballside Block."

02 has the option of making or turning down the pass to 04 on his initial Backdoor Cut to the basket. Another option would be for 02 to then kill his dribble and look to make the "Inside Pass" to 01 (now inverted on the new "Ballside Block.") With 05 now inverted out on the perimeter, the presumed biggest opposing defender, X5, has been pulled away from the basket and outside of the arc where he can no longer be a defensive threat near the basket. In addition, both 02 and 03 are also spread out on the perimeter and have kept their own defenders far from the inverted 01. These actions allow 01 to attack his completely isolated perimeter type defender in the lane.

Four of the five offensive players have moved their defenders and all five players are now in the proper "3-Out/2-In" Spot-Ups, allowing a smooth conversion into the continuity offense. See Diagram 19.1

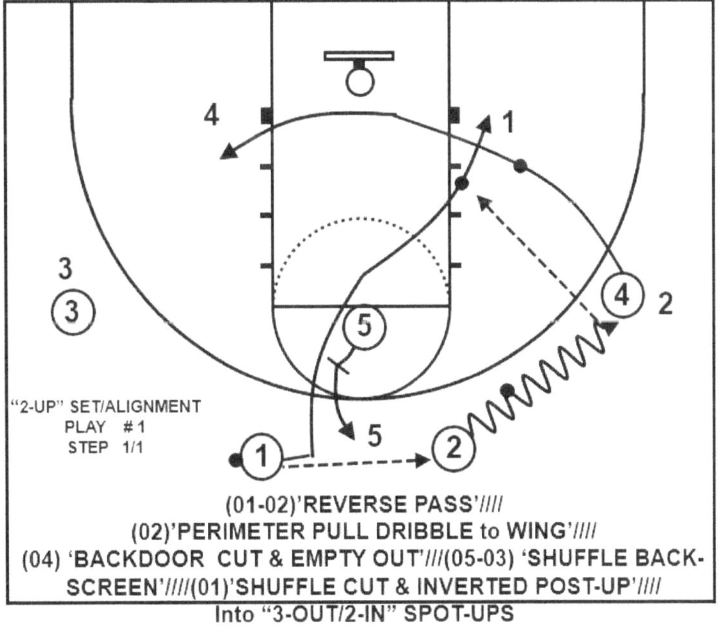

Play # 1   Diagram 19.1.

Diagram 19.2 illustrates this counter play to Play # 1. Play # 2 simply has everyone execute the same actions but has 05 and 01 switch screening and cutting assignments and their ultimate ending spot-up locations. After 01 again reverses the ball to 02, and 02 deciding to make the same dribble and again pushing 04 into the same "Backdoor Cut" (to the "Ballside Block" and out to the opposite side of the lane.) 02 turns down the pass to 04 and kills his dribble, 05 steps out to set the same "Shuffle Back-Screen" for 01. Instead, 01 "bumps the screen" to allow 05 to turn and become the designated cutter to the now empty "Ballside Block." 01 then exchanges positions with 05 and moves over to the top of the key. This allows 05 to become the designated offensive post player that has isolated his own defender in the highly successful scoring area—the "Ballside Block." The same "3-Out/2-In" Spot-Ups are again filled for the continuity offense to again immediately begin. See Diagram 19.2

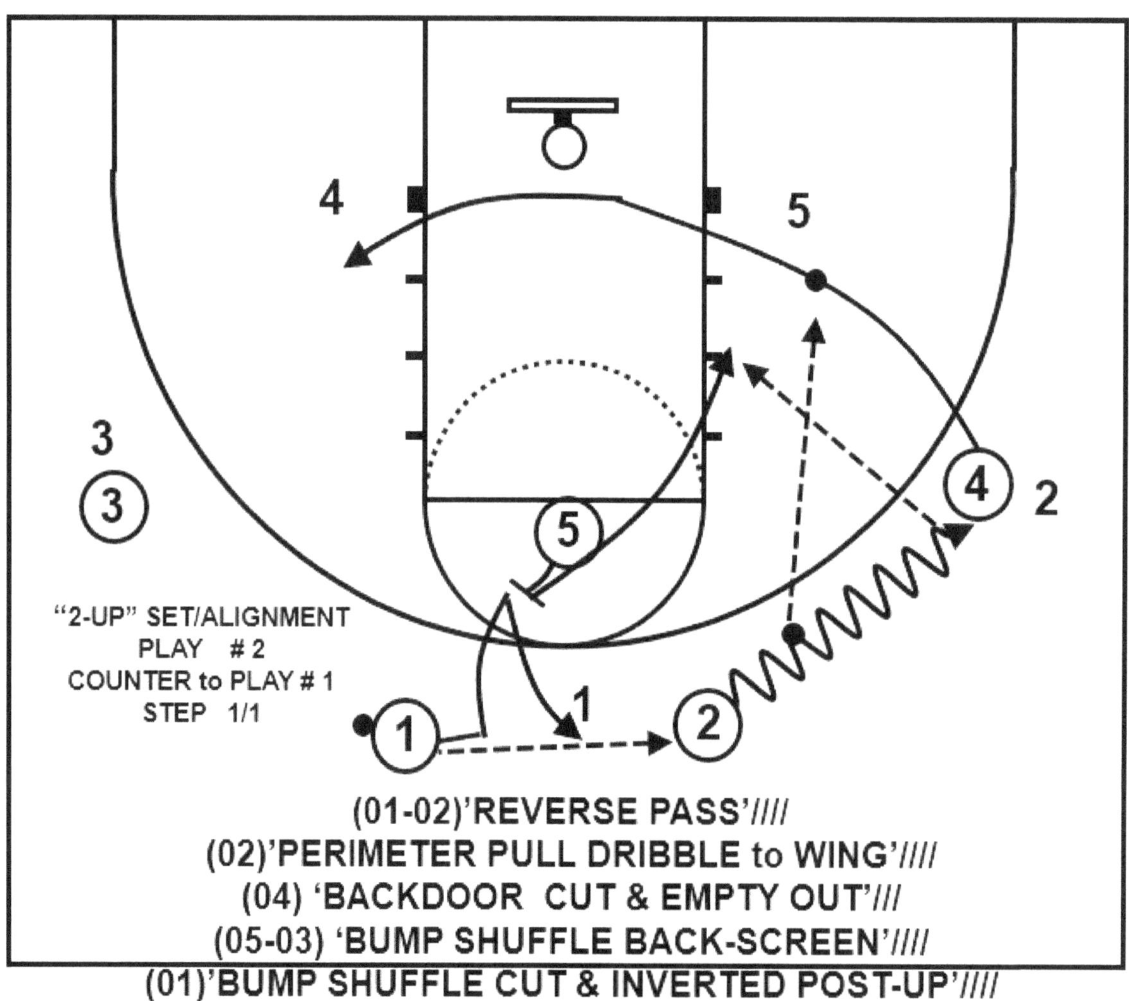

Play # 2   Diagram 19.2

Diagram 19.3 shows the beginning of Play # 3, initially appearing to be the "mirror play of Play # 1, with 02 making the "Reverse Pass" to 01 and 01 immediately pushing 03 into the same type of "Backdoor Cut" that 04 executed in the first two plays. As 01 dribbles to the FT Line extended, he looks to hit 03 on his cut to the basket.

If not open, 03 empties out, 01 kills his dribble and 02 makes his "Shuffle-Cut" off of 05's screen to the new "Ballside Block." Unlike either Play #1 or # 2, 05 then screens for 04 to break to the top of the key while 05 then stays out at the FT Line extended. Once again, a perimeter-type player, 02 gets to attack his perimeter-type defender in an inverted and isolated situation on the new "Ballside Block." In addition, 04 is allowed to "invert his post-type defender" out on the perimeter with 05 screen. This screen also pulls X5 further from the basket, freeing up 02 and 01 to attack the basket more successfully. See Diagram 19.3

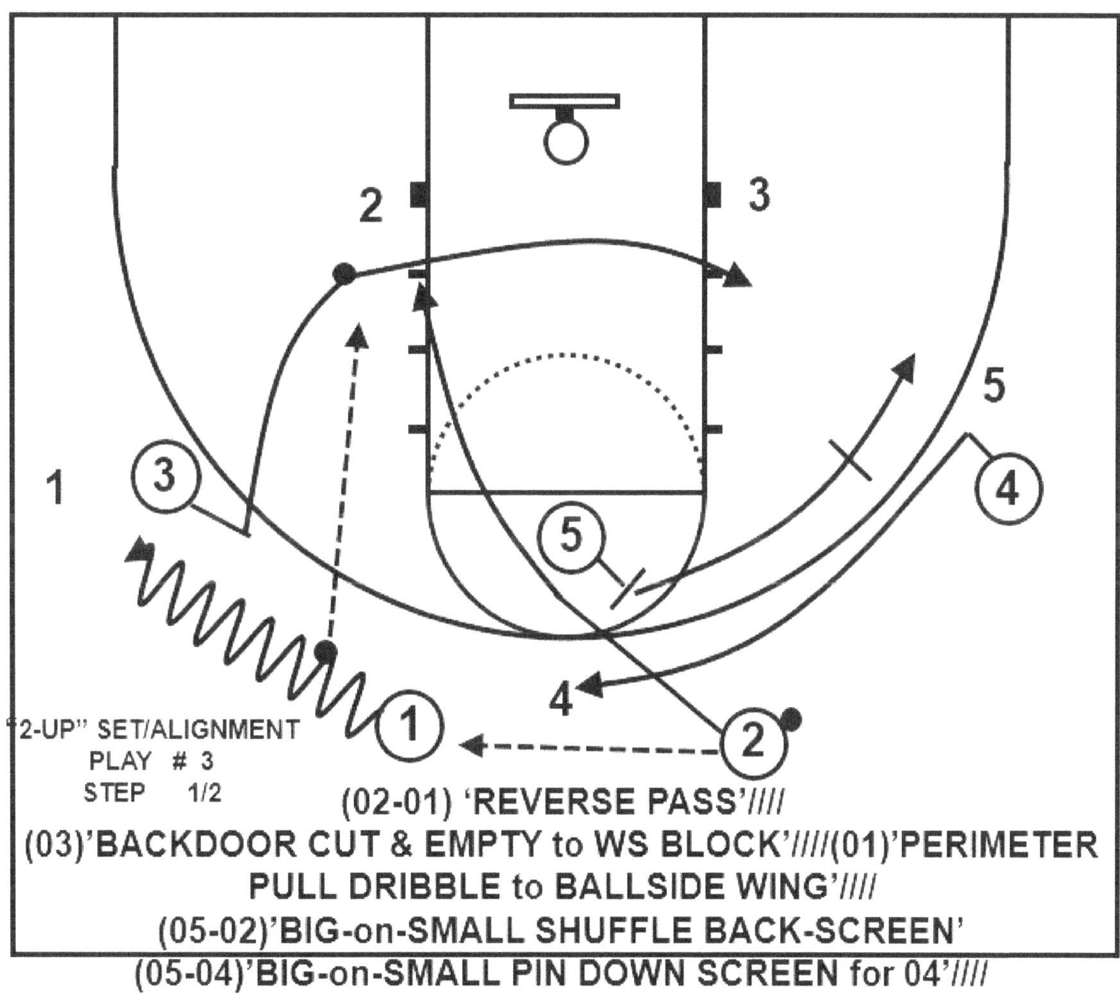

Play # 3   Diagram 19.3.

Diagram 19.4 shows the conclusion of Play # 3 with 01 reversing the ball out to 04. When 04 receives the ball from 01, 03 makes an inverted "Duck-In Cut" into the "Dotted Circle," attacking another perimeter-type defender in the middle of the lane. If not open, 04 swings the ball over to 05 at the FT Line extended. 05 looks to make the "Inside Pass" to 03 as 04 then goes to diagonally "Pin Down-Screen" for 02 to cut towards the top. If 03 or 02 do not have open shots, all players are back in the "3-Out/2-In" Spot-Ups. See Diagram 19.4

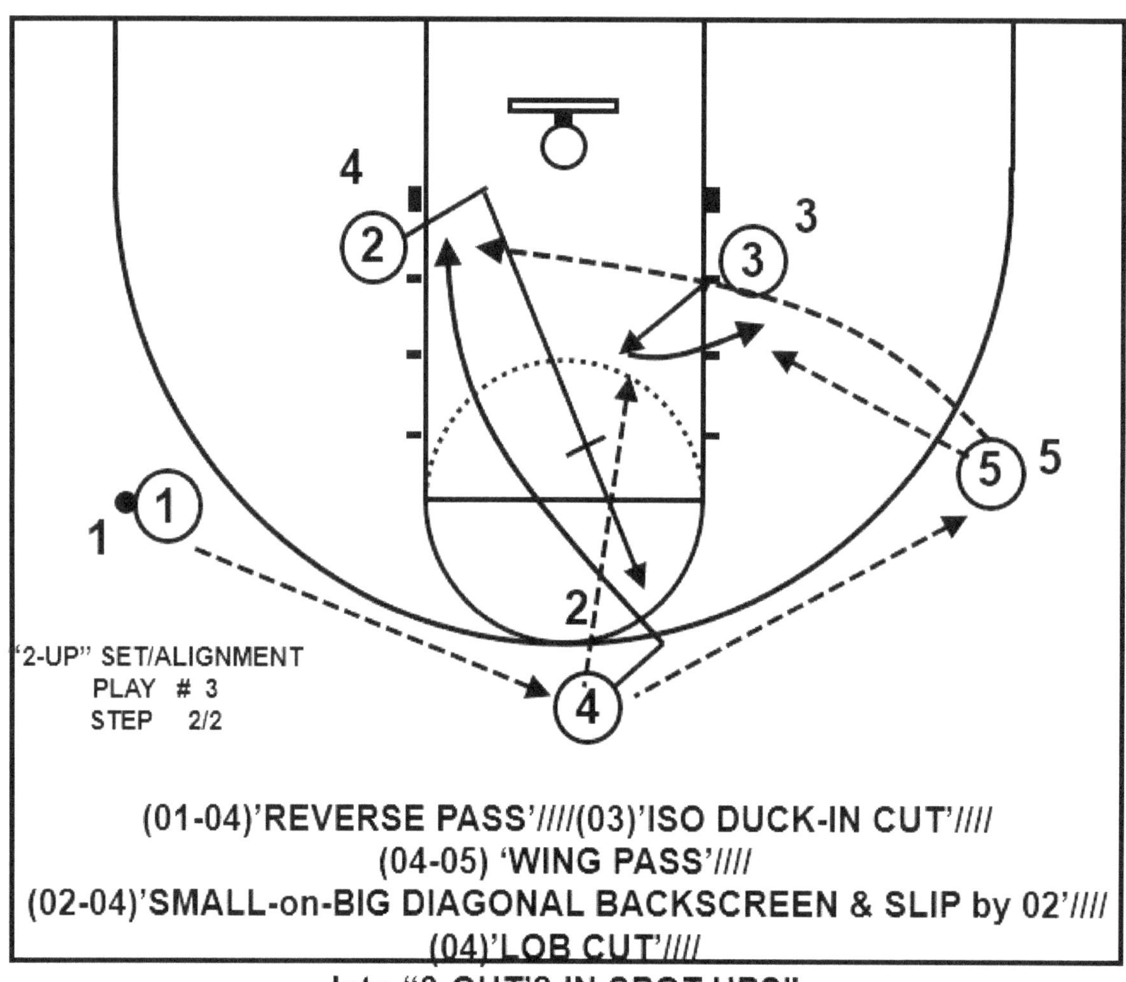

Diagram 19.4

Diagram 19.5 shows the beginning of Play # 4 with a (02-01) "Reverse Pass" that is followed by a (01-03) "Wing Pass." Immediately, 01 follows his pass to 03 to receive the "Flip Pass" back from 03. 03 then makes a "Lob Cut" to the new "Ballside Block." At the same time, 05 breaks over to set a high "Cross Screen" for 04 to break towards 03 and the ball at the "Nail." This action helps eliminate interior support defense for 03 to isolate his perimeter-type defender down on the "Ballside Block." 02 slides over to the new "Ballside Slot" location. See Diagram 19.5

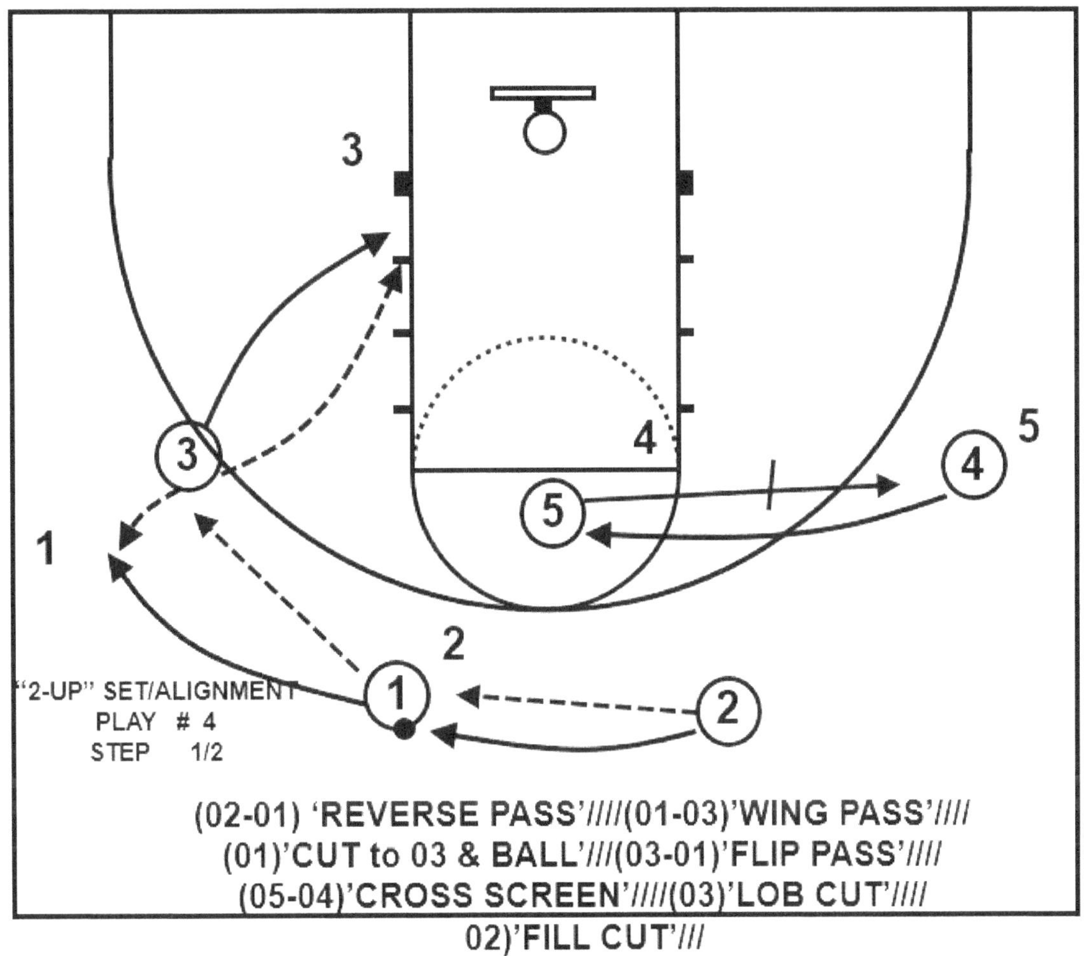

Play # 4   Diagram 19.5

Diagram 19.6 illustrates the conclusion of Play # 4 with 01 turning down the pass to 03 and making the pass out to 02. 04 steps up and out from the "Nail" to set a "Big-on-Small Ball-Screen" for 02 to dribble over to the opposite "Slot." After 02 breaks contact with 04's outside left shoulder, 04 "opens up to the ball with a "reverse pivot off of his lower right foot" and rolls down to the new "Ballside Block."

If 04 is not open, 02 makes the "Wing Pass" to the inverted 05 before then going to set an (02-03) "Pin Down-Screen" for 03 to use to break open at the top of the key. This gives the offense a potential wide open shot at the top of the key for 03 as well as helping to eliminate interior support defense that X4 needs to adequately defend 04 at the new "Ballside Block." These two series of actions attack and move defenders and reposition offensive players into the "3-Out/2-In" Spot-Ups. See Diagram 19.6

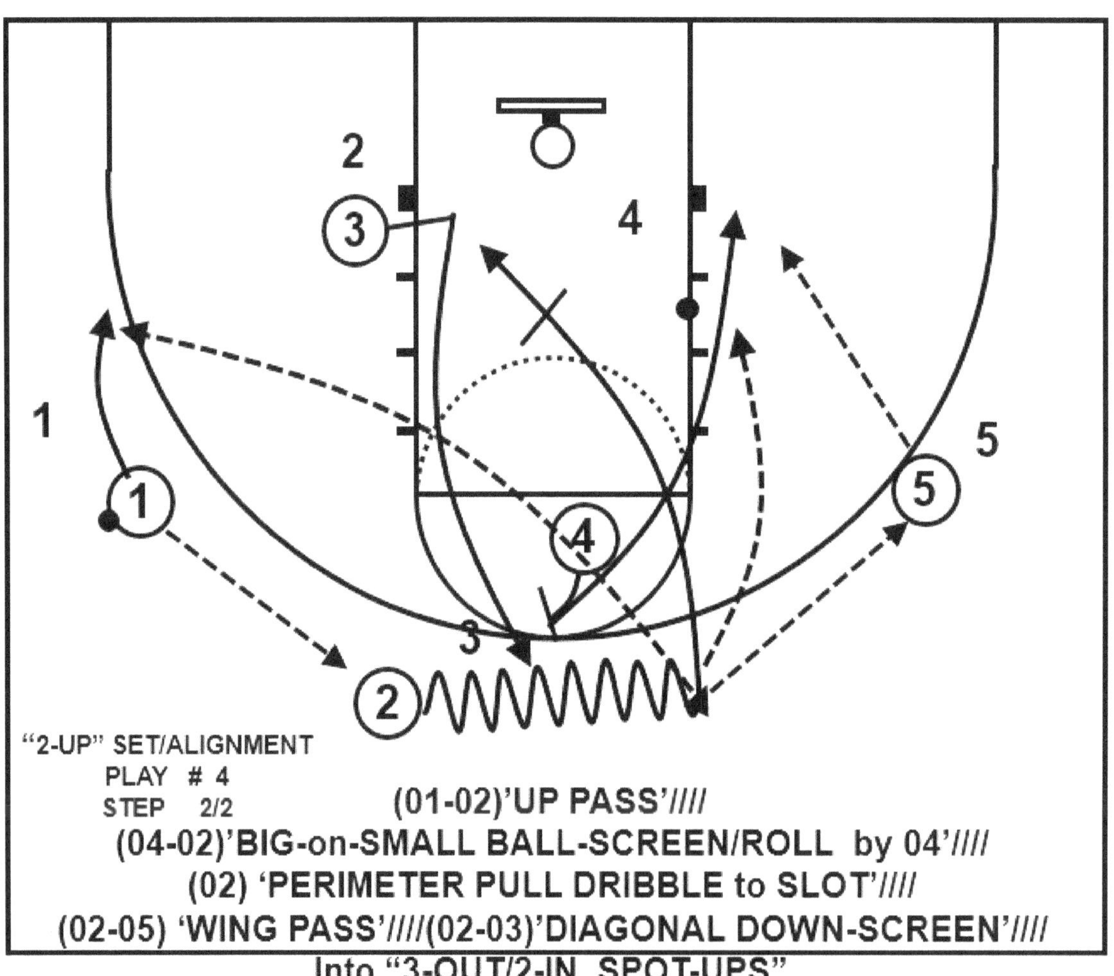

Diagram 19.6

As in all of the plays executed out of the symmetrically balanced "2-UP Set," this play could be executed towards either side of the floor. Diagram 19.7 shows the beginning of Play # 5 being started with 01 dribbling the ball towards 02. 03 makes his "Iverson Cut" over the top of 05 with 04 making his "Barkley Cut" closely cutting underneath 05's "Barkley's Screen at the 'Nail'" position. 03 and 04 can communicate with each other to change up their 'over and under' cuts for a slight change in the initial off-the-ball action.

As the "Iverson and Barkley Cuts" take place, 01 perimeter pull-dribbles directly towards 02 for a Dribble Hand-Off so that 02 can then dribble back to 01's initial side of the floor, thereby having 01 and 02 switching "Slot" locations and having the ball "re-reversed" back to the left side of the floor. See Diagram 19.7

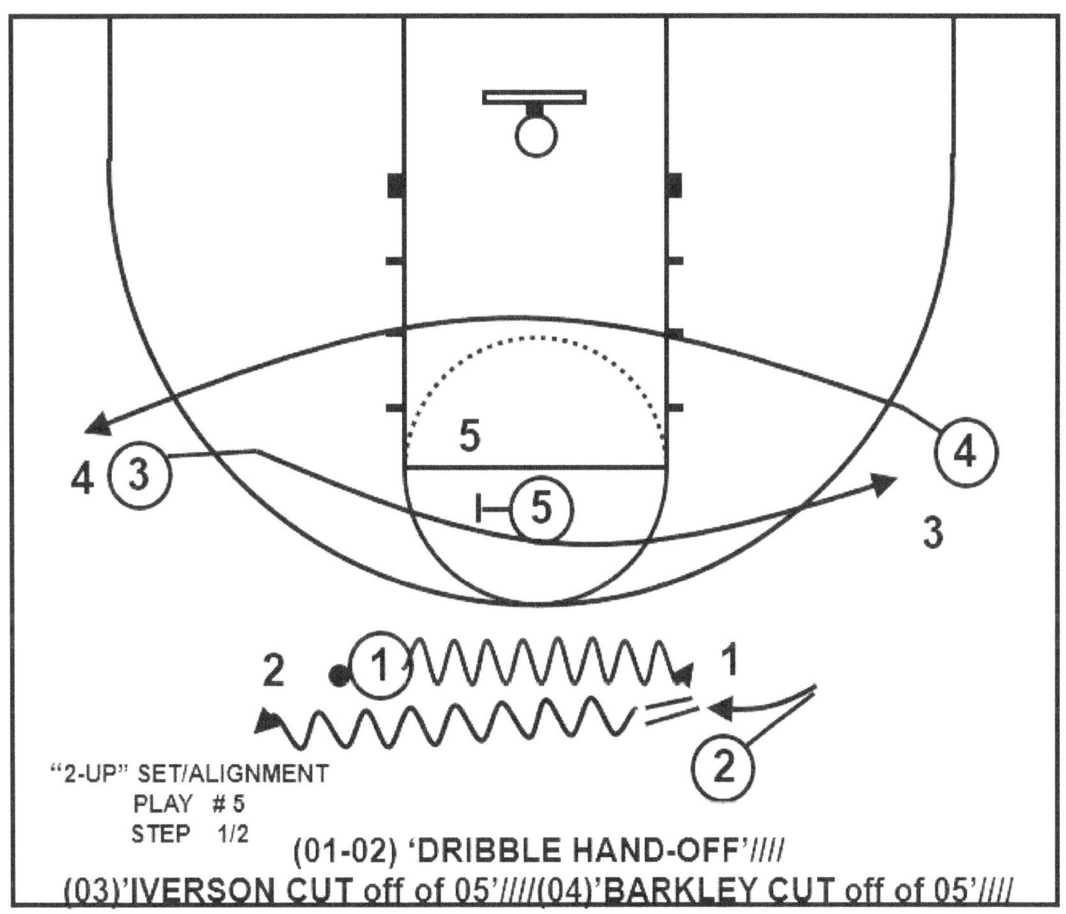

Play # 5   Diagram 19.7

From there 02 could make the "Wing Pass" to 04 with 01 making his "Shuffle-Cut" off of 05's left outside shoulder, and then diagonally across the lane to the new "Ballside Block." While 04 looks to make the "Inside Pass" to the inverted 01, 05 and 02 cut over to set a "Stagger Screen" for 03 to break to the top of the key. This gives the offense a strong perimeter scoring threat at the top of the key while also eliminating helpside defense and making 01 an isolated scoring threat on his perimeter-type defender, X1.

After the stagger-screen, 05 slips down to the "Weakside Block," while 02 curls out to the new "Weakside Wing" area. All offense players have moved into the new "3-Out/2-In" Spot-Ups for the next phase of the offensive attack to begin. See Diagram 19.8

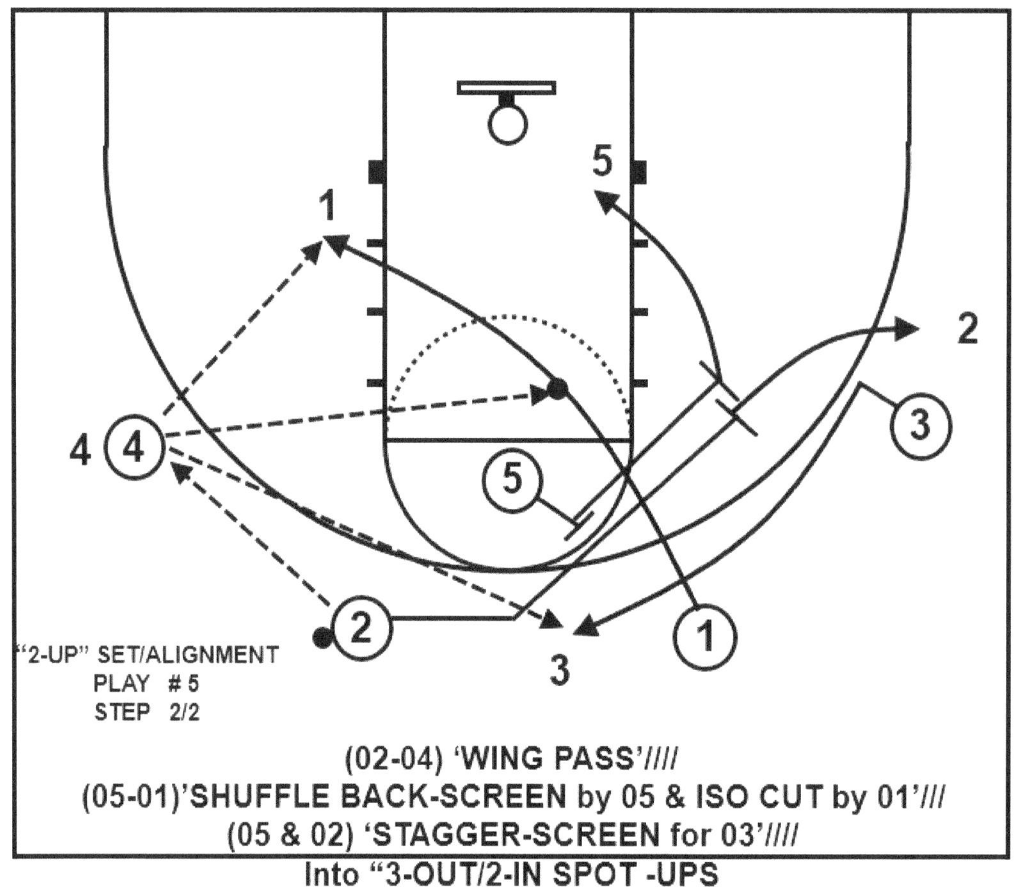

Diagram 19.8

Play # 6 is a Counter to Play # 5 with Diagram 19.9 and its actions being the same as Play # 5's Diagram 19.7. 03 and 04 make the identical "Iverson" and "Barkley" Cuts past 05 as they did in the previous play. 01 and 02 makes the same DHO exchange with 02 again moving the ball over to the same side of the floor. See Diagram 19.9

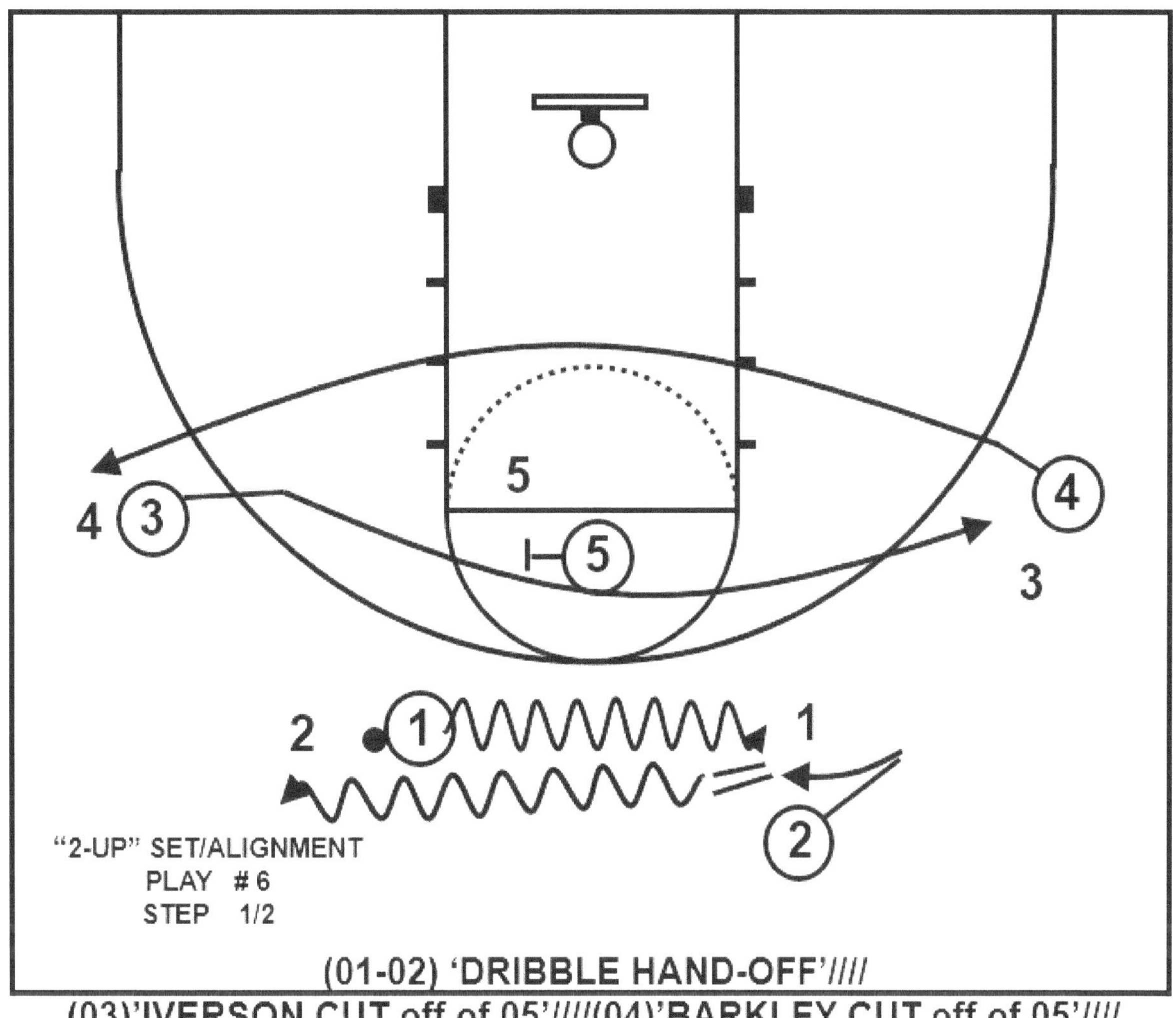

Play # 6   Diagram 19.9

Diagram 19.10 shows the change in the players' cutting responsibilities after the (02-04) "Wing Pass" is again made. 02 and 05 again angle over as if to screen for teammates on the Weakside. Instead, 02 reverses direction to make a delay isolated and inverted "Give-n-Go" Cut towards the new "Ballside Block."

Instead of being the "Shuffle-Cutter" off of 05, 01 and 05 become the "Stagger-Screeners" for 03 to use to break to the top of the key for an open "3." In this Counter Play, 02 becomes the "iso and inverted cutter and post-up player (instead of 01), 05 and 01 become the "Stagger-Screeners" for 03 instead of "05 and 02." 03 remains being the "Stagger-Screen" Cutter and the "top-of-the-key scoring threat." The same "3-Out/2-In Spot-Ups are filled for the designated continuity offense to smoothly begin. See Diagram 19.10

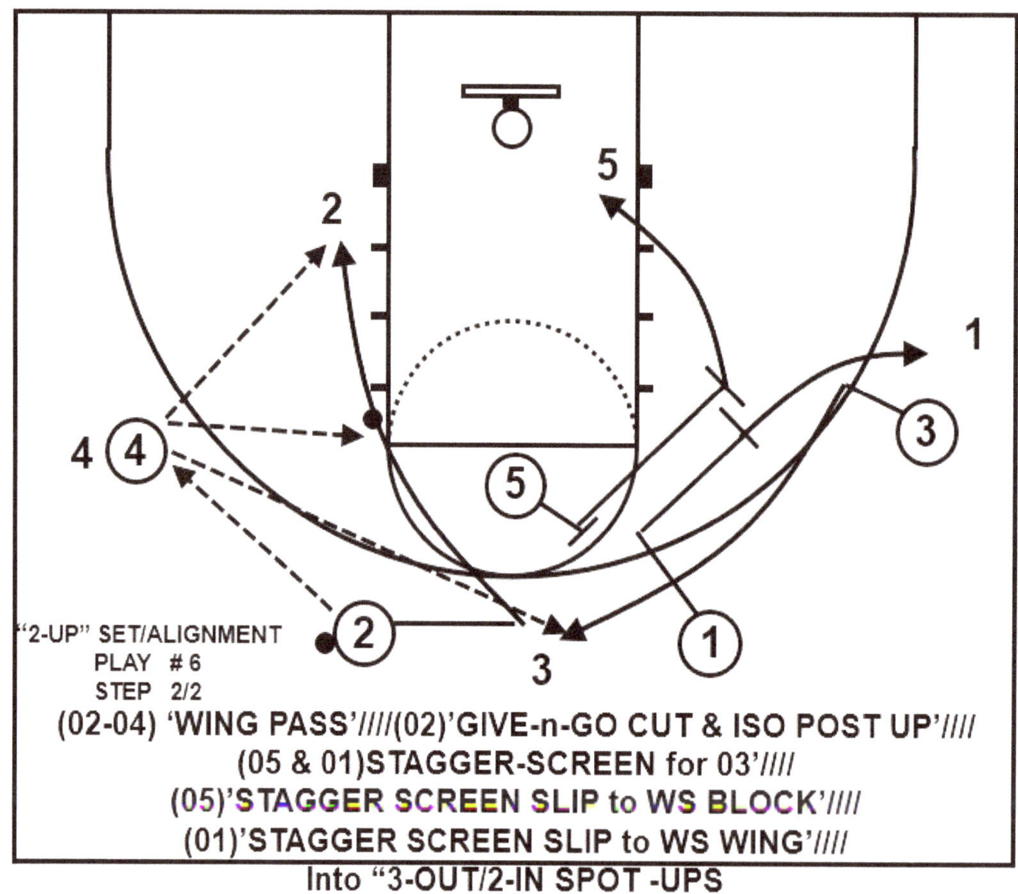

Diagram 19.10

Diagram 19.11 shows Play # 7 being another type of Counter Play to either Play # 5 and/or # 6. In this particular play, both 03 and 04 change routes of going through the middle of the floor with their respective "Iverson" and their "Barkley" Cuts. In addition, instead of an 01-02 DHO, 01 makes the pass to 02, follows his pass and then makes a "Follow (the Pass) Ball-Screen for 02 to use to move the ball to the opposite side of the floor via of a "Drag Dribble" across the top of the floor. See Diagram 19.11

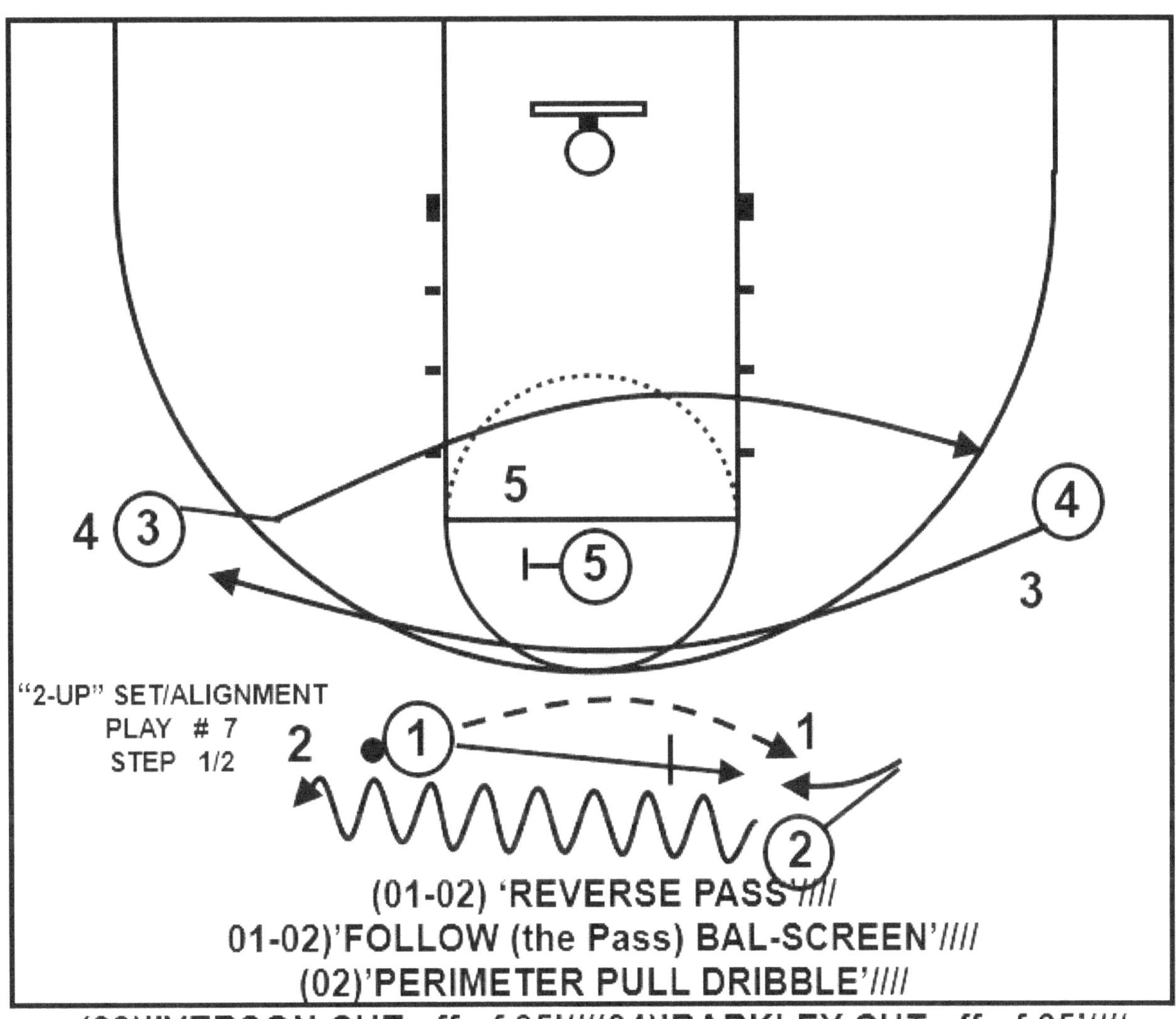

Play # 7   Diagram 19.11

Diagram 19.12 then has the following action. 02 makes the same type of (02-04) "Wing Pass" with 01 setting his defender up to use 05 as a "Shuffle Back-Screener." Instead, 01 "bumps" 05 and therefore makes 05 cutter diagonally going through the lane to iso post up his defender, X5. With 05 taking 02's responsibilities as the cutter, 02 and 01 become the pair of stagger-screeners for (the same) 03 breaking to the top of the key for his open perimeter shot at the top of the key.

After setting his part of the screen, 02 peels back down towards the "Weakside Block" and 01 curling back out to the FT Line extended. This counter-play (Play # 7) places different players in the different cutting and screening roles, but still adjusts all five players into the same "3-Out/2-In" Spot-Ups for the offense to continue. See Diagram 19.12

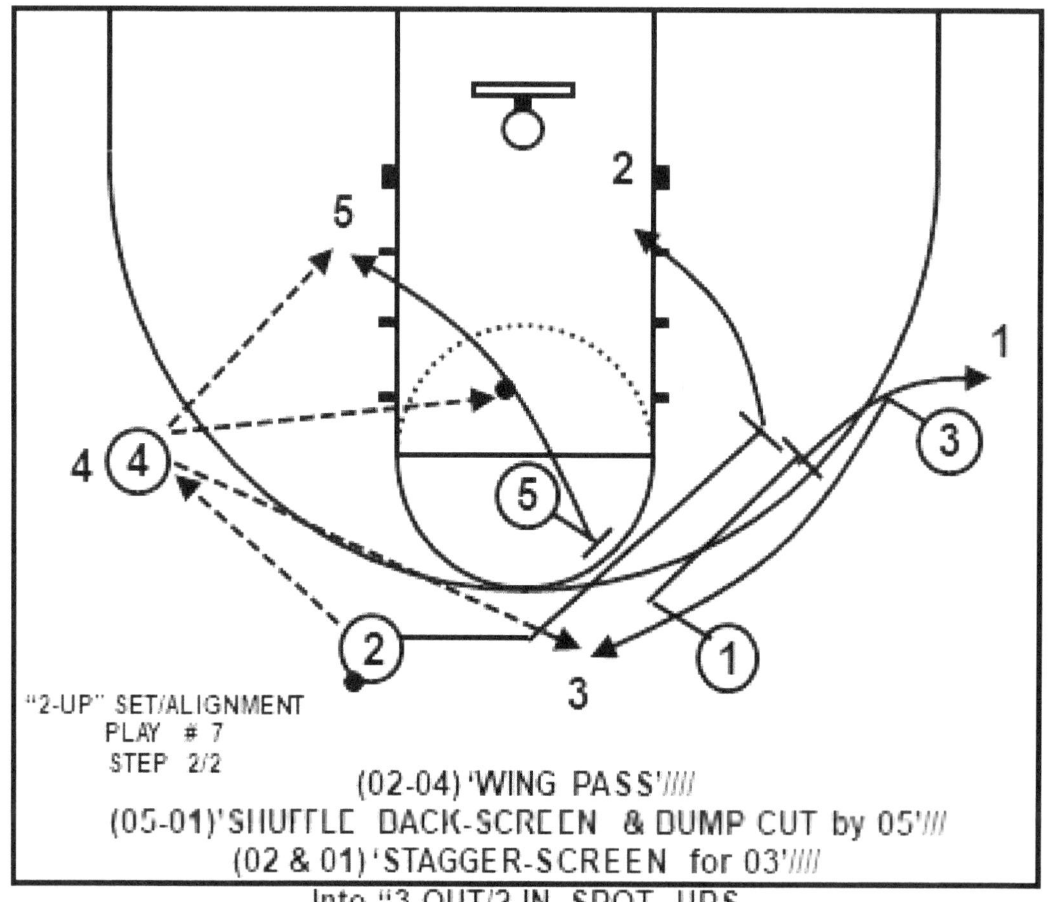

DIAGRAM 19.12

CLOSING

The "2-UP" Offensive Set/Alignment is symmetrically balanced with no clearly declared strong side of the floor. With four the five offensive personnel equally spaced on or above the FT Line extended and also stretched outside of the arc; the spacing gives these offensive players numerous opportunities to attack their defenders in the many different offensive driving gaps as well as the Deep Corner areas that are left vacant on both sides of the floor. Not only can 05 attack the High Post area but can instantly occupy either "Low Post" area on both sides of the lane with one simple and quick "Slash Cut" to the "Block." 04 has immediate access to the empty "Block" area on his specific side of the floor while being a mere two steps or so from the High Post and "Nail" location to become another interior post-up scoring threat. Many different types of plays can be executed for any of the five offensive players located in the five locations with each of those plays having the capabilities of seamlessly flowing into the various types of continuity offenses that provide the offense with a multiple prong style of attack.

CHAPTER 20
PLAYS/ENTRIES EXECUTED FROM
THE "3-ACROSS SET/ALIGNMENT"

There are many different philosophies on how to attack opposing defenses. This multiple-phase offensive system uses more than one phase/layer/wave of attack, with each phase/wave having a seamless and immediate conversion into the next phase/wave. While this system can be confusing to defenses and difficult to defend, this system can be properly taught and (physical talent, mental understand and playing experience.)

In addition, there are several types of offensive schemes and different ways within this system that offenses can attack their defensive counter-parts. Many of these can be integrated within the same offensive system that can attack defenses in various ways. The larger the number of schemes that can be successfully utilized and integrated within the same system, the greater the opportunity an offensive team can find the most efficient and productive schemes that can place both individual and the overall team in the best and most frequent "positions to succeed."

The plays/entries carefully diagrammed down to the small and seemingly unimportant 'V-Cuts' made by countless players before making their more important following cut are also described in detail.

Each play has been carefully studied and evaluated to determine which level of talent and experience must be possessed for that specific team to be able to successfully execute the play. This includes all players' physical skills as well as their mental understanding of the game. Coaches must also have the experience and the associated level of understanding of the game as well as their coaching/teaching of the nuances of each play.

The most sophisticated plays/entries would fall into the first of the three levels all based on the team's physical talents and skills, the mental capacities and the overall team's game experience. In addition, the coaching staff must have a high degree of basketball knowledge as well as very high teaching and coaching skills to educate his/her entire basketball team. The proper breakdown drills must be thoroughly utilized to hone the fundamental skills and techniques needed for individual players and the overall team to execute plays that can be efficient, productive and successful. We define this family of plays as the "Level 3 category" of plays. This "Level 3" family of plays will have a much more complex offensive scheme that would require a very high amount of physical talent as well as requiring a greater amount of the players (to execute) and the coaches (to teach and coach) mental capacities and experience needed for the offense to be efficient, productive and successful. We feel plays in our defined "Level 3" category could possibly be successful for NBA teams, definitely for college teams and also for many high schools and older AAU teams.

The next classification or level of plays would be possibly slightly lower as far as sophistication, complexity and the actual 'length' of the play (and the number of passes, cuts and screens used) in the play's overall scheme. While all "Level 2" plays in each of the chapters in this book remain to be fundamentally sound, these plays may lack the actual number of techniques/methods that are implemented within that play in comparison to the "Level 1" plays/entries. Therefore any team that successfully executes the highest "Level 1" plays/entries could/should easily be able execute any of these so-called lower "Level 2" plays/entries, if so desired. Almost all high school teams should be able to execute successfully all aspects of the "Level 2" plays.

The final grouping of plays would be called "Level 1" plays and are not as difficult for offensive players to master the execution of them, both physically as well as mentally. Even though the techniques are still fundamentally, they may not be as complex to learn and understand in addition to being easier to physically execute.

"Level 1" plays would be lower in the scheme's complexities and the number of techniques used in the execution of this category of plays. Obviously, since these "Level 1" plays are still sound, but lack some of the methods used in the two previous more sophisticated and complex levels; these more elementary plays should be able to be utilized by any teams that use either of the two higher level plays. We feel that Middle School/Junior High teams as well as younger AAU teams or organizations should be able to utilize any of the "Level 1" plays successfully, with a possibility that some of those teams that are slightly more advanced (than other teams) could possibly use some plays located in the immediate next immediate level.

Ideas, concepts and techniques from actual plays from teams of all three levels have been used to modify or to create different combinations of the various techniques and schemes used that will help prove these entries can be successfully used. This allows the author to create numerous plays that use the various schemes to build a library of fundamentally sound plays that will be unique and will be appropriate for the wide range of teams with the various ages and skill levels.

With this book having plays in these three presumed categories or levels, the book will reach out and benefit a much larger group of serious basketball coaches from elementary school age to the highest skilled levels that exists.

In addition, an experienced and resourceful coach may be able to mold some plays that include all of the offensive techniques that he/she desires could reshape a specific play that begins in one specific offensive set/alignment and reshape it so that it could begin in a different offensive/set that is more favorable to that coach and his/her coaching staff's liking.

Conversely, that innovative and creative coach may completely like the specific offensive set/alignment and favor the very same offensive actions included in a certain play, but can modify that play so that the ending spot-ups of all five players are conducive

to being able to begin the final phase of the offensive attack by using a more favorable offensive continuity offense.

The "3-ACROSS SET"

PLAYS/ENTRIES THAT END in the "3-OUT/2-IN" OFFENSIVE SPOT-UPS

After the entry/play/quick-hitter has been executed but no shots have been taken, all five players will end up in a different group of offensive spot-ups. These "3-Out/2-In Spot-Ups" will have players moved about the court with any of the five ending up in the "Ballside Block," the "Ballside Wing," the "Weakside Block," the "Weakside Wing," and the "Point" (at the top of the key). These five positions can provide the offense with safe and easy types of ball-reversals, large gaps for dribble penetration, opportunities to deliver the ball inside to whomever (perimeter-type or post-type players) is posting up their defender on the "Ballside Block," and a player that can be a perimeter-scoring threat and a legitimate offensive rebounding threat from outside of the arc on his "offensive crashing of the boards." The "3-Out/2-In Spot-Ups also provide ample opportunities for constant and effective defensive transition responsibilities.

Diagram 20.1 illustrates the "3-ACROSS" Set with 01 always being the lone primary ball-handler bringing the ball to the top of the key. 03 always starts at the "Wing" area on the left side of the floor at the FT Line extended with 02 always opposite of 03 on the right side of the floor. 04 always begins at the 'Nail' and 05 having the possibilities of starting on either side of the lane at either "Mid-Post" area. With 05 having the luxury of being able to start on either side of the floor, that allows the offense to have different cosmetic appearances and creating higher degrees of unpredictability to opposing defenses.

In the "3-ACROSS" Set, as in every offensive set/alignment, each offensive play/entry will integrate the various types of offensive actions consisting of different cuts, various types of ball-screens, different types of off-the-ball screens, different kinds of dribbles and the various types of passes that all can be used by different players and from various locations on the floor. If these various types of actions do not create the desired shot, these actions will always reposition all players into the necessary locations, called 'spot-ups' will then allow the designated continuity offense(s) chosen to be able to smoothly and instantly flow into that specific continuity offense. Without any hesitation, this multiple phase attack will prevent any opposing defense from being able to regroup, reorganize or readjust, giving the offense another edge to take advantage of.

Diagram 20.1 illustrates a Level 1 play that could be executed both towards 05's side of the floor or to the left side away from 05's initial location. If that were to happen, 05 would simply flash across the lane to the new "Ballside Mid-Post" in an "Iso Post-Up" scenario. In this case, 01 dribbles towards 05's initial side to receive 02's "Big-on-Small Ball-Screen" and continues to the FT Line extended on the new "Ballside Wing." 01 immediately looks for 05 trying to 'shape up' and gain a 'position advantage' over the lone post defender. The next presumed biggest defender is X4 and he is about to see his own man step up to set a (04-02) "Big-on-Small (Back-)Screen the (Ball-)Screener. 02 should rub his perimeter-type defender off of 04's outside right shoulder and curl to the rim, looking for 01's "Lob Pass." To prevent his defender from still trying to help out on the interior and to fill the necessary spot-ups, 04 then slips his screen to invert his defender to the top of the key. 01 looks for 05 inside, for 02 on his cut, then for a possible "Skip Pass" to 03 on the wide open weakside of the floor or the simple and short (01-04) "Reverse Pass." No shots created will still place all players in the necessary proper "3-Out/2-In Spot-Ups" for Play # 1 to have a seamless continuation of the offensive attack. See Diagram 20.1

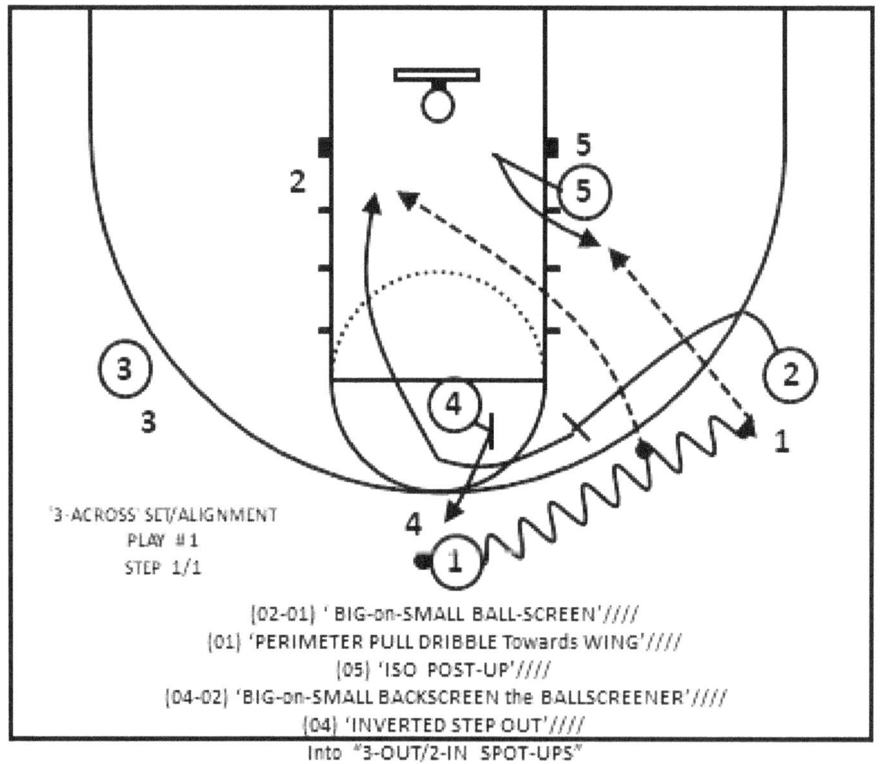

Play # 1   Diagram 20.1

Diagram 20.2 illustrates a second Level 1 play very similar to Play # 1. This shows 02 again setting the "Ball-Screen" for 01 to use to dribble the ball to the FT Line extended. 05 either "iso posts up his defender" or he flashes across the lane to attack his defender on the new "Ballside Block."

After 02 ball-screens for 01, both 02 and 04 break over to the offside wing to then set a "Stagger-Screen" for 03 to get open at the top of the key. 04 then slips his part of the stagger-screen and slides down to the new "Weakside Block" while 02 then slips outside the arc to the new "Weakside Wing." With 01 looking to make passes primarily to 05 and 03, the "3-Out/2-In" Spot-Ups are filled for a smooth transition into the designated continuity offense. See Diagram 20.2

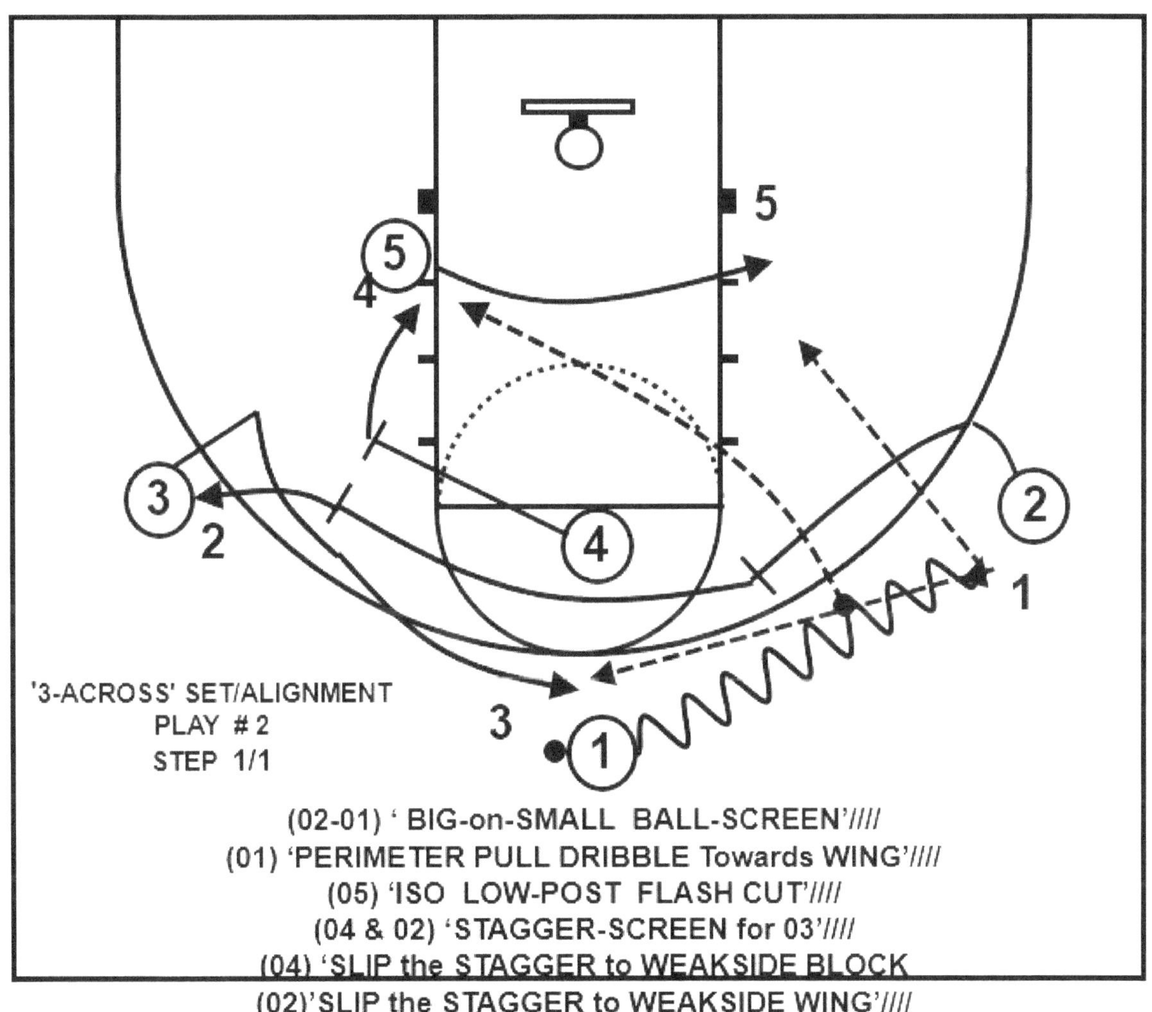

Play # 2   Diagram 20.2

Diagram 20.3 illustrates another Level 1 play with the play having to go towards the side opposite of where 05 begins. In this case 02 again steps up to set a "Ball-Screen" for 01 to use. As 01 "dribble-scrapes" off of 02's outside left shoulder, 02 "reverse pivots" off of his right lower foot and rolls down the lane to invert and isolated his perimeter-type defender, X2. At the same time, 04 breaks diagonally down to set a "Pin Down-Screen" for 05 to use to break up to the top of the key. This two-man option not only gives 05 an opportunity for an open shot, but momentarily eliminates any possible helpside defense that X2 would need to successfully stop 02 from scoring on the (isolated and inverted) "Block." 04 remains at the new "Weakside Block" and 03 floats on the "Weakside Wing," giving 01 multiple passing options. These actions and movements again reposition all five offensive players in the "3-Out/2-In" Spot-Ups. See Diagram 20.3

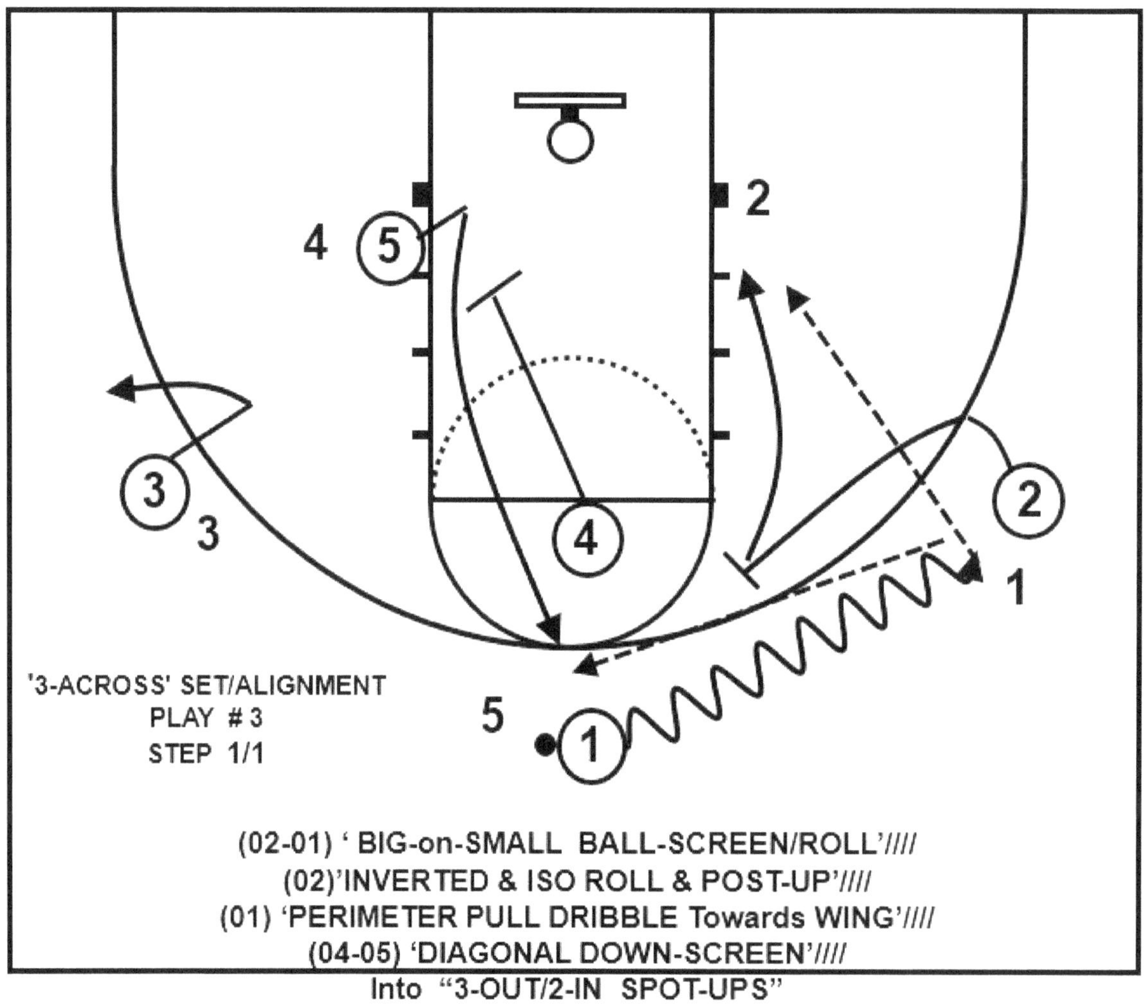

Play # 3   Diagram 20.3

Diagram 20.4 illustrates the first Level 2 play in this package, called Play # 4. With 05 being able to start on either side of the lane, 05 starts on the left side of the lane in this play. 01 must always dribble towards the side that 05 starts. As 01 approaches 03, 05 makes an "Iso Duck-In Cut" into the "Dotted Circle" area, looking to receive 01's pass and attack his isolated and inverted perimeter defender, X3. While maintaining his dribble, if 01 cannot make deliver the ball to 05 with either a "Lob Pass" or "Inside Bounce Pass," 01 continues advancing the ball towards 03. At the same time, 02 breaks diagonally over to align next to 04, now located at the top of the key. See Diagram 20.4

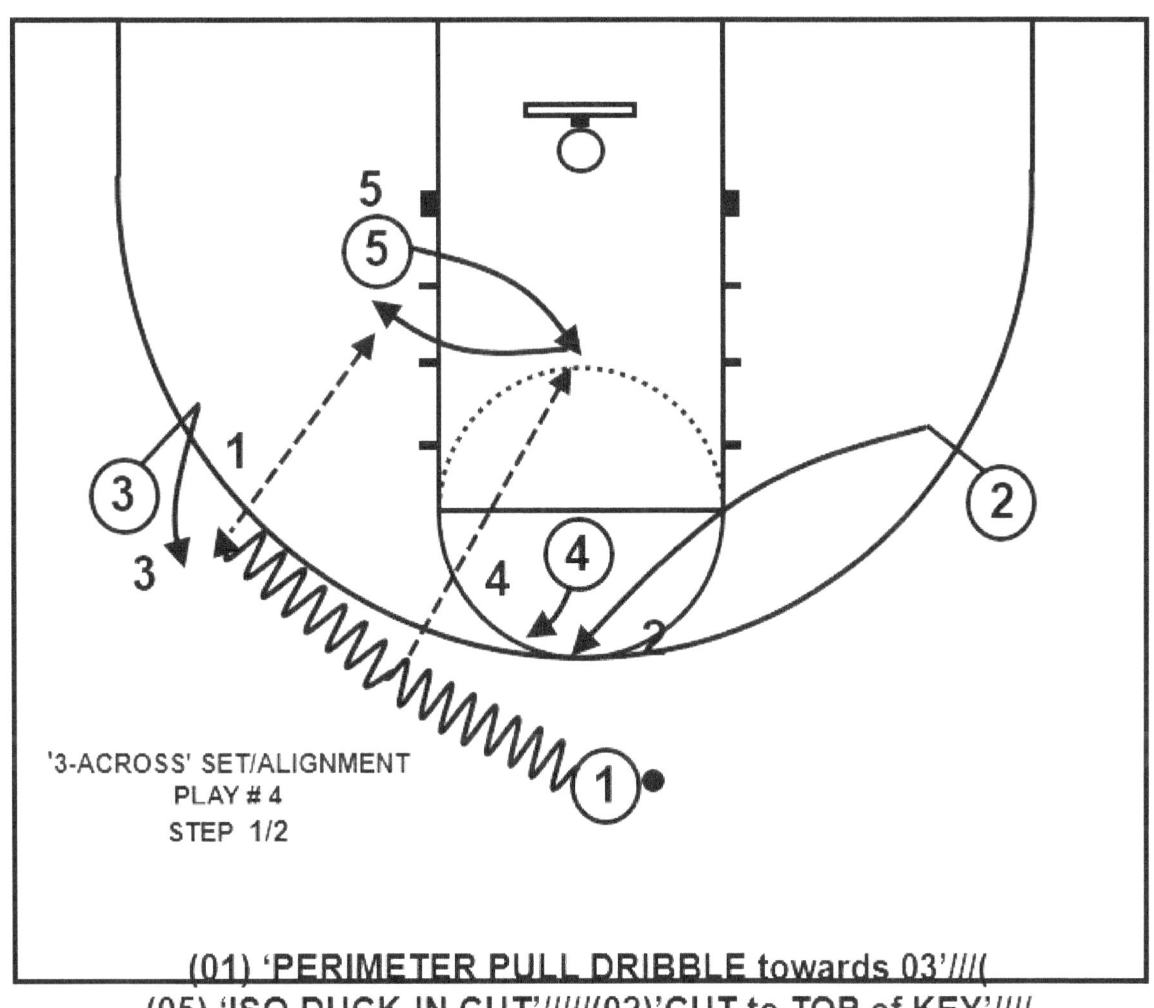

Play # 4   Diagram 20.4

Diagram 20.5 shows 03 faking a possible (01-03) DHO and continuing out to the vacant "Slot" location. If 01 does not make the "Inside Pass" to 05, 01 then makes the "Up Pass" to 03. Upon receiving the (01-03) "Up Pass," 03 starts his dribble out towards the top of the key. 03 continues his dribble and "dribble-scrapes" off of 02's top left shoulder to deflect his defender so he can advance the ball towards the opposite "Wing" area.

As 03 breaks contact with 02, 02 makes a "Reverse Pivot" off of his lower right foot to open up to 02 and the ball and "roll" down the lane. At the same time, 04 makes a "Front Pivot "off of his lower right foot" to diagonally break down to set a "Diagonal Pin Down-Screen" for 05 to use to break to the top of the key. This places 02 on the new "Ballside Block" while 04 remains at the new "Weakside Block," and 05 now at the "top of the key." 03 and 01 end up at the two "Wing" locations; correctly filling the "3-Out/2-In" Spot-Ups. See Diagram 20.5

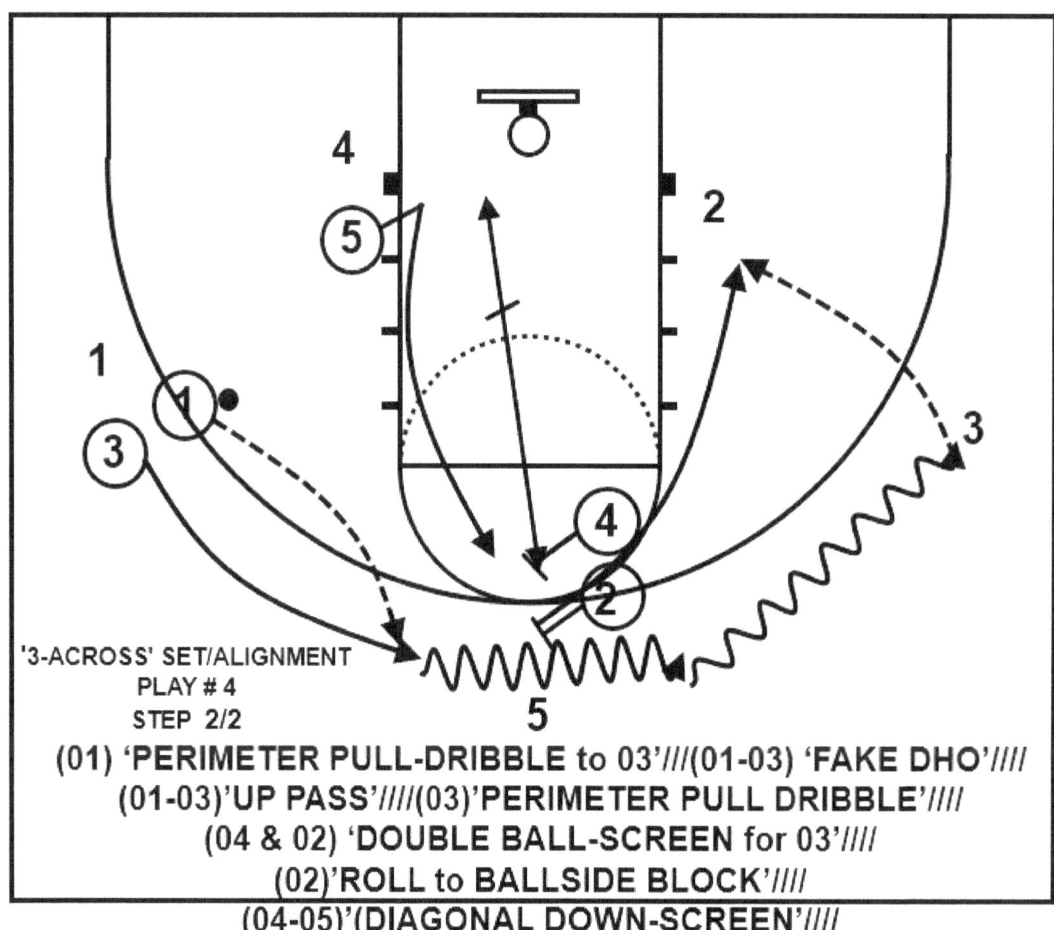

Diagram 20.5

Diagram 20.6 illustrates the beginning of Play #5 as a Level 1 play, with 01 perimeter pull-dribbling towards the right side of the floor. There 02 can step up and set a "Big-on-Small Ball-Screen" for 01 to continue dribbling to the FT Line extended. After setting the screen with 01 "dribble scraping" off of 02's top left shoulder, 02 slips his screen with a "front pivot" off of his lower right foot. There 02 then remains at the top of the key with "getting his feet and hands prepared" for a "catch and shoot." Many coaches define 02's simple action as "Pick and Pop" action.

As 01 'dribble-scrapes' off of 02's outside left shoulder, 04 starts to drift away from the ball before then scraping off of the "Big-on-Small Diagonal Back-Screen" set by 05. While 04 posts up his defender in an isolated situation on the "Ballside Block," with 05 slipping his screen and going to the "Weakside Slot." 01 looks first to deliver the ball to 04 with the closest defensive support defender, X3, near the FT Line on the new weakside of the court. See Diagram 20.6

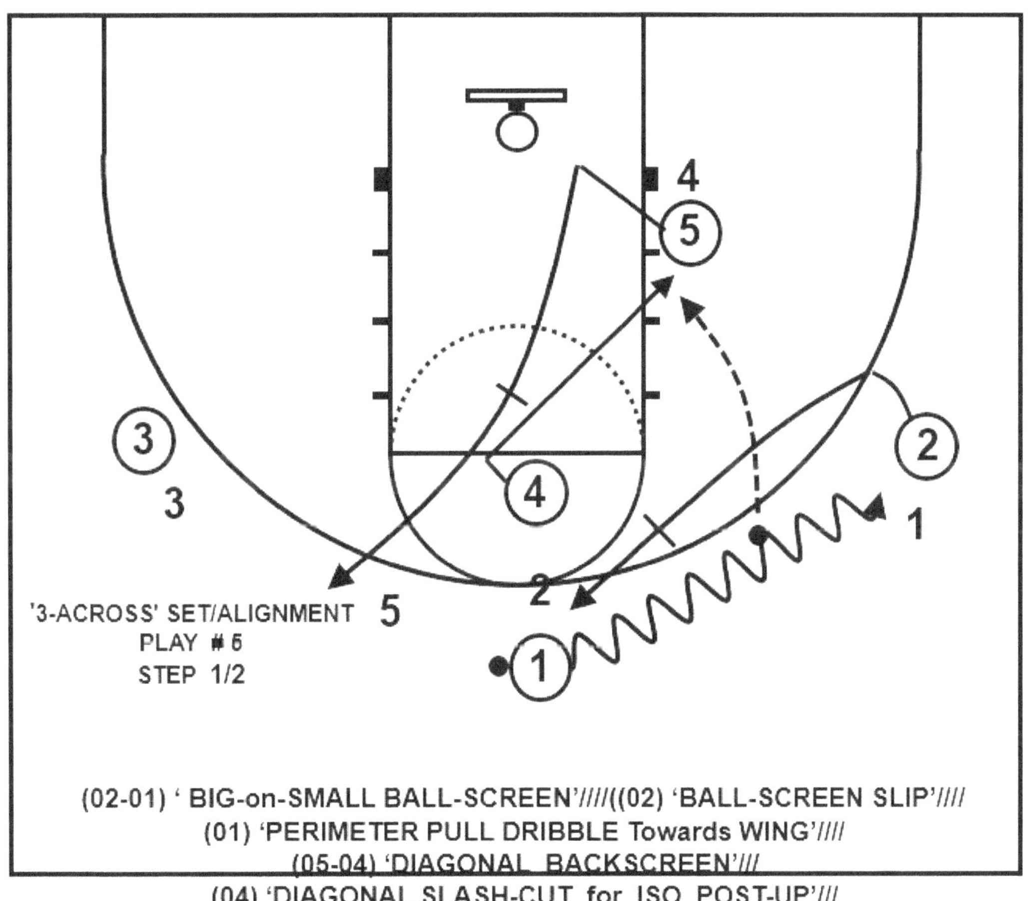

Play # 5   Diagram 20.6

Diagram 20.7 illustrates the continuation of Play # 5. If 01 turns down the "Inside Pass" to 04 as well as a possible "Skip Pass" to 03 on the entirely vacant weakside of the floor, 01 snaps the ball back out to 02 at the top of the key. When the ball first reaches 02 or 03's hands, 04 immediately flashes across the lane to the opposite side of the floor to post up and look to receive the ball from either teammate.

If 02 receives the ball from 01 and does not have an immediate 'catch and shoot' or 'catch and pass' opportunity, 05 steps over from the "Slot" to set a "Big-on-Small Ghost Ball-Screen" for 02. 05 then makes a "Rim-Run" to the basket while 04 has crossed to the other side of the lane. 02 looks to make the "Inside Pass" to 05 and without the use of an actual screen by 05; 02 quickly swings the ball over to 03.

After 02 makes the pass to 03, 01 then steps up to set a "Small-on-Big Flare-Screen" for 02 to use, with 02 "Flare-Cutting to the "Weakside Wing." 01 then slips his flare-screen to remain at the top of the key (with a "front pivot off of his lower right foot" and "gets his hands ready" for a (03-01) "Reverse Pass," allowing for a possible quick "catch and shoot." 03 has his primary pass receivers being 04, now posted up directly below him on the "Block," an (03-02) "Skip Pass" or a safe "Reverse Pass" to 01, now at the top of the key. If either 01 or 02 receive the pass from 03, the actual play is over, but all players are now in the proper "3-Out/2-In Spot-Ups" for the designated continuity offense to seamlessly maintain the attack on the defense. See Diagram 20.7

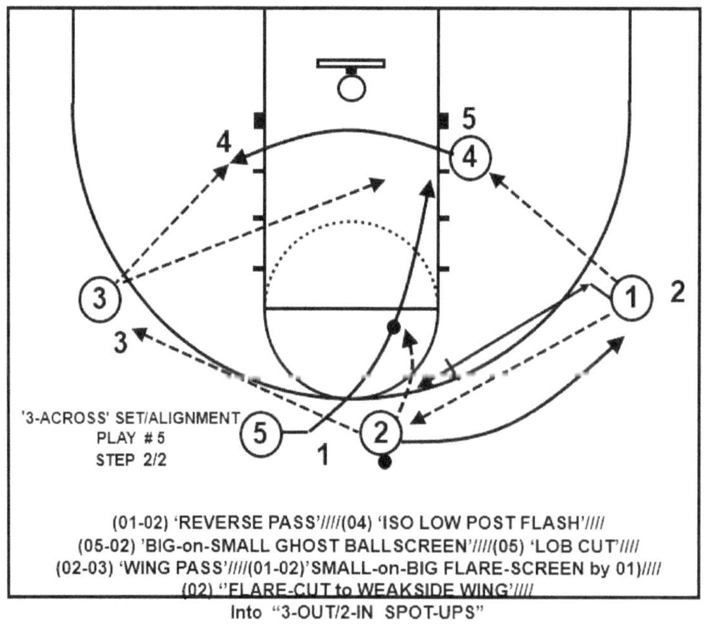

Diagram 20.7

Diagram 20.8 illustrates the beginning of Play # 6, another Level 2 play, with 01 starting to take his dribble towards 02 and with 05 making a "Pipe Cut" up the lane and off of 04's "Pin Screen" at the "Nail." As 01 continues his dribble towards 02, this action forces 02 to make a "Backdoor Cut" to the now empty "Ballside Block." This gives 02 an opportunity to not only "isolate" but to also "invert" his perimeter-type defender, X2, on the completely vacant new "Ballside Block." The two biggest defenders, X5 and X4, are vertically pulled further from the basket and from 02, giving the advantage to the offense. See Diagram 20.8

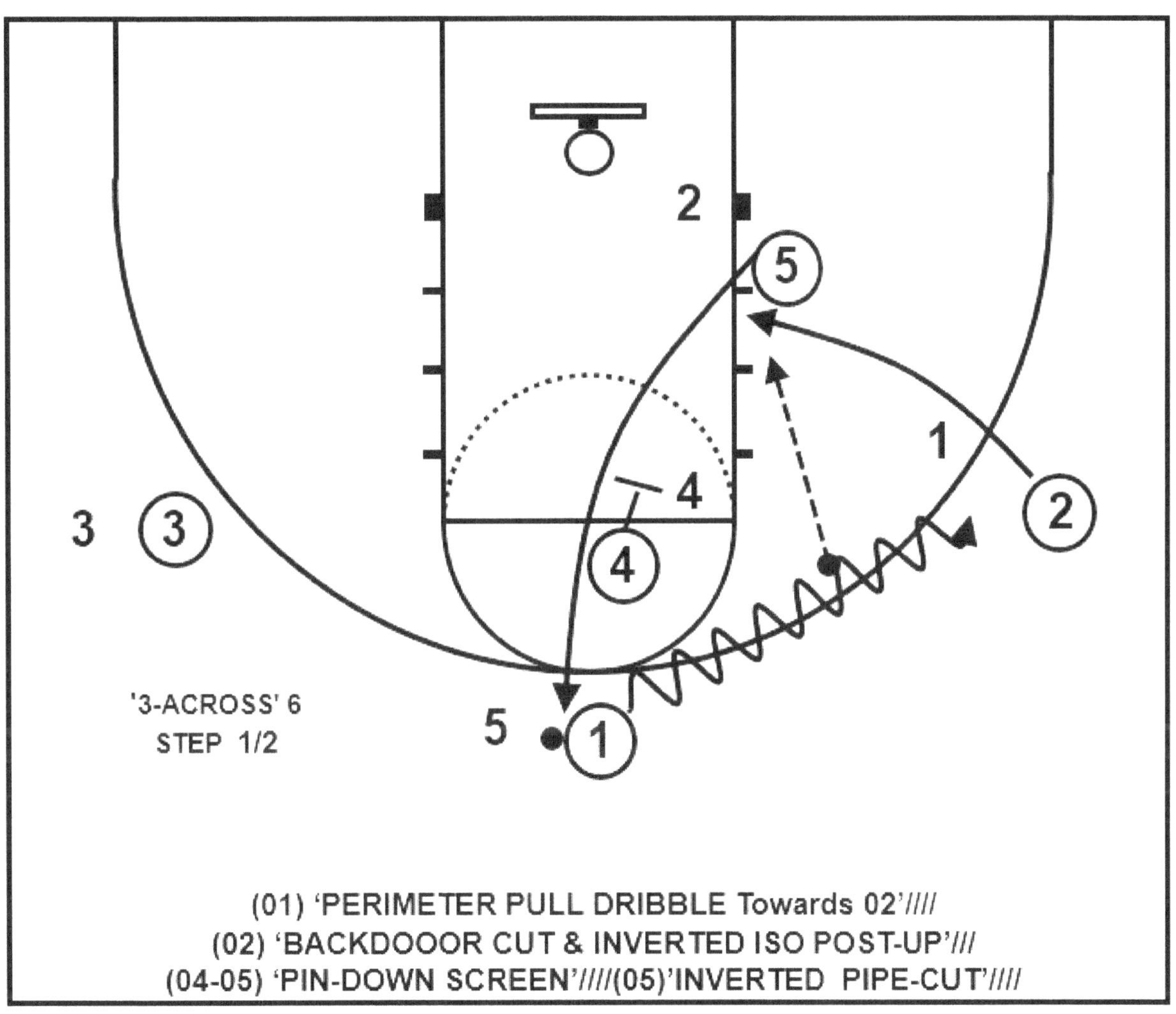

Play # 6   Diagram 20.8

Diagram 20.9 shows how 01 looks to make the "Inside Pass" to 02 (with a "Bounce" or a "Lob Pass" to 02. It then shows 01 having to reverse the ball to 05 at the top of the key, with 05 then quickly swinging the ball on over to 03 on the opposite side of the floor. When 05 makes the "Wing Pass" to 03, 05 and 04 first break towards the ball and 03 for two steps before then cutting diagonally down to set a "Stagger Screen" for 02 to use. 02 sets his defender up before then breaking up and scraping off of 05's right shoulder at the top of the key for an open '3 Pt.' shot. After screening X2, 04 slips to the new "Ballside Block" while 05 moves towards the "Weakside Block." With 03 and 01 horizontally stretching the defense at the two "Wing" positions, the "3-Out/2-In" Spot-Ups are filled for the next phase of the offense to smoothly begin. See Diagram 20.9

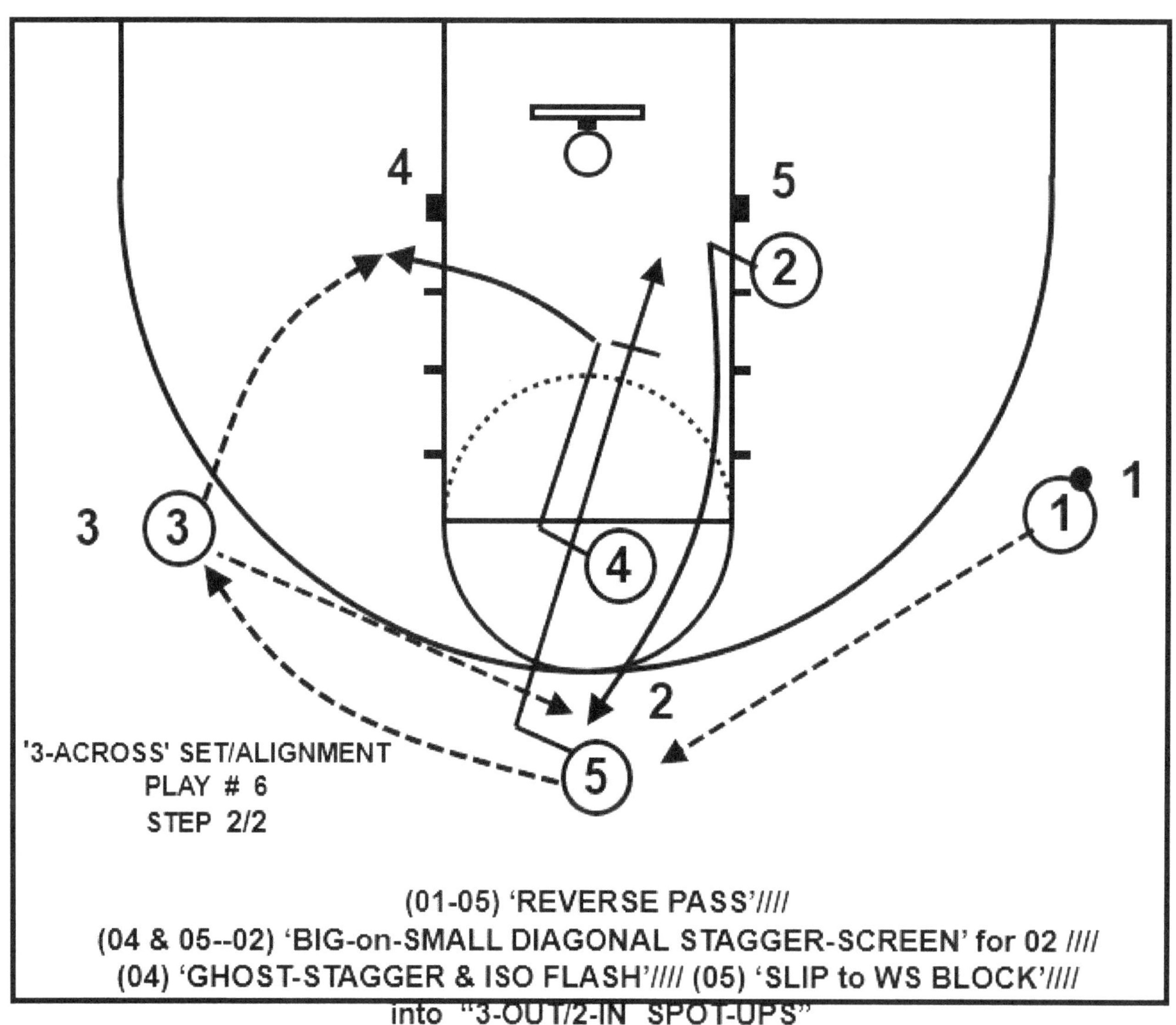

Diagram 20.9

Diagram 20.10 illustrates Play # 7—a Level 2 Play out of the same "3-ACROSS" Set. In this play, 01 dribbles away from 05's initial side of the floor as 03 makes a "Iverson Cut" over the top of 04 and to the opposite "Wing Area." At the same time, 05 flashes across the lane to "Iso Post-Up" his defender. Also, 03's "Iverson Cut" forces 02 to move down to replace 05 at the newly declared "Weakside Block." After 03 scrapes off of 04, 04 then pops out to the top of the key. If 01 does not make the "Inside Pass" to 05, 01 reverses the ball to 04, who has inverted his post-type defender out behind the arc at the top of the key. This action pulls the presumed second biggest defender, X4, further away from the basket, giving 05 an even greater advantage over his defender, X5. Diagram 20.10

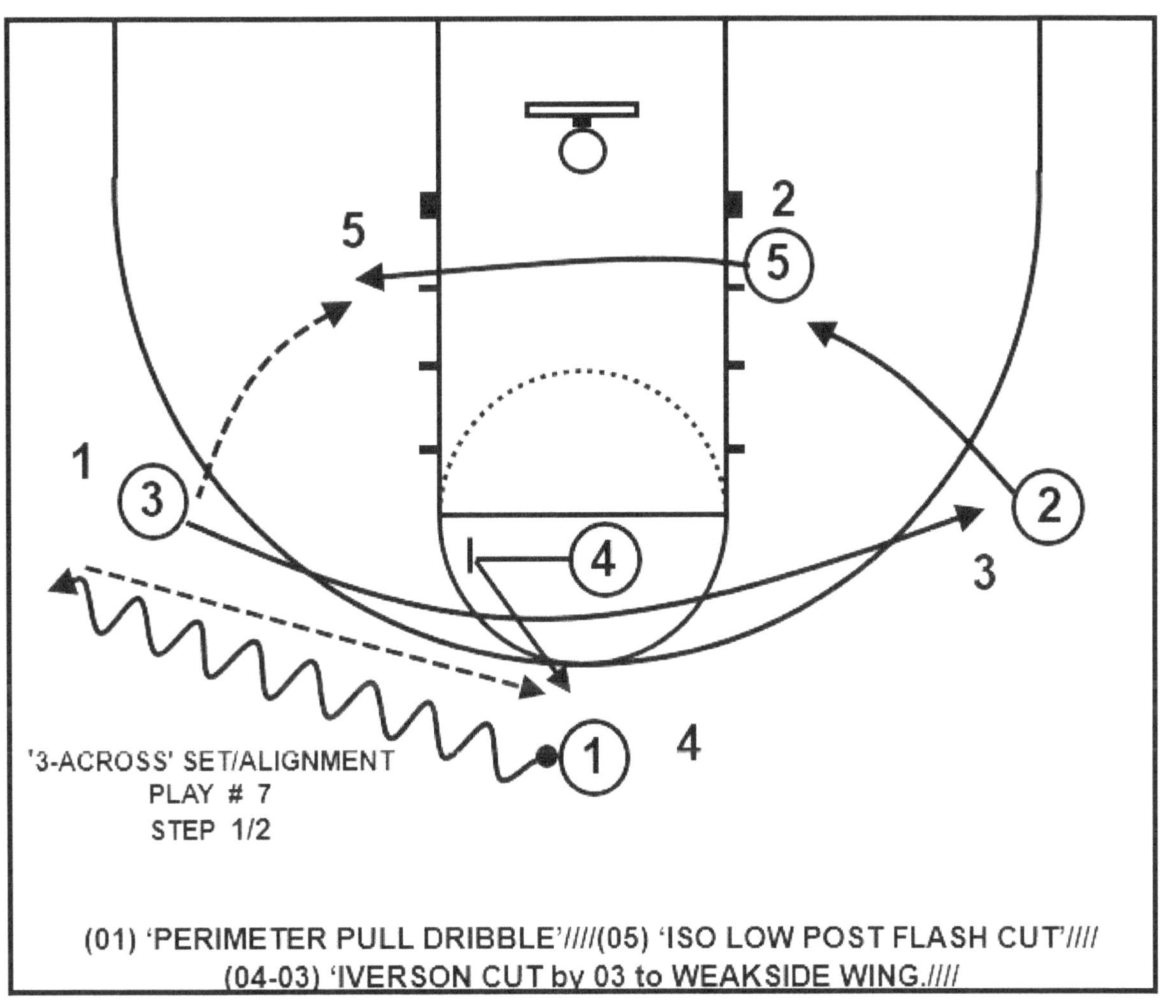

Play # 7   Diagram 20.10

When 01 turns down the pass to 05, 01 should make the quick pass to 04 at the top of the key. 04 should then quickly swing the ball on over to 03 at the "Wing area" on the opposite side of the floor. As the (04-03) pass is made, 02 immediately steps up to set a "Small-on-Big Diagonal Back-Screen" for 04 to use to rub his defender off of the screen and to "Iso Post Up" his defender on the new "Ballside Block." 02 then slips his screen and pops to the top of the key (almost identical to "Pick-n-Pop" action and footwork techniques.

At the same time, to eliminate any helpside defense that X4 will need, 01 sets a "Pin Down-Screen" for 05 to use as 05 pops out to the FT Line extended. This screen extends, vertically and horizontally stretches and pulls the presumed biggest defender further from 04, the basket and the ball. This action also attacks various defenders and also repositions all five offensive players into the "3-Out/2-In" Spot-Ups." See Diagram 20.11

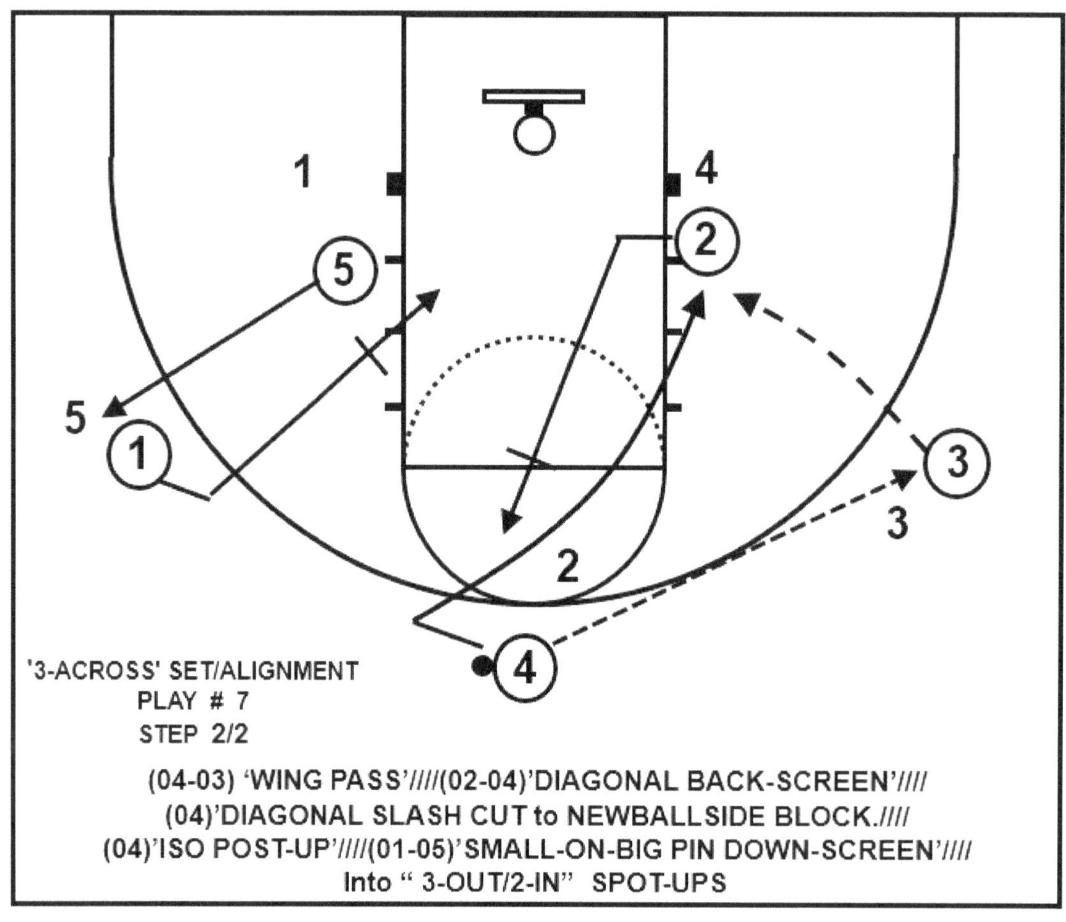

Diagram 20.11

Diagrams 20.12 and 20.13 show the entire Play # 8, another Level 2 play, that is a Counter Play to Play # 7. In this entry, 05 must flash to the side of the ball that 01 dribbles towards if he hasn't already started there. Again, as 01 approaches 03, 03 again makes the same "Iverson Cut" over the top of 04 to the opposite wing. This forces 02 to again move down to the vacated "Block" on the right side of the floor. After "Iverson Screening" for 03, 04 steps out to the top of the key to again invert his post-type defender.

01's first option is to deliver the ball to 05, down on the newly declared "Ballside Block." If 05 is not open, 01's next option is to make a (01-04) "Reverse Pass" out to 04. 04 also looks to hit 05 down low on his "Iso Duck-In Cut" into the middle of the lane or a "Wing Pass" back to 01 on the "Wing." See Diagram 20.12

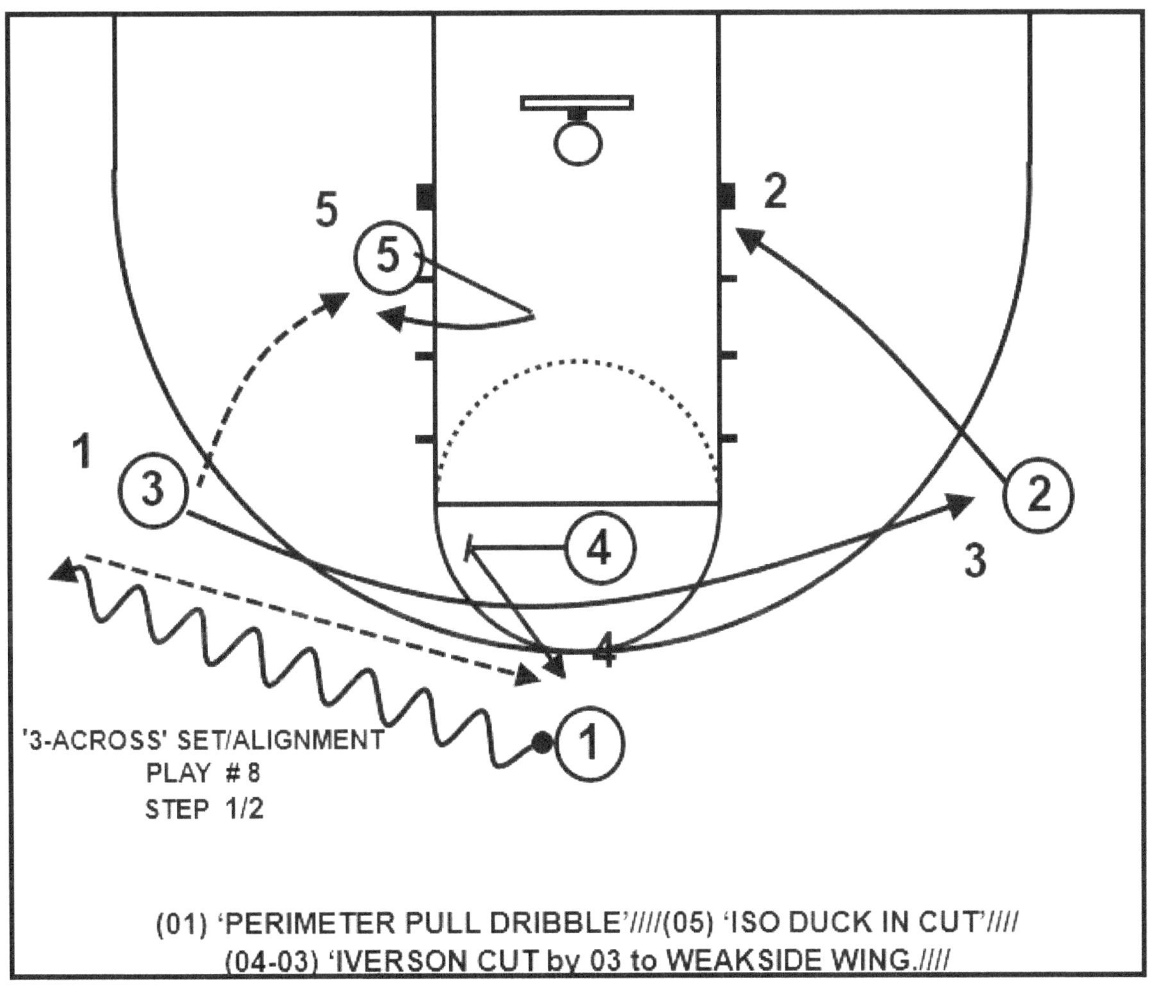

Play # 8   Diagram 20.12

Diagram 20.13 shows 04 turning down an "Inside Pass" to 05 and a pass back to 01. 04 should look then to swing the ball over to 03 on the opposite "Wing" area at the FT Line extended. In a rare sequence of events, 02 then empties out to set a "Small-on-Big Lane Exchange Cross-Screen" for 05 to use to flash to the new "Ballside Block." If the defense switches this "Cross-Screen," 05 would be then defended by X2- a huge mismatch. If the defense does not switch the screen, it is a tough defend for X5 and if there is any support defense, it would be by the presumed second smallest defender, X2.

After the (02-05) "Cross-Screen" has been set for 05 by 02, 04 then diagonally cuts down the lane to set a (04-02) "(Big-on-Small Diagonal Pin-Down) Screen the (Cross-)Screener" action. If none of the interior players (05 or 02 or 04) are open, all three players have switched spot-up locations while 03 and 01 remain at the two perimeter "Wing" areas.

"Screen the screener action with a small player (02) interspersed with two offensive "Bigs" (05 and 04) may be the most difficult off-the-ball screening actions that exists for defensive teams. This action fills the five "3-Out/2-In" Spot-Ups so that the designated continuity offense can fluidly begin. See Diagram 20.13

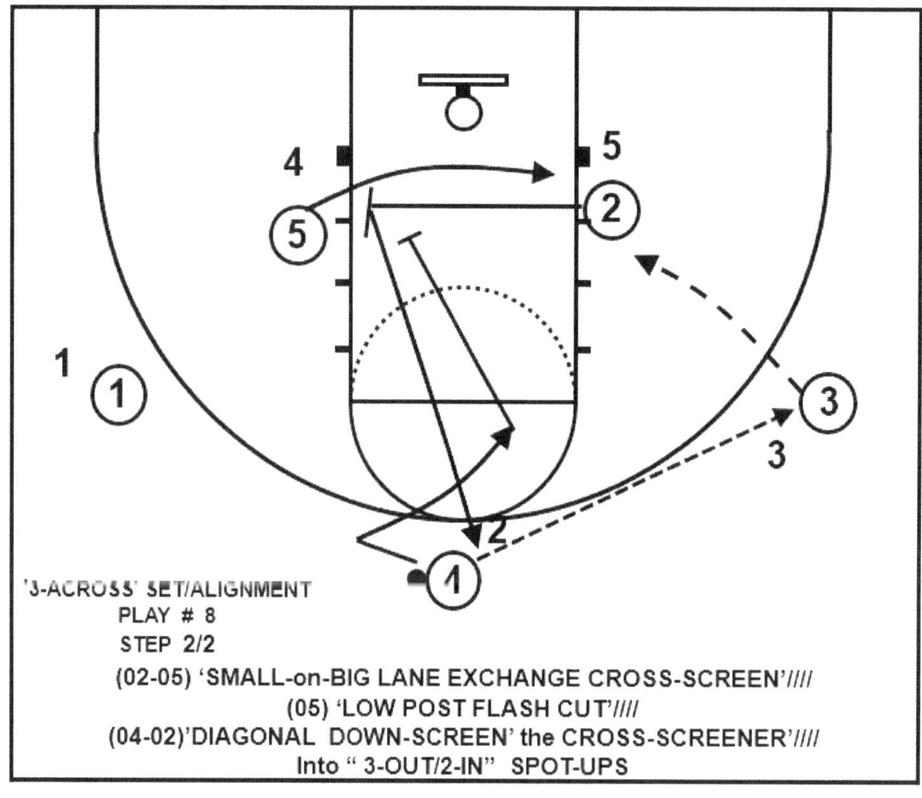

Diagram 20.13

Diagram 20.14 illustrate another counter play to Plays 7 and 8 in Play # 9. This play has 05 begin on the "Mid-Post Block" area on the right side of the lane. The play has 03 make another "Iverson Cut" over the top of 04, with 05 now ending up on the same side of the floor as 03. In addition, 02 also makes an "Iverson Cut" underneath 04 (instead of cutting down to the "Block" as he does in Plays 7 and 8) and breaks out to the "Wing" area on the opposite side of the floor, also away from 05's side. The first phase of Play # 9 ends up with 03 and 02 having exchanged "Wing" locations and 05 being on the "Block" on the right side of the lane, with 04 at the "Nail" and 01 with the ball at the top of the key. See Diagram 20.14

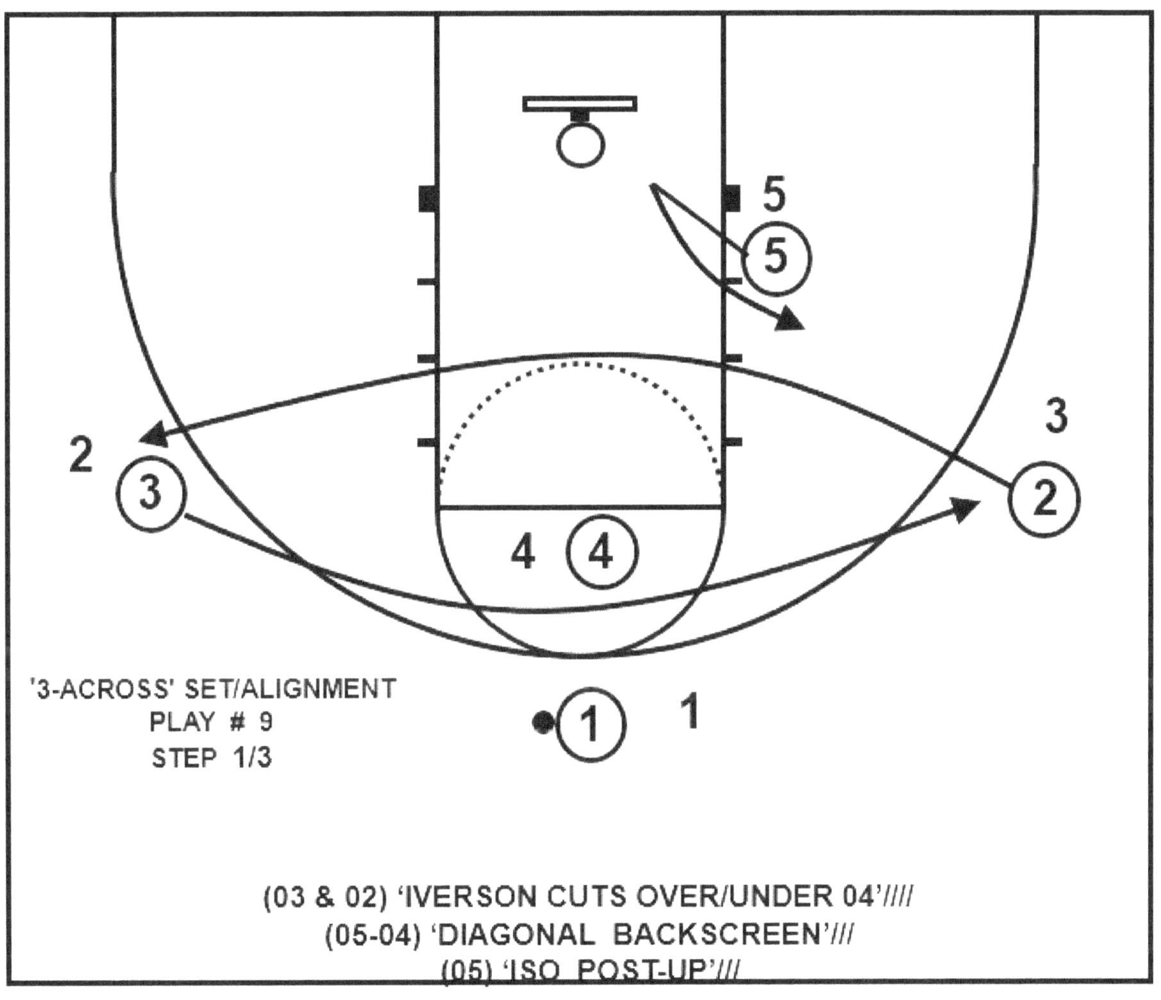

Play # 9   Diagram 20.14

Diagram 20.15 illustrates the second phase of this Level 3 play with 01 making the "Wing Pass" to 03 on the right side of the floor. Immediately after passing the ball to 03, 01 sets his defender up before curling tightly off of 04's outside right shoulder and then towards the "Dotted Circle." 03 should have the advantages of making interior passes to either 01 on his shortened "Lob Cut" or to 05's isolated defender on the "Block."

On the perimeter, 03 could make either perimeter passes to 05 or to 02 and a possible pass to 04 near the "Nail" and the top of the key. See Diagram 20.15

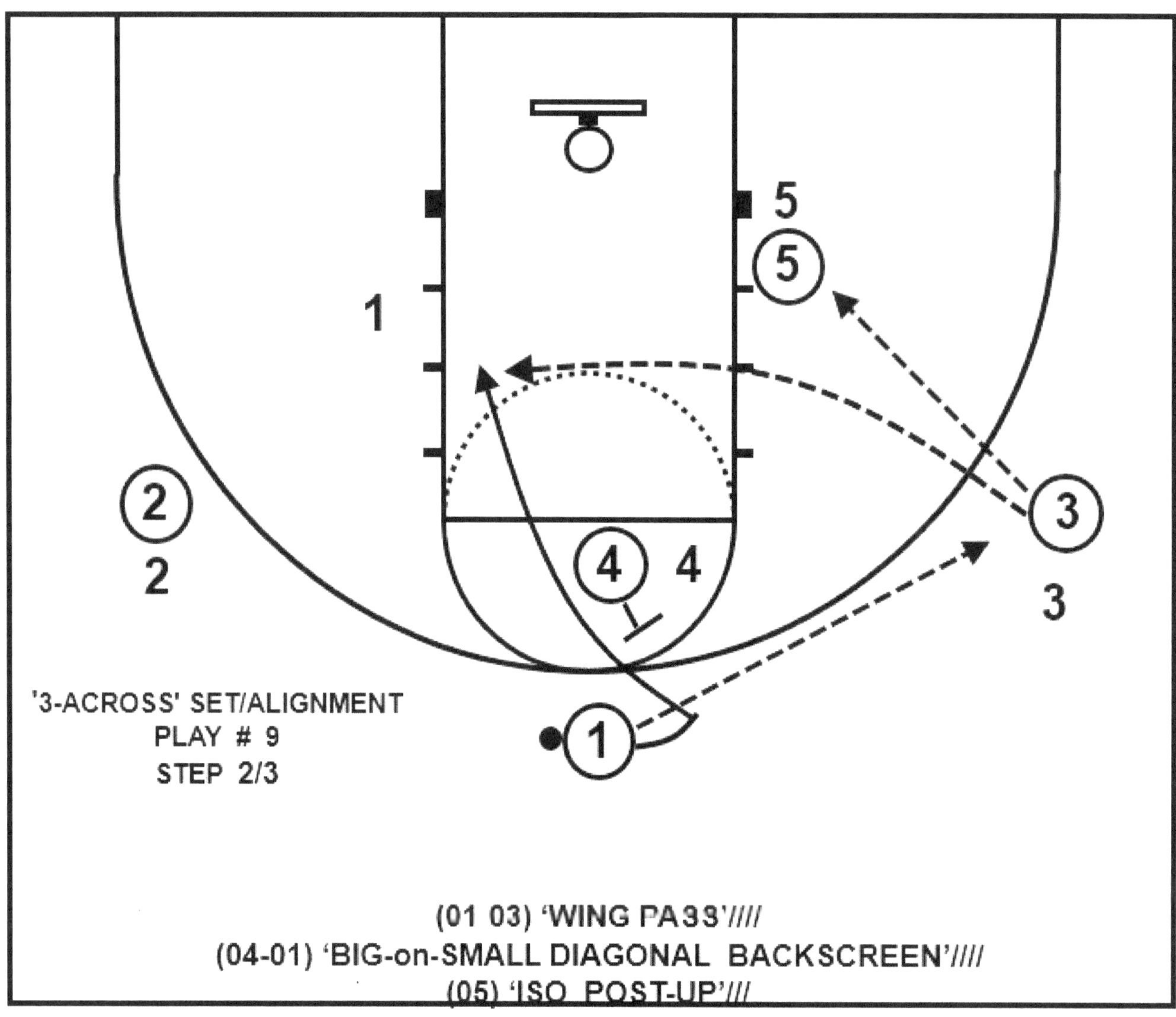

Diagram 20.15

If 03 does not make the quick "Lob Cut" to 01, 01 should stop and break back up to set a "Back-Screen" 04's defender for 04 to become the new "Lob Cutter." This second (01-04) "Back-Screen" with 01 then slipping his screen and breaking to the top of the key acts like a "pin-screen' to free 01 up at the top of the key (and a slip by 04 down low).

The exchanges of 01 and 04 involved between their two "Back-Screens" should free at least one of the cutters open either on the interior (for 04) or at the top of the key (for 01). 03 still has an opportunity to make an "Inside Pass" to 05 on the "Ballside Block" or a possible "Skip Pass" to 02 stretched horizontally out on the weakside wing area. The "3-Out/2-In" Spot-Ups are filled for the final phase of the offense to smoothly begin. See Diagram 20.16

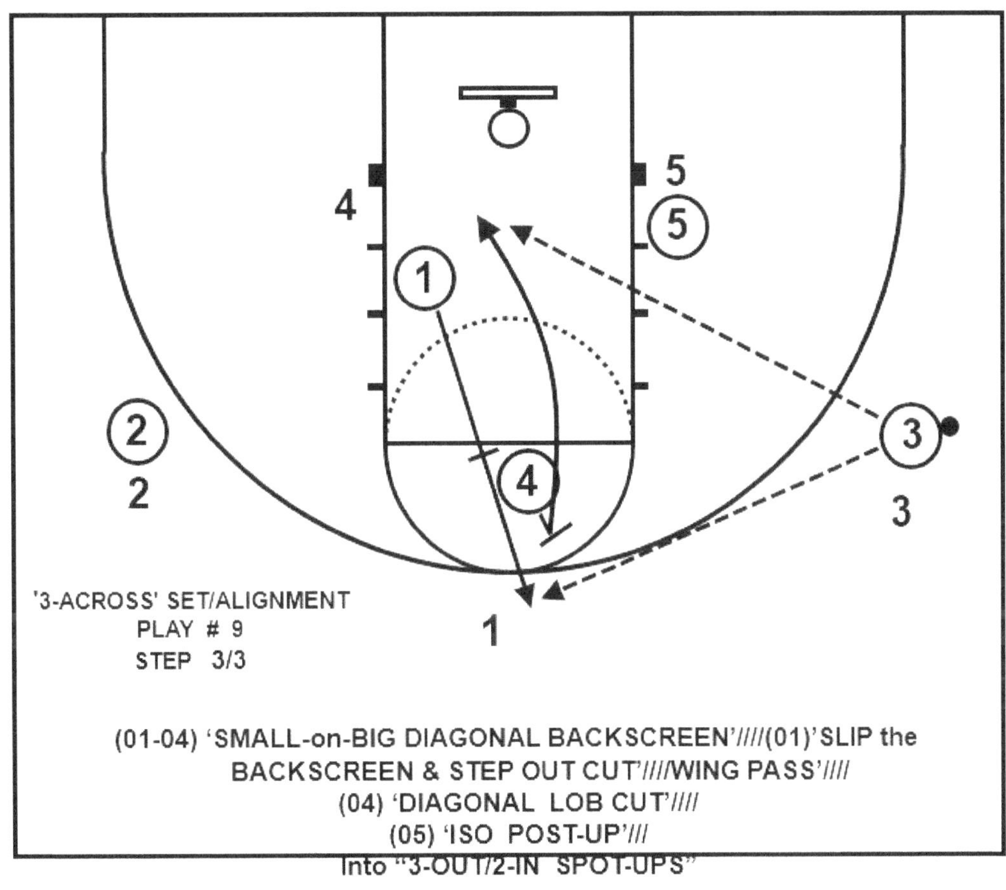

Diagram 20.16

Diagram 20.17 illustrates the beginning of another Level 2 Play, Play # 10. Like Play # 7, 01 dribbles towards 03, who again must be on the opposite side of the floor where 05 begins. During 01's dribble towards 03, 05 flashes up to align next to 04 at the top of the key. This opens up a direct driving avenue for 01 as he approaches the FT Line extended. The action by 01 and 05 vertically and horizontally stretches the overall defense. See Diagram 20.17

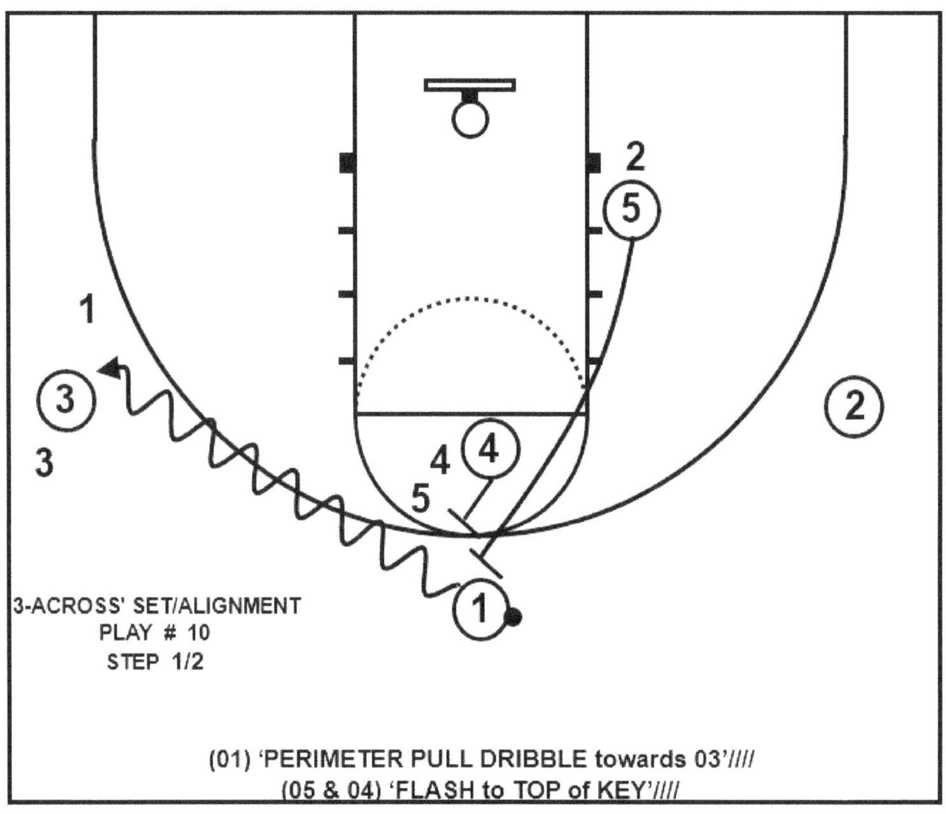

Play # 10   Diagram 20.17

With no dribble drive to the basket, 01 and 03 make a "Small-on-Big Dribble Hand-Off" near the FT Line extended. As 03 then receives the ball, 03 dribbles out towards the top of the key to then use the "Big-on-Small Double Ball-Screen" set by both 05 and 04.

As 03 "dribble-scrapes" off of 05's top left shoulder, 05 rolls down the lane to post up his defender while 04 makes a "Rim-Run" cut through the weakside of the lane.

05 uses a "reverse pivot" off of his lower right foot to open up to 03 and the ball for an "Inside Pass" from 03 (or possibly from 02) on 05's "roll" down the ballside of the lane. 04 makes a "front pivot" off of his right foot and makes a "Lob Cut" to the basket for a potential "Lob Pass" over his inside right shoulder.

If 03 cannot make the pass to 04 or 05, he can either skip the ball back over the top to 01 on the "Weakside Wing" or make the "Reverse Pass" to 02. 02 may have an opportunity for a quick "catch and shoot" opportunity or a possible drive, but most likely will have an improved passing angle to deliver the ball to 05, now posting his defender up down on the new "Ballside Block." If no shots are chosen to be taken, the "3-Out/2-In" Spot-Ups are filled. See Diagram 20.18

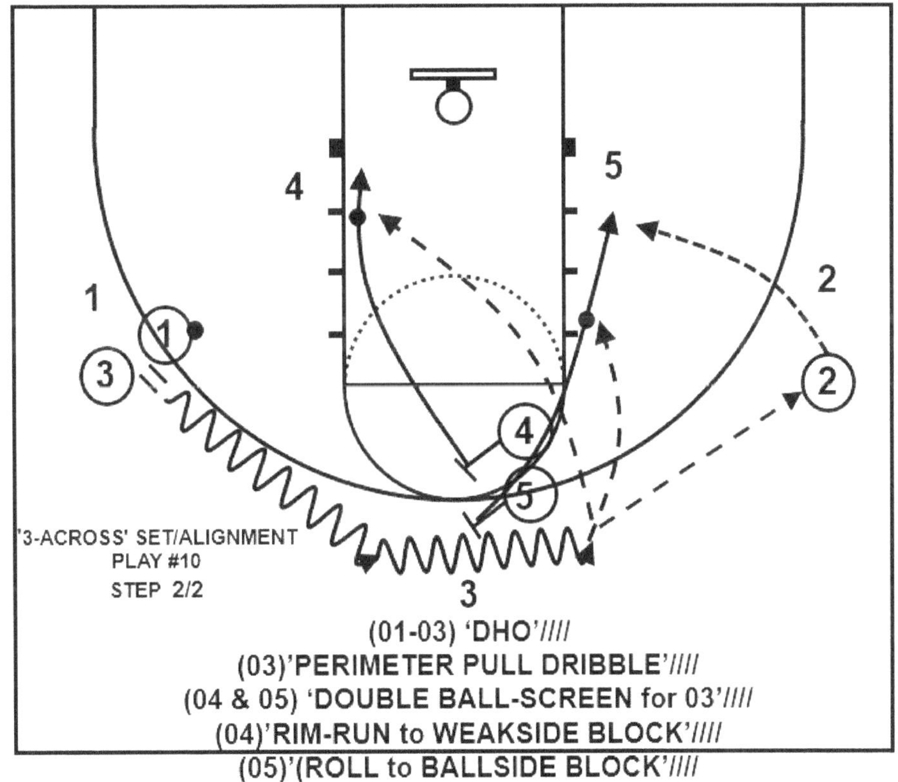

Diagram 20.18

CLOSING

The "3-ACROSS" Set is an offensive alignment that has both an immediate high post and low post threat. The "Low Post threat can be started on either side of the floor, giving the alignment a completely different appearance by declaring that specific side the immediate "strong side" of the set. With wings beginning at both sides of the floor just outside of the arc and a Point Guard out at the top of the key, there is an immediate "outside shot threat" for defenses to contend with. As stated, either side can start or immediately become the overloaded 'high post/low post" side of the floor. Both interior attacking and perimeter attacking plays/entries can be utilized before the various continuity offenses can smoothly begin.

CHAPTER 21
PLAYS/ENTRIES EXECUTED FROM
THE "3-OVER SET/ALIGNMENT"

There are many different philsophies on the most successful methods to attack opponent's man-to-man defenses. The multiple-phase offensive system that is thoroughly described in this book utilizes uses more than one phase/layer/wave of attack within the system, with each phase/wave having a seamless and immediate conversion from the previous phase into the next phase/wave of attack. While this system can be confusing to opposing defenses and difficult for those opponents to defend, this system can be properly taught and coached so that it can be easily understood and ultimately executed by players of many different levels of (physical talent, mental understand and playing experience.)

In addition, there are several types of offensive schemes and different ways within this system that offenses can attack their defensive counter-parts. Many of these can be

integrated within the same offensive system that can attack defenses in various ways. The larger the number of schemes that can be successfully utilized and integrated within the same system, the greater the opportunity an offensive team can find the most efficient and productive schemes that can place both individual and the overall team in the best and most frequent "positions to succeed."

The plays/entries carefully diagrammed down to the small and seemingly unimportant 'V-Cuts' made by countless players before making their more important following cut are also described in detail.

Each play has been carefully studied and evaluated to determine which level of talent and experience must be possessed for that specific team to be able to successfully execute the play. This includes all players' physical skills as well as their mental understanding of the game. Coaches must also have the experience and the associated level of understanding of the game as well as their coaching/teaching of the nuances of each play.

The most sophisticated plays/entries would fall into the first of the three levels all based on the team's physical talents and skills, the mental capacities and the overall team's game experience. In addition, the coaching staff must have a high degree of basketball knowledge as well as very high teaching and coaching skills to educate his/her entire basketball team. The proper breakdown drills must be thoroughly utilized to hone the fundamental skills and techniques needed for individual players and the overall team to execute plays that can be efficient, productive and successful. We define this family of plays as the "Level 3 category" of plays. This "Level 3" family of plays will have a much more complex offensive scheme that would require a very high amount of physical talent as well as requiring a greater amount of the players (to execute) and the coaches (to teach and coach) mental capacities and experience needed for the offense to be efficient, productive and successful. We feel plays in our defined "Level 3" category could possibly be successful for NBA teams, definitely for college teams and also for many high schools and older AAU teams.

The next classification or level of plays would be possibly slightly lower as far as sophistication, complexity and the actual 'length' of the play (and the number of passes, cuts and screens used) in the play's overall scheme. While all "Level 2" plays in each of the chapters in this book remain to be fundamentally sound, these plays may lack the actual number of techniques/methods that are implemented within that play in comparison to the "Level 1" plays/entries. Therefore any team that successfully executes the highest "Level

1" plays/entries could/should easily be able execute any of these so-called lower "Level 2" plays/entries, if so desired. Almost all high school teams should be able to execute successfully all aspects of the "Level 2" plays.

The final grouping of plays would be called "Level 1" plays and are not as difficult for offensive players to master the execution of them, both physically as well as mentally. Even though the techniques are still fundamentally, they may not be as complex to learn and understand in addition to being easier to physically execute.

"Level 1" plays would be lower in the scheme's complexities and the number of techniques used in the execution of this category of plays. Obviously, since these "Level 1" plays are still sound, but lack some of the methods used in the two previous more sophisticated and complex levels; these more elementary plays should be able to be utilized by any teams that use either of the two higher level plays. We feel that Middle School/Junior High teams as well as younger AAU teams or organizations should be able to utilize any of the "Level 1" plays successfully, with a possibility that some of those teams that are slightly more advanced (than other teams) could possibly use some plays located in the immediate next immediate level.

Ideas, concepts and techniques from actual plays from teams of all three levels have been used to modify or to create different combinations of the various techniques and schemes used that will help prove these entries can be successfully used. This allows the author to create numerous plays that use the various schemes to build a library of fundamentally sound plays that will be unique and will be appropriate for the wide range of teams with the various ages and skill levels.

With this book having plays in these three presumed categories or levels, the book will reach out and benefit a much larger group of serious basketball coaches from elementary school age to the highest skilled levels that exists.

In addition, an experienced and resourceful coach may be able to mold some plays that include all of the offensive techniques that he/she desires could reshape a specific play that begins in one specific offensive set/alignment and reshape it so that it could begin in a different offensive/set that is more favorable to that coach and his/her coaching staff's liking.

Conversely, that innovative and creative coach may completely like the specific offensive set/alignment and favor the very same offensive actions included in a certain

play, but can modify that play so that the ending spot-ups of all five players are conducive to being able to begin the final phase of the offensive attack by using a more favorable offensive continuity offense.

The "3-OVER SET"

PLAYS/ENTRIES THAT END in the "3-OUT/2-IN" OFFENSIVE SPOT-UPS

When no shot is taken after any play out of the "3-OVER" Set has been executed, the movement of all five offensive players will have repositioned each individual player into a five positions called the "3-Out/2-In" Spot-Ups. After every different entry has been executed those positions are filled by various different players. The positions are the "Point" (at the top of the key), the "Ballside Block" and the "Weakside Block," (both actually one 'notch' above the actual "Blocks,") the "Ballside Wing" and the "Weakside Wing" (both extended outside of the 3 Pt. arc at the FT Line extended). It must be emphasized that those five locations will be filled by different players dependent upon the actions in the particular play that was just completed without a shot taken.

Various specific continuity offenses are easily and smoothly able to begin immediately after the "3-Out/2-In" Spot-Ups are filled, regardless of which players fill those designated positions. There will always be a fluid transition from the end of the play instantly to the beginning of the continuity offense.

In addition, the five "3-Out/2-In" Spot-Ups offer the offense with many fundamentally sound advantages and benefits. Some of these positives are the ease and quickness of different types of ball-reversals, the many opportunities for perimeter pull dribbles as well as perimeter penetration dribbles (with "penetration and pitch" and "drive and dump" opportunities always available,) regular post-up opportunities for the individual player that ends up on the "Ballside Block,", "3 Pt. Shot" opportunities from both the "Ballside Wing" as well as "catch and shoot" shots after a "Skip" or "Inside-Out Pass" is made, in addition to both a sound offensive rebounding game-plan and also an organized and efficient defensive transition plan.

Diagram 21.1 illustrates the first play from this somewhat unique offensive set/alignment. It could be described as a tight 1-2-2 Box Set with the lower "Block" player on the right side of the floor removed and replaced in the wide "Deep Corner" on the left side of the floor. Both 05 and 04 align at the two higher "Elbow" spots, with 03 on the left

495

"Block," 01 at the top of the key and 02 reinserted at the wide "Deep Corner" on the left side of the floor.

This Play # 1 is a Level 1 play and it shows 04 stepping up to set a "Big-on-Small Ball-Screen for 01 to use to advance the ball to the FT Line extended on the right side of the floor. 04 then turns away from the ball and goes diagonally down to seemingly be a part of a "Triple Stagger-Screen" (first by 03, then 05 and then himself) for what appears to be for 02.

Instead, 05 exits his screening route to become a "Ghost Stagger-Screener" and slashes across the lane to post his isolated defender up on the new "Ballside Block." 04 then slips his initial ball-screen to then "pin-screen 03 before then widening out the to the "Wing" area on the left side of the floor. Instead of 02 coming off of 03's screen, 02 stops and "bump cuts" 03 so that 03 becomes the new cutter who continues higher to then scrape off of 04's outside left shoulder and breaks to the top of the key for an open '3 Pt.' shot. These screens and cuts and misdirection cuts and actions provide 01 with an opportunity for an "Inside Pass" to 05 on the "Ballside Block." If shots are not taken, most likely by 01, 05 or 03; the "3-Out/2-In" Spot-Ups are filled for the next phase of the offense to fluidly begin. Diagram 21.1.

Play # 1   Diagram 21.1

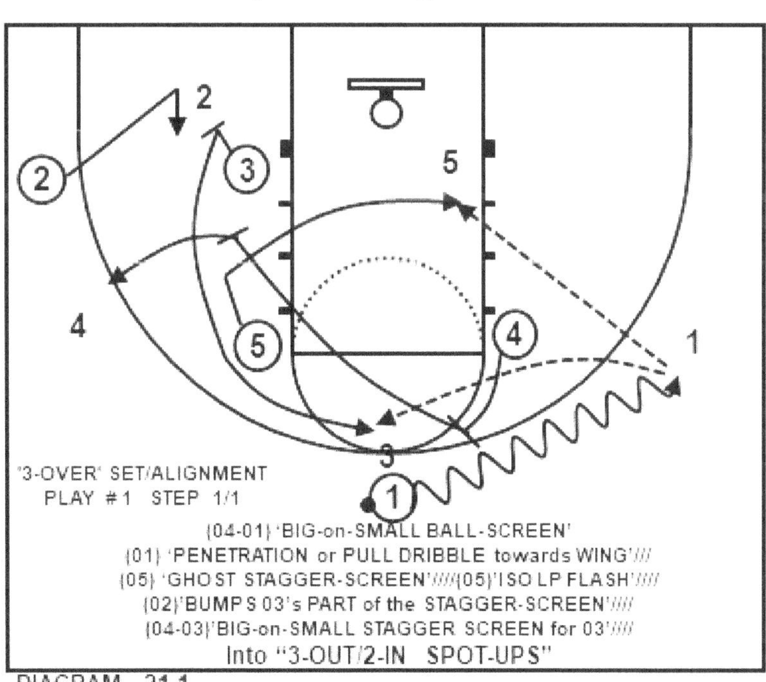

Play # 1   Diagram 21.1

Diagram 21.2 is a counter play to Play # 1 and is also another basic and simple Level 1 play. Again, 01 "dribble-scrapes" off of 04's outside shoulder. 02 appears first to use 03 as a "Pin Down-Screener" to break to the top of the key. Instead, 02 reverses directions and utilizes 03 more as a "Flex-Screener" so that he can make his "Flex-Cut across the lane to post up.

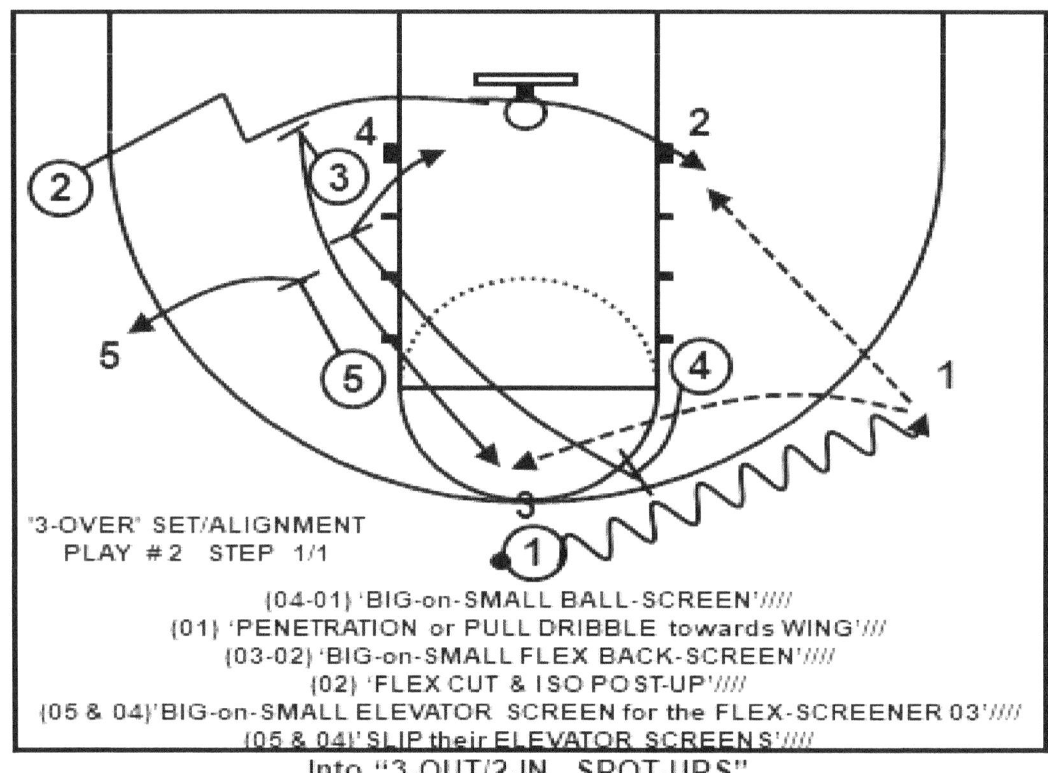

Play # 2   Diagram 21.2

After 01 breaks contact with 04 on the dribble, 04 and 05 both break diagonally down to set a (05 & 04) "(Big-on-Small Elevator-)Screen the ("Flex-)Screener (03)." After 02 scrapes off of 03's shoulder (preferably the lower right shoulder,) 03 makes a cut between 04's left shoulder and 05's right shoulder on his "Elevator Cut" to the top of the key (for an open '3.') After breaking contact with 03, 04 slips to the basket while 05 flares out to the new "Weakside Wing."

This action moves 01 with the ball to the FT Line extended, while moving a perimeter-type cutter (02) inverted and somewhat isolated (with all of the weakside screening action going on) to the new "Ballside Block," and finally 03 to the top of the key, 04 who has slipped his "pin-screen" to step near the basket and 05 now slides out from his part of the

"Elevator Screen" to the new "Weakside Wing" area. This repositions players into the "3-Out/2-In" Spot-Ups for a smooth conversion into the designated continuity offense to begin. Diagram 21.2.

Diagram 21.3 shows a Level 1 play with 04 rolling after setting an identical "Big-on-Small Ball-Screen" for 01 to use to "dribble scrape" off of 04's outside left shoulder. 04's action after the screen are much different than the actions he executes after setting the same 04-01 Ball-Screen that he executes in both Play # 1 and # 2.

In Play # 3, 04 waits until contact is broken with 01 and "reverse-pivots" off of his inside right foot to then open up to the ball and to 01 to look for a pass on his "roll (down the lane) to the basket."

To further give 04 an isolated advantage on the new "Ballside Block" over his defender, both 03 and 05 set delayed "Stagger Screens" for 02 to use to get free for an open '3 Pt' Shot at the top of the key. 03 then slips to the new "Weakside Block," while 05 extends and stretches the presumed biggest defender, X5, further from the basket and from the primary pass receiver, 04.

If shots are not taken by either 04, 02 or by 01; the "3-Out/2-In Spot-Ups" are filled for a quick and immediate transition into the next and final phase of the offense—the designated continuity offense. Diagram 21.3.

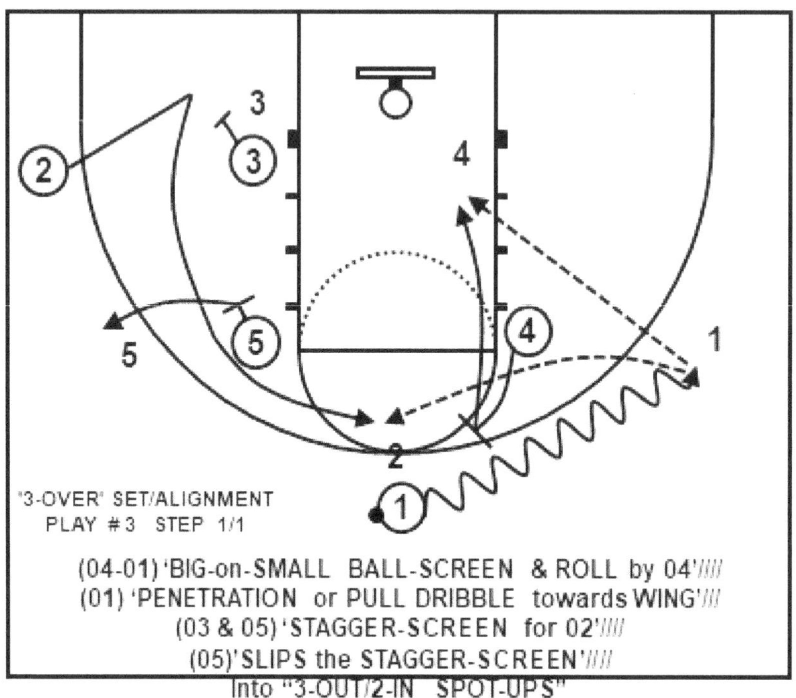

DIAGRAM 21.3

Play # 3   **Diagram 21.3**

Diagram 21.4 explains another Level 1 Play that is both easier to understand as well as to execute. Another advantage of this play/entry is that it is also a counter to both of the two previous plays with 04 setting the same "Ball-Screen" for 01 to utilize to dribble to the FT Line extended. This time, 02 runs pretty much the same "Flex Cut" off of the lower right shoulder of 03 that he does in Play # 2. With X3 trying to help and possibly switch with X2, 03 should have a "position advantage" on his current defender (either X3 or the switching X2) and make a hard "Iso Duck-In Cut" into the "Dotted Circle" area while sealing off his defender.

01 has two teammates that he immediately can make the "Inside Pass" to: 02 in the lane and coming to the "Block" or to 03 in the middle of the lane just inside the "Dotted Circle."

After screening for 01, 04 then should receive the "(05-04) "(Flare-)Screen the (Ball-)Screener" so that 04 can make his "Flare-Cut" to the new "Weakside Wing." After setting the screen, 05 slips the screen and steps to the top of the key. These actions by 05 and 04 vertically and horizontally stretch the defense to force two perimeter-type defenders (X2 and X3) to attempt to guard two players in high percentage scoring areas. It also allows two post-type offensive players to be able to pull their presumed biggest defenders away from the basket into unfamiliar or uncomfortable perimeter areas to defend their men. With 01 at the "Ballside Wing," he now has a high potential passing target (02) at the "Ballside Block," 05 at the top of the key and 04 at the "Weakside Wing." By then, 03 should relocate down to the "Weakside Block." These actions and planned movements by the offense in this play make the first four plays appear to be the same and will make each entry even more difficult to defend with the many similarities and appearances they are share. Regardless of which entry is being executed, all will reposition every one of the five offensive players into the same "3-Out/1-In" Spot-Ups to continue the offensive attack. Diagram 21.4.

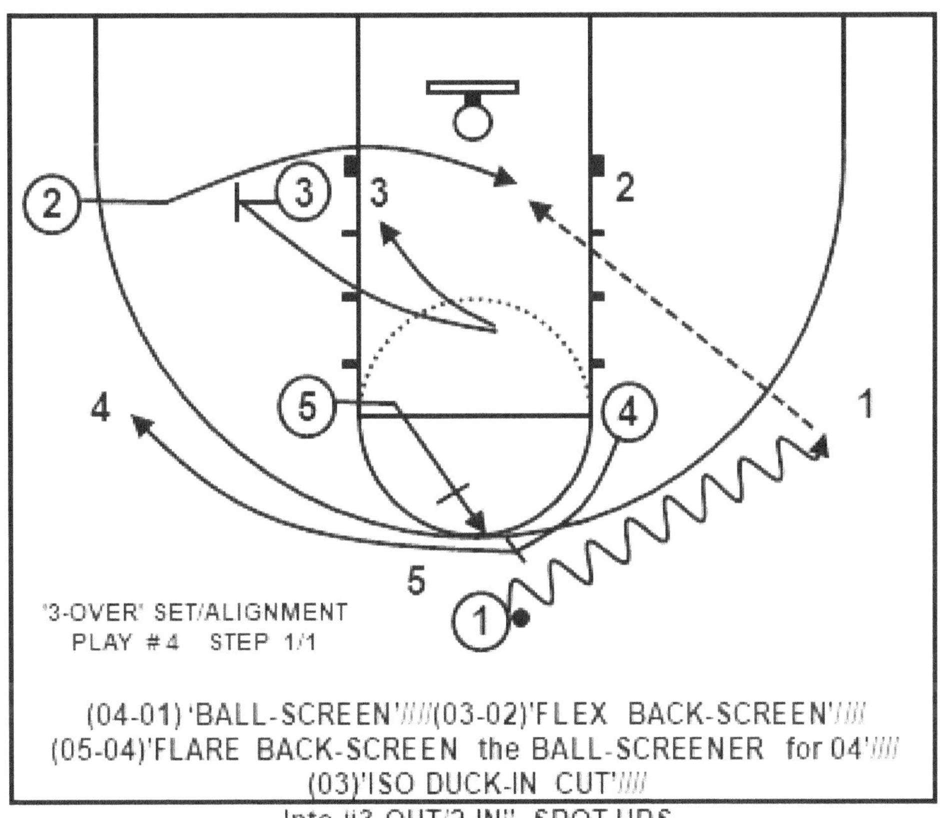

Diagram 21.4

Play # 5 and # 6, two additional Level 1 plays, both appear at the beginning to be the same entries as each other. Therefore, both plays can serve as a counter play to each other. In both entries, 04 makes an inverted "Pop-Out Cut" just outside of the arc midway between the "Slot" and the "Wing" area at the FT Line extended.

In Play # 5, 01 makes the pass to 04 and starts to follow his pass. Instead, he then times his cut with the proper angle break away from 04 and the ball to set a "Small-on-Big Diagonal Brush Screen" for 05 to scrape off of 01's hip to then to make a "Iso Slash Cut" to the new "Ballside Block."

01 continues down towards 03 so that 02 can walk his defender down to the proper angle before then cutting off 03's "Diagonal Pin Down-Screen" to then break up to the top of the key. After screening for 02, 03 slips back up to the FT Line extended, while 01 remains at the new "Weakside Block" area. 04 has one primary interior passing threat at the new "Ballside Block," -05, one primary perimeter threat at the top of the key-02 and a secondary perimeter scoring threat in a possible "Skip Pass" to 03 at the "new Weakside Wing." If shots are not taken, the "3-Out/2-In" Spot-Ups are immediately filled for a smooth transition into the designated continuity offense.

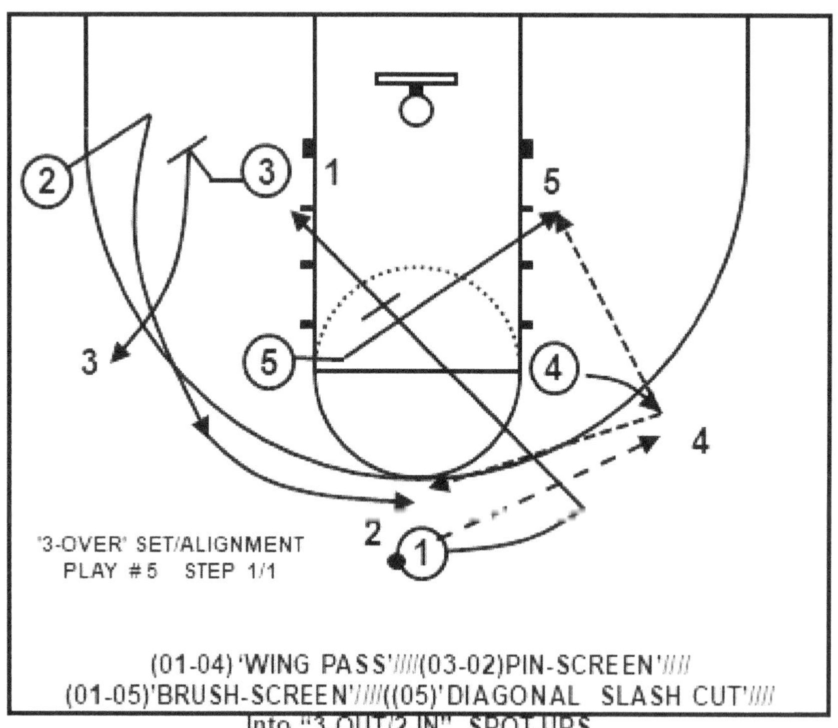

Play # 5   Diagram 21.5

Play # 6 is another Level 1 play similar to the beginning action characteristics as Play # 5. Once again, 01 makes the pass to 04, who has popped outside of the arc on the right side of the floor. This time, 05 has also popped out on his side of the floor to appear to also be a threat to receive 01's initial perimeter pass. In this instance, 01 again makes the pass to 04 and then continues to follow his pass and receive a return (04-01) "Flip Pass" from 04.

At this time, 05 then makes a "Diagonal Slash Cut" near the "Nail" and on through the lane to the new "Ballside Block." 03 "Flex-Screens" 02's defender for 02 to then break diagonally up to set a "Small-on-Big Diagonal Back-Screen" near the "Nail" for 04. After flipping the ball back to 01, 04 spins out to then receive 02's "screen for 04 to use to make a "Lob Cut" to the basket and look for a "Lob Pass" in the lane from 01.

This action occupies all possible helpside defenders and therefore completely isolates X5 down on the "Ballside Block." 01 has primary targets in 05 at the "Block," a possible "Lob Pass" to 04 on the opposite side of the lane, a possible "Skip Pass" to 03 on the opposite side of the floor and a potential '3 Pt.' receiver at the top of the key in 02 after he slipped his (02-04) Back-Screen near the 'Nail.' All the various actions allow the play to reposition all players into the "3-Out/2-In" Spot-Ups for a continuation of the offense— Diagram 21.6.

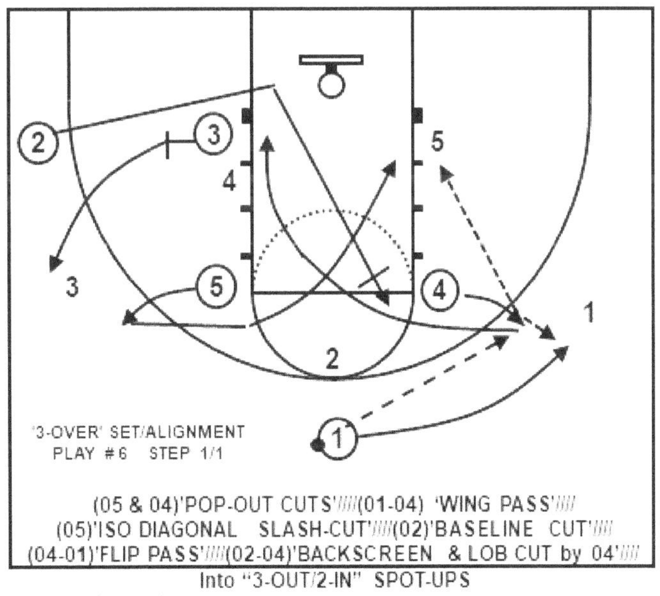

Play # 6   Diagram 21.6

Plays # 7 and # 8 are both Level 2 plays that can easily become counter plays to each other with the same beginning actions of (04-05) "Barkley Screens" by 04 and "Barkley Cuts" by 05. In both plays, it also appears as if 02 is about to "Flex Cut" off of 03 before 03 diagonally pops out to the FT Line extended on his initial side of the floor. In both plays, 02 remains down on the initial "Block" on his side of the floor and actually does not "Flex Cut" across the lane. At this point in time, 01 has potential "Wing Passes" to both 03 on the left side of the floor and 05 on the right side of the floor. An additional pass for 01 could be to 04 now positioned at the 'Nail."

Another potential play could have 01 make the "Wing Pass" to 05 with either 02, 01 or 04 then flashing to the new Ballside Block." These actions are simply hints for a creative coach to make his own offensive plays that would better fit his own philosophies and personnel. Diagram 21.7.

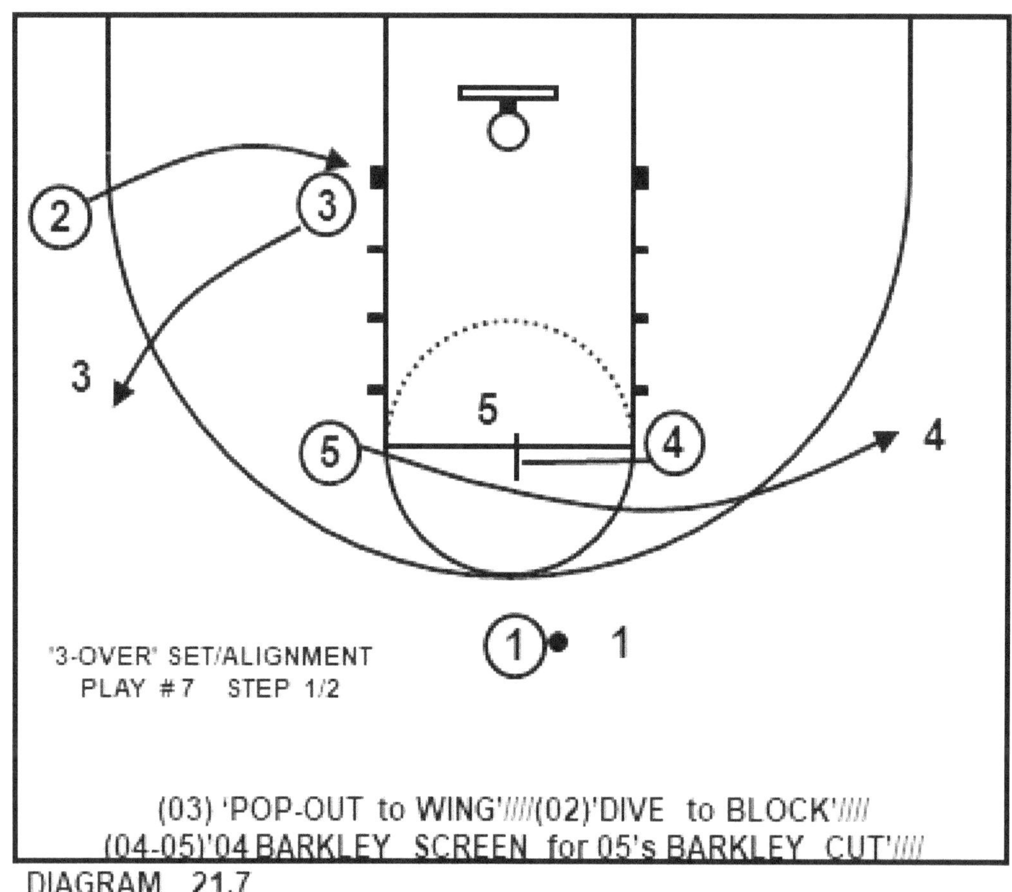

Play # 7   Diagram 21.7

Diagram 21.8 illustrates 01 deciding to make the "Wing Pass" to 03 on the left side of the floor. 02 immediately steps up to set a "Small-on-Big Diagonal Back-Screen" for 04 to use on his "Iso Slash Cut" to the new "Ballside Block." After making the pass to 03, 01 waits one count to then set a (01-02) "(Small-on-Big" Pin Down-)Screen the (Back-)Screener." After setting his screen, 01 drifts down to the new "Weakside Block." 05 ends up on the new "Weakside Wing" and has pulled presumably the biggest opponent away from the scoring and rebounding areas.

03 looks initially to make the "Inside Pass" to 04 on the "Ballside Block" and then on the perimeter to 02 at the top of the key. This places all players in the very same "3-Out/2-In" Spot-Ups where the continuity offense can then smoothly begin. Diagram 21.8.

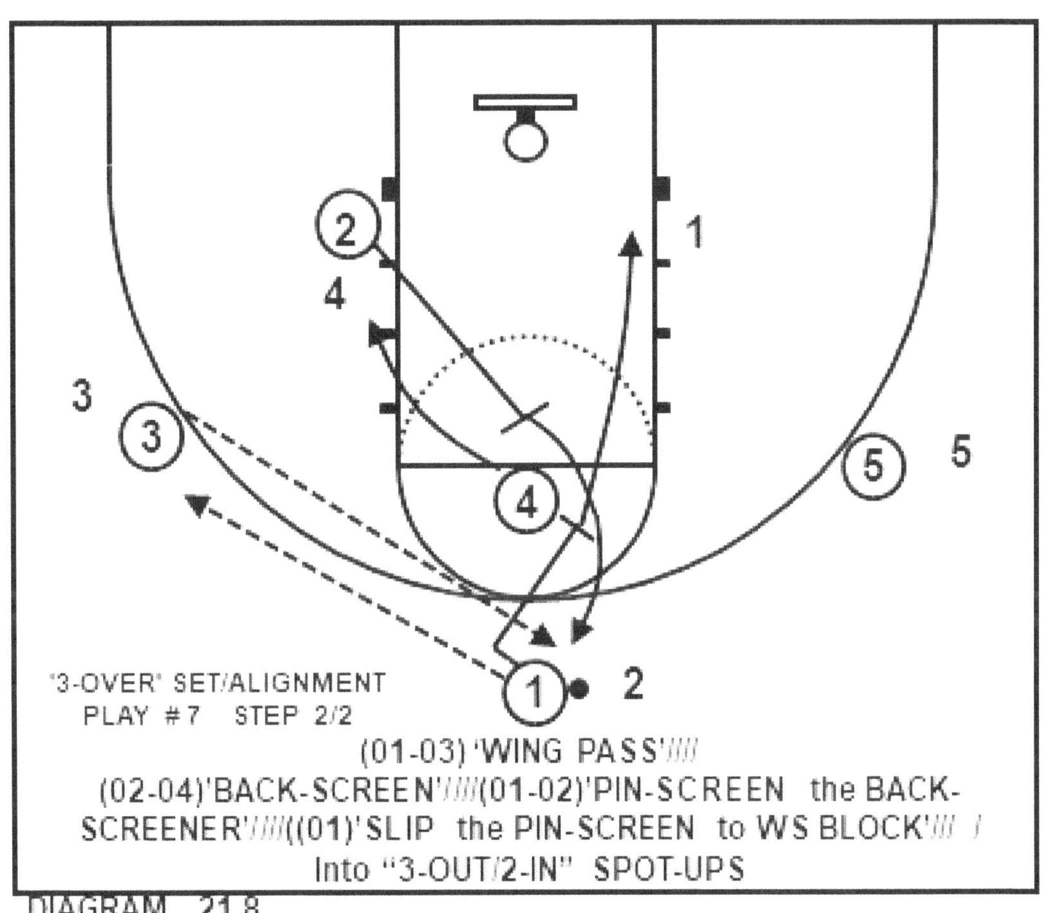

Diagram 21.8

The beginning of Play # 8 is shown in Diagram 21.9 as another simple to understand and execute Level 1 play and is a counter-play to Play 7. Again 04 "Barkley-Screens" for 05, 03 again pops out diagonally to the FT Line extended and 02 dives to the "Block" on the same side of the floor.

At this point, 01 has the same three perimeter pass receivers available. Plays could be created so that the two other receivers in addition to 03 and his two plays (04 at the 'Nail' and 05 at the opposite "Wing" area could also have specific plays created from those two initial beginning passes. Diagram 21.9.

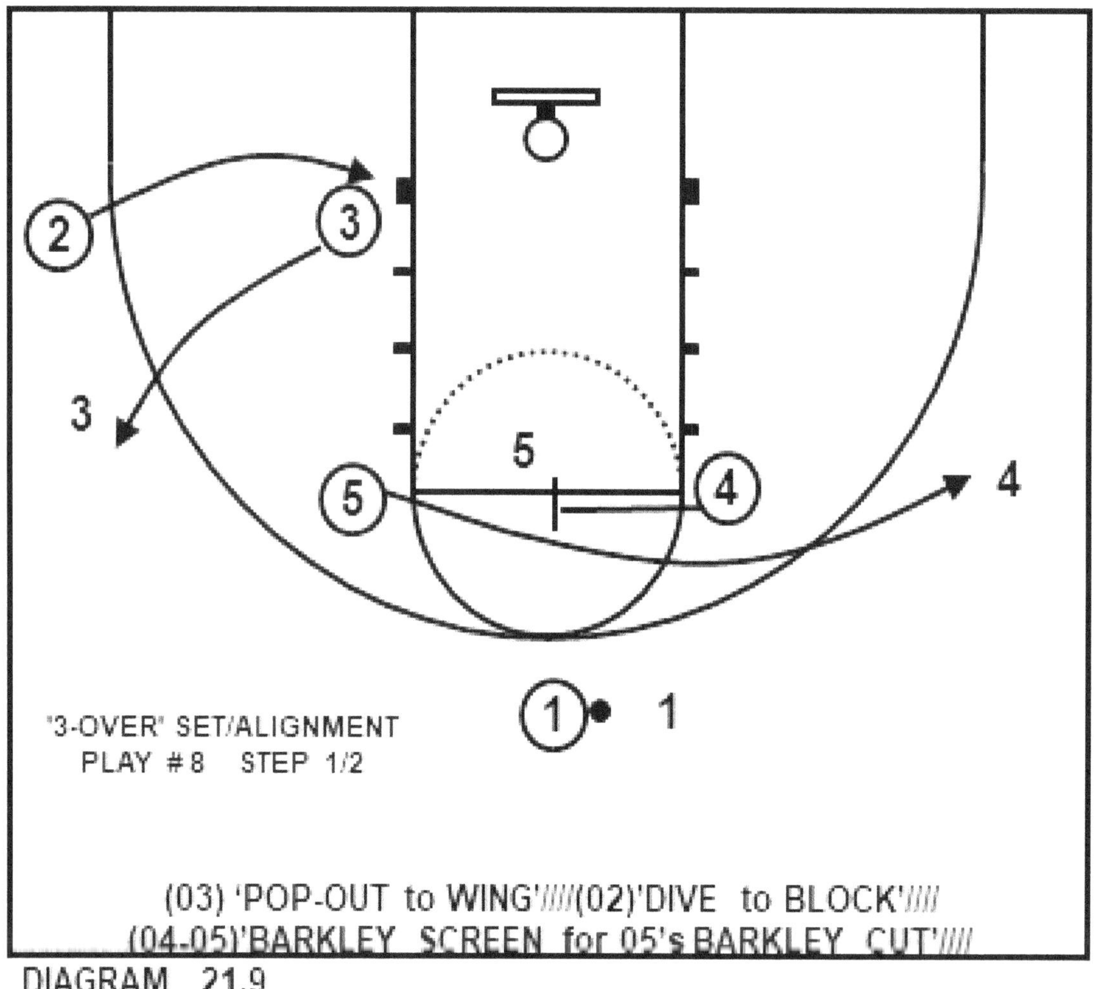

Play # 8   Diagram 21.9

Diagram 21.10 shows the exact action after 01 makes the same "Wing Pass" to 03. While 03 looks to pass to the inverted and isolated perimeter-type player, 02, on the new "Ballside Block;" 04 steps out to set a head-hunting "Big-on-Small Back-Screen" for 01 to use to make a "Lob Cut to the weakside of the lane and to the basket. With 05 being far out from the basket and 04 at the top of the key and X3 involved with the ball, most likely the three biggest defenders are out of the defensive interior with 01 and 02 attacking their perimeter-type defenders on both the "Ballside" and the "Weakside Blocks." This planned action should lead to offensive "personnel advantages" sometimes when it is called for. Regardless, the "3-Out/2-In" Spot-Ups are filled. Diagram 21.10.

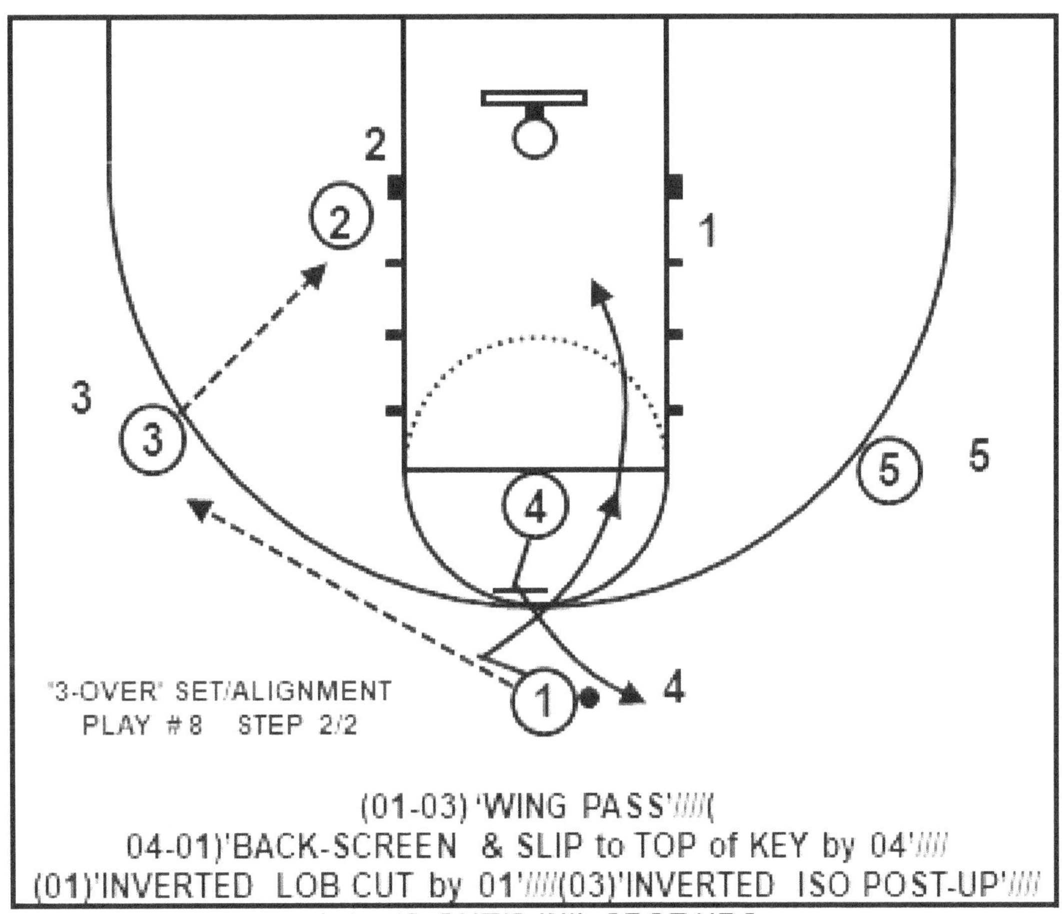

DIAGRAM 21.10

Play # 9 is a Level 3 play that also appears at first to be the same plays as either Play # 7 or # 8. As 01 brings the ball into play, 02 has set up his defender as if to run a "Flex Cut" off of 03 before then receiving 05's "Pin-Screen" towards the "Elbow" area. After setting the screen for 02, 05 receives himself a (04-05) "Barkley Screen" that is then followed by 05's "Barkley Cut" out to the FT Line extended on the opposite side of the floor. This action actually has moved four of the five players for the next series of offensive actions. Diagram 22.11.

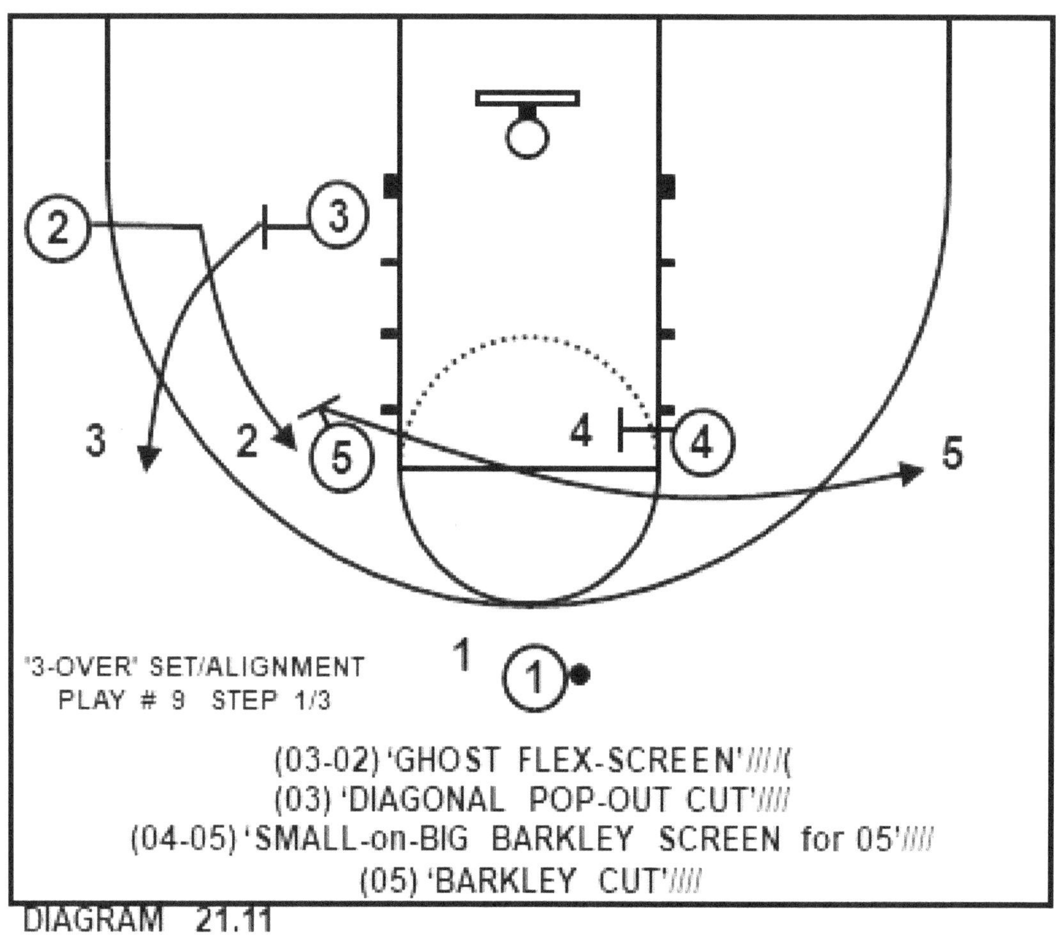

Play # 9   Diagram 21.11

Diagram 22.12 shows 01 turning down three of the four pass receivers and making the (01-02) "Elbow" Pass. As the pass is in mid-air to 02, 03 starts his "Backdoor Cut" to the basket. This initial pass that could then lead to the second and current Backdoor Cut" Pass is called the "Blind Pig" action and is great when facing "Wing Pass" denial pressure.

Once 01 makes the pass, 01 follows his pass to cut to the "Wing" area at the FT Line extended while 03 "Iso Posts Up' his perimeter-type defender and 05 brushes off of 04's short "Cross-Screen." Diagram 21.12.

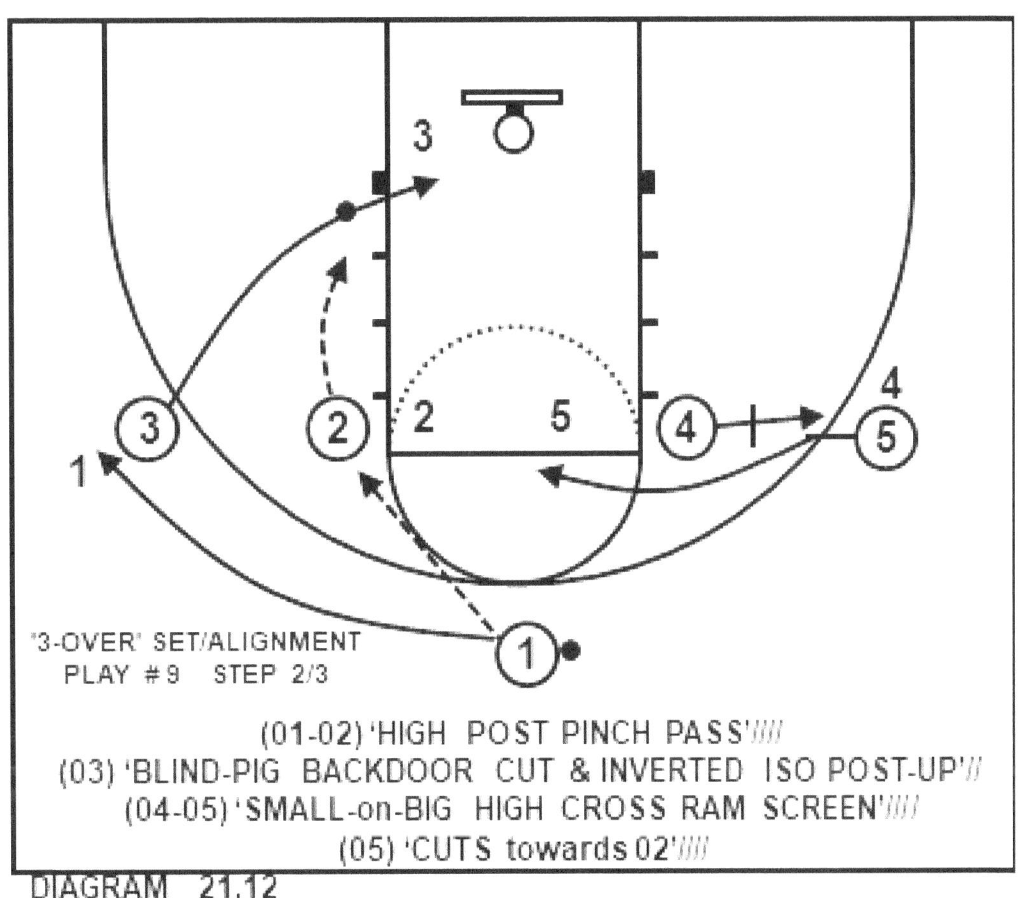

Diagram 21.12

Diagram 21.13 shows 02 not making the quick "Blind Pig Pass" to 03 and waiting for 05 to cut off of 04's screen and break across the FT Line to set a "Big-on-Small Ball-Screen for 02. As 02 dribble pulls near the top of the key and the FT Line and breaks contact with 05's top left shoulder, 05 then makes a "Reverse Pivot" off of his lower right foot and rolls diagonally through the lane while looking for the "Inside Pass" from 02 or possibly from the inverted 04 out at the "Wing" area.

To eliminate helpside defense, 01 will go set a "Small-on-Big Pin Down-Screen" for 03 to break back up to the FT Line extended. 02 could look to make the pass to 02, extend the ball to 04 who could shoot, drive or make the pass to 05. 02 could make a "Throwback Reverse Pass" 03 or look for 01 to seal off his (inexperience in the post) perimeter-type defender with a pass to 01 after 01 slips his own "Pin Screen" (to 03).

Regardless of the many shot opportunities this Level 3 presents, if no shots are taken; the "3-Out/2-In" Spot-Ups are filled. Diagram 21.13.

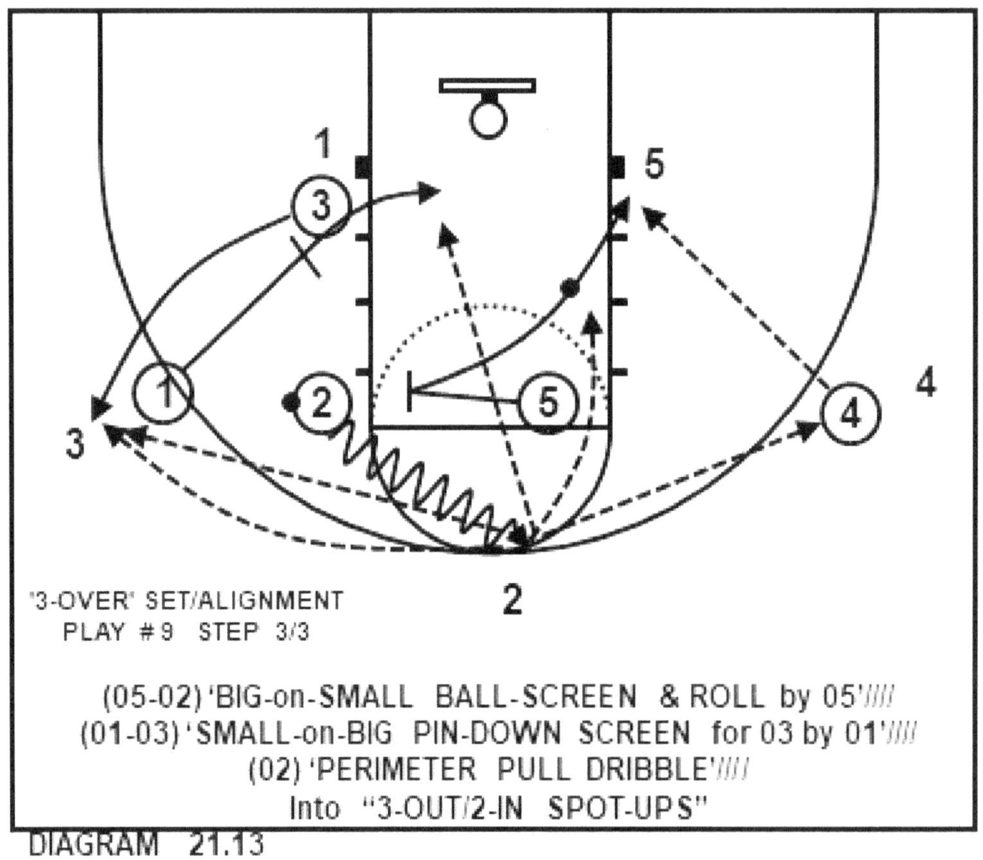

Diagram 21.13

Diagram 21.14 illustrates Play # 10, another Level 3 Play. 02 breaks up and over the top of 05 and 04's "supposed Iverson Screens" respectively. By the time 02 receives 01's "Wing Pass," 05 has slashed diagonally across the lane to post up on the new "Ballside Block" after his "Ghost Iverson Screen" for 02. After 02 receives that same pass, 04 seals off his defender to post him up at the new "Ballside High Post.

After making the "Wing Pass" to 02, 03 should break up to set a "Big-on-Small Flare-Screen" for 01 to use to "Flare-Cut" to the new "Weakside Wing." After screening for 01, 03 slips his screen to step up to the top of the key. Diagram 21.14.

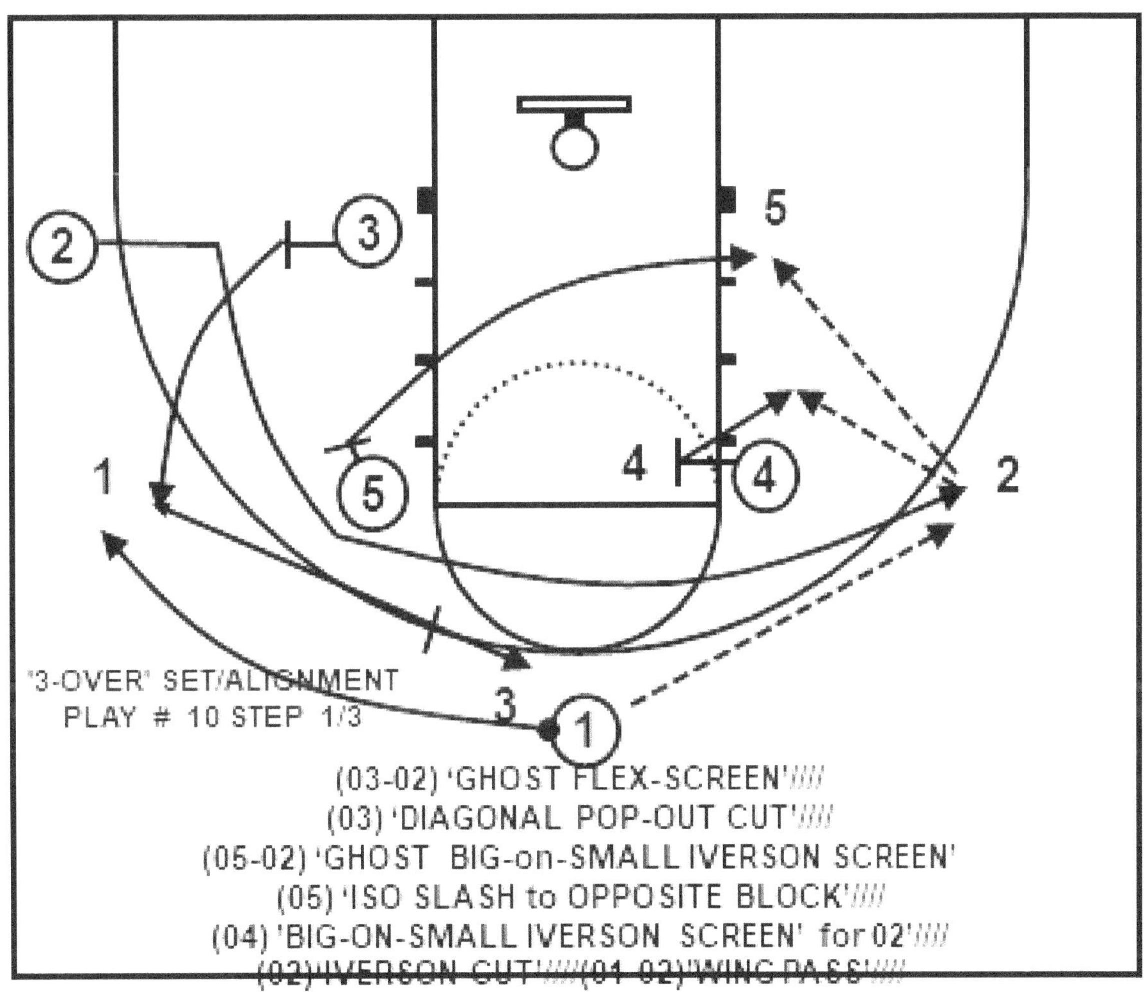

Play 10   Diagram 21.14

Diagram 21.15 illustrates the next phase of Play # 10, where 02 reverses the ball to 03 now out on top of the key. 02 immediately scrapes off of 04's top left shoulder during 04's "Big-on-Small" Shuffle Back-Screen and continues his "Shuffle Cut" through the lane to the opposite side's "Mid-Post" area.

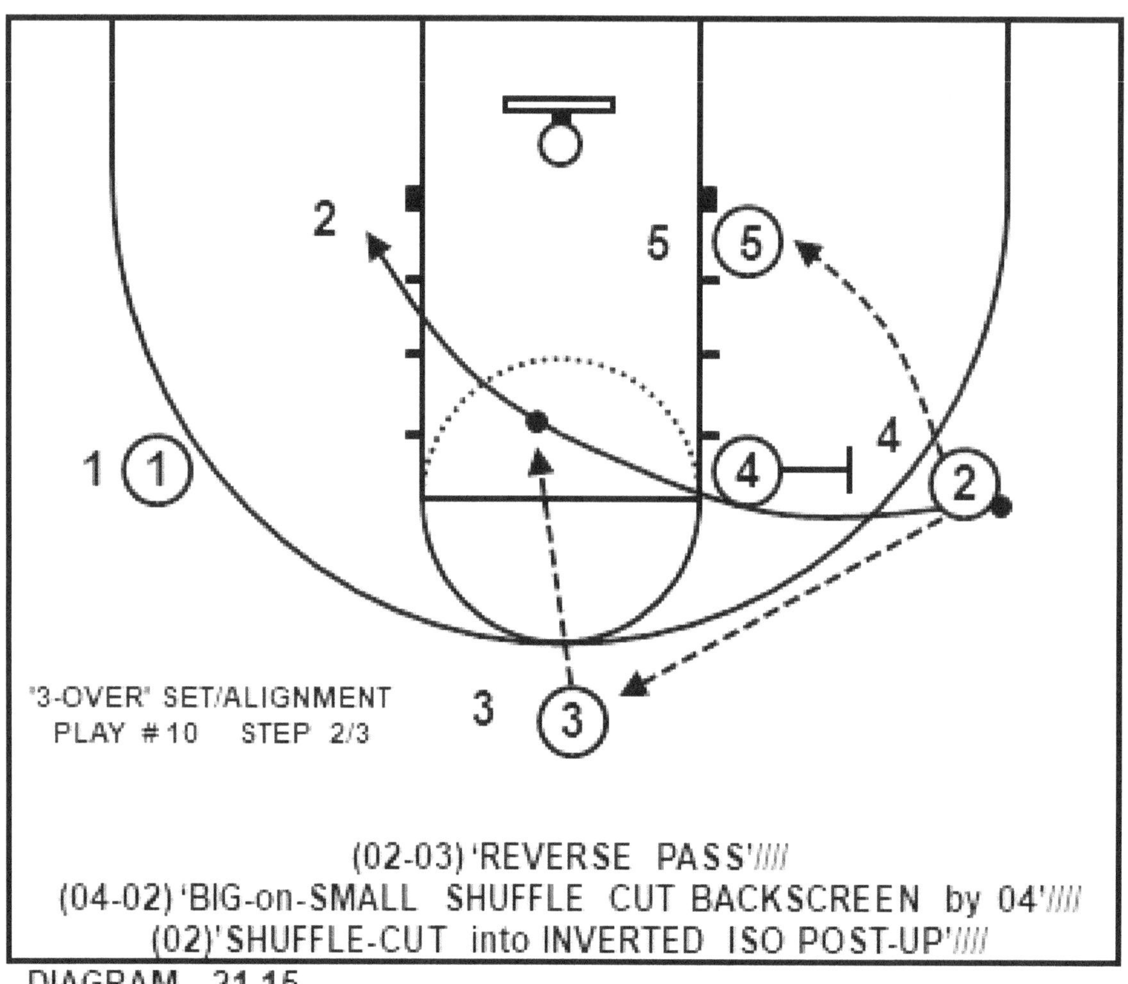

Diagram 21.15

Diagram 21.16 shows the final phase of this Level 3 play with 03 not being able to make the "Inside Pass" to 02 but swinging the ball to 01 (who may have a better passing angle to make an "Inside Pass" to the inverted perimeter-type player, 02. After making the pass, 03 then breaks into the proper location for the proper angle to set a (03-05) "Small-on-Big Diagonal Pin Down-Screen" for 05 to break up to the top of the key. This gives 05 an opportunity for an open '3 Pt.' at the top of the key in addition to helping eliminate the defense's interior support and giving 02 a better opportunity for in "inverted post-up." If no shots are taken, the "3-Out/2-In" Spot-Ups are filled for the last phase of the attack to immediately continue. Diagram 21.16.

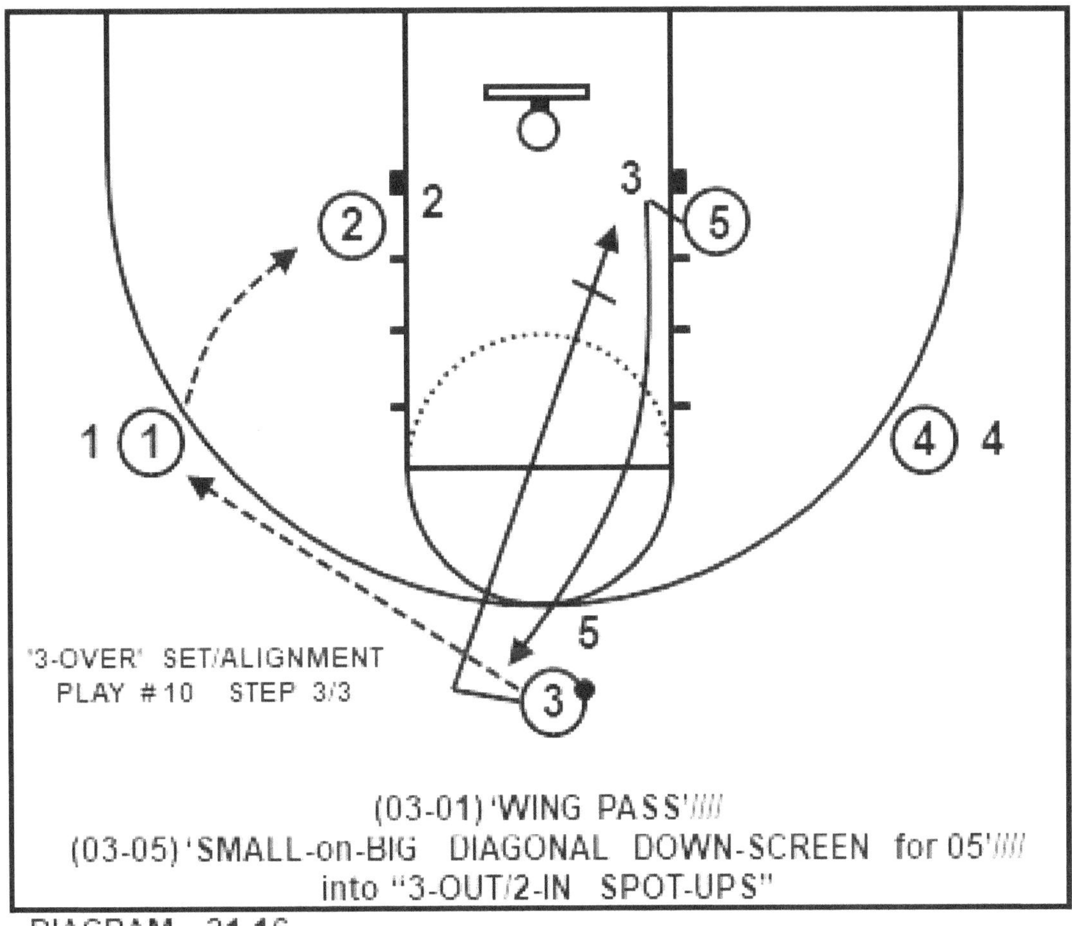

Diagram 21.16

The difference in the following plays/entries are that all five players will end up in one of the different offensive spot-ups. These "4-Out/1-In Spot-Ups" will have players moved about via cuts, screens, dribbles and after every play each player could (and will) result in spotting up in any of the five ending up in the "Ballside Deep Corner" or "Ballside Slot," the Weakside Deep Corner and the Slot," and the "Ballside Mid-Post," and the "Weakside Deep Corner."

These five spot-up positions can also give the offense safe and easy types of ball-reversals, large gaps for dribble penetration, opportunities to deliver the ball inside to whomever (perimeter-type or post-type players) is posting up their defender on the "Ballside Block." The two "Deep Corners" horizontally and vertically spread the opposition's defense to weaken the interior and not allow a complete coverage of both interior and perimeter players. Players that are perimeter-scoring threats and a legitimate offensive rebounding threats from outside of the arc have opportunities for weakside offensive rebounding, defensive transition as well as "skip pass "catch and shoot" possibilities after "skip passes" are made from any of the three locations on the ballside to either "weakside perimeter" location.

21.17 illustrates a Level 3 play out of the same "3-ACROSS" Set with 03 initially stepping out to appear to be setting a "Flex-Screen" for 02 to use on a "Flex-Cut" across the lane, similar to Plays # 4 and # 10. 02 "Bump Cuts" not across the lane but diagonally up and across the lane so 03 could make an "Iverson Cut" off of 04's "Iverson Screen." 03 ends up at the FT Line extended on the opposite side of the floor. After making the pass to 03, 01 makes a "Ballside (Deep) Corner Cut" into the "Deep Corner" on the same side of the floor with 03.

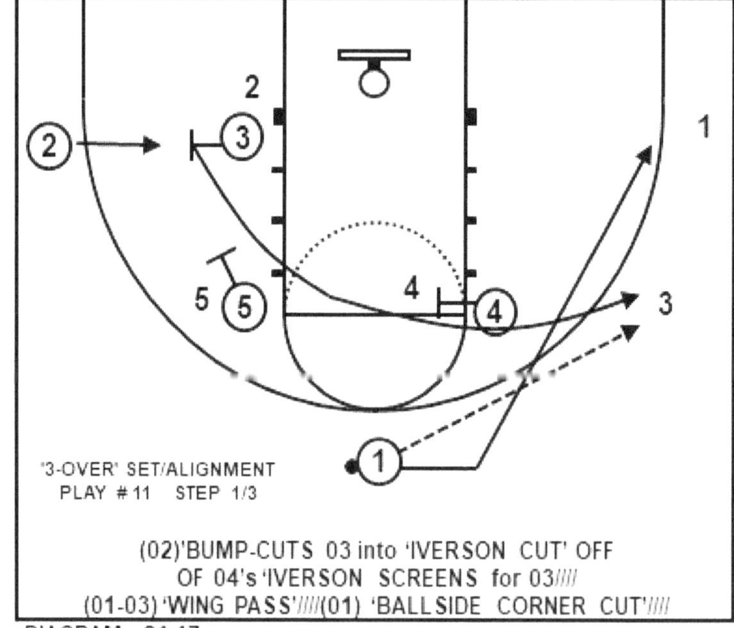

DIAGRAM   21.17

After "Iverson Screening" for 03, 04 then diagonally breaks down to set a "Big-on-Small Diagonal Pin Down-Screen" for 02 to use to flash to the new "Ballside High Post." After screening, 04 steps further out into the "Deep Corner" perimeter area to extend the opposition out horizontally. Also at the same time, 05 stretches the defense vertically by stepping out to the new "Weakside Slot." This action isolates and inverts 02's perimeter-type defender, X2, at the "Ballside High Post." Diagram 21.18.

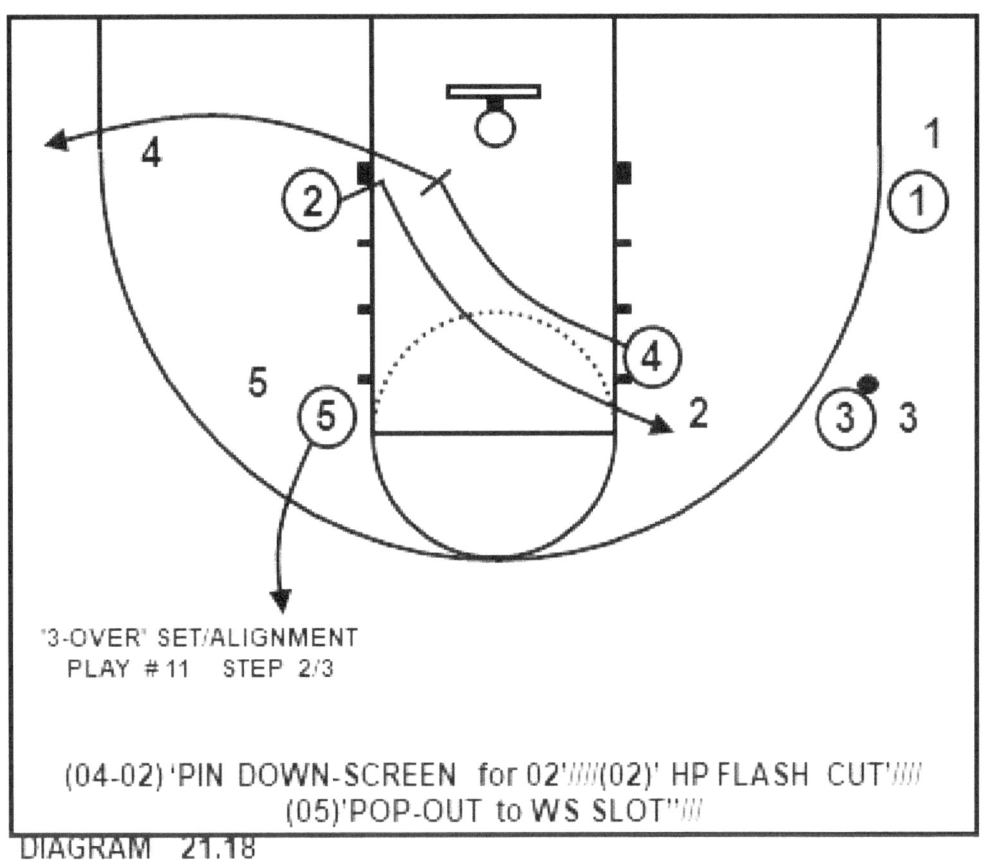

Diagram 21.18

If no shots are taken, 02 steps out to set an "Inside Ball-Screen" for 03 to either "penetrate dribble into the lane" or to "perimeter pull dribble" across the top of the key. 03 uses full advantage of the screen by "dribble-scraping" off of 02's outside right shoulder.

Presumably, the two biggest defenders are 05 and 04 and they both have been manipulated into playing as helpside perimeter players away from the basket. 02 should read the defense and decide whether to "rim-run" or "roll" through the lane to post up his isolated with minimal defensive support and inverted (and most likely inexperienced small post) defender.

If shots are not taken, the "4-Out/1-In" Spot-Ups are filled to continue the offensive attack. Diagram 21.19.

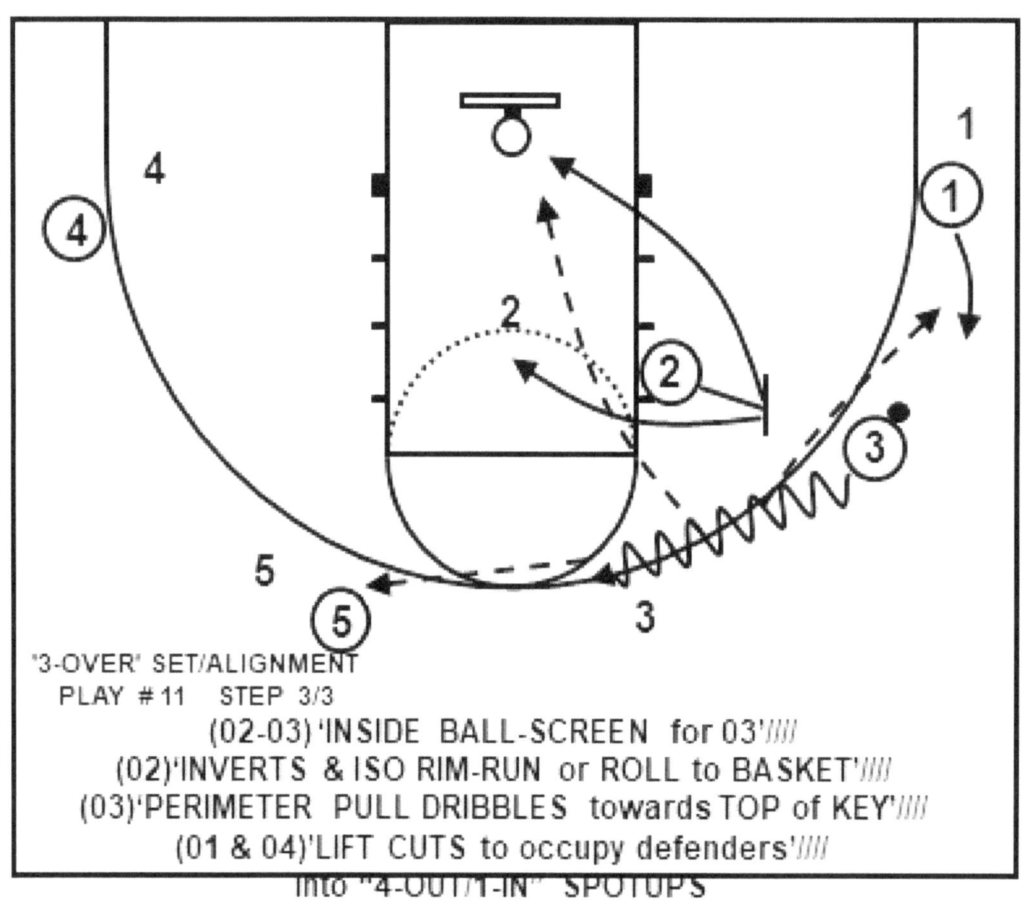

Diagram 21.19

CLOSING

The "3-OVER" Set is a very good and somewhat unique offensive alignment that can use many of the same actions that a "HORNS" Set can use in addition to being able to execute actions such as high "Ball-Screens" and low "Flex-Screens" besides its own set of more unique and less common forms of offensive attack.

Just like every play that is a part of every offensive alignment, there is free-flowing actions of many kinds that always remains fundamentally sound and structured within the framework of the offense. Each play from this offensive set also provides the easy conversion into the final phase of the overall offensive attack, be it a continuity offense or a motion-type offensive phase.

After the entry/play/quick-hitter has been executed but no shots have been taken, all five players will end up in the "3-Out/2-In Spot-Ups" that consist of the following locations/positions: the "Ballside Block," the "Ballside Wing," the "Weakside Block," the "Weakside Wing," and the "Point" (at the top of the key). These five locations/positions will give the offense safe and easy kinds of ball-reversals, large gaps for dribble penetration, ways to deliver the ball inside to whomever (perimeter-type or post-type players) is posting up their defender on the "Ballside Block," and a player that can be a perimeter-scoring threat and a legitimate offensive rebounding threat from outside of the arc on his "offensive crashing of the boards." The "3-Out/2-In Spot-Ups also offer successful methods for constant and effective defensive transition responsibilities.

PLAYS/ENTRIES THAT END in the "4-OUT/1-IN" OFFENSIVE SPOT-UPS

The difference in the following family of plays/entries are that all five players will end up in these "4-Out/1-In Spot-Ups" that could individually called the "Ballside Deep Corner," the "Weakside Deep Corner." the "Ballside Slot," the "Weakside Slot," and the "Ballside Post." "These five positions also can provide the offense with successful ball-reversals, more possibilities for dribble penetration, opportunities to attack the defense with interior passing to either perimeter-type or post-type players. These "4-Out/1-In Spot-Ups will also give the offense strong methods of attacking the defense with offensive rebounds, particularly from the weakside as well as a successful defensive transition scheme.

PLAYS/ENTRIES THAT END in

the "HIGH-POST/LOW POST" OFFENSIVE SPOT-UPS

The main difference in this family of plays plays/entries are that all five players will end up in a different group of offensive spot-ups. These "HIGH-POST/LOW-POST" Spot-Ups will have players moved about the court with any of the five ending up in the "Ballside Block," the "Ballside High Post," the "Ballside Wing," the "Weakside Wing," and the "Point" (or top of the guy)" Though different from the other two sets of offensive spot-ups, these spot-ups can also allow continuity offenses that utilize these spot-ups with the same ball-reversals, driving gaps for dribble penetration, opportunities to deliver the ball inside to two different ballside post pass receiving locations as well as an excellent perimeter shooting location on the weakside of the of the offense. The spot-ups again offer some very strong weakside rebounding opportunities from the perimeter. Defensive conversion should still be good with a fundamentally strong scheme.

The "4-DOWN" SET/ALIGNMENT is a symmetrically balanced offensive set.

With the offense starting in a 1-4 offensive alignment with all four off-the-ball players aligned along the baseline, with two on each side of the lane plus 01 with the ball centered up; there is no designated strong and weak side of the offense.

That means that any entry could actually be executed on both sides of the floor. With that, it means that the number of plays that could be installed within the family of plays doubles without the actual complexity level increasing in a high degree.

Diagram 22.1 is Level 1 play that has 05 step up and out to set a "Big-on-Small Shuffle Back-Screen on their side of the floor with 03 "shuffle-cutting" hard to the basket and 05 then remaining at the now vacant "Wing" area. At the same time, 02 makes an "L-Cut" up and out to the "Wing" on his side of the floor.

01 would make the pass to either side of the floor and execute the "Follow (the Pass) Ball-Screen & Rim Run," but in this instance, 01 makes the pass to 02 on his side of the floor. 01 then follows his pass and sets a "Small-on-Big Ball-Screen" for 02 to "perimeter dribble-pull" out towards the top of the key, while 01(front or reverse) pivots off of his inside left foot to make an inverted "Rim-Run" to the basket. The initial "Ballside Block" player (04 on this side of the floor) breaks diagonally out to the now empty FT Line extended.

If 01 had made the initial pass to 05, 03 would have made the cut that 04 makes and 05 would be the dribbler that 02 is on the right side of the floor.

In either direction, the "3-Out-/2-In" Spot-Ups are filled if no shots are taken (from the interior or the perimeter.) Diagram 22.1

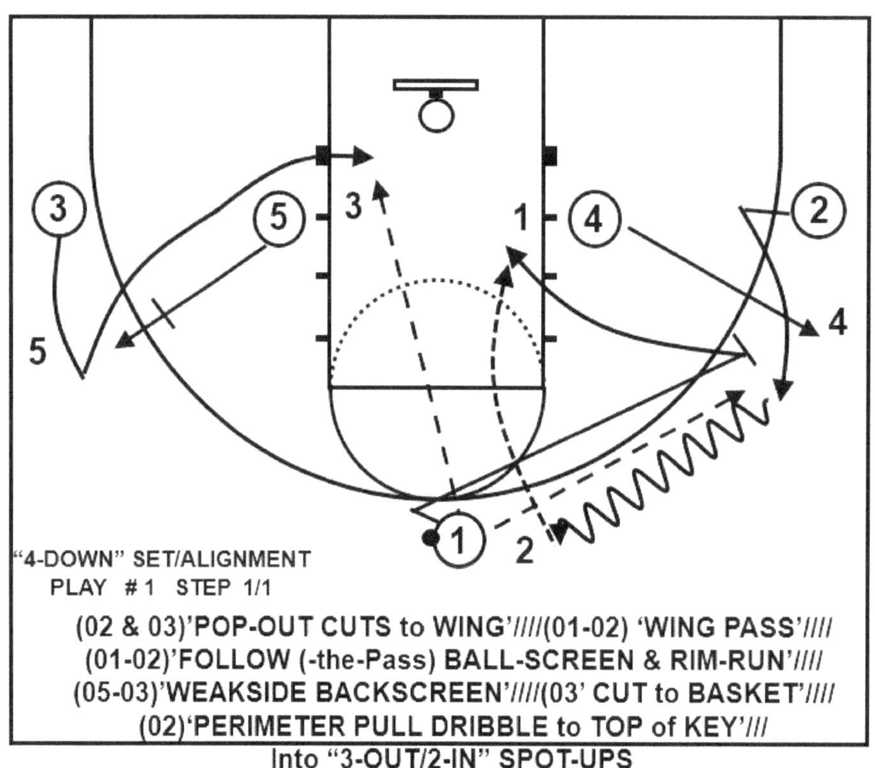

Play # 1   Diagram 22.1

Diagram 22.2 is another Level 1 play that shows the play being run to the left side of the floor. 03 sprints up from his left side "Deep Corner" to set a "Big-on-Small Long Ball-Screen" for 01 to use to dribble off of 03's right shoulder to the "Wing" area on the left side of the floor. Before 01 reaches 03, 04 should break up to set an off-the-ball ("Big-on-Small "Long Flare-) Screen the (Ball-)Screener" for 02 to use to "Flare-Cut" to the opposite side's "Wing" area. As 04 breaks up, 02 should cut off of 05's "Big-on-Small Long Flex-Screen" that takes place on 04's initial location.

01's options are to look to hit 02 on his "Flex Cut," to skip the ball to 03 on the new "Weakside Wing," and to look to create or to reverse the ball to 04 out on top of the key.

Every player has moved himself and therefore his defender into a different location on the floor, looking for defensive breakdowns. The new locations are the exact "3-Out/2-In" Spot-Ups where the offense can transition into the next and final phase of the offense. Diagram 22.2

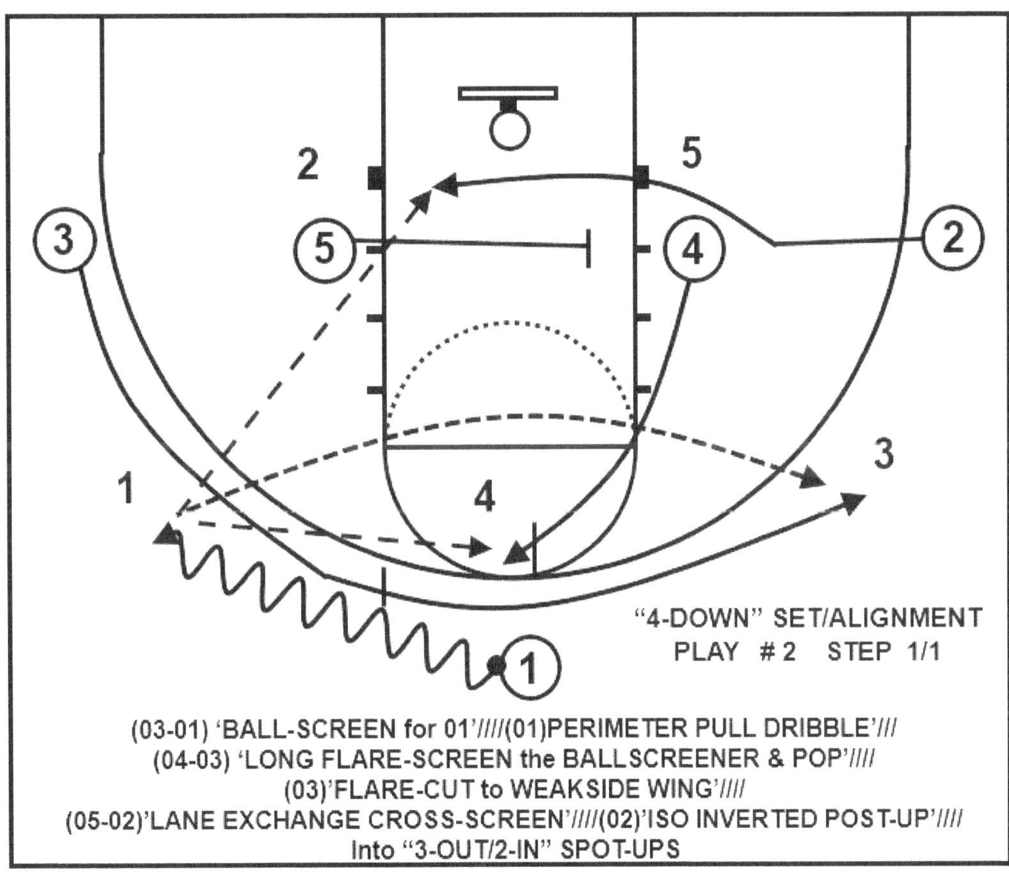

Play # 2   Diagram 22.2

Diagrams 22.3 and 22.4 represent Play #3, another Level 2 play that can be a ""Counter"" to Play 2 with similar action to Play # 2. As 03 breaks up again to set the same "Long Ball-Screen for 01 to use, 05 again sets his "Cross-Screen" but this time for 04 to use to flash to the new "Ballside Block. This time, after 03 sets his screen for 01, he remains at the top of the key and 02 simply rotates up to fill the new "Weakside Wing" area. Diagram 22.3

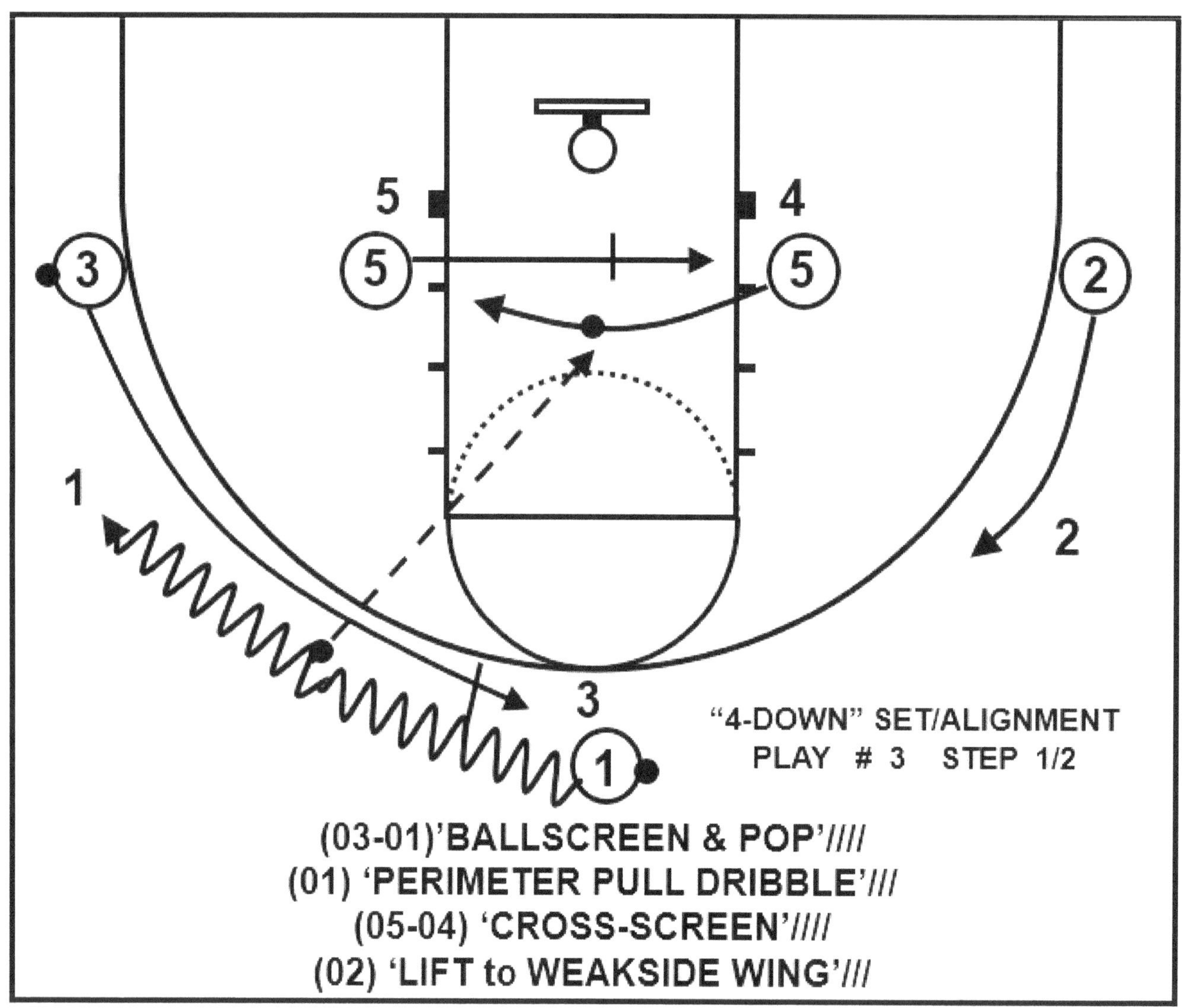

Play # 3   Diagram 22.3

If 01 cannot make the "Inside Pass" to 04 on his new "Ballside Block Post-Up" or his (01-02) "Skip Pass" towards the "Weakside Wing," he simply makes the short and simple "Reverse Pass" to 03, out on top.

Diagram 22.4 illustrates 03 receiving the pass at the top of the key. Upon 03 catching the ball from 01, 04 makes a hard "Iso Duck-In Cut" to receive the "Inside Pass" from 03. If 03 cannot make the pass to 04, X4 would have to be in a "full front" or "3/4 front stance." From the weakside of the lane, 05 must stick his head under the basket to get into the proper screening angle to then set his "Spin Back-Screen" from behind X4. If X4 denies 04 the ball, 04 must "reverse pivot" off of his lower right foot and scrape off of 05's lower right shoulder before curling around him to receive the pass from 03, now at the top of the key. After contact is broken, 05 slips the screen and steps towards 03 and the ball while still in the lane and also looks for the ball from 03 (or possibly from 01.)

If 03 cannot hit either 04 or 05 in the lane, 03 still should be able to make passes to either side of the floor, where 01 and 02 have horizontally stretched the floor and the defense by being in the two "Wing" area locations. Play # 3's action has aggressively attack the interior defense as well as moved all five players into the required "3-Out/2-In" Spot-Up locations for a smooth transition into the designated continuity offense (or motion-type offense). Diagram 22.4

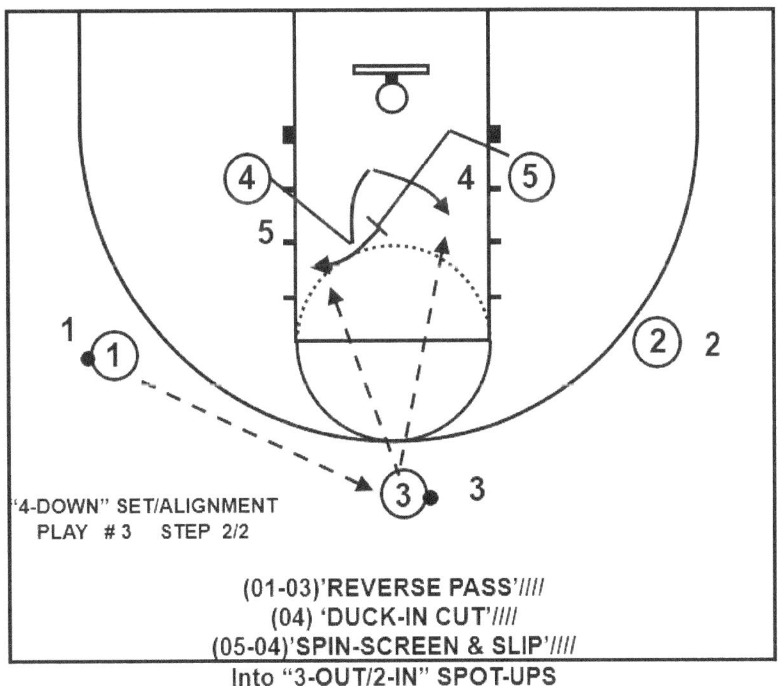

Diagram 22.4

Diagrams 22.5 and 22.6 represent Play #4, another Level 2 play that can be a "Counter" to both Plays 2 and 3.

Diagram 22.5 dribbles towards 03 on the left side of the floor and 03 and 02 both break up from their "Deep Corner" locations. At the same time, 05 empties out to cross the lane to set a "Lane Exchange Cross-Screen" for 04 to use to flash across to the new "Ballside Block." If 04 is not open, 01 continues to meet 03 to receive the DHO. Diagram 22.5

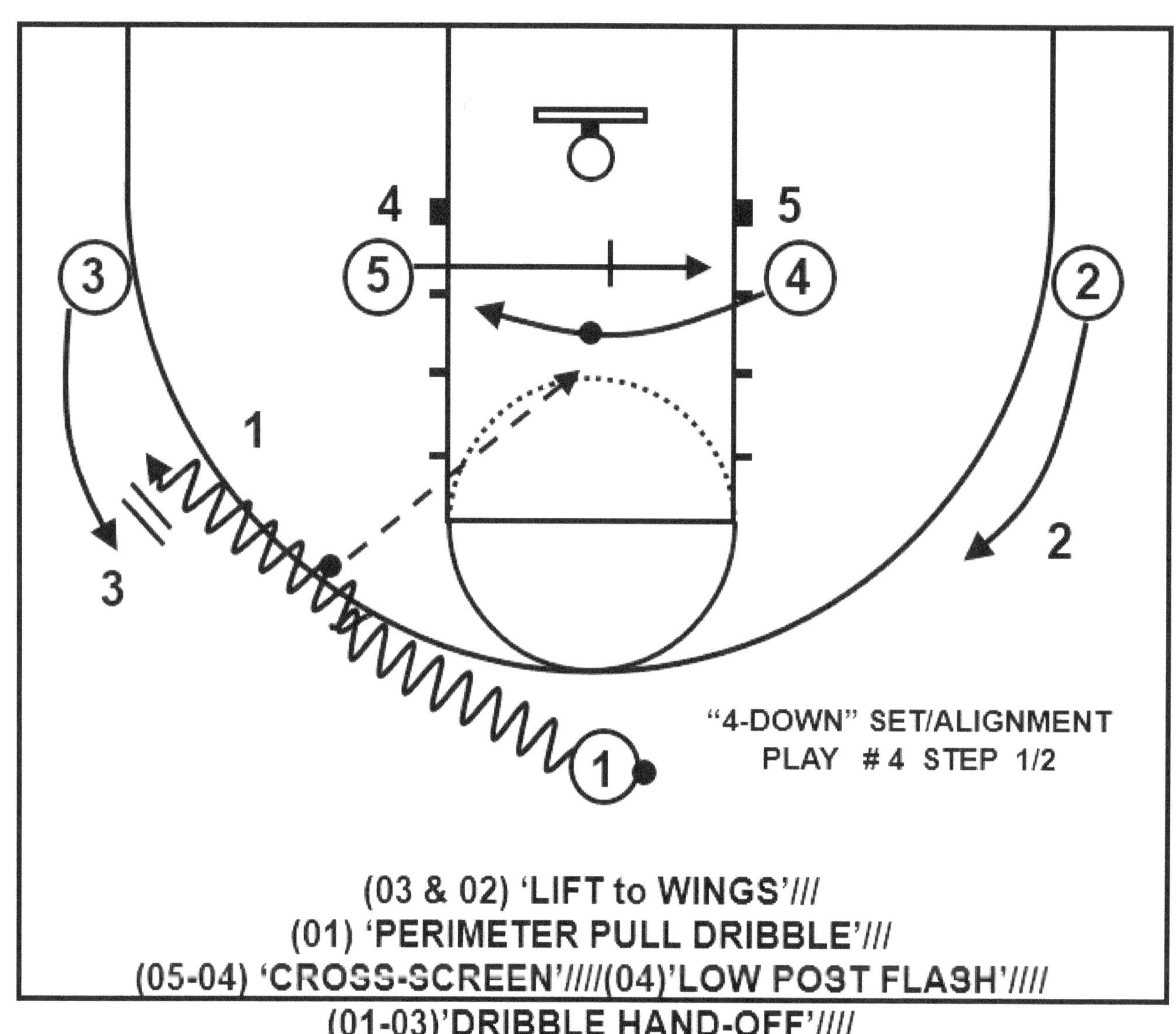

Play # 4   Diagram 22.5

Diagram 22.6 illustrates 03 receiving the DHO and "perimeter pull-dribbling" the ball towards the top of the key. As 03 dribbles out to the top of the key, 04 makes a hard "Iso Duck-In Cut" to receive the ball. For 04 not to receive the ball, X4 would have to "full front" or "3/4 front" 04. This is where, 05 gets into the proper screening angle by cutting up from underneath the basket to set his head-hunter "Spin-(Back)Screen from behind. When fronted by X4 should make a "reverse pivot" off of his lower right foot and then spin tightly off of 05's lower right shoulder before swirling around him to receive the pass from 03 out on top. After 04 breaks contact with 05, 05 slips the screen and steps towards 03 with a "front pivot" towards the ball while still in the lane, ready to catch and attack.

If 03 cannot hit either 04 or 05 in the lane, he still has 01 and 02 floating at each "Wing" area location. This action of Play # 4 has again repositioned all five players into the required "3-Out/2-In" Spot-Up locations for a smooth transition into the designated continuity offense (or motion-type offense). Diagram 22.6

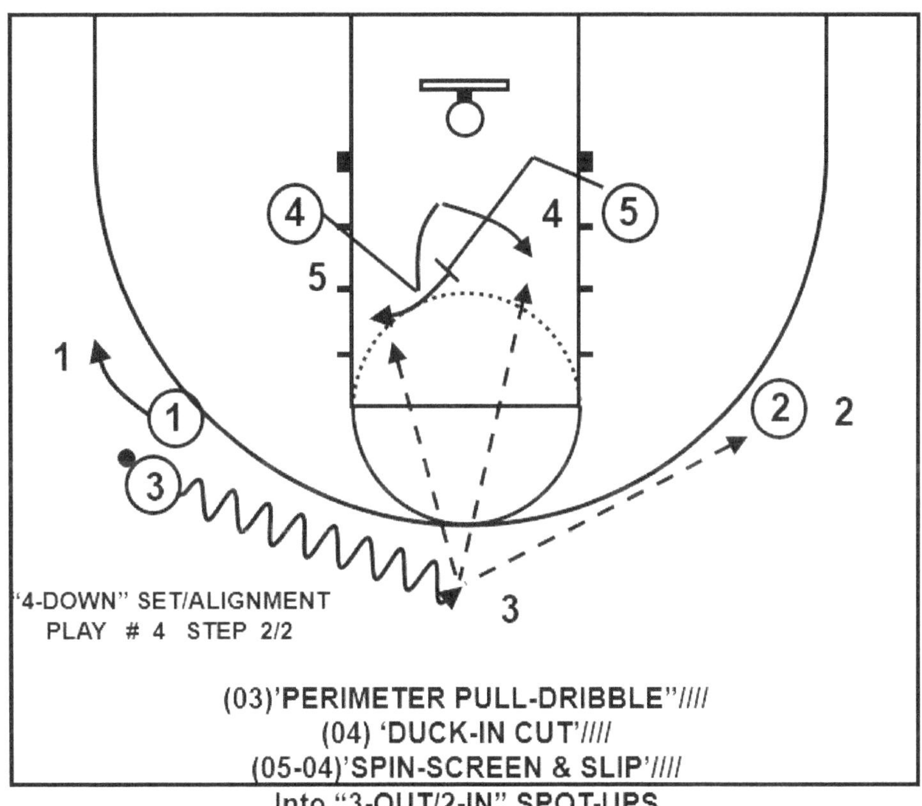

Diagram 22.6

Diagrams 22.7 and 22.8 show the complete Level 2 play numbered # 5. The beginning action has some similarities to Plays # 2, 3 and 4 with the 05-04 "Cross-Screening action and the integral "spin-screening action" that completes each play is identical to each of the three plays.

The slight difference in this play has both 03 and 02 make "Lift Cuts" to the top of the key before 01 then makes a "Wing Pass" to 03 (even though the play could begin with a (01-02) "Wing Pass." 01 then follows his pass to make a "Small-on-Big Follow-the-Pass Ball-Screen" for 03 to use. This action looks different in appearance but gets the same results as a DHO. It requires very little mental effort by the offense and could require a great deal more by the opposition. Diagram 22.7

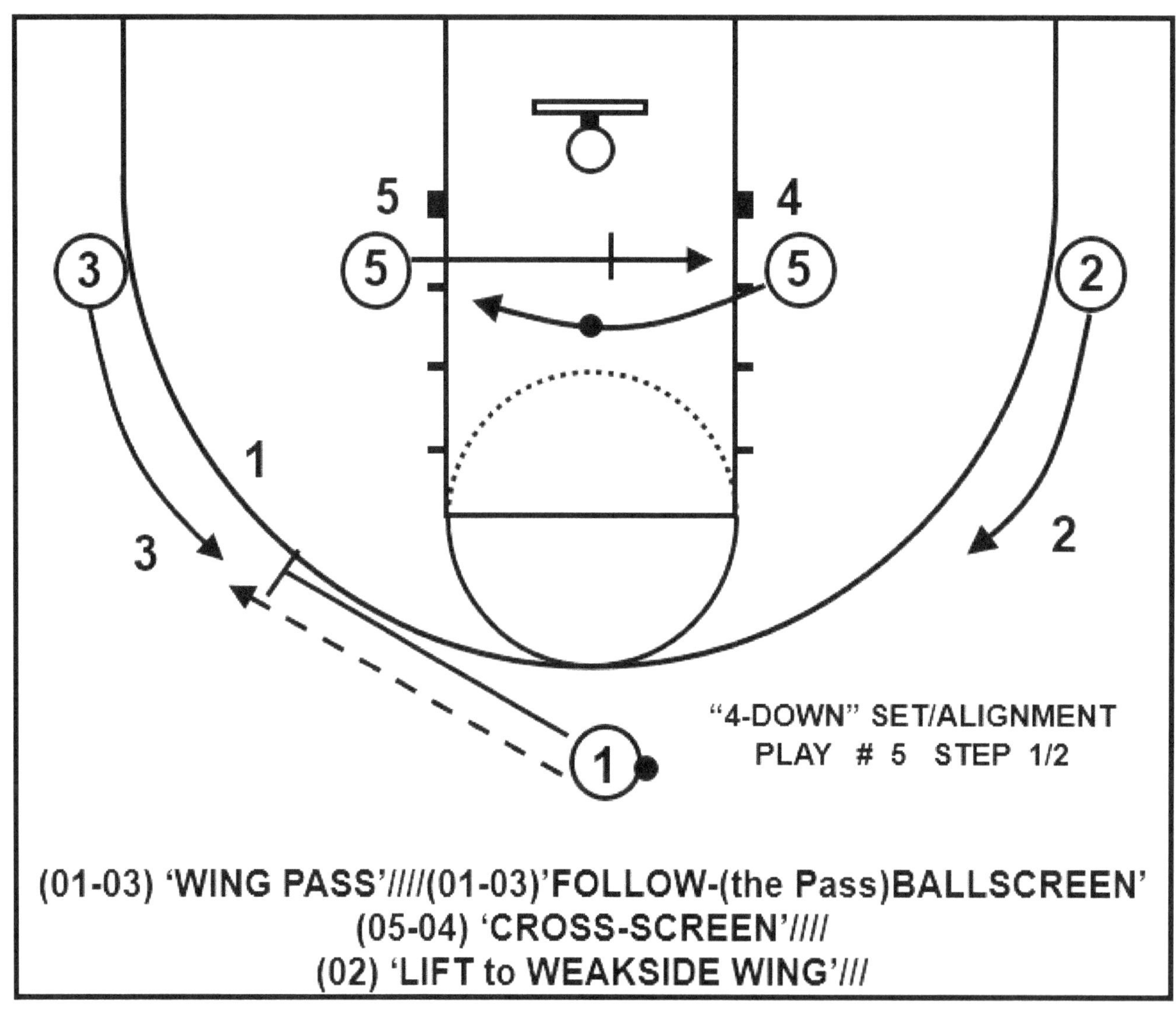

Play # 5   Diagram 22.7

Diagram 22.8 illustrates 03 receiving the pass before then receiving 01's "Ball-Screen." 03 then "dribble-scrapes" off of 01's outside left shoulder and makes his "perimeter pull dribble" towards the top of the key. On 03's trip towards the top of the key, 04 makes the same hard and aggressive "Isolated Duck-In Cut" to be open for the "Interior Pass" made by 03 off of the dribble. If 04 is denied the ball, 05's "Spin-Screen" action should eliminate that defensive problem for both 04 as well as for 05.

Still, if no shots are taken, the "3-Out/2-In" Spot-Ups are filled that will conclude the play but begin the final phase of the attack.

The slight differences in the beginnings of Plays # 2, 3, 4 and 5 should keep opposing defenses off-balance and not know which play is actually being executed (and therefore how it is to be properly defended.) This gives the offense another high level of unpredictability over the opposition—still another offensive advantage over the defense. Diagram 22.8

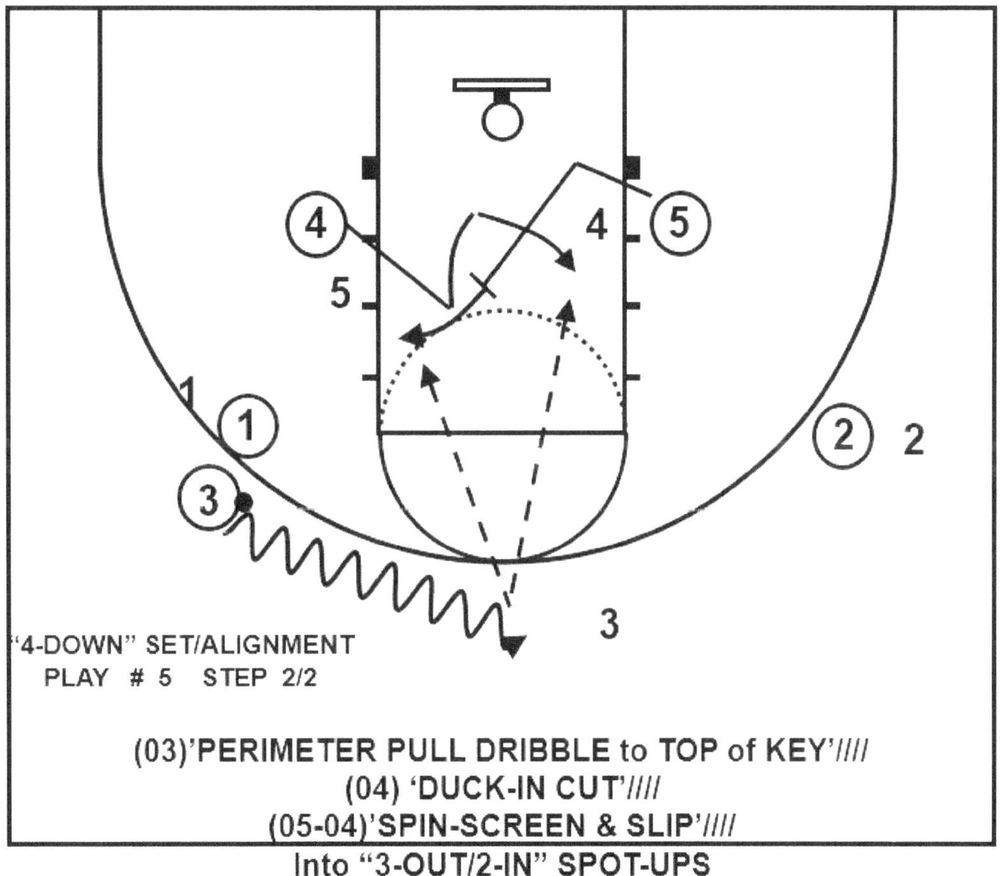

Diagram 22.8

Diagrams 22.9 and 22.10 illustrate the entire Play # 6, a Level 2 play out of the same set. While 01 could dribble towards either "Slot," he has chosen the "Slot" on the right side of the court. 05 and 03 work to sell the fake "Flex Screen & Cut" action before 05 simply makes a vertical "Elbow Cut." 03 acts as if to use 05's screen before remaining in his initial "Deep Corner" area. During this time, 04 makes an aggressive "Iso Duck-In Cut" while 02 remains spotted up in his own "Deep Corner" area.

If 04 is fronted or "3/4 fronted" to prevent him from receiving the ball, 01 could make a "Lob Pass" towards the basket for 04 to seal his defender and receive 01's pass. 01 could also make a "Down Pass" to 02 if 02 has a better passing angle to deliver the ball to 04 or if 02 is wide open for a "catch and shoot" or a "catch and create" situation.

If X4 plays behind 04, 01 should then look to make the "Inside Pass" to 04 in the middle of the lane and attack X4 in a "one on one close to the basket" situation. Diagram 22.9

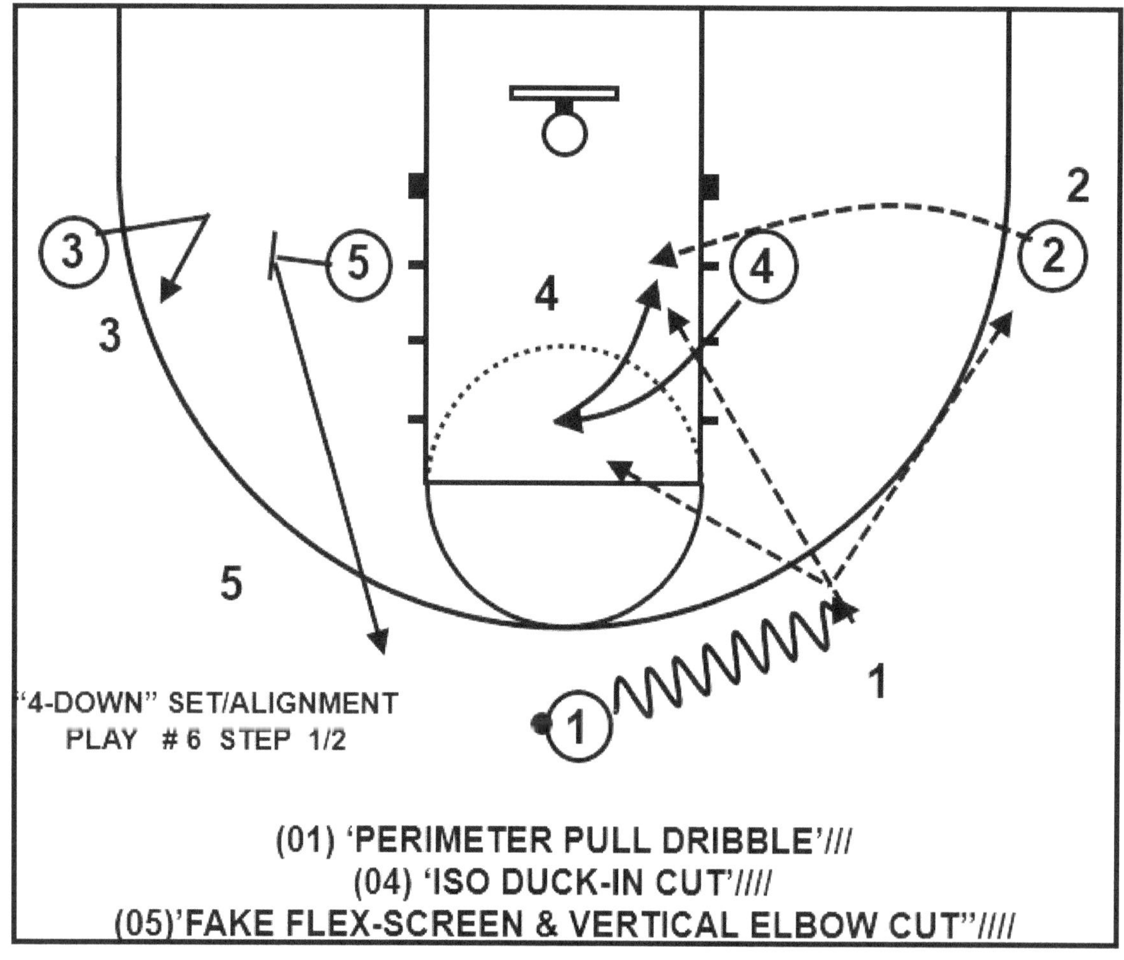

Play # 6   Diagram 22.9

If 01 turns down passes to either 04 or 02, he could easily reverse the ball to the inverted post-type player, 05; who is now spotted up at the new "Weakside Slot." If that pass is made, 04 continues his cut and breaks to the "Nail" to first set an (04-01) "Big-on-Small Shuffle Back-Screen." If 05 does not make the pass to 01 on his "Shuffle Cut," he makes the "Wing Pass" to 03, not spotted up at the FT Line extended.

As soon as the pass is made from 05 to 03, 05 then makes his own "Shuffle-Cut" and scrapes off of 04's left shoulder to make a "Lob Cut" to the basket. 02 occupies the lone helpside defender by repositioning himself to the FT Line extended. 03 could make the "Inside Pass" to 01 on his "Inverted and Iso Post-Up" or the "Lob Pass" to 05 on his cut tightly curling off of 04. After setting the "Scissors Screens" first for 01 and then for 05, 04 makes an inverted "Pop-Out Cut" to the top of the key. This final cut then moves players into the same standard "3-Out/2-In" Spot-Ups. Diagram 22.10

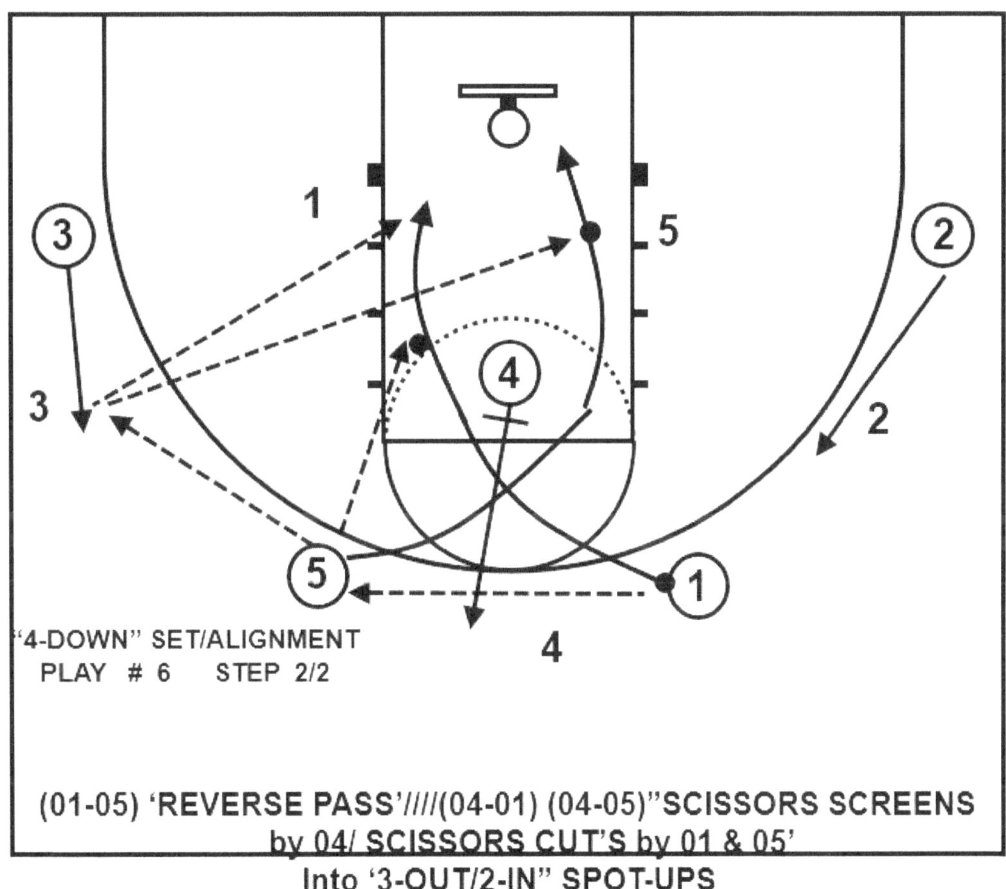

Diagram 22.10

Once again, to emphasize the fact that any entries/plays out of symmetrically balanced offensive sets/alignments such as the "4-DOWN" Set could be designated to begin on both the left or the right side of the floor, Play # 7 is shown to be started on the right side (while 4 of the six entries have currently started on the left side.)

01 starts this particular Level 2 play by both 03 and 02 breaking up to the FT Line extended and 01 then dribbling towards 02 on the right side of the floor. As 01 and 02 appear to meet, 04 makes another "Iso Duck-In Cut." With 03 at the FT Line extended and 05 breaking up to the top of the key, this combined action helps eliminate the defense's interior support defense that X4 would need to deny 04 the ball. Diagram 22.11

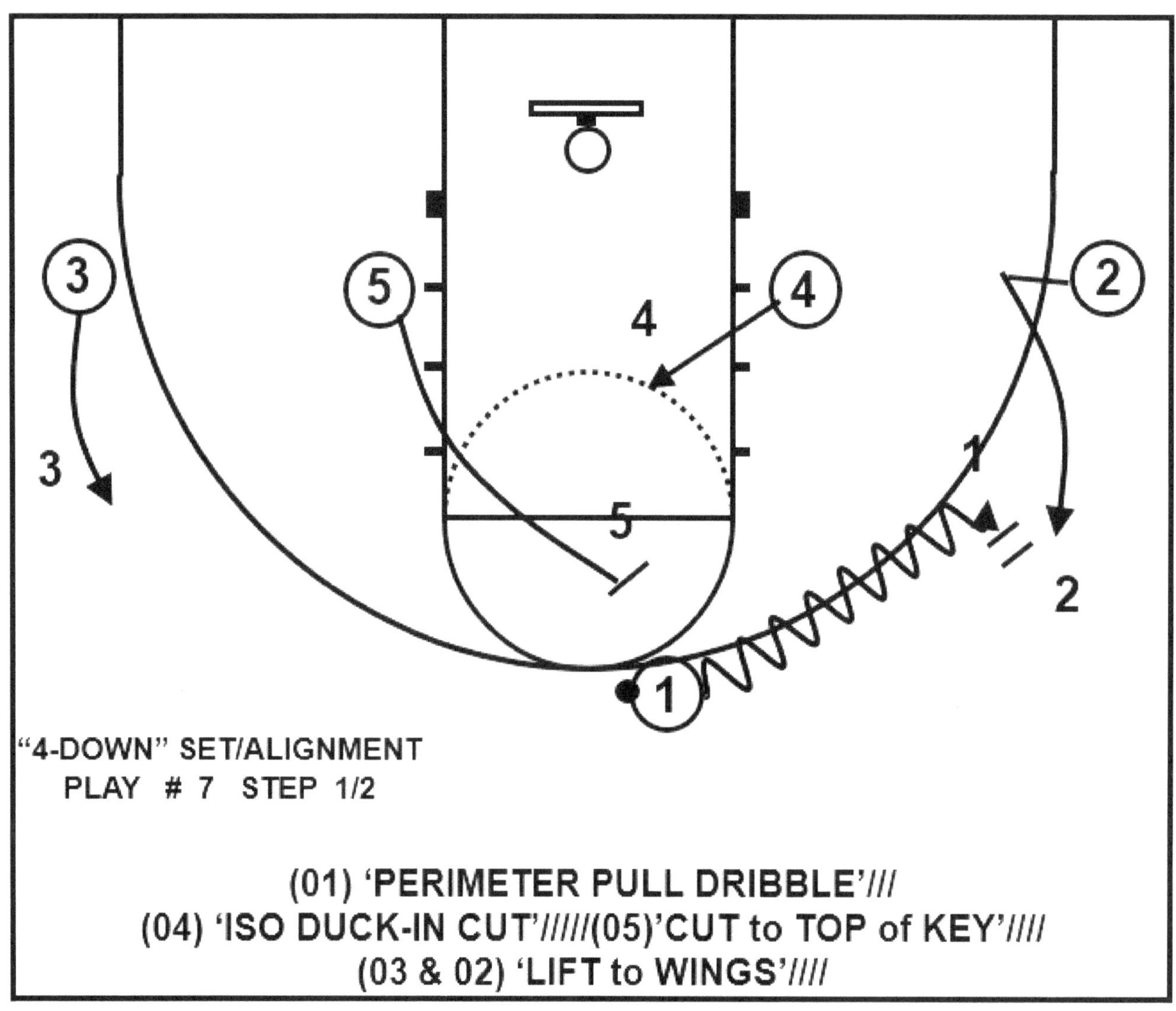

Play # 7   Diagram 22.11

If the ball is not entered to 04, 04 continues cutting across to the other side of the lane. As 02 receives the 01-02 DHO, 02 starts his "perimeter pull-dribble" towards 05 and the top of the key. When 02 reaches the top, he continues to "dribble-scrape" off of 05's top right shoulder and continues across to the opposite side's "Slot." When 01 breaks contact with 05, 05 makes a "front pivot" off of his lower left foot and makes a "Rim-Run Lob Cut" to the basket. 02 would have the opportunity to make an "Inside Pass" to 04 posting up, a "Lob Pass" to 05, a possible "Reverse Throwback Pass" to 01 on the new "Weakside Wing" or a pass to 03 now spotted up on the new "Ballside Wing." 03 would then have scoring or creating opportunities as well as making an "Inside Pass" to 04.

If no shots develop, the "3-Out/2-In" Spot-Ups are filled for a smooth and fluid continuation of the overall offensive attack. Diagram 22.12

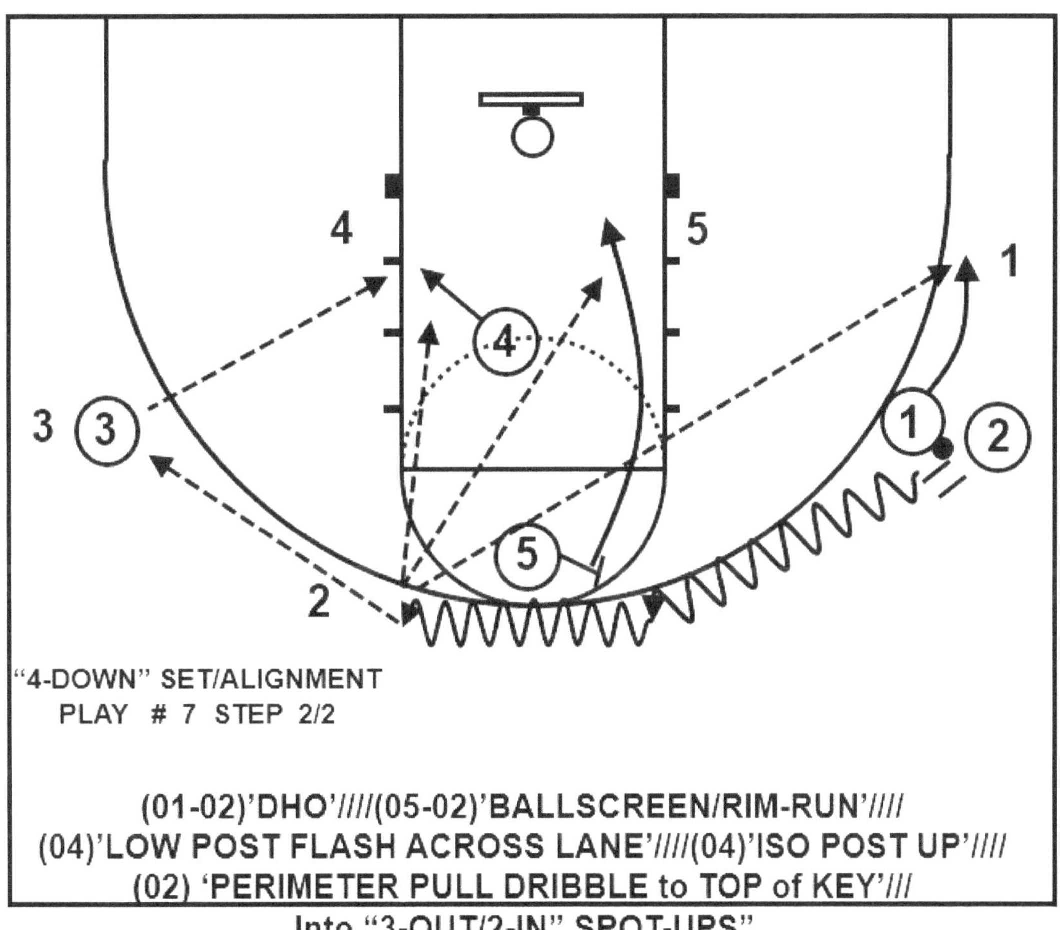

Diagram 22.12

Diagrams 22.13 and 22.14 illustrate the entire Play # 8, another Level 2 play that could be considered a "Counter" to Play # 7. As 03 and 02 both make "Lift Cuts" as they do in Play # 7, and 04 steps into the lane (as he does in the previous play), it appears to be the same play. Instead, 04 starts across as if to set a "Cross-Screen" for 05 to use. 05 starts to use the screen before flashing up (as he does in Play # 7) towards the top of the key. 04 returns to his initial post-up location and looks for an "Inside Pass" from 01 before he reaches 02's destination. If no pass is made to 04, 01 continues to 02 to make the 01-02 DHO. Diagram 22.13

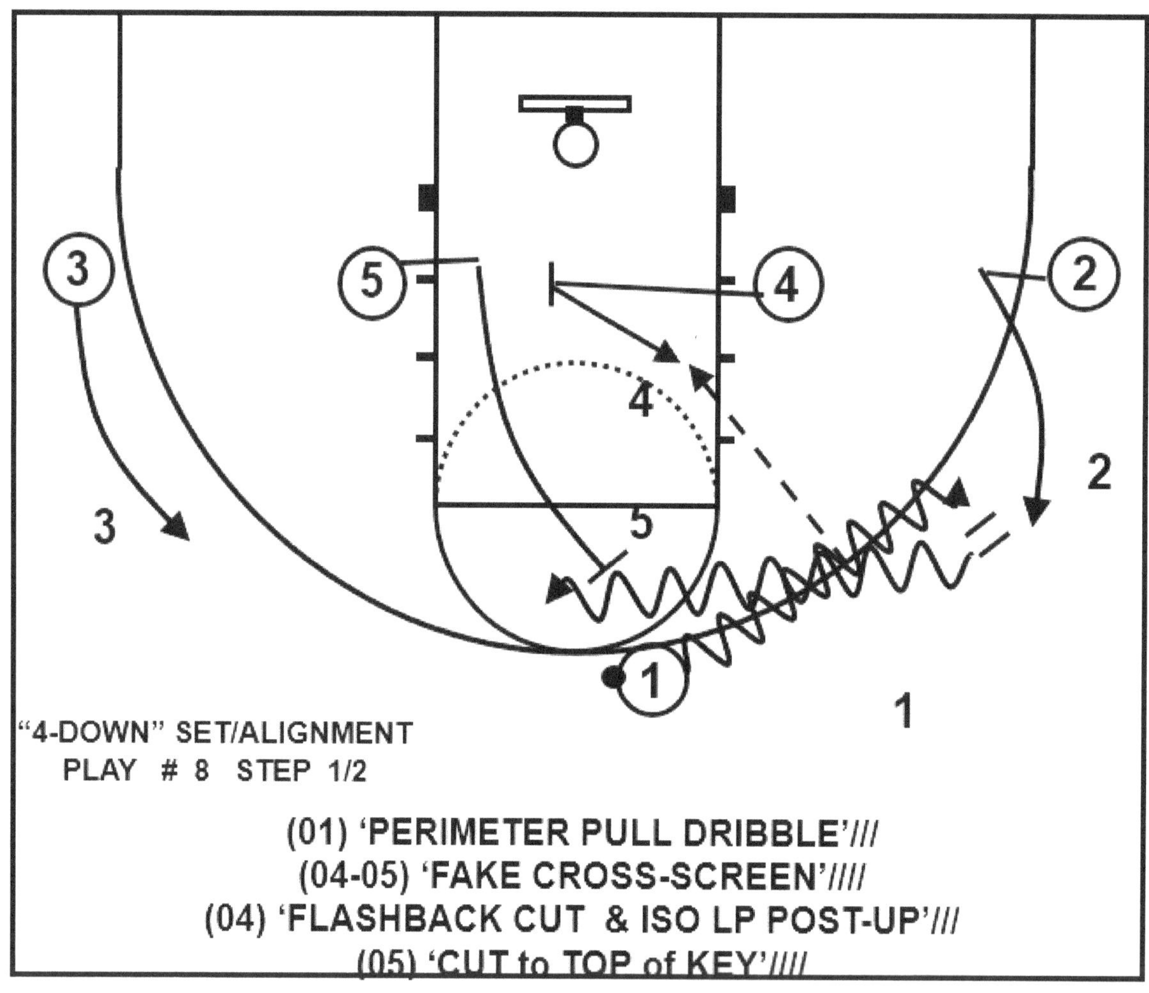

Play # 8   Diagram 22.13

Again, 02 "must dribble tightly off of 05's body to brush his defender off. In this instance, the main difference between Play # 7 and Play # 8 is that upon breaking contact with 02, 05 makes a "reverse pivot" off of his inside left foot and rolls down the lane while looking for an "Inside Pass" from 02 or possibly from 03, now spotted up at the "Weakside Wing" area. With 05 rolling in the opposite direction that he does in Play # 7, 04 returns back to his initial "Block" location to post-up. If no shots are taken, the "3-Out/2-In" Spot-Ups are once again filled for the next phase of the offensive system. Diagram 22.14

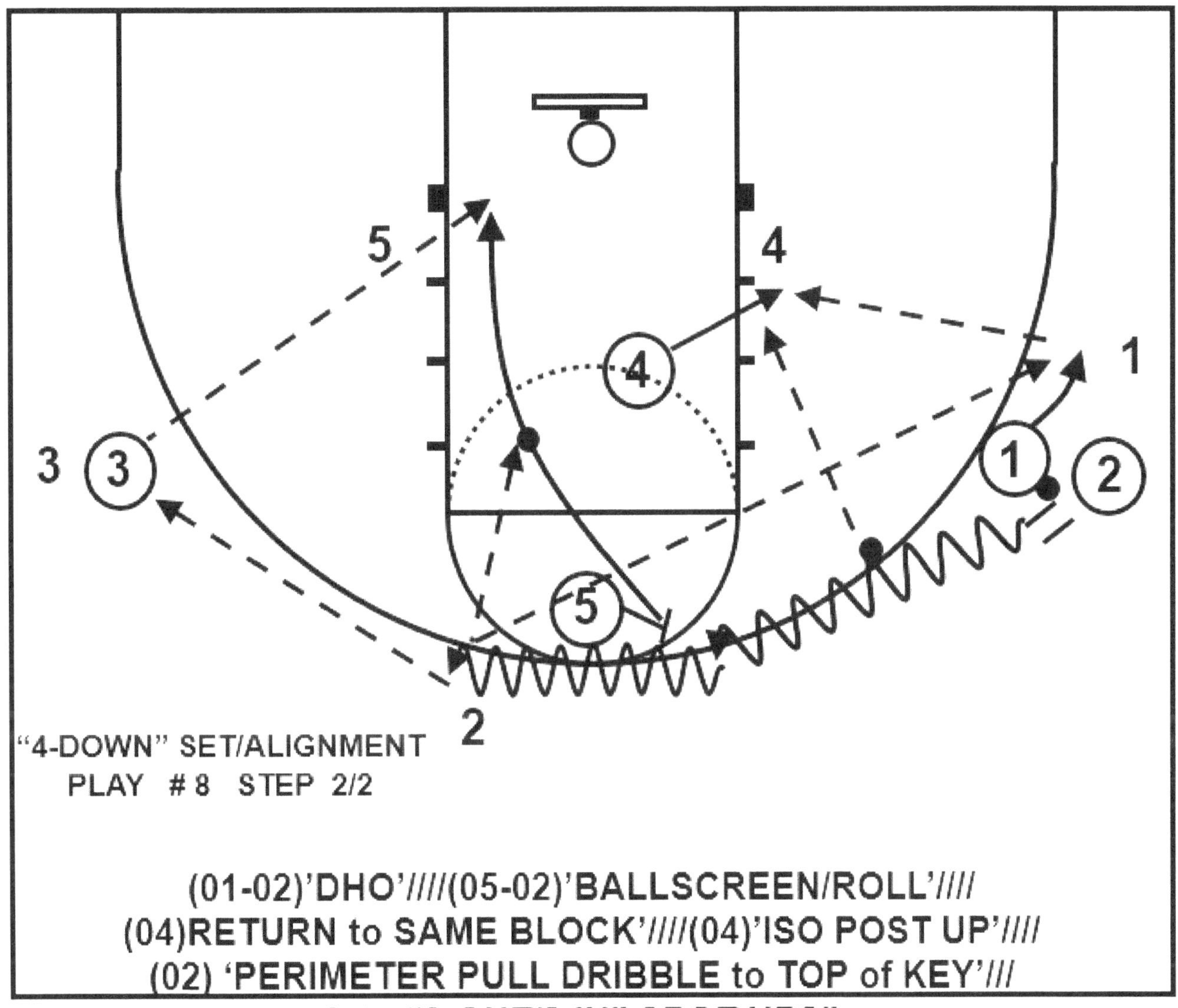

Diagram 22.14

Diagrams 22.15 through 22.17 demonstrate the entire Level 3 play, called Play #9. Again, while the play could be executed towards either side of the floor, 01 has elected to make his "perimeter pull dribble" towards the "Wing" area on the left side of the floor. This dictates that 03 run to the lane before then making a "Zipper Cut" up to the new "Ballside Slot." 01 looks to make an "Inside Pass" to 05 or possibly to 03 on his vertical cut up through the lane. Diagram 22.15

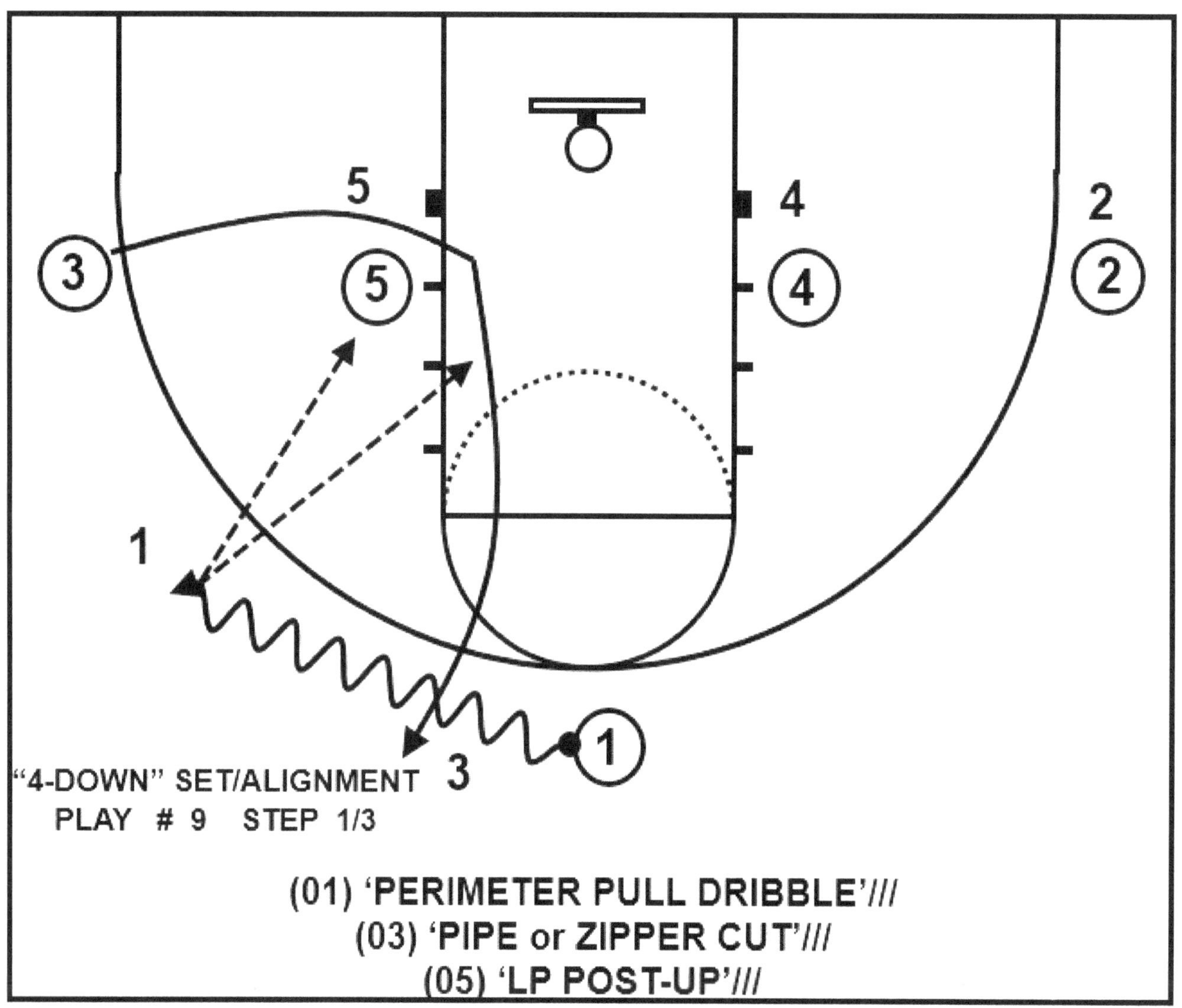

Play # 9   Diagram 22.15

Immediately after 03 has passed by 05, 05 should empty out across the lane to set a (05-04) "Cross-Screen" for 04 to use. 04 should "scrape" off of either shoulder of 04 to flash to the ball, but rubbing off of 05's lower left shoulder will likely give 05 a better opportunity of sealing off of his defender and cutting diagonally up to the top of the key (similar to Plays 7 and 8.)

If 01 cannot make the interior pass to 05, 03 or to 04; 01 waits to make the (01-03) "Reverse Pass" out on the "Slot." Upon receiving 01's pass, 03 should use the (05-03) "Big-on-Small Long Ball-Screen" and start his "perimeter drag dribble" across the top of the key to the opposite "Slot." Diagram 22.16

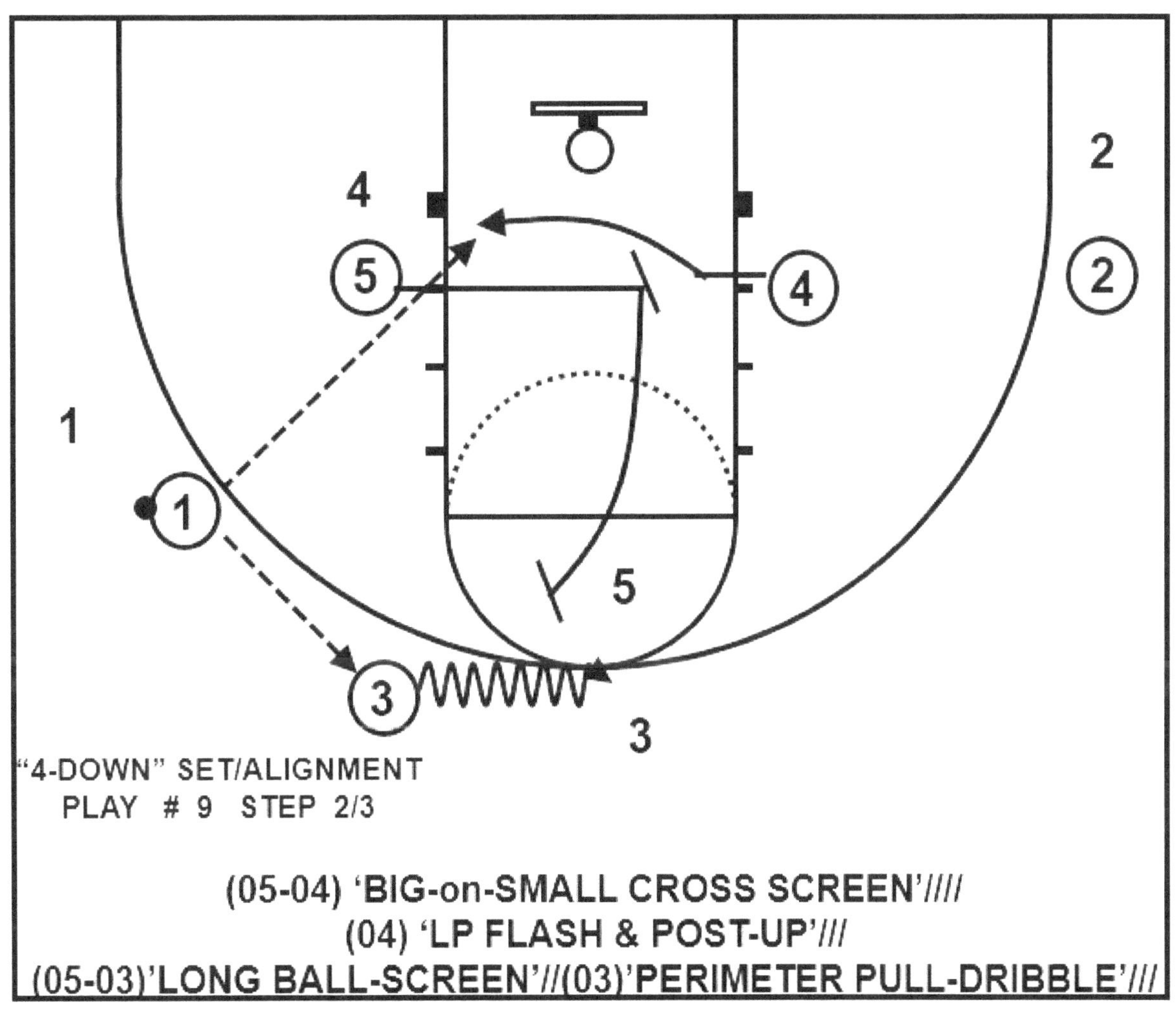

Diagram 22.16

Diagram 22.17 illustrates the conclusion of Play # 9 with 03 "dribble-scraping" off of 05's top left shoulder as he dribbles towards the offense's right "Slot" location. As contact is broken between 05 and 03, 05 makes a "Front Pivot" off of his lower right foot to make a "Rim-Run Lob Cut" towards the basket. As that cut takes place, 04 has flashed across the lane to the opposite side of the floor to post his defender up. Both 01 and 02 stay wide to spread the floor and float around to occupy their individual defenders. This action gives the offense two interior pass receivers (04 and 05) and two potential perimeter pass receivers (02 and 01). This action also repositions all five players into the standard "3-Out/2-In" Spot-Ups. Diagram 22.17

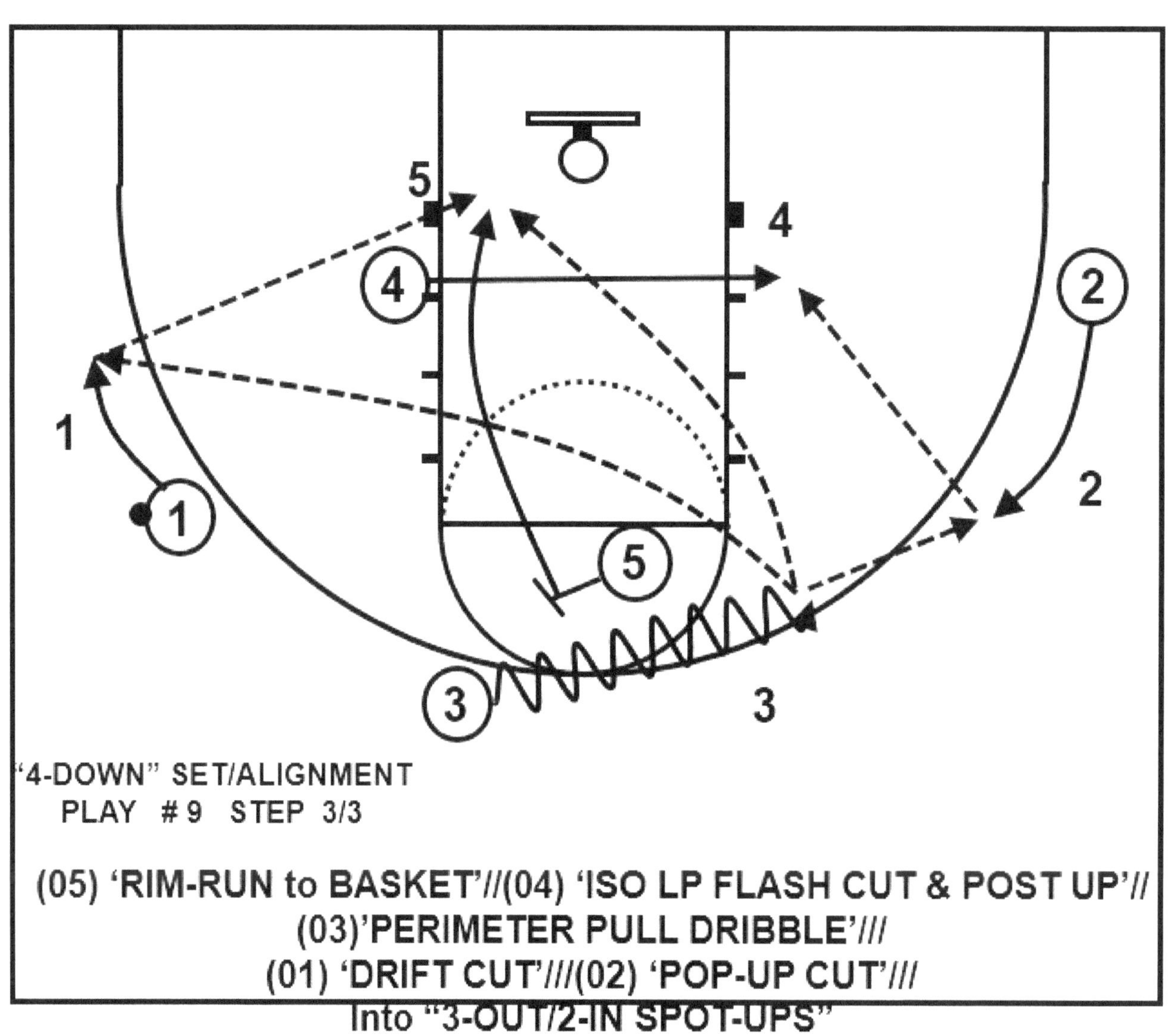

Diagram 22.17

Diagrams 22.18, 22.19 and 22.20 demonstrate all of the different types of action and movement for the Level 3 play that is numbered # 10. 01 starts towards the action by first dribbling towards the right "Slot" area before then reverse dribbling to the opposite "Slot." As 01 dribbles across the imaginary center line, 04 makes an "Iso Duck-In Cut" before then emptying out to the now vacated "Slot" on the right side of the floor. At the same time, 03 sprints to a spot stacked just above 05 while 02 runs the baseline, crosses the lane and then in between 03 and 05 and their "Big-on-Small Elevator Screen" to the opposite side's "Deep Corner" area. Diagram 22.18

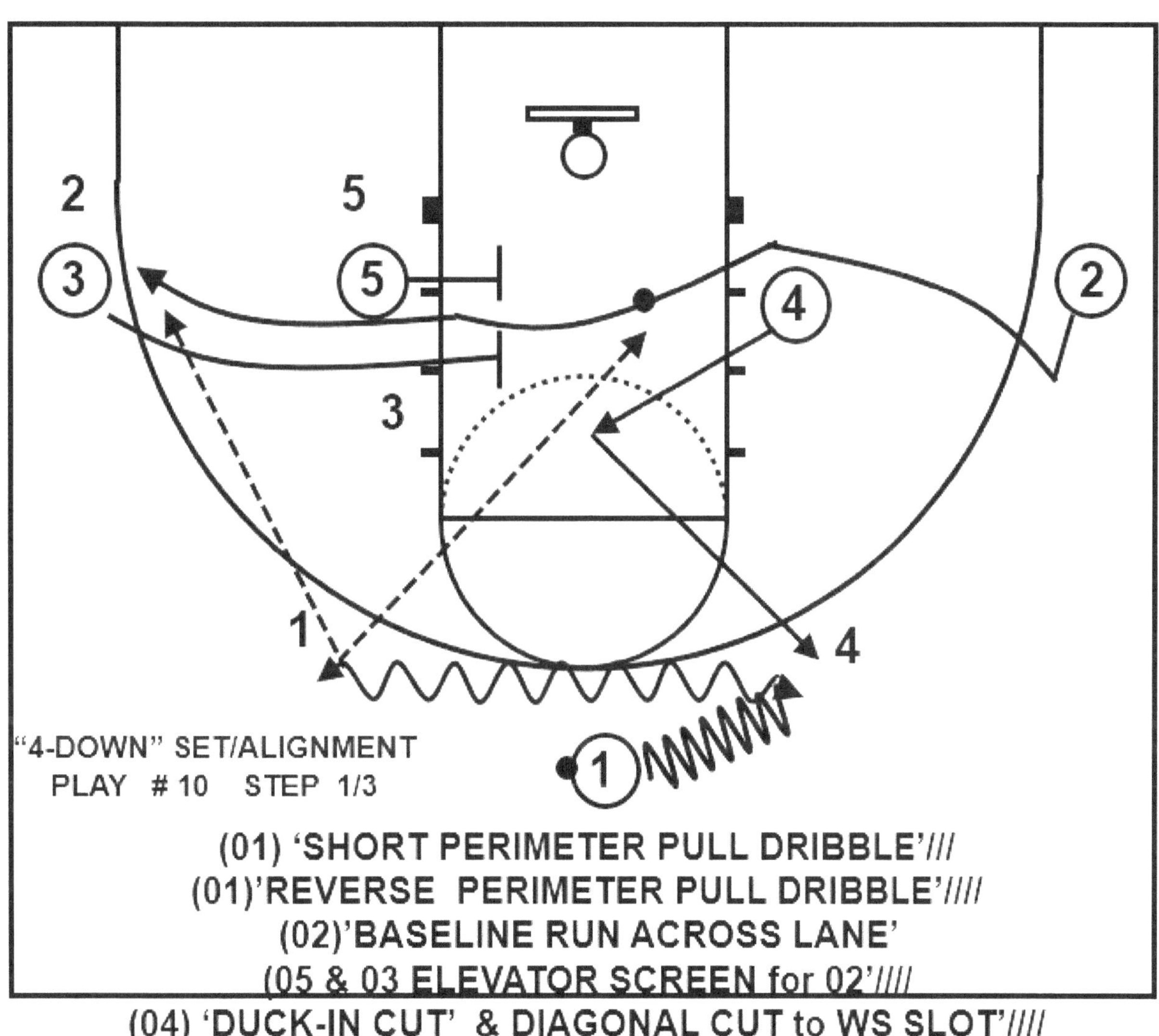

Play # 10   Diagram 22.18

Diagram 22.19 shows how the offense attacks the presumed defensive reaction by X5, X3 and X2. Both 03 and 05 will slip their "Elevator Screens," expecting one or both defenders switching or hard-hedging the screen and therefore sagging off of their own men. This will allow 03 to slip his part of the screen and cut across the lane to post up on the opposite side of the floor. 05 should then scrape off of 03's cut and use it as a "Brush Screen" to make an "Iso Duck-In Cut" on the same side of the floor.

01 can elect to make the "Down Pass" to 02 for an open '3 Pt.' shot in the "Deep Corner." If he looks to go inside to either 05 or 03, he can make that "Inside Pass" or swing the ball over to 04 for his options to make the interior passes. Diagram 22.19

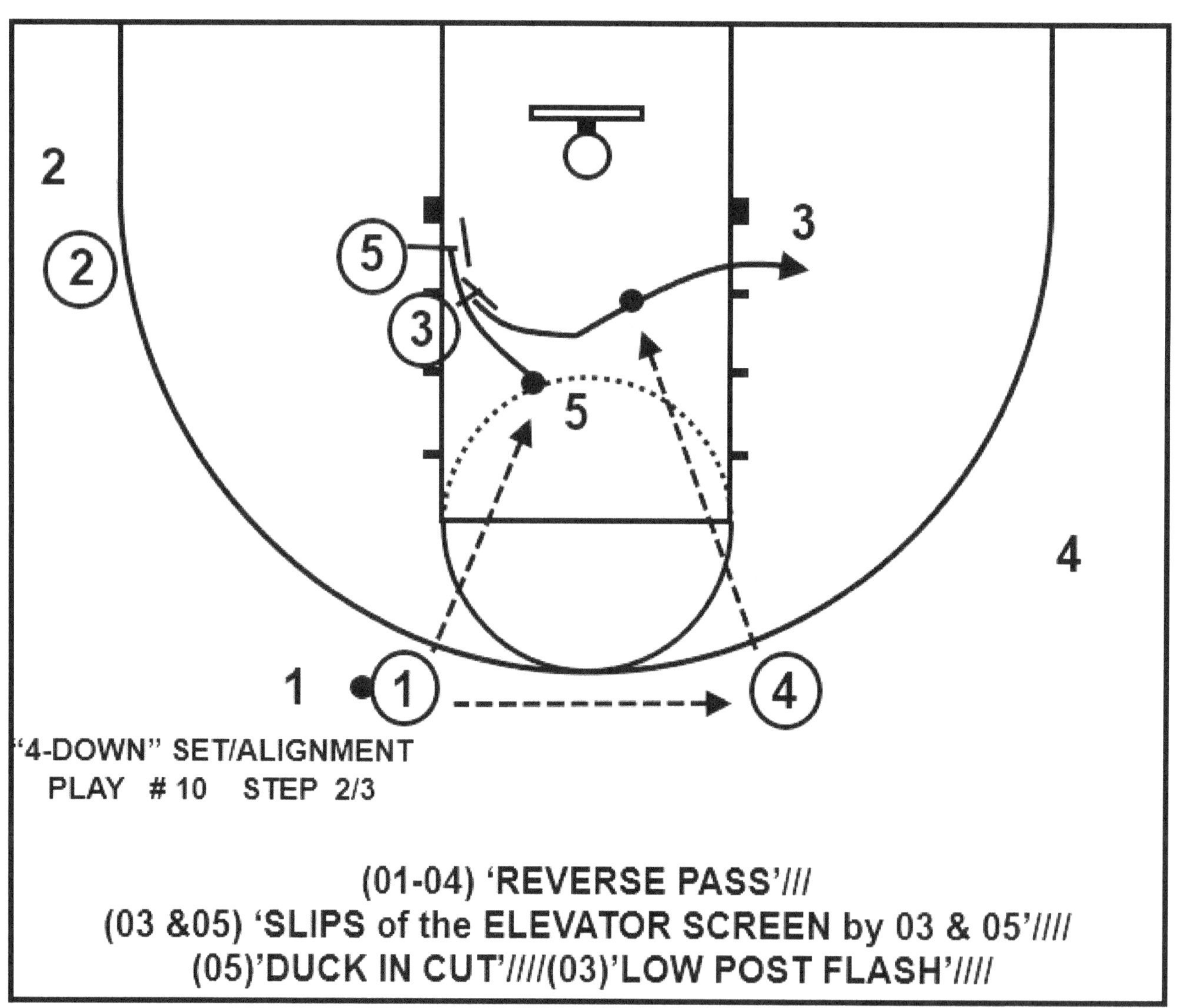

Diagram 22.19

04 can then make a "perimeter pull dribble" against his post-type defender to the "Wing" area to look for better passing angles on the interior—05 at the "Dotted Circle" or 03 on his new Ballside Post-Up." 02 and 01should then rotate up and over to make "Replacement Fill Cuts" to reposition themselves. 04 could easily then reverse the ball back to 01 or skip the ball to 02 on the opposite side of the floor. This allows both 02 and 01 excellent shot and pass opportunities for themselves. This also occupies weakside defenders and also places all players in the "3-Out/2-In" Spot-Ups to continue into the next phase of the offense. Diagram 22.20

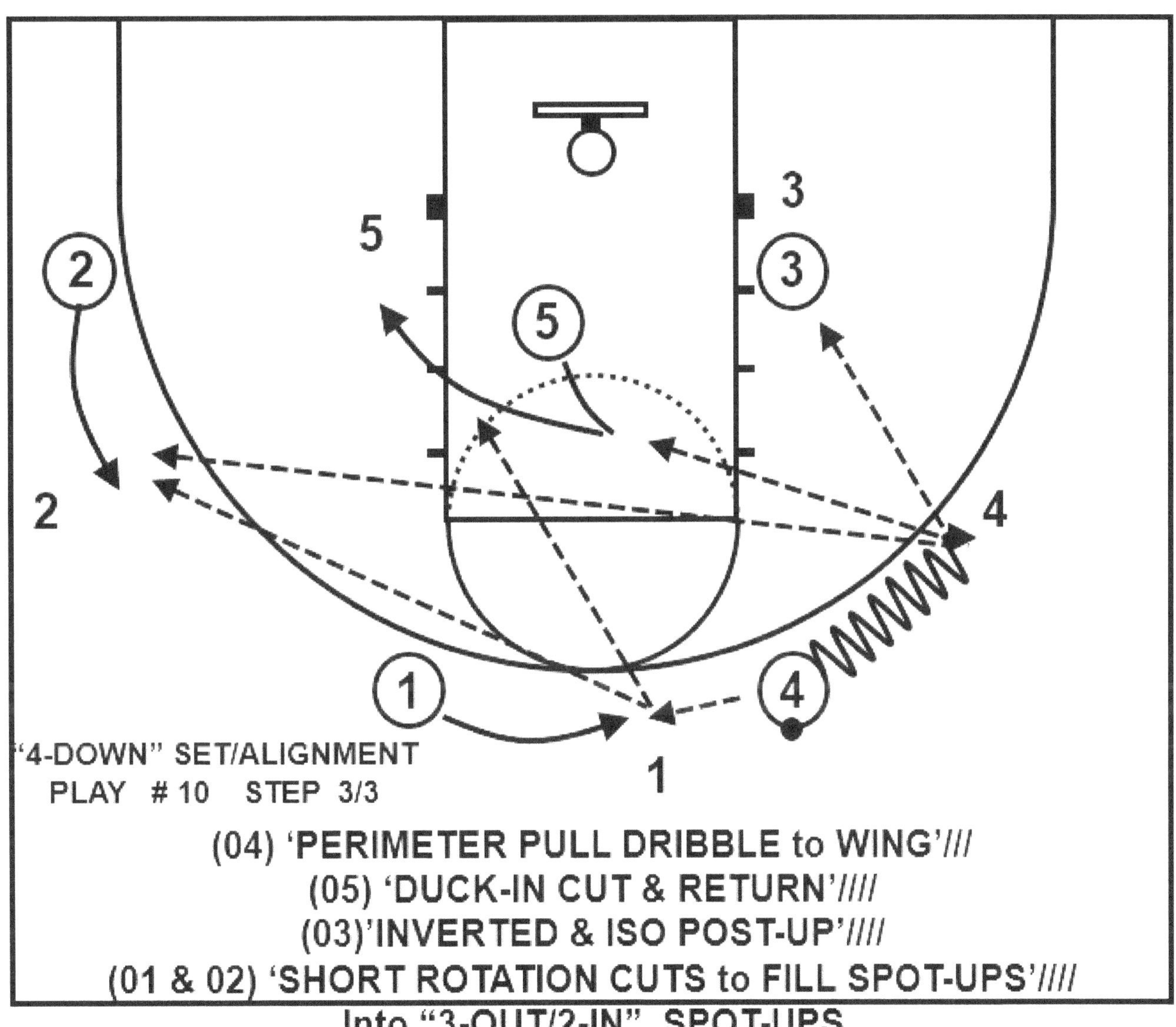

Diagram 22.20

CLOSING

As discussed, the "4-DOWN" Set/Alignment is a symmetrically balanced offensive alignment with one designated post player on each side of the lane with a designated perimeter player "spotted up" on each side's "Deep Corner." Not only does this give true balance to immediately attack either side of the court but to also attack the opposition both on the perimeter and the interior.

Every play/entry can be executed towards either side of the floor with both perimeter and interior scoring threats.

In addition, the action of every play utilizes individual offensive strengths while minimizing any possible offensive weaknesses but also can attack individual opponent's weaknesses as well as overall team defensive weaknesses. Any entry that does not produce the desired shot will have attacked and moved defenders around the court and repositioned offensive players into the desired offensive spot-up positions so that there is a seamless and immediate conversion from the play into the offensive spot-up positions of three different types of continuity offenses.

This makes this "4-DOWN" Offensive Set/Alignment an invaluable offensive weapon.

There are many different philsophies on how to attack opposing defenses. This multiple-phase offensive system uses more than one phase/layer/wave of attack, with each phase/wave having a seamless and immediate conversion into the next phase/wave. While this system can be confusing to defenses and difficult to defend, this system can be properly taught and coached so that it can be easily understood and ultimately executed by players of many different levels of (physical talent, mental understand and playing experience.)

In addition, there are several types of offensive schemes and different ways within this system that offenses can attack their defensive counter-parts. Many of these can be

integrated within the same offensive system that can attack defenses in various ways. The larger the number of schemes that can be successfully utilized and integrated within the same system, the greater the opportunity an offensive team can find the most efficient and productive schemes that can place both individual and the overall team in the best and most frequent "positions to succeed."

The plays/entries carefully diagrammed down to the small and seemingly unimportant 'V-Cuts' made by countless players before making their more important following cut are also described in detail.

Each play has been carefully studied and evaluated to determine which level of talent and experience must be possessed for that specific team to be able to successfully execute the play. This includes all players' physical skills as well as their mental understanding of the game. Coaches must also have the experience and the associated level of understanding of the game as well as their coaching/teaching of the nuances of each play.

The most sophisticated plays/entries would fall into the first of the three levels all based on the team's physical talents and skills, the mental capacities and the overall team's game experience. In addition, the coaching staff must have a high degree of basketball knowledge as well as very high teaching and coaching skills to educate his/her entire basketball team. The proper breakdown drills must be thoroughly utilized to hone the fundamental skills and techniques needed for individual players and the overall team to execute plays that can be efficient, productive and successful. We define this family of plays as the "Level 3 category" of plays. This "Level 3" family of plays will have a much more complex offensive scheme that would require a very high amount of physical talent as well as a greater amount of the players (to execute) and the coaches (to teach and coach) mental capacities and experience needed for the offense to be efficient, productive and successful. We feel plays in our defined "Level 3" category could possibly be successful for NBA teams, definitely for college teams and also for many high schools and older AAU teams.

The next classification or level of plays would possibly be slightly lower as far as sophistication, complexity and the actual 'length' of the play (and the number of passes, cuts and screens used) in the play's overall scheme. While all "Level 2" plays in each of the chapters in this book remain fundamentally sound, these plays may lack the actual number of techniques/methods that are implemented within that play in comparison to the "Level 1" plays/entries. Therefore, any team that successfully executes the highest "Level 1" plays/entries could/should easily be able to execute any of these so-called lower "Level

2" plays/entries, if so desired. Almost all high school teams should be able to execute successfully all aspects of the "Level 2" plays.

The final grouping of plays would be called "Level 1" plays and are not as difficult for offensive players to master the execution of them, both physically as well as mentally. Even though the techniques are still fundamentally, they may not be as complex to learn and understand in addition to being easier to physically execute.

"Level 1" plays would be lower in the scheme's complexities and the number of techniques used in the execution of this category of plays. Obviously, since these "Level 1" plays are still sound, but lack some of the methods used in the two previous more sophisticated and complex levels; these more elementary plays should be able to be utilized by any teams that use either of the two higher level plays. We feel that Middle School/Junior High teams as well as younger AAU teams or organizations, should be able to utilize any of the "Level 1" plays successfully, with a possibility that some of those teams that are slightly more advanced (than other teams) could possibly use some plays located in the immediate next immediate level.

Ideas, concepts and techniques that will help prove these entries can be successfully used. This allows the author to create numerous plays that use the various schemes to build a library of fundamentally sound plays that will be unique and will be appropriate for the wide range of teams with various ages and skill levels.

With this book having plays in these three presumed categories or levels, the book will reach out and benefit a much larger group of serious basketball coaches from elementary school age to the highest skilled levels that exists.

In addition, an experienced and resourceful coach may be able to mold some plays that include all of the offensive techniques that he/she desires could reshape a specific play that begins in one specific offensive set/alignment and reshape it so that it could begin in a different offensive/set that is more favorable to that coach and his/her coaching staff's liking.

Conversely, that innovative and creative coach may completely like the specific offensive set/alignment and favor the very same offensive actions included in a certain play, but can modify that play so that the ending spot-ups of all five players are conducive to being able to begin the final phase of the offensive attack by using a more favorable offensive continuity offense.

The "HORNS SET"

PLAYS/ENTRIES THAT END in the "3-OUT/2-IN" OFFENSIVE SPOT-UPS

After the entry/play/quick-hitter has been executed but no shots have been taken, all five players will end up in a different group of offensive spot-ups. These "3-Out/2-In Spot-Ups" will have players moved about the court with any of the five ending up in the "Ballside Block," the "Ballside Wing," the "Weakside Block," the "Weakside Wing," and the "Point" (at the top of the key). These five positions can provide the offense with safe and easy types of ball-reversals, large gaps for dribble penetration, opportunities to deliver the ball inside to whomever (perimeter-type or post-type players) is posting up their defender on the "Ballside Block," and a player that can be a perimeter-scoring threat and a legitimate offensive rebounding threat from outside of the arc on his "offensive crashing of the boards." The "3-Out/2-In Spot-Ups also provide ample opportunities for constant and effective defensive transition responsibilities.

The "HORNS" SET/ALIGNMENT

The "HORNS" Set is another symmetrically balanced offensive set as the offense positions 03 and 02 in the two opposite "Deep Corners" outside of the arc and along the baseline on an imaginary line that would extend from one side and "Block" to the opposite "Block and out to the sideline. This action spreads those defenders from sideline to sideline and also vertically flattens out the defense, but not so deep towards the baseline that there isn't room for 03 and 02 to create and attack towards the baseline.

The two offensive "Bigs," 05 and 04 start at the "Elbow" positions on both sides of the floor. They immediately are high enough to force the two defensive "Big Counterparts," X5 and X4 to be a good distance from the basket, to also be in positions to easily and quickly set ball-screens for 01 to use, to be able to pin down-screens for their respective teammate below them in the "Deep Corner" as well as to be able to flash (and isolate) their defender to the "Block" on the opposite side of the lane. With two players on each side of the lane plus 01 with the ball centered up; there is no designated initial strong and weak side of the offense, meaning that every quick-hitter/play/entry could actually be run towards either side of the floor. With each play being able to be executed towards either side of the floor, the number within the family of plays doubles without the actual complexity level increasing to a high degree.

543

Diagram 23.1, Play # 1, is a Level 1 play that has 05 step up and out with 03 breaking up also to set a "Big-on-Small Double Ball-Screen for 01 to use to "perimeter-pull dribble to the FT Line extended on the left side of the floor. As 01 "dribble-scrapes" off of 03's right outside shoulder to dribble to the "Wing" area, 05 makes a "Front Pivot" off of his inside left foot so that he can make a "Rim-Run" to the basket. At the same time, 04 makes a "Diagonal Slash Cut" to the newly designated "Ballside Block."

At the same time that 01 breaks contact with 03, 02 steps up to set a "Small-on-Big (Flare-)Screen the (Ball-)Screener" for 03 to "Flare-Cut" to the opposite "Wing" area. 02 then slips his screen and remains at the top of the key.

All of this action not only isolates 04 down on the new "Ballside Block," but gives 01 an opportunity to attack the defense with a "Lob Pass" to 05, a "Skip Pass" to 03 (for a potential '3.') or a "Reverse Pass" and possible open '3' to 02.

If no shots are taken, this action immediately has placed all five players in the appropriate "3-Out/2-In" Spot-Ups for an instant conversion into the designated continuity offense. Diagram 23.1.

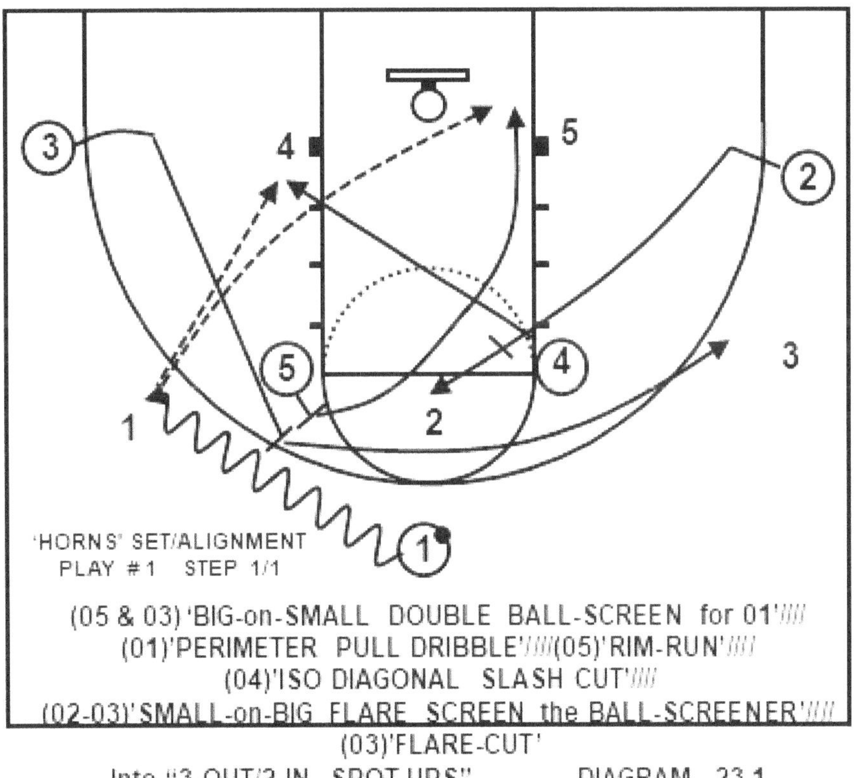

Play # 1   Diagram 23.1

Diagram 23.2 and 23.3 illustrate the first Level 2 play in this family of plays. Play # 2 begins the play with 03 being the designated player that makes the "Iverson Cut" over the top of 05 and 04 to the right wing with 02 being the "Iverson Cutter" that cuts low along the baseline and then out to the opposite wing.

This action moves players but still keeps players in a symmetrically balanced configuration. This means that 01 still could have the freedom and the option to make the "Wing Pass" to either 02 on the left or 03 on the right side of the floor. Diagram 23.2.

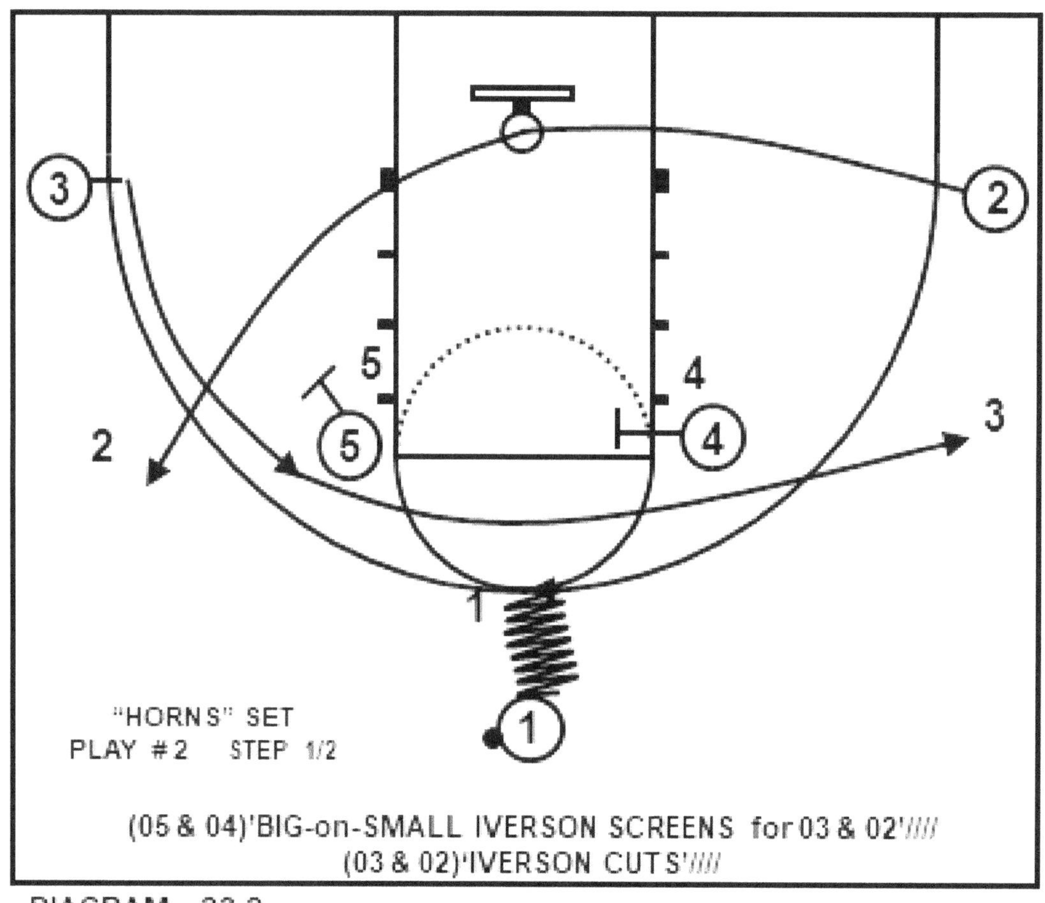

Play # 2   Diagram 23.2

In Diagram 23.3, 01 has elected to make the pass to 02 on the left side of the floor. This dictates that 03 break up and over to set a "Big-on-Small Flare-Screen" for 01 to use to "Flare-Cut" to the wing on the right side of the floor. At the same time, 05 breaks horizontally across the lane to set a "Cross-Screen" for 04 to use to diagonally cut through the lane to the newly declared "Ballside Block. After screening for 04, 05 settles in at the new "Weakside Block" area. 01's primary passing targets are to 04 on the "Block," to 01 on the "Weakside Wing" for a potential open '3' or to 03 at the top of the key also for a possible '3.'

If shots are not taken, the "3-Out/2-In" Spot-Ups are again filled for the desired continuity offense to seamlessly begin. Diagram 23.3.

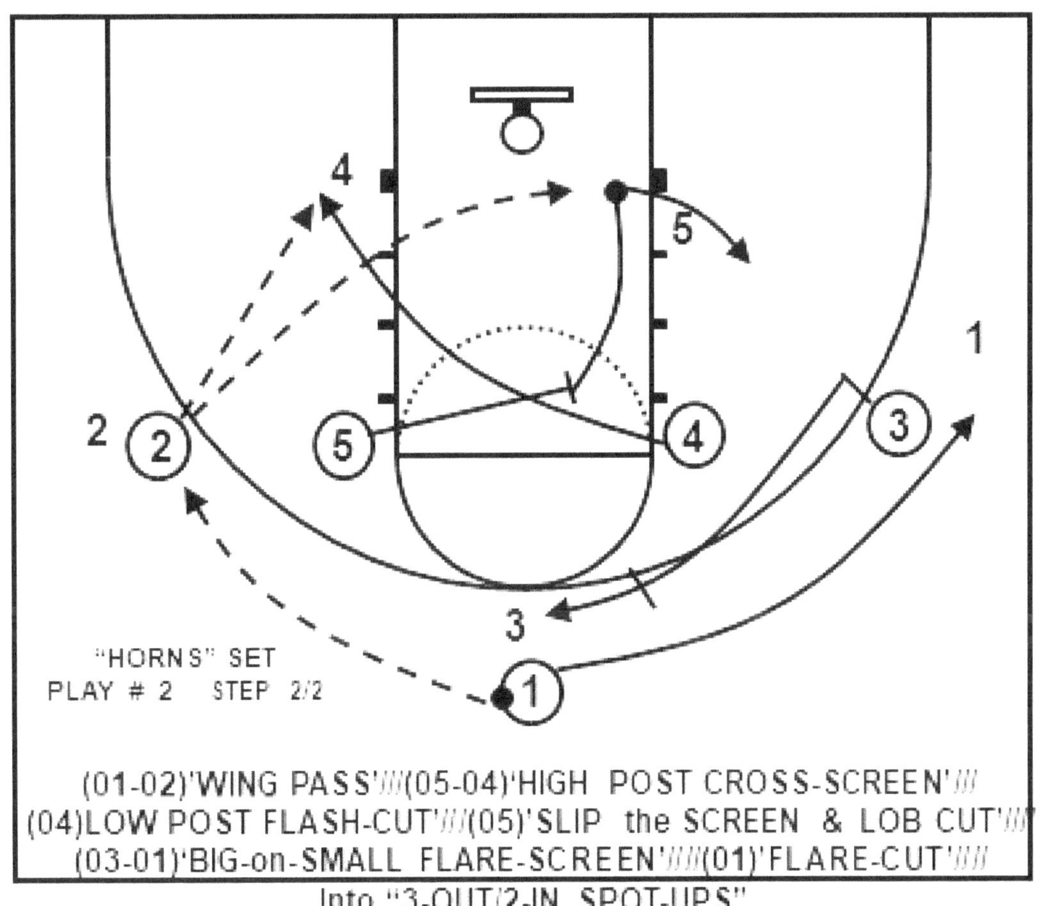

DIAGRAM 23.3

Play # 3, a Level 3 play, is shown in Diagrams 23.4, 23.5 and 23.6. As 01 dribbles towards the top of the key, both 05 and 04 break down diagonally to set "Big-on-Small Pin Down-Screens" for both 03 and 02 to use to break to the vacant "Wing" Spot-Up locations. In this diagram, 04 is the player that slipped his "Pin-Screened" and dove to the basket, looking for a quick "Inside Pass" from 01. Diagram 23.4.

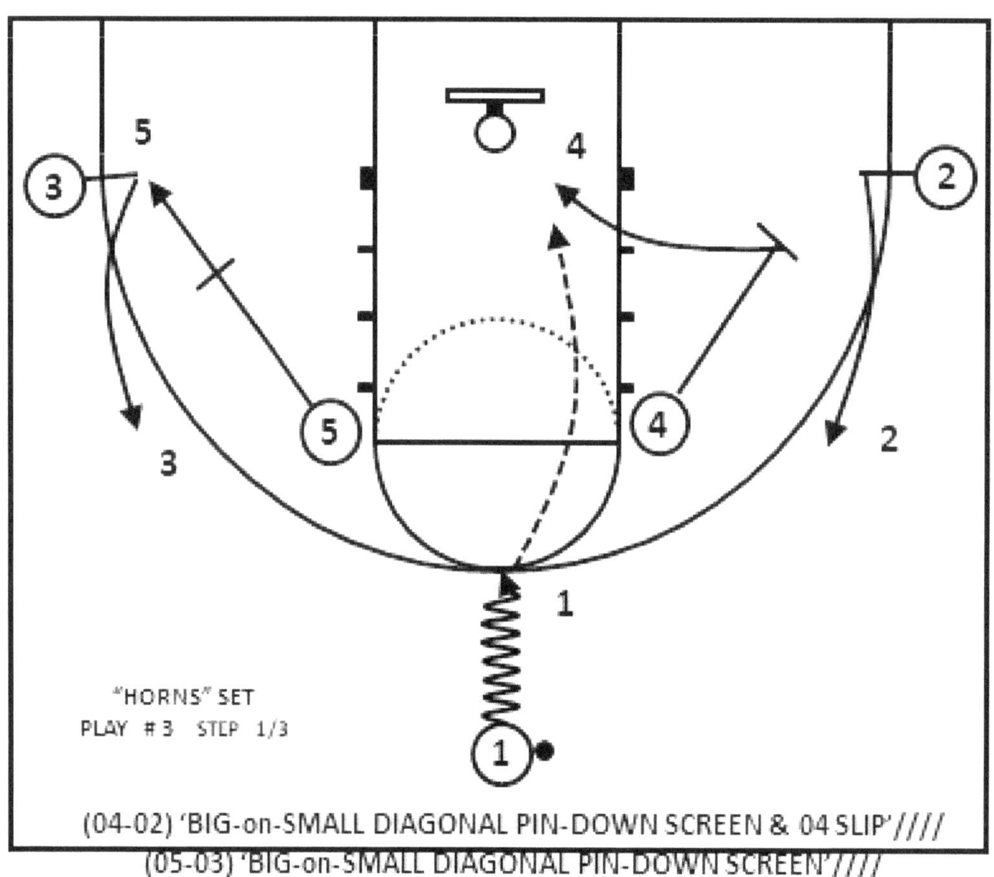

Play # 3   Diagram 23.4

If 04 is not open, 01 has the option of making the "Wing Pass" to 02. 01 breaks down as if to set a "Small-on-Big Diagonal Pin Down-Screen" for 05 to use to break to the top of the key. Instead, 05 slips out to the new "Weakside Wing" and 03 rotates out to the top of the key. After screening for 05, 01 also slips to fill the empty "Block" area. This three-man weakside action between 01, 05 and 03 helps isolate 04 down on the new "Ballside Block" for 02 to deliver the appropriate pass to 04. Diagram 23.5.

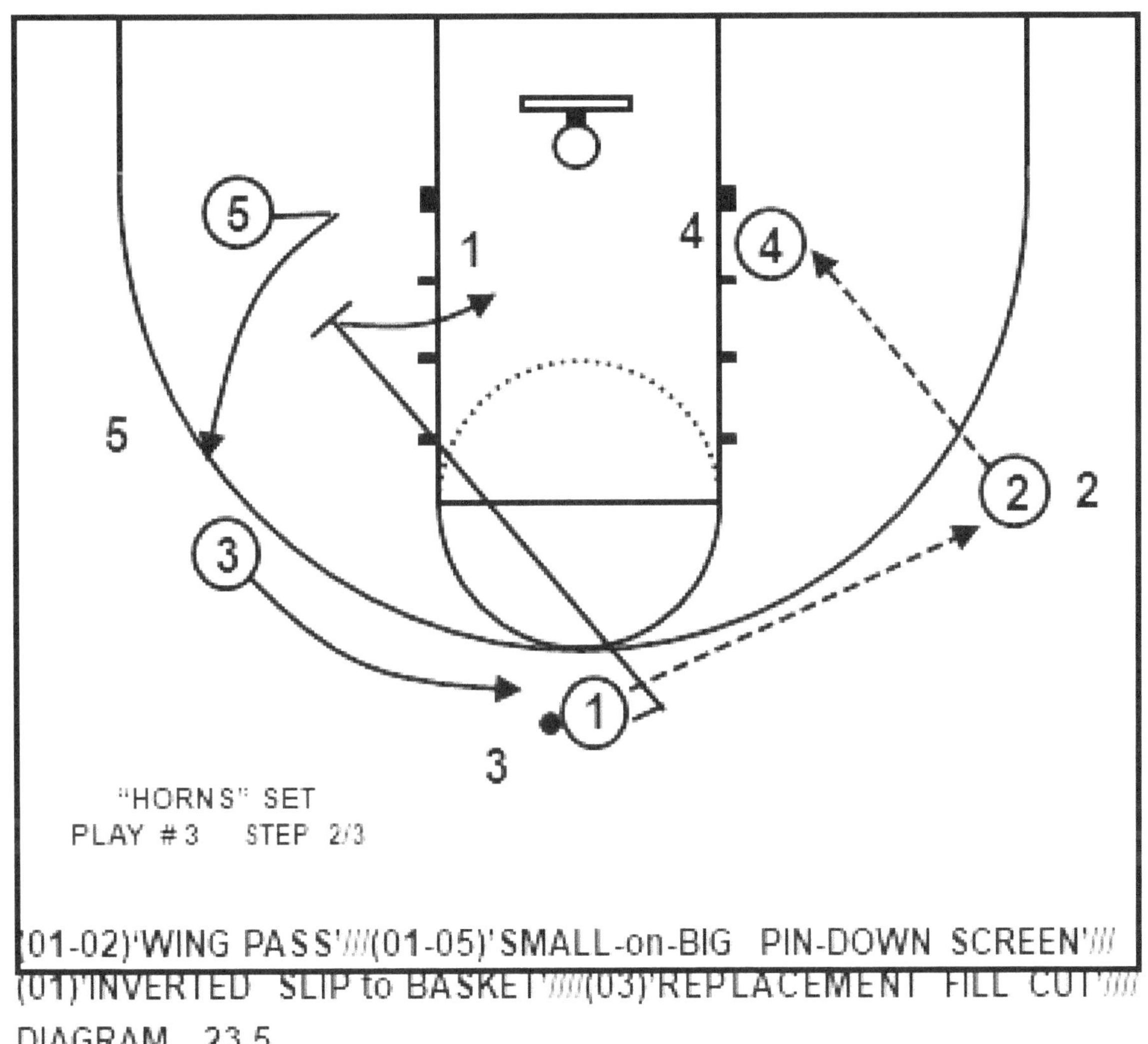

Diagram 23.6. illustrates 02 turning down the pass to 04 and instead making the pass to 03 out on top. 05 immediately steps up and out to set a "Big-on-Small Ball-Screen" for 03 to use to make a "perimeter-pull dribble" to the "Wing" area. After 05 sets the screen for 03, 02 steps up and over to set a "(Flare-)Screen the (Ball-)Screener" for 05 to continue to the opposite side's "wing" area. At the same time that it is determined that 01 is posted up on the new "Ballside Block," 01 spins out away from the ball to set a "Small-on-Big Lane Exchange Cross-Screen" for 04 to use as he cuts across the lane and posts up on the "Ballside Block." If the defense elects to switch the screen, X1 would be stuck with trying to defend 04 and X5 out above the FT Line away from the basket.

03's primary passing targets are first an "Inside Pass" potential with 04 and then a "Reverse Pass" to 02 at the top of the key. If no shots are taken, the "3-Out/2-In" Spot-Ups are filled for the last phase of the offense to instantly begin. Diagram 23.6.

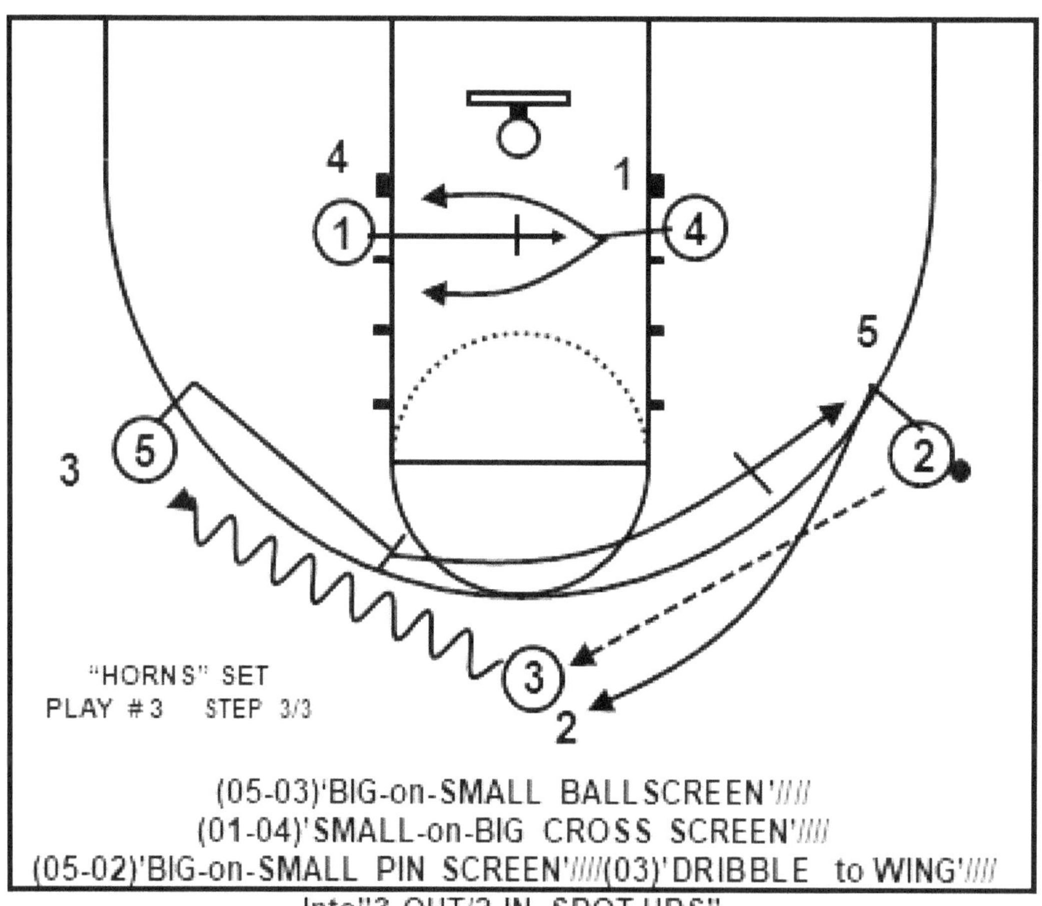

DIAGRAM 23.6

Diagrams 23.7, 23.8, and 23.9 demonstrate Play # 4, another Level 3 play that could also be 'mirrored' on the opposite side of the floor. Even though 03 and 02 could switch up their cuts, 01 declares 04 as the player that steps up to set the "Big-on-Small Ball-Screen" (followed by 05's roll down the lane to post up).

At the same time, 05 sets a stationary "Pin Down Screen" for 03 to break up to the top of the key. Also at the same time, 02 clears out his side of the floor and ends up in the "Deep Corner" on the opposite side of the floor. With 02 staying deep and wide and with 05 at the newly declared "Weakside Elbow," this action completely isolates 04 down on the "Ballside Block." Diagram 23.7.

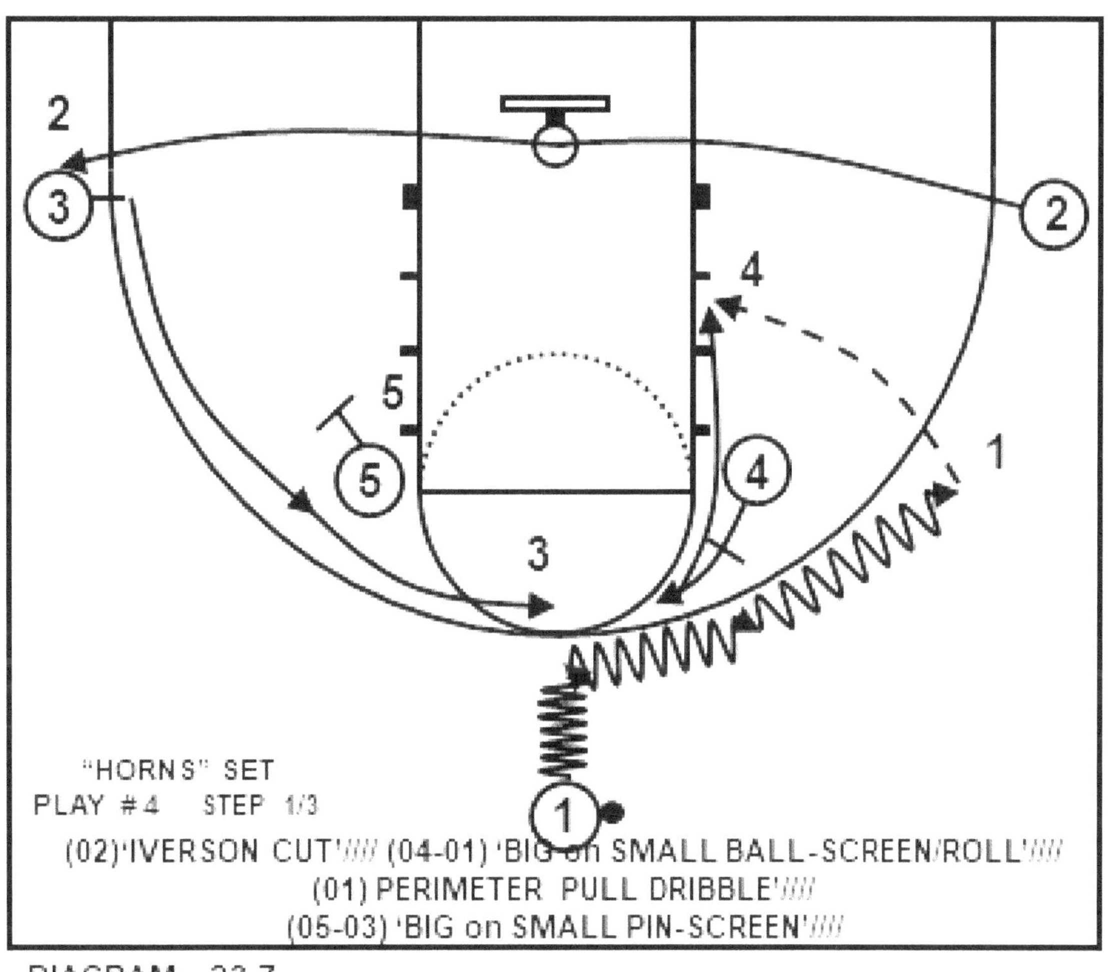

DIAGRAM 23.7

Play # 4   Diagram 23.7

Diagram 23.8 illustrates 01 not making the "Inside Pass" to 04 but reversing the ball to03 out on top. 04 immediately works to gain a "position advantage" over his isolated defender with the proper footwork to break open in the middle of the lane. At the same time, 05 breaks down to set a "Big-on-Small Pin Down-Screen" for 02 to break out of the "Deep Corner" towards 03 and the "Wing" area. In addition to "re-reversing" the ball back to 01, this gives 03 a second perimeter pass target" in 02 on the opposite side of the floor. 04 could always be the primary ("Inside Pass") target as the ball is swung from one side of the floor to the top of the key. Diagram 23.8.

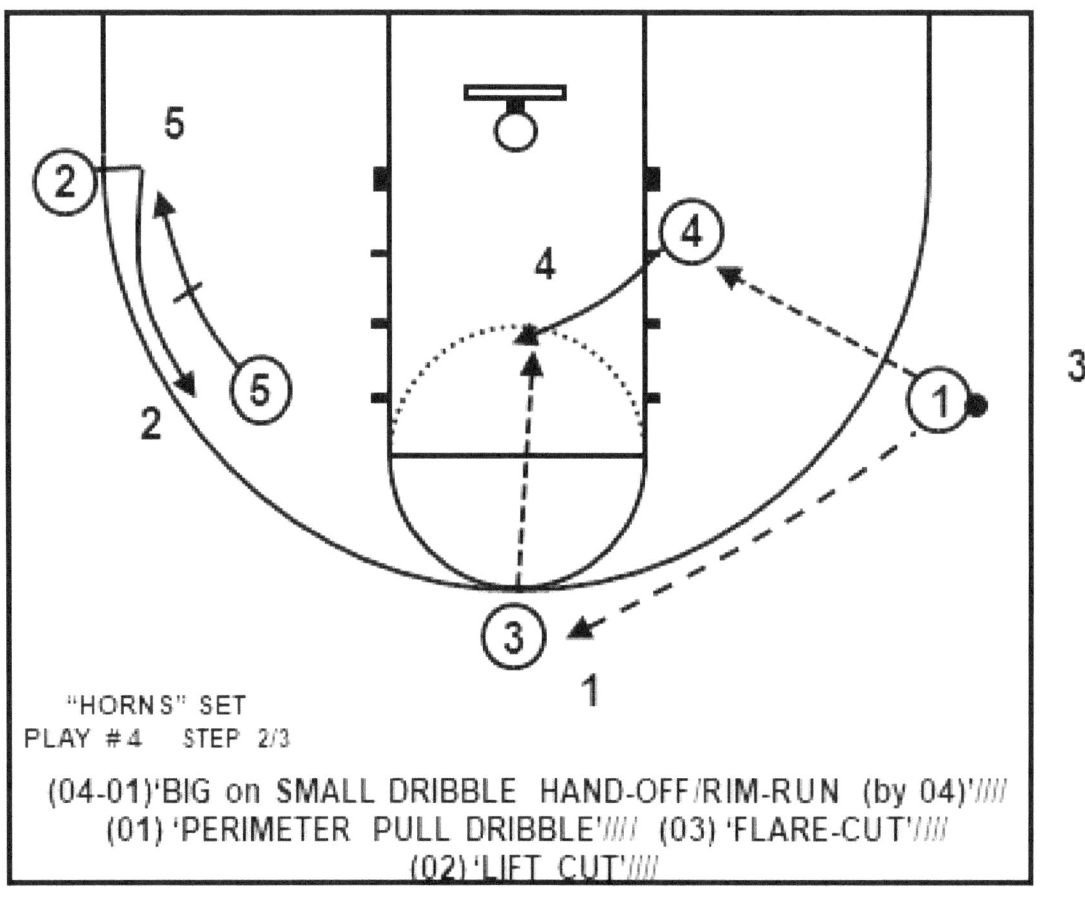

DIAGRAM 23.8

Diagram 23.9 shows 03 not making the pass to 04 in the middle of the lane with 04 then returning to the side of the lane and electing to dribble towards 02 as he breaks up off of 05's screen for the (03-02) DHO. After setting the screen for 02, 05 spins to the new "Ballside Block," looking for a quick pass from 02.

If 02 receives the DHO and does not make the quick pass to 05, he continues his "perimeter-pull dribble" out to the top of the key. With the ball centered up at the top of the key in 02's possession, 02 has two interior scoring threats in 05 and 04. With 01 and 03 spotted up at the two "Wing" areas as perimeter scoring threats, the "3-Out/2-In" Spot-Ups are filled; allowing for a seamless transition into the final phase of the offense. Diagram 23.9.

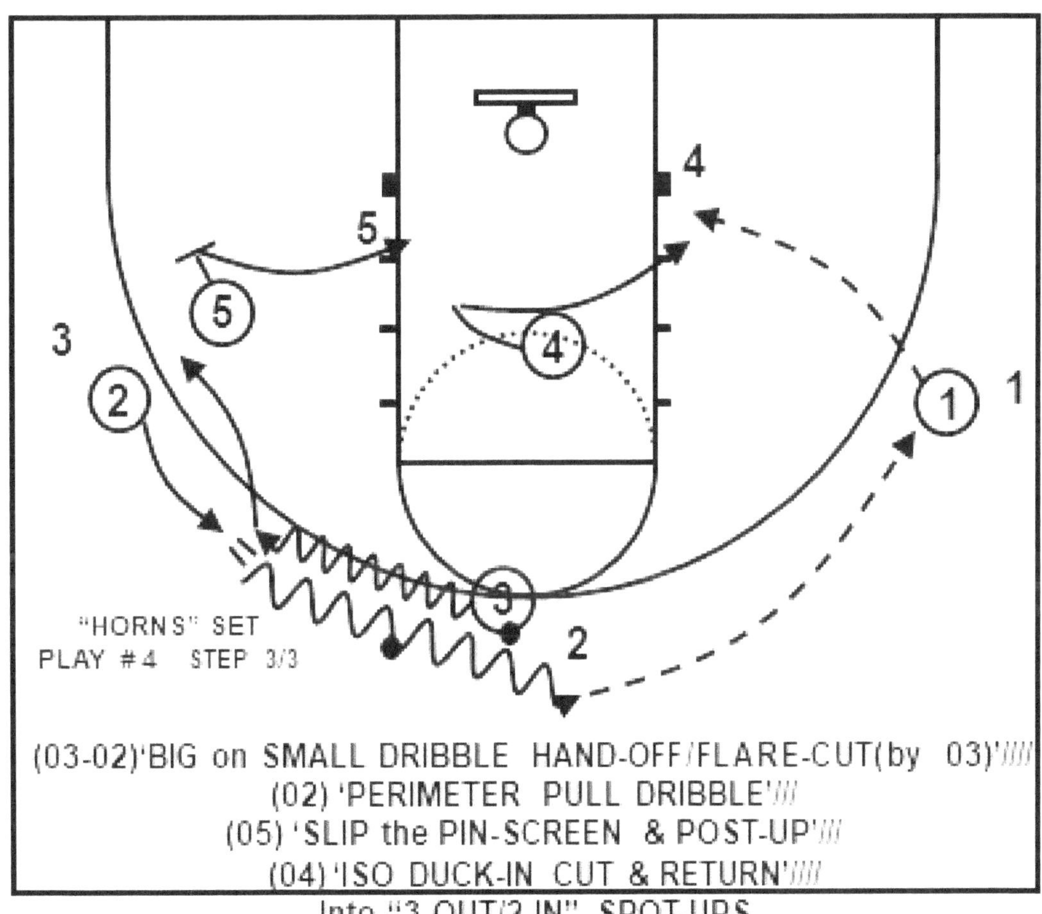

DIAGRAM 23.9

Play # 5 is another Level 3 play that is shown in Diagrams 24.10, 24.11 and 24.12. In this case, it was designated that 02 makes an "Iverson Cut" over the top of both 04 and 05 with 03 stepping up adjacent to 05. 02 ends up at the "Wing" area on the left side of the floor. Diagram 24.10.

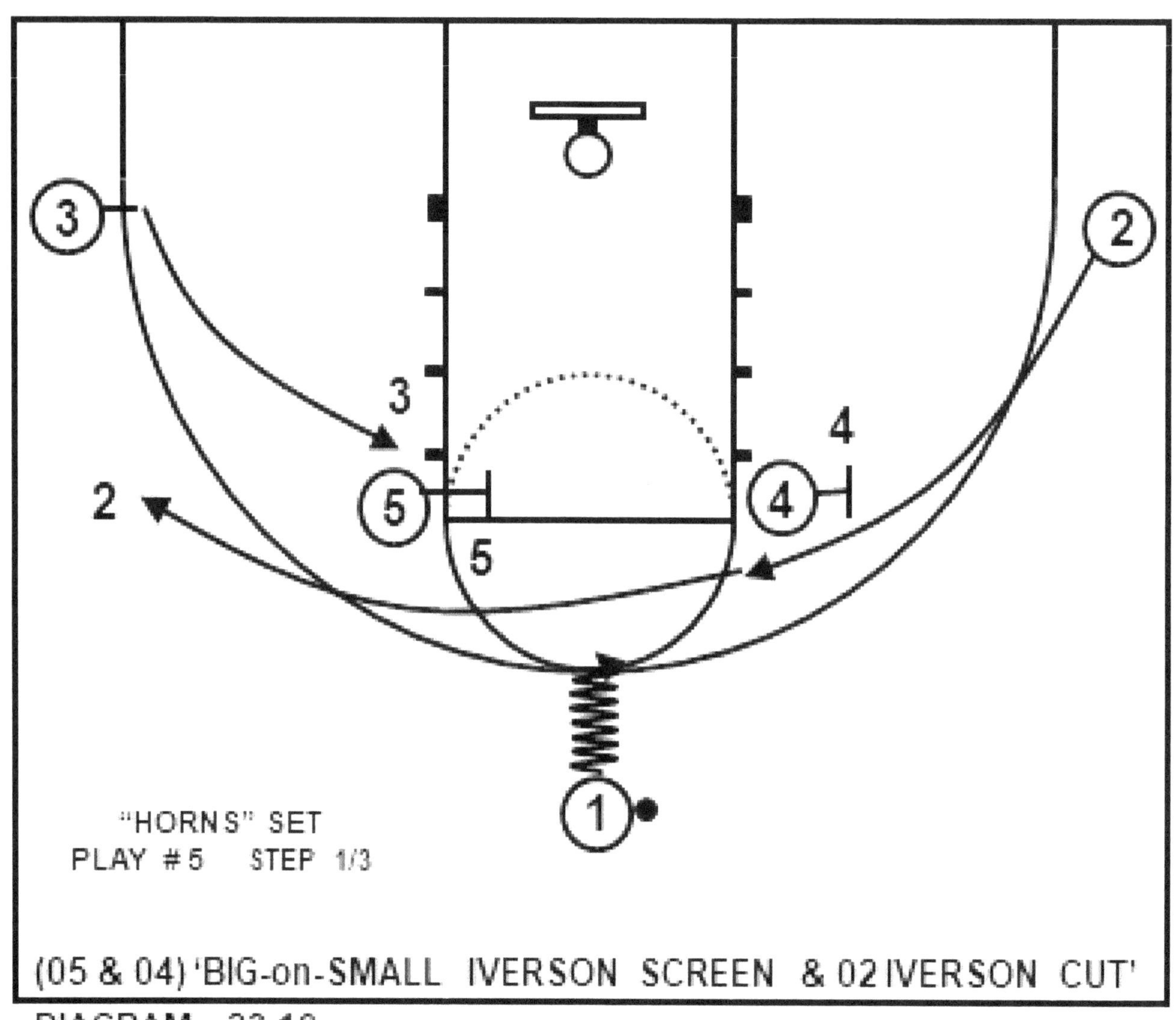

Play # 5   Diagram 23.10

01 makes the "Wing Pass" to 02 on the left wing with 03 immediately stepping in to set a "Small-on-Big Back-Screen" that 05 uses to slide down the lane to "Iso Post-Up" his defender; either X5 who should be delayed in his coverage or by X3 who is a more of a

perimeter-type defender that may have had to defensively switch the screen. After screening for 05, 03 slips his screen to fill the "Ballside Slot."

To fully make 05's post-up even more isolated, 04 steps up and over to set a "Big-on-Small Flare-Screen" for 01 to "Flare-Cut" to the opposite "Wing" area. After setting the screen, 04 slips the screen and fills the "Weakside Slot." This action will keep the presumed next biggest defender, X4, away from the post-up. This gives 02 an excellent pass receiver in 01 not spotted up at the new "Weakside Wing" for a "catch and shoot" opportunity off of the (02-01) "Skip Pass." These actions pull defenders away from 05 and gives 02 a much better chance to deliver the ball inside to 05. Diagram 23.11.

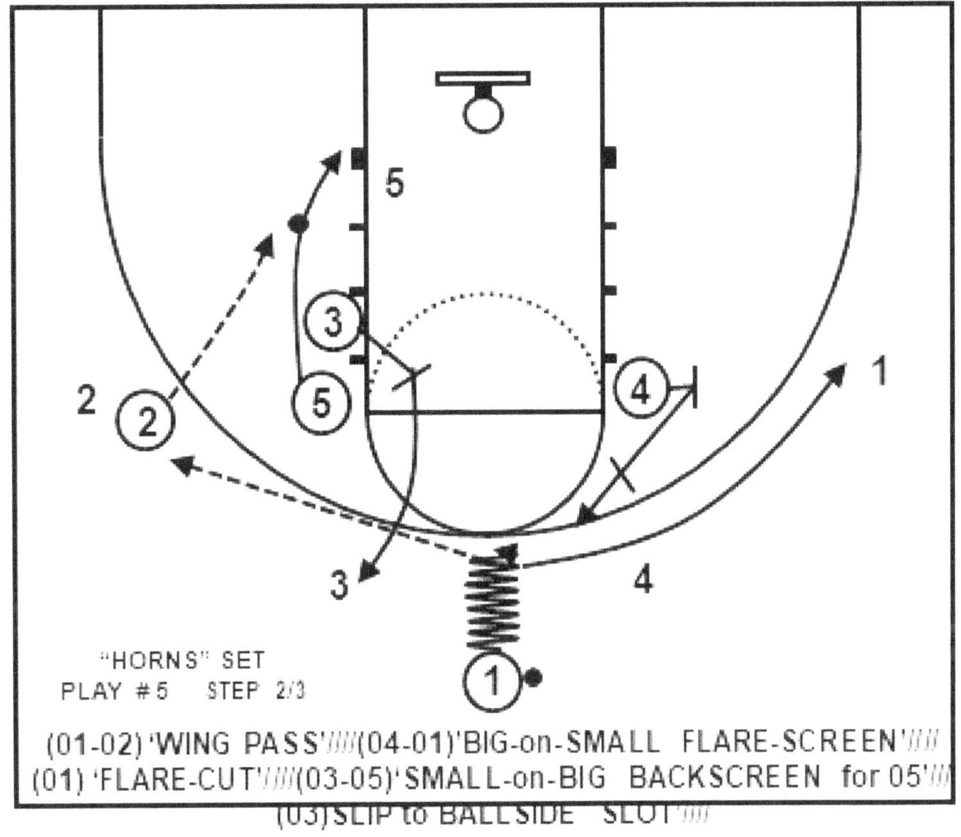

DIAGRAM 23.11

Diagram 23.12 illustrates the action when 02 does not make the "Inside Pass" to 05, 02 swings the ball to 03. After 03 makes the "Reverse Pass" to 04, 03 makes a quick "Given-Go Cut" and continues diagonally through the lane to the opposite side's "Block." If 04 does not make the quick return pass to 03, 04 swings the ball over to 01. After the (04-01) "Wing Pass" is made, 04 immediately cuts to get the proper angle to then set a "Diagonal Down-Screen" for 05 to use to break up to the top of the key. This action then isolates the inverted perimeter player, 03, for 03 to be in an isolated post-up scenario. 05's cut off of 04's screen gives 01 another passing/scoring threat. With 02 spotting up at the new "Weakside Wing," 01 could also have "Skip Pass" opportunities to 02.

If none of the three main scoring opportunities are taken advantage of, the "3-OUT/2-IN" Spot-Ups are filled for the final phase of the offense to immediately and smoothly begin. Diagram 23.12.

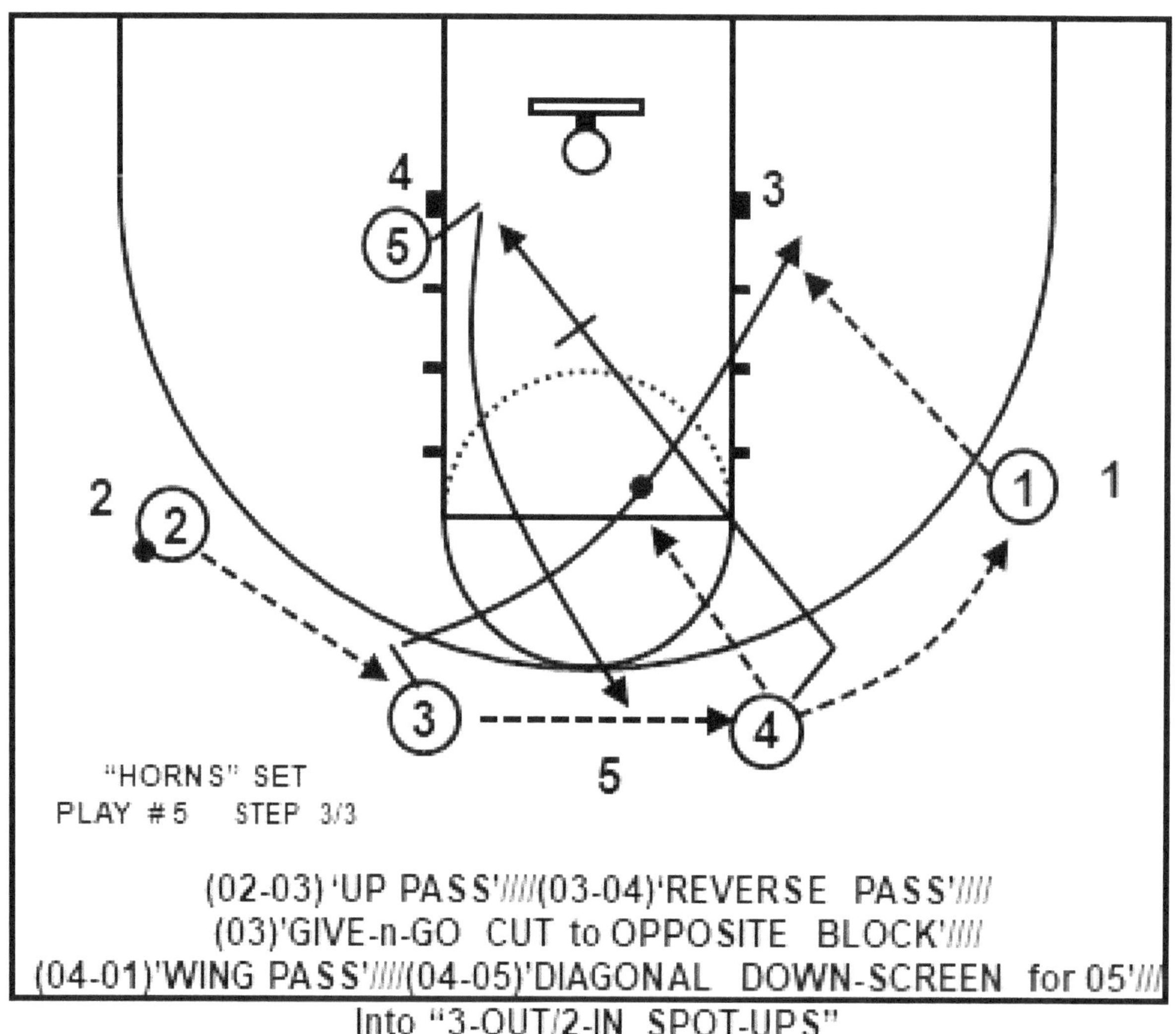

DIAGRAM 23.12

Diagrams 23.13, 23.24 and 23.25 demonstrate Play # 6 out of the "HORNS" Set. This play could be executed towards either side of the floor. In this case, 02 was the designated "Iverson Cutter" to go over the top of both 04 and 05; while 03 dives to the "Block" area on the same side of the floor. Diagram 23.13.

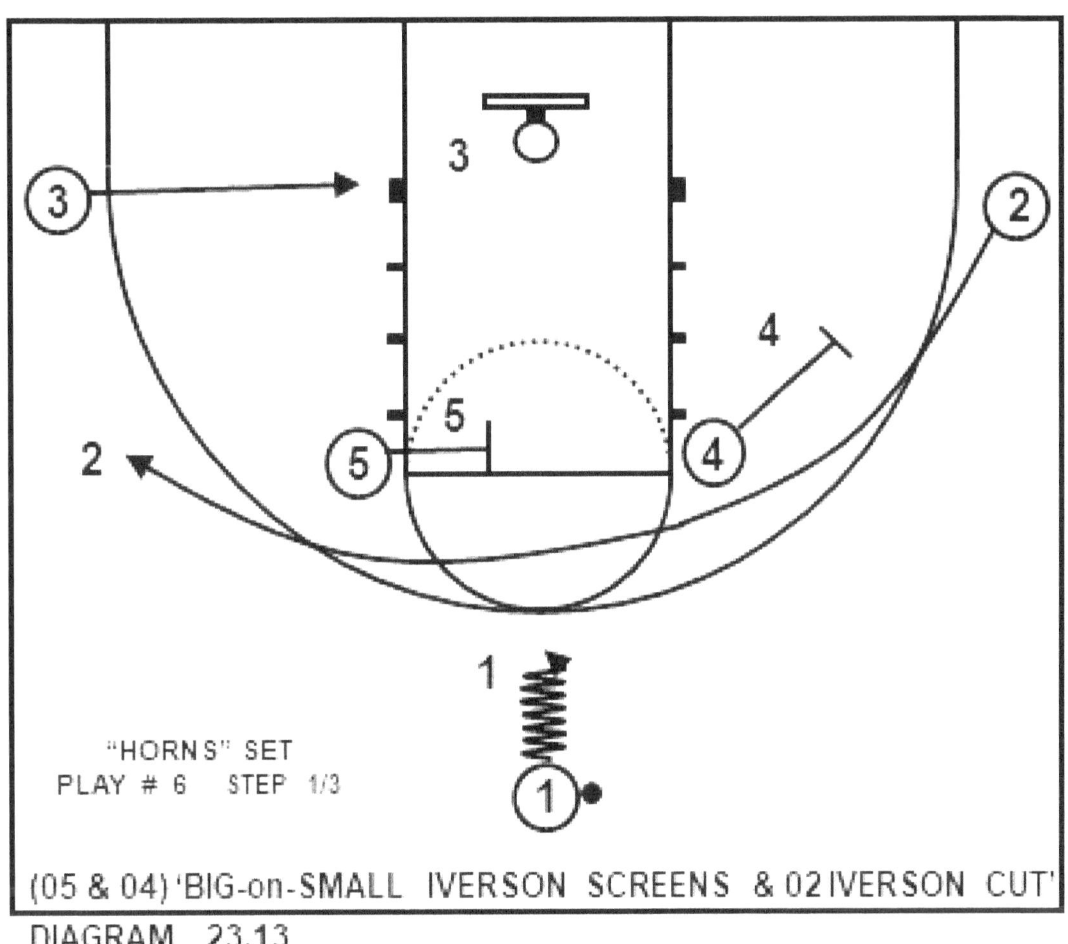

Play # 6   Diagram 23.13

Diagram 23.14 shows 01 making the pass to the new strong side of the alignment; to 02 on the left wing area. 04 immediately sets a "Big-on-Small Flare-Screen" for 01 to "Flare-Cut" to the new "Weakside Wing." After the screen, 04 slips his screen and moves to the new "Weakside Slot."

At the same time of the (01-02), 05 immediately sets a "Big-on-Small Pin Screen" for 03 to use to either make a "Zipper Cut" or a "Pipe Cut" to break out to the new "Ballside Slot." After screening for 03, 05 slips his screen and executes an "Iso Post-Up. Diagram 23.14.

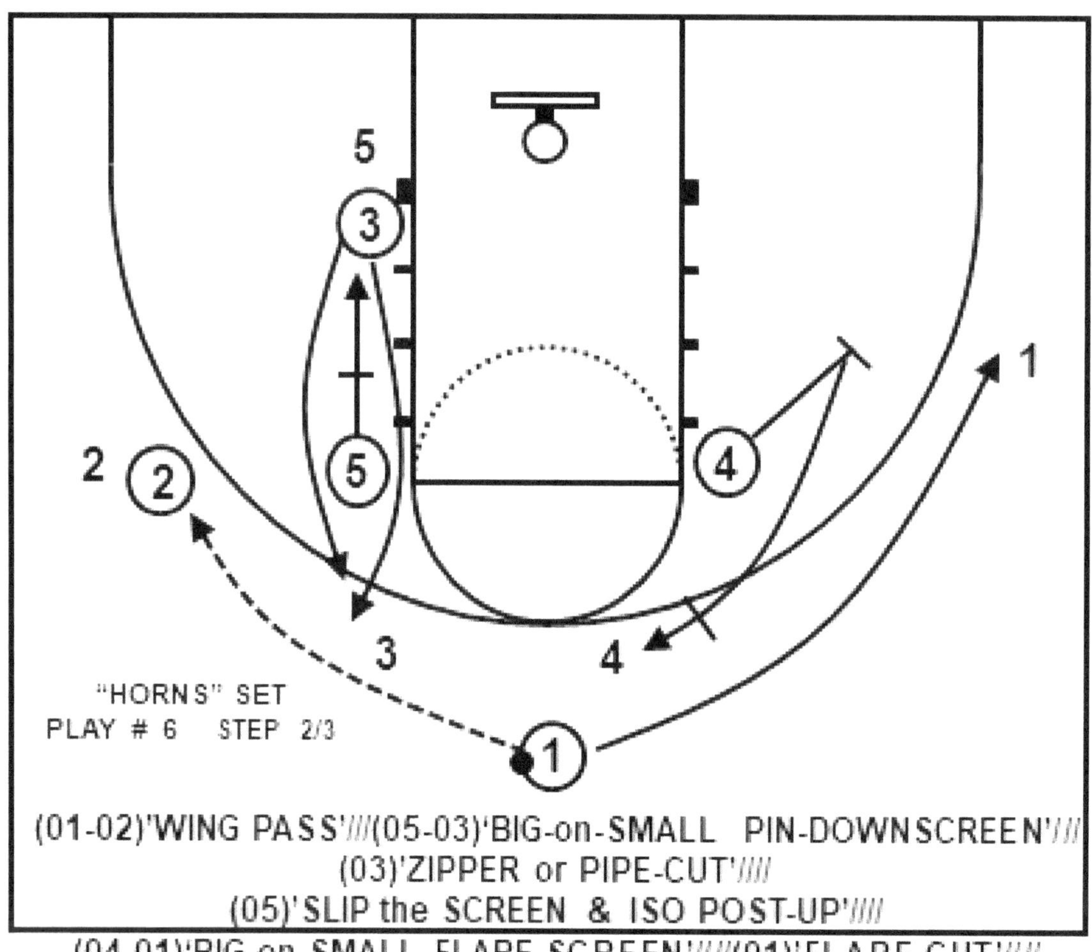

02 first looks to make an "Inside Pass" to 05, who has isolated his defender down on the "Block." If 02 does not make the pass to 05, he passes the ball out to 03 at the "Slot." 05 immediately makes a strong "Iso Duck-In Cut" into the "Dotted Circle" area. If the pass is not made by 03, 05 returns home while 04 breaks across to set a "Big-on-Small (Drag) Ball-Screen" for 03 to "Perimeter Pull (Drag) Dribble" across the top of the floor to the opposite "Slot." As 03 "dribble-scrapes" off of 04's top left shoulder and breaks contact with 04, 04 should "reverse pivot off of his lower right foot and open up to the ball" on his roll down the lane.

As 03 approaches the "Slot," 01 "Drift Cuts" towards the "Deep Corner" to become a potential "catch and shooter/creator/passer (to 04)." One of either 03 or 01 should have the best passing angle to deliver the "Inside Pass" to 04. If no shots are taken, the "3-Out/2-In" Spot-Ups are filled for the smooth transition into the final phase of the offense. Diagram 23.15.

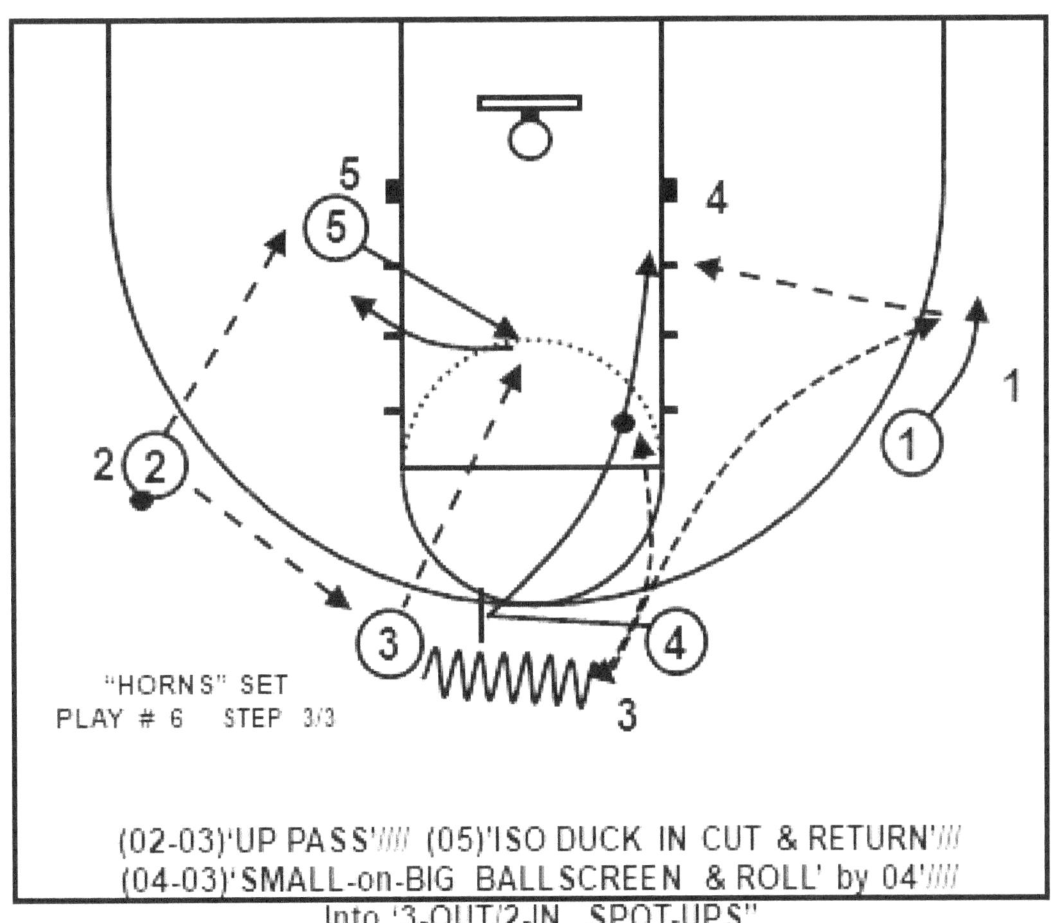

DIAGRAM 23.15

Play # 7 is a Level 3 play that is fully illustrated in Diagrams 23.16 through 23.19. It is a Counter to Play # with the beginning action. These diagrams 'mirror' Diagram 23.10 with 03 (instead of 02) being the "Iverson Cutter" that cuts over the top of 05 and 04.

To counter the play more so (to deceive and confuse the opposition even more so,) when 01 makes the (01-03) "Wing Pass," 02 is the perimeter player that stops his cut at the "Elbow" area and stacks just above 04 (not lower than 04). Diagram 23.16.

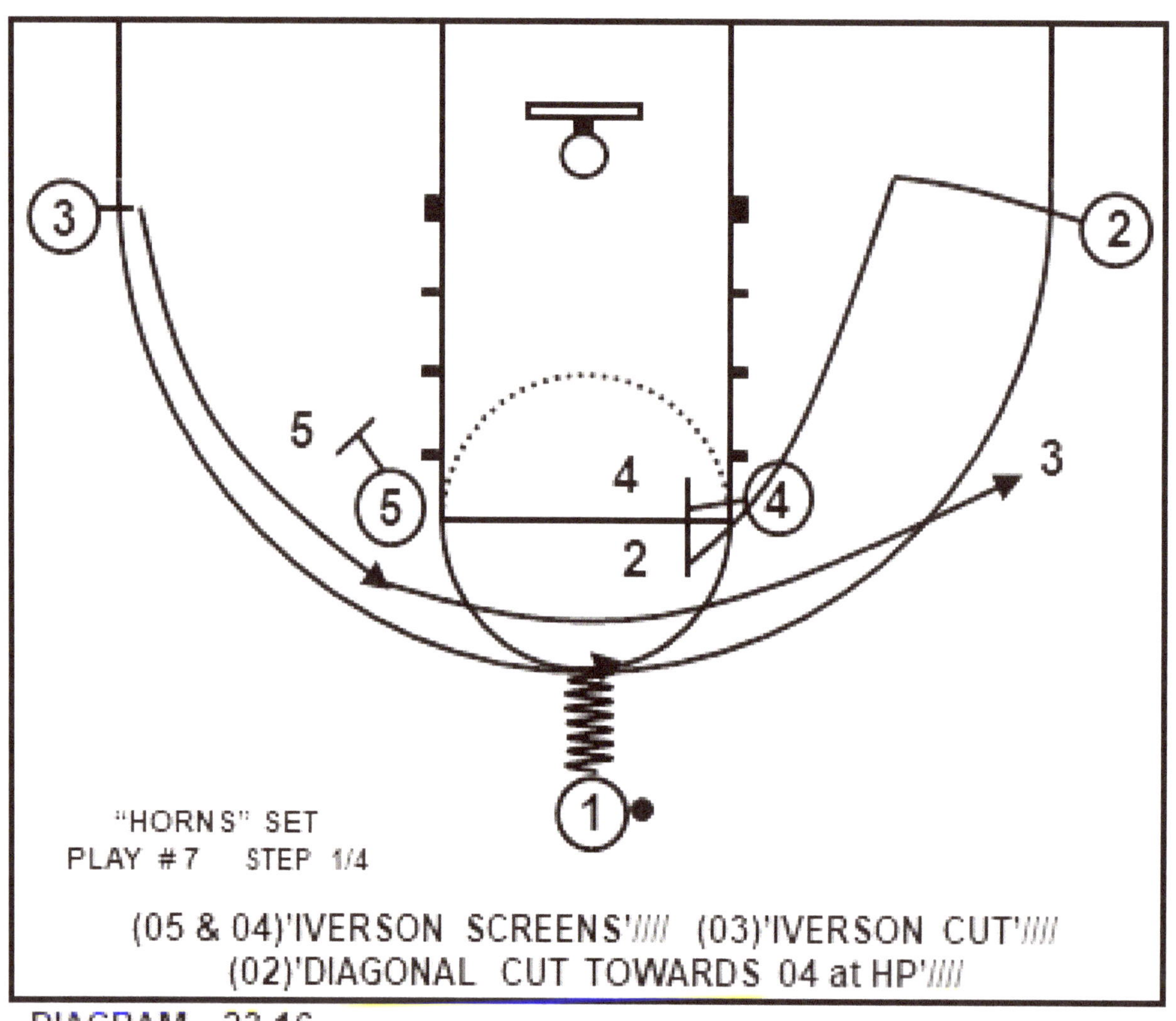

Play # 7   Diagram 23.16

Diagram 23.17 shows 01 making the "Wing Pass" to 03 and 04 setting the quick "Big-on-Small Back-Screen" for 02 to be the player that spins off of the screen and breaks to the newly designated "Ballside Block," while 04 slips out to the new "Ballside Slot." To help eliminate any possible weakside defensive support, particularly by X5, as soon as 01 makes the "Wing Pass" to 03, 05 steps up to set a "Big-on-Small Flare-Screen" for 01 to use to "Flare-Cut" to the new "Weakside Wing." Diagram 23.17.

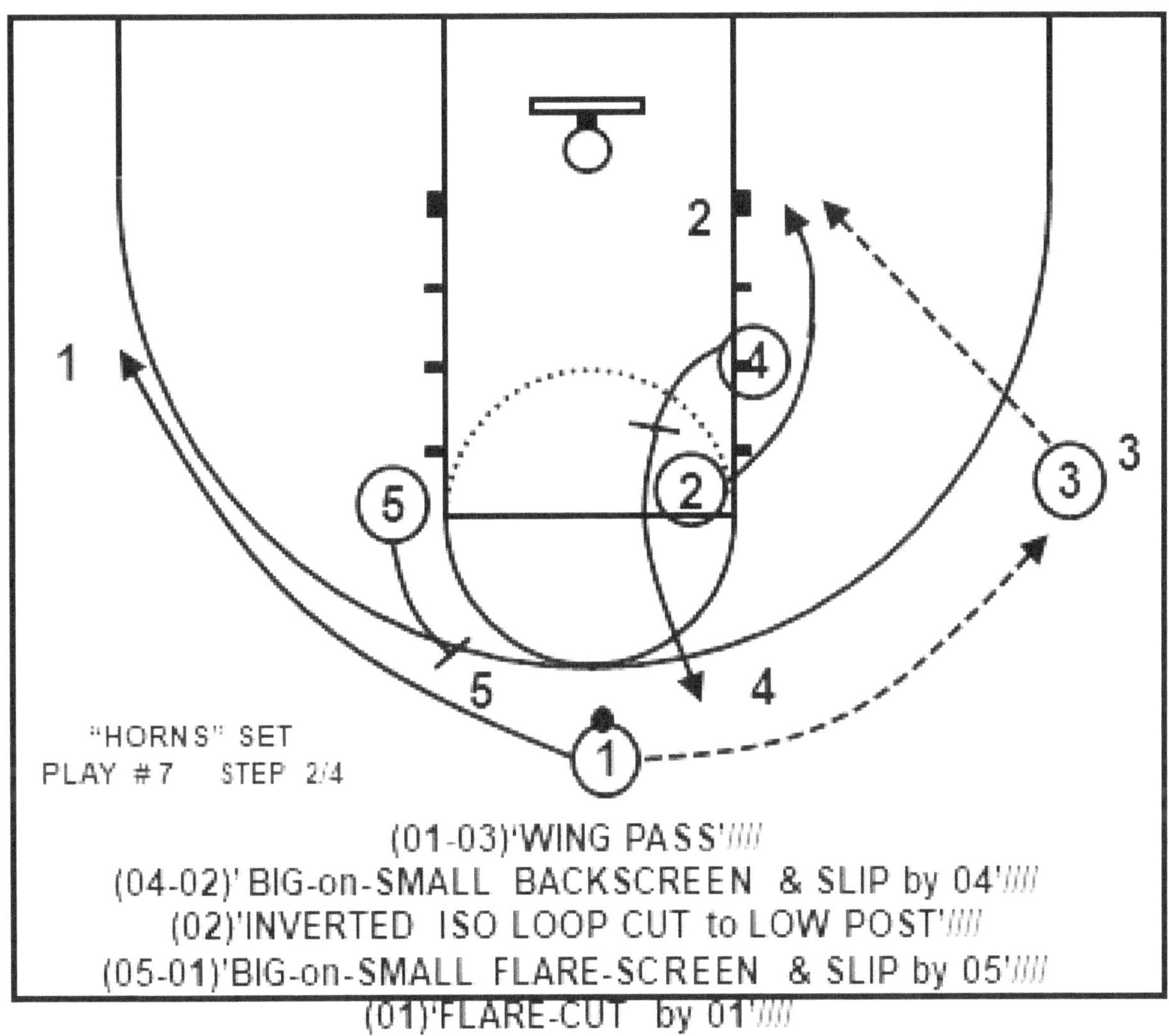

DIAGRAM 23.17

Diagram 23.18 shows the action if 03 does not make the "Inside Pass" to the inverted and isolated 02. 03 would make the "Up Pass" to 04, now inverted out on the perimeter "Slot" position. 02 would make a strong "Inverted and Iso Duck-In Cut" into the "Dotted Circle" area. If 04 cannot make the pass to 02, 04 should swing the ball over to 05, also inverted out on the perimeter's "Weakside Slot." To occupy the support defense to isolate 02 even more so, in addition to giving 05 a pass receiver for a perimeter shot, 04 cuts over to set a "Big-on-Small Pin-Screen for 03. Diagram 23.18.

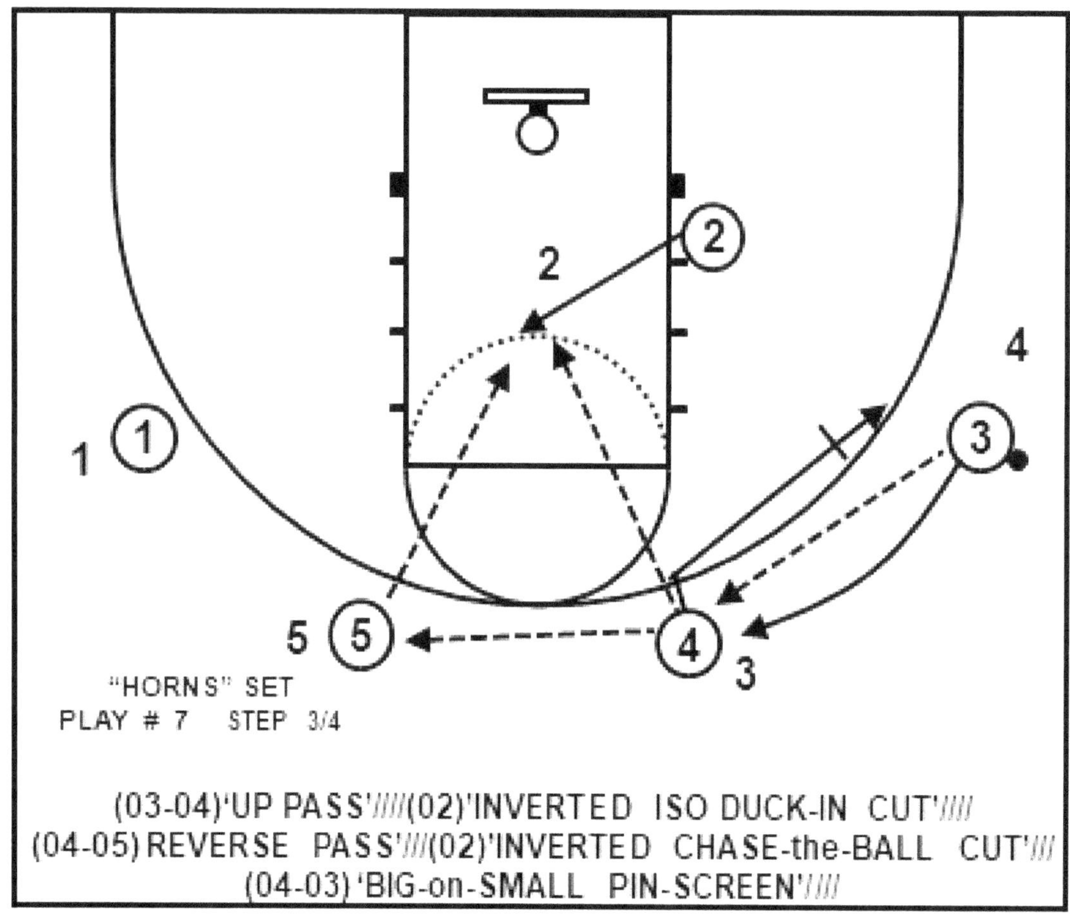

DIAGRAM 23.18

Diagram 23.19 shows 05 not being able to make the pass to 02, but realizing 01 has the ideal passing angle to deliver the ball to 02, 05 swings the ball over to 01. To totally eliminate any possible interior defensive help, both 05 and 03 diagonally cut across the perimeter to set a "Stagger-Screen" for 04 to break to the top of the key. Even if 04 is not a perimeter scoring threat, X5 and X4, (the two presumed biggest defenders) are involved in this off-the-ball weakside action and therefore pull them away from the ball and from 02 on the "Block."

If this action does not create the shot wanted by the offense, the "3-Out/2-In" Spot-Ups are filled for the next immediate phase of the offensive attack to begin. Diagram 23.19.

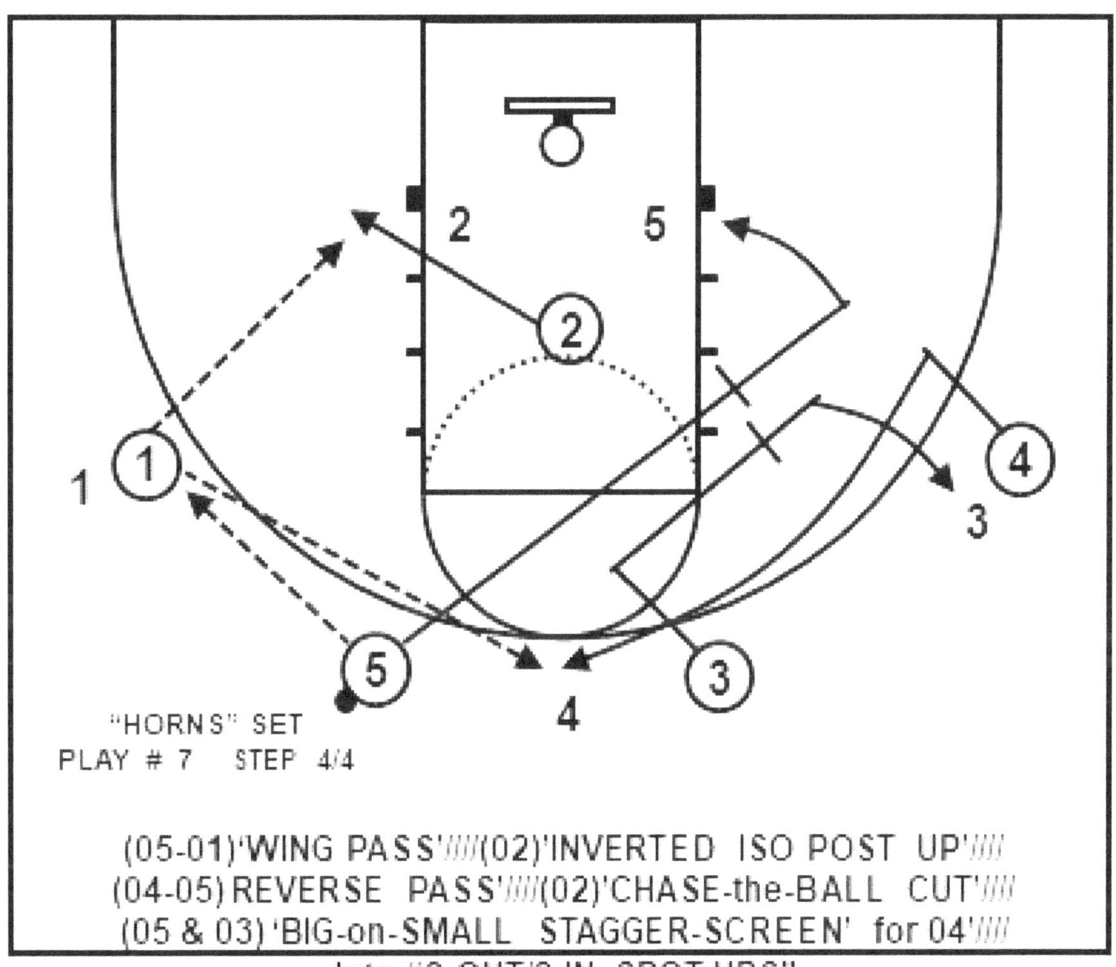

DIAGRAM 23.19

CLOSING

While it has been discussed often, the coaching staff has many decisions to make. They must decide on the most advantageous continuity offense that will meet the skill set of their present players, the coaching staff's offensive philosophies, the type of Primary and Secondary Fastbreaks (Odd-Front or Even-Front Breaks Options, depending on the continuity offense(s) chosen), the best one or two offensive alignments/sets that will be the most efficient and productive for individual and overall team performance, the specific plays and the actual number of plays that should be implemented within the half-court package of plays. In addition, the Baseline and Sideline Plays along with the number of plays chosen must be determined.

It must be emphasized that "Quality trumps Quantity" in the decision in selecting the number of continuity offenses, the number of sets/alignments and the number of plays (from each alignments) that are to be implemented. Don't allow too many plays or alignments to mentally bog down the offensive team.

Again, it must be brought to the coaching staff's attention that the continuity offense(s) chosen will be the main determination of which Secondary Break Options, offensive alignments and plays/entries are incorporated within the current season's offensive arsenal.

There are many different philosophies how to attack opposing defenses. This multiple-phase offensive system uses more than one phase/layer/wave of attack, with each phase/wave having a seamless and immediate conversion into the next phase/wave. While this system can be confusing to defenses and difficult to defend, this system can be properly taught and coached so that it can be easily understood and ultimately executed by players of many different levels of (physical talent, mental understanding and playing experience.)

In addition, there are several types of offensive schemes and different ways within this system that offenses can attack their defensive counter-parts. Many of these can be

integrated within the same offensive system that can attack defenses in various ways. The larger the number of schemes that can be successfully utilized and integrated within the same system, the greater the opportunity an offensive team can find the most efficient and productive schemes that can place both individual and the overall team in the best and most frequent "positions to succeed."

The plays/entries carefully diagrammed down to the small and seemingly unimportant 'V-Cuts' made by countless players before making their more important following cut are also described in detail.

Each play has been carefully studied and evaluated to determine which level of talent and experience must be possessed for that specific team to be able to successfully execute the play. This includes all players' physical skills as well as their mental understanding of the game. Coaches must also have the experience and the associated level of understanding of the game as well as their coaching/teaching of the nuances of each play.

The most sophisticated plays/entries would fall into the last of the three levels all based on the team's physical talents and skills, the mental capacities and the overall team's game experience. In addition, the coaching staff must have a high degree of basketball knowledge as well as very high teaching and coaching skills to educate his/her entire basketball team. The proper breakdown drills must be thoroughly utilized to hone the fundamental skills and techniques needed for individual players and the overall team to execute plays that can be efficient, productive and successful. We define this family of plays as the "Level 3 category" of plays. This "Level 3" family of plays will have a much more complex offensive scheme that would require a very high amount of physical talent as well as requiring a greater amount of the players (to execute) and the coaches (to teach and coach) mental capacities and experience needed for the offense to be efficient, productive and successful. We feel plays in our defined "Level 3" category could possibly be successful for NBA teams, definitely for college teams and also for many high schools and older AAU teams.

The next classification or level of plays would be possibly slightly lower as far as sophistication, complexity and the actual 'length' of the play (and the number of passes, cuts and screens used) in the play's overall scheme. While all "Level 2" plays in each of the chapters in this book remain to be fundamentally sound, these plays may lack the actual number of techniques/methods that are implemented within that play in comparison to the "Level 1" plays/entries. Therefore any team that successfully executes the highest "Level

1" plays/entries could/should easily be able execute any of these so-called lower "Level 2" plays/entries, if so desired. Almost all high school teams should be able to execute successfully all aspects of the "Level 2" plays.

The final grouping of plays would be called "Level 1" plays and are not as difficult for offensive players to master the execution of them, both physically as well as mentally. Even though the techniques are still fundamentally sound, they may not be as complex to learn and understand in addition to being easier to physically execute.

"Level 1" plays would be lower in the scheme's complexities and the number of techniques used in the execution of this category of plays. Obviously, since these "Level 1" plays are still sound, but lack some of the methods used in the two previous more sophisticated and complex levels; these more elementary plays should be able to be utilized by any teams that use either of the two higher level plays. We feel that Middle School/Junior High teams as well as younger AAU teams or organizations should be able to utilize any of the "Level 1" plays successfully, with a possibility that some of those teams that are slightly more advanced (than other teams) could possibly use some plays located in the immediate next immediate level.

Ideas, concepts and techniques from actual plays from teams of all three levels have been used to modify or to create different combinations of the various techniques and schemes used that will help prove these entries can be successfully used. This allows the author to create numerous plays that use the various schemes to build a library of fundamentally sound plays that will be unique and will be appropriate for a wide range of teams with various ages and skill levels.

With this book having plays/entries in these three presumed categories or levels, the book will reach out and benefit a much larger group of serious basketball coaches from elementary school age to the highest skilled levels that exists.

In addition, an experienced and resourceful coach may be able to mold some plays that include all of the offensive techniques that he/she desires could reshape a specific play that begins in one specific offensive set/alignment and reshape it so that it could begin in a different offensive/set that is more favorable to that coach and his/her coaching staff's liking.

Conversely, that innovative and creative coach may completely like the specific offensive set/alignment and favor the very same offensive actions included in a certain

play, but can modify that play so that the ending spot-ups of all five players are conducive to being able to begin the final phase of the offensive attack by using a more favorable offensive continuity offense.

The "HI-LO STAX SET"

PLAYS/ENTRIES THAT END in the "3-OUT/2-IN" OFFENSIVE SPOT-UPS

At the conclusion of every entry/play/quick-hitter where no shots have been taken, all five players will always be repositioned into a different family of offensive spot-ups. One of these groups of spot-ups is called the "3-Out/2-In Spot-Ups." After each play every player will have been repositioned around the court with any one of the five players ending up in the "Ballside Block," the "Ballside Wing," the "Weakside Block," the "Weakside Wing," and the "Point" (at the top of the key). These five positions can provide the offense with safe and easy types of ball-reversals, large gaps for dribble penetration, opportunities to deliver the ball inside to whomever (perimeter-type or post-type players) is posting up their defender on the "Ballside Block," and a player that can be a perimeter-scoring threat and a legitimate offensive rebounding threat from outside of the arc on his "offensive crashing of the boards." The "3-Out/2-In Spot-Ups also provide ample opportunities for constant and effective defensive transition responsibilities and well as maximum offensive rebounding.

Diagram 24.1 illustrates the "HI-LO STAX" Set with 01 always being the lone primary ball-handler bringing the ball to the top of the key. 03 always starts at the "Elbow" area on the left side of the floor stacked just below 05 who is also aligned at the left "Elbow."

On the opposite side of the floor, 04 starts on the "Ballside Notch" above the Block, while 02 stacks just below 04.

Play # 1, a Level 1 Play, begins as 01 approaches the top of the key, 03 steps up closer to 05's defender to set a "Small-on-Big Back-Screen" before then slipping to the top of the key. 05 spins off of 03's outside right shoulder and slides down to the new "Ballside Block." 01 dribbles to the FT Line extended on the left "Wing" area.

On the opposite side of the floor, 04 sets a "Big-on-Small Pin Screen" for 02 to use to rub his defender off of 04's outside right shoulder and to then break out to the FT Line extended on the right side of the floor. After screening for 02, 04 seals his defender off and tries to post up his defender if and when 01 makes the "Wing Pass" to 02.

567

If 01 does not make the "Inside Pass" to 04, he could skip the ball to 02 or he could reverse the ball to 03 out on top. After 01's first pass (to 03 or to 02), the "3-Out/2-In" Spot-Ups are filled and the designated continuity offense can fluidly begin. Diagram 24.1.

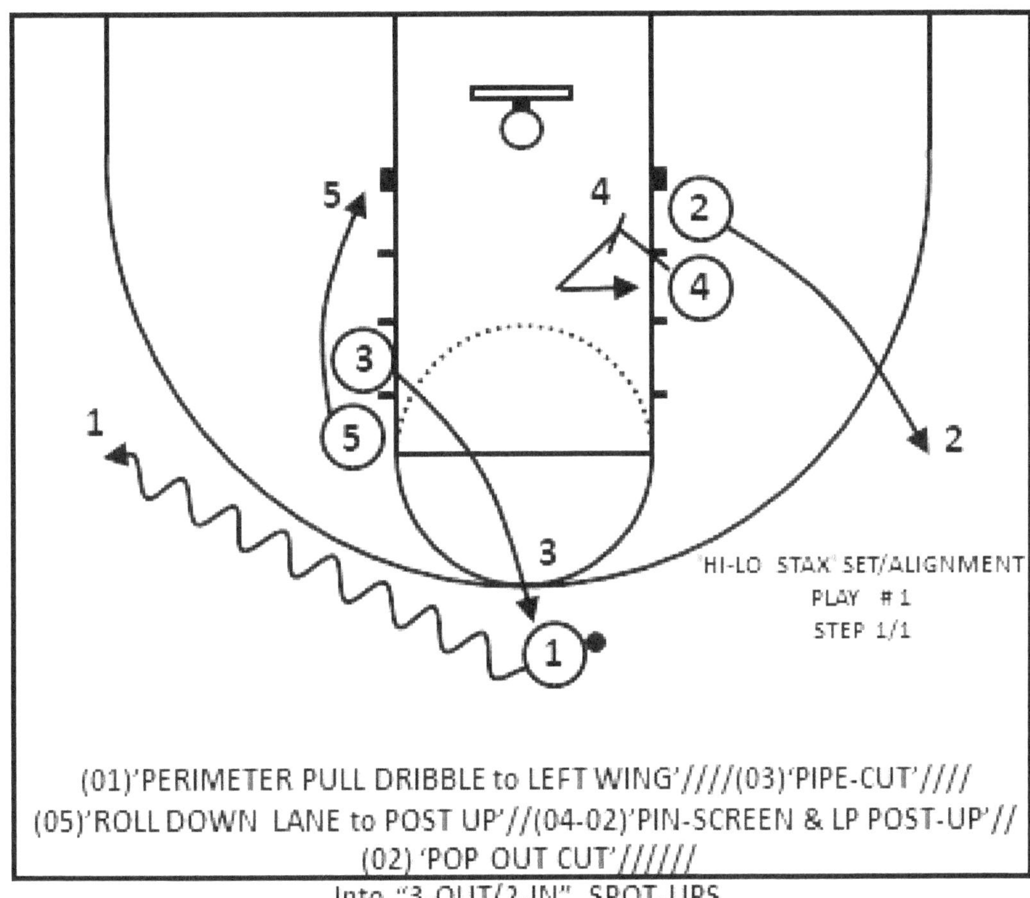

DIAGRAM 24.1

Play# 1   Diagram 24.1

Diagram 24.2 shows a second Level 1 play that describes Play # 2. This play is a Counter to Play # 1. As 01 dribbles towards the left wing, 03 steps up as if to set the same screen for 05, but instead 03 changes direction and slides down the lane to become a perimeter-type player that will post his perimeter-type defender up on the new "Ballside Block." Instead of being the post player, 05 then becomes the post-type player that breaks out to the top of the key. On the opposite side of the floor, the identical weakside action takes place as in Play # 1 and therefore 02 and 04 end up in the same two spot-ups. On the ballside of the floor, 01 remains at the "Ballside Wing" with 05 and 03 exchanging locations, therefore 03 becoming the primary interior pass receiver that is attacking a more of a perimeter-type defender while vertically pulling the presumed biggest defender further from the basket.

Another huge similarity of the two plays is that just after 01's perimeter-pull dribble to the same left side of the floor, the "3-Out/2-In" Spot-Ups are filled for a smooth conversion into the designated continuity offense. Diagram 24.2.

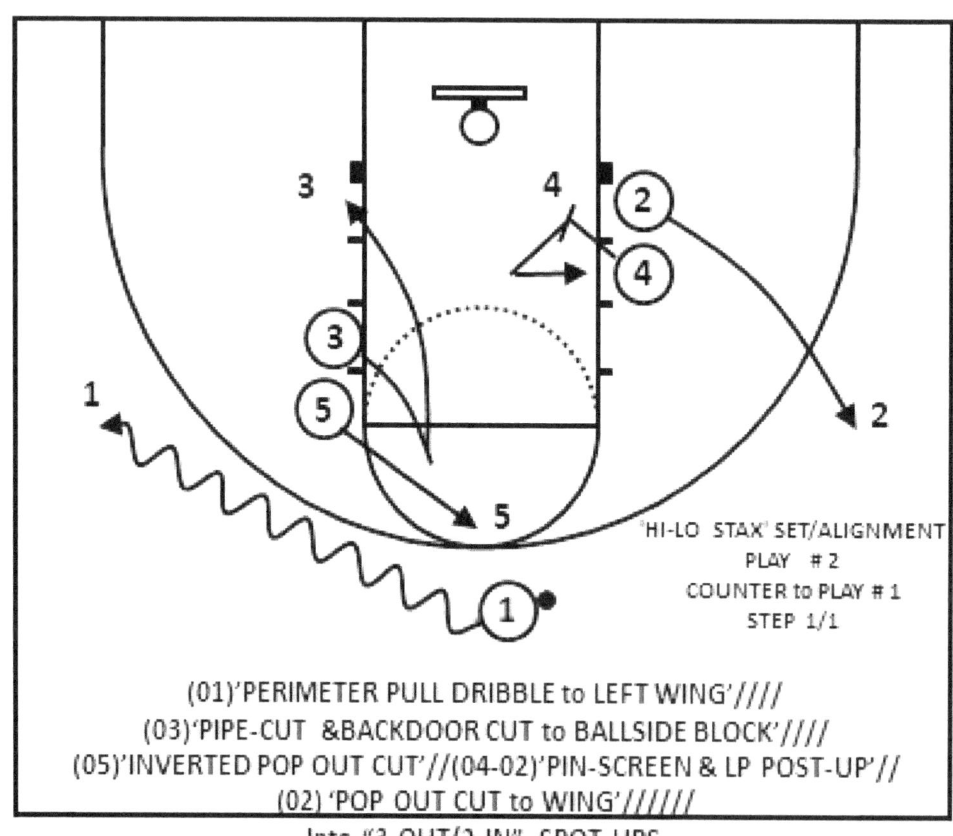

Play # 2   Diagram 24.2

Diagram 24.3 illustrates a Level 2 play called Play # 3 with 01 having to always drive towards the "Wing" area on the right side of the floor. 04 screens for 02 and 02 makes a "Pipe Cut" up the Lane Line to the new "Ballside Slot." On the left side of the floor, 05 "Pin-Screens" for 03 to break out to the left "Wing" area before then slipping that screen and inverting his post-type defender, X5, by stepping out to the "Weakside Slot." After 02 makes his "Pipe Cut" and 0505 makes his inverted "Slot Cut," it allows 04 to isolate his defender, X4, down on the new "Ballside Block."

If 01 cannot make the "Inside Pass" to 04, he should look to make a "Skip Pass" to 03 on the "Weakside Wing." To reverse the ball and attack the opposite side of the floor, 01 should look to make the pass to 02. Diagram 24.3.

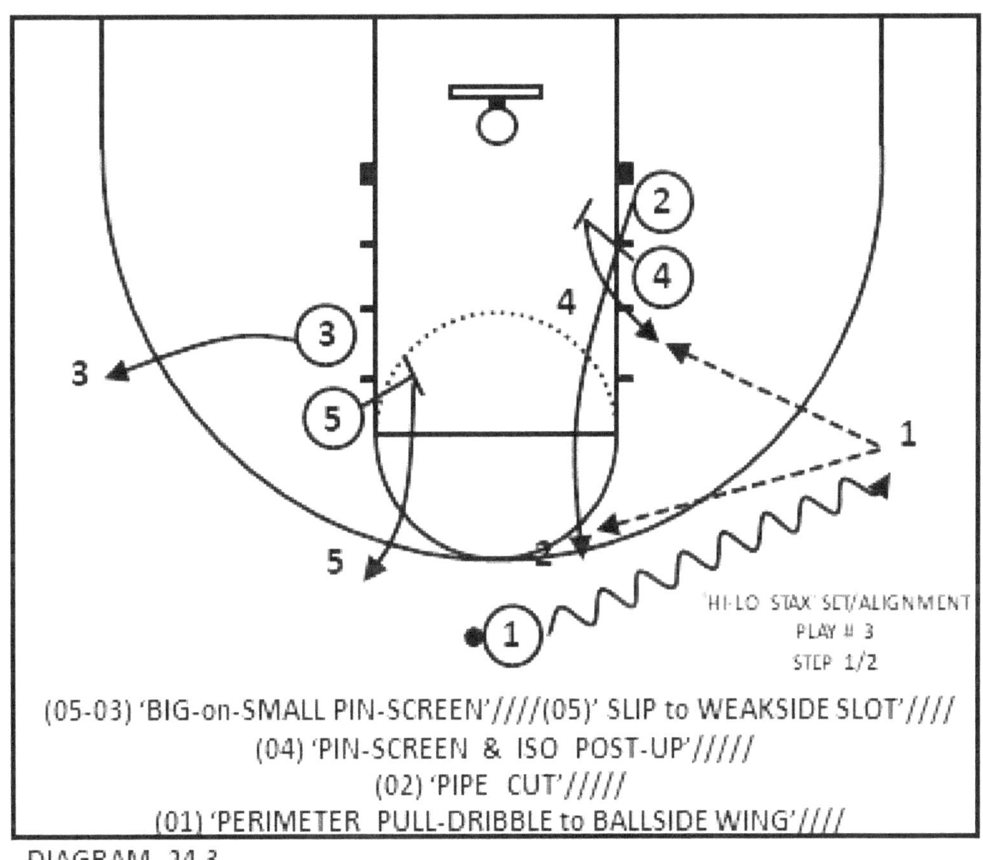

DIAGRAM 24.3

Play # 3   Diagram 24.3

Diagram 24.4 shows 02 receiving the pass from 01. This pass dictates that 04 work on getting open with any techniques and footwork on his direct path towards 02 and the ball. 05 then cuts across to set a "Big-on-Small Ball-Screen" for 02 to perimeter-pull (drag) dribble across the imaginary center line. As 04 continues his "chase of the ball," when 02 breaks contact with 05's top right shoulder, 05 makes a front pivot off of his left foot and "Rim-Runs" to the basket. 02 looks to make a "Lob Pass" to 05 or a pass to 04 now on the opposite side of the lane. 02 could make the "Wing Pass" to 03 for 03 to have his possible "catch/shoot or catch/create or catch/pass" opportunities.

If no shots are taken by any of the many possible shooters on the interior or the perimeter, the "3-Out/2-In" Spot-Ups are filled for a smooth conversion into the last phase of the offense. Diagram 24.4.

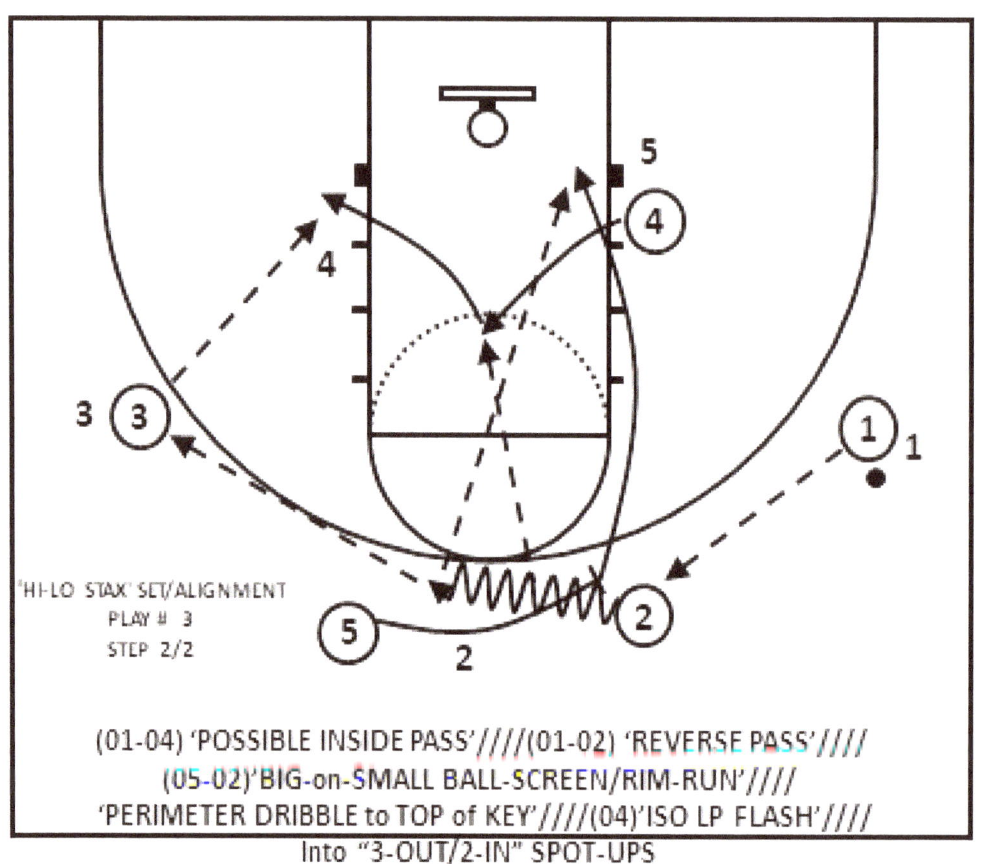

Play # 3   Diagram 24.4

Diagrams 24.5 and 24.6 show sometime of a counter to Play # 3—another Level 2 play that begins with the same action on the same side of the floor with one exception. The exception is that 02 makes a "Zipper Cut," versus a "Pipe Cut." There is just a small difference in the two cuts but will probably be defended in different manners. All other players execute the same methods and end up in the same locations as they do in Play # 3. Diagram 24.5.

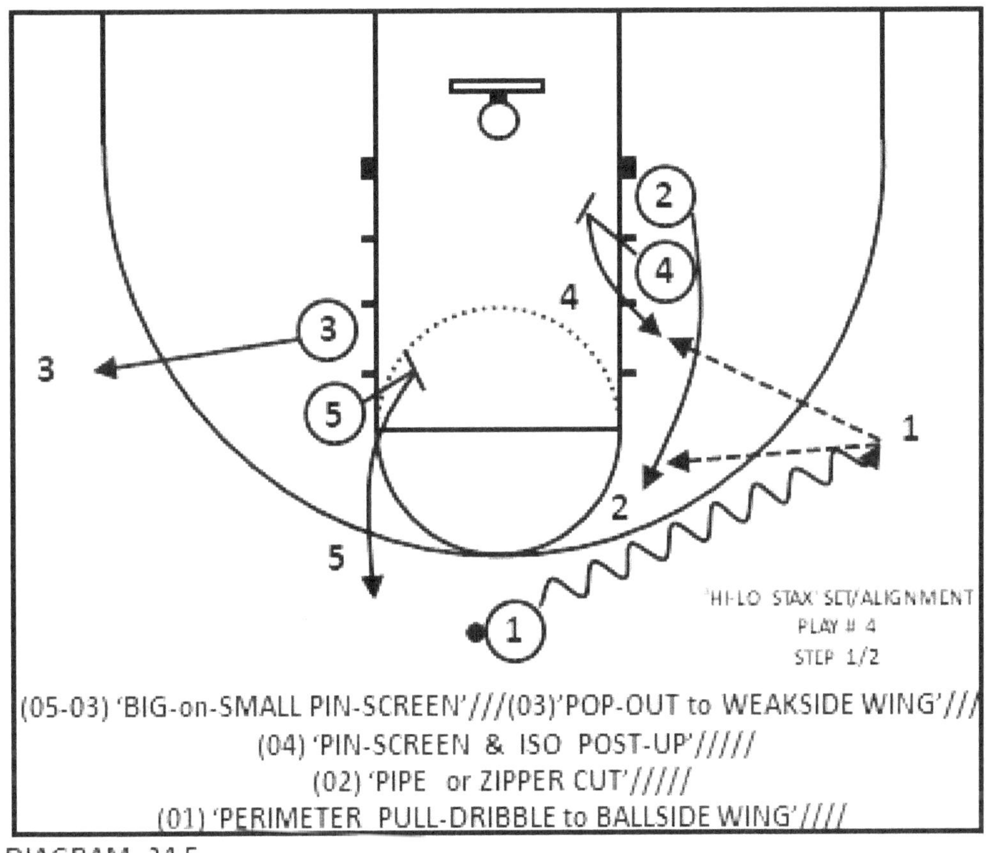

DIAGRAM 24.5

Play # 4   Diagram 24.5

During the second phase of the play, the action is extremely different and can easily catch the opposition off guard. After the pass is made out to 02 (after his "Pipe or Zipper Cut," 04 empties out more quickly by cutting horizontally across the lane. 04 continues emptying of the lane to receive a "Small on Big Pin Down-Screen" by 03, where 04 ends up on the "Wing" area and 03 on the "Mid-Post Block." At the same time, 05 begins breaking towards 02 and the ball for the presumed same "Ball-Screen/Rim-Run" (as executed in Play # 3.) With the time of 04 cutting out of the lane just before 05 ends up cutting through the lane, 05's cut will allow him to isolate his own defender.

With the ball centered up in 02's hands, the attack could go to either side of the floor and attack either on the perimeter or the interior. 02 could make an "Inside Pass" to 05 on his "Ghost Screen Cut" or make a "Throwback Reverse Pass" to 01, who could then deliver the ball to 05 on a post-up.

On the opposite side of the floor, 02 could make a "Wing Pass" to the now inverted 05 or an "Inside Pass" to the now inverted 03 on "Wing" area. Besides having a wide variety of scorers in many different locations, the "3-Out/2-In" Spot-Ups are filled so that the last phase of the offense could immediately begin. Diagram 24.6.

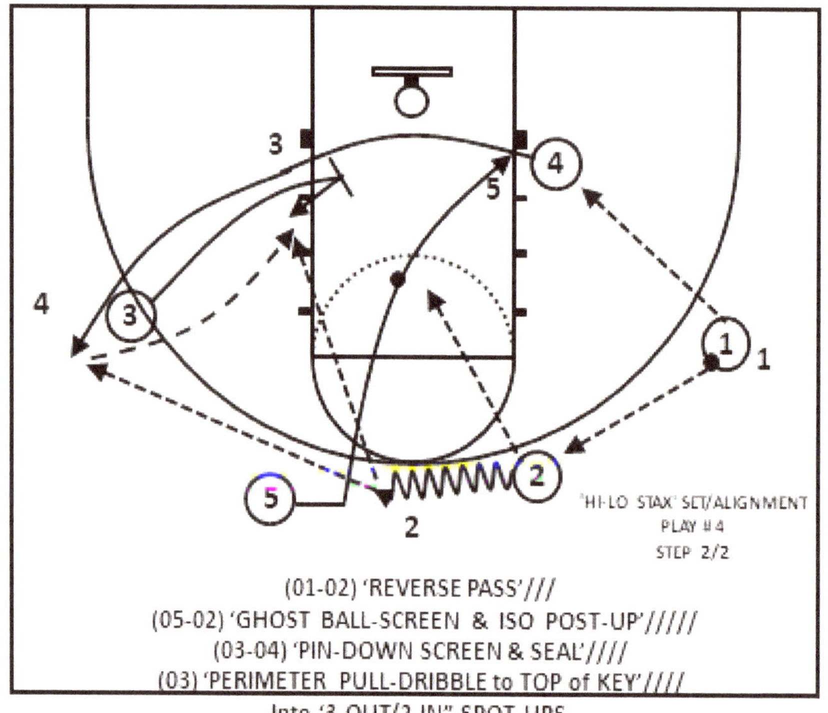

Play 4 Diagram 24.6

Instead, 05 breaks off of his initial route and executes a "Ghost Ball-Screen & Diagonal Slash Cut" across the lane to the opposite side's Mid-Post area.

Play # 5, another Level 2 play, is demonstrated in Diagrams 24.7 and 24.8 with typical "Big-on-Small Pin Screens set by 05 (for 03) and by 04 (for 02). 02 breaks out to the "Wing" area on his side of the floor with 04 immediately sealing off his defender in an isolated post-up.

05 screens for 03 who pops out to his "Wing" area also with 05 remaining at the "Elbow" area. When 01 makes the "Wing Pass" to 02, 01 then makes a "Corner Cut" to the newly declared "Ballside Deep Corner." At the same time, 03 breaks to the top of the key to replace 01 and 05 slips to the new "Weakside Wing" to replace 03. Again, with all four of his teammates spread about the court and all four outside of the arc, 04 should be able to isolate the lone defender, X4.

These current locations: "Ballside Block," "Ballside Deep Corner," "Ballside Wing," "Top of the Key," and the lone "Weakside Wing," are the exact locations for our "ODD-FRONT SECONDARY BREAK" Spot-Ups.

It could be utilized that any time these "BREAK" Spot-Ups are filled, any of the Options for the "Break" could be immediately employed and those options could be additional half-court plays. Diagram 24.7.

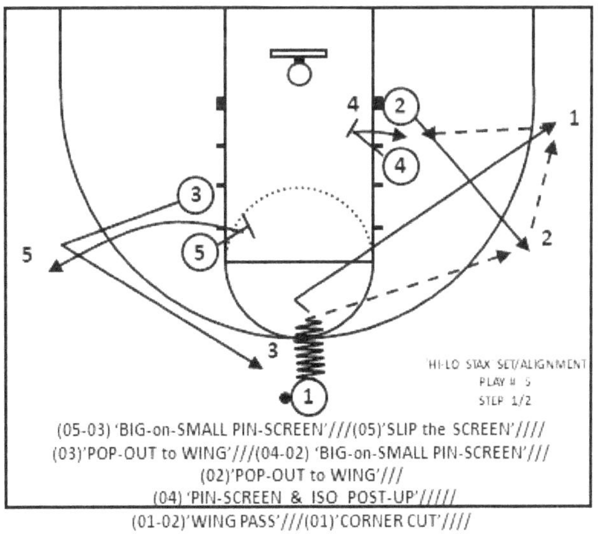

DIAGRAM 24.7

Play # 5   Diagram 24.7

In this particular half-court play/entry, when the "Inside Pass" is not utilized and the ball is "Up-Passed" from 01 to 02 and the ball is "Reverse Passed" from 02 to 03 out on top; 05 steps up and over to set a (05-03) "Big-on-Small Ball-Screen/Roll." As 03 "dribble-scrapes" off of 05's top right shoulder and continues dribbling to the "Wing" area, 05 reverse-pivots off of his lower left foot, opens up to the ball and then slides down the land to post up his defender.

To also give the play a perimeter type scoring threat and to accentuate the inside isolation post-up (for 05), both 04 and 02 diagonally break down to set a "Big-on-Small Elevator Screen" for 01 to use to break to the top of the key for an open '3.'

After screening, 04 slips further to the new "Weakside Block" while 02 moves up to the new "Weakside Wing." With 01 looking for an open '3' at the top of the key, 03 having dribbled to the new "Ballside Wing" and 05 having "rolled" down to the new "Ballside Block;" the same "3-Out/2-In" Spot-Ups are filled not only for the smooth conversion to the designated continuity offense but also for maximum offensive rebounding and defensive transition efficiency. Diagram 24.8.

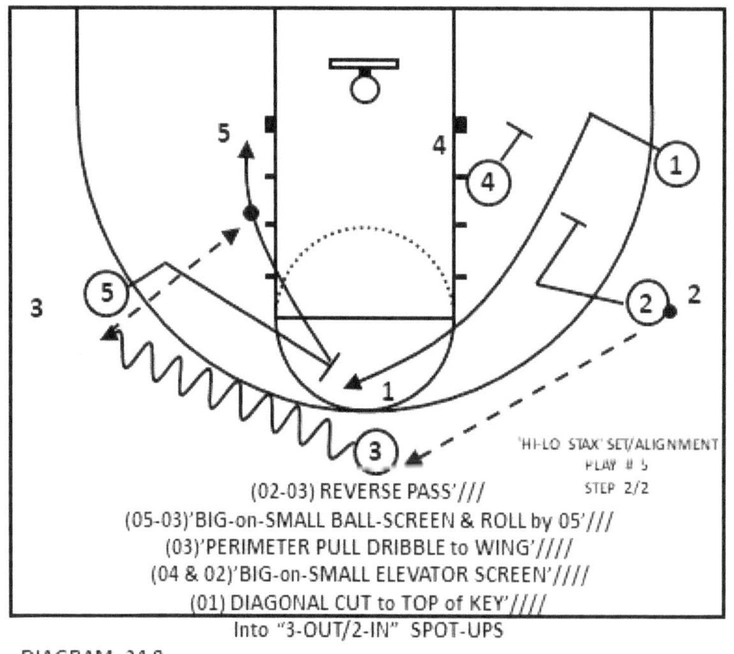

DIAGRAM 24.8

Play # 5   Diagram 24.8

Diagrams 24.9, 24.10 and 24.11 illustrate Play # 6, which is a Level 3 play that can be a Counter to Play # 5. The same (05-03) and (04-02) "Big-on-Small Pin Screens" are set with 03 and 02 both breaking off of the screens to break to the "Wing" areas on their respective sides of the floor. 04 again slips his screen to shape up to "Iso Post" his defender on the same "Ballside Block." As a change in this play, 03 remains at the new "Weakside Wing" while 05 slips his screen and makes an inverted "Pop-Out" Cut to the new "Weakside Slot."

After making the (01-02) "Wing Pass," 01 makes the same "Corner Cut" to the new "Ballside Deep Corner." Once again, this action repositions all four of 04's teammates evenly spread outside of the arc in the same "Secondary Break Spot-Ups." The only change is that 05 and 03 have exchanged their locations away from the ball. Diagram 24.9.

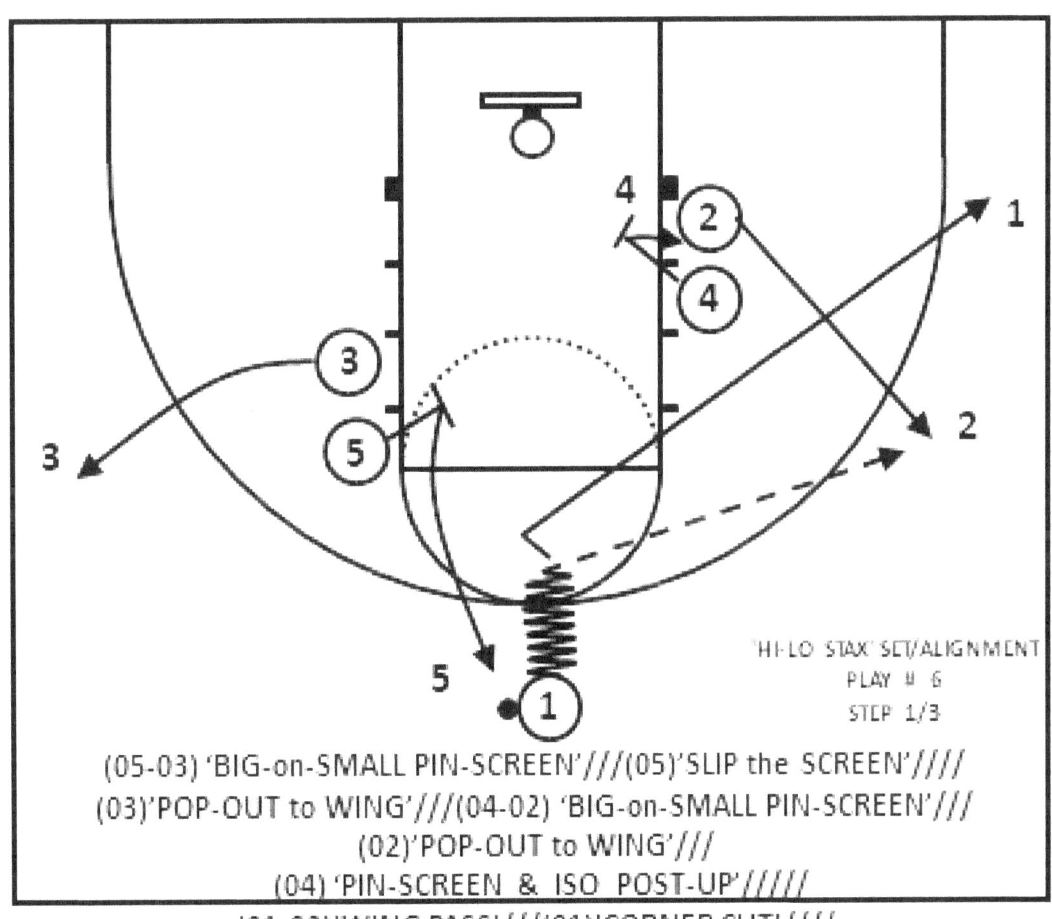

Play # 6   Diagram 24.9

Diagram 24.10 illustrates both 01 and 02 attempting to make any type of "Inside Pass" to 04 that is possible. Again, any of the designed "Odd Front Secondary Break" Options could be used. In this case, when the ball is finally reversed to 05 out on top, 04 again "chases" the ball with an "Iso Duck-In Cut" before then following the path of 05's next "Wing Pass" (to either 03 or to 01). At the same time 04 cuts into the "Dotted Circle" area, 01 has run the baseline towards the basket first for a "Lob Pass." Diagram 24.10.

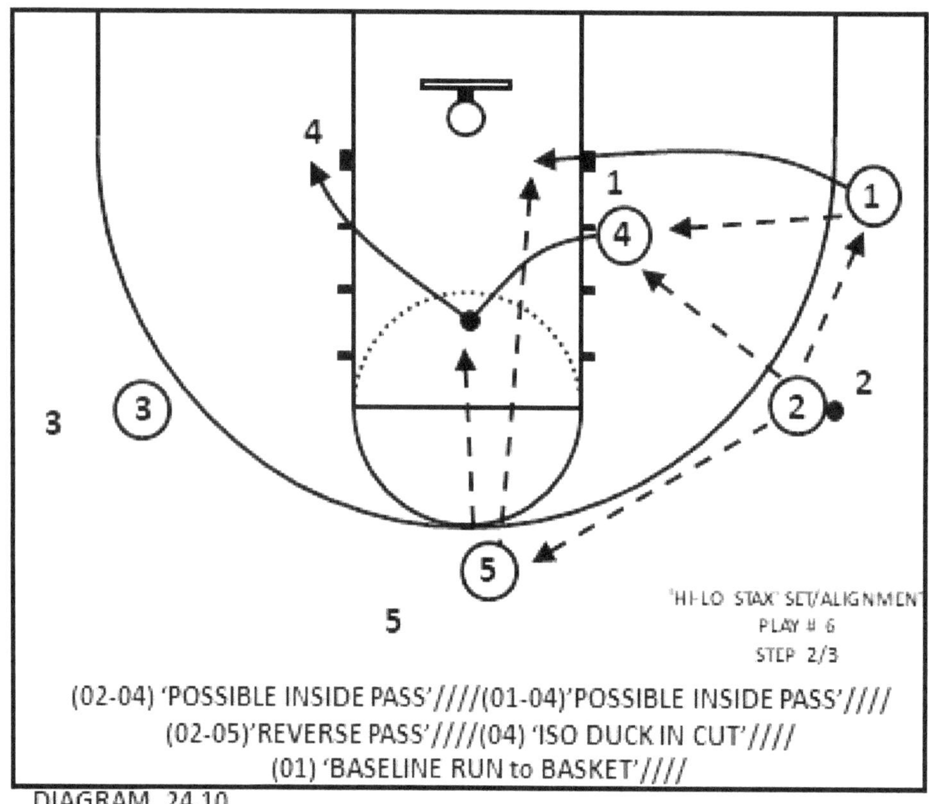

DIAGRAM 24.10

Diagram 24.11 shows 05 not turning down the pass to 04, the "Lob Pass" to 01 or the "Re-reverse Pass" to 02 and instead swinging the ball on over to 03. 03 then looks to make the "Inside Pass" to 04 as 02 breaks diagonally up to set a "Small-on-Big Diagonal Back-Screen" for 05 to use to make his "Lob Cut" to the basket for 03's "Lob Pass" (to 05.)

If shots are not taken, the "3-Out/2-In" Spot-Ups are filled for the designated continuity offense to fluidly begin. Diagram 24.11.

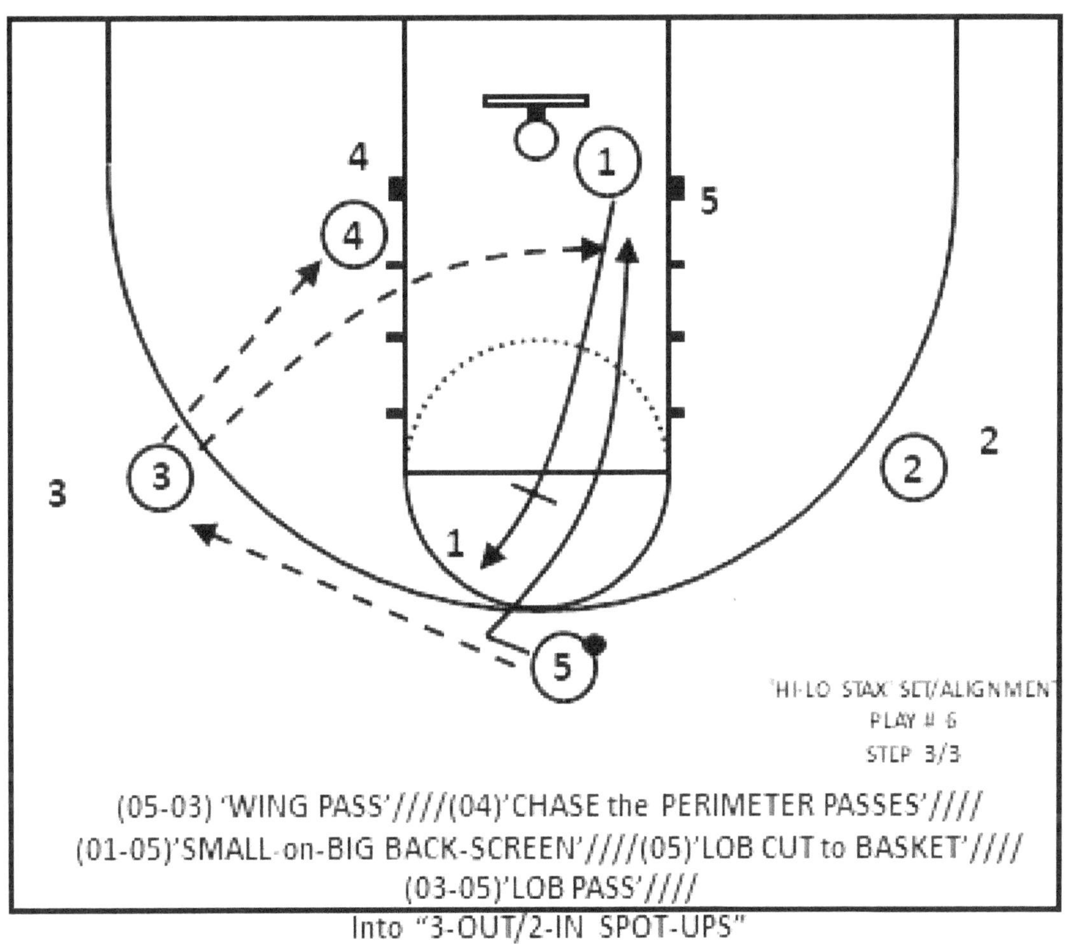

DIAGRAM 24.11

Play # 6   Diagram 24.11

Diagrams 24.12, 24.13 and 24.14 illustrate Play # 7, which is another Level 3 play that can be a Counter to both Play # 5 and Play # 6. Once again, identical (05-03) and (04-02) "Big-on-Small Pin Screens" are set for the same teammates. Again, both 03 and 02 scrape off of the screens to break to the same "Wing" areas on the same sides of the offense. Diagram 24.12.

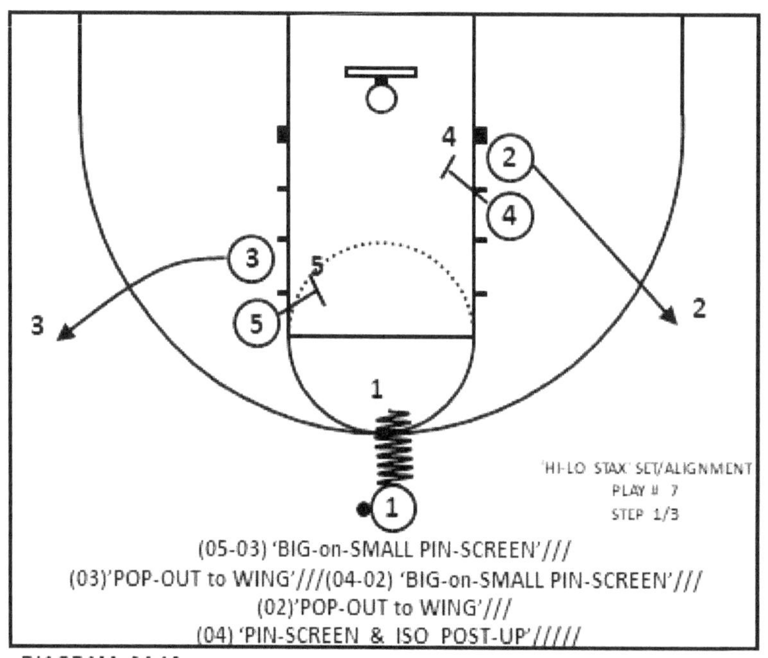

DIAGRAM 24.12

Play # 7   Diagram 24.12

Diagram 24.13 shows the first differences in this play compared to the first two plays in this three-play package. After 02 breaks up to the "Wing" area, he then continues up and over to set a "Ball-Screen" for 01 to move the ball to the FT Line extended via dribble. 03 then breaks up to the top of the key to execute a "Big-on-Small Flare-Screen the Ball-Screener" for 02 to use to then "Flare-Cut" to the new "Weakside Wing," while 03 then slips his screen (for 02) to remain at the top of the key.

At the same time, 04 breaks diagonally up to set a "Diagonal Back-Screen" for 05 to use to "Slash Cut" across the lane" to the now empty "Ballside Block." After screening for 05, 04 then reverses his cut's direction to then flash back to the newly declared "Ballside High Post." Diagram 24.13.

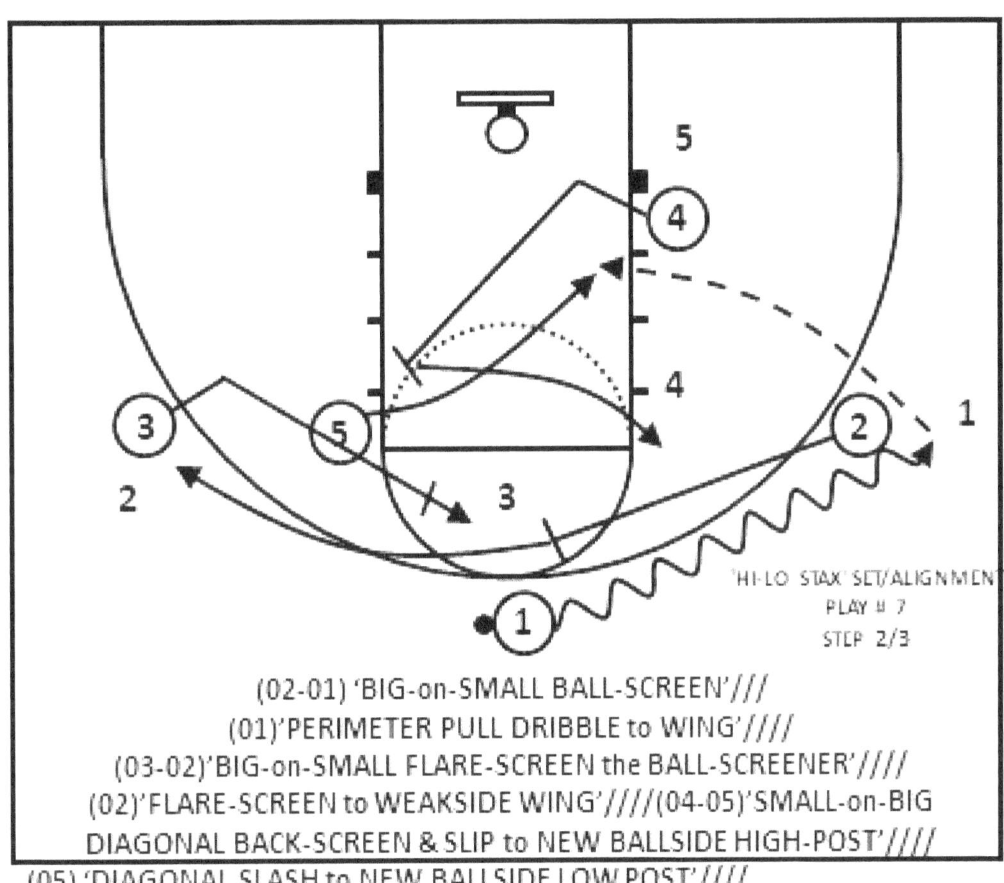

(05) 'DIAGONAL SLASH to NEW BALLSIDE LOW POST'////
DIAGRAM 24.13

Diagram 24.14 shows the final step of the half-court play phase of the attack with 03 making the "Wing Pass" to 02 before starting to set up in the proper (Stagger) Screening angles with 04 for 05 to use to break to the top of the key. As 03 starts his cut, he reads his defender and when appropriate, he changes his direction to slash back towards the new "Ballside Block." 04 continues cutting in the right angle to finish his part of the initial "Stagger-Screen." 05 sets his defender up by "sticking his head under the basket" before changing directions to then scrape off of 04's outside right shoulder and continue cutting to the top of the key. 04 then slips his screen and remains on the new "Weakside Block," while 01 "spots up" on the new "Weakside Wing."

With 02 having possession of the ball on the left side of the floor, his primary receivers are 03 posted up on the "Block," 05 at the top of the key and 01 "floating" around the new "Weakside Wing" and preparing for a possible (02-01) "Skip Pass" (especially if X1 starts to sag off into the lane to help out X3. These spot-ups also are the proper positions so that the designated continuity offense can immediately begin with the next pass made by 02. Diagram 24.14.

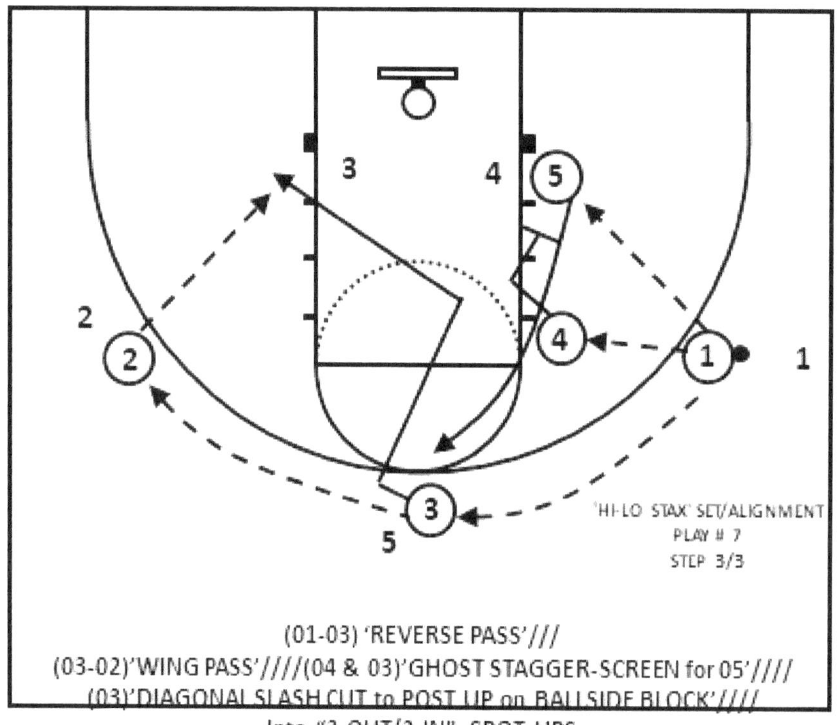

DIAGRAM 24.14

Another Level 3 Play called Play # 8 starts with the identical action of all five players as it does in Play # 4 (even though Play # 4 is a Level 2 Play.) 01 must dribble to the right side at the FT Line extended with 02 making a "Zipper Cut" up the Lane Line to the new "Ballside Slot" and 04 trying to "Iso Post-Up" his defender on the isolated "Ballside Block."

On the weakside, the same action of 05 "Pin-Screening" for 03 to pop out followed by 05 slipping his screen to invert out to the new "Weakside Slot." Diagram 24.15.

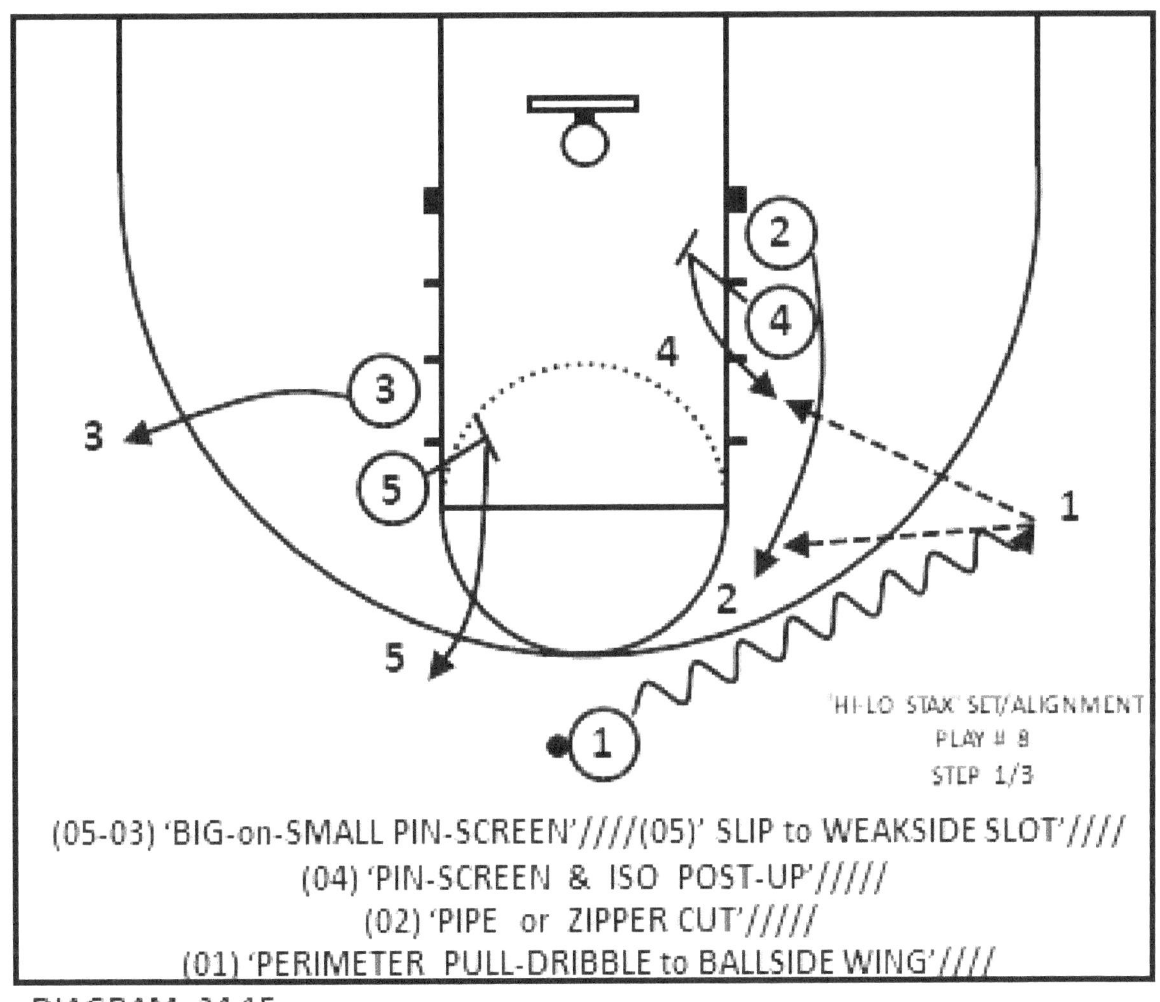

DIAGRAM 24.15

Play # 8   Diagram 24.15.

Diagram 24.16 shows 01 making the "Up Pass" out to 02 at the "Slot." 04 makes a hard "Iso Duck-In Cut" and if not open, 02 reverses the ball to the inverted 05. As the ball reaches 05, 04 continues his cut to the "Nail." 02 then makes a "shuffle-cut" off of 04's right shoulder all the way to the new "Ballside Block." 05 looks to make the quick surprise pass to 02 or a "Wing Pass" to 03 (who may have a better passing angle to deliver the ball to 02 on the "Block." Diagram 24.16.

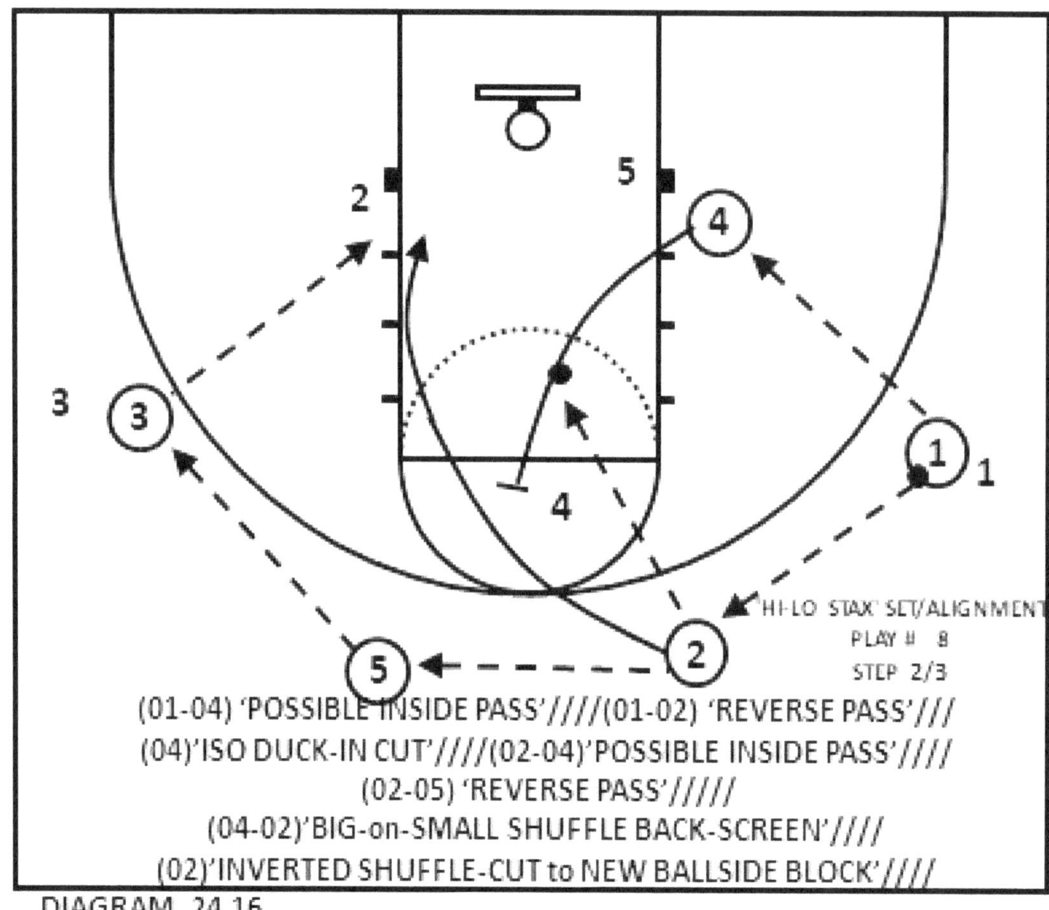

DIAGRAM 24.16

After turning down the pass to 02 and making the pass to 03, 05 then sets up his post-type defender with a (perimeter-type) "Shuffle-Cut" off of 04's left shoulder as 05 then makes a "Lob Cut" to the basket. 03 now has a second interior pass opportunity. After screening for 05, 04 steps to the top of the key to become the second perimeter pass receiver that 03 could utilize. This action repositions all five players in the "3-Out/2-In" Spot-Ups for the final phase of the attack. Diagram 24.17.

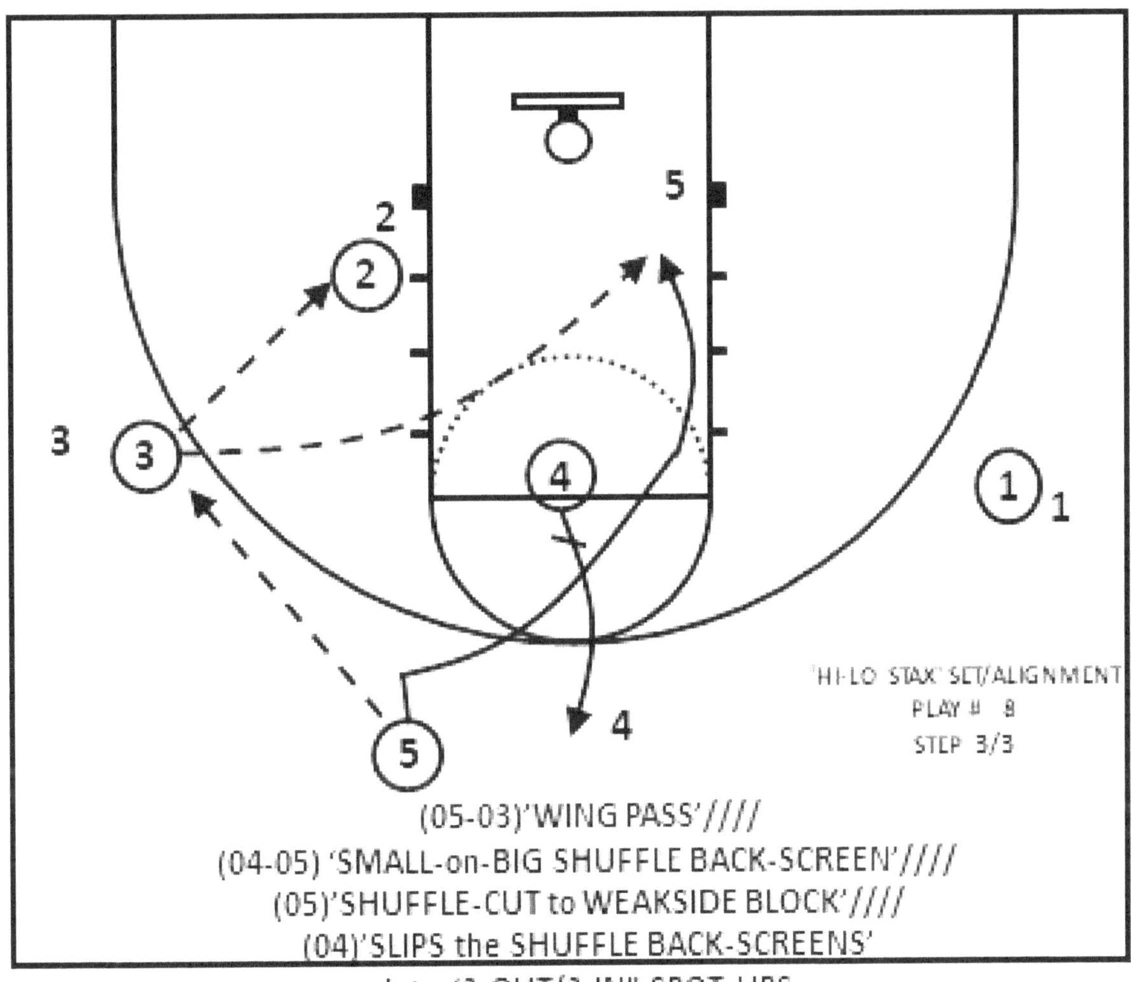

DIAGRAM 24.17

Play # 8   Diagram 24.17

Play # 9 is a Level 3 entry that can be used with Play # 3 as a Counter pair. The initial action of all five players contains identical action to the beginning of Play # 3. Play # 4 and Play # 8 are identical in the first stages also (just with "Zipper Cuts.) Just like Play # 3, this play starts out with 01 dribbling to the right side's "Wing" area with 02 making a "Pipe Cut" up after 04's "Pin Screen" and out to the new "Ballside Slot." After the screen for 02, 04 again "Iso Posts" his defender.

On the opposite side, 05 sets the same "Big-on-Small Pin-Screen" for 03 to use as he again pops out to the "Wing" area on the new "Weakside Wing" location. After setting the screen for 03, 05 slips out to the new "Weakside Slot." Diagram 24.18.

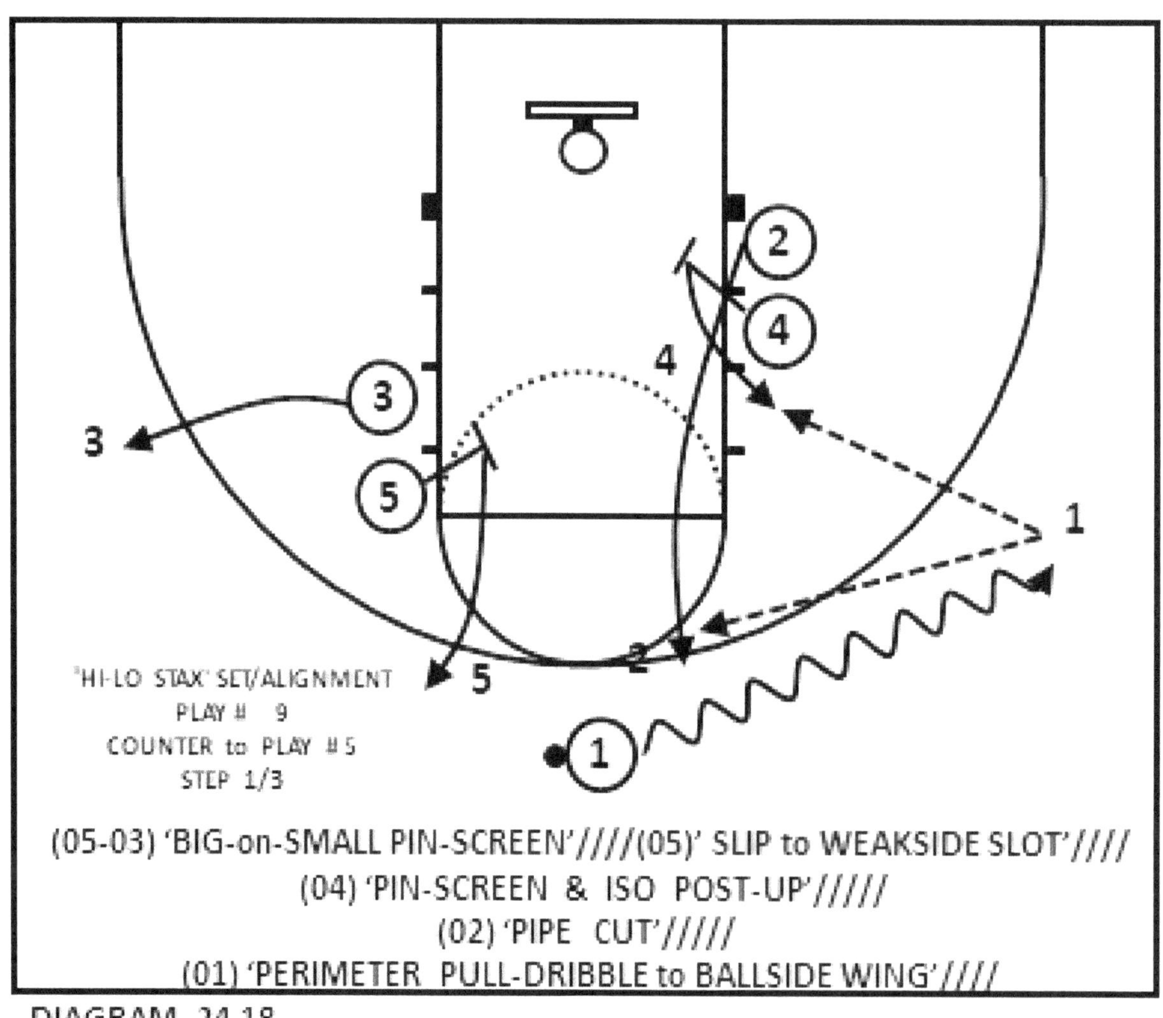

DIAGRAM 24.18

Play # 9   Diagram 24.18.

Play # 9 becomes a different action than Play # 3 when the ball is "Up Passed" from 01 to 02. 02 immediately looks to make a "Lob Pass" to 04 who has stepped towards the rim. At the same time, 05 breaks across the top of the key to set the same type of "Big-on-Small Ball-Screen" for 02. 02 then "dribble-scrapes" off of 05's outside right shoulder to make his perimeter-pull (drag) dribble towards the now vacant "Weakside Slot." So far, this action still remains the same as Play # 3, but it changes when 05 makes a "Reverse Pivot" off of his lower left foot and opens up to 02 and the ball as he rolls down the lane to post up his defender. Diagram 24.19.

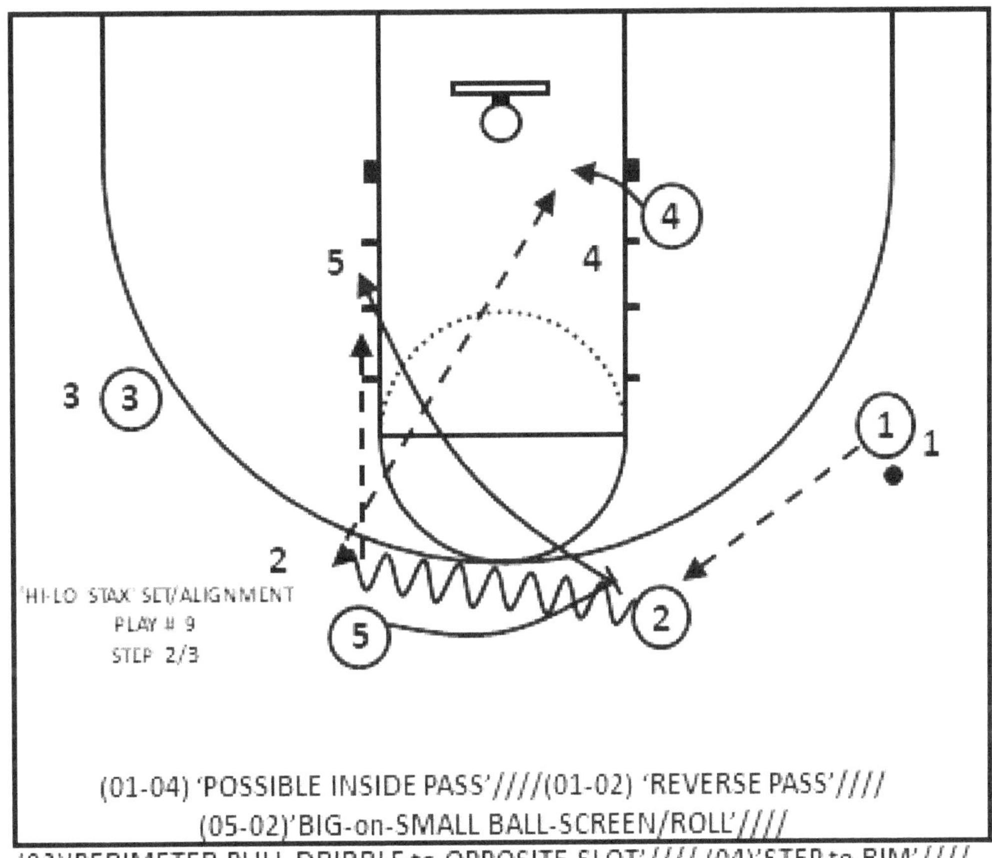

(01-04) 'POSSIBLE INSIDE PASS'/////(01-02) 'REVERSE PASS'/////
(05-02)'BIG-on-SMALL BALL-SCREEN/ROLL'/////
(02)'PERIMETER PULL DRIBBLE to OPPOSITE SLOT'///// (04)'STEP to RIM'/////
DIAGRAM 24.19

Diagram 24.20 shows when 02 successfully utilizes 05's screen and does not make the "Inside Pass" to 05. Instead, 02 makes the "Wing Pass" to 03 who then looks to deliver the ball to 05. To isolate 05 and to give him a position advantage over his defender, 02 makes a "Diagonal Down-Screen" for 04 to use to break to the top of the key (for an open '3.') 03 also has a potential "Skip Pass" receiver in 01 on the "Weakside Wing." If and when 03 makes the pass to 04 out on top, the actual play is over and since the "3-Out/2-In" Spot-Ups are correctly filled, the designated continuity offense can immediately begin. Diagram 24.20.

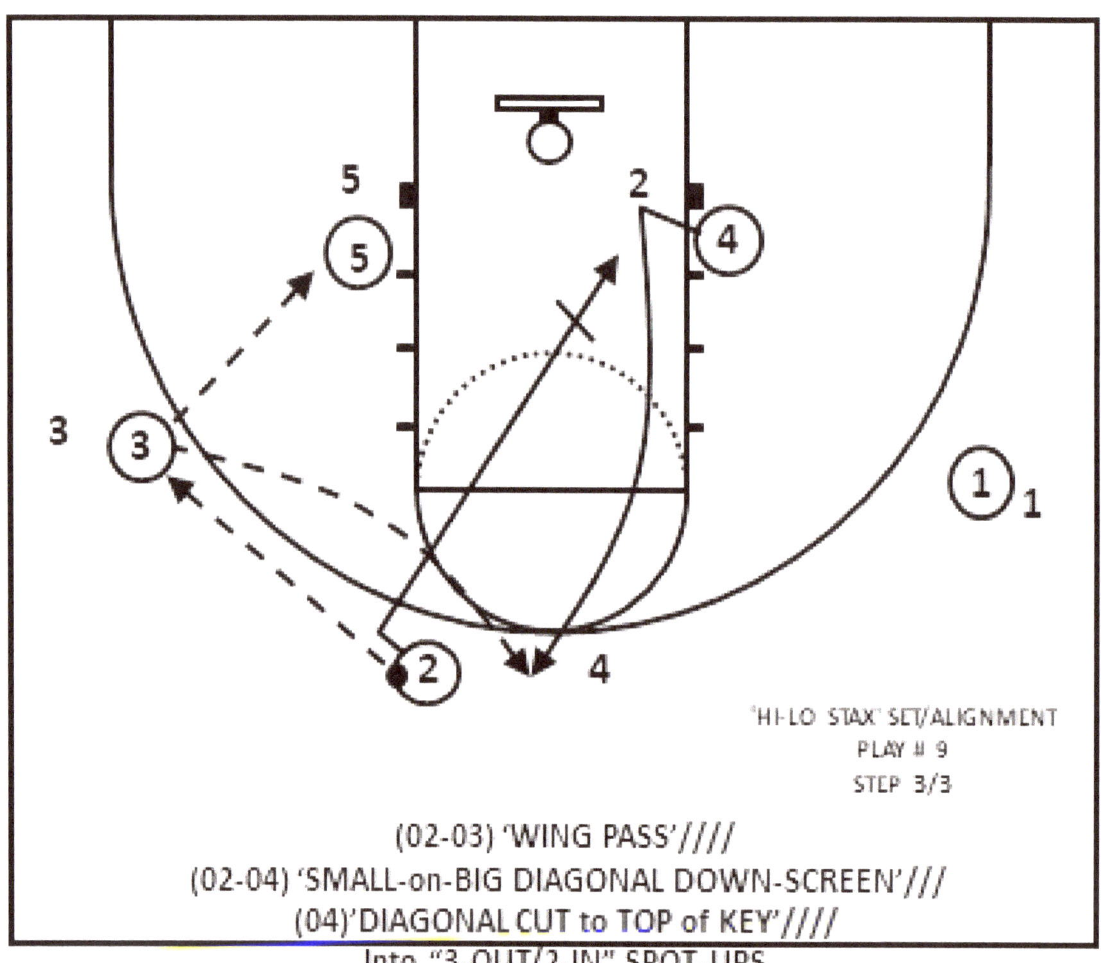

DIAGRAM 24.20

Diagrams 24.21, 24.22 and 24.23 illustrate Play # 10, another Level 3 play. This entry can be one of the three plays (Plays # 5, # 6 and this play.) In this entry, 04 sets the same "Big-on-Small Pin Screen" for 02, but with 02 breaking out to the "Deep Corner." As in several other entries, after 04 has set his screen; again he pivots to gain "position advantage" on his defender to post him up (more than likely in an isolated situation.)

On the opposite side, 05 sets his customary screen for 03 to pop out to the FT Line extended on his own side of the floor. In a different action, 05 then slips his "Pin-Screen" and then makes his "Barkley Cut" across the floor to the opposite side's FT Line extended. Diagram 24.21.

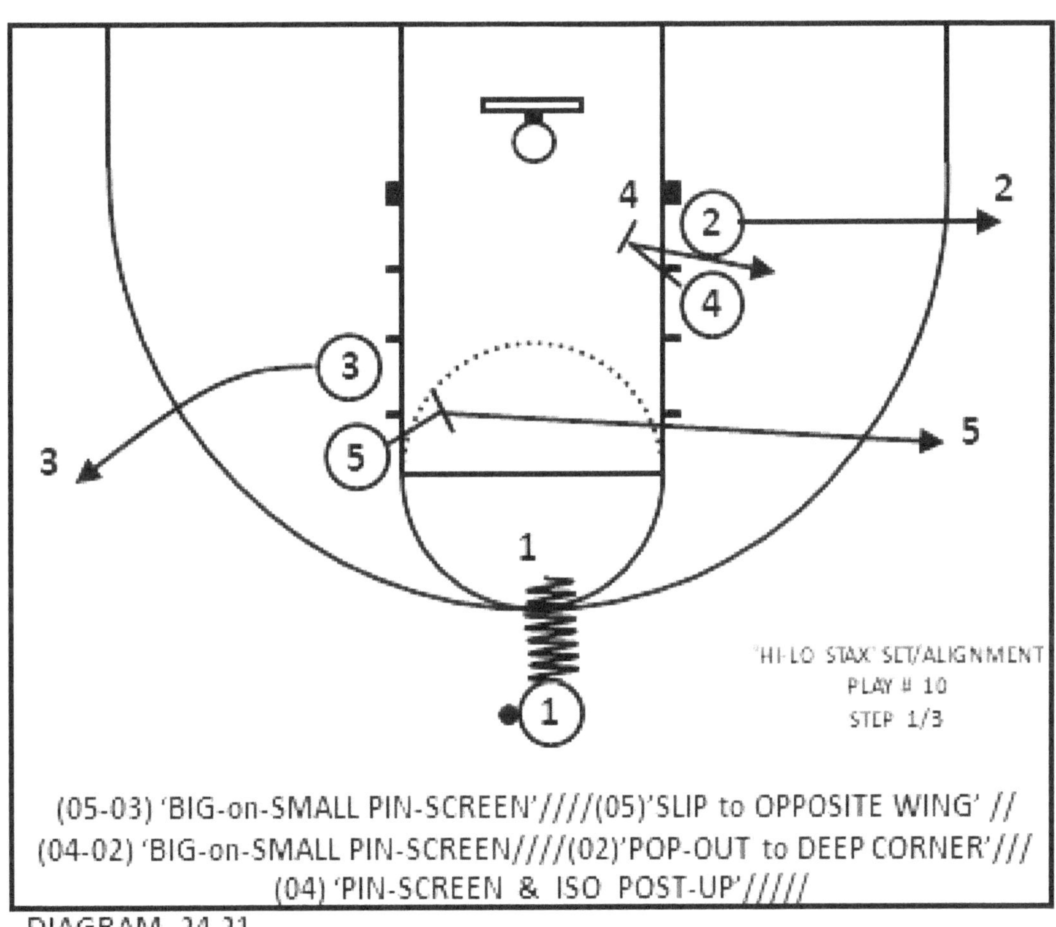

DIAGRAM 24.21

Play # 10   Diagram 24.21

01 makes his "Wing Pass" to 05 with 04 posting his defender up on the new "Ballside Block," with 02 now spotted up in the "Ballside Deep Corner." After the pass is made from 01 to 05, 03 steps up to set a "Big-on-Small Flare-Screen" for 01 to use to "Flare-Cut" to the newly declared "Weakside Wing." Just as in Plays # 5 and # 6, with 05 having the ball at the "Ballside Wing," the spot-ups of the "Odd Front Secondary Break" are filled. As previously stated, any of the "Odd Front Secondary Break" options could be utilized, in addition to any different half-court plays that could be used. Diagram 24.22.

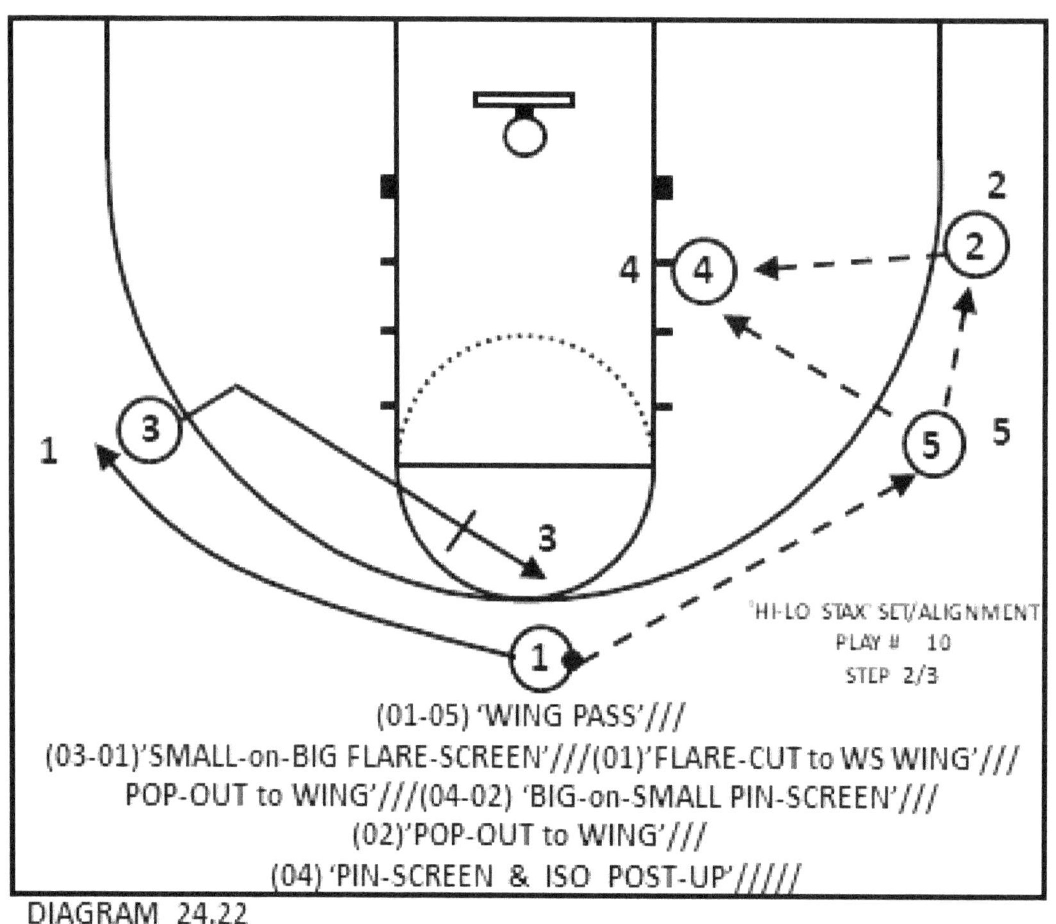

DIAGRAM 24.22

Play # 10   Diagram 24.22

Diagram 24.23 demonstrates the action that could be used in this particular play. If neither 02 or 05 can deliver the ball inside to the isolated 04, the ball should be passed out to 03, causing 04 to use the proper techniques and footwork to make his "Iso Duck-In Cut" into the "Dotted Circle" area.

If 04 is defensively fronted, 03 should lob the ball over X4 and 04 should seal and catch the "Lob Pass." If X4 defends 04 by playing behind, 03 should make the bounce pass directly to 04 and have 04 attack his defender "one on one."

If 03 cannot make the pass to 04, the ball should be swung over to 01; who could have an improved passing angle to make the pass to 04, now on the "Ballside Block."

When the pass is made by 03 to 01, 03 and 05 should break to get the proper angles to set a "Big-on-Small Stagger-Screen" for 02 to use to break to the open and vacant "Top of the Key." The three-man action on the weakside by 03, 05 and 02 not only can produce an open '3' for 02 but also give 04 more of an isolated post-up advantage over his defender, X3.

If shots are not taken, the same "3-Out/2-In" Spot-Ups are correctly filled; giving the offense a smooth transition into the final phase of the attack. Diagram 24.23.

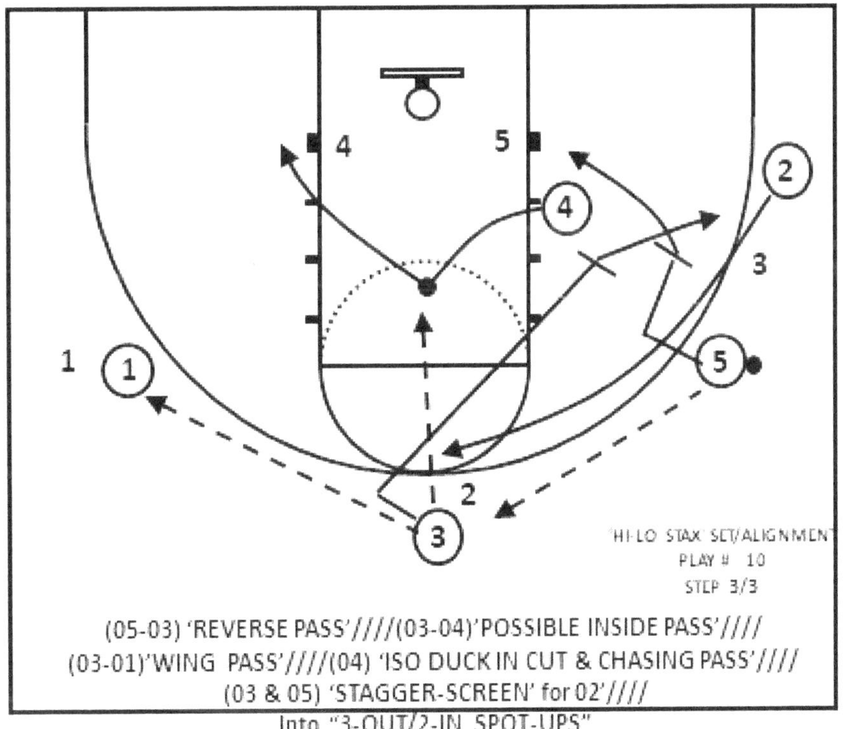

DIAGRAM 24.23

To make the overall play/entry attack package more balanced, Play # 11, another Level 3 play, should be added. 01 dribbles to the left side of the floor, the less frequent action side so far in this entire package of entries out of this "HI-LO STAX" Offensive Set/Alignment. This play has 03 quickly step up to set a "Small-on-Big Back-Screen" for 05 to spin out of the high "Elbow" area and immediately roll down to the new "Ballside Block."

04 sets the frequent "Big-on-Small Pin Down-Screen" for 02 to use to break out to the "Deep Corner." In rare action, 04 then sets his screen and then breaks diagonally out to the "Wing" area near the FT Line extended. Diagram 24.24.

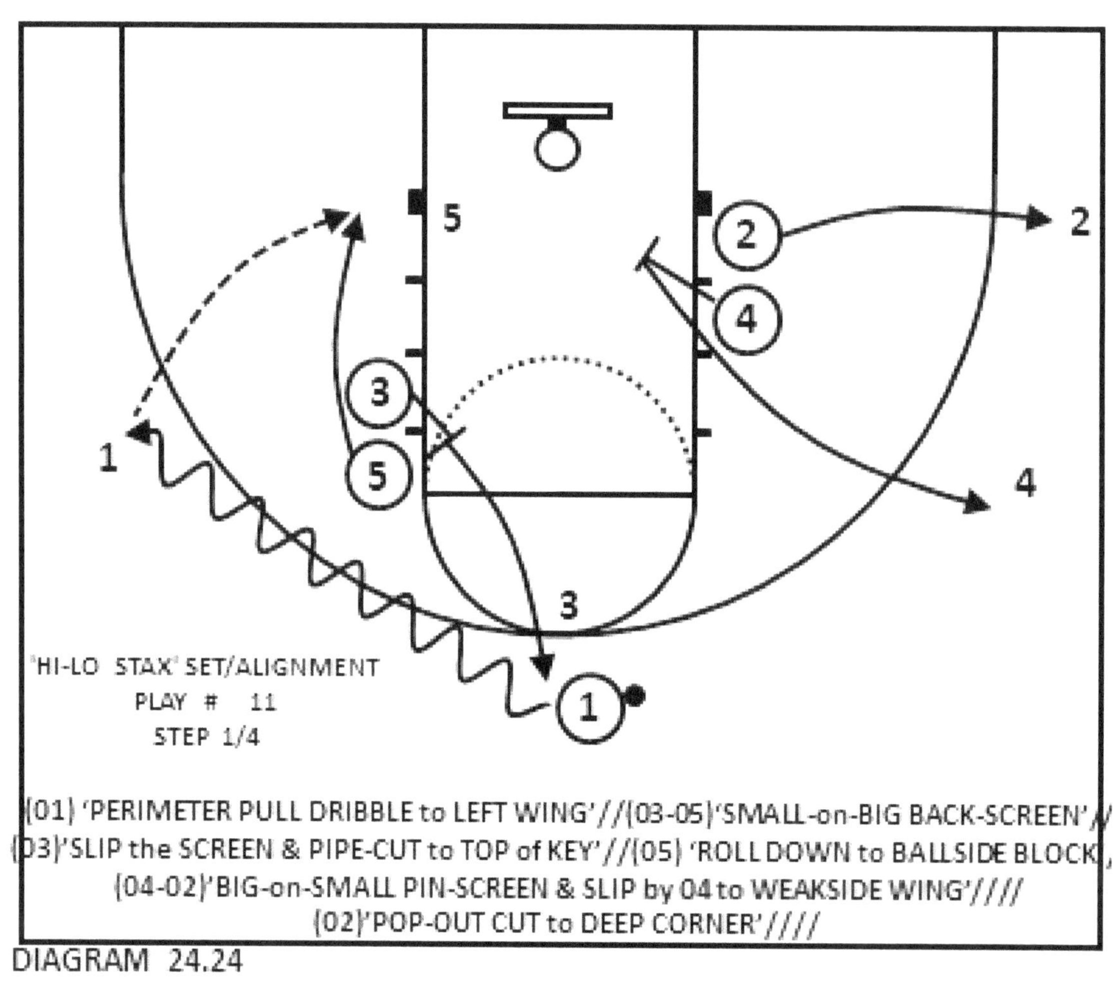

Play # 11   Diagram 24.24

Diagram 24.25 shows 01 not making the pass to 05 down on the "Block," and instead reversing the ball to 03 out on top. 03 takes one dribble towards 04 who has inverted his post-type defender out on the perimeter so that 04 can then attack his post-type defender with a perimeter-oriented action—a (perimeter) "Backdoor Cut." At the same time, 02 makes a hard cut to up replace 04 at the "Wing" area with 04 remaining on the "Block."

For timing purposes and to give 04 some space and time to isolate his defender on the cut to the basket and for the post-up; 05 steps out as if to set a "Shuffle Back-Screen" for 01 to use. Instead, 01 breaks back out from his initial "Wing" location and 05 reverses his direction to go back inside. This (05-01) "Ghost Shuffle Back-Screen" first provides time and space for 04 to attack his defender on the opposite side of the floor and then for 05 to become the secondary pass receiver on the interior and for 01 to become the primary perimeter pass receiver on the left side of the floor. Diagram 24.25.

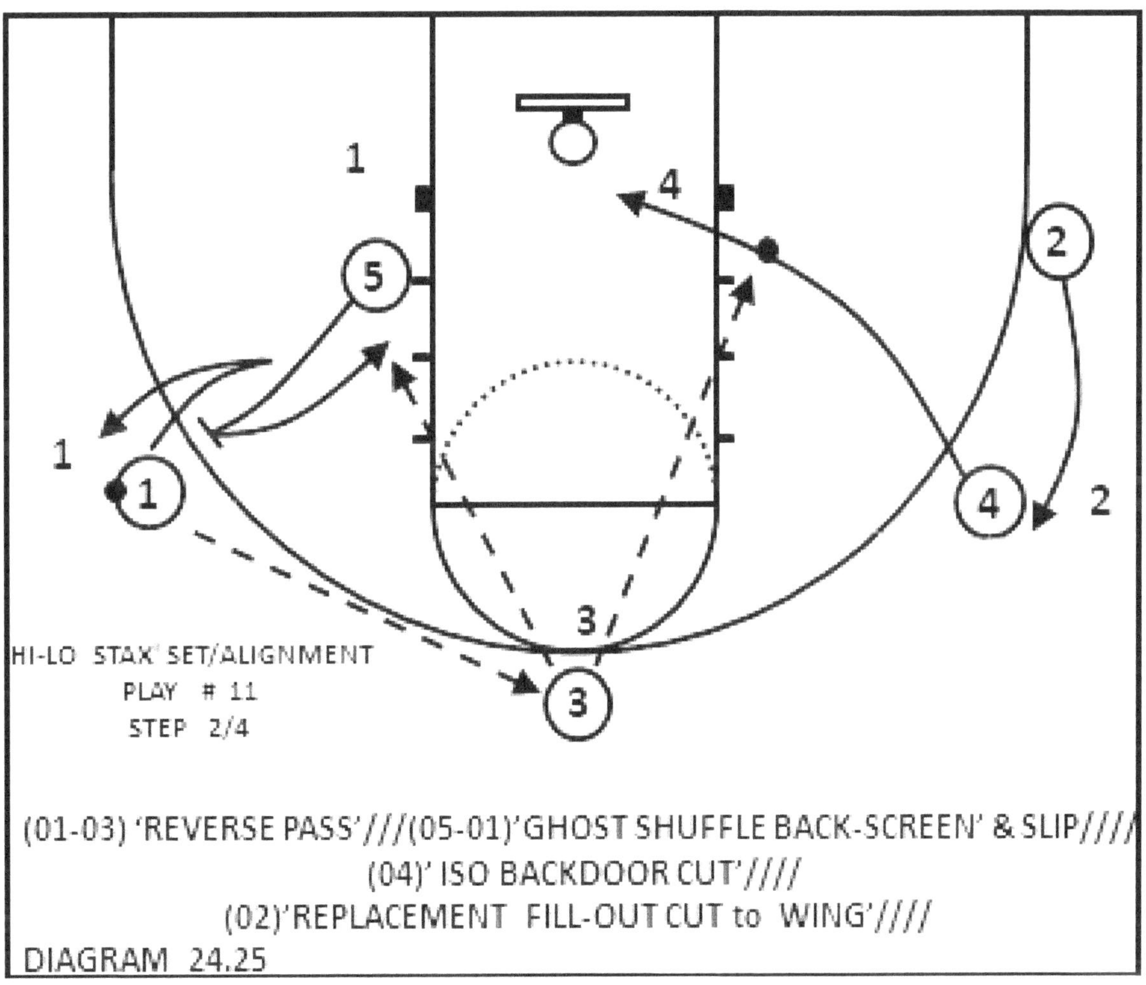

If and when 03 receives the ball from 01, 03 looks to make an "Inside Pass" to 04 on his "Iso Duck-In Cut" and if 04 is not open; 03 should dribble towards 02's side of the floor and meet him near the "Wing" area for a (03-02) DHO. 03 would remain at the "Wing" area while 02 makes a "perimeter-pull dribble" to the top of the key. Diagram 24.26.

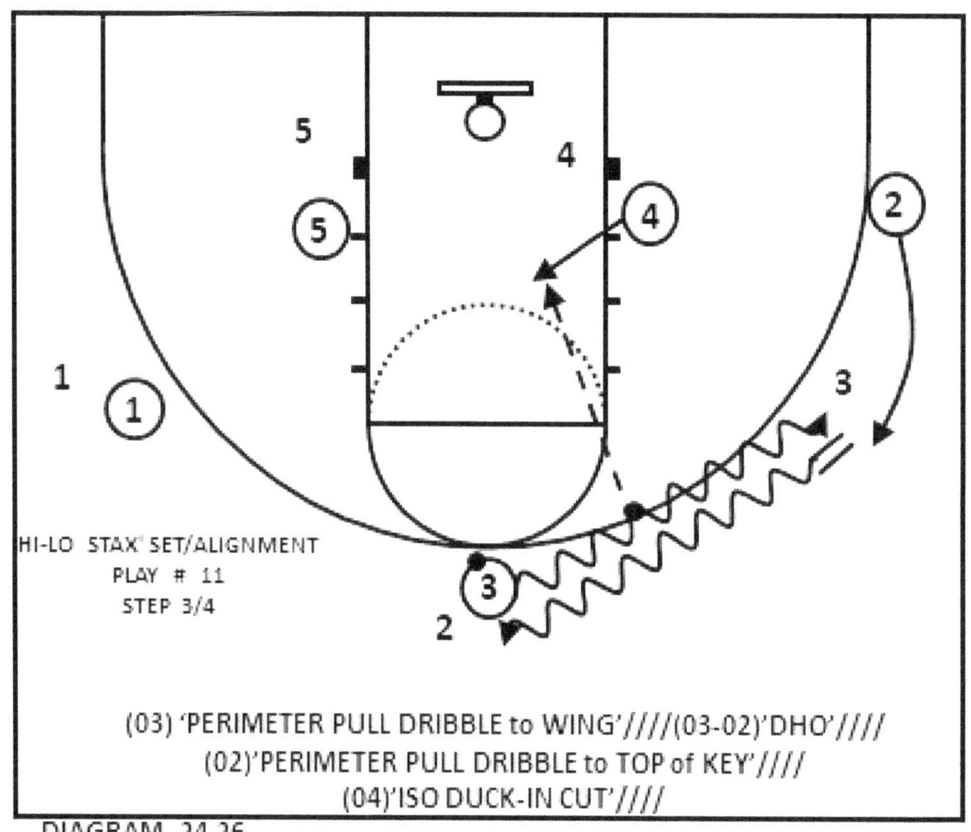

DIAGRAM 24.26

Diagram 24.27 shows the action from the interior weakside when 02 reaches the imaginary center line at the top of the key. For 04 not to have received the ball from either 03 or 02, it should be because of hard defensive denial pressure by X4 near the "Dotted Circle" area. If that is the case, 05 who is lower than the "Dotted Circle," can step up with a short diagonal cut to "head-hunt back-screen" X4 (whose full attention and effort is denying 04 the ball from 02). In this scenario, the contact by X4 and 04 would be made with 04's inside 'contact' right shoulder and X4's body. 04 should tightly reverse pivot off of his 'contact' right foot and swing his 'free' left leg and foot with a tightly 270 degree pivot, while making contact with his left shoulder and 05's right shoulder. This tight curl technique would spin him around from behind to end up facing 02 out on top and 01 out on the wing. This puts him in position to immediately catch the ball and execute a variety of post moves (most likely a "Show and Go Opposite Drop Step with the free right foot, followed by a Power Lay-Up shot with both hands off of the glass."

This same diagram shows that after 05 sets this screen on X4, he should step through with his 'contact right' free foot facing towards 02 and 03. When and if he receives the ball from either teammate, another "Show and Go Opposite Drop Step with his free lower left foot, followed by the same Power Lay-Up will not only cause close shots but also defensive fouls.

If there are perimeter defenders such as X1 or X3 on the "Wing" areas or X2 out on top that have collapsed into the paint, any of those three perimeter players should always be prepared by "having their feet and hands ready" for an open perimeter shot outside of the arc.

If after the strong emphasis on attacking X4 and X5 do not result in the desired shot, the two primary offensive players are on both

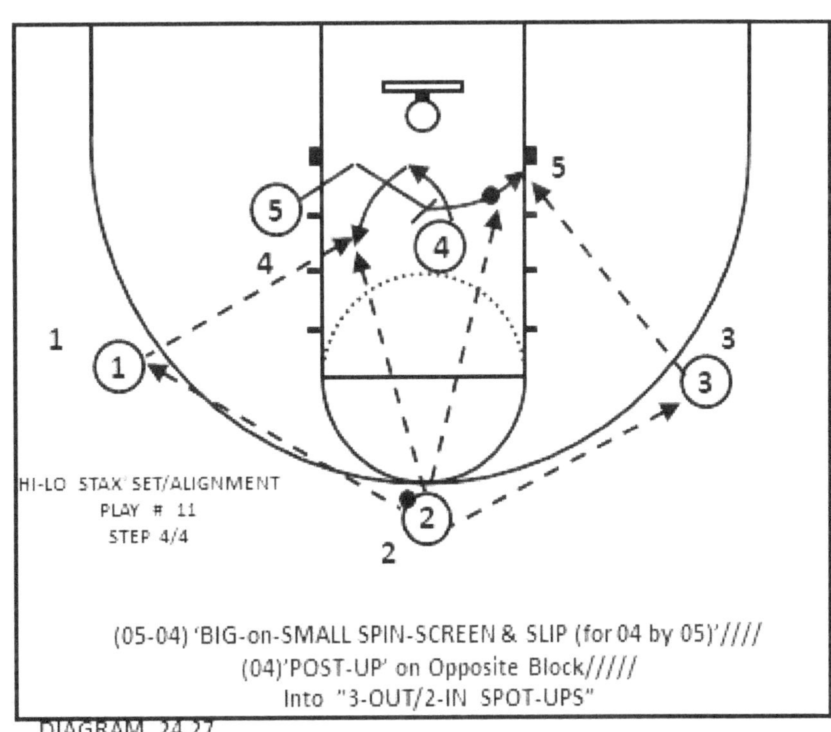

DIAGRAM 24.27

"Blocks" while the three designated defenders are spotted up equally balanced outside of the arc at the two "Wing" areas and the "Top of the Key." These actions have stretched the defense in every possible direction and therefore weakening the overall defense. In addition, the designated continuity offense will immediately be ready to begin its last phase of the overall attack. Diagram 24.27.

CLOSING

This offensive set is more of an unusual set in today's offense since there is a minimal amount of two-man offensive stacks being used. Even more unique is the fact that there are two offensive stacks and that they both are located at different heights on the court. This can cause the first set of problems in that it is harder to prepare.

There will obviously be different forms of "Pin Down-Screens" that can be used a few times or at a majority of the time. Inside action as long as perimeter attacks are available in the twenty plays. Different types of screens, both on-the-ball and off-the-ball screens can and should be utilized at various locations on the floor. Almost every type of offensive cut is available during at least a couple of the plays demonstrated. Both sides of the floor also can and will be used to attack opposing defenses. Along with many other positive attributes comes the fact that there can be numerous types of continuity offense that can seamlessly flow from any of the three sets of offensive spot-ups. This makes this alignment a key and productive offensive set/alignment that should be part of the overall offensive system.

CHAPTER 25

CONCLUSION

It has often been discussed that the coaching staff has many decisions to make regarding the offensive system it is constructing. While half-court plays/entries, out-of-bounds plays and Secondary Fastbreaks are tremendous sources of scoring points and are extremely important, when those initial phases of offense do not produce the shots, the only method remaining is the final phase of the offense to be productive. And that final phase will always be the continuity offense or the motion-type offense that the previous phase(s) place them.

It is important that the Secondary Break, the actual half-court plays and the out-of-bounds plays all score points and are effective during their execution, the continuity offense will very likely be the largest point-producing phase of the overall system. Therefore, it is likely the most important decision that must be made is what is the most productive and efficient continuity or motion-type offense that will meet the skill set of their present players and the coaching staff's overall offensive (and even defensive) philosophies. The proper continuity offense should give the offensive team the proper amount of structure as well (with counter options within the continuity) the freedom, the fluid movement and high levels of unpredictability for opposing defenses to contend with, using many fundamentally sound types of action (including various on-ball screens, off-ball screens, cuts and various forms of dribbling and passing opportunities.)

The desired continuity offense will help determine the type of Primary and Secondary Fastbreaks (Odd-Front or Even-Front Breaks Options) the system needs to utilize, solely based on the required ending spot-up locations. Every Secondary Break Option that is used that does not produce a shot reposition players in the identical spot-ups of the continuity offense for an immediate and seamless transition into that continuity offense.

The ending spot-ups of the designated continuity offense will be a large factor and determine the most productive plays that result in the very same spot-ups every Secondary Break Option ends up in their player movements.

After selecting the half-court plays that are fundamentally sound, fluid and high-scoring, it must be determined that those plays must have the very same spot-ups that are required for the smooth and immediate execution of the continuity offense.

Those half-court quick-hitters/plays/entries that are chosen (directly from the selected continuity offense) would then factor into the best one or two offensive alignments/sets that will allow those plays to be successfully executed.

In addition, the Baseline and Sideline Out-of-Bounds Plays also will be chosen by each play having the play-ending spot-ups locations required by the chosen continuity offense.

It should also be realized that the quicker and more fluid the transitions are between the initial phase (be it the Secondary Break Options phase, the Half-Court Plays/Entries phase or the Out-of-Bounds Plays phase) into the final phase (the designated Continuity Offense or the Motion-type Offense); the productivity and success the final phase will be.

It must be emphasized again that "Quality trumps Quantity" in the decision to select the number of continuity offenses to be executed, the number of sets/alignments and the number of plays (from each of the alignments) that are to be employed. It is very important that coaches don't allow too many plays or alignments to mentally bog down their offensive team.

It must be remembered that the Level order of plays begins with Level 1 plays being the most basic and the actual shorter in length and lesser amount of fundamentally sound types of action. Level 2 plays step in with a greater number of different types of actions that will take longer to execute before spotting up in the proper locations for the same quick transition into the designated Continuity Offense. Level 3 plays reach the maximum in length, sophistication, degrees of difficulty and numbers of the various offensive attacking techniques and methods.

With every play discussed as labeled as a specific Level of play, it must be remembered that older, more skilled and more experienced teams should/could have a variety of different levels of plays; such as Level 1, 2 and 3 plays. Somewhat younger teams and less experienced teams could have only Level 2 and 1 plays; where the very youngest of teams could have only Level 1 plays and a minimal number of those to be successful offensively.

This book will help every coach at every level, regardless of the experience of the coaching staff and/or the players' skill levels and experience. Young, less experienced and less talented players should be coached the Level 1 plays and a variable but minimal number of the many types of offensive cuts, on and off-ball screens that could be utilized in their plays used.

Older, better skilled, and more experienced players can maintain some Level 1 plays while advancing to higher Level 2 plays/entries along with an increased number of cuts and screens that could be added to their offensive attacks.

Older and far better talented and more experienced players have all of the Level 3 plays in addition to retaining some Level 2 plays to keep in their offensive schemes. These players should maximize on the wide number of offensive cuts that could be used on the perimeter as well as the interior. In addition, the number of off-ball screens as well as the number of on-ball screens could be increased dramatically as well as the many actions that can follow both types of screens.

This book also can be the foundation for the younger coaches but also the more veteran coaches to keep adding to their Level 2 and 3 plays. New techniques, different cuts and ways to utilize those cuts can be improvised. Creative coaches can simply use the various cuts, the various screens to create their own Level 1, Level 2 or Level 3 plays as they expand their knowledge and change their philosophies on offense.

This book could be a "starter" and a "progression ladder" book for young coaches that becomes a valuable book as that coach progresses along with the level of his/her teams. As the coach progresses in experience and knowledge, as his/her teams progress in skills and competition levels, so can the offensive schemes, techniques, concepts and plays/entries used in the ever-changing offensive system. The progressions of all of these important components of an offensive system are all included in this detailed and wide range of ideas within this single book.

I feel I would be remiss if I did not strong emphasize again the important of these three levels of plays/entries.

With packages of Level 1 plays that seamlessly flow into the three types of spot-ups that are possessed by almost all types of the many continuity offenses that exist, staffs coaching the lower, younger and inexperience "Level 1" squads have over 40 plays to choose from that could also be modified to even more so fit that particular squad.

In addition, it is entirely possible for at least a limited number of "Level 2" plays could be inserted into that team's offensive package.

An example could be for a team that utilizes the "3-Out/2-In "Spot-Ups (as a Triangle Power Continuity or a 3-Man Interior Motion Offense, a "Level 1" squad has 23 "Level 1" plays plus possibly a small portion of the 33 "Level 2" plays that could be included.

A "Level 1" "Flex Continuity Offense" team could have 7 plays plus a pool of the 24 "Level 2" plays that could be adapted and included in the overall offensive scheme.

Because of a "Level 1" team's inexperience and lower skill level, that number is much more than adequate a for to be able to select just the right specific plays to be efficient and productive.

A "Level 2" team coach would have a tremendous advantage, regardless of the type of continuity of motion-type offense that is utilized because each level excluding "Level 1" teams could actually step lower to possess any or all of those lower level plays."

For instance, "Level 2" teams that use the so-call "4-Out/1-In" Spot-Ups such as the "Flex Continuity Offense uses has it own so-call plays in its group (24 plays in addition to the 7 plays that are labelled as "Level 1" plays . There are 38 "Level 3" plays in this book which a "Level 2" team might be able to incorporate into its system.

This gives a "Level 2" team 24 plays, in addition to 7 different "Level 1" plays and a possible 38 "Level 3" plays that could be implemented. Those could then possibly be fluidly and Smoothly flow into the specific "4-Out/1-In" Spot-Ups Continuity Offense that is being executed.

A "Level 2" team that utilizes the "3-Out/2-In" Spot-Ups would have its own initial 33 plays plus 23 lower level plays and a possibility of a few higher "Level 3" plays (35) for a larger group of 91 different offensive plays/entries. Any of those plays could be inserted or deleted during the same season to fit the current offensive strengths and weaknesses of that specific team.

When it comes to the more skilled and experienced squads, those types of teams have the advantage of utilizing their own classification of plays,35 "Level 3" plays that all flow can be integrated into the various "3-Out/2-In" Spot-Up Continuity Offenses, or the various 38 plays that have the ability to smoothly flow into "4-Out/1-In" Spot-Up Continuity Offenses (with "Flex" being a very often used offense.) or 9 plays that can seamlessly transition to the different "High Post/Low Post Continuity Offenses that exist.

Those "Level 3" teams have the capability to easily convert the lower "Level 1" and/or "Level 2" plays into its overall offensive package, particularly if some of those plays warrant its use.

Adding or deleting plays to more currently "match" the squad's strengths and weaknesses as well as the coaching staff's philosophies would be the reasons to modify the overall offensive plan of attack.

It could be thought to use any of these so-called extra plays as "Counter Plays" (plays that appear to be one play but end up with different forms of action (before players relocate in the same offensive "Spot-Ups. (to then begin the transition into the same continuity offense.) One of two of these additional plays could be used as "Specials" or "ATO s" (After Time-Out Plays or "End-of-Time Periods" plays.

With the temptation of having large quantities of plays, it must be remembered follow the Keep it Simple" and "Quality trumps Quantity" philosophies.

Coach Kimble took the Head Basketball Coaching position at Deland-Weldon (IL) High School where the varsity accumulated a five-year record of 91-43 that included 2 Regional Championships, 2 Regional Runner-Ups and 1 Sectional Tournament Runner-up.

From there, he moved to Dunlap (IL) High School. His five-year record at Dunlap amounted to an overall 90-45 record that included two Regional Runners-up, one Regional Championship, one Sectional and one Super-Sectional Championship and a final 2nd Place Finish in the Illinois Class A State Tournament.

Coach Kimble then moved to Florida where he became an Assistant Basketball Coach at Central Florida Community College in Ocala, FL. The next year, he became the Offensive Coordinator in charge of the team's overall offense. For the next two years, he retained that Offensive Coordinator responsibility while also becoming the Associate Head Basketball Coach, with a 2-year record of 44-22. The four-year overall record while at CFCC was "73 -58".

Coach Kimble then became the Head Basketball Coach at Crestview (FL) High School for the following 10 years. Excluding the initial year, the overall record averaged almost 18 wins each year for the next 9 years.

Coach Kimble has worked over 100 weeks of basketball camps and has spoken at several coaching clinics and camps. He also has had over 100 articles published in the following publications such as: *The Basketball Bulletin of the National Association of Basketball Coaches, The Scholastic Coach and Athletic Journal, Coach and AD, Winning Hoops, and Basketball Sense,* as well as contributing articles submitted and all diagrams drawn for the following books: the *NABC's Coaching Basketball* in two separate editions.

He has authored six other books through Coaches Choice titled, *The Basketball Coaches Complete Guide to the Multiple Match-up Zone Defense," "The Basketball Coaches' Complete Guide to Zone Offenses," "Coaching Basketball's Speed Game, "Coaching Basketball's Multiple 2-1-2 Full-Court Zone Press," The Basketball*

Coaches' Complete Guide to Footwork, Balance and Pivoting" and "Implementing the SPEED GAME."